Advances in System Dynamics and Control

Ahmad Taher Azar
Benha University, Egypt & Nile University, Egypt

Sundarapandian Vaidyanathan
Vel Tech University, India

A volume in the Advances in Systems Analysis, Software Engineering, and High Performance Computing (ASASEHPC) Book Series

Published in the United States of America by
IGI Global
Engineering Science Reference (an imprint of IGI Global)
701 E. Chocolate Avenue
Hershey PA, USA 17033
Tel: 717-533-8845
Fax: 717-533-8661
E-mail: cust@igi-global.com
Web site: http://www.igi-global.com

Library of Congress Cataloging-in-Publication Data

Library of Congress Cataloging-in-Publication Data

Names: Azar, Ahmad Taher, editor. | Vaidyanathan, Sunddarapandian, 1967- editor.
Title: Advances in system dynamics and control / Ahmad Taher Azar and Sundarapandian Vaidyanathan, editors.
Description: Hershey, PA : Engineering Science Reference, [2018] | Author's name spelled Sundarapandian on the title page. | Includes bibliographical references and index.
Identifiers: LCCN 2017028147| ISBN 9781522540779 (hardcover) | ISBN 9781522540786 (ebook)
Subjects: LCSH: Automatic control. | Random dynamical systems.
Classification: LCC TJ213 .A2524 2018 | DDC 629.8--dc23 LC record available at https://lccn.loc.gov/2017028147

This book is published in the IGI Global book series Advances in Systems Analysis, Software Engineering, and High Performance Computing (ASASEHPC) (ISSN: 2327-3453; eISSN: 2327-3461)

British Cataloguing in Publication Data
A Cataloguing in Publication record for this book is available from the British Library.

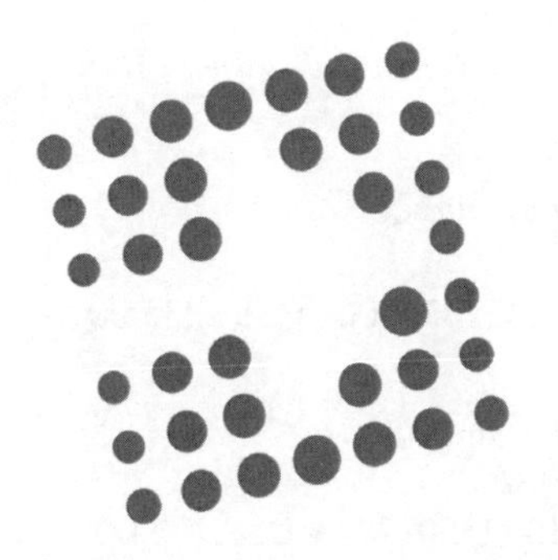

Advances in Systems Analysis, Software Engineering, and High Performance Computing (ASASEHPC) Book Series

Vijayan Sugumaran
Oakland University, USA

ISSN:2327-3453
EISSN:2327-3461

Mission

The theory and practice of computing applications and distributed systems has emerged as one of the key areas of research driving innovations in business, engineering, and science. The fields of software engineering, systems analysis, and high performance computing offer a wide range of applications and solutions in solving computational problems for any modern organization.

The **Advances in Systems Analysis, Software Engineering, and High Performance Computing (ASASEHPC) Book Series** brings together research in the areas of distributed computing, systems and software engineering, high performance computing, and service science. This collection of publications is useful for academics, researchers, and practitioners seeking the latest practices and knowledge in this field.

Coverage

- Human-Computer Interaction
- Parallel Architectures
- Computer graphics
- Engineering Environments
- Network Management
- Enterprise Information Systems
- Distributed Cloud Computing
- Storage Systems
- Software Engineering
- Performance Modelling

IGI Global is currently accepting manuscripts for publication within this series. To submit a proposal for a volume in this series, please contact our Acquisition Editors at Acquisitions@igi-global.com or visit: http://www.igi-global.com/publish/.

The Advances in Systems Analysis, Software Engineering, and High Performance Computing (ASASEHPC) Book Series (ISSN 2327-3453) is published by IGI Global, 701 E. Chocolate Avenue, Hershey, PA 17033-1240, USA, www.igi-global.com. This series is composed of titles available for purchase individually; each title is edited to be contextually exclusive from any other title within the series. For pricing and ordering information please visit http://www.igi-global.com/book-series/advances-systems-analysis-software-engineering/73689. Postmaster: Send all address changes to above address.

Titles in this Series

For a list of additional titles in this series, please visit: www.igi-global.com/book-series

Innovations in Software-Defined Networking and Network Functions Virtualization
Ankur Dumka (University of Petroleum and Energy Studies, India)
Engineering Science Reference • copyright 2018 • 364pp • H/C (ISBN: 9781522536406) • US $235.00 (our price)

Green Computing Strategies for Competitive Advantage and Business Sustainability
Mehdi Khosrow-Pour (Information Resources Management Association, USA)
Business Science Reference • copyright 2018 • 324pp • H/C (ISBN: 9781522550174) • US $185.00 (our price)

Optimizing Contemporary Application and Processes in Open Source Software
Mehdi Khosrow-Pour (Information Resources Management Association, USA)
Engineering Science Reference • copyright 2018 • 318pp • H/C (ISBN: 9781522553144) • US $215.00 (our price)

Formation Methods, Models, and Hardware Implementation of Pseudorandom Number Generators Emerging Research and Opportunities
Stepan Bilan (State Economy and Technology University of Transport, Ukraine)
Engineering Science Reference • copyright 2018 • 301pp • H/C (ISBN: 9781522527732) • US $180.00 (our price)

Aligning Perceptual and Conceptual Information for Cognitive Contextual System Development Emerging Research and Opportunities
Gary Kuvich (IBM, USA)
Engineering Science Reference • copyright 2018 • 172pp • H/C (ISBN: 9781522524311) • US $165.00 (our price)

Applied Computational Intelligence and Soft Computing in Engineering
Saifullah Khalid (CCSI Airport, India)
Engineering Science Reference • copyright 2018 • 340pp • H/C (ISBN: 9781522531296) • US $225.00 (our price)

Enhancing Software Fault Prediction With Machine Learning Emerging Research and Opportunities
Ekbal Rashid (Aurora's Technological and Research Institute, India)
Engineering Science Reference • copyright 2018 • 129pp • H/C (ISBN: 9781522531852) • US $165.00 (our price)

Solutions for Cyber-Physical Systems Ubiquity
Norbert Druml (Independent Researcher, Austria) Andreas Genser (Independent Researcher, Austria) Armin Krieg (Independent Researcher, Austria) Manuel Menghin (Independent Researcher, Austria) and Andrea Hoeller (Independent Researcher, Austria)
Engineering Science Reference • copyright 2018 • 482pp • H/C (ISBN: 9781522528456) • US $225.00 (our price)

701 East Chocolate Avenue, Hershey, PA 17033, USA
Tel: 717-533-8845 x100 • Fax: 717-533-8661
E-Mail: cust@igi-global.com • www.igi-global.com

Table of Contents

Preface xviii

Section 1
Advances in Control and Chaotic Systems

Chapter 1
A Decentralized Control Architecture to Achieve Synchronized Task Behaviors in Autonomous Cooperative Multi-Robot Systems 1
Gen'ichi Yasuda, Nagasaki Institute of Applied Science, Japan

Chapter 2
Proportional Integral Loop Shaping Control Design With Particle Swarm Optimization Tuning 24
Ahmad Taher Azar, Benha University, Egypt & Nile University, Egypt
Fernando E. Serrano, Central American Technical University (UNITEC), Honduras
Sundarapandian Vaidyanathan, Vel Tech University, India

Chapter 3
Control-Based Maximum Power Point Tracking for a Grid-Connected Hybrid Renewable Energy System Optimized by Particle Swarm Optimization 58
Mouna Ben Smida, National Engineering School of Monastir, Tunisia
Anis Sakly, National Engineering School of Monastir, Tunisia
Sundarapandian Vaidyanathan, Vel Tech University, India
Ahmad Taher Azar, Benha University, Egypt & Nile University, Egypt

Chapter 4
Design of Low Order Controllers for Decoupled MIMO Systems With Time Response Specifications 90
Maher Ben Hariz, Université de Tunis El Manar, Ecole Nationale d'Ingénieurs de Tunis, Tunisia
Wassila Chagra, Université de Tunis El Manar, Institut Préparatoire Aux études d'Ingénieurs d'El Manar, Ecole Nationale d'Ingénieurs de Tunis, Tunisia

Faouzi Bouani, Université de Tunis El Manar, Ecole Nationale d'Ingénieurs de Tunis, Tunisia

Chapter 5
Active Control for Multi-Switching Combination Synchronization of Non-Identical Chaotic Systems ... 129
Shikha Singh, Jamia Millia Islamia, India
Ahmad Taher Azar, Benha University, Egypt & Nile University, Egypt
Muzaffar Ahmad Bhat, Jamia Millia Islamia, India
Sundarapandian Vaidyanathan, Vel Tech University, India
Adel Ouannas, University of Larbi Tebessi, Algeria

Chapter 6
Load Frequency Control Based on Modern Techniques in Two Areas Power Systems ... 163
Naglaa Kamel Bahgaat, Canadian International College (CIC), Egypt
Mohamed Ibrahim, Al Azhar University, Egypt
Mohamed Ahmed Moustafa Hassan, Cairo University, Egypt
Fahmy Bendary, Benha University, Egypt

Chapter 7
A Position Control With a Field Programmable Gate Array-Sun-Tracking System for Photovoltaic Panels ... 192
Saber Krim, University of Monastir, Tunisia
Soufien Gdaim, University of Monastir, Tunisia
Abdellatif Mtibaa, University of Monastir, Tunisia
Mimouni Mohamed Faouzi, National Engineering School of Monastir, Tunisia

Chapter 8
Automatic Voltage Regulator System Tuning Using Swarm Intelligence Techniques ... 232
Naglaa K. Bahgaat, Canadian International College (CIC), Egypt
Mohamed Ahmed Moustafa Hassan, Cairo University, Egypt

Chapter 9
Loss of Excitation Protection of Medium Voltage Hydro Generators Using Adaptive Neuro Fuzzy Inference System ... 253
Mohamed Salah El-Din Ahmed Abdel Aziz, Dar Al-Handasah (Shair and Partners) – Cairo, Egypt
Mohamed Ahmed Moustafa Hassan, Cairo University, Egypt
Fahmy Bendary, Benha University, Egypt

Chapter 10
Artificial Neural Network for PWM Rectifier Direct Power Control and DC Voltage Control ... 286
Arezki Fekik, University Mouloud Mammeri of Tizi-Ouzou, Algeria
Hakim Denoun, University Mouloud Mammeri of Tizi-Ouzou, Algeria
Ahmad Taher Azar, Benha University, Egypt & Nile University, Egypt
Mustapha Zaouia, University Mouloud Mammeri of Tizi-Ouzou, Algeria

Nabil Benyahia, University Mouloud Mammeri of Tizi-Ouzou, Algeria
Mohamed Lamine Hamida, University Mouloud Mammeri of Tizi-Ouzou, Algeria
Nacereddine Benamrouche, University Mouloud Mammeri of Tizi-Ouzou, Algeria
Sundarapandian Vaidyanathan, Vel Tech University, India

Chapter 11
Dynamics Analysis and Synchronization in Relay Coupled Fractional Order Colpitts Oscillators ... 317
Kammogne Soup Tewa Alain, Dschang University, Cameroon
Kengne Romanic, Dschang University, Cameroon
Ahmad Taher Azar, Benha University, Egypt & Nile University, Egypt
Sundarapandian Vaidyanathan, Vel Tech University, India
Fotsin Hilaire Bertrand, Dschang University, Cameroon
Ngo Mouelas Adèle, Dschang University, Cameroon

Chapter 12
Analysis and Control of a Dynamical Model for HIV Infection With One or Two Inputs................ 357
Lazaros Moysis, Aristotle University of Thessaloniki, Greece
Ioannis Kafetzis, Aristotle University of Thessaloniki, Greece
Marios Politis, General Hospital of Thessaloniki "G. Papanikolaou", Greece

Chapter 13
A Novel Hyperchaotic System With Adaptive Control, Synchronization, and Circuit Simulation.... 382
Sundarapandian Vaidyanathan, Vel Tech University, India
Ahmad Taher Azar, Benha University, Egypt & Nile University, Egypt
Aceng Sambas, Universitas Muhammadiyah Tasikmalaya, Indonesia
Shikha Singh, Jamia Millia Islamia, India
Kammogne Soup Tewa Alain, Dschang University, Cameroon
Fernando E. Serrano, Central American Technical University (UNITEC), Honduras

Section 2
Applications of Dynamical Systems

Chapter 14
Numerical Analysis for Vehicle Collision Mitigation and Safety Using Dynamics Control Systems 421
Mustafa Elkady, Lebanese International University, Lebanon & Ain Shams University, Lebanon
Muhammad Sheikh, University of Sunderland, UK
Kevin Burn, University of Sunderland, UK

Chapter 15
A Study on the Transportation Mode Choice Behaviour of Individuals With Different Socio-Economic Status.. 476
Arun Bajracharya, Heriot-Watt University Malaysia, Malaysia

Detailed Table of Contents

Section 1
Advances in Control and Chaotic Systems

This chapter describes a method for designing decentralized simulation and control architecture for multiple robot systems based on the discrete event net models. Extended Petri nets are adopted as an effective tool to describe, design, and control cooperative behavior of multiple robots based on asynchronous, concurrent processes. By hierarchical decomposition of the net model of the overall system, global and local Petri net models are assigned to the upper level and the lower level controllers, respectively. For the lower level control, individual net models of robots are executed on separate local controllers. The unified net representation for cooperative control is also proposed. Overall control software is implemented and executed on a general hierarchical and distributed control architecture corresponding to the hardware structure of multiple robot systems.

Backlash is one of several discontinuities found in different kinds of systems. It can be found in actuators of different types, such as mechanical and hydraulic, giving way to unwanted effects in the system behavior. Proportional integral (PI) loop shaping control design implementing a describing function to find the limit cycle oscillations and the appropriate control gain selection by particle swarm optimization is developed. Therefore, a frequency domain approach is implemented for the control of nonlinear system of any kind such as robotics, mechatronics, and other kind of mechanisms, electrical motors, etc. Finally, in order to corroborate the theoretical background explained in this chapter, the stabilization of a cart-pendulum system with the proposed control strategy is shown.

Chapter 3
Control-Based Maximum Power Point Tracking for a Grid-Connected Hybrid Renewable Energy System Optimized by Particle Swarm Optimization 58
Mouna Ben Smida, National Engineering School of Monastir, Tunisia
Anis Sakly, National Engineering School of Monastir, Tunisia
Sundarapandian Vaidyanathan, Vel Tech University, India
Ahmad Taher Azar, Benha University, Egypt & Nile University, Egypt

There has been a great deal of interest in renewable energy sources for electricity generation, particularly for photovoltaic and wind generators. These energy resources have enormous potential and can meet the current global demand for energy. Despite the obvious advantages of renewable energy sources, they have significant disadvantages, such as the discontinuity of their generation, due to their heavy dependence on weather and climate change, which affects their effectiveness in the conversion of renewable energy. Faced with this conflict, it is essential to optimize the performance of renewable systems in order to increase their efficiency. Several unconventional approaches to optimization have been developed in the literature. In this chapter, the management of a hybrid renewable energy system is optimized by intelligent approach based on particle swarm optimization comprising a shaded photovoltaic generator and a wind generator.

Chapter 4
Design of Low Order Controllers for Decoupled MIMO Systems With Time Response Specifications 90
Maher Ben Hariz, Université de Tunis El Manar, Ecole Nationale d'Ingénieurs de Tunis, Tunisia
Wassila Chagra, Université de Tunis El Manar, Institut Préparatoire Aux études d'Ingénieurs d'El Manar, Ecole Nationale d'Ingénieurs de Tunis, Tunisia
Faouzi Bouani, Université de Tunis El Manar, Ecole Nationale d'Ingénieurs de Tunis, Tunisia

The design of a low order controller for decoupled MIMO systems is proposed. The main objective of this controller is to guarantee some closed loop time response performances such as the settling time and the overshoot. The controller parameters are obtained by resolving a non-convex optimization problem. In order to obtain an optimal solution, the use of a global optimization method is suggested. In this chapter, the proposed solution is the GGP method. The principle of this method consists of transforming a non-convex optimization problem to a convex one by some mathematical transformations. So as to accomplish the fixed goal, it is imperative to decouple the coupled MIMO systems. To approve the controllers' design method, the synthesis of fixed low order controller for decoupled TITO systems is presented firstly. Then, this design method is generalized in the case of MIMO systems. Simulation results and a comparison study between the presented approach and a PI controller are given in order to show the efficiency of the proposed controller. It is remarkable that the obtained solution meets the

desired closed loop time specifications for each system output. It is also noted that by considering the proposed approach the user can fix the desired closed loop performances for each output independently.

Shikha Singh, Jamia Millia Islamia, India
Ahmad Taher Azar, Benha University, Egypt & Nile University, Egypt
Muzaffar Ahmad Bhat, Jamia Millia Islamia, India
Sundarapandian Vaidyanathan, Vel Tech University, India
Adel Ouannas, University of Larbi Tebessi, Algeria

This chapter investigates the multi-switching combination synchronization of three non-identical chaotic systems via active control technique. In recent years, some advances have been made with the idea of multi-switching combination synchronization. The different states of the master systems are synchronized with the desired state of the slave system in multi-switching combination synchronization scheme. The relevance of such kinds of synchronization studies to information security is evident in the wide range of possible synchronization directions that exist due to multi-switching synchronization. Numerical simulations justify the validity of the theoretical results discussed.

Naglaa Kamel Bahgaat, Canadian International College (CIC), Egypt
Mohamed Ibrahim, Al Azhar University, Egypt
Mohamed Ahmed Moustafa Hassan, Cairo University, Egypt
Fahmy Bendary, Benha University, Egypt

This chapter gives introduction to evolutionary techniques. Then it presents the problem formulation for load frequency control with evolutionary particle swarm optimization. It gives the application of particle swarm optimization (PSO) in load frequency control; also, it illustrates the use of an adaptive weight particle swarm optimization (AWPSO) and adaptive accelerated coefficients based PSO (AACPSO). Furthermore, it introduces a new modification for AACPSO technique (MAACPSO). The new technique is explained. A well-done comparison will be given in this chapter for these above-mentioned techniques. A reasonable discussion on the obtained results will be displayed. The obtained results are promising.

Saber Krim, University of Monastir, Tunisia
Soufien Gdaim, University of Monastir, Tunisia
Abdellatif Mtibaa, University of Monastir, Tunisia
Mimouni Mohamed Faouzi, National Engineering School of Monastir, Tunisia

Photovoltaic system applications should operate under good conditions. The maximum power point depends on the sunlight angle on the panel surface. In this chapter, an induction motor (IM) controlled with a direct torque control (DTC) is used to control the photovoltaic panel position. The conventional DTC is chosen thanks to its capability to develop the maximum of torque when the motor is standstill. However, the DTC produces a torque with high ripples and it is suffer from the flux demagnetization phenomenon, especially at low speed. To overcome these problems, two DTC approaches are proposed in this chapter: (1) the DTC based on the fuzzy logic and (2) the DTC based on space vector modulation (SVM) and proportional integral (PI) controllers (DTC-SVM-PI). The suggested approaches are implemented on a field programmable gate array (FPGA) Virtex 5 circuit in order to reduce the sampling period of the system and the delay in the control loop. The simulation and hardware implementation results demonstrate that the DTC-SVM-PI offers best the results in terms of ripples.

The voltage regulator may be used to regulate one or more AC or DC voltages in power systems. Voltage regulator may be designed as a simple "feed-forward" or may include "negative feedback" control loops. It may use an electronic components or electromechanical mechanism on the design. AVR is keeping constant output voltage of the generator in a specified range. The PID controller can used to provide the control requirements. This chapter discusses some modern techniques to get the best possible tuning controller parameters for automatic voltage regulator techniques such as particle swarm optimization, adaptive weight particle swarm optimization, adaptive acceleration coefficients, adaptive acceleration coefficients. Also, it presents a new adjustment modified adaptive acceleration coefficients and a discussion of the results of the all methods used. Simulation for comparison between the proposed methods and the obtained results are promising.

This chapter presents a new method for loss of excitation (LOE) faults detection in hydro-generators using adaptive neuro fuzzy inference system (ANFIS). The investigations were done under a complete loss of excitation conditions, and a partial loss of excitation conditions in different generator loading conditions. In this chapter, four different techniques are discussed according to the type of inputs to the proposed ANFIS unit, the generator terminal impedance measurements (R and X) and the generator terminal voltage and phase current (Vtrms and Ia), the positive sequence components of the generator terminal voltage magnitude, phase current magnitude and angle ($|V+ve|$, $|I+ve|$ and $\angle I+ve$) in addition to the stator current 3rd harmonics components (magnitudes and angles). The proposed techniques' results are compared with each other and are compared with the conventional distance relay response in addition to other techniques. The promising obtained results show that the proposed technique is efficient.

In this chapter, a new technique has been proposed for reducing the harmonic content of a three-phase PWM rectifier connected to the networks with a unit power factor and also providing decoupled control of the active and reactive instantaneous power. This technique called direct power control (DPC) is based on artificial neural network (ANN) controller, without line voltage sensors. The control technique is based on well-known direct torque control (DTC) ideas for the induction motor, which is applied to eliminate the harmonic of the line current and compensate for the reactive power. The main idea of this control is based on active and reactive power control loops. The DC voltage capacitor is regulated by the ANN controller to keep it constant and also provides a stable active power exchange. The simulation results are very satisfactory in the terms of stability and total harmonic distortion (THD) of the line current and the unit power factor.

In this chapter, the dynamics of a particular topology of Colpitts oscillator with fractional order dynamics is presented. The first part is devoted to the dynamics of the model using standard nonlinear analysis techniques including time series, bifurcation diagrams, phase space trajectories plots, and Lyapunov exponents. One of the major results of this innovative work is the numerical finding of a parameter region in which the fractional order Colpitts oscillator's circuit experiences multiple attractors' behavior. This phenomenon was not reported previously in the Colpitts circuit (despite the huge amount of related research works) and thus represents an enriching contribution to the understanding of the dynamics

The aim of this chapter is to investigate the effect of vehicle dynamics control systems (VDCS) on both the collision of the vehicle body and the kinematic behaviour of the vehicle's occupant in case of offset frontal vehicle-to-vehicle collision. The study also investigates the full-frontal vehicle-to-barrier crash scenario. A unique 6-degree-of-freedom (6-DOF) vehicle dynamics/crash mathematical model and a simplified lumped mass occupant model are developed. The first model is used to define the vehicle body crash parameters and it integrates a vehicle dynamics model with a vehicle front-end structure model. The second model aims to predict the effect of VDCS on the kinematics of the occupant. It is shown from the numerical simulations that the vehicle dynamics/crash response and occupant behaviour can be captured and analysed quickly and accurately. Furthermore, it is shown that the VDCS can affect the crash characteristics positively and the occupant behaviour is improved in the full and offset crash scenarios.

This chapter presents a study on the transportation mode choice behaviour of individuals with different socio-economic status. A previously developed system dynamics model has been adopted by differentiating the population mass into upper, middle, and lower classes. The simulation experiments with the model revealed that generally the upper class individuals would be more inclined to use a private car (PC) instead of public transportation (PT) when their tendency is compared to middle and lower class individuals. It was also observed that lower class individuals would be more willing to use PT instead of PC when their tendency is compared to middle and upper class individuals. As such, it would be difficult to encourage the upper class individuals to use PT instead of PC, and it would be successively easier to do so in the case of middle and lower class individuals. However, the results also indicated that under certain different circumstances, the upper class individuals would also prefer to go for PT, and the lower class ones could prefer to own and use PC instead of PT.

This chapter describes a system dynamics model developed for forecasting, prioritization, and distribution of critical supplies during relief operations in case of a hurricane event, while integrating GIS information. Development of alternates' routes selection through vehicle routing procedures and the results incorporation into this system dynamics model allows decisions about the operation in case of a major catastrophe and any preparation for future events. The model developed is also able to (1) establish people's decision and transportation characteristics that determine evacuation time; (2) simulate the behavior of key variables due to the relation between hazard level and people's decision to evacuate; (3) estimate for each natural hazard level the time frequency to order and the order size of each relief supply to be needed in shelters and points of distribution; and (4) reveal which routes cause more delays during relief supplies distribution.

In this era of globalization, adoption of information technology (IT) is one of the critical contributing factors of logistics companies' competitiveness and growth. This chapter investigates the investment in IT by an Indian-based logistics company on the logistics performance. Technologies like RFID, EDI, GPS/GIS, and ERP are chosen for improving processes like tracking and tracing, planning and forecasting, transportation automation, coordination with suppliers and customers, and decision optimization. Simulations are carried out using system dynamics modelling. The model is validated and sensitivity analysis is performed. Scenarios are generated under optimistic and pessimistic conditions.

Smallholder African systems operate in harsh environments of climate changes, resource scarcity, environmental degradation, market failures, and weak public and/or donor support. The smallholders must therefore be prepared to survive by self-provisioning. This chapter examines the nature of vulnerability of smallholders' food security caused by above conditions in the context of system dynamics modelling. The results show that smallholders co-exist whereby the non-resilient households offer labor to the resilient households for survival during turbulent seasons irrespective of the magnitude of external shocks and stressors. In addition, non-resilient households cannot be liberated by external handouts but rather through building their capacity for self-reliance. Using simulation evidence, this chapter supports the claim that in the next decade only resilient households will endure the extreme situations highlighted above. Future research that employs similar systems-based methods are encouraged to explore how long-term food security among smallholders can be sustained.

In this chapter, the design and development of a computational model of the cardiovascular system is presented for patients who have undergone the Fontan operation. The model has been built from a physiological basis, considering some of the mechanisms associated to the cardiovascular system of patients with univentricular heart disease. Thus, the model allows the prediction of some hemodynamic variables considering different physiopathological conditions. The original conditions of the model are changed in the Fontan procedure and these new dynamics force the hemodynamic behaviours of the different considered variables. The model has been proved considering the classic Fontan procedure and the techniques from the lateral tunnel and the extracardiac conduit. The results compiled knowledge of several cardiovascular surgeons with many years of experience in such interventions, and have been validated by using other authors' data. In this sense, the participation of a multidisciplinary team has been considered as a key factor for the development of this work.

Compilation of References 607

About the Contributors 668

Index 678

Preface

There are many real systems which can be modelled by dynamical equations. With the increasing requirement for high levels of system performance, it is imperative to deal with more complex systems as dynamical systems used to model reality have become more and more complex. The complexity mainly lies in nonlinearity, uncertainty, time delay, system singularity, strong interconnection, stochastic process, and so forth. The advancement of both scientific technology and control theory has provided the possibility to investigate complex dynamical systems. Study on complex systems becomes increasingly important, which has provided renewed impetus for development of novel techniques and skills for complex control systems.

Complex systems are pervasive in many area of science and we find them every day and everywhere. Examples include financial markets, highway transportation networks, telecommunication networks, world and country economies, social networks, immunological systems, living organisms, computational systems and electrical and mechanical structures. Complex systems are often composed of large number of interconnected and interacting entities exhibiting much richer global scale dynamics than they could be inferred from the properties and behaviour of individual entities. Complex systems are studied in many areas of natural sciences, social sciences, engineering and mathematical sciences.

This book addresses the nonlinear and complex system models considering the dynamical analysis, control, and applications. It involves modeling, non-ideal systems and applications, synchronization, and control for nonlinear systems, such as mechanical, electrical, electromechanical, mechatronic, and very complex systems. This book is intended to be a major reference book for scientists and engineers interested in applying new computational and mathematical tools for solving the complicated problems of mathematical modeling, simulation and control.

This book is mainly focused on the recent achievements and applications in the field of control and analysis for complex systems with a special emphasis on how to solve various control design and/or observer design problems for nonlinear systems, interconnected systems, and singular systems. The considered system is expected to involve at least two of the features such as nonlinearity, disturbances/uncertainty, fault, time delay, interconnections between subsystems, system singularity, stochastic process, and comparison between simulation and experiments.

The main advantage of this book that it is multi-disciplinary and it will attract a lot of researchers working in Control, Automation, system dynamics, simulations, modeling and related fields. With a broad coverage of the contents essential for the analysis and design of various control problems in control engineering practice, this book can also be used as a handy desk top reference during control applications.

This special issue is to improve the dissemination of advanced research in the area of Dynamical Systems and Control Theory that can fulfill the anytime-anywhere access dream. Original research papers are solicited in any aspect of innovative Dynamical Systems and Control Theory.

ORGANIZATION OF THE BOOK

This well-structured book consists of 19 full chapters. They are organized into two sections.

Section 1: Advances in Control and Chaotic Systems
Section 2: Applications of Dynamical Systems

Book Features

- The book presents the dissemination of advanced research in the area of Dynamical Systems and Control Theory
- The book chapters are lucidly illustrated with numerical examples and simulations.
- The book chapters discuss details of engineering applications and future research areas.
- The book chapters give a good literature survey with a long list of references.

The chapters deal with the recent research problems in the areas of system dynamics, automation, control engineering, intelligent control, chaotic systems and applications.

SUMMARY OF THE BOOK CHAPTERS

Section 1 contains Chapters 1-13 focusing on the area "Control and Chaotic Systems."

Chapter 1 describes a method for designing decentralized simulation and control architecture for multiple robot systems based on the discrete event net models. Extended Petri nets are adopted as an effective tool to describe, design and control cooperative behavior of multiple robots based on asynchronous, concurrent processes. By hierarchical decomposition of the net model of the overall system, global and local Petri net models are assigned to the upper level and the lower level controllers, respectively. For the lower level control, individual net models of robots are executed on separate local controllers. The unified net representation for cooperative control is also proposed. Overall control software is implemented and executed on a general hierarchical and distributed control architecture corresponding to the hardware structure of multiple robot systems.

In Chapter 2, a compensation for systems with saturation and backlash in series to the actuator is studied in order to obtain the proposed control strategy. The multivariable Proportional Integral (PI) H_∞ loop shaping design for mechanical systems with backlash is implemented in this chapter due to frequency domain characteristics. This approach is done by implementing the coprime factorization of a linearized model following the loop shaping design procedure. The PI H_∞ control strategy shown in this chapter consists in implementing two weighting functions as a pre-compensator and post compensator considering the linearized model of the nonlinear dynamics of mechanical systems according to their frequency domain properties. One of the main issues overcame in this study, is that the backlash nonlinearity is modeled implementing a describing function, something that it not only allows to ease the design of the proposed control strategy but also to find the limit cycles frequencies and periods. The describing function approach consists in the implementation of Fourier series to obtain a linear model of the backlash and other nonlinearities and to obtain a feasible loop shaping controller design. Also in this chapter, a frequency analysis is explained for this kind of mechanical systems using the Nyquist and the positivity criterion in order to analyze the stability properties of this kind of systems, which can be considered as an important contribution of this study. It is important to remark that the parameter tuning of the PI gains is done by particle swarm optimization (PSO) where an objective function is minimized in order that the system variables reach the equilibrium point faster and accurately. Finally, the stabilization of a cart-pendulum system implementing the proposed control strategy is shown corroborating the effectiveness of this approach.

In Chapter 3, the management of a hybrid renewable energy system is optimized by intelligent approach based on particle swarm optimization comprising a shaded photovoltaic generator and a wind generator. The main objective of this work focuses on thc optimization of the management of multi-source generators by intelligent techniques. Following a bibliographic study on the various hybrid technologies, the study has focused on the development of ordering strategies to meet specific requirements during the operation of photovoltaic and wind generators. In this context, attention was focused on the conversion of wind energy with particular interest to the control of the turbine pitch angle. In fact, this control is a practical technique for regulating the power generated above the nominal wind speed. Since the conventional methods usually uses a PI regulator to control the wind turbine pitch angle, the mathematical model of the system should be well known. As meta-heuristic methods can have potential when the system is non-linear, in this work a new PSO-based regulation technique is developed whose detailed and specific knowledge about the system is not required. Subsequently, the phenomenon of partial shading for photovoltaic generators was addressed. This phenomenon is responsible for the appearance of several peaks in the characteristics of the semi-shaded GPV. In order to circumvent the limitations of conventional techniques, an advanced technique based PSO has been proposed and to differentiate between the global maximum and the local maximum. The comparative study between the different methods developed stressed the robustness and performance of MPPT commands based on meta-heuristics. The studied wind /PV system was then integrated into a conversion chain coupled to the electrical network and controlled by power converters. The results obtained allowed to validate the simulation of the energy behavior of the studied system and to check the performance of the PSO control proposed in particular for the smoothing of the generated power.

In Chapter 4, the design of a low order controller for decoupled MIMO systems is proposed. The main objective of this controller is to guarantee some closed loop time response performances such as the settling time and the overshoot. The controller parameters are obtained by resolving a non-convex optimization problem. In order to obtain an optimal solution, the use of a global optimization method is suggested. In this work, the proposed solution is the GGP method. The principle of this method consists on transforming a non-convex optimization problem to a convex one by some mathematical transformations. So as to accomplish the fixed goal it is imperative to decouple the coupled MIMO systems. To approve the controllers' design method, the synthesis of fixed low order controller for decoupled TITO systems is presented firstly. Then, this design method is generalized in the case of MIMO systems. Simulation results and a comparison study between the presented approach and a PI controller are given in order to show the efficiency of the proposed controller. It is remarkable that the obtained solution meets the desired closed loop time specifications for each system output. It is also noted that by considering the proposed approach the user can fix the desired closed loop performances for each output independently.

Chapter 5 investigates the multi-switching combination synchronization of three non-identical chaotic systems via active control technique. In recent years, some advances have been made with the idea of multi-switching combination synchronization. The different states of the master systems are synchronized with the desired state of the slave system in multi-switching combination synchronization scheme. The relevance of such kinds of synchronization studies to information security is evident in the wide range of possible synchronization directions that exist due to multi-switching synchronization. The idea of multi-switching combination synchronization is implemented on three non-identical recently constructed novel chaotic systems. Brief analysis of the novel chaotic systems is also discussed. Numerical simulations justify the validity of the theoretical results discussed.

Chapter 6 discusses the application of evolutionary techniques in Load Frequency Control (LFC) in power systems. It gives introduction to evolutionary techniques. Then it presents the problem formulation for load frequency control with Evolutionary Particle Swarm Optimization (MAACPSO). It gives the application of Particle Swarm Optimization (PSO) in load frequency control, also it illustrates the use of an Adaptive Weight Particle Swarm Optimization (AWPSO), Adaptive Accelerated Coefficients based PSO, (AACPSO) Adaptive Accelerated Coefficients based PSO (AACPSO). Furthermore, and it introduces a new modification for AACPSO technique (MAACPSO). The new technique will be explained inside the chapter, it is abbreviated to Modified Adaptive Accelerated Coefficients based PSO (MAACPSO). A well-done comparison will be given in this chapter for these above-mentioned techniques. A reasonable discussion on the obtained results will be displayed. The obtained results are promising.

In Chapter 7, an Induction Motor (IM) controlled with a Direct Torque Control (DTC) is used to control the photovoltaic panel position. The conventional DTC is chosen thanks to its capability to develop the maximum of torque when the motor is standstill. However, the DTC produces a torque with high ripples and it is suffer from the flux demagnetization phenomenon, especially at low speed. To overcome these problems, two DTC approaches are proposed in this chapter, which are: (i) the DTC based on the fuzzy logic and (ii) the DTC based on Space Vector Modulation (SVM) and proportional Integral (PI) controllers (DTC-SVM-PI). The suggested approaches are implemented on a Field Programmable Gate Array (FPGA) Virtex 5 circuit in order to reduce the sampling period of the system and the delay in the control loop. The simulation and hardware implementation results demonstrate that the DTC-SVM-PI offers best the results in terms of ripples.

Chapter 8 discusses some modern techniques to get the best possible tuning controller parameters for an automatic voltage regulator (AVR) system of a synchronous generator. It was necessary to use PID controller to increase the stability margin and to improve performance of the system. Some modern techniques were defined. These techniques as Particle Swarm Optimization (PSO), also it explains the use of the Adaptive Weight Particle Swarm Optimization (AWPSO), Adaptive Acceleration Coefficients based PSO, (AACPSO), Adaptive Acceleration Coefficients based PSO (AACPSO). Also, it presents a new adjustment for AACPSO technique, Modified Adaptive Acceleration Coefficients based PSO (MAAPSO) is the new technique which will be conversed in this chapter, A discussion of the results of the all methods used will be given in this chapter. Simulation for comparison between the proposed methods will be displayed. The obtained results are promising.

Chapter 9 presents a new method for Loss of Excitation (LOE) faults detection in Hydro-generators using Adaptive Neuro Fuzzy Inference System (ANFIS). The investigations were done under a complete Loss of Excitation conditions, and a partial Loss of Excitation conditions in different generator loading conditions. In this research work, four different techniques are discussed according to the type of inputs to the proposed ANFIS unit, the generator terminal impedance measurements (R and X) and the generator terminal voltage and phase current (V_{trms} and I_a), the positive sequence components of the generator terminal voltage magnitude, phase current magnitude and angle ($|V_{+ve}|$, $|I_{+ve}|$ and $\angle I_{+ve}$) in addition to the stator current 3rd harmonics components (magnitudes and angles). The proposed techniques' results are compared with each other and are compared with the conventional distance relay response in addition to other techniques. The promising obtained results show that the proposed technique is efficient.

In Chapter 10, a new technique has been proposed for reducing the harmonic content of a three-phase PWM rectifier connected to the networks with a unit power factor and also provide decoupled control of the active and reactive instantaneous power. This technique called direct power control (DPC) is based on artificial neural network (ANN) controller, without line voltage sensors. The control technique is based on well-known direct torque control (DTC) ideas for the induction motor, which is applied to eliminate the harmonic of the line current and compensate for the reactive power. The main idea of this control is based on active and reactive power control loops. The DC voltage capacitor is regulated by the ANN controller to keep it constant and also provides a stable active power exchange. To test the feasibility and functionality and robustness of the Artificial Neural Network Controller (ANN), various simulations scenarios have been performed. The simulation results are very satisfactory in the terms of stability and total harmonic distortion (THD) of the line current and the unit power factor.

In Chapter 11, the dynamics of a particular topology of Colpitts oscillator with fractional order dynamics is presented. The first part is devoted to the dynamics of the model using standard nonlinear analysis techniques including time series, bifurcation diagrams, phase space trajectories plots, and Lyapunov exponents. A PSPICE simulation of the nonlinear dynamics of the oscillator are presented in order to confirm the ability of the proposed Colpitts model to accurately describe/predict both the regular and chaotic behaviors of the oscillator with the fractional order dynamics. One of the major results of this innovative work is the numerical finding of a parameter region in which the fractional order Colpitts oscillator's circuit experiences multiple attractors' behavior (i.e., coexistence of two different periodic and chaotic attractors). This phenomenon was not reported previously in the Colpitts circuit (despite the huge amount of related research works) and thus represents an enriching contribution to the understanding of the dynamics of Chua's oscillator. The second part of this chapter deals with the synchronization of fractional order system. Based on fractional-order Lyapunov stability theory, this chapter provides a novel method to achieve generalized and phase synchronization of two and network fractional-order chaotic Colpitts oscillator's respectively. Finally, simulations are given to verify the effectiveness of the proposed control approach.

In Chapter 12, a dynamical model that describes the interaction between the HIV virus and the human immune system is presented. This model is used to investigate the effect of antiretroviral therapy, consisting of RTI and PI drugs, along with the result of undesired treatment interruption. Furthermore, the effect of both drugs can be combined into a single parameter that further simplifies the model into a single input system. The value of the drug inputs can be adjusted so that the system has the desired equilibrium. Drug administration can also be adjusted by a feedback control law which although linearizes the system, may have issues in its implementation. Furthermore, the system is linearized around the equilibrium, leading to a system of linear differential equations of first order that can be integrated into courses of control systems engineering, linear and nonlinear systems in higher education.

Chapter 13 work announces a new four-dimensional hyperchaotic system having two positive Lyapunov exponents, a zero Lyapunov exponent and a negative Lyapunov exponent. Since the sum of the Lyapunov exponents of the new hyperchaotic system is shown to be negative, it is a dissipative system. The phase portraits of the new hyperchaotic system are displayed with both two-dimensional and three-dimensional phase portraits. Next, the qualitative properties of the new hyperchaotic system are dealt with in detail. It is shown that the new hyperchaotic system has three unstable equilibrium points. Explicitly, it is shown that the equilibrium at the origin is a saddle-point, while the other two equilibrium points are saddle-focus equilibrium points. Thus, it is shown that all three equilibrium points of the new hyperchaotic system are unstable. Dynamical properties such as symmetry and invariance are also discussed for the new hyperchaotic system. Furthermore, Lyapunov exponents and Kaplan-Yorke dimension are derived for the new hyperchaotic system. Next, new results are derived for the global stabilization for the new hyperchaotic system with unknown parameters using adaptive control. Also, new results are derived for the complete hyperchaos synchronization of a pair of identical new hyperchaotic systems with unknown parameters, called as *master* and *slave* systems, using adaptive control. All the new control and synchronization results for the new hyperchaotic system are established using Lyapunov stability theory. Numerical simulations with MATLAB have been shown to validate and demonstrate all the new results derived in this paper. Finally, a circuit design of the new hyperchaotic system is implemented in MultiSim to validate the theoretical model.

Section 2 contains Chapters 14-19 focusing on the area "Applications of Dynamical Systems."

Chapter 14 investigates the effect of vehicle dynamics control systems (VDCS) on both the collision of the vehicle body and the kinematic behaviour of the vehicle's occupant in case of offset frontal vehicle-to-vehicle collision. The study also investigates the full-frontal vehicle-to-barrier crash scenario. A unique 6-Degree-of-Freedom (6-DOF) vehicle dynamics/crash mathematical model and a simplified lumped mass occupant model are developed. The first model is used to define the vehicle body crash parameters and it integrates a vehicle dynamics model with a vehicle front-end structure model. The second model aims to predict the effect of VDCS on the kinematics of the occupant. It is shown from the numerical simulations that the vehicle dynamics/crash response and occupant behaviour can be captured and analysed quickly and accurately. Furthermore, it is shown that the VDCS can affect the crash characteristics positively and the occupant behaviour is improved in the full and offset crash scenarios.

Chapter 15 presents a study on the transportation mode choice behaviour of individuals with different socio-economic status. A previously developed system dynamics model has been adopted by differentiating the population mass into upper, middle and lower classes. The simulation experiments with the model revealed that generally the upper-class individuals would be more inclined in using private car (PC) instead of public transportation (PT) when their tendency is compared to middle and lower-class individuals. It was also observed that lower class individuals would be more willing to use PT instead of PC when their tendency is compared to middle and upper-class individuals. As such, it would be difficult to encourage the upper-class individuals to use PT instead of PC, and it would be successively easier to do so in the case of middle and lower-class individuals. However, the results also indicated that under certain different circumstances, the upper-class individuals would also prefer to go for PT, and the lower-class ones could prefer to own and use PC instead of PT.

Chapter 16 describes a system dynamics model developed for forecasting, prioritization, and distribution of critical supplies during relief operations in case of a hurricane event, while integrating GIS information. Development of alternates' routes selection through vehicle routing procedures and the results incorporation into this system dynamics model allows to make decisions about the operation in case of a major catastrophe and any preparation for future events. The model developed is also able to (1) establish people's decision and transportation characteristics that determine evacuation time; (2) simulate the behavior of key variables due to the relation between hazard level and people's decision to evacuate; (3) estimate for each natural hazard level the time frequency to order and the order size of each relief supply to be needed in shelters and points of distribution; and (4) reveal which routes cause more delays during relief supplies distribution.

Chapter 17 investigates the investment in IT by an Indian based logistics company on the logistics performance. Technologies like RFID, EDI, GPS/GIS and ERP are chosen for improving processes like tracking and tracing, planning and forecasting, transportation automation, coordination with suppliers and customers and decision optimization. Simulations are carried out using system dynamics modelling. The model is validated and sensitivity analysis is performed. Scenarios are generated under optimistic and pessimistic conditions.

Chapter 18 examines the nature of vulnerability of smallholders' food security caused by above conditions in the context of system dynamics modelling. The results show that smallholders co-exist whereby the non-resilient households offer labor to the resilient households for survival during turbulent seasons irrespective of the magnitude of external shocks and stressors. In addition, non-resilient households cannot be liberated by external handouts but rather through building their capacity for self-reliance. Using simulation evidence, this study supports the claim that in the next decade, only resilient households will endure the extreme situations highlighted above. Future research that employ similar systems-based methods are encouraged to explore how long-term food security among smallholders can be sustained.

In Chapter 19, the design and development of a computational model of the cardiovascular system is presented for patients who have undergone the Fontan operation. The model has been built from a physiological basis, considering some of the mechanisms associated to the cardiovascular system of patients with univentricular heart disease. Thus, the model allows the prediction of some hemodynamic variables considering different physiopathological conditions. The original conditions of the model are changed in the Fontan procedure and these new dynamics force the hemodynamic behaviours of the different considered variables. The model has been proved considering the classic Fontan procedure and the techniques from the lateral tunnel and the extracardiac conduit. The results compiled knowledge of several cardiovascular surgeons with many years of experience in such interventions, and have been validated by using other authors' data. In this sense, the participation of a multidisciplinary team has been considered as a key factor for the development of this work.

AUDIENCE

The book is primarily meant for researchers from academia and industry, who are working in the research areas – Computer Science, Information Technology, Engineering, Automation, Chaos and Control Engineering. The book can also be used at the graduate or advanced undergraduate level as a text-book or major reference for courses such as mathematical modeling, computational science, numerical simulation, nonlinear dynamical systems and chaos, control systems, applied artificial intelligence, and many others.

Ahmad Taher Azar
Benha University, Egypt & Nile University, Egypt

Sundarapandian Vaidyanathan
Vel Tech University, India

ACKNOWLEDGMENT

As the editors, we hope that the chapters in this book will stimulate further research in control systems and utilize them in real-world applications. We hope that this book, covering so many different aspects, will be of value for all readers. We would like to thank also the reviewers for their diligence in reviewing the chapters. Special thanks go to IGI Global, especially the book editorial team.

Section 1

Advances in Control and Chaotic Systems

Chapter 1
A Decentralized Control Architecture to Achieve Synchronized Task Behaviors in Autonomous Cooperative Multi-Robot Systems

Gen'ichi Yasuda
Nagasaki Institute of Applied Science, Japan

ABSTRACT

This chapter describes a method for designing decentralized simulation and control architecture for multiple robot systems based on the discrete event net models. Extended Petri nets are adopted as an effective tool to describe, design, and control cooperative behavior of multiple robots based on asynchronous, concurrent processes. By hierarchical decomposition of the net model of the overall system, global and local Petri net models are assigned to the upper level and the lower level controllers, respectively. For the lower level control, individual net models of robots are executed on separate local controllers. The unified net representation for cooperative control is also proposed. Overall control software is implemented and executed on a general hierarchical and distributed control architecture corresponding to the hardware structure of multiple robot systems.

INTRODUCTION

As a wide range of applications emerges in various domains of robotics, multiple robot systems with autonomous cooperative behavior are gaining increasing importance (Lepuschitz et al., 2011; Kantaros & Zavlanos, 2016). A multi-robot system should be realized to achieve an advanced functionality that cannot be realized by a single robot through some kind of cooperation, such as mutual handling of the partner robot or shared object, and map exploration in large-scale fields (Zhou et al., 2013). The key solution for multi-robot systems is to realize the cooperation by autonomous robots, which is different

DOI: 10.4018/978-1-5225-4077-9.ch001

from generic centralized control systems. The control architecture should be intrinsically non-centralized, parallel control architecture. So, the modeling and analysis of multi-robot systems always must meet with difficulties related to the cooperation problem under non-centralized control. In addition to existing frameworks for embedded system design (Gargantini et al., 2009), integrated design environments should support the entire design process from specification to implementation, considering typical features of robotic activities apart from the conventional paradigms for control.

For robots to work together efficiently and reliably to accomplish tasks that are intrinsically distributed in space, time, or functionality, it requires increasing cost and system complexity in control and communication. Currently, every robot carries its own controller and their actions are coordinated by telecommunication among the robots, based on serial architecture just like trees. Autonomous robots are able to cooperate and partition the global task, and then independently plan and execute their own tasks. However, because of time uncertainty, it makes the scheduling problem of the coordinator non-trivial. From a hardware-oriented point of view, a robot itself is composed of modularized components for different functions, such as vehicle, manipulator, end-effector, hand-eye camera, etc., which are computationally independent from each other and are controlled in parallel; independent sub-controller for each component. Current robot sub-controllers are mostly dedicated to centralized motion control at this component level (Melkou & Hamerlain, 2014; Mnasser et al., 2014; Mousa et al., 2015; Rajasekaran et al., 2014), where the communication between the sub-controllers can make cooperation between the components possible through a high-speed bus architecture or point-to-point architecture. Multi-robot systems with a centralized controller can be easily implemented in a well-defined environment, but often perform rather poorly under unknown dynamic environments. The application of model-based techniques is not suitable, because the growing complexity makes the maintenance of a model of the system dynamics unfeasible. Generally, complex control systems are partitioned in multiple components for simpler programming and management, but interrelationships become more complex. If the computer hardware architecture reflects the robot hardware architecture, a clear overview of the system can be provided, making it easier to develop, to debug and to extend. One of the advantages is that each processor can be specialized to its own job and the programmer can concentrate on the control algorithms separated from the input/output functions. Thus, distributed methods are more attractive due to their robustness, flexibility, and adaptability. Although, by allocating one processor to each component, the components can work in parallel and the execution time is reduced, an integral controller with parallel architecture should be implemented to perform the complex coordination tasks for integrated management of multi-robot task execution in lots of situations. A major challenge in distributed control systems is to cope with the distributed nature of events and the lack of central interventions in a dynamic environment.

Continuous advances in hardware, software and communication components increase the expectations on the performance of the robotic systems in terms of flexibility, reliability and responsiveness, by distributed control design that gives more autonomy to robot controllers and other field-level controllers with self-monitoring and maintenance properties. Many natural and manmade systems have hierarchically evolved in such a way that control is exercised in the most economical manner towards hierarchically autonomous self-organizing systems, as a major field of bio-inspired artificial intelligence. However, it is not easy to predict an emerging behavior resulting from a set of local interaction rules in a distributed control system. It is more difficult to identify the rules behind an observed global behavior, such as a component (cell)-based algorithm of self-assembly of arbitrary 3D shapes in analogy with an embryonic development process under gene regulatory networks.

Although there have been many studies on various types of intelligent control methods and control systems have been proposed (Azar & Vaidyanathan, 2015a, b,c; Azar & Vaidyanathan 2016; Zhu & Azar, 2015; Azar & Zhu, 2015; Meghni et al, 2017a,b,c; Boulkroune et al, 2016a,b; Ghoudelbourk et al., 2016; Vaidyanathan & Azar, 2016), there is still no standard representation for multi-robot cooperation as an advanced robot intelligence. So, it is required to develop a unified control methodology that can handle control problems concerned with competitive, collaborative and cooperative behaviors of multiple robots. The unique features of multi-robot cooperation systems are asynchronism, order, and parallelism. Petri nets are capable of representing all of these characteristics effectively (Silva et al., 2014). Ordinary Petri nets are preferred because the Petri net supports powerful analysis techniques and provides needed tools to design, analyze, and evaluate event based robotic systems.

One of inherent advantages of Petri nets over automata is the ability to decompose or modularize complex systems. The combining of two or more interacting asynchronous systems modeled as automata rapidly increases the complexity of the automaton model, hiding some of intuitive structure involved in the combination. Conversely, in a Petri net, the individual components and the level of interaction can be easily discerned to decompose the system into logically distinct modules. Thus, Petri nets form a much more natural framework for these situations, by capturing the concurrent nature of separate processes forming a discrete event system and making it easier to visualize the intuitive structure. If the interacting systems are modeled as Petri nets, the combined system is easy to obtain by leaving the original nets as they are, simply adding and/or merging a few places and/or transitions, such that the Petri net can grow linearly when system components are added. Further, a Petri net is featured, as a runtime simulator, with an intuitive capability in visual representation of the discrete event control logic, and can be employed with other techniques such as object-oriented programming, knowledge-based systems, fuzzy logic, neural networks, etc.

The paper describes the design of decentralized cooperative control architecture for multi-robot systems. Petri nets are used, as an extension of finite state automata, for representing passive or reflexive goal-based robot activities, including parallel execution, synchronization, and resource sharing, with their hierarchical composition and decomposition (Yasuda, 2015; 2016). Since robotic activities have the features of passive, asynchronous, concurrent processes and hierarchically organized into the behavior and the action levels, Petri net based hierarchical and distributed control architecture is proposed, where the process and control software structure reflects the hardware structure of the robot system. A task-oriented, discrete event driven hierarchical and control scheme is presented and discussed for an example multi-robot system.

BACKGROUND

In software based robot control, the behaviors level has the advantage of being easily parallelized. A behavior is a relatively simple, mostly passive sensor-effector connection and the global behavior of the robot is a result of the interactions between the independent behaviors. The advantages include high reactivity by suppressing the chain of sensor-modeling-planning-action. The main problem is to find the different behaviors and arbitrate them. Typically, the behaviors have different priorities, such that the high-level behaviors can inhibit or subsume the behaviors of the lower levels. The original concern in the synthesis of non-centralized systems evolved from a bio-inspired approach proposed in the author's doctoral thesis in the beginning of the 70's was revisited to provide the behavior based synthesis where the distributed autonomous agents have its behavior represented by processes described in Petri nets. For example, our first mobile robots have the capabilities of the three primitive passive or reflexive behaviors: following a colleague, avoiding a colleague, and avoiding other obstacles, according to the rule of detection of the colleagues and obstacles using the infrared sensors module, where the actuation mode for the effectors is selectively determined according to the specified sensing and actuation rule after classification of the sensing results (Yasuda, 1971; Mori, 1975), where the 'following' action is goal-directed, while obstacle avoidance is model-based. Petri nets are suitable for the representation of such passive model-based and goal-based behaviors. When two robots meet within the colleague avoidance region, they wait a specified time and then the 'following' or 'avoiding' action is selected according to the above rule. As an experimental result, small individual differences in hardware for sensing, timer, actuation were amplified so that macroscopic behaviors by associated robots emerged, such as grouping, coalition, separation, etc.

To achieve mobile navigation and manipulation task goals in dynamic, unstructured environments, separate behavior modules, each of which contains some grain of expertise manipulating objects, were arranged in several levels of competence. As a more practical method, appropriate information to provide alternative control paths according to the possible events is specified in real-time robotic assembly applications. As a bottom-up approach, behaviors can be composed on-line from a set of reusable feedback control laws or generic, task-independent control strategies using rule based composition policies that reflect human-like behaviors. The robotic behavior has a standard form consisting of inputs, outputs, pre-conditions, post-conditions, and the behavior activity. The pre-conditions and the post-conditions represent sensory information and determine respectively the conditions to start and end the behavior. The inputs and outputs are used to control the behavior execution and monitor the end status of execution respectively, which allows the execution of any of the behaviors at a time based on the starting pre-conditions of each behavior.

The robotic behavior represents the basic module of the task execution; the composition of the various behaviors will ultimately form the robotic task. Behavior based approaches does not use the task planning based on world modeling and therefore are effective due to fast execution and responsiveness to environmental change for simple tasks such as wall following. However, to perform accurate or optimal behaviors such as parts carrying to goal and soccer playing, an advanced control scheme should be added to achieve such complex tasks, keeping the properties of fast execution and responsiveness. In most cases of robotic control, situations involving concurrent actions in conflict are inevitable. For complex multi-robot systems, because the parallel execution of the behavior modules is important in achieving complex tasks, synchronization for conflict resolution and other cooperation should be supported as the constraint on the task-achieving process. Since difficulties arise due to the conflicts between the behaviors, where the overall complexity emerges from the parallel actions of the independent behaviors, several methods including learning and adaptation, should be added to avoid the deadlock problem (Li et al., 2012). However, any formal design methodology for distributed behavior-based robot control is not yet established.

Since robot systems essentially have the features of concurrency or parallelism at all the hierarchical hardware levels from multiple robots to intelligent devices, first of all, hierarchical discrete event system view should be set up. Further, control software architecture should be matched with the hardware structure at each level of the whole system. Petri net models are suitable to represent behavior modules and the systems that exhibit concurrency, conflict, and synchronization, although behavior modules may need one or more resources. They have well-accepted capabilities of expressing non-determinism and reactive behavior, which are essential features of embedded systems. In robotic systems, net models must have some important structural and behavioral properties, including safeness, liveness, conservativeness, reversibility, and real-time constraints. These properties are validated using reachability analysis, invariant analysis, siphons/traps approach, reduction method, and simulation. For the evaluation of models and the verification of crucial system properties, a wide range of simulation and analysis tools can be used. Further, Petri nets have the ability to represent the concurrency with which the change in conditions related to multiple events is decided according to the timing of these events, which can be used as a multi-task Turing machine.

Because formal methods, such as temporal logic, are hard to understand and manipulate than programming languages, nowadays, most of the works on embedded system design use UML (Unified Modeling Language) as system design language (Ali et al., 2012; Grobelna et al., 2014). The statecharts or state diagrams are adopted to extract the discrete event system dynamics of the UML framework design. Statecharts are designed as state machines and built by initial and final pseudo-states, and transitions having one input state and one output state. Each transition arrow has a label with three optional parts: event, condition, activity; if the current state is the specified source state and the appropriate event occurs with the specified condition, the transition is fired and the specified action is taken. However, UML can be used only for system specification, and not for analysis, synthesis and validation (Brisolara et al., 2009). Although Petri nets are not seen as an alternative to such design language as UML, finite state machines are equivalently represented by a Petri net subclass, where a place having two or more output transitions is referred to as a conflict, decision or choice and the representation of the synchronization of parallel activities does not be allowed. So, Petri nets are seen as a state machine generalization that allows the modeling of resources, parallel and concurrent activities and their synchronization. The translation from a UML statechart to a Petri net is simple such that each statechart state is converted into a Petri net place and each statechart transition into a Petri net transition with corresponding labels and tokens. When the usual Petri net is used to represent a multi-robot cooperation system, the net may be too complex to be managed. So in this approach, the overall control is decomposed into individual robot control and cooperation control information exchange is performed through messages, so that these are independent even though the robot controller is also written using the Petri net.

EXTENSIONS OF EMBEDDED CONTROL SYSTEM DESIGN TO ROBOTIC SYSTEMS

A design approach oriented toward multiple robot system applications, was established for hierarchical and distributed control systems as an extension of conventional embedded system design by identifying design principles for specifying system requirements, partitioning allocating processes to processors, and choosing a communication network. The present robot control architecture is composed of the hardware control level and the robot control level, following a well-established structure. The decomposition policy is based on physical parts of robot body, such as arm, leg, auditory, etc., considering real-time performance and grain size of subsystems. The hardware control level includes a set of procedures, or action control modules, for controlling robot hardware: motors and internal and external sensors, communication devices etc. The robot control level includes procedures for dealing with higher-level system coordination issues or from robotic motion control, multiple sensor data interpretation, navigation, planning and intelligent interfaces, realized as a community of individually acting autonomous cooperating behavior modules that share the information and services with the other modules. Cognitive subsystems can process efficiently information in higher levels of abstraction to detect normal or unexpected events and exceptions during the operation. Each module is aware of its role, learns the specifics of its changing environment locally and makes decisions to pursuit its own goal whereas the system of associated modules altogether pursues the global objectives which are not represented explicitly in any module. The hardware control level is represented as a server component that shares with other modules the information about the current robot state and the set of commands to control this state. In a distributed network system, where information exchange is performed through specific communication mechanisms, different communication strategies such as broadcasting, one-to-one, one-to-many connections, can be employed, with communication protocols to support resource sharing under different situations and conflict resolution schemes such as queues, locking, and priorities.

In a multi-robot system, because input/output peripheral devices are unevenly distributed, it would be more efficient to process in parallel than in serial and it is necessary to achieve both local and global control in real time. Global control means the strategy that controls the whole robot, including communication with other robots for synchronized cooperation, while local control means the execution of algorithms that control low level functions distributed in the robot, locally in real time using peripheral devices, notifying information to the other function modules. To perform global behavior by cooperation of such modules, a robot control system is built as an event driven system; interrupts are used to communicate every exceptional or normal event that occurs among modules through an event handler in each module and communication interfaces among modules are hided in a specific network. For achieving global control, although the planning or scheduling behavior of the robot is necessary, it is prepared as one of the functionally distributed module. The planning module should be operated in parallel with global control to balance the load and cooperate with each other using an intermediate network. Users or any external agents can define, as a global planner, a global task by using abstract commands and situations without being conscious of device control and the functions, just as living things. When the global planner receives events from any distributed module, it updates the corresponding database that manages the states of all modules, process the events, generate global actions, and request commands to the relevant modules, so that the modules perform according to the global task. Otherwise the task plan is locally scheduled by distributed, associated modules and virtual task agents representing the current task status and its goal as packet message routing in the internet.

In the control system development, first, the robotic task and environment requirements are specified to identify functionalities and attributes of the hardware and software architecture needed to complete the task. The control architecture is built based on the client server paradigm, where multiple clients are connected to a server, allowing distributed processing. The applications are composed of master and slave programs. The clients interface the physical elements such as sensors and actuators. Clients at the user site behave as master applications with graphic user interfaces running on smart mobile devices connected to a computer network such as Internet, while several clients at the local site behave as slave applications, executing commands from the master applications or processing data from sensors to provide feedback to the user. The server acts as the message router between the master and slave applications. A customized UML framework is used to describe every component of the robotic system, including class attributes, methods, and their relations of inheritance, composition and association providing a structural view of the software with the hardware locations of the components. Based on the above class diagrams, the interaction sequence and the messages passed among classes are described using UML sequences, collaboration, and use-case diagrams. Finally in the first phase, the statecharts are generated to provide a global view of the inherent states of the software components behavior.

When a robotic task is given, the task name, geometrical parameters of the objects to be used in the task, and the initial/final configuration of the objects (workpieces, parts, products, etc.) are specified. Then the task plan is built by generating task-oriented subtasks, which are arranged in sequential/parallel for achieving the given task goal and can be made autonomously or interactively. A batch of commands is planned to achieve these subtasks and then dispatched to the system coordination level. The system coordination level represents the plan-guided reactive control with functions to plan the required robot-oriented operations tactically and coordinate the lower-level controllers in real time reacting to the environmental change. Behavior commands, typically represented by sensing-actuation pairs, describe the behaviors to be taken to handle the objects in the task executing environment. The lower-level controller decomposes a behavior command into several interconnected executive primitive actions offline and then executes the action plan by activating the actions online, referring to the environment/object model. Actions are the atomic, generic movements of a robot that relate to at most one object in the environment, such as moving, hand opening and closing, holding, putting. Most of these actions are completed in a relatively short period of time by directly triggering the sensory/motor actions of the controllers. In contrast, operations refer to a complete sequence that is composed of different actions. For example, loading a part is an operation that can be decomposed into a number of actions such as reaching for the part on the table, picking up the part, moving the part over the table, and placing the part onto the table. The action/behavior modules are driven by the activated input states and have only one of multiple output states to be used as the activation signals for the other modules. Because the behavior commands are typically performed by coordinating multiple controllers in parallel, it is necessary to define several functional modules describing the control flow of executing modules. Several flow control modules are defined as follows. 'Fork' describes the parallel branches of the program flow, 'Join' triggers the output signal if all of input signals are activated, 'Or' triggers the output signal if one of the input signals is activated at least. Built in a hierarchical fashion, each behavior module can be composed of any combination of other behavior modules and action modules.

MODELING OF ROBOTIC ACTIVITIES USING PETRI NETS

In the next phase of control system design, the dynamics of the UML schematics is translated to Petri nets. For ordinary robotic systems, components are defined as state machines, with initial and final pseudo-states, transitions and simple states, where all transitions have one input state and one output state, representing the flow of control from state to state. Finite state machines are equivalently represented by a Petri net subclass, where a place having two or more output transitions is referred to as a conflict, decision or choice and the representation of the synchronization of parallel activities does not be allowed. The translation from a UML statechart to a Petri net is simple such that each state of the statechart is converted into a Petri net place and each transition into a Petri net transition with corresponding labels and tokens.

In a Petri net model of a robotic activity, an event can be modeled by a transition or by a place. In case that a transition represents an activity event: the start of transition firing indicates the start of the robotic process and the completion of the firing indicates the finishing of the process. In case that a place represents an activity event, a token inside the place indicates that the process goes on and the input and the output transitions represent the start and the completion of the process, respectively. If the activity time is determined by external environment then a place representation should be adopted. For example, in a picking action by a robot, when a robot is ready to work or enabled, the parts or tokens from the input conveyor belt or input place are consumed by the robot and the parts disappear inside the robot or action place during the process. When the action is complete, the parts are deposited into the output conveyor belt or output place.

In this work, for robot systems, a place or condition represents a state of robotic activity or motion, and a transition or event represents a change in robotic activity. The holding of an activity is shown by the token in the place and the activity sequence of a robot is graphically represented by the flow of tokens through the events. In a basic Petri net or condition-event net, a place or condition is represented by a circle, a transition or event is represented by a bar, holding of the condition by a black mark called token. Each element is connected with directed arcs. A marking is a column vector indicating a distribution of tokens among the places. If a sequence of transitions can fire from a marking and results in a new marking then the new marking is reachable from the old marking. The Petri net is said to be reversible if the initial marking is reachable from all markings that are reachable from the initial marking. The Petri net is said to be live if, under any reachable marking from the initial marking, any transition can be made enabled by firing some sequence of transitions. A P-invariant is a set of places, over which the weighted sum of tokens is constant for all markings reachable from any initial marking.

All of the activities are decided according to conditions and events. An event can be activated if and only if all of the pre-conditions and post-conditions are satisfied, demonstrating the sequential nature of the asynchronous concurrent processes. If the input conditions, composed of activity state and sensor state, are satisfied an event is activated, and as a result new output conditions are established. The sensor state in the input conditions can be thought of as a control signal, while the activity state thought as an output to the control system. The activation of an event is called the firing of the transition. Multiple conditions are activated simultaneously, and each event can be individually generated to move multiple tokens. For each transition, an activity is set up, where a subsumption control scheme can be used as the content of the activity, such as following the wall avoiding an obstacle, and carrying the workpiece, while following the guide lane. For example, when a robot is under the activity state of searching and given the sensor state of detecting a workpiece, at the timing of detection the event of activity change is activated to move the tokens to the new activity state of picking the workpiece and the new sensor state of proximity sensing. After the completion of picking, the next activity state is transferring it. By combining the nets of the single robots, cooperative behavior of multiple robots can be made possible.

For a net model to interact with the environment, it should perceive the environment through sensors and make control actions executed through actuators. As a method, sensory data is fed into the places as tokens. When a place is loaded with tokens, it triggers actuators executing the control actions coded in the tokens. As another method for interacting with the environment, a firing transition may trap sensory data and send output data to actuators. The transitions behave as agents for communication with the environment by the use of the pre- and post-processors of a firing transition; an enabled transition can call a pre-processor before it starts firing and after firing it can call a post-processor. The pre-processor also sends signal to the actuator to turn on its effector. Thus, a Petri net for the control have a function mapping the transition set onto a set of logical assertions containing logical variables, predicates, and events, and a function mapping the set of transitions/places onto a set of value assignments to control variables and events. For the use in simulation-based real-time control, Petri nets must be extended so that transition firing can be realized deterministically. The extended Petri net adopts the following elements as input and output interfaces which connect the net to its environment: gate arcs and output arcs. A permissive (inhibitive) gate arc is indicated as an undirected arc from a source to a transition with a small black (white) circle on the end. An output arc is indicated as an undirected arc from a place to a destination. An external permissive gate is interpreted as a relation between an external pre-condition and an element in the system, whereas an external inhibitive gate between an element in the system and an external post-condition. Figure 1 shows an example of extended Petri net model of robotic action control by transition firing with permissive and inhibitive gate arcs.

In the case of complex robotic activities composed of multiple components or subsystems, Petri nets of components are merged to obtain a composed Petri net by adding places, which represent that the signal is sent between Petri nets, and the corresponding input/output transitions of both Petri nets. The procedure to merge two Petri nets to generate a composed net is as follows. For corresponding transitions between two Petri nets, a communication place labeled as "Signal sent" or "Buffer" is built, and an output arc from the transition labeled as "Send" to the place and an input arc from the place to the transition labeled as "Wait" are added. If there is a transition that corresponds to a transition already connected to a communication place, then an input or output arc between the transition and the communication pace is added. Because initial marking of the composed Petri net must be referenced to the Petri nets, numerical labels of places and transitions are reorganized to create a joined marking and transition enumeration for the composed Petri net. Because the number of the input and output places of the corresponding transitions is not one, the composed Petri net no longer represents a state machine. In simple concurrent actions, such as grasping during moving, each action can be independently executed. In more complex concurrent actions, such as object tracking while environment measurement, two actions should communicate with each other through shared memory, which requires conflict-free access control between

Figure 1. Extended Petri net model of robotic activity control by transition firing with gate arcs based on command/reception concept

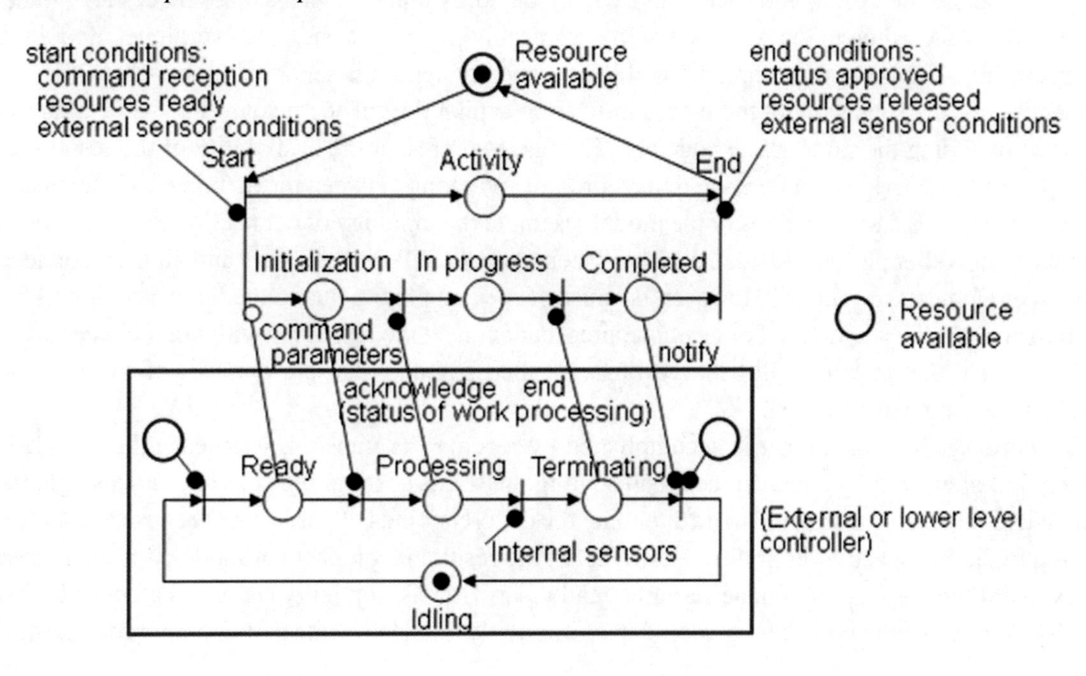

associated actions. The resultant net is also evaluated and merged with another net until it includes the complete robotic system that will operate as an event-based dynamic system.

NET MODELS OF ROBOTIC TASK SPECIFICATIONS

The net model for system control is designed as follows. First, the net model of the task or recipe specifications is constructed using the task-oriented approach. Net models of complex tasks are formed through sequential, concurrent, and conflicting relations among operations. If one operation follows the other, the places and transitions representing them form a sequential relation in the net. If the completion of the last one in a sequence of operations initiates the first one, a cyclic structure is formed. If two or more operations are initiated by an event, they form a concurrent structure starting with a transition, where two or more places are the outputs of the transition. If either of two or more operations can follow an operation, two or more transitions form the outputs from the same place. Two events that have the same pre-conditions and disjoint post-conditions are mutually exclusive, where one of them fires it disables the other. Second, the net model of resource specifications corresponding to each task specification is provided using the mutual exclusion concept. Then, the task and resource models are composed to yield the basic system control model. By analyzing and refining the basic model, a deadlock-free, safe, and reversible model is obtained. The Petri net formalism provides analytical methods for several behavioral properties such as reachability, boundedness, liveness, and coverability. These properties validate that the Petri net is deadlock-free, 1-bounded to avoid signal accumulation or bumping between clients and server, and between master and slaves, indicating that the processes represented by the Petri net are executed as defined by the task specification.

In current robotic tasks, a number of types of parts can be processed in a system concurrently. Each type requires a number of operations according to a prescribed sequence and route. It is straightforward to model such production processes based on Petri nets. For each part type, the activities in processing the part type are identified, and each activity is modeled by a place. Then, these places are connected by transitions according to the sequence of the corresponding operations. The overall net model is built by specifying a subnet representing a possible sequence of activities separately for each part flow, and connecting all the subnets with the places indicating availability of the resources. The resultant net is obtained by fusing the same places together. The places represent the availability of the resources and the status of the activities, while transitions represent switching between the activities. The connections between the places and transitions of the model resemble the topology of connection that exists between the robots and other physical elements in the system, because all the resources and all their connections with other elements are shown. However, because of the complexity due to the large size, it will be difficult to analyze the net model. For example, arcs that connect the resources with other elements induce cycles, which may introduce ill-behaved places, called siphons, that are emptied of tokens, causing deadlocks during net execution.

Reduction in size of the net is accomplished by forging the transitions representing the start and completion of an activity and the place representing the status of on-going activity, into a single transition, where token colors are used to differentiate the different kinds of parts flow because a resource can be used by different activities at different times. In the resultant compact net model, a place represents the availability of a specific unique resource, and a part flow is implicitly shown as a possible flow of activity. By another method, the processes can be implicitly modeled by the paths composed of prescribed resource places, with colors to describe different part flows. For manufacturing machines or buffers, a place plays a role as both resource and operation. A token in a place represents the machine is processing a part, or the buffer holding a part, while a robotic activity is represented by a transition with a self-loop of the resource place. Because the model is compact, some useful structural characteristics, concerning the deadlock avoidance problem, can be revealed (Wu & Zhou, 2009).

If an activity needs two or more specific resources at the same time, some kind of cooperation between resources is needed as constraints for activities by the associated resources. For further compact modeling, the resources are contained in the transitions that represent activities, without explicit representation of resources by places and all the connections between the resource places and the relevant transitions. The activities may reserve, use, and release resources during their operations, and the resource management including conflict resolution, can be accomplished by the underlying system in the background, just as real-time multitasking operating systems for conventional parallel programs._

DECENTRALIZED SYNCHRONIZATION FOR MULTI-ROBOT COOPERATION

In multi-robot systems, since cooperation between robots is the key problem, the net modeling of the associated robotic behaviors and their coordination mechanism is crucial. Since a task specification is provided as some connection of subtasks, the reference net models to coordinate the activities of the robot with respect to other robots are defined as net models of corresponding robotic behaviors. Because a cooperative task consists of several consecutive phases, coordination can be achieved by synchronizing the transitions of consecutive phases, such that the associated robots can end the current phase and start the new phase consistently at the same time by checking for internal and external events to synchronize the different robot activities accordingly for the most relevant phases and transitions.

Based on the hierarchical net modeling, in the behavior level different component behaviors are designed for each robot role. Petri nets are employed to organize these behaviors. From a view of asynchronous concurrent process, each behavior can be enabled if its pre-conditions are met, where pre-conditions and post-conditions are specified at the design stage. Possible sequences of behaviors are organized as extended Petri net according to the overall task plan and the physical constraints of robot itself. Following the behavior level, in the action level a sequence of actions is assembled for a specific behavior. Advanced behaviors such as obstacle avoidance, moving to sub-goal and wandering can be achieved by combining the component behaviors in a specific sequence, while at the lowest level an action control of a robotic mechanism is resolved into parallel control laws of the effectors, such as speed control and orientation control, applying PID control and fuzzy logic control respectively.

In the hierarchical structure, the place representing an activity at the upper level is detailed into a sequence of activities at the lower level, while the transition representing the start or end of the activity at the upper level corresponds to the transition representing the start or end of the sequence of detailed activities at the lower level. The upper level and lower level nets have two events in common and are connected by external gates. Thus, at the upper level, only the names of the events are represented for enabling the activity. Since these associated transitions, called a global transition, should be considered as representing the same global event, they should be fired simultaneously or at the same time in net execution. Thus, global transitions are employed as means to coordinate discrete event activities between levels in the hierarchical structure. The firing of a transition at the upper level invokes the execution of activities at the lower level by adding a token to the input place of the lower-level net. The transition continues its firing at the upper level until a token is added to the corresponding output place at the lower level. In a multi-robot system, a complex behavior or subtask at the upper level is cooperatively executed by two or more robots or independently executed by a single robot. So, in case of cooperative behaviors, the global transition is distributed into the lower level, composed of three or more transitions. For a global transition, if the constituent transitions at the upper and lower levels are enabled, then all the transitions belonging to the global transition are fired.

Further, beside global transitions, synchronization between transitions at the lower level should be performed directly between the lower level controllers, without intervention from the upper level. Such local, mutual coordination is also achieved through communication of the names of enabled transitions or events. All the communication for system coordination can be realized using gate arcs between levels and within the lower level. In parallel control of behaviors or actions, information exchange between components using shared memory may or may not be required. The information required for cooperation is extracted from external sensor. Many examples of local coordination through ad hoc master-slave control without intervention from the upper level are seen in human daily life, such as human conversations, negotiations, quarrel, etc., which represent the features of non-centralized systems. Each adjusts its action selection, generating interlocks, based on the evolution of the ongoing interaction, so that a conditional sequence of actions and goals or a joint plan emerges as a result, involving the temporary master and slaves. The cooperative interaction consists of a series of actions including communication acts such that one causes a change in the environment that triggers the pre-condition of the next action by the others (Taher & Abdeljawad, 2013). For an example robotic task, in handing over an object from a robot to another, the working site for handing over is a shared place, where mutual access control to the site is sequentially performed between the two robots, through external sensors and/or based on message sending and receiving directly without any conflict resolution mechanism such as an arbiter or synchronous timer. The robots independently plan and execute their own actions and the scheduling problem due to time uncertainty of mutual access to the shared place is resolved directly. Similarly, the pick and place operation by a robot from a conveyor site to a station table is directly performed through sequential access control to the shared working sites without the upper-level intervention. Only one action is selected at a time among three actions of picking, placing, and waiting with input and output conditions, using sensory signals or direct messages.

In the hierarchical net based control system composed of one system controller and several local controllers, the upper-level system controller is in charge of global system control based on task specification representing sequential relations between subtasks or robot behaviors, typically cooperative behaviors, together with associated resource assignments. The net models for resource specification with capacity are combined with the subtasks net models for task specification and used for global system control by the system controller. A net model for mutual exclusion consists of a place marked initially with a specified number of tokens to model the shared resource and a set of pairs of transitions to model each activity. The output arc attached to the place calls the function of conflict resolution to the resource as a local coordinator. Transitions competing for the place model the activities sharing the resource. If multiple activities are requested to the multi-robot system, where the robots represent resources shared between the different tasks, since more than one activity may require access to the resource with limited capacity, deadlock between the activities may occur. So, live, bounded, and reversible nets must be synthesized using verification or simulations at the design stage. In case of activities needing some specific resources and/or any other resources at the same time, for optimal management of system resources, the functions

Figure 2. Petri net model execution of individual and cooperative activities using distributed coordinator

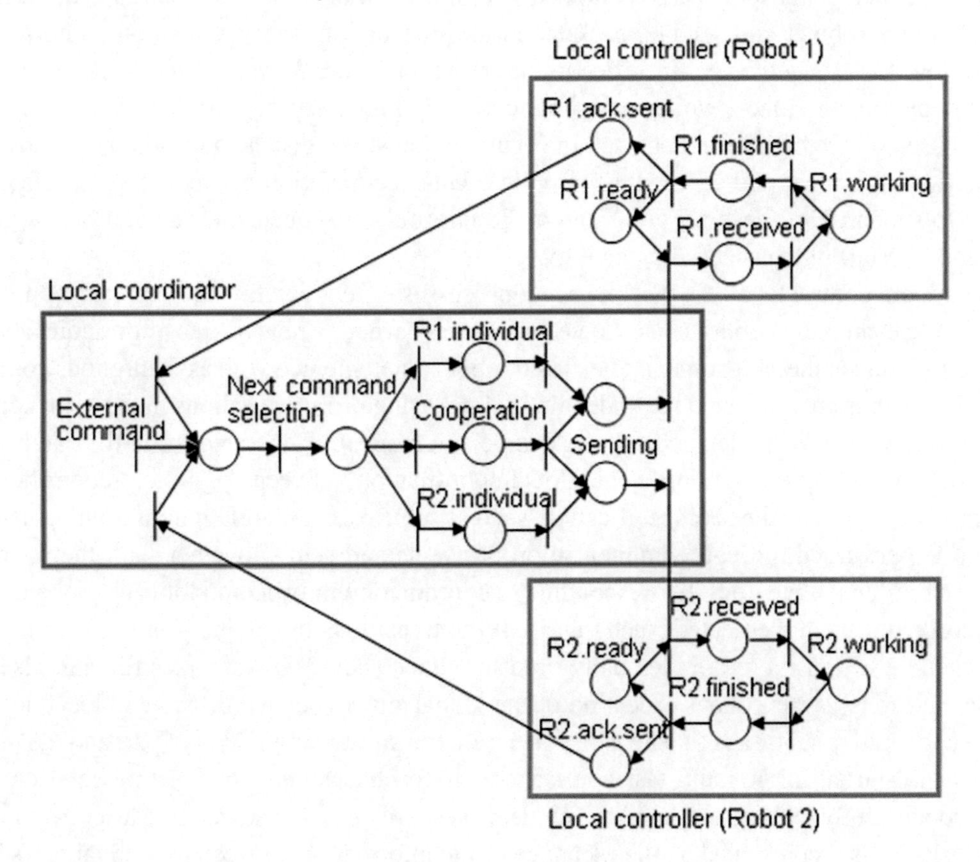

such as requesting and releasing resources, declaring and changing priorities of different transitions, and reporting resource usage time, are provided in the resource specification.

Behavior modules or system components are working in an infinite control loop where there are procedures to read internal and external sensors to avoid unwanted exceptions or failures. For example, when the robot is moving, if it detects an obstacle, it stops (interrupts) the subtask, and until the obstacle is removed or avoided it continues the recovery action. In communication between robots, when messages are transmitted, the acknowledgement should be received to continue its own execution loop; by transmitting the same repeatedly if necessary. Robotic motion tasks generally require exception handling such as recovery from hardware and software failures. The event based control design is appropriate as a way to avoid system failures, because it defines that an event should occur to pass from one system state to the next state, such that the associated sensors assure that the necessary event occurs.

EXAMPLE OF COOPERATIVE MULTI-ROBOT TASK

The example multi-robot task is carrying parts from the factory yard to depository, composed of two robots. Robot 1 picks up and loads the parts into Robot 2, as a robotic crane, equipped with a visual sensor and a force sensor for recognizing, positioning and grasping the parts. On the other hand, Robot

2 is a mobile robot to transport parts, equipped with a radio transceiver for communication receiving commands from Robot 1 and sending back feedback information from its position and obstacle sensors. The flow of parts in the task specification is shown in Figure 3, where each working site of parts is indicated by a macro place, while each robotic activity processed on parts is indicated by a macro transition based on the high-level Petri net. In Figure 3, the working sites indicated by a bold circle are sites shared by preceding and succeeding activities. Thus, cooperation between two associated robots is needed to synchronize these activities and avoid harmful consequence at the end of the preceding activity and the start of the succeeding activity.

At the system control level, the discrete event processes for cooperation are represented by detailed subnets of corresponding subtasks, as shown in Figure 4, where a shared transition indicates that the global event occurs at the same time in associated robots, implemented with asynchronous communication. The operations are translated into a detailed subnet using primitive actions in the local controllers. For the example system, the detailed subnets can be automatically generated using the database of net models of general robotic operations. The global coordination between the system controller and the robot controllers based on the task specification, such as subtasks causal relations and available resource allocation, is performed through communication of events and status together with the coordination information of global transitions. Corresponding to coordination information for each global transition, a local coordinator is implemented, such that if all the transitions belonging to a global transition are enabled, then these transitions are eventually fired simultaneously. The system coordination is achieved through concurrent, asynchronous execution of the global and associated distributed local net models. When the cooperative subtask is finished, the tokens are transmitted to each robot part and the individual operations will start again. In multi-task applications, for each task one global net model is created and executed concurrently with other global net models, as supply chain systems. Because the cooperation between tasks is also represented by the exchange of the information between individual tasks by using the inhibitive and permissive arcs, the interaction of tasks with robots can be clearly represented.

The picking action by Robot 1 is executed in parallel with the transporting action by Robot 2. Because, either of the robots must wait for the partner robot, according to the execution time of picking and transporting, the execution speed of picking and transporting should be optimally adjusted. After the picking action, the identification and the loading actions are executed in parallel in the local controller for Robot 1. Further, for efficient parallel execution in the local controllers, the succeeding actions may be loaded in memory as follows: the loading and the identification actions in the picking action, the picking action in the loading action, and the movement actions to the yard and back to the home in the transporting action to the depository.

Figure 3. Task flow graph of example multi-robot system

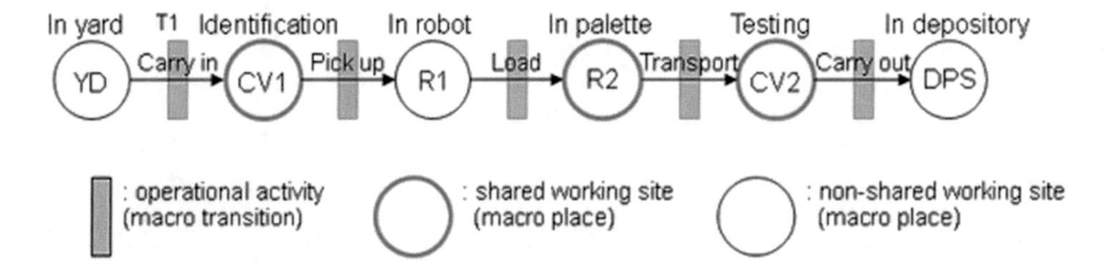

Figure 4. Global net model of example system with cooperative loading and transport operations by two robots

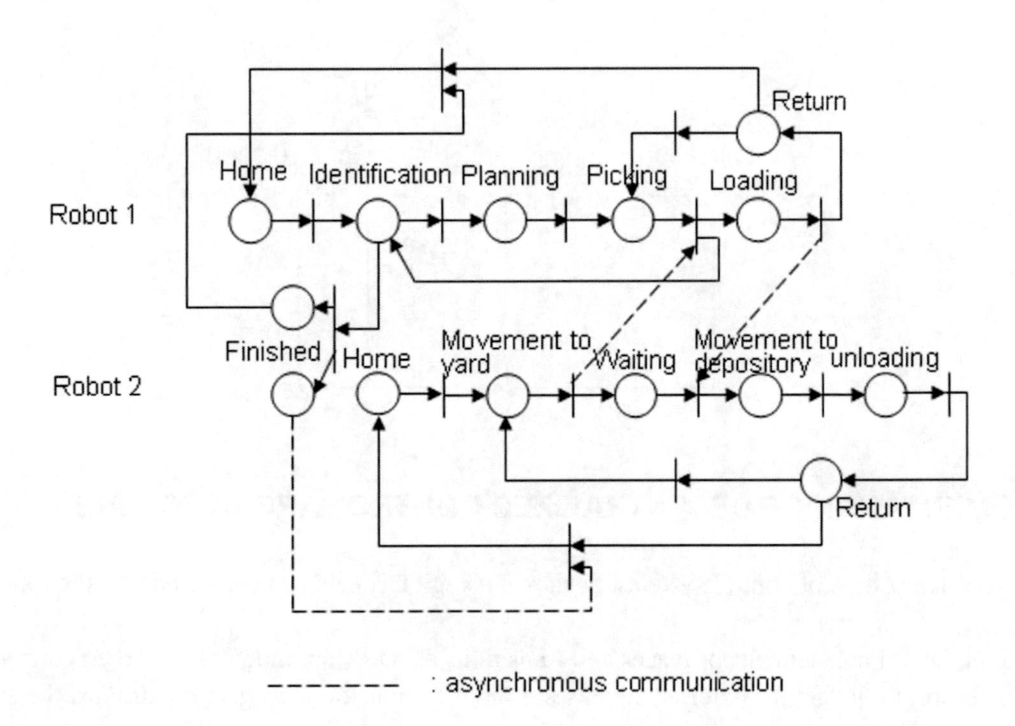

The positional information of reference objects and parts in the environment is shared through a map, which is managed by the map builder in the system controller, for the use in the picking action. The picking and movement actions are goal-directed and detailed into the following primitive actions: path planning, inverse transformation of kinematics, compensation of moment, and path tracking. The tracking action repeatedly executes PID feedback control for a pre-specified desired position. The obstacle avoidance is executed by an interrupt action with ultrasonic sensors during moving, like inhibitive interaction in the behavior based subsumption architecture, and the Petri net is represented as a self-loop output from the place. The detailed net model of transporting movement to a goal, interrupted with obstacle avoidance, is shown in Figure 5.

In the example system, synchronous sending and receiving actions of a part are performed through asynchronous communications without any global synchronization command, called local coordination, as shown in Figure 6 (a), (b). For the handing over behavior, the simple synchronization scheme using the gate arcs can be used, where the sender is a master while the receiver is a slave such that the master informs the slave of the end of waiting. For simultaneous occurrence of actions by two robots, more gate arcs are needed, considering the effective timing of permissive gate arcs, as shown in Figure 6 (c). All the communicating actions are arranged such that the aggregative dynamic behavior of the distributed net models with normal (non-shared) transitions is the same as that of the original centralized, aggregated net model with shared transitions. In case of autonomous, ad hoc cooperation without global coordination, one robot requests another robot to cooperate together, as shown in Figure 7. If the request is accepted, the robots are ready to cooperate and the communicating actions for synchronization are started.

Figure 5. Detailed net model of transport movement to goal with obstacle avoidance

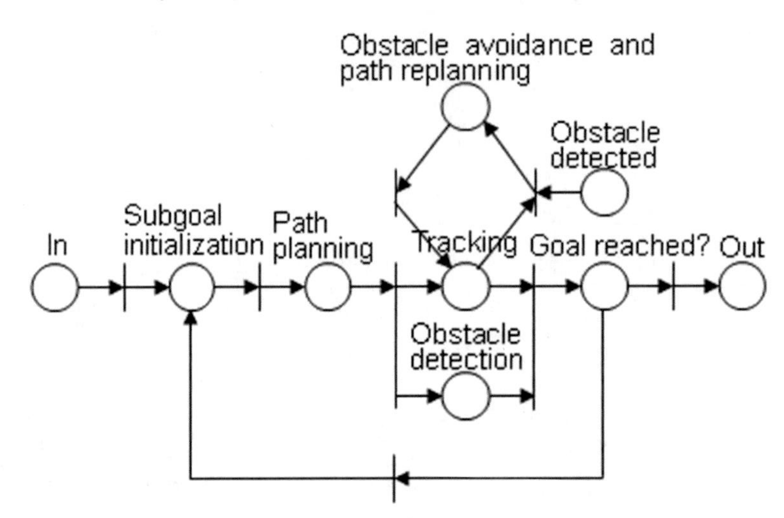

IMPLEMENTATION OF DECENTRALIZED CONTROL ARCHITECTURE

Methods of realization of control systems, designed using Petri nets, are classified into the following:

1. Realize Petri net elements or places and transitions as hardware modules, and then connect them according to the graph. External signals are input to transitions as gate conditions, the states of places are output to the external elements.
2. Decompose the Petri net into state transition diagrams, realize them by hardware, and then connect them with interlock signals.
3. Realize the Petri net execution algorithms by software, and then control the external elements through interface.

Because places and transitions in a Petri net are defined based on local states and events (Costa et al., 2010), decentralized implementation can be naturally realized. The net model of the system controller is designed in a top-down way, including task specification with resources and work types, while the detailed net models of local controllers are composed in a bottom-up way. The global net model for global task control is specified by connecting the resources and/or subtasks, shared places and shared transitions. The net models of the subtasks are decomposed into subnets of sequential processes, which are assigned to local robot controllers or their components and are aggregated into a macro transition with part and processing types as conditions for firing. The system controller executes the global net model, where each macro transition represents the cooperative activities by two or more robots, while each local robot controller executes the respective local net model with communication actions between local controllers, synchronizing the global activities between the system controller and the local controllers with events and status (Yasuda, 2015).

A shared place is implemented as a protected object to manage the synchronized mark (sending) and unmark (receiving) actions. When a shared place has several input or output transitions distributed in different subnets, the conflict is solved by a knowledge based approach as an arbiter or local coordina-

Figure 6. Net representations of synchronization of concurrent activities without global synchronization command: (a) pseudo-synchronous actions using two asynchronous communications, (b) simple representation using permissive gate arcs, and (c) simultaneous actions using gate arcs

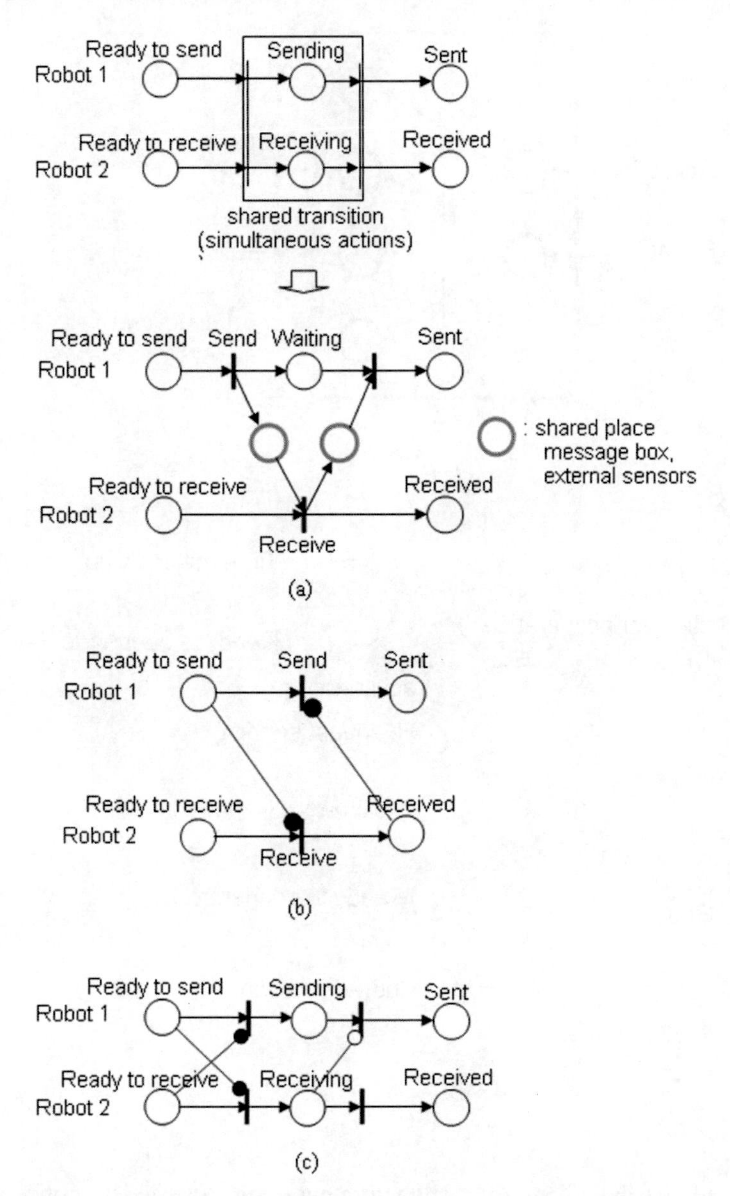

tor, which is also represented as a detailed net of the shared place, such that the transitions are fired in priority order, considering their operational requirements. A shared place may be implemented in one of the associated local controllers and can be created automatically with some rule such as the shortest response time for superficial non-centralized coordination, on the other hand a shared transition is implemented as communicating agents under the global task control or local coordination between local controllers. The aim of the local controller is to generate the synchronization signal that enables transitions in all the synchronized local controllers, for compact decentralized implementation without the system controller at normal operating situations (Costa & Gomes, 2009).

Figure 7. Net representations of ad hoc cooperation without global command: (a) global net model of individual or cooperative activity selection, (b) detailed local net model of negotiation by two robots using request/acknowledge message sending with gate arcs

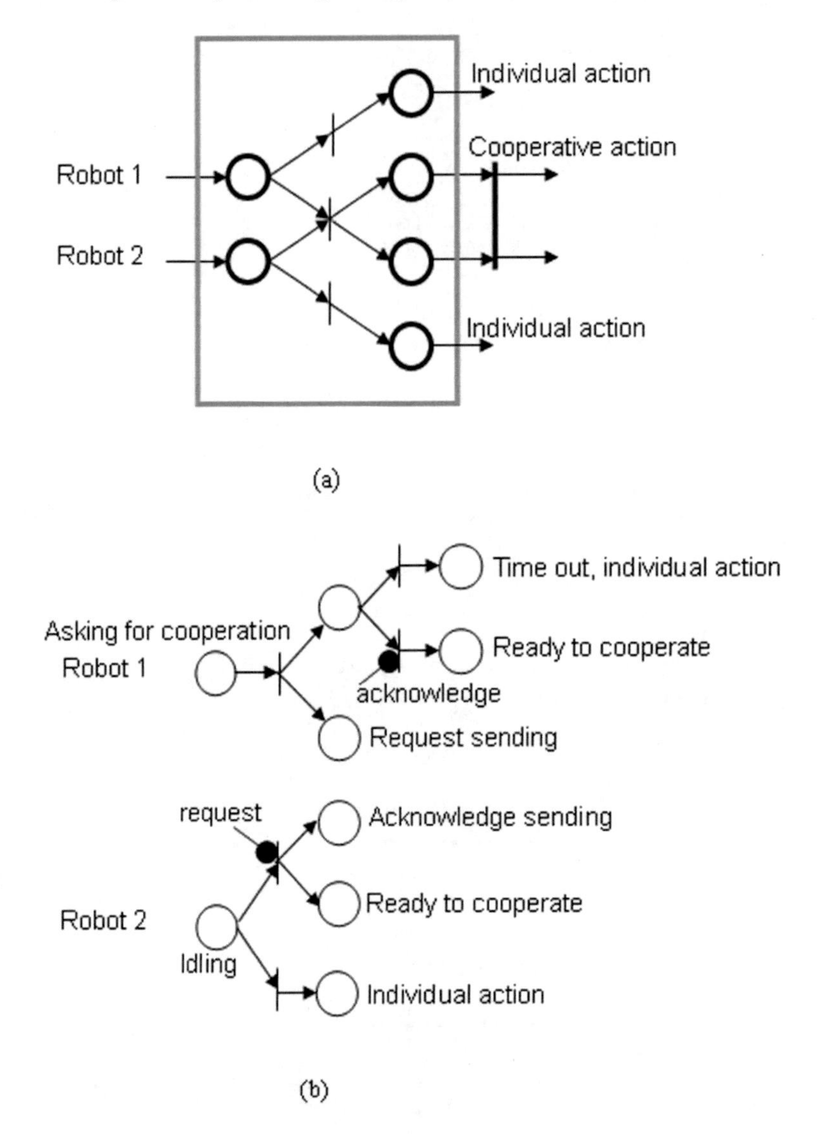

The Petri net based distributed control architecture based on server/client concept is shown in Figure 8. The Petri net simulator is used, as a runtime simulator, to control the real robot system according to the command/reception concept in real time, such that status or marking of the simulator is coincident with the status of the real robot system. The Petri net sends commands to the robot as a message according to the movement of the tokens. The simulator checks for any enabled and completing transitions. If there is any enabled transition, the transition definition file is run to make sure whether it can actually fire, satisfying all the guard conditions defined in the file including reserving resources for use by the activity. If an enabled transition can fire, then it is moved to another queue-like data structure. At the same time, input tokens for this transition are consumed from the respective input places. If there is any transition that is completing, then it is removing the input tokens and the output tokens are deposited into the output places of the end transition. After receiving a command, the firing of an event is determined by investigating the sensory signal of each robot. At the time of event occurrence for token movement, the message from the robot is transmitted to the Petri net. When the robot determines that the token for the current condition can be moved using the sensor information, which is given from the information of each place in advance, the event name is inputted to the Petri net server, which sends the conditions that must be done now and checked next, to the robot by messages. The robot uses this information to change its activity and sends back the occurrence of events judged from sensing of the situation. The simulator can be combined with a conventional real-time OS or multithread OS, where processes and their synchronization are specified by programs (Gharsellaoui et al., 2013).

The elements of the Petri net model and the static connections are defined in the net definition file, and initial inputs to the system and initial tokens are defined in the main simulation file. The interactions between the Petri net model and the environment are defined in the transition definition files. When a transition is enabled, because it has a token in its input place, it calls the files and is waiting for the arrival of start signal from an external sensor. After the transition starts firing, it sends the activating signal to the effector. While the transition is firing or in the in-progress phase, there is no change in the status of

Figure 8. Net model of local controller in Petri net based distributed controllers based on server/client concept

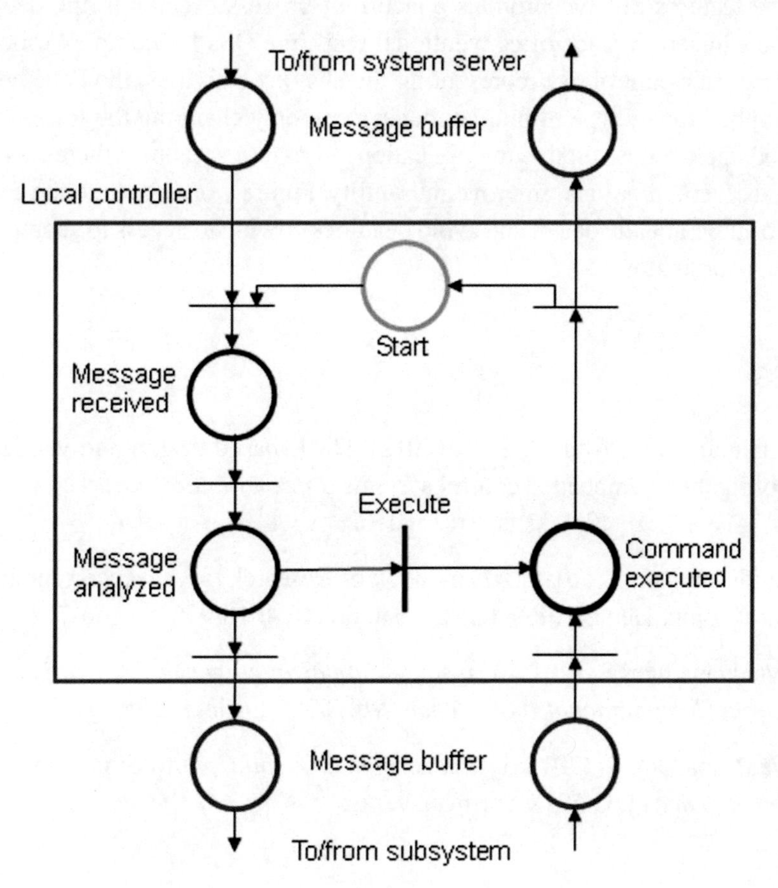

the actuation. When the transition firing has completed or the end transition is fired, the transition sends the inactivating signal to the effector and status report for analyzing to the simulator. The net execution program keeps periodically scanning; in each scan, a Petri net is executed in the similar manner as relay ladder connection diagrams of programmable logic controllers.

CONCLUSION

By separating a large net into several nets, a Petri net representation amenable to a decentralized implementation for multi-robot control systems can be produced. Due to global transition information for hierarchical coordination, decentralized, synchronized task execution in cooperative multi-robot systems has been achieved. The communication protocols for synchronization with other robots and requests of shared resource are simply and similarly realized with gate arcs from the places in the net models of associated local controllers. It is effective to consider the lower-level control of a single robot and the higher-level control of cooperative activity separately. A Petri net is used for the description of the task, so that each robot can get information regarding the task by connecting the robot client to the Petri net server. Further, to realize decentralized control, the Petri net can serve for communication between robots for message exchange of each robot state during cooperation. The applicability of the proposed coordination framework for both example single-robot and multi-robot tasks has been confirmed and successfully evaluated with centralized, nonhierarchical net models on a network of computers.

Because of the features of asynchronous concurrent process execution, the decentralized control framework can be adopted in place of conventional real-time OSs for complex robotic task planning, monitoring and real-time control. By representing the abstract activities, the Petri net based controller can be flexibly applied to any type of multi-robot system, only changing the lower-level control rules. Also, the proposed approach is suitable to applications in robotic systems where models of lower-level control are revised several times and improve reusability. Future works include the design of decentralized algorithms to automatically detect and avoid deadlocks owing to access to shared resources without any global system coordinator.

REFERENCES

Ali, A. B. H., Khalgui, M., & Ahmed, S. B. (2012). UML-based design and validation of intelligent agents-based reconfigurable embedded control systems. *International Journal of System Dynamics Applications*, *1*(1), 17–38. doi:10.4018/ijsda.2012010102

Azar, A. T., & Vaidyanathan, S. (2015a). Handbook of Research on Advanced Intelligent Control Engineering and Automation. Hershey, PA: IGI Global. doi:10.4018/978-1-4666-7248-2

Azar, A. T., & Vaidyanathan, S. (2015b). *Computational Intelligence Applications in Modeling and Control. In Studies in Computational Intelligence* (Vol. 575). Springer-Verlag.

Azar, A. T., & Vaidyanathan, S. (2015c). *Chaos Modeling and Control Systems Design. In Studies in Computational Intelligence* (Vol. 581). Springer-Verlag.

Azar, A. T., & Vaidyanathan, S. (2016). *Advances in Chaos Theory and Intelligent Control. In Studies in Fuzziness and Soft Computing* (Vol. 337). Springer-Verlag. doi:10.1007/978-3-319-30340-6

Azar, A. T., & Zhu, Q. (2015). *Advances and Applications in Sliding Mode Control systems. In Studies in Computational Intelligence* (Vol. 576). Germany: Springer-Verlag.

Boulkroune, A., Bouzeriba, A., Bouden, T., & Azar, A. T. (2016a). Fuzzy Adaptive Synchronization of Uncertain Fractional-order Chaotic Systems. In A. T. Azar & S. Vaidyanathan (Eds.), *Advances in Chaos Theory and Intelligent Control. Studies in Fuzziness and Soft Computing* (Vol. 337). Springer-Verlag. doi:10.1007/978-3-319-30340-6_28

Boulkroune, A., Hamel, S., & Azar, A. T. (2016b). *Fuzzy control-based function synchronization of unknown chaotic systems with dead-zone input. In Advances in Chaos Theory and Intelligent Control. Studies in Fuzziness and Soft Computing* (Vol. 337). Springer-Verlag.

Brisolara, L. C. B., Kreutz, M. E., & Carro, L. (2009). UML as front-end language for embedded systems design. In Behavioral Modeling for Embedded Systems and Technologies: Application for Design and Implementation (pp. 1–23). Hershey, PA: IGI Global.

Costa, A., Barbosa, P., Gomez, L., Ramalho, F., Figueiredo, J., & Junior, A. (2010). Properties preservation in distributed execution of Petri nets models. Emerging Trends in Technological Innovation, 314, 241-250. doi:10.1007/978-3-642-11628-5_26

Costa, A., & Gomes, L. (2009). Petri net partitioning using net splitting operation. In *Proceedings of the 7th IEEE International Conference on Industrial Informatics*, (pp. 204-209). 10.1109/INDIN.2009.5195804

Gargantini, A., Riccobene, E., & Scandurra, P. (2009). Model-driven design and ASM validation of embedded systems. In Behavioral Modeling for Embedded Systems and Technologies: Application for Design and Implementation (pp. 24–54). Hershey, PA: IGI Global.

Gharsellaoui, H., Khalgui, M., & Ahmed, S. B. (2013). Reconfiguration of synchronous real-time operating system. *International Journal of System Dynamics Applications*, *2*(1), 114–132. doi:10.4018/ijsda.2013010106

Ghoudelbourk, S., Dib, D., Omeiri, A., & Azar, A. T. (2016). MPPT Control in wind energy conversion systems and the application of fractional control (PIα) in pitch wind turbine. International Journal of Modelling. *Identification and Control*, *26*(2), 140–151. doi:10.1504/IJMIC.2016.078329

Grobelna, L., Grobelny, M., & Adamski, M. (2014). Model checking of UML activity diagrams in logic controllers design. *Proceedings of the 9th International Conference on Dependability and Complex System*, 233-242. 10.1007/978-3-319-07013-1_22

Kantaros, Y., & Zavlanos, M. M. (2016). Distributed communication-aware coverage control by mobile sensor networks. *Automatica*, *63*, 209–220. doi:10.1016/j.automatica.2015.10.035

Lepuschitz, W., Zoitl, A., Vallee, M., & Merdan, M. (2011). Toward self-reconfiguration of manufacturing systems using automation agents. *IEEE Transactions on Systems, Man, and Cybernetics. Part C*, *41*(1), 52–69.

Li, Z. W., Wu, N. O., & Zhou, M. C. (2012). Deadlock control of automated manufacturing systems based on Petri nets – a literature review. *IEEE Transactions on Systems, Man, and Cybernetics. Part C*, *42*(4), 437–462.

Meghni, B., Dib, D., & Azar, A. T. (2017b). A Second-order sliding mode and fuzzy logic control to Optimal Energy Management in PMSG Wind Turbine with Battery Storage. *Neural Computing & Applications*, *28*(6), 1417–1434. doi:10.100700521-015-2161-z

Meghni, B., Dib, D., Azar, A. T., Ghoudelbourk, S., & Saadoun, A. (2017a). *Robust Adaptive Supervisory Fractional order Controller For optimal Energy Management in Wind Turbine with Battery Storage. In Studies in Computational Intelligence* (Vol. 688, pp. 165–202). Springer-Verlag.

Meghni, B., Dib, D., Azar, A. T., & Saadoun, A. (2017c). *Effective Supervisory Controller to Extend Optimal Energy Management in Hybrid Wind Turbine under Energy and Reliability Constraints. International Journal of Dynamics and Control.* doi:10.100740435-016-0296-0

Melkou, L., & Hamerlain, M. (2014). Classical sliding and generalized variable structure controls for a manipulator robot arm with pneumatic artificial muscles. *International Journal of System Dynamics Applications*, *3*(1), 47–70. doi:10.4018/ijsda.2014010103

Mnasser, A., Bouani, F., & Ksouri, M. (2014). Neural networks predictive controller using an adaptive control rate. *International Journal of System Dynamics Applications*, *3*(3), 127–147. doi:10.4018/ijsda.2014070106

Mori, M. (1975). *The Three-eyed Beatles*. Presented at the International Ocean Exposition, Okinawa, Japan.

Mousa, M. E., Ebrahim, M. A., & Hassan, M. A. M. (2015). Stabilizing and swinging-up the inverted pendulum using PI and PID controllers based on reduced linear quadratic regulator tuned by PSO. *International Journal of System Dynamics Applications*, *4*(4), 52–69. doi:10.4018/IJSDA.2015100104

Rajasekaran, V., Aranda, J., & Casals, A. (2014). Recovering planned trajectories in robotic rehabilitation therapies under the effect of disturbances. *International Journal of System Dynamics Applications*, *3*(2), 34–49. doi:10.4018/ijsda.2014040103

Silva, E., Campos-Rebelo, R., Hirashima, T., Moutinbo, F., Malo, P., Costa, A., & Gomes, L. (2014). Communication support for Petri nets based distributed controllers. *Proceedings of the 2014 IEEE International Symposium on Industrial Electronics*, 1111-1116. 10.1109/ISIE.2014.6864769

Taher, M., & Abdeljawad, M. (2013). A new modular strategy for action sequence automation using neural networks and hidden Markov models. *International Journal of System Dynamics Applications*, *2*(3), 18–35. doi:10.4018/ijsda.2013070102

Vaidyanathan, S., & Azar, A. T. (2016). Takagi-Sugeno Fuzzy Logic Controller for Liu-Chen Four-Scroll Chaotic System. *International Journal of Intelligent Engineering Informatics*, *4*(2), 135–150. doi:10.1504/IJIEI.2016.076699

Wu, N. Q., & Zhou, M. C. (2009). *System Modeling and Control with Resource-oriented Petri Nets*. New York: CRC Press.

Yasuda, G. (1971). *A Fundamental Study on Reproduction - Application of Graph Theory to Self-Reproducing Processes* (Master thesis). The University of Tokyo, Tokyo, Japan.

Yasuda, G. (2015). Distributed coordination architecture for cooperative task planning and execution of intelligent multi-Robot systems. In Handbook of Research on Advanced Intelligent Control Engineering and Automation (pp. 407-426). Hershey PA: IGI Global. doi:10.4018/978-1-4666-7248-2.ch015

Yasuda, G. (2016). Design and implementation of distributed autonomous coordinators for cooperative multi-robot systems. *International Journal of System Dynamics Applications*, *5*(4), 1–15. doi:10.4018/IJSDA.2016100101

Zhou, Y., Xiao, K., Wang, Y., Liang, A., & Hassanien, A. E. (2013). A PSO-inspired multi-robot map exploration algorithm using frontier-based strategy. *International Journal of System Dynamics Applications*, *2*(2), 1–13. doi:10.4018/ijsda.2013040101

Zhu, Q., & Azar, A. T. (2015). *Complex System Modelling and Control through Intelligent Soft Computations. In Studies in Fuzziness and Soft Computing* (Vol. 319). Springer-Verlag.

Chapter 2
Proportional Integral Loop Shaping Control Design With Particle Swarm Optimization Tuning

Ahmad Taher Azar
Benha University, Egypt & Nile University, Egypt

Fernando E. Serrano
Central American Technical University (UNITEC), Honduras

Sundarapandian Vaidyanathan
Vel Tech University, India

ABSTRACT

Backlash is one of several discontinuities found in different kinds of systems. It can be found in actuators of different types, such as mechanical and hydraulic, giving way to unwanted effects in the system behavior. Proportional integral (PI) loop shaping control design implementing a describing function to find the limit cycle oscillations and the appropriate control gain selection by particle swarm optimization is developed. Therefore, a frequency domain approach is implemented for the control of nonlinear system of any kind such as robotics, mechatronics, and other kind of mechanisms, electrical motors, etc. Finally, in order to corroborate the theoretical background explained in this chapter, the stabilization of a cart-pendulum system with the proposed control strategy is shown.

1. INTRODUCTION

Recent decades have witnessed many important developments related to the design of nonlinear systems for many practical applications. Several inspiring approaches have been proposed, such as optimal control, nonlinear feedback control, adaptive control, sliding mode control, nonlinear dynamics, chaos control, chaos synchronization control, fuzzy logic control, fuzzy adaptive control, fractional order control, and

DOI: 10.4018/978-1-5225-4077-9.ch002

robust control and their integrations (Azar & Vaidyanathan, 2015a,b,c, 2016; Azar & Zhu, 2015; Meghni et al, 2017a,b,c; Boulkroune et al, 2016a,b; Ghoudelbourk et al., 2016; Azar & Serrano, 2015a,b,c,d, 2016a,b, 2017; Azar et al., 2017a,b,c,d; Azar 2010a,b, 2012; Mekki et al., 2015; Vaidyanathan & Azar, 2015a,b,c,d, 2016a,b,c,d,e,f,g, 2017a,b,c; Zhu & Azar, 2015; Grassi et al., 2017; Ouannas et al., 2016a,b, 2017a,b,c,d,e,f,g,h,I,j; Singh et al., 2017; Vaidyanathan et al, 2015a,b,c; Wang et al., 2017; Soliman et al., 2017; Tolba et al., 2017).

Backlash is a phenomenon found in different kinds of actuators such as mechanical and hydraulic, generally it occurs when the contact of two mating gears does not match and this give way to many unwanted effects on the systems provoking problems to the whole mechanical system. There are different kinds of mechanical systems to be stabilized (Azar & Serrano, 2014, 2015a,b,c,d, 2016a,b, 2017; Silva & Erraz, 2006), where the stabilization and control of mechanical system with backlash is done by several techniques such as conventional PID control and PI loop shaping control obtaining the optimal outcomes by the proposed strategy. Then another example can be found in Azar & Serrano (2015c) where the stabilization of the Furuta pendulum is done by a second order sliding mode control and adaptive sliding mode control considering that is important to mention these kinds of mechanical systems because of the proposed strategy shown in this chapter can be implemented for any kind of mechanism. Many researchers have proposed several solutions respect to the control and stability issues of these systems with input nonlinearities; taking into account that due to the complexity of the nonlinear model, traditional control strategies fail in most of the cases, and therefore it is necessary to design nonlinear control strategies or implement modified traditional ones. The objective of this chapter is to explain diverse control strategies for systems with this kind of nonlinearity. The intention is to show some nonlinear control techniques that have been developed and propose different approaches to solve this problem.

Robust and output feedback controllers (Barreiro & Baños, 2006; Ismail et. al., 2012; Joshi, 2016; Hariz & Bouani, 2016; Mnasser et. al., 2014) are some approaches that have been used for decades taking into count that most of the mechanical systems are nonlinear and multivariable, thus these techniques are explained as a preamble for some novel control procedures developed for the stabilization of mechanical systems with this kind of nonlinearity.

Adaptive backlash control is another control strategy developed by some authors; this approach has the advantage of cancelling the backlash effects using a backlash inverse model (Tao & Kokotovic, 1993a, b, 1995; Zhou et al., 2005; Jing & Wen, 2007; Guo et al., 2009). There are several mechanical and mechatronic systems that possess backlash nonlinearities, so in this chapter a PI H_∞ loop shaping strategy for n degrees of freedom robotics and multibody systems are developed and analyzed starting with the derivations of the dynamic equations obtained by the Euler Lagrange formulation, including the backlash nonlinearity, then the PI H_∞ loop shaping strategy is obtained for the control and stabilization of these models under the effects of input backlash.

Another example of loop shaping control can be found in Wigren (2017) where an advanced loop shaping feedback and feedforward control for networked systems with saturation and delay is studied. An interesting feature of this technique is that the method adjusts a linear H_2 loop shaping scheme with consistency with a long delay and saturation in the feedback loop, therefore, this controller is implemented in internet data flow control supporting 5G wireless connectivity. Finally, another interesting loop shaping approach and application is shown by Kim et al. (2017) where a practical active control of cavity noise using loop shaping is shown, and a simple loop shaping design technique is implemented to design an optimal and robust controller to reduce the interior noise of an acoustic cavity.

The effect of backlash is common in the above-mentioned systems, considering the contact of different actuators and sensors specially gears; this is a non-desirable characteristic that yields unwanted effects, so it is necessary to devise controllers that deal with this kind of feature in the design process. Some interesting examples of the controller design for different kinds of systems can be found in Liu et al. (2017) where an adaptive control for torsional vibration systems is shown. The studied two masses torsional vibration system dynamic system is obtained first where a frequency response equation is obtained by the modified Lindstedt–Poincare method combined with the multiple scales method, so it is important to consider that the influence of backlash amplitude change of the torsional system is analyzed by the amplitude frequency map. Another interesting reference that must be referred is Si et al. (2017) where an adaptive neural prescribed performance control of a strict-feedback stochastic nonlinear system with hysteresis input is shown. In this paper a robust adaptive neural control scheme is developed to deal with hysteresis where the proposed controller is designed to overcome the problem of over-parameterization. Then, in Rodriguez-Linan & Heath (2017) a backlash compensation technique for plants with saturating actuator is shown, so an inverse backlash with saturation and the backlash model itself is implemented to design a compensator scheme based on traditional anti-windup scheme.

PID and PI controllers are a solid control strategy that has been implemented by decades and the forthcoming years due their simplicity and accuracy. PID and PI controllers have been implemented in the single-input single-output SISO case such as in Azar and Serrano (2014) where an internal model control approach is proposed for PID cascade control systems in the SISO case showing that the approach proposed is accurate and provides an optimal system response with potential implementation in the process control field. Another example can be found in Azar and Serrano (2015b) where an anti-windup scheme for SISO continuous and discrete time systems is developed to stabilize system with input saturation considering that the windup effect deteriorates the system performance and can even drive the system to instability because the controller and compensator shown in this article avoid the windup phenomenon. In the case of multi-input multi-output MIMO system controller design there is a vast number of controller strategies found in the literature, from linear controllers to nonlinear and other kind of complex systems.

In this chapter a compensation for systems with saturation and backlash in series to the actuator is studied in order to obtain the proposed control strategy. Some backlash mathematical models can be implemented for the design of the PI loop shaping controller (Nordin & Gutman, 2002) along with inverse models (Jang et al, 2003), so the designer could select an appropriate mathematical model for the controller design. The multivariable PI H_∞ loop shaping design for mechanical systems with backlash is implemented in this chapter due to their frequency domain characteristics. This approach is done by implementing the coprime factorization of a linearized model following the loop shaping design procedure and it is based on the work of Azar & serrano (2015a). The PI H_∞ control strategy shown in this chapter consists in implementing two weighting functions as a pre-compensator and post compensator considering the linearized model of the nonlinear dynamics of mechanical systems according to their frequency domain properties. One of the main issues overcame in this study, is that the backlash nonlinearity is modeled implementing a describing function, something that it not only allows to ease the design of the proposed control strategy but also to find the limit cycles frequencies and periods. The describing function approach consists in the implementation of Fourier series to obtain a linear model of the backlash and other nonlinearities and to obtain a feasible loop shaping controller design. Also in this chapter, a frequency analysis is explained for this kind of mechanical systems using the Nyquist and the positivity criterion in order to analyze the stability properties of this kind of systems, which can be considered as an important contribution of this study. It is important to remark that the parameter tuning of the PI gains is done by particle swarm optimization (PSO) where an objective function is minimized in order that the system variables reach the equilibrium point faster and accurately (Serrano & Flores, 2015; Mousa et al., 2015). Finally, the stabilization of a cart-pendulum system implementing the proposed control strategy is shown corroborating the effectiveness of this approach (Melkou & Hamerlain, 2014). A conclusion of this book chapter is that these results can be extended to other kinds of physical systems, for example, energy systems as shown in Meghni et al. (2017a,b,c) where an effective supervisory controller to extend energy optimal management in hybrid wind turbine under energy and reliability constraints is shown, and in Ghoudelbourk et al. (2016) where a maximum power point tracking (MPPT) Control in wind energy conversion systems and the application of fractional control (PIα) in pitch wind turbine is implemented. Then, with this proposed approach, the system performance of electrical and energy systems can be improved when the system needs to work in some operating point.

This chapter is organized as follows: In section 2, problem formulation of backlash is introduced. In section 3, backlash models are described. In section 4, loop shaping control of mechanical systems with backlash is presented. In section 5, stabilization of a cart pendulum system with backlash example is shown. Finally in sections 6 and 7, discussions and concluding remarks are given respectively.

2. PROBLEM FORMULATION

Backlash is a phenomenon found in many kinds of system in which for example, there is not a perfect contact between two mating gears. In this study, a PI loop shaping controller for mechanical systems with backlash is proposed where the first part of this study is intended to show different kinds of backlash models. There are two models presented in this book chapter, the first is an approximate model, in which a dead-zone model is implemented to represent the backlash nonlinearity. Even when this model is approximate, the backlash representation provided is acceptably accurate, so it can be implemented for different kinds of controller design taking into account the sector condition. Other kind of backlash representation is an exact model in which a backlash slope is used to provide an exact model, but it is important to consider that this model offers some difficulties for the controller design because it could be intractable. Based on the work of Azar & Serrano (2015a), an extension to this study is provided in which an improvement to this strategy is offered, this improvement is the parameter tuning of the gain matrices K_I and K_P by a particle swarm optimization (PSO) algorithm. The first part of the controller design consists in finding a K_∞ matrix obtained by the robust H_∞ loop shaping controller design, so with this matrix the robust stability and performance of the overall system is obtained. Then by defining the filters $W_1 = I$, where I is the identity matrix, and W_2 is the PI controller dynamics in which K_I and K_P are the integral and proportional gain matrices, the tracking gain $K = W_1 K_\infty W_2$ is obtained. So one critical issue, the robust performance of the system can be improved by implementing a particle swarm optimization algorithm instead of implementing the trial and error selection of the matrices K_I and K_P. It is important to remark that the robust stability and performance of the system are guaranteed by the loop shaping controller design, but the overall system performance is yielded by the PSO to select the optimal matrices values of the PI controller. The particle swarm optimization for the PI controller consists in implementing an objective function selected to reduce the error between the equilibrium point and the measured state variables of the mechanical system. Then by selecting an appropriate number of particles, the particle swarm optimization selects the optimal gain matrices values by finding the particle with the best positions in order to minimize the objective function.

For the PI loop shaping design, it's necessary to select an appropriate model for the backlash nonlinearity, so in order to facilitate the controller design, a describing function representation is implemented. The describing function provides a harmonic decomposition of the backlash nonlinearity implementing the Fourier coefficients and yielding a linear model that is implemented in the loop shaping design procedure. Then, the loop shaping design procedure for mechanical system begins by establishing a nonlinear model of the mechanism, specifically, a dynamic model in the Euler-Lagrange formulation and then linearizing this model by an appropriate methodology. Therefore, in order to obtain the loop shaping design procedure, based on the transfer matrix of the linearized mechanical system a perturbed model is obtained containing all the system uncertainties. The robust loop shaping design is done by meeting the required robust condition and then by selecting appropriate controller, in this case the PI controller dynamics, the frequency characteristics of the open loop system are selected so the closed loop system meets all the required conditions. As explained before, the PI gain matrices in the controller are selected by the particle swarm optimization so the time response and the error between the equilibrium points and the measured variables of the mechanical system are optimized. In order to study the limit cycles yielded by the system, the Nyquist theorem along with the positivity and Popov theorems are used so the characteristics of the oscillations found in the system are analyzed.

In the numerical simulation section of this chapter, the stabilization of a cart-pendulum system is done by the proposed PI loop shaping design procedure, where the state variables such as linear and angular position along with the linear and angular velocities are stabilized to the equilibrium points. The PSO implemented for the PI gain matrices tuning is done using a considerable small number of particles and evolution cycles proving that the PSO algorithm is efficient. The results shown in this section prove and corroborate the theoretical background derived in this study and that can be extended not only for mechanical systems, and it can be extended to hydraulic, electrical and energy systems.

3. BACKLASH MODELS

In this section, some mathematical models of the backlash discontinuity are shown; these models are commonly used before the derivations of suitable controllers when this nonlinearity appears. Backlash occurs when adjacent mechanical parts are not directly connected, for example, when the actuator, that in this case could be a DC motor, and the load do not have a perfect contact. For this reason, it is important to obtain a mathematical model for this non-differentiable nonlinearity. There are some approximated and exact models that could be used in the design of an appropriate controller in mechanical systems where this discontinuity is found. Apart from the backlash models presented in this section, a backlash inverse model is shown due to this mathematical model is used by some control strategies (Tao & Kokotovic, 1993a, b,1995), and it is important to mention this model due to its properties.

3.1. Approximate Model

Sometimes it is necessary to implement approximated backlash models because of its complex characteristics that makes it difficult in the design of appropriate controllers. Therefore, a dead zone model is proposed by some authors (Nordin & Gutman, 2002; Bentsman et al., 2013) because this model is nonlinear and static. The mathematical model is given in (1)

$$D_a(x) = \begin{cases} x-\alpha & x>\alpha \\ 0 & |x|<\alpha \\ x+\alpha & x<-\alpha \end{cases} \quad (1)$$

where $\alpha > 0$

This model is useful and easy to implement in the design of controller with backlash, although it depends on the actuator characteristics of the model.

3.2. Exact Model

Sometimes it is necessary to use an exact backlash model due to the accuracy of the controller design. Therefore a model as represented in Figure 1 is used, where e is the input to the backlash and $n(e)$ is the output of the model (Tao & Kokotovik, 1995). The mathematical description of the backlash model is shown in (2)

$$n(t) = \begin{cases} m_l\left(e(t)-\beta\right) & e(t) \le e_l(t) \\ m_r\left(e(t)-\beta\right) & e(t) \ge e_r(t) \\ n(t-1) & e_l(t) < e(t) < e_r(t) \end{cases} \quad (2)$$

where $\beta > 0$, $m_l, m_r > 0$ are the backlash slope, $e_l(t) = \frac{n(t)}{m_l} + \beta$ and $e_r(t) = \frac{n(t)}{m_r} + \beta$.

The backlash input is *e* and the backlash output is *n(e)*. This backlash model is often used in the design of anti-backlash controllers due to their accuracy in comparison with the dead zone model, but it is quite more difficult than other simplified mathematical models. In the controller design, this mathematical model is implemented, with the derivation of a describing function (Chyung, 1992; Tierno et al., 2000) that is an efficient backlash representation for this complex discontinuity.

4. LOOP SHAPING CONTROL OF MECHANICAL SYSTEMS WITH BACKLASH

Loop shaping is a well-known approach used in the control of multivariable systems. It consists in designing the closed loop specifications of the system in terms of the open loop characteristics (McFarlane & Glover, 1992). This is done by selecting an appropriate control gain with pre-specified closed loop frequency response obtaining the desired performance. The H_∞ loop shaping control design consists of minimizing the infinity norm of the system, therefore some aspects such as sensitivity and disturbance rejection can be included in the controller design (Adams & Baron, 1998).

Figure 1. Backlash model

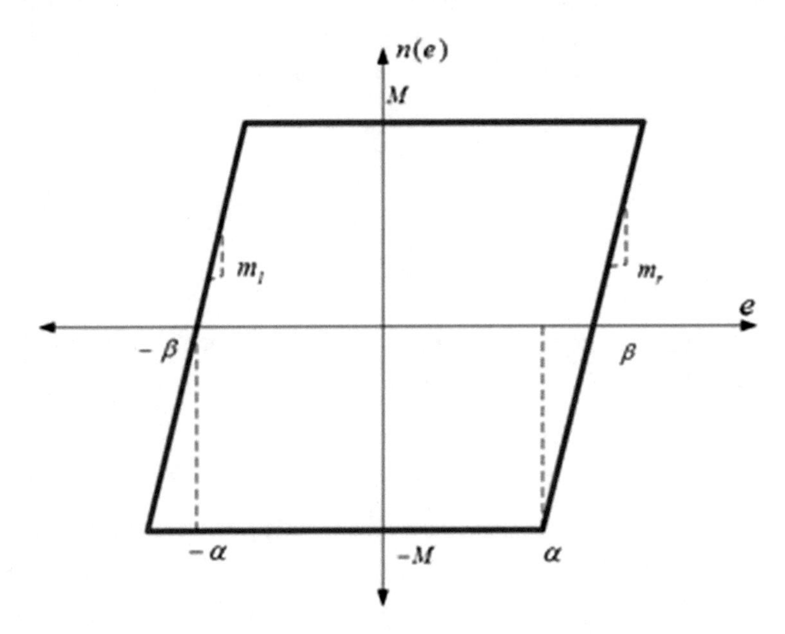

Loop shaping consists of selecting two weight functions W_1 and W_2 that is used as a pre-compensator and post compensator respectively to meet the required bandwidth characteristics. Then a K_∞ gain is calculated based on the minimization of the infinity norm of the system. To implement this control strategy, it is necessary to obtain the coprime factorization of the system (Hippe, 1994; Gao & So, 2003) for multivariable systems. Then each factor is used in the design of the K_∞ gain which stabilizes the system solving the specified Riccati equations (Adams & Bar-on, 1998; Boukhnifer & Ferreira, 2005). In this section, H_∞ loop shaping control approach for mechanical systems with backlash is proposed. Considering the characteristics of mechanical systems, this strategy is suitable for these models due to its frequency domain properties taking into account the backlash effects in the system response. For this purpose, a describing function is implemented to model the backlash nonlinearity with a sinusoidal input, assuming that the system outputs oscillate in the presence of this discontinuity. These oscillations yield a limit cycle that is a non-trivial periodic orbit when there is a neighborhood of the periodic orbit that does not contain any other periodic solution (Haddad & Chellaboina, 2008). This effect is analyzed in this section and then included in the loop shaping design procedure obtaining a controller which deal with backlash with minimal effects on the output of the system.

4.1. Backlash Model by Describing Function

Describing functions are a representation of different kinds of nonlinearities and discontinuities (Brogan, 2005; Tierno et al., 2000; Nordin & Gutman, 2002). It consists of representing a discontinuity by a harmonic decomposition using the Fourier series of this nonlinearity when the input $e(t)$ is a sinusoidal function of time.

The describing function representation consist of deriving a mathematical representation by the Fourier series coefficients of the backlash with a sinusoidal input, as seen in Figure 2, finding the times t_1, t_2, t_3 and t_4. The input signal has a magnitude of E and for this nonlinearity representation the slopes m_r and m_l are assumed to be equal $m_r = m_l$ and then the output of this discontinuity *n(e)* is divided according to their respective time instants. The backlash input is given by:

$$e(t) = E\sin(t) \tag{3}$$

and the backlash output function is defined as:

$$n(t) = \pm\beta + m(e(t)) \tag{4}$$

Figure 2. Backlash representation with a sinusoidal input

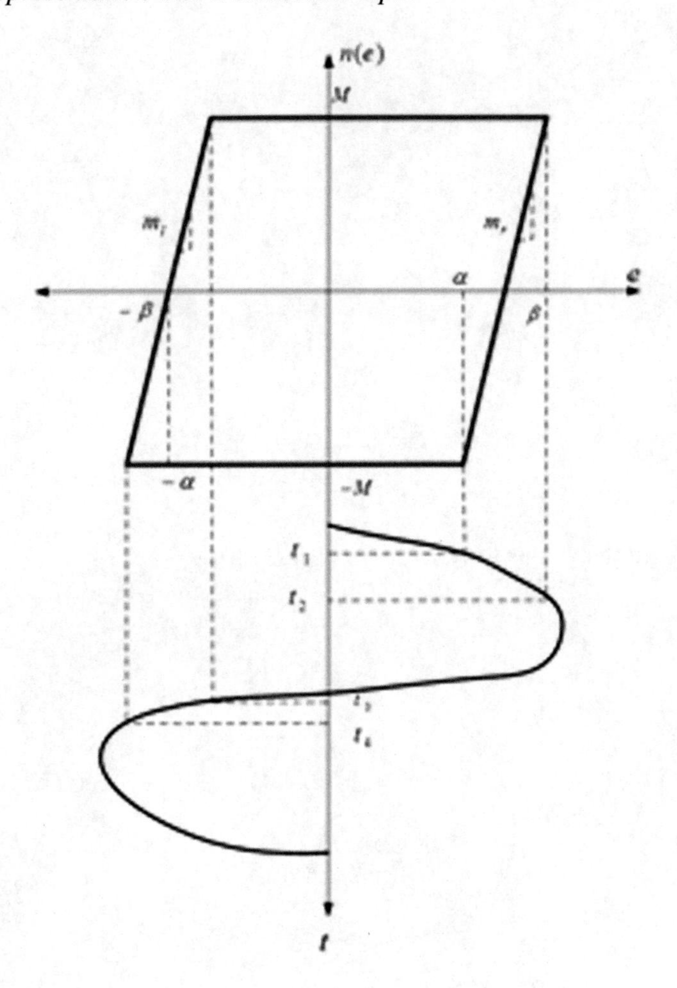

where the sign of β depends if it is the right or the left intersection with the e axis. The Fourier coefficients of $n(t)$ are defined by:

$$a_k = \frac{1}{T}\int_{-T}^{T} sin(k\omega t)\, n(t)\, dt$$

$$b_k = \frac{1}{T}\int_{-T}^{T} cos(k\omega t)\, n(t)\, dt$$

$$b_0 = \frac{1}{2T}\int_{-T}^{T} n(t)\, dt \qquad (5)$$

Usually b_0 is ignored in the describing function, and only a_1 and b_1 are considered for the describing function model. If ω is set as $\omega = 1$, because the signal is 2π periodic, the output backlash function is divided according to the integration time as follow:

$$0 < t < t_1 \quad -M$$

$$t_1 < t < t_2 \quad \beta + msin(t)$$

$$t_2 < t < t_3 \quad M$$

$$t_3 < t < t_4 \quad -(\beta + msin(t))$$

$$t_4 < t < 2\pi \quad -M \qquad (6)$$

where $m = m_r = m_l$ with the values for t_1, t_2, t_3 and t_4

$$t_1 = sin^{-1}\left(\frac{\alpha}{E}\right)$$

$$t_2 = sin^{-1}\left(\frac{M-\beta}{mE}\right)$$

$$t_3 = t_1 + \pi$$

$$t_4 = t_2 + \pi \tag{7}$$

The coefficient a_1 is found using the subdivisions explained in (6) for integration purposes:

$$a_1 = \frac{M}{T}\left(\int sin\left(t\right)dt - \int sin\left(t\right)dt - \int sin\left(t\right)dt\right) \tag{8}$$

Then the coefficient a_1 is:

$$a_1 = \frac{M}{T}\left(2cos\left(t_1\right) + 2cos\left(t_2\right)\right) \tag{9}$$

To find the coefficient b_1 the subdivisions shown in (6) are applied for integration purposes:

$$b_1 = \frac{M}{T}\left(\int cos\left(t\right)dt - \int cos\left(t\right)dt - \int cos\left(t\right)dt\right) \tag{10}$$

Then the following coefficient b_1 is obtained.

$$b_1 = \frac{M}{T}\left(sin\left(t_1\right) + sin\left(t_2\right)\right) + 2\beta sin\left(t_2\right) - 2\beta sin\left(t_1\right) + 2mcos^2\left(t_2\right) - 2mcos^2\left(t_1\right) \tag{11}$$

Then the ratio of the Laplace transform of the input $e\left(t\right)$ and the output $n\left(t\right)$ is given by $N\left(s\right)$ as (Brogan, 2005; Nordin & Gutman, 2002):

$$N\left(s\right) = \frac{a_1\omega + b_1 s}{E\omega} \tag{12}$$

The function (12) is of significant importance for the design of loop shaping controller explained in the next section, it gives a frequency domain based description of the backlash nonlinearity, and therefore it is easier to design a suitable controller with a less complex representation.

4.2. Loop Shaping PI Control of Mechanical Systems With Backlash

In this subsection, a loop shaping PI control for *n* degrees of freedom mechanical systems is developed. As explained before, loop shaping is a control technique which consists in obtaining a controller minimizing the H_∞ norm of the system (McFarlane & Glover, 1992; Zhou et al., 2004; Boukhnifer & Ferreira, 2005) solving a set of Riccati equations (Zhou et al., 2004; Bentsman et al., 2013). The design of loop shaping controllers for this kind of systems consists in implementing a pre-compensator and a post compensator to the plant (the mechanical system) to design a controller that meets the required frequency domain specifications. In order to derive the specified controller, a linearized model of the plant is needed, so the first part of this subsection is devoted to obtain a linearized model by the Jacobian matrix representation of the model. The second part of this subsection consists in the design of the loop shaping PI controller when there is backlash in the system. Consider the following n degrees of freedom mechanical system:

$$D(q)q' + C(q,q')q' + g(q) = \tau \tag{13}$$

where $q \in R^n$ is the joint angle vector, $\tau \in R^n$ is the input vector torque, $D(q) \in R^{nxn}$ is the inertia matrix, $C(q,q')q' \in R^n$ is the coriolis vector and $g(q) \in R^n$ is the gravity vector.

Transforming (13) into state space with $x_1 = q$ and $x_2 = q'$, the following model is obtained:

$$x_1' = x_2$$

$$x_2' = D^{-1}(x_1)\tau - D^{-1}(x_1)C(x_1,x_2)x_2 - D^{-1}(x_1)g(x_1) \tag{14}$$

So, this model is in the following form:

$$X' = f(X,\tau,t) \tag{15}$$

Linearizing this system about the equilibrium point yields (Brogan et al., 2005)

$$\delta X' = A\delta X + B\delta\tau$$

$$\delta Y = C\delta X + D\delta\tau \tag{16}$$

Then the transfer function is defined as:

$$A = \frac{\partial f}{\partial x}$$

$$B = \frac{\partial f}{\partial \tau}$$

$$C = I_n$$

$$D = 0 \tag{17}$$

where

$$G(s) \sim \begin{pmatrix} A\,B \\ C\,D \end{pmatrix} \tag{18}$$

The loop shaping control strategy when there is a backlash consists of implementing the describing function (12) and finding a control gain K_∞ which stabilizes the system with a required closed loop performance. In Figure 3 a block diagram of the proposed control strategy is shown, where the equivalent open loop system is defined as $G_n(s)$, that is, the combination of the describing input function $N(s)$ and the mechanical system transfer matrix $G(s)$.

As explained before, the describing function of the backlash nonlinearity is very helpful for the loop shaping controller design, because, the resulting system can be modeled in the frequency domain. The performance of the system can be obtained by traditional or nonlinear frequency analysis, investigating the limit cycle produced by the backlash discontinuity effects on the model. The describing function implementation avoids the use of a backlash inverse model as explained in (Tierno et al., 2000) and allows a frequency domain analysis of the model.

The resulting transfer matrix G_n is:

$$G_n(s) \sim \begin{pmatrix} A\,b_{1n}ACB + a_{1n}CB \\ I \quad\quad b_{1n}CB \end{pmatrix} \tag{19}$$

where I is the identity matrix, $b_{1n} = \frac{b_1}{E\omega}$ and $a_{1n} = \frac{a_1}{E}$.

The idea behind the loop shaping control is to find a factorized model of the plant and then using a coprime factorization method therefore the resulting model $G_{n\Delta}$ is found as:

$$G_{n\Delta} = M^{-1}N \tag{20}$$

Figure 3. Equivalent closed loop block diagram

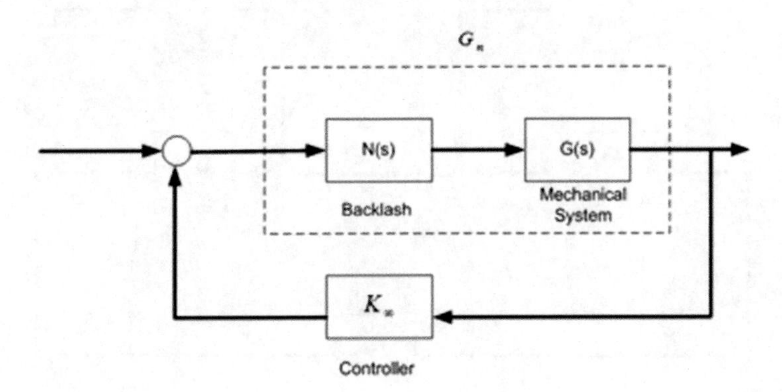

where the condition $MM'+NN'=I$ then N and M are the normalized coprime factorization of G_n. In Figure 4, a perturbed model of the plant is shown where the coprime factors are M and N (Hippe, 1994; Gao & So, 2003). Therefore the perturbed model of the plant is given in (21) as:

$$G_{n\Delta} = \left(M + \Delta M\right)^{-1}\left(N + \Delta N\right) \tag{21}$$

The loop shaping design procedure is divided in two steps. In Step 1 the loop shaping design procedure is described along with the PI controller definition. In Step 2 the robust stabilization of the model is explained with the definition of the system norm.

Step 1: Loop Shaping PI Controller Design

The first step in the loop shaping design is to establish the pre compensator and post compensator functions, to be used in the controller design. The objective is to specify the closed loop characteristics in terms of the requirements of the weighted transfer matrix. Usually the weighting matrices are described as W_1 and W_2 for the pre compensator and post compensator respectively. In Figure 5 the loop shaping design procedure is shown.

The weighted transfer matrix, denoted as $G_s = W_1 G_n\left(s\right) W_2$, is used to specify the open loop performance of the system, then it is implemented later in the design of the K_∞ controller gain. The loop shaping procedure has the property that the design specifications are valid for all frequencies, while the open loop shaping are restricted to frequencies of low and high gain (McFarlane & Glover, 1992). The loop shaping procedure consist in finding the optimal K_∞ closed loop gain by weighting the transfer matrix $G_n\left(s\right)$ as shown in Figure 6:

After finding the optimal closed loop gain K_∞, this gain is weighted with the functions W_1 and W_2 to obtain the final controller gain K as shown in Figure 7, where $K = W_1 K_\infty W_2$ and it is the definitive controller gain.

Figure 4. Perturbed model of the plant

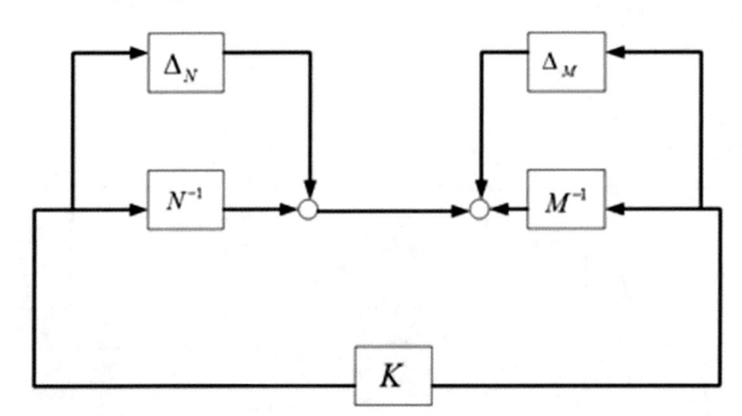

Figure 5. Loop shaping design procedure: Weighted transfer matrix

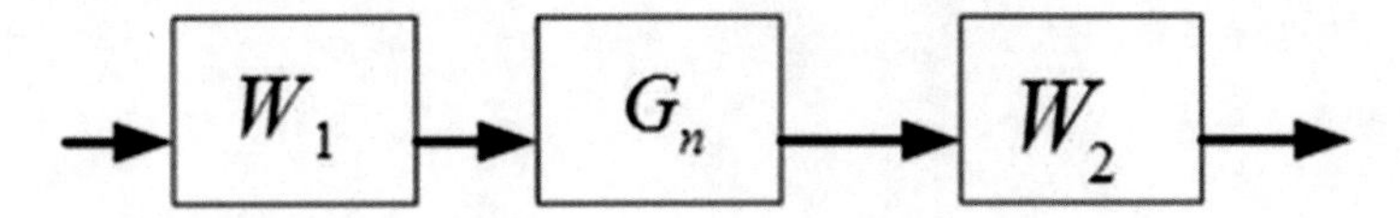

Figure 6. Loop shaping design procedure: Weighted transfer matrix with K_∞ *gain*

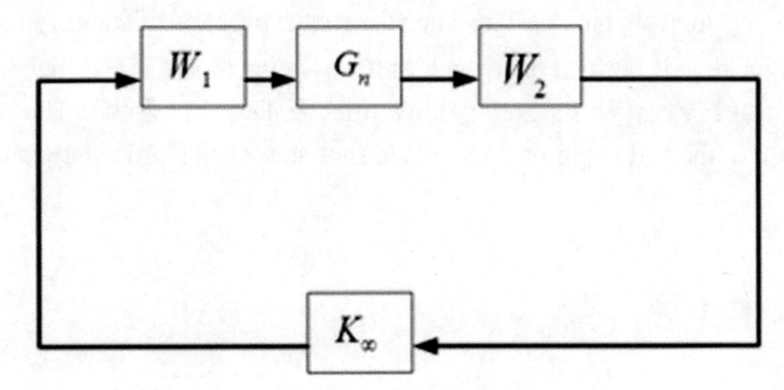

Figure 7. Loop shaping design procedure: Weighted K_∞ *gain*

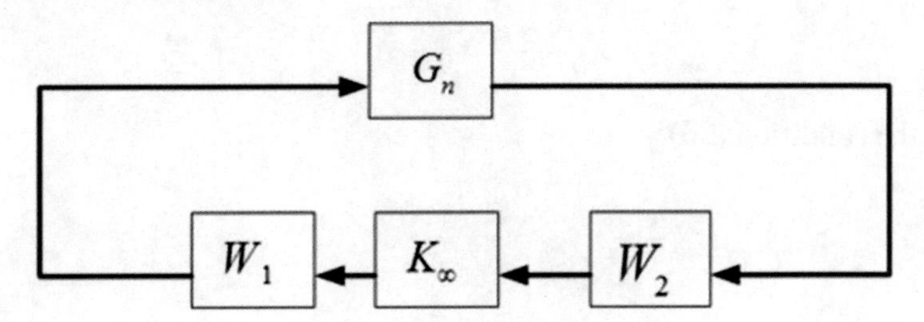

The selected weighting functions for this loop shaping procedure are for the sake of simplicity $W_1 = I$, where I is the identity matrix, and W_2 is the PI controller given by the following state space representation:

$$W_2 = \begin{cases} x_c' = K_I u \\ y_c = x_c + K_p u \end{cases} \tag{22}$$

where K_I is the integral $R^{n\times n}$ gain matrix and K_p is the proportional $R^{n\times n}$ gain matrix. The corresponding transfer matrix for W_2 is defined as:

$$W_2(s) = \begin{pmatrix} 0_n & K_I \\ I_n & K_p \end{pmatrix} \tag{23}$$

Step 2: Robust Stabilization

With the definition of the specified weighting functions, W_1 and W_2, the robust stabilization of the system is done by a H_∞ loop shaping design. Then the robust problem of stability is to find the greatest value of $\varepsilon = \varepsilon_{max}$, where ε is defined later, such as the systems model is stabilized by a gain K (McFarlane & Glover, 1992; Zhou et al., 2004; Boukhnifer & Ferreira, 2005). The robust stabilization problem is described in the following procedure, the first step of this procedure is to calculate ε_{max} by (24)

$$\varepsilon_{\max}^{-1} \triangleq \underset{StabilizingK}{Inf} \| \begin{pmatrix} I \\ K \end{pmatrix} (I - G_s K)^{-1} \|_\infty \tag{24}$$

where

$$\gamma_{min} \varepsilon_{max}^{-1} = \sqrt{1 - \| N - M \|_H^2} < 1 \tag{25}$$

or (24) must meet the condition (26)

$$\| \begin{pmatrix} I \\ K_\infty \end{pmatrix} (I - G_{n\Delta} K_\infty)^{-1} M^{-1} \|_\infty \leq \varepsilon^{-1} \tag{26}$$

If $\varepsilon_{max} \ll 1$, then go back (24) and adjust W_2. γ_{min} and ε_{max} can be found by:

$$\gamma_{min} \varepsilon_{max}^{-1} = \sqrt{1 - \lambda_{max}(XZ)} \tag{27}$$

where $\left\| \left[\Delta_N \Delta_M \right] \right\|_\infty < \gamma^{-1}$, X and Z are the solutions of the following Riccati equations (Zhou et al., 2004; Boukhnifer & Ferreira, 2005; Bentsman et al., 2013)

$$\left(A_n - B_n S^{-1} D_n^T C_n\right)^T X + X\left(A_n - B_n S^{-1} D_n^T C_n\right) - X B_n S^{-1} B_n^T X + C_n^T R^{-1} C_n = 0$$

$$\left(A_n - B_n S^{-1} D_n^T C_n\right) Z + Z\left(A_n - B_n S^{-1} D_n^T C_n\right)^T - Z C_n^T R^{-1} C_n Z + B_n S^{-1} B_n^T = 0 \tag{28}$$

where $S = I + D^T D$, $A_n = A$, $B_n = b_{1n} ACB + a_{1n} CB$, $C_n = I$ and $D_n = b_{1n} CB$ from the transfer matrix realization of $G_n(s) = C_n (SI - A_n)^{-1} B_n + D_n$. Then after selecting the appropriate values of γ, ε, Z and X; a robust control gain K_∞ can be found for the stabilization of the mechanical system as shown in (29) (Zhou et al., 2004; Boukhnifer & Ferreira, 2005).

$$K_\infty = \left(\begin{array}{c|c} A_n + B_n F + \gamma^2 (L^T)^{-1} Z C_n (C_n + D_n F) & \gamma^2 (L^T)^{-1} Z C_n \\ \hline B_n^T X & -D_n \end{array} \right) \tag{29}$$

where $F = -S^{-1} (D_n^T C_n + B_n^T X)$ and $L = (1 - \gamma^2) I + XZ$.

The robust control gain K_∞ shown in (29) can be expressed in transfer matrix form as shown in (30)

$$K_\infty = \left(\begin{array}{c|c} A_k & B_k \\ \hline C_k & D_k \end{array} \right) \tag{30}$$

Then with the gain K_∞, the controller gain K is obtained as shown in Figure 7 with $K = W_1 K_\infty W_2$. After obtaining the appropriate gain by the loop shaping procedure of an n degrees of freedom mechanical system, it is necessary to attain a frequency domain analysis to study the limit cycles produced by the backlash nonlinearity modeled by a describing function. In the next subsection, this analysis is done by the implementation of the positivity theorem and the Nyquist theorem, finding the limit cycle frequency for a mechanical system implementing a describing function to model the backlash discontinuity with defined oscillation amplitude.

4.3. Frequency Analysis of Mechanical Systems With Backlash

In this subsection, the analysis of an n degrees of freedom mechanical system with backlash is done. There are several approaches to analyze the limit cycles produced by the backlash nonlinearities, such as the Nyquist theorem, Popov theorem and positivity theorem. The idea behind this analysis is to find analytically the oscillatory behavior of the systems. This objective is reached implementing two important theorems to analyze nonlinear systems in the frequency domain. These approaches used to analyze the absolute stability of nonlinear systems are the positivity theorem and the Nyquist theorem. To analyze the absolute stability of the system, the limit cycle analysis is necessary to use the positivity theorem along with the Nyquist theorem. These theorems are derived assuming the following statements. Taking into account the following state matrix representation of the mechanical system (58):

$$G(s) = \left(\begin{array}{c|c} A & B \\ \hline C & D \end{array} \right) \textit{is minimum} \tag{31}$$

where $I+N(s)G(s)$ is strictly positive real. $N(s)$ of (12) is the backlash describing function which could be considered as a gain for the mechanical system transfer matrix representation $G(s)$. Then the closed loop system $I+N(s)K(s)G(s)$ is strictly positive real and the following theorem applies (Haddad & Chellaboina, 2008).

Theorem 1

Consider the mechanical system with the following state space realization

$$x'(t)=Ax(t)+B\tau(t)$$

$$y(t)=Cx(t)+D\tau(t) \tag{32}$$

and

$$G(s)=\left(\begin{array}{c|c} A & B \\ \hline C & D \end{array}\right) is\ minimum \tag{33}$$

If $I+N(s)K(s)G(s)$ is strictly positive real. Then the zero solution $x(t)=0$ of the negative feedback interconnection is asymptotically stable. Then by the Nyquist and positivity theorems the limit cycle oscillation frequency can be found analyzing the critical point:

$$\frac{-1}{N(s)K(s)} \tag{34}$$

Then the number of the closed loop unstable poles Z_r is:

$$Z_r=P_r-N_c \tag{35}$$

where P_r is the number of RHP open loop poles and N_c is the number of counterclockwise rounding around the critical point $\frac{-1}{N(s)K(s)}$ as established by the Nyquist and positivity theorem. Then the frequency of the limit cycle oscillations yielded by the backlash nonlinearity in the input of an n degrees of freedom mechanical system is obtained by solving the equation (36) as established by the Nyquist and positivity theorem to obtain a suitable controller which assures the asymptotical stability of the system.

$$\left|I+N(s)K(s)G(s)\right|=0 \tag{36}$$

4.4. Parameter Tuning by Particle Swarm Optimization

The tuning of the parameters K_I and K_p is done by a particle swarm optimization technique as shown in (Serrano & Flores, 2015) and (Mousa et. al., 2015) where the following algorithm is implemented to find the optimal parameter values in order to drive the system variables to the equilibrium point. The algorithm is as shown in (Serrano & Flores, 2015) with the following objective or fitness function

$$F=\sum_{i=1}^{n}\left(x_i-x_e\right)^2\Delta t \tag{37}$$

where the function (37) must be minimized in order to drive the variables to the equilibrium point. x_i and v_i are the respective position and velocity variables of each particle, while F_{pbest} and p_{best} are the best objective function value and the best position value. So, the number of parameters used in the numerical simulation section are two, one for K_I and the other for K_p, then the number of particle used is one with five evolution cycles. Consider the position P and velocity matrix V_e:

$$P=\left[\varphi^1,\varphi^2,\ldots,\varphi^{ns}\right]$$

$$P_{best}=\left[\widehat{\varphi^1},\widehat{\varphi^2},\ldots,\widehat{\varphi^{ns}}\right]$$

$$V_e=\left[v^1,v^2,\ldots,v^{ns}\right]$$

$$v^l=\left[v_1^l,v_2^l,\ldots,v_{n-1}^l\right] \tag{38}$$

so F_l is the fitness value of the l particle defined as:

$$F_l=Fit\left(A^l\right)=Fit\left(S\left(\varphi^l\right)\right)l=1,2,\ldots,ns \tag{39}$$

where the l column of P_b is updated with (39). Then the optimal velocity and position are given by v' and φ' respectively. The actual position and velocities are obtained by:

$$v_j^l(t+1)=wv_j^l(t)+c_1r_1\left(\widehat{\varphi_l^j}-\varphi_j^l(t)\right)+c_2r_2\left(\varphi_l'-\varphi_j^l(t)\right)$$

$$\varphi_j^l\left(t+1\right)=\varphi_j^l\left(t\right)+v_l^j\left(t+1\right)$$

$$r_1=r_2=rand\left(0,1\right)$$

$$l=1,2,\ldots,nsj=1,2,\ldots,n-1t=1,2,\ldots,M \quad (40)$$

5. EXAMPLE: STABILIZATION OF A CART PENDULUM SYSTEM WITH BACKLASH

In this subsection, the design of controller by the loop shaping procedure for a cart pendulum (Iqbal et al., 2007; Glück et al., 2013) system with input backlash is shown. The simulations and calculations were done using MATLAB ® and SimMechanics ® obtaining the following results. The dynamic equations of the cart pendulum system are:

$$\left(M+m\right)x'+ml\left(\theta'+\theta'^2 sin\left(\theta\right)\right)=u+dcos\left(\theta\right)$$

$$m\left(x'cos\left(\theta\right)+l\theta'-gsin\left(\theta\right)\right)=d \quad (41)$$

The parameters of the mechanical system and the respective values used in this example as shown in Figure 8 are shown in Table 1.

The cart is moved by a rotating actuator so the measurement is converted from translational force (N) to rotational torque (N.m).

The linearized model about the equilibrium point $\left(0,0\right)$ on $\left(x,\theta\right)$ is shown in (42):

Table 1. Parameters of the cart pendulum system

Parameter	Description	Value
M	Mass of the cart.	*1 Kg*
M	Mass of the Pendulum	*1 Kg*
l	Length of the pendulum	*0.85 m*
θ	Pendulum rotating angle	*Degrees*
X	Cart displacement	*(m)*
U	Cart force	*N*
D	Pendulum torque	*N.m*
G	Gravity constant	$9.81\ m/s^2$

Figure 8. Cart pendulum system

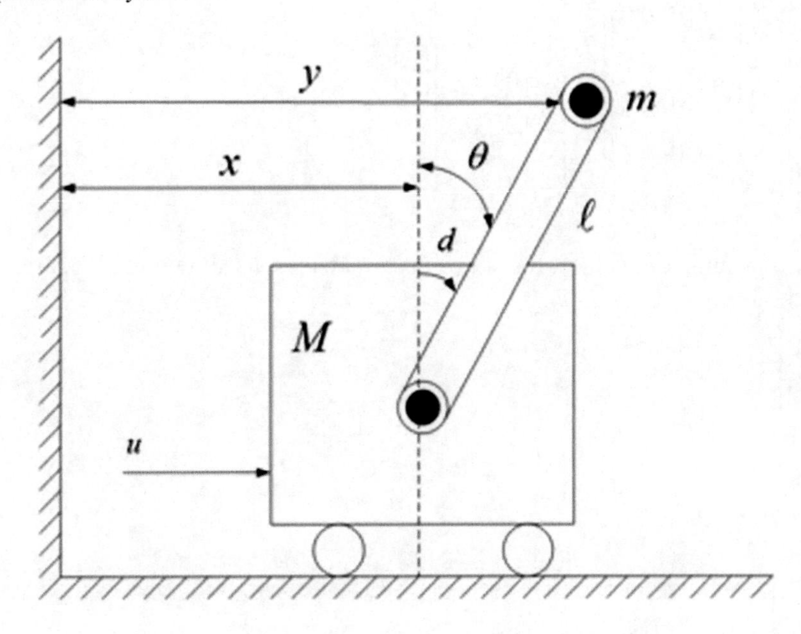

$$\left(M+m\right)x'+ml\theta'=u+d$$

$$x'+l\theta'-g\theta=\frac{1}{m}d \tag{42}$$

Then using the following phase variables, the system is converted to state space form:

$$q_1=x$$

$$q_2=x'$$

$$q_3=\theta$$

$$q_4=\theta' \tag{43}$$

Then the following state space matrix is obtained:

$$\begin{pmatrix} 0 & (M+m) & 0 & ml \\ 1 & 0 & 0 & 0 \\ 0 & 1 & 0 & l \\ 0 & 0 & 1 & 0 \end{pmatrix} \begin{pmatrix} q_1' \\ q_2' \\ q_3' \\ q_4' \end{pmatrix} = \begin{pmatrix} 0 & 0 & 0 & 0 \\ 0 & 1 & 0 & 0 \\ 0 & 0 & g & 0 \\ 0 & 0 & 0 & 1 \end{pmatrix} \begin{pmatrix} q_1 \\ q_2 \\ q_3 \\ q_4 \end{pmatrix} + \begin{pmatrix} 1 & 1 \\ 0 & 0 \\ 0 & 1/m \\ 0 & 0 \end{pmatrix} \begin{pmatrix} u \\ d \end{pmatrix} \tag{44}$$

Substituting the parameters values, the state space matrices, as shown in (18), are:

$$A = \begin{pmatrix} 0 & 0 & 0 & 0 \\ 0 & 0 & -2.45 & 0 \\ 0 & 0 & 0 & 1 \\ 0 & 0 & 14.43 & 0 \end{pmatrix}$$

$$B = \begin{pmatrix} 0 & 0 \\ 0.25 & 0 \\ 0 & 1/m \\ -0.29 & 1.17 \end{pmatrix}$$

$$C = \begin{pmatrix} 1 & 0 & 0 & 0 \\ 0 & 1 & 0 & 0 \\ 0 & 0 & 1 & 0 \\ 0 & 0 & 0 & 1 \end{pmatrix}$$

$$D = 0 \tag{45}$$

Then the equivalent system with input backlash $G_n(s)$ is given by (19). Therefore, applying (36) and solving for ω and E, the following oscillation limit cycle frequency is $\omega = 1$, $E = 1$; and the time values for the description function as shown in (7) are $t_1 = 0.0945$, $t_2 = 0.3869$, $t_3 = 3.2361$ and $t_4 = 3.5285$. Then the constant values are $a_1 = 7.3400$ and $b_1 = -0.0358$ as shown in (9) and (11) and applied in the model (19). The PI controller function W_2 has the following gains obtained by the particle swarm optimization:

$$K_I = \begin{pmatrix} 10000 & 0 \\ 0 & 1000 \end{pmatrix}$$

$$K_p = \begin{pmatrix} 10000 & 0 \\ 0 & 10000 \end{pmatrix} \quad (46)$$

Then the matrices for the K_∞ gain function shown in (30) are:

$$A_k = \begin{pmatrix} -2.0440 & 0.6075 & 0.0118 & -0.3488 \\ -0.3925 & -21.2334 & -4.3115 & -19.0145 \\ 0.0118 & -1.8590 & -3.6897 & -0.8334 \\ -0.3488 & -19.0145 & 12.5930 & -17.9578 \end{pmatrix}$$

$$B_k = \begin{pmatrix} -2.0440 & -0.3925 & 0.0118 & -0.3488 \\ -0.3925 & -21.2334 & -1.8590 & -19.0145 \\ 0.0118 & -1.8590 & -3.6897 & -1.8334 \\ -0.3488 & -19.0145 & -1.8334 & -17.9578 \end{pmatrix}$$

$$C_k = \begin{pmatrix} 0.9911 & 2.8877 & -7.9548 & -1.6685 \\ -0.1334 & -0.5685 & 23.5952 & 6.1909 \end{pmatrix}$$

$D_k = 0$ (47)

The respective matrices A_k, B_k, C_k and D_k were obtained by solving the Riccati equations shown in (28), obtaining the expected results for X and Z. The PSO algorithm implements 2 particles with 10 evolution cycles where if the number of particles and evolution cycles are increased the system response could be improved.

The value of γ_{min} is $\gamma_{min} = 14.67$, then the selected value of γ for the design of the loop shaping controller is $\gamma = 19.7$, therefore the selection of the PI controller W_2 meets the requirements and it is not necessary a redesign of K_∞ because the obtained γ and ϵ are greater than the expected values. In Figure 9 and Figure 10, the linear displacement along with the linear displacement velocity are shown and as can be noticed, the results obtained by tuning the parameters K_I and K_p with the PSO approach (proposed strategy) are superior to the variables response when they are not tuned by PSO (compared strategy) so the equilibrium point is reached faster and accurately by the proposed approach.

Then in Figure 11 and Figure 12 the angular position and angular velocity of the cart are shown where the controlled system with the tuned parameters by particle swarm optimization provides better results in comparison when particle swarm optimization is not used because the equilibrium point is reached faster and accurately with the proposed tuning approach.

Finally, in Figure 13 and Figure 14, the linear force and torque applied to the cart are shown where a better control effort is obtained by the proposed approach in comparison with the compared approach considering that a lower control effort avoids the actuator saturation.

Figure 9. Linear displacement of the cart

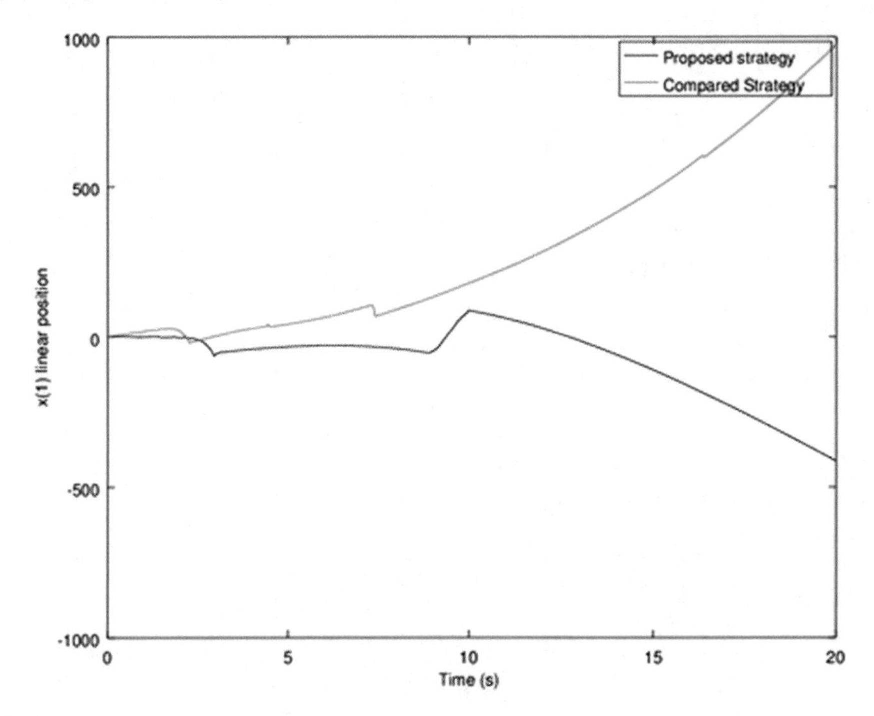

Figure 10. Linear velocity of the cart

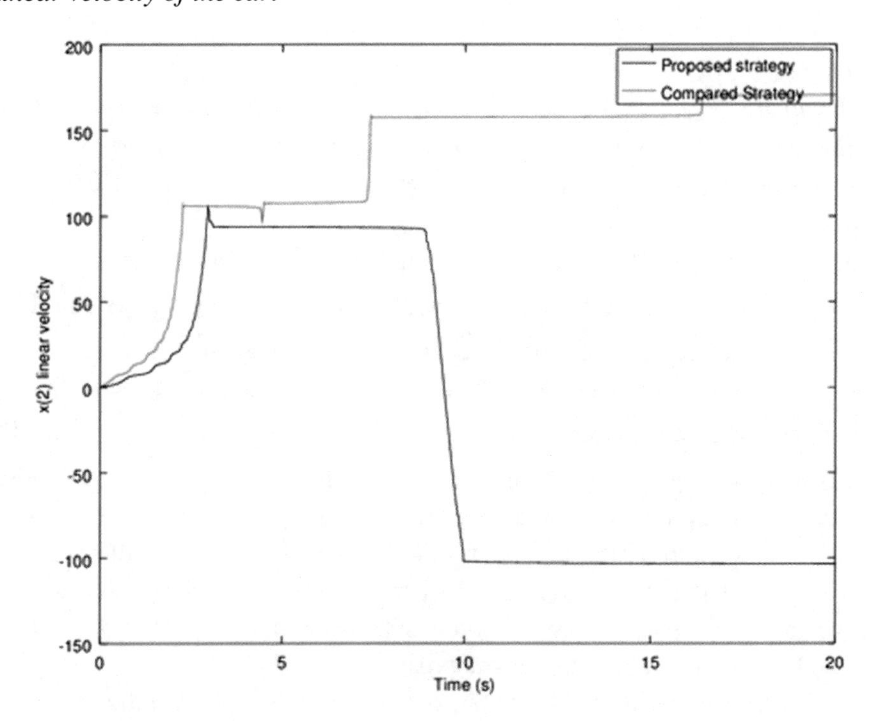

Figure 11. Angular position of the cart

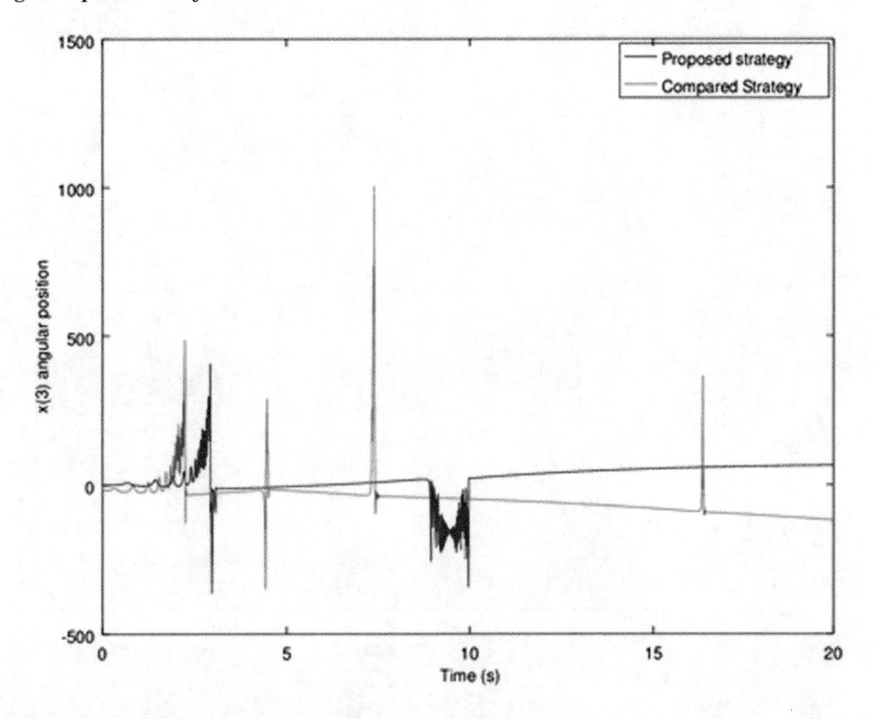

Figure 12. Angular velocity of the cart

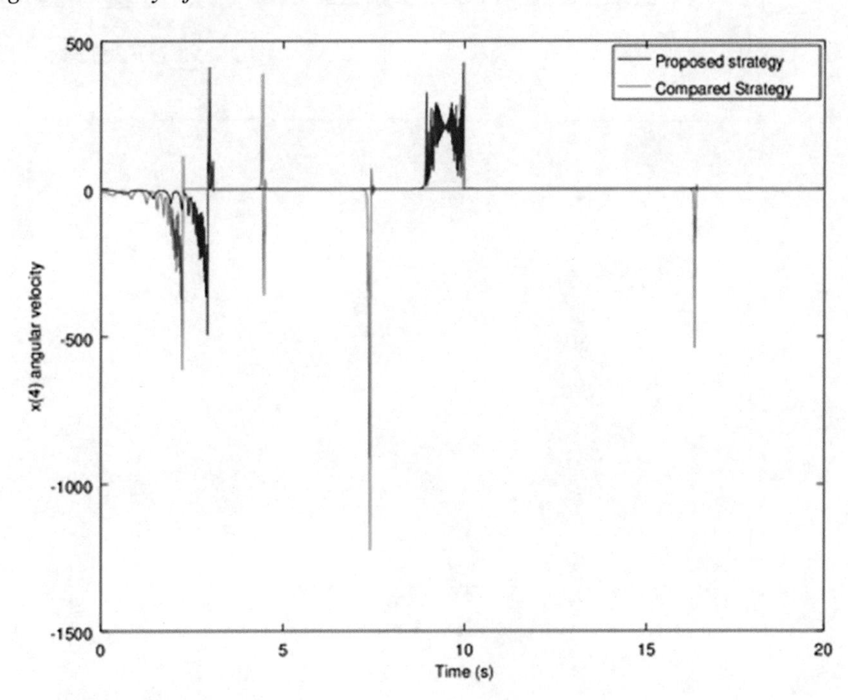

Figure 13. Linear force of the cart

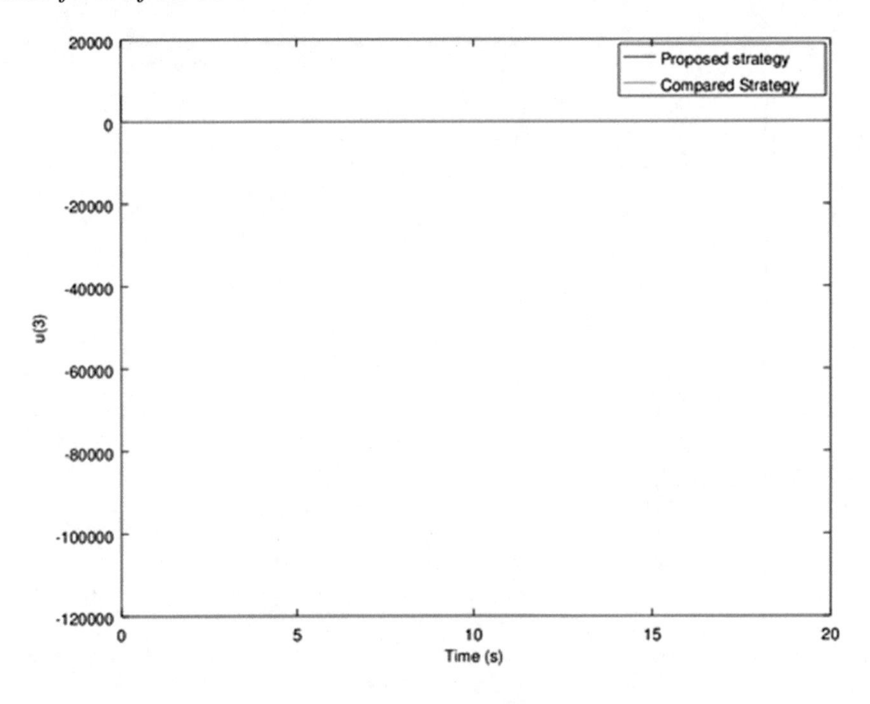

Figure 14. Torque of the cart

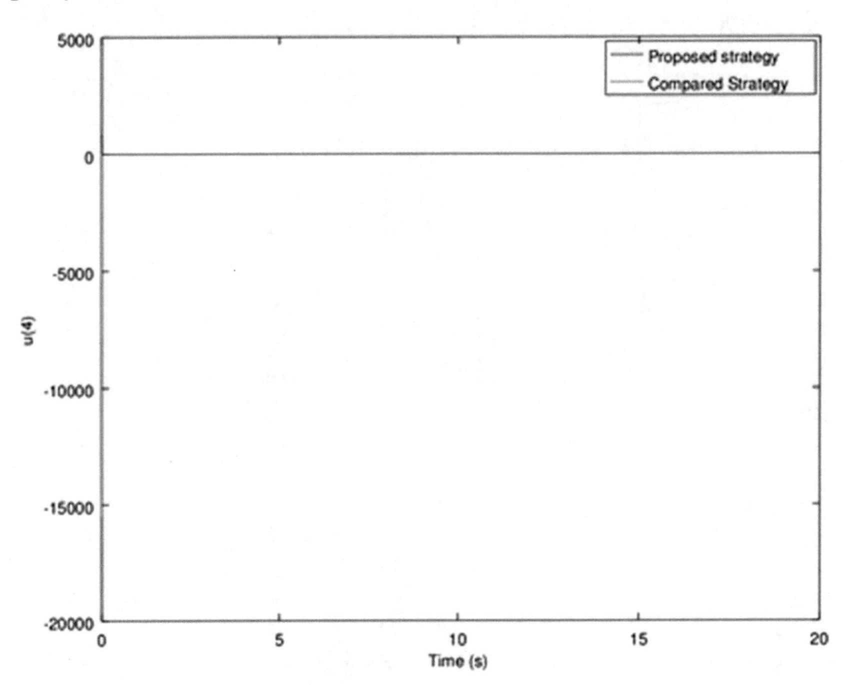

6. DISCUSSIONS

The H_∞ PI loop shaping controller for mechanical system with backlash design described in this chapter offers an excellent contribution due to the robustness and optimality of this technique. The results shown in this chapter, theoretical and experimental, prove that the controller can be implemented in many kinds of mechanical systems such as inverted pendulums, ball and plate systems that are mostly used in laboratories, but as explained in the introduction, there are many practical systems in applications such as mechanical, aeronautical, renewable energy, chemical and acoustic systems.

The proposed strategy is designed first by considering a performance index for the plant and then the loop shaping design is done by taking into account the frequency characteristics of the systems represented by a state-space model. The backlash model is obtained by a describing function which is advantageous because the frequency domain representation of a state-space model and therefore the loop shaping controller design is done easily in order to obtain the desired frequency characteristic of the open loop plant. Something that is important to remark is that the PSO algorithm to find the PI gain matrices used in the controller yields optimal results and improves the system performance in comparison with other strategies found in literature avoiding the gain matrix selection by trial and error. It is important to notice that the PSO algorithm implements a small number of particles and evolution cycles but increasing the number of particles and evolution cycles can improve the system performance considering that PSO is a non-convex optimization technique.

The numerical results obtained by implementing the obtained theoretical results in the cart-pendulum system demonstrated that the system is stabilized in the equilibrium point efficiently in comparison with other techniques, so variables such as the linear and angular position and velocities respectively reach the desired position. In comparison with previous studies, the PI controller parameter tuning done by the PSO provides the desired outcomes related to the optimal parameter selection in order to stabilize the system variables in the equilibrium point. One of the main advantages of the parameter tuning by PSO is that this algorithm is relatively simple and provides an optimal or a near to the optimal system performance that is an advantage with other strategies such as linear matrix inequalities (LMI's).

7. CONCLUSION

In this chapter, a PI H_∞ loop shaping controller for the stabilization of mechanical systems in the presence of backlash is proposed. These approaches offer different point of views when this nonlinearity is present in different kinds of n degrees of freedom mechanical systems. A simple and straightforward independent control approach is proved to be an effective control strategy to deal with this discontinuity avoiding unwanted effects and the decline of the system output. A multivariable control loop shaping approach is implemented with the use of a describing function model; this control strategy has the advantage that allows the designer to select the desired frequency domain characteristics of the closed loop system making it ideal to be implemented along with describing functions. The PSO provides the optimal system response in order to drive the system variables of the mechanical system to the equilibrium point. An absolute stability test is performed to check if the system is asymptotically stable and to find the limit cycle oscillations parameters. The parameter tuning of the PI controller gain is done by PSO algorithm where as it is corroborated in the numerical simulation section, this algorithm provided an optimal controller tuning along with the loop shaping design. For future direction, this study can be extended to other kinds of physical and practical systems such as electrical and energy systems in which this phenomenon is found taking into account that this is a robust control strategy. Moreover, other systems with input nonlinearities such as saturation and dead-zone could be considered in order to design efficient loop shaping control strategies with dynamics. Selecting other appropriate gain matrices tuning with evolutionary algorithms and linear matrix inequalities LMI's for example is also suggested as a future direction.

REFERENCES

Adams, R. J., & Baron, J. R. (1998). Loop Shaping to Improve the Multi-variable Phase Margin. *Proceedings of the 37th IEEE Conference on Decision & Control.* DOI: 10.1109/CDC.1998.757872

Azar, A. T. (2010a). *Fuzzy Systems.* Vienna, Austria: IN-TECH.

Azar, A. T. (2010b). Adaptive Neuro-Fuzzy Systems. In A. T. Azar (Ed.), *Fuzzy Systems.* Vienna, Austria: IN-TECH. doi:10.5772/7220

Azar, A. T. (2012). Overview of Type-2 Fuzzy logic systems. *International Journal of Fuzzy System Applications*, *2*(4), 1–28. doi:10.4018/ijfsa.2012100101

Azar, A. T., Kumar, J., Kumar, V., & Rana, K. P. S. (2017d). Control of a Two Link Planar Electrically-Driven Rigid Robotic Manipulator Using Fractional Order SOFC. *Proceedings of the International Conference on Advanced Intelligent Systems and Informatics 2017, 639*, 47-56.

Azar, A. T., Ouannas, A., & Singh, S. (2017c). Control of New Type of Fractional Chaos Synchronization. *Proceedings of the International Conference on Advanced Intelligent Systems and Informatics 2017, 639*, 47-56.

Azar, A. T., & Serrano, F. E. (2014). Robust IMC-PID tuning for cascade control systems with gain and phase margin specifications. *Neural Computing and Applications, 25*(5), 983-995. DOI: 10.1007/s00521-014-1560-x

Azar, A. T., & Serrano, F. E. (2015a). Stabilization and Control of Mechanical Systems with Backlash. IGI Global. doi:10.4018/978-1-4666-7248-2.ch001

Azar, A. T., & Serrano, F. E. (2015b). Design and Modeling of Anti Wind Up PID Controllers. In Complex system modelling and control through intelligent soft computations (vol. 319, pp. 1-44). Springer-Verlag. doi:10.1007/978-3-319-12883-2_1

Azar, A. T., & Serrano, F. E. (2015c). Adaptive Sliding mode control of the Furuta pendulum. In Studies in Computational Intelligence (vol. 576, pp. 1-42). Springer-Verlag GmbH Berlin/Heidelberg. doi:10.1007/978-3-319-11173-5_1

Azar, A. T., & Serrano, F. E. (2015d). Deadbeat Control for Multivariable Systems with Time Varying Delays. In Chaos Modeling and Control Systems Design (vol. 581, pp. 97-132). Springer-Verlag GmbH Berlin/Heidelberg. DOI doi:10.1007/978-3-319-13132-0_6

Azar, A. T., & Serrano, F. E. (2016a) Robust control for asynchronous switched nonlinear systems with time varying delays. *Proceedings of the International Conference on Advanced Intelligent Systems and Informatics 2016*, 533, 891-899. 10.1007/978-3-319-48308-5_85

Azar, A. T., & Serrano, F. E. (2016b). Stabilization of Mechanical Systems with Backlash by PI Loop Shaping. *International Journal of System Dynamics Applications*, *5*(3), 20–47. doi:10.4018/IJSDA.2016070102

Azar, A. T., & Serrano, F. E. (2017). Passivity Based Decoupling of Lagrangian Systems. *Proceedings of the International Conference on Advanced Intelligent Systems and Informatics 2016*, 533, 891-899. 10.1007/978-3-319-48308-5_85

Azar, A. T., & Vaidyanathan, S. (2015a). Handbook of Research on Advanced Intelligent Control Engineering and Automation. IGI Global. doi:10.4018/978-1-4666-7248-2

Azar, A. T., & Vaidyanathan, S. (2015b). *Computational Intelligence applications in Modeling and Control. In Studies in Computational Intelligence* (Vol. 575). Springer-Verlag.

Azar, A. T., & Vaidyanathan, S. (2015c). *Chaos Modeling and Control Systems Design. In Studies in Computational Intelligence* (Vol. 581). Springer-Verlag.

Azar, A. T., & Vaidyanathan, S. (2016). *Advances in Chaos Theory and Intelligent Control. In Studies in Fuzziness and Soft Computing* (Vol. 337). Springer-Verlag. doi:10.1007/978-3-319-30340-6

Azar, A. T., Vaidyanathan, S., & Ouannas, A. (2017a). *Fractional Order Control and Synchronization of Chaotic Systems. In Studies in Computational Intelligence* (Vol. 688). Springer-Verlag. doi:10.1007/978-3-319-50249-6

Azar, A. T., Volos, C., Gerodimos, N. A., Tombras, G. S., Pham, V. T., Radwan, A. G., … Munoz-Pacheco, J. M. (2017b). A novel chaotic system without equilibrium: Dynamics, synchronization and circuit realization. *Complexity*. doi:10.1155/2017/7871467

Azar, A. T., & Zhu, Q. (2015). *Advances and Applications in Sliding Mode Control systems. In Studies in Computational Intelligence* (Vol. 576). Springer-Verlag.

Barreiro, A., & Baños, A. (2006). Input output stability of systems with backlash. *Automatica*, *42*(6), 1017–1024. doi:10.1016/j.automatica.2006.02.017

Bentsman, J., Orlov, Y., & Aguilar, L. T. (2013). *Nonsmooth H-infinity Output Regulation with Application to a Coal-Fired Boiler/Turbine Unit with Actuator Deadzone. 2013 American Control Conference (ACC)*, Washington, DC. DOI: 10.1109/ACC.2013.6580434

Boukhnifer, M., & Ferreira, A. (2005). H Infinity Loop Shaping for Stabilization and Robustness of a Tele-Micromanipulation System. *IEEE/RSJ International Conference on Intelligent Robots and Systems. Intelligent Robots and Systems*, 778-783.

Boulkroune, A., Bouzeriba, A., Bouden, T., & Azar, A. T. (2016a). Fuzzy Adaptive Synchronization of Uncertain Fractional-order Chaotic Systems. In A. T. Azar & S. Vaidyanathan (Eds.), *Advances in Chaos Theory and Intelligent Control. Studies in Fuzziness and Soft Computing* (Vol. 337). Springer-Verlag. doi:10.1007/978-3-319-30340-6_28

Boulkroune, A., Hamel, S., & Azar, A. T. (2016b). *Fuzzy control-based function synchronization of unknown chaotic systems with dead-zone input. In Advances in Chaos Theory and Intelligent Control. Studies in Fuzziness and Soft Computing* (Vol. 337). Springer-Verlag.

Brogan, W. L. (2005). *Modern Control Theory*. Prentice Hall.

Chyung, D. H. (1992). Output Feedback Controller for Systems Containing a Backlash. *Proceedings of the 31st Conference on Decision and Control*. 10.1109/CDC.1992.371218

Gao, Z. W., & So, A. T. (2003). A general doubly coprime factorization for descriptor systems. *Systems & Control Letters*, *49*(3), 213–224. doi:10.1016/S0167-6911(02)00325-0

Ghoudelbourk, S., Dib, D., Omeiri, A., & Azar, A. T. (2016). MPPT Control in wind energy conversion systems and the application of fractional control (PIα) in pitch wind turbine. *International Journal of Modelling, Identification and Control*, *26*(2), 140–151. doi:10.1504/IJMIC.2016.078329

Glück, T., Eder, A., & Kugi, A. (2013). Swing-up control of a triple pendulum on a cart with experimental validation. *Automatica*, *49*(3), 801–808. doi:10.1016/j.automatica.2012.12.006

Grassi, G., Ouannas, A., Azar, A. T., Radwan, A. G., Volos, C., Pham, V. T., . . . Stouboulos, I. N. (2017). *Chaos Synchronisation Of Continuous Systems Via Scalar Signal*. The 6th International Conference on Modern Circuits and Systems Technologies (MOCAST), Thessaloniki Greece. 10.1109/MOCAST.2017.7937629

Guo, J., Yao, B., Chen, Q., & Wu, X. (2009). High Performance Adaptive Robust Control for Nonlinear System with Unknown Input Backlash. *Proceedings of the 48th IEEE Conference on Decision and Control, 2009 held jointly with the 2009 28th Chinese Control Conference*. 10.1109/CDC.2009.5399543

Haddad, W. M., & Chellaboina, V. (2008). *Nonlinear Dynamical Systems and Control - a Lyapunov Based Approach*. Princeton University Press.

Hariz, M. B., & Bouani, F. (2016). Synthesis and Implementation of a Fix Low Order Controller on an Electronic System. *International Journal of System Dynamics Applications*, *5*(4), 42–63. doi:10.4018/IJSDA.2016100103

Hippe, P. (1994). Strictly Doubly Coprime Factorizations and all Stabilizing Compensators Related to Reduced-order Observer. *Automatica*, *30*(12), 1955–1959. doi:10.1016/0005-1098(94)90056-6

Iqbal, S., Bhatti, A. I., Akhtar, M., & Ullah, S. (2007). Design and Robustness Evaluation of an H Infinity Loop Shaping Controller for a 2DOF Stabilized Platform. *Proceedings of the European Control Conference. Proceedings of the European Control Conference 2007*, 2098-2104.

Ismail, M. M., Abdel Fattah, H. A., & Bhagat, A. (2012). Adaptive Output Feedback Voltage-Based Control of Magnetically-Saturated Induction Motors. *International Journal of System Dynamics Applications*, *1*(3), 1–53. doi:10.4018/ijsda.2012070101

Jang, J. O., Lee, P. G., Chung, H. T., & Jeon, G. J. (2003). Output Backlash Compensation of Systems Using Fuzzy Logic. *Proceedings of the 2003 American Control Conference*. 10.1109/ACC.2003.1243449

Jing, Z., & Wen, C. (2007). Adaptive Inverse Control of a Magnetic Suspension System with Input Backlash. *16th IEEE International Conference on Control Applications*. DOI: 10.1109/CCA.2007.4389423

Joshi, S., & Talange, D. B. (2016). Fault Tolerant Control of an UAV Using Periodic Output Feedback with Multi Model Approach. *International Journal of System Dynamics Applications*, *5*(2), 41–62. doi:10.4018/IJSDA.2016040103

Kim, S.-M., Pereira, J. A., Lopes, V. Jr, Turra, A. E., & Brennan, M. J. (2017). Practical active control of cavity noise using loop shaping: Two case studies. *Applied Acoustics*, *121*, 65–73. doi:10.1016/j.apacoust.2016.12.004

Liu, S., Ai, H., Lin, Z., & Meng, Z. (2017). Analysis of vibration characteristics and adaptive continuous perturbation control of some torsional vibration system with backlash. *Chaos, Solitons, and Fractals*, *103*, 151–158. doi:10.1016/j.chaos.2017.06.001

McFarlane, D., & Glover, K. (1992). A Loop Shaping Design Procedure Using H Infinity Synthesis. *IEEE Transactions on Automatic Control*, *37*(6), 759–769. doi:10.1109/9.256330

Meghni, B., Dib, D., & Azar, A. T. (2017c). A Second-order sliding mode and fuzzy logic control to Optimal Energy Management in PMSG Wind Turbine with Battery Storage. *Neural Computing & Applications*, *28*(6), 1417–1434. doi:10.100700521-015-2161-z

Meghni, B., Dib, D., Azar, A. T., Ghoudelbourk, S., & Saadoun, A. (2017a). *Robust Adaptive Supervisory Fractional order Controller For optimal Energy Management in Wind Turbine with Battery Storage. In Studies in Computational Intelligence* (Vol. 688, pp. 165–202). Springer-Verlag.

Meghni, B., Dib, D., Azar, A. T., & Saadoun, A. (2017b). *Effective Supervisory Controller to Extend Optimal Energy Management in Hybrid Wind Turbine under Energy and Reliability Constraints. International Journal of Dynamics and Control*. doi:10.100740435-016-0296-0

Mekki, H., Boukhetala, D., & Azar, A. T. (2015). Sliding Modes for Fault Tolerant Control. In Advances and Applications in Sliding Mode Control systems (vol. 576, pp. 407-433). Springer-Verlag GmbH Berlin/Heidelberg. doi:10.1007/978-3-319-11173-5_15

Melkou, L., & Hamerlain, M. (2014). Classical Sliding and Generalized Variable Structure Controls for a Manipulator Robot Arm with Pneumatic Artificial Muscles. *International Journal of System Dynamics Applications*, *3*(1), 47–70. doi:10.4018/ijsda.2014010103

Mnasser, A., Bouani, F., & Ksouri, M. (2014). Neural Networks Predictive Controller Using an Adaptive Control Rate. *International Journal of System Dynamics Applications*, *3*(3), 127–147. doi:10.4018/ijsda.2014070106

Mousa, M. E., Ebrahim, M. A., & Moustafa, M. A. (2015). Stabilizing and Swinging-Up the Inverted Pendulum Using PI and PID Controllers Based on Reduced Linear Quadratic Regulator Tuned by PSO. *International Journal of System Dynamics Applications*, *4*(4), 52–69. doi:10.4018/IJSDA.2015100104

Nordin, M., & Gutman, P.-O. (2002). Controlling mechanical systems with backlash—a survey. *Automatica*, *38*(10), 1633–1649. doi:10.1016/S0005-1098(02)00047-X

Ouannas, A., Azar, A. T., & Abu-Saris, R. (2016a). A new type of hybrid synchronization between arbitrary hyperchaotic maps. *International Journal of Machine Learning and Cybernetics*. doi:10.100713042-016-0566-3

Ouannas, A., Azar, A. T., & Radwan, A. G. (2016b) On Inverse Problem of Generalized Synchronization Between Different Dimensional Integer-Order and Fractional-Order Chaotic Systems. *The 28th International Conference on Microelectronics*. 10.1109/ICM.2016.7847942

Ouannas, A., Azar, A. T., & Vaidyanathan, S. (2017f). On A Simple Approach for Q-S Synchronization of Chaotic Dynamical Systems in Continuous-Time. *Int. J. Computing Science and Mathematics*, *8*(1), 20–27.

Ouannas, A., Azar, A. T., & Vaidyanathan, S. (2017g). New Hybrid Synchronization Schemes Based on Coexistence of Various Types of Synchronization Between Master-Slave Hyperchaotic Systems. *International Journal of Computer Applications in Technology*, *55*(2), 112–120. doi:10.1504/IJCAT.2017.082868

Ouannas, A., Azar, A. T., & Vaidyanathan, S. (2017i). A Robust Method for New Fractional Hybrid Chaos Synchronization. *Mathematical Methods in the Applied Sciences*, *40*(5), 1804–1812. doi:10.1002/mma.4099

Ouannas, A., Azar, A. T., & Ziar, T. (2017h). *On Inverse Full State Hybrid Function Projective Synchronization for Continuous-time Chaotic Dynamical Systems with Arbitrary Dimensions*. Differential Equations and Dynamical Systems. doi:10.100712591-017-0362-x

Ouannas, A., Azar, A. T., Ziar, T., & Radwan, A. G. (2017d). *Study On Coexistence of Different Types of Synchronization Between Different dimensional Fractional Chaotic Systems. In Studies in Computational Intelligence* (Vol. 688, pp. 637–669). Springer-Verlag.

Ouannas, A., Azar, A. T., Ziar, T., & Radwan, A. G. (2017e). *Generalized Synchronization of Different Dimensional Integer-order and Fractional Order Chaotic Systems. In Studies in Computational Intelligence* (Vol. 688, pp. 671–697). Springer-Verlag.

Ouannas, A., Azar, A. T., Ziar, T., & Vaidyanathan, S. (2017a). *On New Fractional Inverse Matrix Projective Synchronization Schemes. In Studies in Computational Intelligence* (Vol. 688, pp. 497–524). Springer-Verlag.

Ouannas, A., Azar, A. T., Ziar, T., & Vaidyanathan, S. (2017b). *Fractional Inverse Generalized Chaos Synchronization Between Different Dimensional Systems. In Studies in Computational Intelligence* (Vol. 688, pp. 525–551). Springer-Verlag.

Ouannas, A., Azar, A. T., Ziar, T., & Vaidyanathan, S. (2017c). *A New Method To Synchronize Fractional Chaotic Systems With Different Dimensions. In Studies in Computational Intelligence* (Vol. 688, pp. 581–611). Springer-Verlag.

Ouannas, A., Grassi, G., Azar, A. T., Radwan, A. G., Volos, C., Pham, V. T., . . . Stouboulos, I. N. (2017j). *Dead-Beat Synchronization Control in Discrete-Time Chaotic Systems*. The 6th International Conference on Modern Circuits and Systems Technologies (MOCAST), Thessaloniki, Greece. 10.1109/MOCAST.2017.7937628

Rodriguez-Linan, M. C., & Heath, W. P. (2017). Backlash compensation for plants with saturating actuators. *Proceedings of the Institution of Mechanical Engineers. Part I, Journal of Systems and Control Engineering*, *231*(6), 471–480. doi:10.1177/0959651817692471

Serrano, F. E., & Flores, M. A. (2015). C++ Library for Fuzzy Type-2 Controller Design With Particle Swarm Optimization Tuning. IEEE CONCAPAN 2015, Tegucigalpa, Honduras.

Si, W., Dong, X., & Yang, F. (2017). Adaptive neural prescribed performance control for a class of strict-feedback stochastic nonlinear systems with hysteresis input. *Neurocomputing*, *251*, 35–44. doi:10.1016/j.neucom.2017.04.017

Silva, E. I., & Erraz, D. A. (2006). An LQR Based MIMO PID Controller Synthesis Method for Unconstrained Lagrangian Mechanical Systems. *Proceedings of the 45th IEEE Conference on Decision & Control. Decision and Control.* 10.1109/CDC.2006.377348

Singh, S., Azar, A. T., Ouannas, A., Zhu, Q., Zhang, W., & Na, J. (2017). Sliding Mode Control Technique for Multi-switching Synchronization of Chaotic Systems. *9th International Conference on Modelling, Identification and Control (ICMIC 2017)*, Kunming, China.

Soliman, N. S., Said, L. A., Azar, A. T., Madian, A. H., Radwan, A. G., & Ouannas, A. (2017). *Fractional Controllable Multi-Scroll V-Shape Attractor with Parameters Effect*. The 6th International Conference on Modern Circuits and Systems Technologies (MOCAST), Thessaloniki, Greece.

Tao, G., & Kokotovic, P. V. (1993a). Adaptive Control of Systems with Backlash. *Automatic*, *29*(2), 323–335. doi:10.1016/0005-1098(93)90126-E

Tao, G., & Kokotovic, P. V. (1993b). Continuous-time Adaptive Control of Systems with Unknown Backlash. In *Proceedings of the American Control Conference*. IEEE.

Tao, G., & Kokotovik, P. (1995). Adaptive Control of Systems with Unknown Output Backlash. *IEEE Transactions on Automatic Control*, *40*(2), 326–330. doi:10.1109/9.341803

Tierno, J. E., Kim, K. Y., Lacy, S. L., & Bernstein, D. S. (2000). Describing Function Analysis of an Anti-Backlash Controller. *Proceedings of the American Control Conference*. 10.1109/ACC.2000.877005

Tolba, M. F., AbdelAty, A. M., Soliman, N. S., Said, L. A., Madian, A. H., Azar, A. T., & Radwan, A. G. (2017). FPGA implementation of two fractional order chaotic systems. *International Journal of Electronics and Communications*, *28*, 162–172. doi:10.1016/j.aeue.2017.04.028

Vaidyanathan, S., & Azar, A. T. (2015a) Anti-Synchronization of Identical Chaotic Systems using Sliding Mode Control and an Application to Vaidyanathan-Madhavan Chaotic Systems. In Advances and Applications in Sliding Mode Control systems (vol. 576, pp. 527-547). Springer-Verlag GmbH Berlin/Heidelberg. doi:10.1007/978-3-319-11173-5_19

Vaidyanathan, S., & Azar, A. T. (2015b). Hybrid Synchronization of Identical Chaotic Systems using Sliding Mode Control and an Application to Vaidyanathan Chaotic Systems. In Advances and Applications in Sliding Mode Control systems (vol. 576, pp. 549-569). Springer-Verlag GmbH Berlin/Heidelberg. doi:10.1007/978-3-319-11173-5_20

Vaidyanathan, S., & Azar, A. T. (2015c). Analysis, Control and Synchronization of a Nine-Term 3-D Novel Chaotic System. In Chaos Modeling and Control Systems Design (vol. 581, pp. 3-17). Springer-Verlag GmbH Berlin/Heidelberg. DOI doi:10.1007/978-3-319-13132-0_1

Vaidyanathan, S., & Azar, A. T. (2015d). Analysis and Control of a 4-D Novel Hyperchaotic System. In Chaos Modeling and Control Systems Design (vol. 581, pp. 19-38). Springer-Verlag GmbH Berlin/Heidelberg. DOI doi:10.1007/978-3-319-13132-0_2

Vaidyanathan, S., & Azar, A. T. (2016a). Takagi-Sugeno Fuzzy Logic Controller for Liu-Chen Four-Scroll Chaotic System. *International Journal of Intelligent Engineering Informatics*, *4*(2), 135–150. doi:10.1504/IJIEI.2016.076699

Vaidyanathan, S., & Azar, A. T. (2016b). *Dynamic Analysis, Adaptive Feedback Control and Synchronization of an Eight-Term 3-D Novel Chaotic System with Three Quadratic Nonlinearities. In Studies in Fuzziness and Soft Computing* (Vol. 337, pp. 155–178). Springer-Verlag.

Vaidyanathan, S., & Azar, A. T. (2016c). *Qualitative Study and Adaptive Control of a Novel 4-D Hyperchaotic System with Three Quadratic Nonlinearities. In Studies in Fuzziness and Soft Computing* (Vol. 337, pp. 179–202). Springer-Verlag.

Vaidyanathan, S., & Azar, A. T. (2016d). *A Novel 4-D Four-Wing Chaotic System with Four Quadratic Nonlinearities and its Synchronization via Adaptive Control Method. Advances in Chaos Theory and Intelligent Control. In Studies in Fuzziness and Soft Computing* (Vol. 337, pp. 203–224). Springer-Verlag.

Vaidyanathan, S., & Azar, A. T. (2016e). *Adaptive Control and Synchronization of Halvorsen Circulant Chaotic Systems. Advances in Chaos Theory and Intelligent Control. In Studies in Fuzziness and Soft Computing* (Vol. 337, pp. 225–247). Springer-Verlag.

Vaidyanathan, S., & Azar, A. T. (2016f). *Adaptive Backstepping Control and Synchronization of a Novel 3-D Jerk System with an Exponential Nonlinearity. In Advances in Chaos Theory and Intelligent Control* (Vol. 337, pp. 249–274). Springer-Verlag.

Vaidyanathan, S., & Azar, A. T. (2016g). *Generalized Projective Synchronization of a Novel Hyperchaotic Four-Wing System via Adaptive Control Method. In Advances in Chaos Theory and Intelligent Control* (Vol. 337, pp. 275–296). Springer-Verlag.

Vaidyanathan, S., Azar, A. T., & Ouannas, A. (2017a). *An Eight-Term 3-D Novel Chaotic System with Three Quadratic Nonlinearities, its Adaptive Feedback Control and Synchronization. In Studies in Computational Intelligence* (Vol. 688, pp. 719–746). Springer-Verlag.

Vaidyanathan, S., Azar, A. T., & Ouannas, A. (2017c). *Hyperchaos and Adaptive Control of a Novel Hyperchaotic System with Two Quadratic Nonlinearities. In Studies in Computational Intelligence* (Vol. 688, pp. 773–803). Springer-Verlag.

Vaidyanathan, S., Azar, A. T., Rajagopal, K., & Alexander, P. (2015b). Design and SPICE implementation of a 12-term novel hyperchaotic system and its synchronization via active control (2015). International *Journal of Modelling, Identification and Control*, *23*(3), 267–277. doi:10.1504/IJMIC.2015.069936

Vaidyanathan, S., Idowu, B. A., & Azar, A. T. (2015c). Backstepping Controller Design for the Global Chaos Synchronization of Sprott's Jerk Systems. In Chaos Modeling and Control Systems Design (vol. 581, pp. 39-58). Springer-Verlag GmbH Berlin/Heidelberg. doi:10.1007/978-3-319-13132-0_3

Vaidyanathan, S., Sampath, S., & Azar, A. T. (2015a). Global chaos synchronisation of identical chaotic systems via novel sliding mode control method and its application to Zhu system. International Journal of Modelling. *Identification and Control*, *23*(1), 92–100. doi:10.1504/IJMIC.2015.067495

Vaidyanathan, S., Zhu, Q., & Azar, A. T. (2017b). *Adaptive Control of a Novel Nonlinear Double Convection Chaotic System. In Studies in Computational Intelligence* (Vol. 688, pp. 357–385). Springer-Verlag.

Wang, Z., Volos, C., Kingni, S. T., Azar, A. T., & Pham, V. T. (2017). Four-wing attractors in a novel chaotic system with hyperbolic sine nonlinearity. *Optik - International Journal for Light and Electron Optics, 131*(2017), 1071-1078.

Wigren, T. (2017). Loop-Shaping Feedback and Feedforward Control for Networked Systems With Saturation and Delay. *Asian Journal of Control*, *19*(4), 1329–1349. doi:10.1002/asjc.1442

Zhou, J., Er, M. J., & Wen, C. (2005). Adaptive Control of Nonlinear Systems with Uncertain Dead-zone Nonlinearity. *Proceedings of the 44th IEEE Conference on Decision and Control, and the European Control Conference*. DOI: 10.1109/CDC.2005.1582254

Zhou, S.-L., Han, P., Wang, D.-F., & Liu, Y.-Y. (2004). A Kind of Multivariable PID Design Method for Chaos System using H infinity loop shaping design procedure. *Proceedings of the Third International Conference on Machine Learning and Cybernetics. Machine Learning and Cybernetics*. DOI: 10.1109/ICMLC.2004.1382294

Zhu, Q., & Azar, A. T. (2015). *Complex system modelling and control through intelligent soft computations. In Studies in Fuzziness and Soft Computing* (Vol. 319). Springer-Verlag.

Chapter 3
Control-Based Maximum Power Point Tracking for a Grid-Connected Hybrid Renewable Energy System Optimized by Particle Swarm Optimization

Mouna Ben Smida
National Engineering School of Monastir, Tunisia

Anis Sakly
National Engineering School of Monastir, Tunisia

Sundarapandian Vaidyanathan
Vel Tech University, India

Ahmad Taher Azar
Benha University, Egypt & Nile University, Egypt

ABSTRACT

There has been a great deal of interest in renewable energy sources for electricity generation, particularly for photovoltaic and wind generators. These energy resources have enormous potential and can meet the current global demand for energy. Despite the obvious advantages of renewable energy sources, they have significant disadvantages, such as the discontinuity of their generation, due to their heavy dependence on weather and climate change, which affects their effectiveness in the conversion of renewable energy. Faced with this conflict, it is essential to optimize the performance of renewable systems in order to increase their efficiency. Several unconventional approaches to optimization have been developed in the literature. In this chapter, the management of a hybrid renewable energy system is optimized by intelligent approach based on particle swarm optimization comprising a shaded photovoltaic generator and a wind generator.

DOI: 10.4018/978-1-5225-4077-9.ch003

1. INTRODUCTION

The energy consumption has extensively augmented due to the considerable industrial development. Dealing with this problem a major interest is oriented to the use of renewable energy sources (Zhu & Azar, 2015; Azar & Zhu, 2015; Azar & Vaidyanathan, 2015a,b,c). Firstly, wind power generation is considered the most economically viable alternative within the portfolio of renewable energy resources. It is one of the most promising renewable energy resources for producing electricity due to its cost competitiveness compared to other conventional types of energy resources (Suvire & Mercado, 2012). On the other hand, solar energy has an increasing importance in the field of electrical applications, since it is considered to be an inexhaustible and widely available source (Lalouni et al., 2009). In fact, photovoltaic (PV) generators have been applied in various fields such as electrification of isolated sites, installation in buildings and direct connection to medium and low voltage networks (Billel et al, 2017, 2016; Ghoudelbourk et al., 2016). To optimize the utilization of large arrays of PV modules, maximum power point tracker (MPPT) is normally employed in conjunction with the power converter (DC-DC converter and/or inverter). Due to the varying environmental condition, as temperature and solar insolation, the PV characteristic curve exhibits a maximum power point (MPP) that varies nonlinearly with these conditions, thus posing a challenge for the tracking method. Various MPP tracking methods have been proposed (Lyden & Haque, 2015; Saravanan & Babu, 2016; Liu et al., 2016). Most commonly used techniques of MPPT are perturb and observation (P&O), incremental conductance (IC), hill-climbing method (HC); Constant Voltage and Current, Parasitic Capacitance along with some digital signal processing (DSP) based methods (Joshi & Arora, 2017; Ramli et al., 2017; Liu et al., 2015).

While the above alternative energy systems are considered as promising power sources, they have a main drawback given their strong dependence on the weather and climate conditions affecting their efficiency during energy conversion (Ramli et al., 2017; Joshi & Arora, 2017). Also, when partially shaded conditions (PSC) occurs, the power voltage characteristic curve of the PV modules becomes complex, exhibiting multiple peak values. Therefore, traditional MPPT methods are not suitable for use in PSC (Liu et al., 2015; Jordehi, 2016). A Combination of sources to form a single renewable energy system called as hybrid renewable energy system (HRES), is considered as a suitable solution for this conflict (Wang & Singh, 2009). HRESs are usually more reliable and less costly than other type of renewable systems that rely on a single source of energy. It is true that, from an economic point of view, the results appear quite convincing as to the profitability of the above-mentioned hybrid system, but this does not exclude the fact that the combination of the two sources constitutes a rather complex system from a technological point of view. In this framework, several researchers have investigated the design, optimization, operation and control of HRES. Recent years, many important developments related to the design of nonlinear systems for many practical applications have been proposed such as optimal control, nonlinear feedback control, adaptive control, sliding mode control, nonlinear dynamics, chaos control, chaos synchronization control, fuzzy logic control, fuzzy adaptive control, fractional order control, and robust control and their integrations (Azar & Vaidyanathan, 2016; Boulkroune et al, 2016a,b; Azar et al., 2017a,b,c,d; Azar 2010a,b, 2012; Meghni et al, 2017a,b,c; Mekki et al., 2015; Vaidyanathan & Azar, 2015a,b,c,d, 2016a,b,c,d,e,f,g, 2017a,b,c; Grassi et al., 2017; Ouannas et al., 2016a,b, 2017a,b,c,d,e,f,g,h,I,j; Singh et al., 2017; Vaidyanathan et al, 2015a,b,c; Wang et al., 2017; Soliman et al., 2017; Tolba et al., 2017).

Various aspects and problems must be taken into account when the major concern is about the optimization of a hybrid solar/wind energy system (Celik, 2002). Evaluating the general performance of hybrid photovoltaic/wind energy system and generating acceptable power quality are some of these problems (Nehrir et al., 2000) even if there are many research works that discussed the optimization of a HRES. However, few works consider more than one object in optimization problem of a HRES by using evolutionary algorithm (EA). Some research suggested the use of adaptive neuro-fuzzy inference system to model the hybrid systems (Rajkumar et al., 2011). Yang et al. (2008) studied an optimal sizing method for stand-alone hybrid solar/wind system with the loss of power supply probability technology by using a genetic algorithm (GA). The above-mentioned algorithm was also developed for optimal placement of a hybrid PV–wind system (Masoum et al., 2010).

In fact, due to the high complexity and high nonlinearity of the renewable systems, this work suggests a meta-heuristic method called particle swarm optimization (PSO) (Khare & Rangnekar, 2013) to control a grid connected hybrid solar/wind system. Metaheuristics have proved to be efficient techniques for solving difficult optimization problems (Jordehi, 2016). They are even efficient in cases where a clear mathematical formulation of objective function versus decision variables does not exist. They are equipped with exploration capability, so unlike P&O, IC and HC, they may find global MPP in partial shading conditions (PSC). Unlike conventional MPPT techniques, metaheuristic MPPT strategies do not oscillate around MPP (Jordehi, 2016). This works discusses also the control of the pitch angle of the wind turbine system and the maximum power point tracking (MPPT) of a shaded PV system via the PSO algorithm.

The remaining of this chapter is organized as follows: Section 2 gives the model of the studied PV/wind system. Modeling of the proposed hybrid renewable energy systems is discussed in Section 3. Section 4 focuses on the application of intelligent techniques in the field of renewable energy sources and the concept of using PSO method in controlling the wind turbine pitch angle and global maximum power point (GMPP) tracking. The performance of the developed control strategies is discussed in Section 5 using simulation results and finally Section 6 concludes the chapter.

2. STUDY OF HYBRID RENEWABLE ENERGY SYSTEMS

A Hybrid Renewable Energy System (HRES) is defined as an electrical system consisting of several sources of energy, at least one of which is renewable. The architecture of a hybrid system may include a device of storage (Stoyanov, 2011). Several distributions of hybrid systems are carried out according to the criterion adopted. In this section a development of the most common classifications is presented. A classification of the HRES according to their mode of operation can be established. In fact, the first group includes hybrid systems that pump their power to the grid also called network grid, this type helps to satisfy the need of the country's electrical system. The second group comprises the HRESs operation in stand-alone or isolated mode. They must meet consumption requirements in remote locations on the electricity grid.

The classification of hybrid systems according to their structure can be carried out taking into account three criteria. In fact, the first model is based on the presence of a conventional energy source, which can be a micro-gas turbine, a diesel generator, and an entire power station in the case of a complete electrical network study (Vechiu, 2005). The second criterion is linked to the presence of the storage device, in fact the presence of this element during the absence of a primary resource makes it possible to ensure better satisfaction. Storage devices can be rechargeable batteries, flywheels, electrolysers with hydrogen tanks, etc. The third classification relates to the type of renewable energy sources present in the chain. In fact, the hybrid system may include a photovoltaic source, a wind turbine or a combination of both, the choice of source depends on the potential energy available at the HRES facility. The block diagram in Figure 1 summarizes the classification criteria for hybrid systems.

2.1. Different Configurations of Hybrid Systems

Several techniques are adopted in the literature to integrate different alternatives energy power generation sources to form a hybrid system. Generally, these methods are classified into three configurations: dc-coupled architecture, ac-coupled architecture, and hybrid-coupled architecture (Agbossou et al., 2004, 2001; Ko et al., 2006; Farret & Simoes 2006). These configurations are briefly described in the next subsections.

1. DC-Coupled Systems

The DC-coupled configuration is given in Figure 2. In fact, the different renewable sources are connected to a DC bus via appropriate power electronic interfacing circuits. The DC sources may be directly connected to the DC bus if appropriate. In the presence of DC loads, they can be linked through a DC-DC converter, to achieve appropriate DC voltage for the DC loads. The entire system can supply power to the AC loads, or be interfaced to the utility grid via a DC/AC converter that can be designed to control the bidirectional power flow. In spite of the simplicity of the studied DC coupling configuration, it also presents drawbacks. In fact, certain amount of energy is dissipated at the converters, which affects the overall efficiency of the system. Also, the entire system is highly dependent on the state of the inverter to supply AC power. To avoid this situation, it is possible to connect in parallel several inverters with lower power rating but in this case a suitable power sharing control scheme is required to achieve a desired load distribution among the different (Maharjan et al., 2008).

Figure 1. Block diagram of hybrid renewable energy systems

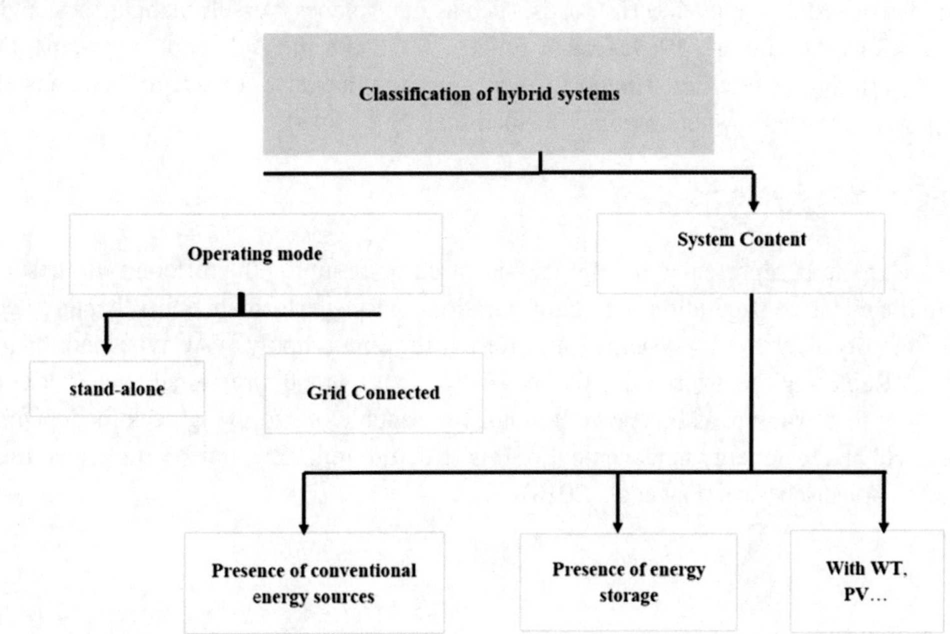

Figure 2. Block diagram of the DC coupled hybrid energy system

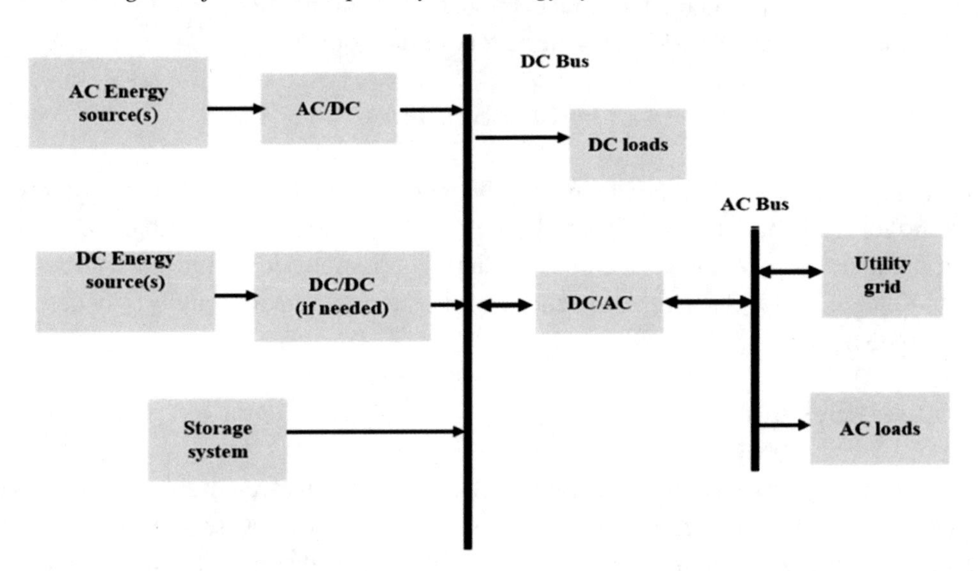

2. AC-Coupled Systems

The AC-coupled configuration can be classified into two subcategories: the power frequency AC (PFAC)-coupled and the high-frequency AC (HFAC)-coupled systems (Nehrir & Wang, 2009).

For the PFAC configuration, given in Figure 3 (a), the different energy sources are integrated via their own power electronic interfacing circuits to a power frequency AC bus. This architecture can also contain coupling inductors between the power electronic circuits and the AC bus to achieve desired power flow management. In HFAC-coupled system, shown in Figure 3 (b), the different energy sources are connected to a HFAC bus, to which HFAC loads are linked. This configuration has been used mostly in applications with HFAC (e.g., 400 Hz) loads, such as in airplanes, vessels, submarines, and in space station applications (Sood et al., 1987; Cha & Enjeti, 2003). For the AC coupled systems, DC power can be obtained through a rectifier. The HFAC configuration may also include a PFAC bus and utility grid using power converters, where regular AC loads can be coupled.

3. Hybrid-Coupled Systems

The hybrid architecture, represented by Figure 4, is based on grouping the different sources to a DC or an AC bus of the mixed configuration. This configuration is more performant than other architectures. In fact, the profitability of the hybrid system is improved by the direct supply of AC type loads by renewable energy source. Replacing the inverter and the rectifier by using of a bidirectional converter emphasizes the efficiency of this structure as this power topology is capable of supplying peak loads. On the other hand, the control and the energy management of this structure might be more complicated than for the DC- and AC-coupled schemes (Fay et al., 2010).

Figure 3. Configuration of AC-coupled hybrid energy system: (a) PFAC; (b) HFAC

A)

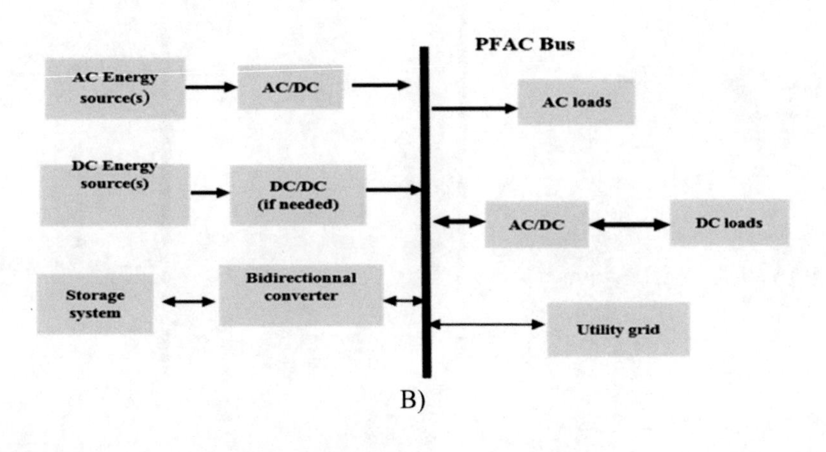

B)

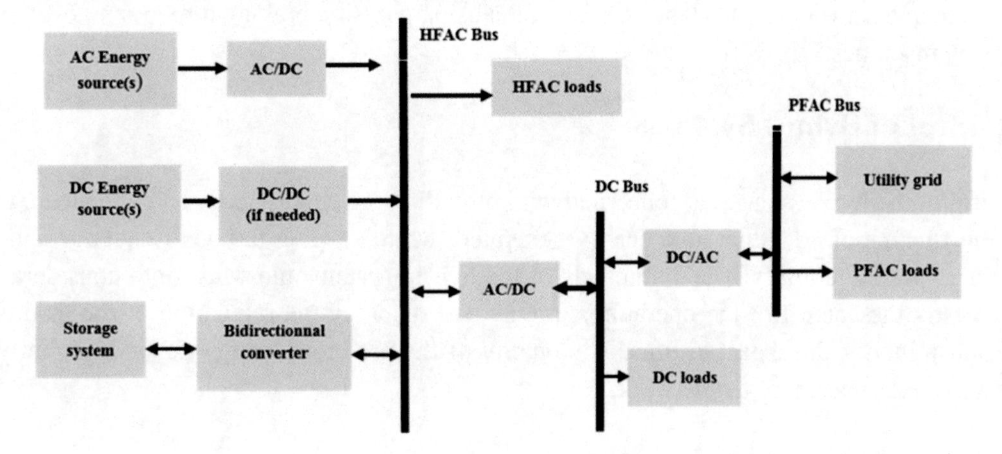

2.2. Problems Encountered in Operation of Hybrid Systems

The main constraint encountered in the functioning of the hybrid systems is related to the random nature of renewable energy sources. In fact, these resources are incapable of instantly producing the required energy by the load. This requires a parallel operation between the sources and the storage system. For this functioning, diesel generators for example operate at a low power and renewable energy sources proceed as a negative source by reducing the average load of the generators (Nema et al., 2009). Other operational problems are also related to the dynamics of the renewable sources generators', particularly in the case of wind turbines. Indeed, when starting a turbine at a high wind speed, the power generated reaches practically the nominal power of the generator. Which causes a sudden change in voltage and frequency and even the shutdown of the system. A hybrid system connected to the insulated three-phase network faces a major problem related to voltage unbalance between phases. In fact, the nature of the electrical receiver, three-phase or unbalanced single phase powered by the isolated three-phase

Figure 4. Block diagram of the hybrid-coupled systems configuration

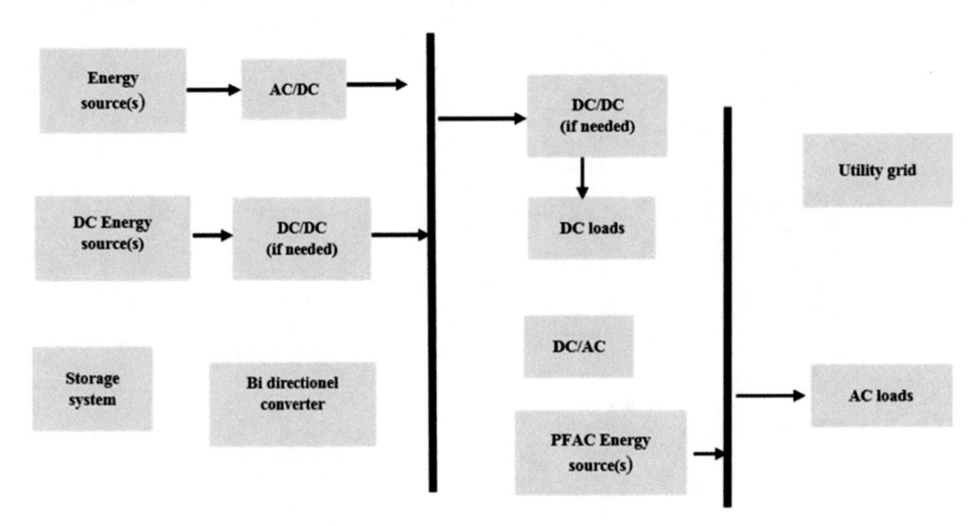

network, generates a voltage unbalance capable of causing parasitic braking torques and overheating in AC rotating machines.

2.3. Control of Hybrid Systems

The control of the hybrid system is concerned with providing the energy required by the load, irrespective of the fluctuations of renewable energy generated, while keeping the bus frequency and voltage within the appropriate limits. The commands of the hybrid systems must take into consideration two aspects, firstly the control of the operating strategy and secondly the regulation of the quality of the energy transmitted with respect to time. The quality of the produced energy depends strongly on the voltage and the frequency of the network.

3. PROPOSED HYBRID RENEWABLE ENERGY SYSTEMS MODELING

3.1 Wind Turbine Model

The output power of the wind turbine is given by:

$$\begin{cases} V_{g_d} = V_{i_d} - R_g i_{g_d} - L\dfrac{di_{g_d}}{dt} + \omega l_g i_{g_q} \\ V_{g_q} = V_{i_q} - R_g i_{g_q} - L\dfrac{di_{g_q}}{dt} - \omega l_g i_{g_d} \end{cases} \quad (1)$$

where: ρ is the air density, A is the turbine swept area and V_W is the wind speed

The power coefficient C_P is a non-linear function depending on the tip speed ratio λ and β the blade pitch angle. It is expressed by:

$$C_p(\lambda,\beta) = 0.53\left[\frac{151}{\lambda_i} - 0.58\beta - 0.002\beta^{2.14} - 13.2\right]\times \exp\left(\frac{-18.4}{\lambda_i}\right) \tag{2}$$

where:

$$\lambda_i = \frac{1}{\frac{1}{\lambda - 0.02\beta} - \frac{0.003}{\beta^3 + 1}} \tag{3}$$

The tip speed ratio (TSR) is explicit by the following expression:

$$\lambda = \frac{R\Omega}{V_w} \tag{4}$$

By using (2), the typical C_p versus λ curve is shown in Figure 5.
The turbine torque is expressed by:

$$T_m = \frac{P_w}{\Omega} \tag{5}$$

The mechanical speed of the turbine is derived from the fundamental equation of the dynamics as:

$$J\frac{d\Omega}{dt} = T_m - T_{em} - f\Omega \tag{6}$$

Figure 5. Power coefficient (Cp) versus tip speed ratio (λ) curve

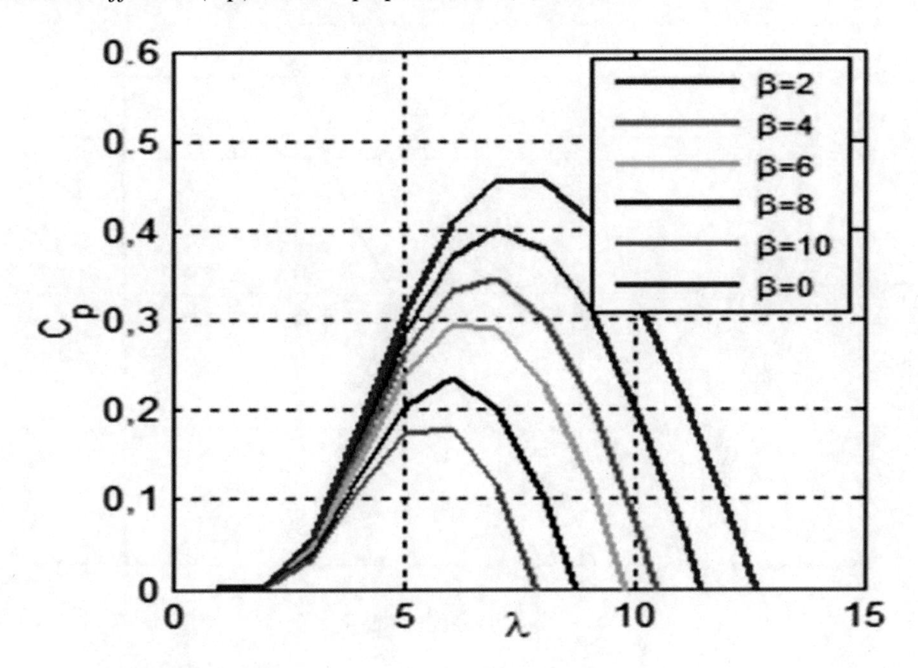

3.1.1 Different Operating Zones of Wind Turbine

The power of the wind turbine depends essentially on the wind speed, and there are mainly three power control regions as shown in Figure 6. Three wind speeds are considered as limits of this division, the minimum wind speed V_{cut-in}, the nominal wind speed V_{nom} and the wind speed limit $V_{cut-out}$.

In region I, the wind turbine is in the off state while the wind speed is less than $V_{cut-in,}$ so the generator torque is zero and the wind turbine cannot produce energy.

In the second region, region II, the wind speed is limited between V_{cut-in} and V_{nom}. The main objective of the control in this region is to maximize the power generated by the wind turbine via an MPPT control.

Considering Region III, the wind speed is greater than V_{nom} but lower than the $V_{cut-out}$ limit speed. The main objective of control in this region is to maintain the power of the generator around the nominal power of the alternator. In fact, in the case of high wind speed, it is necessary to limit the speed of rotation of the turbine in order to avoid damage to the electrical machine. This limitation is obtained by checking the pitch angle. In region IV where the wind speed is greater than $V_{cut-out,}$ the wind turbine must be stopped in order to protect the wind turbine from the damage of the pressure. In this case, the setting angle is generally set at 90 ° and the energy production is stopped.

3.2. Shaded PV System Model

The studied photovoltaic system consists of two PV array connected in series where one of them is shaded. Each PV array comprises 5 modules where each one contains 54 serial cells. The whole system delivers under uniform climatic situations 2000W. The P-V and I-V characteristics of the system are given in Figure 7.

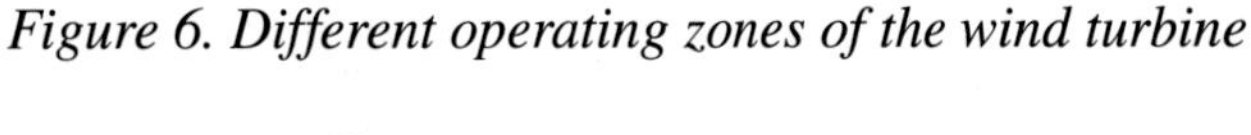

Figure 6. Different operating zones of the wind turbine

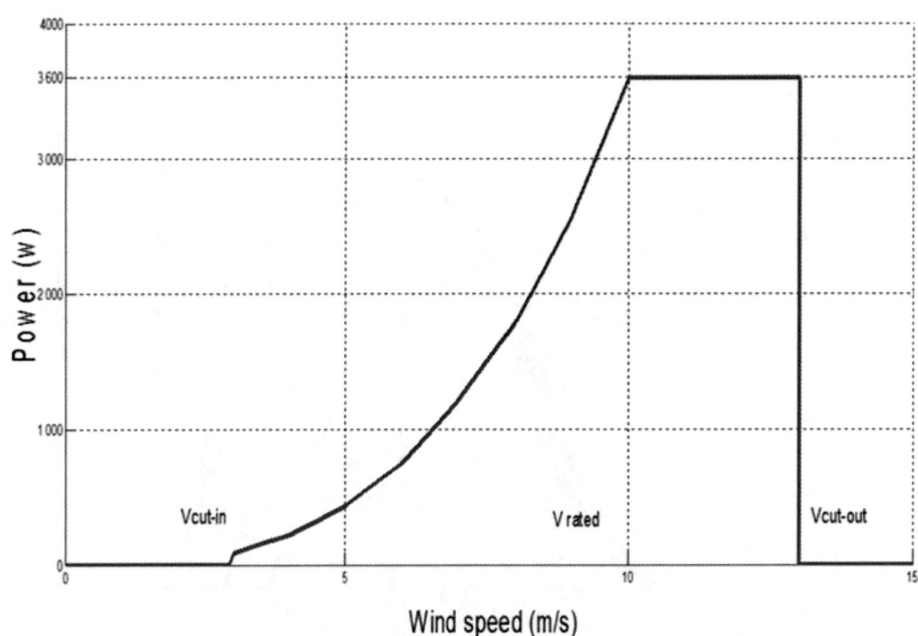

Figure 7. Characteristics of the PV system studied under nominal conditions

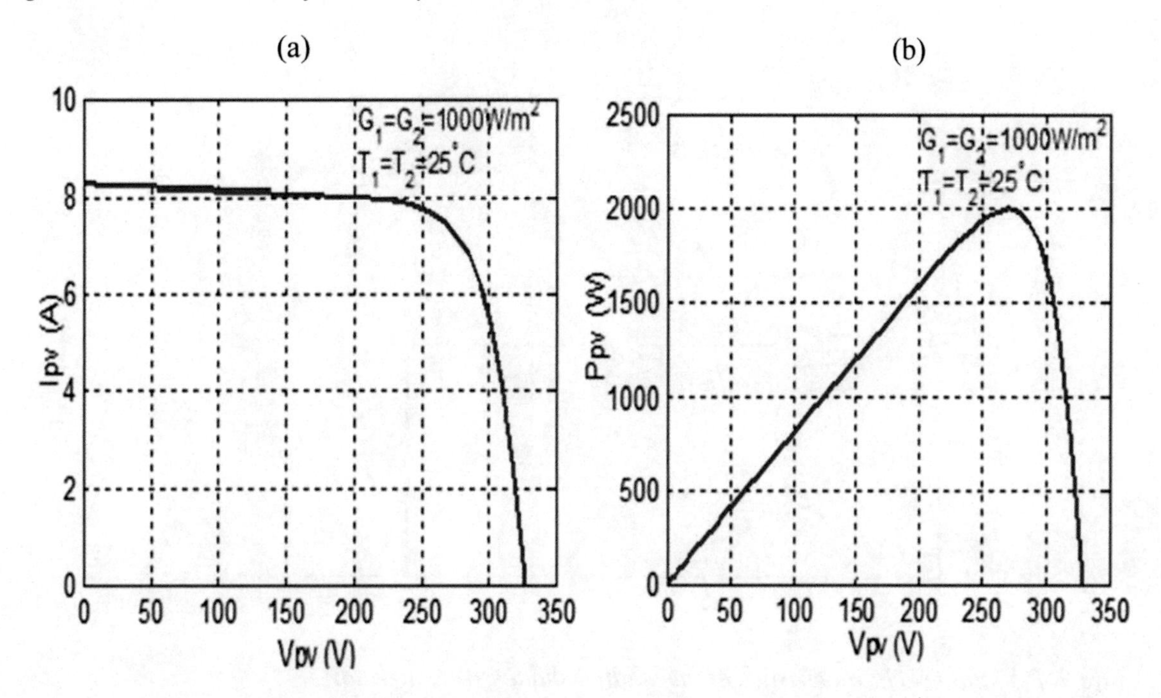

Partial shading occurs due to the exposure of the photovoltaic system under different illumination conditions. In fact, the electrical performance of the system will be based on the cell specifications as well as on the irradiation's conditions because the shaded modules use an amount of the generated power and behave as a load (Zegaoui et al., 2011). This affects the overall behavior of the system and can cause a hot spot problem. Therefore, additional bypass diodes are used in the PV configuration to avoid the self-heating of solar modules.

Many researches have been developed to implement the shaded PV model. The studied photovoltaic system under partial shading conditions when two bypass diodes are used is illustrated in Figure 8. The mathematical model of a solar module with Ns series cells is given by equation (7):

$$I_{pv} = I_{ph} - I_0(\exp(V_{pv} + \frac{N_s R_s I_{pv}}{N_s V_T}) - 1) - V_{pv} + \frac{N_s R_s I_{pv}}{R_{shg}} \qquad (7)$$

The studied system is simulated under two irradiations: G1 and G2. The I-V and P-V characteristics are given in Figure 9 and comprises of two peaks: a local maximum and a global one.

The illumination received by the second generator influences on the overall appearance of the system, particularly on the second extremum, which can be either a Local Maximum (LM) or a Global Maximum (GM) as shown in Figure 9. The next section is devoted to the justification of the position of the extremum.

3.2.1. Position of the Extremum in the Shaded Panel Characteristic

The characteristics of the non-shaded photovoltaic generator, first exposed to G = 1000W/m^2 illumination and secondly to G = 500W / m illumination, are shown in Figure 10. Some research work (Shaiek

Figure 8. Equivalent scheme of the studied photovoltaic system under partial shading conditions

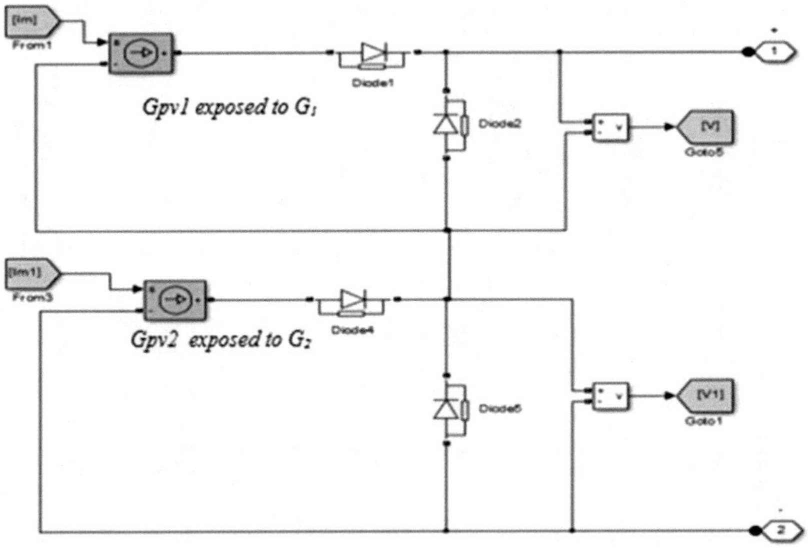

Figure 9. P-V and I-V characteristics of the studied shaded PV generator

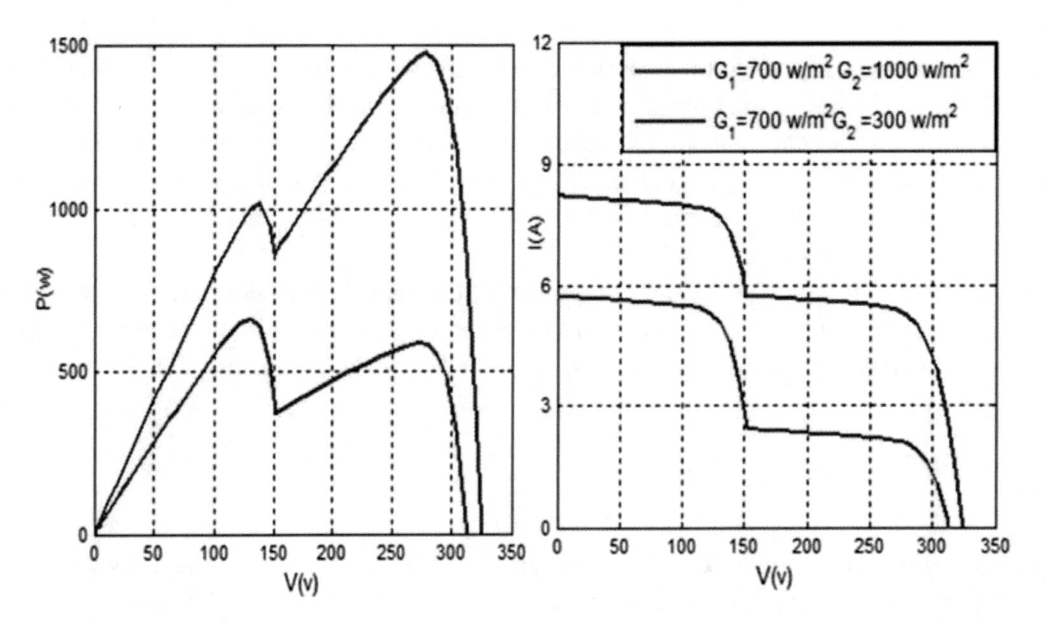

et al., 2013) have approved that the inflection point of the P-V characteristic of the shaded photovoltaic generator corresponds to the intersection between the characteristic of the panel exposed to the illumination G_1 and that of the generator under the illumination G_2. The following part will be devoted to the mathematical justification.

In order to calculate the coordinates of the point of intersection of the two characteristics, the straight lines (D_1) and (D_2) are considered as represented in Figure 10 whose equations are respectively given by:

$$D_1 : a_1 V_{pv} + b_1 \tag{8}$$

$$D_2 : a_2 V_{pv} + b_2 \tag{9}$$

where:

$$a_1 = \frac{510.5 - 103.2}{155.4 - 162.6} = -56.56 \; ; \; a_2 = \frac{314.2 - 82.05}{80.02 - 20.21} = 3.87 \; ; \; b_1 = 9.2910^3 \text{ and } b_2 = 4.52$$

The coordinates of the point of intersection of the two straight lines are obtained by the resolution of the equation $D_1 = D_2$, they are given by:

$$\begin{cases} V_{pv_I} = 153.65 \text{ V} \\ P_{pv_I} = 599.14 \text{ W} \end{cases} \tag{10}$$

The results indicate that the coordinates obtained are in agreement with those of the inflection point I given in Figure 11.

Local Maximum (LM) is M_1 and Global Maximum (GM) is M_3. In fact, M_3 is obtained by dragging the generator characteristic for G = 500W/m² at point I, hence:

Figure 10. The P-V characteristics of the unshaded PV system for different illuminations

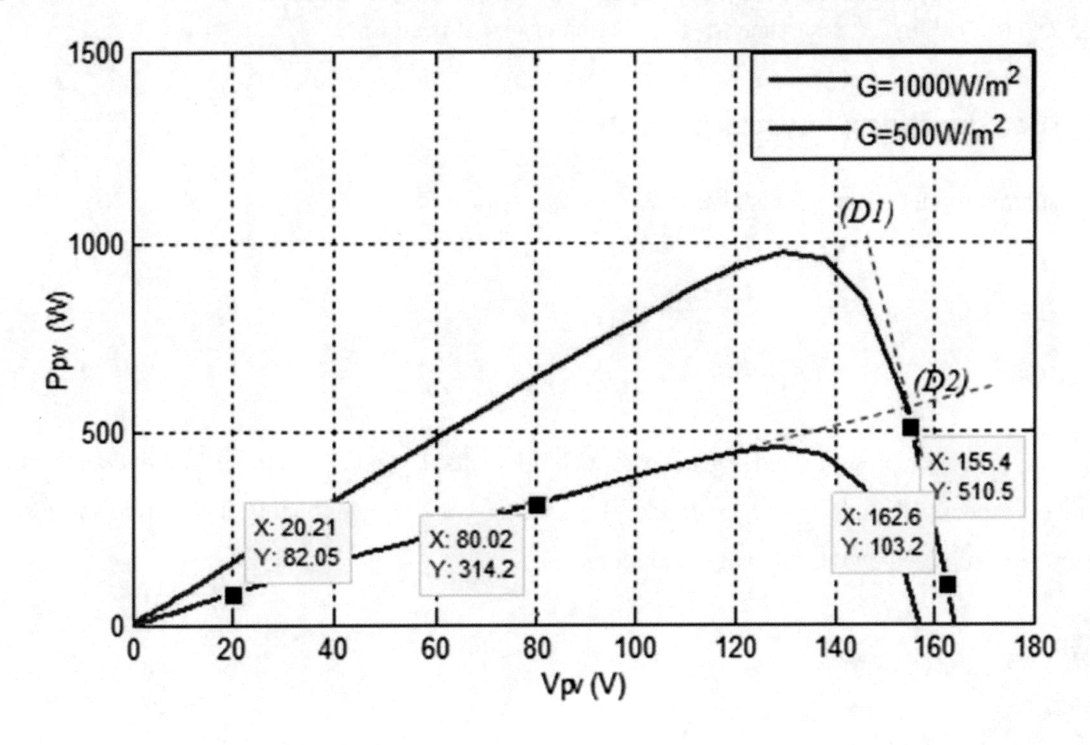

Figure 11. The P-V characteristics of partially shaded PV system under different illuminations

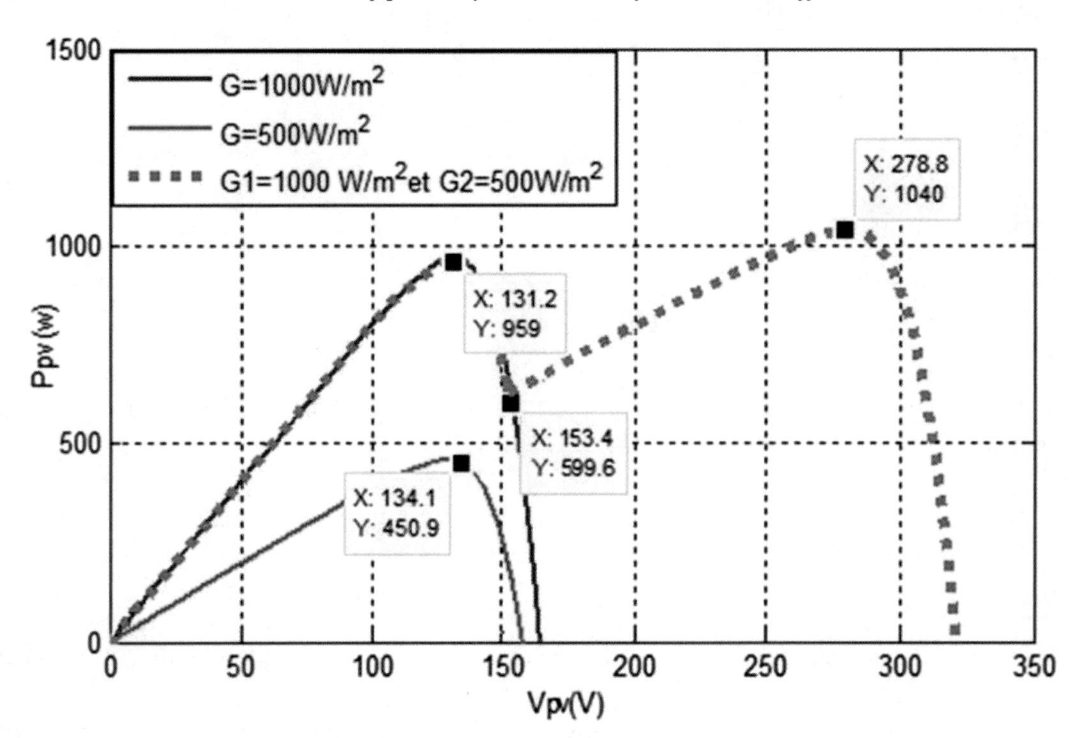

$$P_{pv}(M_2) + P_{pv}(I) = P_{pv}(M_3) \tag{11}$$

The overall appearance of the system depends heavily on the G_2 illumination:
If $P_{pv}(M_2) + P_{pv}(I) > P_{pv}(M_1)$ then M_3 is a GM otherwise it is an LM.

3.3. The Line-Side Converter's Control

The dynamic model of the grid is given by:

$$\begin{cases} V_{g_d} = V_{i_d} - R_g i_{g_d} - L\dfrac{di_{g_d}}{dt} + \omega l_g i_{g_q} \\ V_{g_q} = V_{i_q} - R_g i_{g_q} - L\dfrac{di_{g_q}}{dt} - \omega l_g i_{g_d} \end{cases} \tag{12}$$

where i_{g_d} and i_{g_q} represent the d-q grid current components, L_g and R_g are the grid inductance and resistance, respectively and V_{i_d} and V_{i_q} are the d-q inverter voltage components. The active and reactive powers are expressed by the following equations:

$$P = \frac{3}{2}\left(V_{g_d} i_{g_d} + V_{g_q} i_{g_q}\right) \tag{13}$$

$$Q = \frac{3}{2}\left(V_{g_q} i_{g_d} - V_{g_d} i_{g_q}\right) \tag{14}$$

The grid-side converter's power transmission is regulated in order to keep the DC-link voltage at its reference value, 400v. As the increase in output power than the input power of the DC-link capacitor causes a decrease in DC-link voltage and vice versa, the output power will be controlled to maintain the DC-link voltage approximately constant. Controlling the DC-link voltage and regulating the transmission of the active and reactive power to the grid is assured via the d-q vector control approach. The dc-link voltage is regulated at the desired value by using a PI-controller and the change in the DC-link voltage represents a change in the q-axis current component. The developed structure to control the grid side converter is given in Figure 12; two PI controllers are available to regulate the injected power flow. A d-axis conventional PI regulator controls the active power, while a q-axis one assures the regulation of the reactive power. In this work, the total extracted power from the hybrid system is transmitted to the network.

4. APPLICATION OF INTELLIGENT TECHNIQUES IN THE FIELD OF RENEWABLE ENERGY SOURCES

4.1. Application of Intelligent Techniques in the Field of Wind Energy

The literature has addressed the use of intelligent techniques in the field of wind energy. In fact, several works have dealt with the problem of controlling the tail angle of the turbine via evolutionary methods.

Figure 12. The different grid side control loops

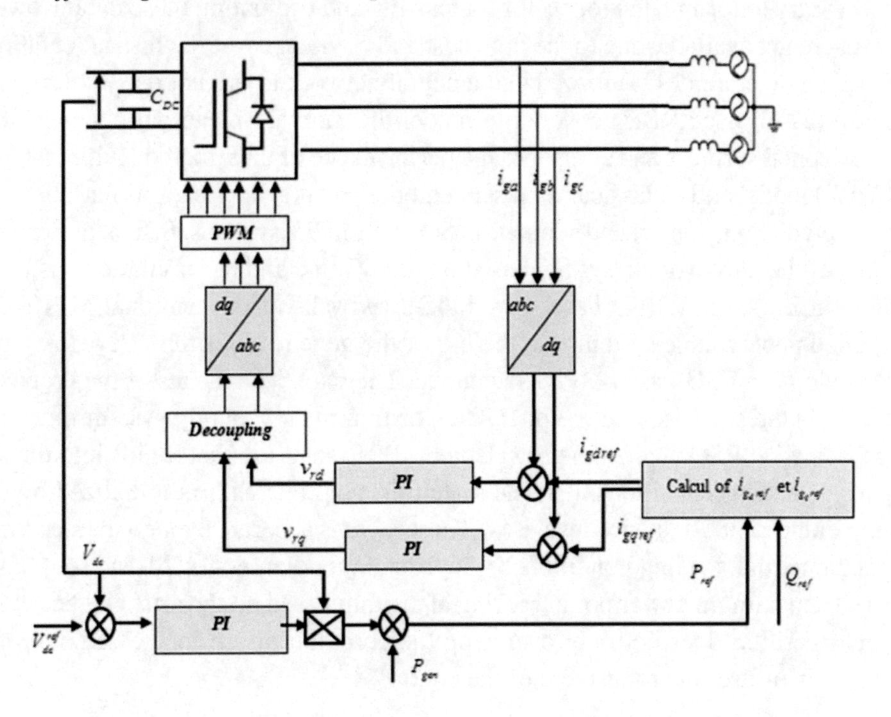

In Chowdhury et al. (2012), modeling of the variable-speed wind turbine connected to the grid has been carried out as well as the control of the pitch angle via a fuzzy logic controller is studied. Ishaque et al. (2012) proposed the design of a robust fuzzy controller to minimize the loss of speed of a Permanent Magnet Synchronous Generator (GSAP) and develops a recursive neural network (RNN) algorithm for controlling the pitch angle of the turbine. The back-propagation learning algorithm is used to regulate the RNN controller. The control of the pitch angle by two mutually exclusive fuzzy logic systems is presented by Chen et al. (2012). The main role of the studied controller is to regulate the output power during high wind speeds and the smoothing of wind energy fluctuations. Poultangari et al. (2012) developed a PSO algorithm to provide a suitable terrain to determine the optimum PI gains for controlling the pitch angle of high power wind turbine blades. In order to provide a set of optimal data to form the neural network, an optimization by the evolutionary algorithm PSO is used. The proposed process does not need the complexity, non-linearities and uncertainties of the system under control. Other research has developed the so-called intelligent techniques to extract the maximum power from the wind generator. In fact, an identification procedure capable of generating an adaptive fuzzy controller for variable-speed wind systems is presented and tested. This methodology, based on digital input-output data generates the best fuzzy Takagi-Sugeno-Kang (TSK) model able to estimate with maximum precision the maximum power extractable from a variable speed wind turbine. The study of the PSO algorithm made it possible by Kongnam & Nuchprayoon (2010) to determine the maximum coefficient of power for each of the two types of wind turbines, that of fixed speed and the other with variable speed so that the energy output can be maximized.

4.2. Application of Intelligent Techniques in the Field of Photovoltaic Energy

Meteorological data such as solar radiation, ambient temperature and duration of sunshine are recognized as reliable variables for renewable energy sources. They play an important role in PV systems. It is therefore necessary to formulate models for forecasting and estimating these data. However, in many cases these data are not available due to the high cost and complexity of the instrumentation required to record them. Elizondo et al. (1994) formulated a neural network to predict daily solar radiation, while Mohandes et al. (2000) used RBF networks to model the monthly mean daily values of global solar radiation on horizontal surfaces and compared the performance of their method with that of a multilayer perceptron (MLP) model and a classical regression model. Several applications have been developed in the literature for prediction, control and simulation of MPPT in PV systems. In fact, in Ben smida & Sakly (2016), a model of the photovoltaic system based on fuzzy logic and its simulation has been developed and the authors in Liu et al. (2016) have solved the drawbacks of conventional MPPT commands in the case of shaded photovoltaic systems via the use of the genetic algorithm. Seyedmahmoudian et al. (2014) have developed a PSO-based MPPT technique. The main advantages of the proposed technique are as follows: ''(1) the stochastic nature of PSO algorithm made a purely system-independent MPPT technique. (2) Using the PSO algorithm protects the MPPT, ensuring that it falls into the local maxima during the partial shading conditions. (3) The system is adaptive; as it is initialized by detecting any changes in temperature and irradiance levels. (4) The system is accurate enough to track the global MPP even during acute partial shading conditions'' (Seyedmahmoudian et al., 2014). Soufyane Benyoucef (2015) proposed a maximum power point tracking algorithm based on the artificial bee colony method. The developed algorithm does not only overcome the common disadvantage of conventional MPPT methods, but also it ensures the robustness of the control.

4.3. PSO Technique Applied to the Studied Hybrid Renewable System

4.3.1. Basic PSO Algorithm

Particle Swarm Optimization (PSO) is considered as an example of evolutionary algorithms. This method imitates the comportment of some natural social organizations as the swarm of bees or colony and a group of birds. It is based on their behavior (Zhan et al., 2009). Particle Swarm Optimization investigates the search-space, and can be used to determine the components and settings required to optimize a special objective function.

The operation begins with a random selection, continues with a search for optimal solutions through earlier iterations, and evaluates the solution qualities through the fitness. In fact, each individual or particle in a swarm performs in a spread approach via its own intelligence and the collective one of the swarm. Consequently, if one particle finds the direction to food, the others individuals will also be able to follow it instantly whatever their positions (Hung, 2013). The PSO algorithm is suited for the derivation of the global optimum. It is also simple in principle, and has a high tracing accuracy as well as fast convergence. For multivariable optimization structure like renewable systems, swarm is supposed to be fixed with each particle located initially at random positions in multi-dimensional space. Each particle possesses a position and a velocity (Clerc & Kennedy, 2002; Seo et al., 2006). It stochastically moves in the design space and remembers the best-encountered position. The particles communicate good positions to each other and adjust their individual positions and velocities based on the information received. As described earlier, the PSO algorithm first selects a number of particles, given as N, at random from a D dimensional search space; the dimension, D, is determined by number of decision variables. Every particle represents one candidate solution, each running stochastically with a certain velocity (V_i) in the search space. The movements of particles are in accordance with their best (P_{best}) position and their Global best (g_{best}) position. To be more precise, P_{best} is the best position experienced by the ith particle throughout all previous iterations, while g_{best} is the best position experienced by the sum of all particles within all past iterations. During the optimization process, the particles adopt the objective function's values, whilst their g_{best} and are P_{best} recorded. The basic PSO algorithm that defines the next position of the candidate solution is as follows:

For the standard algorithm, the velocity v and position x of each particle in iteration k can be expressed as follows:

$$v_k^{(m)} = W\, V_{k-1}^{(m)} + C_1 r_1 \left(p_{best}^{(m)} - x_{k-1}^{(m)} \right) + C_2 r_2 \left(g_{best} - x_{k-1}^{(m)} \right) \quad (15)$$

$$x_k^{(m)} = x_{k-1}^{(m)} + v_k^{(m)} \quad (16)$$

where: i represents the variable of the optimization vector,

k is the number of iterations,

V_{ik} and X_{ik} are the velocity and the position of the ith variable within k iterations,

W is the inertia weight factor,
C_1 is the cognitive coefficient of individual particles,
C_2 is the social coefficient of all particles,
and r_1 as well as r_2 are the random selected variables in the range [0, 1].

The main purpose of these random parameters is to maintain the stochastic movement within iterations. To keep the search space in a certain area, the values of the velocity are set to the range of [0, V_{max}]. The parameters C_1 and C_2 set the relative pull of p_{best} and g_{best}. The parameters r_1 and r_2 are uniformly distributed random variables in the range of [0, 1] .

4.3.2. Pitch Angle Control Using PSO

In this part, the pitch angle regulation of the wind turbine is based on PSO technique is proposed. In fact, the proposed controller calculates the appropriate pitch angle by the adjustment of the reference angle β_{ref}. The angle β_{ref} is considered the particle. The fitness function is expressed using the following equation:

$$FIT = \left|P_{g,\mathrm{nom}} - P_g\right| \tag{17}$$

The initial positions of the evolutionary parameters, particles, are given by a vector comprising βref_j^k . Where j = (1,2,3,4) is the index of the particles.

For each iteration k, the j reference angle values are transmitted to the turbine system imposing a specified torque and therefore a generated power. The studied algorithm is tuned online and the developed algorithm is described by the flowchart shown in Figure 13.

4.3.3. PSO Method for GMPP Tracking

In this work, the MPPT of the studied shaded PV system is based on the PSO technique. In fact, the algorithm tunes the cyclic ratio of the converter by controlling the output voltage of the generator. The cyclic ratio is considered as the particle at each iteration. For the studied algorithm, 4 particles are considered. The initial position of the population is given by the vector below:

$$x=[0.2\ 0.4\ 0.6\ 0.8]\times 2V_{oc} \tag{18}$$

The fitness function to be maximized presents the generated PV power. It is developed as in (19):

$$\mathrm{Fitness}=V_{pv}*I_{pv} \tag{19}$$

Due to the change in operations conditions, the GA algorithm is modified in order to search the new MPP again by resetting the initial population whenever it detects a variation of solar irradiance, temperature, and load.

Accordingly, the GA is reinitialized while the following two conditions are satisfied:

Figure 13. Flowchart of pitch angle control using PSO

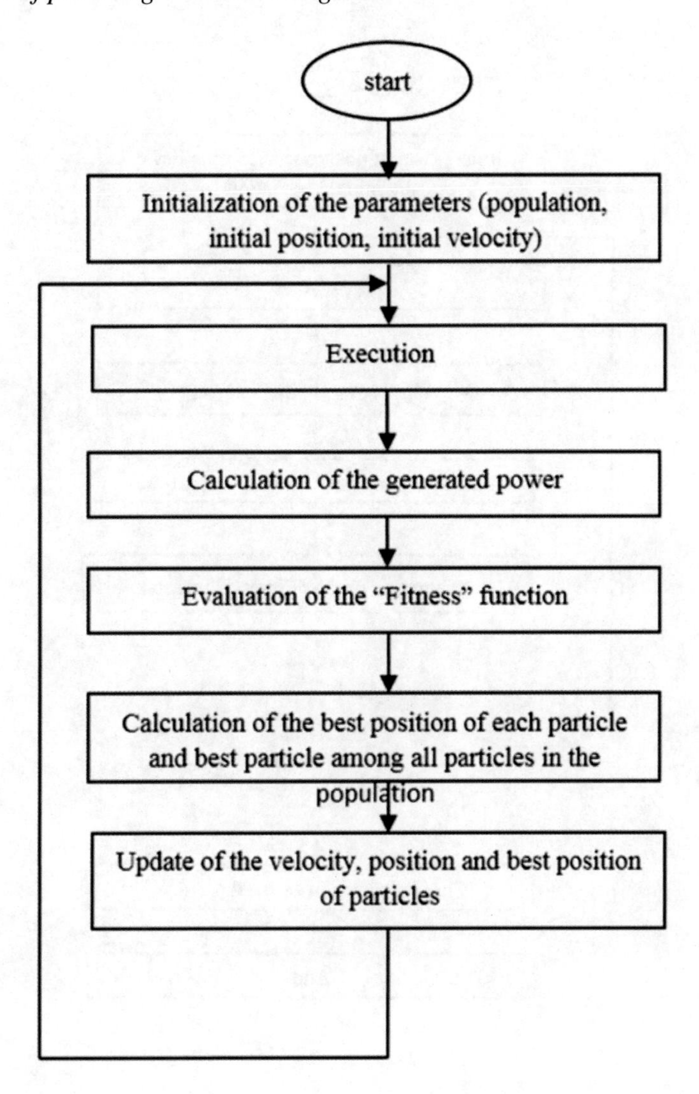

$$\left|V_{pv}(k+1)\right| \langle -\Delta V \tag{20}$$

$$\frac{P_{pv}(k+1)-P_{pv}(k)}{P_{pv}(k)} \rangle \Delta P \tag{21}$$

The flowchart of the proposed PSO algorithm for GMPP tracking is given in Figure 14.

Figure 14. Flowchart of GMPP tracking using PSO

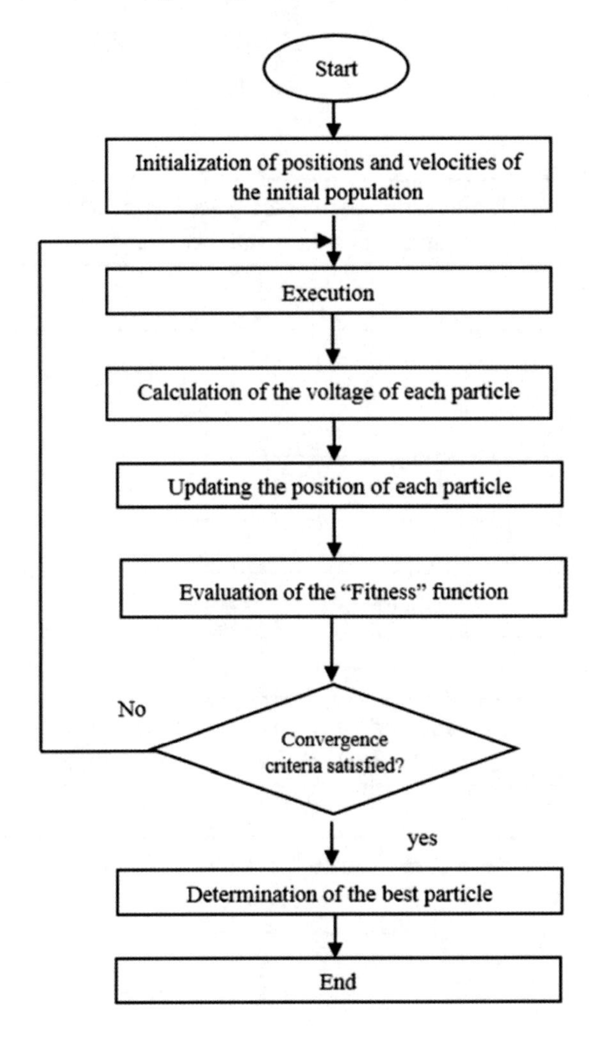

Figure 15. Wind profile

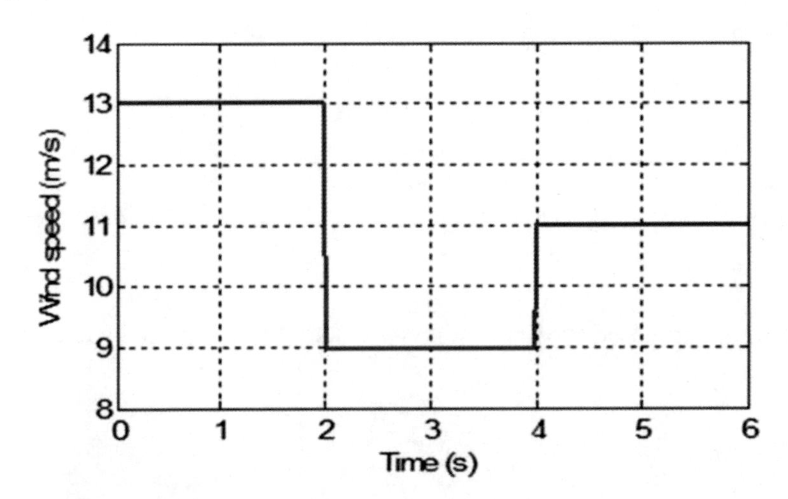

Figure 16. Wind turbine generated power

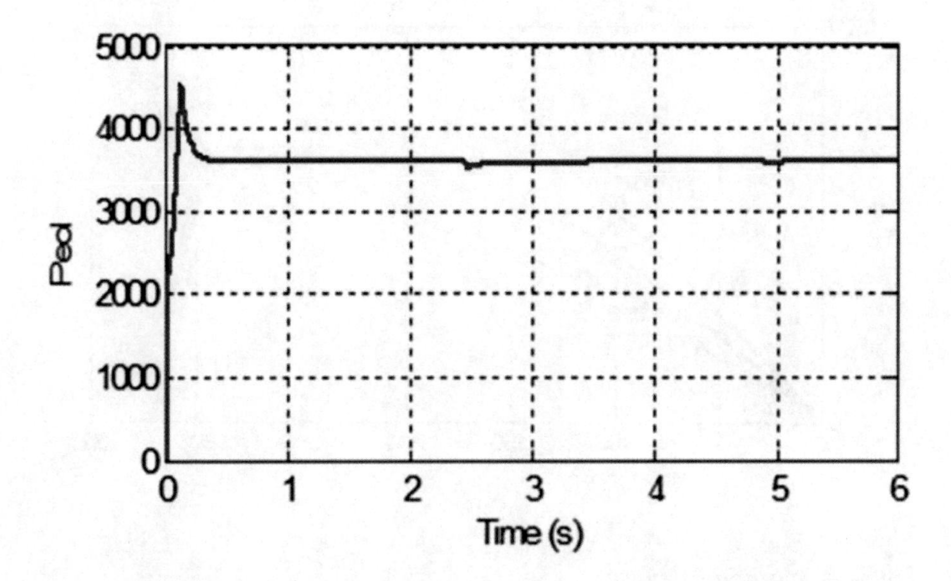

Figure 17. Illumination profile

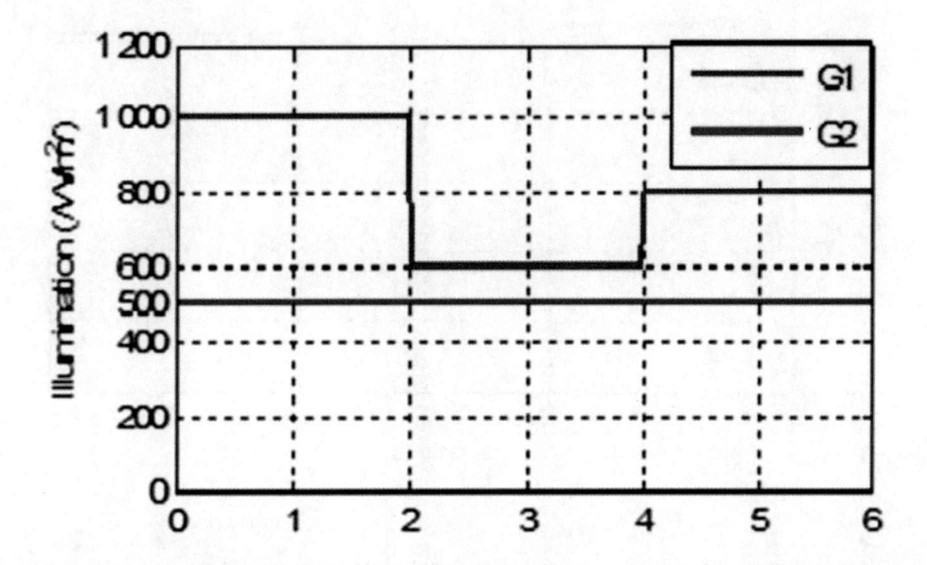

5. SIMULATIONS RESULTS

The behavior of the studied hybrid renewable system is illustrated using numerical simulations carried out under Matlab -Simulink. The variable wind profile is given in Figure 15. The wind turbine generates power P_{eol} is shown in Figure 16. The shaded PV generator is exposed to a variable illumination illustrated in Figure 17. Figure 19 shows its generated power. The P-V characteristic of the GPV is illustrated in Figure 18. It is clear that the PSO algorithm follows the maximum power point for the different states.

Figure 18. P-V characteristics for different studied scenarios

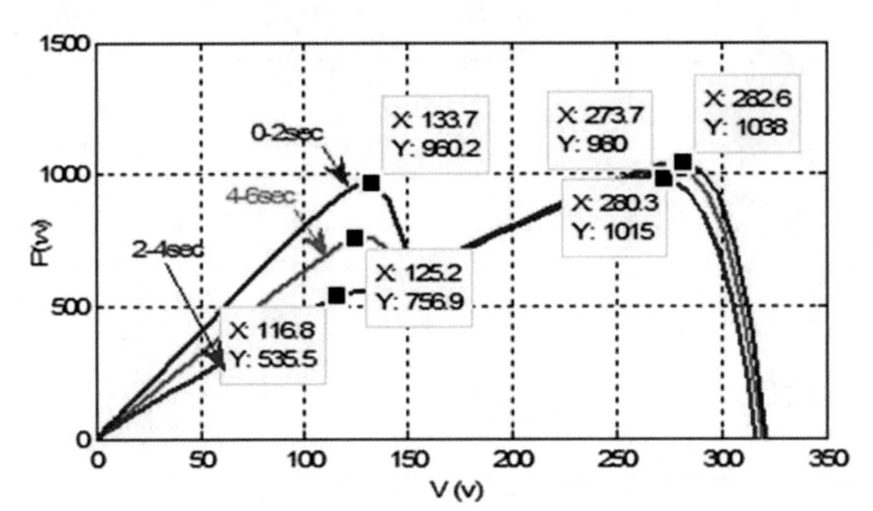

Figure 19. Photovoltaic generated power

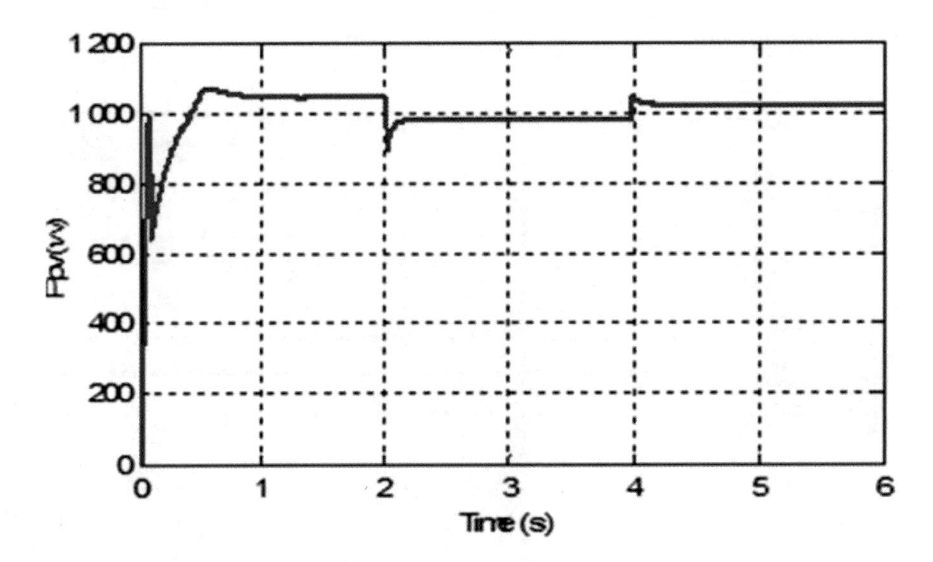

Figure 20 shows the evolution of the power generated by renewable energy sources. The DC bus voltage given in Figure 21 is constant and well-regulated at its 400V set point and thus proves the efficiency of the implanted regulator. Figure 22 and Figure 23 illustrate the evolution of the currents and the voltages injected into the grid.

In this section, the PSO approach described above is firstly applied for the design of the pitch angle controller. The wind allure as considered includes a variation of the wind speed in the form of steps in order to highlight the robustness of the control method following the sudden change of the weather conditions. In fact, the pitch angle control is intended to improve the response of the system during wind speeds above the nominal speed. Thus, operating conditions below 10 ms^{-1} are not taken into account

Figure 20. generated power by the hybrid system

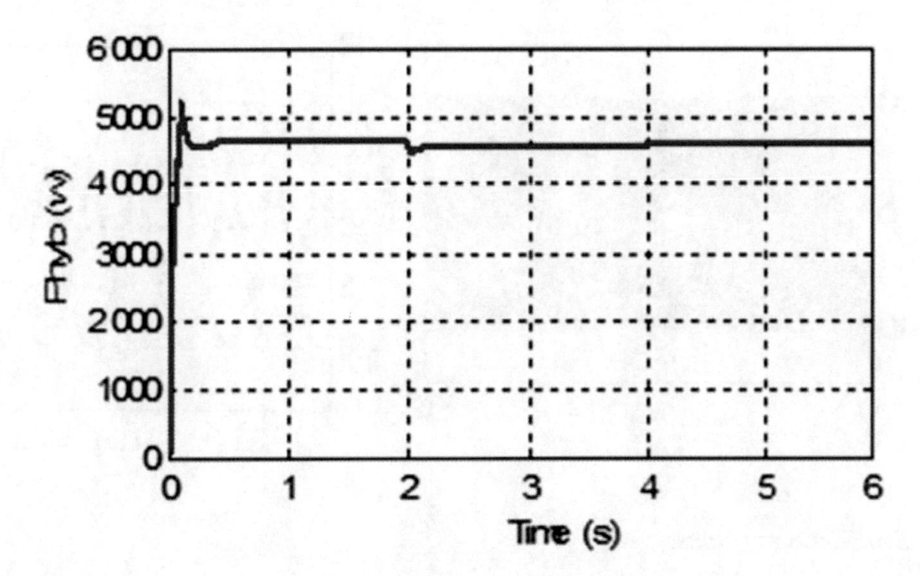

Figure 21. Response of the DC bus voltage

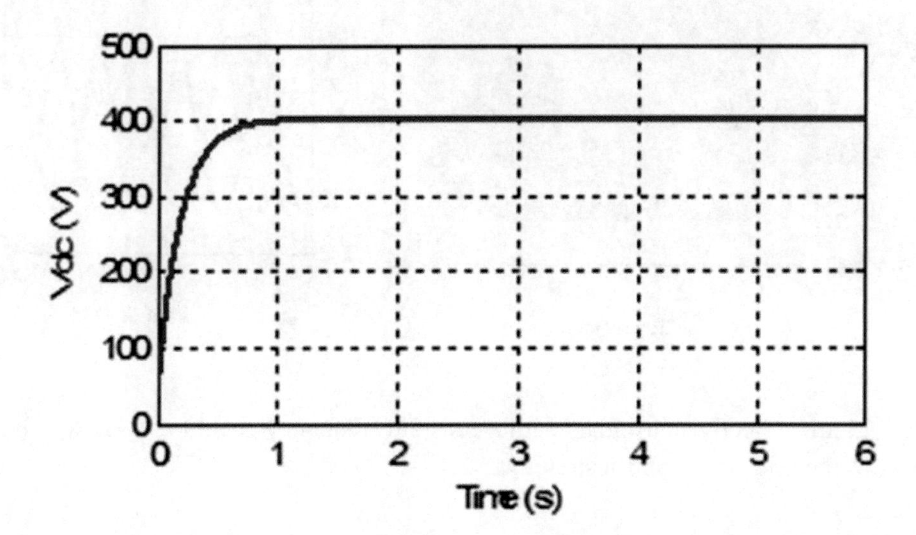

during the simulations. The response, given by Figure 16, indicates that the generated power is limited at its rated value, 3600W, which highlights the efficiency of the proposed method.

The PSO approach is applied after that to the MPPT control of the studied shaded PV generator. It's clear that this method is able to track the GM of the PV characteristic for each illumination variation. For example, in the case of the first interval of time, the overall maximum of the PV characteristic, as indicated in Figure 18, is of the order of 1038 W. The response the generated power, given in Figure 19, converges appropriately to this value.

The hybrid generated power, given in Figure 20, is the sum of the powers generated by renewable sources. Finally, the currents and the voltages injected into the network, represented respectively, in Figure

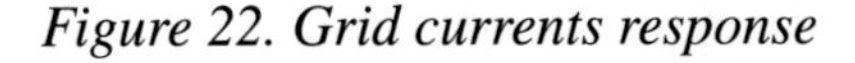

Figure 22. Grid currents response

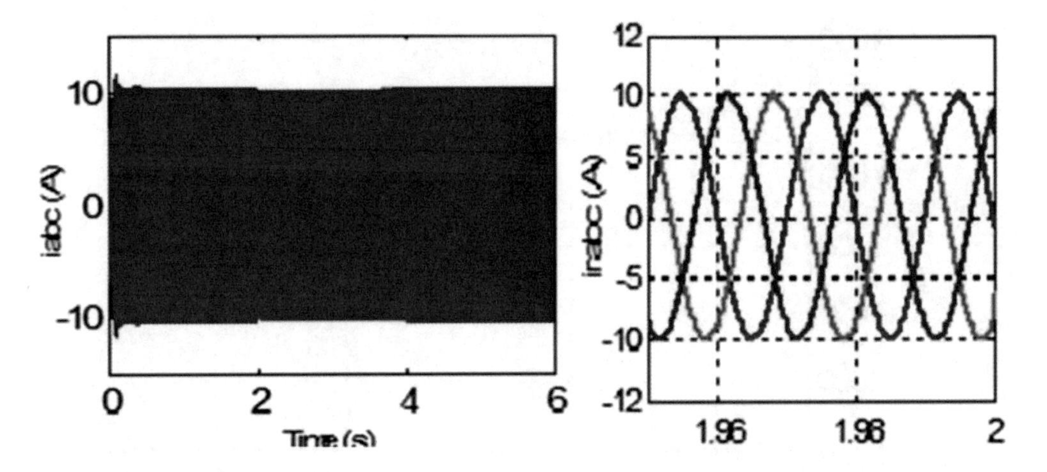

Figure 23. Grid voltage response

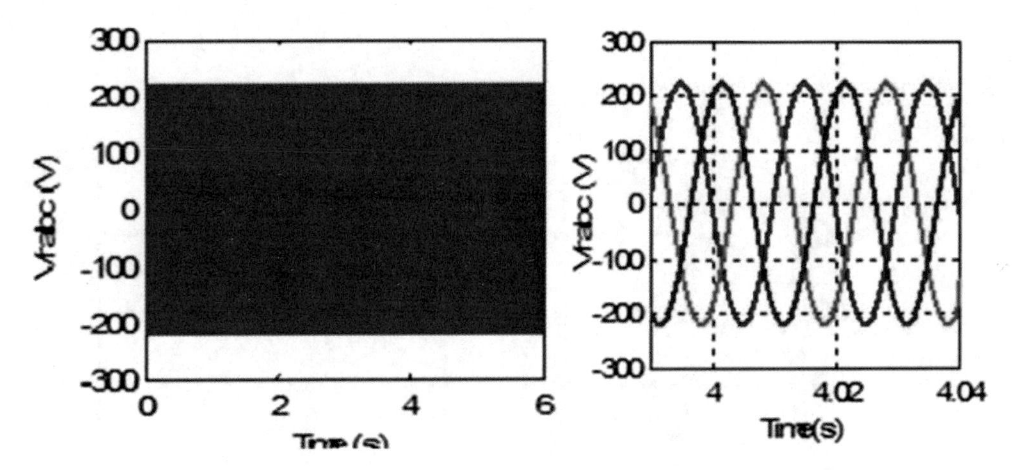

22 and Figure 23 are perfectly sinusoidals with a constant frequency equal to 50 Hz which emphasizes the robustness of the grid sides control strategy.

6. CONCLUSION

Improvements in the functioning of photovoltaic and wind generators are essential in order to make the integration of these alternative energy sources more competitive in the balance sheet of the global energy production systems. In this framework, the main objective of this work focuses on the optimization of the management of multi-source generators by intelligent techniques. Following a bibliographic study on the various hybrid technologies, the study has focused on the development of ordering strategies to meet specific requirements during the operation of photovoltaic and wind generators. In this context, attention was focused on the conversion of wind energy with particular interest to the control of the turbine pitch angle. In fact, this control is a practical technique for regulating the power generated above the nominal wind speed. Since the conventional methods usually uses a PI regulator to control the wind turbine pitch angle, the mathematical model of the system should be well known. As meta-heuristic methods can have potential when the system is non-linear, in this work a new PSO-based regulation technique is developed whose detailed and specific knowledge about the system is not required. Subsequently, the phenomenon of partial shading for photovoltaic generators was addressed. This phenomenon is responsible for the appearance of several peaks in the characteristics of the semi-shaded GPV. In order to circumvent the limitations of conventional techniques, an advanced technique based PSO has been proposed and to differentiate between the global maximum and the local maximum. The comparative study between the different methods developed stressed the robustness and performance of MPPT commands based on meta-heuristics. The studied wind /PV system was then integrated into a conversion chain coupled to the electrical network and controlled by power converters. The results obtained allowed to validate the simulation of the energy behavior of the studied system and to check the performance of the PSO control proposed in particular for the smoothing of the generated power.

REFERENCES

Agbossou, K., Chahine, R., Hamelin, J., Laurencelle, F., Anouar, A., St-Arnaud, J. M., & Bose, T. K. (2001). Renewable energy systems based on hydrogen for remote applications. *Journal of Power Sources*, *96*(1), 168–172. doi:10.1016/S0378-7753(01)00495-5

Agbossou, K., Kolhe, M., Hamelin, J., & Bose, T. K. (2004). Performance of a stand-alone renewable energy system based on energy storage as hydrogen. *IEEE Transactions on Energy Conversion*, *19*(3), 633–640. doi:10.1109/TEC.2004.827719

Azar, A. T. (2010a). *Fuzzy Systems*. Vienna, Austria: IN-TECH.

Azar, A. T. (2010b). Adaptive Neuro-Fuzzy Systems. In A. T. Azar (Ed.), *Fuzzy Systems*. Vienna, Austria: IN-TECH. doi:10.5772/7220

Azar, A. T. (2012). Overview of Type-2 Fuzzy logic systems. *International Journal of Fuzzy System Applications*, *2*(4), 1–28. doi:10.4018/ijfsa.2012100101

Azar, A. T., Kumar, J., Kumar, V., & Rana, K. P. S. (2017d). Control of a Two Link Planar Electrically-Driven Rigid Robotic Manipulator Using Fractional Order SOFC. *Proceedings of the International Conference on Advanced Intelligent Systems and Informatics 2017*, *639*, 47-56.

Azar, A. T., Ouannas, A., & Singh, S. (2017c). Control of New Type of Fractional Chaos Synchronization. *Proceedings of the International Conference on Advanced Intelligent Systems and Informatics 2017*, *639*, 47-56.

Azar, A. T., & Serrano, F. E. (2014). Robust IMC-PID tuning for cascade control systems with gain and phase margin specifications. *Neural Computing and Applications*, *25*(5), 983-995. DOI 10.1007/s00521-014-1560-x

Azar, A. T., & Serrano, F. E. (2015a). Stabilization and Control of Mechanical Systems with Backlash. In Advanced Intelligent Control Engineering and Automation. IGI Global. doi:10.4018/978-1-4666-7248-2.ch001

Azar, A. T., & Serrano, F. E. (2015b). Design and Modeling of Anti Wind Up PID Controllers. In Complex system modelling and control through intelligent soft computations (vol. 319, pp. 1-44). Springer-Verlag. doi:10.1007/978-3-319-12883-2_1

Azar, A. T., & Serrano, F. E. (2015c). Adaptive Sliding mode control of the Furuta pendulum. In Advances and Applications in Sliding Mode Control systems (vol. 576, pp. 1-42). Springer-Verlag GmbH Berlin/Heidelberg. doi:10.1007/978-3-319-11173-5_1

Azar, A. T., & Serrano, F. E. (2015d). Deadbeat Control for Multivariable Systems with Time Varying Delays. In Chaos Modeling and Control Systems Design (vol. 581, pp. 97-132). Springer-Verlag GmbH Berlin/Heidelberg. DOI doi:10.1007/978-3-319-13132-0_6

Azar, A. T., & Serrano, F. E. (2016a). Robust control for asynchronous switched nonlinear systems with time varying delays. *Proceedings of the International Conference on Advanced Intelligent Systems and Informatics 2016*, 533, 891-899. 10.1007/978-3-319-48308-5_85

Azar, A. T., & Serrano, F. E. (2016b). Stabilization of Mechanical Systems with Backlash by PI Loop Shaping. *International Journal of System Dynamics Applications*, *5*(3), 20–47. doi:10.4018/IJSDA.2016070102

Azar, A. T., & Serrano, F. E. (2017). Passivity Based Decoupling of Lagrangian Systems. *Proceedings of the International Conference on Advanced Intelligent Systems and Informatics 2016*, 533, 891-899. 10.1007/978-3-319-48308-5_85

Azar, A. T., & Vaidyanathan, S. (2015a). Handbook of Research on Advanced Intelligent Control Engineering and Automation. IGI Global. doi:10.4018/978-1-4666-7248-2

Azar, A. T., & Vaidyanathan, S. (2015b). *Computational Intelligence applications in Modeling and Control. In Studies in Computational Intelligence* (Vol. 575). Springer-Verlag.

Azar, A. T., & Vaidyanathan, S. (2015c). *Chaos Modeling and Control Systems Design. In Studies in Computational Intelligence* (Vol. 581). Springer-Verlag.

Azar, A. T., & Vaidyanathan, S. (2015c). *Computational Intelligence applications in Modeling and Control. In Studies in Computational Intelligence* (Vol. 575). Springer-Verlag.

Azar, A. T., & Vaidyanathan, S. (2016). *Advances in Chaos Theory and Intelligent Control. In Studies in Fuzziness and Soft Computing* (Vol. 337). Springer-Verlag. doi:10.1007/978-3-319-30340-6

Azar, A. T., Vaidyanathan, S., & Ouannas, A. (2017a). *Fractional Order Control and Synchronization of Chaotic Systems. In Studies in Computational Intelligence* (Vol. 688). Springer-Verlag. doi:10.1007/978-3-319-50249-6

Azar, A. T., Volos, C., Gerodimos, N. A., Tombras, G. S., Pham, V. T., Radwan, A. G., … Munoz-Pacheco, J. M. (2017b). A novel chaotic system without equilibrium: Dynamics, synchronization and circuit realization. *Complexity*. doi:10.1155/2017/7871467

Azar, A. T., & Zhu, Q. (2015). *Advances and Applications in Sliding Mode Control systems. In Studies in Computational Intelligence* (Vol. 576). Springer-Verlag.

Ben Smida, M., & Sakly, A. (2016). A Comparative Study of Different MPPT Methods for Grid-Connected Partially Shaded Photovoltaic Systems. *International Journal of Renewable Energy Research, 6*(3).

Boulkroune, A., Bouzeriba, A., Bouden, T., & Azar, A. T. (2016a). Fuzzy Adaptive Synchronization of Uncertain Fractional-order Chaotic Systems. In A. T. Azar & S. Vaidyanathan (Eds.), *Advances in Chaos Theory and Intelligent Control* (Vol. 337). Springer-Verlag. doi:10.1007/978-3-319-30340-6_28

Boulkroune, A., Hamel, S., & Azar, A. T. (2016b). *Fuzzy control-based function synchronization of unknown chaotic systems with dead-zone input. In Advances in Chaos Theory and Intelligent Control* (Vol. 337). Springer-Verlag.

Celik, A. N. (2002). Optimization and techno-economic analysis of autonomous photovoltaic–wind hybrid energy systems in comparison to single photovoltaic and wind systems. *Energy Conversion and Management, 43*(18), 2453–2468. doi:10.1016/S0196-8904(01)00198-4

Cha, H. J., & Enjeti, P. N. (2003, June). A three-phase AC/AC high-frequency link matrix converter for VSCF applications. In *Power Electronics Specialist Conference, 2003. PESC'03. 2003 IEEE 34th Annual* (Vol. 4, pp. 1971-1976). IEEE.

Chen, C. H., Hong, C. M., & Ou, T. C. (2012). Hybrid fuzzy control of wind turbine generator by pitch control using RNN. *International Journal of Ambient Energy, 33*(2), 56–64. doi:10.1080/01430750.2011.630754

Chowdhury, M. A., Hosseinzadeh, N., & Shen, W. X. (2012). Smoothing wind power fluctuations by fuzzy logic pitch angle controller. *Renewable Energy, 38*(1), 224–233. doi:10.1016/j.renene.2011.07.034

Clerc, M., & Kennedy, J. (2002). The particle swarm-explosion, stability, and convergence in a multidimensional complex space. *IEEE Transactions on Evolutionary Computation, 6*(1), 58–73. doi:10.1109/4235.985692

Elizondo, D., Hoogenboom, G., & McClendon, R. W. (1994). Development of a neural network model to predict daily solar radiation. *Agricultural and Forest Meteorology, 71*(1-2), 115–132. doi:10.1016/0168-1923(94)90103-1

Farret, F. A., & Simoes, M. G. (2006). *Integration of alternative sources of energy*. John Wiley & Sons.

Fay, G., Schwoerer, T., & Keith, K. (2010). *Alaska isolated wind-diesel systems: performance and economic analysis*. Prepared for Alaska Energy Authority and Denali Commission, Institute of Social and Economic Research, University of Alaska, Anchorage.

Ghoudelbourk, S., Dib, D., Omeiri, A., & Azar, A. T. (2016). MPPT Control in wind energy conversion systems and the application of fractional control (PIα) in pitch wind turbine. *International Journal of Modelling, Identification and Control, 26*(2), 140–151. doi:10.1504/IJMIC.2016.078329

Grassi, G., Ouannas, A., Azar, A. T., Radwan, A. G., Volos, C., Pham, V. T., . . . Stouboulos, I. N. (2017). *Chaos Synchronisation Of Continuous Systems Via Scalar Signal*. The 6th International Conference on Modern Circuits and Systems Technologies (MOCAST), Thessaloniki, Greece. 10.1109/MOCAST.2017.7937629

Hung, J. C. (2013). Modified particle swarm optimization structure approach to direction of arrival estimation. *Applied Soft Computing*, *13*(1), 315–320. doi:10.1016/j.asoc.2012.08.006

Ishaque, K., Salam, Z., Shamsudin, A., & Amjad, M. (2012). A direct control based maximum power point tracking method for photovoltaic system under partial shading conditions using particle swarm optimization algorithm. *Applied Energy*, *99*, 414–422. doi:10.1016/j.apenergy.2012.05.026

Jordehi, A. R. (2016). Maximum power point tracking in photovoltaic (PV) systems: A review of different approaches. *Renewable & Sustainable Energy Reviews*, *65*, 1127–1138. doi:10.1016/j.rser.2016.07.053

Joshi, P., & Arora, S. (2017). Maximum power point tracking methodologies for solar PV systems – A review. *Renewable & Sustainable Energy Reviews*, *70*, 1154–1177. doi:10.1016/j.rser.2016.12.019

Khare, A., & Rangnekar, S. (2013). A review of particle swarm optimization and its applications in solar photovoltaic system. *Applied Soft Computing*, *13*(5), 2997–3006. doi:10.1016/j.asoc.2012.11.033

Ko, S. H., Lee, S. R., Dehbonei, H., & Nayar, C. V. (2006). Application of voltage-and current-controlled voltage source inverters for distributed generation systems. *IEEE Transactions on Energy Conversion*, *21*(3), 782–792. doi:10.1109/TEC.2006.877371

Kongnam, C., & Nuchprayoon, S. (2010). A particle swarm optimization for wind energy control problem. *Renewable Energy*, *35*(11), 2431–2438. doi:10.1016/j.renene.2010.02.020

Lalouni, S., Rekioua, D., Rekioua, T., & Matagne, E. (2009). Fuzzy logic control of stand-alone photovoltaic system with battery storage. *Journal of Power Sources*, *193*(2), 899–907. doi:10.1016/j.jpowsour.2009.04.016

Liu, L., Meng, X., & Liu, C. (2016). A review of maximum power point tracking methods of PV power system at uniform and partial shading. *Renewable & Sustainable Energy Reviews*, *53*, 1500–1507. doi:10.1016/j.rser.2015.09.065

Liu, Y. H., Chen, J. H., & Huang, J. W. (2015). A review of maximum power point tracking techniques for use in partially shaded conditions. *Renewable & Sustainable Energy Reviews*, *41*, 436–453. doi:10.1016/j.rser.2014.08.038

Lyden, S., & Haque, M. E. (2015). Maximum Power Point Tracking techniques for photovoltaic systems: A comprehensive review and comparative analysis. *Renewable & Sustainable Energy Reviews*, *52*, 1504–1518. doi:10.1016/j.rser.2015.07.172

Maharjan, L., Inoue, S., & Akagi, H. (2008). A transformerless energy storage system based on a cascade multilevel PWM converter with star configuration. *IEEE Transactions on Industry Applications*, *44*(5), 1621–1630. doi:10.1109/TIA.2008.2002180

Masoum, M. A. S., Seyed, M., Badejani, M., & Kalantar, M. (2010). *Optimal placement of hybrid PV-wind systems using genetic algorithm*. IEEE 2010 Innovative Smart Grid Technologies (ISGT), Gaithersburg, MD. DOI: 10.1109/ISGT.2010.5434746

Meghni, B., Dib, D., & Azar, A. T. (2017c). A Second-order sliding mode and fuzzy logic control to Optimal Energy Management in PMSG Wind Turbine with Battery Storage. *Neural Computing & Applications*, *28*(6), 1417–1434. doi:10.100700521-015-2161-z

Meghni, B., Dib, D., Azar, A. T., Ghoudelbourk, S., & Saadoun, A. (2017a). *Robust Adaptive Supervisory Fractional order Controller For optimal Energy Management in Wind Turbine with Battery Storage. In Studies in Computational Intelligence* (Vol. 688, pp. 165–202). Springer-Verlag.

Meghni, B., Dib, D., Azar, A. T., & Saadoun, A. (2017b). *Effective Supervisory Controller to Extend Optimal Energy Management in Hybrid Wind Turbine under Energy and Reliability Constraints. International Journal of Dynamics and Control.* doi:10.100740435-016-0296-0

Mekki, H., Boukhetala, D., & Azar, A. T. (2015). Sliding Modes for Fault Tolerant Control. In Advances and Applications in Sliding Mode Control systems (vol. 576, pp. 407-433). Springer-Verlag GmbH Berlin/Heidelberg. doi:10.1007/978-3-319-11173-5_15

Mohandes, M. K. S. R. M., Balghonaim, A., Kassas, M., Rehman, S., & Halawani, T. O. (2000). Use of radial basis functions for estimating monthly mean daily solar radiation. *Solar Energy*, *68*(2), 161–168. doi:10.1016/S0038-092X(99)00071-7

Nehrir, M. H., LaMeres, B. J., Venkataramanan, G., Gerez, V., & Alvarado, L. A. (2000). An approach to evaluate the general performance of stand-alone wind/photovoltaic generating systems. *IEEE Transactions on Energy Conversion*, *15*(4), 433–439. doi:10.1109/60.900505

Nehrir, M. H., & Wang, C. (2009). *Modeling and control of fuel cells: Distributed generation applications* (Vol. 41). John Wiley & Sons. doi:10.1109/9780470443569

Nema, P., Nema, R. K., & Rangnekar, S. (2009). A current and future state of art development of hybrid energy system using wind and PV-solar: A review. *Renewable & Sustainable Energy Reviews*, *13*(8), 2096–2103. doi:10.1016/j.rser.2008.10.006

Ouannas, A., Azar, A. T., & Abu-Saris, R. (2016a). A new type of hybrid synchronization between arbitrary hyperchaotic maps. *International Journal of Machine Learning and Cybernetics*. doi:10.100713042-016-0566-3

Ouannas, A., Azar, A. T., & Radwan, A. G. (2016b). *On Inverse Problem of Generalized Synchronization Between Different Dimensional Integer-Order and Fractional-Order Chaotic Systems*. The 28th International Conference on Microelectronics, Cairo, Egypt. 10.1109/ICM.2016.7847942

Ouannas, A., Azar, A. T., & Vaidyanathan, S. (2017f). On A Simple Approach for Q-S Synchronization of Chaotic Dynamical Systems in Continuous-Time. *Int. J. Computing Science and Mathematics*, *8*(1), 20–27.

Ouannas, A., Azar, A. T., & Vaidyanathan, S. (2017g). New Hybrid Synchronization Schemes Based on Coexistence of Various Types of Synchronization Between Master-Slave Hyperchaotic Systems. *International Journal of Computer Applications in Technology*, *55*(2), 112–120. doi:10.1504/IJCAT.2017.082868

Ouannas, A., Azar, A. T., & Vaidyanathan, S. (2017i). A Robust Method for New Fractional Hybrid Chaos Synchronization. *Mathematical Methods in the Applied Sciences*, *40*(5), 1804–1812. doi:10.1002/mma.4099

Ouannas, A., Azar, A. T., & Ziar, T. (2017h). *On Inverse Full State Hybrid Function Projective Synchronization for Continuous-time Chaotic Dynamical Systems with Arbitrary Dimensions*. Differential Equations and Dynamical Systems; doi:10.100712591-017-0362-x

Ouannas, A., Azar, A. T., Ziar, T., & Radwan, A. G. (2017d). *Study On Coexistence of Different Types of Synchronization Between Different dimensional Fractional Chaotic Systems. In Studies in Computational Intelligence* (Vol. 688, pp. 637–669). Springer-Verlag.

Ouannas, A., Azar, A. T., Ziar, T., & Radwan, A. G. (2017e). *Generalized Synchronization of Different Dimensional Integer-order and Fractional Order Chaotic Systems. In Studies in Computational Intelligence* (Vol. 688, pp. 671–697). Springer-Verlag.

Ouannas, A., Azar, A. T., Ziar, T., & Vaidyanathan, S. (2017a). *On New Fractional Inverse Matrix Projective Synchronization Schemes. In Studies in Computational Intelligence* (Vol. 688, pp. 497–524). Springer-Verlag.

Ouannas, A., Azar, A. T., Ziar, T., & Vaidyanathan, S. (2017b). *Fractional Inverse Generalized Chaos Synchronization Between Different Dimensional Systems. In Studies in Computational Intelligence* (Vol. 688, pp. 525–551). Springer-Verlag.

Ouannas, A., Azar, A. T., Ziar, T., & Vaidyanathan, S. (2017c). *A New Method To Synchronize Fractional Chaotic Systems With Different Dimensions. In Studies in Computational Intelligence* (Vol. 688, pp. 581–611). Springer-Verlag.

Ouannas, A., Grassi, G., Azar, A. T., Radwan, A. G., Volos, C., Pham, V. T., . . . Stouboulos, I. N. (2017j). *Dead-Beat Synchronization Control in Discrete-Time Chaotic Systems*. The 6th International Conference on Modern Circuits and Systems Technologies (MOCAST), Thessaloniki, Greece. 10.1109/MOCAST.2017.7937628

Poultangari, I., Shahnazi, R., & Sheikhan, M. (2012). RBF neural network based PI pitch controller for a class of 5-MW wind turbines using particle swarm optimization algorithm. *ISA Transactions*, *51*(5), 641–648. doi:10.1016/j.isatra.2012.06.001 PMID:22738782

Rajkumar, R. K., Ramachandaramurthy, V. K., Yong, B. L., & Chia, D. B. (2011). Techno-economical optimization of hybrid pv/wind/battery system using Neuro-Fuzzy. *Energy*, *8*(36), 5148–5153. doi:10.1016/j.energy.2011.06.017

Ramli, M. A. M., Twaha, S., Ishaque, K., & Al-Turki, Y. A. (2017). A review on maximum power point tracking for photovoltaic systems with and without shading conditions. *Renewable & Sustainable Energy Reviews*, *67*, 144–159. doi:10.1016/j.rser.2016.09.013

Saravanan, S., & Babu, R. (2016). Maximum power point tracking algorithms for photovoltaic system – A review. *Renewable & Sustainable Energy Reviews*, *57*, 192–204. doi:10.1016/j.rser.2015.12.105

Seo, J. H., Im, C. H., Heo, C. G., Kim, J. K., Jung, H. K., & Lee, C. G. (2006). Multimodal function optimization based on particle swarm optimization. *IEEE Transactions on Magnetics*, *42*(4), 1095–1098. doi:10.1109/TMAG.2006.871568

Seyedmahmoudian, M., Mekhilef, S., Rahmani, R., Yusof, R., & Asghar Shojaei, A. (2014). Maximum power point tracking of partial shaded photovoltaic array using an evolutionary algorithm: A particle swarm optimization technique. *Journal of Renewable and Sustainable Energy, 6*(2), 1-13.

Shaiek, Y. B., Smida, M., Sakly, A., & Mimouni, M. F. (2013). Comparison between conventional methods and GA approach for maximum power point tracking of shaded solar PV generators. *Solar Energy, 90*, 107–122. doi:10.1016/j.solener.2013.01.005

Singh, S., Azar, A. T., Ouannas, A., Zhu, Q., Zhang, W., & Na, J. (2017). *Sliding Mode Control Technique for Multi-switching Synchronization of Chaotic Systems. 9th International Conference on Modelling, Identification and Control (ICMIC 2017)*, Kunming, China.

Soliman, N. S., Said, L. A., Azar, A. T., Madian, A. H., Radwan, A. G., & Ouannas, A. (2017). *Fractional Controllable Multi-Scroll V-Shape Attractor with Parameters Effect.* The 6th International Conference on Modern Circuits and Systems Technologies (MOCAST), Thessaloniki, Greece.

Sood, P., Lipo, T., & Hansen, I. (1987, March). A versatile power converter for high frequency link systems. In Applied Power Electronics Conference and Exposition, 1987 IEEE (pp. 249-256). IEEE. doi:10.1109/APEC.1987.7067159

Soufyane Benyoucef, A., Chouder, A., Kara, K., & Silvestre, S. (2015). Artificial bee colony based algorithm for maximum power point tracking (MPPT) for PV systems operating under partial shaded conditions. *Applied Soft Computing, 32*, 38–48.

Stoyanov, L. (2011). *Etude de différentes structures de systèmes hybrides à sources d'énergie renouvelables* (Doctoral dissertation). Université Pascal Paoli.

Suvire, G. O., & Mercado, P. E. (2012). Active power control of a flywheel energy storage system for wind energy applications. *IET Renewable Power Generation, 6*(1), 9–16. doi:10.1049/iet-rpg.2010.0155

Tolba, M. F., AbdelAty, A. M., Soliman, N. S., Said, L. A., Madian, A. H., Azar, A. T., & Radwan, A. G. (2017). FPGA implementation of two fractional order chaotic systems. *International Journal of Electronics and Communications, 28*, 162–172. doi:10.1016/j.aeue.2017.04.028

Vaidyanathan, S., & Azar, A. T. (2015a). Anti-Synchronization of Identical Chaotic Systems using Sliding Mode Control and an Application to Vaidyanathan-Madhavan Chaotic Systems. In Advances and Applications in Sliding Mode Control systems (vol. 576, pp. 527-547). Springer-Verlag GmbH Berlin/Heidelberg. doi:10.1007/978-3-319-11173-5_19

Vaidyanathan, S., & Azar, A. T. (2015b). Hybrid Synchronization of Identical Chaotic Systems using Sliding Mode Control and an Application to Vaidyanathan Chaotic Systems. In Advances and Applications in Sliding Mode Control systems (vol. 576, pp. 549-569). Springer-Verlag GmbH Berlin/Heidelberg. doi:10.1007/978-3-319-11173-5_20

Vaidyanathan, S., & Azar, A. T. (2015c). Analysis, Control and Synchronization of a Nine-Term 3-D Novel Chaotic System. In Chaos Modeling and Control Systems Design (vol. 581, pp. 3-17). Springer-Verlag GmbH Berlin/Heidelberg. DOI doi:10.1007/978-3-319-13132-0_1

Vaidyanathan, S., & Azar, A. T. (2015d). Analysis and Control of a 4-D Novel Hyperchaotic System. In Chaos Modeling and Control Systems Design (vol. 581, pp. 19-38). Springer-Verlag GmbH Berlin/Heidelberg. DOI doi:10.1007/978-3-319-13132-0_2

Vaidyanathan, S., & Azar, A. T. (2016a). Takagi-Sugeno Fuzzy Logic Controller for Liu-Chen Four-Scroll Chaotic System. *International Journal of Intelligent Engineering Informatics*, *4*(2), 135–150. doi:10.1504/IJIEI.2016.076699

Vaidyanathan, S., & Azar, A. T. (2016b). *Dynamic Analysis, Adaptive Feedback Control and Synchronization of an Eight-Term 3-D Novel Chaotic System with Three Quadratic Nonlinearities. In Studies in Fuzziness and Soft Computing* (Vol. 337). Springer-Verlag.

Vaidyanathan, S., & Azar, A. T. (2016c). *Qualitative Study and Adaptive Control of a Novel 4-D Hyperchaotic System with Three Quadratic Nonlinearities. In Studies in Fuzziness and Soft Computing* (Vol. 337). Springer-Verlag.

Vaidyanathan, S., & Azar, A. T. (2016d). *A Novel 4-D Four-Wing Chaotic System with Four Quadratic Nonlinearities and its Synchronization via Adaptive Control Method. In Advances in Chaos Theory and Intelligent Control* (Vol. 337). Springer-Verlag.

Vaidyanathan, S., & Azar, A. T. (2016e). *Adaptive Control and Synchronization of Halvorsen Circulant Chaotic Systems. In Advances in Chaos Theory and Intelligent Control* (Vol. 337). Springer-Verlag.

Vaidyanathan, S., & Azar, A. T. (2016f). *Adaptive Backstepping Control and Synchronization of a Novel 3-D Jerk System with an Exponential Nonlinearity. In Advances in Chaos Theory and Intelligent Control* (Vol. 337). Springer-Verlag.

Vaidyanathan, S., & Azar, A. T. (2016g). *Generalized Projective Synchronization of a Novel Hyperchaotic Four-Wing System via Adaptive Control Method. In Advances in Chaos Theory and Intelligent Control* (Vol. 337). Springer-Verlag.

Vaidyanathan, S., Azar, A. T., & Ouannas, A. (2017a). *An Eight-Term 3-D Novel Chaotic System with Three Quadratic Nonlinearities, its Adaptive Feedback Control and Synchronization. In Studies in Computational Intelligence* (Vol. 688, pp. 719–746). Springer-Verlag.

Vaidyanathan, S., Azar, A. T., & Ouannas, A. (2017c). *Hyperchaos and Adaptive Control of a Novel Hyperchaotic System with Two Quadratic Nonlinearities. In Studies in Computational Intelligence* (Vol. 688, pp. 773–803). Springer-Verlag.

Vaidyanathan, S., Azar, A. T., Rajagopal, K., & Alexander, P. (2015b). Design and SPICE implementation of a 12-term novel hyperchaotic system and its synchronization via active control (2015). *International Journal of Modelling, Identification and Control*, *23*(3), 267–277. doi:10.1504/IJMIC.2015.069936

Vaidyanathan, S., Idowu, B. A., & Azar, A. T. (2015c). Backstepping Controller Design for the Global Chaos Synchronization of Sprott's Jerk Systems. In Chaos Modeling and Control Systems Design, Studies in Computational Intelligence (vol. 581, pp 39-58). Springer-Verlag GmbH Berlin/Heidelberg. doi:10.1007/978-3-319-13132-0_3

Vaidyanathan, S., Sampath, S., & Azar, A. T. (2015a). Global chaos synchronisation of identical chaotic systems via novel sliding mode control method and its application to Zhu system. *International Journal of Modelling, Identification and Control, 23*(1), 92–100. doi:10.1504/IJMIC.2015.067495

Vaidyanathan, S., Zhu, Q., & Azar, A. T. (2017b). *Adaptive Control of a Novel Nonlinear Double Convection Chaotic System. In Studies in Computational Intelligence* (Vol. 688, pp. 357–385). Springer-Verlag.

Vechiu, I. (2005). *Modélisation et analyse de l'intégration des énergies renouvelables dans un réseau autonome* (Doctoral dissertation). Université du Havre.

Wang, L., & Singh, C. (2009). Multicriteria design of hybrid power generation systems based on a modified particle swarm optimization algorithm. *IEEE Transactions on Energy Conversion, 24*(1), 163–172. doi:10.1109/TEC.2008.2005280

Wang, Z., Volos, C., Kingni, S. T., Azar, A. T., & Pham, V. T. (2017). Four-wing attractors in a novel chaotic system with hyperbolic sine nonlinearity. *Optik - International Journal for Light and Electron Optics, 131*(2017), 1071-1078.

Yang, H., Zhou, W., Lu, L., & Fang, Z. (2008). Optimal sizing method for stand-alone hybrid solar–wind system with LPSP technology by using a genetic algorithm. *Solar Energy, 82*(4), 354–367. doi:10.1016/j.solener.2007.08.005

Zegaoui, A., Aillerie, M., Petit, P., Sawicki, J. P., Charles, J. P., & Belarbi, A. W. (2011). Dynamic behaviour of PV generator trackers under irradiation and temperature changes. *Solar Energy, 85*(11), 2953–2964. doi:10.1016/j.solener.2011.08.038

Zhan, Z. H., Zhang, J., Li, Y., & Chung, H. S. H. (2009). Adaptive particle swarm optimization. *IEEE Transactions on Systems, Man, and Cybernetics. Part B, Cybernetics, 39*(6), 1362–1381. doi:10.1109/TSMCB.2009.2015956 PMID:19362911

Zhu, Q., & Azar, A. T. (2015). *Complex system modelling and control through intelligent soft computations. In Studies in Fuzziness and Soft Computing* (Vol. 319). Springer-Verlag.

Chapter 4

Design of Low Order Controllers for Decoupled MIMO Systems With Time Response Specifications

Maher Ben Hariz
Université de Tunis El Manar, Ecole Nationale d'Ingénieurs de Tunis, Tunisia

Wassila Chagra
Université de Tunis El Manar, Institut Préparatoire Aux études d'Ingénieurs d'El Manar, Ecole Nationale d'Ingénieurs de Tunis, Tunisia

Faouzi Bouani
Université de Tunis El Manar, Ecole Nationale d'Ingénieurs de Tunis, Tunisia

ABSTRACT

The design of a low order controller for decoupled MIMO systems is proposed. The main objective of this controller is to guarantee some closed loop time response performances such as the settling time and the overshoot. The controller parameters are obtained by resolving a non-convex optimization problem. In order to obtain an optimal solution, the use of a global optimization method is suggested. In this chapter, the proposed solution is the GGP method. The principle of this method consists of transforming a non-convex optimization problem to a convex one by some mathematical transformations. So as to accomplish the fixed goal, it is imperative to decouple the coupled MIMO systems. To approve the controllers' design method, the synthesis of fixed low order controller for decoupled TITO systems is presented firstly. Then, this design method is generalized in the case of MIMO systems. Simulation results and a comparison study between the presented approach and a PI controller are given in order to show the efficiency of the proposed controller. It is remarkable that the obtained solution meets the desired closed loop time specifications for each system output. It is also noted that by considering the proposed approach the user can fix the desired closed loop performances for each output independently.

DOI: 10.4018/978-1-5225-4077-9.ch004

1. INTRODUCTION

Recent years, several inspiring control system approaches have been proposed, such as optimal control, nonlinear feedback control, adaptive control, sliding mode control, nonlinear dynamics, chaos control, chaos synchronization control, fuzzy logic control, fuzzy adaptive control, fractional order control, and robust control and their integrations (Azar & Vaidyanathan, 2015a,b,c, 2016; Azar & Zhu, 2015; Billel et al, 2017, 2016; Boulkroune et al, 2016a,b; Ghoudelbourk et al., 2016; Meghni et al, 2017a,b,c; Azar et al., 2017a,b,c,d; Azar 2010a,b, 2012; Mekki et al., 2015; Vaidyanathan & Azar, 2015a,b,c,d, 2016a,b,c,d,e,f,g, 2017a,b,c; Zhu & Azar, 2015; Grassi et al., 2017; Ouannas et al., 2016a,b, 2017a,b,c,d,e,f,g,h,I,j; Singh et al., 2017; Vaidyanathan et al, 2015a,b,c; Wang et al., 2017; Soliman et al., 2017; Tolba et al., 2017). In the industrial environment, engineers are in several applications facing multivariable systems, such as refinery process, chemical reactor (Skogestad & Postlethwaite, 2005). Because of interactions between the input/output variables, MIMO processes present, usually, difficulties to design controllers. So in order to deal with this problem, control engineers have used the decoupling system techniques. These techniques have been discussed in the literature over the years (Wang, 2003; Ogunnaike & Harmor, 1994). The choice of a decoupling method is not obvious because each technique possesses some benefits and limitations. It should be noted that in practice the simplified decoupling is the most used method. In fact, its principal advantage is the simplicity of its elements. Although it facilitates the determination of the controller transfer matrix, the ideal decoupling is rarely implemented in real applications. In addition, the inverted decoupling is uncommonly employed in practice. It has the principal benefits of the simplified and ideal decoupling techniques. Some research works have already made comparisons between different decoupling types. Luyben (1970) and Weischedel and McAvoy (1980) have made a comparison between ideal and simplified decoupling methods. They concluded that simplified decoupling is more robust with regards to ideal decoupling. Shinskey (1988) described both simplified and inverted decoupling techniques which are also detailed by Seborg et al., (1989). Gagnon et al., (1998) proposed a comparative study between simplified, ideal and inverted decoupling. They also demonstrated some drawbacks such as the implementation problem of inverted decoupling compared to other techniques. A centralized multivariable control based on simplified decoupling was presented by Garrido et al., (2012). Jevtovic and Matausek (2010) proposed the design of PID controller for TITO system based on ideal decoupler. Thanks to its former advantages, the simplified decoupling the simplified decoupling will be exploited in this work. In this research, the objective is to design a controller for MIMO systems with time response specifications. It should be noted that the controller parameters are obtained by resolving a non-convex optimization problem. In fact, the optimization is found at the heart of several real problem-solving processes. Therefore, the resolution of optimization problems has attracted the attention of many researchers in various fields. Toksari (2009) proposed an ant colony optimization algorithm to find the global minimum. This algorithm was tested on some standard functions and it was compared with other algorithms. Zhou, et al. (2013) used the PSO in the control algorithm in order to allow robots to navigate towards the remote frontier after exploring the region. The PSO is also applied by Abu-Seada, et al. (2013) to obtain an optimal tuning of proportional integral derivative controller parameters for an automatic voltage regulator system of a synchronous generator. Mousa, et al. (2015) exploited the PSO in order to determine PI and PID controllers parameters. These controllers with a feed forward gain are used with a reduced linear quadratic regulator for stabilizing swinging-up the inverted pendulum. Shahin, et al. (2014) proposed the improvement of the steady state and dynamic performance of the power grids by using the advanced flexible AC transmission systems based on evolutionary computing methods. The control of the electric power system can be achieved by using the PSO method applied to this subject to enhance the characteristics of the controller performance. Bahgaat, et al. (2014) used different methods such as the PSO, the adaptive weight PSO, the adaptive acceleration coefficients based PSO and the adaptive neuro fuzzy inference system to determine the PID controller parameters. They concluded that time performances such as the overshoots and settling times with their proposed controllers are better than the outputs of the conventional PID controllers. GA with hierarchically structured population was applied by Toledo, Oliveira and França (2014) with the aim of solving unconstrained optimization problems. The implementation of GA in an embedded microcontroller based polarization control system was proposed by Mamdoohi et al. (2012). The controller measures the signal intensity. These measures will be exploited in the estimation of the genetic value. Then, the GA controls this process. To attain the optimum performance, the best genetic parameters optimize the code such that the fastest execution time can be obtained. Valdez et al., (2014) presented a hybrid approach for optimization, combining PSO and GAs using fuzzy logic so as to integrate the results. They affirmed that the proposed method, in their work, combines the advantages of PSO and GA to get an improved FPSO and FGA hybrid method. Fuzzy logic is employed with the objective of combining the results of the GA and PSO in the best possible way. Fuzzy logic is also used with an aim of adjusting parameters in FPSO and FGA. Jiang et al., (2014) proposed a hybrid approach in order to solve economic emission load dispatch problems considering various practical constraints by employing Hybrid PSO and GSA. Their algorithm provided a combination between the PSO and the GSA and adopted co-evolutionary technique to update its particle position in the swarm with the cooperation of PSO and GSA. With the aim of finding the global minimum in the numerical, Servet Kiran et al., (2012) proposed a hybrid algorithm which is based on PSO and ACO. This algorithm is named hybrid ant particle optimization algorithm. The ACO and the PSO work, at each iteration, independently and give rise to their solutions. The best solution is, subsequently, chosen as the global best solution of the system and its parameters are used to choose the new position of particles and ants at the next iteration. Tabakhi et al., (2014) presented a method based on ACO, manned unsupervised feature selection method based on ACO so as to find an optimal solution to the feature selection problem. Geometric branch and bound techniques are usually known solution algorithms for non-convex continuous global optimization problems. Several approaches can be found in the literature. Schöbel & Scholz (2014) proposed an extension of geometric branch and bound methods for mixed integer optimization problems. As a matter of fact, they presented some general bounding operations. Hence, with the objective of solving mixed integer optimization problems they provided a general algorithm.

In this work, the GGP will be applied as a global optimization method in order to resolve the optimization problem. The principle of this method is to transform a non- convex optimization problem to a convex one by means of variable transformations. The overall organization of this paper is as follows: Section 2 provides a quick review on the global optimization and the design of controllers with time response specifications. Besides, section 3 presents firstly the decoupling system technique for TITO systems then in the case of MIMO systems. Afterwards, the problem statement is exposed in section 4. In section 5, the controller's design procedure is developed. Then the GGP method is introduced in section 5. In order to illustrate the effectiveness of the fixed low controller some simulation results are given in section 6. Also, a comparative study between the proposed controller and the PI controller is made. Then section 7 discusses and analyzes the simulation results. The last section is dedicated to conclude this chapter and to present future directions.

2. RELATED WORK

Pörn et al., (2007) presented an approach in order to obtain the global solution for non convex MINLP problems that include signomial expressions. They proved that it is possible to decompose any non convex optimization problem composed by an objective function and inequality constraints to a convex MINLP problem by applying some variable transformation techniques. Tsai et al., (2007) proposed a technique for treating both positive and non positive variables with integer powers in GGP problems. Choi & Briker (1996) demonstrated the effectiveness of the geometric programming approach in machining economics problems compared with the results of generalized reduced gradient. Tsai (2009) proposed an approach for the treatment of free variables in GGP problems. A deterministic global optimization algorithm was proposed by Manaras & Floudas (1997) so as to find the global minimum of generalized geometric (signomial) problems. The GGP method was used by Kheriji et al., (2011a) in order to solve a non-convex min–max optimization problem to compute a predictive controller for a class of constrained linear MIMO systems in presence of parametric uncertainties in the state space model. Bjork et al., (2003) presented an optimization technique based on the convexification of signomial terms. The proposed approach is based on the solution of a sequence of convexified sub problems.

Because the controller parameters are obtained by resolving a non-convex optimization problem, the use of a global optimization method is recommended. In this work, the GGP method will be exploited so as to resolve this optimization problem. The principle of this method is to transform a non-convex optimization problem to a convex one by means of some variable transformations.

The synthesis of a fixed low-order controller for linear time invariant, SISO systems with some step response specifications such as the settling time and the overshoot was presented in previous work (Ben Hariz, Bouani & Ksouri, 2012). The synthesis and the implementation of a fixed low order controller in an electronic system have been done by Ben Hariz & Bouani (2016) and Ben Hariz, Bouani & Ksouri, (2014). They used the STM32 microcontroller in order to control a real system. Ben Hariz, Chagra & Bouani (2013) and Ben Hariz, Chagra & Bouani (2014) proposed the design of fixed low order controller for decoupled TITO systems. In this research, an extension of these works in the case of MIMO systems will be proposed. The controller design is formulated as an optimization problem which takes into account the desired closed loop performances. Kim, Keel and Bhattacharyya (2003) presented the methodology to fix the desired closed loop characteristic equation by the user.

3. DECOUPLING SYSTEM TECHNIQUE

The existence of interactions between the inputs and the outputs of a MIMO system is a form of coupling when the system is represented by a transfer matrix. In practice, the coupling presents a difficulty to be able to control a given system that is why it is recommended to decouple the system. The decoupling can be described as the conversion of MIMO problems to SISO problems when the system is represented by a transfer matrix.

3.1. Decoupling TITO Systems

Let consider the following Two Input Two Output (TITO) process *G(s)* described by:

$$G(s)=\begin{bmatrix} G_{11}(s) & G_{12}(s) \\ G_{21}(s) & G_{22}(s) \end{bmatrix} \tag{1}$$

The process *G(s)* is represented by Figure 1.

The elements $G_{11}(s)$, $G_{12}(s)$, $G_{21}(s)$ and *G22(s)*, which represent the transfer functions of the process, are supposed to be known. According to configuration depicted in Figure 1, the system outputs are given by:

$$\begin{cases} Y_1(s)=G_{11}(s)U_1(s)+G_{12}(s)U_2(s) \\ Y_2(s)=G_{21}(s)U_1(s)+G_{22}(s)U_2(s) \end{cases} \tag{2}$$

The algebraic decoupling upstream of the multivariable *G*(*s*) process requires the design of a transfer matrix *D*(*s*) such that *D*(*s*) in series with *G*(*s*) produces a diagonal transfer matrix *T*(*s*).

$$D(s)=\begin{bmatrix} D_{11}(s) & D_{12}(s) \\ D_{21}(s) & D_{22}(s) \end{bmatrix} \tag{3}$$

and

Figure 1. TITO process representation

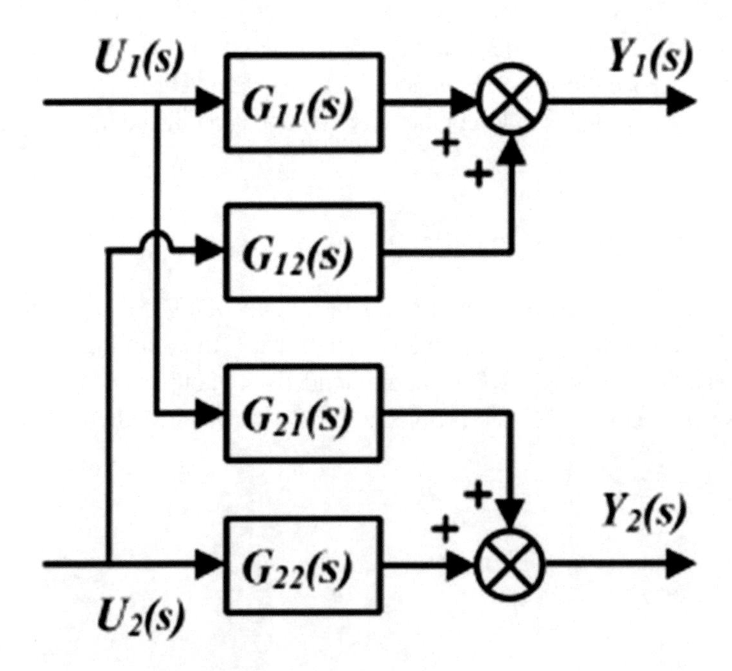

$$T(s) = \begin{bmatrix} T_1(s) & 0 \\ 0 & T_2(s) \end{bmatrix} = G(s)D(s) = T(s) \tag{4}$$

A simplified decoupling system design for a TITO process is depicted in Figure 2.

The variables V_1(s) and $V_2(s)$ are the controller outputs, $U_1(s)$ and U_2(s) represent the control signals and Y_1(s) and $Y_2(s)$ are the process outputs.

The controller transfer matrix $C(s)$ is diagonal and it is defined by:

$$C(s) = \begin{bmatrix} C_1(s) & 0 \\ 0 & C_2(s) \end{bmatrix} \tag{5}$$

By using Eqs. 1 and 3, the Eq. 4 provides:

$$\begin{aligned} D(s) &= G(s)^{-1}T(s) \\ &= \frac{1}{G_{11}(s)G_{22}(s) - G_{12}(s)G_{21}(s)} \begin{bmatrix} G_{22}(s)T_1(s) & -G_{12}(s)T_2(s) \\ -G_{21}(s)T_1(s) & G_{11}(s)T_2(s) \end{bmatrix} \end{aligned} \tag{6}$$

The only unknown elements are $T_1(s)$ and $T_2(s)$. They constitute the desired dynamics of the decoupled system. In this work, the simplified decoupling will be applied.

3.2. Generalized Decoupling Technique for MIMO Systems

The decoupling control design, called "simplified decoupling" by Luyben (1970), is commonly used in the literature. For *nxn* process $G(s)$ the decoupler can be selected as (Garrido *et al*., 2012)

Figure 2. Block diagram of the simplified decoupling

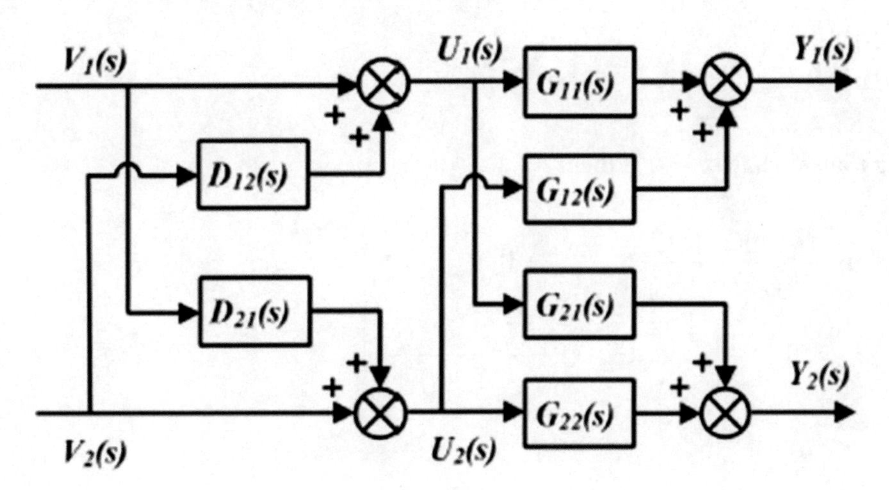

$$D(s)=\begin{pmatrix} 1 & \dfrac{adjG_{12}}{adjG_{22}} & \cdots & \dfrac{adjG_{1n}}{adjG_{nn}} \\ \dfrac{adjG_{21}}{adjG_{11}} & 1 & \cdots & \dfrac{adjG_{2n}}{adjG_{nn}} \\ \vdots & \vdots & \ddots & \vdots \\ \dfrac{adjG_{n1}}{adjG_{11}} & \dfrac{adjG_{n2}}{adjG_{22}} & \cdots & 1 \end{pmatrix} \tag{7}$$

The transfer matrix $T(s)$ is given by:

$$T(s)=\begin{pmatrix} \dfrac{|G|}{adjG_{11}} & 0 & \cdots & 0 \\ 0 & \dfrac{|G|}{adjG_{22}} & \cdots & 0 \\ \vdots & \vdots & \ddots & \vdots \\ 0 & 0 & \cdots & \dfrac{|G|}{adjG_{nn}} \end{pmatrix} \tag{8}$$

where $|G|$ is the determinant of $G(s)$, $adjG$ is the adjugate matrix of $G(s)$ that represents the transpose of the cofactore matrix of $G(s)$.

3.3. Simplified Decoupling for TITO Systems

$$D(s)=\begin{bmatrix} 1 & -\dfrac{G_{12}(s)}{G_{11}(s)} \\ -\dfrac{G_{21}(s)}{G_{22}(s)} & 1 \end{bmatrix} \tag{9}$$

The resulting transfer matrix $T(s)$ is then:

$$T(s)=\begin{bmatrix} G_{11}(s)-\dfrac{G_{12}(s)G_{21}(s)}{G_{22}(s)} & 0 \\ 0 & G_{22}(s)-\dfrac{G_{12}(s)G_{21}(s)}{G_{11}(s)} \end{bmatrix} \tag{10}$$

where

$$T_1(s) = G_{11}(s) - \frac{G_{12}(s)G_{21}(s)}{G_{22}(s)} \tag{11}$$

and

$$T_2(s) = G_{22}(s) - \frac{G_{12}(s)G_{21}(s)}{G_{11}(s)} \tag{12}$$

The system inputs are given by:

$$\begin{cases} U_1(s) = V_1(s) + D_{12}(s)V_2(s) \\ U_2(s) = V_2(s) + D_{21}(s)V_1(s) \end{cases} \tag{13}$$

By using Eqs. 2, 11, 12 and 13, the following expressions of the system outputs can be found:

$$\begin{cases} Y_1(s) = \left(G_{11}(s) - \dfrac{G_{12}(s)G_{21}(s)}{G_{22}(s)} \right) V_1(s) \\ Y_2(s) = \left(G_{22}(s) - \dfrac{G_{12}(s)G_{21}(s)}{G_{11}(s)} \right) V_2(s) \end{cases} \tag{14}$$

3.4. Simplified Decoupling for 3x3 Systems

For 3x3 process the decoupler can be chosen as follows (Garrido *et al.*, 2012).

$$D(s) = \begin{pmatrix} 1 & \dfrac{adjG_{12}}{adjG_{22}} & \dfrac{adjG_{13}}{adjG_{33}} \\ \dfrac{adjG_{21}}{adjG_{11}} & 1 & \dfrac{adjG_{23}}{adjG_{33}} \\ \dfrac{adjG_{31}}{adjG_{11}} & \dfrac{adjG_{32}}{adjG_{22}} & 1 \end{pmatrix} \tag{15}$$

The resulting transfer matrix can be deduced:

$$T(s)=\begin{pmatrix} \frac{|G|}{adjG_{11}} & 0 & 0 \\ 0 & \frac{|G|}{adjG_{22}} & 0 \\ 0 & 0 & \frac{|G|}{adjG_{33}} \end{pmatrix} \quad (16)$$

4. PROBLEM STATEMENT

For *nxn* systems, the simplified decoupling technique allows us to obtain the following configuration which is constituted by *n* SISO systems as shown in Figure 3. Each system is composed by a controller $C_i(s)$ and a transfer function $T_i(s)$ for $i=1,...,n$.

The system transfer function is given by

$$\begin{aligned} T_i(s) &= \frac{N_i(s)}{D_i(s)} \\ &= \frac{n_m s^m + n_{m-1}{}^{m-1} s^{m-1} + \cdots + n_0}{d_l s^l + d_{l-1} s^{l-1} + \cdots + d_0} \end{aligned} \quad (17)$$

The controller transfer function is defined by:

$$C_i(s) = \frac{B_i(s)}{A_i(s)} \quad (18)$$

where the polynomials Ai(s) and Bi(s) that represent, respectively, the denominator and the numerator of the controller are expressed as follows:

$$\begin{aligned} A_i(s) &= s^t + a_{t-1} s^{t-1} + \cdots + a_1 s + a_0 \\ B_i(s) &= b_r s^r + b_{r-1} s^{r-1} + \cdots + b_1 s + b_0 \end{aligned} \quad (19)$$

Figure 3. A feedback control system

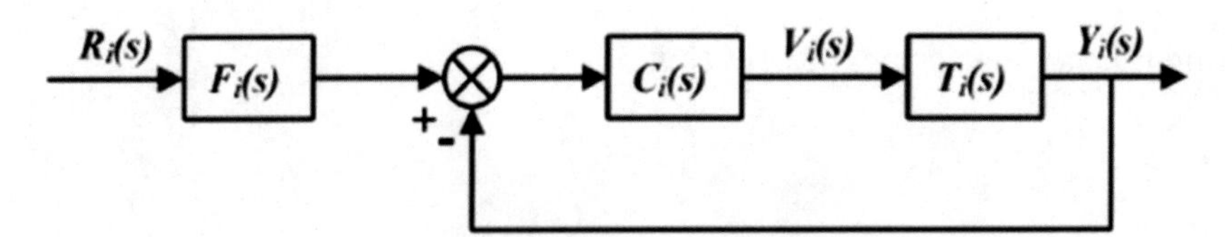

In the case of low-order controller, suppose that: $r \leq t < l - 1$.

In order to obtain a closed loop transfer function with a unit static gain, a polynomial $F_i(s)$ is introduced as follows:

$$F_i(s) = f_q s^q + f_{q-1} s^{q-1} + \cdots + f_1 s + f_0 \quad (20)$$

By using Eqs. 17, 18 and 20 the closed loop transfer function will be given by the following expression:

$$H_i(s) = \frac{F_i(s) B_i(s) N_i(s)}{A_i(s) D_i(s) + B_i(s) N_i(s)} \quad (21)$$

The closed loop characteristic equation is given by the following relation:

$$\begin{aligned} \delta_i(s) &= A_i(s) D_i(s) + B_i(s) N_i(s) \\ &= \delta_n s^n + \delta_{n-1} s^{n-1} + \cdots + \delta_1 s + \delta_0 \end{aligned} \quad (22)$$

where $n = l + t$

The methodology of fixing the desired closed loop characteristic equation which was detailed by Kim, Keel and Bhattacharyya (2003), Jin and Kim (2008) and Ben Hariz, Bouani and Ksouri (2012) will be explained subsequently.

Let consider the following polynomial:

$$\delta(s) = \delta_n s^n + \delta_{n-1} s^{n-1} + \cdots + \delta_1 s + \delta_0 = \sum_{j=0}^{n} \delta_j s^j \quad (23)$$

The characteristic ratios α_j $(j = 1, \ldots, n-1)$ and the generalized time constant τ are defined by Kim, Keel and Bhattacharyya (2003) and Jin and Kim (2008):

$$\alpha_j = \frac{\delta_j^2}{\delta_{j-1} \delta_{j+1}}, \; j = 1, \ldots, n-1 \quad (24)$$

$$\tau = \frac{\delta_1}{\delta_0} \quad (25)$$

Then, the coefficients of the polynomial $\delta(s)$ can be expressed as a function of α_j and τ as follows:

$$\delta_1 = \delta_0\tau,\ \delta_2 = \frac{\delta_0\tau^2}{\alpha_1},\ldots,\delta_n = \frac{\delta_0\tau^n}{\alpha_{n-1}\alpha_{n-2}^2\ldots\alpha_1^{n-1}} \tag{26}$$

The characteristic polynomial is defined as the polynomial having the following characteristic ratios:

$$\begin{cases} \alpha_1 > 2 \\ \alpha_k = \dfrac{\sin\left(\dfrac{k\pi}{n}\right) + \sin\left(\dfrac{\pi}{n}\right)}{2\sin\left(\dfrac{k\pi}{n}\right)}\alpha_1 \ \ for\ \ k = 2,\ldots,n-1 \end{cases} \tag{27}$$

So the characteristic polynomial is determined by fixing only α_1 for a given τ and δ_0 by using relations 26 and 27.

The objective, now, is to design a controller which guaranties some step response performances such as the overshoot and the settling time.

5. CONTROLLERS DESIGN METHOD

The controller parameters vector is described by the following expression:

$$x = \begin{bmatrix} b_0 & \cdots & b_r & a_0 & \cdots & a_{t-1} \end{bmatrix}^T \tag{28}$$

In is noted that each controller $C_i(s)$ has $(r+t+1)$ parameters.

The coefficients vectors of the closed loop characteristic polynomial δ and the closed loop desired polynomial $\bar{\delta}$ are defined respectively as follows:

$$\delta = \begin{bmatrix} \delta_0 & \delta_1 & \cdots & \delta_{n-1} & \delta_n \end{bmatrix}^T \tag{29}$$

$$\bar{\delta} = \begin{bmatrix} \overline{\delta_0} & \overline{\delta_1} & \cdots & \overline{\delta_{n-1}} & \overline{\delta_n} \end{bmatrix}^T \tag{30}$$

At this stage, the coefficient vector of the closed loop characteristic polynomial δ $\delta(x)$. $\delta(x)$c be expressed as a function of x by:

$$\delta = Px + q \tag{31}$$

where the matrix P and the vector q depend on the transfer function $T_i(s)$ parameters and are given by:

$$P = \begin{bmatrix} n_0 & 0 & \cdots & 0 & d_0 & 0 & \cdots & 0 \\ n_1 & n_0 & \cdots & 0 & d_1 & d_0 & \cdots & 0 \\ \vdots & \vdots & & \vdots & d_2 & d_1 & \cdots & 0 \\ n_m & n_{m-1} & \cdots & n_{m-r} & \vdots & \vdots & & \vdots \\ \vdots & \vdots & & \vdots & d_l & d_{l-1} & \cdots & d_{l-t+1} \\ 0 & 0 & \cdots & n_m & \vdots & \vdots & & \vdots \\ \vdots & \vdots & & \vdots & 0 & 0 & \cdots & d_l \\ 0 & 0 & \cdots & 0 & 0 & 0 & \cdots & 0 \end{bmatrix}$$

$$q = \begin{bmatrix} 0 & \cdots & 0 & d_0 & \cdots & d_{l-t} & \cdots & d_l \end{bmatrix}^T$$

where $P \in R^{(n+1)\times(r+t+1)}$, $x \in R^{r+t+1}$, $q \in R^{n+1}$

The controller parameters are calculated such that the difference between δ and $\overline{\delta}$ is minimum. This can be given by the following weighted cost function:

$$f(x) = \left[\delta - \overline{\delta}\right]^T W \left[\delta - \overline{\delta}\right]$$

where W is a weighting matrix.

By using (31), the cost function can be rewritten as:

$$f(x) = x^T\left[P^T W P\right]x + 2\left[\left(q-\overline{\delta}\right)^T W P\right]x + \left[\left(q-\overline{\delta}\right)^T W\left(q-\overline{\delta}\right)\right] \quad (32)$$

It was mentioned by Kim, Keel and Bhattacharyya (2003) and Kim, Kim and Manabe (2004) that the coefficients of lower powers of s in the transfer function are the most related to the step response. So, the weighting matrix may be chosen so that the weights for the low powers of s have greater values than those for higher powers.

The Diophantine Eq. 33 cannot be resolved as long as any low-order controller is employed. So, the PMM approach will be used with the purpose of obtaining an approximate solution. The PMM method can be regarded as a least square estimation problem in the sense of minimizing $f(x)$ with regards to x.

The controller parameters can be obtained by resolving the following problem:

$$\min_x f(x) \quad (33)$$

This non convex optimization problem can be resolved by local approach which might result local solutions. Accordingly, the use of a global optimization method is suggested so as to obtain an optimal control law. In this work, the exploited method is the GGP. Consequently, the presentation of the GGP method is the subject of the next section.

6. GENERALIZED GEOMETRIC PROGRAMMING METHOD

6.1 Mathematical Formulation of the GGP Method

GGP problems are commonly used in engineering design, management and chemical process industry (see e.g. Nand, 1995; Chul & Dennis, 1996; Maranas & Floudas, 1997; Porn, Bjork & Westerlund, 2008; Tsai, 2009; Kheriji, Bouani & Ksouri, 2011). The distinctive peculiarity of this method is that it is dedicated to solve a class of non convex non-linear programming problems with the objective function and constraints are in polynomial forms. The mathematical formulation of a GGP problem with free variables is expressed as follows (Tsai, Lin & Hu, 2007):

$$\min_{X} Z(X) = \sum_{p=1}^{T_0} c_p z_p \tag{34}$$

where

$$z_p = x_1^{\alpha_{p1}} x_2^{\alpha_{p2}} \dots x_n^{\alpha_{pn}}, \; p = 1,\dots,T_0 ,$$
$$X = (x_1, x_2, \dots, x_m, x_{m+1}, \dots, x_n), \; \underline{x_i} \le x_i \le \overline{x_i}, \; x_i > 0, \text{ for } 1 \le i \le m \text{ and } x_i \le 0, \text{ for } m+1 \le i \le n, \tag{35}$$

$c_p \in \Re$ $\alpha_{pi} \in \Re$ for $1 \le i \le m$, α_{pi} is integer for $m+1 \le i \le n$ and $\underline{x_i}$ and $\overline{x_i}$ are, respectively, lower and upper bounds of continuous variables x_i. It should be noted that convexification strategy that will be introduced later is only applied to positive variables x_i because of the logarithmic/exponential transformation. Accordingly, this transformation necessitates substituting x_i by $\exp(y_i)$. Therefore, x_i must be strictly positive. Nevertheless, this is not a handicap because simple translations of the variables to accomplish specifications for variables originally having negative values can be used (Bjork, Lindberg & Westerlund, 2003).

The GGP method has been suggested to find the global optimum based on variable transformations. This transformation technique allows the convexification of the objective function and the constraints. To begin with, some definitions are needed before presenting the convexification propositions and property.

Definition 1: A "*monomial*" function is a product of power terms and it can be given by:

$$f(X) = c \prod_{i=1}^{n} x_i^{p_i} \tag{36}$$

where c is a real constant and p_i can be negative or positive power for $1 \le i \le n$.

Definition 2: A "*signomial*" function is constituted of a sum with products of power terms, where each product with power terms is multiplied by a real constant (Liberti & Maculan, 2006):

$$f(X) = \sum_{j=1}^{T} c_j \prod_{i=1}^{n} x_i^{p_{i,j}} \tag{37}$$

The constants c_j and powers $p_{i,j}$ for $1 \le i \le n$ and $1 \le j \le T$ can be positive or negative.

Definition 3: The function *f(X)* is called a "*posynomial*", when all constants c_j, for $1 \le j \le T$, in a signomial function of Eq. 33 are positive.

Optimization problems that possess only signomial terms are called GGP problems.

Before exposing the convexification rules, some convex analysis results will be introduced in the next subsection:

Proposition 1 (Tsai, Lin & Hu, 2007): A twice-differential function $f(X) = c\prod_{i=1}^{n} x_i^{p_i}$ is convex in $\Re_+^n$ for $c \ge 0$ if $p_i \le 0$.

Proposition 2 (Tsai, Lin & Hu, 2007): A twice-differential function $f(X) = c\prod_{i=1}^{n} x_i^{p_i}$ is convex in $\Re_+^n$ for $c \le 0$ if $p_i \ge 0$ and $(1 - \sum_{i=1}^{n} p_i) \ge 0$.

Property (Porn, Bjork & Westerlund, 2008): The function $f(X) = c\exp\left(\sum_{i=1}^{n} p_i x_i\right)$ is convex in $\Re_+^n$ if $c \ge 0$ and $p_i \in \Re$.

6.2 Convexification Strategy of the GGP Method

The fundamental concept in the convexification strategy is to perform variable transformations to problem (34) that permits to convexify each monomial of the signomial depending on their signs. Since the objective function of the controller possesses only variables with positive powers, just the following transformation rules will be taken into account.

Positively signed term (c>0): Let consider the function $f(X) = c\prod_{i=1}^{n} x_i^{p_i}$, where $p_i>0$. This function is non convex. An exponential transformation is introduced according to $x_i = \exp(y_i)$, for *i=1,2,...,n.* Then, the following equivalence can be established:

$$f(X) = c\prod_{i=1}^{n} x_i^{p_i} = c\exp\left(\sum_{i=1}^{n} p_i y_i\right) \tag{38}$$

According to the property previously presented, the signomial in the right hand of Eq. 38 is now convex relatively to y_i.

Negatively signed term (c<0): Let consider the function $f(X) = c\prod_{i=1}^{n} x_i^{p_i}$, where $p_i>0$ and $\left(1 - \sum_{i=1}^{n} p_i\right) < 0$. In order to transform this function to a convex one, power transformation is used according to $x_i = z_i^{\frac{1}{\beta}}$, for *i=1,2,...,n,* where $\beta = \sum_{i-1}^{n} p_i$.

Then, the resulting equality will be given by:

$$f(X) = c\prod_{i=1}^{n} x_i^{p_i} = c\prod_{i=1}^{n} z_i^{\frac{p_i}{\beta}} \tag{39}$$

According to Proposition 2, the signomial in the right hand of Eq. 39 is now convex with respect to z_i, since all exponents are positive and their sum is equal to 1. Another solution to convexify *f(X)* is to simply choose $\beta > \sum_{i=1}^{n} p_i$.

In this work, the objective function to be optimized given by Eq. 32 is non convex. So, in order to convexify it and to obtain a global solution the GGP method will be applied. Thereafter, the simulation results will be illustrated in order to highlight the proposed approach.

7. SIMULATION RESULTS

In this section simulation examples are proposed to shed light on the efficiency of the synthesis method presented in section 5. A comparison study between the proposed controller and a PI controller for TITO and MIMO systems is presented.

7.1 Design of Controllers for TITO Systems

In this part, two TITO systems are considered.

First System Presentation

The TITO process is defined by:

$$G(s) = \begin{bmatrix} \dfrac{2s+1}{11s^2+6s+1} & \dfrac{5}{3s+1} \\ \dfrac{7}{8s+1} & \dfrac{7s+2}{9s^2+8s+1} \end{bmatrix} \tag{40}$$

So, by using Eq. 6, the simplified decoupler will be given by:

$$D(s) = \begin{bmatrix} 1 & \dfrac{-2s^2-16s-10}{2s^2+3s+1} \\ \dfrac{-4s^2-24s-8}{3s^2+15s+3} & 1 \end{bmatrix} \tag{41}$$

The resulted transfer matrix functions $T_1(s)$ and $T_2(s)$ that are expressed in Eq. 11 and Eq. 12 are given by:

$$T_1(s) = \frac{-3129s^4 - 4552s^3 - 2197s^2 - 457s - 33}{1848s^5 + 2383s^4 + 1237s^3 + 321s^2 + 41s + 2} \tag{42}$$

and

$$T_2(s) = \frac{-3129s^4 - 4552s^3 - 2197s^2 - 457s - 33}{432s^5 + 798s^4 + 533s^3 + 159s^2 + 21s + 1} \tag{43}$$

Fixed Low Order Controller

The synthesis of fixed low order controllers for the previously defined system with different time response specifications is the subject of this part of the work.

Assume that the objective is to design a controller $C_1(s)$ for $T_1(s)$ which will satisfy the following specifications:

1. Overshoot $\leq 2\%$
2. 2% settling time ≤ 10 s

The controller is described by the following polynomials:

$$\begin{cases} A(s) = s^2 + a_1 s + a_0 \\ B(s) = b_1 s + b_0 \end{cases} \tag{44}$$

By fixing the step response time specifications, the characteristic ratio α_1 and the generalized time constant τ are determined and will be given by $\alpha_1 = 2.6$ and $\tau = 11$. Then, by using the procedure presented by Kim, Keel and Bhattacharyya (2003) the desired characteristic polynomial coefficients can be computed. So the desired characteristic polynomial $\bar{\delta}$ will be given by:

$$\bar{\delta}_1 = [0.0037 \quad 0.0814 \quad 0.6888 \quad 2.8831 \quad 6.4243 \quad 7.6202 \quad 4.4714 \quad 1]$$

Subsequently, the objective function to be optimized can be found. Then, the resolution of the non convex optimization problem by applying the GGP method leads to the following low order controller:

$$C_1(s) = \frac{-0.58s - 0.177}{s^2 + 2.77s + 1.35} \tag{45}$$

Let the objective, now, be to design a controller $C_2(s)$ for $T_2(s)$ which will satisfy the following performances:

1. Overshoot $\leq 2\%$
2. 2% settling time ≤ 25 s

By using these specifications, the parameters α_1 and τ are determined and are given by $\alpha_1 = 2.7$ and $\tau = 20$. Then, the same procedure of the first example is used so as to find the following desired characteristic polynomial $\bar{\delta}$:

$$\bar{\delta}_2 = \begin{bmatrix} 0.0158 & 0.3160 & 2.3407 & 8.2598 & 14.9406 & 13.8533 & 6.1191 & 1 \end{bmatrix}$$

As a result, the following controller $C_2(s)$ is obtained by adopting the same strategy applied to system described by the transfer function $T_1(s)$:

$$C_2(s) = \frac{-0.028134s - 0.040745}{s^2 + 2.5235s + 2.9715} \tag{46}$$

The output signals given in Figure 4 and the control signals represented in Figure 5 are obtained by applying these two controllers with the coupled TITO system defined by Eq. 40.

Figure 4. Evolution of set points and outputs for the first TITO system

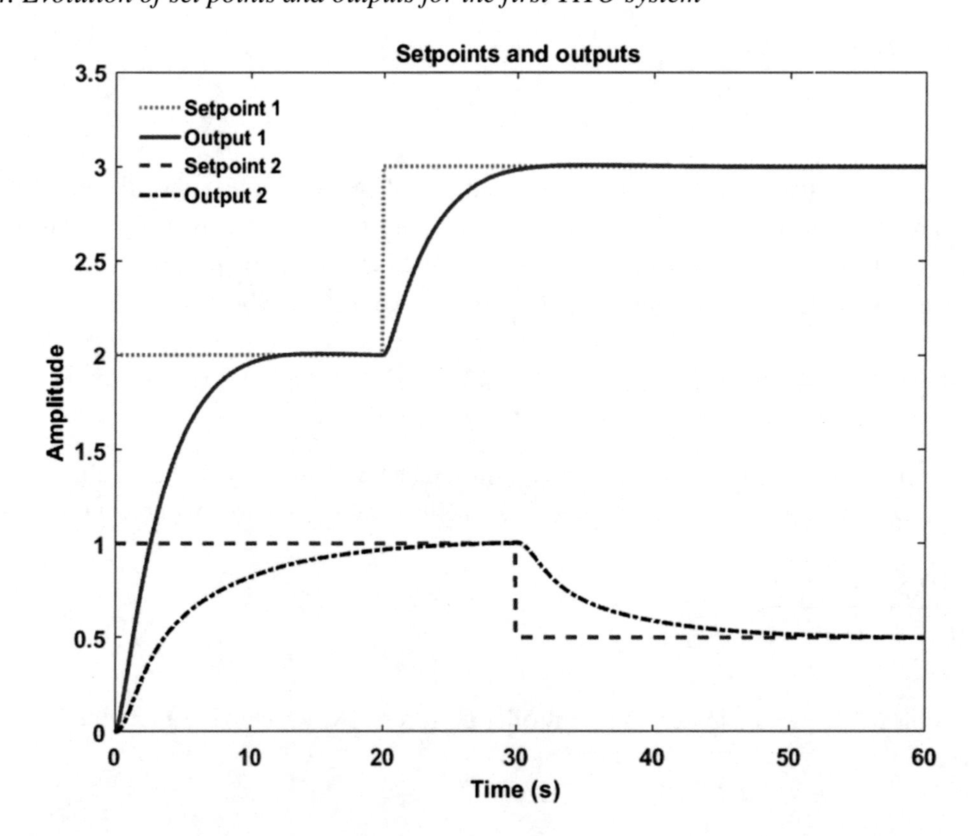

Figure 5. Evolution of control signals for the first TITO system

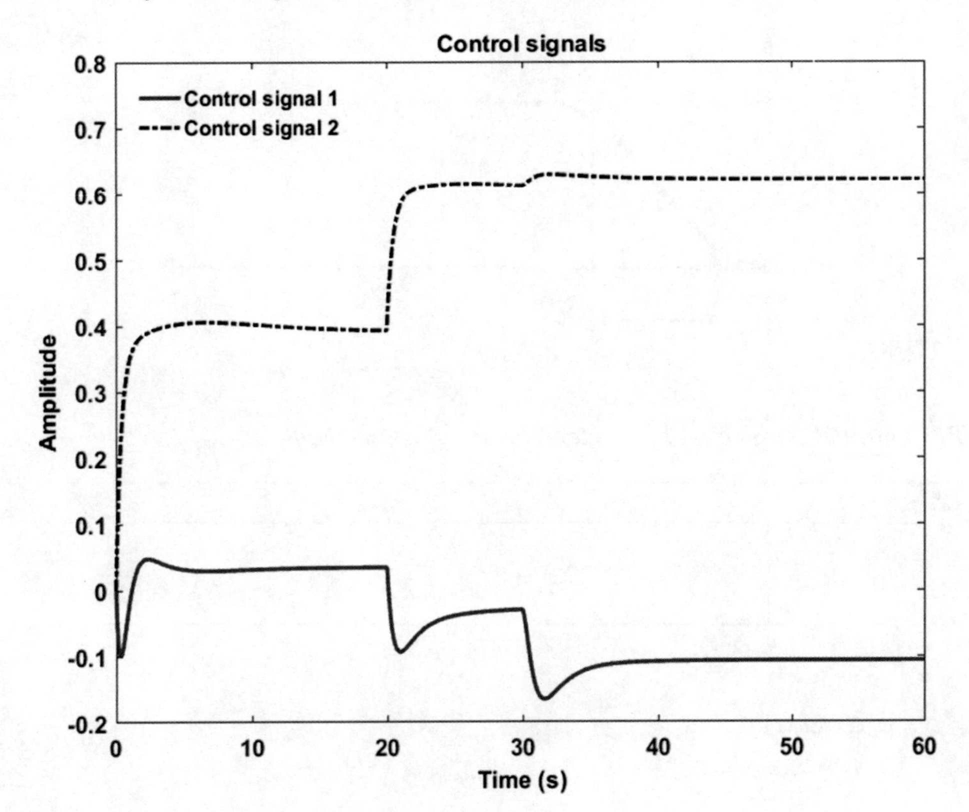

According to Figure 4, it is noted that the design fixed low order controllers assume the desired requirements for the two system outputs.

PI Controller

With an aim of determining the PI controller parameters, the first method of Ziegler-Nichols which takes into account the step response of the open loop system (Lequesne, 2006) as shown in Figure 6 is used.

In order to find T and L values, the tangent to the response curve at the point of inflection is drawn. From these found values, the controller parameters K_p and K_i can be determined as mentioned in Table 1.

The PI controller is described by the following expression:

$$C(s) = K_p + K_i \frac{1}{s} \tag{47}$$

By applying this method, the PI controllers transfer functions will be given by:

$$C_{PI1}(s) = 2.658 + 4.347 \frac{1}{s} \tag{48}$$

Figure 6. Response curve for Ziegler-Nichols first method

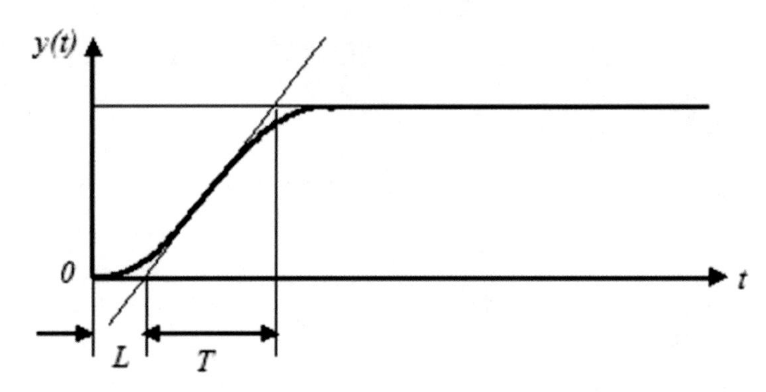

Table 1. PI Controller parameters by Ziegler–Nichols's first method

Controller	Kp	Ti=K_p/K_i
PI	$0.9\frac{T}{L}$	$\frac{L}{0.3}$

$$C_{PI2}(s) = 9.649 + 168.947\frac{1}{s} \tag{49}$$

The evolutions of the set points, the output signals and the control signals, obtained with the PI controllers are depicted in Figure 7 and Figure 8 respectively.

It is observed from Figure 7 that the control signals present peaks with high amplitude. It is also remarkable from Figure 8 that with the PI controller does not allow us to meet the required response time specifications. In fact the first system output, for example, presents an important overshoot value (about 38%) and a 2% settling time about 11.5 s.

Second System Presentation

Let consider the following second TITO system described by:

$$G(s) = \begin{bmatrix} \dfrac{s^2+2s+2}{s^4+3s^3+7.5s^2+5s+1} & \dfrac{1}{s^2+8s+3} \\ \dfrac{1}{s^2+6s+2} & \dfrac{s^2+2s+1}{s^4+3s^3+6s^2+4s+1} \end{bmatrix} \tag{50}$$

So, by using Eq. 6, the simplified decoupler will be given by:

Figure 7. Evolution of set points and outputs for the first TITO system obtained with the PI controller

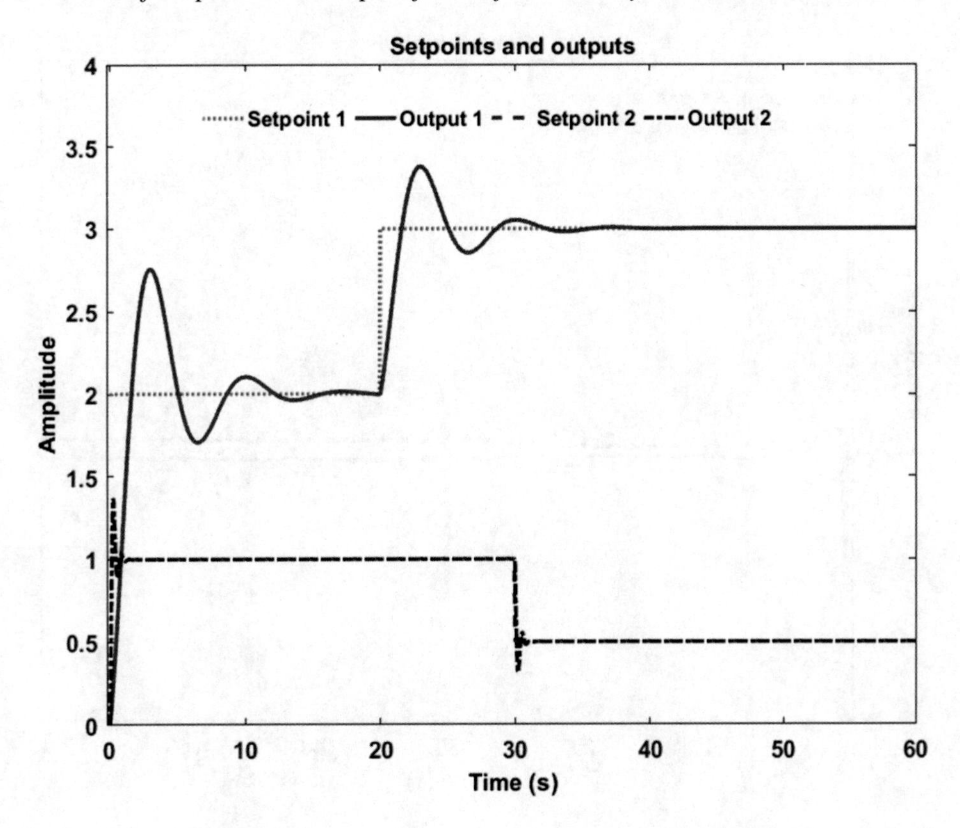

$$D(s)=\begin{bmatrix} 1 & -\dfrac{s^4+3s^3+7.5s^2+5s+1}{s^4+10s^3+21s^2+22s+6} \\ -\dfrac{s^4+3s^3+6s^2+4s+1}{s^4+8s^3+15s^2+10s+2} & 1 \end{bmatrix} \tag{51}$$

Then the transfer matrix functions $T_1(s)$ and $T_2(s)$ can be calculated and given by:

$$T_1(s)=\frac{12s^7+93.5s^6+300.5s^5+525s^4+542s^3+318.5s^2+95s+11}{s^{10}+19s^9+137.5s^8+525s^7+1285s^6+2008s^5+1948.5s^4+1152s^3+402s^2+76s+6} \tag{52}$$

and

$$T_2(s)=\frac{12s^7+93.5s^6+300.5s^5+525s^4+542s^3+318.5s^2+95s+11}{s^{10}+19s^9+137s^8+517s^7+1247s^6+1976s^5+2087s^4+1404s^3+572s^2+128s+12} \tag{53}$$

Figure 8. Evolution of control signals for the first TITO system obtained with the PI controller

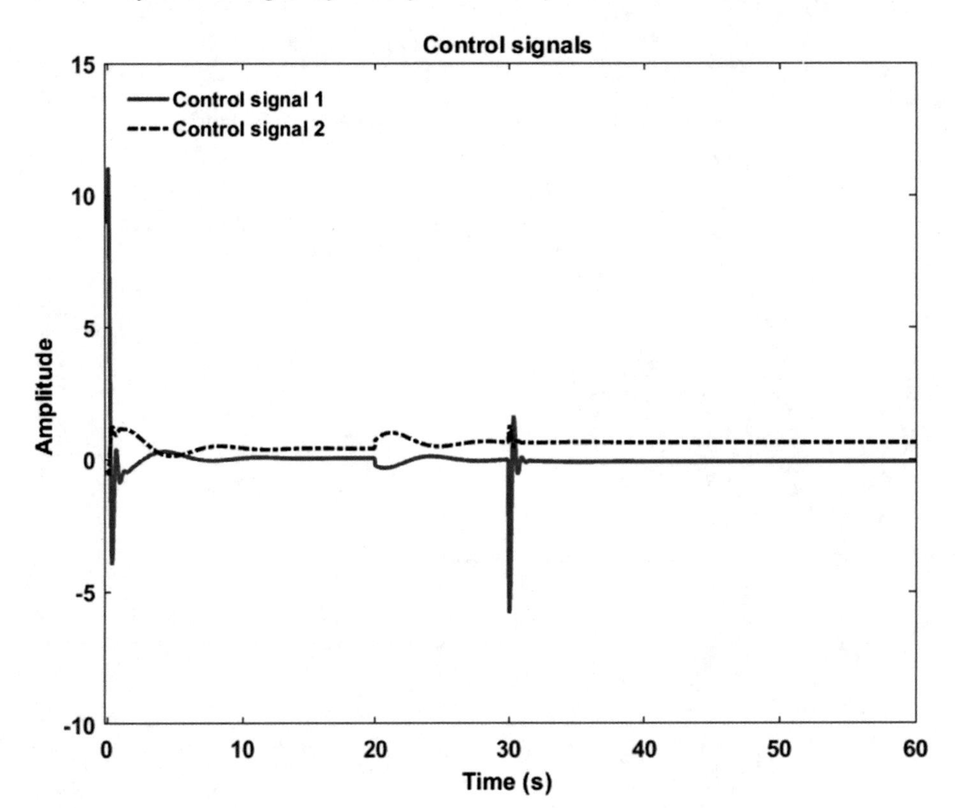

Fixed Low Order Controller

After decoupling the TITO system, let the objective be the design of a fixed low order controller that will be able to ensure the following time performance for the first output:

1. Overshoot $\leq 2\%$
2. 2% settling time ≤ 10 s

The controller is defined by the following polynomials:

$$\begin{cases} A(s) = s^5 + a_4 s^4 + a_3 s^3 + a_2 s^2 + a_1 s + a_0 \\ B(s) = b_3 s^3 + b_2 s^2 + b_1 s + b_0 \end{cases} \tag{54}$$

By fixing the desired time specifications, the characteristic ratio α_1 and the generalized time constant τ are given by $\alpha_1 = 2.27$ and $\tau = 16$. Then, by adopting the same procedure as in the case of the first example the following desired characteristic polynomial $\overline{\delta}$ can be computed:

$$\bar{\delta}_1 = [265.6 \quad 4249.6 \quad 29953.1 \quad 123091.2 \quad 329220.6 \quad 606203.2 \quad 793058.9 \quad 750121.4 \quad 517029.2 \quad 259690.4 \quad 94305.2 \quad 24331.6 \quad 4321.9 \quad 499.64 \quad 33.67 \quad 1]$$

Let the x vector, the vector x containing the controller parameters be defined by:

$$x = [x_1 \quad x_2 \quad x_3 \quad x_4 \quad x_5 \quad x_6 \quad x_7 \quad x_8 \quad x_9]^T = [b_0 \quad b_1 \quad b_2 \quad b_3 \quad a_0 \quad a_1 \quad a_2 \quad a_3 \quad a_4]^T$$

Then, a non convex optimization problem is formulated. Then, the minimization of this optimization problem by applying the GGP method leads to the following controller:

$$C_1(s) = -\frac{96.016s^3 + 272.119s^2 + 180.423s + 36.408}{s^5 + 14.629s^4 + 83.022s^3 + 196.464s^2 + 208.364s + 111.114} \quad (55)$$

Let the objective be now the synthesis of a controller to guarantee the following specifications for the second system output:

1. Overshoot $\leq 6\%$
2. 2% settling time ≤ 9 s

By considering these specifications, the parameters α_1 and τ are determined and given by $\alpha_1 = 2.23$ and $\tau = 14.2$. Then, the following the following desired characteristic polynomial $\bar{\delta}$ can be calculated:

$$\bar{\delta}_2 = [246.05 \quad 3493.9 \quad 22248.2 \quad 84079.5 \quad 210514.3 \quad 369373.1 \quad 468733.3 \quad 437770.3 \quad 303280.9 \quad 155855.5 \quad 58946.7 \quad 16124 \quad 3090.86 \quad 392.538 \quad 29.58 \quad 1]$$

Hence, by using the GGP method, the following controller transfer function $C_2(s)$ is determined:

$$C_2(s) = -\frac{11.98s^3 + 88.717s^2 + 72.67s + 20.255}{s^5 + 10.428s^4 + 54.42s^3 + 102.119s^2 + 101.851s + 39.016} \quad (56)$$

By applying these two controllers $C_1(s)$ and $C_2(s)$ to the decoupled TITO system, it is possible to obtain the evolution of the system outputs that are shown in Figure 9. The evolutions of the control signals are given in Figure 10.

It can be seen from Figure 9 that the designed low order controllers allows us to achieve the desired closed loop performances. In fact, the first output does not present an overshoot and it is characterized by a 2% settling time less than 10 s while the second output has an overshoot less than 6% and a 2% settling time less than 9 s that represent the objective defined previously.

Figure 9. Evolution of set points and outputs for the second TITO system

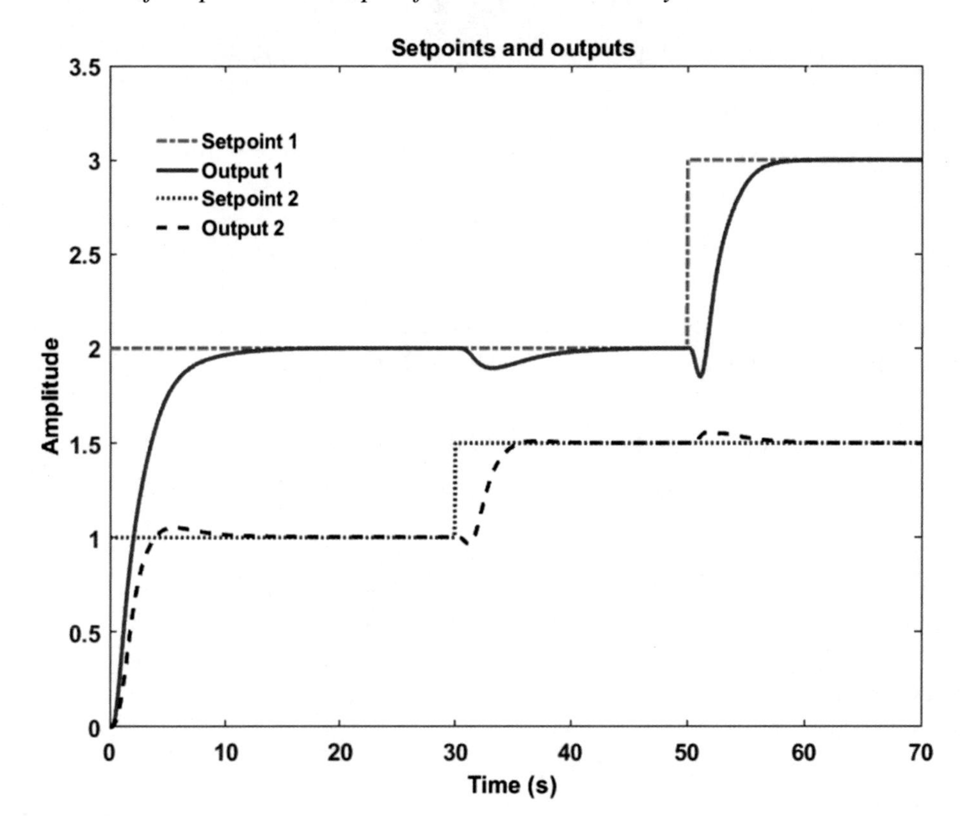

PI Controller

So as to highlight the performance of the fixed low order controller the synthesis of a PI controller will be the subject of this part of the work.

By applying the first method of Ziegler-Nichols, previously presented to the system described by the transfer functions $T_1(s)$ and $T_2(s)$ that are described by Eq. (53) and Eq. (54) respectively. It is possible to obtain the controllers given by the following transfer functions:

$$C_{PI1}(s) = 6.705 + 1.133\frac{1}{s} \tag{57}$$

$$C_{PI2}(s) = 6.17 + 2.145\frac{1}{s} \tag{56}$$

The evolutions of the set points and of the output signals obtained by applying these two controllers PI to the coupled system are represented in Figure 11. The evolution of the control signals are plotted in Figure 12.

Figure 10. Evolution of control signals for the second TITO system

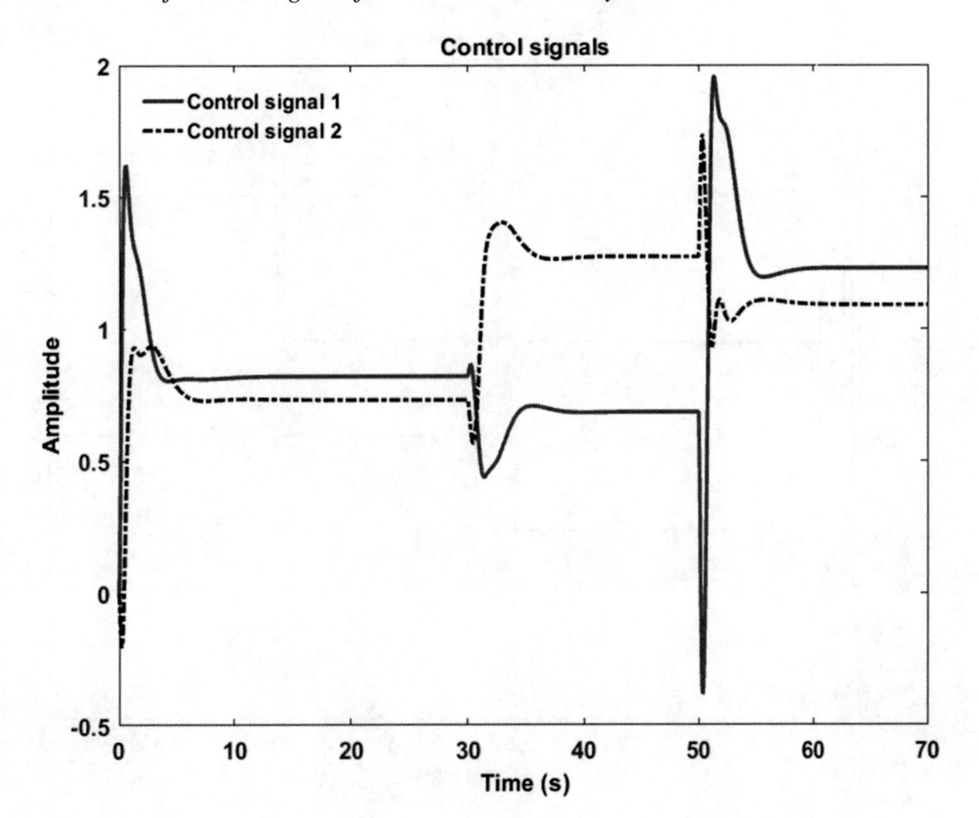

From Figure 11, it is noted that the first system output presents a significant overshoot and a few oscillations before reaching the steady state.

From this example, it can be seen that the proposed fixed low order controller allows us to guarantee the response time specifications imposed by the user, while the PI controller does not allow it. Indeed, it is difficult to adjust the parameters of the latter one in order to achieve the desired objective.

The design of low order controllers for TITO systems with fixed parameter was presented. The main objective of these controllers is to ensure certain closed-loop temporal performances. The parameters of the proposed controllers are obtained by solving a convex optimization problem. So as to obtain a global solution and consequently an optimal control law the GGP method is used as a global optimization method, A comparison between the fixed low order controller and the PI controller has been carried out. The simulations showed the effectiveness of the control law developed in this work.

In this part, the study focused on the design of the controllers for the decoupled TITO systems.

An extension of the proposed approach in the case of decoupled MIMO systems will be discussed in the next paragraph.

7.2 Design of Controllers for MIMO Systems

In order to generalize the proposed approach, the design of fixed low order controllers for decoupled three input three output systems will be the object of this part of the work.

Let consider the MIMO system described by the following transfer matrix:

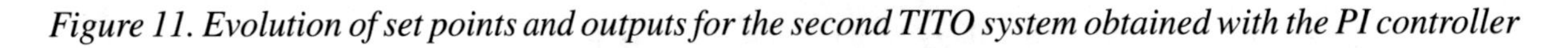

Figure 11. Evolution of set points and outputs for the second TITO system obtained with the PI controller

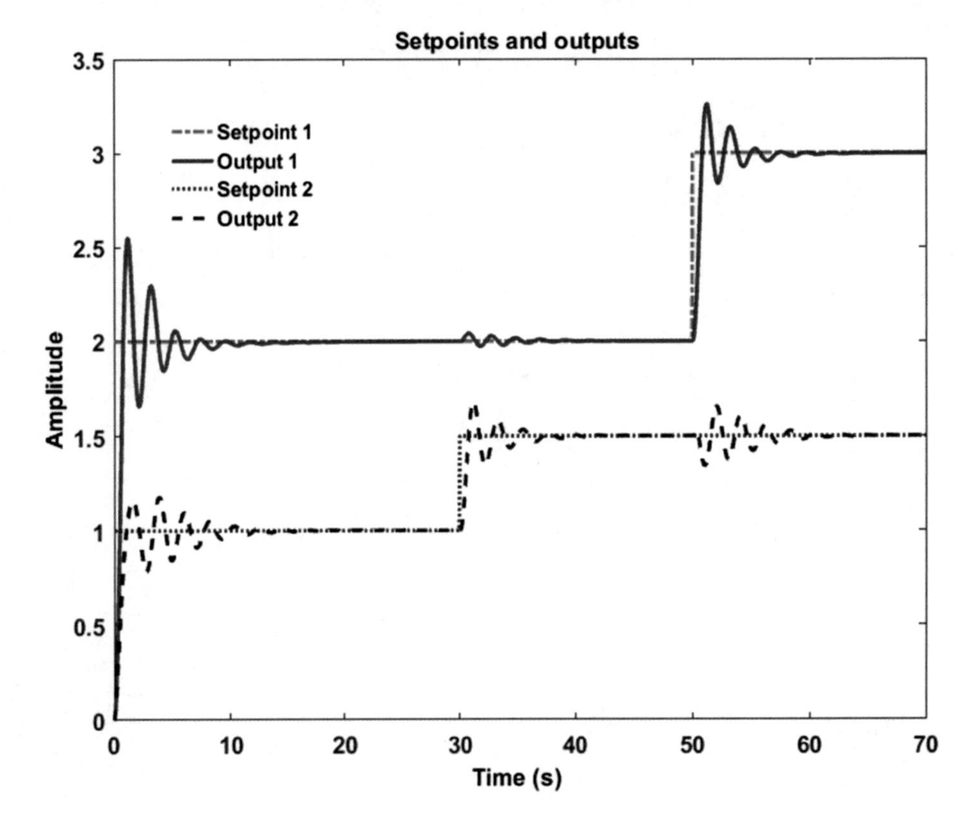

$$G(s) = \begin{bmatrix} \dfrac{-6}{3s+1} & \dfrac{2}{3s+1} & \dfrac{3}{s+2} \\ \dfrac{3}{2s+1} & \dfrac{-4}{4s+2} & \dfrac{5}{4s+3} \\ \dfrac{4}{7s+2} & \dfrac{2}{2s+1} & \dfrac{5}{4s+1} \end{bmatrix} \tag{51}$$

By considering Eq. 6, the simplified decoupler can be computed and given by the following relations:

$$D_{12}(s) = \frac{-1828s^3 - 24s^2 + 57s + 14}{354s^3 + 741s^2 + 414s + 66} \tag{51}$$

$$D_{13}(s) = \frac{46s^2 + 64s + 19}{12s^2 + 33s + 18} \tag{52}$$

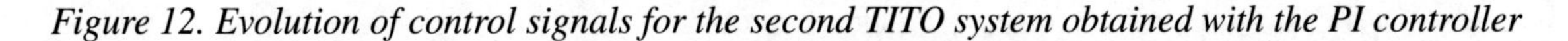

Figure 12. Evolution of control signals for the second TITO system obtained with the PI controller

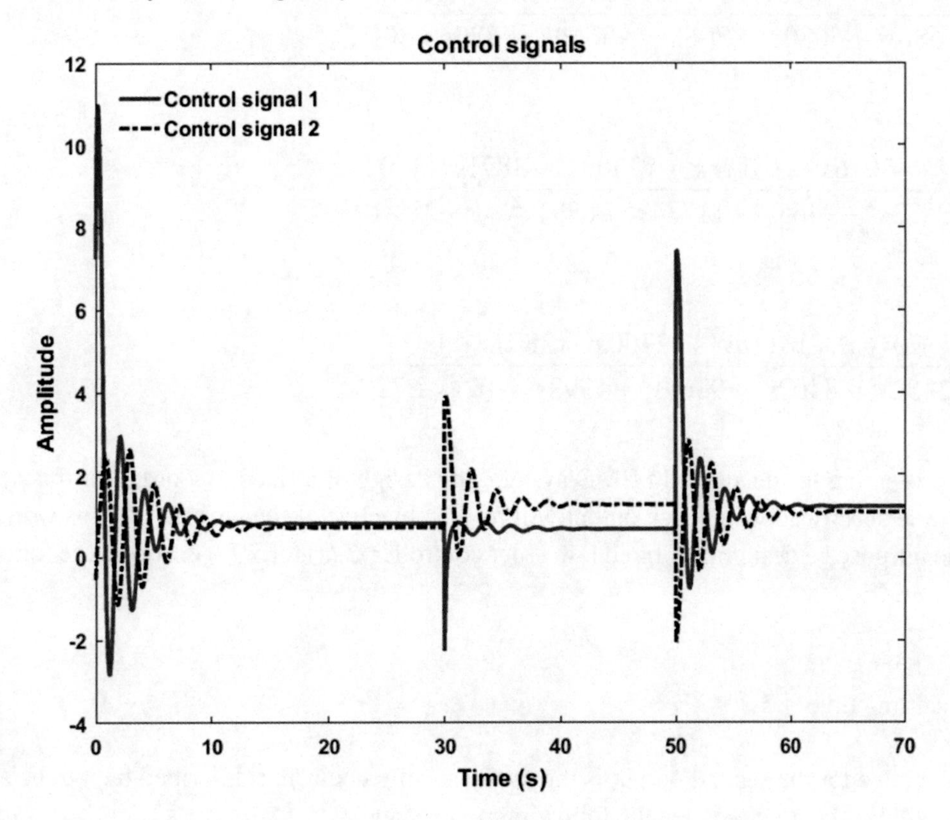

$$D_{21}(s)=\frac{52s^2+63s+14}{112s^2+88s+16} \tag{53}$$

$$D_{23}(s)=\frac{56s^2+89s+29}{8s^2+22s+12} \tag{54}$$

$$D_{31}(s)=\frac{-464s^3-624s^2-247s-30}{560s^3+720s^2+300s+40} \tag{55}$$

$$D_{32}(s)=\frac{-200s^3-514s^2-244s-32}{354s^3+741s^2+414s+66} \tag{56}$$

It should be noted that: $D_{11}(s) = D_{22}(s) = D_{33}(s) = 1$

By taking into account the decoupler previously calculated, the three following transfer functions can be deduced as follows:

$$T_1(s) = \frac{-7016s^4 - 16118s^3 - 12300s^2 - 3871s - 430}{1680s^5 + 6080s^4 + 7060s^3 + 3660s^2 + 880s + 80} \quad (57)$$

$$T_2(s) = \frac{-7016s^4 - 16118s^3 - 12300s^2 - 3871s - 430}{2832s^5 + 9468s^4 + 11784s^3 + 6891s^2 + 1902s + 198} \quad (58)$$

$$T_3(s) = \frac{7016s^4 + 16118s^3 + 12300s^2 + 3871s + 430}{2352s^5 + 8400s^4 + 9369s^3 + 4398s^2 + 924s + 72} \quad (59)$$

After presenting the decoupled MIMO system, the design of a fixed low order for this system with different time specifications of each output will be the objective of the next part of this work.

Let the purpose be designing a fixed low order controller $C_1(s)$ for $T_1(s)$ ensuring the following time specifications:

1. Overshoot $\leq 2\%$
2. 2% settling time ≤ 5s

The objective for the second output is the synthesis of a controller described by a transfer function $C_2(s)$ that will be able to guarantee the following performances:

1. Overshoot $\leq 2\%$
2. 2% settling time ≤ 3s

For the third output, the following closed loop time specifications are required:

i) Overshoot $\leq 2\%$
ii) 2% settling time ≤ 15s

The three controllers are described by the following polynomials:

$$\begin{cases} A(s) = s^3 + a_2 s^2 + a_1 s + a_0 \\ B(s) = b_1 s + b_0 \end{cases} \quad (60)$$

In order to achieve the objective previously fixed for the first output, the desired characteristic polynomial $\overline{\delta}$ is determined by considering $\alpha_1 = 2.52$ and $\tau = 11$. Thus, this characteristic polynomial will be given by the following vector:

$$\overline{\delta_1} = \begin{bmatrix} 1.437 & 15.807 & 68.998 & 155.097 & 195.651 & 141.667 & 57.566 & 12.046 & 1 \end{bmatrix}$$

By minimizing the non convex optimization problem via GGP method the following controller can be obtained:

$$C_1(s) = \frac{-3.118s - 3.56}{s^3 + 8.71s^2 + 21.814s + 10.953} \tag{61}$$

For the second subsystem described by the transfer function $T_2(s)$, the desired characteristic polynomial $\bar{\delta}$ is calculated by considering $\alpha_1 = 2.58$ and $\tau = 11$. As a result, this characteristic polynomial is obtained and given by the following coefficients:

$$\bar{\delta}_2 = [2.776 \quad 30.536 \quad 130.192 \quad 279.196 \quad 328.194 \quad 216.291 \quad 78.134 \quad 14.197 \quad 1]$$

Then the controller $C_2(s)$ obtained by minimizing the objective function is, thus, given by:

$$C_2(s) = \frac{-14.581s - 15.266}{s^3 + 10.964s^2 + 37.304s + 4.411} \tag{62}$$

In order to reach the predefined objectives for the third output, the desired characteristic polynomial is calculated by choosing $\bar{\delta}$ is determined by considering $\alpha_1 = 2.9$ and $\tau = 16$. Thus, this $\bar{\delta}$ is, then, computed and given by:

$$\bar{\delta}_3 = [3.66 \quad 58.560 \quad 323.089 \quad 797.662 \quad 960.356 \quad 576.706 \quad 168.886 \quad 22.131 \quad 1]$$

By applying the GGP method to solve the non convex optimization problem, the following controller is obtained:

$$C_3(s) = \frac{0.541s + 1.515}{s^3 + 19.177s^2 + 97.085s + 148.747} \tag{63}$$

The evolutions of set points, output signals and control signals obtained by applying these three controllers to the coupled MIMO system are represented in Figure 13 and Figure 14 respectively.

As shown in Fig. 9, it is remarkable that the synthesis low order controllers allow the system outputs to meet accurately the desired specifications. It is also noted that it is possible to specify the desired time performances for each output independently.

8. DISCUSSION

In the first part of this work the synthesis of low order controller for decoupled Two Input Two Output (TITO) systems is presented. Then, this design method is generalized in the case of MIMO systems.

Figure 13. Evolution of set points and outputs for the MIMO system

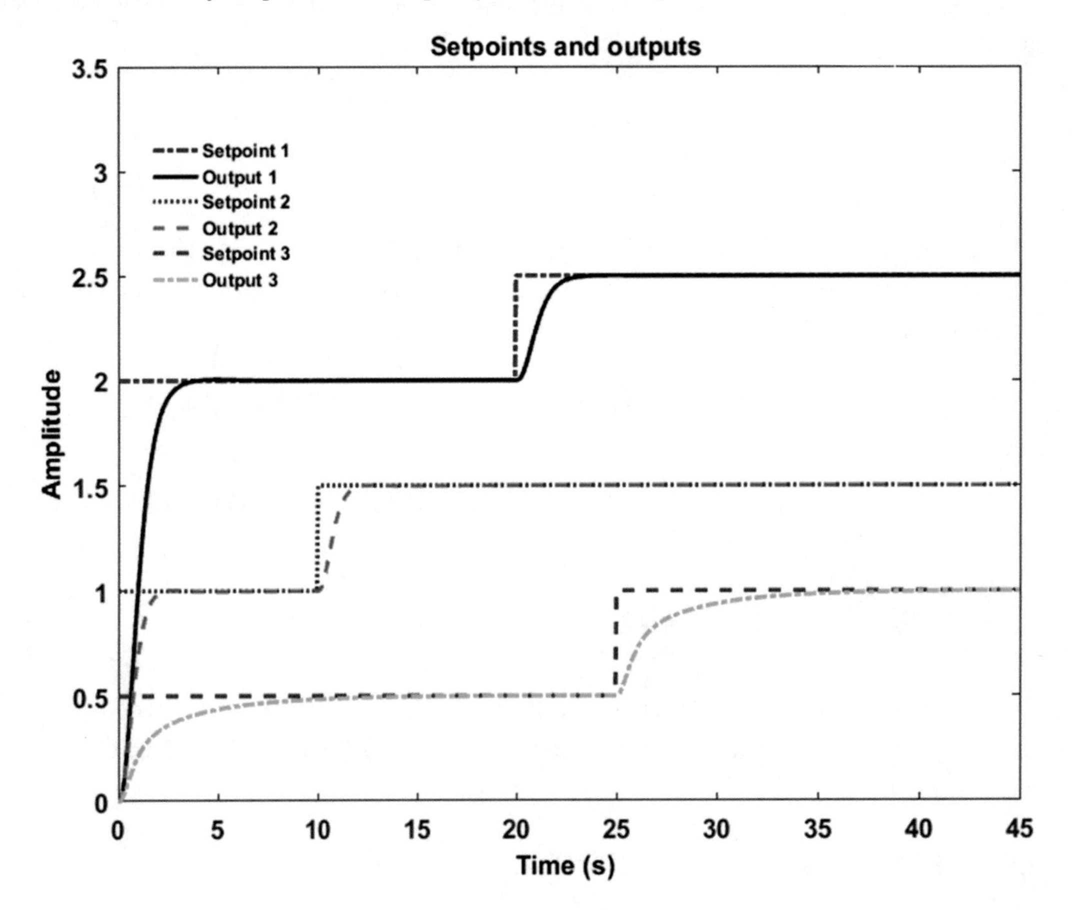

After presenting its advantages, the simplified decoupling was used as decoupling technique. So as to determine the controller parameters, a non convex optimization problem must be solved. The resolution by a local optimization method of such kind of problem may lead to a local solution. And then, the obtained control law is not optimal. Therefore, with the purpose of overcoming this problem and obtaining a global solution the GGP method was used. This method allows us to establish the optimal control law. From simulation results it is remarkable that the proposed controller allows us to guarantee the desired closed loop time specifications (the overshoot and the settling time) for each system output. The developed approach in this work has several advantages. In fact, the obtained solution is independent of the initialization and it leads to an optimal control law. Moreover, by adopting this approach, the designer can fix the desired closed loop performances of the outputs independently.

In order to highlight its efficiency a comparison between the proposed fixed low controller and a PI controller has been made. Simulation results show that the PI controller may not guarantee the required performances. It is noted that it is difficult to find the PI controller parameters values to achieve the desired performances. Control signals obtained with the PI controller present peaks with high amplitude when varying set-points in contrast to those obtained with the proposed controller.

Figure 14. Evolution of control signals for the MIMO system

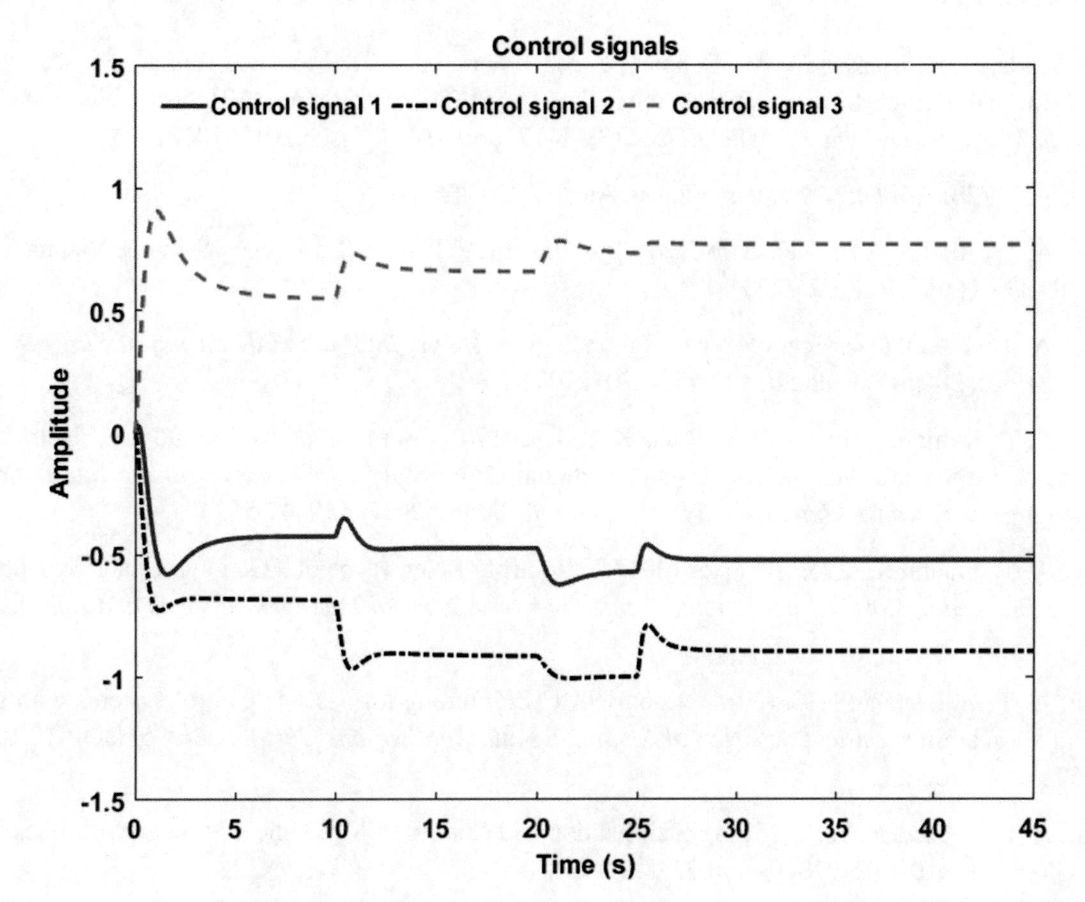

9. CONCLUSION AND FUTURE WORK

In this work, the design of low order controllers for MIMO systems is presented. The main objective of these controllers is to guarantee some step response performances. The controller parameters are obtained by solving non convex optimization problem. In order to obtain a global solution and so to design an optimal control law, a global optimization method was used. The study of TITO systems was the subject of the first part of this work and then a generalization in the case of MIMO systems was proposed. Besides, in order to achieve the defined objective, the simplified decoupling is exploited as decoupling system technique. A comparison between the proposed controller and a PI controller has been made. Simulation results showed the effectiveness of the presented controller.

The system transfer matrix function parameters adopted in this work did not change over the time. But, real physical system cannot be defined by an only one model with fixed parameters. So, in order to describe their exact behavior, systems with uncertain parameters will be considered in later works. Parametric uncertainties will be adopted to describe the real system behavior. Then, the main objective of the control law will be the guarantee, in presence of model uncertainties, some time response performances.

REFERENCES

Abu-Seada, H. F., Mansor, W. M., Bendary, F. M., Emery, A. A., & Moustafa Hassan, M. A. (2013). Application of Particle Swarm Optimization in Design of PID Controller for AVR System. *International Journal of System Dynamics Applications*, *2*(3), 1–17. doi:10.4018/ijsda.2013070101

Azar, A. T. (2010a). *Fuzzy Systems*. Vienna, Austria: IN-TECH.

Azar, A. T. (2010b). Adaptive Neuro-Fuzzy Systems. In A. T. Azar (Ed.), *Fuzzy Systems*. Vienna, Austria: IN-TECH. doi:10.5772/7220

Azar, A. T. (2012). Overview of Type-2 Fuzzy logic systems. *International Journal of Fuzzy System Applications*, *2*(4), 1–28. doi:10.4018/ijfsa.2012100101

Azar, A. T., Kumar, J., Kumar, V., & Rana, K. P. S. (2017d). Control of a Two Link Planar Electrically-Driven Rigid Robotic Manipulator Using Fractional Order SOFC. *Proceedings of the International Conference on Advanced Intelligent Systems and Informatics 2017, 639*, 47-56.

Azar, A. T., Ouannas, A., & Singh, S. (2017c). Control of New Type of Fractional Chaos Synchronization. *Proceedings of the International Conference on Advanced Intelligent Systems and Informatics 2017, 639*, 47-56.

Azar, A. T., & Serrano, F. E. (2014). Robust IMC-PID tuning for cascade control systems with gain and phase margin specifications. *Neural Computing and Applications, 25*(5), 983-995. DOI: 10.1007/s00521-014-1560-x

Azar, A. T., & Serrano, F. E. (2015a). Stabilization and Control of Mechanical Systems with Backlash. IGI Global. doi:10.4018/978-1-4666-7248-2.ch001

Azar, A. T., & Serrano, F. E. (2015b). Design and Modeling of Anti Wind Up PID Controllers. In Complex system modelling and control through intelligent soft computations (vol. 319, pp. 1-44). Springer-Verlag. doi:10.1007/978-3-319-12883-2_1

Azar, A. T., & Serrano, F. E. (2015c). Adaptive Sliding mode control of the Furuta pendulum. In Studies in Computational Intelligence (vol. 576, pp. 1-42). Springer-Verlag GmbH Berlin/Heidelberg. doi:10.1007/978-3-319-11173-5_1

Azar, A. T., & Serrano, F. E. (2015d). Deadbeat Control for Multivariable Systems with Time Varying Delays. In Chaos Modeling and Control Systems Design (vol. 581, pp. 97-132). Springer-Verlag GmbH Berlin/Heidelberg. DOI doi:10.1007/978-3-319-13132-0_6

Azar, A. T., & Serrano, F. E. (2016a) Robust control for asynchronous switched nonlinear systems with time varying delays. *Proceedings of the International Conference on Advanced Intelligent Systems and Informatics 2016*, 533, 891-899. 10.1007/978-3-319-48308-5_85

Azar, A. T., & Serrano, F. E. (2016b). Stabilization of Mechanical Systems with Backlash by PI Loop Shaping. *International Journal of System Dynamics Applications*, *5*(3), 20–47. doi:10.4018/IJSDA.2016070102

Azar, A. T., & Serrano, F. E. (2017). Passivity Based Decoupling of Lagrangian Systems. *Proceedings of the International Conference on Advanced Intelligent Systems and Informatics 2016*, 533, 891-899. 10.1007/978-3-319-48308-5_85

Azar, A. T., & Vaidyanathan, S. (2015a). Handbook of Research on Advanced Intelligent Control Engineering and Automation. IGI Global. doi:10.4018/978-1-4666-7248-2

Azar, A. T., & Vaidyanathan, S. (2015b). *Computational Intelligence applications in Modeling and Control. In Studies in Computational Intelligence* (Vol. 575). Springer-Verlag.

Azar, A. T., & Vaidyanathan, S. (2015c). *Chaos Modeling and Control Systems Design. In Studies in Computational Intelligence* (Vol. 581). Springer-Verlag.

Azar, A. T., & Vaidyanathan, S. (2016). *Advances in Chaos Theory and Intelligent Control. In Studies in Fuzziness and Soft Computing* (Vol. 337). Springer-Verlag. doi:10.1007/978-3-319-30340-6

Azar, A. T., Vaidyanathan, S., & Ouannas, A. (2017a). *Fractional Order Control and Synchronization of Chaotic Systems. In Studies in Computational Intelligence* (Vol. 688). Springer-Verlag. doi:10.1007/978-3-319-50249-6

Azar, A. T., Volos, C., Gerodimos, N. A., Tombras, G. S., Pham, V. T., Radwan, A. G., … Munoz-Pacheco, J. M. (2017b). A novel chaotic system without equilibrium: Dynamics, synchronization and circuit realization. *Complexity*. doi:10.1155/2017/7871467

Azar, A. T., & Zhu, Q. (2015). *Advances and Applications in Sliding Mode Control systems. In Studies in Computational Intelligence* (Vol. 576). Springer-Verlag.

Ben Hariz, M., & Bouani, F. (2016). Synthesis and Implementation of a Fixed Low Order Controller on an Electronic System. *International Journal of System Dynamics Applications*, *5*(4), 42–63. doi:10.4018/IJSDA.2016100103

Ben Hariz, M., Bouani, F., & Ksouri, M. (2012). Robust controller for uncertain parameters systems. *ISA Transactions*, *51*(5), 632–640. doi:10.1016/j.isatra.2012.04.007 PMID:22749294

Ben Hariz, M., Bouani, F., & Ksouri, M. (2014). Implementation of a fixed low order controller on STM32 microcontroller. *International Conference on Control, Engineering and Information Technologies (CEIT)*, 244-252.

Ben Hariz, M., Chagra, W., & Bouani, F. (2013). Controllers design for MIMO systems with time response specifications. *International Conference on Control, Decision and Information Technologies (CoDIT)*, 573-578. 10.1109/CoDIT.2013.6689607

Ben Hariz, M., Chagra, W., & Bouani, F. (2014). Synthesis of Controllers for MIMO Systems with Time Response Specifications. *International Journal of System Dynamics Applications*, *3*(3), 25–52. doi:10.4018/ijsda.2014070102

Bjork, K., Lindberg, P., & Westerlund, T. (2003). Some convexifications in global optimization of problems containing signomial terms. *Computers & Chemical Engineering*, *27*(5), 669–679. doi:10.1016/S0098-1354(02)00254-5

Boulkroune, A., Bouzeriba, A., Bouden, T., & Azar, A. T. (2016a). Fuzzy Adaptive Synchronization of Uncertain Fractional-order Chaotic Systems. In A. T. Azar & S. Vaidyanathan (Eds.), *Advances in Chaos Theory and Intelligent Control. Studies in Fuzziness and Soft Computing* (Vol. 337). Springer-Verlag. doi:10.1007/978-3-319-30340-6_28

Boulkroune, A., Hamel, S., & Azar, A. T. (2016b). *Fuzzy control-based function synchronization of unknown chaotic systems with dead-zone input. In Advances in Chaos Theory and Intelligent Control* (Vol. 337). Germany: Springer-Verlag.

Chul, C., & Dennis, L. (1996). Effectiveness of a geometric programming algorithm for optimization of machining economics models. *Computers & Operations Research, 23*(10), 957–961. doi:10.1016/0305-0548(96)00008-1

Gagnon, E., Pomerleau, A., & Desbiens, A. (1998). Simplified, ideal or inverted decoupling? *ISA Transactions, 37*(4), 265–276. doi:10.1016/S0019-0578(98)00023-8

Garrido, J., Vazquez, F., & Morilla, F. (2012). Centralized multivariable control by simplified decoupling. *Journal of Process Control, 22*(6), 1044–1062. doi:10.1016/j.jprocont.2012.04.008

Ghoudelbourk, S., Dib, D., Omeiri, A., & Azar, A. T. (2016). MPPT Control in wind energy conversion systems and the application of fractional control (PIα) in pitch wind turbine. International Journal of Modelling [IJMIC]. *Identification and Control, 26*(2), 140–151. doi:10.1504/IJMIC.2016.078329

Grassi, G., Ouannas, A., Azar, A. T., Radwan, A. G., Volos, C., Pham, V. T., . . . Stouboulos, I. N. (2017). *Chaos Synchronisation Of Continuous Systems Via Scalar Signal.* The 6th International Conference on Modern Circuits and Systems Technologies (MOCAST), Thessaloniki, Greece. 10.1109/MOCAST.2017.7937629

Jevtovic, B. T., & Matauvsek, M. R. (2010). PID controller design of TITO system based on ideal decoupler. *Journal of Process Control, 20*(7), 869–876. doi:10.1016/j.jprocont.2010.05.006

Jiang, S., Ji, Z., & Shen, Y. (2014). A novel hybrid particle swarm optimization and gravitational search algorithm for solving economic emission load dispatch problems with various practical constraints. *Electrical Power and Energy Systems, 55*(1), 628–644. doi:10.1016/j.ijepes.2013.10.006

Jin, L., & Kim, Y. C. (2008). Fixed, low-order controller design with time response specifications using non-convex optimization. *ISA Transactions, 47*(4), 429–438. doi:10.1016/j.isatra.2008.05.001 PMID:18606409

Kheriji, A., Bouani, F., & Ksouri, M. (2011). A GGP approach to solve non convex min-max predictive controller for a class of constrained MIMO systems described by state-space models. *International Journal of Control, Automation, and Systems, 9*(3), 452–460. doi:10.100712555-011-0304-2

Kim, Y., Kim, K., & Manabe, S. (2004). Sensitivity of time response to characteristic ratios. *Proceeding of the 2004 American Control Conference Boston*, 2723-2728.

Kim, Y. C., Keel, L. H., & Bhattacharyya, S. P. (2003). Transient response control via characteristic ratio assignment. *IEEE Transactions on Automatic Control, 48*(12), 2238–2244. doi:10.1109/TAC.2003.820153

Lequesne, D. (2006). Régulation PID Analogique-numérique-floue. Paris: Hermès, Lavoisier.

Liberti, L., & Maculan, N. (2006). *Global Optimization From Theory to Implementation*. Springer.

Luyben, W. L. (1970). Distillation decoupling. *AIChE Journal. American Institute of Chemical Engineers*, *16*(2), 198–203. doi:10.1002/aic.690160209

Mamdoohi, G., Abas, A. F., & Samsudin, K. (2012). Implementation of genetic algorithm in an embedded microcontroller based polarization control system. *Engineering Applications of Artificial Intelligence*, *25*(4), 869–873. doi:10.1016/j.engappai.2012.01.018

Maranas, C., & Floudas, C. (1997). Global optimization in generalized geometric programming. *Computers & Chemical Engineering*, *21*(4), 351–369. doi:10.1016/S0098-1354(96)00282-7

Meghni, B., Dib, D., & Azar, A. T. (2017c). A Second-order sliding mode and fuzzy logic control to Optimal Energy Management in PMSG Wind Turbine with Battery Storage. *Neural Computing & Applications*, *28*(6), 1417–1434. doi:10.100700521-015-2161-z

Meghni, B., Dib, D., Azar, A. T., Ghoudelbourk, S., & Saadoun, A. (2017a). *Robust Adaptive Supervisory Fractional order Controller For optimal Energy Management in Wind Turbine with Battery Storage. In Studies in Computational Intelligence* (Vol. 688, pp. 165–202). Springer-Verlag.

Meghni, B., Dib, D., Azar, A. T., & Saadoun, A. (2017b). *Effective Supervisory Controller to Extend Optimal Energy Management in Hybrid Wind Turbine under Energy and Reliability Constraints. International Journal of Dynamics and Control*. doi:10.100740435-016-0296-0

Mekki, H., Boukhetala, D., & Azar, A. T. (2015). Sliding Modes for Fault Tolerant Control. In Advances and Applications in Sliding Mode Control systems (vol. 576, pp. 407-433). Springer-Verlag GmbH Berlin/Heidelberg. doi:10.1007/978-3-319-11173-5_15

Mousa, M. E., Ebrahim, M. A., & Moustafa Hassn, M. A. (2015). Stabilizing and Swinging-Up the Inverted Pendulum Using PI and PID Controllers Based on Reduced Linear Quadratic Regulator Tuned by PSO. *International Journal of System Dynamics Applications*, *4*(4), 52–69. doi:10.4018/IJSDA.2015100104

Nand, K. (1995). Geometric programming based robot control design. *Computers & Industrial Engineering*, *29*(1), 631–635.

Ogunnaike, B., & Harmor, W. (1994). *Process Dynamics, Modelling and Control*. New York: Oxford University Press.

Ouannas, A., Azar, A. T., & Abu-Saris, R. (2016a). A new type of hybrid synchronization between arbitrary hyperchaotic maps. *International Journal of Machine Learning and Cybernetics*. doi:10.100713042-016-0566-3

Ouannas, A., Azar, A. T., & Radwan, A. G. (2016b) On Inverse Problem of Generalized Synchronization Between Different Dimensional Integer-Order and Fractional-Order Chaotic Systems. *The 28th International Conference on Microelectronics*. 10.1109/ICM.2016.7847942

Ouannas, A., Azar, A. T., & Vaidyanathan, S. (2017f). On A Simple Approach for Q-S Synchronization of Chaotic Dynamical Systems in Continuous-Time. *Int. J. Computing Science and Mathematics*, *8*(1), 20–27.

Ouannas, A., Azar, A. T., & Vaidyanathan, S. (2017g). New Hybrid Synchronization Schemes Based on Coexistence of Various Types of Synchronization Between Master-Slave Hyperchaotic Systems. *International Journal of Computer Applications in Technology*, *55*(2), 112–120. doi:10.1504/IJCAT.2017.082868

Ouannas, A., Azar, A. T., & Vaidyanathan, S. (2017i). A Robust Method for New Fractional Hybrid Chaos Synchronization. *Mathematical Methods in the Applied Sciences*, *40*(5), 1804–1812. doi:10.1002/mma.4099

Ouannas, A., Azar, A. T., & Ziar, T. (2017h). *On Inverse Full State Hybrid Function Projective Synchronization for Continuous-time Chaotic Dynamical Systems with Arbitrary Dimensions*. Differential Equations and Dynamical Systems. doi:10.100712591-017-0362-x

Ouannas, A., Azar, A. T., Ziar, T., & Radwan, A. G. (2017d). *Study On Coexistence of Different Types of Synchronization Between Different dimensional Fractional Chaotic Systems. In Studies in Computational Intelligence* (Vol. 688, pp. 637–669). Springer-Verlag.

Ouannas, A., Azar, A. T., Ziar, T., & Radwan, A. G. (2017e). *Generalized Synchronization of Different Dimensional Integer-order and Fractional Order Chaotic Systems. In Studies in Computational Intelligence* (Vol. 688, pp. 671–697). Springer-Verlag.

Ouannas, A., Azar, A. T., Ziar, T., & Vaidyanathan, S. (2017a). *On New Fractional Inverse Matrix Projective Synchronization Schemes. In Studies in Computational Intelligence* (Vol. 688, pp. 497–524). Springer-Verlag.

Ouannas, A., Azar, A. T., Ziar, T., & Vaidyanathan, S. (2017b). *Fractional Inverse Generalized Chaos Synchronization Between Different Dimensional Systems. In Studies in Computational Intelligence* (Vol. 688, pp. 525–551). Springer-Verlag.

Ouannas, A., Azar, A. T., Ziar, T., & Vaidyanathan, S. (2017c). *A New Method To Synchronize Fractional Chaotic Systems With Different Dimensions. In Studies in Computational Intelligence* (Vol. 688, pp. 581–611). Springer-Verlag.

Ouannas, A., Grassi, G., Azar, A. T., Radwan, A. G., Volos, C., Pham, V. T., . . . Stouboulos, I. N. (2017j). *Dead-Beat Synchronization Control in Discrete-Time Chaotic Systems*. The 6th International Conference on Modern Circuits and Systems Technologies (MOCAST), Thessaloniki, Greece. 10.1109/MOCAST.2017.7937628

Porn, R., Bjork, K., & Westerlund, T. (2008). Global solution of optimization problems with signomial parts. *Discrete Optimization*, *5*(1), 108–120. doi:10.1016/j.disopt.2007.11.005

Schöbel, A., & Scholz, D. (2014). A solution algorithm for non-convex mixed integer optimization problems with only few continuous variables. *European Journal of Operational Research*, *232*(1), 266–275. doi:10.1016/j.ejor.2013.07.003

Seborg, D. E., Edgar, T. F., & Mellichamp, D. A. (1989). *Process Dynamics & Control*. New York: John Wiley and Sons.

Servet Kiran, M., Gunduz, M., & Kaan Baykan, O. (2012). A novel hybrid algorithm based on particle swarm and ant colony optimization for finding the global minimum. *Applied Mathematics and Computation*, *219*(1), 1515–1521. doi:10.1016/j.amc.2012.06.078

Shahin, M., Saied, E., Moustafa Hassan, M. A., Liang, A., & Bendary, F. (2014). Voltage Swell Mitigation Using Flexible AC Transmission Systems Based on Evolutionary Computing Methods. *International Journal of System Dynamics Applications*, *3*(3), 73–95. doi:10.4018/ijsda.2014070104

Shinskey, F. G. (1988). *Process Control Systems: Application, Design and Adjustment*. New York: McGraw- Hill.

Singh, S., Azar, A. T., Ouannas, A., Zhu, Q., Zhang, W., & Na, J. (2017). *Sliding Mode Control Technique for Multi-switching Synchronization of Chaotic Systems. 9th International Conference on Modelling, Identification and Control (ICMIC 2017)*, Kunming, China.

Skogestad, S., & Postlethwaite, I. (2006). *Multivariable Feedback Control: Analysis and Design*. New York: John Wiley and Sons.

Soliman, N. S., Said, L. A., Azar, A. T., Madian, A. H., Radwan, A. G., & Ouannas, A. (2017). *Fractional Controllable Multi-Scroll V-Shape Attractor with Parameters Effect*. The 6th International Conference on Modern Circuits and Systems Technologies (MOCAST), Thessaloniki, Greece.

Tabakhi, S., Moradi, P., & Akhlaghian, F. (2014). An unsupervised feature selection algorithm based on ant colony optimization. *Engineering Applications of Artificial Intelligence*, *32*(1), 112–123. doi:10.1016/j.engappai.2014.03.007

Tolba, M. F., AbdelAty, A. M., Soliman, N. S., Said, L. A., Madian, A. H., Azar, A. T., & Radwan, A. G. (2017). FPGA implementation of two fractional order chaotic systems. *International Journal of Electronics and Communications*, *28*, 162–172. doi:10.1016/j.aeue.2017.04.028

Toledo, C. F. M., Oliveira, L., & França, P. M. (2014). Global optimization using a genetic algorithm with hierarchically structured population. *Journal of Computational and Applied Mathematics*, *261*, 341–351. doi:10.1016/j.cam.2013.11.008

Tsai, J. (2009). Treating free variables in generalized geometric programming problems. *Computers & Chemical Engineering*, *33*(1), 239–243. doi:10.1016/j.compchemeng.2008.08.011

Tsai, J., Lin, M., & Hu, Y. (2007). On generalized geometric programming problems with non positive variables. *European Journal of Operational Research*, *178*(1), 10–19. doi:10.1016/j.ejor.2005.11.037

Vaidyanathan, S., & Azar, A. T. (2015a) Anti-Synchronization of Identical Chaotic Systems using Sliding Mode Control and an Application to Vaidyanathan-Madhavan Chaotic Systems. In Advances and Applications in Sliding Mode Control systems (vol. 576, pp. 527-547). Springer-Verlag GmbH Berlin/Heidelberg. doi:10.1007/978-3-319-11173-5_19

Vaidyanathan, S., & Azar, A. T. (2015b). Hybrid Synchronization of Identical Chaotic Systems using Sliding Mode Control and an Application to Vaidyanathan Chaotic Systems. In Advances and Applications in Sliding Mode Control systems (vol. 576, pp. 549-569). Springer-Verlag GmbH Berlin/Heidelberg. doi:10.1007/978-3-319-11173-5_20

Vaidyanathan, S., & Azar, A. T. (2015c). Analysis, Control and Synchronization of a Nine-Term 3-D Novel Chaotic System. In Chaos Modeling and Control Systems Design (vol. 581, pp. 3-17). Springer-Verlag GmbH Berlin/Heidelberg. DOI doi:10.1007/978-3-319-13132-0_1

Vaidyanathan, S., & Azar, A. T. (2015d). Analysis and Control of a 4-D Novel Hyperchaotic System. In Chaos Modeling and Control Systems Design (vol. 581, pp. 19-38). Springer-Verlag GmbH Berlin/Heidelberg. DOI doi:10.1007/978-3-319-13132-0_2

Vaidyanathan, S., & Azar, A. T. (2016a). Takagi-Sugeno Fuzzy Logic Controller for Liu-Chen Four-Scroll Chaotic System. *International Journal of Intelligent Engineering Informatics*, *4*(2), 135–150. doi:10.1504/IJIEI.2016.076699

Vaidyanathan, S., & Azar, A. T. (2016b). *Dynamic Analysis, Adaptive Feedback Control and Synchronization of an Eight-Term 3-D Novel Chaotic System with Three Quadratic Nonlinearities. In Studies in Fuzziness and Soft Computing* (Vol. 337, pp. 155–178). Springer-Verlag.

Vaidyanathan, S., & Azar, A. T. (2016c). *Qualitative Study and Adaptive Control of a Novel 4-D Hyperchaotic System with Three Quadratic Nonlinearities. In Studies in Fuzziness and Soft Computing* (Vol. 337, pp. 179–202). Springer-Verlag.

Vaidyanathan, S., & Azar, A. T. (2016d). *A Novel 4-D Four-Wing Chaotic System with Four Quadratic Nonlinearities and its Synchronization via Adaptive Control Method. Advances in Chaos Theory and Intelligent Control. In Studies in Fuzziness and Soft Computing* (Vol. 337, pp. 203–224). Springer-Verlag.

Vaidyanathan, S., & Azar, A. T. (2016e). *Adaptive Control and Synchronization of Halvorsen Circulant Chaotic Systems. Advances in Chaos Theory and Intelligent Control. In Studies in Fuzziness and Soft Computing* (Vol. 337, pp. 225–247). Springer-Verlag.

Vaidyanathan, S., & Azar, A. T. (2016f). *Adaptive Backstepping Control and Synchronization of a Novel 3-D Jerk System with an Exponential Nonlinearity. In Advances in Chaos Theory and Intelligent Control* (Vol. 337, pp. 249–274). Springer-Verlag.

Vaidyanathan, S., & Azar, A. T. (2016g). *Generalized Projective Synchronization of a Novel Hyperchaotic Four-Wing System via Adaptive Control Method. In Advances in Chaos Theory and Intelligent Control* (Vol. 337, pp. 275–296). Springer-Verlag.

Vaidyanathan, S., Azar, A. T., & Ouannas, A. (2017a). *An Eight-Term 3-D Novel Chaotic System with Three Quadratic Nonlinearities, its Adaptive Feedback Control and Synchronization. In Studies in Computational Intelligence* (Vol. 688, pp. 719–746). Springer-Verlag.

Vaidyanathan, S., Azar, A. T., & Ouannas, A. (2017c). *Hyperchaos and Adaptive Control of a Novel Hyperchaotic System with Two Quadratic Nonlinearities. In Studies in Computational Intelligence* (Vol. 688, pp. 773–803). Springer-Verlag.

Vaidyanathan, S., Azar, A. T., Rajagopal, K., & Alexander, P. (2015b). Design and SPICE implementation of a 12-term novel hyperchaotic system and its synchronization via active control (2015). International *Journal of Modelling, Identification and Control*, *23*(3), 267–277. doi:10.1504/IJMIC.2015.069936

Vaidyanathan, S., Idowu, B. A., & Azar, A. T. (2015c). Backstepping Controller Design for the Global Chaos Synchronization of Sprott's Jerk Systems. In Chaos Modeling and Control Systems Design (vol. 581, pp. 39-58). Springer-Verlag GmbH Berlin/Heidelberg. doi:10.1007/978-3-319-13132-0_3

Vaidyanathan, S., Sampath, S., & Azar, A. T. (2015a). Global chaos synchronisation of identical chaotic systems via novel sliding mode control method and its application to Zhu system. International Journal of Modelling. *Identification and Control*, *23*(1), 92–100. doi:10.1504/IJMIC.2015.067495

Vaidyanathan, S., Zhu, Q., & Azar, A. T. (2017b). *Adaptive Control of a Novel Nonlinear Double Convection Chaotic System. In Studies in Computational Intelligence* (Vol. 688, pp. 357–385). Springer-Verlag.

Valdez, F., Melin, P., & Castillo, O. (2014). Modular Neural Networks architecture optimization with a new nature inspired method using a fuzzy combination of Particle Swarm Optimization and Genetic Algorithms. *Information Sciences*, *270*(20), 143–153. doi:10.1016/j.ins.2014.02.091

Vijay Kumar, V., Rao, V. S. R., & Chidambaram, M. (2012). Centralized PI controllers for interacting multivariable processes by synthesis method. *ISA Transactions*, *51*(3), 400–409. doi:10.1016/j.isatra.2012.02.001 PMID:22405751

Wang, Q. W. (2003). *Decoupling Control.* New York: Springer-Verlag.

Wang, Z., Volos, C., Kingni, S. T., Azar, A. T., & Pham, V. T. (2017). Four-wing attractors in a novel chaotic system with hyperbolic sine nonlinearity. Optik - International Journal for Light and Electron Optics, 131(2017): 1071-1078.

Weischedel, K., & McAvoy, T. J. (1980). Feasibility of decoupling in conventionally controlled distillation columns. *Industrial & Engineering Chemistry Fundamentals*, *19*(4), 379–384. doi:10.1021/i160076a010

Zhou, Y., Xiao, K., Wang, Y., Liang, A., & Hassanien, A. E. (2013). A PSO-Inspired Multi-Robot Map Exploration Algorithm Using Frontier-Based Strategy. *International Journal of System Dynamics Applications*, *2*(2), 1–13. doi:10.4018/ijsda.2013040101

Zhu, Q., & Azar, A. T. (2015). *Complex system modelling and control through intelligent soft computations. In Studies in Fuzziness and Soft Computing* (Vol. 319). Springer-Verlag.

APPENDIX: LIST OF ABBREVIATIONS

FGA: Fuzzy Genetic Algorithm
FPSO: Fuzzy Practical Swarm Optimization
GA: Genetic Algorithm
GGP: Generalized Geometric Programming
GSA: Gravitational Search Algorithm
MIMO: Multi Input Multi Output
MINLP: Mixed Integer Non-Linear Programming
PI: Proportional Integral
PMM: Partial Model Matching
PSO: Practical Swarm Optimization
SISO: Singe Input Single Output
TITO: Two Input Two Output

Chapter 5
Active Control for Multi-Switching Combination Synchronization of Non-Identical Chaotic Systems

Shikha Singh
Jamia Millia Islamia, India

Ahmad Taher Azar
Benha University, Egypt & Nile University, Egypt

Muzaffar Ahmad Bhat
Jamia Millia Islamia, India

Sundarapandian Vaidyanathan
Vel Tech University, India

Adel Ouannas
University of Larbi Tebessi, Algeria

ABSTRACT

This chapter investigates the multi-switching combination synchronization of three non-identical chaotic systems via active control technique. In recent years, some advances have been made with the idea of multi-switching combination synchronization. The different states of the master systems are synchronized with the desired state of the slave system in multi-switching combination synchronization scheme. The relevance of such kinds of synchronization studies to information security is evident in the wide range of possible synchronization directions that exist due to multi-switching synchronization. Numerical simulations justify the validity of the theoretical results discussed.

DOI: 10.4018/978-1-5225-4077-9.ch005

1. INTRODUCTION

Over the last decades there has been a great interest to harness the very peculiar chaotic behavior in deterministic systems. Chaotic attractor can be defined as deterministic random behavior in bounded phase space of the underlying nonlinear dynamical system that has extreme sensitiveness to infinitesimal perturbations in initial conditions. Deterministic because it arises from intrinsic causes and not from some extraneous noise or interference and random due to irregular, unpredictable behavior, which is characterized by exponential divergence of nearby trajectories on average. Chaos theory, once considered to be the third revolution in physics following relativity theory and quantum mechanics, has been studied extensively in the past thirty years. During the last few decades, chaotic dynamics has moved from mystery to familiarity. Chaotic attractor can also be defined as having deterministic random behavior in bounded phase space of the underlying nonlinear dynamical system that has extreme sensitiveness to infinitesimal perturbations in initial conditions. Deterministic because it arises from intrinsic causes and not from some extraneous noise or interference and random due to irregular, unpredictable behavior, which is characterized by exponential divergence of nearby trajectories on average. In the last few decades or so a large number of theoretical investigations, numerical simulations and experimental works have been carried out on various dynamical systems in an effort to understand the different features associated with the occurrence of chaotic behavior.

A lot of chaotic phenomena have been found and enormous mathematical strides have been taken. Nowadays, it has been agreed by scientists and engineers that chaos is ubiquitous in natural sciences and social sciences, such as in physics, chemistry, mathematics, biology, ecology, physiology, economics, and so on. Wherever nonlinearity exists, chaos may be found. For a long time, chaos was thought of as a harmful behavior that could decrease the performance of a system and therefore should be avoided when the system is running. One remarkable feature of a chaotic system distinguishing itself from other non-chaotic systems is that the system is extremely sensitive to initial conditions. Any tiny perturbation of the initial conditions will significantly alter the long-term dynamics of the system. This fact means that when one wants to control a chaotic system one must make sure that the measurement of the needed signals is absolutely precise. Otherwise any attempt of controlling chaos would make the dynamics of the system go to an unexpected state. Chaos control refers to purposefully manipulating chaotic dynamical behaviors of some complex nonlinear systems. As a new and young discipline, chaos control has in fact come into play with many traditional scientific and technological advances today. Automatic control theory and practice, on the other hand, is a traditional and long-lasting engineering discipline. It has recently rapidly evolved and expanded, to overlap with and sometimes completely encompass many new and emerging technical areas of developments, and chaos control is one of them.

Chaos synchronization involves the coupling of two chaotic systems so that both systems achieve identical dynamics asymptotically with time. There are two forms of coupling: mutual (bidirectional) coupling and the drive-response (unidirectional) coupling. In mutual coupling, the two systems influence or alter each others dynamics until both systems achieve identical dynamics. In the unidirectional coupling, control functions are designed to force the dynamics of one system referred to as the response system to track the unaltered dynamics of the other system referred to as the drive system. The history of synchronization goes back to the 17th century when the Dutch physicist Christiaan Huygens reported on his observation of phase synchronization of two pendulum clocks (Field and Gyorgyi, 1993). Huygens briefly, but extremely precisely, described his observation of synchronization as follows:

It is quite worth noting that when we suspended two clocks so constructed from two hooks imbedded in the same wooden beam, the motions of each pendulum in opposite swings were so much in agreement that they never receded the lease bit from each other and the sound of each was always heard simultaneously. Further, if this agreement was disturbed by some interference, it reestablished itself in a short time. For a long time I was amazed at this unexpected result, but after a careful examination finally found that the cause of this is due to the motion of the beam, even though this is hardly perceptible, The cause is that the oscillations of the pendula, in proportion to their weight, communicate some motion to the clocks. This motion, impressed onto the beam, necessarily has the effect of making the pendula come to a state of exactly contrary swings if it happened that they moved otherwise at first, and from this finally the motion of the beam completely ceases. But this cause is not sufficiently powerful unless the opposite motions of the clocks are exactly equal and uniform.

Since the work of Pecora and Carroll in 1990 (Pecora and Carroll, 1990), chaos control and chaos synchronization have attracted great interest and received extensive studies in many disciplines such as secure communication, information processing, chemical reaction, and high-performance circuits, etc. Chaos has shown great potential to be useful and brought forth great fascination. The problems of control of chaos attract attention of the researchers and engineers since the early 1990s. Several thousand publications have appeared over the recent decade. In recent years, the control of chaotic and hyper chaotic systems has received great attention due to its potential applications in physics, chemical reactor, biological networks, artificial neural networks, telecommunications, etc. Basically, chaos controlling is the stabilization of an unstable periodic orbit or equilibria by means of tiny perturbations of the system. In 1990 Ott et al. (Ott et al., 1990) introduced the OGY method for controlling chaos.E. Ott, C. Grebogi and J. A. Yorke were the first to make the key observation that the infinite number of unstable periodic orbits typically embedded in a chaotic attractor could be taken advantage of for the purpose of achieving control by means of applying only very small perturbations. After making this general point, they illustrated it with a specific method, since called the OGY method (Ott, Grebogi and Yorke) of achieving stabilization of a chosen unstable periodic orbit. In the OGY method, small, wisely chosen, kicks are applied to the system once per cycle, to maintain it near the desired unstable periodic orbit (Aleksandr et al., 1998).

In search of better methods for chaos control and synchronization different types of methods have been developed for controlling chaos and synchronization of non identical and identical systems for instance linear feedback (Becker and Packard, 1994), optimal control (Zhang et al., 2011, Khan and Tyagi, 2016), adaptive control (Azar, & Vaidyanathan, 2015a,b,c; Azar, & Vaidyanathan, 2016; Vaidyanathan 2012; Vaidyanathan 2015a,b,c,d,e,f; Vaidyanathan 2016a,b,c,d,e,f,g,h,I; Vaidyanathan et al., 2017a,b,c; Vaidyanathan and Azar, 2016a,b,d,e), active control (Vaidyanathan 2011; Vaidyanathan et al., 2015a), active sliding mode control (Vaidyanathan 2016j,k,l,m,n; Zhang et al., 2004), passive control (Wang and Liu, 2007), impulsive control (Yang and Chua, 1997), backstepping control (Rasappan and Vaidyanathan, 2012a,b,c, 2013, 2014; Suresh and Sundarapandian, 2013; Vaidyanathan et al., 2015b,c, Vaidyanathan and Azar, 2016f), sliding mode control (Sampath and Vaidyanathan 2016, Vaidyanathan 2016j,k,l,m,n, Vaidyanathan et al., 2015c), adaptive sliding mode control (Khan and Shahzad, 2013, Khan and Shikha, 2017a), Fuzzy Adaptive Synchronization (Boulkroune et al., 2016a,b; Vaidyanathan and Azar, 2016g) etc. In past few years, active control have been extensively used as vigorous control method for controlling chaos and synchronization. This control method gives the flexibility to establish a control law to use it widely for controlling chaos and synchronization of various chaotic and hyperchaotic nonlinear dynamical system.

As a result of fast growing interest in chaos control and synchronization various synchronization types and schemes have been proposed and reported, for instance complete synchronization (Mahmoud and Mahmoud, 2010; Khan and Pal, 2013), phase synchronization (Rosenblum et al., 1996), generalized synchronization (Ouannas et al., 2017b,d; Khan and Shikha, 2017b), generalized projective synchronization (Sarasu and Sundarapandian, 2011a,b, 2012a,b,c, Vaidyanathan and Azar, 2016c), lag synchronization (Shahverdiev et al., 2002), anti-synchronization (Vaidyanathan and Azar, 2015b), projective synchronization (Mainieri and Rehacek, 1999), modified projective synchronization (Li, 2007), function projective synchronization (Du et al., 2008), modified-function projective synchronization (Du et al., 2009), hybrid synchronization (Ouannas et al., 2017a,g; Ouannas et al., 2016a; Vaidyanathan and Azar, 2015c), hybrid function projective synchronization (Ouannas et al., 2017e; Khan and Shikha, 2016] and different order synchronization (Ahmad et al., 2016a,b; Khan et al., 2017b). Over the last decade, several synchronization schemes have been proposed, but often in an ad hoc way. Specifically, synchronization of nonlinear dynamical systems gives the capability to gain an accurate and deep understanding of collective dynamical behavior in physical, chemical and biological and other systems. The presence of synchronous behavior has been observed in different mathematical, physical, sociology, physiology, biological and other systems (Koronovskii et al., 2013).

2. RECENT WORK

Recently many studies focuses on construction and analysis of chaotic and hyperchaotic systems (Pham et al., 2017; Ouannas et al., 2017a,b,c,d,e,f,g,h,i,j; Azar et al., 2017b; Wang et al., 2017; Vaidyanathan and Azar, 2015a,d; Vaidyanathan, 2016; Soliman et al., 2017; Tolba et al., 2017; Singh et al., 2017; Grassi et al., 2017). These novel systems can be later used for performing synchronization which have vast applications in secure communication, image processing etc. Fractional order chaotic system shows more complex dynamics than the integer order chaotic systems. So, to study its behavior and analysing the dynamics is a crucial issue which attracted attention of many researchers nowadays (Ouannas et al., 2016b; Azar et al., 2017a,b,c,d; Meghni et al., 2017a,b,c; Zhu & Azar, 2015; Azar & Zhu, 2015). In 2008, Ahmet Ucar proposed the multi-switching synchronization of coupled chaotic systems via active controls, and has achieved the multi-switching synchronization of the Lorenz system (Ucar et al., 2008). Several manuscripts have investigate multi-switching synchronization (Khan and Bhat, 2016; Khan and Bhat, 2017; Khan and Shikha, 2017c]. The relevance of such kinds of synchronization studies to information security is evident in the wide range of possible synchronization directions that exist due to multi switching synchronization. Despite of these schemes clearly providing improved resistance and anti attack ability for secure communication, only a few studies of this kind has been reported in the literature. Combination synchronization scheme [Khan and Shikha 2017a,b,c; Khan et al., 2017a,b; Runzi et al., 2011; Wu and Fu, 2013; Sun et al., 2015) has been generalized in such a manner that other forms of synchronization scheme can be achieved form it. As a result, combination synchronization and combination-combination synchronization scheme is more flexible and applicable to the real world systems. In addition, the combination synchronization also gives better insight into the complex synchronization and several pattern formations that take place in real world systems since synchronization in real world systems are complex. Motivated by the above discussions, in this chapter we have described the combination multi-switching synchronization of non-identical chaotic systems via active control technique. This chapter is categorize as follows: In section 2 problem formulation for combination multi-switching synchronization of chaotic system via active control technique is introduced. In section 3 system description of three non-identical chaotic systems which are recently published and analysed is described. In section 4 multi-switching combination synchronization of non-identical chaotic systems via active control technique is attained. In section 5, numerical simulations are given. Finally in section 6 concluding remarks are given.

3. PROBLEM FORMULATION

In this section, we propose the generalized technique for multi-switching combination synchronization of non-identical using active control technique.

To perform this technique, we consider the two master system as follows:

$$\dot{X} = f(X) \tag{1}$$

and

$$\dot{Y} = g(Y) \tag{2}$$

The slave system defined by

$$\dot{Z} = h(Z) + U \tag{3}$$

where $X = (x_1, x_2, \ldots, x_n) \in \mathrm{R}^n$, $Y = (y_1, y_2, \ldots, y_n) \in \mathrm{R}^n$, $Z = (z_1, z_2, \ldots, z_n) \in \mathrm{R}^n$ are the state variables and $U = (u_1, u_2, \ldots, u_n) \in \mathrm{R}^n$ is the controller to be determined.

Definition 1. *The two master systems described by (1) and (2) and a slave system described by (3) are said to in combination synchronization if there exists three nonzero scaling matrices P, Q, $R \in \mathrm{R}^{n\times n}$ such that*

$$\lim_{t\to\infty} \| \mathrm{PZ - QX - RY} \| = 0 \tag{4}$$

where $\mathrm{P.P}$ represents a vector norm induced by the matrix norm. Remark: If $P = diag(\gamma_1, \gamma_2, \ldots, \gamma_3)$, $Q = diag(\alpha_1, \alpha_2, \ldots, \alpha n)$ and $R = diag(\beta_1, \beta_2, \ldots, \beta_n)$. Then from definition 1, we can obtain the error vector

$$e_{ijk} = \gamma_k z_k - \alpha_i x_i - \beta_j y_j \tag{5}$$

where the indices of the error vector are strictly chosen to satisfy $i = j = k, \; i, j, k = 1, 2, ..., n$.

Definition 2. *The master systems (1) and (2) and the slave system (3) are said to obtain multi-switching combination synchronization, if the error states (5) are redefined such that*

$$\lim_{t \to \infty} \left\| \gamma_k z_k - \alpha_i x_i - \beta_j y_j \right\| = 0 \tag{6}$$

and $i = j \neq k \; or \; i = k \neq j \; or \; j = k \neq i \; or \; i \neq k \neq j \; or \; i \neq j = k$, where $i, j, k = 1, 2, ..., n$ and $\left\| \bullet \right\|$ is a vector norm.

4. SYSTEMS DESCRIPTION

In 2016, a 3D novel chaotic (Vaidyanathan and Azar, 2015a) system was formulated which is given by

$$\begin{cases} \dot{x}_1 = a_1(x_2 - x_1) + 30x_2x_3 \\ \dot{x}_2 = b_1x_1 + c_1x_2 - x_1x_3 \\ \dot{x}_3 = 0.5x_1x_3 - d_1x_3 + x_1^2 \end{cases} \tag{7}$$

where $x_1, x_2, x_3 \in \mathrm{R}$ are the state variables and $a_1, b_1, c_1, d_1 \in \mathrm{R}$ are parameters. For the parameter values $a_1 = 25, b_1 = 33, c_1 = 11 \; and \; d_1 = 6$ and initial condition $(x_1(0), x_2(0), x_3(0)) = (1.2, 0.6, 1.8)$ the system shows chaotic attractor displayed in Figure (1). It can be clearly seen that the nine-term novel chaotic system exhibits an attractor, which may be named as umbrella attractor. Also, the Lyapunov exponents for the given parameters values are $\gamma_1 = 9.45456, \gamma_2 = 0, \gamma_3 = -30.50532$. Thus the maximum Lyapunov exponent (MLE) of the system 4 is obtained as $\gamma_1 = 9.45456$.

Further, since $\sum_{i=1}^{3} \gamma_i = -21.05076 < 0$, so the system is dissipative.

Also, the Kaplan-Yorke dimension of the system is calculated as

$$\begin{aligned} D_{KY} &= 2 + \frac{\gamma_1 + \gamma_2}{|\gamma_3|} \\ &= 2.1095 \end{aligned}$$

This means that the chaotic attractor has fractal dimension.

The system has three equilibrium points $E_0 = (0,0,0)$, $E_1 = (8.0776, 0.1974, 33.2688)$ and $E_2 = (-24.7120, -0.6039, 33.2688)$ and the corresponding eigenvalues are $(-6, -40.8969, 26.8969)$, $(27.8120 + 55.1509\iota, 27.8120 - 55.1509\iota, -71.5851)$ and $(37.63 + 79.67\iota, 37.63 - 79.67\iota, -107.62)$ respectively. Since corresponding to each equilibrium point there is at least one positive real part of eigenvalue so, each equilibrium point is unstable. Since the system has three equilibrium points, so the system orbits around the three unstable equilibrium points where E_0 is a saddle point and E_1 , E_2 are saddle-focus points.

Since the system is invariant under the transformation $(x_1, x_2, x_3) \to (-x_1, -x_2, x_3)$, so the system is symmetric about x_3-axis. The detailed description of system (7) is given in (Vaidyanathan and Azar, 2015a).

The Vaidyanathan and Madhavan chaotic system (Vaidyanathan and Azar, 2015b) is a described by the 3-D dynamics

$$\begin{cases} \dot{y}_1 = a_2(y_2 - y_1) + y_2 y_3 \\ \dot{y}_2 = b_2 y_1 + c_2 y_1 y_3 \\ \dot{y}_3 = -d_2 y_3 - y_1 y_2 - y_1^2 \end{cases} \tag{8}$$

where $y_1, y_2, y_3 \in \mathrm{R}$ are the state variables and $a_2, b_2, c_2, d_2 \in \mathrm{R}$ are parameters. For the parameter values

$$a_2 = 22, b_2 = 400, c_2 = 50 \textit{ and } d_2 = 0.5$$

Figure 1. Phase portraits of a novel 3D chaotic system

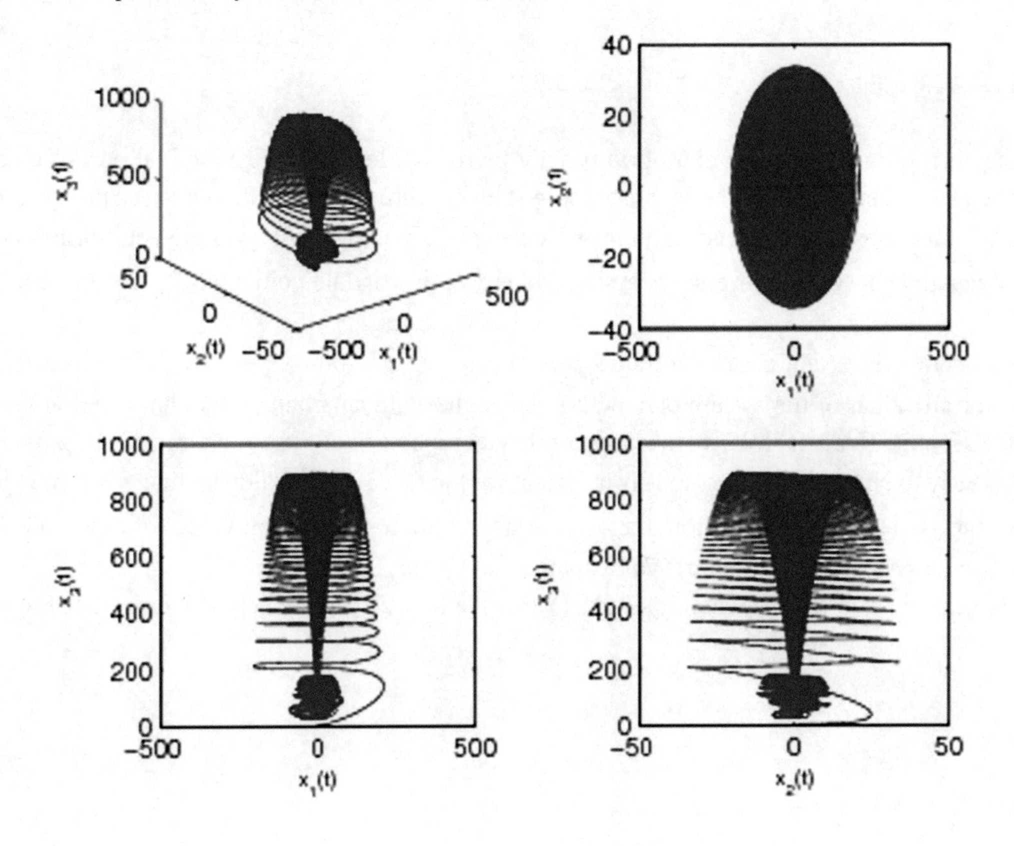

and initial condition $(y_1(0), y_2(0), y_3(0)) = (0.6, 1.8, 1.2)$ the system shows strange chaotic attractor displayed in Figure (2). The system is a seven-term polynomial chaotic system with three quadratic nonlinearities. Also, the Lyapunov exponents for the given parameters values are $\gamma_1 = 3.3226, \gamma_2 = 0, \gamma_3 = -30.3406$. Thus the maximum Lyapunov exponent (MLE) of the system 4 is obtained as $\gamma_1 = 3.3226$.

Further, since $\sum_{i=1}^{3} \gamma_i = -27.018 < 0$, so the system is dissipative.

Also, the Kaplan-Yorke dimension of the system is calculated as

$$\begin{aligned} D_{KY} &= 2 + \frac{\gamma_1 + \gamma_2}{|\gamma_3|} \\ &= 2.1095 \end{aligned}$$

This means that the chaotic attractor has fractal dimension.

The system has three equilibrium points $E_0 = (0,0,0)$, $E_1 = (1.2472, 1.9599, -8)$ and $E_2 = (-1.2472, -1.9599, -8)$ and the corresponding eigenvalues are

$$(-0.5, -105.451, 83.451)$$

$$(2.1011 + 14.3283\iota, 2.1011 - 14.3283\iota, -26.7022)$$

and

$$(2.1011 + 14.3283\iota, 2.1011 - 14.3283\iota, -26.7022)$$

Since corresponding to each equilibrium point there is at least one positive real part of eigenvalue so, each equilibrium point is unstable. Since the system has three equilibrium points, so the system orbits around the three unstable equilibrium points. Hence E_0, E_1, E_2 are all unstable equilibrium points of the Vaidyanathanâ€"Madhavan chaotic system, where E_0 is a saddle point and E_0, E_0 are saddle focus points.

The system is invariant under the transformation $(x_1, x_2, x_3) \rightarrow (-x_1, -x_2, x_3)$. The transformation persists for all values of the system parameters. Thus, the Vaidyanathan system has rotation symmetry about the x3-axis. Hence, it follows that any non-trivial trajectory of the system must have a twin trajectory. It is easy to check that the x_3-axis is invariant for the flow of the Vaidyanathan system. Hence, all orbits of the system (26) starting from the x_3 axis stay in the x_3 axis for all values of time. The detailed description of system (8) is given in (Vaidyanathan and Azar, 2015b).

In 2016, an eight-term novel chaotic system (Vaidyanathan, 2016o), which is given by the 3D dynamics

Figure 2. Phase portrait of Vaidyanathan Madhavan chaotic system

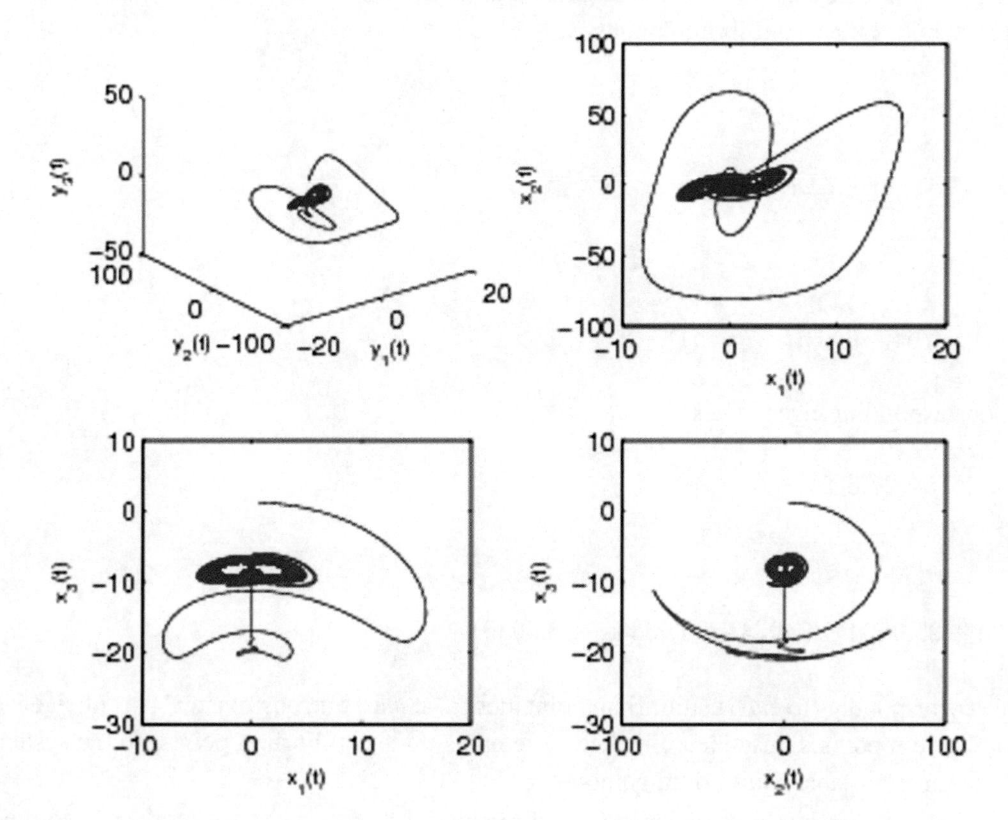

$$
\begin{cases}
\dot{z}_1 = a_3(z_2 - z_1) + z_2 z_3 \\
\dot{z}_2 = b_3(z_1 + z_2) - z_1 z_3 \\
\dot{z}_3 = -cz_3 + z_1^2
\end{cases}
\tag{9}
$$

where $z_1, z_2, z_3 \in \mathrm{R}$ are the state variables and $a_3, b_3, c_3 \in \mathrm{R}$ are parameters. For the parameter values $a_3 = 32, b_3 = 18, c_3 = 9$ and initial condition $(z_1(0), z_2(0), z_3(0)) = (0.3, 0.2, 0.3)$ the system shows chaotic attractor displayed in figure (3). This is an eight-term polynomial system with three quadratic nonlinearities. Also, the Lyapunov exponents for the given parameters values are $\gamma_1 = 6.34352, \gamma_2 = 0, \gamma_3 = -29.26796$. Thus the maximum Lyapunov exponent (MLE) of the system 4 is obtained as $\gamma_1 = 6.34352$.

Further, since $\sum_{i=1}^{3} \gamma_i = -22.9244 < 0$, so the system is dissipative.

Also, the Kaplan-Yorke dimension of the system is calculated as

$$
\begin{aligned}
D_{KY} &= 2 + \frac{\gamma_1 + \gamma_2}{|\gamma_3|} \\
&= 2.2167
\end{aligned}
$$

This means that the chaotic attractor has fractal dimension.

The system has three equilibrium points

$$E_0 = (0,0,0)$$

$$E_1 = (15.7765, 8.4627, 27.6554)$$

and

$$E_2 = (-15.7765, -8.4627, 27.6554)$$

and the corresponding eigenvalues are

$$(-9, -41.6554, 27.6554)$$

and

$$(10.4974 + 25.9534\iota, 10.4974 - 25.9534\iota, -43.9949)$$

Since corresponding to each equilibrium point there is at least one positive real part of eigenvalue so, each equilibrium point is unstable. Since the system has three equilibrium points, so the system orbits around the three unstable equilibrium points .

Since the system is invariant under the transformation $(x_1, x_2, x_3) \rightarrow (-x_1, -x_2, x_3)$, so the system is symmetric about x_3-axis. The detailed description of system (9) is given in (Vaidyanathan, 2016).

5. MULTI-SWITCHING COMBINATION SYNCHRONIZATION OF NON-IDENTICAL CHAOTIC SYSTEMS

In this section, we perform the multi-switching combination synchronization of non-identical chaotic systems via active control technique. For this purpose, we consider (7) and (8) as the master systems and the slave system is obtained by adding controller to the (9) which is given as:

$$\begin{cases} \dot{z}_1 &= a_3(z_2 - z_1) + z_2 z_3 + u_1 \\ \dot{z}_2 &= b_3(z_1 + z_2) - z_1 z_3 + u_2 \\ \dot{z}_3 &= -cz_3 + z_1^2 + u_3 \end{cases} \tag{10}$$

where u_1, u_2, u_3 are the controllers which are to be determined by using active control technique. By the conditions on indices $i, j, k = 1,2,3$ stated in Definition 2, several switching combinations exists for defining the error states for the master slave systems (1)-(3) which are listed as follow:

Figure 3. Phase portrait of an eight term novel 3D chaotic system

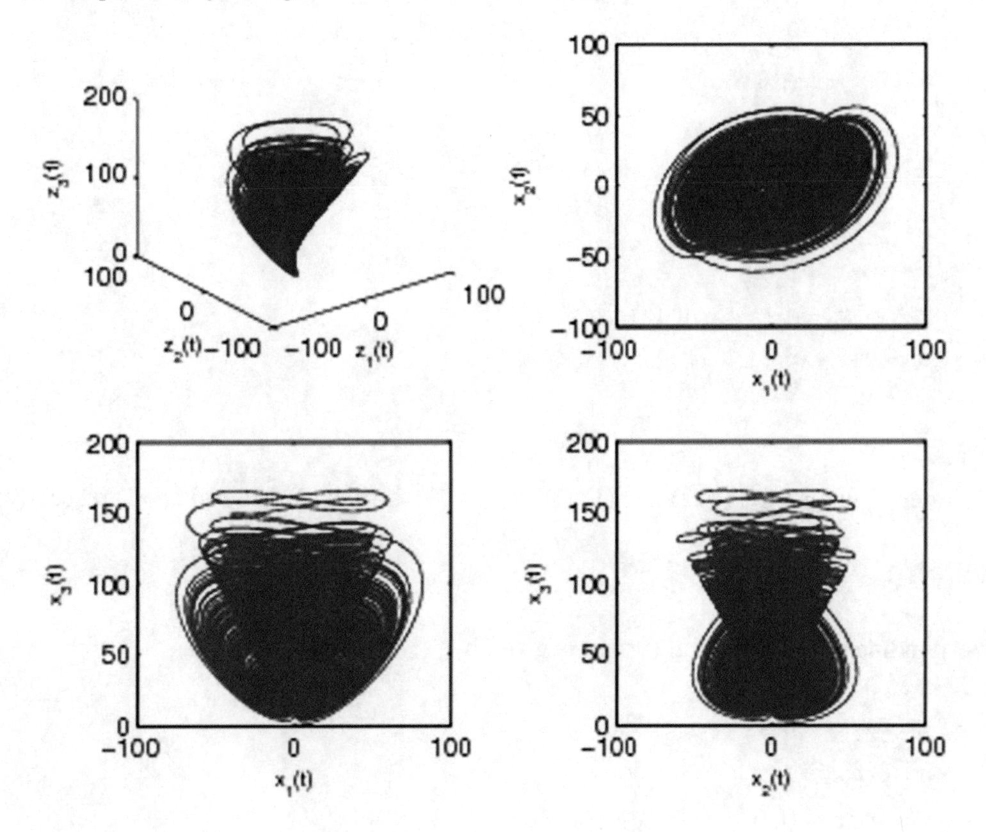

For $i = j \neq k$, we have e_{112}, e_{113}, e_{221}, e_{223}, e_{331} and e_{332}.
For $i = k \neq j$, we have e_{121}, e_{131}, e_{212}, e_{232}, e_{313} and e_{323}.
For $j = k \neq i$, we have e_{122}, e_{133}, e_{211}, e_{233}, e_{311} and e_{322}.
For $j \neq k \neq i$, we have e_{123}, e_{132}, e_{213}, e_{231}, e_{312} and e_{321}.
For $i \neq j = k$, we have e_{122}, e_{133}, e_{211}, e_{233}, e_{311} and e_{322}.

In this chapter, we present some results for three randomly selected error space vector combination formed out of several switching possibilities.

Let the switched error states be given by:

$$\begin{cases} e_{123} = \gamma_1 z_1 - \alpha_2 x_2 - \beta_3 y_3 \\ e_{231} = \gamma_2 z_2 - \alpha_3 x_3 - \beta_1 y_1 \qquad \textit{Switch } 1 \\ e_{312} = \gamma_3 z_3 - \alpha_1 x_1 - \beta_2 y_2 \\ \end{cases} \tag{11}$$

$$\begin{cases} e_{132} &= \gamma_1 z_1 - \alpha_3 x_3 - \beta_2 y_2 \\ e_{213} &= \gamma_2 z_2 - \alpha_1 x_1 - \beta_3 y_3 \qquad Switch\ 2 \\ e_{321} &= \gamma_3 z_3 - \alpha_2 x_2 - \beta_1 y_1 \end{cases} \tag{12}$$

$$\begin{cases} e_{132} &= \gamma_2 z_2 - \alpha_3 x_3 - \beta_1 y_1 \\ e_{213} &= \gamma_1 z_1 - \alpha_2 x_1 - \beta_2 y_2 \qquad Switch\ 3 \\ e_{321} &= \gamma_3 z_3 - \alpha_1 x_1 - \beta_3 y_3 \end{cases} \tag{13}$$

where we refer equations (11), (12) and (13) as switch (1), switch (2) and switch (3) respectively.

5.1. Switch 1

The corresponding error dynamical system is given by:

$$\begin{cases} \dot{e}_{123} &= \gamma_1 \dot{z}_1 - \alpha_2 \dot{x}_2 - \beta_3 \dot{y}_3 \\ \dot{e}_{231} &= \gamma_2 \dot{z}_2 - \alpha_3 \dot{x}_3 - \beta_1 \dot{y}_1 \\ \dot{e}_{312} &= \gamma_3 \dot{z}_3 - \alpha_1 \dot{x}_1 - \beta_2 \dot{y}_2 \end{cases} \tag{14}$$

Using equations (7) - (9), the error dynamical system (28) becomes

$$\begin{cases} \dot{e}_{123} &= \gamma_1 (a_3(z_2 - z_1) + z_2 z_3 + u_1) - \alpha_2 (b_1 x_1 + c_1 x_2 - x_1 x_3) - \beta_3 (-d_2 y_3 - y_1 y_2 - y_1^2) \\ \dot{e}_{231} &= \gamma_2 (b_3 (z_1 + z_2) - z_1 z_3 + u_2) - \alpha_3 (0.5 x_1 x_3 - d_1 x_3 + x_1^2) - \beta_1 (a_2 (y_2 - y_1) + y_2 y_3) \\ \dot{e}_{312} &= \gamma_3 (-c z_3 + z_1^2 + u_3) - \alpha_1 (a_1 (x_2 - x_1) + 30 x_2 x_3) - \beta_2 (b_2 y_1 + c_2 y_1 y_3) \end{cases} \tag{15}$$

Theorem 1. *The drive systems (7) and (8) will achieve multi-switching combination synchronization with the response system (9) if the controllers are chosen such that*

$$\begin{cases} u_1 &= \frac{1}{\gamma_1}(\alpha_2(b_1x_1 + c_1x_2 - x_1x_3) + \beta_3(-d_2y_3 - y_1y_2 - y_1^2)) - a_3(z_2 - z_1) - z_2z_3 - K_1e_{123} \\ u_2 &= \frac{1}{\gamma_2}(\alpha_3(0.5x_1x_3 - d_1x_3 + x_1^2) - \beta_1(a_2(y_2 - y_1) + y_2y_3)) - b_3(z_1 + z_2) + z_1z_3 - K_2e_{231} \\ u_3 &= \frac{1}{\gamma_3}(\alpha_1(a_1(x_2 - x_1) + 30x_2x_3) - \beta_2(b_2y_1 + c_2y_1y_3)) + cz_3 - z_1^2 - K_3e_{312} \end{cases} \quad (16)$$

where $K_i > 0,\ i = 1,2,3.$

Proof: We choose Lyapunov function in such a way that it satisfies the conditions of Lyapunov stability theory for the controllers designed above, which in turn shows the stability of error dynamical system and hence required synchronization is obtained.

So, we choose the following Lyapunov function candidate for the error system as follows:

$$V(t) = \frac{1}{2}(E_1^2 + E_2^2 + E_3^2)$$

where $E_1 = e_{123}, E_2 = e_{231}, E_3 = e_{312}$ Obviously, $V(t) > 0$. The time derivative of V(t) along the trajectories of the error system (29) is

$$\begin{aligned} \dot{V}(t) &= E_1\dot{E}_1 + E_2\dot{E}_2 + E_3\dot{E}_3 \\ &= E_1(\gamma_1(a_3(z_2 - z_1) + z_2z_3 + u_1) - \alpha_2(b_1x_1 + c_1x_2 - x_1x_3) - \beta_3(-d_2y_3 - y_1y_2 - y_1^2)) \\ &+ E_2(\gamma_2(b_3(z_1 + z_2) - z_1z_3 + u_2) - \alpha_3(0.5x_1x_3 - d_1x_3 + x_1^2) - \beta_1(a_2(y_2 - y_1) + y_2y_3)) \\ &+ E_3(\gamma_3(-cz_3 + z_1^2 + u_3) - \alpha_1(a_1(x_2 - x_1) + 30x_2x_3) - \beta_2(b_2y_1 + c_2y_1y_3)) \end{aligned} \quad (17)$$

Substituting (15) and (16) into 17 we obtain

$$\begin{aligned} \dot{V}(t) &= E_1(\gamma_1(a_3(z_2 - z_1) + z_2z_3) - \alpha_2(b_1x_1 + c_1x_2 - x_1x_3) - \beta_3(-d_2y_3 - y_1y_2 - y_1^2)) \\ &+ \alpha_2(b_1x_1 + c_1x_2 - x_1x_3) + \beta_3(-d_2y_3 - y_1y_2 - y_1^2)) - \gamma_1(a_3(z_2 - z_1) + z_2z_3 + K_1e_{123}) \\ &+ E_2(\gamma_2(b_3(z_1 + z_2) - z_1z_3) - \alpha_3(0.5x_1x_3 - d_1x_3 + x_1^2) - \beta_1(a_2(y_2 - y_1) + y_2y_3)) \\ &+ \alpha_3(0.5x_1x_3 - d_1x_3 + x_1^2) + \beta_1(a_2(y_2 - y_1) + y_2y_3)) - \gamma_2(b_3(z_1 + z_2) - z_1z_3 - K_2e_{231}) \\ &+ E_3(\gamma_3(-cz_3 + z_1^2) - \alpha_1(a_1(x_2 - x_1) + 30x_2x_3) - \beta_2(b_2y_1 + c_2y_1y_3)) \\ &+ \alpha_1(a_1(x_2 - x_1) + 30x_2x_3) + \beta_2(b_2y_1 + c_2y_1y_3)) - \gamma_3(-cz_3 + z_1^2 - K_3e_{312}) \\ &= -K_1E_1^2 - K_2E_2^2 - K_3E_3^2 \\ &= EKE < 0 \end{aligned}$$

where $E = (E_1, E_2, E_3)$ and $K = diag(K_1, K_2, K_3)$

Since $\dot{V}$ (t) < 0,, on the basis of the Lyapunov stability theory, the error vector **E** asymptotically converges to zero, i.e., $\lim_{t\to\infty}\|E(t)\| = 0$. It implies that the master and slave systems attains globally and asymptotically combination synchronization. This completes the proof. The following Corollaries can easily be obtained from Theorem 1, the proofs of these Corollaries are similar to Theorem 1. So, the proofs are omitted.

Corollary 1. *For* $\beta_1 = \beta_2 = \beta_3 = 0$, $\gamma_1 = \gamma_2 = \gamma_3 = 1$ *and controllers:*

$$\begin{cases} u_1 &= \alpha_2(b_1x_1 + c_1x_2 - x_1x_3) - a_3(z_2 - z_1) - z_2z_3 - K_1e_{123} \\ u_2 &= \alpha_3(0.5x_1x_3 - d_1x_3 + x_1^2 - b_3(z_1 + z_2) + z_1z_3 - K_2e_{231} \\ u_3 &= \alpha_1(a_1(x_2 - x_1) + 30x_2x_3) + cz_3 - z_1^2 - K_3e_{312} \end{cases} \tag{18}$$

where $K_i > 0,\ i = 1,2,3.$ the master systems (7) and (8) will achieve modified projective synchronization with the slave system (9).

Corollary 2. *For* $\alpha_1 = \alpha_2 = \alpha_3 = 0$, $\gamma_1 = \gamma_2 = \gamma_3 = 1$ *and controllers:*

$$\begin{cases} u_1 &= \beta_3(-d_2y_3 - y_1y_2 - y_1^2) - a_3(z_2 - z_1) - z_2z_3 - K_1e_{123} \\ u_2 &= -\beta_1(a_2(y_2 - y_1) + y_2y_3) - b_3(z_1 + z_2) + z_1z_3 - K_2e_{231} \\ u_3 &= -\beta_2(b_2y_1 + c_2y_1y_3) + cz_3 - z_1^2 - K_3e_{312} \end{cases} \tag{19}$$

where $K_i > 0$, i = 1, 2, 3. the master systems (7) and (8) will achieve modified projective synchronization with the slave system (9).

Corollary 3. *For* $\beta_1 = \beta_2 = \beta_3 = 0$, $\alpha_1 = \alpha_2 = \alpha_3 = 0$, $\gamma_1 = \gamma_2 = \gamma_3 = 1$ *and controllers:*

$$\begin{cases} u_1 &= -a_3(z_2 - z_1) - z_2z_3 - K_1e_{123} \\ u_2 &= -b_3(z_1 + z_2) + z_1z_3 - K_2e_{231} \\ u_3 &= cz_3 - z_1^2 - K_3e_{312} \end{cases} \tag{20}$$

where $K_i > 0,\ i = 1,2,3.$ then the equilibrium point of the response system (9) becomes asymptotically stable.

5.1.1. Numerical Simulations

Numerical simulation is performed to illustrate the validity and feasibility of the presented synchronization technique. The parameters values of all three chaotic systems are chosen so that system shows chaotic behavior in the absence of controllers as shown in Figures (1), (2) and (3). The initial conditions of the master systems and slave system are chosen as

$$(x_1(0),\ x_2(0),\ x_3(0)) \ = \ (1.2, 0.6, 1.8) \ \textit{and} \ (y_1(0), y_2(0), y_3(0)) = (0.6, 1.8, 1.2)$$

The initial condition for slave system is chosen as $(z_1(0), z_2(0), z_3(0)) = (0.3, 0.2, 0.3)$.

Suppose that $\gamma_1 = \gamma_2 = \gamma_3 = \alpha_1 = \alpha_2 = \alpha_3 = \xi_1 = \xi_2 = \xi_3 = 1$. The corresponding initial condition for error system is obtained as $(e_{132}, e_{213}, e_{321}) = (-3.3, -2.8, -0.9)$. The convergence of error state variables in figure (8) shows that the combination synchronization among chaotic systems (7), (8) and (9) is achieved when controllers are activated at $t > 0$. Figure (9) shows the trajectory of master and slave state variables when controller are activated at $t > 0$, this again confirms combination synchronization among time delay chaotic systems (7), (8) and (9).

5.2. Switch 2

The corresponding error dynamical system is given by:

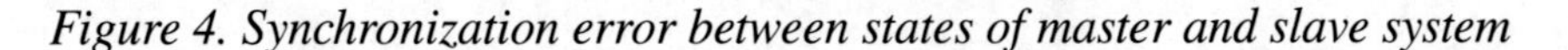

Figure 4. Synchronization error between states of master and slave system

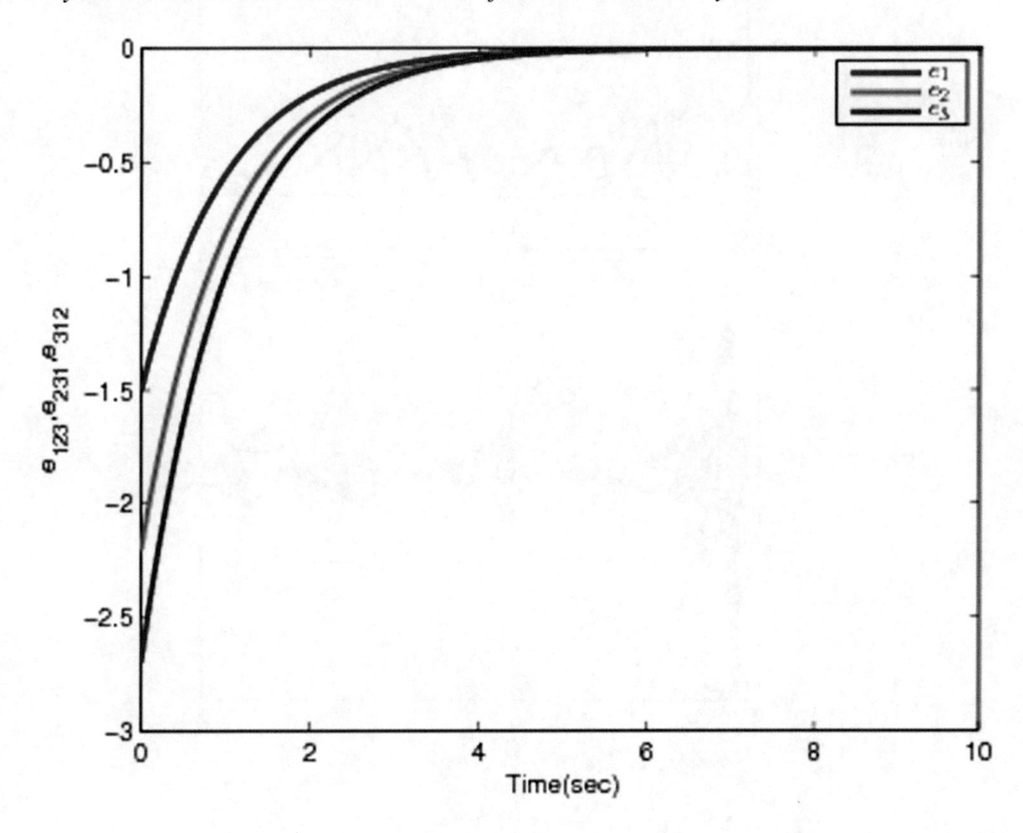

Figure 5. Time series showing combination synchronization (a,b,c)

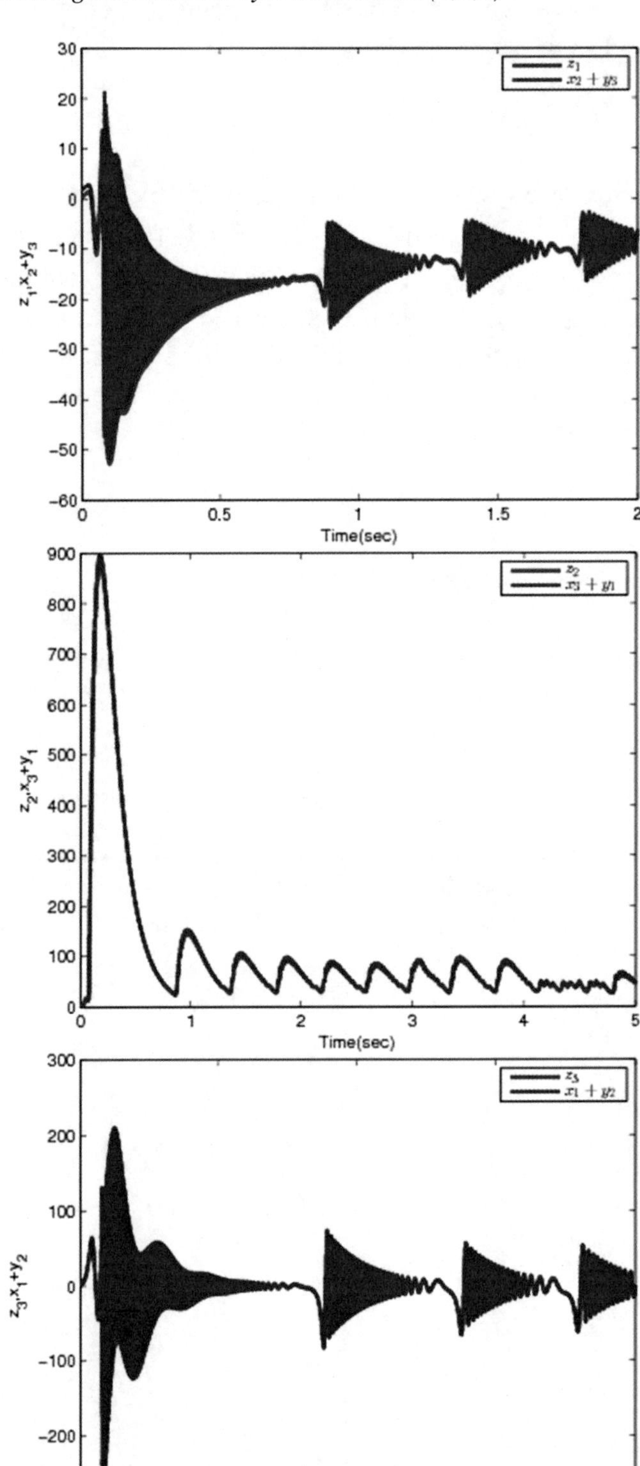

$$\begin{cases} \dot{e}_{132} &= \gamma_1\dot{z}_1 - \alpha_3\dot{x}_3 - \beta_2\dot{y}_2 \\ \dot{e}_{213} &= \gamma_2\dot{z}_2 - \alpha_1\dot{x}_1 - \beta_3\dot{y}_3 \\ \dot{e}_{321} &= \gamma_3\dot{z}_3 - \alpha_2\dot{x}_2 - \beta_1\dot{y}_1 \end{cases} \tag{21}$$

Using equations (7) - (9), the error dynamical system (21) becomes

$$\begin{cases} \dot{e}_{132} &= \gamma_1(a_3(z_2 - z_1) + z_2z_3 + u_1) - \alpha_3(0.5x_1x_3 - d_1x_3 + x_1^2) - \beta_2(b_2y_1 + c_2y_1y_3) \\ \dot{e}_{213} &= \gamma_2(b_3(z_1 + z_2) - z_1z_3 + u_2) - \alpha_1(a_1(x_2 - x_1) + 30x_2x_3) - \beta_3(-d_2y_3 - y_1y_2 - y_1^2) \\ \dot{e}_{312} &= \gamma_3(-c_3z_3 + z_1^2 + u_3) - \alpha_2(b_1x_1 + c_1x_2 - x_1x_3) - \beta_1(a_2(y_2 - y_1) + y_2y_3) \end{cases} \tag{22}$$

Theorem 2. *The drive systems (7) and (8) will achieve multi-switching combination synchronization with the response system (9) if the controllers are chosen such that*

$$\begin{cases} u_1 &= \frac{1}{\gamma_1}(\alpha_3(0.5x_1x_3 - d_1x_3 + x_1^2) + \beta_2(b_2y_1 + c_2y_1y_3) - a_3(z_2 - z_1) - z_2z_3) - K_1e_{123} \\ u_2 &= \frac{1}{\gamma_2}(\alpha_1(a_1(x_2 - x_1) + 30x_2x_3) + \beta_3(-d_2y_3 - y_1y_2 - y_1^2) - b_3(z_1 + z_2) + z_1z_3) - K_2e_{231} \\ u_3 &= \frac{1}{\gamma_3}(\alpha_2(b_1x_1 + c_1x_2 - x_1x_3) + \beta_1(a_2(y_2 - y_1) + y_2y_3) + c_3z_3 - z_1^2) - K_3e_{312} \end{cases} \tag{23}$$

where $K_i > 0,\ i = 1,2,3.$

Proof: We choose Lyapunov function in such a way that it satisfies the conditions of Lyapunov stability theory for the controllers designed above, which in turn shows the stability of error dynamical system and hence required synchronization is obtained.

So, we choose the following Lyapunov function candidate for the error system as follows:

$$V(t) = \frac{1}{2}(E_1^2 + E_2^2 + E_3^2)$$

where $E_1 = e_{132}, E_2 = e_{213}, E_3 = e_{321}$ Obviously, $V(t) > 0$. The time derivative of V(t) along the trajectories of the error system (22) is

$$\begin{aligned}\dot{V}(t) &= E_1\dot{E}_1 + E_2\dot{E}_2 + E_3\dot{E}_3 \\ &= E_1(\gamma_1(a_3(z_2 - z_1) + z_2z_3 + u_1) - \alpha_3(0.5x_1x_3 - d_1x_3 + x_1^2) - \beta_2(b_2y_1 + c_2y_1y_3)) \\ &+E_2(\gamma_2(b_3(z_1 + z_2) - z_1z_3 + u_2) - \alpha_1(a_1(x_2 - x_1) + 30x_2x_3) - \beta_3(-d_2y_3 - y_1y_2 - y_1^2)) \\ &+E_3(\gamma_3(-c_3z_3 + z_1^2 + u_3) - \alpha_2(b_1x_1 + c_1x_2 - x_1x_3) - \beta_1(a_2(y_2 - y_1) + y_2y_3))\end{aligned} \tag{24}$$

Substituting (22) and (23) into (24), we obtain

$$\begin{aligned}\dot{V}(t) &= E_1(\gamma_1(a_3(z_2 - z_1) + z_2z_3) - \alpha_3(0.5x_1x_3 - d_1x_3 + x_1^2) - \beta_2(b_2y_1 + c_2y_1y_3)) \\ &+\alpha_3(0.5x_1x_3 - d_1x_3 + x_1^2) + \beta_2(b_2y_1 + c_2y_1y_3) - \gamma_1(a_3(z_2 - z_1) + z_2z_3) - K_1e_{123} \\ &+E_2(\gamma_2(b_3(z_1 + z_2) - z_1z_3) - \alpha_1(a_1(x_2 - x_1) + 30x_2x_3) - \beta_3(-d_2y_3 - y_1y_2 - y_1^2)) \\ &\alpha_1(a_1(x_2 - x_1) + 30x_2x_3) + \beta_3(-d_2y_3 - y_1y_2 - y_1^2) - \gamma_2(b_3(z_1 + z_2) - z_1z_3) - K_2e_{231} + \\ &+E_3(\gamma_3(-cz_3 + z_1^2) - \alpha_2(b_1x_1 + c_1x_2 - x_1x_3) - \beta_1(a_2(y_2 - y_1) + y_2y_3)) \\ &\alpha_2(b_1x_1 + c_1x_2 - x_1x_3) + \beta_1(a_2(y_2 - y_1) + y_2y_3) - \gamma_3(-c_3z_3 + z_1^2) - K_3e_{312} \\ &= -K_1E_1^2 - K_2E_2^2 - K_3E_3^2 \\ &= EKE < 0\end{aligned}$$

where $E = (E_1, E_2, E_3)$ and $K = diag(K_1, K_2, K_3)$

Since $\dot{V}$ (t) < 0,, on the basis of the Lyapunov stability theory, the error vector **E** asymptotically converges to zero, i.e., $\lim_{t\to\infty}\|E(t)\| = 0$. It implies that the master and slave systems attains globally and asymptotically combination synchronization. This completes the proof. The following Corollaries can easily be obtained from Theorem 1, the proofs of these Corollaries are similar to Theorem 1. So, the proofs are omitted.

Corollary 1. *For* $\beta_1 = \beta_2 = \beta_3 = 0$, $\gamma_1 = \gamma_2 = \gamma_3 = 1$ *and controllers:*

$$\begin{cases} u_1 &= \alpha_3(0.5x_1x_3 - d_1x_3 + x_1^2) - a_3(z_2 - z_1) - z_2z_3 - K_1e_{123} \\ u_2 &= \alpha_1(a_1(x_2 - x_1) + 30x_2x_3) - b_3(z_1 + z_2) + z_1z_3 - K_2e_{231} \\ u_3 &= \alpha_2(b_1x_1 + c_1x_2 - x_1x_3) + c_3z_3 - z_1^2 - K_3e_{312} \end{cases} \tag{25}$$

where $K_i > 0$, $i = 1,2,3.$ the master systems (7) and (8) will achieve modified projective synchronization with the slave system (9).

Corollary 2. *For* $\alpha_1 = \alpha_2 = \alpha_3 = 0$, $\gamma_1 = \gamma_2 = \gamma_3 = 1$ *and controllers:*

$$\begin{cases} u_1 &= \beta_2(b_2y_1 + c_2y_1y_3) - a_3(z_2 - z_1) - z_2z_3 - K_1e_{123} \\ u_2 &= \beta_3(-d_2y_3 - y_1y_2 - y_1^2) - b_3(z_1 + z_2) + z_1z_3 - K_2e_{231} \\ u_3 &= \beta_1(a_2(y_2 - y_1) + y_2y_3) + c_3z_3 - z_1^2 - K_3e_{312} \end{cases} \tag{26}$$

where $K_i > 0$, i = 1, 2, 3. the master systems (7) and (8) will achieve modified projective synchronization with the slave system (9).

Corollary 3. *For* $\beta_1 = \beta_2 = \beta_3 = 0$, $\alpha_1 = \alpha_2 = \alpha_3 = 0$, $\gamma_1 = \gamma_2 = \gamma_3 = 1$ *and controllers:*

$$\begin{cases} u_1 &= -a_3(z_2 - z_1) - z_2 z_3 - K_1 e_{123} \\ u_2 &= -b_3(z_1 + z_2) + z_1 z_3 - K_2 e_{231} \\ u_3 &= c_3 z_3 - z_1^2 - K_3 e_{312} \end{cases} \tag{27}$$

where $K_i > 0$, $i = 1,2,3.$ then the equilibrium point of the response system (9) becomes asymptotically stable.

5.2.1. Numerical Simulations

Numerical simulation is performed to illustrate the validity and feasibility of the presented synchronization technique. The parameters values of all three chaotic systems are chosen so that system shows chaotic behavior in the absence of controllers as shown in Figures (1), (2) and (3). The initial conditions of the master systems and slave system are chosen as

$$(x_1(0),\ x_2(0),\ x_3(0)) = (1.2, 0.6, 1.8)\ \textit{and}\ (y_1(0), y_2(0), y_3(0)) = (0.6, 1.8, 1.2)$$

The initial condition for slave system is chosen as $(z_1(0), z_2(0), z_3(0)) = (0.3, 0.2, 0.3)$.

Suppose that $\gamma_1 = \gamma_2 = \gamma_3 = \alpha_1 = \alpha_2 = \alpha_3 = \xi_1 = \xi_2 = \xi_3 = 1$. The corresponding initial condition for error system is obtained as $(e_{123}, e_{231}, e_{312}) = (-1.5, -2.2, -2.7)$. The convergence of error state variables in figure (8) shows that the combination synchronization among chaotic systems (7), (8) and (9) is achieved when controllers are activated at $t > 0$. Figure (9) shows the trajectory of master and slave state variables when controller are activated at $t > 0$, this again confirms combination synchronization among time delay chaotic systems (7), (8) and (9).

5.3. Switch 3

The corresponding error dynamical system is given by:

$$\begin{cases} \dot{e}_{231} &= \gamma_2 \dot{z}_2 - \alpha_3 \dot{x}_3 - \beta_1 \dot{y}_1 \\ \dot{e}_{122} &= \gamma_1 \dot{z}_1 - \alpha_2 \dot{x}_2 - \beta_2 \dot{y}_2 \\ \dot{e}_{313} &= \gamma_3 \dot{z}_3 - \alpha_1 \dot{x}_1 - \beta_3 \dot{y}_3 \end{cases} \tag{28}$$

Using equations (7) - (9), the error dynamical system (28) becomes

Figure 6. Synchronization error between states of master and slave system

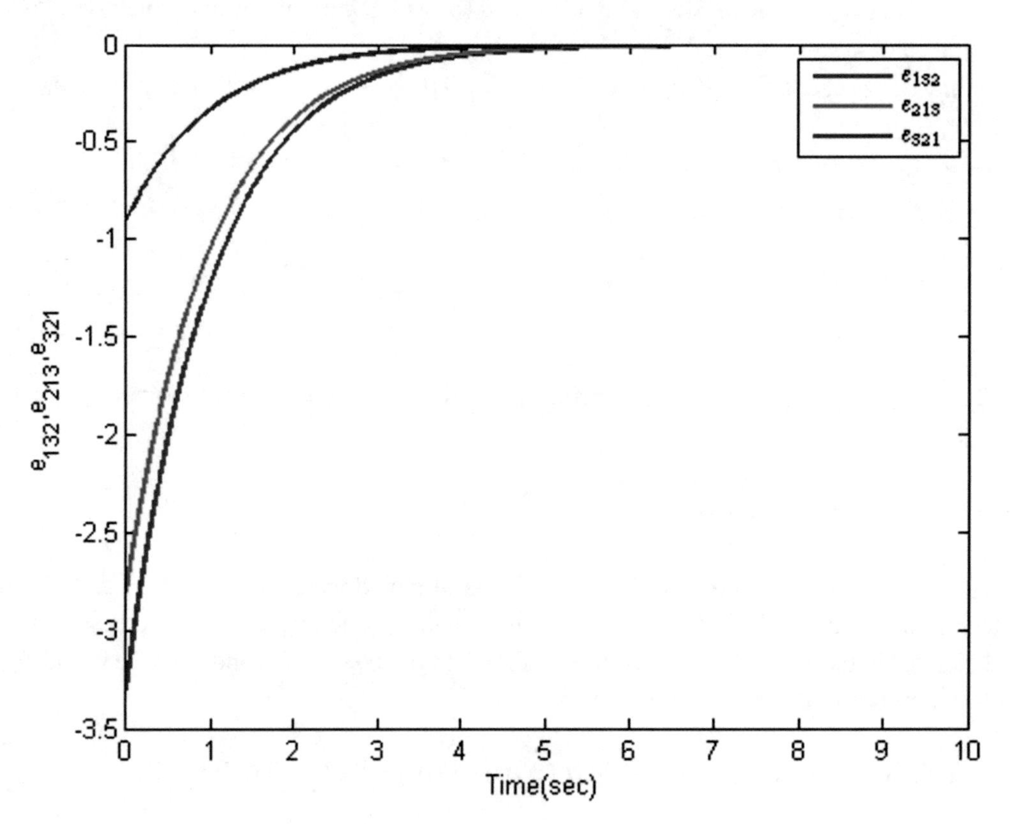

$$\begin{cases} \dot{e}_{231} &= \gamma_2(b_3(z_1+z_2)-z_1z_3+u_2)-\alpha_3(0.5x_1x_3-d_1x_3+x_1^2)-\beta_1(a_2(y_2-y_1)+y_2y_3) \\ \dot{e}_{122} &= \gamma_1(a_3(z_2-z_1)+z_2z_3+u_1)-\alpha_2(b_1x_1+c_1x_2-x_1x_3)-\beta_2(b_2y_1+c_2y_1y_3) \\ \dot{e}_{313} &= \gamma_3(-c_3z_3+z_1^2+u_3)-\alpha_1(a_1(x_2-x_1)+30x_2x_3)-\beta_3(-d_2y_3-y_1y_2-y_1^2) \end{cases} \tag{29}$$

Theorem 3. *The drive systems (7) and (8) will achieve multi-switching combination synchronization with the response system (9) if the controllers are chosen such that*

$$\begin{cases} u_2 &= \dfrac{1}{\gamma_2}(\alpha_3(0.5x_1x_3-d_1x_3+x_1^2)+\beta_1(a_2(y_2-y_1)+y_2y_3)-b_3(z_1+z_2)+z_1z_3)-K_1e_{231} \\ u_1 &= \dfrac{1}{\gamma_1}(\alpha_2(b_1x_1+c_1x_2-x_1x_3)+\beta_2(b_2y_1+c_2y_1y_3)-a_3(z_2-z_1)-z_2z_3)-K_2e_{122} \\ u_3 &= \dfrac{1}{\gamma_3}(\alpha_1(a_1(x_2-x_1)+30x_2x_3)+\beta_3(-d_2y_3-y_1y_2-y_1^2)+c_3z_3-z_1^2)-K_3e_{313} \end{cases} \tag{30}$$

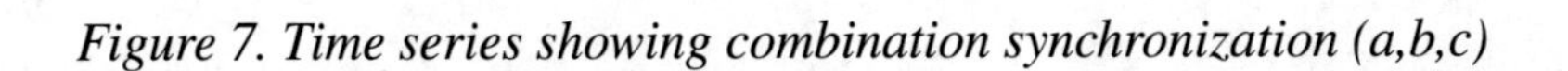

Figure 7. Time series showing combination synchronization (a,b,c)

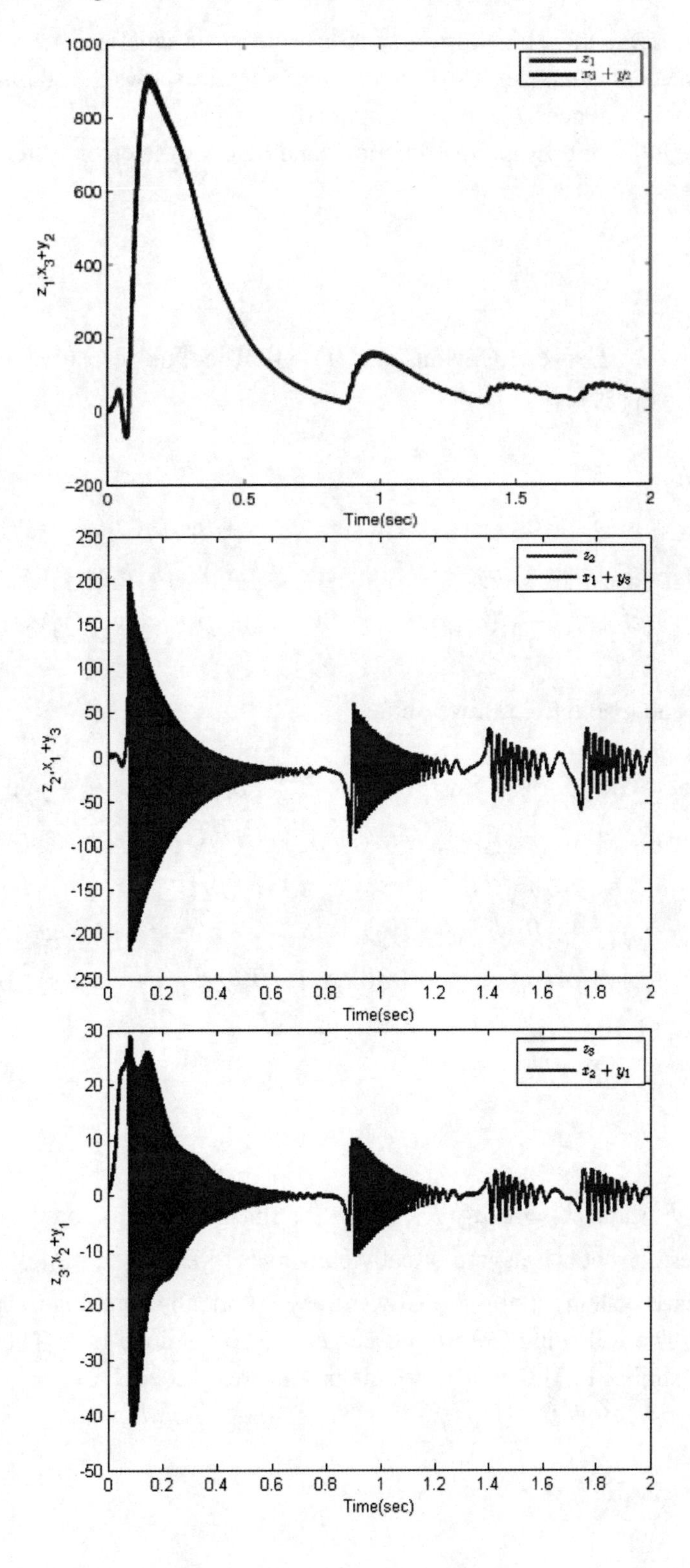

where $K_i > 0,\ i = 1,2,3.$

Proof: We choose Lyapunov function in such a way that it satisfies the conditions of Lyapunov stability theory for the controllers designed above, which in turn shows the stability of error dynamical system and hence required synchronization is obtained.

So, we choose the following Lyapunov function candidate for the error system as follows:

$$V(t) = \frac{1}{2}(E_1^2 + E_2^2 + E_3^2)$$

where $E_1 = e_{132}, E_2 = e_{213}, E_3 = e_{321}$ Obviously, $V(t) > 0$. The time derivative of V(t) along the trajectories of the error system (29) is

$$\begin{aligned} \dot{V}(t) &= E_1\dot{E}_1 + E_2\dot{E}_2 + E_3\dot{E}_3 \\ &= E_1(\gamma_2((z_1 + z_2) - z_1 z_3 + u_2) - \alpha_3(0.5x_1x_3 - d_1x_3 + x_1^2) - \beta_1(a_2(y_2 - y_1) + y_2y_3) \\ &+ E_2(\gamma_1(a_3(z_2 - z_1) + z_2z_3 + u_1) - \alpha_2(b_1x_1 + c_1x_2 - x_1x_3) - \beta_2(b_2y_1 + c_2y_1y_3)) \\ &+ E_3(\gamma_3(-c_3z_3 + z_1^2 + u_3) - \alpha_1(a_1(x_2 - x_1) + 30x_2x_3) - \beta_3(-d_2y_3 - y_1y_2 - y_1^2)) \end{aligned} \quad (31)$$

Substituting (29) and (30) into (31), we obtain

$$\begin{aligned} \dot{V}(t) &= E_1(\gamma_2 z_1 + z_2) - z_1z_3) - \alpha_3(0.5x_1x_3 - d_1x_3 + x_1^2) - \beta_1(a_2(y_2 - y_1) + y_2y_3) \\ &+ \alpha_3(0.5x_1x_3 - d_1x_3 + x_1^2) + \beta_1(a_2(y_2 - y_1) + y_2y_3) - b_3(z_1 + z_2) + z_1z_3 - K_1e_{231} \\ &+ E_2(\gamma_1(a_3(z_2 - z_1) + z_2z_3) - \alpha_2(b_1x_1 + c_1x_2 - x_1x_3) - \beta_2(b_2y_1 + c_2y_1y_3)) \\ &+ \alpha_2(b_1x_1 + c_1x_2 - x_1x_3) + \beta_2(b_2y_1 + c_2y_1y_3) - a_3(z_2 - z_1) - z_2z_3 - K_2e_{122} \\ &+ E_3(\gamma_3(-c_3z_3 + z_1^2) - \alpha_1(a_1(x_2 - x_1) + 30x_2x_3) - \beta_3(-d_2y_3 - y_1y_2 - y_1^2)) \\ &+ \alpha_1(a_1(x_2 - x_1) + 30x_2x_3) + \beta_3(-d_2y_3 - y_1y_2 - y_1^2) + c_3z_3 - z_1^2) - K_3e_{313} \\ &= -K_1E_1^2 - K_2E_2^2 - K_3E_3^2 \\ &= EKE < 0 \end{aligned}$$

where $E = (E_1, E_2, E_3)$ and $K = diag(K_1, K_2, K_3)$. Since $\dot{V}$ (t) < 0,, on the basis of the Lyapunov stability theory, the error vector **E** asymptotically converges to zero, i.e., $\lim_{t\to\infty}\|E(t)\| = 0$. It implies that the master and slave systems attains globally and asymptotically combination synchronization. This completes the proof. The following Corollaries can easily be obtained from Theorem 1, the proofs of these Corollaries are similar to Theorem 1. So, the proofs are omitted.

Corollary 1. *For* $\beta_1 = \beta_2 = \beta_3 = 0$, $\gamma_1 = \gamma_2 = \gamma_3 = 1$ *and controllers:*

$$\begin{cases} u_2 &= \alpha_3(0.5x_1x_3 - d_1x_3 + x_1^2) - b_3(z_1 + z_2) + z_1z_3 - K_1e_{231} \\ u_1 &= \alpha_2(b_1x_1 + c_1x_2 - x_1x_3) - a_3(z_2 - z_1) - z_2z_3 - K_2e_{122} \\ u_3 &= \alpha_1(a_1(x_2 - x_1) + 30x_2x_3) + c_3z_3 - z_1^2 - K_3e_{313} \end{cases} \tag{32}$$

where $K_i > 0,\ i = 1,2,3.$ the master systems (7) and (8) will achieve modified projective synchronization with the slave system (9).

Corollary 2. *For* $\alpha_1 = \alpha_2 = \alpha_3 = 0$, $\gamma_1 = \gamma_2 = \gamma_3 = 1$ *and controllers:*

$$\begin{cases} u_2 &= \beta_1(a_2(y_2 - y_1) + y_2y_3) - b_3(z_1 + z_2) + z_1z_3 - K_1e_{231} \\ u_1 &= \beta_2(b_2y_1 + c_2y_1y_3) - a_3(z_2 - z_1) - z_2z_3 - K_2e_{122} \\ u_3 &= \beta_3(-d_2y_3 - y_1y_2 - y_1^2) + c_3z_3 - z_1^2 - K_3e_{313} \end{cases} \tag{33}$$

where $K_i > 0$, i = 1, 2, 3. the master systems (7) and (8) will achieve modified projective synchronization with the slave system (9).

Corollary 3. *For* $\beta_1 = \beta_2 = \beta_3 = 0$, $\alpha_1 = \alpha_2 = \alpha_3 = 0$, $\gamma_1 = \gamma_2 = \gamma_3 = 1$ *and controllers:*

$$\begin{cases} u_2 &= -b_3(z_1 + z_2) + z_1z_3 - K_1e_{231} \\ u_1 &= -a_3(z_2 - z_1) - z_2z_3 - K_2e_{122} \\ u_3 &= c_3z_3 - z_1^2 - K_3e_{313} \end{cases} \tag{34}$$

where $K_i > 0,\ i = 1,2,3.$ then the equilibrium point of the response system (9) becomes asymptotically stable.

5.3.1. Numerical Simulations

Numerical simulation is performed to illustrate the validity and feasibility of the presented synchronization technique. The parameters values of all three chaotic systems are chosen so that system shows chaotic behavior in the absence of controllers as shown in Figures (1), (2) and (3). The initial conditions of the master systems and slave system are chosen as $(x_1(0), x_2(0), x_3(0)) = (1.2, 0.6, 1.8)$ *and* $(y_1(0), y_2(0), y_3(0)) = (0.6, 1.8, 1.2)$. The initial condition for slave system is chosen as $(z_1(0), z_2(0), z_3(0)) = (0.8, 0.2, 0.5)$.

Suppose that $\gamma_1 = \gamma_2 = \gamma_3 = \alpha_1 = \alpha_2 = \alpha_3 = \xi_1 = \xi_2 = \xi_3 = 1$. The corresponding initial condition for error system is obtained as $(e_{123}, e_{231}, e_{312}) = (-1.6, -2.2, -1.9)$. The convergence of error state variables in figure (8) shows that the combination synchronization among chaotic systems (7), (8) and (9) is achieved when controllers are activated at $t > 0$. Figure (9) shows the trajectory of master and slave state variables when controller are activated at $t > 0$, this again confirms combination synchronization among time delay chaotic systems (7), (8) and (9).

6. CONCLUSION

In this chapter, we have accomplished multi-switching combination synchronization scheme among three non-identical chaotic systems by considering one arbitrary switch. Using active control technique, suitable controllers are constructed and then based on the stability of Lyapunov stability theory, the multi-switching combination synchronization among three non-identical chaotic systems has been investigated. Finally, simulations are displayed to show the viability of the multi-switching combination synchronization scheme. Computational and analytical results are in excellent agreement. We have shown from the theoretical analysis that various controllers which are suitable for different type of synchronization scheme can be obtained from the general results. The typical synchronization between one master and one slave is a special case of combination synchronization. Combination synchronization of non-identical chaotic systems using active control has many applications in secure communication, neural network and other important areas. For future scope other synchronization techniques like combination-combination synchronization, compound synchronization, compound-combination synchronization of time delay chaotic system is an important issue which can be discussed.

Figure 8. Synchronization error between states of master and slave system

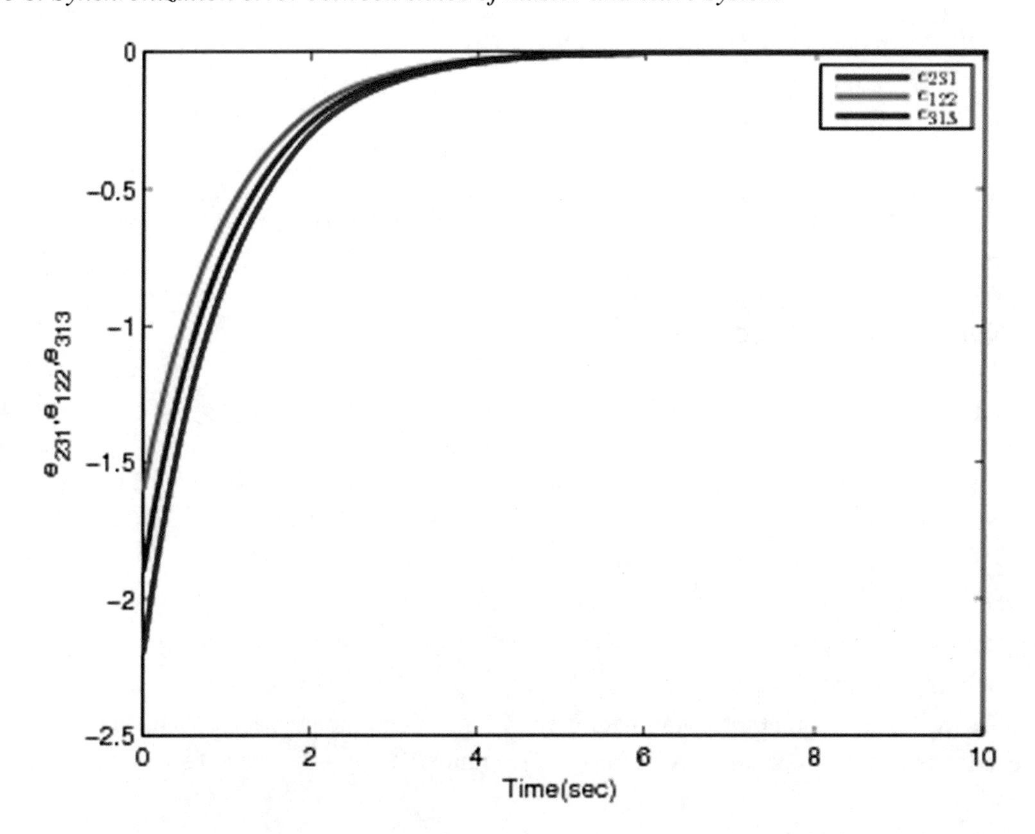

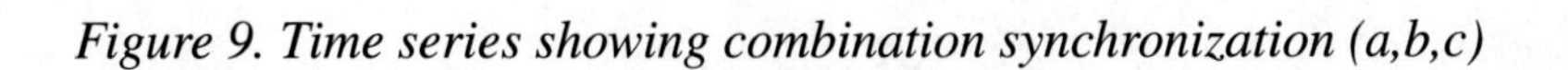
Figure 9. Time series showing combination synchronization (a,b,c)

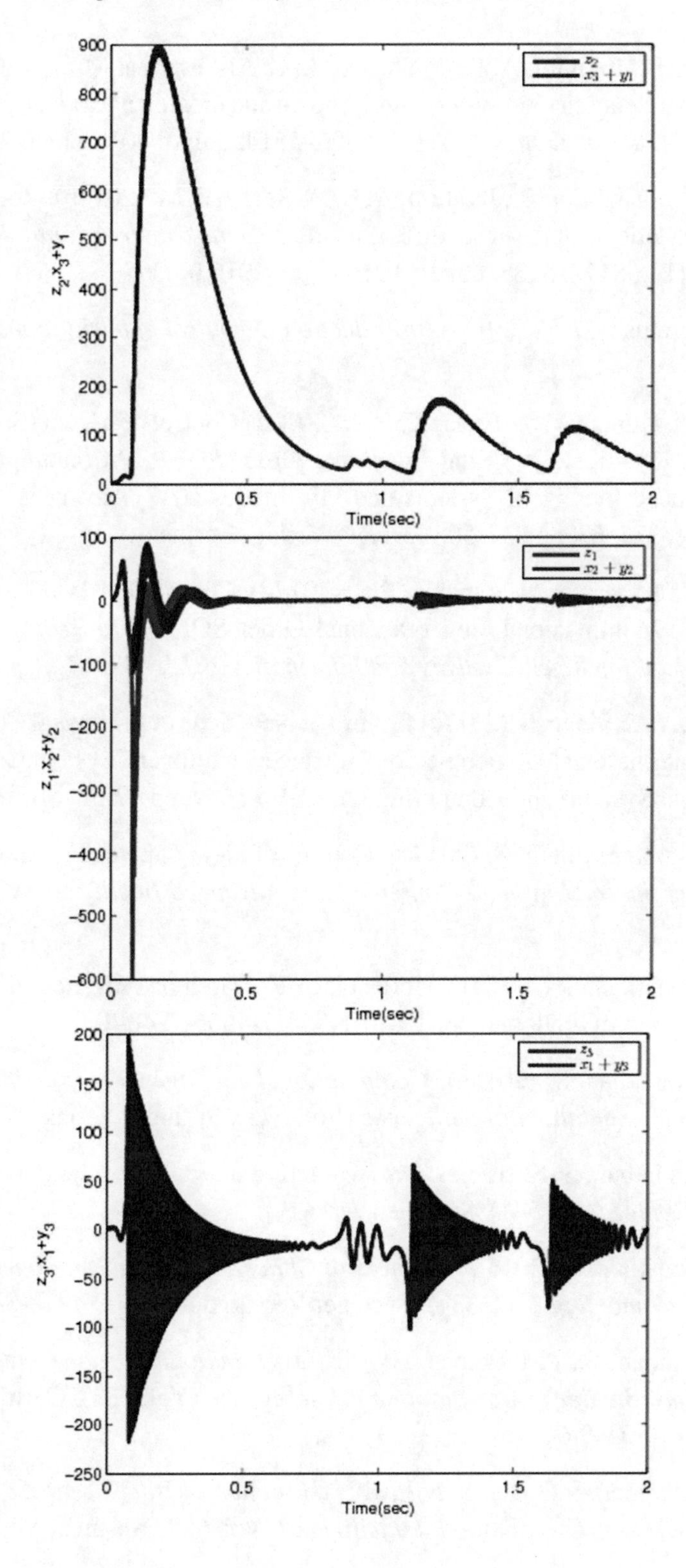

REFERENCES

Ahmad, I., Saaban, A. B., Ibrahim, A. B., Shahzad, M., & Al-Sawalha, M. M. (2016a). Reduced-order synchronization of time-delay chaotic systems with known and unknown parameters. *Optik-International Journal for Light and Electron Optics*, *127*(13), 5506–5514. doi:10.1016/j.ijleo.2016.02.078

Ahmad, I., Shafiq, M., Saaban, A. B., Ibrahim, A. B., & Shahzad, M. (2016b). Robust finite-time global synchronization of chaotic systems with different orders. *Optik-International Journal for Light and Electron Optics*, *127*(19), 8172–8185. doi:10.1016/j.ijleo.2016.05.065

Aleksandr, L., & Pogromsky, A. Y. (1998). *Introduction to control of oscillations and chaos* (Vol. 35). World Scientific.

Azar, A. T., Kumar, J., Kumar, V., & Rana, K. P. S. (2017d) Control of a Two Link Planar Electrically-Driven Rigid Robotic Manipulator Using Fractional Order SOFC. Proceedings of the International Conference on Advanced Intelligent Systems and Informatics 2017, Advances in Intelligent Systems and Computing series, Vol. 639, pp 47-56. Springer-Verlag, Germany.

Azar, A. T., Kumar, J., Kumar, V., & Rana, K. P. S. (2017d). Control of a Two Link Planar Electrically-Driven Rigid Robotic Manipulator Using Fractional Order SOFC. *Proceedings of the International Conference on Advanced Intelligent Systems and Informatics 2017, 639*, 47-56.

Azar, A. T., Ouannas, A., & Singh, S. (2017c) Control of New Type of Fractional Chaos Synchronization. Proceedings of the International Conference on Advanced Intelligent Systems and Informatics 2017, Advances in Intelligent Systems and Computing series, Vol. 639, pp 47-56. Springer-Verlag, Germany.

Azar, A. T., Ouannas, A., & Singh, S. (2017c). Control of New Type of Fractional Chaos Synchronization. *Proceedings of the International Conference on Advanced Intelligent Systems and Informatics 2017, 639*, 47-56.

Azar, A. T., & Vaidyanathan, S. (2015a). Handbook of Research on Advanced Intelligent Control Engineering and Automation. IGI Global. doi:10.4018/978-1-4666-7248-2

Azar, A. T., & Vaidyanathan, S. (2015b). *Computational Intelligence applications in Modeling and Control. In Studies in Computational Intelligence* (Vol. 575). Springer-Verlag.

Azar, A. T., & Vaidyanathan, S. (2015c). *Chaos Modeling and Control Systems Design. In Studies in Computational Intelligence* (Vol. 581). Springer-Verlag.

Azar, A. T., & Vaidyanathan, S. (2016). *Advances in Chaos Theory and Intelligent Control. In Studies in Fuzziness and Soft Computing* (Vol. 337). Springer-Verlag. doi:10.1007/978-3-319-30340-6

Azar, A. T., Vaidyanathan, S., & Ouannas, A. (2017a). *Fractional Order Control and Synchronization of Chaotic Systems. Studies in Computational Intelligence* (Vol. 688). Germany: Springer-Verlag. doi:10.1007/978-3-319-50249-6

Azar, A. T., Vaidyanathan, S., & Ouannas, A. (2017a). *Fractional Order Control and Synchronization of Chaotic Systems. In Studies in Computational Intelligence* (Vol. 688). Springer-Verlag. doi:10.1007/978-3-319-50249-6

Azar, A. T., Volos, C., Gerodimos, N. A., Tombras, G. S., Pham, V. T., Radwan, A. G., ... Munoz-Pacheco, J. M. (2017b). A novel chaotic system without equilibrium: Dynamics, synchronization and circuit realization. *Complexity*. doi:10.1155/2017/7871467

Azar AT, Volos C, Gerodimos NA, Tombras GS, Pham VT, Radwan AG, Vaidyanathan S, Ouannas A, and Munoz-Pacheco JM (2017b) A novel chaotic system without equilibrium: Dynamics, synchronization and circuit realization. Complexity, vol. 2017, Article ID 7871467, 11 pages, 2017. doi:.10.1155/2017/7871467

Becker, G., & Packard, A. (1994). Robust performance of linear parametrically varying systems using parametrically-dependent linear feedback. *Systems & Control Letters*, *23*(3), 205–215. doi:10.1016/0167-6911(94)90006-X

Boulkroune, A., Bouzeriba, A., Bouden, T., & Azar, A. T. (2016a). *Fuzzy Adaptive Synchronization of Uncertain Fractional-order Chaotic Systems. In Studies in Fuzziness and Soft Computing* (Vol. 337, pp. 681–697). Springer-Verlag.

Boulkroune, A., Hamel, S., & Azar, A. T. (2016b). *Fuzzy control-based function synchronization of unknown chaotic systems with dead-zone input. In Studies in Fuzziness and Soft Computing* (Vol. 337, pp. 699–718). Springer-Verlag.

Du, H., Zeng, Q., & Wang, C. (2008). Function projective synchronization of different chaotic systems with uncertain parameters. *Physics Letters. [Part A]*, *372*(33), 5402–5410. doi:10.1016/j.physleta.2008.06.036

Du, H., Zeng, Q., & Wang, C. (2009). Modified function projective synchronization of chaotic system. *Chaos, Solitons, and Fractals*, *42*(4), 2399–2404. doi:10.1016/j.chaos.2009.03.120

Field, R. J., & Györgyi, L. (1993). *Chaos in chemistry and biochemistry*. World Scientific. doi:10.1142/1706

Grassi, G., Ouannas, A., Azar, A. T., Radwan, A. G., Volos, C., Pham, V. T., . . . Stouboulos, I. N. (2017). *Chaos Synchronisation Of Continuous Systems Via Scalar Signal*. The 6th International Conference on Modern Circuits and Systems Technologies (MOCAST), Thessaloniki, Greece. 10.1109/MOCAST.2017.7937629

Khan, A., & Shikha. (2016) Hybrid function projective synchronization of chaotic systems via adaptive control. *International Journal of Dynamics and Control*, 1–8. DOI: 10.1007/s40435-016-0258-6

Khan, A., & Bhat, M. A. (2016). Hyper-chaotic analysis and adaptive multi-switching synchronization of a novel asymmetric non-linear dynamical system. *International Journal of Dynamics and Control*, 1–11.

Khan, A., & Bhat, M. A. (2017). Multi-switching combination–combination synchronization of non-identical fractional-order chaotic systems. *Mathematical Methods in the Applied Sciences*, *40*(15), 5654–5667. doi:10.1002/mma.4416

Khan, A., Khattar, D., & Prajapati, N. (2017a). Adaptive multi switching combination synchronization of chaotic systems with unknown parameters. *International Journal of Dynamics and Control*. doi:10.100740435-017-0320-z

Khan, A., Khattar, D., & Prajapati, N. (2017b). Reduced order multi switching hybrid synchronization of chaotic systems. *Journal of Mathematical and Computational Science*, *7*(2), 414.

Khan, A., & Pal, R. (2013). Complete synchronization, anti-synchronization and hybrid synchronization of two identical parabolic restricted three body problem. *Asian Journal of Current Engineering and Maths*, *2*(2), 118–126.

Khan, A., & Shahzad, M. (2013). Synchronization of circular restricted three body problem with lorenz hyper chaotic system using a robust adaptive sliding mode controller. *Complexity*, *18*(6), 58–64. doi:10.1002/cplx.21459

Khan, A., & Shikha. (2017b). Combination synchronization of time-delay chaotic system via robust adaptive sliding mode control. *Pramana*, *88*(6), 91. doi:10.100712043-017-1385-0

Khan, A., & Shikha. (2017c). Increased and reduced order synchronisations between 5d and 6d hyperchaotic systems. *Indian Journal of Industrial and Applied Mathematics*, *8*(1), 118–131. doi:10.5958/1945-919X.2017.00010.X

Khan, A., & Shikha, S. (2017a) Combination synchronization of genesio time delay chaotic system via robust adaptive sliding mode control. *International Journal of Dynamics and Control*, 1–10. DOI: 10.1007/s40435-017-0339-1

Khan, A., & Tyagi, A. (2016). Analysis and hyper-chaos control of a new 4-d hyper-chaotic system by using optimal and adaptive control design. *International Journal of Dynamics and Control*. doi:10.1007/s40435-016-0265-7

Koronovskii, A. A., Moskalenko, O. I., Shurygina, S. A., & Hramov, A. E. (2013). Generalized synchronization in discrete maps. new point of view on weak and strong synchronization. *Chaos, Solitons, and Fractals*, *46*, 12–18. doi:10.1016/j.chaos.2012.10.004

Li, G.-H. (2007). Modified projective synchronization of chaotic system. *Chaos, Solitons, and Fractals*, *32*(5), 1786–1790. doi:10.1016/j.chaos.2005.12.009

Mahmoud, G. M., & Mahmoud, E. E. (2010). Complete synchronization of chaotic complex nonlinear systems with uncertain parameters. *Nonlinear Dynamics*, *62*(4), 875–882. doi:10.100711071-010-9770-y

Mainieri, R., & Rehacek, J. (1999). Projective synchronization in three-dimensional chaotic systems. *Physical Review Letters*, *82*(15), 3042–3045. doi:10.1103/PhysRevLett.82.3042

Meghni, B., Dib, D., & Azar, A. T. (2017c). A Second-order sliding mode and fuzzy logic control to Optimal Energy Management in PMSG Wind Turbine with Battery Storage. *Neural Computing & Applications*, *28*(6), 1417–1434. doi:10.100700521-015-2161-z

Meghni, B., Dib, D., Azar, A. T., Ghoudelbourk, S., & Saadoun, A. (2017a). *Robust Adaptive Supervisory Fractional order Controller For optimal Energy Management in Wind Turbine with Battery Storage. In Studies in Computational Intelligence* (Vol. 688, pp. 165–202). Springer-Verlag.

Meghni, B., Dib, D., Azar, A. T., & Saadoun, A. (2017b). *Effective Supervisory Controller to Extend Optimal Energy Management in Hybrid Wind Turbine under Energy and Reliability Constraints. International Journal of Dynamics and Control*. doi:10.100740435-016-0296-0

Ott, E., Grebogi, C., and Yorke, J. A. (1990). Controlling chaos. *Physical Review Letters*, *64*(11), 1196-1199.

Ouannas, A., Azar, A. T., & Abu-Saris, R. (2016a). A new type of hybrid synchronization between arbitrary hyperchaotic maps. *International Journal of Machine Learning and Cybernetics*. doi:10.100713042-016-0566-3

Ouannas, A., Azar, A. T., & Radwan, A. G. (2016b) On Inverse Problem of Generalized Synchronization Between Different Dimensional Integer-Order and Fractional-Order Chaotic Systems. *The 28th International Conference on Microelectronics*. 10.1109/ICM.2016.7847942

Ouannas, A., Azar, A. T., & Vaidyanathan, S. (2017f). On A Simple Approach for Q-S Synchronization of Chaotic Dynamical Systems in Continuous-Time. *Int. J. Computing Science and Mathematics*, *8*(1), 20–27.

Ouannas, A., Azar, A. T., & Vaidyanathan, S. (2017g). New Hybrid Synchronization Schemes Based on Coexistence of Various Types of Synchronization Between Master-Slave Hyperchaotic Systems. *International Journal of Computer Applications in Technology*, *55*(2), 112–120. doi:10.1504/IJCAT.2017.082868

Ouannas, A., Azar, A. T., & Vaidyanathan, S. (2017i). A Robust Method for New Fractional Hybrid Chaos Synchronization. *Mathematical Methods in the Applied Sciences*, *40*(5), 1804–1812. doi:10.1002/mma.4099

Ouannas, A., Azar, A. T., & Ziar, T. (2017h). *On Inverse Full State Hybrid Function Projective Synchronization for Continuous-time Chaotic Dynamical Systems with Arbitrary Dimensions*. Differential Equations and Dynamical Systems. doi:10.100712591-017-0362-x

Ouannas, A., Azar, A. T., Ziar, T., & Radwan, A. G. (2017d). *Study On Coexistence of Different Types of Synchronization Between Different dimensional Fractional Chaotic Systems. In Studies in Computational Intelligence* (Vol. 688, pp. 637–669). Springer-Verlag.

Ouannas, A., Azar, A. T., Ziar, T., & Radwan, A. G. (2017e). *Generalized Synchronization of Different Dimensional Integer-order and Fractional Order Chaotic Systems. In Studies in Computational Intelligence* (Vol. 688, pp. 671–697). Springer-Verlag.

Ouannas, A., Azar, A. T., Ziar, T., & Vaidyanathan, S. (2017a). *On New Fractional Inverse Matrix Projective Synchronization Schemes. In Studies in Computational Intelligence* (Vol. 688, pp. 497–524). Springer-Verlag.

Ouannas, A., Azar, A. T., Ziar, T., & Vaidyanathan, S. (2017b). *Fractional Inverse Generalized Chaos Synchronization Between Different Dimensional Systems. In Studies in Computational Intelligence* (Vol. 688, pp. 525–551). Springer-Verlag.

Ouannas, A., Azar, A. T., Ziar, T., & Vaidyanathan, S. (2017c). *A New Method To Synchronize Fractional Chaotic Systems With Different Dimensions. In Studies in Computational Intelligence* (Vol. 688, pp. 581–611). Springer-Verlag.

Ouannas, A., Grassi, G., Azar, A. T., Radwan, A. G., Volos, C., Pham, V. T., . . . Stouboulos, I. N. (2017j). *Dead-Beat Synchronization Control in Discrete-Time Chaotic Systems*. The 6th International Conference on Modern Circuits and Systems Technologies (MOCAST), Thessaloniki, Greece. 10.1109/MOCAST.2017.7937628

Pecora, L. M., & Carroll, T. L. (1990). Synchronization in chaotic systems. *Physical Review Letters*, *64*(8), 821–825. doi:10.1103/PhysRevLett.64.821 PMID:10042089

Pham, V.-T., Vaidyanathan, S., Volos, C. K., Azar, A. T., Hoang, T. M., & Van Yem, V. (2017). *A Three-Dimensional No-equilibrium chaotic system: Analysis, synchronization and its fractional order form. In Studies in Computational Intelligence* (Vol. 688, pp. 449–470). Springer-Verlag.

Rasappan, S., & Vaidyanathan, S. (2012a). Global chaos synchronization of WINDMI and Coullet chaotic systems by backstepping control. *Far East Journal of Mathematical Sciences*, *67*(2), 265–287.

Rasappan, S., & Vaidyanathan, S. (2012b). Synchronization of hyperchaotic Liu system via backstepping control with recursive feedback. *Communications in Computer and Information Science*, *305*, 212–221. doi:10.1007/978-3-642-32112-2_26

Rasappan, S., & Vaidyanathan, S. (2012c). Hybrid synchronization of n-scroll Chua and Lur'e chaotic systems via backstepping control with novel feedback. *Archives of Control Sciences*, *22*(3), 343–365.

Rasappan, S., & Vaidyanathan, S. (2013). Hybrid synchronization of n-scroll Chua circuits using adaptive backstepping control design with recursive feedback. *Malaysian Journal of Mathematical Sciences*, *7*(2), 219–246.

Rasappan, S., & Vaidyanathan, S. (2014). Global chaos synchronization of WINDMI and Coullet chaotic systems using adaptive backstepping control design. *Kyungpook Mathematical Journal*, *54*(1), 293–320. doi:10.5666/KMJ.2014.54.2.293

Rosenblum, M. G., Pikovsky, A. S., & Kurths, J. (1996). Phase synchronization of chaotic oscillators. *Physical Review Letters*, *76*(11), 1804–1807. doi:10.1103/PhysRevLett.76.1804 PMID:10060525

Runzi, L., Yinglan, W., & Shucheng, D. (2011). Combination synchronization of three classic chaotic systems using active backstepping design. *Chaos (Woodbury, N.Y.)*, *21*(4), 043114. doi:10.1063/1.3655366 PMID:22225351

Sampath, S., & Vaidyanathan, S. (2016). Hybrid synchronization of identical chaotic systems via novel sliding control method with application to Sampath four-scroll chaotic system. *International Journal of Control Theory and Applications*, *9*(1), 221–235.

Sarasu, P., & Sundarapandian, V. (2011a). Active controller design for generalized projective synchronization of four-scroll chaotic systems. *International Journal of Systems Signal Control and Engineering Application*, *4*(2), 26–33.

Sarasu, P., & Sundarapandian, V. (2011b). The generalized projective synchronization of hyperchaotic Lorenz and hyperchaotic Qi systems. *International Journal of Soft Computing*, *6*(5), 216–223. doi:10.3923/ijscomp.2011.216.223

Sarasu, P., & Sundarapandian, V. (2012a). Adaptive controller design for the generalized projective synchronization of 4-scroll systems. *International Journal of Systems Signal Control and Engineering Application*, *5*(2), 21–30.

Sarasu, P., & Sundarapandian, V. (2012b). Generalized projective synchronization of two-scroll systems via adaptive control. *International Journal of Soft Computing*, *7*(4), 146–156. doi:10.3923/ijscomp.2012.146.156

Sarasu, P., & Sundarapandian, V. (2012c). Generalized projective synchronization of three-scroll chaotic systems via adaptive control. *European Journal of Scientific Research*, *72*(4), 504–522.

Shahverdiev, E., Sivaprakasam, S., & Shore, K. (2002). Lag synchronization in time-delayed systems. *Physics Letters. [Part A]*, *292*(6), 320–324. doi:10.1016/S0375-9601(01)00824-6

Singh, S., Azar, A. T., Ouannas, A., Zhu, Q., Zhang, W., & Na, J. (2017). *Sliding Mode Control Technique for Multi-switching Synchronization of Chaotic Systems. 9th International Conference on Modelling, Identification and Control (ICMIC 2017)*, Kunming, China.

Soliman, N. S., Said, L. A., Azar, A. T., Madian, A. H., Radwan, A. G., & Ouannas, A. (2017). *Fractional Controllable Multi-Scroll V-Shape Attractor with Parameters Effect*. The 6th International Conference on Modern Circuits and Systems Technologies (MOCAST), Thessaloniki, Greece.

Sun, J., Cui, G., Wang, Y., & Shen, Y. (2015). Combination complex synchronization of three chaotic complex systems. *Nonlinear Dynamics*, *2*(79), 953–965. doi:10.100711071-014-1714-5

Suresh, R., & Sundarapandian, V. (2013). Global chaos synchronization of a family of n-scroll hyperchaotic Chua circuits using backstepping control with recursive feedback. *Far East Journal of Mathematical Sciences*, *73*(1), 73–95.

Tolba, M. F., AbdelAty, A. M., Soliman, N. S., Said, L. A., Madian, A. H., Azar, A. T., & Radwan, A. G. (2017). FPGA implementation of two fractional order chaotic systems. *International Journal of Electronics and Communications*, *28*, 162–172. doi:10.1016/j.aeue.2017.04.028

Ucar, A., Lonngren, K. E., & Bai, E.-W. (2008). Multi-switching synchronization of chaotic systems with active controllers. *Chaos, Solitons, and Fractals*, *38*(1), 254–262. doi:10.1016/j.chaos.2006.11.041

Vaidyanathan, S. (2011). Hybrid chaos synchronization of Liu and Lü systems by active nonlinear control. *Communications in Computer and Information Science*, *204*, 1–10. doi:10.1007/978-3-642-24043-0_1

Vaidyanathan, S. (2012). Adaptive controller and synchronizer design for the Qi-Chen chaotic system. *Lecture Notes of the Institute for Computer Sciences. Social-Informatics and Telecommunications Engineering*, *85*, 124–133.

Vaidyanathan, S. (2015a). Adaptive synchronization of novel 3-D chemical chaotic reactor systems. *International Journal of Chemtech Research*, *8*(7), 159–171.

Vaidyanathan, S. (2015b). Synchronization of 3-cells cellular neural network (CNN) attractors via adaptive control method. *International Journal of Pharm Tech Research*, *8*(5), 946–955.

Vaidyanathan, S. (2015c). Chaos in neurons and synchronization of Birkhoff-Shaw strange chaotic attractors via adaptive control. *International Journal of Pharm Tech Research*, *8*(6), 1–11.

Vaidyanathan, S. (2015d). Output regulation of the forced Van der Pol chaotic oscillator via adaptive control method. *International Journal of Pharm Tech Research*, *8*(6), 106–116.

Vaidyanathan, S. (2015e). Adaptive control of the FitzHugh-Nagumo chaotic neuron model. *International Journal of Pharm Tech Research*, *8*(6), 117–127.

Vaidyanathan, S. (2015f). Global chaos synchronization of the forced Van der Pol chaotic oscillators via adaptive control method. *International Journal of Pharm Tech Research*, *8*(6), 156–166.

Vaidyanathan, S. (2016a). Mathematical analysis, adaptive control and synchronization of a ten-term novel three-scroll chaotic system with four quadratic nonlinearities. *International Journal of Control Theory and Applications*, *9*(1), 1–20.

Vaidyanathan, S. (2016b). An eleven-term novel 4-D hyperchaotic system with three quadratic nonlinearities, analysis, control and synchronization via adaptive control method. *International Journal of Control Theory and Applications*, *9*(1), 21–43.

Vaidyanathan, S. (2016c). A novel 3-D conservative chaotic system with a sinusoidal nonlinearity and its adaptive control. *International Journal of Control Theory and Applications*, *9*(1), 115–132.

Vaidyanathan, S. (2016d). A novel 3-D jerk chaotic system with two quadratic nonlinearities and its adaptive backstepping control. *International Journal of Control Theory and Applications*, *9*(1), 199–216.

Vaidyanathan, S. (2016e). A novel hyperchaotic hyperjerk system with two nonlinearities, its analysis, adaptive control and synchronization via backstepping control method. *International Journal of Control Theory and Applications*, *9*(1), 257–278.

Vaidyanathan, S. (2016f). A highly chaotic system with four quadratic nonlinearities and its adaptive backstepping control. *International Journal of Control Theory and Applications*, *9*(1), 279–297.

Vaidyanathan, S. (2016g). Hybrid synchronization of the generalized Lotka-Volterra three-species biological systems via adaptive control. *International Journal of Pharm Tech Research*, *9*(1), 179–192.

Vaidyanathan, S. (2016h). Anti-synchronization of novel coupled Van der Pol conservative chaotic Systems via adaptive control method. *International Journal of Pharm Tech Research*, *9*(2), 106–123.

Vaidyanathan, S. (2016i). Anti-synchronization of enzymes-substrates biological systems via adaptive backstepping control. *International Journal of Pharm Tech Research*, *9*(2), 193–205.

Vaidyanathan, S. (2016j). Anti-synchronization of Duffing double-well chaotic oscillators via integral sliding mode control. *International Journal of Chemtech Research*, *9*(2), 297–304.

Vaidyanathan, S. (2016k). Global chaos regulation of a symmetric nonlinear gyro system via integral sliding mode control. *International Journal of Chemtech Research*, *9*(2), 462–469.

Vaidyanathan, S. (2016l). Anti-synchronization of 3-cells cellular neural network attractors via integral sliding mode control. *International Journal of Pharm Tech Research*, *9*(1), 193–205.

Vaidyanathan, S. (2016m). Anti-synchronization of 3-cells cellular neural network attractors via integral sliding mode control. *International Journal of Pharm Tech Research*, *9*(1), 193–205.

Vaidyanathan, S. (2016n). Global chaos control of the generalized Lotka-Volterra three-species system via integral sliding mode control. *International Journal of Pharm Tech Research*, *9*(4), 399–412.

Vaidyanathan, S. (2016o). Analysis, control and synchronization of a novel highly chaotic system with three quadratic nonlinearities. In *Advances and Applications in Nonlinear Control Systems* (pp. 211–234). Springer. doi:10.1007/978-3-319-30169-3_11

Vaidyanathan, S., & Azar, A. T. (2015a). Analysis, control and synchronization of a nine-term 3-d novel chaotic system. In *Chaos modeling and control systems design* (pp. 19–38). Springer. doi:10.1007/978-3-319-13132-0_2

Vaidyanathan, S., & Azar, A. T. (2015b). Anti-synchronization of identical chaotic systems using sliding mode control and an application to vaidyanathan–madhavan chaotic systems. In *Advances and Applications in Sliding Mode Control systems* (pp. 527–547). Springer. doi:10.1007/978-3-319-11173-5_19

Vaidyanathan, S., & Azar, A. T. (2015c). Hybrid synchronization of identical chaotic systems using sliding mode control and an application to vaidyanathan chaotic systems. In *Advances and applications in sliding mode control systems* (pp. 549–569). Springer. doi:10.1007/978-3-319-11173-5_20

Vaidyanathan, S., & Azar, A. T. (2015d). Analysis and Control of a 4-D Novel Hyperchaotic System. In Chaos Modeling and Control Systems Design (vol. 581, pp. 19-38). Springer-Verlag GmbH Berlin/Heidelberg. DOI doi:10.1007/978-3-319-13132-0_2

Vaidyanathan, S., & Azar, A. T. (2016a). *Adaptive Control and Synchronization of Halvorsen Circulant Chaotic Systems. In Advances in Chaos Theory and Intelligent Control. Studies in Fuzziness and Soft Computing* (Vol. 337, pp. 225–247). Springer-Verlag.

Vaidyanathan, S., & Azar, A. T. (2016b). *Dynamic Analysis, Adaptive Feedback Control and Synchronization of an Eight-Term 3-D Novel Chaotic System with Three Quadratic Nonlinearities. In Studies in Fuzziness and Soft Computing* (Vol. 337, pp. 155–178). Springer-Verlag.

Vaidyanathan, S., & Azar, A. T. (2016c). *Generalized Projective Synchronization of a Novel Hyperchaotic Four-Wing System via Adaptive Control Method. Advances in Chaos Theory and Intelligent Control. In Studies in Fuzziness and Soft Computing* (Vol. 337, pp. 275–296). Springer-Verlag.

Vaidyanathan, S., & Azar, A. T. (2016d). A novel 4-d four-wing chaotic system with four quadratic nonlinearities and its synchronization via adaptive control method. In *Advances in Chaos Theory and Intelligent Control* (pp. 203–224). Springer. doi:10.1007/978-3-319-30340-6_9

Vaidyanathan, S., & Azar, A. T. (2016e). *Qualitative Study and Adaptive Control of a Novel 4-D Hyperchaotic System with Three Quadratic Nonlinearities. In Studies in Fuzziness and Soft Computing* (Vol. 337, pp. 179–202). Springer-Verlag.

Vaidyanathan, S., & Azar, A. T. (2016f). *Adaptive Backstepping Control and Synchronization of a Novel 3-D Jerk System with an Exponential Nonlinearity. In Advances in Chaos Theory and Intelligent Control* (Vol. 337, pp. 249–274). Springer-Verlag.

Vaidyanathan, S., & Azar, A. T. (2016g). Takagi-Sugeno Fuzzy Logic Controller for Liu-Chen Four-Scroll Chaotic System. *International Journal of Intelligent Engineering Informatics*, *4*(2), 135–150. doi:10.1504/IJIEI.2016.076699

Vaidyanathan, S., Azar, A. T., & Ouannas, A. (2017a). *An Eight-Term 3-D Novel Chaotic System with Three Quadratic Nonlinearities, its Adaptive Feedback Control and Synchronization. In Studies in Computational Intelligence* (Vol. 688, pp. 719–746). Springer-Verlag.

Vaidyanathan, S., Azar, A. T., & Ouannas, A. (2017c). *Hyperchaos and Adaptive Control of a Novel Hyperchaotic System with Two Quadratic Nonlinearities. In Studies in Computational Intelligence* (Vol. 688, pp. 773–803). Springer-Verlag.

Vaidyanathan, S., Azar, A. T., Rajagopal, K., & Alexander, P. (2015a). Design and spice implementation of a 12-term novel hyperchaotic system and its synchronisation via active control. *International Journal of Modelling, Identification and Control, 23*(3), 267–277. doi:10.1504/IJMIC.2015.069936

Vaidyanathan, S., Idowu, B. A., & Azar, A. T. (2015b) Backstepping Controller Design for the Global Chaos Synchronization of Sprott's Jerk Systems. In Chaos Modeling and Control Systems Design (vol. 581, pp. 39-58). Springer-Verlag GmbH Berlin/Heidelberg. doi:10.1007/978-3-319-13132-0_3

Vaidyanathan, S., Sampath, S., & Azar, A. T. (2015c). Global chaos synchronisation of identical chaotic systems via novel sliding mode control method and its application to Zhu system. *International Journal of Modelling, Identification and Control, 23*(1), 92–100. doi:10.1504/IJMIC.2015.067495

Vaidyanathan, S., Zhu, Q., & Azar, A. T. (2017b). *Adaptive Control of a Novel Nonlinear Double Convection Chaotic System. In Studies in Computational Intelligence* (Vol. 688, pp. 357–385). Springer-Verlag.

Wang, F., & Liu, C. (2007). Synchronization of unified chaotic system based on passive control. *Physica D. Nonlinear Phenomena, 225*(1), 55–60. doi:10.1016/j.physd.2006.09.038

Wang, Z., Volos, C., Kingni, S. T., Azar, A. T., & Pham, V.-T. (2017). Four-wing attractors in a novel chaotic system with hyperbolic sine nonlinearity. *Optik-International Journal for Light and Electron Optics, 131*, 1071–1078. doi:10.1016/j.ijleo.2016.12.016

Wu, Z., & Fu, X. (2013). Combination synchronization of three different order nonlinear systems using active backstepping design. *Nonlinear Dynamics, 3*(73), 1863–1872. doi:10.100711071-013-0909-5

Yang, T., & Chua, L. O. (1997). Impulsive stabilization for control and synchronization of chaotic systems: Theory and application to secure communication. *IEEE Transactions on Circuits and Systems. I, Fundamental Theory and Applications, 44*(10), 976–988. doi:10.1109/81.633887

Zhang, H., Lewis, F. L., & Das, A. (2011). Optimal design for synchronization of cooperative systems: State feedback, observer and output feedback. *IEEE Transactions on Automatic Control, 56*(8), 1948–1952. doi:10.1109/TAC.2011.2139510

Zhang, H., Ma, X.-K., & Liu, W.-Z. (2004). Synchronization of chaotic systems with parametric uncertainty using active sliding mode control. *Chaos, Solitons, and Fractals, 21*(5), 1249–1257. doi:10.1016/j.chaos.2003.12.073

Zhu, Q., & Azar, A. T. (2015). *Complex system modelling and control through intelligent soft computations. In Studies in Fuzziness and Soft Computing* (Vol. 319). Springer-Verlag.

Chapter 6
Load Frequency Control Based on Modern Techniques in Two Areas Power Systems

Naglaa Kamel Bahgaat
Canadian International College (CIC), Egypt

Mohamed Ibrahim
Al Azhar University, Egypt

Mohamed Ahmed Moustafa Hassan
Cairo University, Egypt

Fahmy Bendary
Benha University, Egypt

ABSTRACT

This chapter gives introduction to evolutionary techniques. Then it presents the problem formulation for load frequency control with evolutionary particle swarm optimization. It gives the application of particle swarm optimization (PSO) in load frequency control; also, it illustrates the use of an adaptive weight particle swarm optimization (AWPSO) and adaptive accelerated coefficients based PSO (AACPSO). Furthermore, it introduces a new modification for AACPSO technique (MAACPSO). The new technique is explained. A well-done comparison will be given in this chapter for these above-mentioned techniques. A reasonable discussion on the obtained results will be displayed. The obtained results are promising.

1. INTRODUCTION

Frequency is an important factor to describe the stability criterion in power systems (Ismail & Hassan, 2012; Salami et al., 2006). To provide the stability of power system, the balance of power and steady frequency is required. In case of change occurs in active power demand or the generation in power systems, oscillations increase in both power and frequency. Frequency depends on active power balance so it cannot be hold in its rated value (Azar, 2010, 2012a and 2012b). Thus, system suffering from a

DOI: 10.4018/978-1-5225-4077-9.ch006

serious of instability problem. Load Frequency Control (LFC) is an important issue in power system operation and control for supplying stable (Skogestad, 2003). The principle aspect of Automatic Load Frequency Control is to maintain the generator power output and frequency within the prescribed limits (Bahgaat et al., 2013).

There are many studies that have been conducted to reach the fastest and best control methods that achieve stability of the electrical power systems (Azar & Serrano, 2014; Azar & Serrano, 2015a,b,c,d; Zhu & Azar, 2015; Azar & Zhu, 2015; Boulkroune et al, 2016a,b; Ghoudelbourk et al., 2016; Mekki et al., 2015; Meghni et al, 2017a,b,c). Recently, many important developments related to the design of nonlinear systems for many practical applications have been proposed, such as optimal control, nonlinear feedback control, adaptive control, sliding mode control, nonlinear dynamics, chaos control, chaos synchronization control, fuzzy logic control, fuzzy adaptive control, fractional order control, and robust control and their integrations (Azar & Vaidyanathan, 2015a,b,c, 2016; Azar & Serrano, 2015a,b,c,d, 2016a,b, 2017; Azar et al., 2017a,b,c,d; Azar 2010, 2012; Vaidyanathan & Azar, 2015a,b,c,d, 2016a,b,c,d,e,f,g, 2017a,b,c; Zhu & Azar, 2015; Grassi et al., 2017; Ouannas et al., 2016a,b, 2017a,b,c,d,e,f,g,h,I,j; Singh et al., 2017; Vaidyanathan et al, 2015a,b,c; Wang et al., 2017; Soliman et al., 2017; Tolba et al., 2017).

One of the famous controllers used in power system are Proportional Integral (PI) (Azar & Serrano, 2016a,b), Proportional Derivative (PD) and Proportional Integral Derivative (PID) controllers, PID will be used for the stabilization of the frequency in the load frequency control problems (Hassanien et al., 2014; Zhu & Azar, 2015; Azar & Zhu, 2015; Ismail & Hassan, 2012; Salami et al., 2006; Skogestad, 2003). When changes the loads each control area is responsible for specific load changes and scheduled interchanges with neighboring areas. The changes of the loads and abnormal conditions leads to incompatibilities in frequency and tie line power exchanges which are to be kept in the allowable limits, for the strong operation of the power system. For simplicity, the effects of governor dead band are neglected in the Load Frequency Control studies. To study the analysis of the system performance, the governor dead band effect is to be combined. To improve the stability of the power networks, it is necessary to design LFC system that controls the power generation and active power at tie lines (Bahgaat et al., 2014, 2015; Ali et al., 2015).

There are many studies done in the past the load frequency control. As stated in some literature (Rama Sudha et al., 2010; Bevrani, 2009; Ismail, 2006), its objective is to minimize the transient deviations in area frequency and tie-line power exchange and to ensure their steady state errors to be zeros. This chapter discusses the application of modern techniques in Load Frequency Control (LFC) in power systems. such that Particle Swarm Optimization (PSO), Adaptive Weighted Particle Swarm Optimization techniques (AWPSO), Adaptive Accelerated Coefficients based on PSO (AACPSO) and Evolutionary Particle Swarm Optimization (MAACPSO) (Ali, et.al, 2016).will be used to control the parameters of a PID controller according to the system dynamics. Using the two identical PID controllers for the two different areas (Bahgaat et al., 2014b; Panigrahi et al., 2008). To choose best parameters of PID Controller many techniques are used, Particle Swarm Optimization and Adaptive Weight Particle Swarm Optimization Techniques (PSO) and (AWPSO) (Rania, 2012; Naik et al., 2005; Gaing, 2004) and Also using Adaptive Accelerated Coefficients based PSO, (AACPSO), then a new modification for AACPSO technique will be discuss called evolutionary techniques based on Particle Swarm Optimization (MAACPSO).

This chapter is planned as follow: Section one introduces the chapter. The second section presents literature review of the study. Section three introduces Particle Swarm (PSO), AWPSO, the Adaptive Accelerated Coefficients based PSO (AACPSO) and Modified Adaptive Accelerated Coefficients based PSO (MAACPSO). Section four displays the case study and a comparative study between these methods, while Section five concludes the chapter. Finally a list of references and Appendix of this chapter are given at the end of the chapter.

2. LITERATURE REVIEW

The PID controller was first described by Minorsky (Amjady and Nasiri-Rad, 2009). It has been confirmed that in control applications more than 95% of the controllers are PID type. The choice of appropriate PID parameters can be achieved manually by trial and error, using as guidelines the transient and steady response characteristic of each of the three terms. However, this procedure is very time consuming and requires certain skills (Bahgaat et al., 2014b; Ang et al., 2005).

The structure of PID controllers as shown in Figure 1 is very simple. They operate on the error signal, which is the difference between the desired output and the actual output, and generate the actuating signal that efforts the plant. They have three basic terms: proportional action, which the actuating signal is proportional to the error signal, integral action, the signal is proportional to the time integral of the error signal; and derivative action, where the actuating signal is proportional to the time derivative of the error signal as shown in (Bahgaat et al., 2016; Darrell, 2005; Reeves and Rowe, 2002).

The PID standard form is given by:

$$u = K_p.e + K_i \int e.dt + K_d.\frac{de}{dt} \tag{1}$$

where:

e Is the error signal.
u Is the control action.
Kp Is the proportional gain

Figure 1. Structure of PID Controller

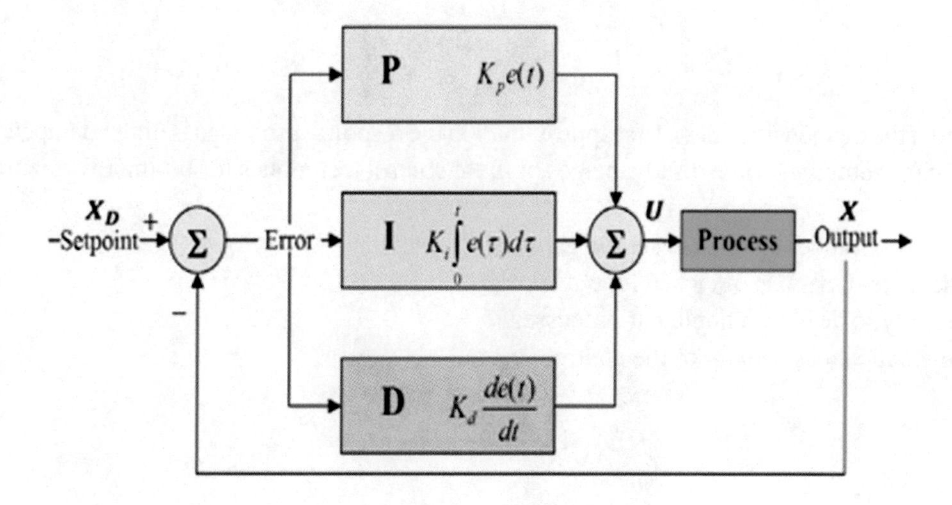

Ki Is the integral gain
Kd Is the derivative gain

The controller used in power systems should provide some degree of strength under different operating conditions. (Ismail & Hassan, 2012; Salami, et al., 2006; Skogestad, 2003). So many methods used since 1890s till now to tune the controller. First method is the manual tuning, this method

As described in (Bahgaat et al., 2015).Second method is an automatic method called Ziegler–Nichols method which introduced by John G. Ziegler and Nathaniel B. Nichols in the 1940s (Skogestad, 2003). It is recognized that the step response of most process control systems has an S-shaped curve called the process reaction curve and can be generated experimentally or from dynamic simulation of the plant (Bahgaat et al., 2014), the shape of the curve is characteristic of high order systems, and the plant behavior may be approximated by the following transfer function (Bahgaat et al., 2014 a,b):

$$\frac{Y(S)}{U(S)} = \frac{K.e^{-t_d.s}}{\tau.S+1} \quad (2)$$

Which is simply; a first order system plus a transportation lag. The constants in the above equation can be determined from the unit step response of the process. Ziegler and Nichols applied the PID controller to plants without integrator or dominant complex-conjugate poles, whose unit-step response resemble an S shaped curve with no overshoot. This S-shaped curve is called the reaction curve as shown in Figure 1:

The following PID controller parameters were suggested:

$$K_P = {}^{1.2T}\!/_{L} \quad (3)$$

$$K_i = {}^{K_P}\!/_{2L} \quad (4)$$

$$K_d = 0.5.L.K_P \quad (5)$$

Although the method provides a first approximation the response produced is under damped and needs further manual retuning. Some disadvantages of these control techniques for tuning PID controllers are:

1. Excessive number of rules to set the gains.
2. Inadequate dynamics of closed loop responses.
3. Difficulty to deal with nonlinear processes.
4. Mathematical complexity of the control design.

Figure 2. Reaction Curve used by Ziegler and Nichols

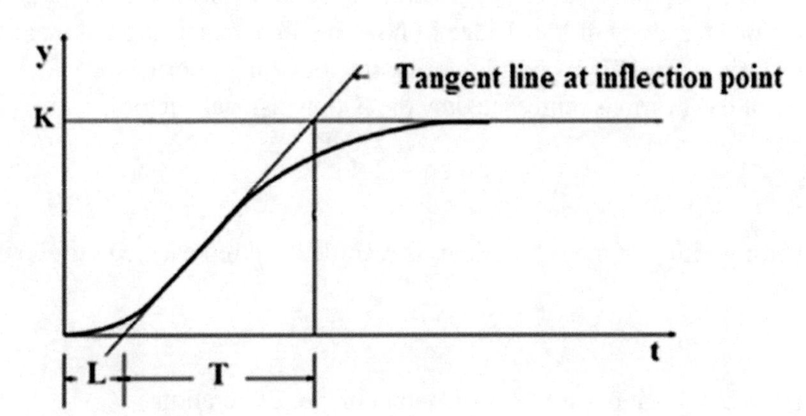

Therefore, it is interesting for academic and industrial communities the aspect of tuning for PID controllers, especially with a reduced number of parameters to be selected and a good performance to be achieved when dealing with complex processes.

The manual calculation methods no longer are used to tune loops in most modern industrial facilities. Instead, PID tuning and loop optimization software are used to guarantee dependable results (Bahgaat et al., 2013; Ismail, 2006; Kumar, 1998). These software packages will gather the data, develop process models, and suggest optimal tuning.

Some software packages can even develop tuning by collecting data from reference changes, such as PSO, AWPSO (Rania, 2012; Panigrahi, et al., 2008; Naik et al., 2005), AACPSO (Bahgaat, et al., 2014; Ahmed et al., 2013). And this chapter will discuss the design of the PID controller by using modern method PSO, AWPSO, AACPSO and MAACPSO. These methods are simulated on MATLAB software program. This computer program which written on MATLAB had loops and run many times until reaching to a solution of the transfer function to have a value of PID parameters. These parameters lead to have the smallest value of settling time and over shoot. Therefore, these values of PID parameters are the best values to reach to the best controller parameters. Moreover, a good comparison between the results of each used method will be done to choose the best one of them which will be suitable to use in the power system model used.

3. PRACTICAL SWARM OPTIMIZATION TECHNIQUES

A Particle Swarm Optimization (PSO) is one of Artificial Intelligence (AI) Techniques. It's an optimization algorithm modeled. From the fields of AI with those of control engineering to design independent systems that can sense, reason, learn and act in an intelligent method. PSO depends on the simulation of the social behavior of bird and fish school (Fakhry et al., 2016; Bahgaat et al., 2014; Rania, 2012). PSO is developed through the simulation of a bird flocking in two-dimension space by X-Y axis position where Vx and Vy express the velocity in X direction and Y direction. The flow chart described in Figure 2, presented the steps of PSO. Modification of the agent position is realized by the position and velocity information (Abu-Seada et al., 2013; Rania, 2012; Panigrahi et al., 2008; Naik et al., 2005; Gaing, 2004). This information is analogy of personal experiences of each agent. Each agent knows its best value so far (P_{best}) and its XY position; each agent knows the best value so far in the group (g_{best}) among P_{best}. This information is analogy of knowledge of how the other agents around them have performed. Namely, each agent tries to modify its position using the following information:

Let the particle of the swarm is represented by the N dimensional vector i^{th}

$$X_i = (X_1, X_2, X_3, \ldots, X_N) \tag{6}$$

The previous best position of the Nth particles is recorded and represented as follows:

$$P_{besti} = P_{best1}, P_{best2}, \ldots, P_{bestN}) \tag{7}$$

where P_{best} is Particle best position (m), N is the total number of iterations.

The best position of the particle among all particles in the swarm is represented by g_{best} the velocity of the particle is represented as follows:

$$V_i = (V_1, V_2, \ldots, V_N) \tag{8}$$

where V_i is the velocity of each i particle.

The modified velocity and position of each particle can be calculated from the current velocity and the distance from particle current position to particle best position P_{best} and to global best position g_{best} as shown in the following Equations (Bahgaat et al., 2014):

$$V_i(t) = W.\ V_i(t\text{-}1) + C_1.\text{rand}(0,1).(P_{best} - X_i(t\text{-}1)) + C_2.\text{rand}(0,1).(g_{best} - X_i(t\text{-}1)) \tag{9}$$

Figure 3. General Flow Chart of PSO

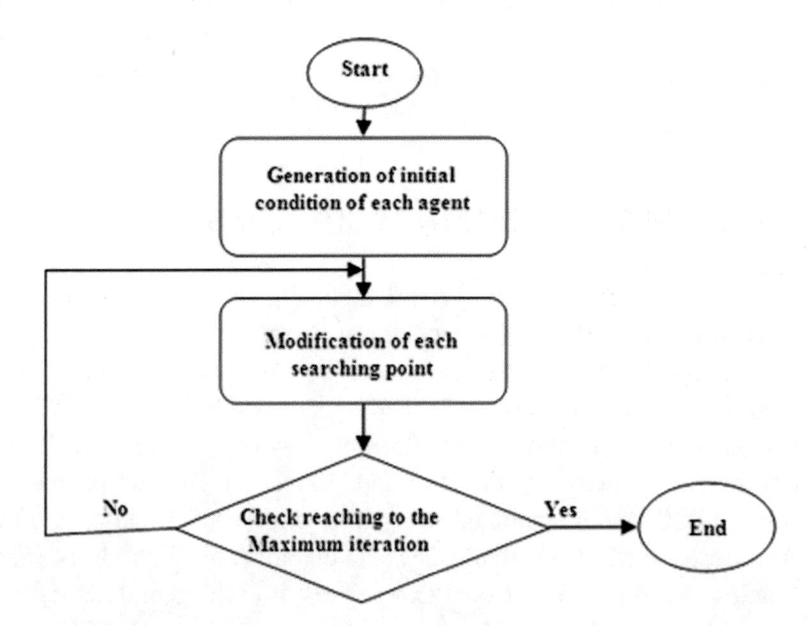

$X_i(t)=X_i(t-1)+V_i(t)$ (10)

$i=1, 2, 3...N$ (11)

$j=1, 2, 3...D$ (12)

where:

Vi(t) Velocity of the particle i at iteration t (m/s)
Xi(t) The Current position of particle i at iteration t (m)
D The Dimension
C_1 The cognitive acceleration coefficient and it is a positive number
C_2 Social acceleration coefficient and it is a positive number
rand [0,1] A random number obtained from a uniform random distribution function in the interval [0,1]
g_{best} The Global best position (m)
W The Inertia weight

3.1. Adaptive Weighted Particle Swarm Optimization

Adaptive Weighted Particle Swarm Optimization (AWPSO) technique has been estimated for improving the performance of PSO in multi-objective optimization problems (Panigrahi et al., 2008; Naik et al., 2005). AWPSO is consists of two terms which are: inertia weigh (W) and Acceleration factor (A) (Rania, 2012). The inertia weight (W) function is to balance global exploration and local exploration. It controls previous velocities effect on the new velocity. Larger the inertia weight, larger exploration of search space while smaller the inertia weights, the search will be limited and focused on a small region in the search space . The inertia weight formula is as follows which makes W value changes randomly from W_o to 1 (Bahgaat et al., 2014; Salem et al., 2014; Azar, 2012b; Azar, 2010).

$W=W_o+ rand(0,1)(1-W_o)$ (13)

where:

Wo The initial positive constant in the interval chosen from [0,1]

Particle velocity at i^{th} iteration as follows:

$V_i(t) = W. V_i(t-1) + AC_1.rand(0,1).(P_{best} -X_i(t-1)) + AC_2.rand(0,1).(g_{best} -X_i(t-1)$ (14)

Additional term denoted by A called acceleration factor is added in the original velocity equation to improve the swarm search.

The acceleration factor formula is given as follows (Rania, 2012):

$$A = A_o + \frac{i}{n} \tag{15}$$

where:

A_o: Is the initial positive constant in the interval [0.5, 1].
n: Is the number of iteration
C_1 andC_2: Are the constant representing the weighing of the stochastic acceleration terms that pull each particle towards P_{best} and g_{best} positions.

As shown in acceleration factor formula, that the acceleration term will increase as the number of iterations increases. This will increase the global search ability at the end of the run and help the algorithm to get far from the local optimum region. In this chapter, the term A_O is set at 0.5. Low values of $C_1$and C_2 allow particles to roam far from the target region before being tugged back. However, high values result in abrupt movement toward, or past, target regions.

3.2. Adaptive Accelerated Coefficients Based PSO

In Section (3.1) the value of W can be located a good solution at a considerably faster rate but its ability to fine tune the optimum solution is weak, due to the lack of diversity at the end of the search. It has been observed by most researchers that in PSO, problem based tuning of parameters is a key factor to find the optimum solution accurately and efficiently (Vlachogiannis and Lee, 2009). New researches have emerged to improve PSO Algorithms, as Time-Varying Acceleration Coefficients (TVAC), where C_1 and C_2 in (Hamid et al., 2010) change linearly with time, in the way that the cognitive component is reduced while the social component is increased as the search proceeds (Ahmed et al., 2013). This method studies how to deal with inertia weight and acceleration factors and how to change acceleration coefficients exponentially (with inertia weight) in the time, with respect to their minimal and maximal values. The choice of the exponential function is justified by the increasing or decreasing speed of such a function to accelerate the convergence process of the algorithm and to get better search in the exploration s pace. Furthermore, C_1 and C_2 vary adaptively according to the fitness value of g_{best} and P_{best}, (Bahgaat et al., 2014; Hamid et al., 2010) becomes:

$$V_i^{(t+1)} = w^{(t)} V_i^{(t)} + C_1^{(t)} r_1 * \left(P_{best\,i}^{(t)} - X_i^{(t)}\right) + C_2^{(t)} r_2 * \left(g_{best}^{(t)} - X_i^{(t)}\right) \tag{16}$$

$$w^{(t)} = w_o * exp\left(- \propto_w *t\right) \tag{17}$$

$$C_1^{(t)} = C_{1o} * \exp\left(- \propto_c *t * k_c^{(t)}\right) \tag{18}$$

$$C_2^{(t)} = C_{2o} * \exp\left(\propto_c *t * k_c^{(t)}\right) \tag{19}$$

$$\propto_c = \frac{-1}{t_{max}} \ln\left(\frac{C_{2o}}{C_{1o}}\right) \tag{20}$$

$$k_c^{(t)} = \frac{\left(F_m^{(t)} - g_{best}^{(t)}\right)}{F_m^{(t)}} \tag{21}$$

where:

$w^{(t)}$ The inertia weight factor
$C_1^{(t)}$ Acceleration coefficient at iteration t
i Equal 1 or 2
t The iteration number
ln The neperian logarithm
α_w Is determined with respect to initial and final values of ω with the same manner as αc described in (Amjady et al., 2009).
$k_c^{(t)}$ Determined based on the fitness value of g_{best} and P_{best} at iteration t
ω_o, c_{io} c_{io} initial values of inertia weight factor and acceleration coefficients respectively with i=1or 2.
$F_m^{(t)}$ The mean value of the best positions related to all particles at iteration t

3.3. Modified Adaptive Accelerated Coefficients PSO

In this section, a new approach called Modified Adaptive Accelerated Coefficients PSO will be described as illustrated in (Khalifa, 2015). A suggestion will be show how to choose the acceleration factors. The new approach will be make modification on the values of C_1 and C_2 which described in the last section (3.2). The first coefficient changes exponentially (with inertia weight) in the time, with respect to their minimal and maximal values. While, the other one changes as a factor of the first coefficient. The choice of the exponential function is justified by the increasing or decreasing speed of such a function to accelerate the convergence process of the algorithm and to get better search in the exploration s pace.

Instead of the equation (18) the parameter $C_2(t)$ is suggested to be equal (Khalifa, 2015):

$C_2(t) = C_t\text{-}C_1(t)$ where $C_t = 4$ then:

$$C_2(t) = 4\text{-}C_1(t) \tag{22}$$

The results of the program are shown in Table 1, 2 and 3

4. CASE STUDY

The case study is consists of two power system networks connected with each other's by tie transmission line as shown in Figures 3 and 4 (Bahgaat et al., 2014, 2016). Simulations are done by using MATLAB / SIMULINK the parameters of the networks are shown in the Appendix. Electric power system components are non-linear; therefore a linearization around a nominal operating point is usually performed to get a linearized system model which is used in the controller design process.

The LFC function is to minimize the transient deviation of the frequency and maintains their values to steady state values and to restore the planned exchanges between different areas.

The operating conditions of power systems are continuously changing. Accordingly, the real plant usually differs from the assumed one. Therefore, classical algorithms to design an automatic generation controller using an assumed plant may not ensure the stability of the overall real system (Bahgaat et al., 2014). MATLAB programs are used all techniques used to make tuning of the PID controller's parameters. These parameters adjusted to have minimum integrated error value with shorted settling time. The objective function is defined as follows (Bahgaat et al., 2014):

For Integral of Absolute Error (IAE):

$$IAE = \int_0^\infty \left|e\left(t\right)\right| dt \tag{23}$$

$$f = IAE_1 + IAE_2 + IAE_{Ptie} \tag{24}$$

Integral of Squared Error (ISE)

$$ISE = \int_0^\infty e^2\left(t\right) dt \tag{25}$$

$$f = ISE_1 + ISE_2 + ISE_{Ptie} \tag{26}$$

Integral of Time Weighted Absolute Error (ITAE)

$$ITAE = \int_0^\infty t\left|e\left(t\right)\right| dt \tag{27}$$

$$f = ITAE_1 + ITAE_2 + ITAE_{Ptie} \tag{28}$$

where:

e Is the error
f Is the objective function
$IAE_1, IAE_2, IAE_{Ptie1}$ The Integral of Absolute Error of area 1, area 2 and the tie line of the System
$ISE_1, ISE_2, ISE_{Ptie1}$ The Integral of Squared Error of area 1, area2 and the tie line of the System
$ITAE_1, ITAE_2, ITAE_{Ptie1}$ Integral of Time Weighted Absolute Error of area 1, area 2 and the tie line of the System

For the two power system areas, step loading disturbance has been applied for each area, 0.07 p.u load throw has been withdrawn from the first area and 0.05 p.u loading added for the second area. The control objective is to control the frequency deviation for each area.

4.1. Steps of the Study

The steps of the study by using MATLAB / SIMULINK for all intelligent techniques and finally by using MAACPSO technique on the two areas as the following:

1. Using MATLAB / SIMULINK model of the system with its parameters.
2. Select the type of error used in the equations in the beginning of the MATLAB program (IAE, ISE, or ITAE).
3. Using PSO program with the equations of the chosen type of error.
4. Repeat using AWPSO program for the same type of error used.
5. Repeat using AACPSO program for the same type of error used.
6. Repeat using MAACPSO program for the same type of error used.
7. Compare the results of the four methods used and determine the best which has a less value of settling time and frequency deviation.
8. Assign the value of the PID controller for the best method results.
9. Conclude the results.

The performance index selected by the user in the beginning of the program. Based on this performance index (f) optimization problem can be stated as: Minimize f the nominal system description and parameters are describing in the following:

4.2. Model Description and Parameters

The block diagram of the two areas power system model using PID controller presented at Fig.3as obtained in (Bahgaat et al., 2016). The description for the system parameters is displayed in Table 1 and the parameters values of the system are presented in Table 2.

So the transfer function of governors, turbine, mass and load becomes as given in (Bahgaat et al., 2016):

$$G_{h1}\left(S\right) = G_{h2}\left(S\right) = \frac{1}{0.08s + 1} \tag{29}$$

Table 1. Parameter Description

Parameter	Description
Tg1, Tg2	Time constant for area 1 governor and area 2 governor in (seconds)
Tt1,Tt2	Turbine time delay between switching the valve and output turbine torque (seconds)
Tl1, Tl2	Generator 1 and generator 2 inertia constant
Kl1, Kl2	Power system gain constant (HZ/ MW p.u)
R1, R2	Speed regulation constant of the governor (HZ/ MW p.u)
B1,B2	Frequency bias p.u. MW/HZ
T12	Tie line synchronizing coefficient with area 2 MW p.u /HZ
a12	Gain
$\Delta f_1 or df_1$	Area 1 frequency deviation
$\Delta f_2 or df_2$	Area 2 frequency deviation
dPL1, dPL2	Frequency sensitive load change for Area1 and Area2
ΔPtie or dPtie	Net Tie line power flow
Vi	Area interface
ACE1	Area 1 control error
ACE2	Area 2 control error

$$G_{t1}\left(S\right) = G_{t2}\left(S\right) = \frac{1}{0.3s + 1} \tag{30}$$

$$G_{y1}\left(S\right) = G_{y2}\left(S\right) = \frac{120}{20s + 1} \tag{31}$$

Table 2. Parameters Values

System Parameters	Value
Tg1, Tg2	0.08 seconds
Tt1,Tt2	0.3 seconds
Tl1, Tl2	20 seconds
Kl1, Kl2	100 HZ/MW p.u
R1, R2	2.4 HZ/MW p.u
B1,B2	0.425 MW p.u /HZ
T12	0.05 MW p.u /HZ
a12	1

To optimize the performance of a PID controlled system, the PID gains KP, Ki, and Kdof the two-area electric power system shown in Fig. 3are adjusted to minimize a certain performance index. The performance index is calculated over a time interval; T, normally in the region of 0 < T < ts where ts is the settling time of the system. By using different techniques in conjunction with Equations: 22-30 the optimal controller parameters under various performance indices were obtained as shown in Table 1, 2 and 3 show the results of the different methods used based PID controller.

4.3 Results in Case of IAE Error

A MATLAB code was written to carry out the PSO, AWPSO, AACPSO and MAACPSO algorithms. The Integral of Absolute Error (IAE) is considered as a choice in the run of the program. Table 3 illustrates The Results of the Program Using PSO, AWPSO, AACPSO and MAACPSO

Figures 5 and 6 present the frequency deviation of area1 and area2 without using PID controller.

Furthermore, there are the Figures describe the output of the system after controlling the error on area1 and area 2. Figure 7 presents the frequency deviation of area 1 with PSO based PID Controller, Figure 8 presents the frequency deviation of area1 with AWPSO based PID controller and Figure 9 illustrates the frequency deviation of area 1 with AACPSO based PID controller and finally Figure 10 presented the frequency deviation of area 1 using MAACPSO based PID controller.

Figure 11 presents the frequency deviation of area2 with PSO based PID controller using IAE performance indices; Figure 12 shows the behavior of the frequency deviation of area 2 in case of using AWPSO, while; Figure 13 displays The frequency deviation of area 2 with AACPSO based PID controller, finally Figure 14 presents the frequency deviation of area 2 with MAACPSO based PID controller using IAE performance indices.

From the results shown in Table 3 and also the above Figures from 7 to 14 all these show that:

1. The settling time by using AACPSO is the smallest value of all the techniques used in the comparison. While, the settling time using MAACPSO comes next.

Table 3. The Results of the Program Using PSO, AWPSO, AACPSO and MAACPSO

Items of Comparison	PSO	AWPSO	AACPSO	MAACPSO
Number of iterations	500	500	500	500
Error IAE (Integrated Error)	0.0611	0.0252	0.0149	0.0267
Settling time _Area 1 (sec)	5.4281	1.9323	1.6514	1.7267
Settling time _Area 2 (sec)	7.6946	4.1854	3.569	2.5288
Settling time _Tie line (sec)	7.7624	4.2082	3.6553	2.5696
Kp1	2.4283	8.1472	9.1995	3.7517
Ki1	1.5555	7.5774	9.4936	6.0754
Kd1	1.3753	2.7603	3.2393	0.8947
Kp2	2.9522	3.4998	4.7149	4.9802
Ki2	9.2078	1.6218	0.876	1.2982
Kd2	5.7955	8.6869	2.1397	8.4839

Figure 4. Two-Area Power System SIMULINK Model Using PID Controller

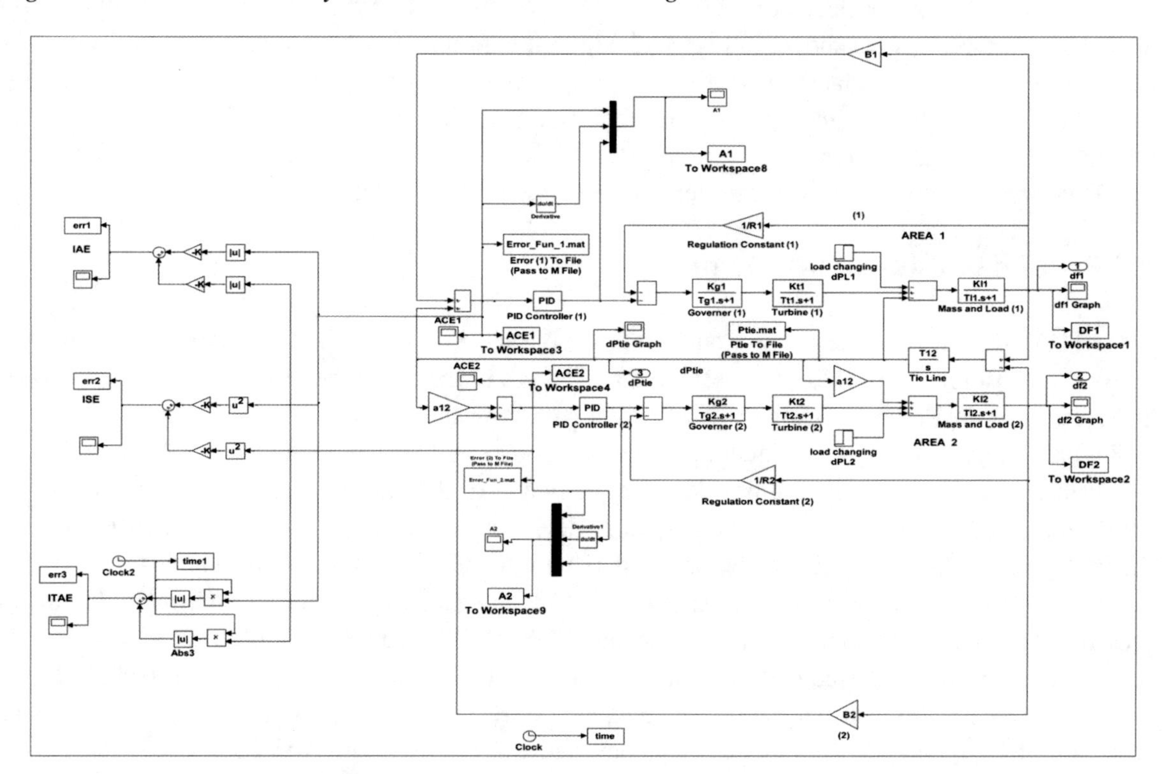

Figure 5. The Frequency Deviation of Area 1 without Controller

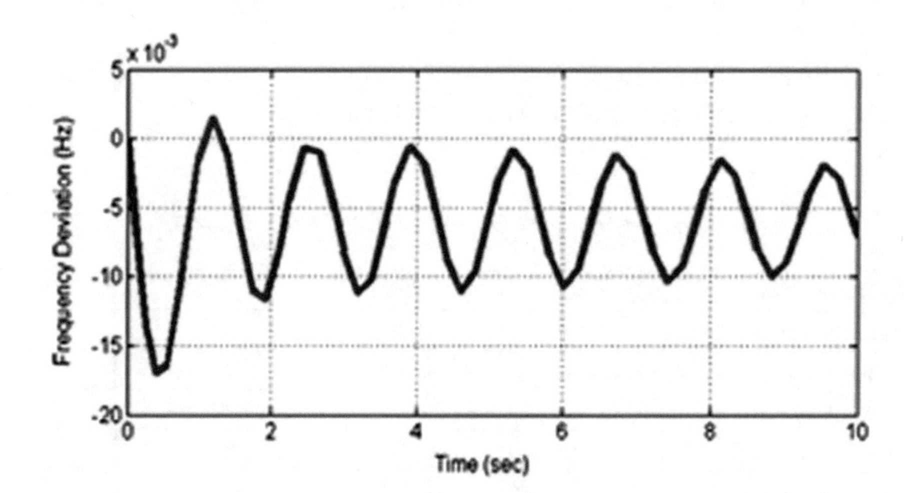

2. The difference value between the settling time values using two methods “AACPSO, MAACPSO” is very small and equal nearly 0.08 sec.
3. All these results present that: the best method used to reach the minimum value of settling time in area 1 is AACPSO.
4. The value of settling time of area 2 by using MAACPSO is less than all values using other methods.

Figure 6. The Frequency Deviation of Area 2 without Controller

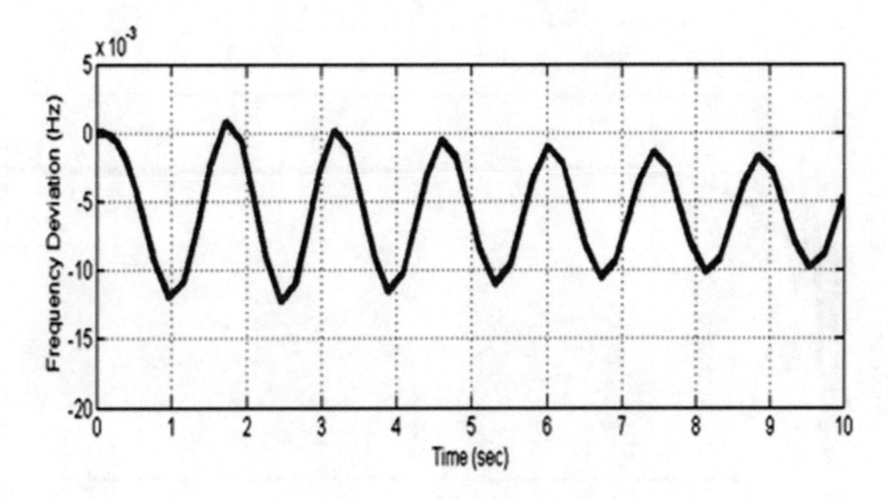

Figure 7. The Frequency Deviation of Area 1 with PSO Based PID Controller Using IAE Performance Indices

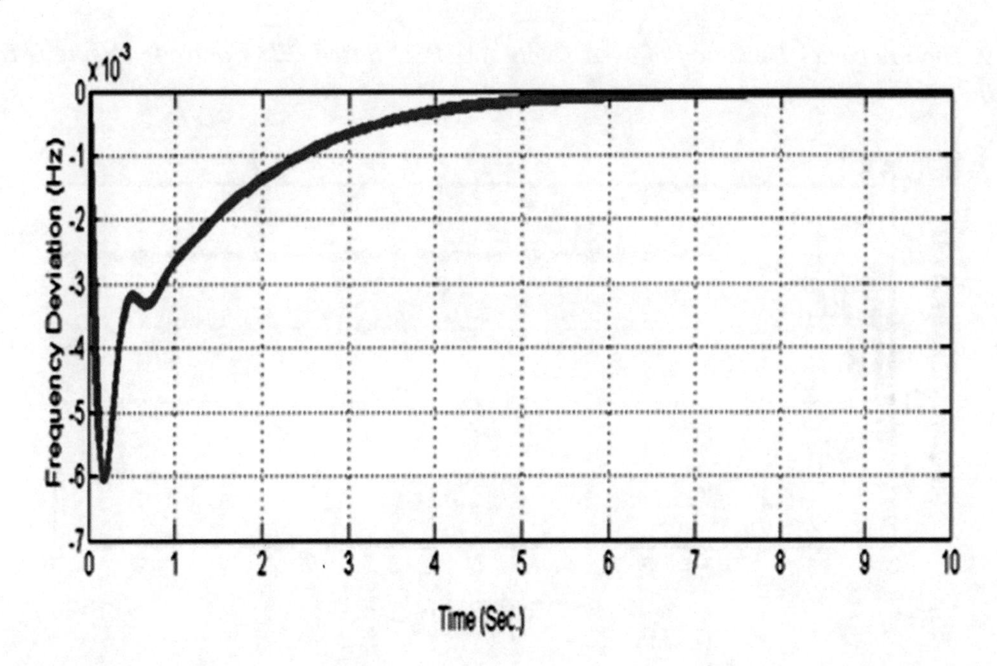

5. The difference between the value of settling time using MAACPSO and the nearest value using AACPSO is equal approximately 1.04 sec.
6. The value of settling time of the tie line using MAACPSO technique is the smallest compared to all methods used.
7. The difference between the values of settling time of the tie line using MAACPSO technique is less than the nearest value of settling time using AAPSO by approximately 1.08 sec.

Figure 8. The Frequency Deviation of Area 1 with AWPSO Based PID Controller Using IAE Performance Indices

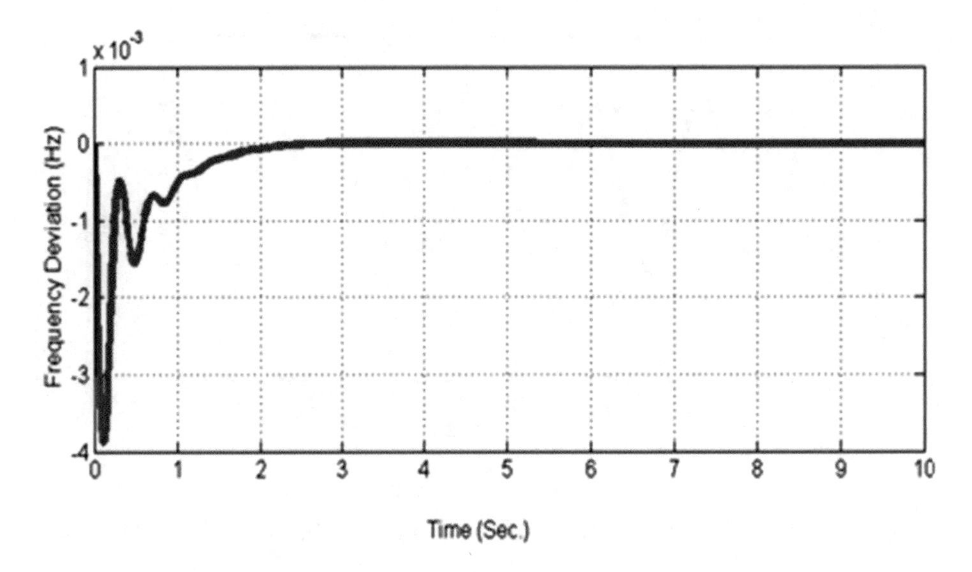

Figure 9. The Frequency Deviation of Area 1 with AACPSO Based PID Controller Using IAE Performance Indices

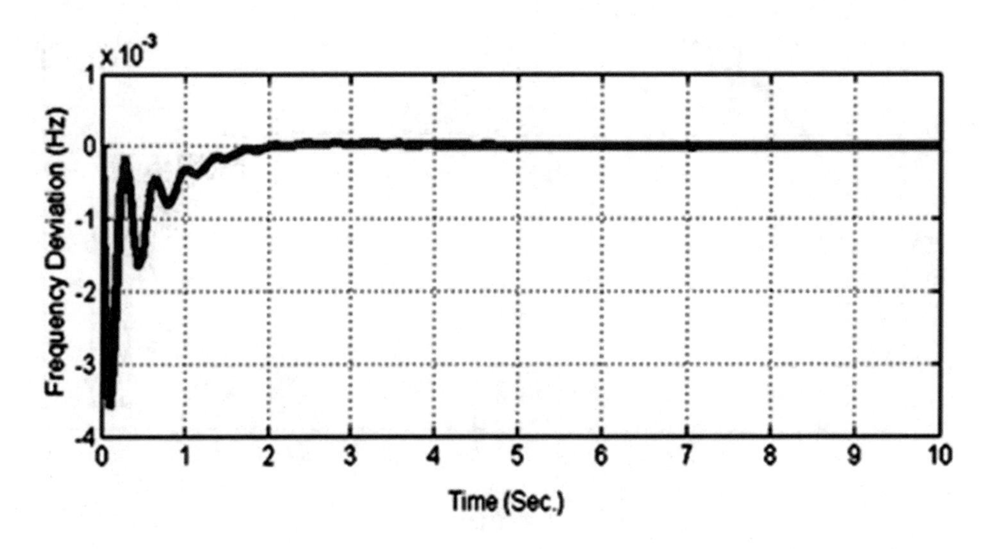

In the following sections, there is Table 4 and Figure 15 of Tie Line which describes the effects of using different techniques.

Table 5 shows Comparison of the value of Overshoot (Hz) and settling time (sec.) of the best two methods used MAACPSO and AACPSO.

The illustrated results in Table 5 and Figure 15 show that:

Figure 10. The Frequency Deviation of Area 1 with MAACPSO Based PID Controller Using IAE Performance Indices

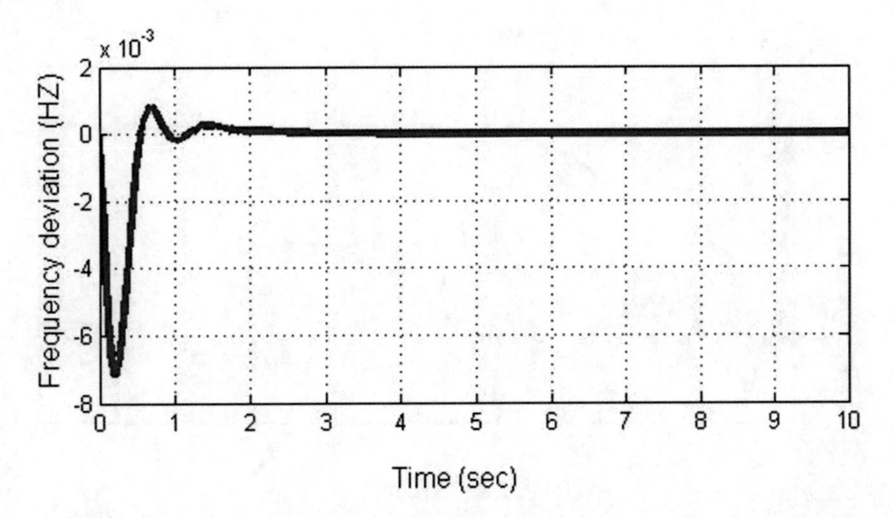

Figure 11. The Frequency Deviation of Area 2 with PSO Based PID Controller Using IAE Performance Indices

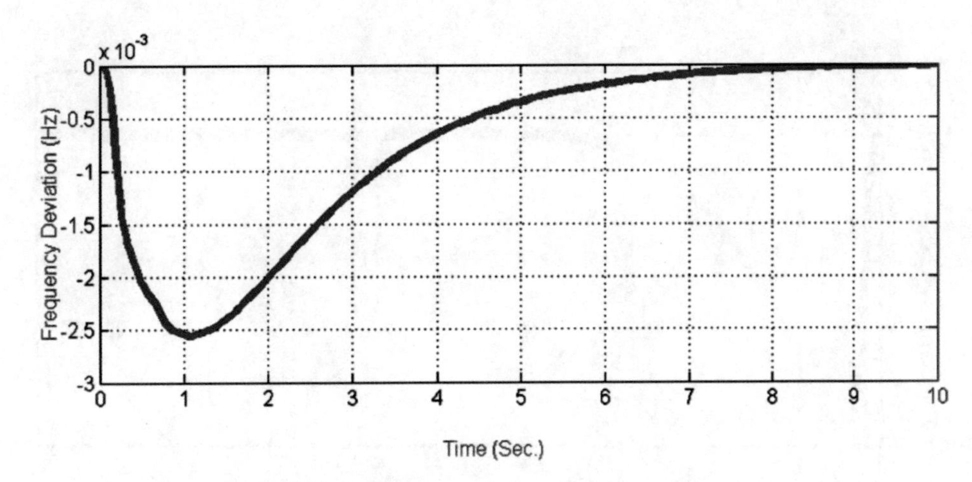

1. Table 4 and Table 5 indicate that on the Tie line power, the value of settling time in case of using MAACPSO is the best results and has a smaller value comparing with the other methods used (PSO, AWPSO and AACPSO).
2. The settling time of Tie line in case of using MAACPSO is less than its value in case of using AACPSO by about 1.5 seconds, and less than its value when using AWPSO by about 1.6 seconds.
3. Settling time by AWPSO is smaller than using PSO by 0.0359 seconds.
4. The maximum frequency of Tie line power in case of using MAACPSO is less than its value of the other methods of controller used by a very small value.
5. In general the maximum frequency of Tie line power is construed to be zero.

Figure 12. The Frequency Deviation of Area 2 with AWPSO Based PID Controller Using IAE Performance Indices

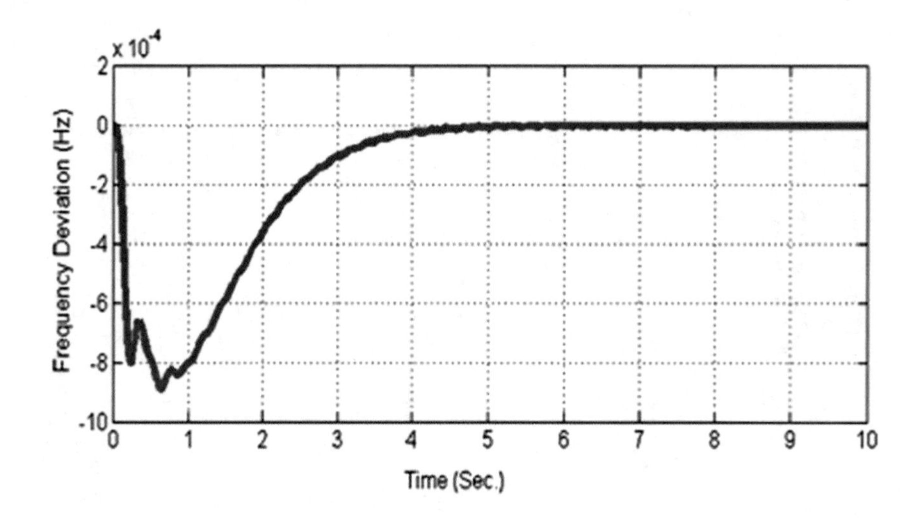

Figure 13. The Frequency Deviation of Area 2 with AACPSO Based PID Controller Using IAE Performance Indices

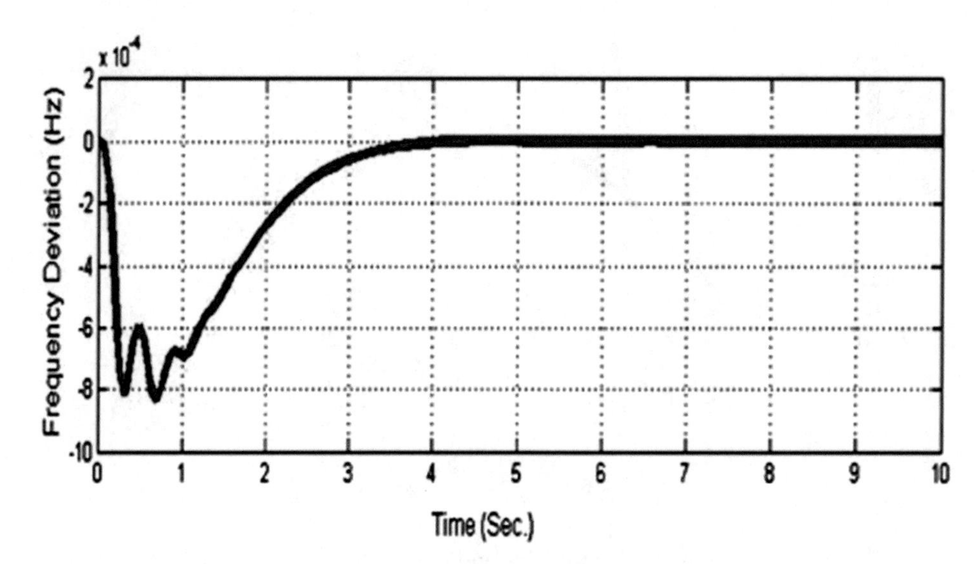

6. Time at maximum power in case of using MAACPSO is less than the its value by using AACPSO by about 8%, and the value of that time by using AACPSO is less than the other values of PSO and AWPSO. This value is less than the time of maximum power in case of using PSO by about 23.4% and less than its value in case of using AWPSO by about 21.5% .
7. The minimum Tie line power in case of using MAACPSO is very small comparing with another methods, and its value in case of using AWPSO and AACPSO are almost equal and less than its value in case of using PSO.

Figure 14. The Frequency Deviation of Area 2 with MAACPSO Based PID Controller Using IAE Performance Indices

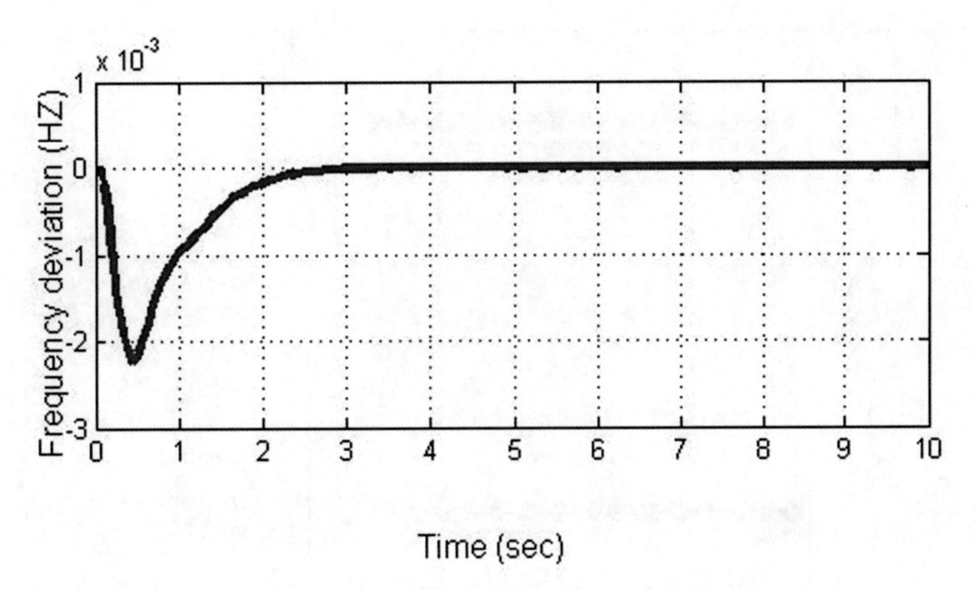

Table 4. Tie line behavior at different typed of control

Items of comparison	PSO	AWPSO	AACPSO	MAACPSO
Settling time _Tie line (sec.)	7.7624	4.2082	3.6553	2.5696
Maximum frequency of Tie line power (Hz)	3.00E-07	4.24E-07	1.06E-06	4.98E-07
Time at Maximum frequency of Tie line power (sec.)	20.502	22.2727	4.8003	4.0135
Minimum frequency of Tie line power (Hz)	-0.0011	-3.66E-04	-3.20E-04	-9.13E-04
Time at minimum frequency of Tie line power (sec.)	1.0319	0.612	0.5743	0.442

8. Time at minimum power in case of using MAACPSO is less than the other values of PSO, AWPSO and AACPSO.
9. The Overshoot and settling time of area 1 by using MAACPSO is greater than that values by using AACPSO by a very small value.
10. The Overshoot and settling time of area 2 by using MAACPSO is smaller than that values by using AACPSO.
11. The Overshoot and settling time of tie line by using MAACPSO is very small than that values by using AACPSO.

All these results present that: the best method used to reach the minimum value of settling time is MAACPSO and AACPSO comes next.

Figure 15. Displays the Frequency Change of the Tie Line Power with Using PSO, AWPSO and AAPSO Based PID Controller

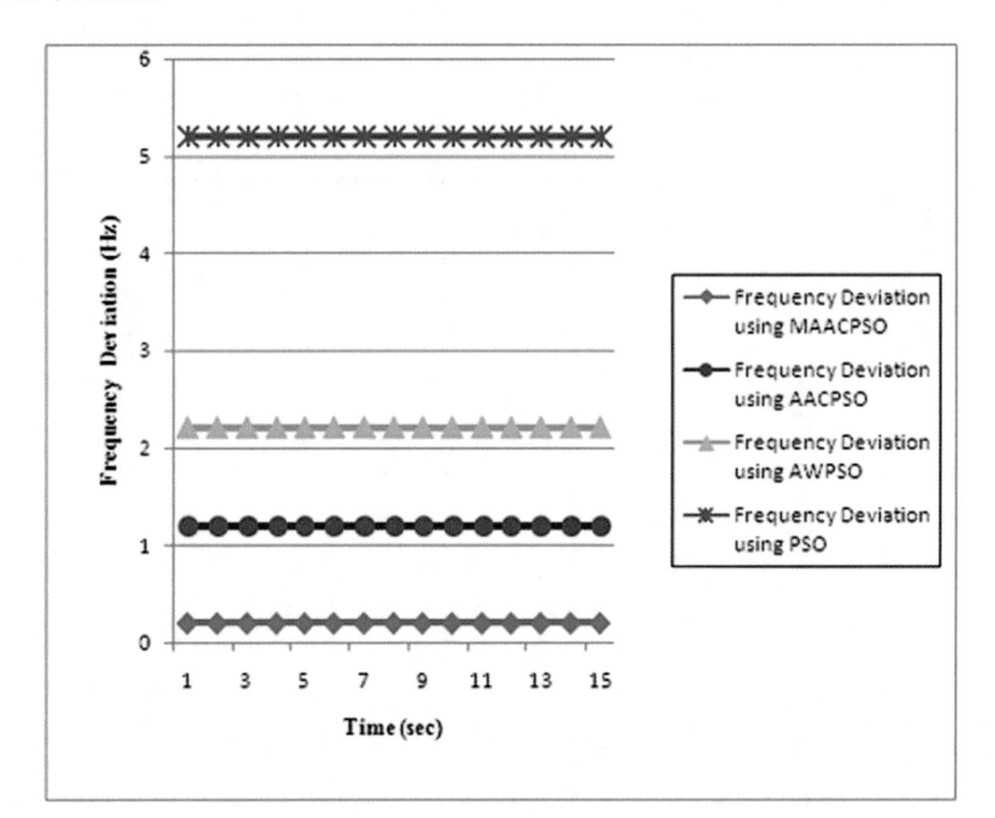

Table 5. Comparison between (MAACPSO) and (AACPSO)

Controller	Overshoot (Hz)	Settling Time (Sec.)
MAACPSO with IAE on Aera 1	5.5E-05	1.7267
AACPSO with IAE on Aera 1	4.10E-05	1.6514
MAACPSO with IAE on Aera 2	2.2E-03	2.5288
AACPSO with IAE on Aera 2	4.14E-06	3.6553
MAACPSO with IAE on tie line	4.98E-07	2.5696
AACPSO with IAE on tie line	1.06E-06	3.6553

5. CONCLUSION

The evolutionary technique explained in this chapter of the proposed controllers indicate that the Modified Adaptive Accelerated Coefficients based on PSO (MAACPSO) is the best method comparing with all other techniques used in this chapter. Then AACPSO comes next. The value of the settling time of area 1 using MAACPSO is near its value by using AACPSO, as shown from the results the difference was 0.07 sec, which is very small value. While the settling time in area 2 by using MAACPSO gives a value smaller than the value using AACPSO, the difference about 1.13 sec, this is a very good result of MAACPSO. The settling time in tie line using MAACPSO gives very good value comparing with AACPSO, the difference was about 1.08 sec., as shown in Table 4 and Table 5 the frequency deviation values of area 1 of the best two methods MAACPSO and AACPSO was nearly equal, and the value using MAACPSO of tie tine is smaller than its value using AACPSO by about 5.6E-7 Hz.

As a future work it's recommended to complete this study by studding the load frequency control for many different areas more than two areas connected together by using the modern techniques like MAACPSO and make a comparison between the results of settling time and overshoot frequency which obtained using some techniques like Fuzzy, Adaptive Neuro-Fuzzy or other modern techniques.

REFERENCES

Abu-Seada, H. F., Mansor, W. M., Bendary, F. M., Emery, A. A., & Hassan, M. M. (2013). Application of Particle Swarm Optimization in Design of PID Controller for AVR System. *International Journal of System Dynamics Applications*, *2*(3), 1–17. doi:10.4018/ijsda.2013070101

Ahmed, S., Tarek, B., & Djemai, N. (2013). Economic Dispatch Resolution using Adaptive Accelerated Coefficients based PSO considering Generator Constraints. *International Conference on Control, Decision and Information Technologies (CoDIT'13).*

Ali, A., Ebrahim, M.A., & Hassan, M.M. (2015). Control of Single Area Power System Based on Evolutionary Computation Techniques. *MEPCON*, *16*, 19.

Ali, A. M., Ebrahim, M. A., & Hassan, M. M. (2016). Automatic Voltage Generation Control for Two Area Power System Based on Particle Swarm Optimization. *Indonesian Journal of Electrical Engineering and Computer Science*, *2*(1), 132–144. doi:10.11591/ijeecs.v2.i1.pp132-144

Amjady, N., & Nasiri-Rad, H. (2009). Nonconvex economic dispatch with AC constraints by a new real coded genetic algorithm. *Power Systems' IEEE Transactions on*, *24*(3), 1489–1502.

Ang, K. H., Chong, G. C. Y., & Li, Y. P. I. D. (2005). Control system analysis, design, and technology. *IEEE Transactions on Control Systems Technology*, *13*(4), 559–576. doi:10.1109/TCST.2005.847331

Azar, A. T. (2010). Adaptive Neuro-Fuzzy Systems. In A. T. Azar (Ed.), *Fuzzy Systems*. Vienna, Austria: IN-TECH. doi:10.5772/7220

Azar, A. T. (2010). *Fuzzy Systems*. IN-TECH.

Azar, A. T. (2012a). System Dynamics as a Useful Technique for Complex Systems. *International Journal of Industrial and Systems Engineering*, *10*(4), 377–410. doi:10.1504/IJISE.2012.046298

Azar, A. T. (2012b). Overview of Type-2 Fuzzy logic systems. *International Journal of Fuzzy System Applications*, *2*(4), 1–28.

Azar, A.T., & El-Said, S.A. (2013). Superior Neuro-Fuzzy Classification Systems. *Neural Computing and Applications, 23*(1), 55-72. DOI: 10.1007/s00521-012-1231-8

Azar, A. T., Kumar, J., Kumar, V., & Rana, K. P. S. (2017d). Control of a Two Link Planar Electrically-Driven Rigid Robotic Manipulator Using Fractional Order SOFC. *Proceedings of the International Conference on Advanced Intelligent Systems and Informatics 2017, 639*, 47-56.

Azar, A. T., Ouannas, A., & Singh, S. (2017c). Control of New Type of Fractional Chaos Synchronization. *Proceedings of the International Conference on Advanced Intelligent Systems and Informatics 2017, 639*, 47-56.

Azar, A.T., & Serrano, F.E. (2014). Robust IMC-PID tuning for cascade control systems with gain and phase margin specifications. *Neural Computing and Applications, 25*(5), 983-995. DOI .10.1007/s00521-014-1560-x

Azar, A. T., & Serrano, F. E. (2015a). Adaptive Sliding mode control of the Furuta pendulum. In Advances and Applications in Sliding Mode Control systems (vol. 576, pp. 1-42). Springer-Verlag GmbH Berlin/Heidelberg. doi:10.1007/978-3-319-11173-5_1

Azar, A. T., & Serrano, F. E. (2015b). Deadbeat Control for Multivariable Systems with Time Varying Delays. In Chaos Modeling and Control Systems Design (vol. 581, pp. 97-132). Springer-Verlag GmbH Berlin/Heidelberg. DOI doi:10.1007/978-3-319-13132-0_6

Azar, A. T., & Serrano, F. E. (2015c). Design and Modeling of Anti Wind Up PID Controllers. In Complex system modelling and control through intelligent soft computations (vol. 319, pp. 1-44). Springer-Verlag. . 1. doi:10.1007/978-3-319-12883-2_1

Azar, A. T., & Serrano, F. E. (2015d). Stabilization and Control of Mechanical Systems with Backlash. In Advanced Intelligent Control Engineering and Automation. IGI Global. doi:10.4018/978-1-4666-7248-2.ch001

Azar, A. T., & Serrano, F. E. (2016a). Robust control for asynchronous switched nonlinear systems with time varying delays. *Proceedings of the International Conference on Advanced Intelligent Systems and Informatics 2016*, 533, 891-899. 10.1007/978-3-319-48308-5_85

Azar, A. T., & Serrano, F. E. (2016b). Stabilization of Mechanical Systems with Backlash by PI Loop Shaping. *International Journal of System Dynamics Applications*, *5*(3), 20–47. doi:10.4018/IJSDA.2016070102

Azar, A. T., & Vaidyanathan, S. (2015a). *Chaos Modeling and Control Systems Design, Studies in Computational Intelligence* (Vol. 581). Springer-Verlag.

Azar, A. T., & Vaidyanathan, S. (2015b). *Computational Intelligence applications in Modeling and Control. Studies in Computational Intelligence* (Vol. 575). Springer-Verlag.

Azar, A. T., & Vaidyanathan, S. (2015c). Handbook of Research on Advanced Intelligent Control Engineering and Automation. IGI Global. doi:10.4018/978-1-4666-7248-2

Azar, A. T., & Vaidyanathan, S. (2016). *Advances in Chaos Theory and Intelligent Control. Studies in Fuzziness and Soft Computing* (Vol. 337). Springer-Verlag. doi:10.1007/978-3-319-30340-6

Azar, A. T., Vaidyanathan, S., & Ouannas, A. (2017a). *Fractional Order Control and Synchronization of Chaotic Systems. Studies in Computational Intelligence* (Vol. 688). Springer-Verlag. doi:10.1007/978-3-319-50249-6

Azar, A.T., Volos, C., Gerodimos, N.A., Tombras, G.S., Pham, V.T., Radwan, A.G., … Munoz-Pacheco, J.M. (2017b). A novel chaotic system without equilibrium: Dynamics, synchronization and circuit realization. *Complexity*. doi:10.1155/2017/7871467

Azar, A. T., & Zhu, Q. (2015). *Advances and Applications in Sliding Mode Control systems. Studies in Computational Intelligence* (Vol. 576). Springer-Verlag.

Bevrani, H. (2009). *Robust power system frequency control*. Brisbane, Australia: Springer Science and Business Media, LLC. doi:10.1007/978-0-387-84878-5

Boulkroune, A., Bouzeriba, A., Bouden, T., & Azar, A. T. (2016a). Fuzzy Adaptive Synchronization of Uncertain Fractional-order Chaotic Systems. In A. T. Azar & S. Vaidyanathan (Eds.), *Advances in Chaos Theory and Intelligent Control. Studies in Fuzziness and Soft Computing* (Vol. 337). Springer-Verlag. doi:10.1007/978-3-319-30340-6_28

Boulkroune, A., Hamel, S., & Azar, A. T. (2016b). *Fuzzy control-based function synchronization of unknown chaotic systems with dead-zone input. Advances in Chaos Theory and Intelligent Control. Studies in Fuzziness and Soft Computing* (Vol. 337). Springer-Verlag.

Darrell, W. (2005). *A Genetic Algorithm Tutorial* [Report]. Computer Science Department, Colorado State University.

Fakhry, A. M., Ammar, M. E., & Hassan, M. M. (2016). Two Area Load Frequency Control Based On Evolutionary. *Computing Techniques*.

Gaing, Z. L. (2004). 'A Particle Swarm Optimization approach for optimum design of PID controller in AVR system. *Energy Conversion. IEEE Transactions on*, *19*(2), 384–391.

Ghoudelbourk, S., Dib, D., Omeiri, A., & Azar, A. T. (2016). MPPT Control in wind energy conversion systems and the application of fractional control (PIa) in pitch wind turbine. *International Journal of Modelling, Identification and Control*, *26*(2), 140–151. doi:10.1504/IJMIC.2016.078329

Grassi, G., Ouannas, A., Azar, A. T., Radwan, A. G., Volos, C., Pham, V. T., . . . Stouboulos, I. N. (2017). *Chaos Synchronisation Of Continuous Systems Via Scalar Signal*. The 6th International Conference on Modern Circuits and Systems Technologies (MOCAST), Thessaloniki, Greece. 10.1109/MOCAST.2017.7937629

Hamid, A., & Abdul-Rahman, T. K. (2010). Short Term Load Forecasting Using an Artificial Neural Network Trained by Artificial Immune System Learning Algorithm in Computer Modeling and Simulation (UKSim). *IEEE, 12th International Conference on*, 408-413.

Hassanien, A. E., Tolba, M., & Azar, A. T. (2014). *Advanced Machine Learning Technologies and Applications: Second International Conference, AMLTA 2014*. Springer-Verlag GmbH Berlin/Heidelberg. 10.1007/978-3-319-13461-1

Ismail, A. (2006). Improving UAE power systems control performance by using combined LFC and AVR. *7th UAE University Research Conference*, 50-60.

Ismail, M. M., & Moustafa Hassan, M. A. (2012). Load Frequency Control Adaptation Using Artificial Intelligent Techniques for One and Two Different Areas Power System. *International Journal of Control, Automation, and Systems*, *1*(1), 12–23.

Khalifa, F., Moustafa Hassan, M. A., Abul-Haggag, O., & Mahmoud, H. (2015). The Application of Evolutionary Computational Techniques in Medium Term Forecasting. In *MEPCON'2015*. Mansoura, Egypt: Mansoura University.

Kumar, D. V. (1998). Intelligent controllers for automatic generation control. *TENCON' 98. IEEE Region, 10 International Conference on Global Connectivity in Energy, Computer, Communication and Control*, *2*, 557-574.

Mansour. (2012). *Development of advanced controllers using adaptive weighted PSO algorithm with applications* (M.Sc. Thesis). Faculty of Engineering, Cairo University, Cairo, Egypt.

Meghni, B., Dib, D., & Azar, A. T. (2017c). A Second-order sliding mode and fuzzy logic control to Optimal Energy Management in PMSG Wind Turbine with Battery Storage. *Neural Computing & Applications*, *28*(6), 1417–1434. doi:10.100700521-015-2161-z

Meghni, B., Dib, D., Azar, A. T., Ghoudelbourk, S., & Saadoun, A. (2017a). *Robust Adaptive Supervisory Fractional order Controller For optimal Energy Management in Wind Turbine with Battery Storage. Studies in Computational Intelligence* (Vol. 688). Springer-Verlag.

Meghni, B., Dib, D., Azar, A. T., & Saadoun, A. (2017b). *Effective Supervisory Controller to Extend Optimal Energy Management in Hybrid Wind Turbine under Energy and Reliability Constraints. International Journal of Dynamics and Control*. Springer; doi:10.100740435-016-0296-0

Mekki, H., Boukhetala, D., & Azar, A. T. (2015). Sliding Modes for Fault Tolerant Control. In Advances and Applications in Sliding Mode Control systems (vol. 576, pp. 407-433). Springer-Verlag GmbH Berlin/Heidelberg. DOI doi:10.1007/978-3-319-11173-5_15

Mousa, M. E., Ebrahim, M. A., & Hassan, M. M. (2015). Stabilizing and swinging-up the inverted pendulum using PI and PID controllers based on reduced linear quadratic regulator tuned by PSO. *International Journal of System Dynamics Applications*, *4*(4), 52–69. doi:10.4018/IJSDA.2015100104

Naglaa & Hassan. (2016). Swarm Intelligence PID Controller Tuning for AVR System. Springer-Verlag.

Naglaa, K., Bahgaat, El-Sayed, M.I., Moustafa Hassan, M.A., & Bendary, F.A. (2013). Artificial Intelligence Based Controller for Load Frequency Control in Power System. *Al-Azhar University Engineering sector*, *8*(28), 1215-1226.

Naglaa, K., Bahgaat, El-Sayed, M.I., Moustafa Hassan, M.A., & Bendary, F.A. (2014a). Load Frequency Control in Power System via Improving PID Controller Based on Particle Swarm Optimization and ANFIS Techniques. *International Journal of System Dynamics Applications*.

Naglaa, K., Bahgaat, El-Sayed, M.I., Moustafa Hassan, M.A., & Bendary, F.A. (2014b). Control of Load Frequency on Power System Based on Particle Swarm Optimization Techniques and ANFIS. *Al-Azhar University Engineering sector*, *9*(30), 287-294.

Naglaa, K., Bahgaat, El-Sayed, M.I., Moustafa Hassan, M.A., & Bendary, F.A. (2015). Application of Some Modern Techniques in Load Frequency Control in Power Systems. Chaos Modeling and Control Systems Design, 581, 163-211.

Naglaa, K., Bahgaat, El-Sayed, M.I., Moustafa Hassan, M.A., & Bendary, F.A. (2015). Application of Some Modern Techniques in Load Frequency Control in Power Systems. In Computational Intelligence applications in Modeling and Control. Springer-Verlag.

Naglaa, K., Bahgaat, El-Sayed, M.I., Moustafa Hassan, M.A., & Bendary, F.A. (2016). Load Frequency Control Based on Evolutionary Techniques in Electrical Power Systems. Springer-Verlag.

Naglaa, K., Bahgaat, El-Sayed, M.I., Moustafa Hassan, M.A., & Bendary, F.A. (2014). Load Frequency Control in Power System via Improving PID Controller Based on Particle Swarm Optimization and ANFIS Techniques. *International Journal of System Dynamics Applications, 3*(3), 1-24.

Naik, R.S., ChandraSekhar, K., & Vaisakh, K. (2005). Adaptive PSO based optimal fuzzy controller design for AGC equipped with SMES and SPSS. *Journal of Theoretical and Applied Information Technology, 7*(1), 8-17.

Ouannas, A., Azar, A. T., & Abu-Saris, R. (2016a). A new type of hybrid synchronization between arbitrary hyperchaotic maps. *International Journal of Machine Learning and Cybernetics*. doi:10.100713042-016-0566-3

Ouannas, A., Azar, A. T., & Radwan, A. G. (2016b). *On Inverse Problem of Generalized Synchronization Between Different Dimensional Integer-Order and Fractional-Order Chaotic Systems*. The 28th International Conference on Microelectronics, Cairo, Egypt. 10.1109/ICM.2016.7847942

Ouannas, A., Azar, A. T., & Vaidyanathan, S. (2017f). On A Simple Approach for Q-S Synchronization of Chaotic Dynamical Systems in Continuous-Time. Int. J. *Computing Science and Mathematics*, *8*(1), 20–27.

Ouannas, A., Azar, A. T., & Vaidyanathan, S. (2017g). New Hybrid Synchronization Schemes Based on Coexistence of Various Types of Synchronization Between Master-Slave Hyperchaotic Systems. *International Journal of Computer Applications in Technology*, *55*(2), 112–120. doi:10.1504/IJCAT.2017.082868

Ouannas, A., Azar, A. T., & Vaidyanathan, S. (2017i). A Robust Method for New Fractional Hybrid Chaos Synchronization. *Mathematical Methods in the Applied Sciences*, *40*(5), 1804–1812. doi:10.1002/mma.4099

Ouannas, A., Azar, A. T., & Ziar, T. (2017h). *On Inverse Full State Hybrid Function Projective Synchronization for Continuous-time Chaotic Dynamical Systems with Arbitrary Dimensions*. Differential Equations and Dynamical Systems. doi:10.100712591-017-0362-x

Ouannas, A., Azar, A. T., Ziar, T., & Radwan, A. G. (2017d). *Study On Coexistence of Different Types of Synchronization Between Different dimensional Fractional Chaotic Systems. Studies in Computational Intelligence* (Vol. 688). Springer-Verlag.

Ouannas, A., Azar, A. T., Ziar, T., & Radwan, A. G. (2017e). *Generalized Synchronization of Different Dimensional Integer-order and Fractional Order Chaotic Systems. Studies in Computational Intelligence* (Vol. 688). Springer-Verlag.

Ouannas, A., Azar, A. T., Ziar, T., & Vaidyanathan, S. (2017a). *On New Fractional Inverse Matrix Projective Synchronization Schemes. Studies in Computational Intelligence* (Vol. 688). Springer-Verlag.

Ouannas, A., Azar, A. T., Ziar, T., & Vaidyanathan, S. (2017b). *Fractional Inverse Generalized Chaos Synchronization Between Different Dimensional Systems. Studies in Computational Intelligence* (Vol. 688). Springer-Verlag.

Ouannas, A., Azar, A. T., Ziar, T., & Vaidyanathan, S. (2017c). *A New Method To Synchronize Fractional Chaotic Systems With Different Dimensions. Studies in Computational Intelligence* (Vol. 688). Springer-Verlag.

Ouannas, A., Grassi, G., Azar, A. T., Radwan, A. G., Volos, C., Pham, V. T., . . . Stouboulos, I. N. (2017j). *Dead-Beat Synchronization Control in Discrete-Time Chaotic Systems.* The 6th International Conference on Modern Circuits and Systems Technologies (MOCAST), Thessaloniki, Greece. 10.1109/MOCAST.2017.7937628

Panigrahi, B. K., Ravikumar Pandi, V., & Das, S. (2008). Adaptive particle swarm optimization approach for static and dynamic economic load dispatch. *Energy Conversion and Management*, *49*(6), 1407–1415. doi:10.1016/j.enconman.2007.12.023

RamaSudha, K., Vakula, V.S., & Shanthi, R.V. (2010). PSO Based Design of Robust Controller for Two Area Load Frequency Control with Nonlinearities. *International Journal of Engineering Science*, *2*(5), 1311–1324.

Reeves, C. R., & Rowe, J. E. (2002). *Genetic algorithm Principles and perspective, A Guide to GA theory*. Kluwer Academic Publishers.

Salami, A., Jadid, S., & Ramezani, N. (2006). The Effect of load frequency controller on load pickup during restoration. *Power and Energy Conference, PECon'06, IEEE International*, 225-228. 10.1109/PECON.2006.346651

Salem, A., Hassan, M. M., & Ammar, M. E. (2014). Tuning PID Controllers Using Artificial Intelligence Techniques Applied To DC-Motor and AVR System. *Asian Journal of Engineering and Technology, 2*(2).

Singh, S., Azar, A. T., Ouannas, A., Zhu, Q., Zhang, W., & Na, J. (2017). Sliding Mode Control Technique for Multi-switching Synchronization of Chaotic Systems. *9th International Conference on Modelling, Identification and Control (ICMIC 2017)*, Kunming, China.

Skogestad, S. (2003). Simple analytic rules for model reduction and PID controller tuning. *Journal of Process Control*, *13*(4), 291–309. doi:10.1016/S0959-1524(02)00062-8

Soliman, N. S., Said, L. A., Azar, A. T., Madian, A. H., Radwan, A. G., & Ouannas, A. (2017). *Fractional Controllable Multi-Scroll V-Shape Attractor with Parameters Effect.* The 6th International Conference on Modern Circuits and Systems Technologies (MOCAST), Thessaloniki, Greece.

Tolba, M. F., AbdelAty, A. M., Soliman, N. S., Said, L. A., Madian, A. H., Azar, A. T., & Radwan, A. G. (2017). FPGA implementation of two fractional order chaotic systems. *International Journal of Electronics and Communications*, *28*, 162–172. doi:10.1016/j.aeue.2017.04.028

Vaidyanathan, S., & Azar, A. T. (2015a) Anti-Synchronization of Identical Chaotic Systems using Sliding Mode Control and an Application to Vaidyanathan-Madhavan Chaotic Systems. In Advances and Applications in Sliding Mode Control systems. Springer-Verlag GmbH Berlin/Heidelberg. doi:10.1007/978-3-319-11173-5_19

Vaidyanathan, S., & Azar, A. T. (2015b) Hybrid Synchronization of Identical Chaotic Systems using Sliding Mode Control and an Application to Vaidyanathan Chaotic Systems. In Advances and Applications in Sliding Mode Control systems. Springer-Verlag GmbH Berlin/Heidelberg. DOI doi:10.1007/978-3-319-11173-5_20

Vaidyanathan, S., & Azar, A. T. (2015c). Analysis, Control and Synchronization of a Nine-Term 3-D Novel Chaotic System. In Chaos Modeling and Control Systems Design. Springer-Verlag GmbH Berlin/Heidelberg. DOI doi:10.1007/978-3-319-13132-0_1

Vaidyanathan, S., & Azar, A. T. (2015d). Analysis and Control of a 4-D Novel Hyperchaotic System. In Chaos Modeling and Control Systems Design. Springer-Verlag GmbH Berlin/Heidelberg. DOI doi:10.1007/978-3-319-13132-0_2

Vaidyanathan, S., & Azar, A. T. (2016a). Takagi-Sugeno Fuzzy Logic Controller for Liu-Chen Four-Scroll Chaotic System. *International Journal of Intelligent Engineering Informatics*, *4*(2), 135–150. doi:10.1504/IJIEI.2016.076699

Vaidyanathan, S., & Azar, A. T. (2016b). *Dynamic Analysis, Adaptive Feedback Control and Synchronization of an Eight-Term 3-D Novel Chaotic System with Three Quadratic Nonlinearities. Studies in Fuzziness and Soft Computing* (Vol. 337). Springer-Verlag.

Vaidyanathan, S., & Azar, A. T. (2016c). *Qualitative Study and Adaptive Control of a Novel 4-D Hyperchaotic System with Three Quadratic Nonlinearities. Studies in Fuzziness and Soft Computing* (Vol. 337). Springer-Verlag.

Vaidyanathan, S., & Azar, A. T. (2016d). *A Novel 4-D Four-Wing Chaotic System with Four Quadratic Nonlinearities and its Synchronization via Adaptive Control Method. Advances in Chaos Theory and Intelligent Control. Studies in Fuzziness and Soft Computing* (Vol. 337). Springer-Verlag.

Vaidyanathan, S., & Azar, A. T. (2016e). *Adaptive Control and Synchronization of Halvorsen Circulant Chaotic Systems. Advances in Chaos Theory and Intelligent Control. Studies in Fuzziness and Soft Computing* (Vol. 337). Springer-Verlag.

Vaidyanathan, S., & Azar, A. T. (2016f). *Adaptive Backstepping Control and Synchronization of a Novel 3-D Jerk System with an Exponential Nonlinearity. Advances in Chaos Theory and Intelligent Control. Studies in Fuzziness and Soft Computing* (Vol. 337). Springer-Verlag.

Vaidyanathan, S., & Azar, A. T. (2016g). *Generalized Projective Synchronization of a Novel Hyperchaotic Four-Wing System via Adaptive Control Method. Advances in Chaos Theory and Intelligent Control. Studies in Fuzziness and Soft Computing* (Vol. 337). Springer-Verlag.

Vaidyanathan, S., Azar, A. T., & Ouannas, A. (2017a). *An Eight-Term 3-D Novel Chaotic System with Three Quadratic Nonlinearities, its Adaptive Feedback Control and Synchronization. Studies in Computational Intelligence* (Vol. 688). Springer-Verlag.

Vaidyanathan, S., Azar, A. T., & Ouannas, A. (2017c). *Hyperchaos and Adaptive Control of a Novel Hyperchaotic System with Two Quadratic Nonlinearities. Studies in Computational Intelligence* (Vol. 688). Springer-Verlag.

Vaidyanathan, S., Azar, A. T., Rajagopal, K., & Alexander, P. (2015b). Design and SPICE implementation of a 12-term novel hyperchaotic system and its synchronization via active control (2015). *International Journal of Modelling, Identification and Control, 23*(3), 267–277. doi:10.1504/IJMIC.2015.069936

Vaidyanathan, S., Idowu, B. A., & Azar, A. T. (2015c) Backstepping Controller Design for the Global Chaos Synchronization of Sprott's Jerk Systems. In Chaos Modeling and Control Systems Design. Springer-Verlag GmbH Berlin/Heidelberg. doi:10.1007/978-3-319-13132-0_3

Vaidyanathan, S., Sampath, S., & Azar, A. T. (2015a). Global chaos synchronisation of identical chaotic systems via novel sliding mode control method and its application to Zhu system. *International Journal of Modelling, Identification and Control, 23*(1), 92–100. doi:10.1504/IJMIC.2015.067495

Vaidyanathan, S., Zhu, Q., & Azar, A. T. (2017b). *Adaptive Control of a Novel Nonlinear Double Convection Chaotic System. Studies in Computational Intelligence* (Vol. 688). Springer-Verlag.

Wang, Z., Volos, C., Kingni, S.T., Azar, A.T., & Pham, V.T. (2017). Four-wing attractors in a novel chaotic system with hyperbolic sine nonlinearity. *Optik - International Journal for Light and Electron Optics, 131*(2017), 1071-1078.

Zhu, Q., & Azar, A. T. (2015). *Complex system modelling and control through intelligent soft computations. Studies in Fuzziness and Soft Computing* (Vol. 319). Springer-Verlag.

APPENDIX

Transmission line 1 parameters

Kg1=1
Kt1=1
Tg1=0.08
Tt1=20
R1=2.4
T11=20
Kl1=120
a12=1

Transmission line 2 parameters

Kg2=1
Kt2=1
Tg2=0.08
Tt2=0.33
R2=2.4
T12=20
Kl2=120
N = 25 number of swarm beings
d = 6 two dimensional problem
n = 500 number of iterations
W0 = 0.15 percentage of old velocity
A0 = 0.5 Acceleration factor constant between [0 1]
C1 = 2.05 percentage towards personal optimum
C2 = 2.05 percentage towards
x0range = [0 10] range of uniform initial distributon of positions
vstddev = 1 std. deviation of initial velocities
C11 = 2 percentage towards personal optimum used in ACC
C22 = 2.05 percentage towards used in ACC

Chapter 7
A Position Control With a Field Programmable Gate Array-Sun-Tracking System for Photovoltaic Panels

Saber Krim
University of Monastir, Tunisia

Soufien Gdaim
University of Monastir, Tunisia

Abdellatif Mtibaa
University of Monastir, Tunisia

Mimouni Mohamed Faouzi
National Engineering School of Monastir, Tunisia

ABSTRACT

Photovoltaic system applications should operate under good conditions. The maximum power point depends on the sunlight angle on the panel surface. In this chapter, an induction motor (IM) controlled with a direct torque control (DTC) is used to control the photovoltaic panel position. The conventional DTC is chosen thanks to its capability to develop the maximum of torque when the motor is standstill. However, the DTC produces a torque with high ripples and it is suffer from the flux demagnetization phenomenon, especially at low speed. To overcome these problems, two DTC approaches are proposed in this chapter: (1) the DTC based on the fuzzy logic and (2) the DTC based on space vector modulation (SVM) and proportional integral (PI) controllers (DTC-SVM-PI). The suggested approaches are implemented on a field programmable gate array (FPGA) Virtex 5 circuit in order to reduce the sampling period of the system and the delay in the control loop. The simulation and hardware implementation results demonstrate that the DTC-SVM-PI offers best the results in terms of ripples.

DOI: 10.4018/978-1-5225-4077-9.ch007

INTRODUCTION

The induction motor drive is widely used in several industrial applications, such as the elevators, pumps, electric vehicle, steel and cement mills, chip propulsion, fans, and subway transportation, etc., thanks to its low cost, mechanical robustness and low rate of maintenance relative to the DC motors, several information about the induction motor can be found in Bimal (2002) and Enany et al. (2014). The DC motor disadvantages are the high cost, the important rate of maintenance due to the existence of the brushes and commutators, see Bimal (2002). However, from control point of view, the induction motor is considered as the one of the most challenging topics. The control of the induction motor is complex because its dynamic is nonlinear, multivariable, and highly coupled. Recently, several control strategies are utilized to control the induction motor drive, like the scalar control, Field Oriented Control (FOC) and the Direct Torque Control (DTC). The scalar control has been widely used to industry thanks to its easy implementation. The major drawback of the scalar control is the poor performance during transients. However, the importance of this control approach is diminished recently because of the superior performance offered by the FOC approach, as given in Bimal (2002). According to the Takahashi & Noguchi (1986), Baader et al. (1992) the DTC on AC drives was developed by Takahashi in 1986 and then by Depenbrock in 1992. The DTC is featured by its simple structure relative to the FOC, as given in Ai et al. (2010) and Casadei et al. (2002). The DTC provides a high dynamic speed response and a good tracking control in the torque and the flux; see Lekhchine et al. (2013). With these strong points, the DTC can be considered as an alternative solution to replace the FOC in several industrial applications.

Traditionally, position control applications are based on a Permanent-Magnet Synchronous Motor (PMSM), as given in Vittek et al. (2005), Vittek et al. (2008), and Shin et al. (2012), thanks to its high efficiency, high torque and low inertia, as given in Tomohiro et al. (2014). The disadvantage of the PMSM is its high cost relative to the Induction Motor (IM). Thanks to the DTC, it is possible to use the IMs in position control applications. According to Rakesh (2003), The IM is more popular thanks to its robust performance, low maintenance and low cost. Utilizing an IM is equivalent to minimizing the cost of a control system.

Nowadays, the DTC has become the best candidate in several industrial applications especially where a high torque at a low speed range is required, in particular position control applications that require a maximum of torque when the motor is off, which favors the use of the DTC approach. Nevertheless, the basic DTC suffers from several drawbacks, like torque and flux ripples, stator current distortions, demagnetization problem at low speed, and commutation losses in the inverter. Referring to the researches works presented in Sivaprakasam & Manigandan (2013), Pham et al. (2016), Bhim et al. (2008), Atia (2009), and Rashag et al. (2013), these drawbacks are caused by the hysteresis controllers and the switching table used in its structure as well as the variation of the switching frequency. In fact, the conventional DTC uses two hysteresis controllers to control the torque and the stator flux. These controllers generate two states, which produce the same results for the small and the big error of the torque and the stator flux. As consequence, the generated switching states of the inverter cannot produce the best voltages vectors to make the flux and the torque errors both zero. This leads in ripples of torque and flux, and variations of the switching frequency as given in Kaboli et al. (2003), Sanila, (2012), Mohanty (2009), and Idris & Yatim (2004). Kang & Sul (2001) present an analysis of the switching frequency variation which is caused by the hysteresis band, the motor speed and torque slope. This leads in additional switching losses in the inverter.

During the last decade, a lot of modifications in conventional DTC scheme have been developed, including Casadei et al. (2000), Reddy et al. (2006), Chen et al. (2005), Grabowski et al. (2000), Romeral et al. (2003), and Ortega et al. (2005). The proposed modifications aimed to reduce the torque and flux ripples, the stator current distortions, the mechanical noises and avoid the variations of the inverter switching frequency, which consequently improves the motor performances especially at low speed operations and increases its service life. Kouro et al. (2007), Zhang et al. (2009), and Rahmati et al. (2011) propose an increasing of in the inverter levels to reduce the ripples. However, this rise consists in increasing the number of inverter switches, hence raising the system cost. Nevertheless, higher implementation cost would not be generally justified by an improvement in performance. Other studies for the DTC have been developed, like the combination between the multilevel inverter and the SVM, as presented in Wang et al. (2006), as well as the predictive control, see Uddin at al. (2014), in order to select the desired voltage vector, which provides a significant improvement in terms of ripples. In this case, the algorithm is based on a complex mathematical model that depends on several machine parameters, especially in applications with high-level inverters, as given in Rodriguez et al. (2003). According to Messaif et al. (2007), Zaimeddine & Undeland (2010), Escalante et al. (2002), and Gholinezhad & Noroozian (2012), the main technologies of a multilevel inverter used in industrial applications are the Neutral Point Clamped (NPC), the Flying Capacitors (FCs), and the Cascaded H-Bridge (CHB). Yet, using a multilevel inverter with an SVM, the system complexity increases, its reliability declines and the price goes up.

Many other researchers are oriented to combine the DTC and the space vector modulation to provide an operation with a constant frequency, including Taib et al. (2010), and Jidin et al. (2012). Zhang et al. (2013) present a DTC with space vector modulation to improve the DTC conventional DTC performances. This method internally contains a deadbeat controller that operates with torque and flux errors. It offers a good dynamic response of speed and torque and a reduction in distortion and ripples. On the other hand, the main limitation factor of this method is that it is computationally intensive. Other method is known as the oriented stator flux control, as given in Lai & Chen (2001). This method is based on two PI controllers, which provide good performances in terms of ripples. Nevertheless, the PI controllers used in the DTC-SVM structure are more suitable for the linear system and are sensitive to motor parameter variation and external disturbances and it is not easy to obtain the appropriate PI parameters. Nonlinear controls like the sliding mode control are proposed by several researchers to improve the systems performances, including Azar & Zhu (2015), Azar & Serrano (2015). Referring to Ahammad et al. (2013), and Bharatirajal et al. (2011), the modified DTC schemes based on Sliding Mode Controllers (SMCs) have been used to improve the DTC performances and reject perturbations. However, the main limitation of the sliding mode control is the chattering phenomenon, due to the discontinuous nature of the control law.

Nowadays, many researchers have used the intelligent and nonlinear techniques in several applications domain such as optimal control, nonlinear feedback control, adaptive control, sliding mode control, nonlinear dynamics, chaos control, chaos synchronization control, fuzzy logic control, fuzzy adaptive control, fractional order control, and robust control and their integrations (Azar & Vaidyanathan, 2015a,b,c, 2016; Azar & Zhu, 2015; Meghni et al, 2017a,b,c; Boulkroune et al, 2016a,b; Ghoudelbourk et al., 2016; Azar & Serrano, 2015a,b,c,d, 2016a,b, 2017; Azar et al., 2017a,b,c,d; Azar 2010, 2012; Mekki et al., 2015; Vaidyanathan & Azar, 2015a,b,c,d, 2016a,b,c,d,e,f,g, 2017a,b,c; Zhu & Azar, 2015; Grassi et al., 2017; Ouannas et al., 2016a,b, 2017a,b,c,d,e,f,g,h,I,j; Singh et al., 2017; Vaidyanathan et al, 2015a,b,c; Wang et al., 2017; Soliman et al., 2017; Tolba et al., 2017; Abdel Aziz et al., 2017; Ali & Hassan, 2012; El-Ghazaly, 2012; Abdel Aziz et al., 2016; Shereen et al., 2016). The Fuzzy Logic Control (FLC) based on the language rules can be used to solve the ripples problem of the DTC, as given in Youb

& Craciunescu (2009). Referring to Zidani & Said (2005), fuzzy logic uses the experience knowledge to release the rule base and it is based on intuition and simulation. It is more suitable for the imprecise processes and does not require any mathematical models (Azar, 2010a, b, 2012). Also, the FLS is a more effective technique when the system is based on a severely nonlinear mathematical model (Lokriti et al., 2013). The FLC has been proposed in several researches work to select the optimal voltage vectors in conventional DTC and improve the DTC performances, including Adam et al. (2007), Romeral et al. (2003), Liu et al. (2004) and Ismail (2012).

In this chapter, two DTC schemes are proposed for an IM position control, to overcome the conventional DTC limitations. The first one is defined by a combination between the DTC and the SVM with one PI controller of the torque and a predictive controller for the reference voltage vector components. This modified scheme offers an operation with a constant switching frequency which reduces considerably the ripples. The second one consists to use the Fuzzy Logic System (FLS) to replace the switching table and the hysteresis controllers. Referring to the conventional DTC scheme, the torque and the flux errors, and the stator flux vector position are fuzzified into several fuzzy subsets in order to select a more suitable space voltage vector to smooth the torque and flux ripples and control the switching frequency variations. With the Fuzzy DTC (FDTC) method, the transistors are only switched when it is needed which consequently reduces ripples and the inverter switching losses.

To improve the Photo-voltaic (PV) panel performances and efficiency, two main solutions are utilized. The first one consists to use the Maximum Power Point Tracking (MPPT) algorithms to control the DC/DC converter associated with the PV panel (Reisi et al., 2013; Babu et al., 2015; Hadji et al., 2014; Krim et al., 2015). The second solution consists to control the PV position to track the sun during the day which improves its efficiency. This solution is developed by Rhif (2014) utilizing a DC motor. The DC motors are very expensive relative to the IM and require an important rate of maintenance, which consequently increases the system const. In this chapter, the IM is chosen to control the PV panel position. A PV panel has two freedom degrees within latitudes and meridians. The first freedom degree is realized by a mechanical system entrained by an IM controlled with the DTC approach. The second freedom degree is realized according to the period of the year and the geographical site where the photovoltaic panel is located. This chapter consists in studying the first freedom degree. A comparative study between the proposed schemes is presented at the end of this chapter.

The second contribution of this chapter is to reduce the period of the system utilizing the FPGA because of its higher computation power. Nowadays, to make a marketing difference, the developed control systems must be highly performing and reliable at the same time; the system cost is a key issue as well. To reduce this cost, the time to market a control system must be shortened. It is too difficult to reduce this cost because these new control systems are based on control algorithms with high performances, which require a low execution time and a lot of computing resources. To cope with this problem and get a control with high performances, two main families of digital devices can be exploited by the designer. The first family integrates the software platform, like microcontrollers and Digital Signal Processor (DSP) controllers. These components integrate a microprocessor and several peripherals to communicate with the external environment. The microcontrollers include a 16-bit or 32- bit Reduced Instruction Set Computer (RISC) core and different peripherals, such as the ST Microcontrollers (STM32F3, STM32F4, STM32F1…), which can be utilized to control the electrical systems, as presented in Rao et al. (2016). The main limitation of these controllers is the computing power which allows fixing the sampling period. The DSP controller integrates a high performing processor core based on a hardware accelerator computing block and few peripherals. In the field of controlling an IM the digital signal processor dSPACE (dSPACE

1102(DSP TMS320), dSPACE 1103(DSP TMS320 F240), and dSPACE 1104 (DSP TMS320 F240)) is so much used, but the main limitations of this solution is the low processing speed due to sequential processing, this require a sampling more than 100us, as demonstrated in Boussak & Jarray (2006), Hmidet et al. (2010), and Abbou et al. (2012). The second family integrates the hardware platform like the Field Programmable Gate Arrays (FPGAs). As demonstrated in Monmasson et al. (2011), and Naouar et al. (2013), the FPGA is considered as a primordial solution for implementing control algorithms of electrical systems as the IM. The internal architecture of FPGAs consists of elementary cells that are interconnected by programming. Utilizing the VHSIC Hardware Description Language (VHDL) code, the end user builds the specific hardware architecture that matches the control algorithm. The FPGA is featured by parallel processing which lets the designer implement complex control algorithms in real time and with a very low execution time, as given in Monmasson & Cirstea (2007).

Configuring the FPGAs, a VHDL or Verilog is necessary, but programming a VHDL needs knowledge of VHDL instructions and an important development time; the same problem is for the Verilog code. To face out this problem, the Xilinx System Generator (XSG) tool is proposed in this chapter as a low-cost solution to design, simulate and automatically generate the VHDL or Verilog code with rapid prototyping and without any knowledge of the hardware description language (Bossoufi et al., 2015), The FPGA design methodology using the XSG tool is illustrated in Figure 1.

- After modular partitioning of the control algorithm, a functional simulation step must be realized, which consists in validating the algorithm functionality in a time-continuous mode utilizing a Matlab-Simulink environment.
- The digital redesign step redesigns the algorithm from the XSG in order to choose the sampling period and the fixed-point formats of coefficients and variables and to generate the VHDL code.
- The third step presents the VHDL code of the control algorithm, which is presented in the previous step.
- The fourth step presents the implementation on the FPGA, which maps, places, routes the algorithm design, and analyzes the performances in terms of execution time.
- The final step validates the control algorithm using the FPGA board, either a real or Hardware-In-the-Loop (HIL) system, as presented in Myaing and Dinavahi (2011).

In the rest of the chapter a fair comparative study between the DTC approaches is presented at zero speed and important torque. This comparison aims to indicate to the user which approach can be effectively used in controlling position applications. Moreover, this chapter aims also to illustrate the interest of FPGA devices for AC drive applications by presenting some practical examples utilizing an FPGA Virtex 5-ML507.

This chapter is organized as follows: Section 2 presents a mathematical model of the induction motor and the conventional DTC principle. Section 3 presents a simplified description of the DTC-SVM strategy. The principle of the DTC based on the fuzzy logic is presented in section 4. The architecture of the proposed DTC schemes from the XSG tool and the simulation results are presented in section 5. The implementation and the hardware co-simulation results are presented in sections 6 and 7, respectively. Section 8 presents the evaluation of the system cost. Finally, a conclusion is given in Section 9.

Figure 1. Design methodology

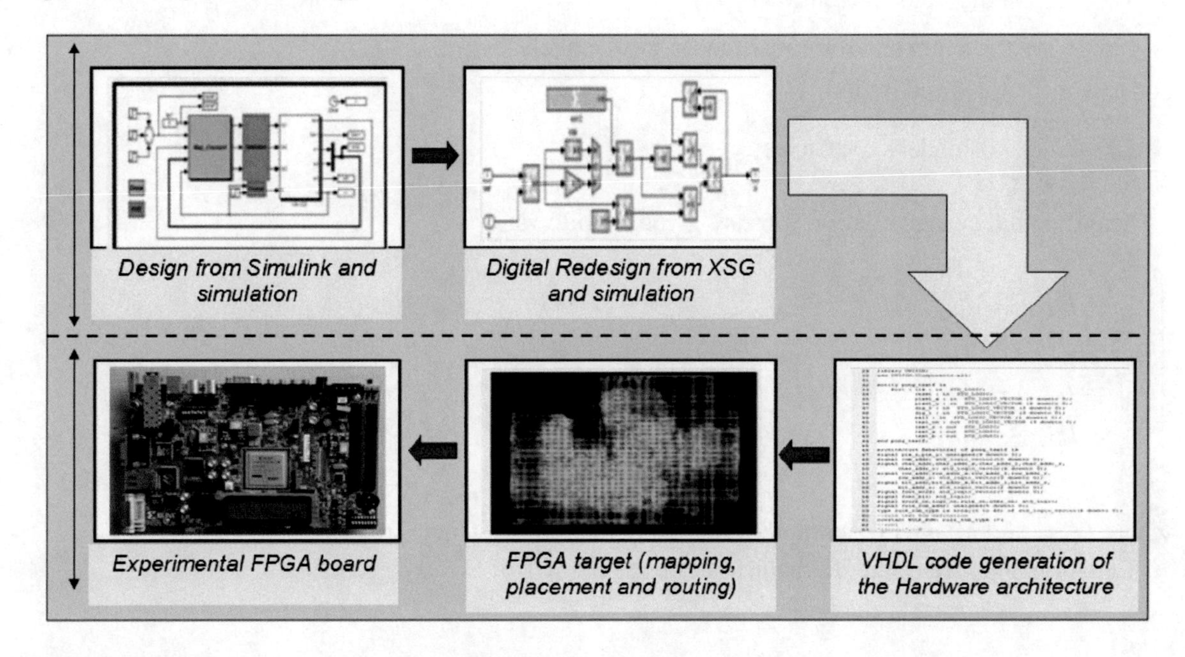

CONVENTIONAL DTC FORMULATION

In the (α, β) reference of Concordia, the IM model is described in system (1):

$$\begin{cases} \dot{i}_{s\alpha} = -\dfrac{1}{\sigma}\left(\dfrac{R_S}{L_S} + \dfrac{R_r}{L_r}\right) i_{s\alpha} - \omega i_{s\beta} + \dfrac{R_r}{\sigma L_r L_S}\varphi_{s\alpha} + \dfrac{\omega}{\sigma L_S}\varphi_{s\beta} + \dfrac{1}{\sigma L_S} v_{S\alpha} \\ \dot{i}_{S\beta} = \omega i_{s\alpha} - \dfrac{1}{\sigma}\left(\dfrac{R_S}{L_S} + \dfrac{R_r}{L_r}\right) i_{s\beta} - \dfrac{\omega}{\sigma L_S}\varphi_{s\alpha} + \dfrac{R_r}{\sigma L_r L_S}\varphi_{s\beta} + \dfrac{1}{\sigma L_S} v_{S\beta} \\ \dfrac{d\varphi_{s\alpha}}{dt} = -R_s i_{s\alpha} + v_{s\alpha} \\ \dfrac{d\varphi_{s\beta}}{dt} = -R_s i_{s\beta} + v_{s\beta} \\ 0 = \dfrac{d\varphi_{r\alpha}}{dt} + R_r i_{r\alpha} + \omega\varphi_{r\beta} t_1 \\ 0 = \dfrac{d\varphi_{r\beta}}{dt} + R_r i_{r\beta} - \omega\varphi_{r\alpha} \end{cases} \tag{1}$$

where:

$\overline{v}_s = (v_{s\alpha} v_{s\beta})^T$ is the voltage vector,

$\overline{\varphi}_s = (\varphi_{s\alpha}\varphi_{s\beta})^T$ is the stator flux vector,

$\overline{\varphi}_r = (\varphi_{r\alpha}\varphi_{r\beta})^T$ is the rotor flux vector,

$\bar{i}_s = (i_{s\alpha} i_{s\beta})^T$ is the stator current vector,

R_s and R_r are the stator and rotor resistances, respectively.

and ω is the rotor speed (rad/s).

$\sigma = 1 - \frac{M^2}{L_r L_s}$: Blondel's coefficient.

The flux and current relationships are given as follows:

$$\begin{cases} \varphi_{s\alpha} = L_s i_{s\alpha} + M i_{r\alpha} \\ \varphi_{s\beta} = L_s i_{s\beta} + M i_{r\beta} \\ \varphi_{r\alpha} = L_r i_{r\alpha} + M i_{s\alpha} \\ \varphi_{r\beta} = L_r i_{r\beta} + M i_{s\beta} \end{cases} \tag{2}$$

where L_s, L_r and M: are the stator, the rotor and mutual inductances, respectively.

Equation 3 describes the mechanical behavior of the IM:

$$J \frac{d\Omega}{dt} = T_{em} - T_l - f\Omega \tag{3}$$

where J and f are respectively the motor inertia and the viscous friction coefficient, Ω and T_l are respectively the mechanical rotor speed and the load torque, T_{em} is the electromagnetic torque, which is expressed by the following equation:

$$Tem = \frac{3}{2} Np\left(\varphi_{s\alpha} i_{s\alpha} - \varphi_{s\beta} i_{s\alpha}\right) \tag{4}$$

With N_p is number of the poles pairs. To feed the IM, a two-level voltage inverter is used. According to Gholinezhad & Noroozian (2012), the selected voltage vector is expressed as:

$$v_S = \sqrt{\frac{2}{3}} U_{dc}(S_A + S_B e^{j\frac{2\pi}{3}} + S_C e^{j\frac{4\pi}{3}}) \tag{5}$$

where S_A, S_B and S_C are the inverter switching states, and U_{dc} is the continuous voltage produced by the rectifier.

The basic idea of the DTC is to control of the stator flux and the electromagnetic torque through the selection of an optimal voltage vector. This consists in keeping the electromagnetic torque and the stator flux within hysteresis bands, as given in Takahashi & Noguchi (1986), and Buja et al. (1997). The stator flux vector is described by the following equation:

$$\overrightarrow{\varphi_s} = \overrightarrow{\varphi_{so}} + \int \left(\overrightarrow{v_S} - R_s \overrightarrow{i_s}\right) dt \tag{6}$$

If the voltage drop (Rs* is) is neglected and the voltage vector is kept constant in each sampling period T_s, then the stator flux vector variation is proportional to the voltage vector, as shown in the following equation:

$$\overrightarrow{\Delta\varphi}(k) = \vec{\varphi}(k+1) - \vec{\varphi}(k) \approx \overrightarrow{v_S} * T_S \quad (7)$$

The following equation presents the amplitude of the stator flux:

$$|\varphi_S| = \sqrt{\varphi_{S\alpha}^2 + \varphi_{S\beta}^2} \quad (8)$$

where $\varphi_{s\alpha}$ and $\varphi_{s\beta}$ are the components of the stator flux vector in the Concordia reference. The stator flux position Θ_S is calculated by the following equation:

$$\theta_S = a\tan\left(\frac{\varphi_{S\beta}}{\varphi_{S\alpha}}\right) \quad (9)$$

As depicted in Figure 2, the DTC is based on two hysteresis controllers which are used to detect the stator flux and the electromagnetic torque errors. The outputs of the two hysteresis controllers and the position of the stator flux are used to calculate the inverter switching states utilizing the switching table presented in Figure 2.

PROPOSED DTC SCHEME 1: DTC-SVM -PI

The SVM is a good technique that can be used to control the voltage inverter, with less harmonic and commutation losses, as given in Holtz (1994). Figure 3 describes the position of the generated voltage vectors for each sampling period. There are eight voltage vectors from V_0 to V_7. As presented in this figure, each voltage vector is generated through the inverter switching states.

As shown in Figure 3, the determination of the voltage vector consists in projecting this vector on the two nearest adjacent vectors, as indicated in sector 1. Equation (10) can be utilized to determine the sector number and the voltage vector position.

$$\theta_{Sv} = a\tan\left(\frac{v_{S\beta}}{v_{S\alpha}}\right) \quad (10)$$

The commutation times of the inverters T_i and T_{i+1} can be calculated using the components ($V_{s\alpha}$, $V_{s\beta}$) of the inverter. For example, for sector 1, the commutation times, the voltage vectors and the cyclic reports are expressed in system (12):

Figure 2. DTC Diagram of an IM

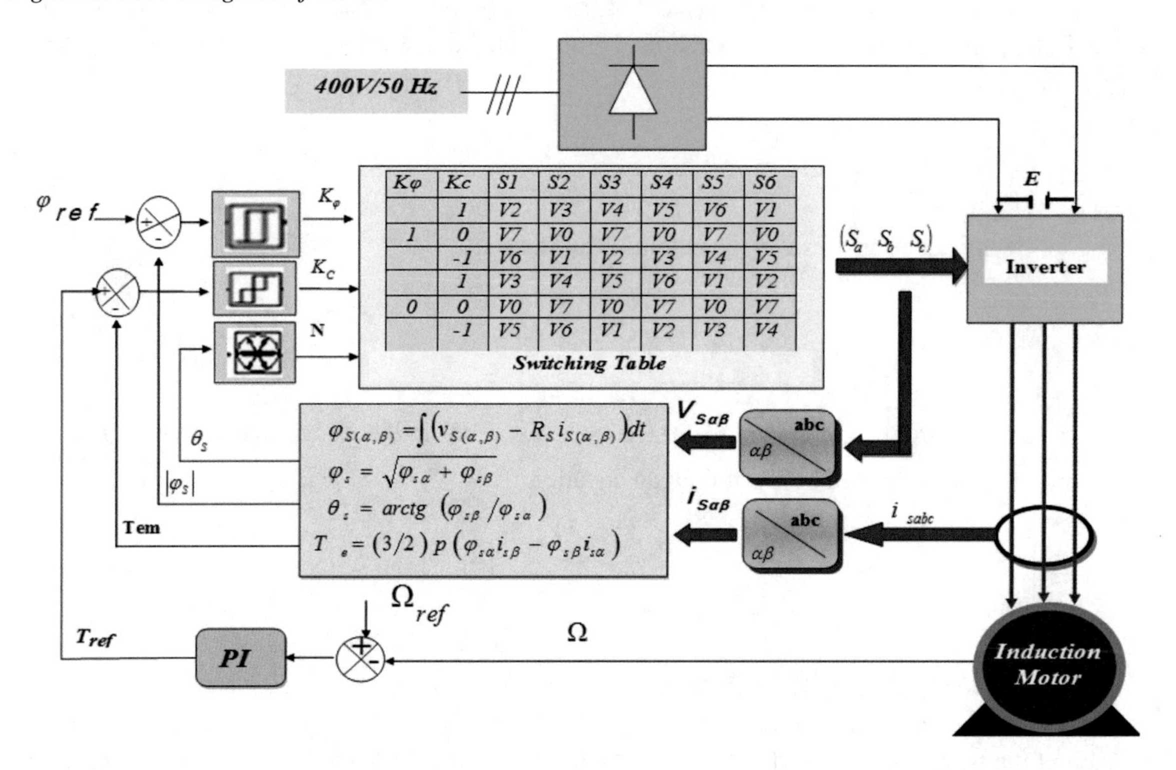

Figure 3. Diagram of DTC-SVM-PI for position control

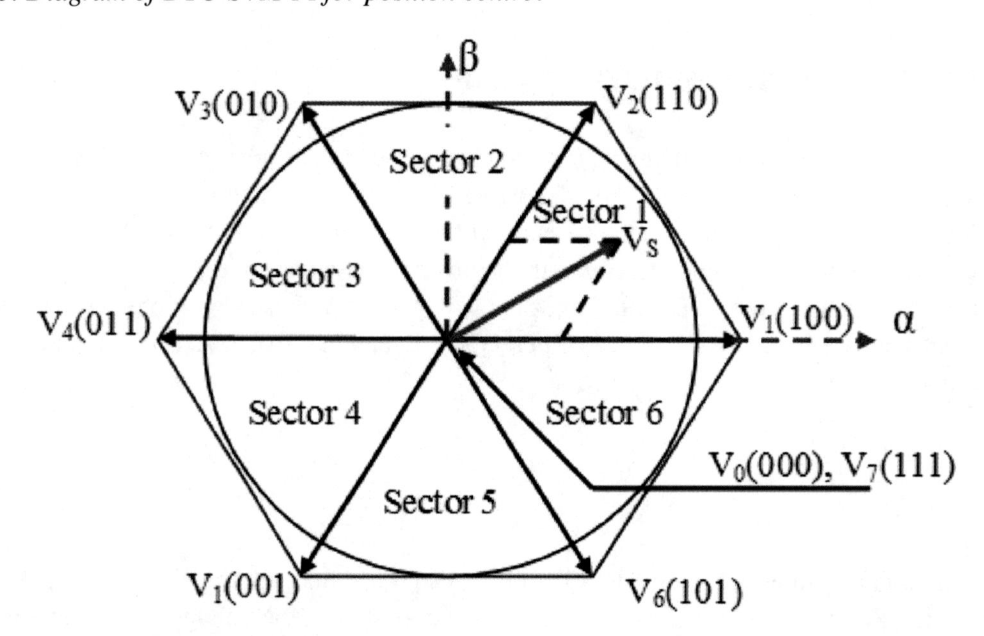

$$\begin{cases} \vec{v_s} = v_{s\alpha} + j v_{s\alpha} = \dfrac{T_1}{T_{\text{mod}}} \vec{v_1} + \dfrac{T_2}{T_{\text{mod}}} \vec{v_2} \\ \vec{v_1} = \sqrt{\dfrac{2}{3}} E \left(\cos(0) + j \sin(0) \right) = \sqrt{\dfrac{2}{3}} E \\ \vec{v_2} = \sqrt{\dfrac{2}{3}} E \left(\cos\left(\dfrac{\pi}{3}\right) + j \sin\left(\dfrac{\pi}{3}\right) \right) \\ T_{\text{mod}} = T_1 + T_2 + T_0 \\ T_1 = \left(\sqrt{\dfrac{2}{3}} v_{s\alpha} + \dfrac{1}{\sqrt{2}} v_{s\beta} \right) \dfrac{T\,\text{mod}}{E} \\ T_1 = \sqrt{2} v_{s\alpha} \dfrac{T\,\text{mod}}{E} \\ D_1 = \sqrt{\dfrac{3}{2}} \dfrac{v_{s\alpha}}{E} - \dfrac{1}{\sqrt{2}} \dfrac{v_{s\beta}}{E} \\ D_2 == \sqrt{2} \dfrac{v_{s\beta}}{E} \end{cases} \tag{12}$$

Figure 4 demonstrates the inverter switching states in sector N_1. The time duration of each nonzero vector is equally divided into two parts. The time duration of the zero vectors is equally distributed from V_0 to V_7, and thus the switching sequence of the space vector is V_0, V_1, V_2, V_7, V_7, V_2, V_1, and V_0 during the period modulation. The duties of the three phases of the inverter are expressed as follows:

$$\begin{cases} D_a = D_1 + D_2 + \frac{1}{2} D_0 \\ D_b = D_2 + \frac{1}{2} D_0 \\ D_c = \frac{1}{2} D_0 \\ D_1 + D_2 + D_0 = 1 \end{cases} \tag{13}$$

Figure 4. Sequences of inverter switching states in sector one (N_1)

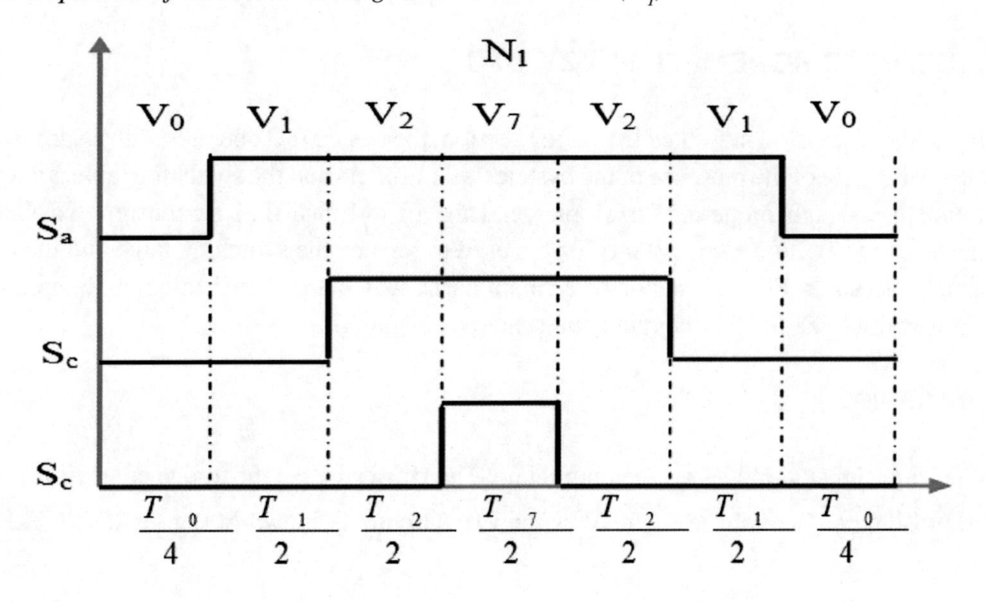

Referring to expressions D_1 and D_2, presented in system 12, system 13 can be rewritten as given by system 14:

$$\begin{cases} D_a = \frac{1}{2}(1 + \sqrt{\frac{3}{2}}\frac{V_{s\alpha}}{E_0} + \frac{1}{\sqrt{2}}\frac{V_{s\beta}}{E_0} \\ D_b = \frac{1}{2}(1 - \sqrt{\frac{3}{2}}\frac{V_{s\alpha}}{E_0} + \frac{1}{\sqrt{2}}\frac{V_{s\beta}}{E_0} \\ D_c = \frac{1}{2}(1 - \sqrt{\frac{3}{2}}\frac{V_{s\alpha}}{E_0} + \frac{1}{\sqrt{2}}\frac{V_{s\beta}}{E_0} \end{cases} \tag{14}$$

According to Srirattanawichaikul et al. (2010), the components $\varphi^*_{s\alpha}$ and $\varphi^*_{s\beta}$ of the reference are given by Equation 15.

$$\begin{cases} \varphi^*_{s\alpha} = |\varphi^*_s| \cos(\theta^*_s) \\ \varphi^*_{s\beta} = |\varphi^*_s| \sin(\theta^*_s) \end{cases} \tag{15}$$

The components $V^*_{s\alpha}$ and $V^*_{s\beta}$ of the voltage vector are expressed below:

$$\begin{cases} V^*_{s\alpha} = \dfrac{\varphi^*_{s\alpha} - \varphi_{s\alpha}}{T_e} + R_s i_{s\alpha} \\ V^*_{s\beta} = \dfrac{\varphi^*_{s\beta} - \varphi_{s\beta}}{T_e} + R_s i_{s\beta} \end{cases} \tag{16}$$

where T_e is the sampling period. Finally, the obtained components presented in (16) are used in the SVM block to determine the states ($S_a S_b S_c$) of the inverter. The control system of the panel position based on the DTC-SVM-PI is described by Figure 5.

PROPOSED DTC SCHEME 2: FUZZY DTC

According to the discussion presented in the first section, the basic DTC operates with a variable switching frequency because of the presence of the hysteresis controllers and the switching table, which creates commutation losses, high torque and flux ripples, and high distortion in the stator current. To obtain better performances, a Fuzzy Inference System (FIS) is used to replace the switching table and the hysteresis controllers. Generally, a FIS is based on three main parts, which are fuzzification, an inference engine and defuzzification. The FDTC diagram is presented by Figure 6.

Fuzzy Variables

The FIS has three input variables and an output one. The flux error e_φ, the torque error e_T and the angle θ_S are the FIS inputs. The voltage vector V_i is the FIS output. As shown in Figure 8, The FIS is based

Figure 5. Diagram of the DTC-SVM-PI for position control

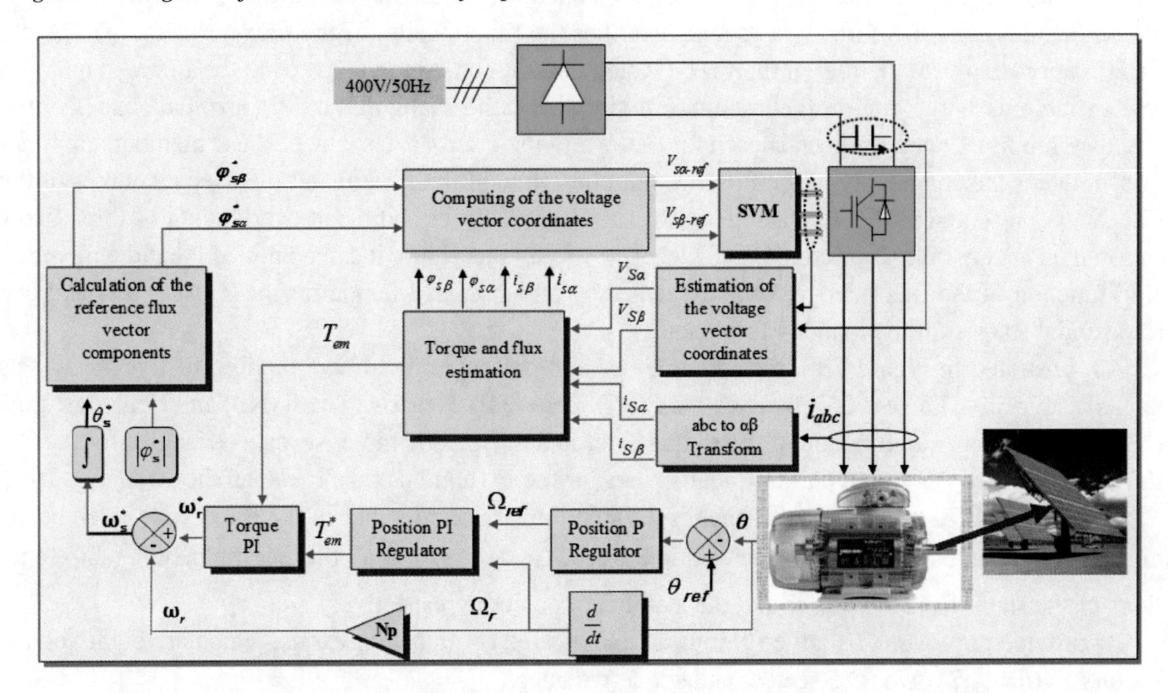

Figure 6. FDTC diagram for position control

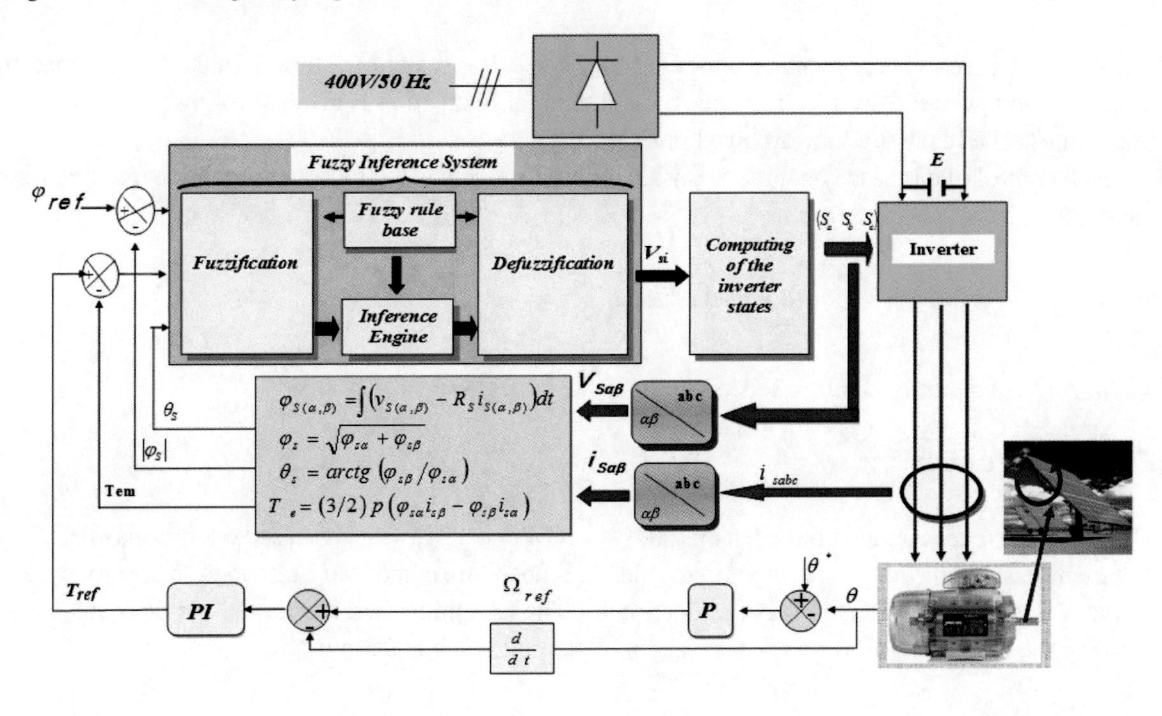

on three steps: *i*) the fuzzification step consists in converting input analog variables into fuzzy ones, *ii*) a base of rules consists of fuzzy rules and describes the functionality of the fuzzy system. *iii*) The defuzzification step is to the reason the fuzzy system, and it consists in converting the fuzzy output to a real variable usable to control the system. For simplicity, the triangular and trapezoidal shapes of the membership functions have been chosen for fuzzy linguistic sets. The shape of these membership functions reduces the complexity of the FIS, the sampling time of the system and the used resources of the FPGA. As presented in Figure 7(a), the stator flux error is described by an overlapping of three fuzzy sets named as: Positive (P), Zero (Z) and Negative (N). In this figure it can be noticed that the membership function of the stator flux error is described by an isosceles triangle for the Z fuzzy sets and two trapezoidal shapes for the P and N fuzzy sets.

As illustrated in Figure 7(b), the torque error is represented by an overlapping of five fuzzy sets named as: Positive Large (PL), Positive Small (PS), Zero (ZE), Negative Small (NS) and Negative Large (NL). The membership function of the torque error is described by three isosceles triangles for the PS, ZE and NS fuzzy sets and two trapezoidal shapes for the PL and NL fuzzy sets, as shown in Fig. 7(b).

In the basic DTC, the (α, β) reference is divided into six sectors, but in the FDTC this reference is divided into twelve fuzzy sets, as depicted in Figure 7(c). μ_{φ}, μ_T and $\mu_{\theta s}$ present the membership functions of the stator flux, the torque and the stator flux position, respectively.

As provided in Figure 7(d), the FIS output is indicated by eight singletons, which are eight voltage vectors V_i (i=0…7): two zero vectors and six active ones.

Fuzzy Control Rules

The FIS has three inputs which are presented by Figure 7(a, b and c). These inputs are described by three, five and twelve fuzzy sets. Thus, the total number of fuzzy rules is given as follows: 3×5×12=180 fuzzy rules. The fuzzy rules are archived in Table 1.

Each control rule is based on three fuzzy-set inputs, as given by the following equation that describes the fuzzy rules R_i.

$$R_i : if\ e_{\varphi}\ is\ A_i, e_T\ is\ B_i\ and\ \theta_s\ is\ C_i\ then\ v\ is\ v_i \tag{17}$$

where A_i, B_i and C_i are the fuzzy sets of the input variables.

Fuzzy Inferences

The fuzzy inference method utilized in this study is of Mamdani's, which is based on min-max decision. The membership functions of the inputs variables A, B and C are noted by μ_A, μ_B and μ_C, respectively. The output V is defined by the membership function μ_V. The weighting factor α_i for the ith rule is calculated utilizing the minimum (min) function, as given by the following equation:

$$\alpha_i = \min\left(\mu_{Ai}\left(e_{\varphi}\right), \mu_{Bi}\left(e_T\right), \mu_{Ci}\left(\theta_s\right)\right) \tag{18}$$

Figure 7. (a) Fuzzy membership functions of flux error e_φ, (b): Fuzzy membership functions of torque error e_T, (c): Fuzzy membership functions of angle Θ_S, (d): Fuzzy membership functions of output

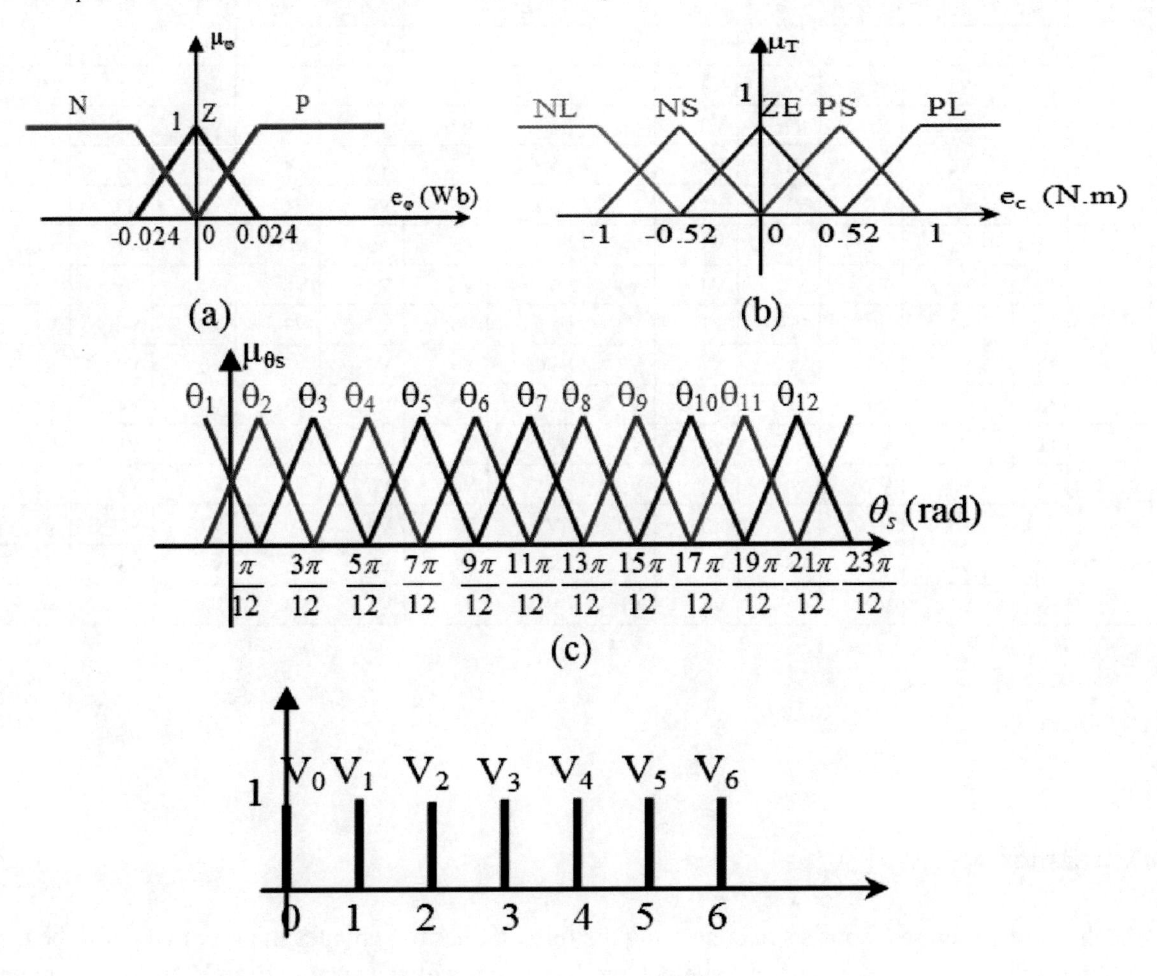

Figure 8. Fuzzy logic system diagram

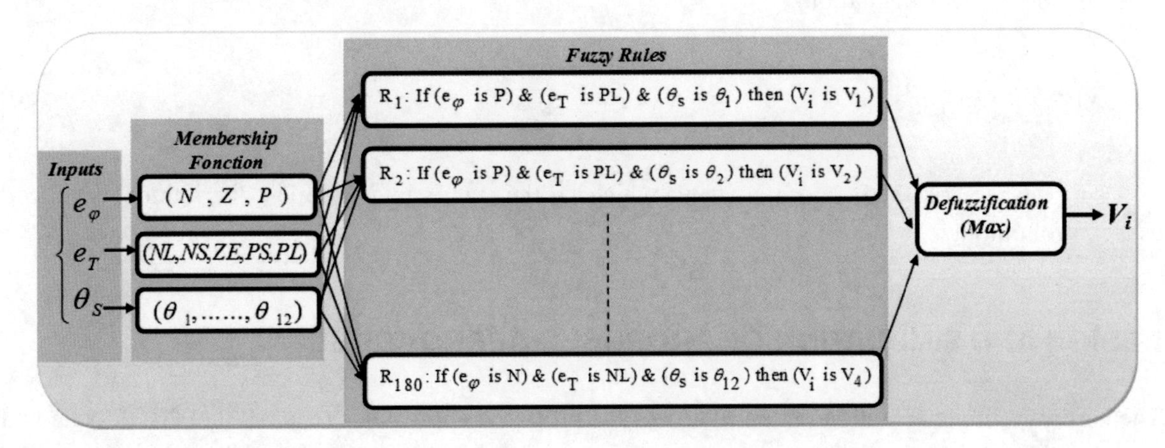

Table 1. Fuzzy control rules table

e_φ	e_T	θ_1	θ_2	θ_3	θ_4	θ_5	θ_6	θ_7	θ_8	θ_9	θ_{10}	θ_{11}	θ_{12}
P	PL	V1	V2	V2	V3	V3	V4	V4	V5	V5	V6	V6	V1
	PS	V2	V2	V3	V3	V4	V4	V5	V5	V6	V6	V1	V1
	Z	V0	V7	V7	V0	V0	V7	V7	V0	V0	V7	V7	V0
	NS	V6	V6	V1	V1	V2	V2	V3	V3	V4	V4	V5	V5
	NL	V6	V6	V1	V1	V2	V2	V3	V3	V4	V4	V5	V5
Z	PL	V2	V2	V3	V3	V4	V4	V5	V5	V6	V6	V1	V1
	PS	V2	V3	V3	V4	V4	V5	V5	V6	V6	V1	V1	V2
	Z	V7	V0	V0	V7	V7	V0	V0	V7	V7	V0	V0	V7
	NS	V7	V0	V0	V7	V7	V0	V0	V7	V7	V0	V0	V7
	NL	V5	V6	V6	V1	V1	V2	V2	V3	V3	V4	V4	V5
N	PL	V2	V3	V3	V4	V4	V5	V5	V6	V6	V1	V1	V2
	PS	V3	V3	V4	V4	V5	V5	V6	V6	V1	V1	V2	V2
	Z	V0	V7	V7	V0	V0	V7	V7	V0	V0	V7	V7	V0
	NS	V4	V5	V5	V6	V6	V1	V1	V2	V2	V3	V3	V4
	NL	V5	V5	V6	V6	V1	V1	V2	V2	V3	V3	V4	V4

$$\mu'_{v_i}(v) = \max\left(\alpha_i, \mu_{v_i}(v)\right) \tag{19}$$

Deffuzifier

The defuzzification step consists in converting the fuzzy values to real ones in order to control the real system. In this study the defuzzification block produces eight voltage vectors from V_0 to V_7. The membership functions of the output are illustrated in Figure 7(d). In this step, the Max method is chosen, as given by the following equation:

$$\mu'_{out}(v) = \max_{i=1}^{180}\left(\mu'_{Vi}(V)\right) \tag{20}$$

Using this method, the fuzzy output value which has the maximum possibility distribution, is utilized as a control output.

DESIGN AND SIMULATION OF PROPOSED APPROACHES

The hardware implementation on the FPGA of the proposed approaches requires the VHDL code and then the Bitstream file, which can be automatically, generated using the developed design from the XSG tool, as described in Figure 1.

The first step consists in designing the control algorithms from the XSG tool with 16 bits and a fixed point format is used in all XSG blocks. For example, the full architectures of the FDTC and the DTC-SVM-PI from the XSG tool are depicted in Figure 9 (a and b), respectively.

As presented in Figure 9 (a, b), the FDTC and the DTC-SVM-PI consist of several blocks. For example, the internal architectures the negative fuzzy set (N) of the stator flux error from the XSG tool is presented by Figure 10. As shown in Figure 7(a), the error of the stator flux is presented by three fuzzy sets: N, Z and P. Each membership function is defined by a mathematical model. The fuzzy set N is given by equation 21. Figure 10 presents the architecture of (21) from the XSG tool.

Figure 9. Architecture from the XSG tool of the: (a) FDTC, (b) DTC-SVM-PI

(a)

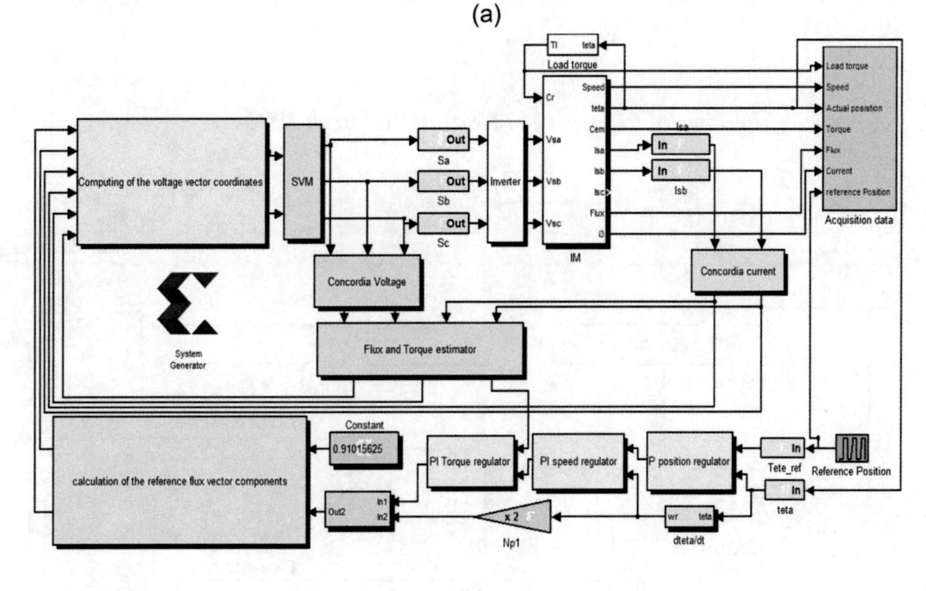

(b)

$$\begin{cases} if\ \mu_{\varphi} < -0.02\ then\ N(e_{\varphi}) = 1 \\ if\ \mu_{\varphi} > 0\ then\ N(e_{\varphi}) = 0 \\ else\ N(e_{f}) = -50\, e_{\varphi} \end{cases} \tag{21}$$

To determine the internal design of the other fuzzy sets, it is possible to follow the same manner presented in Figure 10.

The proposed approaches are verified by digital simulation before being tested in the test bench. This section presents a comparative study between the basic DTC, the FDTC and the DTC-SVM-PI. The IM parameters are given in Table 6. The position set-point θ^* varies as follows:

From 0 to 1s: $\theta^* = \frac{\pi}{6}$ (rad) then load torque:

$T_l = 10\sin(\frac{\pi}{6}) = 5Nm$

From 1s to 1.5 s: $\theta^* = \frac{\pi}{9}t + \frac{\pi}{18}$ then the load torque:

$T_l = 10\sin(\frac{\pi}{9}t + \frac{\pi}{18})$

From 1.5 s to 2.5s: $\theta^* = \frac{\pi}{3}$ (rad) then load torque:

$T_l = 10\sin(\frac{\pi}{3}) = 8.66Nm$.

The obtained results are reported as follows.

Figure 10. Internal architecture of fuzzy set N of stator flux from XSG

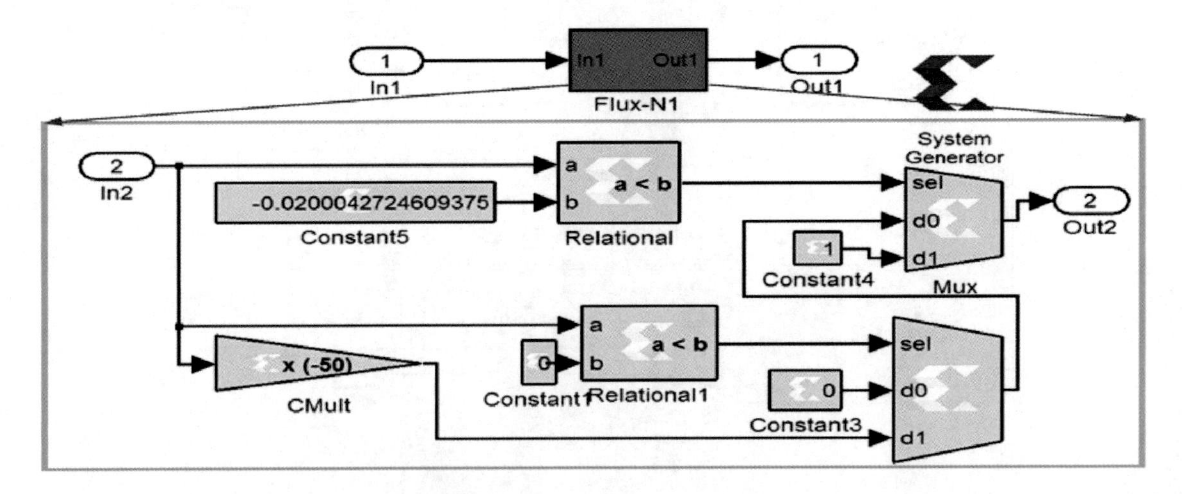

Referring to Figure 11 and Figure 12, the basic DTC, the FDTC and the DTC-SVM-PI offer the same performances in terms of position and speed dynamics. The rotor position reaches quickly its reference value thanks to the high dynamics response of the DTC approaches. In the basic DTC, the rotor speed has several ripples, which reduce the control system performances. The speed ripples are removed in the FDTC and DTC-SVM-PI approaches.

Figure 13 (a) shows that the electromagnetic torque has high ripples, which are reduced in the FDTC (Figure 13 (b)) and which are considerably reduced when the motor is controlled with the DTC-SVM-PI (Figure 13(c)). It is clear that the DTC-SVM-PI offers a better performance in terms of ripples.

Figure 14 (a) demonstrates that the stator current is characterized by high ripples and distortions, which are reduced in the FDTC (Figure 14 (b)) and which are considerably decreased in case of DTC-DVM-PI, as depicted in Figure 14 (c).

As indicated in Figure 15 (a), the stator flux in the basic DTC has high ripples and the DTC is affected by a demagnetization problem. Referring to Figure 15 (b), these ripples will decline in case of a FDTC. As given in Figure 15 (c), the flux ripples are significantly removed and the demagnetization phenomenon is discarded.

The evolution of the stator flux vector extremity is presented by the circular trajectory, as shown in Figure 16. It is clear that the DTC-SVM-PI offers the smoothest circular locus. A comparative study between the proposed approaches is provided in Table 2.

Figure 11. Evolution of rotor position: (a) Basic DTC, (b) FDTC, and (c) DTC-SVM-PI

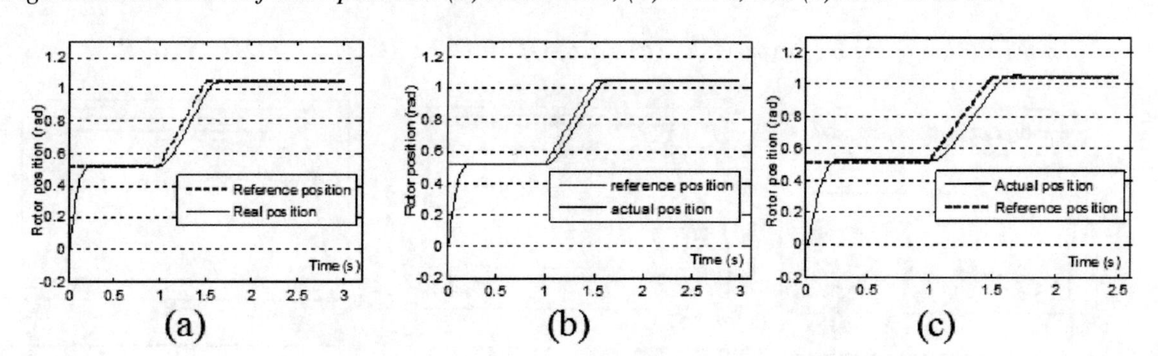

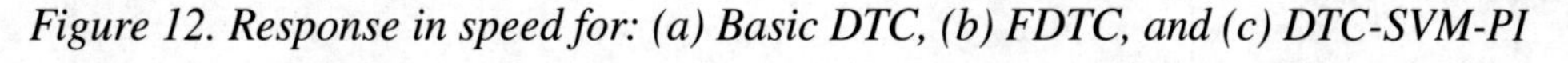
Figure 12. Response in speed for: (a) Basic DTC, (b) FDTC, and (c) DTC-SVM-PI

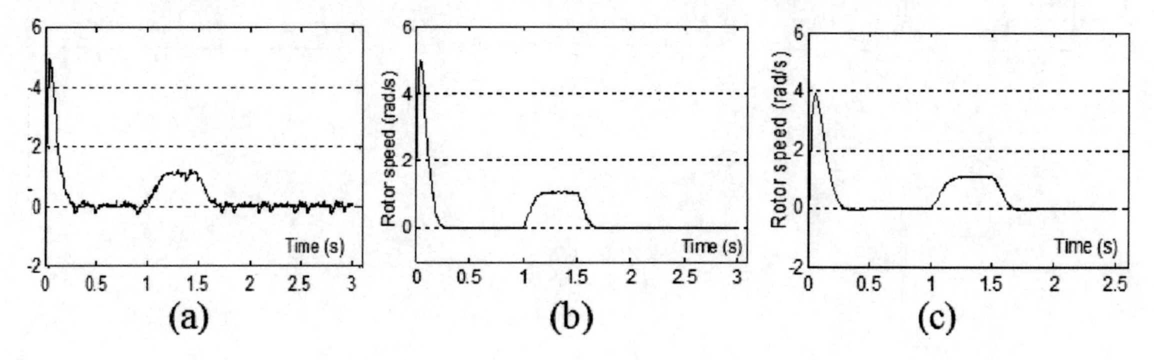

Figure 13. Torque response: (a) Basic DTC, (b) FDTC, and (c) DTC-SVM-PI

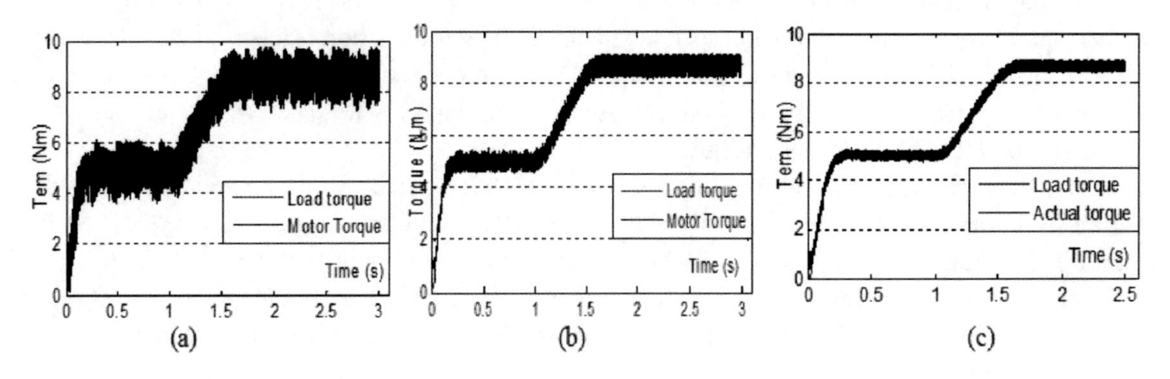

Figure 14. Stator current variation: (a) Basic DTC, (b) FDTC, and (c) DTC-SVM-PI

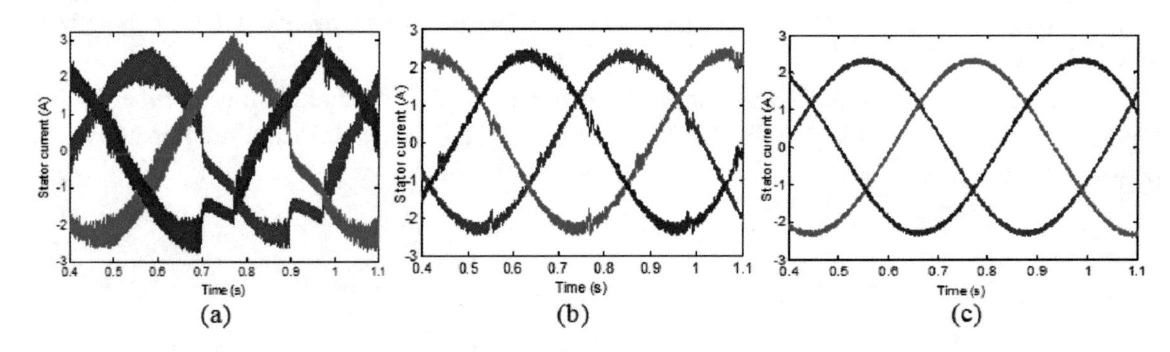

Figure 15. Evolution of stator flux module: (a) Basic DTC, (b) FDTC, and (c) DTC-SVM-PI

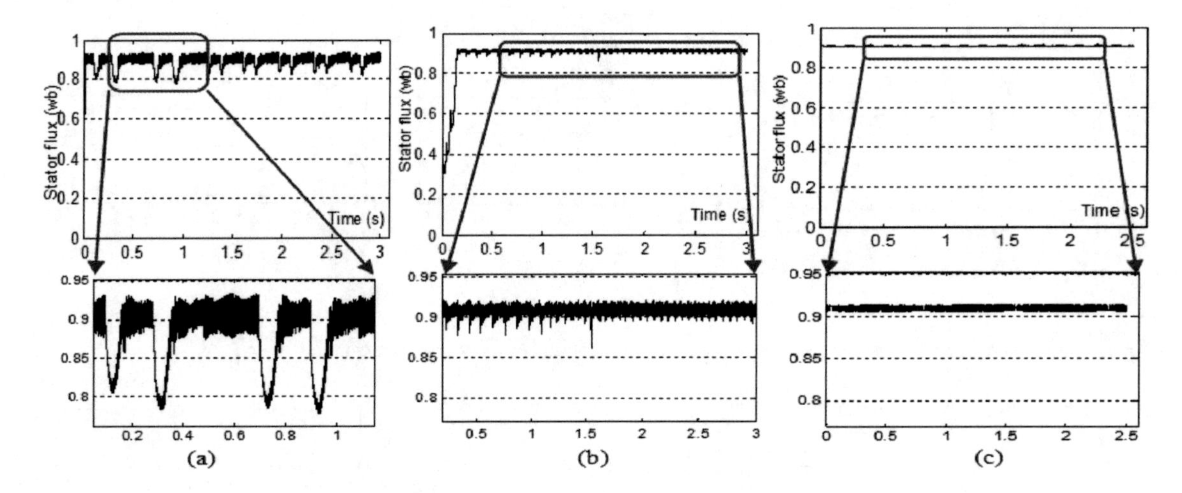

Figure 16. Evolution of stator flux vector trajectory: (a) Basic DTC, (b) FDTC, and (c) DTC-SVM-PI

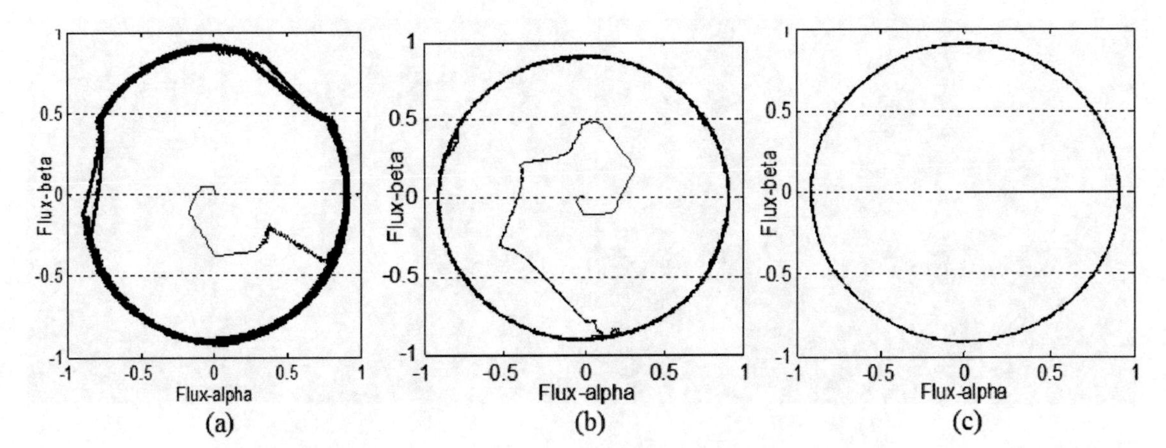

Table 2. A comparative study in terms of ripples between Basic DTC, FDTC and DTC-SVM-PI

Type of controller	Basic DTC		FDTC		DTC-SVM -PI	
	Max-Min	%	Max-Min	%	Max-Min	%
Electromagnetic torque ripples (Nm)	2	23	0.7	8.62	0.35	4.041
Stator flux ripples (wb)	0.145	15.93	0.02	2.197	0.007	0.769
Stator current ripples	0.7	15.48	0.225	4.97	0.1	2.21

FPGA IMPLEMENTATION STEP

Once the control algorithm is verified by digital simulation, this step will present the implementation on the FPGA, which maps, places, routes the algorithm design, and analyzes the performances in terms of execution time. For instance, the Register Transfer Level (RTL) schematic and the routing results of the DTC-SVM-PI are illustrated in Figure 17. The FPGA execution time performance of the DTC-SVM-PI is archived in Table 3.

T_{ADC} is the analog-to-digital conversion time of the stator current. The FPGA offers high performances in terms of execution time, for the three DTC approaches. As presented in Table 3, the execution time is evaluated as 0.78µs, which allows the user to choose a sampling time equal to 5µs with a sampling frequency equal to 200 kHz. However, utilizing a software solution like the DSP, the execution time is evaluated by tens or even hundreds of microseconds, as given in Nahid-Mobarakeh et al.(2004), Bendjedia et al. (2007), and Brandstetter et al. (2006). According to Idkhajine et al. (2010), the same algorithms were implemented on a DSP and an FPGA and the execution time was evaluated to 66 µs and 6µs, respectively. Naouar et al. (2007) present the execution time influence on the control system performances. In the case of an execution time with 50µs, the total harmonic distortion would be equal to 11.1%, which would reduce to 8.4% when the execution time was equal to 2.64 µs. The execution time problem was solved utilizing the FPGA.

Figure 17. Implementation results from XSG using FPGA Virtex 5: (a) RTL schematic, (b) Routing results

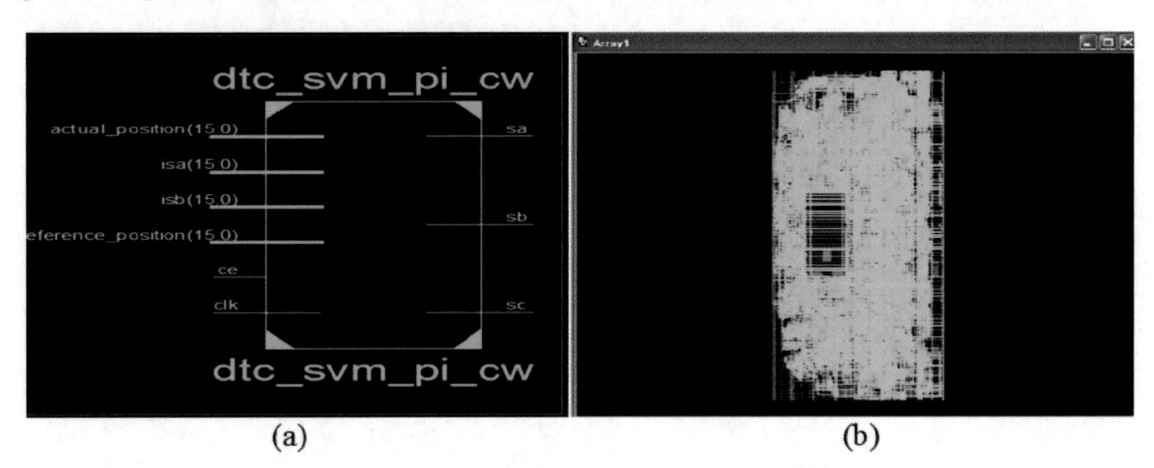

Table 3. FPGA performances in terms of execution time for DTC-SVM-PI

Modules	Computation time (µs)
Concordia	T_C= 0.06
Stator Flux Estimator	T_F= 0.1
PI speed controller and P position controller	T_{PIs} =0.16
PI torque controller	T_{PI} =0.14
Calculation of the stator Flux Reference	T_{RF} =0.06
Calculation of the Reference Voltage vector components	T_{RV} =0.12
SVM	T_{SVM} =0.14
Execution Time of DTC-SVM-PI	0.78 µs
Total control time of DTC-SVM-PI	T_{ADC}+ 0.78
Consumed resources	29%

HARDWARE IN THE LOOP VALIDATION OF THE DTC-SVM-PI AND THE FDTC APPROACHES ON REAL FPGA-VIRTEX 5-ML507

In order to verify a first operating attempt, it is highly recommended to start the experimentation by a HIL validation. The HIL is considered as an intermediate step between a fully computer-based development validation (simulation tools and FPGA design tools) and a fully experimental validation (actual system platform). This step investigates an experimental one of the proposed control algorithms utilizing an FPGA Virtex 5, which consists in: ***i)*** generating a JTAG block; the DTC-SVM-PI architecture presented in Figure 9(b) is replaced by the generated JTAG block as shown in Figure 18(a), and ***ii)*** connecting the FPGA to a PC computer through the JTAG cable. When the start simulation is clicked on, the FPGA board will exchange the data with full synchronization with Simulink. In this step, the FPGA receives the stator current and the rotor position, and then sends the inverter switching states to Simulink through the JTAG cable, as given in Figure 18(b).

The HIL validation results of the DTC-SVM-PI and the FDTC are illustrated in Figures 19 and 20.

The HIL validation results of the DTC-SVM-PI and the FDTC are given by Figure 19 and Figure 20 respectively, which present the evolution of the rotor position, the rotor speed, the electromagnetic torque and the stator flux.

The DTC-SVM-PI and the FDTC provide similar results in terms of speed and position control, but the FDTC has more speed ripples, as given in Figure 19 (a,b) and Figure 20(a,b).

In the DTC-SVM-PI, the torque and the flux ripples are evaluated to 4.59% and 0.989%, respectively, as shown in Figure 19 (c,d). However, in the FDTC, the torque and the flux ripples are evaluated to 9.19% and 2.417% respectively, as presented in Figure 20(c,d).

Figure 18. (a) Generation of hardware JTAG block, (b) HIL validation environment

(a)

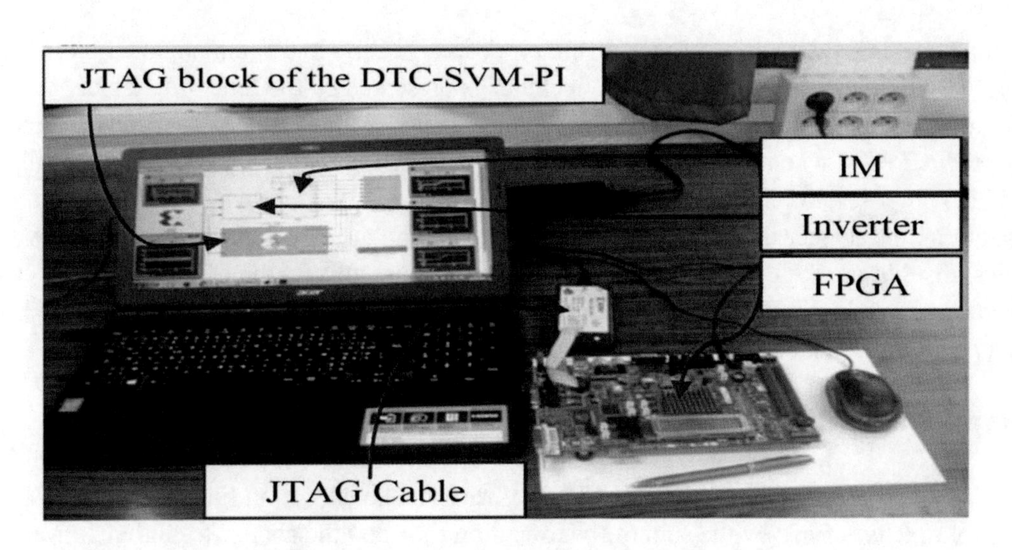

(b)

Figure 19. HIL results of DTC-SVM-PI: (a) Induction motor position, (b) Rotor speed, (c) Electromagnetic torque, (d) Stator flux

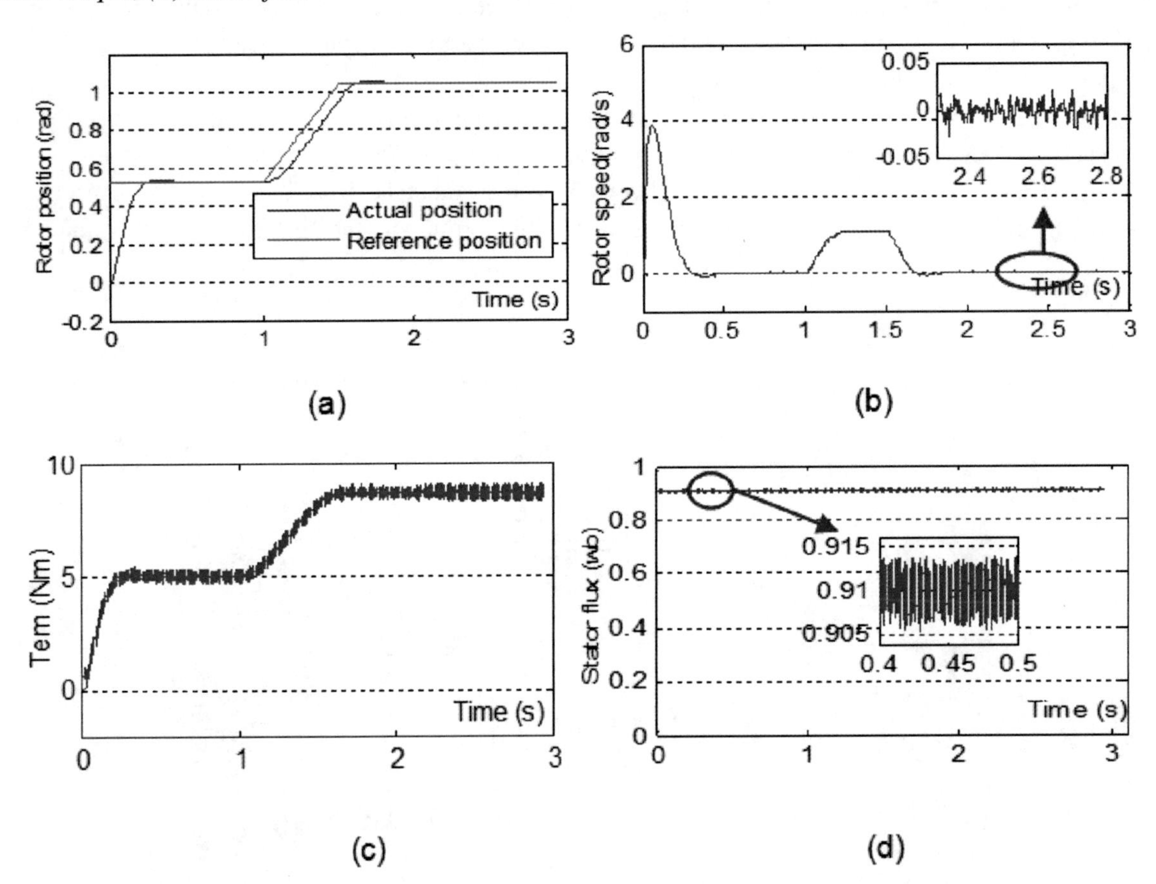

A Comparative Study With Other Methods

To demonstrate again the performances of the proposed DTC-SVM-PI implemented on the FPGA, a comparative study with other existing DTC methods is presented by the following table.

According to Kızılkaya & Gülez (2016), the stator flux was evaluated as 2%, which will be reduced in this chapter to 0.989% when the motor is controlled with the DTC-SVM-PI despite at standstill. Ramesh et al. (2015) propose a DTC approach, referred to as DTFC-SVPWM, provided a torque with 4.75% of ripples, but in this chapter the DTC-SVM-PI implemented on the FPGA provides a torque with 4.59% of ripples. In addition, the DTFC-SVPWM is more complex relative to the DTC-SVM-PI. Referring to the results presented in Table 4, the proposed solution based on the DTC-SVM-PI designed from the XSG tool and implemented on the FPGA offers the best results in terms of torque ripples.

A Comparison With Other FPGA Implementation Work About DTC

The DTC-SVM-PI is implemented on an FPGA Virtex 5. The execution time is evaluated to 0.78µs. The control time is defined by the sum of the execution time and the analog-to-digital conversion time t_{ADC}. For this reason, the sampling time is limited to 5µs with a sampling frequency equal to 200 kHz.

Figure 20. HIL results of FDTC: (a) Induction motor position, (b) Rotor speed, (c) Electromagnetic torque, (d) Stator flux

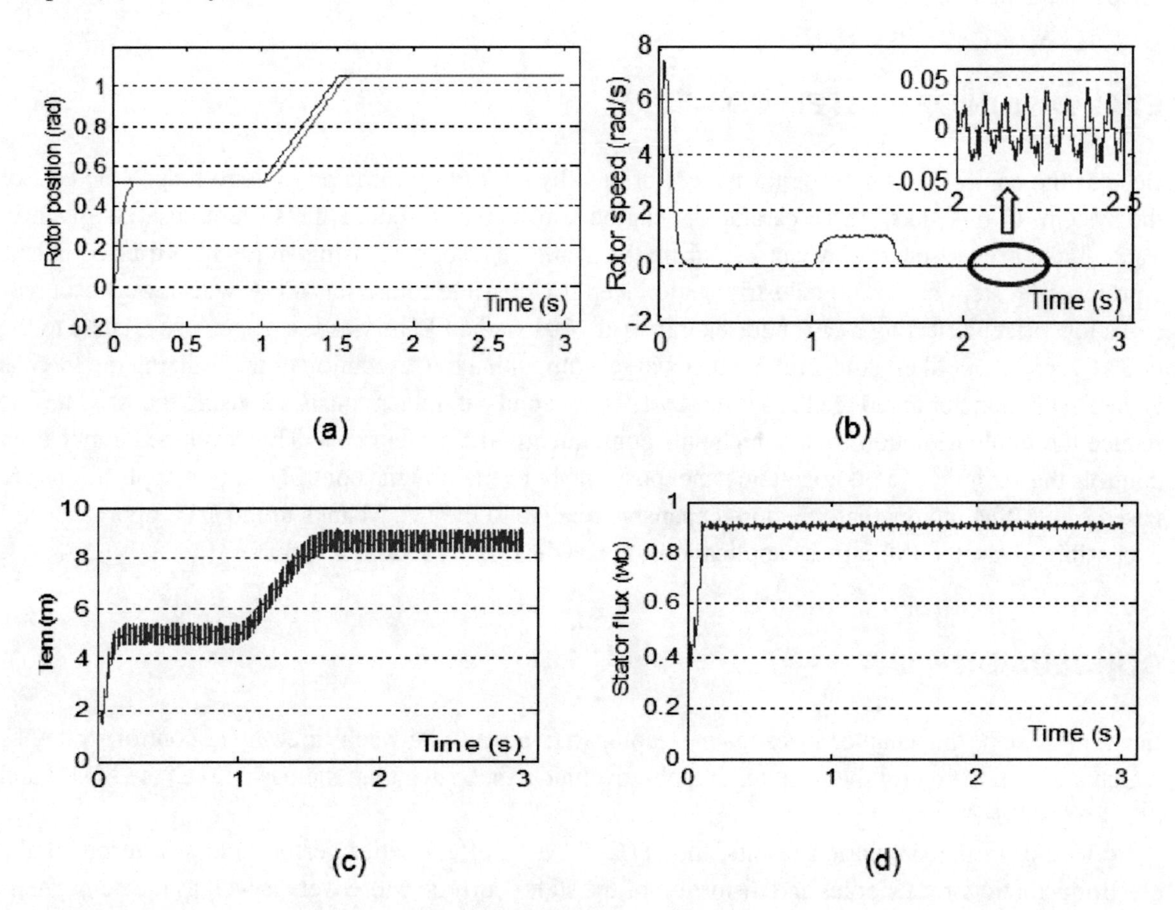

Table 4. A comparative study between DTC-SVM implemented on FPGA and other existing methods

DTC method	Speed Range	Flux Ripples	Torque Ripples	Percentage of the Torque
Proposed DTC-SVM-PI	Standstill	0.989%	0.4 Nm	4.59%
DTC-SVM and fuzzy logic: T1FLC (Ramesh et al., 2015)	From 0 to 1200 rpm	---	1.98 Nm	9.9%
DTC-SVM and fuzzy logic: T2FLC (Ramesh et al., 2015)	From 0 to 1200 rpm	---	0.95 Nm	4.75%
Five-level inverter using DTC (Gholinezhad & Noroozian, 2013)	2000 rpm	---	2 Nm	80%
Five-level inverter using DTCSVM (Gholinezhad & Noroozian, 2013)	2000 rpm	---	0.95 Nm	38%
Predictive DTC with conventional weighting factor (Uddin et al., 2015)	Rated speed	---	4.8 Nm	9.41%
DTC-SVPWM (Kızılkaya & Gülez, 2016)	Steady state	2%	---	---

A comparative study in terms of sampling time reduction and growth of the sampling frequency is presented in the next table.

EVALUATION OF SYSTEM COST

Besides the control with high performances offered by the FPGAs, it is possible to reduce the cost of the system. In this study, three parameters can be considered to reduce the system cost. As given in Table 3, the used resources present 29% from the available resources, using an FPGA Virtex 5. This is a prototyping step, but in the industrialization step it is feasible to use an FPGA with fewer resources and a low price. Referring to Chandrasekaran et al. (2013), the FPGA was less expensive relative to the dSPACE and it could execute a full complex algorithm with a low execution time. Utilizing the FPGAs is the first parameter to reduce the system cost. The second parameter consists in using the XSG tool to reduce the implementation time, which cuts consequently the system cost. The developed application controls the position of a photovoltaic panel position, but generally the control position applications are based on PMSM motors that are more expensive relative to the IM. Thanks to the DTC approaches, it is possible to use the IM in these applications, hence decreasing the system cost.

CONCLUSION

In the first step, this chapter investigates a comparative study between three DTC control strategies which are used to control the position of a photovoltaic panel, such that, the basic DTC, the FDTC and the DTC-SVM-PI.

Referring to the simulation results, the DTC-SVM-PI offers better performances in terms of the electromagnetic torque ripples and distortion of the stator current. Moreover, as well as the demagnetization problem when the motor is at very low speed is discarded. The DTC-SVM-PI is more complex to implement, which promotes the use of the FPGA as an alternative digital device.

The second contribution in this chapter consists implementing the DTC strategies on the FPGA. Referring to the implementation results, the FPGA provides good performances in terms of execution time relative to the dSPACE. Using the FPGA, the execution time is evaluated as 0.78 μs. However, utilizing the dSPACE, the execution time is estimated by tens or even hundreds of microseconds.

Table 5. Comparison in terms of sampling frequency

<table>
<tr><th>N°</th><th colspan="2">Reference</th><th>DTC sampling frequency (kHz)</th></tr>
<tr><td>1</td><td colspan="2">Proposed DTC-SVM-SMC</td><td>200</td></tr>
<tr><td>2</td><td colspan="2">(Bossoufi et al., 2011)</td><td>20</td></tr>
<tr><td rowspan="2">3</td><td rowspan="2">(Utsumi et al., 2006)</td><td>Type A controller</td><td>20</td></tr>
<tr><td>Type B controller</td><td>40</td></tr>
<tr><td>4</td><td colspan="2">(Llor et al., 2004)</td><td>40</td></tr>
<tr><td>5</td><td colspan="2">(Ferreira et al., 2003)</td><td>40</td></tr>
</table>

Table 6. IM parameters

Parameters		Values
P_N	Nominal power	1.5 kW
V_N	Nominal voltage	230/400 v
I_N	Nominal current	3.2 /5.5 A
n_N	Nominal speed	1435 rpm
F	Frequency	50 Hz
P	Pair pole	2
R_s	Stator resistance	5.717 Ω
R_r	Rotor resistance	4.282 Ω
L_s	Stator inductance	0.464 H
L_r	Rotor inductance	0.464 H
M	Mutual inductance	0.441 H
J	Moment of inertia	0.0049 Kg.m^2
f	Viscous friction coefficient	0.0029 N.m.s/rad

The third contribution of the FPGA consists in using the XSG tool to automatically generate the VHDL code of the DTC algorithms, which enormously reduces the prototyping time and then the system cost.

The DTC-SVM-PI is validated utilizing the physical FPGA Virtex 5 with an xc5vfx70t-3ff1136 package.

REFERENCES

Abbou, A., Nasser, T., Mahmoudi, H., Akherraz, M., & Essadki, A. (2012). dSPACE IFOC Fuzzy Logic Controller Implementation for Induction Motor Drive. *Journal of Electrical Systems*, *8*(3), 317–327.

Abdel Aziz, M. S., El Samahy, M., Hassan, M. A., & El Bendary, F. (2016). Applications of ANFIS in Loss of Excitation Faults Detection in Hydro-Generators. *International Journal of System Dynamics Applications*, *5*(2), 63–79. doi:10.4018/IJSDA.2016040104

Abdel Aziz, M. S., Elsamahy, M., Hassan, M. A., & Bendary, F. M. (2017). Enhancement of Turbo-Generators Phase Backup Protection Using Adaptive Neuro Fuzzy Inference System. *International Journal of System Dynamics Applications*, *6*(1), 58–76. doi:10.4018/IJSDA.2017010104

Adam, A. A., Gulez, K., & Erdogan, N. (2007, August). Minimum torque ripple algorithm with fuzzy logic controller for DTC of PMSM. In *International Conference on Intelligent Computing* (pp. 511-521). Springer. 10.1007/978-3-540-74171-8_51

Ahammad, T., Beig, A. R., & Al-Hosani, K. (2013, May). An improved direct torque control of induction motor with modified sliding mode control approach. In Electric Machines & Drives Conference (IEMDC), 2013 IEEE International (pp. 166-171). IEEE. doi:10.1109/IEMDC.2013.6556249

Ai, Y., Wang, Y., & Marrten, K. (2010). Modelling and control of six-phase induction machine under special current waveform. *International Journal of Modelling, Identification and Control, 10*(1), 4–11. doi:10.1504/IJMIC.2010.033838

Ali, M. M., & Hassan, M. A. (2012). Parameter Identification Using ANFIS for Magnetically Saturated Induction Motor. *International Journal of System Dynamics Applications, 1*(2), 28–43. doi:10.4018/ijsda.2012040103

Azar, A. T. (2010a). *Fuzzy Systems*. Vienna, Austria: IN-TECH.

Azar, A. T. (2010b). Adaptive Neuro-Fuzzy Systems. In A. T. Azar (Ed.), *Fuzzy Systems*. Vienna, Austria: IN-TECH. doi:10.5772/7220

Azar, A. T. (2012). Overview of Type-2 Fuzzy logic systems. *International Journal of Fuzzy System Applications, 2*(4), 1–28. doi:10.4018/ijfsa.2012100101

Azar, A. T., Kumar, J., Kumar, V., & Rana, K. P. S. (2017d) Control of a Two Link Planar Electrically-Driven Rigid Robotic Manipulator Using Fractional Order SOFC. *Proceedings of the International Conference on Advanced Intelligent Systems and Informatics 2017, 639*, 47-56.

Azar, A. T., Ouannas, A., & Singh, S. (2017c). Control of New Type of Fractional Chaos Synchronization. *Proceedings of the International Conference on Advanced Intelligent Systems and Informatics 2017, 639*, 47-56.

Azar, A.T., & Serrano, F.E. (2014). Robust IMC-PID tuning for cascade control systems with gain and phase margin specifications. *Neural Computing and Applications, 25*(5), 983-995. DOI .10.1007/s00521-014-1560-x

Azar, A. T., & Serrano, F. E. (2015a). Stabilization and Control of Mechanical Systems with Backlash. In Advanced Intelligent Control Engineering and Automation. IGI Global. doi:10.4018/978-1-4666-7248-2.ch001

Azar, A. T., & Serrano, F. E. (2015b). Design and Modeling of Anti Wind Up PID Controllers. In Complex system modelling and control through intelligent soft computations. Springer-Verlag. . 1. doi:10.1007/978-3-319-12883-2_1

Azar, A. T., & Serrano, F. E. (2015c). Adaptive Sliding mode control of the Furuta pendulum. In Advances and Applications in Sliding Mode Control systems. Springer-Verlag GmbH Berlin/Heidelberg. doi:10.1007/978-3-319-11173-5_1

Azar, A. T., & Serrano, F. E. (2015d). Deadbeat Control for Multivariable Systems with Time Varying Delays. In Chaos Modeling and Control Systems Design. Springer-Verlag GmbH Berlin/Heidelberg. DOI doi:10.1007/978-3-319-13132-0_6

Azar, A. T., & Serrano, F. E. (2016a). Robust control for asynchronous switched nonlinear systems with time varying delays. *Proceedings of the International Conference on Advanced Intelligent Systems and Informatics 2016*, 533, 891-899. 10.1007/978-3-319-48308-5_85

Azar, A. T., & Serrano, F. E. (2016b). Stabilization of Mechanical Systems with Backlash by PI Loop Shaping. *International Journal of System Dynamics Applications, 5*(3), 20–47. doi:10.4018/IJSDA.2016070102

Azar, A. T., & Serrano, F. E. (2017). Passivity Based Decoupling of Lagrangian Systems. *Proceedings of the International Conference on Advanced Intelligent Systems and Informatics 2016*, 533, 891-899. 10.1007/978-3-319-48308-5_85

Azar, A. T., & Vaidyanathan, S. (2015a). Handbook of Research on Advanced Intelligent Control Engineering and Automation. IGI Global. doi:10.4018/978-1-4666-7248-2

Azar, A. T., & Vaidyanathan, S. (2015b). *Computational Intelligence applications in Modeling and Control. Studies in Computational Intelligence* (Vol. 575). Springer-Verlag.

Azar, A. T., & Vaidyanathan, S. (2015c). *Chaos Modeling and Control Systems Design, Studies in Computational Intelligence* (Vol. 581). Springer-Verlag.

Azar, A. T., & Vaidyanathan, S. (2016). *Advances in Chaos Theory and Intelligent Control. Studies in Fuzziness and Soft Computing* (Vol. 337). Springer-Verlag. doi:10.1007/978-3-319-30340-6

Azar, A. T., Vaidyanathan, S., & Ouannas, A. (2017a). *Fractional Order Control and Synchronization of Chaotic Systems. Studies in Computational Intelligence* (Vol. 688). Springer-Verlag. doi:10.1007/978-3-319-50249-6

Azar, A.T., Volos, C., Gerodimos, N.A., Tombras, G.S., Pham, V.T., Radwan, A.G., … Munoz-Pacheco, J.M. (2017b). A novel chaotic system without equilibrium: Dynamics, synchronization and circuit realization. *Complexity*. doi:10.1155/2017/7871467

Azar, A. T., & Zhu, Q. (2015). *Advances and Applications in Sliding Mode Control systems. Studies in Computational Intelligence* (Vol. 576). Springer-Verlag.

Baader, M., Depenbrock, U., & Gierse, G. (1992). Direct self-control (DSC) of inverter-fed induction machine: A basis for speed control without speed measurement. *IEEE Transactions on Industry Applications*, *28*(3), 581–588. doi:10.1109/28.137442

Babu, T. S., Rajasekar, N., & Sangeetha, K. (2015). Modified particle swarm optimization technique based maximum power point tracking for uniform and under partial shading condition. *Applied Soft Computing*, *34*, 613–624. doi:10.1016/j.asoc.2015.05.029

Bendjedia, M., Ait-Amirat, Y., Walther, B., & Berthon, A. (2007, September). Sensorless control of hybrid stepper motor. In *Power Electronics and Applications, 2007 European Conference on* (pp. 1-10). IEEE.

Bharatirajal, C., Raghu, S., Jeevananthan, S., & Latha, R. (2011). *Implementation of variable structure DTC-SVM based VWF for an induction motor drive using FPGA-SPARTEN III*. Academic Press.

Bhim, S., Pradeep, J., Mittal, A. P., & Gupta, J. R. P. (2008). Torque Ripples Minimization of DTC IPMSM Drive for the EV Propulsion System using a Neural Network. *Journal of Power Electronics*, *8*(1), 23–34.

Bose. (2002). Modern power electronics and AC drives. Academic Press.

Bossoufi, B., Karim, M., Lagrioui, A., Taoussi, M., & Derouich, A. (2015). Observer backstepping control of DFIG-Generators for wind turbines variable-speed: FPGA-based implementation. *Renewable Energy*, *81*, 903–917. doi:10.1016/j.renene.2015.04.013

Bossoufi, B., Karim, M., Silviu, I., & Lagrioui, A. (2011, June). FPGA-based implementation by direct torque control of a PMSM machine. In Compatibility and Power Electronics (CPE), 2011 7th International Conference-Workshop (pp. 464-469). IEEE.

Boulkroune, A., Bouzeriba, A., Bouden, T., & Azar, A. T. (2016a). Fuzzy Adaptive Synchronization of Uncertain Fractional-order Chaotic Systems. In A. T. Azar & S. Vaidyanathan (Eds.), *Advances in Chaos Theory and Intelligent Control. Studies in Fuzziness and Soft Computing* (Vol. 337). Springer-Verlag. doi:10.1007/978-3-319-30340-6_28

Boulkroune, A., Hamel, S., & Azar, A. T. (2016b). *Fuzzy control-based function synchronization of unknown chaotic systems with dead-zone input. Advances in Chaos Theory and Intelligent Control. Studies in Fuzziness and Soft Computing* (Vol. 337). Springer-Verlag.

Boussak, M., & Jarray, K. (2006). A high-performance sensorless indirect stator flux orientation control of induction motor drive. *IEEE Transactions on Industrial Electronics*, *53*(1), 41–49. doi:10.1109/TIE.2005.862319

Brandstetter, P., Kuchar, M., & Vinklarek, D. (2006, July). Estimation techniques for sensorless speed control of induction motor drive. In *Industrial Electronics, 2006 IEEE International Symposium on* (Vol. 1, pp. 154-159). IEEE.

Buja, G., Casadei, D., & Serra, G. (1997, July). Direct torque control of induction motor drives. In *Industrial Electronics, 1997. ISIE'97., Proceedings of the IEEE International Symposium on* (*Vol. 1*, pp. TU2-TU8). IEEE. 10.1109/ISIE.1997.651717

Casadei, D., Profum, F., Serra, G., & Tani, A. (2002). FOC and DTC: Two viable schemes for induction motors torque control. *IEEE Transactions on Power Electronics*, *17*(5), 779–787. doi:10.1109/TPEL.2002.802183

Casadei, D., Serra, G., & Tani, K. (2000). Implementation of a direct control algorithm for induction motors based on discrete space vector modulation. *IEEE Transactions on Power Electronics*, *15*(4), 769–777. doi:10.1109/63.849048

Chandrasekaran, V., Dalley, B., Ned Mohan, S. K., & Posbergh, T. (2013). Low Cost FPGA Based Replacement for dSPACE Units in the Electric Drives Laboratory. Laboratory to accompany 4701. *Simulink-based simulations of electric machines/drives in applications such as energy conservation and motion control in robotics*. Retrieved from http://cusp. umn.edu/Napa_2013/Friday/Tom_P_Napa.pdf

Chen, L., Fang, K. L., & Hu, Z. F. (2005, August). A scheme of fuzzy direct torque control for induction machine. In *Machine Learning and Cybernetics, 2005. Proceedings of 2005 International Conference on* (*Vol. 2*, pp. 803-807). IEEE.

El-Ghazaly, G. (2012). Adaptive Synchronization of Unknown Chaotic Systems Using Mamdani Fuzzy Approach. *International Journal of System Dynamics Applications*, *1*(3), 122–138. doi:10.4018/ijsda.2012070104

Enany, T. A., Wahba, W. I., & Hassan, M. A. (2014). A Remote and Sensorless Stator Winding Temperature Estimation Method for Thermal Protection for Induction Motor. *International Journal of System Dynamics Applications*, *3*(3), 53–72. doi:10.4018/ijsda.2014070103

Escalante, M. F., Vannier, J. C., & Arzandé, A. (2002). Flying capacitor multilevel inverters and DTC motor drive applications. *IEEE Transactions on Industrial Electronics*, *49*(4), 809–815. doi:10.1109/TIE.2002.801231

Ferreira, S., Haffner, F., Pereira, L. F., & Moraes, F. (2003, September). Design and prototyping of direct torque control of induction motors in FPGAs. In Integrated Circuits and Systems Design, 2003. SBCCI 2003. Proceedings. doi:10.1109/SBCCI.2003.1232814

Gholinezhad, J., & Noroozian, R. (2012, February). Application of cascaded H-bridge multilevel inverter in DTC-SVM based induction motor drive. In Power Electronics and Drive Systems Technology (PEDSTC), (pp. 127-132). IEEE.

Gholinezhad, J., & Noroozian, R. (2013). Analysis of cascaded H-bridge multilevel inverter in DTC-SVM induction motor drive for FCEV. *Journal of Electrical Engineering & Technology*, *8*(2), 304–315. doi:10.5370/JEET.2013.8.2.304

Grabowski, P. Z., Kazmierkowski, M. P., Bose, B. K., & Blaabjerg, F. (2000). A simple direct-torque neuro-fuzzy control of PWM-inverter-fed induction motor drive. *IEEE Transactions on Industrial Electronics*, *47*(4), 863–870. doi:10.1109/41.857966

Grassi, G., Ouannas, A., Azar, A. T., Radwan, A. G., Volos, C., Pham, V. T., . . . Stouboulos, I. N. (2017). *Chaos Synchronisation Of Continuous Systems Via Scalar Signal*. The 6th International Conference on Modern Circuits and Systems Technologies (MOCAST), Thessaloniki, Greece. 10.1109/MOCAST.2017.7937629

Hadji, S., Gaubert, J. P., & Krim, F. (2014, October). Experimental analysis of genetic algorithms based MPPT for PV systems. *In Renewable and Sustainable Energy Conference (IRSEC), 2014 International* (pp. 7-12). IEEE. 10.1109/IRSEC.2014.7059887

Hassan, F. R. (2013). Modified Direct Torque Control using Algorithm Control of Stator Flux Estimation and Space Vector Modulation Based on Fuzzy Logic Control for Achieving High Performance from Induction Motors. *Journal of Power Electronics*, *13*(3), 369–380. doi:10.6113/JPE.2013.13.3.369

Hmidet, A., Dhifaoui, R., & Hasnaoui, O. (2010). Development, implementation and experimentation on a dSPACE DS1104 of a direct voltage control scheme. *Journal of Power Electronics*, *10*(5), 468–476. doi:10.6113/JPE.2010.10.5.468

Holtz, J. (1994). Pulsewidth modulation for electronic power conversion. *Proceedings of the IEEE*, *82*(8), 1194–1214. doi:10.1109/5.301684

Idkhajine, L., Monmasson, E., & Maalouf, A. (2010, July). Extended Kalman filter for AC drive sensorless speed controller-FPGA-based solution or DSP-based solution. In *Industrial Electronics (ISIE), IEEE International Symposium on* (pp. 2759-2764). IEEE.

Idris, N. R. N., & Yatim, A. H. M. (2004). Direct torque control of induction machines with constant switching frequency and reduced torque ripple. *IEEE Transactions on Industrial Electronics*, *51*(4), 758–767. doi:10.1109/TIE.2004.831718

Ismail, M. M. (2012). Applications of ANFIS and Fuzzy Algorithms for Improvement of the DTC Performance for the Three Phase Saturated Model of Induction Motor. *International Journal of System Dynamics Applications*, *1*(3), 54–83. doi:10.4018/ijsda.2012070102

Jidin, A. B., Idris, N. R. B. N., Yatim, A. H. B. M., Elbuluk, M. E., & Sutikno, T. (2012). A wide-speed high torque capability utilizing overmodulation strategy in DTC of induction machines with constant switching frequency controller. *IEEE Transactions on Power Electronics*, *27*(5), 2566–2575. doi:10.1109/TPEL.2011.2168240

Kaboli, S., Zolgbadri, M. R., & Emadi, A. (2003). Hysteresis Band Determination of Direct Torque Controlled Induction Motor Drives with Torque Ripple and Motor-Inverter Loss Considerations. *IEEE 34th annual, power electronics specialist conference*, (Vol. 3, pp. 1107-1111). IEEE.

Kang, J. W., & Sul, S. K. (2001). Analysis and prediction of inverter switching frequency in direct torque control of induction machine based on hysteresis bands and machine parameters. *IEEE Transactions on Industrial Electronics*, *48*(3), 545–553. doi:10.1109/41.925581

Kanungo, B. M. (2009). A Direct Torque Controlled Induction Motor with Variable Hysteresis Band. *11th International Conference on Computer Modelling and Simulation*, 405-410.

Kızılkaya, M. Ö., & Gülez, K. (2016). Feed-Forward Approach in Stator-Flux-Oriented Direct Torque Control of Induction Motor with Space Vector Pulse-Width Modulation. *Journal of Power Electronics*, *16*(3), 994–1003. doi:10.6113/JPE.2016.16.3.994

Kouro, S., Bernal, R., Miranda, H., Silva, C. A., & Rodríguez, J. (2007). High-performance torque and flux control for multilevel inverter fed induction motors. *IEEE Transactions on Power Electronics*, *22*(6), 2116–2123. doi:10.1109/TPEL.2007.909189

Krim, S., Gdaim, S., Mtibaa, A., & Mimouni, M. F. (2016). FPGA Contribution in Photovoltaic Pumping Systems: Models of MPPT and DTC-SVM Algorithms. *International Journal of Renewable Energy Research*, *6*(3), 866–879.

Lai, Y. S., & Chen, J. H. (2001). A new approach to direct torque control of induction motor drives for constant inverter switching frequency and torque ripple reduction. *IEEE Transactions on Energy Conversion*, *16*(3), 220–227. doi:10.1109/60.937200

Lekhchine, S., Bahi, T., & Soufi, Y. (2013). Direct Torque Control of Dual Star Induction Motor. *International Journal of Renewable Energy Research*, *3*(1), 121–125.

Liu, J., Wu, P., Bai, H., & Huang, X. (2004, June). Application of fuzzy control in direct torque control of permanent magnet synchronous motor. In *Intelligent Control and Automation, 2004. WCICA 2004. Fifth World Congress on* (Vol. 5, pp. 4573-4576). IEEE.

Llor, A., Allard, B., Lin-Shi, X., & Retif, J. M. (2004, June). Comparison of DTC implementations for synchronous machines. In *Power Electronics Specialists Conference, 2004. PESC 04. 2004 IEEE 35th Annual* (Vol. 5, pp. 3581-3587). IEEE. 10.1109/PESC.2004.1355109

Lokriti, A., Salhi, I., Doubabi, S., & Zidani, Y. (2013). Induction motor speed drive improvement using fuzzy IP-self-tuning controller. A real time implementation. *ISA Transactions*, *52*(3), 406–417. doi:10.1016/j.isatra.2012.11.002 PMID:23317661

Meghni, B., Dib, D., & Azar, A. T. (2017c). A Second-order sliding mode and fuzzy logic control to Optimal Energy Management in PMSG Wind Turbine with Battery Storage. *Neural Computing & Applications*, *28*(6), 1417–1434. doi:10.100700521-015-2161-z

Meghni, B., Dib, D., Azar, A. T., Ghoudelbourk, S., & Saadoun, A. (2017a). *Robust Adaptive Supervisory Fractional order Controller For optimal Energy Management in Wind Turbine with Battery Storage. Studies in Computational Intelligence* (Vol. 688). Springer-Verlag.

Meghni, B., Dib, D., Azar, A. T., & Saadoun, A. (2017b). *Effective Supervisory Controller to Extend Optimal Energy Management in Hybrid Wind Turbine under Energy and Reliability Constraints. International Journal of Dynamics and Control.* Springer. doi:10.100740435-016-0296-0

Mekki, H., Boukhetala, D., & Azar, A. T. (2015). Sliding Modes for Fault Tolerant Control. In Advances and Applications in Sliding Mode Control systems. Springer-Verlag GmbH Berlin/Heidelberg. doi:10.1007/978-3-319-11173-5_15

Messaif, I., Berkouk, E. M., & Saadia, N. (2007, December). Ripple reduction in DTC drives by using a three-level NPC VSI. In *Electronics, Circuits and Systems, 2007. ICECS 2007. 14th IEEE International Conference on* (pp. 1179-1182). IEEE. 10.1109/ICECS.2007.4511206

Monmasson, E., & Cirstea, M. N. (2007). FPGA design methodology for industrial control systems—A review. *IEEE Transactions on Industrial Electronics*, *54*(4), 1824–1842. doi:10.1109/TIE.2007.898281

Monmasson, E., Idkhajine, L., Cirstea, M. N., Bahri, I., Tisan, A., & Naouar, M. W. (2011). FPGAs in industrial control applications. *IEEE Transactions on Industrial Informatics*, *7*(2), 224–243. doi:10.1109/TII.2011.2123908

Myaing, A., & Dinavahi, V. (2011, July). FPGA-based real-time emulation of power electronic systems with detailed representation of device characteristics. In *Power and Energy Society General Meeting, 2011 IEEE* (pp. 1-11). IEEE.

Nahid-Mobarakeh, B., Meibody-Tabar, F., & Sargos, F. M. (2004). Mechanical sensorless control of PMSM with online estimation of stator resistance. *IEEE Transactions on Industry Applications*, *40*(2), 457–471. doi:10.1109/TIA.2004.824490

Naouar, M. W., Monmasson, E., Naassani, A. A., & Slama-Belkhodja, I. (2013). FPGA-based dynamic reconfiguration of sliding mode current controllers for synchronous machines. *IEEE Transactions on Industrial Informatics*, *9*(3), 1262–1271. doi:10.1109/TII.2012.2220974

Naouar, M. W., Monmasson, E., Naassani, A. A., Slama-Belkhodja, I., & Patin, N. (2007). FPGA-based current controllers for AC machine drives—A review. *IEEE Transactions on Industrial Electronics*, *54*(4), 1907–1925. doi:10.1109/TIE.2007.898302

Ortega, M., Restrepo, J., Viola, J., Gimenez, M. I., & Guzman, V. (2005, November). Direct torque control of induction motors using fuzzy logic with current limitation. In *Industrial Electronics Society, 2005. IECON 2005. 31st Annual Conference of IEEE* (pp. 6-pp). IEEE. 10.1109/IECON.2005.1569107

Ouannas, A., Azar, A. T., & Abu-Saris, R. (2016a). A new type of hybrid synchronization between arbitrary hyperchaotic maps. *International Journal of Machine Learning and Cybernetics*. doi:10.100713042-016-0566-3

Ouannas, A., Azar, A. T., & Radwan, A. G. (2016b) *On Inverse Problem of Generalized Synchronization Between Different Dimensional Integer-Order and Fractional-Order Chaotic Systems.* The 28th International Conference on Microelectronics, Cairo, Egypt. 10.1109/ICM.2016.7847942

Ouannas, A., Azar, A. T., & Vaidyanathan, S. (2017f). On A Simple Approach for Q-S Synchronization of Chaotic Dynamical Systems in Continuous-Time. *Int. J. Computing Science and Mathematics*, *8*(1), 20–27.

Ouannas, A., Azar, A. T., & Vaidyanathan, S. (2017g). New Hybrid Synchronization Schemes Based on Coexistence of Various Types of Synchronization Between Master-Slave Hyperchaotic Systems. *International Journal of Computer Applications in Technology*, *55*(2), 112–120. doi:10.1504/IJCAT.2017.082868

Ouannas, A., Azar, A. T., & Vaidyanathan, S. (2017i). A Robust Method for New Fractional Hybrid Chaos Synchronization. *Mathematical Methods in the Applied Sciences*, *40*(5), 1804–1812. doi:10.1002/mma.4099

Ouannas, A., Azar, A. T., & Ziar, T. (2017h). *On Inverse Full State Hybrid Function Projective Synchronization for Continuous-time Chaotic Dynamical Systems with Arbitrary Dimensions.* Differential Equations and Dynamical Systems. doi:10.100712591-017-0362-x

Ouannas, A., Azar, A. T., Ziar, T., & Radwan, A. G. (2017d). *Study On Coexistence of Different Types of Synchronization Between Different dimensional Fractional Chaotic Systems. Studies in Computational Intelligence* (Vol. 688). Springer-Verlag.

Ouannas, A., Azar, A. T., Ziar, T., & Radwan, A. G. (2017e). *Generalized Synchronization of Different Dimensional Integer-order and Fractional Order Chaotic Systems. Studies in Computational Intelligence* (Vol. 688). Springer-Verlag.

Ouannas, A., Azar, A. T., Ziar, T., & Vaidyanathan, S. (2017a). *On New Fractional Inverse Matrix Projective Synchronization Schemes. Studies in Computational Intelligence* (Vol. 688). Springer-Verlag.

Ouannas, A., Azar, A. T., Ziar, T., & Vaidyanathan, S. (2017b). *Fractional Inverse Generalized Chaos Synchronization Between Different Dimensional Systems. Studies in Computational Intelligence* (Vol. 688). Springer-Verlag.

Ouannas, A., Azar, A. T., Ziar, T., & Vaidyanathan, S. (2017c). *A New Method To Synchronize Fractional Chaotic Systems With Different Dimensions. Studies in Computational Intelligence* (Vol. 688). Springer-Verlag.

Ouannas, A., Grassi, G., Azar, A. T., Radwan, A. G., Volos, C., Pham, V. T., . . . Stouboulos, I. N. (2017j). *Dead-Beat Synchronization Control in Discrete-Time Chaotic Systems.* The 6th International Conference on Modern Circuits and Systems Technologies (MOCAST), Thessaloniki, Greece. 10.1109/MOCAST.2017.7937628

Pham, V., Trillion, Q., Zheng, Z. Y., Fei, L., & Viet-dung, D. (2016). A DTC Stator Flux Algorithm for the Performance Improvement of Induction Traction Motors. *Journal of Power Electronics*, *16*(2), 572–583. doi:10.6113/JPE.2016.16.2.572

Rahmati, A., Arasteh, M., Farhangi, S., & Abrishamifar, A. (2011). Flying Capacitor DTC Drive with Reductions in Common Mode Voltage and Stator Overvoltage. *Journal of Power Electronics*, *11*(4), 512–519. doi:10.6113/JPE.2011.11.4.512

Rakesh, P. (2003). *AC Induction Motor Fundamentals*. Microchip Technology Inc, AN887, DS00887A, 1-24.

Ramesh, T., Panda, A. K., & Kumar, S. S. (2015). MRAS speed estimator based on type-1 and type-2 fuzzy logic controller for the speed sensorless DTFC-SVPWM of an induction motor drive. *Journal of Power Electronics*, *15*(3), 730–740. doi:10.6113/JPE.2015.15.3.730

Rao, K., Vaghela, D. J., & Gojiya, M. V. (2016, July). Implementation of SPWM technique for 3-Φ VSI using STM32F4 discovery board interfaced with MATLAB. In *Power Electronics, Intelligent Control and Energy Systems (ICPEICES), IEEE International Conference on* (pp. 1-5). IEEE.

Reddy, T. B., Reddy, B. K., Amarnath, J., Rayudu, D. S., & Khan, M. H. (2006, April). Sensorless direct torque control of induction motor based on hybrid space vector pulsewidth modulation to reduce ripples and switching losses-A variable structure controller approach. In *Power India Conference*. IEEE.

Reisi, A. R., Moradi, M. H., & Jamasb, S. (2013). Classification and comparison of maximum power point tracking techniques for photovoltaic system: A review. *Renewable & Sustainable Energy Reviews*, *19*, 433–443. doi:10.1016/j.rser.2012.11.052

Rodriguez, J., Pontt, J., Kouro, S., & Correa, P. (2003, June). Direct torque control with imposed switching frequency and torque ripple minimization in an 11-level cascaded inverter. In *Power Electronics Specialist Conference, 2003. PESC'03. 2003 IEEE 34th Annual* (Vol. 2, pp. 501-506). IEEE. 10.1109/PESC.2003.1218106

Romeral, L., Arias, A., Aldabas, E., & Jayne, M. G. (2003). Novel direct torque control (DTC) scheme with fuzzy adaptive torque-ripple reduction. *IEEE Transactions on Industrial Electronics*, *50*(3), 487–492. doi:10.1109/TIE.2003.812352

Sanila, C. M. (2012). Direct Torque Control of Induction Motor With Constant Switching Frequency. In *IEEE International Conference on Power Electronics, Drives and Energy Systems* (pp. 1-6). Bengaluru, India: IEEE. 10.1109/PEDES.2012.6484352

Shereen, A. (2016). Classification of EEG Signals for Motor Imagery based on Mutual Information and Adaptive Neuro Fuzzy Inference System. *International Journal of System Dynamics Applications*, *5*(4), 64–82. doi:10.4018/IJSDA.2016100104

Shin, S., Choi, C., Youm, J., Lee, T., & Won, C. (2012). Position Control of PMSM using Jerk-Limited Trajectory for Torque Ripple Reduction in Robot Applications. *IECON - 38th Annual Conference on IEEE Industrial Electronics Society*, 2400 – 2405. DOI: 10.1109/IECON.2012.6388868

Singh, S., Azar, A. T., Ouannas, A., Zhu, Q., Zhang, W., & Na, J. (2017). *Sliding Mode Control Technique for Multi-switching Synchronization of Chaotic Systems. 9th International Conference on Modelling, Identification and Control (ICMIC 2017)*, Kunming, China.

Sivaprakasam, A., & Manigandan, T. (2013). Novel Switching Table for Direct Torque Controlled Permanent Magnet Synchronous Motors to Reduce Torque Ripple. *Journal of Power Electronics*, *13*(6), 939–954. doi:10.6113/JPE.2013.13.6.939

Soliman, N. S., Said, L. A., Azar, A. T., Madian, A. H., Radwan, A. G., & Ouannas, A. (2017). *Fractional Controllable Multi-Scroll V-Shape Attractor with Parameters Effect.* The 6th International Conference on Modern Circuits and Systems Technologies (MOCAST), Thessaloniki, Greece.

Srirattanawichaikul, W., Kumsuwan, Y., & Premrudeepreechacharn, S. (2010). Reduction of torque ripples in direct torque control for induction motor drives using decoupled amplitude and angle of stator flux control. *ECTI Trans. on Electrical Engineering, Electronics, and Communications*, *8*(2), 187–196.

Taib, N., Rekioua, T., & François, B. (2010). *An improved fixed switching frequency direct torque control of induction motor drives fed by direct matrix converter.* arXiv preprint arXiv:1004.1745.

Takahashi, I., & Noguchi, T. (1986). A new quick-response and high-efficiency control strategy of an induction motor. *IEEE Transactions on Industry Applications*, *22*(5), 820–827. doi:10.1109/TIA.1986.4504799

Texas Instruments Europe. (1997). *Sensorless Control with Kalman Filter on TMS320 Fixed-Point DSP.* TI. Literature no. BPRA057.

Tolba, M. F., AbdelAty, A. M., Soliman, N. S., Said, L. A., Madian, A. H., Azar, A. T., & Radwan, A. G. (2017). FPGA implementation of two fractional order chaotic systems. *International Journal of Electronics and Communications*, *28*, 162–172. doi:10.1016/j.aeue.2017.04.028

Tomohiro, N., Shinji, D., & Masami, F. (2014). Position Sensorless control of PMSM with a low-frequency signal injection. *International Power Electronics Conference (IPEC-Hiroshima - ECCE ASIA)*, 3079 – 3084. DOI: 10.1109/IPEC.2014.6870124

Uddin, M., Mekhilef, S., Mubin, M., Rivera, M., & Rodriguez, J. (2014). Model predictive torque ripple reduction with weighting factor optimization fed by an indirect matrix converter. *Electric Power Components and Systems*, *42*(10), 1059–1069. doi:10.1080/15325008.2014.913739

Uddin, M., Mekhilef, S., Rivera, M., & Rodriguez, J. (2015). Imposed weighting factor optimization method for torque ripple reduction of IM fed by indirect matrix converter with predictive control algorithm. *Journal of Electrical Engineering & Technology*, *10*(1), 227–242. doi:10.5370/JEET.2015.10.1.227

Utsumi, Y., Hoshi, N., & Oguchi, K. (2006). Comparison of FPGA-based Direct Torque Controllers for Permanent Magnet Synchronous Motors. *Journal of Power Electronics*, *6*(2), 114–120.

Vaidyanathan, S., & Azar, A. T. (2015a). Anti-Synchronization of Identical Chaotic Systems using Sliding Mode Control and an Application to Vaidyanathan-Madhavan Chaotic Systems. In Advances and Applications in Sliding Mode Control systems. Springer-Verlag GmbH Berlin/Heidelberg. doi:10.1007/978-3-319-11173-5_19

Vaidyanathan, S., & Azar, A. T. (2015b). Hybrid Synchronization of Identical Chaotic Systems using Sliding Mode Control and an Application to Vaidyanathan Chaotic Systems. In Advances and Applications in Sliding Mode Control systems. Springer-Verlag GmbH Berlin/Heidelberg. doi:10.1007/978-3-319-11173-5_20

Vaidyanathan, S., & Azar, A. T. (2015c). Analysis, Control and Synchronization of a Nine-Term 3-D Novel Chaotic System. In Chaos Modeling and Control Systems Design. Springer-Verlag GmbH Berlin/Heidelberg. DOI doi:10.1007/978-3-319-13132-0_1

Vaidyanathan, S., & Azar, A. T. (2015d). Analysis and Control of a 4-D Novel Hyperchaotic System. In Chaos Modeling and Control Systems Design. Springer-Verlag GmbH Berlin/Heidelberg. DOI doi:10.1007/978-3-319-13132-0_2

Vaidyanathan, S., & Azar, A. T. (2016a). Takagi-Sugeno Fuzzy Logic Controller for Liu-Chen Four-Scroll Chaotic System. *International Journal of Intelligent Engineering Informatics*, *4*(2), 135–150. doi:10.1504/IJIEI.2016.076699

Vaidyanathan, S., & Azar, A. T. (2016b). *Dynamic Analysis, Adaptive Feedback Control and Synchronization of an Eight-Term 3-D Novel Chaotic System with Three Quadratic Nonlinearities. Studies in Fuzziness and Soft Computing* (Vol. 337). Springer-Verlag.

Vaidyanathan, S., & Azar, A. T. (2016c). *Qualitative Study and Adaptive Control of a Novel 4-D Hyperchaotic System with Three Quadratic Nonlinearities. Studies in Fuzziness and Soft Computing* (Vol. 337). Springer-Verlag.

Vaidyanathan, S., & Azar, A. T. (2016d). *A Novel 4-D Four-Wing Chaotic System with Four Quadratic Nonlinearities and its Synchronization via Adaptive Control Method. Advances in Chaos Theory and Intelligent Control. Studies in Fuzziness and Soft Computing* (Vol. 337). Springer-Verlag.

Vaidyanathan, S., & Azar, A. T. (2016e). *Adaptive Control and Synchronization of Halvorsen Circulant Chaotic Systems. Advances in Chaos Theory and Intelligent Control. Studies in Fuzziness and Soft Computing* (Vol. 337). Springer-Verlag.

Vaidyanathan, S., & Azar, A. T. (2016f). *Adaptive Backstepping Control and Synchronization of a Novel 3-D Jerk System with an Exponential Nonlinearity. Advances in Chaos Theory and Intelligent Control. Studies in Fuzziness and Soft Computing* (Vol. 337). Springer-Verlag.

Vaidyanathan, S., & Azar, A. T. (2016g). *Generalized Projective Synchronization of a Novel Hyperchaotic Four-Wing System via Adaptive Control Method. Advances in Chaos Theory and Intelligent Control. Studies in Fuzziness and Soft Computing* (Vol. 337). Springer-Verlag.

Vaidyanathan, S., Azar, A. T., & Ouannas, A. (2017a). *An Eight-Term 3-D Novel Chaotic System with Three Quadratic Nonlinearities, its Adaptive Feedback Control and Synchronization. Studies in Computational Intelligence* (Vol. 688). Springer-Verlag.

Vaidyanathan, S., Azar, A. T., & Ouannas, A. (2017c). *Hyperchaos and Adaptive Control of a Novel Hyperchaotic System with Two Quadratic Nonlinearities. Studies in Computational Intelligence* (Vol. 688). Springer-Verlag.

Vaidyanathan, S., Azar, A. T., Rajagopal, K., & Alexander, P. (2015b). Design and SPICE implementation of a 12-term novel hyperchaotic system and its synchronization via active control (2015). International Journal of Modelling. *Identification and Control, 23*(3), 267–277. doi:10.1504/IJMIC.2015.069936

Vaidyanathan, S., Idowu, B. A., & Azar, A. T. (2015c). Backstepping Controller Design for the Global Chaos Synchronization of Sprott's Jerk Systems. In Chaos Modeling and Control Systems Design. Springer-Verlag GmbH Berlin/Heidelberg. doi:10.1007/978-3-319-13132-0_3

Vaidyanathan, S., Sampath, S., & Azar, A. T. (2015a). Global chaos synchronisation of identical chaotic systems via novel sliding mode control method and its application to Zhu system. International Journal of Modelling. *Identification and Control, 23*(1), 92–100. doi:10.1504/IJMIC.2015.067495

Vaidyanathan, S., Zhu, Q., & Azar, A. T. (2017b). *Adaptive Control of a Novel Nonlinear Double Convection Chaotic System. Studies in Computational Intelligence* (Vol. 688). Springer-Verlag.

Vittek, J., Bris, P., Štulrajter, M., Makyš, P., Comnac, V., & Cernat, M. (2008). Chattering free sliding mode control law for the drive employing PMSM position control. *International Conference on Optimization of Electrical and Electronic Equipment*, 115-120. 10.1109/OPTIM.2008.4602466

Vittek, J., Stulrajter, M., Makys, P., Vavrus, V., Dodds, J. S., & Perryman, R. (2005). Near-time-optimal position control of an actuator with PMSM. *European Conference on Power Electronics and Applications, 21*(2), 1-10. DOI: 10.1109/EPE.2005.219516

Wang, Y., Li, H., & Shi, X. (2006, November). Direct torque control with space vector modulation for induction motors fed by cascaded multilevel inverters. In *IEEE Industrial Electronics, IECON 2006-32nd Annual Conference on* (pp. 1575-1579). IEEE. 10.1109/IECON.2006.347240

Wang, Z., Volos, C., Kingni, S.T., Azar, A.T., & Pham, V.T. (2017). Four-wing attractors in a novel chaotic system with hyperbolic sine nonlinearity. *Optik - International Journal for Light and Electron Optics, 131*(2017), 1071-1078.

Youb, L., & Craciunescu, A. (2009). Direct torque control of induction motors with fuzzy minimization torque ripple. In *Proceedings of the world congress on engineering and computer science* (*Vol. 2*, pp. 713-717). Academic Press.

Yousry, A. (2009). Torque Ripple Minimization for Induction Motor Driven by a Photovoltaic Inverter. *Journal of Power Electronics, 9*(5), 679–690.

Zaimeddine, R., & Undeland, T. (2010, June). DTC control schemes for induction motor fed by three-level NPC-VSI using space vector modulation. In *Power Electronics Electrical Drives Automation and Motion (SPEEDAM), 2010 International Symposium on* (pp. 966-971). IEEE. 10.1109/SPEEDAM.2010.5545036

Zhang, Y., Yang, H., & Li, Z. (2013, October). A simple SVM-based deadbeat direct torque control of induction motor drives. In *Electrical Machines and Systems (ICEMS), 2013 International Conference on* (pp. 2201-2206). Academic Press.

Zhang, Y., Zhu, J., Guo, Y., Xu, W., Wang, Y., & Zhao, Z. (2009, September). A sensorless DTC strategy of induction motor fed by three-level inverter based on discrete space vector modulation. *In Power Engineering Conference, 2009. AUPEC 2009. Australasian Universities* (pp. 1-6). IEEE.

Zhu, Q., & Azar, A. T. (2015). *Complex system modelling and control through intelligent soft computations. Studies in Fuzziness and Soft Computing* (Vol. 319). Springer-Verlag.

Zidani, F., & Said, R. N. (2005). Direct torque control of induction motor with fuzzy minimization torque ripple. *Journal of Electrical Engineering-Bratislava*, *56*(7/8), 183.

APPENDIX

The abbreviations cited in the text are listed as follows:

DTC: Direct Torque Control.
SVM: Space Vector Modulation.
FLC: Fuzzy Logic Control.
FDTC: Fuzzy Direct Torque Control.
IM: Induction Motor.
XSG: Xilinx System Generator.
FPGA: Field Programmable Gate Array.
RTL: Register Transfer Level.
JTAG: Joint Test Action Group.
FLS: Fuzzy Logic System.
FIS: Fuzzy Inference System.
VHDL: VHSIC Hardware Description Language.
HIL: Hardware In the Loop.
PI: Proportional Integral.
FOC: Field Oriented Control.
DSPACE: Digital Signal Processing and Control Engineering.
DSP: Digital Signal Processor.
RISC: Reduced Instruction Set Computer.
PMSM: Permanent-Magnet Synchronous Motor.
UDC: Direct Voltage to fed he inverter.
NPC: Neutral Point Clamped.
FCs: Flying Capacitors.
CHB: Cascaded H-Bridge.
($i_{s\alpha}$ $i_{s\beta}$): α and β components of the stator currents.
($V_{s\alpha}$ $V_{s\beta}$): α and β components of the voltage.
($\varphi_{s\alpha}, \varphi_{s\beta}$): α and β components of stator flux.
($\varphi_{r\alpha}, \varphi_{r\beta}$): α and β components of rotor flux.
R_r, R_s: rotor and stator resistances, respectively.
L_r, L_s and M: rotor stator and mutual inductances, respectively.
T_{em}: Electromagnetic torque.
ω: electric Rotor speed.
J: Inertia moment.
f: Coefficient of friction.
T_L: Load torque.
N_p: number of the poles pairs.
$\sigma = 1 - \frac{M^2}{L_r L_s}$: Blondel's coefficient.
Ω_{ref}: Rotor speed reference.

φ_{ref} : Stator flux reference.
θ_s : Stator flux position.
θ_{sv} : voltage vector position.
Ts: sampling period.
PV: Photo-Voltaic
AC drive: Alternating Current drive

Chapter 8
Automatic Voltage Regulator System Tuning Using Swarm Intelligence Techniques

Naglaa K. Bahgaat
Canadian International College (CIC), Egypt

Mohamed Ahmed Moustafa Hassan
Cairo University, Egypt

ABSTRACT

The voltage regulator may be used to regulate one or more AC or DC voltages in power systems. Voltage regulator may be designed as a simple "feed-forward" or may include "negative feedback" control loops. It may use an electronic components or electromechanical mechanism on the design. AVR is keeping constant output voltage of the generator in a specified range. The PID controller can used to provide the control requirements. This chapter discusses some modern techniques to get the best possible tuning controller parameters for automatic voltage regulator techniques such as particle swarm optimization, adaptive weight particle swarm optimization, adaptive acceleration coefficients, adaptive acceleration coefficients. Also, it presents a new adjustment modified adaptive acceleration coefficients and a discussion of the results of the all methods used. Simulation for comparison between the proposed methods and the obtained results are promising.

1. INTRODUCTION

Automatic Voltage Regulator is a very important part of the power system generation, the main aim of the Automatic Voltage Regulator (AVR) loop is to control the amount of the terminal voltage V of the generator in the power system. The Dc signal, being proportional to |V|, is compared with a dc reference $\backslash V\backslash_{ref}$, the result of the comparison is the value of the "error voltage", after amplification and signal shaping, serves as the input to the exciter which finally delivers the voltage V_f to the generator field winding (Naglaa, 2013; Tammam,2011; Ingemar, 1983). A simple AVR circuit consists of many parts: amplifier, exciter, generator and sensor. In order to maintain the normal operation of AVR in the power

DOI: 10.4018/978-1-5225-4077-9.ch008

system to control the value of the generator output voltage, there are many types of controllers used. In Previous works on AVR system with self-tuning control was initiated in the years of 1990s. Sweden bank and coworkers carried out the classical self-tuning control techniques to the AVR system in 1999 (Bhati & Nitnawwre, 2012; Swidenbank et al., 1999). After this study, Fitch used a generalized projecting control technique as a self-tuning control algorithm in the same year (Fitch et al., 1999). Several nonlinear system approaches have been proposed for many practical applications such as optimal control, nonlinear feedback control, adaptive control, sliding mode control, nonlinear dynamics, chaos control, chaos synchronization control, fuzzy logic control, fuzzy adaptive control, fractional order control, and robust control and their integrations (Azar & Vaidyanathan, 2015a,b,c, 2016; Azar & Zhu, 2015; Meghni et al, 2017a,b,c; Boulkroune et al, 2016a,b; Ghoudelbourk et al., 2016; Azar & Serrano, 2015a,b,c,d, 2016a,b, 2017; Azar et al., 2017a,b,c,d; Azar 2010a,b, 2012; Mekki et al., 2015; Vaidyanathan & Azar, 2015a,b,c,d, 2016a,b,c,d,e,f,g, 2017a,b,c; Zhu & Azar, 2015; Grassi et al., 2017; Ouannas et al., 2016a,b, 2017a,b,c,d,e,f,g,h,I,j; Singh et al., 2017; Vaidyanathan et al, 2015a,b,c; Wang et al., 2017; Soliman et al., 2017; Tolba et al., 2017). The usage of artificial intelligence based self-tuning controllers was preferred by researchers from the beginning of 2000 (Azar & Zhu Q, 2015). In particular, self-tuning PID type controllers which were tuned with the optimization methods based on artificial intelligence have been initiated to carry out the AVR system since as described in (Azar & Vaidyanathan, 2015b; Azar & Vaidyanathan, 2015c), then Gaing suggested a PSO based self-tuning PID controller for AVR in 2006, Kim and colleagues developed the hybrid method which contains genetic algorithm and bacterial foraging optimization technique in order to improve the performance of self-tuning PID controller in AVR system (Kim & Cho, 2006). In 2007, Mukherjee and Goshen reported the Surgeon fuzzy logic self-tuning algorithm based on crazy-PSO for PID controller (RamaSudha, et al., 2010; Bevrani, 2009; Ismail, 2006).

This chapter presents the application of some modern techniques used for tuning the parameters of the controller for an automatic voltage regulator (AVR) system. Such as Particle Swarm Optimization (PSO) technique as described in (Rania, 2012; Naik et al., 2005; Gaing, 2004), Adaptive Weighted Particle Swarm Optimization techniques (AWPSO), Adaptive Accelerated Coefficients based on PSO (AACPSO) and Evolutionary Particle Swarm Optimization (MAACPSO). It will be used to determine the parameters of a PID controller according to the system dynamics (Bahgaat et al., 2014; Azar & Vaidyanathan, 2015c; Panigrahi, et al., 2008). The comparison of all the results in each method used and the preferred method which gives the more suitable and stable ranges of voltages will be discussed.

This chapter is arranged as follow: Section one introduction about the chapter. The second section presents literature review of the study. Section three introduces the automatic voltage regulation equations and brief explanation and equations of the modern techniques used in the study which are: Particle Swarm Optimization (PSO), AWPSO, the Adaptive Accelerated Coefficients based PSO (AACPSO) and Modified Adaptive Accelerated Coefficients based PSO (MAACPSO). While Section four shows the case study and presents all the results in each method used and a comparative study between these methods and results, Also, Section five concludes the chapter, and finally discusses the future work. A list of references and Appendix of this chapter are given at the end of the chapter.

2. LITERATURE REVIEW

2.1. Linear Model of an AVR System

AVR used in power systems to keep constant output voltage of the generator in a specified range. A simple AVR model consists of amplifier, exciter, generator and sensor. The model and the block diagram of AVR with PID controller are shown in Figure 1.

The linear models of the elements of the AVR are given as the following (Kumar & Gupta, 2014):

a. PID Controller Model

The transfer function of PID controller is

$$G_c(S) = K_p + K_d S + \frac{K_i}{S} \quad (1)$$

where: k_p, k_d, and k_i are the proportion coefficient, Differential coefficient, and integral coefficient, respectively.

b. Amplifier Model

The transfer function of amplifier model is:

$$\frac{V_R(s)}{V_e(S)} = \frac{K_A}{1+\tau_A S} \quad (2)$$

where K_A is an amplifier gain and τ_A is a time constant.

Figure 1. The block diagram of the AVR

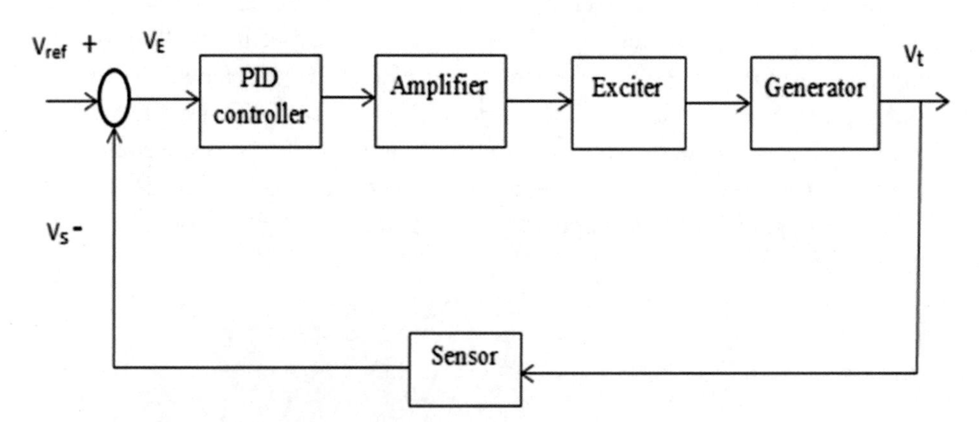

c. Exciter Model

The transfer function of exciter model is:

$$\frac{V_F(s)}{V_R(S)} = \frac{K_E}{1+\tau_E S} \tag{3}$$

Where K_E is an amplifier gain and τ_E is a time constant.

d. Generator Model

The transfer function of generator model is:

$$\frac{V_t(s)}{V_F(S)} = \frac{K_G}{1+\tau_G S} \tag{4}$$

Where K_G is an amplifier gain and τ_G is a time constant.

e. Sensor Model

The transfer function of sensor model is:

$$\frac{V_S(s)}{V_t(S)} = \frac{K_R}{1+\tau_R S} \tag{5}$$

where K_R is an amplifier gain and τ_R is a time constant.

Figure 2 presents the block diagram of an AVR system with PID controller as the following:

2.2. PID Controller

PID controller used more than 95% in control applications. Also, they state that 30% of the PID loops operate in the manual mode and 25% of PID loops really operate under default factory settings. PID parameters can be realized manually by trial and error, and by using many modern techniques as presented in (Bahgaat et. al., 2014; Ang et al., 2005).

As presented before the PID control described as a linear control. Which consists of three parameters, these parameters activate on the error signal, which is the difference between the desired output and the actual output, and generate the actuating signal that drives the plant. They have three basic terms: the first one is the proportional action, in which the actuating signal is proportional to the error signal, the second on is the integral action, where the actuating signal is proportional to the time integral of the error signal; the last one is the derivative action, where the actuating signal is proportional to the time

Figure 2. Block diagram of an AVR system with a PID controller

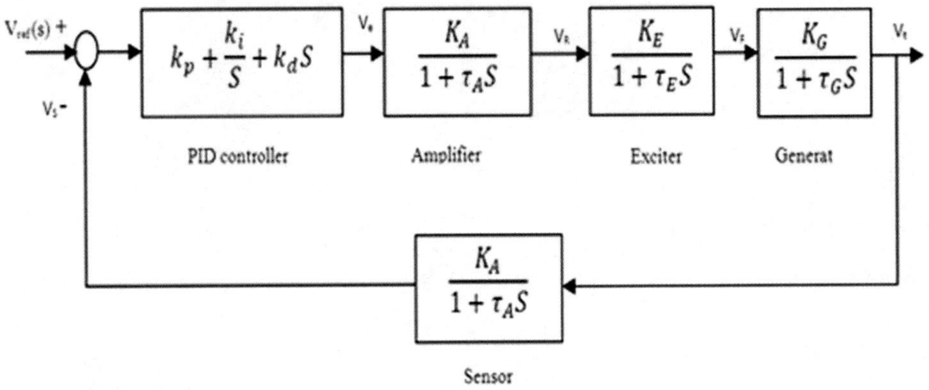

derivative of the error signal as existing in (Azar & Vaidyanathan, 2015c; Tammam et al., 2011; Reeves & Rowe, 2002; Darrell, 2005).The PID standard form is given by the following equations:

$$u = K_p.e + K_i \int e.dt + K_d.\frac{de}{dt} \tag{6}$$

where:

e: Is the error signal.
u: Is the control action.
K_p: Is the proportional gain
K_i: Is the integral gain
K_d: Is the derivative gain

Using conventional PD, PI, PID controllers does not provide sufficient control performance with the effect of governor dead band (Ismail & Hassan, 2012; Salami et al., 2006; Skogestad, 2003; Wang et al., 1993). So many other methods used since 1890s till now to tune the controller. First method is the manual tuning. In this method the parameters (K_p, K_i and K_d) have to be adjusted to arrive at acceptable performance. Second method is an automatic method called Ziegler–Nichols method which introduced by John G. Ziegler and Nathaniel B. Nichols in the 1940s (Skogestad, 2003; Wang et al., 1993). In this technique, the control systems has an S-shaped curve called the process reaction curve and can be generated experimentally or from dynamic simulation of the plant as presented in (Bahgaat, et. al., 2014; Tammam, 2011)

Some software can used to tuning the PID controller, such as PSO, AWPSO (Rania, 2012; Panigrahi et al., 2008; Naik et al., 2005), AACPSO and MAACPSO (Bahgaat et al., 2014; Azar et al., 2013; Azar & Serrano, 2014). This chapter will present the design of the PID controller by using Particle Swarm Optimization (PSO), Adaptive Weighted Particle Swarm Optimization (AWPSO), Adaptive Accelerated Coefficients based PSO (AACPSO) and Modified Adaptive Accelerated Coefficients PSO (MAACPSO) by using the simulation based on MATLAB software program. This program run many times until reaching to the best result of the transfer function to have a value of PID parameters. These parameters produce the smallest value of settling time and over shoot. So, these values of PID parameters are the best values to reach. In the following there are a little review of these modern techniques and the equation of each one of them.

2.3. Particle Swarm Optimization (PSO)

PSO as illustrated in (Soundarrajan and Sumathi, 2010), is a technique based on the behavior of the birds, particle acts individually and accelerates toward the best personal location (P_{best}) while checking the fitness value of its current position. Fitness value of a position is obtained by evaluating the so-called fitness function at that location. If a particles' current location has a better fitness value than that of its current (P_{best}), then the (P_{best}) is replaced by the current location (Naglaa, 2015; Azar & Vaidyanathan, 2015b). Each particle in the swarm has knowledge of the location with best fitness value of the whole swarm which is called the global best or (g_{best}) . At each point along their path, each particle also compares the fitness value of their (P_{best}) to that of (g_{best}) . If any particle has a (P_{best}) with better fitness value than that of current (g_{best}), then the current (g_{best}) is replaced by that particle's (P_{best}) . The movement of particles is stopped once all particles reach close to the position with best fitness value of the swarm.

Let the particle of the swarm is represented by the N dimensional vector ith then the equations of the swarm as the following:

$$X_i = (X_1, X_2, X_3, \ldots\ldots X_N) \quad (7)$$

The previous best position of the Nth particles is recorded and represented as follows:

$$P_{besti} = (P_{best1}, P_{best2}, \ldots, P_{bestN}) \quad (8)$$

where P_{best} is Particle best position (m), N is the total number of iterations.

The best position of the particle among all particles in the swarm is represented by gbest the velocity of the particle is represented as follows:

$$V_i = (V_1, V_2, \ldots, V_N) \quad (9)$$

where V_i is the velocity of each i particle

The modified velocity and position of each particle can be calculated from the current velocity and the distance from particle current position to particle best position P_{best} and to global best position g_{best} as shown in the following Equations (Bahgaat et al., 2014)

$$V_{i(t)} = W.\, V_{i(t-1)} + C_1.rand(0,1).(P_{best} - X_{i(t-1)}) + C_2.rand(0,1).(g_{best} - X_{i(t-1)}) \quad (10)$$

$$X_{i(t)} = X_{i(t-1)} + V_{i(t)} \quad (11)$$

$$i = 1,2,3\ldots,N \quad (12)$$

$j=1,2,3...,D$ (13)

Where:

$V_i(t)$: Velocity of the particle i at iteration t (m/s)
$X_i(t)$: The Current position of particle i at iteration t (m)
D: The Dimension
C_1: The cognitive acceleration coefficient and it is a positive number
C_2: Social acceleration coefficient and it is a positive number
rand [0,1]: A random number obtained from a uniform random distribution function in the interval [0,1]
gbest: The Global best position (m)
W: The Inertia weight

2.4. Adaptive Weighted Particle Swarm Optimization

Adaptive Weighted Particle Swarm Optimization (AWPSO) technique used is a modification of PSO in multi-objective optimization problems as presented in (Panigrahi, et al., 2008; Naik, et al., 2005). AWPSO is consists of two terms which are: inertia weigh (W) and Acceleration factor (A) as illustrated in (Bahgaat et al., 2015; Rania, 2012). The inertia weight formula is as follows which makes W value changes randomly from Wo to 1 as shown in (Bahgaat et al., 2014;Azar, 2012; Azar, 2010).

$$W=Wo+ rand(0,1)(1-Wo) \quad (14)$$

where:

Wo: The initial positive constant in the interval chosen from [0, 1]

Particle velocity at *i*th iteration as follows:

$$V_i(t) = W.\ V_i(t-1) + AC_1.rand(0,1).(P_{best} - X_i(t-1)) + AC_2.rand(0,1).(g_{best} - X_i(t-1)) \quad (15)$$

Additional term denoted by *A* called acceleration factor is added in the original velocity equation to improve the swarm search.

The acceleration factor formula is given as follows (Rania, 2012):

$$A = A_o + \frac{i}{n} \quad (16)$$

where:

Ao: Is the initial positive constant in the interval [0.5, 1].
n: is the number of iteration.

C_1 *and* C_2: Are the constant representing the weighing of the stochastic acceleration terms that pull each particle towards P_{best} and g_{best} positions.

2.5. Adaptive Accelerated Coefficients Based PSO

This modification have emerged to advance AWPSO Algorithms, as Time-Varying Acceleration Coefficients (TVAC), where C_1 and C_2which described in (Hamid et al., 2010) ; C_1 and C_2 values will be change linearly with time, This method deal with inertia weight and acceleration factors and how to change acceleration coefficients exponentially as presented in (Azar & Serrano, 2014; Vlachogiannis & Lee, 2009; Hassanien, 2014). The parameters C_1 and C_2 vary adaptively according to the fitness value of G_{best} and P_{best}, as presented in (Bahgaat et al., 2014; Hamid et al., 2010) becomes:

$$V_i^{(t+1)} = w^{(t)}V_i^{(t)} + C_1^{(t)}r_1 * \left(P_{best}^{(t)} - X_i^{(t)}\right) + C_2^{(t)}r_2 * \left(G_{best}^{(t)} - X_i^{(t)}\right) \quad (17)$$

$$w^{(t)} = w_o * exp\left(- \propto_w * t\right) \quad (18)$$

$$C_1^{(t)} = C_{1o} * \exp\left(- \propto_c * t * k_c^{(t)}\right) \quad (19)$$

$$C_2^{(t)} = C_{2o} * \exp\left(\propto_c * t * k_c^{(t)}\right) \quad (20)$$

$$\propto_c = \frac{-1}{t_{max}} \ln\left(\frac{C_{2o}}{C_{1o}}\right) \quad (21)$$

$$k_c^{(t)} = \frac{\left(F_m^{(t)} - G_{best}^{(t)}\right)}{F_m^{(t)}} \quad (22)$$

where:

$w^{(t)}$: The inertia weight factor
$C_1^{(t)}$: Acceleration coefficient at iteration t
i: Equal 1 or 2
t: The iteration number

ln: The neperian logarithm

αw: Is determined with respect to initial and final values of ω with the same manner as αc described in (Amjady, et al., 2009).

$k_c^{(t)}$: Determined based on the fitness value of G_{best} and Pbest at iteration t

ω_o, c_{io} c_{io}: initial values of inertia weight factor and acceleration coefficients respectively with i=1or 2.

$F_m^{(t)}$: The mean value of the best positions related to all particles at iteration t

2.6 Modified Adaptive Accelerated Coefficients PSO

Modified Adaptive Accelerated Coefficients PSO will be described as presented in (Khalifa, et al 2015). In this modification the first choice the value of C_1 and C_2 which described in the last section. Then C_1 will be changes exponentially (with inertia weight) in the time, with respect to their minimal and maximal values. While, the other one C_2 changes as a factor of the first coefficient. The choice of the exponential function is justified by the increasing or decreasing speed of such a function to accelerate the process of the algorithm and to get better search in the exploration s pace.

In this technique the value of C_1 as presented in the equation (20) the parameter $C_2(t)$ is suggested to be equal the following as described in (Khalifa, 2015):

$$C_2(t) = 4-C_1(t) \quad (23)$$

3. CASE STUDY

The detection of the performance of AVR system working on the SIMULINK model to obtain the Simulation result using MATLAB program. Figure 3 shows the SIMULINK of the model used (Musa et al., 2013).

The parameters value of the system presented in Table 1.

Figure 3. SIMULINK model of AVR with PID Controller

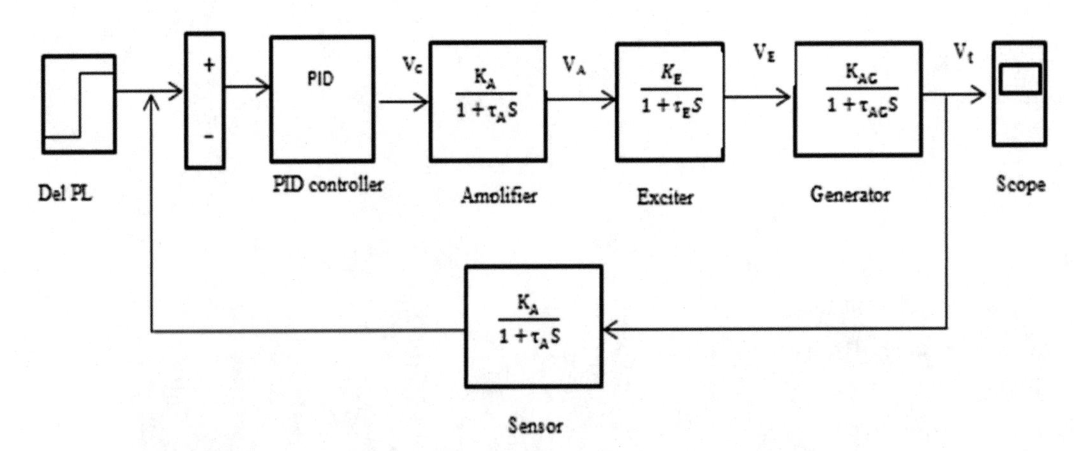

Table 1. The value of the parameters in the system

Parameter	The value
K_g	1
K_a	10
K_e	1
K_r	1
T_g	0.02
T_a	0.1
T_e	0.4
T_r	0.05

The load differs by 0.8 percent; by using MATLAB program and choice the type of error which used in the program, there are three types of error described as the following:

Integral of Absolute Error (IAE):

$$IAE = \int_0^{\infty} \left|e(t)\right| dt \tag{24}$$

Integral of Squared Error (ISE)

$$ISE = \int_0^{\infty} e^2(t)\, dt \tag{25}$$

Integral of Time Weighted Absolute Error (ITAE)

$$ITAE = \int_0^{\infty} t\left|e(t)\right| dt \tag{26}$$

where:

e: Is the error
f : Is the objective function

In this chapter the ITAE error was used in the program

The program used the equations for PSO as shown above, and then the program was repeated using the equations of AWPSO, AACPSO and finally using MAACPSO, the results of the PID controller using different methods are shown in Table 2 and Figure 5

Table 2. The Results of the Program Using PSO, AWPSO, AACPSO and MAACPSO

Items of Comparison	PSO	AWPSO	AACPSO	MAACPSO
Number of iterations	100	100	100	100
Error ITAE	0.0611	0.0252	0.0149	0.0267
Settling time (sec)	18.4281	13.9323	8.6514	3.7267
Over shoot	0.85	0.98	0.97	0.985
K_p	2.4	8.1	9.1	3.7
K_i	1.5	7.5	8.46	5.07
K_d	1.3	2.7	3.2	1.8

Figure 4. The power system response before using the controller

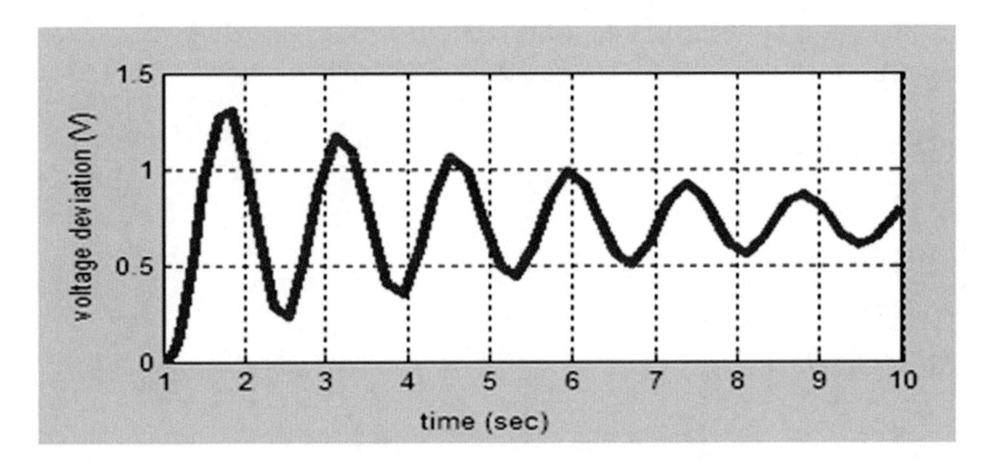

Figure 4 presents the power system response before using the controller and Figures 5-9 show the terminal voltage response for change in load and regulation which obtained. It could be observed that the response settles in about 3.7 seconds with very small overshoot. These results indicate that the PID controller using the modified MAACPSO controller reduces the steady state error to zero. It is practical that the settling time of AVR with PID controller using MAAPSO is less and there is no transient peak overshoot. Other methods used above give good results also, but the best results got by using MAAPSO which give the smallest value of settling time and over shoot value.

4. DISCUSSION AND CONCLUSION

The quality of controller used in power system is determined by constancy of frequency and voltage. Minimum frequency deviation and good terminal voltage level are required. The characteristic of a reliable power system must be considered. The AVR loop control is very important to study, to control the output voltage of the generator and make the deviation of it smaller as possible. It can be concluded that, the PID controllers provide an acceptable stability between overshoot and transient oscillations with zero steady state error. The simulation results presented the difference between the methods used to tune the

Figure 5. AVR Based PID controller using PSO

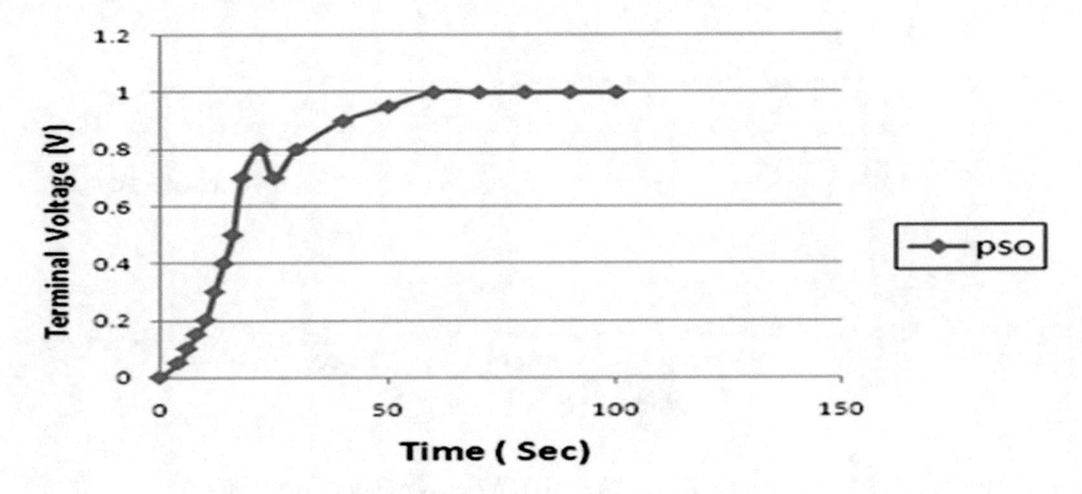

Figure 6. AVR Based PID controller using AWPSO

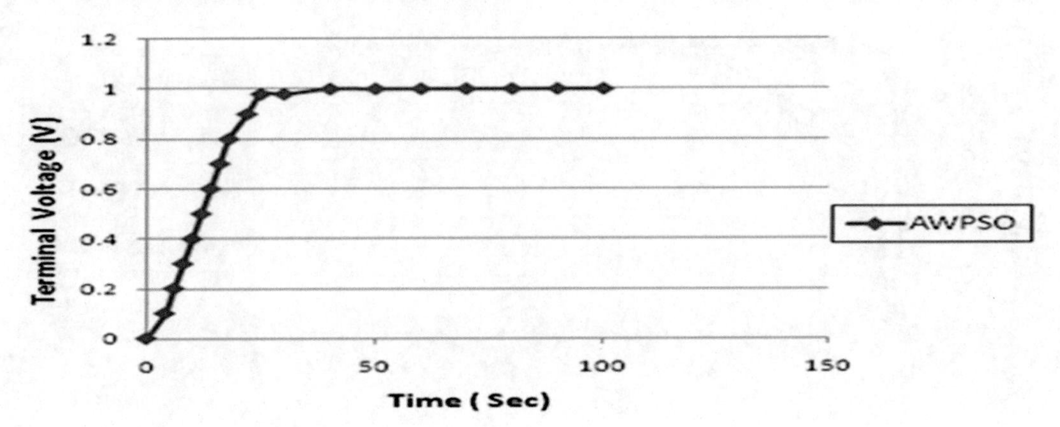

Figure 7. AVR Based PID controller using AAPSO

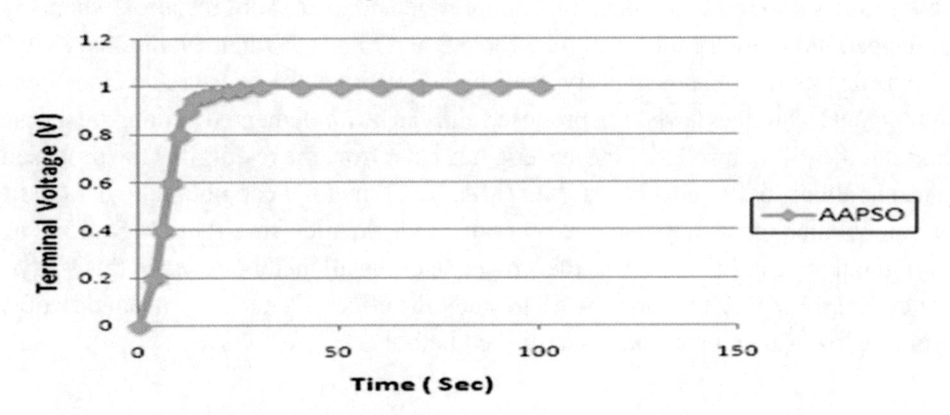

Figure 8. AVR Based PID controller using MAAPSO

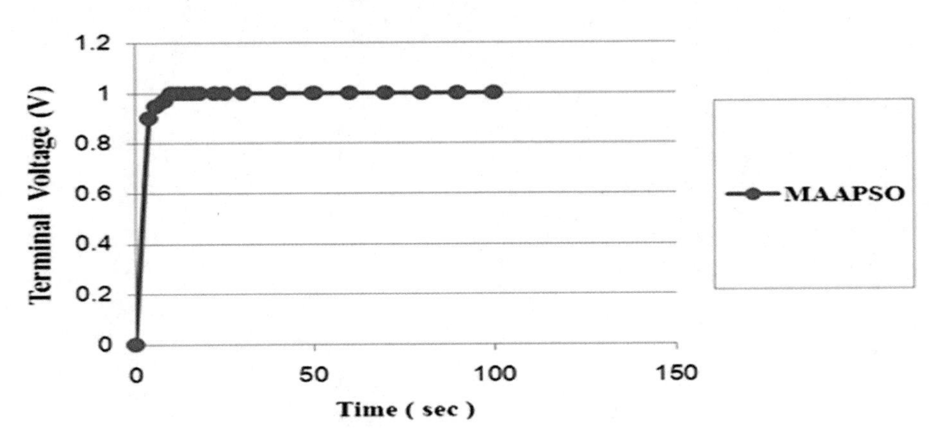

Figure 9. AVR Based PID controller using PSO, AWPSO, AAPSO and MAAPSO

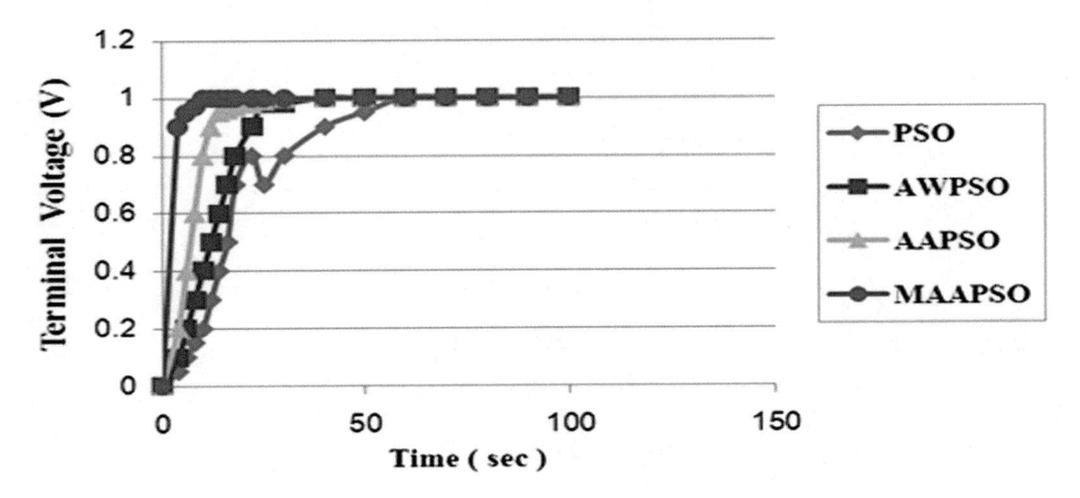

PID controller to reach to the best values of settling time and over shoot response when any changing of the load happen. From the results shown in Table 2 and Figure 5 when evolutionary algorithms are applied to control system problems, their typical characteristics show a faster and smoother response.

Some intelligent techniques have been proposed and can be implemented to improve the performance characteristics of the PID controller of the system. It is clear from the results that the proposed Modified Adaptive Acceleration Coefficients based PSO (MAAPSO) method can obtain higher quality solution with better computation efficiency than the other methods. While using Particle Swarm Optimization (PSO) only without any modification was the worst one of the all methods used in this study. AVR with load frequency control will be the future work to study the effect of changing the load frequency on the AVR control loop by using all methods as described before.

REFERENCES

Allaoua, B., Abdessalam, A., Brahim, G., & Abdelfatah, N. (2008). The efficiency of Particle Swarm Optimization applied on Fuzzy Logic DC motor speed control. *Serbian Journal of Electrical Engineering*, *5*(2), 247–262. doi:10.2298/SJEE0802247A

Azar, A. T. (2010a). *Fuzzy Systems*. Vienna, Austria: IN-TECH.

Azar, A. T. (2010b). Adaptive Neuro-Fuzzy Systems. In A. T. Azar (Ed.), *Fuzzy Systems*. Vienna, Austria: IN-TECH. doi:10.5772/7220

Azar, A. T. (2012). Overview of Type-2 Fuzzy logic systems. *International Journal of Fuzzy System Applications*, *2*(4), 1–28. doi:10.4018/ijfsa.2012100101

Azar, A. T., Kumar, J., Kumar, V., & Rana, K. P. S. (2017d). Control of a Two Link Planar Electrically-Driven Rigid Robotic Manipulator Using Fractional Order SOFC. *Proceedings of the International Conference on Advanced Intelligent Systems and Informatics 2017, 639*, 47-56.

Azar, A. T., Ouannas, A., & Singh, S. (2017c). Control of New Type of Fractional Chaos Synchronization. *Proceedings of the International Conference on Advanced Intelligent Systems and Informatics 2017, 639*, 47-56.

Azar, A.T., & Serrano, F.E. (2014). Robust IMC-PID tuning for cascade control systems with gain and phase margin specifications. *Neural Computing and Applications, 25*(5), 983-995. DOI 10.1007/s00521-014-1560-x

Azar, A. T., & Serrano, F. E. (2015a). Stabilization and Control of Mechanical Systems with Backlash. In Advanced Intelligent Control Engineering and Automation. IGI Global. doi:10.4018/978-1-4666-7248-2.ch001

Azar, A. T., & Serrano, F. E. (2015b). Design and Modeling of Anti Wind Up PID Controllers. In Complex system modelling and control through intelligent soft computations. Springer-Verlag. . 1. doi:10.1007/978-3-319-12883-2_1

Azar, A. T., & Serrano, F. E. (2015c). Adaptive Sliding mode control of the Furuta pendulum. In Advances and Applications in Sliding Mode Control systems. Springer-Verlag GmbH Berlin/Heidelberg. doi:10.1007/978-3-319-11173-5_1

Azar, A. T., & Serrano, F. E. (2015d). Deadbeat Control for Multivariable Systems with Time Varying Delays. In Chaos Modeling and Control Systems Design. Springer-Verlag GmbH Berlin/Heidelberg. DOI doi:10.1007/978-3-319-13132-0_6

Azar, A. T., & Serrano, F. E. (2016a). Robust control for asynchronous switched nonlinear systems with time varying delays. *Proceedings of the International Conference on Advanced Intelligent Systems and Informatics 2016*, 533, 891-899. 10.1007/978-3-319-48308-5_85

Azar, A. T., & Serrano, F. E. (2016b). Stabilization of Mechanical Systems with Backlash by PI Loop Shaping. *International Journal of System Dynamics Applications*, *5*(3), 20–47. doi:10.4018/IJSDA.2016070102

Azar, A. T., & Serrano, F. E. (2017). Passivity Based Decoupling of Lagrangian Systems. *Proceedings of the International Conference on Advanced Intelligent Systems and Informatics 2016*, 533, 891-899. 10.1007/978-3-319-48308-5_85

Azar, A. T., & Vaidyanathan, S. (2015a). Handbook of Research on Advanced Intelligent Control Engineering and Automation. IGI Global. doi:10.4018/978-1-4666-7248-2

Azar, A. T., & Vaidyanathan, S. (2015b). *Computational Intelligence applications in Modeling and Control. Studies in Computational Intelligence* (Vol. 575). Springer-Verlag.

Azar, A. T., & Vaidyanathan, S. (2015c). *Chaos Modeling and Control Systems Design, Studies in Computational Intelligence* (Vol. 581). Springer-Verlag.

Azar, A. T., & Vaidyanathan, S. (2016). *Advances in Chaos Theory and Intelligent Control. Studies in Fuzziness and Soft Computing* (Vol. 337). Springer-Verlag. doi:10.1007/978-3-319-30340-6

Azar, A. T., Vaidyanathan, S., & Ouannas, A. (2017a). *Fractional Order Control and Synchronization of Chaotic Systems. Studies in Computational Intelligence* (Vol. 688). Springer-Verlag. doi:10.1007/978-3-319-50249-6

Azar, A.T., Volos, C., Gerodimos, N.A., Tombras, G.S., Pham, V.T., Radwan, A.G., … Munoz-Pacheco, J.M. (2017b). A novel chaotic system without equilibrium: Dynamics, synchronization and circuit realization. *Complexity*. doi:10.1155/2017/7871467

Azar, A. T., & Zhu, Q. (2015). *Advances and Applications in Sliding Mode Control systems. Studies in Computational Intelligence* (Vol. 576). Springer-Verlag.

Bahgaat, N. K. (2013). *Artificial intelligent based controller for frequency control in power systems* (Ph.D. thesis). Faculty of Engineering at Al- Azhar University, Cairo, Egypt.

Bahgaat, N. K., El-Sayed, M. I., Moustafa Hassan, M. A., & Bendary, F. A. (2014). Load Frequency Control in Power System via Improving PID Controller Based on Particle Swarm Optimization and ANFIS Techniques. International Journal of System Dynamics Applications, 3(3), 1-24.

Bahgaat, N. K., El-Sayed, M. I., Moustafa Hassan, M. A., & Bendary, F. A. (2015). *'Application of Some Modern Techniques in Load Frequency Control in Power Systems', Chaos Modeling and Control Systems Design* (Vol. 581). Springer-Verlag.

Bevrani, H. (2009). *Robust power system frequency control.* Brisbane, Australia: Springer Science and Business Media, LLC. doi:10.1007/978-0-387-84878-5

Bhati, S., & Nitnawwre, D. (2012). Genetic Optimization Tuning of an Automatic Voltage Regulator System. *International Journal of Scientific Engineering and Technology, 1*, 120–124.

Bhatt, V. K., & Bhongade, S. (2013). Design Of PID Controller In Automatic Voltage Regulator (AVR) System Using PSO Technique. *International Journal of Engineering Research and Applications, 3*(4), 1480–1485.

Boulkroune, A., Bouzeriba, A., Bouden, T., & Azar, A. T. (2016a). Fuzzy Adaptive Synchronization of Uncertain Fractional-order Chaotic Systems. In A. T. Azar & S. Vaidyanathan (Eds.), *Advances in Chaos Theory and Intelligent Control. Studies in Fuzziness and Soft Computing* (Vol. 337). Springer-Verlag. doi:10.1007/978-3-319-30340-6_28

Boulkroune, A., Hamel, S., & Azar, A. T. (2016b). *Fuzzy control-based function synchronization of unknown chaotic systems with dead-zone input. Advances in Chaos Theory and Intelligent Control. Studies in Fuzziness and Soft Computing* (Vol. 337). Springer-Verlag.

Cheng, G. (1997). *Genetic Algorithms and Engineering Design*. New York: Wiley.

Coello, C. A. C., Pulido, G. T., & Lechuga, M. S. (2004). Handling multiple objectives with particle swarm optimization. *IEEE Transactions on Evolutionary Computation*, *8*(3), 256–279. doi:10.1109/TEVC.2004.826067

Eberhart, R. C., & Shi, Y. (1998). Comparison between genetic algorithms and particle swarm optimization. *Proc. IEEE Int. Conf. Evol. Comput.*, 611–616.

Fitch, J. W., Zachariah, K. J., & Farsi, M. (1999). Turbo generator Self-Tuning Automatic Voltage Regulator. *IEEE Transactions on Energy Conversion*, *14*(3), 843–848. doi:10.1109/60.790963

Gaing, Z. L. (2004). A Particle Swarm Optimization approach for optimum design of PID controller in AVR system. *Energy Conversion. IEEE Transactions on*, *19*(2), 384–391.

Ghoudelbourk, S., Dib, D., Omeiri, A., & Azar, A. T. (2016). MPPT Control in wind energy conversion systems and the application of fractional control (PIα) in pitch wind turbine. International Journal of Modelling *Identification and Control*, *26*(2), 140–151. doi:10.1504/IJMIC.2016.078329

Grassi, G., Ouannas, A., Azar, A. T., Radwan, A. G., Volos, C., Pham, V. T., . . . Stouboulos, I. N. (2017). *Chaos Synchronisation Of Continuous Systems Via Scalar Signal*. The 6th International Conference on Modern Circuits and Systems Technologies (MOCAST), Thessaloniki, Greece. 10.1109/MOCAST.2017.7937629

Hamid, A., & Abdul-Rahman, T. K. (2010). Short Term Load Forecasting Using an Artificial Neural Network Trained by Artificial Immune System Learning Algorithm in Computer Modeling and Simulation (UKSim). *IEEE, 12th International Conference on*, 408-413.

Hassanien, A. E., Tolba, M., & Azar, A. T. (2014). *Advanced Machine Learning Technologies and Applications: Second International Conference, AMLTA 2014*. Springer-Verlag GmbH Berlin/Heidelberg. 10.1007/978-3-319-13461-1

Ingemar, E. O. (1983). *Electric Energy Systems Theory*. London: McGraw Hill Book Company.

Ismail, A. (2006). Improving UAE power systems control performance by using combined LFC and AVR. *7th UAE University Research Conference*, 50-60.

Kennedy, J., & Eberhart, R. C. (1995). A new optimizer using particle swarm theory. *Proc. of 6th International symposium Micro machine Human Sci.*, 39-43.

Khalifa, F., Moustafa Hassan, M., Abul-Haggag, O., & Mahmoud, H. (2015). The Application of Evolutionary Computational Techniques in Medium Term Forecasting. In *MEPCON'2015*. Mansoura, Egypt: Mansoura University.

Kim, D. H., & Cho, J. H. (2006). A Biologically Inspired Intelligent PID Controller Tuning for AVR Systems. *International Journal of Control, Automation, and Systems*, *4*, 624–636.

Kumar, A., & Gupta, R. (2013). Compare the results of Tuning of PID controller by using PSO and GA Technique for AVR system. *International Journal of Advanced Research in Computer Engineering & Technology, 2*(6).

Kumar, D. V. (1998). Intelligent controllers for automatic generation control. *TENCON' 98. IEEE Region, 10 International Conference on Global Connectivity in Energy, Computer, Communication and Control*, 2, 557-574.

Mansour. (2012). *Development of advanced controllers using adaptive weighted PSO algorithm with applications* (M.Sc Thesis). Faculty of Engineering, Cairo University, Cairo, Egypt.

Meghni, B., Dib, D., & Azar, A. T. (2017c). A Second-order sliding mode and fuzzy logic control to Optimal Energy Management in PMSG Wind Turbine with Battery Storage. *Neural Computing & Applications*, *28*(6), 1417–1434. doi:10.100700521-015-2161-z

Meghni, B., Dib, D., Azar, A. T., Ghoudelbourk, S., & Saadoun, A. (2017a). *Robust Adaptive Supervisory Fractional order Controller For optimal Energy Management in Wind Turbine with Battery Storage. Studies in Computational Intelligence* (Vol. 688). Springer-Verlag.

Meghni, B., Dib, D., Azar, A. T., & Saadoun, A. (2017b). *Effective Supervisory Controller to Extend Optimal Energy Management in Hybrid Wind Turbine under Energy and Reliability Constraints. International Journal of Dynamics and Control*. Springer. doi:10.100740435-016-0296-0

Mekki, H., Boukhetala, D., & Azar, A. T. (2015). Sliding Modes for Fault Tolerant Control. In Advances and Applications in Sliding Mode Control systems. Springer-Verlag GmbH Berlin/Heidelberg. doi:10.1007/978-3-319-11173-5_15

Musa, B. U., Kalli, B. M., & Kalli, S. (2013). Modeling and Simulation of LFC and AVR with PID Controller. *International Journal of Engineering Science Invention*, *2*, 54–57.

Naik, R.S., ChandraSekhar, K., & Vaisakh, K. (2005). Adaptive PSO based optimal fuzzy controller design for AGC equipped with SMES and SPSS. *Journal of Theoretical and Applied Information Technology, 7*(1), 8-17.

Ouannas, A., Azar, A. T., & Abu-Saris, R. (2016a). A new type of hybrid synchronization between arbitrary hyperchaotic maps. *International Journal of Machine Learning and Cybernetics*. doi:10.100713042-016-0566-3

Ouannas, A., Azar, A. T., & Radwan, A. G. (2016b). *On Inverse Problem of Generalized Synchronization Between Different Dimensional Integer-Order and Fractional-Order Chaotic Systems*. The 28th International Conference on Microelectronics, Cairo, Egypt. 10.1109/ICM.2016.7847942

Ouannas, A., Azar, A. T., & Vaidyanathan, S. (2017f). On A Simple Approach for Q-S Synchronization of Chaotic Dynamical Systems in Continuous-Time. *Int. J. Computing Science and Mathematics*, *8*(1), 20–27.

Ouannas, A., Azar, A. T., & Vaidyanathan, S. (2017g). New Hybrid Synchronization Schemes Based on Coexistence of Various Types of Synchronization Between Master-Slave Hyperchaotic Systems. *International Journal of Computer Applications in Technology*, *55*(2), 112–120. doi:10.1504/IJCAT.2017.082868

Ouannas, A., Azar, A. T., & Vaidyanathan, S. (2017i). A Robust Method for New Fractional Hybrid Chaos Synchronization. *Mathematical Methods in the Applied Sciences*, *40*(5), 1804–1812. doi:10.1002/mma.4099

Ouannas, A., Azar, A. T., & Ziar, T. (2017h). *On Inverse Full State Hybrid Function Projective Synchronization for Continuous-time Chaotic Dynamical Systems with Arbitrary Dimensions*. Differential Equations and Dynamical Systems; doi:10.100712591-017-0362-x

Ouannas, A., Azar, A. T., Ziar, T., & Radwan, A. G. (2017d). *Study On Coexistence of Different Types of Synchronization Between Different dimensional Fractional Chaotic Systems. Studies in Computational Intelligence* (Vol. 688). Springer-Verlag.

Ouannas, A., Azar, A. T., Ziar, T., & Radwan, A. G. (2017e). *Generalized Synchronization of Different Dimensional Integer-order and Fractional Order Chaotic Systems. Studies in Computational Intelligence* (Vol. 688). Springer-Verlag.

Ouannas, A., Azar, A. T., Ziar, T., & Vaidyanathan, S. (2017a). *On New Fractional Inverse Matrix Projective Synchronization Schemes. Studies in Computational Intelligence* (Vol. 688). Springer-Verlag.

Ouannas, A., Azar, A. T., Ziar, T., & Vaidyanathan, S. (2017b). *Fractional Inverse Generalized Chaos Synchronization Between Different Dimensional Systems. Studies in Computational Intelligence* (Vol. 688). Springer-Verlag.

Ouannas, A., Azar, A. T., Ziar, T., & Vaidyanathan, S. (2017c). *A New Method To Synchronize Fractional Chaotic Systems With Different Dimensions. Studies in Computational Intelligence* (Vol. 688). Springer-Verlag.

Ouannas, A., Grassi, G., Azar, A. T., Radwan, A. G., Volos, C., Pham, V. T., . . . Stouboulos, I. N. (2017j). *Dead-Beat Synchronization Control in Discrete-Time Chaotic Systems*. The 6th International Conference on Modern Circuits and Systems Technologies (MOCAST), Thessaloniki, Greece. 10.1109/MOCAST.2017.7937628

RamaSudha, K., Vakula, V.S., & Shanthi, R.V. (2010). PSO Based Design of Robust Controller for Two Area Load Frequency Control with Nonlinearities. *International Journal of Engineering Science*, *2*(5), 1311–1324.

Shabib, G., Abdel Gayed, M., & Rashwan, A. M. (2010). Optimal Tuning of PID Controller for AVR System using Modified Particle Swarm Optimization. *Proceedings of the 14th International Middle East Power Systems Conference (MEPCON'10).*

Singh, S., Azar, A. T., Ouannas, A., Zhu, Q., Zhang, W., & Na, J. (2017). *Sliding Mode Control Technique for Multi-switching Synchronization of Chaotic Systems. 9th International Conference on Modelling, Identification and Control (ICMIC 2017)*, Kunming, China.

Skogestad, S. (2003). Simple analytic rules for model reduction and PID controller tuning. *Journal of Process Control, 13*(4), 291–309. doi:10.1016/S0959-1524(02)00062-8

Soliman, N. S., Said, L. A., Azar, A. T., Madian, A. H., Radwan, A. G., & Ouannas, A. (2017). *Fractional Controllable Multi-Scroll V-Shape Attractor with Parameters Effect*. The 6th International Conference on Modern Circuits and Systems Technologies (MOCAST), Thessaloniki, Greece.

Soundarrajan, A., & Sumathi, S. (2010). *Particle Swarm Optimization Based LFC and AVR of Autonomous Power Generating System*. IAENG International Journal of Computer Science.

Swidenbank, E., Brown, M. D., & Flynn, D. (1999). Self-Tuning Turbine Generator Control for Power Plant. *Mechatronics, 9*(5), 513–537. doi:10.1016/S0957-4158(99)00009-4

Tammam, M. A. (2011). *Multi objective genetic algorithm controllers Tuning for load frequency control in Electric power systems* (M. Sc. Thesis). Faculty of Engineering at Cairo University, Cairo, Egypt.

Tolba, M. F., AbdelAty, A. M., Soliman, N. S., Said, L. A., Madian, A. H., Azar, A. T., & Radwan, A. G. (2017). FPGA implementation of two fractional order chaotic systems. *International Journal of Electronics and Communications, 28*, 162–172. doi:10.1016/j.aeue.2017.04.028

Vaidyanathan, S., & Azar, A. T. (2015a). Anti-Synchronization of Identical Chaotic Systems using Sliding Mode Control and an Application to Vaidyanathan-Madhavan Chaotic Systems. In Advances and Applications in Sliding Mode Control systems. Springer-Verlag GmbH Berlin/Heidelberg. doi:10.1007/978-3-319-11173-5_19

Vaidyanathan, S., & Azar, A. T. (2015b). Hybrid Synchronization of Identical Chaotic Systems using Sliding Mode Control and an Application to Vaidyanathan Chaotic Systems. In Advances and Applications in Sliding Mode Control systems. Springer-Verlag GmbH Berlin/Heidelberg. doi:10.1007/978-3-319-11173-5_20

Vaidyanathan, S., & Azar, A. T. (2015c). Analysis, Control and Synchronization of a Nine-Term 3-D Novel Chaotic System. In Chaos Modeling and Control Systems Design. Springer-Verlag GmbH Berlin/Heidelberg. DOI doi:10.1007/978-3-319-13132-0_1

Vaidyanathan, S., & Azar, A. T. (2015d). Analysis and Control of a 4-D Novel Hyperchaotic System. In Chaos Modeling and Control Systems Design. Springer-Verlag GmbH Berlin/Heidelberg. DOI doi:10.1007/978-3-319-13132-0_2

Vaidyanathan, S., & Azar, A. T. (2016a). Takagi-Sugeno Fuzzy Logic Controller for Liu-Chen Four-Scroll Chaotic System. *International Journal of Intelligent Engineering Informatics*, *4*(2), 135–150. doi:10.1504/IJIEI.2016.076699

Vaidyanathan, S., & Azar, A. T. (2016b). *Dynamic Analysis, Adaptive Feedback Control and Synchronization of an Eight-Term 3-D Novel Chaotic System with Three Quadratic Nonlinearities. Studies in Fuzziness and Soft Computing* (Vol. 337). Springer-Verlag.

Vaidyanathan, S., & Azar, A. T. (2016c). *Qualitative Study and Adaptive Control of a Novel 4-D Hyperchaotic System with Three Quadratic Nonlinearities. Studies in Fuzziness and Soft Computing* (Vol. 337). Springer-Verlag.

Vaidyanathan, S., & Azar, A. T. (2016d). *A Novel 4-D Four-Wing Chaotic System with Four Quadratic Nonlinearities and its Synchronization via Adaptive Control Method. Advances in Chaos Theory and Intelligent Control. Studies in Fuzziness and Soft Computing* (Vol. 337). Springer-Verlag.

Vaidyanathan, S., & Azar, A. T. (2016e). *Adaptive Control and Synchronization of Halvorsen Circulant Chaotic Systems. Advances in Chaos Theory and Intelligent Control. Studies in Fuzziness and Soft Computing* (Vol. 337). Springer-Verlag.

Vaidyanathan, S., & Azar, A. T. (2016f). *Adaptive Backstepping Control and Synchronization of a Novel 3-D Jerk System with an Exponential Nonlinearity. Advances in Chaos Theory and Intelligent Control. Studies in Fuzziness and Soft Computing* (Vol. 337). Springer-Verlag.

Vaidyanathan, S., & Azar, A. T. (2016g). *Generalized Projective Synchronization of a Novel Hyperchaotic Four-Wing System via Adaptive Control Method. Advances in Chaos Theory and Intelligent Control. Studies in Fuzziness and Soft Computing* (Vol. 337). Springer-Verlag.

Vaidyanathan, S., Azar, A. T., & Ouannas, A. (2017a). *An Eight-Term 3-D Novel Chaotic System with Three Quadratic Nonlinearities, its Adaptive Feedback Control and Synchronization. Studies in Computational Intelligence* (Vol. 688). Springer-Verlag.

Vaidyanathan, S., Azar, A. T., & Ouannas, A. (2017c). *Hyperchaos and Adaptive Control of a Novel Hyperchaotic System with Two Quadratic Nonlinearities. Studies in Computational Intelligence* (Vol. 688). Springer-Verlag.

Vaidyanathan, S., Azar, A. T., Rajagopal, K., & Alexander, P. (2015b). Design and SPICE implementation of a 12-term novel hyperchaotic system and its synchronization via active control (2015). International Journal of Modelling *Identification and Control, 23*(3), 267–277. doi:10.1504/IJMIC.2015.069936

Vaidyanathan, S., Idowu, B. A., & Azar, A. T. (2015c). Backstepping Controller Design for the Global Chaos Synchronization of Sprott's Jerk Systems. In Chaos Modeling and Control Systems Design. Springer-Verlag GmbH Berlin/Heidelberg. doi:10.1007/978-3-319-13132-0_3

Vaidyanathan, S., Sampath, S., & Azar, A. T. (2015a). Global chaos synchronisation of identical chaotic systems via novel sliding mode control method and its application to Zhu system. International Journal of Modelling *Identification and Control, 23*(1), 92–100. doi:10.1504/IJMIC.2015.067495

Vaidyanathan, S., Zhu, Q., & Azar, A. T. (2017b). *Adaptive Control of a Novel Nonlinear Double Convection Chaotic System. Studies in Computational Intelligence* (Vol. 688). Springer-Verlag.

Vlachogiannis, J. G., & Lee, K. Y. (2009). Economic load dispatch - A comparative study on heuristic optimization techniques with an improved coordinated aggregation based PSO. *Power Systems. IEEE Transactions on, 24*(2), 991–1001.

Wang, Z., Volos, C., Kingni, S.T., Azar, A.T., & Pham, V.T. (2017). Four-wing attractors in a novel chaotic system with hyperbolic sine nonlinearity. *Optik - International Journal for Light and Electron Optics, 131*(2017), 1071-1078.

Wong, C. C., An Li, S., & Wang, H. (2009). Optimal PID Controller Design for AVR System. *Tamkang Journal of Science and Engineering*, *12*(3), 259–270.

Yoshida, H., Kawata, K., Fukuyama, Y., Takayama, S., & Nakanishi, Y. (2000). A particle swarm optimization for reactive power and voltage control considering voltage security assessment. *IEEE Transactions on Power Systems*, *15*(4), 1232–1239. doi:10.1109/59.898095

Zhu, Q., & Azar, A. T. (2015). *Complex system modelling and control through intelligent soft computations. Studies in Fuzziness and Soft Computing* (Vol. 319). Springer-Verlag.

Chapter 9
Loss of Excitation Protection of Medium Voltage Hydro Generators Using Adaptive Neuro Fuzzy Inference System

Mohamed Salah El-Din Ahmed Abdel Aziz
Dar Al-Handasah (Shair and Partners) – Cairo, Egypt

Mohamed Ahmed Moustafa Hassan
Cairo University, Egypt

Fahmy Bendary
Benha University, Egypt

ABSTRACT

This chapter presents a new method for loss of excitation (LOE) faults detection in hydro-generators using adaptive neuro fuzzy inference system (ANFIS). The investigations were done under a complete loss of excitation conditions, and a partial loss of excitation conditions in different generator loading conditions. In this chapter, four different techniques are discussed according to the type of inputs to the proposed ANFIS unit, the generator terminal impedance measurements (R and X) and the generator terminal voltage and phase current (Vtrms and Ia), the positive sequence components of the generator terminal voltage magnitude, phase current magnitude and angle (| V+ve |, | I+ve | and ∟I+ve) in addition to the stator current 3rd harmonics components (magnitudes and angles). The proposed techniques' results are compared with each other and are compared with the conventional distance relay response in addition to other techniques. The promising obtained results show that the proposed technique is efficient.

DOI: 10.4018/978-1-5225-4077-9.ch009

INTRODUCTION

Loss of Excitation is a very common fault in synchronous generators. It happens due to short circuit of the field winding, unexpected field breaker open or Loss of Excitation relay incorrect-operation. According to the statistics, the generator failure due to Loss of Excitation represents about 69.5% of all generator failures as described in (Wang, 2002; Shi, 2010). Loss of Excitation causes severe damages to the generator and the system. When a generator loses its excitation, it overspeeds and operates as an induction generator. It continues to supply power to the system and receives its excitation from the system in the form of reactive power, as such; the stator may suffer over heating because of this large current. On the other hand, for the system; its voltage will be reduced after the generator loses its excitation, since the generator operates as an induction generator and absorbs reactive power from the system. For a weak system, the system voltage possibly will collapse due to the Loss of Excitation condition as described in (Ghandhari, 2008). Moreover, when a generator loses its excitation, the rest of generators in the system will boost their reactive power output. This might cause overloading to the transmission lines or transformers and the over-current protection may consider this overloading as a fault and trip the power system (Benmouyal, 2007; Paithankar and Bhide 2003; Blackburn and Domin 2015; Mozina et al. 2008; Ebrahimi and Ghorbani 2016; Mozina, 2010). The above reasons motivated this research work to propose an advanced solution for this problem.

The most widely applied method for detecting a generator loss of excitation condition is the use of impedance relays to sense the variation of impedance as viewed from the generator terminals. A two-zone impedance relay approach is generally used within the industry to provide high speed detection. Figure 1 shows this impedance approach as adopted from (NERC, 2008). It consists of two impedance circles. The first impedance circle (zone 2) diameter equals to the generator synchronous reactance (Xd) and offset downward by half of the generator transient reactance (Xd'/2). The operation of this element is delayed approximately 0.5 s and is used to detect loss of excitation conditions during light loading conditions. The second impedance circle (zone 1) is set at a diameter of 1.0 per unit (on the generator base), with the same offset of half of the generator transient reactance. This zone is delayed approximately 0.1 s and is used to detect loss of excitation conditions during heavy loading conditions (Vancouver and Mozina 1995).

This impedance relay was developed to provide improved selectivity between Loss of Excitation conditions and other normal or abnormal operating conditions. This relay confirmed its capability of detecting some of the excitation system failures. But some few cases of incorrect operation that have occurred due to incorrect relay setting, blown potential transformer fuses have initiated user's worry about the performance of this type of relaying for loss of excitation protection. In addition, the performance of this impedance relay is found to be time delayed and is depending on the generator loading conditions and the percentage loss of excitation in the detection process (Benmouyal, 2007; Patel et al. 2004). Moreover; some loss of excitation cases are not detected by these impedance relays. As a result, widespread studies were recently proposed to overcome the problems associated with the performance of this relay. Therefore, several techniques and schemes have been recently proposed to enhance the generators Loss of Excitation relay performance. Some of these techniques are arranged historically and are based on:

- Artificial Neural Network (Sharaf and Lie 1994).
- Time-Derivatives of Impedance (Tambay and Paithankar 2005).
- Fuzzy Inference Mechanism (De Morais et al. 2010).

Figure 1. Conventional loss of excitation protection scheme

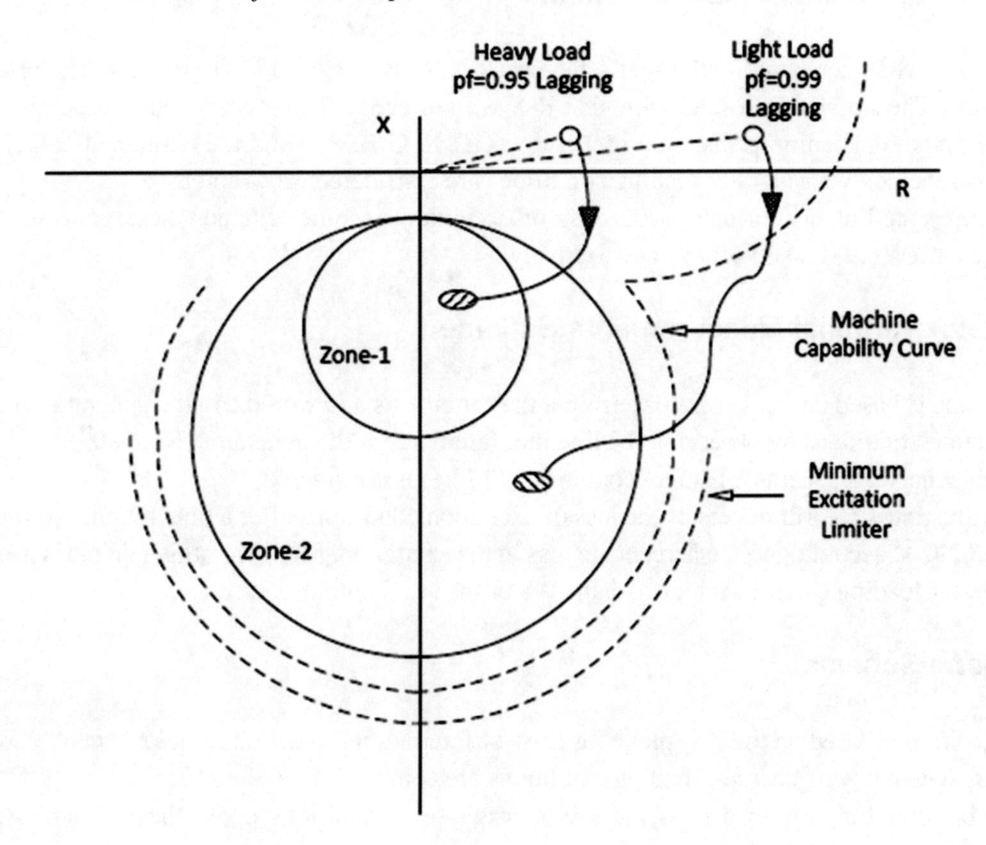

- Steady-State Stability Limit (Liu et al. 2013).
- Derivative of the terminal voltage and the output reactive power of the generator (Amini et al. 2015).

LOSS OF EXCITATION PROTECTION SCHEMES SURVEY

This section presents some the existing schemes for the Loss of Excitation protection function.

Usually, the generator field voltage cannot be measured directly, in order to detect the Loss of Excitation condition. As such, any Loss of Excitation protection scheme applies the generator terminal voltage, current, active power or reactive power output as the input value and calculates the generator characteristic values to determine the Loss of Excitation fault (Shi, 2010).

Generator Reactive Power Output Scheme

This scheme is based on measuring of the three phase reactive power output of the generator and monitors the direction and magnitude of leading reactive power at the generator terminal (Usta et al. 2007).

In this scheme, two generator loading conditions are considered (10% and 50%).

This described algorithm detects the loss of excitation events within 1.12 s.

R-X With Directional Element Scheme

This scheme when compared with other schemes (R-X, G-B, P-Q and U-I) gives the best results (Shi et al. 2012). The simulation results show that R-X with directional element scheme responds faster for Loss of Excitation conditions than other schemes as (R-X, G-B, P-Q and U-I) (Shi et al. 2012).

In this scheme, two generator loading conditions are considered (40% and 80%).

This presented algorithm detects the loss of excitation conditions under these generator loading conditions after (6.931 s and 4.175 s) respectively.

Generator Terminal Measurements Scheme

This scheme is based on the generator terminal measurements and would trip the generator under Loss of Excitation conditions by observing the line measurements at the generator (Xu, 2009).

In this scheme, a generator loading condition of (78%) is considered.

This illustrated algorithm detects the loss of excitation conditions after a time ranging from (1.276 s up to 15.6792 s) according to the percentage loss in the excitation. Moreover, this scheme is useful only for generator loading conditions higher than 50% of the rated output power.

P-Q Plane Scheme

This algorithm is based on the P-Q plane for Loss of Excitation protection (Sandoval et al. 2007).

In this scheme, two generator loading conditions are considered (20% and 75%).

This presented algorithm detects the loss of excitation conditions under these generator loading conditions after (14 s and 2.9 s) respectively.

Derivative of the Terminal Voltage and the Output Reactive Power of the Generator Scheme

This algorithm employs a combined scheme based on the derivative of both the terminal voltage and the output reactive power of the generator (Amini et al. 2015).

In this scheme, two generator loading conditions are considered (25% and 78%).

This described algorithm detects the loss of excitation conditions under thesegenerator loading conditions after (1.66 s and 1.6 s) respectively.

Comments on the Loss of Excitation Protection Schemes

From the above discussed different Loss of Excitation schemes, it is clear that the response time for these schemes is long and the performance of these schemes is depending on the generator loading conditions.

Accordingly, the need for this research work came into sight to propose a pioneer scheme for the Loss of Excitation faults detection. As the shortage of the Loss of Excitation impedance relays in addition to the long response time of the above presented schemes became obvious.

THE SYSTEM UNDER STUDY

The system used in the investigations is depicted in Figure 2. It comprises of two hydro-generator sets (G1 and G2), which are connected through transformers to a system through a 300 km, 345 kV transmission line. The generators and system data are illustrated in Appendix 1, and are cited from (Elsamahy et al. 2010). Hydro-generators are chosen for this study, as the hydro-generators can operate as synchronous condensers and are allowed to operate in the under excited region of the generator capability curve. Therefore, they are subjected to the Loss of Excitation conditions. The generator set (G1) is considered to be subjected to the Loss of Excitation conditions and is supervised by an under voltage relay as per the North American Electric Reliability Corporation (NERC) recommendations (NERC, 2008). This under voltage relay is used to prevent unnecessary operation of the loss of excitation relay. It is used as the hydro generators are often run as synchronous condensers and loss of excitation relays may experience incorrect operations in this mode of operation if the Var loading is near the rating of the generator. This problem can be eliminated if these relays are supervised by under voltage relays (Elmore, 2003). Another concern is the load rejection that can cause hydro generators' speed and frequency to exceed 200% of its' value. This makes the relay diameter to increase about 200% to 300%, with this increase in the relay characteristic it is possible for the loss of excitation relays to operate for temporary over speed and overvoltage conditions. To avoid this problem, the loss of excitation relays on hydro units shall be supervised by an under voltage relay which is used with the impedance functions to detect a complete loss of excitation condition (Elmore, 2003). The model used for this study has the facility to change the generator loading conditions and the percentage loss in the excitation to simulate all possible cases using the PSCAD/EMTDC simulation package (PSCAD, 2003), for the type and the number of the used membership functions, see Appendix 2.

ADAPTIVE NEURO FUZZY INFERENCE SYSTEM (ANFIS)

A Fuzzy Logic System (FLS) can be viewed as a non-linear mapping from the input space to the output space. A FLS consists of five main components: Fuzzy Sets, fuzzifiers, fuzzy rules, an inference engine and defuzzifiers. However fuzzy inference system is limited in its application to only modeling ill defined systems.

These systems have rule structure which is essentially predetermined by the user's interpretation of the characteristic of the variables in the model. It has been considered only fixed membership functions that were chosen arbitrarily. However, in some modeling situations, it cannot be distinguished what the membership functions should look like simply from looking at data. Rather than choosing the parameters associated with a given membership function arbitrarily, these parameters could be chosen so as to tailor the membership functions to the input/output data in order to account for these types of variations in the data values. In such case the necessity of the ANFIS becomes obvious. Adaptive Neuro-Fuzzy networks are enhanced FLSs with learning, generalization, and adaptive capabilities. These networks encode the fuzzy if-then rules into a neural network-like structure and then use appropriate learning algorithms to minimize the output error based on the training/validation data sets (Aziz et al. 2011; Aziz et al. 2012; Aziz et al. 2012; Aziz et al. 2011; Kamel et al. 2011; Kamel et al. 2012; Azar and El-Said 2013).

There are many recent applications of neuro-fuzzy systems as in (Ismail and Hassan 2012; Hussein et al. 2017; Ali and Hassan 2012; Ismail 2012).

Figure 2. One-line diagram of the system under study in PSCAD

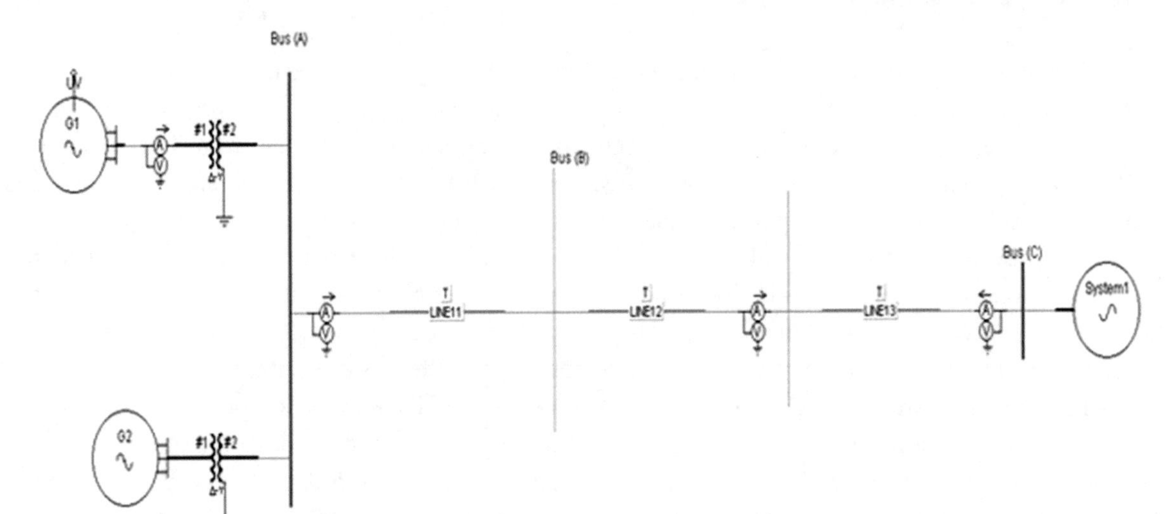

Neuro-adaptive learning techniques provide a method for the fuzzy modeling procedure to learn information about a data set. It computes the membership function parameters that best allow the associated fuzzy inference to track the given input/output data.

A network-type structure similar to that of an Artificial Neural Network (ANN) can be used to interpret the input/output map. Therefore, it maps inputs through input membership functions and associated parameters, and then through output membership functions and associated parameters to outputs. These parameters change through the learning process.

The used ANFIS is assumed to have the following properties (Kamel et al. 2011; Kamel et al. 2012):

- It is zeroth order sugeno-type system.
- It has a single output, obtained using weighted average defuzzification. All output membership functions are constant.
- It has no rule sharing. Different rules do not share the same output membership function; the number of output membership functions must be equal to the number of rules.
- It has unity weight for each rule.

The architecture of the ANFIS, comprising by input, Fuzzification, Inference and Defuzzification layers could be obtained from the Graphical User Interface (GUI) of the Matlab dealing with ANFIS. The network can be visualized as consisting of inputs, with N neurons in the input layer and F input membership functions for each input, with F * N neurons in the Fuzzification layer. There are F^N rules with F^N neurons in the inference and Defuzzification layers. It is assumed one neuron in the output layer.

THE LOSS OF EXCITATION RELAY BASED ON CONVENTIONAL METHOD

This section discusses the performance of the conventional Loss of Excitation impedance relay. Two fault cases are explained and the relay performance is illustrated.

Case-1 discusses when the two generators are operating at 80% loading condition and a 50% loss in the excitation of the generator (G1) occurs at $T_f = 5$ s. Figure 3 shows the waveforms of generator (G1) (active power, reactive power, terminal voltage, phase current, under voltage relay reference, the under voltage relay trip signal and the field voltage (E_{f1})) when it is subjected to the Loss of Excitation condition. It is clear that the generator terminal voltage will decrease, the stator current will increase and the

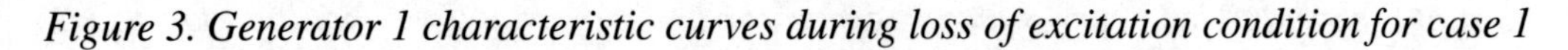

Figure 3. Generator 1 characteristic curves during loss of excitation condition for case 1

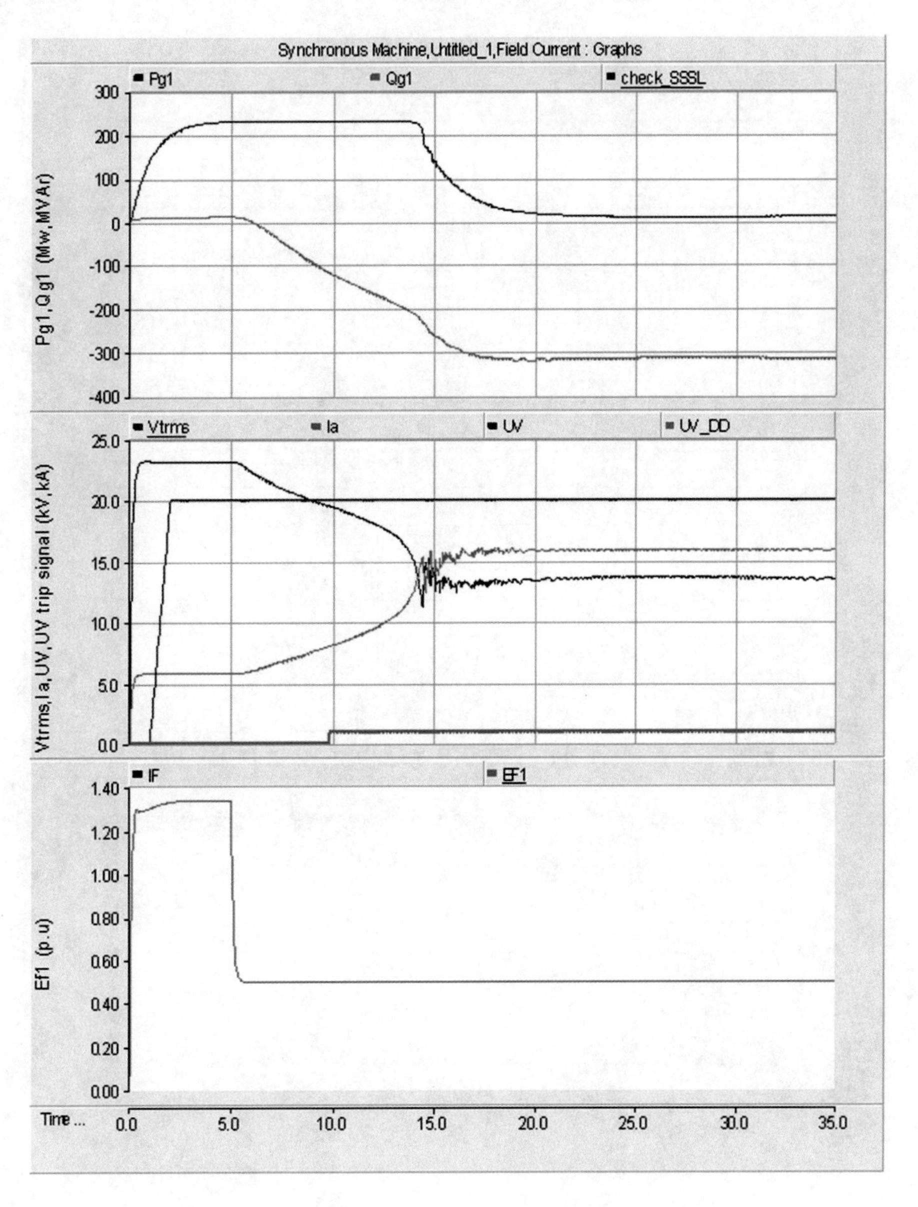

generator will absorb reactive power from the system instead of supplying reactive power to it. Also, the under voltage relay trip signal will be generated at "9.8 s" when the generator terminal voltage becomes less than 20.01 kV. Furthermore, Figure 4 explains the waveforms of generator (G2) which increases its' output reactive power to supply generator (G1). Figure 5 presents the impedance trajectory which will penetrate the relay circle. Finally, the relay trip signal is as indicated in Figure 6. This trip signal is generated at approximately "14.5 s" and is considered very delayed compared to the fault inception time which is "5 s". This means that the trip signal triggers after a time of "9.5 s" from fault occurrence.

Case-2 explains when the two generators are lightly loaded and are operating at 25% loading condition and a 80% loss in the excitation of the generator (G1) takes place at $T_f = 5$ s. Figure 7 highlights the

Figure 4. Generator 2 characteristic curves during generator 1 loss of excitation condition for case 1

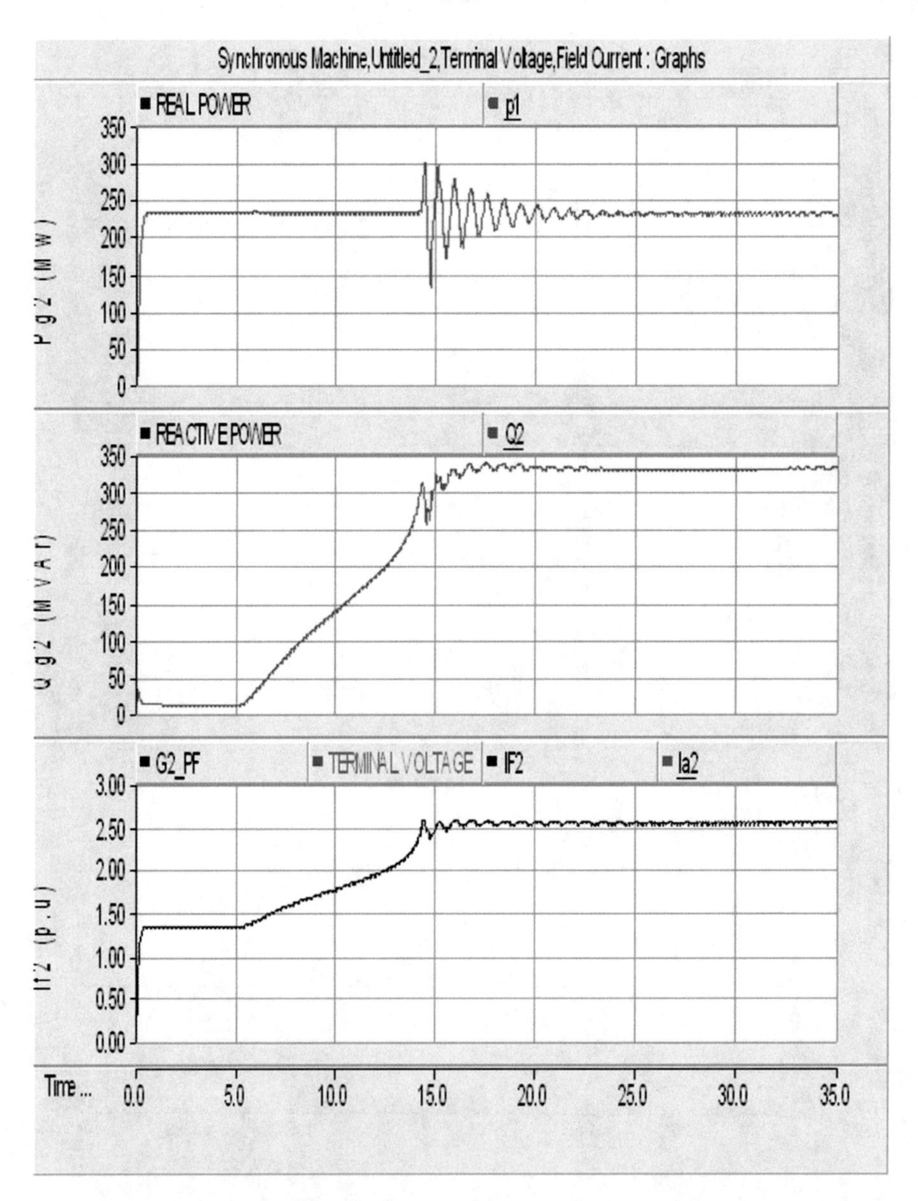

Figure 5. Impedance trajectory measured by the conventional loss of excitation relay for case 1

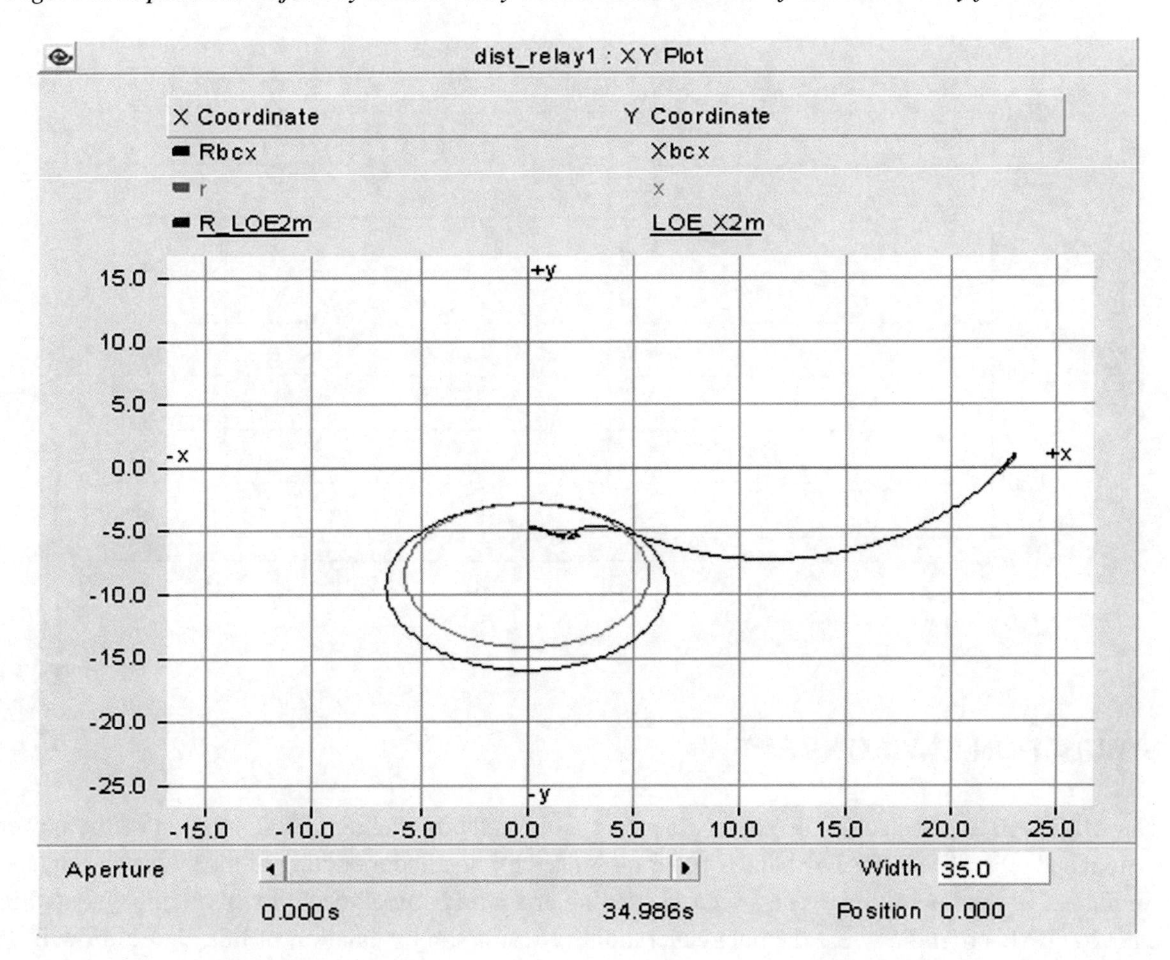

waveforms of generator (G1) when it is subjected to the Loss of Excitation condition. It is obvious that the generator terminal voltage will decrease, the stator current will increase slightly and the generator will absorb reactive power from the system instead of supplying reactive power to it. Also, the under voltage relay trip signal will be generated at "24 s" when the generator terminal voltage becomes less than 20.01 kV. In addition, Figure 8 discusses the waveforms of generator 2 which increases its' output reactive power to supply generator 1. Figure 9 presents the impedance trajectory which will not penetrate the relay circle. Lastly, no relay trip signal will be initiated as indicated in Figure 10.

From the above discussed two cases, it is clear that the performance of the impedance relay to different Loss of Excitation conditions is completely depending on the generator loading and the percentage loss of excitation. In addition, many Loss of Excitation conditions may not be detected by these relays. Therefore, the necessity for developing an Artificial Intelligent (AI) based relay to overcome these problems appeared.

Figure 6. Conventional loss of excitation relay trip signal for case 1

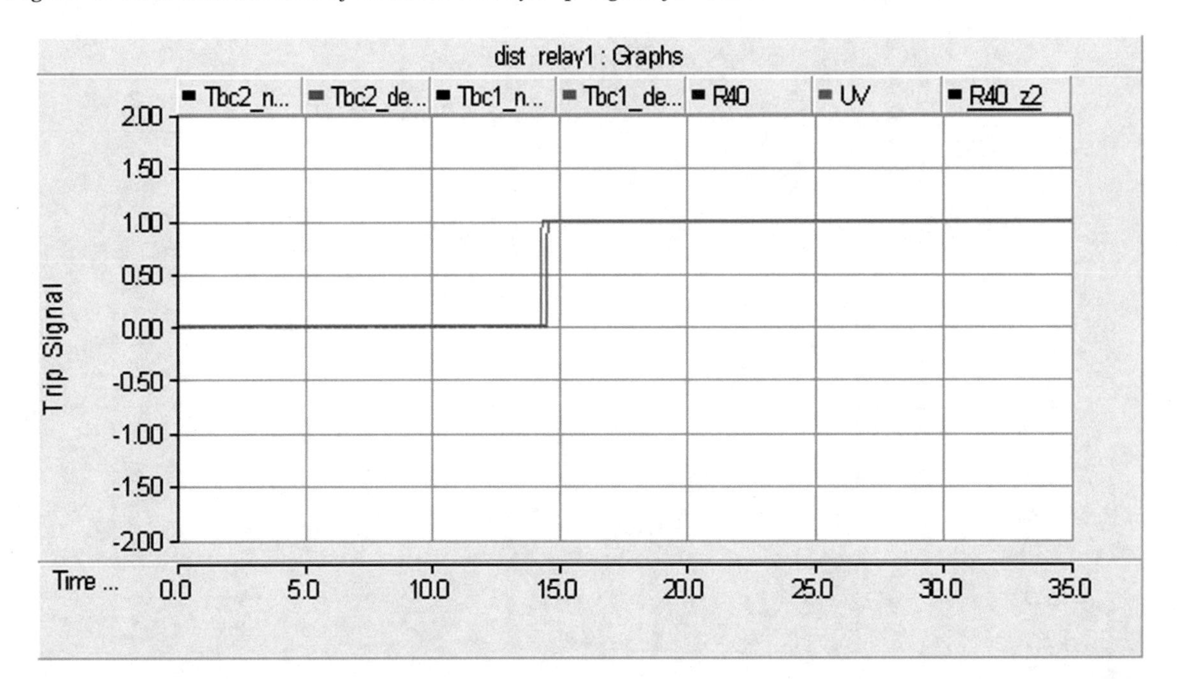

SIMULATION ENVIRONMENT

The MATLAB is selected as the key engineering tool for the modeling and simulation of the power system and relay. The PSCAD/EMTDC program is used for detailed modeling of the power system and simulation of the interesting events. Scenario setting and a relaying algorithm will be implemented in the MATLAB program, while the data generation for testing and validation of this algorithm will be carried out by the PSCAD/EMTDC program.

The training data used to train the ANFIS are taken at different Loss of Excitation fault conditions and no-fault conditions.

The fault conditions are representing different Loss of Excitation fault types:

- Partial Loss of Excitation conditions,
- Complete Loss of Excitation condition.

The fault conditions are implemented at a wide range of generators loading conditions (assuming that the two generators are equally loaded) (18.5%, 25%, 35%, 40%, 50%, 55%, 60%, 65%, 70% and up to 80%) with fault inception time $T_f = 5$ s and at different Loss of Excitation percentage cases (20%, 25%, 50%, 60%, 70%, 75%, 80% and 100%). However, less than (18.5%) generator loading conditions lead to bad results.

All loss of excitation cases are predicted to give an output index of "1", while the no fault conditions are expected to provide an output index of "0".

In this research work, four different types are used as inputs to the ANFIS unit for the loss of excitation faults detection task. The obtained results from these schemes are compared with each other and

Figure 7. Generator 1 characteristic curves during loss of excitation condition for case 2

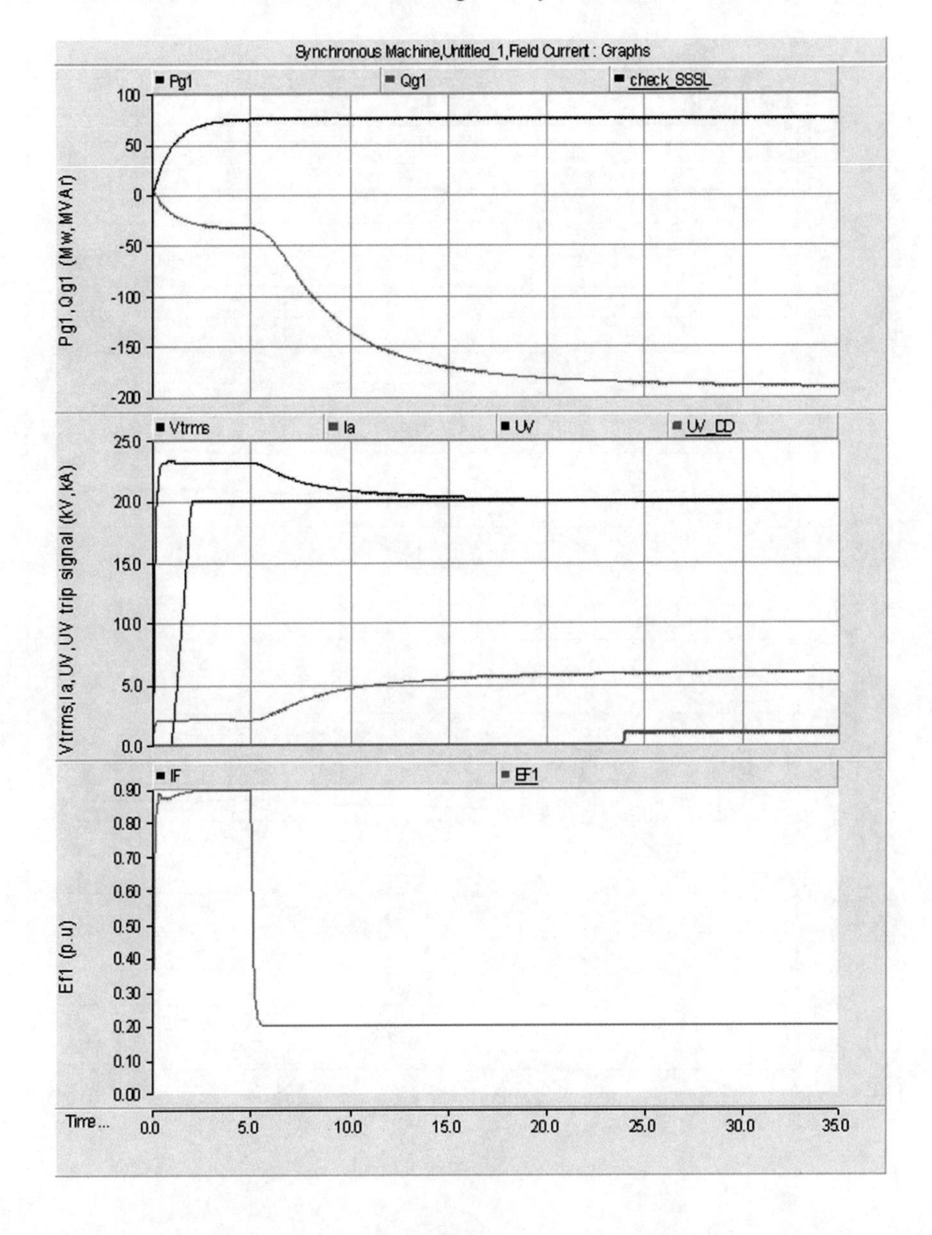

are compared with other schemes to prove the effectiveness of the proposed ANFIS solution. Training using ANFIS is done using the command "anfisedit" on the Matlab. However, the file of the training data should be loaded. Furthermore, some parameters should be selected as "Number of Epoches", the "Tolerance" and Fuzzy Inference System (FIS). The last parameter could be selected either "Grid Partition" or "Sub clustering".

These inputs to the loss of excitation ANFIS unit can be classified as follows:

- The generator terminal impedance measurements (R and X) (Aziz et al. 2017; Aziz et al. 2016; Aziz et al. 2016),

Figure 8. Generator 2 characteristic curves during generator 1 loss of excitation condition for case 2

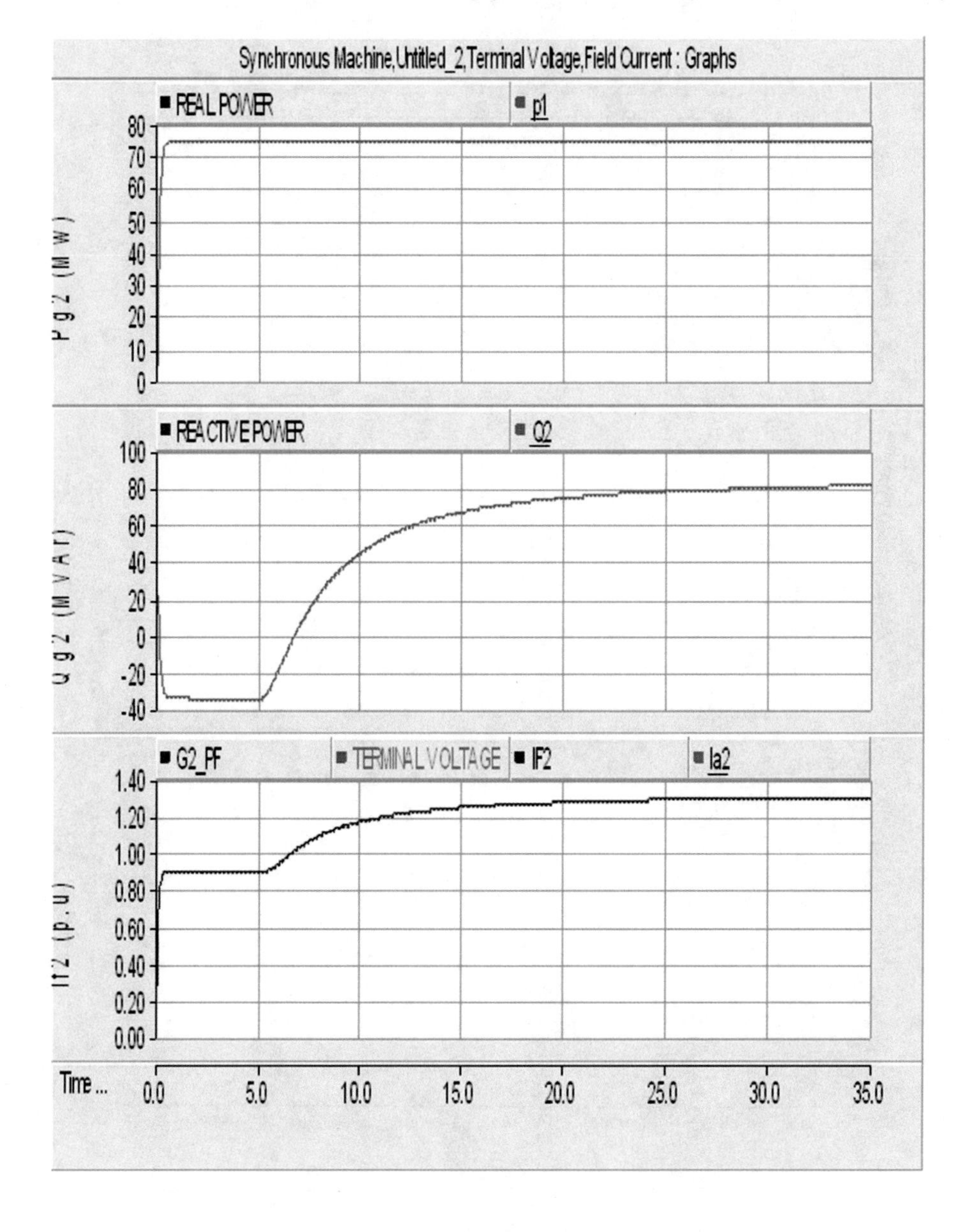

- The generator RMS Line to Line voltage and Phase current (V_{trms} and I_a) (Aziz et al. 2017; Aziz et al. 2016; Aziz et al. 2016),
- The positive sequence components of the terminal voltage (magnitude) and stator current (magnitude and angle) ($|V_{+ve}|$, $|I_{+ve}|$ and $\angle I_{+ve}$), also it is considered as the strongest indicator to the presence of the fault as displayed in (Aziz et al. 2017; Aziz et al. 2016),
- The stator current 3rd harmonic components (magnitudes and angles) (Kamel et al. 2011; Kamel et al. 2012; Aziz et al. 2017; Aziz et al. 2016; Aziz et al. 2016; Aziz et al. 2016; Kamel et al. 2009; Kamel et al. 2009; Aziz et al. 2016).

Figure 9. Impedance trajectory measured by the conventional loss of excitation relay for case 2

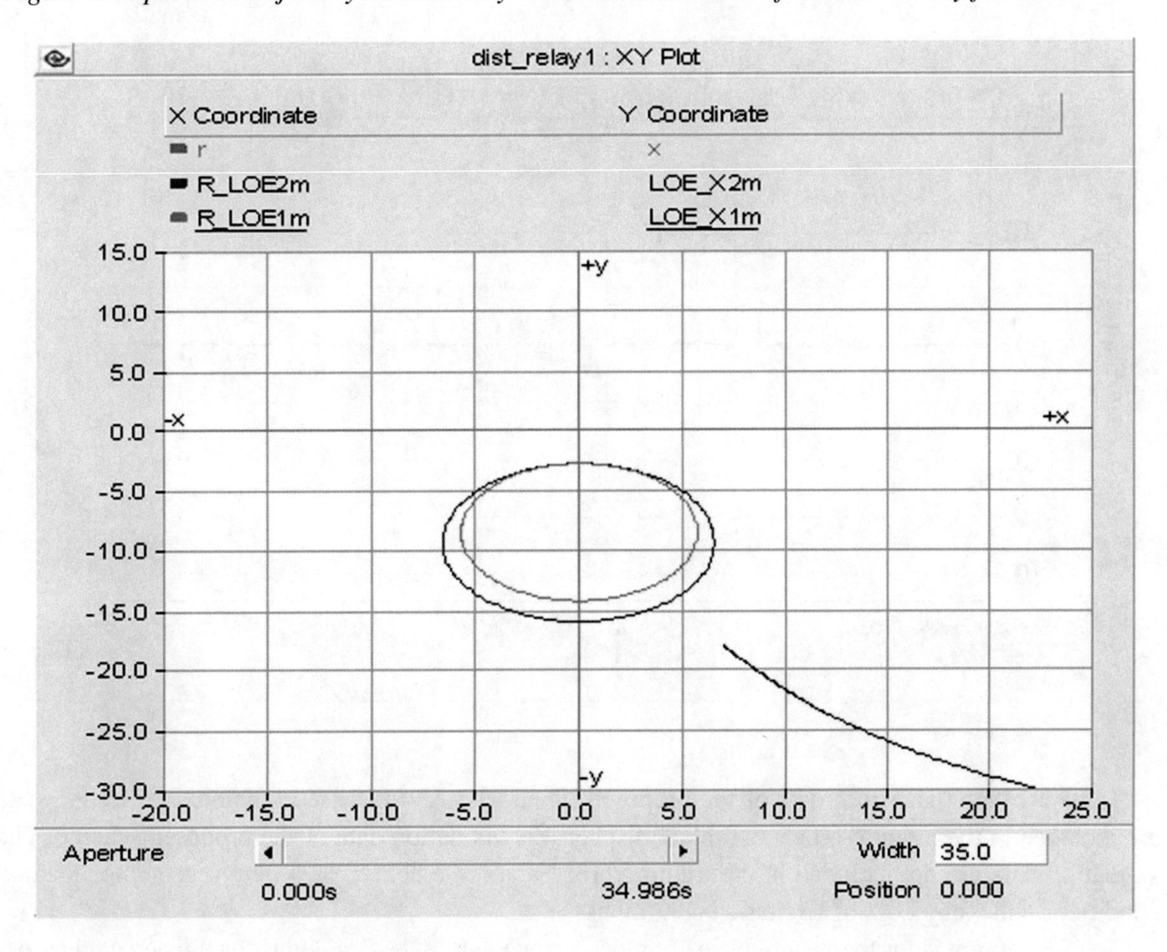

The testing data are chosen arbitrarily from the data included in the training process, on the other hand, the validation data are chosen from data that were not included in the training process to ensure that the proposed scheme is robust.

RESULTS AND DISCUSSION

The following paragraphs describe how to construct, train and test this unit according to the type of input to the ANFIS unit.

The Proposed (R And X) Protection Scheme

In this scheme, the inputs to the ANFIS unit are the generator terminal impedance measurements (R and X), these measurements are obtained from the generator terminal voltage and stator current values. Figure 11 illustrates the flowchart for the process of Loss of Excitation detection of the proposed (R and X) ANFIS protection scheme.

Figure 10. Conventional loss of excitation relay trip signal for case 2

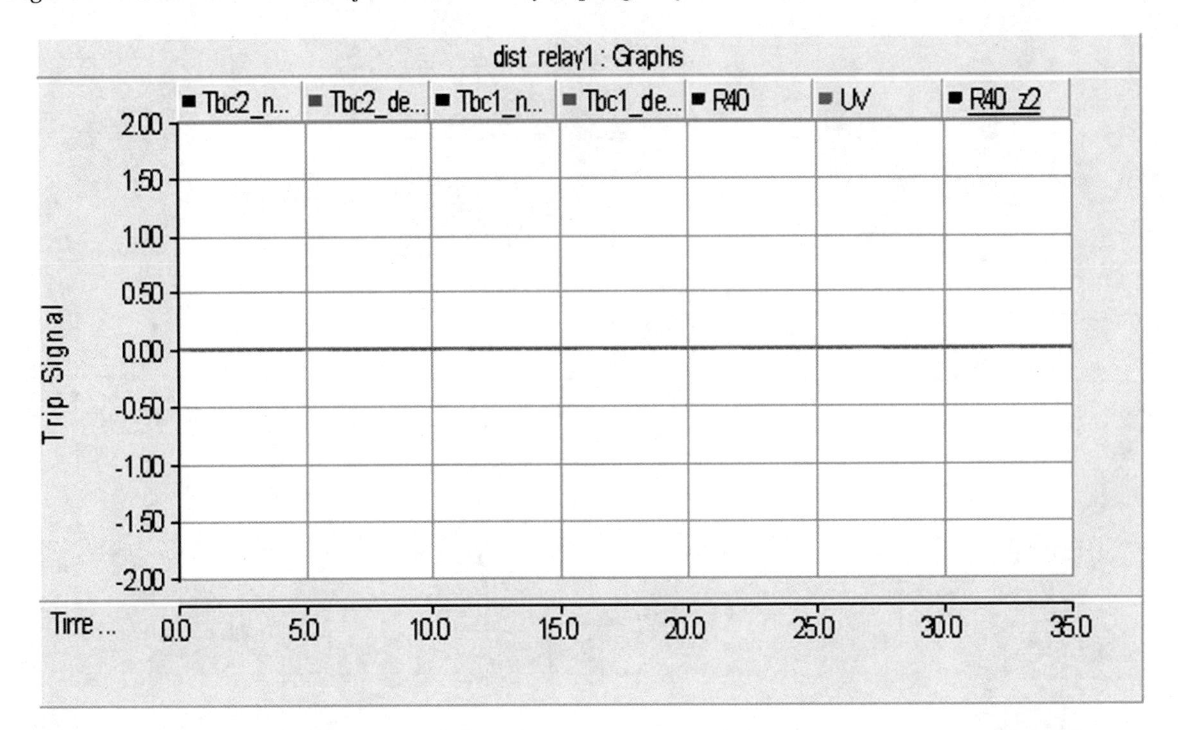

Table 1 offers the testing data of the proposed (R and X) ANFIS based scheme. The testing data are included in the training process. Table 2 displays the validation data of the proposed scheme. The validation data are not included in the training process and are chosen at different generator loading conditions and many Loss of Excitation conditions.

The 2nd column is for the generator loading percentage, while the 3rd one is for the percentage loss of excitation in the generator field circuit. Moreover; the 4th column illustrates the loss of excitation fault inception time which is considered to be $T_f = 5$ s. Furthermore, the 5th column (Testing Time) belongs to the time when the test is applied on the proposed ANFIS relay. Additionally, the 6th and 7th columns are showing the (R and X) values at a specific time which is the "Testing Time". Moreover; the 8th column indicates the calculated index from the ANFIS unit. Finally, the 9th column indicates the expected index from the ANFIS unit.

Tables 1 and 2 demonstrate the successful accuracy of the proposed (R and X) ANFIS based relay in detecting the generator Loss of Excitation conditions under a wide range of generator loading conditions in a reasonable small time.

For example, the first row in Table 2 explains when the generator excitation losses 50% of its excitation at $T_f = 5$ s, while the generator is loaded by 80% of its' full load, the proposed (R and X) ANFIS based scheme will detect this fault condition. This detection takes place at "6 s" by means of the calculated index "I_{R40}" which is larger than the threshold value "0.85". This means that this fault condition will be detected after its inception time by "1 s".

Also, the ninth row in Table 2 presents when the generator losses 75% of its excitation at $T_f = 5$ s on the other hand the generator is loaded by 35% of its' full load, the proposed (R and X) ANFIS based

Figure 11. Flowchart for the detection process of loss of excitation relay based on (R and X)

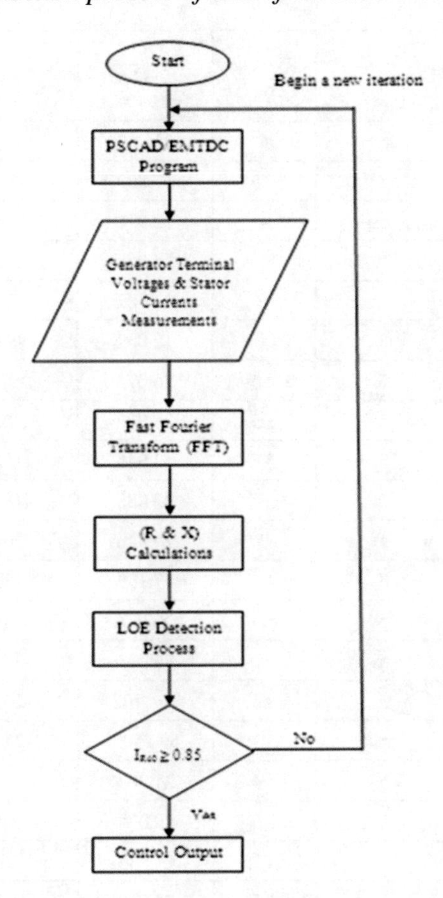

Table 1. Testing data for the proposed (R and X) ANFIS based scheme

Row No.	Generator Loading %	LOE %	LOE Fault Inception Time (s)	TestingTime (s)	R value	X value	Calculated Index "I_{R40}"	Expected Index
1	80%	75%	5	6	21.702	-1.188	0.874	1
2	80%	75%	5	8	14.431	-6.603	1.001	1
3	80%	75%	5	7	17.985	-4.819	1.003	1
4	80%	75%	5	6.5	19.959	-3.258	1.009	1
5	50%	25%	5	7.5	33.2204	-10.388	0.865	1
6	50%	25%	5	8	31.748	-11.653	0.987	1
7	50%	25%	5	2	38.9802	-1.9002	0.166	0
8	50%	25%	5	3.5	39.0941	-1.662	0.103	0
9	70%	25%	5	6.1	25.007	-2.155	0.853	1
10	70%	25%	5	7	23.364	-4.304	0.995	1
11	70%	25%	5	8.5	20.559	-6.882	1.002	1
12	70%	25%	5	3	26.072	-0.2803	0.105	0
13	70%	25%	5	4	26.071	-0.2695	0.1	0

Table 2. Validation data for the proposed (R and X) ANFIS based scheme

Row No.	Generator Loading %	LOE %	LOE Fault Inception Time (s)	Testing Time (s)	R value	X value	Calculated Index "I_{R40}"	Expected Index
1	80%	50%	5	6	21.759	-1.129	0.856	1
2	80%	50%	5	7.5	17.802	-5.163	1.002	1
3	80%	50%	5	4	22.976	1.0601	0.143	0
4	70%	75%	5	5.8	24.968	-2.245	0.869	1
5	70%	75%	5	6	24.187	-3.163	0.97	1
6	70%	75%	5	8	16.062	-8.486	1.002	1
7	70%	75%	5	2.5	26.073	-0.292	0.11	0
8	70%	75%	5	3.5	26.072	-0.273	0.1	0
9	35%	75%	5	5.7	43.946	-16.859	0.882	1
10	35%	75%	5	6	40.488	-18.725	1.059	1
11	35%	75%	5	9	16.946	-20.803	0.996	1
12	35%	75%	5	4.5	47.169	-13.993	0.08	0
13	25%	80%	5	5.3	58.2303	-28.216	0.934	1
14	25%	80%	5	6	46.223	-31.995	1.038	1
15	25%	80%	5	8.5	16.3102	-26.806	0.993	1
16	25%	80%	5	4	59.2503	-27.336	0.094	0
17	80%	20%	5	6.4	21.787	-1.217	0.865	1
18	80%	20%	5	7.5	20.024	-3.526	1.006	1
19	80%	20%	5	15	11.944	-7.434	0.9987	1
20	80%	20%	5	1.5	23.048	1.1004	0.118	0
21	80%	20%	5	3	23.055	1.247	0.103	0

scheme will detect this fault condition. This detection happens at "5.7 s", this means that this fault condition will be detected after its inception time by only "0.7 s".

From the calculated indices (I_{R40}) in the below Tables 1 and 2, it is easy to conclude that the output of the proposed (R and X) ANFIS based scheme should be reasonably chosen as:

- $I_{R40} \geq 0.85$ for Loss of Excitation (LOE) conditions,
- $I_{R40} \leq 0.2$ for no-fault conditions.

The proposed (R and X) ANFIS based relay detects the different Loss of Excitation fault conditions within about (300-1400 ms) after the fault occurrence under a wide range of generator loading conditions from (18.5% to 80%) (Aziz et al. 2017; Aziz et al. 2016; Aziz et al. 2016).

The Proposed (V_{trms} And I_a) Protection Scheme

On this scheme, the generator RMS Line to Line voltage and the Phase current (V_{trms} and I_a) are the inputs to the ANFIS unit.

Figure 12 demonstrates the flowchart for the process of Loss of Excitation detection of the proposed (V_{trms} and I_a) ANFIS protection scheme.

Table 3 shows the testing data of the proposed (V_{trms} and I_a) ANFIS based scheme, also, Table 4 presents the validation data of this proposed ANFIS scheme.

Tables 3 and 4 show that the proposed (V_{trms} and I_a) ANFIS based scheme is fast in detecting the generator Loss of Excitation conditions during the generator heavy loading conditions only (larger than 50% of its rating) compared to the other (R and X) ANFIS based scheme.

For example, the fifth row in Table 3 indicates that, when the generator losses about 25% of its excitation at $T_f = 5$ s while the generator is loaded by 50% of its' full rated power, the proposed (V_{trms} and I_a) ANFIS based scheme will detect this Loss of Excitation condition. This detection occurs at "9.7 s". This is too delayed compared to the other proposed (R and X) ANFIS based scheme which will detect the same fault condition at "7.5 s".

Figure 12. Flowchart for the detection process of loss of excitation relay based on (Vtrms and Ia)

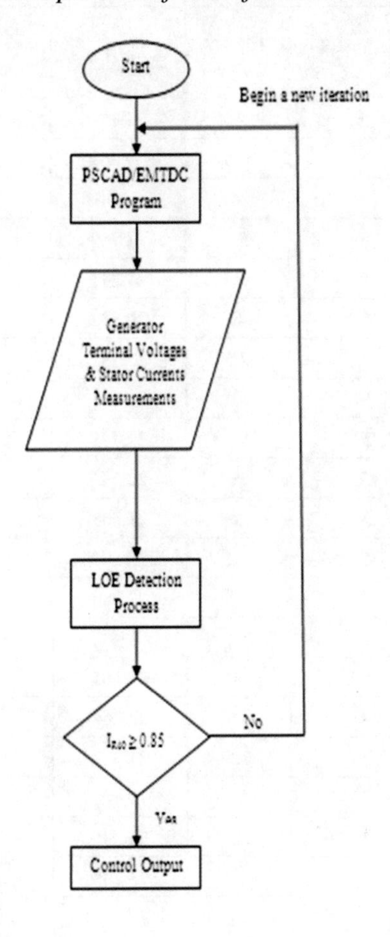

Table 3. Testing data for the proposed (Vtrms and Ia) ANFIS based scheme

Row No.	Generator Loading %	LOE %	LOE Inception Time (s)	Testing Time (s)	V_{trms} (kV)	I_a (kA)	Calculated Index "I_{R40}"	Expected Index
1	80%	75%	5	6	22.103	6.154	0.913	1
2	80%	75%	5	8	19.949	7.597	0.9917	1
3	80%	75%	5	7	20.938	6.798	0.962	1
4	80%	75%	5	6.5	21.545	6.397	0.936	1
5	50%	25%	5	9.7	22.815	4.263	0.86	1
6	50%	25%	5	2	24.185	3.556	0.22	0
7	50%	25%	5	3.5	24.173	3.555	0.23	0
8	70%	25%	5	6.1	22.586	5.267	0.913	1
9	70%	25%	5	7	22.138	5.4705	0.929	1
10	70%	25%	5	8.5	21.571	5.829	0.952	1
11	70%	25%	5	3	23.128	5.106	0.13	0
12	70%	25%	5	4	23.128	5.103	0.129	0

Table 4. Validation data for the proposed (Vtrms and Ia) ANFIS based scheme

Row No.	Generator Loading %	LOE %	LOE Inception Time (s)	Testing Time (s)	V_{trms} (kV)	I_a (kA)	Calculated Index "I_{R40}"	Expected Index
1	80%	50%	5	5.6	22.732	5.8702	0.89	1
2	80%	50%	5	7.5	20.969	6.739	0.963	1
3	80%	50%	5	4	23.1301	5.785	0.077	0
4	70%	75%	5	5.5	22.769	5.172	0.877	1
5	70%	75%	5	6	22.241	5.4102	0.925	1
6	70%	75%	5	8	20.344	6.737	1.019	1
7	70%	75%	5	2.5	23.131	5.105	0.123	0
8	70%	75%	5	3.5	23.128	5.103	0.131	0
9	35%	75%	5	5.7	22.711	2.946	0.85	1
10	35%	75%	5	6	22.531	3.069	0.902	1
11	35%	75%	5	9	21.003	4.664	1.019	1
12	35%	75%	5	4.5	23.15001	2.706	0.2	0
13	25%	80%	5	6.5	22.086	2.936	0.863	1
14	25%	80%	5	8.5	21.1905	4.074	1.019	1
15	25%	80%	5	4	23.165	2.042	0.157	0
16	80%	20%	5	5.9	22.764	5.9173	0.86	1
17	80%	20%	5	7.5	21.826	6.301	0.923	1
18	80%	20%	5	15	19.601	8.115	0.988	1
19	80%	20%	5	1.5	23.2802	5.792	0.076	0
20	80%	20%	5	3	23.244	5.795	0.076	0

The same is for the thirteenth row in Table 4, as the (V_{trms} and I_a) ANFIS based scheme will detect this Loss of Excitation fault condition at "6.5 s". Which is too much compared to the other proposed (R and X) ANFIS scheme which will detect the same fault condition at "5.3 s".

On the other hand, when the generator is heavy loaded, as illustrated in the first, fourth and sixteenth rows on Table 4, it is clear that the (V_{trms} and I_a) ANFIS based scheme will detect the Loss of Excitation fault conditions faster than the proposed (R and X) ANFIS scheme. As an example, the first row in Table 4 shows when the generator losses about 50% of its excitation at $T_f = 5$ s while it is loaded by 80% of its' full rated power, the proposed (V_{trms} and I_a) ANFIS based scheme will detect this Loss of Excitation fault condition. This detection takes place at "5.6 s". Which is quicker than the proposed (R and X) ANFIS based scheme which will detect this fault condition at "6 s".

From the calculated indices (I_{R40}) in Tables 3 and 4, it is easy to suggest that the output of the proposed (V_{trms} and I_a) ANFIS unit should be selected as:

- $I_{R40} \geq 0.85$ for Loss of Excitation (LOE) conditions,
- $I_{R40} \leq 0.25$ for no-fault conditions.

From the above derivations, it is apparent that the proposed (V_{trms} and I_a) ANFIS based scheme detects the Loss of Excitation fault conditions in a time period of (500-900 ms) after the fault occurrence, this only happens when the generator loading is higher than 50% of its' rated power (Aziz et al. 2017; Aziz et al. 2016; Aziz et al. 2016).

The Proposed Positive Sequence Components Protection Scheme

In this scheme, the positive sequence components of the generator terminal voltage (magnitude) and stator current (magnitude and angle) ($|V_{+ve}|$, $|I_{+ve}|$ and $\angle I_{+ve}$) are considered as inputs to the ANFIS unit. The phase angle of the voltage positive sequence component ($\angle V_{+ve}$) is not considered in this scheme as it is not an effective factor in all loss of excitation conditions as indicated in Figure 13. The phase angle of the current positive sequence component (red waveform) varies clearly with the loss of excitation condition (which occurs at T = 5 s) while the phase angle of the voltage positive sequence component (green waveform) is not affected obviously. As such, the phase angle of the voltage positive sequence component ($\angle V_{+ve}$) is excluded from this scheme. These measurements are obtained from a sequence filter.

Figure 14 depicts the flowchart for the process of Loss of Excitation detection of the proposed positive sequence components ANFIS based protection scheme.

Table 5 offers the testing data of the proposed positive sequence components ANFIS based scheme. Moreover; Table 6 shows the validation data of this proposed ANFIS scheme.

Tables 5 and 6 present the talented results obtained from the proposed positive sequence components ANFIS scheme in the generator Loss of Excitation conditions detection under a wide range of generator loading conditions in a very small time compared to other ANFIS based schemes.

The first row in Table 6 describes when the generator losses about 50% of its excitation at $T_f = 5$ s while it's loaded by about 80% of its' full rated power, the proposed positive sequence components ANFIS based scheme will detect this fault condition. This detection occurs at "5.6 s". This means that this fault condition will be detected after fault occurrence by "0.6 s" by the calculated index "I_{R40}" which is greater than the threshold value "0.85".

Figure 13. Phase angle waveforms of the positive sequence component of the generator stator current and terminal voltage with loss of excitation condition

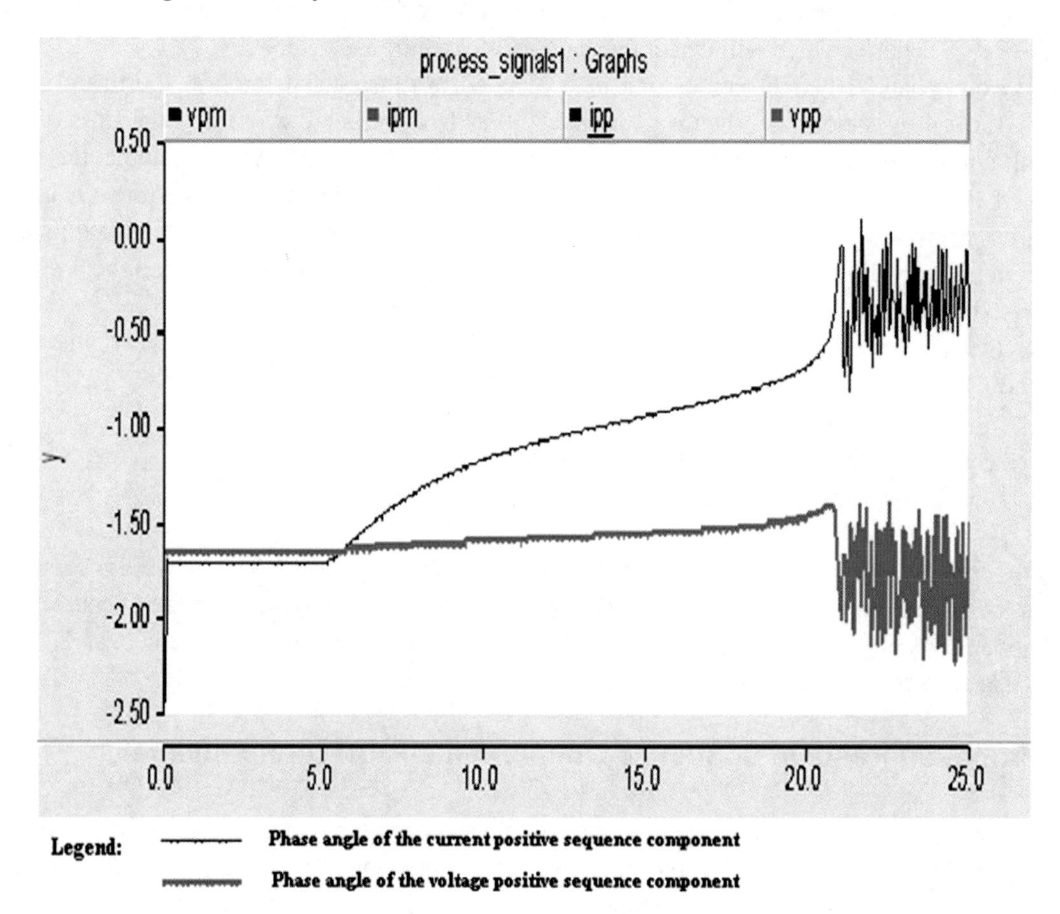

Also, the fourth row in Table 6 illustrates when the generator losses about 75% of its excitation at T_f = 5 s while the generator is loaded by about 70% of its' full rated power, the proposed positive sequence components ANFIS based scheme will detect this fault condition. This detection takes place at "5.5 s". This means that this fault condition will be detected after its occurrence by only "0.5 s".

From the calculated indices (I_{R40}) in Tables 5 and 6, it is easy to say that the output of the proposed positive sequence components ANFIS based scheme should be sensibly chosen as:

- $I_{R40} \geq 0.85$ for Loss of Excitation (LOE) conditions,
- $I_{R40} \leq 0.24$ for no-fault conditions.

From the obtained results indicated in Tables 5 and 6, it is evident that the proposed positive sequence components ANFIS based scheme detects the different Loss of Excitation conditions within about (500-1000 ms) after the fault inception time under a wide range of generator loading conditions from about (18.5% to 80%) of its' rated power and under various Loss of Excitation percentages conditions. This is better than the other (R and X) and (V_{trms} and I_a) ANFIS schemes (Aziz et al. 2017; Aziz et al. 2016).

Figure 14. Flowchart for the detection process of loss of excitation relay based on positive sequence components of voltage and current

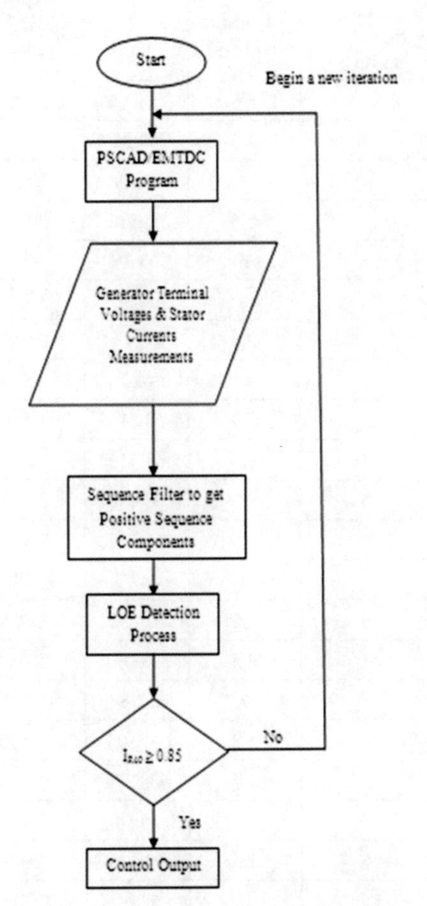

Table 5. Testing data for the proposed positive sequence components ANFIS based scheme

Row No.	Generator Loading %	LOE %	LOE Inception Time (s)	Testing Time (s)	$\lvert V_+ \rvert$ (Volt)	$\lvert I_+ \rvert$ (Ampere)	$\angle I_+$ (rad)	Calculated Index "I_{R40}"	Expected Index
1	80%	75%	5	6	63.652	3.088	-1.491	1.128	1
2	80%	75%	5	8	57.256	3.841	-1.087	0.965	1
3	80%	75%	5	7	60.05	3.438	-1.256	0.998	1
4	80%	75%	5	6.5	61.749	3.24	-1.364	1.063	1
5	50%	25%	5	7.5	66.992	1.97	-1.53	1.233	1
6	50%	25%	5	8	66.633	2.012	-1.486	1.203	1
7	50%	25%	5	2	69.714	1.78	-1.848	0.095	0
8	50%	25%	5	3.5	69.689	1.7808	-1.847	0.09	0
9	70%	25%	5	6.1	65.011	2.645	-1.591	0.949	1
10	70%	25%	5	7	63.687	2.749	-1.482	1.043	1
11	70%	25%	5	8.5	62.098	2.929	-1.345	1.005	1
12	70%	25%	5	3	66.675	2.557	-1.721	0.109	0
13	70%	25%	5	4	66.676	2.557	-1.721	0.106	0

Table 6. Validation data for the proposed positive sequence components ANFIS based scheme

Row No.	Generator Loading %	LOE %	LOE Inception Time (s)	Testing Time (s)	$\|V_+\|$ (Volt)	$\|I_+\|$ (Ampere)	$\angle I_+$ (rad)	Calculated Index "I_{R40}"	Expected Index
1	80%	50%	5	5.6	65.361	2.955	-1.617	0.882	1
2	80%	50%	5	7.5	60.24	3.401	-1.265	1.002	1
3	80%	50%	5	4	66.68	2.899	-1.707	0.122	0
4	70%	75%	5	5.5	65.312	2.621	-1.615	0.874	1
5	70%	75%	5	6	63.76	2.737	-1.502	1.048	1
6	70%	75%	5	8	58.447	3.404	-1.128	0.974	1
7	70%	75%	5	2.5	66.68	2.556	-1.721	0.109	0
8	70%	75%	5	3.5	66.675	2.556	-1.721	0.107	0
9	35%	75%	5	5.9	64.812	1.554	-1.441	0.855	1
10	35%	75%	5	6	64.513	1.591	-1.406	0.884	1
11	35%	75%	5	9	60.468	2.352	-1.039	1.015	1
12	35%	75%	5	4.5	66.737	1.356	-1.689	0.028	0
13	25%	80%	5	6	64.73	1.29	-1.31	0.865	1
14	25%	80%	5	7.5	62.052	1.808	-1.048	1.054	1
15	25%	80%	5	8.5	61.0001	2.06	-0.976	1.023	1
16	25%	80%	5	4	66.783	1.023	-1.615	0.24	0
17	80%	20%	5	5.8	65.5917	2.9675	-1.618	0.859	1
18	80%	20%	5	7.5	62.7272	3.1756	-1.405	1.095	1
19	80%	20%	5	15	56.44	4.077	-1.006	0.984	1
20	80%	20%	5	1.5	67.094	2.899	-1.718	0.002	0
21	80%	20%	5	3	67.01	2.903	-1.715	0.022	0

The Proposed Stator Current 3rd Harmonic Components Protection Scheme

This scheme employs the 3rd harmonic components (magnitudes and angles) of the generator stator current as inputs to the ANFIS unit.

Figure 15 affords the flow chart for the proposed stator current 3rd harmonic components ANFIS based scheme for the process of Loss of Excitation detection.

Tables 7 and 8 indicate the testing and validation data of the proposed 3rd harmonic components ANFIS based scheme respectively. These Tables highlight the promising results of the proposed 3rd harmonic components ANFIS based scheme. This proposed ANFIS scheme detects all the generator Loss of Excitation fault conditions under all the generator loading conditions in a very small time compared to other proposed ANFIS schemes.

As an example, the first row in Table 8 shown when the generator losses about 50% of its excitation at $T_f = 5$ s while it is loaded by 80% of its' full rated power, the proposed 3rd harmonic components ANFIS based scheme will detect this fault at "5.2 s". This means that this fault condition will be detected after its occurrence by about "0.2 s", this happens through the calculated index "I_{R40}" which is higher than

Figure 15. Flowchart for the detection process of loss of excitation relay based on 3rd harmonic components

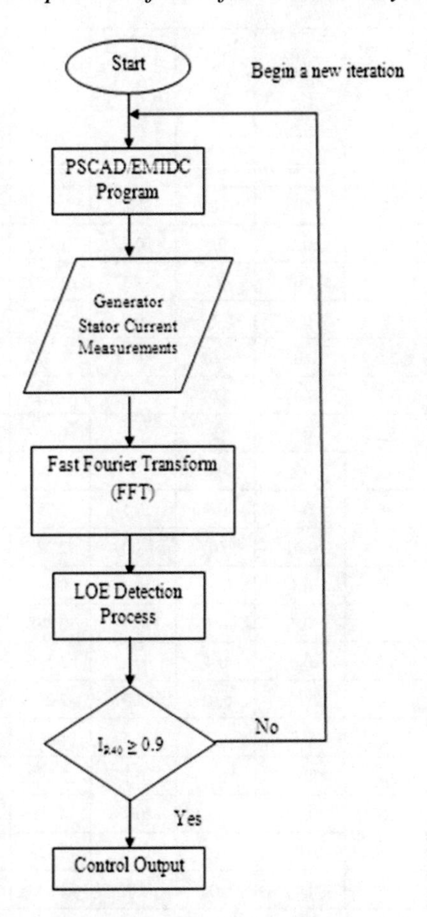

Table 7. Testing data for the proposed 3rd harmonic components of stator current ANFIS based scheme

Row No.	Generator Loading %	LOE %	LOE Inception Time (s)	Testing Time (s)	$\lvert I_a \rvert$ (mA)	$\lvert I_b \rvert$ (mA)	$\lvert I_c \rvert$ (mA)	$\angle I_a$ (rad)	$\angle I_b$ (rad)	$\angle I_c$ (rad)	Calculated Index "I_{R40}"	Expected Index
1	80%	75%	5	6	1.1	0.9	1.8	-1.558	-2.57	1.15	0.992	1
2	80%	75%	5	8	0.5	1.3	1	-1.99	1.905	-0.843	0.948	1
3	80%	75%	5	7	0.4	1.3	1.4	-1.976	2.938	0.123	0.948	1
4	80%	75%	5	6.5	1.2	0.8	1.8	-1.595	-2.637	1.135	0.993	1
5	50%	25%	5	7.5	0.2	0.2	0.4	-2.598	2.804	0.04	0.956	1
6	50%	25%	5	8	0.1	0.3	0.3	-2.622	1.826	-0.932	0.956	1
7	50%	25%	5	2	0.01	0.01	0.02	-2.445	-0.421	2.047	0.317	0
8	50%	25%	5	3.5	0.02	0.01	0.01	-2.1804	0.297	1.824	0.154	0
9	70%	25%	5	6.1	0.5	0.3	0.79	-1.55	-2.607	1.15	0.992	1
10	70%	25%	5	7	0.2	0.5	0.65	-2.186	2.927	0.109	0.95	1
11	70%	25%	5	8.5	0.1	0.4	0.41	-2.4288	1.859	-0.894	0.954	1
12	70%	25%	5	3	0.03	0.02	0.02	-2.2433	0.095	1.766	0.215	0
13	70%	25%	5	4	0.03	0.02	0.01	-2.2605	0.464	2.025	0.094	0

Table 8. Validation data for the proposed 3rd harmonic components of stator current ANFIS based scheme

Row No.	Generator Loading %	LOE %	LOE Inception Time (s)	Testing Time (s)	$\lvert I_a \rvert$ (mA)	$\lvert I_b \rvert$ (mA)	$\lvert I_c \rvert$ (mA)	$\angle I_a$ (rad)	$\angle I_b$ (rad)	$\angle I_c$ (rad)	Calculated Index "I_{R40}"	Expected Index
1	80%	50%	5	5.2	0.3	0.5	0.7	-1.361	-2.232	1.253	0.98	1
2	80%	50%	5	7.5	0.42	0.9	1.1	-2.253	2.898	0.09	0.952	1
3	80%	50%	5	4	0.03	0.03	0.02	-2.251	0.477	1.982	0.096	0
4	70%	75%	5	5.2	0.4	0.5	0.9	-1.425	-2.292	1.227	0.98	1
5	70%	75%	5	6	1.07	0.7	1.5	-1.587	-2.625	1.137	0.993	1
6	70%	75%	5	8	0.4	1	0.8	-2.15	1.883	-0.87	0.95	1
7	70%	75%	5	2.5	0.03	0.02	0.02	-2.329	0.149	1.845	0.17	0
8	70%	75%	5	3.5	0.03	0.02	0.02	-2.253	0.116	1.73	0.232	0
9	35%	75%	5	5.1	0.3	1	0.4	-0.637	-2.004	2.204	0.902	1
10	35%	75%	5	6	0.8	0.4	1	-1.68	-2.882	1.091	0.997	1
11	35%	75%	5	9	0.1	0.3	0.4	-2.794	1.823	-0.95	0.958	1
12	35%	75%	5	4.5	0.01	0.01	0.009	-2.226	0.5305	1.924	0.097	0
13	25%	80%	5	5.04	0.1	0.03	0.13	-0.691	-2.195	2.177	0.937	1
14	25%	80%	5	7.5	0.3	0.4	0.7	-2.678	2.709	-0.00	0.957	1
15	25%	80%	5	8.5	0.1	0.4	0.4	-3.119	1.776	-1.01	0.96	1
16	25%	80%	5	4	0.01	0.01	0.007	-2.271	0.415	1.818	0.13	0
17	80%	20%	5	5.2	0.2	0.3	0.5	-1.405	-2.19	1.268	0.98	1
18	80%	20%	5	7.5	0.2	0.5	0.7	-2.329	2.898	0.087	0.953	1
19	80%	20%	5	10	0.31	0.4	0.2	-2.72	0.762	-1.85	0.959	1
20	80%	20%	5	1.5	0.02	0.03	0.01	-3.138	-0.313	2.385	0.26	0
21	80%	20%	5	3	0.03	0.02	0.02	-2.228	0.068	1.731	0.24	0

the threshold value "0.9". Furthermore, the fourth row in Table 8 describes when the generator losses about 75% of its excitation at $T_f = 5$ s while it is loaded by 70% of its' full rated power, the proposed 3rd harmonic components ANFIS based scheme will detect this fault at "5.2 s".

From the calculated indices (I_{R40}) in Tables 7 and 8, it is easy to conclude that the output of this proposed ANFIS based scheme should be logically chosen as:

- $I_{R40} \geq 0.9$ for Loss of Excitation (LOE) conditions,
- $I_{R40} \leq 0.325$ for no-fault conditions.

The illustrated results in Tables 7 and 8, explain that the proposed 3rd harmonic components of the stator currents ANFIS based scheme detects the Loss of Excitation fault conditions within about (40-200 ms) after the fault occurrence, this happens under all generator loading conditions and under a variety of Loss of Excitation percentage conditions. These results are better than those obtained from the other ANFIS based schemes (Aziz et al. 2016).

It is obvious that the generator stator current 3rd harmonic components as inputs for the ANFIS based unit gives superior results more professional than the other ANFIS based schemes and better than other techniques as in (Amini et al. 2015; Usta et al. 2007; Shi et al. 2012; Xu, 2009; Sandoval et al.

2007). Also, the calculated indices "IR40" are very near to the expected indices. As a final point, Table 9 summarizes a comparison between the different proposed Loss of Excitation ANFIS based schemes and other techniques. This comparison is classifying the techniques according to the generator loading conditions, threshold values and the response time of each technique. The first five methods are based on the current research.

CONCLUSION

This Chapter explains the shortage in the performance of the conventional Loss of Excitation impedance relay. Moreover; this chapter presents the Loss of Excitation protection relay based on ANFIS scheme. From all of the above obtained results and discussion, it can be concluded that the proposed Loss of Excitation protection ANFIS based relay is robust and proved its' high efficiency. The generator stator current 3rd harmonic components (magnitudes and angles) perform the necessary role in the Loss of Excitation faults detection process. As it gives advanced results, very near to the expected indices when used as inputs to the ANFIS scheme. These results coincide with the obtained results from different protection techniques like HIF, Distance relay.

Table 9. Comparison between loss of excitation ANFIS based techniques and other techniques

Loss of Excitation Based Technique	Generator Loading %	Threshold Values	Response Time (s)
ANFIS relay based on (R and X) (Aziz et al. 2017; Aziz et al. 2016; Aziz et al. 2016).	All loading conditions (from 18.5% to 80%).	• $I_{R40} \geq 0.85$ for Loss of Excitation (LOE) conditions. • $I_{R40} \leq 0.2$ for no-fault conditions.	(300-1400 ms).
ANFIS relay based on (Vtrms and Ia) (Aziz et al. 2017; Aziz et al. 2016; Aziz et al. 2016).	Higher than 50%.	• $I_{R40} \geq 0.85$ for Loss of Excitation (LOE) conditions. • $I_{R40} \leq 0.25$ for no-fault conditions.	(500-900 ms).
ANFIS relay based on ($\lvert V_{+ve} \rvert$, $\lvert I_{+ve} \rvert$ and $\angle I_{+ve}$) (Aziz et al. 2017 ; Aziz et al. 2016).	All loading conditions (from 18.5% to 80%).	• $I_{R40} \geq 0.85$ for Loss of Excitation (LOE) conditions. • $I_{R40} \leq 0.24$ for no-fault conditions.	(500-1000 ms).
ANFIS relay based on stator current 3rd harmonics (magnitudes and angles) (Aziz et al. 2016).	All loading conditions (from 18.5% to 80%).	• $I_{R40} \geq 0.9$ for Loss of Excitation (LOE) conditions. • $I_{R40} \leq 0.325$ for no-fault conditions.	(40-200 ms).
Conventional Impedance relay (Aziz et al. 2017; Aziz et al. 2016; Aziz et al. 2016; Aziz et al. 2016).	All loading conditions (from 18.5% to 80%).	-	Minimum 7-8 s and some LOE conditions are not detected.
Other technique based on "generator reactive power output and its pull out curve" (Usta et al. 2007).	10% and 50%.	-	Within 1.12 s.
Other technique based on "R-X with directional element scheme" (Shi et al. 2012).	40% and 80%.	-	6.931 s and 4.175 s.
Other technique based on "generator terminal measurements" (Xu, 2009).	78%. (This scheme is useful for generator loading conditions ≥ 50%).	-	From 1.276 s up to 15.6792 s.
Other technique based on "P-Q plane" (Sandoval et al. 2007).	20% and 75%.	-	14 s and 2.9 s.
Other technique based on "Derivative of the terminal voltage and the output reactive power of the generator" (Amini et al. 2015).	25% and 78%.	-	1.66 s and 1.6 s.

The obtained indices are the output values of the ANFIS unit. It is the best ever when utilizing the stator current 3rd harmonic components (magnitudes and angles) with this proposed ANFIS scheme, as it detects the Loss of Excitation fault conditions in about (40-200 ms) after the fault occurrence. This happens under all generator loading conditions and under a different Loss of Excitation percentage conditions. The calculated indices are almost near to the expected values for fault and no fault conditions. The expected value for Loss of Excitation fault conditions is (1) and the expected value for no fault conditions is (0). However, for the matter of reducing any possible errors these indices could be reasonably chosen as:

- $I_{R40} \geq 0.9$ for Loss of Excitation (LOE) conditions and
- $I_{R40} \leq 0.325$ for no-fault conditions.

ACKNOWLEDGMENT

The authors are pleased to acknowledge Dr. Mohamed ElSamahy for the help and support that he provided to this research work.

REFERENCES

Abdel Aziz, M. S., Elsamahy, M., Moustafa Hassan, M. A., & Bendary, F. M. A. (2017). A novel study for hydro-generators loss of excitation faults detection using ANFIS. *International Journal of Modelling and Simulation*, *37*(1), 36–45.

Ali, M. M. I., & Hassan, M. M. (2012). Parameter identification using ANFIS for magnetically saturated induction motor. *International Journal of System Dynamics Applications*, *1*(2), 28–43. doi:10.4018/ijsda.2012040103

Amini, M., Davarpanah, M., & Sanaye-Pasand, M. (2015). A novel approach to detect the synchronous generator loss of excitation. *IEEE Transactions on Power Delivery*, *30*(3), 1429–1438. doi:10.1109/TPWRD.2014.2370763

Azar, A. T., & El-Said, S. A. (2013). Superior neuro-fuzzy classification systems. *Neural Computing & Applications*, 1–18.

Aziz, M. A., Hassan, M. A., & Zahab, E. A. (2011, October). *An Artificial Intelligence Based Approach for High Impedance Faults Analysis in Distribution Networks under Different Loading Conditions*. In *The 21st International conference on Computer Theory and Applications*, Alexandria, Egypt.

Aziz, M. A., Hassan, M. M., & El-Zahab, E. A. (2012). An artificial intelligence based approach for high impedance faults analysis in distribution networks. *International Journal of System Dynamics Applications*, *1*(2), 44–59. doi:10.4018/ijsda.2012040104

Aziz, M. A., Hassan, M. M., & Zahab, E. A. (2011, September). Applications of ANFIS in high impedance faults detection and classification in distribution networks. In *Diagnostics for Electric Machines, Power Electronics & Drives (SDEMPED), 2011 IEEE International Symposium*, (pp. 612-619). IEEE.

Aziz, M. A., Hassan, M. M., & Zahab, E. A. (2012). High-impedance faults analysis in distribution networks using an adaptive neuro fuzzy inference system. *Electric Power Components and Systems, 40*(11), 1300–1318. doi:10.1080/15325008.2012.689418

Aziz, M. S. E. D. A., El Samahy, M., Hassan, M. A. M., & El Bendary, F. (2016). Applications of ANFIS in Loss of Excitation Faults Detection in Hydro-Generators. *International Journal of System Dynamics Applications, 5*(2), 63–79. doi:10.4018/IJSDA.2016040104

Aziz, M. S. E. D. A., Elsamahy, M., Moustafa, M., & Bendary, F. (2016). Loss of Excitation Faults Detection in Hydro-Generators Using an Adaptive Neuro Fuzzy Inference System. *Indonesian Journal of Electrical Engineering and Computer Science, 1*(2), 300–309. doi:10.11591/ijeecs.v1.i2.pp300-309

Aziz, M. S. E. D. A., Elsamahy, M., Moustafa, M., & Bendary, F. (2016). Loss of Excitation Detection in Hydro-Generators Based on ANFIS Approach Using Positive Sequence Components. *The XIX IEEE International Conference on Soft Computing and Measurements SCM'2016*, 309-312. 10.1109/SCM.2016.7519765

Aziz, M. S. E. D. A., Elsamahy, M., Moustafa, M., & Bendary, F. (2016). Detecting the Loss of Excitation in Hydro Generators Using a Neuro-Fuzzy Technique. The Annals of "Dunarea De Jos". *University of Galati, 39*(1), 34–43.

Benmouyal, G. (2007). *The impact of synchronous generators excitation supply on protection and relays*. Schweitzer Engineering Laboratories, Inc., Tech. Rep. TP6281-01, 20070912.

Blackburn, J. L., & Domin, T. J. (2015). *Protective relaying: principles and applications*. CRC press.

De Morais, A. P., Cardoso, G., & Mariotto, L. (2010). An innovative loss-of-excitation protection based on the fuzzy inference mechanism. *IEEE Transactions on Power Delivery, 25*(4), 2197–2204. doi:10.1109/TPWRD.2010.2051462

Ebrahimi, S. Y., & Ghorbani, A. (2016). Performance comparison of LOE protection of synchronous generator in the presence of UPFC. *Engineering Science and Technology, an International Journal, 19*(1), 71-78.

Elmore, W. A. (2003). *Protective relaying: theory and applications* (Vol. 1). CRC Press. doi:10.1201/9780203912850

Elsamahy, M., Faried, S. O., & Ramakrishna, G. (2010, July). Impact of midpoint STATCOM on the coordination between generator distance phase backup protection and generator capability curves. *Power and Energy Society General Meeting*, 1-7. 10.1109/PES.2010.5590134

Ghandhari, M. (2008). *Dynamic Analysis of Power Systems. PART II.* Royal Institute of Technology.

Hussein, H. T., Ammar, M. E., & Hassan, M. M. (2017). Three Phase Induction Motor's Stator Turns Fault Analysis Based on Artificial Intelligence. *International Journal of System Dynamics Applications, 6*(3), 1–19. doi:10.4018/IJSDA.2017070101

Ismail, M. M. (2012). Applications of anfis and fuzzy algorithms for improvement of the DTC performance for the three phase saturated model of induction motor. *International Journal of System Dynamics Applications, 1*(3), 54–83. doi:10.4018/ijsda.2012070102

Ismail, M. M., & Hassan, M. M. (2012). Using positive and negative sequence components of currents and voltages for high impedance fault analysis via ANFIS. *International Journal of System Dynamics Applications*, *1*(4), 132–157. doi:10.4018/ijsda.2012100106

Kamel, T. S., El-Morshedy, A. K., & Moustafa, M. A. (2009). *A novel approach to distance protection of transmission lines using adaptive neuro fuzzy inference system* (Doctoral dissertation). Cairo University.

Kamel, T. S., Hassan, M. M. A., & El-Morshedy, A. (2011). An ANFIS based distance relay protection for transmission lines in EPS. *International Journal of Innovations in Electrical Power Systems.*

Kamel, T. S., Moustafa, M. A. & El-Morshedy, A. K. (2009). Application of Artificial Intelligent Approach in Distance Relay for Transmission line Protection. *The International Scientific & Technical Conference' Actual Trends in Development of Power System Protection and Automation*, 28-36.

Kamel, T. S., Moustafa Hassan, M. A., & El-Morshedy, A. (2012). Advanced distance protection technique based on multiple classified ANFIS considering different loading conditions for long transmission lines in EPS. International Journal of Modelling. *Identification and Control, 16*(2), 108–121. doi:10.1504/IJMIC.2012.047119

Liu, Y. D., Wang, Z. P., Zheng, T., Tu, L. M., Su, Y., & Wu, Z. Q. (2013, December). A novel adaptive loss of excitation protection criterion based on steady-state stability limit. *Power and Energy Engineering Conference (APPEEC), IEEE PES Asia-Pacific*, 1-5. 10.1109/APPEEC.2013.6837140

Mozina, C. J. (2010, March). Coordinating generator protection with transmission protection and generator control—NERC standards and pending requirements. *Protective Relay Engineers, 2010 63rd Annual Conference for IEEE*, 1-12.

Mozina, C. J., Reichard, M., Bukhala, Z., Conrad, S., Crawley, T., Gardell, J., . . . Johnson, G. (2008, June). Coordination of generator protection with generator excitation control and generator capability. *Pulp and Paper Industry Technical Conference, 2008. PPIC 2008. Conference Record of 2008 54th Annual IEEE*, 62-76.

Paithankar. T. G., & Bhide S. R. (2003). *Fundamentals of Power System Protection*. Prentice-Hall of India Private Limited.

Patel, S., Stephan, K., Bajpai, M., Das, R., Domin, T. J., Fennell, E., ... King, H. J. (2004). Performance of generator protection during major system disturbances. *IEEE Transactions on Power Delivery*, *19*(4), 1650–1662. doi:10.1109/TPWRD.2003.820613

PSCAD/EMTDC User's Manual. (2003). Manitoba HVDC Research Centre.

Sandoval, R., Guzman, A., & Altuve, H. J. (2007, March). Dynamic simulations help improve generator protection. *Power Systems Conference: Advanced Metering, Protection, Control, Communication, and Distributed Resources, 2007. PSC 2007*, 16-38. 10.1109/PSAMP.2007.4740896

Sharaf, A. M., & Lie, T. T. (1994). ANN based pattern classification of synchronous generator stability and loss of excitation. *IEEE Transactions on Energy Conversion*, *9*(4), 753–759. doi:10.1109/60.368331

Shi, Z. (2010). *Investigation on generator loss of excitation protection in generator protection coordination*. Academic Press.

Shi, Z. P., Wang, J. P., Gajic, Z., Sao, C., & Ghandhari, M. (2012). The comparison and analysis for loss of excitation protection schemes in generator protection. *Developments in Power Systems Protection, 11th International Conference on IET*, 1-6. 10.1049/cp.2012.0071

Tambay, S. R., & Paithankar, Y. G. (2005, June). A new adaptive loss of excitation relay augmented by rate of change of reactance. *Power Engineering Society General Meeting*, 1831-1835. 10.1109/PES.2005.1489421

Usta, Ö., Musa, M. H., Bayrak, M., & Redfern, M. A. (2007). A new relaying algorithm to detect loss of excitation of synchronous generators. *Turkish Journal of Electrical Engineering and Computer Sciences*, *15*(3), 339–349.

Wang, W. (2002). *Principle and Application of Electric Power Equipment Protection. China Electric.* Power Press.

Xu, R. (2009). *Loss of field protection and its impact on power system stability* (Doctoral dissertation). Washington State University.

APPENDIX 1

Data of the System Used for Loss of Excitation Study

Generators

Rating = 300 MVA
Rated Voltage = 23 kV
$X_d = j1.15$ p.u.
$X_q = j0.75$ p.u.

Generator Step Up (GSU) Transformers

300 MVA, 23 kVΔ / 345 kV Yg
Leakage reactance = j0.1 p.u.

Transmission Line

Length = 300 km
Positive sequence impedance Z1 = 0.51 ∟85.98° Ω /km.

System

Represented by three phase voltage source at 60 Hz.
Rated voltage = 345 kV.
Positive sequence impedance Z1 = 15 ∟85° Ω.

Under Voltage Relay

Setting = 0.87 x 23 = 20.01 kV.
Time delay = 0.9 s.

Loss of Excitation Impedance Relay Setting

Zone 1

Diameter of the circle is set at 1.0 p.u or at $Z_{base} = [V_{Gen} / (R_v \times \sqrt{3})] / [I / (R_c) = [23 / (200 \times \sqrt{3})] / [7.54 / 2000] = 17.61\Omega$.
Zone1 radius = 8.805 Ω.
Offset of the circle = $-X_d' / 2 = -0.314 / 2 = -2.76\ \Omega$.
Time delay = 0.1 s.

Zone 2

Diameter of the circle is set at $X_d = 1.15$ p.u = 20.2515 Ω.
Zone 2 radius = 10.15 Ω.
Offset of the circle is set the same as for Zone 1.
Offset of the circle = $-X_d'/2 = -2.76\ \Omega$.
Time delay = 0.5 s.

APPENDIX 2

The different membership functions and the corresponding calculated error values for the proposed (R and X) ANFIS based scheme are shown in Figure 16.
The different membership functions and the corresponding calculated error values for the proposed (V_{trms} and I_a) ANFIS based scheme are indicated in Figure 17.

Figure 16. The Different Membership Functions and the Corresponding Errors for the (R and X) ANFIS Based Scheme

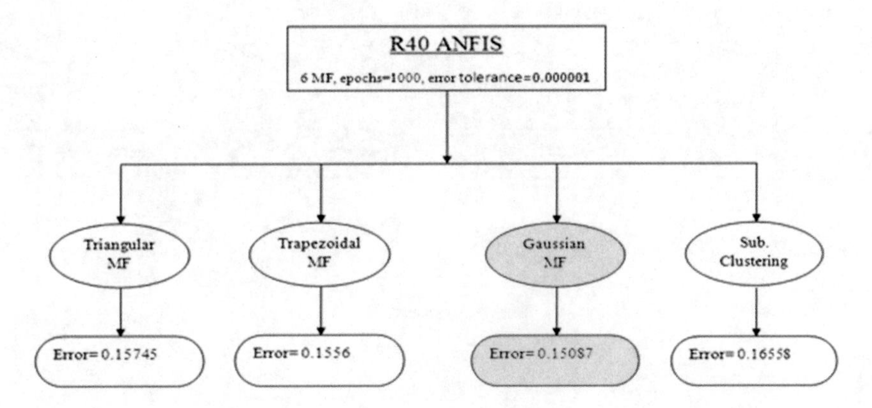

Figure 17. The Different Membership Functions and the Corresponding Errors for the (Vtrms and Ia) ANFIS Based Scheme

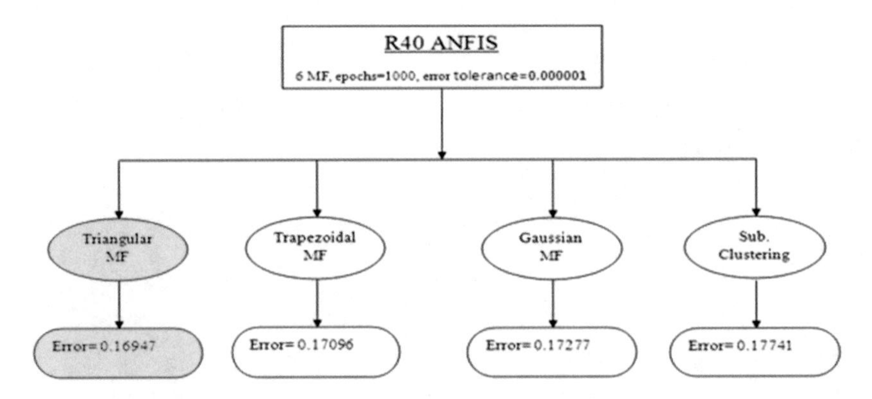

The different membership functions and the corresponding calculated error values for the proposed positive sequence components ANFIS based scheme are clarified in Figure 18.
The different membership functions and the corresponding calculated error values for the proposed 3rd harmonics components ANFIS based scheme are illustrated in Figure 19.

Figure 18. The Different Membership Functions and the Corresponding Errors for the Positive Sequence Components ANFIS Based Scheme

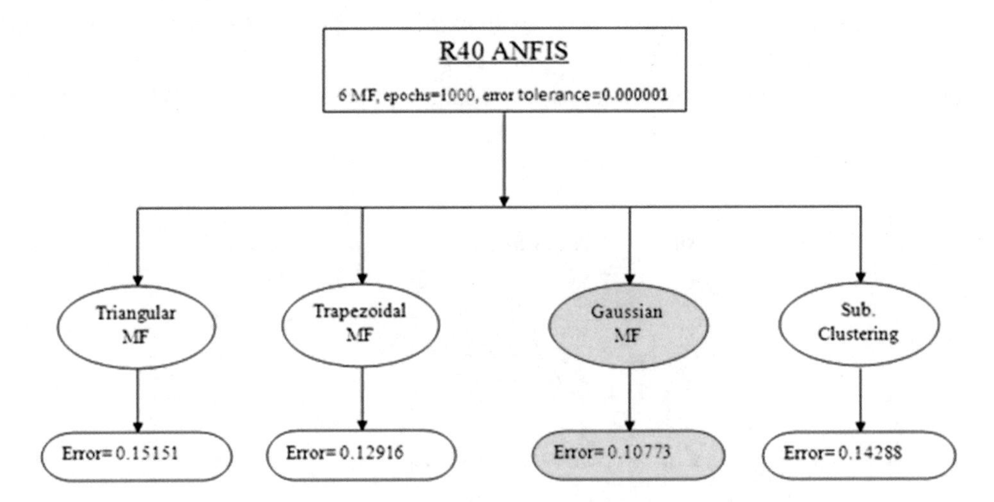

Figure 19. The Different Membership Functions and the Corresponding Errors for the 3rd Harmonic Components ANFIS Based Scheme

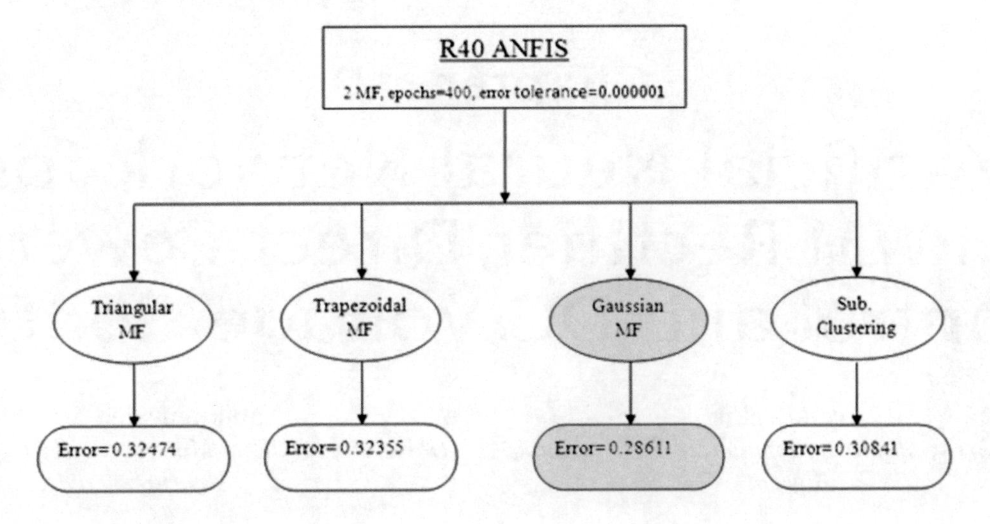

Chapter 10
Artificial Neural Network for PWM Rectifier Direct Power Control and DC Voltage Control

Arezki Fekik
University Mouloud Mammeri of Tizi-Ouzou, Algeria

Nabil Benyahia
University Mouloud Mammeri of Tizi-Ouzou, Algeria

Hakim Denoun
University Mouloud Mammeri of Tizi-Ouzou, Algeria

Mohamed Lamine Hamida
University Mouloud Mammeri of Tizi-Ouzou, Algeria

Ahmad Taher Azar
Benha University, Egypt & Nile University, Egypt

Nacereddine Benamrouche
University Mouloud Mammeri of Tizi-Ouzou, Algeria

Mustapha Zaouia
University Mouloud Mammeri of Tizi-Ouzou, Algeria

Sundarapandian Vaidyanathan
Vel Tech University, India

ABSTRACT

In this chapter, a new technique has been proposed for reducing the harmonic content of a three-phase PWM rectifier connected to the networks with a unit power factor and also providing decoupled control of the active and reactive instantaneous power. This technique called direct power control (DPC) is based on artificial neural network (ANN) controller, without line voltage sensors. The control technique is based on well-known direct torque control (DTC) ideas for the induction motor, which is applied to eliminate the harmonic of the line current and compensate for the reactive power. The main idea of this control is based on active and reactive power control loops. The DC voltage capacitor is regulated by the ANN controller to keep it constant and also provides a stable active power exchange. The simulation results are very satisfactory in the terms of stability and total harmonic distortion (THD) of the line current and the unit power factor.

DOI: 10.4018/978-1-5225-4077-9.ch010

1. INTRODUCTION

Recently, different control approaches have been proposed for designing nonlinear systems for many practical applications, such as optimal control, nonlinear feedback control, adaptive control, sliding mode control, nonlinear dynamics, chaos control, chaos synchronization control, fuzzy logic control, fuzzy adaptive control, fractional order control, and robust control and their integrations (Azar & Vaidyanathan, 2015a,b,c, 2016; Azar & Zhu, 2015; Azar & Serrano, 2015a,b,c,d, 2016a,b, 2017; Boulkroune et al, 2016a,b; Ghoudelbourk et al., 2016; Meghni et al, 2017a,b,c; Azar et al., 2017a,b,c,d; Azar 2010a,b, 2012; Mekki et al., 2015; Vaidyanathan & Azar, 2015a,b,c,d, 2016a,b,c,d,e,f,g, 2017a,b,c; Zhu & Azar, 2015; Grassi et al., 2017; Ouannas et al., 2016a,b, 2017a,b,c,d,e,f,g,h,I,j; Singh et al., 2017; Vaidyanathan et al, 2015a,b,c; Wang et al., 2017; Soliman et al., 2017; Tolba et al., 2017).

The increasing use of electronically powered and controllable systems in the industrial sector, motivated by improved performance, has led to a proliferation of static converters. Today, the number of these devices connected to electricity grids is constantly increasing. The switching operation of the semiconductor components constituting these converters is the reason why their behavior with respect to the power source is non-linear. Indeed, they take non-sinusoidal currents and for the most part consume reactive power, which poses serious problems for electrical networks. Static converters have become the most important sources of harmonics on the network. The uncontrolled diode and controlled thyristor rectifier is the most polluting and widespread static converter in both industry and domestic appliances. Under certain operating conditions, it can introduce a harmonic distortion rate (THDi) of current greater than 30%. For this reason, some recent adapted international standards, such as IEEE Standard 519, IEC 61000 and EN 50160, impose limits on the THD of currents and voltages within the supply network (5% for currents and 3% for voltages). In view of this state of affairs, and in order to limit the harmonic disturbance caused by the power electronics systems connected to the network, it is necessary to develop curative devices such as active filtering on one side and the other to design preventive actions such as non-polluting converters, equipped with a control device making the current drawn on the network as sinusoidal as possible.

In this context and over the past few years, high-power static converters have started to appear on the market mainly concerning AC / DC conversion. Indeed, changes have been made on conventional bridge rectifiers modifying their structure or their control system in order to reduce their injection of harmonic currents into the network. These new AC / DC converters are distinguished by their structure and how to handle the currents absorbed. They can be divided into three classes: diode rectifier with power factor correction (PFC), rectifier with current injection and PWM-rectifier with voltage or current structure. Among these most popular and attractive structures are the voltage PWM-rectifier. It is characterized by a quasi-resistive behavior with respect to the supply network. In addition to its ability to control the currents absorbed and to operate with a power factor close to one unit, the voltage Pulse Width Modulation (PWM) rectifier can also operate in two modes: rectification and regeneration. Thus, it controls the flow of active and reactive power in both directions. This advantage enables it to be used in a wide range of applications, particularly in regeneration mode and bidirectional power flow control (variable speed drives). This converter currently a key research theme for specialists in the field. The research is carried out mainly on so-called advanced strategies (predictive, fuzzy, Neurons, etc.) as well as on the selection and sizing of the input filter. To solve this problem, several research works have been done on PWM rectifiers due to some of their important advantage such as power regeneration capabilities, control of DC-bus voltage, low harmonic distortion of input currents, and high-power factor (Bouafia

& Krim, 2008; Sanjuan, 2010; Escobar et al., 2003; Malinowski et al., 2004; Malinowski et al., 2003; Cichowlas et al., 2005). Various control strategies have being proposed in recent works on this type of PWM rectifier. A well know method of indirect active and reactive power control is Voltage Oriented Control (VOC) (Sanjuan, 2010; Fekik et al., 2015a). Voltage Oriented Control guarantees high dynamic and static performance via internal current control loop (Fekik et al., 2015b), however, the final configuration and performance of the VOC system largely depends on the quality of the applied current control strategy (Bouafia & Krim, 2008; Sanjuan, 2010).

Another less known method based on instantaneous direct active and reactive power control is called direct power control (DPC) (Escobar et al., 2003; Malinowski et al., 2004; Cichowlas et al., 2005). In this method, there are no internal current control loops and no PWM modulator block because the converter switching states are appropriately selected by a switching table based on the instantaneous errors between the commanded and estimated values of active and reactive power. This method requires a good estimate of the active and reactive powers (Bouafia & Krim, 2008; Fekik et al., 2015a,b; Lamterkati et al., 2014a,b; Fekik et al., 2016). In Bouafia et al. (2009), the selection of the control vectors is based on the fuzzy logic, whose switching table is replaced by a fuzzy controller and in this structure, there are no hysteresis regulators. Recently, predictive control model theories have grown (Antoniewicz & Kazmierkowski, 2008; Vazquez et al., 2014, 2008; Vazquez & Salmeron, 2003; Karamanakos et al., 2014; Geyer & Quevedo, 2015) and have been introduced for direct power control in order to improve system performance (Hu et al., 2013; Zhang, et al., 2013; Fischer et al., 2014; Song et al., 2016). Based on the predictive control theory of the model, another type of direct power controllers called predictive control of direct power control has been proposed (Larrinaga et al., 2007). During its implementation process, a sequence of voltage vectors must first be selected. The corresponding application time for these vectors is then determined by minimizing the cost function, which is constructed as a function of predicted values and power references. In most cases, excellent control performance can be achieved when the predictive direct power control strategy is adopted. Fekik et al. (2015a) presented a VOC for the control of the PWM-rectifier, and for the control of the DC bus voltage and it's compared with conventional PI regulator and Fuzzy logic controller. On the other hand, the researchers are interested in the application of the different DC bus voltage regulators (e.g. Fuzzy Sliding mode control) of the PWM-rectifier control by direct power control (Jiang, 2010).

In this chapter, a new control method called direct power control (DPC) of three phase PWM rectifier is proposed based on the artificial neural network (ANN) controller; which makes it possible to achieve unity power factor operation by directly controlling its instantaneous active and reactive power, without any power source voltage captor. The DC-voltage is controlled by ANN-controller which provides active power reference P_{ref}, while the reactive power reference Q_{ref} is set to zero to achieve unity power factor operation. The simulation results show the feasibility and efficiency of neural networks and voltage regulation under transient or steady state with a nearly sinusoidal current source and side THD standards-compliant standards.

This chapter is organized as follows: In section 2 modeling of a PWM rectifier is introduced. In section 3, direct power control (DPC) is described. In section 4, brief overview of neural network principle is presented. In section 5, DC-voltage regulation based on neural network controller is shown. Results and simulation are shown in section 6. Finally in section 7, concluding remarks with future directions are given.

2. MODELING OF A PWM RECTIFIER

The power circuit of the PWM rectifier contains a bridge of six power transistors with anti-parallel diodes, which is used to carry out the PWM generation as well as the power bidirectional conversion, the general diagram of the PWM rectifier is shown in Figure 1. The converter is supplied by a voltage source in series with an inductance and a resistance, which models the network. Generally, the network inductance is insufficient (Bouafia & Krim, 2008; Sanjuan, 2010; Fekik et al., 2017) to eliminate all the harmonics present in the current and voltage waveforms. To attenuate the ripples due to the switching operation of the PWM rectifier, a series filter having a more significant inductance is needed. A load and a capacitor are connected simultaneously at the output of the converter. The capacitor is used as a voltage source and allows the rectifier to also operate as an inverter (Escobar et al., 2003; Malinowski et al., 2004; Cichowlas et al., 2005; Fekik et al., 2015a,b, 2016, 2017):

The logical states impose the rectifier input voltages, are given as (Fekik et al., 2016, 2017)

$$\begin{aligned} u_{ea} &= S_a.V_{dc} \\ u_{eb} &= S_b.V_{dc} , \\ u_{ec} &= S_c.V_{dc} \end{aligned} \tag{1}$$

Thus, the operation principle of the rectifier is illustrated by the following matrix system (Fekik et al., 2016, 2017):

Figure 1. General diagram of the PWM rectifier

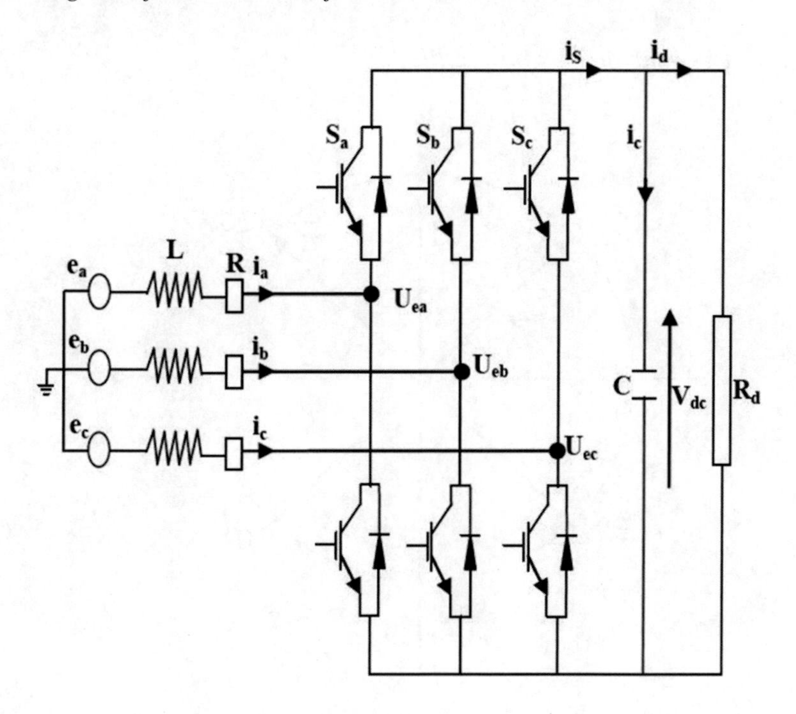

$$\begin{bmatrix} u_{ea} \\ u_{eb} \\ u_{ec} \end{bmatrix} = V_{dc} \begin{pmatrix} \frac{2}{3} & -\frac{1}{3} & -\frac{1}{3} \\ -\frac{1}{3} & \frac{2}{3} & -\frac{1}{3} \\ -\frac{1}{3} & -\frac{1}{3} & \frac{2}{3} \end{pmatrix} \begin{pmatrix} S_a \\ S_b \\ S_c \end{pmatrix}, \tag{2}$$

The AC side can be modeled by the following equations (Fekik et al., 2016, 2017)

$$\begin{cases} u_{ea} = e_a - Ri_a - L\frac{di_a}{dt} \\ u_{eb} = e_b - Ri_b - L\frac{di_b}{dt} \\ u_{ec} = e_c - Ri_c - L\frac{di_c}{dt} \end{cases}, \tag{3}$$

AC currents i_a, i_b and i_c are generated by voltage drops at impedances network boundaries (e_a-u_{ea}), (e_b-u_{eb}) and (e_c-u_{ec}), and then these currents will be modulated through the switches to provide the D.C.current i_s such as (Fekik et al., 2016, 2017):

$$i_s = S_a i_a + S_b i_b + S_c i_c, \tag{4}$$

The vector representation of voltages generated by the rectifier is illustrated in Figure 2.

Figure 2. Voltage vectors generated by the rectifier

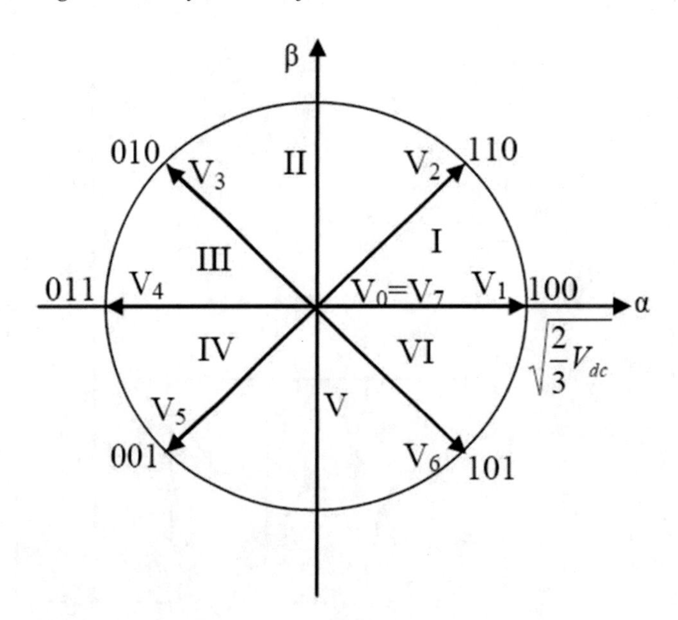

3. DIRECT POWER CONTROL (DPC) STRATEGY

Direct Power Control (DPC) of PWM rectifiers can be generally classified into two types of estimation (Bouafia & Krim, 2008; Sanjuan, 2010):

- Voltage estimation,
- Virtual flux estimation,

Different control strategies of a PWM rectifier are shown in Figure 3.

The main idea of DPC is similar to the well-known Direct Torque Control (DTC) for induction motors. It is based on instantaneous active and reactive power control loops (Bouafia & Krim, 2008; Sanjuan, 2010; Fekik et al., 2016, 2017). In DPC there are no internal current control loops and no PWM modulator block because the converter switching states are selected by a switching table based on the instantaneous errors between the reference and estimated values of active and reactive power as shown in Table 1.

3.1 DPC Based on Voltage Estimation

In order to remove the sensors from the alternating voltage, an instantaneous active and reactive power estimator has been made as a function of the switching states and the DC voltage as indicated by (Bouchakour, 2005; Fekik et al., 2016, 2017):

$$\begin{aligned} \hat{P} &= L\left(\frac{di_a}{dt} + \frac{di_b}{dt} + \frac{di_C}{dt}\right) + V_{dc}(S_a i_a + S_b i_b + S_c i_c) \\ \hat{Q} &= \frac{1}{\sqrt{3}}\left[L\left(\frac{di_a}{dt} i_c - \frac{di_c}{dt} i_a\right) + V_{dc}(S_a(i_b - i_c) + S_b(i_c - i_a) + S_c(i_a - i_b))\right] \end{aligned} \tag{5}$$

Figure3. Different control strategies of a PWM rectifier

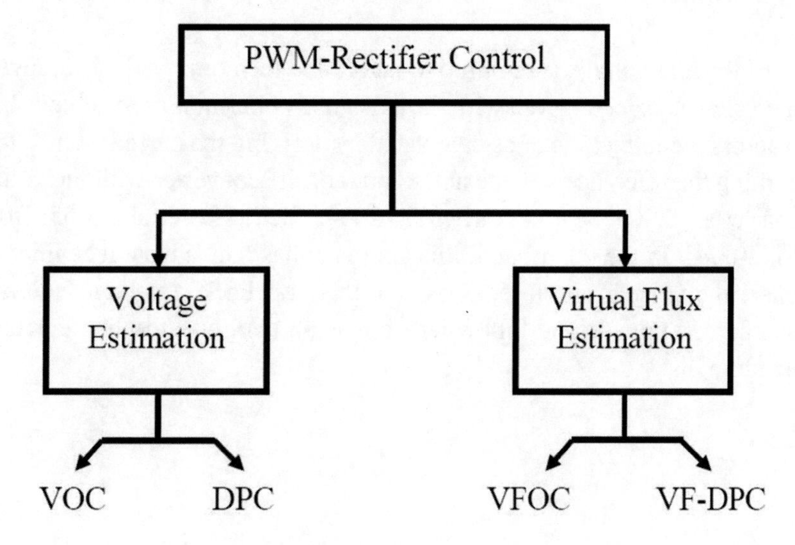

Table 1. Different switches configurations and the corresponding voltage vectors

S_a	S_b	S_c	U_{ea}	U_{eb}	U_{ec}	V_i
0	0	0	0	0	0	V_0
0	0	1	$-\frac{V_{dc}}{3}$	$-\frac{V_{dc}}{3}$	$\frac{2V_{dc}}{3}$	V_5
0	1	0	$-\frac{V_{dc}}{3}$	$\frac{2V_{dc}}{3}$	$-\frac{V_{dc}}{3}$	V_3
0	1	1	$-\frac{2V_{dc}}{3}$	$\frac{V_{dc}}{3}$	$\frac{V_{dc}}{3}$	V_4
1	0	0	$\frac{2V_{dc}}{3}$	$\frac{V_{dc}}{3}$	$\frac{V_{dc}}{3}$	V_1
1	0	1	$\frac{V_{dc}}{3}$	$-\frac{2V_{dc}}{3}$	$\frac{V_{dc}}{3}$	V_6
1	1	0	$\frac{V_{dc}}{3}$	$\frac{V_{dc}}{3}$	$-\frac{2V_{dc}}{3}$	V_2
1	1	1	0	0	0	V_7

The first parts of the two expressions shown above show the power in the line inductors. It's noted that the internal resistances of these inductances are negligible because the active power dissipated in these resistors is much lower in comparison with the power involved. Other parts represent the power in the converter (Bouchakour, 2005).

3.2 Estimated Voltage

The working area of the line voltage is required to determine the commands. Moreover, it is important to estimate the line voltage correctly, even with the existence of harmonics to achieve high power factor. The voltage drop across the inductor can be calculated by deriving the current. Thus, the voltage can be calculated by summing the reference voltage at the input of the converter with the voltage drop already calculated (Escobar et al., 2003; Malinowski et al., 2004; Cichowlas et al., 2005; Bouchakour, 2005; Fekik et al., 2016, 2017). On the other hand, this approach has a disadvantage which is the derivative of the current, where the noise is amplified. To avoid this drawback, a voltage estimator based on the power calculation can be applied. The following expression (6) gives the line currents i_a, i_b, i_c in the stationary coordinates a_β:

$$\begin{bmatrix} i_\alpha \\ i_\beta \end{bmatrix} = \sqrt{\tfrac{2}{3}} \begin{bmatrix} 1 & \frac{-1}{2} & \frac{-1}{2} \\ 0 & \frac{\sqrt{3}}{2} & \frac{-\sqrt{3}}{2} \end{bmatrix} \begin{bmatrix} i_a \\ i_b \\ i_c \end{bmatrix} \tag{6}$$

The expressions of the active and reactive powers can be written as:

$$\begin{aligned} \hat{p} &= v_\alpha i_\alpha + v_\beta i_\beta \\ \hat{p} &= v_\alpha i_\beta - v_\beta i_\alpha \end{aligned} \tag{7}$$

The matrix writing of the preceding expressions is given as:

$$\begin{bmatrix} \hat{p} \\ \hat{q} \end{bmatrix} = \begin{bmatrix} v_\alpha & v_\beta \\ -v_\beta & v_\alpha \end{bmatrix} \begin{bmatrix} i_\alpha \\ i_\beta \end{bmatrix} \tag{8}$$

The matrix equation (8) can be rewritten as a function of the line current (measured) and the (estimated) power as follows:

$$\begin{bmatrix} \hat{v}_\alpha \\ \hat{v}_\beta \end{bmatrix} = \frac{1}{i_\alpha^2 + i_\beta^2} \begin{bmatrix} i_\alpha & -i_\beta \\ i_\beta & i_\alpha \end{bmatrix} \begin{bmatrix} \hat{P} \\ \hat{Q} \end{bmatrix} \tag{9}$$

Concordia's inverse transform of line tensions is written as:

$$\begin{bmatrix} \hat{v}_a \\ \hat{v}_b \\ \hat{v}_c \end{bmatrix} = \sqrt{\tfrac{2}{3}} \cdot \begin{bmatrix} 1 & 0 \\ -\frac{1}{2} & \frac{\sqrt{3}}{2} \\ -\frac{1}{2} & \frac{\sqrt{3}}{2} \end{bmatrix} \cdot \begin{bmatrix} \hat{v}_\alpha \\ \hat{v}_\beta \end{bmatrix} \tag{10}$$

3.3 Number of Sectors

The area of the voltage vector can be divided into twelve or six sectors, as shown in Figure 2. These sectors can be expressed numerically as follows (Bouchakour, 2005; Fekik et al., 2016, 2017):

$$(n-2)\frac{\pi}{6} < \theta_n < (n-1)\frac{\pi}{6} \tag{11}$$

where n=1,2,3…12 and indicates the sector number. It is instantaneously given by the voltage vector position and is computed as follows:

$$\theta_n = arct(\frac{v_\beta}{v_\alpha}) \tag{12}$$

where *n* is the number of all pass filters. It is clearly noted that by changing the value of resistor *R*, the amount of delay can vary and as the result the resolution of the delay block can be controlled easily.

3.4 Hysteresis Regulator

The great simplicity of the implementation of this control approach is also an important element in the choice of the two-level comparator. Moreover, the energy considerations on the converter impose a limited number of commutations. However, for the same control hysteresis width, the two-level comparator requires a smaller number of commutations (Chapuis, 1996; Escobar et al., 2003; Malinowski et al., 2004; Cichowlas et al., 2005). The width of the hysteresis regulators band has a considerable effect on the performance of the converter, particularly the current distortion, the average switching frequency of the converter and the pulsation of the power. In addition, the losses are strongly affected by the hysteresis band. The controller proposed in the DPC is the two-stage controller for active and reactive power. The regulator hysteresis at three levels can be considered for more improvement (Noguchi et al., 1998). The output of the hysteresis regulators given by the Boolean variables S_p and S_q, indicates the upper or lower amplitude exceedances of the powers according to the following expressions:

$$\begin{aligned}
\hat{q} &\prec q_{ref} - h_q \Rightarrow S_q = 1 \\
\hat{q} &\succ q_{ref} - h_q \Rightarrow S_q = 0 \\
\hat{p} &\prec p_{ref} - h_p \Rightarrow S_p = 1 \\
\hat{p} &\succ p_{ref} - h_p \Rightarrow S_p = 0
\end{aligned} \tag{13}$$

3.5 Switching Table

As shown in Figure 4, the instantaneous active and reactive powers depend on the position of the voltage vector Us because the voltage vector Us allows the phase and amplitude (linear) indirect control of the line current (Malinowski et al., 2001; Bouchakour, 2005). Figure 4 presents the four different situations, which illustrate the variations in instantaneous power. Point M shows the reference value of the active and reactive powers. The four possible situations of the instantaneous powers are schematized, in the case where the voltage vector is in the third sector (Bouchakour, 2005). The line current is ahead of the voltage U_L for the first two cases (a) and (b). However, its amplitude is greater in (a) and lower in (b) than in the reference current. In the last two cases (c) and (d), the current is lagging behind the voltage U_L, with a lower amplitude in (c) and greater in (d) (Malinowski & Kazmierkowski, 2000). The selection of the control vector must be chosen so that the error between the estimate and the reference is restricted in a hysteresis band. When the estimated voltage vector is close to the boundaries of a sector, two out of six possibilities are bad. These vectors can guarantee only the control of the instantaneous active power without being able to make correction on the error of the reactive power.

Some methods to improve the behavior of DPC within the boundaries of a sector are well known. One of them is to increase the number of sectors or to use comparators with hysteresis at several levels (Chen & Joos, 2001, 2008; Bouchakour, 2005). Generally, the switching table is constructed taking into account the number of sectors, dynamic performance and two or three stage hysteresis regulators. Table 2 gives the switchboard of the direct power control. The digitized errors S_p, S_q and the working sector θ_n are the inputs of this table, where the switching states S_a, S_b and S_c of the converter are stored. The optimum switching state of the converter is chosen in each switching state according to the combination of the digital signals S_p, S_q and number of sector. Thus, the choice is made so that the error of the active

Figure 4. Variation of instantaneous powers

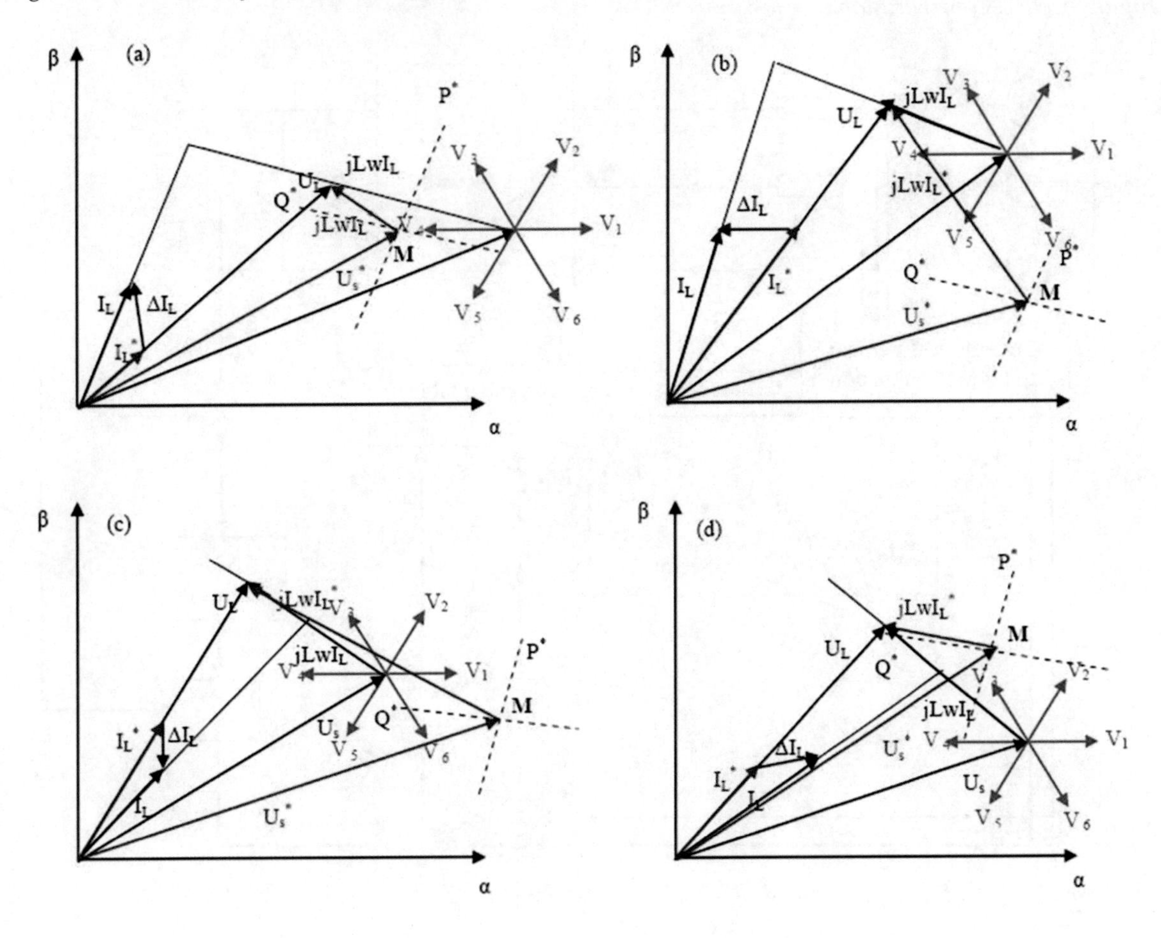

Table 2. Logical states of the rectifier switches are generated basing on the switching table

S_p	S_q	θ_1	θ_2	θ_3	θ_4	θ_5	θ_6	θ_7	θ_8	θ_9	θ_{10}	θ_{11}	θ_{12}
0	0	101	100	100	110	110	010	010	011	011	001	001	101
0	1	100	110	110	010	010	011	011	001	001	101	101	100
1	0	001	001	101	101	100	100	110	110	010	010	011	011
1	1	010	010	011	011	001	001	101	101	100	100	110	110

power can be restricted in a band with hysteresis of width $2\Delta h_p$ and the same for the error of the reactive power with a Band of width $2\Delta h_q$.

Figure 5 shows the configuration of direct instantaneous active and reactive power control based on neural network controller for three-phase PWM rectifier (Fekik et al., 2017). The controller is relay control of the active and reactive power by using hysteresis comparators and a switching table. In this configuration, the DC-voltage is regulated by controlling the active power using neural network controller, and the unity power factor operation is achieved by controlling the reactive power to be zero.

Figure 5.DPC configuration

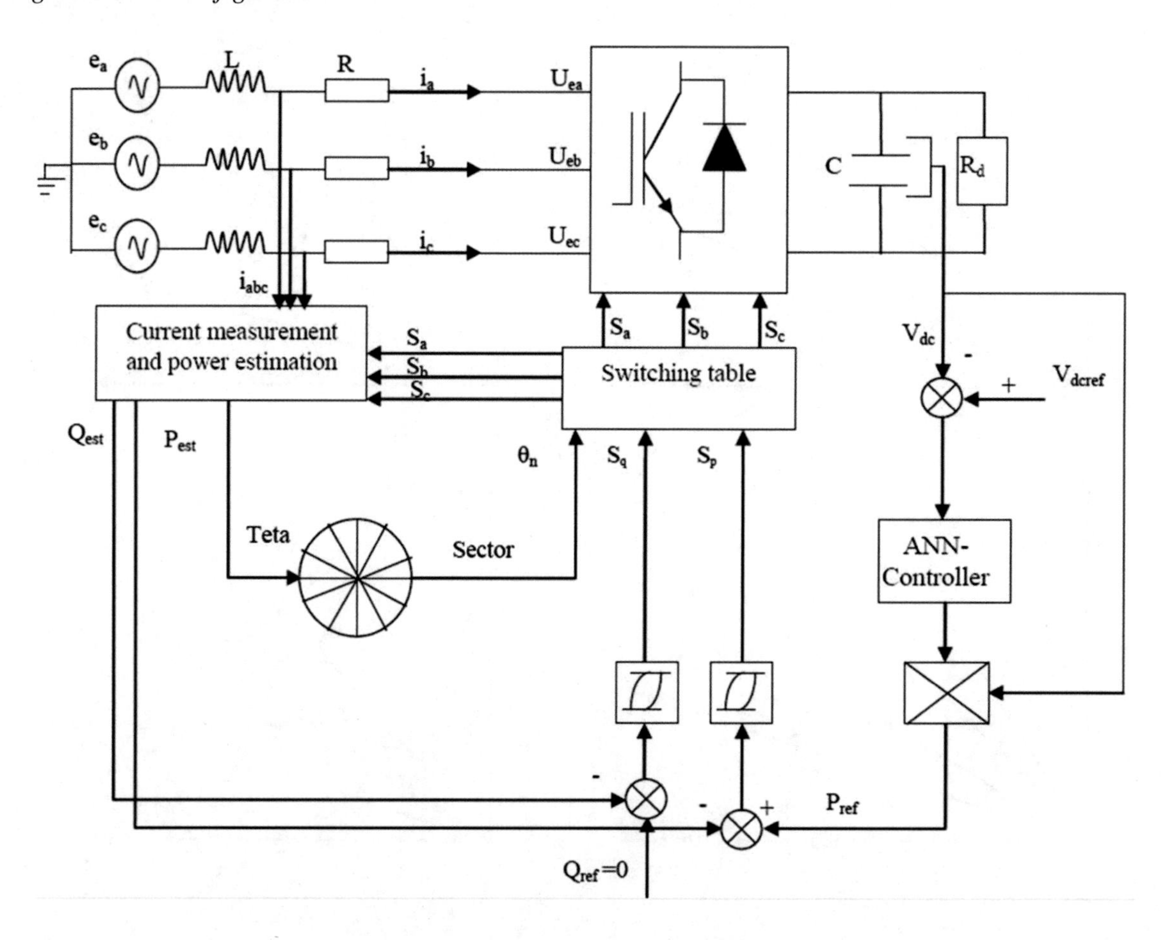

4. PRINCIPLE AND DEFINITION OF NEURAL NETWORKS

Neural networks form a set of nonlinear functions, allowing to build, by learning, a large family of models and nonlinear correctors (Mondal et al., 2002) A network of neurons is a system of interconnected nonlinear operators, receiving signals from the outside through its inputs, and delivering output signals, which are in fact the activities of certain neurons (Azar, 2013; Azar & El-Said, 2013; Hassanien et al., 2014). The formal neuron model presented here, from Mac Culloch and Pitts (Baghli, 1999), is a very simple mathematical model derived from an analysis of biological reality. It begins with a simple summation of the signals arriving at the neuron. These signals are commonly referred to as the neuron inputs (see Figure 6) (Mezache & Betto, 1997). The sum obtained is then compared with a threshold and the output of the neuron is deduced from the comparison. More formally, it is sufficient to obtain this behavior to subtract the threshold considered to the sum of the inputs (Mezache & Betto, 1997), and to pass the result by the transfer function of the neuron. The result after transfer function is the output of the neuron. This "summation" and then "nonlinearity" sequence finally represents the "physical" properties of the neuron.

4.1 General Modeling of a Neuron

From a mathematical point of view, a formal neuron is a processing element having n inputs x_1, x_2, ..., x_n (are the external inputs or outputs of the other neurons), and an output. Signals are passed between neurons over connection links. Each connection link has an associated weight, which, in a typical neural net, multiplies the signal transmitted. Each neuron applies an activation function *f* (usually nonlinear) to its net input (sum of weighted input signals) to determine its output signal y (Baghli, 1999; Constant, 2000; Bimal & Bos, 1994).

$$y_i = f\left(\sum_{i=1}^{m} w_{ij} x_i\right) \tag{14}$$

Figure 6. The formal neuron of MacCulloch and Pitts

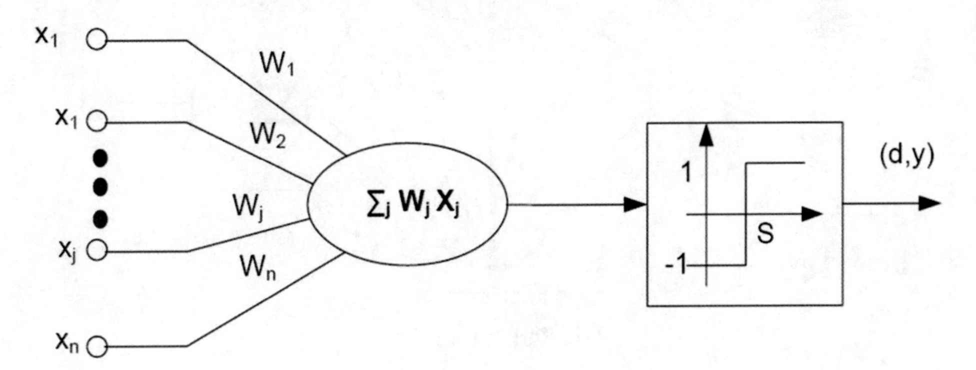

Where W_{ij} is the weight (or weight) associated with the ith input of the neuron j. Sometimes there is an additional term b_j representing the internal threshold of the neuron, this term is considered as a weight W_{0j} associated with a constant input (Baghli, 1999; Constant, 2000). The expression can be modified to:

$$y_i = f\left(\sum_{i=1}^{m} w_{ij}x_i - b_j\right) \tag{15}$$

4.2 Multilayer Perceptron

Multi-Layer perceptron (MLP) is a feedforward neural network with one or more layers between input and output layer. Feedforward means that data flows in one direction from input to output layer (forward). The hidden neurons are controlled by the inputs and are distributed in one layer but are not connected to one another; The output neurons are only controlled by the hidden neurons (Baghli, 1999). Figure 7 is an example of a 3-layer perceptron. This type of network is trained with the backpropagation learning algorithm. MLPs are widely used for pattern classification, recognition, prediction and approximation (Azar & Zhu, 2015; Azar & Vaidyanathan, 2015b). Multi-Layer Perceptron can solve problems which are not linearly separable.

4.3 Learning by Error Retro-Propagation

The efficient function optimization algorithms generally use the differential of the function considered (i.e. its gradient because it has real values). When the transfer functions used in neurons are differentiable, and when the distance function is also differentiable, the error committed by a MLP is a differentiable

Figure 7. Structure of a multilayer neural network with forward propagation

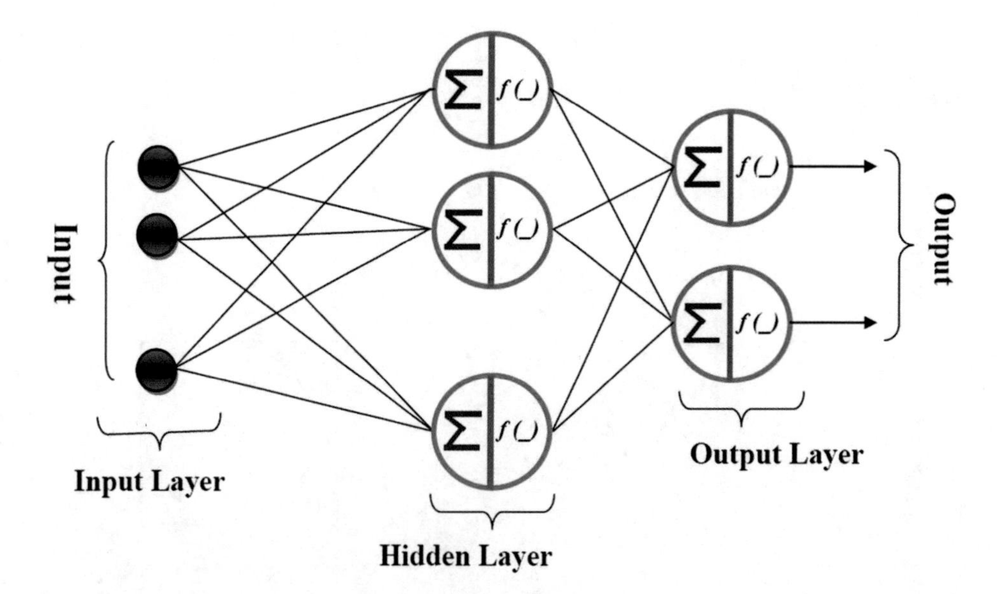

function of the network synaptic coefficients (Baghli, 1999). The retro-propagation algorithm makes it possible to calculate the gradient of this error efficiently. The number of operations (multiplications and additions) to be made is indeed proportional to the number of connections of the network, as in the case of calculating the output of this one. This algorithm makes it possible to learn A MLP (Baghli, 1999).

Let the vector W contain the synaptic weights, *m* the number of outputs of the network, y_k and d_k the respective components of Y and D on the output k. The quadratic error committed in Example i is therefore:

$$E_w(i) = \frac{1}{2}\sum_{K=1}^{m}\left|y_k - d_k\right|^2 \qquad (16)$$

On the learning set, we have:

$$E_w(i) = \frac{1}{2}\sum_{i=1}^{m}E_w(i) \qquad (17)$$

The retrograde propagation is a gradient descent, which therefore modifies the weights by an amount proportional to the opposite of the gradient:

$$\Delta w_{ij} = -h\frac{\partial E}{\partial w_{ij}} \qquad (18)$$

where *h* is the learning step.

The algorithm consists of calculating an error term ε and makes the weight changes from the top layers to the lower layers. This method of learning is the most used in the training of neural networks, because of its simplicity. However, it has the disadvantage of having a very slow convergence (Baghli, 1999; Bose, 2001)

5. DC-VOLTAGE REGULATION BASED ON NEURAL NETWORK CONTROLLER

In this chapter, the neuron DC voltage regulation system is proposed. The PWM rectifier used in the work is designed around a Multi-Layer Perceptron (MLP) which can replace the conventional PI controller. The regulator is used to control the terminal voltage of the condenser C in order to keep it constant around a value of V_{dcref} = 300V. The architecture adopted for this network is a MLP which has three layers: an input layer corresponding to an error between V_{dc} and V_{dcref}, and an output layer corresponding to the identified output. The number of neurons in the hidden layer can be selected by performing several learning tests. In this study, six neurons are used and the LOG-sigmoid learning function of the network is realized with the Levenberg-Marquardt back-propagation algorithm (Bose, 2001). Other optimization methods like genetic algorithms can be used to determine neuron numbers. Figure 8 shows a block diagram of the ANN controller (Artificial Neural Network) used for DC voltage adjustment:

Figure 8. The external block of ANN-controller

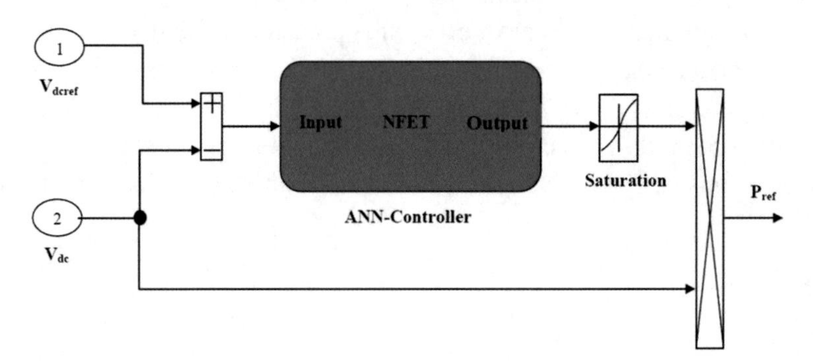

6. RESULTS AND SIMULATION

To validate the effectiveness of the control strategy studied in this paper, a digital simulation was carried out under MATLAB/SIMULINK environment. The system parameters studied in this chapter are given in Table 3.

6.1 Test Variation of DC-Voltage

The DC voltage control system is tested as well as the DPC using the ANN controller method following a DC voltage variation at t = 0.5 s from 300V to 380V. DC control of DC voltage is shown in Figure 9.

Figure 9 shows that the response of the system is fast (t <0.1s) and follows its reference without overflow according to the proposed controller based on neural networks.

It is noted that the system has become stable and robust. The system response is acceptable and does not exceed. Figure 10 shows that when the DC voltage reaches the new reference value, the line current increases. In this case, the power increase is limited, which avoids dangerous risks for the operation of the system.

It is observed from Figure 10 that the current and the voltage of phase (a) are in phase, which guarantees a unit power factor.

Figure 11 shows that the DPC technique responds very quickly with respect to the variation of power reference according to to the regulator proposed in this work.

It's noted that the estimated active voltage follows its reference correctly based on the neuro-controller.

Table 3. System parameters

	R	0.25 Ω
	L	0.016 H
	C	0.0047 F
	R_{load}	100 Ω
Peak amplitude of line voltage		120 V
Source voltage frequency		50 Hz
DC-Voltage V_{dcref}		300 V

Figure 9. Control system step response

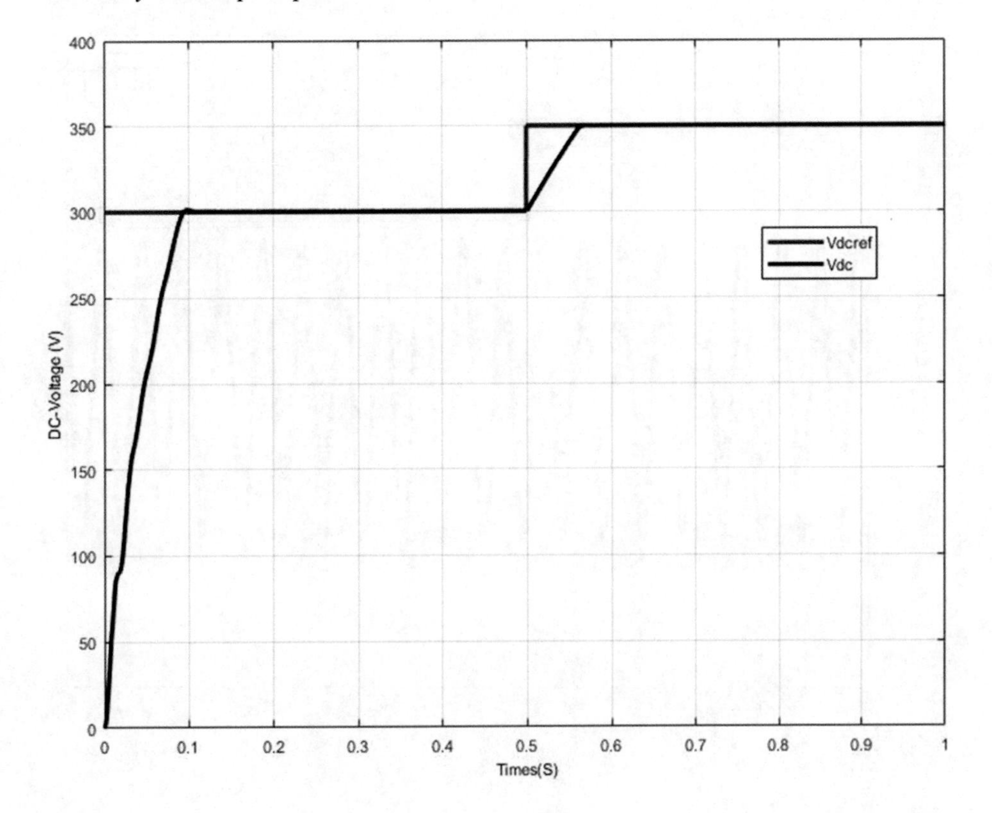

It can be observed from Figure 12 that the reactive power flow is low, which is very beneficial for the performance of the system.

It can be noted that the estimated reactive power imposed reference equal to zero, even in the case of a change in the reference DC voltage (the active power) (see Figures 9 and 11) Which guarantees a decoupled control of the instantaneous power.

The waveform of the line current is very close to the sinusoid and hence THD (total harmonic distortion) has been reduced to 3.47% (see Figure 13). Which guarantees a non-polluting system and therefore a very good quality of electrical energy. In order to keep the DC bus loaded, the DC voltage variation involves a reference variation in the instantaneous active power.

Figure 14 shows the estimated voltage V_{aest} and the detected voltage V_a. It can be observed that the estimated voltage follows the voltage captured on the side of the AC source. This is useful for estimating the two control variables accurately (active and reactive power).

6.2 Test Variation of the Load Resistance

To test the performance of the regulator, the load resistance (R_d) varies from 100 Ω to 150 Ω at time t = 0.5 s. Figure 15 illustrates the results of the simulation after a sudden change in load (t = 0.5 s) and the DC bus voltage during the load variation. It can be observed that the voltage follows the reference signal with a very good precision even at the moment of the abrupt change of the load which demonstrates the robustness of the proposed regulator.

Figure 10. Line voltage and line current

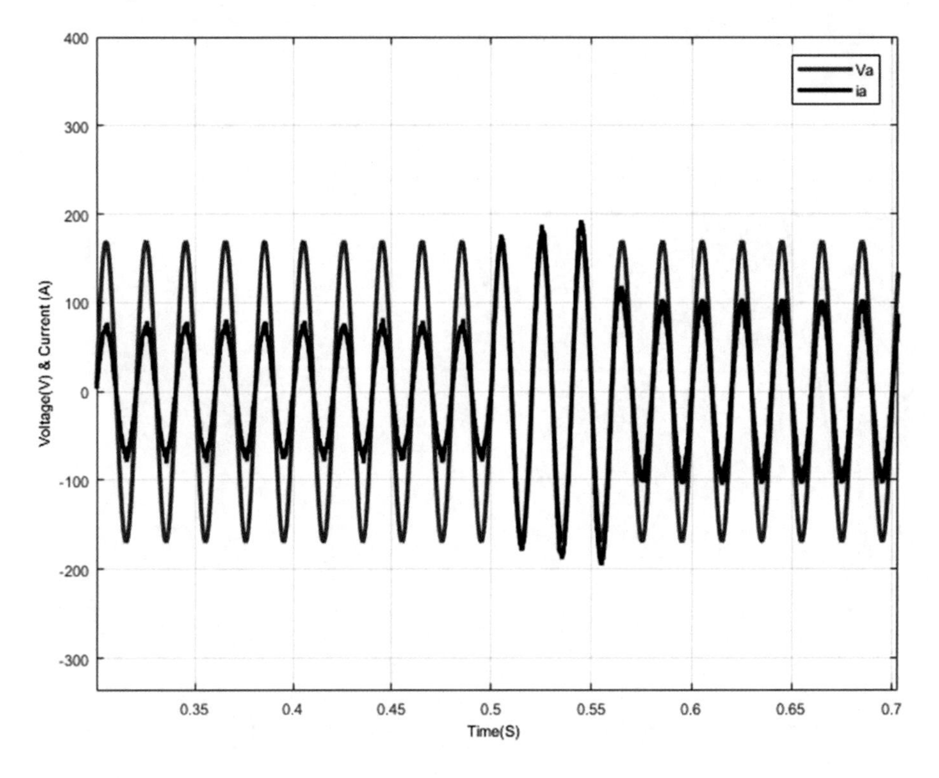

Figure 11. Reference and estimation active power

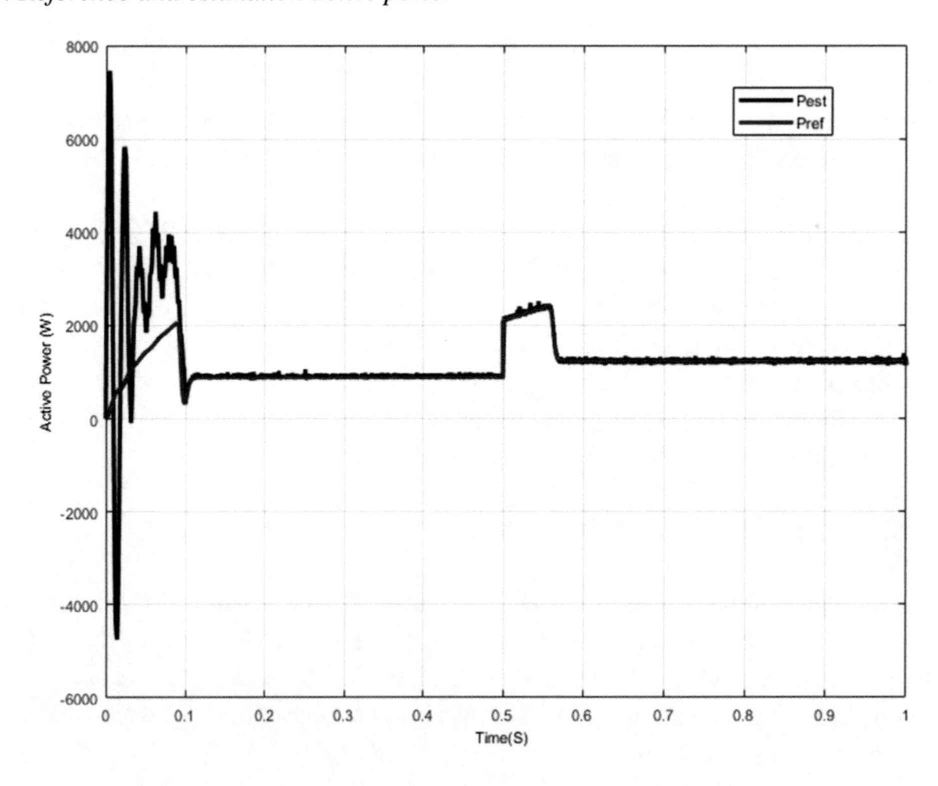

Figure 12. Estimated and reference instantaneous reactive power

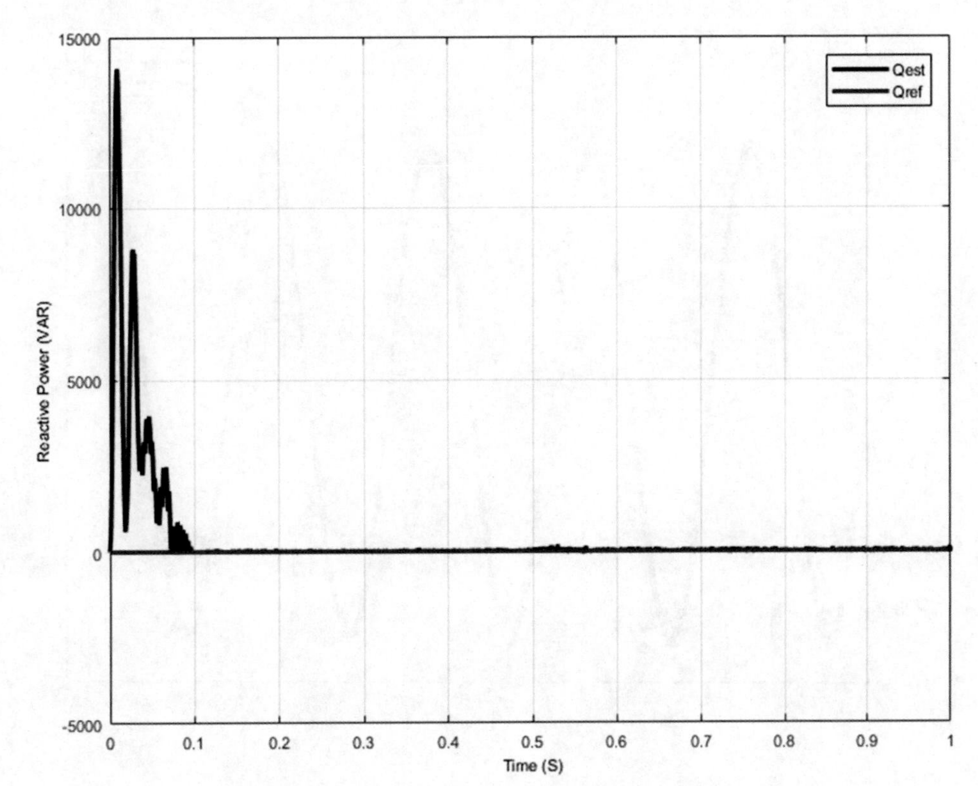

Figure 13. Harmonic spectrum and THD of the current with an ANN-controller

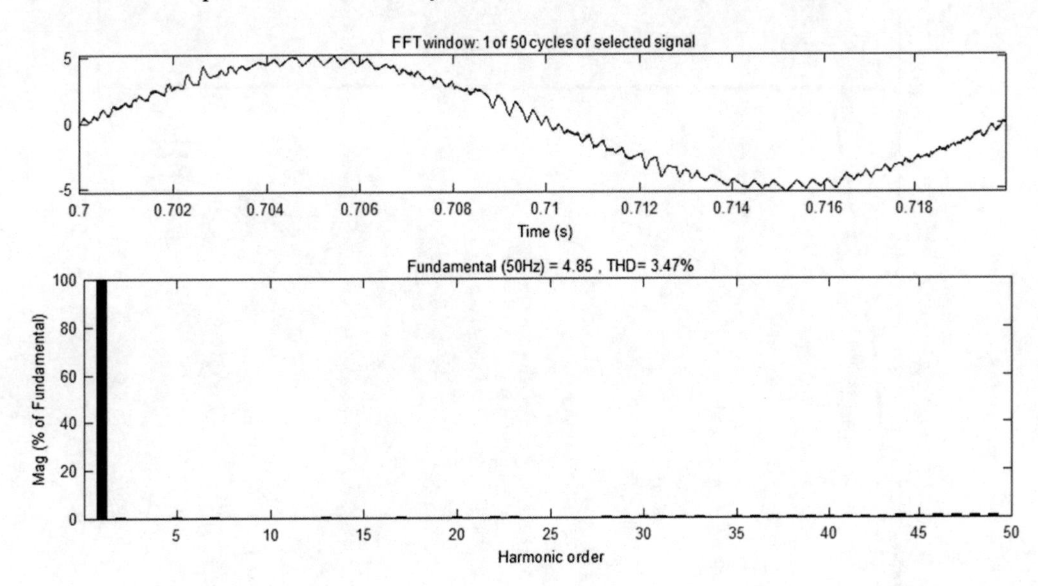

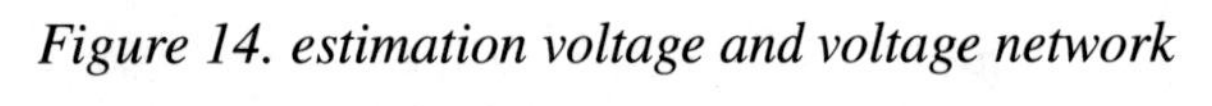

Figure 14. estimation voltage and voltage network

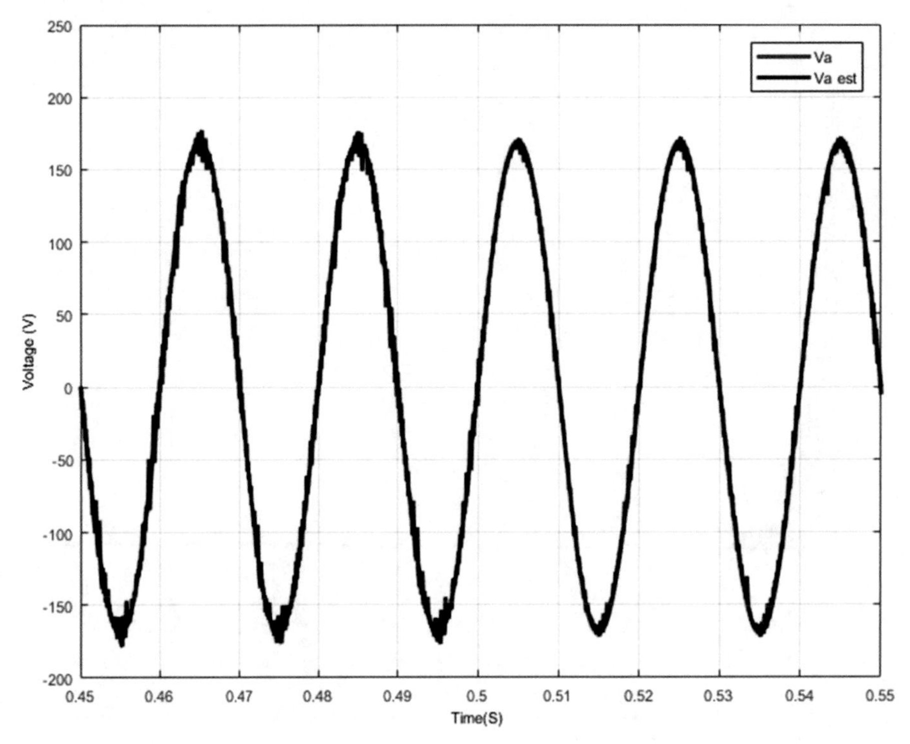

Figure 15. Control system step response

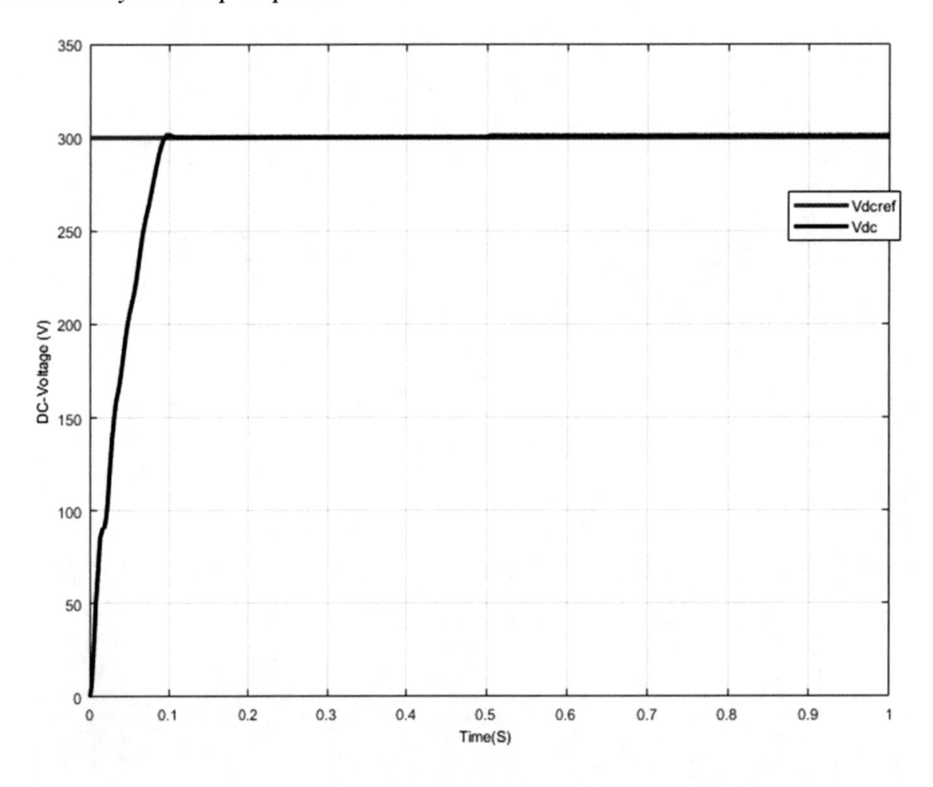

Figure 16. Line voltage and line current

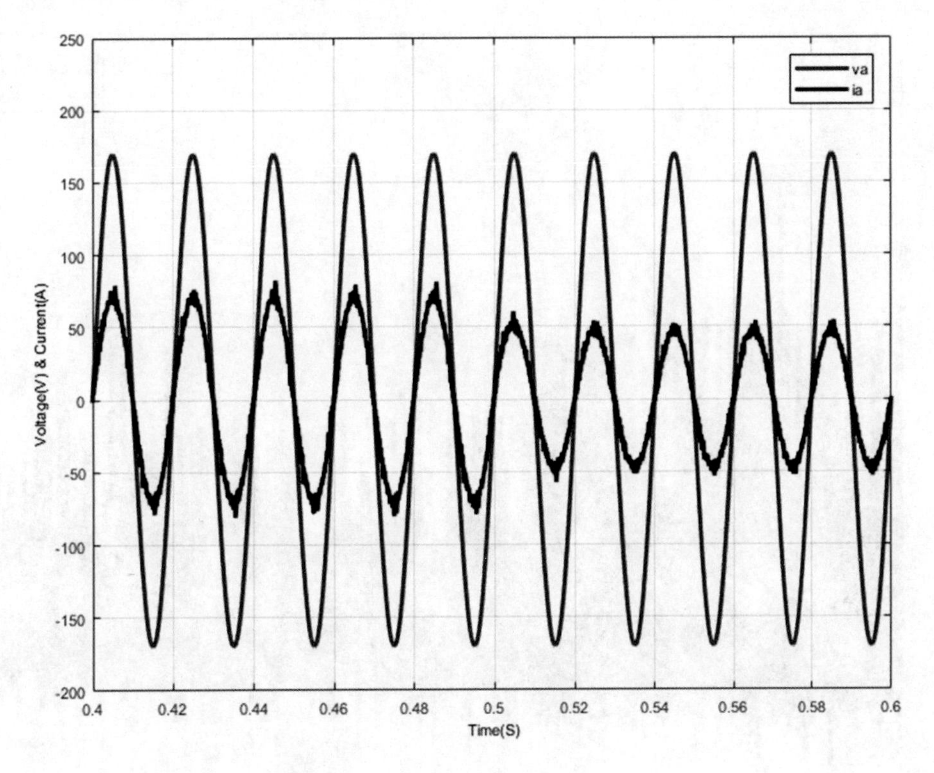

Figure 17. Reference and estimation active power

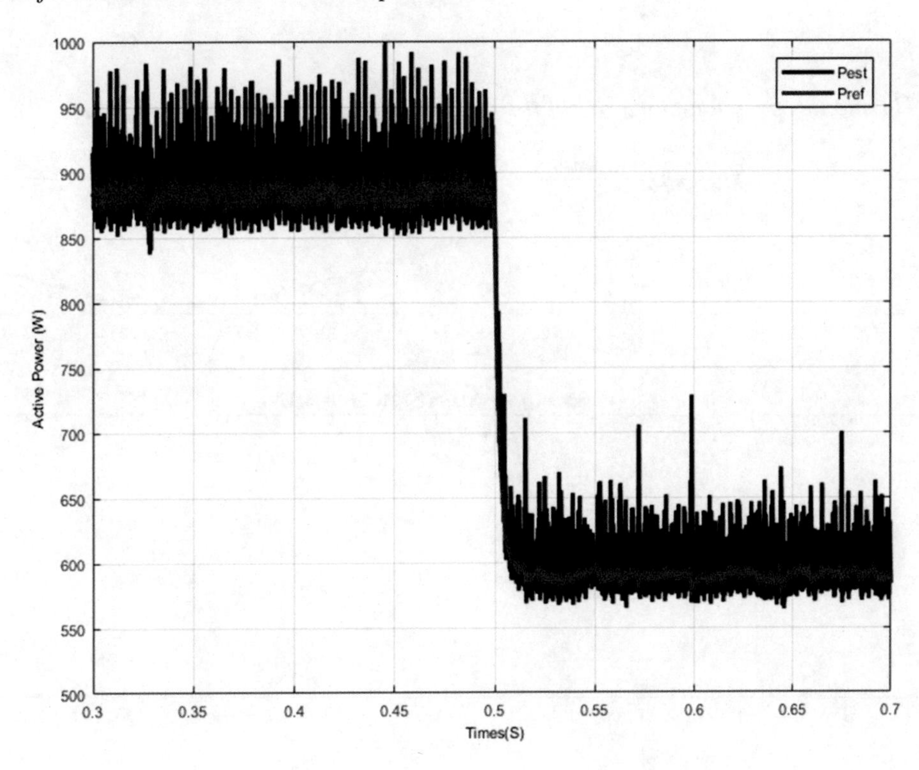

Figure 18. Estimated and reference instantaneous reactive power

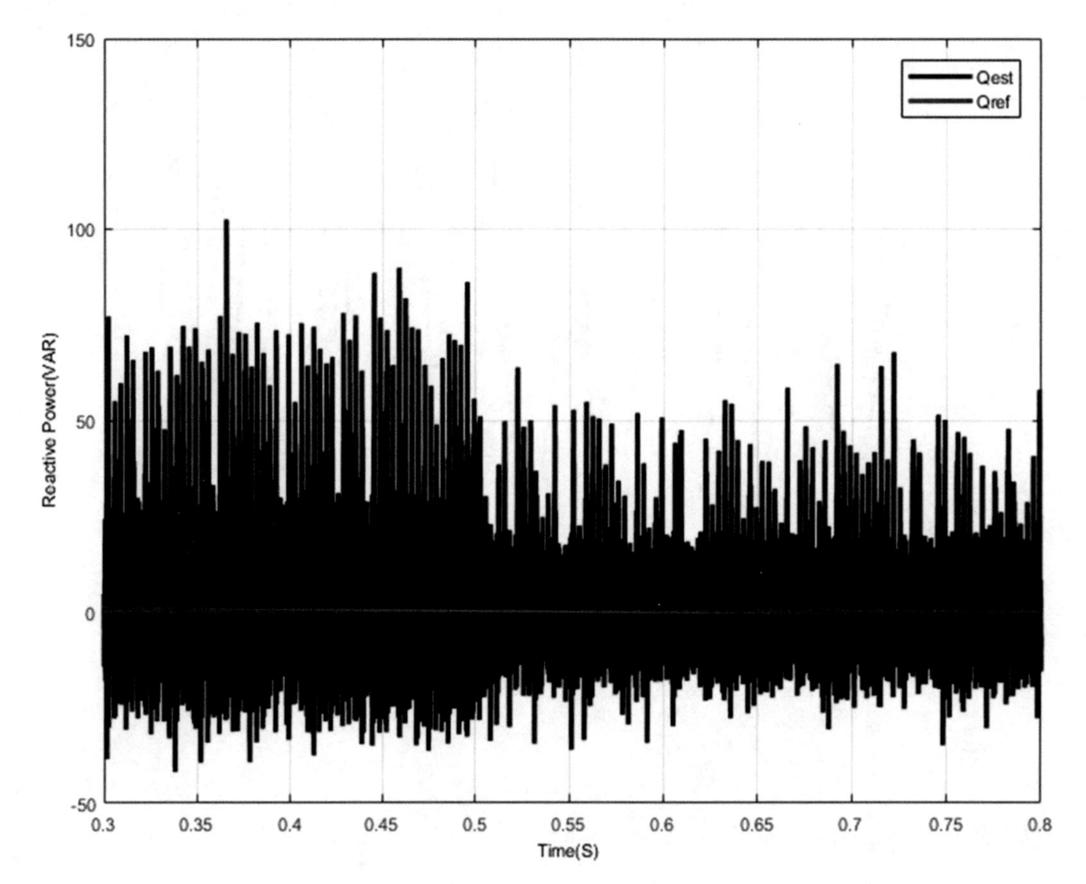

Figure 19. Harmonic spectrum and THD of the current with an ANN-controller

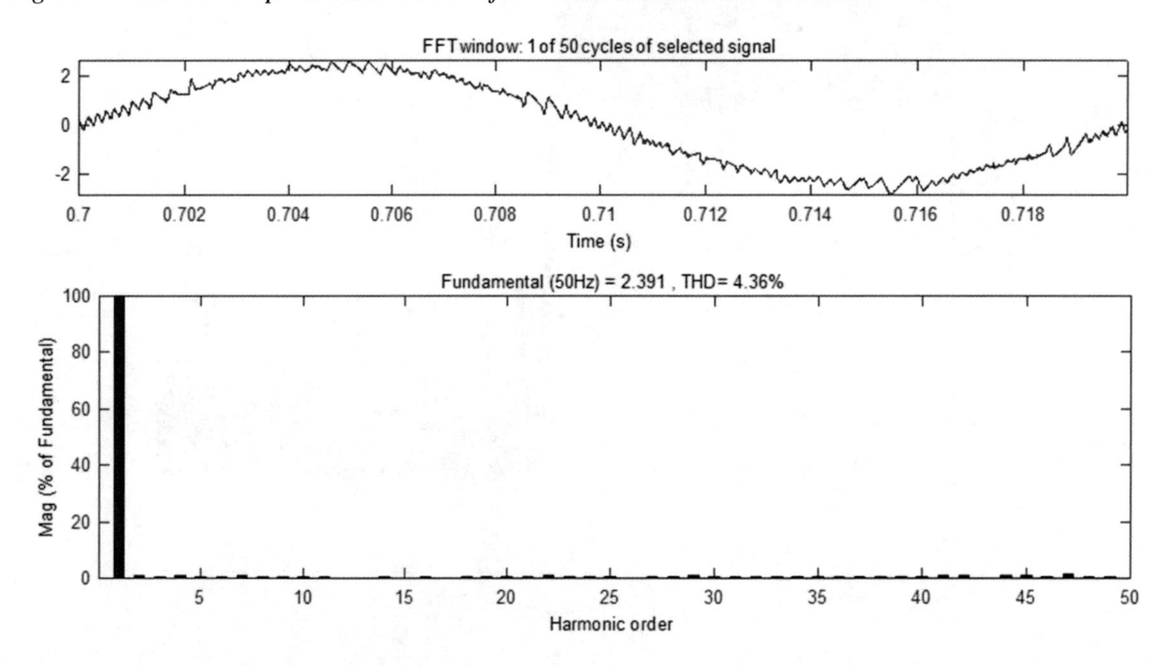

Figure 16 illustrates the voltage and the current of the phase (a) during the variation of the load. It is found that the current remains always in phase with the voltage and that the current decreases with the decrease of the load to ensure a continuous voltage at the desired reference by agitation on the active reference power.

Figure 17 illustrates the reference active power and the estimated power. During the variation of the load, it can be noted that the power reference is reduced when the load is demined with a very good result of the estimated value.

Figure 18 illustrates the reference and estimated reactive power. During the variation of the load, it can be seen that the reactive power follows its imposed reference equal to zero, which allows us to obtain a decoupled control of the two-instantaneous power which reveals the good regulation of the DC voltage.

The reactive power estimated remains always at its imposed value (equal to zero), so a unit power factor is achieved successfully. This regulator also guarantees a low current THD even in case of load variation as shown in Figure 19 (THDi = 4.36%).

Figure 20. shows the estimated voltage V_{aest} and the voltage V_a during the variation of the load R_d. It can be observed that the estimated voltage follows the voltage captured on the side of the AC source; this confirms a control without sensor voltage in side grid.

Figure 20. Estimation voltage and voltage network

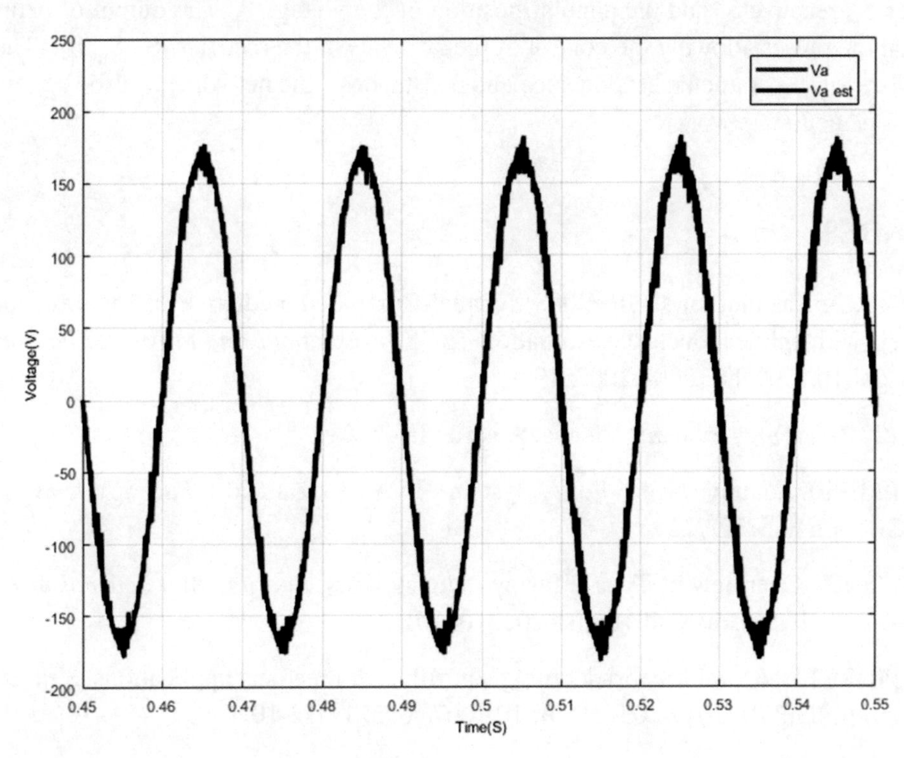

7. CONCLUSION

In this chapter, a new technique is proposed for controlling PWM-three-phase rectifier and harmonic content reduction to ensure a non-polluting system operates under a unit power factor. This control technique is analogous to direct torque control of the induction machine (DTC). Instead of torque and stator flux, the active and reactive instantaneous powers are the controlled quantities. This is known as Direct Control of Power. It consists in selecting a control vector according to a switching table and it's based on the digitized error S_p, S_q of the instantaneous active and reactive power, as well as the angular position of the estimated voltage. The plane ($\alpha\beta$) is divided into twelve sectors to determine the work area. In this work, a new control strategy is presented for PWM Rectifier. It concerns the use of direct power control principle via an Artificial Neural Network control system on the DC side; it reduces the number of sensors and offers a very good stability in the presence of disturbance. To obtain a stable exchange of the flow of active power between the converter and the electric network, the DC voltage is controlled by an ANN controller. Simulation results show that the technique combined with DPC voltage, ANN control improves system performance. These improvements affect the performance of the stability and response of the system on the DC side (and exceeded the response time), a unit power factor is achieved successfully, and THD is reduced to the lower line currents. For future work, the conventional switching table can be replaced by a multilayer neural network (MLP) for the selection of the optimum control vector. The inputs of the neuro-controller can be selected as the digitized errors of the active power S_p, reactive S_q and the angular position of the voltage θ_n. The output of neuro-controller can represent the pulses allowing the control of the switches of the rectifier (S_a, S_b, S_c). The adaptation of the PWM-rectifier parameters (inductance and resistance of the network) is also suggested using an ADALINE type neural network

REFERENCES

Antoniewicz, P., & Kazmierkowski, P. (2008). Virtual-flux-based predictive direct power control of AC/DC converters with online inductance estimation. *IEEE Transactions on Industrial Electronics*, *55*(12), 4381–4390. doi:10.1109/TIE.2008.2007519

Azar, A. T. (2010a). *Fuzzy Systems*. Vienna, Austria: IN-TECH.

Azar, A. T. (2010b). Adaptive Neuro-Fuzzy Systems. In A. T. Azar (Ed.), *Fuzzy Systems*. Vienna, Austria: IN-TECH. doi:10.5772/7220

Azar, A. T. (2012). Overview of Type-2 Fuzzy logic systems. *International Journal of Fuzzy System Applications*, *2*(4), 1–28. doi:10.4018/ijfsa.2012100101

Azar, A.T. (2013). Fast neural network learning algorithms for medical applications. *Neural Computing and Applications, 23*(3-4), 1019-1034. DOI: 10.1007/s00521-012-1026-y

Azar, A.T., & El-Said, S.A. (2013). Probabilistic neural network for breast cancer classification. *Neural Computing and Applications, 23*(6), 1737-1751. DOI: 10.1007/s00521-012-1134-8

Azar, A.T., & Serrano, F.E. (2014). Robust IMC-PID tuning for cascade control systems with gain and phase margin specifications. *Neural Computing and Applications, 25*(5), 983-995. DOI 10.1007/s00521-014-1560-x

Azar, A. T., & Serrano, F. E. (2015a). Stabilization and Control of Mechanical Systems with Backlash. In Advanced Intelligent Control Engineering and Automation. IGI Global. doi:10.4018/978-1-4666-7248-2.ch001

Azar, A. T., & Serrano, F. E. (2015b). Design and Modeling of Anti Wind Up PID Controllers. In Complex system modelling and control through intelligent soft computations. Springer-Verlag. . 1. doi:10.1007/978-3-319-12883-2_1

Azar, A. T., & Serrano, F. E. (2015c). Adaptive Sliding mode control of the Furuta pendulum. In Advances and Applications in Sliding Mode Control systems. Springer-Verlag GmbH Berlin/Heidelberg. doi:10.1007/978-3-319-11173-5_1

Azar, A. T., & Serrano, F. E. (2015d). Deadbeat Control for Multivariable Systems with Time Varying Delays. In Chaos Modeling and Control Systems Design. Springer-Verlag GmbH Berlin/Heidelberg. DOI doi:10.1007/978-3-319-13132-0_6

Azar, A. T., & Serrano, F. E. (2016a). Robust control for asynchronous switched nonlinear systems with time varying delays. *Proceedings of the International Conference on Advanced Intelligent Systems and Informatics 2016*, 533, 891-899. 10.1007/978-3-319-48308-5_85

Azar, A. T., & Serrano, F. E. (2016b). Stabilization of Mechanical Systems with Backlash by PI Loop Shaping. *International Journal of System Dynamics Applications*, *5*(3), 20–47. doi:10.4018/IJSDA.2016070102

Azar, A. T., & Serrano, F. E. (2017). Passivity Based Decoupling of Lagrangian Systems. *Proceedings of the International Conference on Advanced Intelligent Systems and Informatics 2016*, 533, 891-899. 10.1007/978-3-319-48308-5_85

Azar, A. T., & Vaidyanathan, S. (2015a). Handbook of Research on Advanced Intelligent Control Engineering and Automation. IGI Global. doi:10.4018/978-1-4666-7248-2

Azar, A. T., & Vaidyanathan, S. (2015b). *Computational Intelligence applications in Modeling and Control. Studies in Computational Intelligence* (Vol. 575). Springer-Verlag.

Azar, A. T., & Vaidyanathan, S. (2015c). *Chaos Modeling and Control Systems Design, Studies in Computational Intelligence* (Vol. 581). Springer-Verlag.

Azar, A. T., & Vaidyanathan, S. (2016). *Advances in Chaos Theory and Intelligent Control. Studies in Fuzziness and Soft Computing* (Vol. 337). Springer-Verlag. doi:10.1007/978-3-319-30340-6

Azar, A. T., Vaidyanathan, S., & Ouannas, A. (2017a). *Fractional Order Control and Synchronization of Chaotic Systems. Studies in Computational Intelligence* (Vol. 688). Springer-Verlag. doi:10.1007/978-3-319-50249-6

Azar, A.T., Volos, C., Gerodimos, N.A., Tombras, G.S., Pham, V.T., Radwan, A.G., … Munoz-Pacheco, J.M. (2017b). A novel chaotic system without equilibrium: Dynamics, synchronization and circuit realization. *Complexity*. doi:10.1155/2017/7871467

Azar, A. T., Ouannas, A., & Singh, S. (2017c). Control of New Type of Fractional Chaos Synchronization. *Proceedings of the International Conference on Advanced Intelligent Systems and Informatics 2017, 639*, 47-56.

Azar, A. T., Kumar, J., Kumar, V., & Rana, K. P. S. (2017d). Control of a Two Link Planar Electrically-Driven Rigid Robotic Manipulator Using Fractional Order SOFC. *Proceedings of the International Conference on Advanced Intelligent Systems and Informatics 2017, 639*, 47-56.

Azar, A. T., & Zhu, Q. (2015). *Advances and Applications in Sliding Mode Control systems. Studies in Computational Intelligence* (Vol. 576). Springer-Verlag.

Baghli, L. (1999). *Contribution à la Commande de la Machine Asynchrone, Utilisation de la Logique Floue, des Réseaux de Neurones et des Algorithmes Génétiques* (Thèse de Doctorat). Département de Génie Electrique Université Henri Poincaré, Nancy-I.

Bimal, & Bos, K. (1994). Expert system, fuzzy logic, and neural network applications in power electronics and motion control. *Proceedings of the IEEE, 82*(8), 1303 – 1323.

Bose, B. (2001). *Artificial neural network applications in power electronics*. The 27th Annual Conférence of the IEEE Industrial Electronics Society, Denver, CO. 10.1109/IECON.2001.975533

Bouchakour, S. (2005). *Commande Directe de Puissance d'un Convertisseur AC/DC Triphasé Sans Capteurs de Tension*. Memory of Magister Ecole Militaire Polytechnique Algeria.

Bouafia, A., & Krim, F. (2008). A fuzzy-Logic-Based Controller for Three-Phase PWM Rectifier with Unity Power Factor Operation. J. *Electrical Systems*, *4*(1), 36–50.

Bouafia, A., Krim, F., & Gaubert, J. P. (2009). Fuzzy-Logic-Based Switching State Selection for Direct Power Control of Three-Phase PWM Rectifier. *IEEE Transactions on Industrial Electronics*, *56*(6), 1984–1992. doi:10.1109/TIE.2009.2014746

Boulkroune, A., Bouzeriba, A., Bouden, T., & Azar, A. T. (2016a). Fuzzy Adaptive Synchronization of Uncertain Fractional-order Chaotic Systems. In A. T. Azar & S. Vaidyanathan (Eds.), *Advances in Chaos Theory and Intelligent Control. Studies in Fuzziness and Soft Computing* (Vol. 337). Springer-Verlag. doi:10.1007/978-3-319-30340-6_28

Boulkroune, A., Hamel, S., & Azar, A. T. (2016b). *Fuzzy control-based function synchronization of unknown chaotic systems with dead-zone input. Advances in Chaos Theory and Intelligent Control. Studies in Fuzziness and Soft Computing* (Vol. 337). Springer-Verlag.

Cichowlas, M., Malinowski, M., Kazmierkowski, P., Sobczuk, D., & Pou, J. (2005). Active filtering function of three-phase PWM boost rectifier under different line voltage conditions. *IEEE Transactions on Industrial Electronics*, *52*(2), 410–419. doi:10.1109/TIE.2005.843915

Chapuis, Y. A. (1996). *Contrôle directe du couple d'une machine asynchrone par l'orientation de son flux statorique* (Doctoral thesis). INP-Grenoble, France.

Chen, B., & Joos, G. (2008). Direct power control of active filters with averaged switching frequency regulation. *IEEE Transactions on Power Electronics*, *23*(6), 2729–2737. doi:10.1109/TPEL.2008.2004958

Chen, S., & Joos, G. (2001) Direct Power Control of Three Active filer with Minimum Energy Storage Components. *APEC 2001. Sixteenth Annual IEEE Applied Power Electronics Conference and Exposition*. DOI: 10.1109/APEC.2001.911703

Constant, L. (2000). *Modélisation de Dispositifs Electriques par Réseaux de Neurones en Vue de L'émulation Temps Réel* (Thesis Doctorate). Toulouse, France.

Escobar, G., Stankovic, A., Carrasco, M., Galvan, E., & Ortega, R. (2003). Analysis and design of direct power control (DPC) for a three phase synchronous rectifier via output regulation subspaces. *IEEE Transactions on Power Electronics*, *18*(3), 823–830. doi:10.1109/TPEL.2003.810862

Fekik, A., Denoun, H., Benamrouche, N., Benyahia, N., Zaouia, M., & Haddad, S. (2015a) Comparative study of PI and FUZZY DC- voltage control for Voltage Oriented Control-PWM rectifier. *The 14th International Conference on Circuits, Systems, Electronics, Control & Signal Processing 2015.*

Fekik, A., Denoun, H., Benamrouche, N., Benyahia, N., & Zaouia, M. (2015b). A Fuzzy Logic Based Controller For Three Phase PWM Rectifier With Voltage Oriented Control Strategy. *International Journal of Circuits, Systems and Signal Processing*, *9*, 412–419.

Fekik, A., Denoun, H., Benamrouche, N., Benyahia, N., Badji, A., & Zaouia, M. (2016*)* Comparative Analysis of Direct Power Control and Direct power control with space vector modulation of PWM rectifier. 4th IEEE *International Conference on Control Engineering & Information Technology (CEIT-2016).* 10.1109/CEIT.2016.7929058

Fekik, A., Denoun, H., Benamrouche, N., Benyahia, N., Zaouia, M., Badji, A., & Vaidyanathan, S. (2017). Improvement of the Performances of the Direct Power Control Using Space Vector Modulation of Three Phases PWM-Rectifier. *International Journal of Control Theory and Applications*, *10*, 125–137.

Fischer, J. R., González, S. A., Carugat, I., Herrán, M. A., Judewicz, M. G., & Carrica, D. O. (2014). Robust predictive control of grid-tied converters based on direct power control. *IEEE Transactions on Power Electronics*, *29*(10), 5634–5643. doi:10.1109/TPEL.2013.2294919

Geyer, T., & Quevedo, E. (2015). Performance of multistep finite control set model predictive control for power electronics. *IEEE Transactions on Power Electronics*, *30*(3), 1633–1644. doi:10.1109/TPEL.2014.2316173

Ghoudelbourk, S., Dib, D., Omeiri, A., & Azar, A. T. (2016). MPPT Control in wind energy conversion systems and the application of fractional control (PIα) in pitch wind turbine. International Journal of Modelling *Identification and Control*, *26*(2), 140–151. doi:10.1504/IJMIC.2016.078329

Grassi, G., Ouannas, A., Azar, A. T., Radwan, A. G., Volos, C., Pham, V. T., . . . Stouboulos, I. N. (2017). *Chaos Synchronisation Of Continuous Systems Via Scalar Signal*. The 6th International Conference on Modern Circuits and Systems Technologies (MOCAST), Thessaloniki, Greece. 10.1109/MOCAST.2017.7937629

Hassanien, A.E., Moftah, H.M., Azar, A.T., & Shoman, M. (2014). MRI Breast cancer diagnosis hybrid approach using adaptive Ant-based segmentation and Multilayer Perceptron neural networks classifier. *Applied Soft computing, 14*(Part A), 62-71.

Hu, J., Zhu, J., Zhang, Y., Platt, G., Ma, Q., & Dorrell, D. G. (2013). Predictive direct virtual torque and power control of doubly fed induction generators for fast and smooth grid synchronization and flexible power regulation. *IEEE Transactions on Power Electronics, 28*(7), 3182–3194. doi:10.1109/TPEL.2012.2219321

Jiang, W. (2010) Sliding-mode Control of Single-phase PWM Rectifier for DC Microgrid Applications. *International Conference on Computer and Electrical Engineering*, 53, 82-90. DOI: 10.7763/IPCSIT.2012.V53.No.1.82

Karamanakos, P., Geyer, T., Oikonomou, N., Kieferndorf, F., & Manias, S. (2014). Direct model predictive control: A review of strategies that achieve long prediction intervals for power electronics. *IEEE Industrial Electronics Magazine, 8*(1), 32–43. doi:10.1109/MIE.2013.2290474

Lamterkati, J., Khafallah, M., & Ouboubker, L. (2014a). A New DPC for Three-phase PWM rectifier with unity power factor operation. *International Journal of Advanced Research in Electrical Electronics and Instrumentation Engineering, 3*(4), 8273–8285.

Lamterkati, J., Khafallah, M., & Ouboubker, L. (2014b). Comparison of PI and Fuzzy logic DC-Link Voltage Controller for DPC PWM-Rectifier. *International Journal of Enhanced Research in Science Technology & Engineering, 3*(4), 321–332.

Larrinaga, S. A., Vidal, M. A. R., Oyarbide, E., & Apraiz, J. R. T. (2007). Predictive control strategy for DC/AC converters based on direct power control. *IEEE Transactions on Industrial Electronics, 54*(3), 1261–1271. doi:10.1109/TIE.2007.893162

Larrinaga, S., Vidal, M., Oyarbide, E., & Apraiz, J. (2007). Predictive control strategy of DC/AC converters based on direct power control. *IEEE Transactions on Industrial Electronics, 54*(3), 1261–1271. doi:10.1109/TIE.2007.893162

Malinowski, M., Kazmierkowski, M. P., & Trzynadlowski, A. M. (2003). A Comparative Study of Control Techniques for PWM Rectifiers in AC Adjustable Speed Drives. *IEEE Transactions on Power Electronics, 18*(6), 1390–1396. doi:10.1109/TPEL.2003.818871

Malinowski, M., Jasinski, M., & Kazmierkowski, P. (2004). Simple Direct power control of three phase PWM rectifier using space vector modulation (DPC-SVM). *IEEE Transactions on Industrial Electronics, 51*(2), 447–454. doi:10.1109/TIE.2004.825278

Malinowski, M., Kaz'mierkowski, M. P., Hansen, S., Blaabjerg, F., & Marques, G. D. (2001). Virtual flux based direct power control of three-phase PWM rectifiers. *IEEE Transactions on Industry Applications, 37*(4), 1019–1027. doi:10.1109/28.936392

Malinowski, M., & Kazmierkowski, M.P. (2000). *Simulation Study of Virtual Flux Based Direct Power Control for Three-Phase PWM Rectifiers*. 26th Annual Confjerence of the IEEE Industrial Electronics Society, Nagoya, Japan. DOI: 10.1109/IECON.2000.972411

Meghni, B., Dib, D., Azar, A. T., Ghoudelbourk, S., & Saadoun, A. (2017a). *Robust Adaptive Supervisory Fractional order Controller For optimal Energy Management in Wind Turbine with Battery Storage. Studies in Computational Intelligence* (Vol. 688). Springer-Verlag.

Meghni, B., Dib, D., Azar, A. T., & Saadoun, A. (2017b). *Effective Supervisory Controller to Extend Optimal Energy Management in Hybrid Wind Turbine under Energy and Reliability Constraints. International Journal of Dynamics and Control*. Springer. doi:10.100740435-016-0296-0

Meghni, B., Dib, D., & Azar, A. T. (2017c). A Second-order sliding mode and fuzzy logic control to Optimal Energy Management in PMSG Wind Turbine with Battery Storage. *Neural Computing & Applications*, *28*(6), 1417–1434. doi:10.100700521-015-2161-z

Mekki, H., Boukhetala, D., & Azar, A. T. (2015). Sliding Modes for Fault Tolerant Control. In Advances and Applications in Sliding Mode Control systems. Springer-Verlag GmbH Berlin/Heidelberg. doi:10.1007/978-3-319-11173-5_15

Mondal, S. K., Pinto, J. O. P., & Bose, B. K. (2002). A Neural-Network-Based Space-Vector PWM Controller for a three-Level Voltage-Fed Inverter Induction Motor Drive. *Industry Applications. IEEE Transactions on.*, *38*(3), 660–669.

Mezache, A., & Betto, K. (1997). *Estimation et Commande d'un Réacteur de Fabrication de Pâte a Papier par les Réseaux de Neurones Flous. Memory of Engineer*. University of Constantine.

Noguchi, T., Tomiki, H., Kondo, S., & Takahashi, I. (1998). Direct power control of PWM converter without power-source voltage sensors. *IEEE Transactions on Industry Applications*, *34*(3), 473–479. doi:10.1109/28.673716

Ouannas, A., Azar, A. T., & Abu-Saris, R. (2016a). A new type of hybrid synchronization between arbitrary hyperchaotic maps. *International Journal of Machine Learning and Cybernetics*. doi:10.100713042-016-0566-3

Ouannas, A., Azar, A. T., & Radwan, A. G. (2016b). *On Inverse Problem of Generalized Synchronization Between Different Dimensional Integer-Order and Fractional-Order Chaotic Systems*. The 28th International Conference on Microelectronics, Cairo, Egypt. 10.1109/ICM.2016.7847942

Ouannas, A., Azar, A. T., Ziar, T., & Vaidyanathan, S. (2017a). *On New Fractional Inverse Matrix Projective Synchronization Schemes. Studies in Computational Intelligence* (Vol. 688). Springer-Verlag.

Ouannas, A., Azar, A. T., Ziar, T., & Vaidyanathan, S. (2017b). *Fractional Inverse Generalized Chaos Synchronization Between Different Dimensional Systems. Studies in Computational Intelligence* (Vol. 688). Springer-Verlag.

Ouannas, A., Azar, A. T., Ziar, T., & Vaidyanathan, S. (2017c). *A New Method To Synchronize Fractional Chaotic Systems With Different Dimensions. Studies in Computational Intelligence* (Vol. 688). Springer-Verlag.

Ouannas, A., Azar, A. T., Ziar, T., & Radwan, A. G. (2017d). *Study On Coexistence of Different Types of Synchronization Between Different dimensional Fractional Chaotic Systems. Studies in Computational Intelligence* (Vol. 688). Springer-Verlag.

Ouannas, A., Azar, A. T., Ziar, T., & Radwan, A. G. (2017e). *Generalized Synchronization of Different Dimensional Integer-order and Fractional Order Chaotic Systems. Studies in Computational Intelligence* (Vol. 688). Springer-Verlag.

Ouannas, A., Azar, A. T., & Vaidyanathan, S. (2017f). On A Simple Approach for Q-S Synchronization of Chaotic Dynamical Systems in Continuous-Time. *Int. J. Computing Science and Mathematics*, *8*(1), 20–27.

Ouannas, A., Azar, A. T., & Vaidyanathan, S. (2017g). New Hybrid Synchronization Schemes Based on Coexistence of Various Types of Synchronization Between Master-Slave Hyperchaotic Systems. *International Journal of Computer Applications in Technology*, *55*(2), 112–120. doi:10.1504/IJCAT.2017.082868

Ouannas, A., Azar, A. T., & Ziar, T. (2017h). *On Inverse Full State Hybrid Function Projective Synchronization for Continuous-time Chaotic Dynamical Systems with Arbitrary Dimensions*. Differential Equations and Dynamical Systems; doi:10.100712591-017-0362-x

Ouannas, A., Azar, A. T., & Vaidyanathan, S. (2017i). A Robust Method for New Fractional Hybrid Chaos Synchronization. *Mathematical Methods in the Applied Sciences*, *40*(5), 1804–1812. doi:10.1002/mma.4099

Ouannas, A., Grassi, G., Azar, A. T., Radwan, A. G., Volos, C., Pham, V. T., . . . Stouboulos, I. N. (2017j). *Dead-Beat Synchronization Control in Discrete-Time Chaotic Systems*. The 6th International Conference on Modern Circuits and Systems Technologies (MOCAST), Thessaloniki, Greece. 10.1109/MOCAST.2017.7937628

Sanjuan, S. (2010). Voltage Oriented Control of Three-Phase Boost PWM Converters Design, simulation and implementation of a 3-phase boost battery Charger. Chalmers University of Technologie.

Singh, S., Azar, A. T., Ouannas, A., Zhu, Q., Zhang, W., & Na, J. (2017). *Sliding Mode Control Technique for Multi-switching Synchronization of Chaotic Systems. 9th International Conference on Modelling, Identification and Control (ICMIC 2017)*, Kunming, China.

Soliman, N. S., Said, L. A., Azar, A. T., Madian, A. H., Radwan, A. G., & Ouannas, A. (2017). *Fractional Controllable Multi-Scroll V-Shape Attractor with Parameters Effect*. The 6th International Conference on Modern Circuits and Systems Technologies (MOCAST), Thessaloniki, Greece.

Song, Z., Tian, Y., Chen, W., Zou, Z., & Chen, Z. (2016). Predictive duty cycle control of three-phase active-front-end rectifier. *IEEE Transactions on Power Electronics*, *31*(1), 698–710. doi:10.1109/TPEL.2015.2398872

Tolba, M. F., AbdelAty, A. M., Soliman, N. S., Said, L. A., Madian, A. H., Azar, A. T., & Radwan, A. G. (2017). FPGA implementation of two fractional order chaotic systems. *International Journal of Electronics and Communications*, *28*, 162–172. doi:10.1016/j.aeue.2017.04.028

Vaidyanathan, S., Sampath, S., & Azar, A. T. (2015a). Global chaos synchronisation of identical chaotic systems via novel sliding mode control method and its application to Zhu system. International Journal of Modelling *Identification and Control*, *23*(1), 92–100. doi:10.1504/IJMIC.2015.067495

Vaidyanathan, S., Azar, A. T., Rajagopal, K., & Alexander, P. (2015b). Design and SPICE implementation of a 12-term novel hyperchaotic system and its synchronization via active control (2015). International Journal of Modelling *Identification and Control, 23*(3), 267–277. doi:10.1504/IJMIC.2015.069936

Vaidyanathan, S., Idowu, B. A., & Azar, A. T. (2015c). Backstepping Controller Design for the Global Chaos Synchronization of Sprott's Jerk Systems. In Chaos Modeling and Control Systems Design. Springer-Verlag GmbH Berlin/Heidelberg. doi:10.1007/978-3-319-13132-0_3

Vaidyanathan, S., & Azar, A. T. (2015a). Anti-Synchronization of Identical Chaotic Systems using Sliding Mode Control and an Application to Vaidyanathan-Madhavan Chaotic Systems. In Advances and Applications in Sliding Mode Control systems. Springer-Verlag GmbH Berlin/Heidelberg. doi:10.1007/978-3-319-11173-5_19

Vaidyanathan, S., & Azar, A. T. (2015b). Hybrid Synchronization of Identical Chaotic Systems using Sliding Mode Control and an Application to Vaidyanathan Chaotic Systems. In Advances and Applications in Sliding Mode Control systems. Springer-Verlag GmbH Berlin/Heidelberg. doi:10.1007/978-3-319-11173-5_20

Vaidyanathan, S., & Azar, A. T. (2015c). Analysis, Control and Synchronization of a Nine-Term 3-D Novel Chaotic System. In Chaos Modeling and Control Systems Design. Springer-Verlag GmbH Berlin/Heidelberg. DOI doi:10.1007/978-3-319-13132-0_1

Vaidyanathan, S., & Azar, A. T. (2015d). Analysis and Control of a 4-D Novel Hyperchaotic System. In Chaos Modeling and Control Systems Design. Springer-Verlag GmbH Berlin/Heidelberg. DOI doi:10.1007/978-3-319-13132-0_2

Vaidyanathan, S., & Azar, A. T. (2016a). Takagi-Sugeno Fuzzy Logic Controller for Liu-Chen Four-Scroll Chaotic System. *International Journal of Intelligent Engineering Informatics, 4*(2), 135–150. doi:10.1504/IJIEI.2016.076699

Vaidyanathan, S., & Azar, A. T. (2016b). *Dynamic Analysis, Adaptive Feedback Control and Synchronization of an Eight-Term 3-D Novel Chaotic System with Three Quadratic Nonlinearities. Studies in Fuzziness and Soft Computing* (Vol. 337). Springer-Verlag.

Vaidyanathan, S., & Azar, A. T. (2016c). *Qualitative Study and Adaptive Control of a Novel 4-D Hyperchaotic System with Three Quadratic Nonlinearities. Studies in Fuzziness and Soft Computing* (Vol. 337). Springer-Verlag.

Vaidyanathan, S., & Azar, A. T. (2016d). *A Novel 4-D Four-Wing Chaotic System with Four Quadratic Nonlinearities and its Synchronization via Adaptive Control Method. Advances in Chaos Theory and Intelligent Control. Studies in Fuzziness and Soft Computing* (Vol. 337). Springer-Verlag.

Vaidyanathan, S., & Azar, A. T. (2016e). *Adaptive Control and Synchronization of Halvorsen Circulant Chaotic Systems. Advances in Chaos Theory and Intelligent Control. Studies in Fuzziness and Soft Computing* (Vol. 337). Springer-Verlag.

Vaidyanathan, S., & Azar, A. T. (2016f). *Adaptive Backstepping Control and Synchronization of a Novel 3-D Jerk System with an Exponential Nonlinearity. Advances in Chaos Theory and Intelligent Control. Studies in Fuzziness and Soft Computing* (Vol. 337). Springer-Verlag.

Vaidyanathan, S., & Azar, A. T. (2016g). *Generalized Projective Synchronization of a Novel Hyperchaotic Four-Wing System via Adaptive Control Method. Advances in Chaos Theory and Intelligent Control. Studies in Fuzziness and Soft Computing* (Vol. 337). Springer-Verlag.

Vaidyanathan, S., Azar, A. T., & Ouannas, A. (2017a). *An Eight-Term 3-D Novel Chaotic System with Three Quadratic Nonlinearities, its Adaptive Feedback Control and Synchronization. Studies in Computational Intelligence* (Vol. 688). Springer-Verlag.

Vaidyanathan, S., Zhu, Q., & Azar, A. T. (2017b). *Adaptive Control of a Novel Nonlinear Double Convection Chaotic System. Studies in Computational Intelligence* (Vol. 688). Springer-Verlag.

Vaidyanathan, S., Azar, A. T., & Ouannas, A. (2017c). *Hyperchaos and Adaptive Control of a Novel Hyperchaotic System with Two Quadratic Nonlinearities. Studies in Computational Intelligence* (Vol. 688). Springer-Verlag.

Vazquez, S., Sanchez, J., Carrasco, J., Leon, J., & Galvan, E. (2008). A model-based direct power control for three-phase power converters. *IEEE Transactions on Industrial Electronics*, *55*(4), 1647–11657. doi:10.1109/TIE.2008.917113

Vazquez, S., Leon, J. I., Franquelo, L. G., Rodriguez, J., Young, H., Marquez, A., & Zanchetta, P. (2014). Model predictive control: A review of its applications in power electronics. *IEEE Industrial Electronics Magazine*, *8*(1), 16–31. doi:10.1109/MIE.2013.2290138

Vazquez, J., & Salmeron, P. (2003). Active power filter control using neural network technologies. *IEE Proceedings. Electric Power Applications*, *150*(2), 139–145. doi:10.1049/ip-epa:20030009

Wang, Z., Volos, C., Kingni, S.T., Azar, A.T., & Pham, V.T. (2017). Four-wing attractors in a novel chaotic system with hyperbolic sine nonlinearity. *Optik - International Journal for Light and Electron Optics, 131*(2017), 1071-1078.

Zhang, Y., Xie, W., Li, Z., & Zhang, Y. (2013). Model predictive direct power control of a PWM rectifier with duty cycle optimization. *IEEE Transactions on Power Electronics*, *28*(11), 5343–5351. doi:10.1109/TPEL.2013.2243846

Zhu, Q., & Azar, A. T. (2015). *Complex system modelling and control through intelligent soft computations. Studies in Fuzziness and Soft Computing* (Vol. 319). Springer-Verlag.

Chapter 11
Dynamics Analysis and Synchronization in Relay Coupled Fractional Order Colpitts Oscillators

Kammogne Soup Tewa Alain
Dschang University, Cameroon

Sundarapandian Vaidyanathan
Vel Tech University, India

Kengne Romanic
Dschang University, Cameroon

Fotsin Hilaire Bertrand
Dschang University, Cameroon

Ahmad Taher Azar
Benha University, Egypt & Nile University, Egypt

Ngo Mouelas Adèle
Dschang University, Cameroon

ABSTRACT

In this chapter, the dynamics of a particular topology of Colpitts oscillator with fractional order dynamics is presented. The first part is devoted to the dynamics of the model using standard nonlinear analysis techniques including time series, bifurcation diagrams, phase space trajectories plots, and Lyapunov exponents. One of the major results of this innovative work is the numerical finding of a parameter region in which the fractional order Colpitts oscillator's circuit experiences multiple attractors' behavior. This phenomenon was not reported previously in the Colpitts circuit (despite the huge amount of related research works) and thus represents an enriching contribution to the understanding of the dynamics of Chua's oscillator. The second part of this chapter deals with the synchronization of fractional order system. Based on fractional-order Lyapunov stability theory, this chapter provides a novel method to achieve generalized and phase synchronization of two and network fractional-order chaotic Colpitts oscillators, respectively.

DOI: 10.4018/978-1-5225-4077-9.ch011

INTRODUCTION

Fractional calculus is a mathematical topic that deals with derivatives and integration of arbitrary order (Miller & Ross, 1993). The commonly used definitions are those of Riemann–Liouville and Grünwald-Letnikov (Herrmann, 2011; Gorenflo & Mainardi, 1997; Samko et al., 1993). An important history of fractional calculus can be found in Machado et *al.* (2011). Although the subject is as old as the conventional calculus, it did not attract enough attention until recent decades. Nowadays, it has been known that many systems in interdisciplinary fields, such as viscoelastic materials, (Bagley & Calico 1991), electrode electrolyte polarization (Ichise et al., 1971), thermoelectric systems (Ezzat & El-Karamany 2012), finance systems (Laskin, 2000), dielectric polarization (Sun et al., 1984), Control systems (Azar et al., 2017a,b,c,d; Meghni et al., 2017a,b,c; Boulkroune et al, 2016a,b; Azar & Zhu, 2015), synchronization (Wang et al., 2017; Soliman et al., 2017; Tolba et al., 2017 ; Singh et al., 2017 ; Grassi et al., 2017), boundary layer effects in ducts, Electromagnetic waves, signal processing, and bio-engineering, can be elegantly described by fractional differential derivatives. The fractional calculus provides effective tools for the description of the memory and hereditary properties of various materials and processes.

The application of fractional-order calculus to nonlinear physics and its applications is only a recent focus of interest (Azar et al., 2017a; Ouannas et al., 2017a,b,c,d,e,i; Pham et al., 2017a; Ouannas et al., 2016a,b). Chaotic systems are deterministic and nonlinear dynamical systems which are exponentially sensitive to initial conditions (Yang et al., 2009; Lamamra et al., 2017; Vaidyanathan & Azar, 2017a,b,c; Vaidyanathan & Azar, 2016a,b,c,d,e,f). It's well-known that chaos is ubiquitous in most nonlinear systems which have some additional properties, such as chaotic attractors and fractal motion (Azar et al., 2017b; Azar, & Vaidyanathan, 2015a,b,c; Azar, & Vaidyanathan, 2016). Moreover, many studies have demonstrated that many fractional-order differential systems, such as the fractional-order Lorenz system (Grigorenko & Grigorenko 2003), fractional order Duffling system (Ge & Ou, 2007), fractional-order Chua's system (Hartley, et al., 1995), and fractional-order Chen's system (Deng & Li, 2005) exhibit chaotic behaviors. Recently, Li et al. (2010) have studied the definition of Lyapunov exponents of fractional differential systems, which are often used to detect chaos in fractional differential systems. On the other hand, both frequency-domain methods and time-domain methods are used for computing the fractional differential systems (Li & Peng, 2004; Li et al., 2011). It was noted that using the frequency-domain approximation methods can conceal chaotic behaviour for a chaotic fractional order system or display chaos for a non-chaotic one (Tavazoei & Haeri, 2007). In comparison, the time-domain approximation method provides more effective numerical simulations to recognize chaos in fractional differential systems (Li et al., 2010).

In the pioneering work of Pecora and Carroll (1990) have shown that the chaotic systems can be synchronized by introducing appropriate coupling. Synchronization of chaotic systems is a phenomenon that occurs when two or more chaotic systems are coupled or when a chaotic system drives another chaotic system (Vaidyanathan et al., 2015a,b,c; Vaidyanathan & Azar, 2015a,b,c,d; Ouannas et al., 2017f,g,h,j). Because of the butterfly effect which causes exponential divergence of the trajectories of two identical chaotic systems started with nearly the same initial conditions, the synchronization of chaotic systems is a challenging research problem in the chaos literature. Major works on synchronization of chaotic systems deal with the complete synchronization of a pair of chaotic systems called the master and slave systems. The design goal of the complete synchronization is to apply the output of the master system to control the slave system so that the output of the slave system tracks the output of the master system asymptotically with time. Active feedback control is used when the system parameters are available for measurement. Adaptive feedback control is used when the system parameters are unknown. On the order hand, the first attempt concerning the synchronization of fractional systems was by Li et *al.* (2011) in which they showed by means of a control law that fractional order chaotic systems can be synchronized by using the similar scheme as that of their integer counterparts. Aghababa (2012) used the finite-time theory to realize finite-time synchronization of chaotic systems. More recently Li and coworkers presented the dynamics, synchronization and fractional order form of a chaotic system without equilibrium (Li et al. 2012). This research provides the systematic procedure to analyses the fractional system without equilibrium point. In the purpose to complete some dynamical aspects of the researches in fractional order of chaotic systems, Ouannas *et al.* developed many problematics in this topic. They first presented a fractional inverse generalized chaos synchronization between different dimensional systems (Ouannas et al., 2017b), secondly, they proposed a new method to synchronize fractional chaotic systems with different dimensions (Ouannas et al., 2017c). Wu et *al.* (2016) proposed a Global Mittag-Leffler projective synchronization for fractional-order neural networks: an LMI-based approach. Razminia *et al.* (2011) considered the synchronization of fractional-order Rössler system via active control. By using the approach in Yu et al. (2014), Bao and Cao (2015) considered the projective synchronization of fractional-order memristor-based neural networks, and some sufficient criteria were derived to ensure the synchronization goal. More recently, Azar et al. (2017a) presented the control and synchronization of fractional-order chaotic systems. The authors provide a general scheme of control, switching and generalized synchronization of fractional-order chaotic systems. On the other hand, Zhuxiang et al (2016) proposed an adaptive synchronization of the fractional order chaotic system based on passive control. In this work, the problem is firstly transformed into stability analysis of the integer order error system. Secondly, the error system could be asymptotically stabilized by designing adaptive passive state feedback controllers. Ouannas and coworkers presented a new approach to investigate the coexistence of some synchronization types between non-identical systems characterized by different dimensions and different orders (Ouannas et al., 2017f). A robust method for new fractional hybrid chaos synchronization is developed by the same author with others researchers (Ouannas et al., 2017g) in which they a robust mathematical method is proposed to study a new hybrid synchronization type, which is a combining generalized synchronization and inverse generalized synchronization. Among all the works previously mentioned, little provides a systematic procedure for the control of generalized chaotic system to the best of authors' knowledge. In fact, the nonlinearities in many systems used in the literature are simply a cubic function or a continuous (but not differentiable) piecewise-linear function. More systems topology different to common systems encountered in the literature presents many important features (fractals, bifurcations, coexistence and so on) and leads to many applications such as random bits generation and chaos theory which is aimed to provide security in the transmission of information performed through telecommunications technologies. These circuits are Colpitts oscillators' family in which the nonlinear term is an exponential with many arguments.

The linear transformation of the Modified Colpitts Oscillator (further called MCO) which first introduced by Ababei and Marculescu (2000) is investigated prior to the more detailed study by Kammogne and Fotsin (2011). Recently, there have been many efforts for the study of dynamical properties of this oscillator which was used in the qualitative numerical transmission of information. The particular feature of this oscillator is the real possibility to control chaos using a single resistor, without varying any parameter of the intrinsic Colpitts oscillator, which offers the possibility of an electronic analog or digital control on the system dynamics. Therefore, most of previous studies in the literature have predominantly concentrated on standard systems such as the Lorentz, the classic Colpitts oscillator, the Chua system, the Chen system, the Lu system, or the Rossler system with their fractional order associated either in the studies of their stability analysis and periodic oscillations or of their synchronization. It has been shown that the MCO can exhibit complicated dynamics with reference to the classical Colpitts oscillator linked to its nonlinearity topology which is a great advantage in telecommunication. In general, the security of chaos-based communication systems is dependent on the complexity degree of master's dynamics, carrying signal as well as the encryption scheme used (Wang & Su, 2004). There are few studies in the synchronization of the integer-fractional MCO (Kammogne & Fotsin, 2011; Kammogne et al, 2013), though these systems are widely encountered in practice, in particular in communication. To the best of authors' knowledge, dynamical properties of fractional Colpitts system can be rarely found in the literature. Based on aforementioned observations, stability analysis and synchronization of fractional MCO are investigated in this chapter. Roughly speaking, the Colpitts oscillator's family provides better spectral properties which are suitable for communication application. Some of the motivations for considering this circuit including the following:

1. The frequency of operation can vary from a few hertz up to the microwave region (gigahertz), depending on the technology;
2. The system possesses an intrinsic nonlinearity given by the exponential characteristic of the active device;
3. Generic system because of its non-symmetry;
4. The Colpitts oscillator exhibits rich dynamical behaviors like many other third-order oscillator configurations analyzed in the literature (Lindberg, 2004; Rhea, 2004).

Similar to the nonlinear Colpitts oscillators, the nonlinear fractional Colpitts oscillators may also have complex dynamics. These studies are useful in the design and implementation of fractional-order modified Colpitts oscillators. The configuration of the MCO provides a systematic procedure to highlight the simplicity and flexibility of the suggested control approach.

In this chapter, a detailed study of dynamical fractional-order modified Colpitts oscillator is provided. The multistability and coexistence of attractors are introduced that has two regimes of amplitude control with constant or linearly rescaled Lyapunov exponents. Also, a new procedure is proposed using the relay network coupled MCO with fractional-order. As far as to the best of authors' knowledge, in the literature this class of control scheme has not be used.

The rest of this chapter is organized as follows. In section 2, some basic concepts of chaos in fractional order MCO are introduced. In section 3, Spice model of fractional-order modified Colpitts oscillator is presented. Dynamical properties of Fractional-order MCO is discussed in section 4. Numerical study is discussed in section 5 to show the effectiveness of the proposed method. Occurrence of multiple attractors is provided in section 6. In section 7, occurrence of transient chaos is discussed while Synchronization of relay coupled fractional-order systems is presented in section 8. Finally, section 9 concludes the chapter.

2. SOME BASIC CONCEPTS OF FRACTIONAL CALCULUS

2.1. Preliminaries

The operator ${}_tD_0^{\alpha}$, called differ-integral operator, is commonly used in fractional calculus as notation for taking both fractional derivative and fractional integral in a single expression. This operator is defined as follows:

$$ {}_tD_0^{\alpha} = \begin{cases} \dfrac{d^{\alpha}}{dt^{\alpha}}, & \alpha > 0 \\ 1, & \alpha = 0 \\ \int_0^t (d\tau)^{\alpha}, & \alpha < 0 \end{cases} \tag{1} $$

There are several definitions of a fractional derivative of order $\alpha \in (0,1)$, we will use the Caputo fractional operator in the definition of fractional order systems, because the meaning of the initial conditions for the systems described using this operator is the same as for integer order systems.

Definition 1. The uniform formula of a fractional derivative with $\alpha \in (0,1)$ of a function *x* is defined as:

$$ x^{(\alpha)} = {}_{t_0}D_t^{\alpha} x(t) = \frac{1}{\Gamma(m-\alpha)} \int_{t_0}^{t} \frac{d^m x(\varphi)}{d\varphi^m} (t-\varphi)^{m-\alpha-1} d\varphi \tag{2} $$

where: $m - 1 \leq \alpha < m$, $\dfrac{d^m x(\varphi)}{d\varphi^m}$ is the mth derivative of x in the usual sense, $m \in IN$ and Γ is the gamma function.

2.2. The Fractional-Order MCO

An integer-order autonomous MCO chaotic system in Ref. (Kammogne et al, 2013), which is described by the following nonlinear differential equations:

$$ \begin{aligned} \frac{dx}{d\tau} &= z - \alpha \exp(-az - by) \\ \frac{dy}{d\tau} &= -\beta - \beta y + z \\ \frac{dz}{d\tau} &= 1 - x - y - \gamma z \end{aligned} \tag{3} $$

where x, y and z are state variables; and $a, b, \alpha, \beta, \gamma$ are systems parameters. When $a = 2.251362$, $b = 192.3$, $\beta = 0.1064814815, \gamma = 0.934$, $\alpha = 8.518518.10^{-11}$, system (3) exhibits a chaotic behaviour. Its attractor is similar to Chen's attractor, as depicted in Figure 1.

The equations of the fractional-order MCO are given by:

$$\begin{aligned} \frac{d^{q_1} x}{d\tau^{q_1}} &= z - \alpha \exp(-az - by) \\ \frac{d^{q_2} y}{d\tau^{q_2}} &= -\beta - \beta y + z \\ \frac{d^{q_3} z}{d\tau^{q_3}} &= 1 - x - y - \gamma z \end{aligned} \tag{4}$$

where q_i is the fractional order, $0 < q_i \leq 1\ (i = 1, 2, 3)$

The equations of system (4) are derived from the integer-order counterpart, but the value of system parameters of the original integer-order system cannot be applied to the fractional-order system directly. In the following sections, the choices of system parameters and the order q_i, which cause the systems to be of chaos, need a large amount of trial and error by numerical simulations and nonlinear dynamical analyses. In what follows, the nonlinear dynamical behaviors of system (4) are studied by using the bifurcation diagrams, the largest Lyapunov exponents, the phase portraits and the power spectrum diagrams.

2.3. Existence and Uniqueness of the Solution

Let us remember that system of equations (4) can be generalized to the following n-dimensional fractional dynamical system:

Figure 1. Trajectories and chaotic attractors of MCO

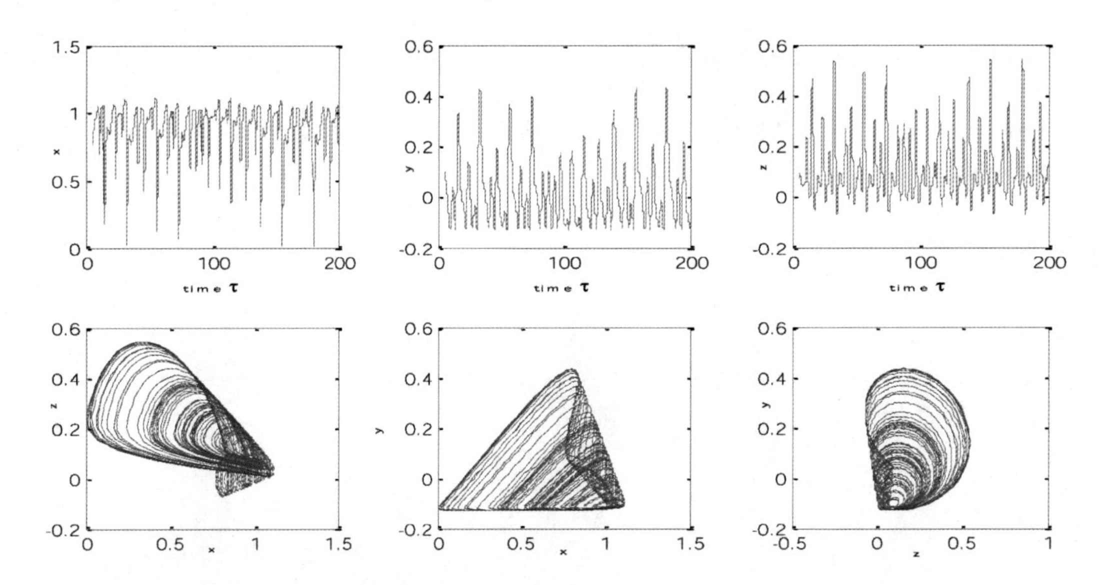

$$\frac{d^q X(t)}{dt^q} = F(t, X(t)), \quad \forall t \in (0, T]$$
$$X_0(0) = X_0 \tag{5}$$

where $X(t) = \left(x_1(t), ..., x_n(t)\right)^T$ and $q = (q_1, ...q_n)$, $q_i \in (0,1)$ for $i = 1, 2, ...n$ is said to be a commensurate order if $q_1 = q_2 = ... = q_n$, otherwise it is said to be an incommensurate order.

Assumption 1. The states of the chaotic system describe by the equations (4) are bounded, and the nonlinear function with two variables $f(a'v_3, b'v_2)$ is locally Lipschitz, i.e., there exists a positive constant k_f such that

$$\left\| f(a'v_3, b'v_2) - f(a'\tilde{v}_3, b'\tilde{v}_2) \right\| \le a'k_f \left\| \tilde{v}_3 - v_3 \right\| + b'k_f \left\| \tilde{v}_2 - v_2 \right\| \tag{6}$$

where $v = (v_1, v_3, v_2)$, a' and b' are positive constants. The relation (6) can be put in the following form

$$\left\| f(a'v_3, b'v_2) - f(a'\tilde{v}_3, b'\tilde{v}_2) \right\| \le M(a', b')e_\perp \tag{7}$$

where $e_\perp = \left(\left\| \tilde{v}_1 - v_1 \right\|, \left\| \tilde{v}_2 - v_2 \right\|, \left\| \tilde{v}_3 - v_3 \right\| \right)^T$, $M(a', b') = \begin{bmatrix} 0 & 0 & 0 \\ 0 & \varepsilon' & 0 \\ 0 & 0 & \varepsilon'' \end{bmatrix}$ with $\varepsilon' = b'k_f$ and $\varepsilon'' = a'k_f$

Theorem 1. (Matignon, 1996). *Suppose that* $D = \left[0, T^*\right] \times \left[x_0 - \rho, x_0 + \rho\right]$ *with some* $T^* > 0$ *and some* $\rho > 0$ *Let* $F : D \to R$ *be a continuous function. Define*

$$T := \min \left\{ T^*, \left(\frac{\rho \Gamma(\alpha + 1)}{\left\| F \right\|_\infty} \right)^{1/\alpha} \right\} \tag{8}$$

Then there exists a function $x : \left[0, T\right] \to R$ *which solves the initial problem (5).*

Theorem 2. (Matignon, 1996). *Assume that* $D = \left[0, T^*\right] \times \left[x_0 - \rho, x_0 + \rho\right]$ *with some* $T^* > 0$ *and some* $\rho > 0$. *Let* $\rho > 0$. *Let* $F : D \to R$ *be a bounded function that satisfies the Lipschitz condition with respect to second component. Then, there exist only one function* $x : \left[0, T\right] \to R$ *which solves the initial value problem (5) where T is defined at (8).*

For the sake of clarity, let's represent the system (5) in the explicit following form:

$$\frac{d^q x(\tau)}{dt^q} = Ax(\tau) + f(x(\tau)) + C$$

where

$$A = \begin{bmatrix} 0 & 0 & 1 \\ 0 & -\beta & 1 \\ -1 & -1 & -\gamma \end{bmatrix}, C = \begin{bmatrix} -1 & 0 & 0 \\ 0 & 0 & 0 \\ 0 & 0 & 0 \end{bmatrix}, f(x) = \begin{bmatrix} f(x_2, x_3) \\ -\beta \\ 0 \end{bmatrix} \tag{9}$$

Theorem 3. Let $0 \leq t \leq T$ for some $T \in R_+$. The initial value problem of commensurate order fractional MCO represented as in (4) has unique solution.

Proof. Define $F(X(t)) = Ax(\tau) + f(x(\tau)) + C$ where A and C are defined at (9). It is clear that $F(X(t))$ defined in this way is a continuous and bounded function on the interval $\left[x_0 - \rho, x_0 + \rho\right]$ for some $\rho \in R_+$. Now, it's shown that $F(X(t))$ satisfies the Lipschitz condition with respect to X.

$$\begin{aligned} \left|F(X(t)) - F(X(t))\right| &= \left|Ax(\tau) + f(x(\tau)) + C - Ay(\tau) - f(y(\tau)) - C\right| \\ &= \left|Ax(\tau) - Ay(\tau) + f(x(\tau)) - f(y(\tau))\right| \\ &\leq \left\|A\right\| \left\|x(\tau) - y(\tau)\right\| + \left|M(a,b)\right| \left\|e_\perp\right\| \\ &\leq K \left\|x(\tau) - y(\tau)\right\| \end{aligned} \tag{10}$$

where $K = \left\|A\right\| + \left\|M(a,b)\right\| > 0$ with $M(a,b) = \max_{t \in [0,T]} \left(2\left\|x_0\right\| + \rho\right) \begin{bmatrix} 0 & 0 & 0 \\ 0 & a & 0 \\ 0 & 0 & b \end{bmatrix}$

This proves that $F(x(t))$ satisfies the Lipschitz condition with respect to $x(t)$. Therefore, it's concluded from theorem 2 that the solution of the initial value problem of commensurate order fractional MCO dynamical uniquely exists.

2.4. Approximated Solutions of MCO With Fractional Order-Derivative

Let's recall that MCO is first of all and electrical circuit and a fractional analysis cannot be perform without considering behaviour of their electrical components under different range of frequencies. If it's assumed that all the parasitic devices of the electrical circuit (See figure 2) are ignored and it's assumed that $dc_2/dt = 0$ and $dL/dt = 0$ (These assumptions are observed in low frequencies). Linearity can be considered in the analysis and hence the active device whose characteristic is $f(V_{BE})$ simply modeled by an ideal linear current source, controlled by the instantaneous voltage V_{BE} on c_1. As a result,

$$\beta_F f(V_{BE}) = a_1 V_{BE}, \tag{11}$$

where a_1 is the transconductance of the active device (the assumption here is that a_1 is constant). The equation (4) moves one step forward in providing a somewhat more practical representation of the VCO oscillator. This is done dealing with a third-order oscillator system. The common method of varying the frequency of a Colpitts is by changing the tuned circuit parameters (Sarafian,1993). This is achieved by employing a varactor and/or an electronic inductor, in the oscillator tuned circuit. A third-order oscilla-

Figure 2. Circuit model: (a) Schematic of the Colpitts oscillator. (b) BJT model in the common base configuration

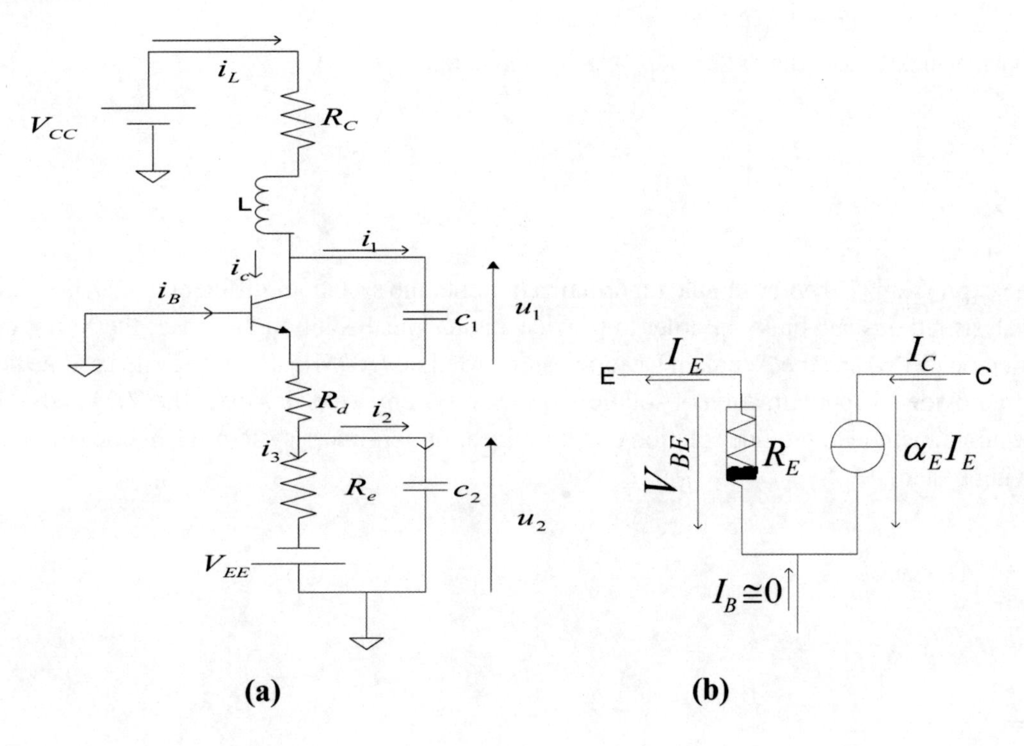

tor model in its linear approximation can be represented as consisting of a double imaginary pole together with a simple pole which stands for an exponentially decaying parasitic bias mode (Behagi, 1992). The linear analysis is not the aims of this chapter and will not be developed in the present document. Now let consider the present MCO with fractional derivatives. The MCO system given by Eq. (4) is a perfect non-linear system. Therefore, providing an analytical solution to this system is a real big challenge. It should be noted that the evaluation provides an analytical expression for the oscillator dynamics in the vicinity of the limit cycle. The linear analysis and its nonlinear extension is a strongly recommended mechanism for controlling the frequency. An unpleasant consequence of the linear analysis methods is that they are to some extent inaccurate, and unfortunately, precise nonlinear symbolic analysis methods do not exist. Dynamical systems are mathematically studied in books such as Andronov et al. (2011), but the focus is on mathematical methods and remains mainly qualitative. It is difficult to draw conclusions for practical purposes on the basis of this material. In some cases simplified nonlinear solutions are found but in general, oscillators design relies heavily on computer-aided simulation methods. It is well known that an oscillator cannot be implemented as a linear circuit. This is due to the fact that the amplitude of the sinusoidal waveform (in the linear model) is dependent on initial conditions and thus sensitive to noise. The analysis taken into account assumes that the function (11) is nonlinear function of the voltage.

The nonlinearity is associated here with the source as follows (see the Figure 2):

$$\beta_F f(V_{BE}) = a_{11} V_{BE} + a_{22} V_{BE}^2 + a_{33} V_{BE}^3 + \ldots + a_{nn} V_{BE}^n \quad (12)$$

where $a_{nn} = \frac{\beta_F I_{SBE}}{n!}\left(\frac{e}{k_B T}\right)^n$

Considering, the fact that $V_{BE} = -u_2 - R_d i_L$ one obtains:

$$\beta_F f(V_{BE}) = \sum_{i=0}^{n} (-1)^i \frac{\beta_F I_{SBE}}{i!}\left(\frac{e}{k_B T}\right)^i \left(u_2 + R_d i_L\right)^i \tag{13}$$

The expression (13) with suitable renormalization into the system of differential equations (4) leads his analysis tedious and bulky in order to provide an analytical solution, however, the Variation Iterative Method (VIM) and the Adomain Decomposition Method (ADM), are among others some powerful tools to provide an approximation of solution to such a system. Thus, it's clear the VIM is the simplest and accurate method to provide solution either to linear or non-linear system. Then, the solution of the following system:

$$\begin{aligned} \frac{d^q x}{dt^q} &= f_1\left(t, x, y, z\right) \\ \frac{d^q y}{dt^q} &= f_2\left(t, x, y, z\right) \\ \frac{d^q z}{dt^q} &= f_3\left(t, x, y, z\right) \end{aligned} \tag{14}$$

can be built as follows:

$$\begin{aligned} x^{k+1}(t) &= x^k(t) - \int_0^t \left(D^q x^k(\tau) - f_1\left(\tau, x^k(\tau), y^k(\tau), z^k(\tau)\right)\right) d\tau \\ y^{k+1}(t) &= y^k(t) - \int_0^t \left(D^q y^k(\tau) - f_2\left(\tau, x^k(\tau), y^k(\tau), z^k(\tau)\right)\right) d\tau \\ z^{k+1}(t) &= z^k(t) - \int_0^t \left(D^q z^k(\tau) - f_3\left(\tau, x^k(\tau), y^k(\tau), z^k(\tau)\right)\right) d\tau \end{aligned} \tag{15}$$

where

$$\begin{aligned} f_1\left(\tau, x^k(\tau), y^k(\tau), z^k(\tau)\right) &= z - \alpha \exp(-az - by) \\ f_2\left(\tau, x^k(\tau), y^k(\tau), z^k(\tau)\right) &= -\beta - \beta y + z \\ f_3\left(\tau, x^k(\tau), y^k(\tau), z^k(\tau)\right) &= 1 - x - y - \gamma z \end{aligned} \tag{16}$$

By using system (15) and the definition of Caputo derivative and keeping the same initial conditions of the proposed commensurate system, the solution up to 2rd order of system (4) can be given by:

$$\begin{aligned} x^0 &= x_0 \\ y^0 &= y_0 \\ z^0 &= z_0 \end{aligned} \tag{17}$$

$$\begin{aligned} x^1 &= x_0 + a_x t \\ y^1 &= y_0 + a_y t \\ z^1 &= z_0 + a_z t \end{aligned} \tag{18}$$

with

$$\begin{aligned} a_x &= z_0 - a_2 \exp\left(-a_1 z_0 - b_1 y_0\right) \\ a_y &= -b_2 - b_2 y_0 + z_0 \\ a_z &= 1 - x_0 - y_0 - c z_0 \end{aligned} \tag{19}$$

by setting

$$\begin{aligned} \alpha &= a_1 a_z + b_1 a_y \\ \beta &= a_1 z_0 + b_1 y_0 \end{aligned} \tag{20}$$

Ones obtain

$$\begin{aligned} x^2 &= x_0 + \left(a_x + z_0\right)t + \frac{a_z}{2}t^2 - \frac{a_x \Gamma(2)}{(2-q)\Gamma(2-q)}t^{2-q} + \frac{a_2}{\alpha}\exp\left(-\alpha t - \beta\right) \\ y^2 &= y_0 + 2a_y t + \frac{1}{2}\left(a_z - b_2 a_y\right)t^2 - \frac{a_y \Gamma(2)}{(2-q)\Gamma(2-q)}t^{2-q} \\ z^2 &= z_0 + 2a_z t - \frac{1}{2}\left(a_x + a_y + c a_z\right)t^2 - \frac{a_z \Gamma(2)}{(2-q)\Gamma(2-q)}t^{2-q} \end{aligned} \tag{21}$$

The approximated solution provided presented in this chapter leads us to conclude that one can approximate the solution of such a system by simple power-series function which can be handle easily. These results reveal that the proposed method is very effective,

simple and leads to accurate, approximately convergent solutions of non-linear equations. These approximated solutions preserve the non-linearity and give an additional insight into the dynamic of the simulated system.

3. SPICE MODEL OF FRACTIONAL-ORDER MODIFIED COLPITTS OSCILLATOR

3.1. Integer-Order MCO Model

The Colpitts circuit is easily modelled, easily realized and scalable in frequency. In 1994, the occurrence of chaos was first demonstrated in the Colpitts oscillator by Kennedy (1994). Actually the chaotic dynamics produced by this oscillator is relatively well understood. The configuration of the Colpitts circuit which dimensionless equations are derived in (4) is presented in Figure 2. This circuit uses a bipolar junction transistor (BJT) as the gain element and a resonant network consisting of an inductor (L) and a pair of capacitors (C_1 and C_2). The resistor R_d is the additive element compared to the classical system. This resistance renders elegant and attractive the integer-order MCO. The unique feature of this oscillator is the real possibility of controlling chaos using a single resistor, without varying any parameter of the intrinsic Colpitts oscillator, which offers the possibility of an electronic analog or digital control on the system dynamics. It's also noted that there exists an important difference between existing MCO topologies and the classical Colpitts oscillator, which confers on each one specific synchronization properties.

3.2. Circuit Implementation of Fractional-Order MCO

Although the MCO is a relatively simple oscillator, access to some state variables of the system can practically turn to a delicate task, because of the high frequency of operation. In addition, the literature lacks to deal a systematic procedure to construct the fractional-order nonlinear system in Pspice which

Figure 3. Electrical analog model of FOMCO on Pspice for $q = 1$

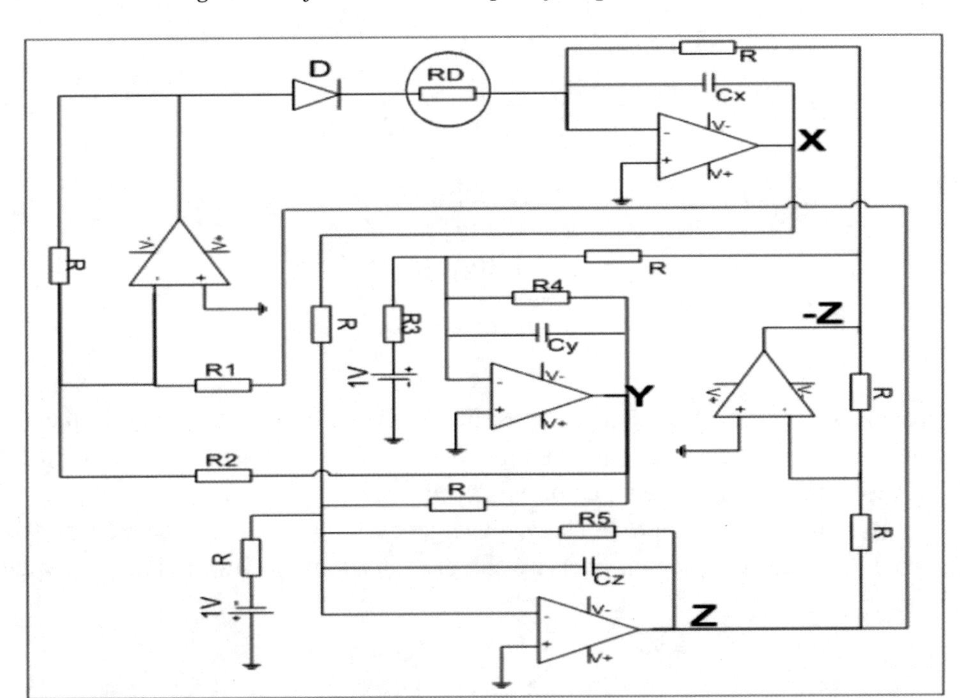

remains a hard task. It should be noted that the Ref. (Jakubowska & Szymczak, 2016) presented the simulations studies on the synthesis of new fractional-order components, such as supercapacitors and real coils with ferromagnetic cores. They restricted their works on the realization of new fractional-order elements using a generalized impedance converter GIC in Spice A/D program. This approach although good, do not enables best understanding of the design of fractional-order nonlinear system. In order to simplify access and manipulation of the three state variables *x, y* and *z* of the fractional-order MCO, in this section an electronic analog operational amplifiers-based model of the fractional-order MCO (referred to as the FOMCO hereafter) is proposed. The circuit includes five operational amplifiers for integration and inversion operations. The device features are high slew rates, low input bias and offset currents and low offset voltage temperature coefficient. This is significant to reduce sensitivity to circuit parameter values. Hence a particularly elegant circuit is obtained (See Figure 4) in which the required nonlinearity is provided by a single silicon diode. This diode model is here taken as

$$\begin{aligned} f(y,z) &= \tfrac{R}{R_D} I_0 \exp[\tfrac{0.026(-az-by)}{V_T} - 1] \\ &\approx \tfrac{R}{R_D} I_0 \exp[\tfrac{0.026(-az-by)}{V_T}] \end{aligned} \tag{21}$$

with $I_0 = 10^{-12} A$ and $V_T = 0.026V$, giving a forward voltage drop of approximately $0.6V$ at room temperature, as it is well-known for normal silicon diodes.

The components values and the voltage sources of this circuit are taken as $C_X = C_Y = C_Z = 100\mu F$, (we recall that the voltages V_{Cx}, V_{Cy}, and V_{Cz} represents the variables x, y and z, respectively). R=10KΩ, R_D= 117.39Ω, R_1=170.837KΩ, R_2=2KΩ, R_3=R_4=93.913KΩ, R_5=10.7KΩ, V_1=V_2=1V. The operational amplifiers are supplied with Vcc=+15V and Vss=-15V. The system parameters are given by $a_2 = \frac{R}{R_D} I_0$, $a = \frac{R}{0.026R_1}$, $b = \frac{R}{0.026R_2}$, $c_{11} = \frac{1}{10^4 R_5 C_3}$, $b_0 = \frac{1}{10^4 R_3 C_2} = \frac{1}{10^4 R_4 C_2}$. The metalized paper capacitors are used C_X, C_Y and C_Z with the real order $q_1 = q_2 = 0.99$ and it's assumed that the real order of inductor is $q_3 = 0.98$. The total order of the system is $\bar{q} \approx 3$. The resulting phase space plot of this circuit is obtained using Pspice program. The time history of the trajectories and phase portrait are provided in Figure 4.

4. DYNAMICAL PROPERTIES OF FRACTIONAL-ORDER MCO.

4.1. Stability Analysis

The study of circuit dynamics is started by analysing the possible states of equilibrium, their stability, and the bifurcations which occur on monitoring the parameters corresponding to the circuit's components. Stability of the fractional-order nonlinear system is very complex and is different from the fractional-order linear system. The main difference is that for a nonlinear system it is necessary to investigate steady states having two types: equilibrium point and limit cycle. Nonlinear systems may have several equilibrium points. For nonlinear systems, there are many definitions of stability (asymptotic, global, orbital, etc.). The basic idea was formulated by A.M. Lyapunov. As mentioned in Matignon (1998),

Figure 4. Phase portraits of the FOMCO

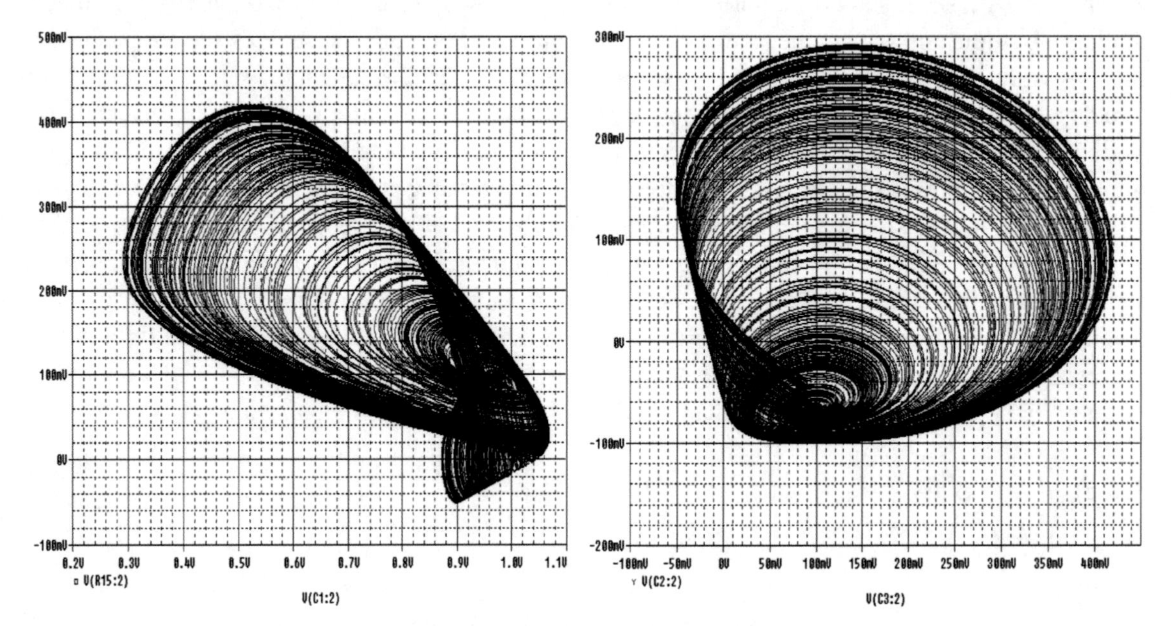

exponential stability cannot be used to characterize asymptotic stability of fractional-order systems. A new definition was introduced (Oustaloup, 2008).

Definition 2. Trajectory $x(t) = 0$ of the system (4) is t^{-q} asymptotically stable if there is a positive real q so that:

$$\forall \left\|x(t)\right\| \text{ with } t \le t_0,\ \exists N(x(t)),\ \text{such that } \forall t \ge t_0,\ \left\|x(t)\right\| \le N t^{-q} \tag{22}$$

The fact that the components of $x(t)$ slowly decay towards following t^{-q} leads to fractional systems sometimes called long memory systems. Power law stability t^{-q} is a special case of the Mittag-Leffler stability (Li et al, 2008).

Theorem 3. According to stability theorem defined in Tavazoei & Haeri, (2008), *the equilibrium points are asymptotically stable for* $q_1 = q_2 = \ldots = q_n = q$ *if all the eigenvalues* λ_i $(i = 1,2,3\ldots n)$ *of the Jacobian matrix* $J = \partial f / \partial x$, *where* $f = \left[f_1, f_2, \ldots f_n\right]^T$, *evaluated at the equilibrium* E^*, *satisfy the condition:*

$$\left|\arg(eig(J)) = \left|\arg(\lambda_i)\right|\right| > q\frac{\pi}{2},\ \ i = 1,2,\ldots,n \tag{23}$$

This theorem deals with the necessary stability condition for fractional order systems (4) to remain chaotic is keeping at least one eigenvalue λ in the unstable region. Assume that a 3D chaotic system has only one equilibria. Let denoted the unstable eigenvalues saddle points are: $\lambda = \alpha \pm j\beta$. The condition for commensurate derivatives order is

$$q > \frac{2}{\pi}\operatorname{atan}\left(\frac{\beta}{\alpha}\right) \tag{24}$$

Figure 5 shows stable and unstable regions of the complex plane for such case.

4.2. Fixed Points

The equilibriums constitute the simplest cases of steady state, thus through the study of their bifurcations, it is possible to detect the existence of other more complicated dynamic regimes (Azar et al., 2017a). In other words, the equilibrium points play a crucial role on the nonlinear dynamics of the circuit. The fixed points of system (5) can be found by solving the following nonlinear system:

$$F(t, X(t)) = 0 \tag{25}$$

After some algebraic manipulations and, it turns out that the fixed point is given by:

$$X_{eq} = (1.020374922; -0.109430898; 0.095088709)^T \tag{26}$$

By performing a Taylor expansion of second order of the exponential expression around the stationary solutions, the Jacobean of Eq. (4) is derived by:

$$DF(X_{eq}) = \begin{bmatrix} 0 & a_2 b \exp\left(-az_0 - by_0\right) & 1 + aa_2 \exp(-az_0 - by_0) \\ 0 & -b_0 & 1 \\ -1 & -1 & -c_{11} \end{bmatrix} \tag{27}$$

Figure 5. Stability regions of the fractional-order system with $0 < q < 1$

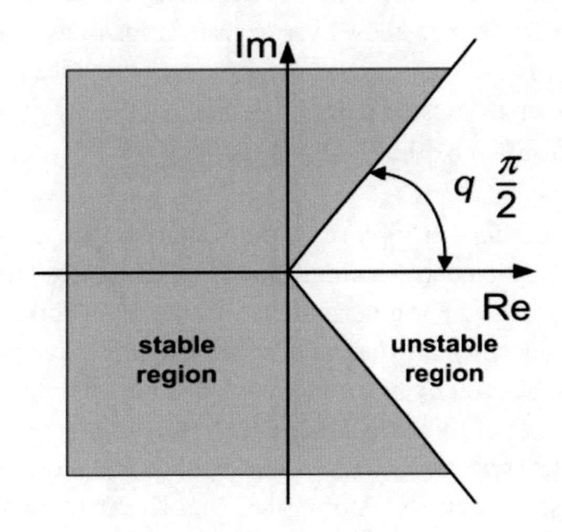

Let's $R_d = 0.5\Omega$. The eigenvalues of the matrix $DF(X_{eq})$ are

$\lambda_1 = -2.6965,\ \lambda_2 = 0.828 + 2.466\,i,\ \lambda_3 = 0.8280 - 2.466\,i$.

We can obtain $\arg(\lambda_1) = \pi,\ \arg(\lambda_2) = 1.246$ and $\arg(\lambda_3) = -1.246$. Using theorem 3, it can be concluded that at the equilibrium point (26), the system will never be stable for any $q \in (0,1)$.

5. NUMERICAL STUDY

To investigate various transitions to chaos in the fractional-order MCO, system (4) is integrated numerically using the classical fourth-order Runge-Kutta integration algorithm. For the each set of parameters used in this work, the time step is always $\Delta t = 0.005$ and the calculations are performed using variables and parameters in extended precision mode. For each parameters setting, the system is integrated for a sufficiently long time and the transient is deleted. Two indicators are judiciously exploited to define the type of scenario giving rise to chaos. The bifurcation diagram stands as the first indicator, the second indicator being the graph of the largest Lyapunov exponents. In the latter case, the sign of the largest Lyapunov exponent determines the rate of almost all small perturbations to the system's state, and consequently, the nature of the underlined dynamical attractor. For $\lambda_{\max} < 0$, all perturbations vanish and trajectories starting sufficiently close to each other converge to the same stable equilibrium point in state space; for $\lambda_{\max} = 0$, initially close orbits remain close but distinct, corresponding to oscillatory dynamics on a limit cycle or torus; and finally for $\lambda_{\max} > 0$, small perturbations grow exponentially, and the system evolves chaotically within the folded space of a strange attractor. To focus on the effects of biasing on the dynamics of the oscillator, R_d and q are chosen as control parameters and the rest of system parameters are assigned as state above. Therefore, a scanning process is performed to investigate the sensitivity of the oscillator to tiny changes in R_d and q. The range $0 \le R_d \le 8$ and $0 \le q \le 1$ are considered to monitor the bifurcation control parameter. It is found that the FOMCO can exhibit complex dynamical motions including periodic, multiperiodic, and chaotic states. Indeed, for the values of system parameters defined above, various scenarios/routes to chaos are observed such as period doubling and crisis scenarios to chaos. Sample results are provided in Figure 6 and Figure 7 where a bifurcation diagrams is shown associated with the corresponding graphs of 1D largest numerical Lyapunov exponents. Clearly justified by the small values of $\lambda_{\max} < 0$ (largest 1D numerical Lyapunov exponent) that are always less than 0.01.

With the same parameters settings in Figure 1, various numerical computations of the phase portraits of the oscillator associated with their corresponding power spectra were obtained confirming transitions/routes to chaos depicted previously. For a periodic steady state, all spikes in the power spectrum are harmonically related to the fundamental whereas a broadband noise like power spectrum is associated to a chaotic steady state. The periodicity of the attractor (i.e., total number of frequencies in a wave) is deduced by counting the number of spikes located at the left-hand side of the highest spike (the latter is included). Indeed, the complete scenarios to chaos are obtained and presented in Figure 8. Specifically, the following scenario was observed when monitoring the control parameter q: fixed point behavior→period-

Figure 6. Fractional-order MCO diagrams. Bifurcation diagram (for $R_d = 3\Omega$) and corresponding largest Lyapunov exponent

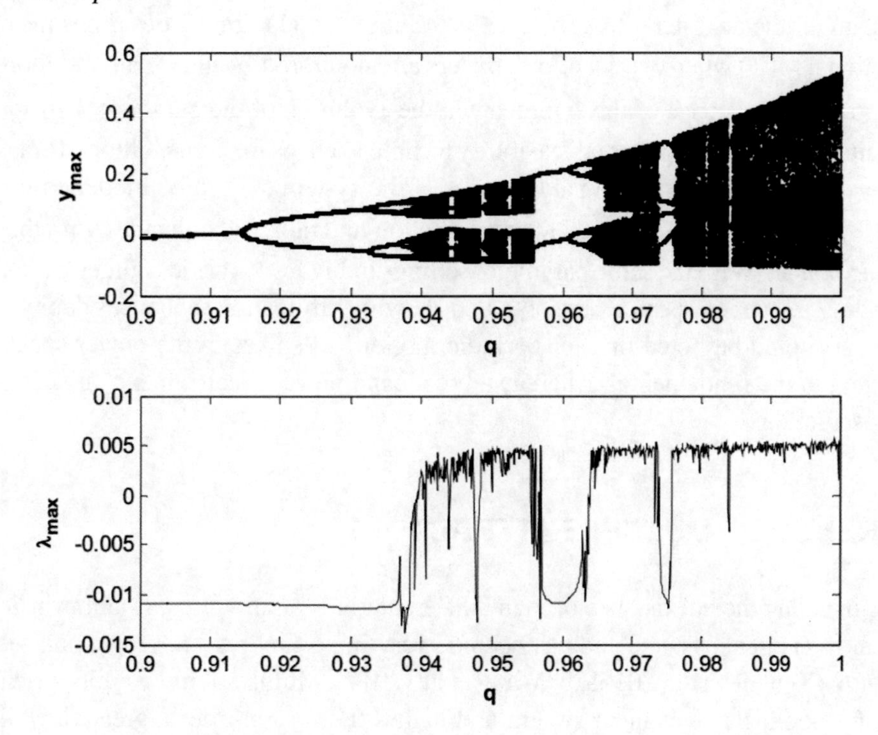

Figure 7. Fractional-order MCO diagrams. Bifurcation diagram (for $R_d = 0.95$) and corresponding largest Lyapunov exponent

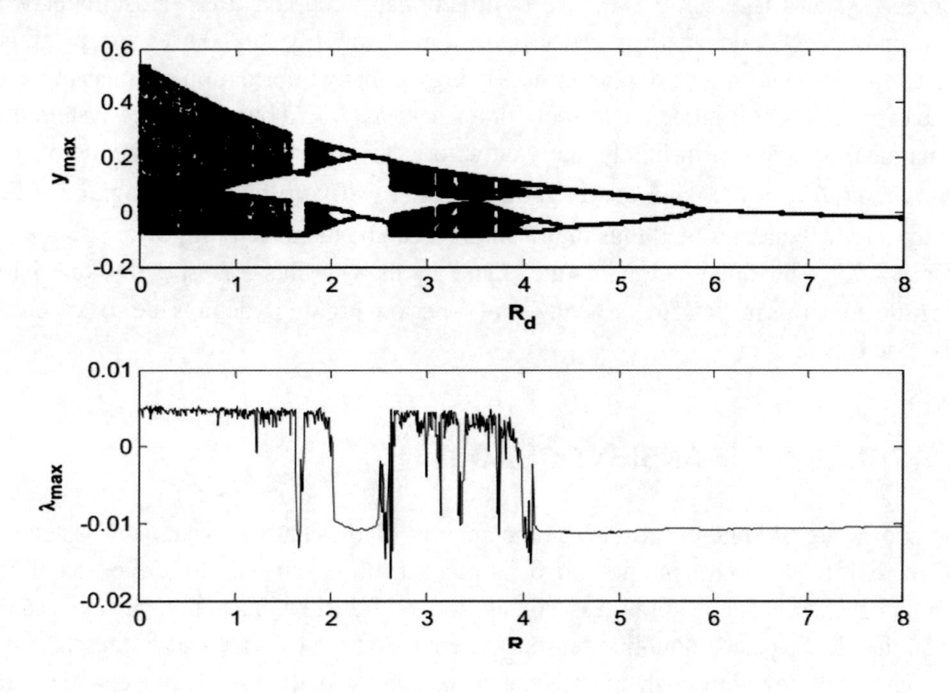

1→period-2→period-4→period-5→chaos→period-6→chaos→period-4→chaos→period-4→chaos→period-2→period-3→chaos. The final state at each iteration of the control parameter serves as the initial state for the next iteration. The graphs of Fiure. 6 and Figure 7 describes the entire behavior of the Fractional MCO when two set of parameters are monitored q and R_d are monitored. A simple observation shows the existence of the symmetry in the evolution of the parameters q and R_d respectively. This feature provides the potential feasibility technic to chaos implementation of fractional MCO. Indeed, for $q = 1$, the complete fractional behavior of the system (4) can be modelled for a set of parameters $R_d \in (0\Omega, 6\Omega)$. It can be seen that the bifurcation diagram well coincides with the spectrum of the Lyapunov exponent. With the same parameter settings in Figure 1, various numerical phase portraits and corresponding frequency spectra were obtained showing bifurcation sequences depicted by Eqs. (4) (see Figure 8). It should be noted that for periodic motion, all spikes in the power spectrum are harmonically related to the fundamental, whereas a broadband power spectrum is characteristic of a chaotic mode of oscillations.

6. OCCURRENCE OF MULTIPLE ATTRACTORS

Multistability, meaning the coexistence of many different kinds of attractors, is an intrinsic property of many nonlinear dynamical systems and has become very important research topic and received much attention recently (Kengne et al., 2016a, b; Wang et al., 2017). Multistability exhibits a rich diversity of stable states of a nonlinear dynamical system and makes the system offer a great flexibility. Particularly, when the number of coexisting attractors generating from a dynamical system tends to infinite, the coexistence of infinitely many attractors depending on the initial condition of a certain state variable is alleged extreme multistability (Kengne et al., 2017), which has been reported in two unidirectional coupled Lorenz systems (Feudel, 2008), two bi-directionally coupled Rössler oscillator with partial synchronization (Azar & Vaidyanathan, 2015a). Since multistability can be used for image processing or regarded as an additional source of randomness using for many information engineering applications (Kammogne et al, 2013), it is attractive to seek for a fractional MCO based chaotic system that has the striking dynamical behavior of infinitely many attractors. To observe the phenomenon of multiple attractors, R_d is fixed ($R_d = 3\Omega$) and the diagram is plotted $(z(0), y(0))$ In the diagram of Figure 9, a window of hysteretic dynamics (and thus multistability) can be identified for power spectra (*right*): (**a**) period-1 for $q = 0.9$. The cloud region in which there are many points correspond to the chaos and the region with little points correspond to the behavior of 4-period. Figure 10 depicts the coexistence between the period-4 and chaos.

7. OCCURRENCE OF TRANSIENT CHAOS

Periodic windows are ubiquitous in the chaotic regime of dissipative dynamical systems (Azar & Vaidyanathan, 2015b). In such windows, chaos is present in the sense that there exists an infinity of periodic orbits but their union is not necessarily attractive. Transient chaos thus always occurs in such windows both inside the period doubling regime, where the attractor is a cycle of length 2^n with an integer n, and outside these regimes where transient chaos coexists with a small size chaotic attractor*: the*

Figure 8. Computer generated phase portraits (left) of the system projected onto the plane $(y(\tau), z(\tau))$ showing routes to chaos (in terms of the control parameter q) and corresponding (b) period-2 for $q = 0.93$, (c) period-4 for $q = 0.97$, (e) period-6 for $R_d = 0.981$, (d) Chaotic attractor for $q = 0.99$

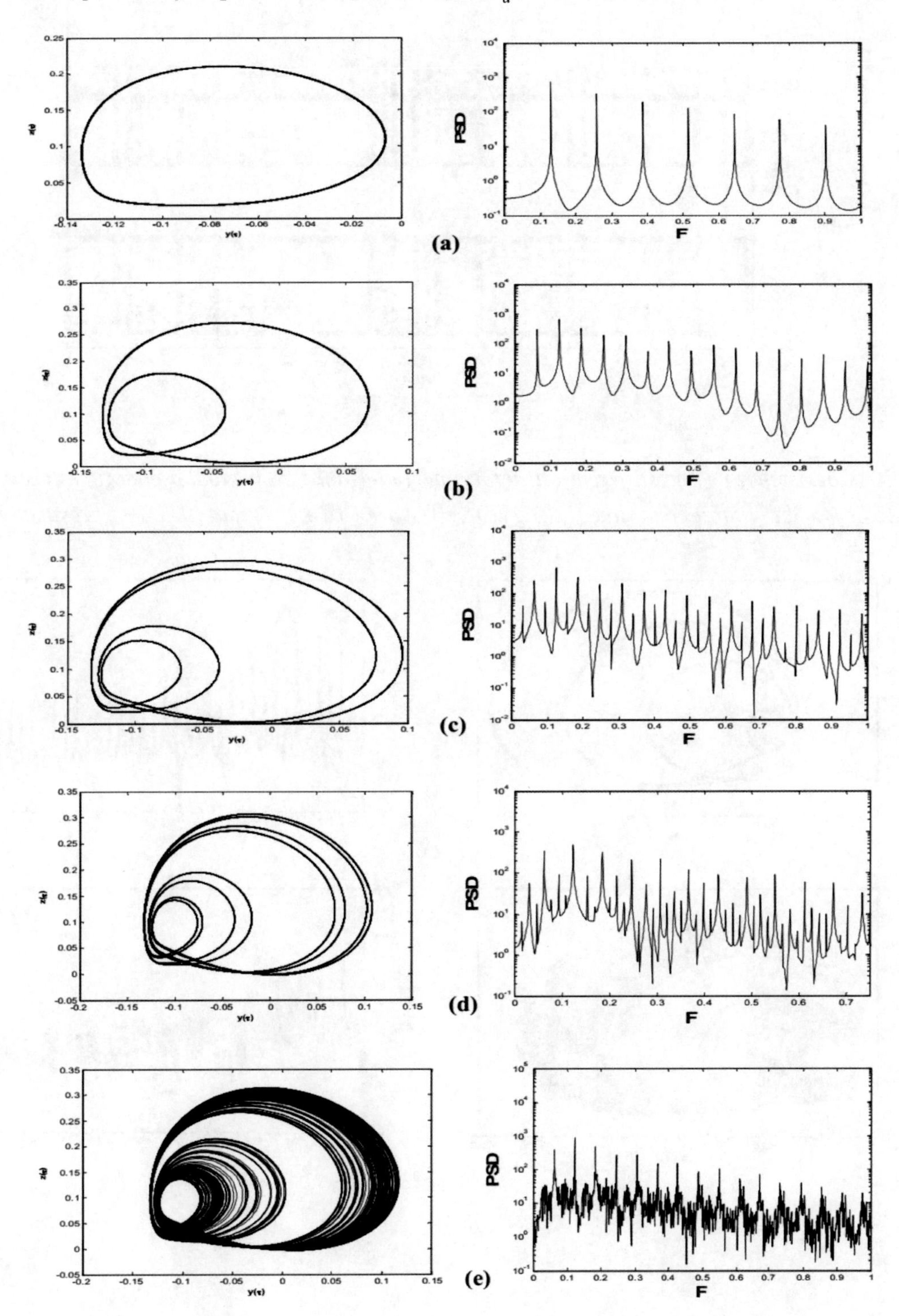

Figure 9. 1D diagram of $(z(0), y(0))$

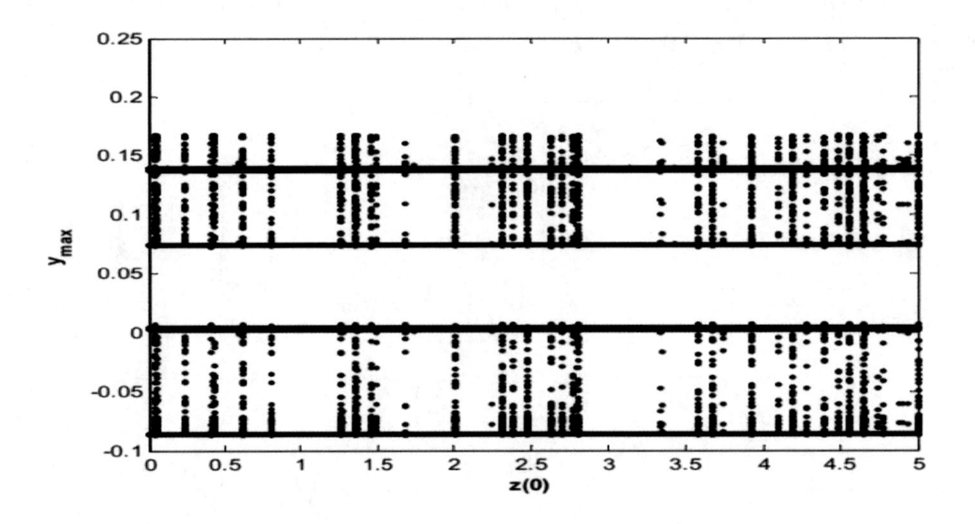

Figure 10. Coexistence of four different attractors (period-4 limit cycles and a chaotic attractors) for $q = 0.95, R_d = 3\Omega$. *Initial conditions* $(x(0), y(0), z(0))$ *are (-014, 0,1) and (0.14, 0,5) respectively*

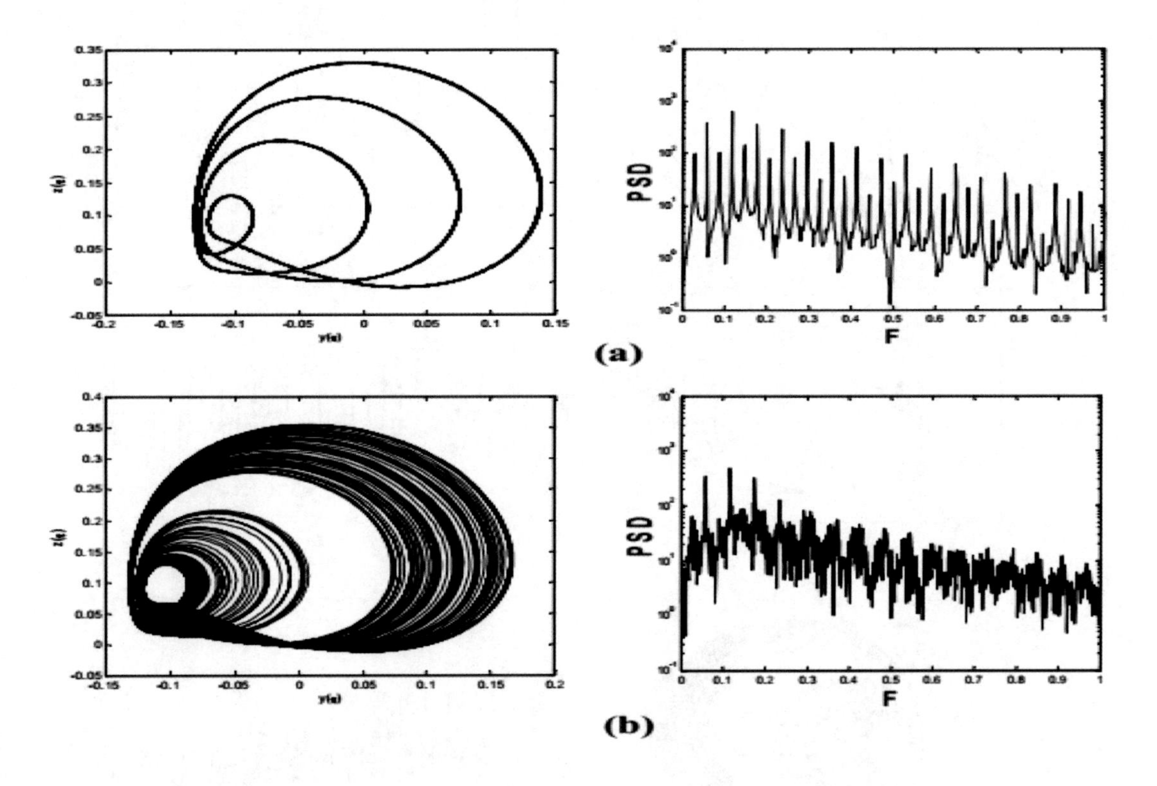

topological entropy is positive everywhere in the window (Tamás, 2015). Since the total measure of windows is known to be finite in the parameter space, just like that of strictly chaotic parameter values, the probability to find transient chaos is comparable to that of permanent chaos even in systems known to be chaotic in a traditional sense. With some initial condition, complex transient chaotic transition behaviors occur in the system (4). By taking $R_d = 3\Omega$ and the following initial conditions $(-0.14, 0, 0.16)$, the trajectories of the system have a transition from a transient chaotic attractor to another steady chaotic attractor with two different dynamic amplitudes of the state variable $y(\tau)$ with the time evolutions. The Figure 11 shows the transient chaos depicted by the FOMCO. Two different behavior zones of the MCO are observed with fractional derivatives.

1. For $\tau \in \left[0, 525\right]$

The trajectory is chaotic. The Figure (12.a) present the corresponding attractor and spectra of the system.

2. For $\tau \in \left[525, 1500\right]$

When the time increase the system, a stable period-4 cycle born from the Hopf bifurcation culminating to a band spiralling chaotic attractor. See Figure 12(b).

Figure 11. Experimental wave forms showing unstable chaos and two orbits within the chaotic time series data for Rd=3Ω. The first range of the plot shows an unstable period-one orbit starting shortly after t==00 s. The second range of the plot shows an unstable period-four orbit starting just before t==−=s. The plots themselves are taken from different datasets

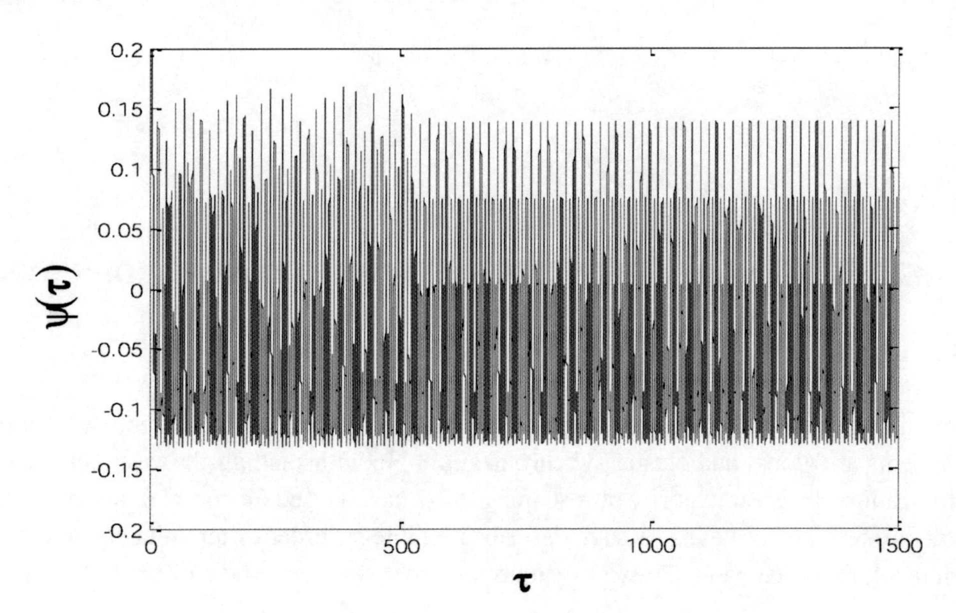

Figure 12. Phase portraits for a value of the resistance R_d plotted with their corresponding spectral density

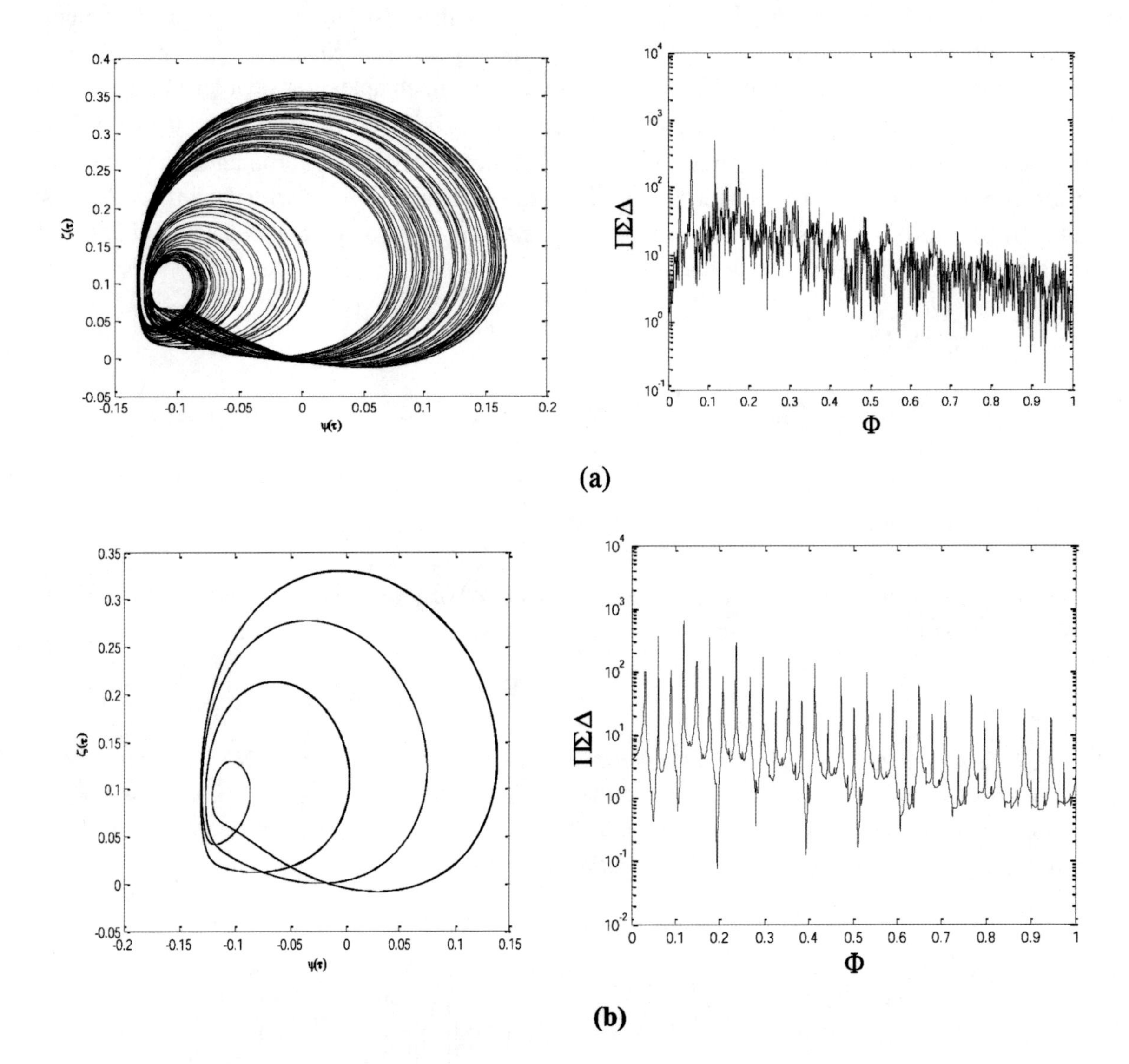

8. SYNCHRONIZATION OF RELAY COUPLED FRACTIONAL-ORDER SYSTEMS

8.1. Introduction

One of the major collective coherent behaviors in ensembles of identical and non-identical fractional-order chaotic elements are global and cluster synchronization. Notwithstanding the vast technical literature on synchronization, the great majority of research efforts has focused on complex networks of coupled integer-order systems, whose dynamics are described by integer-order differential equations. However, it has been recognized that many physical systems are more suitable to be modeled by fractional-order differential equations (*i.e.*, differential equations involving fractional-order derivatives) rather than the classic integer-order ones (Kilbas et al., 2006). Analytical studies of these synchronization phenomena meet some problems, where currently there are only few results in this direction (Ouannas et al., 2017b) and the references therein. In the context of coupled chaotic elements, many different types of synchronization have been studied in the past two decades. The most important ones are complete or identical synchronization (CS), phase synchronization (PS) (Rosenblum et al., 1997, 1998), lag synchronization (LS) (Azar & Vaidyanathan, 2016) and generalized synchronization (GS).

This part focuses on CS in ensembles of non-symmetrically fractional-order coupled chaotic cells. CS was first discovered and is the simplest form of synchronization in chaotic systems. It consists of a perfect hooking of the chaotic trajectories of two or many identical systems even though their initial conditions may be different. In arrays of coupled systems CS can take the forms of global (full) and cluster (partial) synchronization. In global synchronization all the elements of the ensemble are mutually synchronized. The phenomenon of cluster synchronization is observed when an ensemble of oscillators splits into groups of synchronized elements (Zhu & Azar, 2015). The analytical and numerical study of the conditions for existence and stability of CS are presented.

8.2. Generalize Synchronization of Coupled MCO Using Fractional Derivatives

As mentioned in the introduction part, chaotic systems are dynamical systems that defy synchronization, due to their essential feature of displaying high sensitivity to initial conditions. Almost all fractional systems depicts the same observation. As a result, two identical fractional chaotic systems starting at nearly the same initial points in phase space develop onto trajectories which become uncorrelated in the course of the time. Nevertheless, it has been shown that it is possible to synchronize these kinds of systems, to make them evolving on the same chaotic trajectory. When one deals with coupled identical systems, synchronization appears as the equality of the state variables while evolving in time. This type of synchronization is referred as complete synchronization (CS). Other names were given in the literature, such as conventional synchronization (Pyragas, 1996) or identical synchronization.

In this section, the main properties of this kind of synchronization are presented. While our discussion will focus on continuous systems, most of the exposed ideas can be easily extended to discrete systems, such as chaotic mappings.

Let us consider the following coupled chaotic systems

$$D^q x(t) = f(t,x), \tag{28}$$

$$D^q y(t) = g(t,x), \tag{29}$$

where $x = \left(x_1, x_2, ..., x_n\right)^T \in \mathbb{R}^n$ and $y = \left(y_1, y_2, ..., y_n\right)^T \in \mathbb{R}^n$ denote the master and the slave equations respectively. f and g are two vectors functions so that $\left(f, g\right) : \mathbb{R}^n \to \mathbb{R}^n$, consequently, $g : \mathbb{R}^n \to \mathbb{R}^n$. It's important to notice that f and g are continuous non-linear functions that fulfill the Lipschitz condition.

$u(t,x,y)$ is the external output defined such that $u = \left(u_1, u_2, \ldots, u_n\right)^T \in \mathbb{R}^n$. Let's define the error vector function as follows: $e(t) = \left(e_1(t), e_2(t), \ldots, e_n(t)\right)^T \in \mathbb{R}^n$, with $e_i(t) = x_i(t) - y_i(t)$. The synchronization is achieved when $\lim_{t\to\infty} e(t) = \lim_{t\to\infty} \left\|x(t) - y(t)\right\| \to 0$

The generalized synchronization errors between systems (27) and (28) are defined as follows

$$D^q e_i(t) = f_i(t, x_1, x_2, \ldots, x_n) - g_i(t, y_1, y_2, \ldots, y_n) - u_i \tag{30}$$

Synchronization implies stabilization of the systems (27) and (28). So, from the partial region stability theory, one can construct the Lyapunov function from where the controller can be designed.

Let's consider a function *V (x)*: $V(x) : \mathbb{R}^n \to \mathbb{R}^n$ such that, the following conditions:

1. $V(x)$ *Positive definite function, radially unbounded*
2. $D^q V(x)$ *is negative semi-definite along the trajectories of the system (30) (* $D^q V(x) \le 0$ *) with additional property like boundedness, then V(x) will decrease as time goes forward.*

The study of the stability of these systems leads to the conclusion that, taking into consideration the fractional derivative can lead to more stability of the system. On the other hand, the synchronization scheme proposed in this Section shows that, compared to other methods, the synchronization by the GYC partial region stability theory is very appropriated. The GYC partial region stability theory is used by Ge and Li studied the synchronization of new Mathieu-Van der Pol systems with new Duffing-Van der Pol systems (Ge & Li, 2011).

8.2.1. Numerical Simulations

Let us consider as the unidirectional master and slave (or response) systems, the FOMCO both defined as follows:

$$\text{Master equation} \begin{cases} \dfrac{d^{q_1} x_1}{dt^{q_1}} = x_3 - \alpha \exp(-a x_3 - b x_2) \\ \dfrac{d^{q_2} x_2}{dt^{q_2}} = -\beta - \beta x_2 + x_3 \\ \dfrac{d^{q_3} x_3}{dt^{q_3}} = 1 - x_1 - x_2 - \gamma x_3 \end{cases} \tag{31}$$

and

Slave equation $$\begin{cases} \dfrac{d^{q_1}y_1}{dt^{q_1}} = y_3 - \alpha \exp(-ay_3 - by_2) + u_1 \\ \dfrac{d^{q_2}y_2}{dt^{q_2}} = -\beta - \beta y_2 + y_3 + u_2 \\ \dfrac{d^{q_3}y_3}{dt^{q_3}} = 1 - y_1 - y_2 - \gamma y_3 + u_3 \end{cases} \tag{32}$$

where u_1, u_2, u_3 are control parameters to be designed. α, a, b, β and γ are the parameters which the corresponding values are given in the previous section 2. The initial conditions are defined by $(x_{10}, x_{20}, x_{30})^T = (0.01, -0.5, 0.1)^T$ for the master and $(y_{10}, y_{20}, y_{30})^T = (0.1, -0.5, 0.1)^T$. The goal is to be able to synchronize the system introducing a control. That is, the generalized synchronization as developed in the previous section.

Knowing that $e_i(t) = x_i(t) - y_i(t) \quad \forall i = 1,2,3$, to make this error always exist in the first quadrant:

$$e_i(t) = x_i(t) - y_i(t) + \lambda \quad \forall i = 1,2,3. \tag{33}$$

where λ is the constant that regulate the stability of the system (30). Using this, the following error dynamical system is derived using Eqs. (27) and (28):

$$\begin{cases} \dfrac{d^{q_1}e_1}{dt^{q_1}} = x_3 - y_3 - \alpha\left[\exp(-ax_3 - bx_2) - \exp(-ay_3 - by_2)\right] - u_1 \\ \dfrac{d^{q_2}e_2}{dt^{q_2}} = -\beta(x_2 - y_2) + x_3 - y_3 - u_2 \\ \dfrac{d^{q_3}e_3}{dt^{q_3}} = -(x_1 - y_1) - (x_2 - y_2) - \gamma(x_3 - y_3) - u_3 \end{cases} \tag{34}$$

By GYC partial region stability, one can choose a Lyapunov function in the form of a positive definite function in first quadrant. The relevant candidate for the incommensurate $\left(q_1 = q_2 = q_3 = q\right)$ case can be:

$$D^q V(t, e_i(t)) = e_1 + e_2 + e_3 \tag{35}$$

One obtains

$$\begin{aligned} D^q V(t, e_i(t)) = {} & \left[x_3 - y_3 - \alpha\left[\exp(-ax_3 - bx_2) - \exp(-ay_3 - by_2)\right] - u_1\right] + \left[-\beta(x_2 - y_2) + x_3 - y_3 - u_2\right] \\ & + \left[-(x_1 - y_1) - (x_2 - y_2) - \gamma(x_3 - y_3) - u_3\right] \end{aligned} \tag{36}$$

In order to have $D^q V(t, e_i(t))$ as a negative semi-definite function, let's choose the control parameters as follows:

$$\begin{cases} u_1 = x_3 - y_3 - \alpha\left[\exp(-ax_3 - bx_2) - \exp(-ay_3 - by_2)\right] + e_1 \\ u_2 = -\beta(x_2 - y_2) + x_3 - y_3 + e_2 \\ u_3 = -(x_1 - y_1) - (x_2 - y_2) - \gamma(x_3 - y_3) + e_3 \end{cases} \tag{37}$$

Substituting Eqs. (37) in Eqs. (36), yields:

$$D^q V(t, e_i(t)) = -e_1 - e_2 - e_3 < 0 \tag{38}$$

which is negative definite function in the first quadrant.

The parameter λ is a positive constant to be specified by the designer. In the numerical simulations, the parameters of drive system (31) are known as in the previous section such that the system exhibits chaotic behavior and remains chaotic for slight variations of the systems parameter. However, large variation can make the system to switch to periodic or chaotic motions changing qualitatively its dynamics. In this case, the discrepancy between master and slave exponentially increases. We note this gap in this chapter by $e_q(t)$. Without loss of generality, it's assumed that the parameters of the drive and response systems are the same, that is, with no parameter mismatch. Suppose the initial values of systems (31) and (32) are, respectively, to characterize the degree of synchronization, the following error quantity is used: $(x_{10}, y_{10}, z_{10})^T = (0.02, 0.34, 0.2)^T$ and $(x_{20}, y_{20}, z_{20})^T = (0.2, 0.4, 0.5)^T$ and $\lambda = 30$.

The relationship between the states of the drive and response systems under the feedback coupling is depicted in Figure 13.

From these figures, one can conclude that the chaotic oscillations of the drive and response systems are synchronized completely, so that our synchronization objective has been attained.

To characterize the degree of synchronization, the following error quantity is used:

$$e_q(t) = \sqrt{\left(x_1(t) - x_2(t)\right)^2 + \left(y_1(t) - y_2(t)\right)^2 + \left(z_1(t) - z_2(t)\right)^2} \tag{39}$$

As shown in figure 14, it is obvious that $\lim_{t\to\infty} e_q(t) \approx 0$ which implies that synchronization is achieved with very short time **t=8.5s.** The average value is computed $\langle e_q(t)\rangle$ over time.

8.2. Output Feedback Control of Complex Network MCO Fractional-Order System

Let us consider the following problem of an ensemble of identical oscillators, which in the absence of interaction exhibit qualitatively similar dynamics. For different initial conditions the oscillators show different dynamical trajectories, while for identical initial conditions the trajectories coincide. On the other hand, when considering interaction between the oscillators, one may achieve alignment of a certain

Figure 13. (a). $x_1(t) - x_2(t)$; (b). $y_2(t) - y_1(t)$; (c) $z_1(t) - z_2(t)$ depicts the time evolution of the master and the slave systems trajectories superimposed on the same graph for comparison, although these both curves are not distinguishable after a short transient time

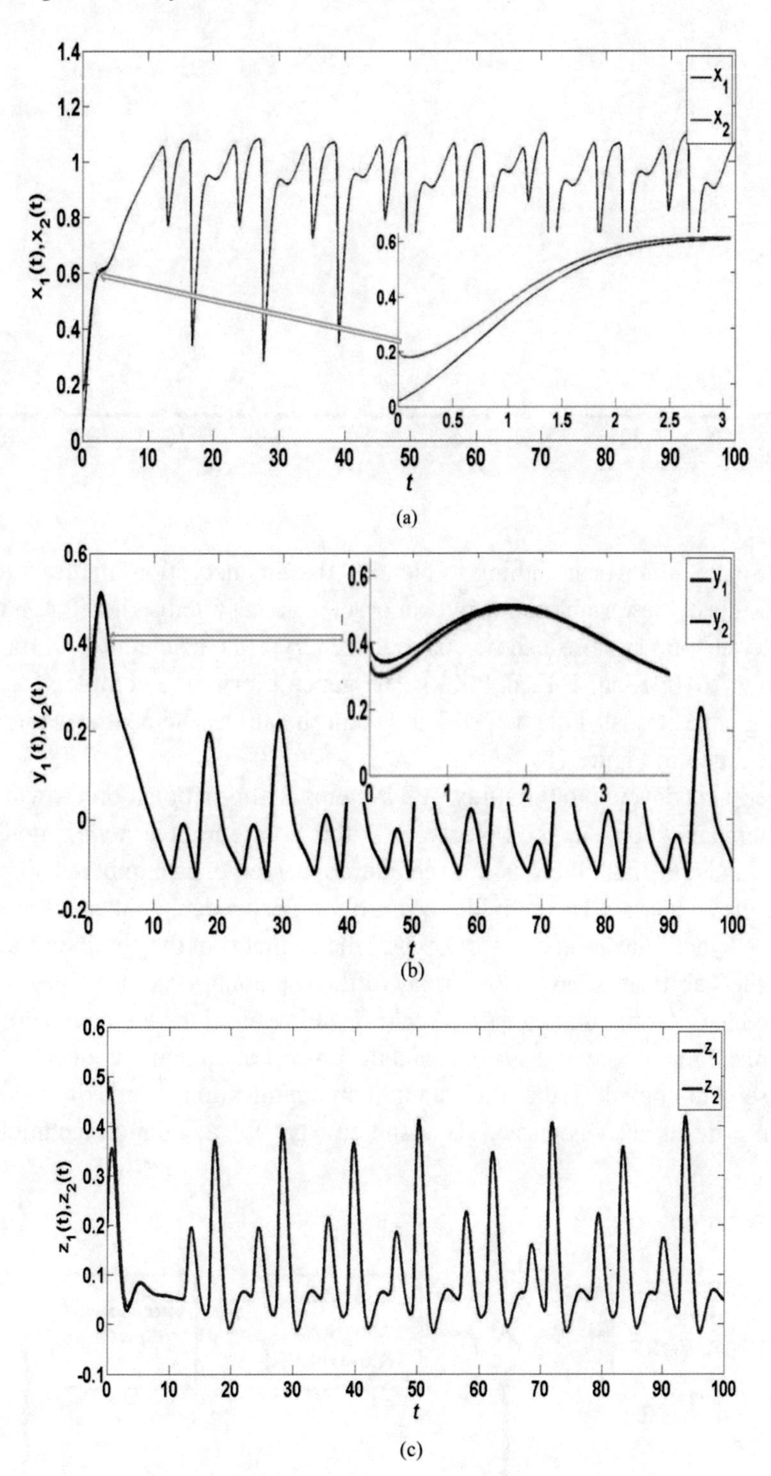

Figure 14. Time series of the error norm dynamics

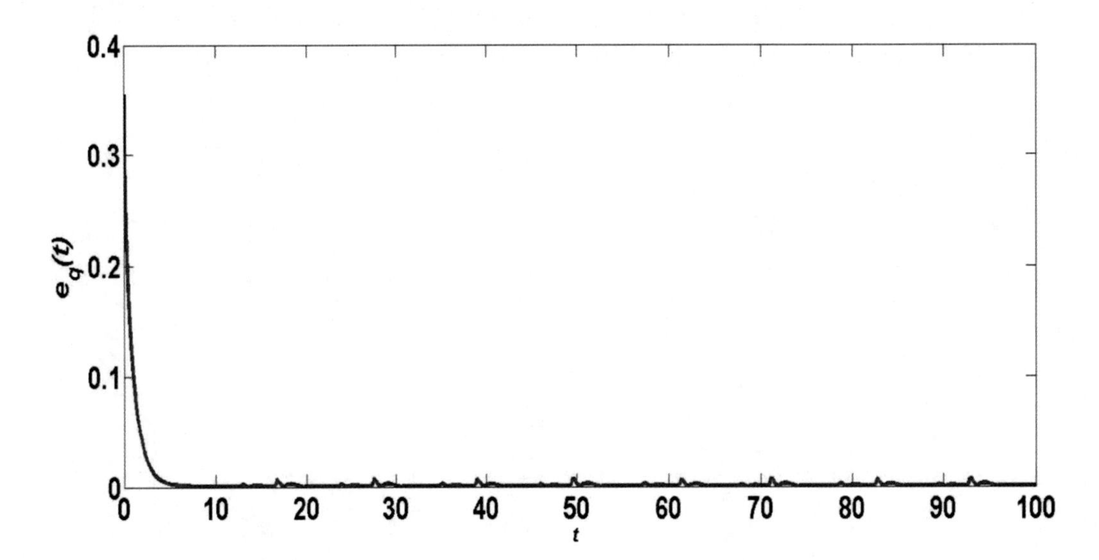

state with all other ones. It is worth nothing to mention that in encryption, the fractional order chaotic systems have more adjustable variables than integer order chaotic systems, therefore it is widely believed that fractional-order chaotic systems can be applied in encryption efficiently and thus enlarge the key space (Tang & Fang, 2010; Kiani-B et al. 2009). The general form of a complex fractional network is proposed consisting of fractional-order MCO. The synchronization scheme that is presented in this Section is roughly illustrated in Figure 15.

That is, this section is devoted to the study of 9 systems with fractional order, which are interacting under a certain interconnection, see the Figure 16. In this configuration, node1, node2 and node3 are the ring oscillators and constitute the relay of the interconnected ones numbered simple as (1,2), (3,4) and (4,5) usually called *embassy*. The individual controls are dependent on the master system and on the network topology. A synchronization error for each of the elements of the complex fractional network is defined, and then the stabilization around the relay of the fractional-order nonlinear dynamical system of the error is tested in order to guarantee the synchronization of all the elements within the network.

Remark. Let's recall that the central systems and the corresponding interconnected are the fractional MCO. This proposed topology describes the standard communication scheme in real world. The use of multiple agents (in patterns such as master-slave and embassy) is a common technique in agent-based

Figure 15. Synchronization scheme

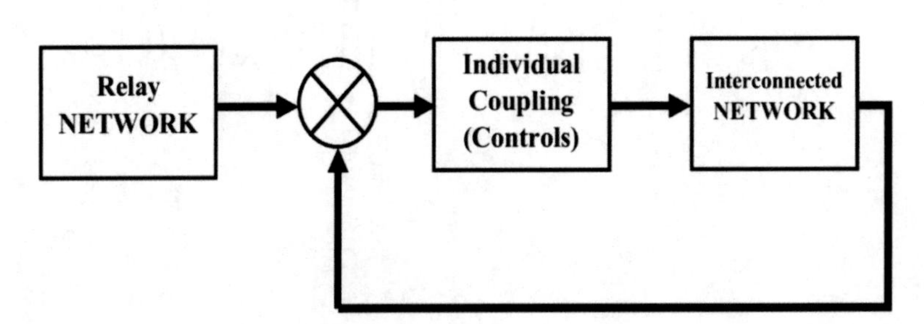

systems. Maintaining coordination and communication between groups of agents, whilst relatively simple in the non-distributed paradigm, cannot impose a significant overhead on the developers of distributed/ mobile agent systems since the MCO are relatively simple in term of cost and power consumption. Security protocols are a must for communication between parties which in this case is ensured by the rich dynamical behavior depicted by the MCO.

With the aim of determining whether CS is behind the role played by the relay system, the case of three interacting MCO is considered with fractional-order oscillators diffusively (systems denoted by 1,2,3) coupled according to the configuration scheme of Figure 16. The generic route to complete synchronization of two integer-order MCO is well known in the literature (Kammogne & Fotsin, 2011). Here, instead, a relay configuration is considered in which oscillators 2 and 3 are identical, whereas the central system (the relay unit) is set to have (one or more) different parameters with respect to them. The coupling is assumed to be unidirectional and instantaneous. It should be noticed that system 1, 2, 3 constitutes the relay for interconnected oscillators systems represented by a small circle (Osc1, Osc2, Osc3).

The objectives of this part can be stated as follow:

1. Established the complete synchronization between oscillators 2 and 3 and the relay unit.
2. Achieved the completed synchronization between the interconnected oscillators (*embassy*). For example the synchronization between *Osc.i* and *Osc.j* must be observed. with $i=1,2,....,6; j=1,2,.....,6.$

The second objective of this work is not deal in the present chapter for the sake to keep in mind the purpose mentioned in the introduction. Nevertheless, the generality is considered as an application of MCO with fractional derivative. The equations of motion of the full system are:

Figure 16. Fractional Complex network consisting of fractional-order MCO

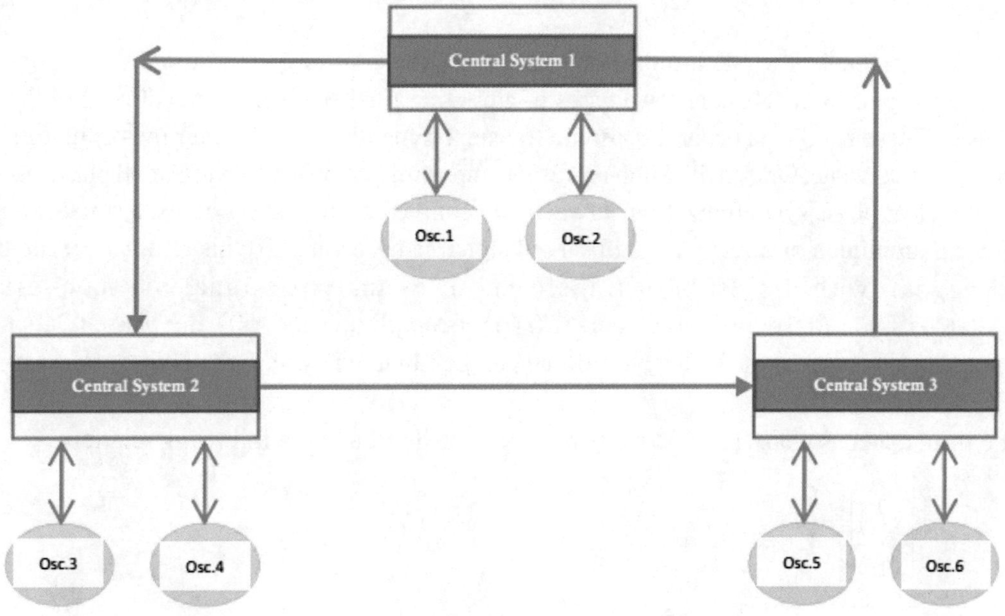

Relay Systems (i=1,2,3).

$$\begin{aligned}
\frac{d^q x_{(i,0)}}{dt^q} &= z_{(i,0)} - a_2 \exp\left(-a_1 z_{(i,0)} - b_1 y_{(i,0)}\right) - k\left(2x_{(i,0)} - y_{(i,1)} - y_{(i,2)}\right) - k\left(x_{(i,0)} - x_{(i-1,0)}\right) \\
\frac{d^q y_{(i,0)}}{dt^q} &= -b_{2i} - b_{2i} y_{(i,0)} + z_{(i,0)} \\
\frac{d^q z_{(i,0)}}{dt^q} &= 1 - x_{(i,0)} - y_{(i,0)} - c z_{(i,0)}
\end{aligned} \tag{40}$$

Note that essentially for the coupling, *i≠0*
Interconnected systems (i=1,2,3)

$$\begin{aligned}
\frac{d^q x_{(i,j)}}{dt^q} &= z_{(i,j)} - a_2 \exp\left(-a_1 z_{(i,j)} - b_1 y_{(i,j)}\right) - k\left(x_{(i,j)} - x_{(i,0)}\right) \\
\frac{d^q y_{(i,j)}}{dt^q} &= -b_{2i} - b_{2i} y_{(i,j)} + z_{(i,j)} \\
\frac{d^q z_{(i,j)}}{dt^q} &= 1 - x_{(i,j)} - y_{(i,j)} - c z_{(i,j)}
\end{aligned} \tag{41}$$

In addition, the synchronization error $< e >_{i,j}$ is defined as

$$\lim_{T\to\infty} \int_0^T \left\| x_{i,0}(t) - x_{i,j}(t) \right\| dt \tag{40}$$

where T is considered as a synchronization time and k the control gain adjusted by the designer to achieved synchronization. There are two types of attracting final states for the evolution of the oscillators' phases. These equilibria occur after some transient dynamics, that is, after the oscillators' phases converge to a final value. One equilibrium represents the complete phase-locking of all phase oscillators. In order to detect phase synchronization between two coupled oscillatory systems, a suitable definition of phase and amplitude of a real valued observed signal is necessary. To this aim, let $s(t)$ be the real-valued signal with its Hilbert transform. The analytic signal is then given by $\psi(t) = s(t) + i\hat{s}(t) = R(t)\exp(i\phi(t))$, where $R(t)$ is its amplitude and $\phi(t)$ the phase (Gabor, 1947). The imaginary counterpart of the analytic signal can be obtained by, e.g. the Hilbert transform of the signal (Sharma et al., 2011).

If the instantaneous phase is $\phi_i(t)$, it can be determined through the following relation

$$\phi_i(t) = \tan^{-1}\left[\frac{\tilde{s}_i(t)}{s_i(t)}\right] \tag{41}$$

Figure 17. Phase synchronization of the relay systems

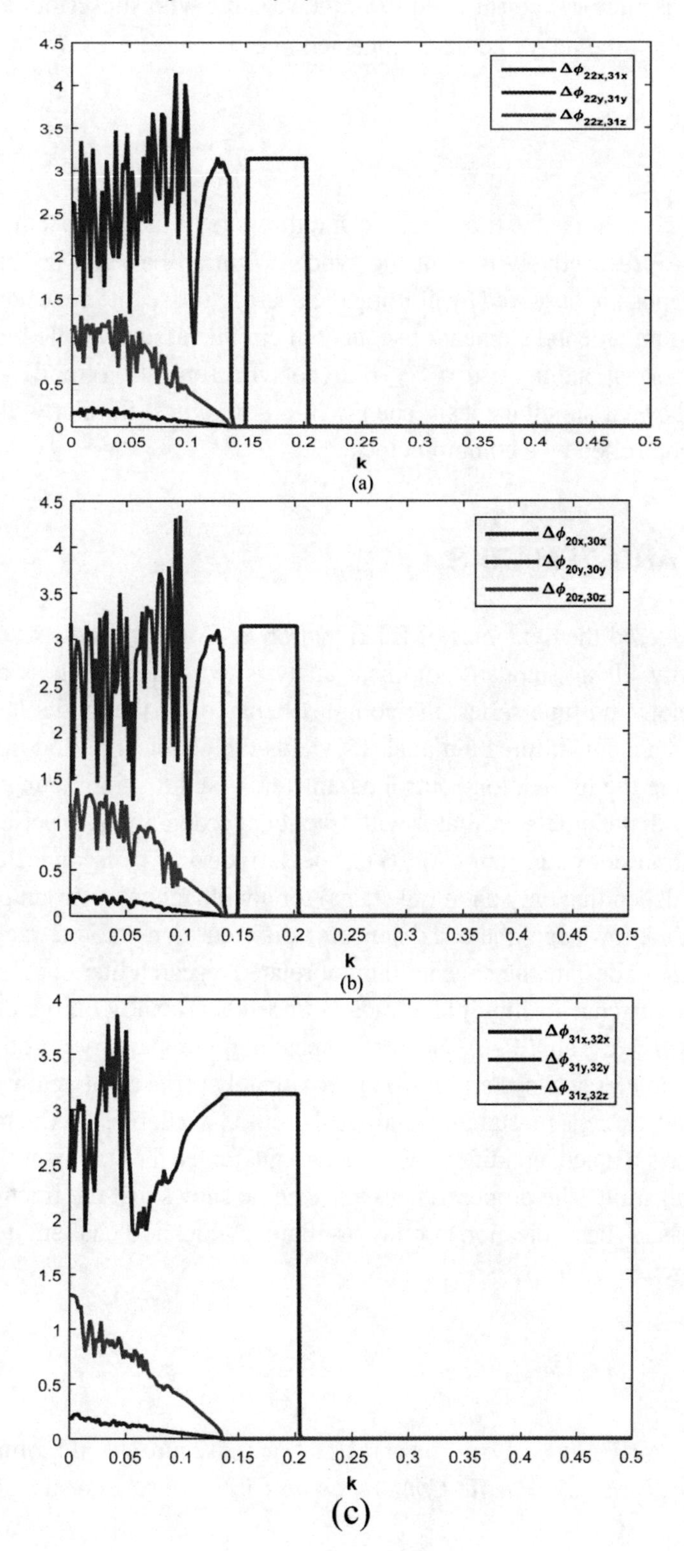

The phase of each oscillator is constructed from the variable with subscript *i* and the average phase difference $\Phi_{i,j}(t)$ between the relay and interconnected ones is:

$$\Delta\phi_{i,j}(t) = \langle|\phi_{i,j}(t) - \phi_{k,n}|\rangle \quad (42)$$

where $\langle\bullet\rangle$ and *(k,n)≠(i,j)* denotes the time average and the state of the all system.

Figure 17 (a)–(b)-(c) respectively present the synchronization between the combinations of users (oscillators). These graphs are observed by plotting the average phase difference over the variation of *k*. Our results presents a fundamental element of sequential circuits ussually called *Flip-flops.* The transition from *bad region* corresponding to $0 < k \leq 0.2$ (no synchronization) to the *good region* for (zone of synchronization) shows a simultaneously change in all variables. Similarly, the timing of all state transitions seems be controlled by a common clock.

9. CONCLUSION AND REMARKS

This chapter has considered the dynamics of fractional order Colpitts oscillator circuit with a smooth exponential nonlinearity. Using standard nonlinear analysis techniques such as bifurcation diagrams, Lyapunov exponent plots and time series, the complex behavior of the model has been characterized in terms of its parameters. The bifurcation analysis yields the classical period-doubling, and periodic windows when adjusting the bifurcation control parameters q and R_d in tiny ranges. As a major result, it is found numerically that Colpitts oscillator with fractional order circuit experiences the unusual and striking feature of multiple coexisting attractors (i.e., coexistence of two disconnected non-static periodic and chaotic attractors depending only on initial states) for a wide range of circuit parameters values. To the best of the author's knowledge, the coexistence of different non-static attractors has not yet been reported in Colpitts circuit despite the huge amount of related research literature. However, it should be pointed out that the occurrence of multiple attractors depends crucially on the choice of nonlinearity as well as parameters (Li & Yao, 2016). Normally speaking, compared with other synchronizations, phase synchronization in classical systems most approximately reflects the real world so attracts much more attention, although there is no suitable analytical method available. On the basis of the Lyapunov stability theorem, some sufficient conditions are given to guarantee the stabilization and then to achieve master-slave synchronization. The proposed network scheme shows that the fractional Colpitts oscillators can undergoes phase synchronization in relay oscillators which is a challenging topic that needs far more attention in future research.

REFERENCES

Ababei, C., & Marculescu, R. (2000). Low-power realizations of secure chaotic communication Schemes. In: *Proceedings of the IEEE Asia-Pacific Conference on Circuits and Systems*, 30–33. 10.1109/APCCAS.2000.913397

Aghababa, M. P. (2012). Finite-time chaos control and synchronization of fractional-order nonautonomous chaotic (hyperchaotic) systems using fractional nonsingular terminal sliding mode technique. *Nonlinear Dynamics*, *69*(1-2), 247–267. doi:10.100711071-011-0261-6

Andronov, A., Vitt, A.A., & Khaikin, S.E. (2011). *Theory of Oscillators.* Dover Publications.

Azar, A. T., Kumar, J., Kumar, V., & Rana, K. P. S. (2017d). Control of a Two Link Planar Electrically-Driven Rigid Robotic Manipulator Using Fractional Order SOFC. *Proceedings of the International Conference on Advanced Intelligent Systems and Informatics 2017, 639*, 47-56.

Azar, A. T., Ouannas, A., & Singh, S. (2017c). Control of New Type of Fractional Chaos Synchronization. *Proceedings of the International Conference on Advanced Intelligent Systems and Informatics 2017, 639*, 47-56.

Azar, A. T., & Vaidyanathan, S. (2015a). *Chaos Modeling and Control Systems Design.* Springer-Verlag.

Azar, A. T., & Vaidyanathan, S. (2015b). Handbook of research on advanced intelligent control engineering and automation. IGI Global. doi:10.4018/978-1-4666-7248-2

Azar, A. T., & Vaidyanathan, S. (2015c). *Computational Intelligence applications in Modeling and Control. Studies in Computational Intelligence* (Vol. 575). Springer-Verlag.

Azar, A. T., & Vaidyanathan, S. (2016). *Advances in Chaos Theory and Intelligent Control. Studies in Fuzziness and Soft Computing* (Vol. 337). Springer-Verlag. doi:10.1007/978-3-319-30340-6

Azar, A. T., Vaidyanathan, S., & Ouannas, A. (2017a). *Fractional Order Control and Synchronization of Chaotic Systems. Studies in Computational Intelligence* (Vol. 688). Springer-Verlag. doi:10.1007/978-3-319-50249-6

Azar, A.T., Volos, C., Gerodimos, N.A., Tombras, G.S., Pham, V.T., Radwan, A.G., ... Munoz-Pacheco, J.M. (2017b). A novel chaotic system without equilibrium: Dynamics, synchronization and circuit realization. *Complexity.* doi:10.1155/2017/7871467

Azar, A. T., & Zhu, Q. (2015). *Advances and Applications in Sliding Mode Control systems. Studies in Computational Intelligence* (Vol. 576). Springer-Verlag.

Bagley, R. L., & Calico, R. A. (1991). Fractional order state equations for the control of viscoelastically damped structures. *Journal of Guidance, Control, and Dynamics*, *14*(2), 304–311. doi:10.2514/3.20641

Bao, H., & Cao, J. (2015). Projective synchronization of fractional-order memristor-based neural networks. *Neural Networks*, *63*, 1–9. doi:10.1016/j.neunet.2014.10.007 PMID:25463390

Behagi. (1992). Piece-wise Linear Modeling of Solid-state Varactor-tuned Microwave Oscillators. *Proceedings of the IEEE Frequency Control Symposium*, 415–519.

Boulkroune, A., Bouzeriba, A., Bouden, T., & Azar, A. T. (2016a). Fuzzy Adaptive Synchronization of Uncertain Fractional-order Chaotic Systems. In A. T. Azar & S. Vaidyanathan (Eds.), *Advances in Chaos Theory and Intelligent Control. Studies in Fuzziness and Soft Computing* (Vol. 337). Springer-Verlag. doi:10.1007/978-3-319-30340-6_28

Boulkroune, A., Hamel, S., & Azar, A. T. (2016b). *Fuzzy control-based function synchronization of unknown chaotic systems with dead-zone input. Advances in Chaos Theory and Intelligent Control. Studies in Fuzziness and Soft Computing* (Vol. 337). Springer-Verlag.

Deng, W. H., & Li, C. P. (2005). Synchronization of chaotic fractional Chen system. *Journal of the Physical Society of Japan, 74*(6), 1645–1648. doi:10.1143/JPSJ.74.1645

Ezzat, M. A., & El-Karamany, A. S. (2012). Fractional thermoelectric viscoelastic materials. *Journal of Applied Polymer Science, 124*(3), 2187–2199. doi:10.1002/app.35243

Feudel, U. (2008). Complex dynamics in multistable systems. *International Journal of Bifurcation and Chaos in Applied Sciences and Engineering, 18*(06), 1607–1626. doi:10.1142/S0218127408021233

Gabor, D. (1947). Theory of Communication. *Journal of the Institution of Electrical Engineers, 94*(73), 429–441.

Ge, Z. M., & Li, S. Y. (2011). Chaos generalized synchronization of new Mathieu-VAN der POL systems with new Dufng-VAN der POL systems as functional system by GYC partial region stability theory. *Applied Mathematical Modelling, 35*(11), 5245–5264. doi:10.1016/j.apm.2011.03.022

Ge, Z. M., & Ou, C. Y. (2007). Chaos in a fractional order modified Duffing system. *Chaos, Solitons, and Fractals, 34*(2), 262–291. doi:10.1016/j.chaos.2005.11.059

Gorenflo, R., & Mainardi, F. (1997). Fractional calculus: Integral and differential equations of fractional order. In A. Carpinteri & F. Mainardi (Eds.), *Fractals and fractional calculus in continuum mechanics*. Springer. doi:10.1007/978-3-7091-2664-6_6

Grassi, G., Ouannas, A., Azar, A. T., Radwan, A. G., Volos, C., Pham, V. T., . . . Stouboulos, I. N. (2017). *Chaos Synchronisation Of Continuous Systems Via Scalar Signal*. The 6th International Conference on Modern Circuits and Systems Technologies (MOCAST), Thessaloniki, Greece. 10.1109/MOCAST.2017.7937629

Grigorenko, I., & Grigorenko, E. (2003). Chaotic dynamics of the fractional Lorenz system. *Physical Review Letters, 91*(3), 034101. doi:10.1103/PhysRevLett.91.034101 PMID:12906418

Hartley, T. T., Lorenzo, C. F., & Killory, Q. H. (1995). Chaos in a fractional order Chua's system. *IEEE Trans. CAS-I, 42*(8), 485–490. doi:10.1109/81.404062

Herrmann, R. (2011). *Fractional calculus* (1st ed.). World Scientific publishing Co. doi:10.1142/8072

Ichise, M., Nagayanagi, Y., & Kojima, T. (1971). An analog simulation of non-integer order transfer functions for analysis of electrode process. *Journal of Electroanalytical Chemistry and Interfacial Electrochemistry, 33*(2), 253–265. doi:10.1016/S0022-0728(71)80115-8

Jakubowska, A., & Szymczak, M. (2016). Electronic realizations of fractional-order elements: II. Simulation studies. Poznan University of Technology Academic Journals. *Electrical Engineering*, (85): 149–159.

Kammogne, S. T., & Fotsin, H. B. (2011). Synchronization of modified Colpitts oscillators with structural perturbations. *Physica Scripta, 83*(6), 065011. doi:10.1088/0031-8949/83/06/065011

Kammogne, S. T., Fotsin, H. B., Kontchou, M., & Louodop, P. (2013). A robust observer design for passivity-based synchronization of uncertain modifed Colpitts oscillators and circuit simulation. *Asian Journal of Science and Technology*, *5*(1), 29–41.

Kengne, J., Negou, A. N., & Tchiotsop, D. (2017). Antimonotonicity, chaos and multiple attractors in a novel autonomous memristor-based jerk circuit. *Nonlinear Dynamics*, *88*(4), 2589–2608. doi:10.100711071-017-3397-1

Kengne, J., Njitacke, T., & Fotsin, H. B. (2016b). Coexistence of multiple attractors and crisis route to chaos in autonomous third order Duffing-Holmes type chaotic oscillators. *Communications in Nonlinear Science and Numerical Simulation*, *36*, 29–44. doi:10.1016/j.cnsns.2015.11.009

Kengne, J., Njitacke, Z. T., & Fotsin, H. B. (2016a). Dynamical analysis of a simple autonomous jerk system with multiple attractors. *Nonlinear Dynamics*, *83*(1-2), 751–765. doi:10.100711071-015-2364-y

Kennedy, M. P. (1994). Chaos in the Colpitts Oscillator. *Fundamental Theory and Applications*, *41*(11), 771–778.

Kiani-B, A., Fallahi, K., Pariz, N., & Leung, H. (2009). A chaotic secure communication scheme using fractional chaotic systems based on an extended fractional Kalman filter. *Commun. Nonlinear Sci.*, *14*(3), 863–879. doi:10.1016/j.cnsns.2007.11.011

Kilbas, A. A., Srivastava, H. M., & Trujillo, J. J. (2006). Theory and applications of fractional differential equations, vol. 204. North-Holland mathematics studies. Elsevier.

Lamamra, K., Azar, A. T., & Ben Salah, C. (2017). *Chaotic system modelling using a neural network with optimized structure. Studies in Computational Intelligence* (Vol. 688). Springer-Verlag.

Laskin, N. (2000). Fractional market dynamics. *Physica A*, *2875*(3), 482–492. doi:10.1016/S0378-4371(00)00387-3

Li, C., Chen, A & Ye, J. (2011). Numerical approaches to fractional calculus and fractional ordinary differential equation. *J. Comput. Phys.*, *230*(9), 3352–3368. doi:.2011.01.03010.1016/j.jcp

Li, C., Gong, Z., Qian, D., & Chen, Y. (2010). On the bound of the Lyapunov exponents for the fractional differential systems. *Chaos (Woodbury, N.Y.)*, *20*(1), 013127. doi:10.1063/1.3314277 PMID:20370282

Li, C. P., & Peng, G. J. (2004). Chaos in Chen's system with a fractional order. *Chaos Solit. Frac.*, *22*(2), 443–450.

Li, F., & Yao, C. (2016). The infinite-scroll attractor and energy transition in chaotic circuit. *Nonlinear Dynamics*, *84*(4), 2305–2315. doi:10.100711071-016-2646-z

Li, H., Liao, X., & Luo, M. (2012). A novel non-equilibrium fractional-order chaotic system and its complete synchronization by circuit implementation. *Nonlinear Dynamics*, *68*(1-2), 137–149. doi:10.100711071-011-0210-4

Li, Y., Chen, Y. Q., Podlubny, I., & Cao, Y. (2008). Mittag-Leffler stability of fractional order nonlinear dynamic system. *Automatica*, *45*(8), 1965–1969. doi:10.1016/j.automatica.2009.04.003

Lindberg, E. (2004). Is the Quadrature Oscillator a Multivibrator? *IEEE Circuits & Devices Magazine*, *20*(6), 23–28. doi:10.1109/MCD.2004.1364772

Machado, J. T., Kiryakova, V., & Mainardi, F. (2011). Recent history of fractional calculus. *Communications in Nonlinear Science and Numerical Simulation*, *16*(3), 1140–1153. doi:10.1016/j.cnsns.2010.05.027

Matignon, D. (1996). Stability results of fractional differential equations with applications to control processing. In *IMACS* (pp. 963–968). Lille, France: IEEE–SMC.

Matignon, D. (1998). Stability properties for generalized fractional differential systems. Proc. of Fractional Differential Systems, 5, 145-158. doi:10.1051/proc:1998004

Meghni, B., Dib, D., & Azar, A. T. (2017c). A Second-order sliding mode and fuzzy logic control to Optimal Energy Management in PMSG Wind Turbine with Battery Storage. *Neural Computing & Applications*, *28*(6), 1417–1434. doi:10.100700521-015-2161-z

Meghni, B., Dib, D., Azar, A. T., Ghoudelbourk, S., & Saadoun, A. (2017a). *Robust Adaptive Supervisory Fractional order Controller For optimal Energy Management in Wind Turbine with Battery Storage. Studies in Computational Intelligence* (Vol. 688). Springer-Verlag.

Meghni, B., Dib, D., Azar, A. T., & Saadoun, A. (2017b). *Effective Supervisory Controller to Extend Optimal Energy Management in Hybrid Wind Turbine under Energy and Reliability Constraints. International Journal of Dynamics and Control*. Springer. doi:10.100740435-016-0296-0

Miller, K. S., & Ross, B. (1993). *Introduction to the Fractional Calculus and Fractional Differential Equations*. New York: John Wiley.

Ouannas, A., Azar, A. T., & Abu-Saris, R. (2016a). A new type of hybrid synchronization between arbitrary hyperchaotic maps. *International Journal of Machine Learning and Cybernetics*. doi:10.100713042-016-0566-3

Ouannas, A., Azar, A. T., & Radwan, A. G. (2016b). *On Inverse Problem of Generalized Synchronization Between Different Dimensional Integer-Order and Fractional-Order Chaotic Systems*. The 28th International Conference on Microelectronics, Cairo, Egypt. 10.1109/ICM.2016.7847942

Ouannas, A., Azar, A. T., & Vaidyanathan, S. (2017f). On A Simple Approach for Q-S Synchronization of Chaotic Dynamical Systems in Continuous-Time. *Int. J. Computing Science and Mathematics*, *8*(1), 20–27.

Ouannas, A., Azar, A. T., & Vaidyanathan, S. (2017g). New Hybrid Synchronization Schemes Based on Coexistence of Various Types of Synchronization Between Master-Slave Hyperchaotic Systems. *International Journal of Computer Applications in Technology*, *55*(2), 112–120. doi:10.1504/IJCAT.2017.082868

Ouannas, A., Azar, A. T., & Vaidyanathan, S. (2017i). A Robust Method for New Fractional Hybrid Chaos Synchronization. *Mathematical Methods in the Applied Sciences*, *40*(5), 1804–1812. doi:10.1002/mma.4099

Ouannas, A., Azar, A. T., & Ziar, T. (2017h). *On Inverse Full State Hybrid Function Projective Synchronization for Continuous-time Chaotic Dynamical Systems with Arbitrary Dimensions*. Differential Equations and Dynamical Systems. doi:10.100712591-017-0362-x

Ouannas, A., Azar, A. T., Ziar, T., & Radwan, A. G. (2017d). *Study On Coexistence of Different Types of Synchronization Between Different dimensional Fractional Chaotic Systems. Studies in Computational Intelligence* (Vol. 688). Springer-Verlag.

Ouannas, A., Azar, A. T., Ziar, T., & Radwan, A. G. (2017e). *Generalized Synchronization of Different Dimensional Integer-order and Fractional Order Chaotic Systems. Studies in Computational Intelligence* (Vol. 688). Springer-Verlag.

Ouannas, A., Azar, A. T., Ziar, T., & Vaidyanathan, S. (2017a). *On New Fractional Inverse Matrix Projective Synchronization Schemes. Studies in Computational Intelligence* (Vol. 688). Springer-Verlag.

Ouannas, A., Azar, A. T., Ziar, T., & Vaidyanathan, S. (2017b). *Fractional Inverse Generalized Chaos Synchronization Between Different Dimensional Systems. Studies in Computational Intelligence* (Vol. 688). Springer-Verlag.

Ouannas, A., Azar, A. T., Ziar, T., & Vaidyanathan, S. (2017c). *A New Method To Synchronize Fractional Chaotic Systems With Different Dimensions. Studies in Computational Intelligence* (Vol. 688). Springer-Verlag.

Ouannas, A., Grassi, G., Azar, A. T., Radwan, A. G., Volos, C., Pham, V. T., . . . Stouboulos, I. N. (2017j). *Dead-Beat Synchronization Control in Discrete-Time Chaotic Systems.* The 6th International Conference on Modern Circuits and Systems Technologies (MOCAST), Thessaloniki, Greece. 10.1109/MOCAST.2017.7937628

Oustaloup, A., Sabatier, J., Lanusse, P., Malti, R., Melchior, P., Moreau, X., & Moze, M. (2008). An overview of the CRONE approach in system analysis, modeling and identification, observation and control. *Proc. of the 17th World Congress IFAC*, 14254–14265. 10.3182/20080706-5-KR-1001.02416

Pecora, L. M., & Carroll, T. L. (1990). Synchronization in chaotic systems. *Physical Review Letters*, *64*(8), 821–824. doi:10.1103/PhysRevLett.64.821 PMID:10042089

Pham, V. T., Vaidyanathan, S., Volos, C. K., Azar, A. T., Hoang, T. M., & Yem, V. V. (2017a). A Three-Dimensional No-equilibrium chaotic system: Analysis, synchronization and its fractional order form. Studies in Computational Intelligence, 688, 449-470.

Pyragas, K. (1996). Weak and strong synchronization of chaos. *Physical Review E: Statistical Physics, Plasmas, Fluids, and Related Interdisciplinary Topics*, *54*(5), R4508–R4511. doi:10.1103/PhysRevE.54.R4508 PMID:9965792

Razminia, A., Majd, V. J., & Baleanu, D. (2011). Chaotic incommensurate fractional order Rössler system: Active control and synchronization. *Advances in Difference Equations*, *15*. doi:10.1186/1687-1847-2011-15

Rhea, R. (2004). A new class of oscillators. *IEEE Microwave Magazine*, *5*(2), 72–83. doi:10.1109/MMW.2004.1306839

Rosenblum, M. G., Pikovsky, A. S., & Kurths, J. (1996). Phase synchronization of chaotic oscillators. *Physical Review Letters*, *76*(11), 1804–1807. doi:10.1103/PhysRevLett.76.1804 PMID:10060525

Rosenblum, M. G., Pikovsky, A. S., & Kurths, J. (1997). Phase synchronization in driven and coupled chaotic oscillators. *IEEE Transactions on circuits and Systems I. Fundamental Theory and Applications*, *44*(10), 874–881.

Samko, S. G., Klibas, A. A., & Marichev, O. I. (1993). *Fractional integrals and derivatives: theory and applications*. Gordan and Breach.

Sarafian, G., & Kaplan, B.-Z. (1993). A New approach to the modeling of the dynamics of RF VCOs and Some of Its Practical Implications. *IEEE Transactions on Circuits and Systems–Fundamental Theory and Applications*, *40*(12), 895–901. doi:10.1109/81.269030

Sharma, A., Shrimali, M., Prasad, A., Ramaswamy, R., & Feudel, U. (2011). Phase-flip transition in relay-coupled nonlinear oscillators. *Physical Review. E*, *84*(016226), 1–5. PMID:21867292

Singh, S., Azar, A. T., Ouannas, A., Zhu, Q., Zhang, W., & Na, J. (2017). *Sliding Mode Control Technique for Multi-switching Synchronization of Chaotic Systems. 9th International Conference on Modelling, Identification and Control (ICMIC 2017)*, Kunming, China.

Soliman, N. S., Said, L. A., Azar, A. T., Madian, A. H., Radwan, A. G., & Ouannas, A. (2017). *Fractional Controllable Multi-Scroll V-Shape Attractor with Parameters Effect*. The 6th International Conference on Modern Circuits and Systems Technologies (MOCAST), Thessaloniki, Greece.

Sun, H., Abdelwahab, A., & Onaral, B. (1984). Linear approximation of transfer function with a pole of fractional power. *IEEE Transactions on Automatic Control*, *29*(5), 441–444. doi:10.1109/TAC.1984.1103551

Tamás, T. (2015). The joy of transient chaos. *Chaos*, *25*(2015). doi: 1728710.1063/1.49

Tang, Y., & Fang, J.-A. (2010). Synchronization of n-coupled fractional order chaotic systems with ring connection. *Commun. Nonlinear Sci.*, *15*(2), 401–412. doi:10.1016/j.cnsns.2009.03.024

Tavazoei, M. S., & Haeri, M. (2007). Unreliability of frequency-domain approximation in recognizing chaos in fractional-order systems. *IET Signal Processing*, *1*(4), 171–181. doi:10.1049/iet-spr:20070053

Tavazoei, M. S., & Haeri, M. (2008). Limitations of frequency domain approximation for detecting chaos in fractional order systems. *Nonlinear Analysis*, *69*(4), 1299–1320. doi:10.1016/j.na.2007.06.030

Tolba, M. F., AbdelAty, A. M., Soliman, N. S., Said, L. A., Madian, A. H., Azar, A. T., & Radwan, A. G. (2017). FPGA implementation of two fractional order chaotic systems. *International Journal of Electronics and Communications*, *28*, 162–172. doi:10.1016/j.aeue.2017.04.028

Vaidyanathan, S., & Azar, A. T. (2015a). Anti-Synchronization of Identical Chaotic Systems using Sliding Mode Control and an Application to Vaidyanathan-Madhavan Chaotic Systems. In Advances and Applications in Sliding Mode Control systems. Springer-Verlag GmbH Berlin/Heidelberg. doi:10.1007/978-3-319-11173-5_19

Vaidyanathan, S., & Azar, A. T. (2015b). Analysis, Control and Synchronization of a nine-term 3-D novel chaotic system. In Chaos Modeling and Control Systems Design. Springer-Verlag GmbH Berlin/Heidelberg. DOI doi:10.1007/978-3-319-13132-0_1

Vaidyanathan, S., & Azar, A. T. (2015b). Hybrid Synchronization of Identical Chaotic Systems using Sliding Mode Control and an Application to Vaidyanathan Chaotic Systems. In Advances and Applications in Sliding Mode Control systems. Springer-Verlag GmbH Berlin/Heidelberg. doi:10.1007/978-3-319-11173-5_20

Vaidyanathan, S., & Azar, A. T. (2015c). Analysis, Control and Synchronization of a Nine-Term 3-D Novel Chaotic System. In Chaos Modeling and Control Systems Design. Springer-Verlag GmbH Berlin/Heidelberg. DOI doi:10.1007/978-3-319-13132-0_1

Vaidyanathan, S., & Azar, A. T. (2015d). Analysis and Control of a 4-D Novel Hyperchaotic System. In Chaos Modeling and Control Systems Design. Springer-Verlag GmbH Berlin/Heidelberg. DOI doi:10.1007/978-3-319-13132-0_2

Vaidyanathan, S., & Azar, A. T. (2016a). *Dynamic Analysis, Adaptive Feedback Control and Synchronization of an Eight-Term 3-D Novel Chaotic System with Three Quadratic Nonlinearities. Studies in Fuzziness and Soft Computing* (Vol. 337). Springer-Verlag.

Vaidyanathan, S., & Azar, A. T. (2016b). *Qualitative Study and Adaptive Control of a Novel 4-D Hyperchaotic System with Three Quadratic Nonlinearities. Studies in Fuzziness and Soft Computing* (Vol. 337). Springer-Verlag.

Vaidyanathan, S., & Azar, A. T. (2016c). *A Novel 4-D Four-Wing Chaotic System with Four Quadratic Nonlinearities and its Synchronization via Adaptive Control Method. Advances in Chaos Theory and Intelligent Control. Studies in Fuzziness and Soft Computing* (Vol. 337). Springer-Verlag.

Vaidyanathan, S., & Azar, A. T. (2016d). *Adaptive Control and Synchronization of Halvorsen Circulant Chaotic Systems. Advances in Chaos Theory and Intelligent Control. Studies in Fuzziness and Soft Computing* (Vol. 337). Springer-Verlag.

Vaidyanathan, S., & Azar, A. T. (2016e). *Adaptive Backstepping Control and Synchronization of a Novel 3-D Jerk System with an Exponential Nonlinearity. Advances in Chaos Theory and Intelligent Control. Studies in Fuzziness and Soft Computing* (Vol. 337). Springer-Verlag.

Vaidyanathan, S., & Azar, A. T. (2016f). *Generalized Projective Synchronization of a Novel Hyperchaotic Four-Wing System via Adaptive Control Method. Advances in Chaos Theory and Intelligent Control. Studies in Fuzziness and Soft Computing* (Vol. 337). Springer-Verlag.

Vaidyanathan, S., Azar, A. T., & Ouannas, A. (2017a). *An Eight-Term 3-D Novel Chaotic System with Three Quadratic Nonlinearities, its Adaptive Feedback Control and Synchronization. Studies in Computational Intelligence* (Vol. 688). Springer-Verlag.

Vaidyanathan, S., Azar, A. T., & Ouannas, A. (2017c). *Hyperchaos and Adaptive Control of a Novel Hyperchaotic System with Two Quadratic Nonlinearities. Studies in Computational Intelligence* (Vol. 688). Springer-Verlag.

Vaidyanathan, S., Idowu, B. A., & Azar, A. T. (2015c). Backstepping Controller Design for the Global Chaos Synchronization of Sprott's Jerk Systems. In Chaos Modeling and Control Systems Design. Springer-Verlag GmbH Berlin/Heidelberg. doi:10.1007/978-3-319-13132-0_3

Vaidyanathan, S., Sampath, S., & Azar, A. T. (2015a). Global chaos synchronization of identical chaotic systems via novel sliding mode control method and its application to Zhu system. *International Journal of Modelling Identification and Control, 23*(1), 92–100. doi:10.1504/IJMIC.2015.067495

Vaidyanathan, S., Zhu, Q., & Azar, A. T. (2017b). *Adaptive Control of a Novel Nonlinear Double Convection Chaotic System. Studies in Computational Intelligence* (Vol. 688). Springer-Verlag.

Wang, C., & Su, J. P. (2004). A new adaptive variable structure control for chaotic synchronization and secure communication. *Chaos, Solitons, and Fractals, 20*(5), 967–977. doi:10.1016/j.chaos.2003.10.026

Wang, Z., Volos, C., Kingni, S.T., Azar, A.T., & Pham, V.T. (2017). Four-wing attractors in a novel chaotic system with hyperbolic sine nonlinearity. *Optik - International Journal for Light and Electron Optics, 131*(2017), 1071-1078.

Wu, H., Wang, L., Wang, Y., Niu, P., & Fang, B. (2016). Global Mittag-Leffler projective synchronization for fractional-order neural networks: An LMI-based approach. *Advances in Difference Equations, 2016*(1), 132. doi:10.118613662-016-0857-8

Yang, T., Jian-an, F., & Qingying, M. (2009). On the exponential synchronization of stochastic jumping chaotic neural networks with mixed delays and sector-bounded non-linearities. *Neurocomputing, 72*(7–9), 1694–1701.

Yu, J., Hu, C., Jiang, H., & Fan, X. (2014). Projective synchronization for fractional neural networks. *Neural Networks, 49*, 87–95. doi:10.1016/j.neunet.2013.10.002 PMID:24184824

Zhu, Q., & Azar, A. T. (2015). *Complex system modelling and control through intelligent soft computations. Studies in Fuzziness and Soft Computing* (Vol. 319). Springer-Verlag.

Zhuxiang, D., Tao, L., & Yu, W. (2016). *Adaptive synchronization of the fractional order chaotic system based on passive control. 2016 Chinese Control and Decision Conference (CCDC)*, Yinchuan, China. 10.1109/CCDC.2016.7531689

Chapter 12
Analysis and Control of a Dynamical Model for HIV Infection With One or Two Inputs

Lazaros Moysis
Aristotle University of Thessaloniki, Greece

Ioannis Kafetzis
Aristotle University of Thessaloniki, Greece

Marios Politis
General Hospital of Thessaloniki "G. Papanikolaou", Greece

ABSTRACT

A dynamical model that describes the interaction between the HIV virus and the human immune system is presented. This model is used to investigate the effect of antiretroviral therapy, consisting of RTI and PI drugs, along with the result of undesired treatment interruption. Furthermore, the effect of both drugs can be combined into a single parameter that further simplifies the model into a single input system. The value of the drug inputs can be adjusted so that the system has the desired equilibrium. Drug administration can also be adjusted by a feedback control law, which although it linearizes the system, may have issues in its implementation. Furthermore, the system is linearized around the equilibrium, leading to a system of linear differential equations of first order that can be integrated into courses of control systems engineering, linear and nonlinear systems in higher education.

1. INTRODUCTION

The infection from the human immunodeficiency virus constitutes a global pandemic. According to the recent report of the Joint United Nations Programme on HIV/AIDS (UNAIDS, 2014), from its first occurrence until today, more than 78 million people have been infected with HIV and 39 million have died from causes related to HIV/AIDS. By the end of 2014, 36.99 million people were living with HIV,

DOI: 10.4018/978-1-5225-4077-9.ch012

of which 3.2 million are children, 2.1 million are young adults and 4.2 million are over 50 years old. Around 70% of HIV positive persons live in regions of sub-Saharan Africa.

The number of people being infected with HIV is decreasing in most countries. In 2015 there was an accounting of 2.1 million new HIV infections, a number that is 38% lower than the 3.4 million infections reported in 2001. There is also a steady decrease in the number of deaths from AIDS. In 2013 for example, 1 million deaths from AIDS have been reported, which corresponds to a 35% decrease compared with 2005.

Results regarding antiretroviral therapy are positive and reflect the steps forward that have been taken in the last years. The number of persons with no access to therapy in 2006 was as high as 90%, while in 2013 they have been decreased to 63%. In 2015, the number of people with access to therapy was 15.8 million, while today they are about 17 million, which is 2 million higher than the aim that the United Nations had set for 2015.

An important part in the epidemiological analysis of HIV infection is the high risk groups. By that, we refer to population groups where the infection occurs with a higher frequency than that of the general population. These groups have a higher infection risk all around the globe. More specifically, men who have sex with men are 19 times more likely to be infected with HIV. Injecting drug users have 28 times higher likelihood than the general population. Around 12.7 million injecting drug users are reported worldwide, of which 13% are HIV positive. Another risk group is the one of sex industry workers, with 12 times higher likelihood than the general population. In addition, transgender women are 49 times more likely to live with the HIV virus than other adults of the same age.

Specifically, in Greece, according to the recent HIV/AIDS surveillance report on October of 2015 (H.C.D.C.P., 2015), the Hellenic Center For Disease Control & Prevention (H.C.D.C.P.) has so far reported 15.109 positive HIV infections. Of these, 3.782 have already developed AIDS and around 7.700 are subject to antiretroviral therapy (ART). The number of deaths resulting from the infection amounts to 2.562. According to the H.C.D.C.P. 2014 report (H.C.D.C.P., 2014), the largest portion of HIV cases has been diagnosed in men who had sex with men (46.2%), followed by the categories of heterosexual sexual contact (21.3%) and injecting drug users (10.8%).

More specifically, during the period of 2011-2013, there was a big rise in the number of cases regarding injecting drug users. This rise, that amounted in 2012 to 9.6 new infections per 100000 people is strongly contributed to the economic crisis in Greece, and is a testament to the key part that social (homelessness, imprisonment) and economic factors (austerity) play in the disease transmission in high risk groups (Hatzakis et al. 2015; Tsang et al. 2015). The role that Big Events, such as the economic crisis, play in the creation of hazardous environments that promote infectious diseases like HIV by causing economic instability, population displacement, inter-communal violence, drug consumption and youth alienation where investigated in (Nikolopoulos et al. 2015).

This HIV outbreak was followed by a steady decrease during the last two years (2014-2015) with around 6.2 infections per 100000 people. This was possibly the result of various prevention and awareness programs that were implemented, focusing on high risk groups (Nikolopoulos et al. 2016; Nikolopoulos & Fotiou, 2015; Sypsa et al. 2017). Yet, as the Office for HIV and Sexually Transmitted Diseases emphasizes, although the last data on the decrease infections are positive, they should not be considered comforting. There must be constant actions to raise the awareness of both the high risk groups and the general population.

Motivated by similar and even more alarming statistics in South Africa, the University of Pretoria, being aware of the fact that the student population generally falls into the high risk groups, mainly due to a lack of awareness, decided to organize an action to inform their students about the problem. The department of Electrical, Electronic and Computer Engineering, the department of Telematic Learning and Education Innovation and the Center for the Study of AIDS came together and developed a CD (Craig & Xia, 2005; Craig et al. 2005), with the aim of presenting a model for the HIV infection from a control theory perspective. Their aim was to present the problem through a mathematical model that would introduce the students to the field of control systems engineering, motivating them at the same time to learn more about this sensitive subject.

Based on this innovative idea by the University of Pretoria, we propose an analytical description of the dynamic model for HIV infection, with the purpose of fulfilling two different objectives. First, to present a detailed control engineering problem that can be implemented in a vast variety of undergraduate courses in the field of dynamical systems, thus making the syllabus much more interesting through the perspective of real life applications. This study, as will be shown later, is subject to extensive research (Barão & Lemos, 2007; Barman & Mukhopadhyay, 2015; Callaway & Perelson, 2002; Department of Pathology, 2012; Gonçalves & Kamdem, 2016; Ho & Ling, 2010; Jeffrey et al. 2002, 2003; Kramer, 1999; Mhawej et al. 2010; Mhawej et al. 2009; Moysis et al. 2016; Perelson & Nelson, 1999; Perelson & Ribeiro, 2013; Radisavljevic-Gajic, 2009; Rivadeneira & Moog, 2012; Rivadeneira et al. 2014; SMART study group, 2006; Xia, 2007). Secondly, raising the awareness among students on the subject should be a natural consequence of taking such a subject.

The rest of this work is outlined as follows. In section 2, a nonlinear model for the HIV infection consisting of three differential equations is presented and explained. In Section 3, the influence of two types of drugs is described. The two drugs can also be combined two a single parameter to obtain a system with only one input. In addition, a feedback control method to linearize the system is given. In Section 4, a method to compute a linearized state space model for the system around it equilibrium is given. In Section 5 a discussion is given based on the simulation results and Section 6 concludes the paper. Each section is accompanied by model simulations.

2. A DYNAMIC MODEL FOR HIV INFECTION

The *Human Immunodeficiency Virus (HIV)* acts by attacking the immune system, causing its progressive failure over time and its collapse after years (when no treatment is administered). The virus can be transmitted mainly through sexual intercourse without protection. In addition, the virus can be spread through sharing needles in drug users and in health care accidents, through blood, organ or sperm donations and from mother to child during pregnancy or birth (Department of Internal Medicine, 2012; Mayo clinic, 2010).

The virus acts by infecting (mainly) the *CD4+ T cells*, but also aims at other cells in the body, such as the plasmacytoid dendritic cells and the NK-natural killer cells. In the initial days of the infection, the virus rapidly multiplies and as a result, in the first 2-12 weeks, 70% of the patients develop general flu-like symptoms like fever, chills, rashes, night sweats, sore throat, fatigue and swollen lymph nodes. This is called the *acute HIV infection stage* and in general the severity of the clinical picture of a patient may vary significantly from person to person, from asymptomatic to having the symptoms described above (*Acute retroviral syndrome*) and can last up to six months. The spread of the virus activates the immune system to fight of the infection. This leads, after a period of 12-15 weeks, to the suppression of the virus spread and the stabilization of the immune system.

Now, the patient enters the *clinical latency stage*, also called the *chronic HIV infection*. During this stage there is a balance between healthy CD4+ cells and viral load, so the virus is still active but its reproductive cycle is repressed by the immune system. At this stage there are no AIDS related clinical conditions and the patients are affected by other infections at the same rate as the general population. Some conditions that may rise but are not pathognomonic to HIV are Herpes zoster, seborrhoeic dermatitis, Angular cheilitis, recurrent oral ulcerations and a mediocre but unexplainable loss of weight. This stage may last as long as 10 years for patients who do not take medication and up to many decades for patients who are properly administered antiretroviral therapy. Eventually, through chronic deterioration, the immune system becomes weak and vulnerable, making the individual vulnerable to opportunistic infections. This is the final stage of the HIV infection and is called the *Acquired ImmunoDeficiency Syndrome (AIDS)*. Some characteristic opportunistic infections and tumors include Kaposi's sarcoma, Lymphoma (cerebral or B cell non-Hodgkin), Pneumocystis pneumonia, Extrapulmonary TB, Central nervous system (CNS) toxoplasmosis and Cytomegalovirus (CMV) retinitis (World Health Organization, 2007). It should be noted though that not all HIV positive patients advance to this stage.

A simple model that describes the effect of the HIV to the immune system can be constructed by describing the interactions between healthy CD4+ T cells, infected CD4+ cells and the viral load, see Figure 1. Healthy CD4+ cells are produced by the thymus at a constant rate of s and die at a rate d. They are infected by the virus at a rate that is proportional to the product of their number and the viral load. The effectiveness of the infection is given by a constant β. The infected CD4+ cells result from the infection of healthy cells and die at a constant rate m_2. Free virus particles, known as virions are produced from infected CD4+ cells at a rate k and die at a rate m_1 (Barão & Lemos, 2007; Craig et al. 2007; Craig & Xia, 2005; Mhawej et al. 2009; Mhawej et al. 2010; Nowak & May, 2000).

Figure 1. Interaction of HIV and CD4+ cells

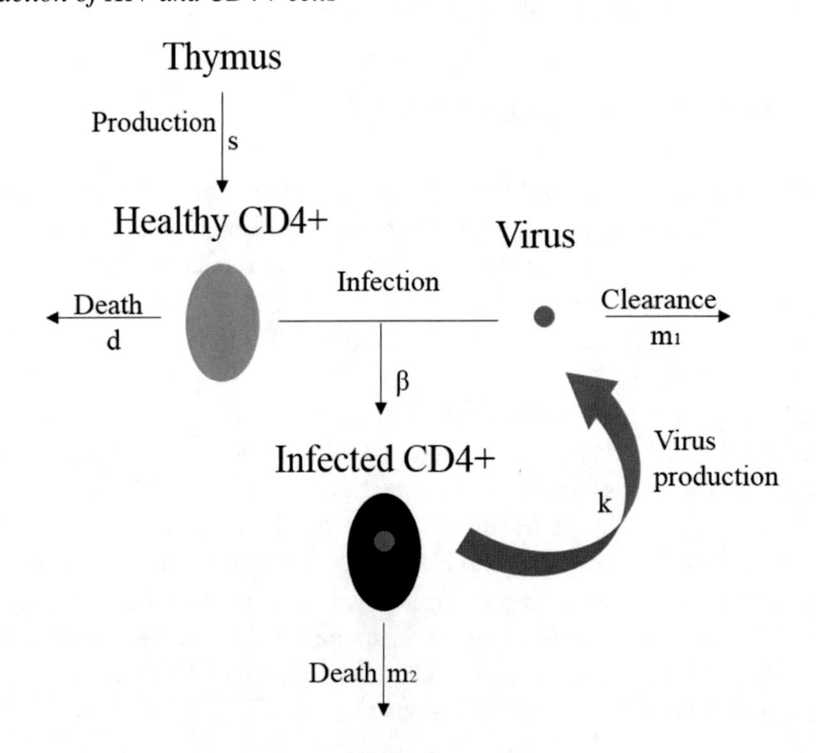

These interactions between healthy CD4+ cells, infected CD4+ and free virions can be described by the following system of nonlinear equations

$$\dot{T}(t) = s - dT(t) - \beta T(t)v(t) \tag{1a}$$

$$\dot{T}^*(t) = \beta T(t)v(t) - m_2 T^*(t) \tag{1b}$$

$$\dot{v}(t) = kT^*(t) - m_1 v(t) \tag{1c}$$

where *T(t)* the number of healthy CD4+, $T^*(t)$ the number of infected CD4+ and *v(t)* the number of virions, also known as the viral load. Typical values for the parameters of the system are given in Table 1, according to (Barão & Lemos, 2007; Craig & Xia, 2005; Craig et al. 2004).

The first step in understanding the dynamical behavior of the system would be to compute its equilibrium points. As defined in (Sastry, 2013), a point $x^* \in R^n$ is an equilibrium point for the system $\dot{x} = f(t,x)$ if $f(x^*) = 0$, for all $t \geq 0$. So, in order to specify the equilibrium points of (1) we solve the system of equations

$$0 = s - dT(t) - \beta T(t)v(t) \tag{2a}$$

$$0 = \beta T(t)v(t) - m_2 T^*(t) \tag{2b}$$

$$0 = kT^*(t) - m_1 v(t) \tag{2c}$$

In case where $T^* = v = 0$, the equilibrium is

Table 1. Typical values for the disease parameters

t	Time	Days
d	Death rate of healthy CD4+	0.02/day
k	Number of virions produced per infected CD4+	100/cell
s	Production rate of healthy CD4+	10mm^3/day
β	Viral infection rate	2.4×10^{-5}mm^3/day
m_1	Virus death rate	2.4/day
m_2	Infected CD4+ death	0.24/day

$$\begin{pmatrix} T_{eq_1} & T^*_{eq_1} & v_{eq_1} \end{pmatrix} = \begin{pmatrix} \frac{s}{d} & 0 & 0 \end{pmatrix} = \begin{pmatrix} 500 & 0 & 0 \end{pmatrix} \quad (3)$$

and in case where $v \neq 0$ the equilibrium is

$$\begin{pmatrix} T_{eq_2} & T^*_{eq_2} & v_{eq_2} \end{pmatrix} = \begin{pmatrix} \frac{m_1 m_2}{k\beta} & \frac{s}{m_2} - \frac{dm_1}{\beta k} & \frac{ks}{m_1 m_2} - \frac{d}{\beta} \end{pmatrix} = \begin{pmatrix} 240 & 21.6667 & 902.778 \end{pmatrix} \quad (4)$$

It should be clear that the first equilibrium corresponds to a healthy uninfected individual. The second equilibrium corresponds to the equilibrium point after the patient enters the clinical latency stage. The Jacobian of the system is given by

$$J(f) = \left.\frac{df}{dx}\right|_{x=x_{eq}} = \begin{pmatrix} -d - \beta v_{eq} & 0 & -\beta T_{eq} \\ \beta v_{eq} & -m_2 & \beta T_{eq} \\ 0 & k & -m_1 \end{pmatrix} \quad (5)$$

Computing the eigenvalues of the Jacobian for each equilibrium point, we find that for the first point, the Jacobian has a positive eigenvalue, while for the second point the eigenvalues of the Jacobian are all negative. Thus, the first equilibrium point is unstable, while the second is stable and hyperbolic (Khalil, 2002). The fact that the first equilibrium, which corresponds to an uninfected individual is unstable, is compatible with the underlying theory of the biological model, since the smallest amount of virions inserting the body will cause the system to diverge from the healthy status towards the second equilibrium point.

A typical progression for the disease is shown in Figure 2. It is clear that after initial infection, there is a rise in the viral load and the infected CD4+ cells and after the immune system's reaction, the system is stabilized and the patient enters the clinical latency stage.

It should also be noted that the system always ends up in the same equilibrium point, regardless of the initial conditions of the patient. This is expected since this equilibrium is hyperbolic. This can be seen in Figure 3, which shows multiple trajectories for varying initial conditions (note that some may correspond to unrealistic data). So eventually, the patient's system will in every case go through the same stages of a high overshoot in its viral load, before entering the clinical latency stage.

The Simulink model for system (1) is given in Figure 4a.

3. METHODS FOR ANTIRETROVIRAL TREATMENT

Antiretroviral treatment describes the ensemble of drugs that are used in the therapy against the immunodeficiency virus. The combination of different drugs in order to achieve better therapeutic results is called highly active antiretroviral therapy (HAART) and constitutes a milestone in the history of the disease. The drugs constitute a causative therapy, acting on multiple stages of the virus' life cycle. From 1996 when HAART was first introduced, it is usually administered as a combination of three drugs.

Figure 2. Time response of the HIV infection

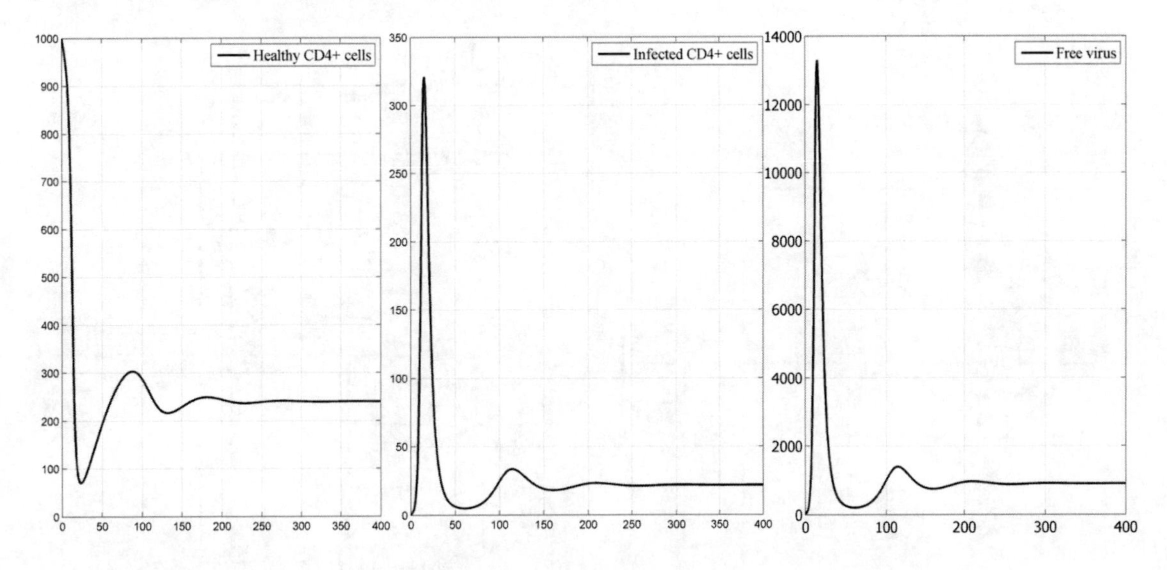

Figure 3. System trajectories for different initial conditions

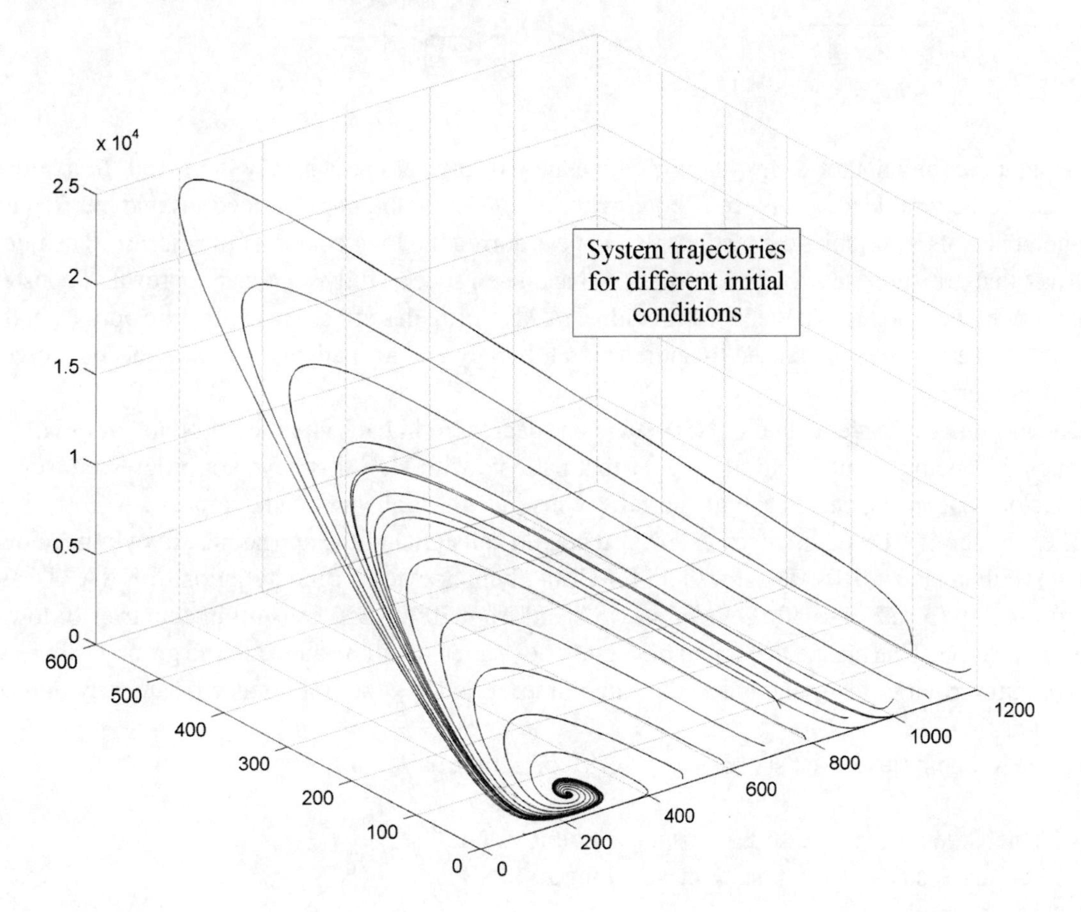

Figure 4. Simulink model for the system (1). (a) System without inputs, (b) System with inputs

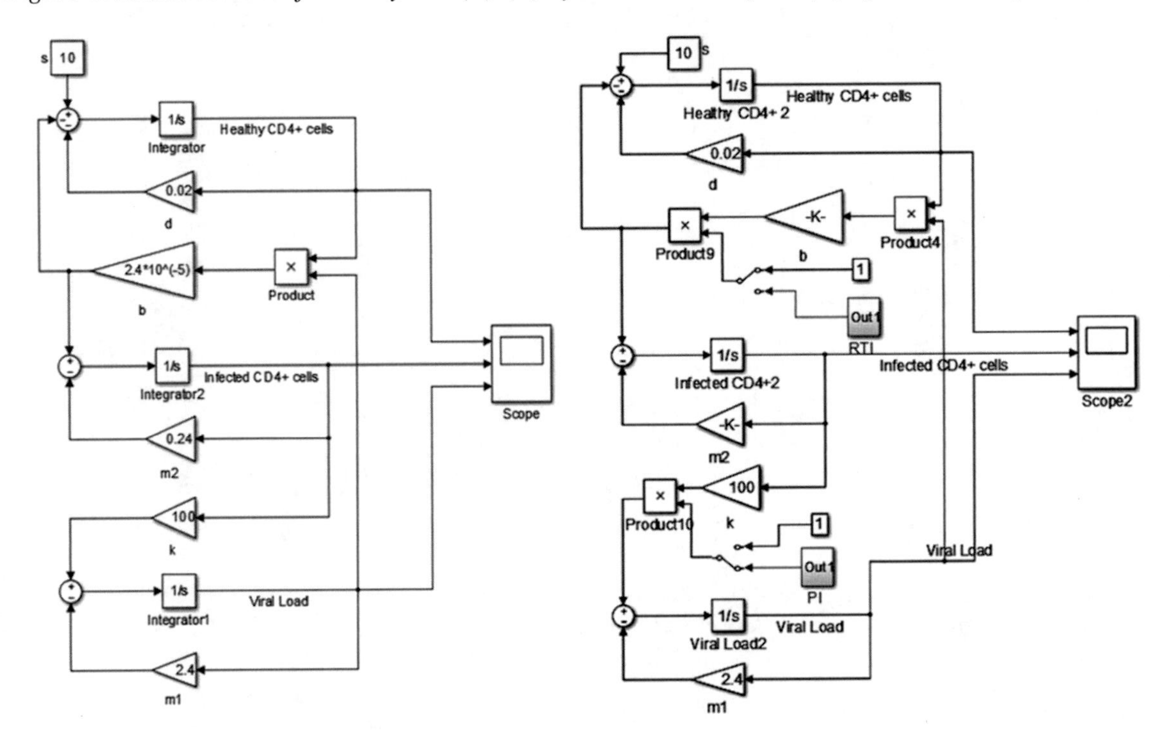

By using a combination of drugs, the life expectancy of the patient is highly increased. In addition, a decrease in the viral load is achieved, along with its impact on the body's functions and the frequency of emergence of opportunistic infections that appear during the long course of the disease. The number of drugs that are subjected to clinical trials or have been successfully received approval is constantly rising, giving new hopes to patients worldwide. HAART provides effective therapeutic options both for patients who are newly introduced to antiretroviral therapy and for patients who have been receiving a combined therapy.

The mortality of patients in the AIDS stage has decreased in half with the introduction of HAART, although still being about five times higher that patients with HIV that have not progressed to AIDS. Risk factors that are connected to high mortality constitute the high viral load of more than 400 particles/ml, the number of CD4+ lymphocytes lower than 200 cells/ml and the appearance of cytomegalovirus (CMV) (Puhan et al. 2010). The threshold for CD4+ lymphocytes for the initiation of HAART has recently risen up from 350 to 500 cells/ml in USA and from 200 to 350 cells/ml in countries of low and medium income. This means that a notable number of patients will be added to the group of those who receive antiretroviral treatment and at the same time, it denotes the importance of an early diagnosis (Lodi et al. 2011).

At the moment there exist six basic categories of antiretroviral drugs

- Nucleoside analog reverse-transcriptase inhibitors NRTIs.
- Non-nucleoside reverse-transcriptase inhibitors NNRTIs.
- Protease inhibitors PIs.

- Integrase inhibitors INSTIs.
- Fusion inhibitors FIs.
- Chemokine receptor antagonists CCR5 antagonists.

3.1. Two Input Model

We will focus on the two basic categories of antiretroviral drugs, the reverse transcriptase inhibitors (RTIs) and protease inhibitors (PIs). RTIs act by blocking the infection of new T cells while PIs prevent the production of new virions. More specifically:

- NRTIs where the first agents to be used in HIV therapy. NRTIs affect the multiplication of the virus, terminating the production of the DNA chain through the blockade of the reverse transcriptase of the virus. The inverse transcriptase is an HIV polymerase that is used in the production of the viral single stranded and the double stranded DNA from the initial viral RNA. In this form the viral genetic material can connect with that of the host. The NRTI drugs constitute analogs of the nucleotides that are used from the inverse transcriptase in the synthesis of the viral DNA. When they connect to the inverse transcriptase they block the production of the viral DNA.
- NNRTIs are highly drastic against HIV-1 and are agents that are used in the initiation of antiretroviral therapy. Reverse transcriptase is a dimer consisting of two subunits (p66 and p51). NNRTIs connect to the p66 subunit, in a less active region of the enzyme. This less competitive sort of connection results in structural changes in the enzyme that affect its active site and decrease its activity.
- HIV protease inhibitors are an integral part of therapy. HIV protease is a homodimer, with 99 amino acids. They attach to the enzyme's active site and block the proteolytic maturation of the viral precursor polypeptides.

Taking into consideration the effect of these antiretroviral drugs, model (1) takes the form (Barão & Lemos, 2007; Craig & Xia, 2005; Craig et al. 2004; Mhawej et al. 2009; Mhawej et al. 2010):

$$\dot{T}(t) = s - dT(t) - \left(1 - u_1(t)\right)\beta T(t)v(t) \tag{6a}$$

$$\dot{T}^*(t) = \left(1 - u_1(t)\right)\beta T(t)v(t) - m_2 T^*(t) \tag{6b}$$

$$\dot{v}(t) = \left(1 - u_2(t)\right)kT^*(t) - m_1 v(t) \tag{6c}$$

Where the terms $\left(1 - u_1(t)\right)$ and $\left(1 - u_2(t)\right)$ represent the effectiveness of RTIs and PIs respectively (for $u_{\{1,2\}} = 0$ the drug is not administered, while for $u_{\{1,2\}} = 1$ the treatment is 100% effective, which of course is not achievable). Here, by trying different combinations of intensity for the two drugs we can observe their effect on the viral load, as shown in Figures 5 and 6. Indeed, it can be seen that the viral load can be successfully suppressed. The aim of the antiretroviral treatment is to reduce the viral load to less than 50 copies/mm^3 (Radisavljevic-Gajic, 2009; Stephens, 2008). The Simulink model of system (6) is given in Figure 4b.

For the simulation shown in Figures 5 and 6, the treatment is initiated at the 150th day, at the end of the acute infection stage, when the viral load is near its equilibrium. This is based on the premise that the patient was tested and diagnosed during the acute infection stage, when he or she developed the first signs of infection. This is a good case scenario, since the earlier the infection is diagnosed, the less chances the virus has to mutate and become resistant to drugs. For various drug variations, we observe

Figure 5. Viral load for different drug dosages (treatment at day 150)

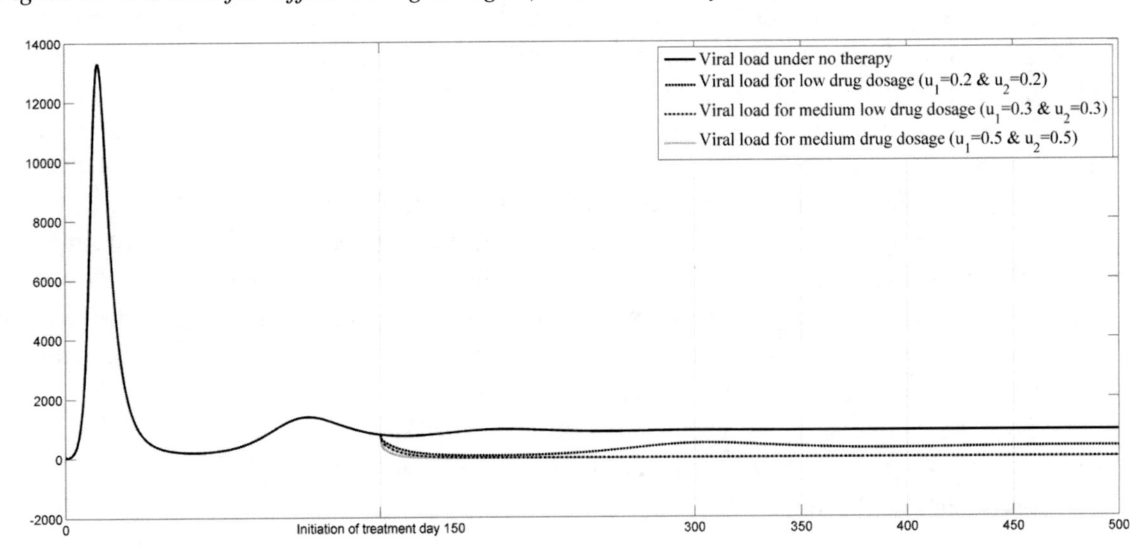

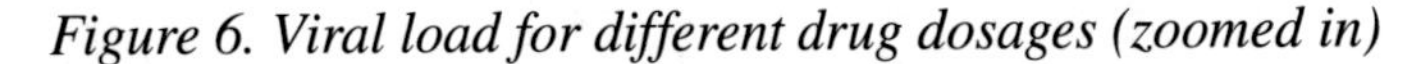
Figure 6. Viral load for different drug dosages (zoomed in)

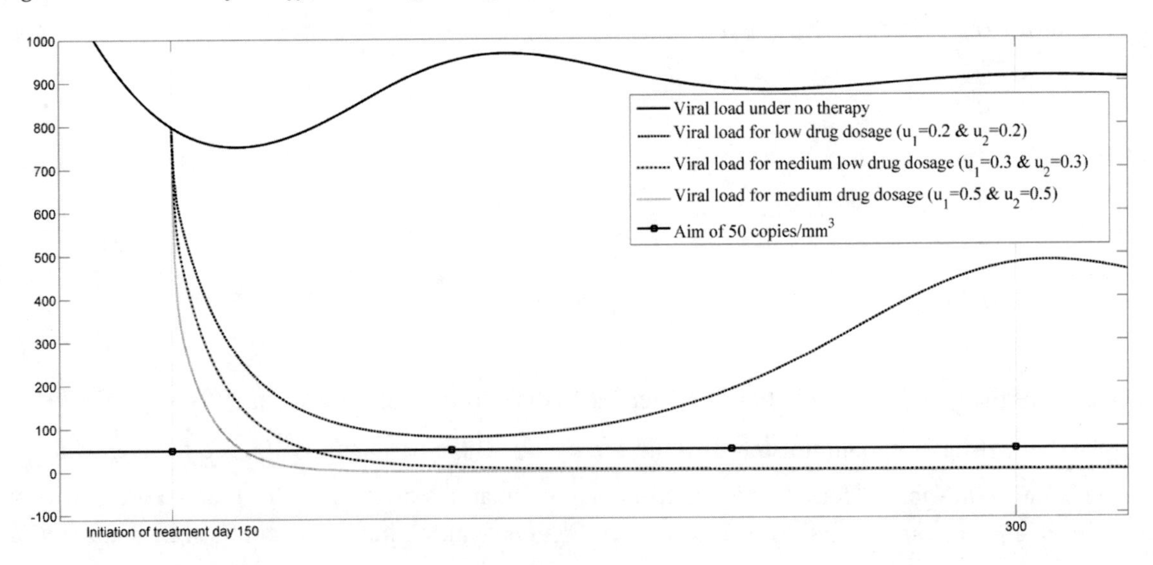

in Figures 5 and 6 that an effectiveness of at least 0.3 is required for both inputs to reach the desired goal for the viral load.

Another good case scenario is when the patient gets tested immediately after a potentially dangerous contact. This can lead to an immediate diagnosis, which gives doctors more options as to how the treatment will proceed. The administration of higher dosages of drugs, before the emergence of the high viral overshoot in the acute infection stage, may lead to a suppression of the overshoot, but can also lead to a lot of undesirable side effects, as well as an early emergence of viral resistance (Perelson & Nelson, 1999). Thus, the doctor who monitors a patient may choose not to administer high dosages immediately, since the high overshoot stage is more or less inevitable, but rather choose moderate doses, so as to moderately suppress the high overshoot in the acute infection stage and keep administering the same drug dosages for a longer period of time. This can be seen in Figure 7 where the treatment begins at day 10. A higher dose of 0.5 effectiveness can completely suppress the viral load overshoot.

What should also be noted is that the drugs should be taken continuously and with no interruptions, so that the virus is always suppressed and is not given the chance to mutate. In case the treatment is interrupted, there is a great possibility that the virus will rebound back to high levels, which also favors the development of drug resistant mutations. This can be confirmed from the model (6). Indeed, as can be seen in Figure 8, if the treatment starts at day 150 but is terminated at day 400, the viral load may stay low for at best a number of 150-180 more days, depending on the effectiveness of the drugs, but rises back up afterwards. The issue of treatment interruption has been clinically studied in (SMART study group, 2006).

Since for the system (6) the values of the inputs are considered constant, we can compute the new equilibrium point for the system, which is given by

$$\begin{pmatrix} T_{eq_2} & T^*_{eq_2} & v_{eq_2} \end{pmatrix} = \begin{pmatrix} \dfrac{m_1 m_2}{k\beta(1-u_1)(1-u_2)} & \dfrac{s}{m_2} - \dfrac{dm_1}{k\beta(1-u_1)(1-u_2)} & \dfrac{ks(1-u_2)}{m_1 m_2} - \dfrac{d}{\beta(1-u_1)} \end{pmatrix} \quad (7)$$

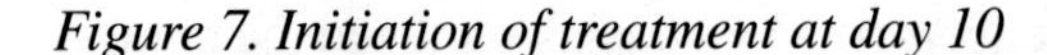

Figure 7. Initiation of treatment at day 10

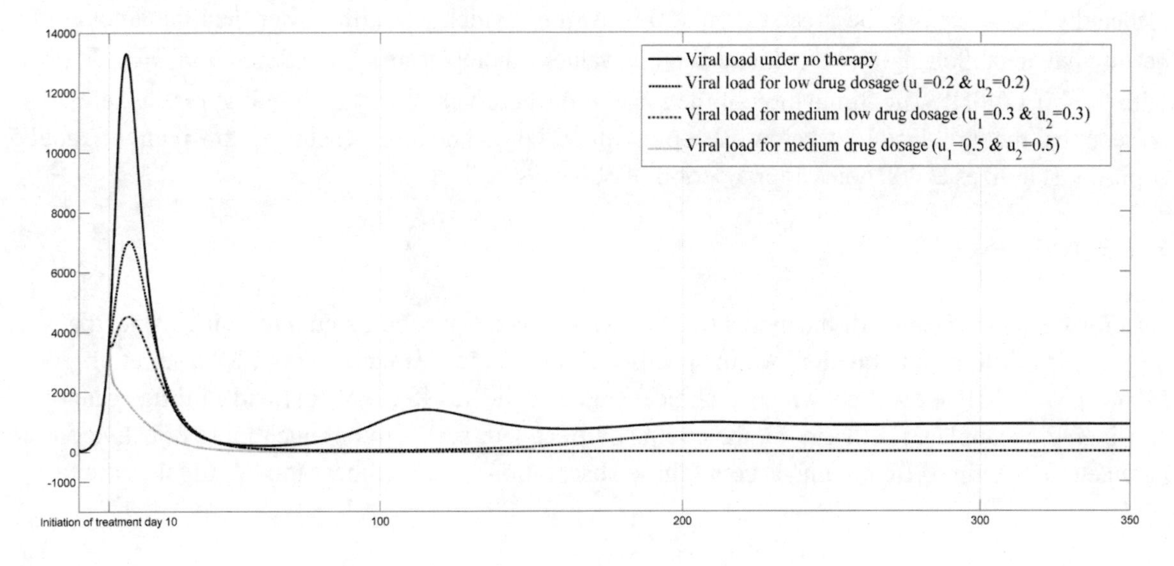

Figure 8. Viral load after treatment interruption

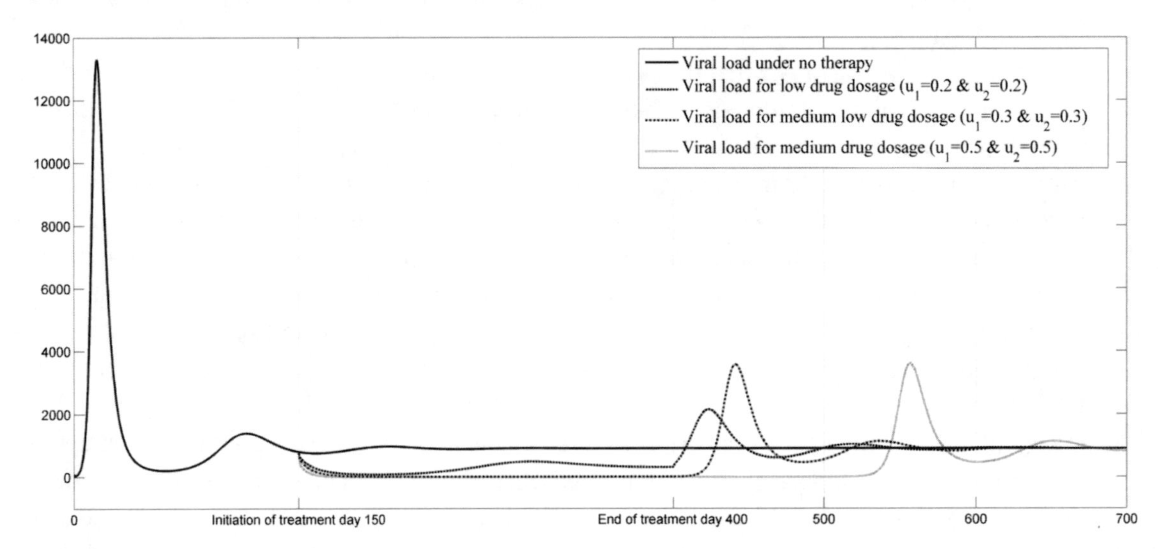

Using the above formula, it is possible to choose a desired value for the healthy CD4+ cells and the viral load, according to the standard guidelines and compute the input values that should be used to achieve the desired equilibrium. This method was used in (Karagiannis et al. 2016). As a more general approach, we can consider this as a minimization problem

$$\begin{array}{ll} \min & J = u_1^2 + u_2^2 \\ \text{under} & \begin{array}{l} -T_{eq_2} \le -450 \quad v_{eq_2} \le 40 \\ 0 \le u_1, u_2 \le 1 \end{array} \end{array} \tag{8}$$

where the objective function was chosen to be the sum of the squares of the two inputs and for the desired equilibrium points we chose the value of the viral load to be lower than 40 copies/mm^3 and the number of healthy CD4+ cells to be greater than 450 cells/mm^3, which is a little lower than the amount of a healthyindividual.Solving(8),wefindthattheoptimalvaluesoftheinputsare $u_1 = 0.286866$, $u_2 = 0.303875$, with $J = 0.174632$. The Simulation of the system for these values is shown in Figure 9, where it can be seen that the viral load falls below 50 copies after 25 days and after reaching a low point of about 5 copies, it stabilizes at 40 copies after a period of 800 days.

3.2. Single Input Model

As a further simplification of the model (6), the two inputs can be combined into a single one, that acts on the third differential equation. More specifically in (Barão & Lemos, 2007; Mhawej et al. 2009; Mhawej et al. 2010) it was shown after clinical studies that the effects of RTI and PI drugs cannot be considered decoupled. Furthermore, the combined treatment seems to be much more effective on the parameter *k* than in *β*. Taking into account these observations, the nonlinear model (6) takes the form

Figure 9. Viral load for inputs given by (8)

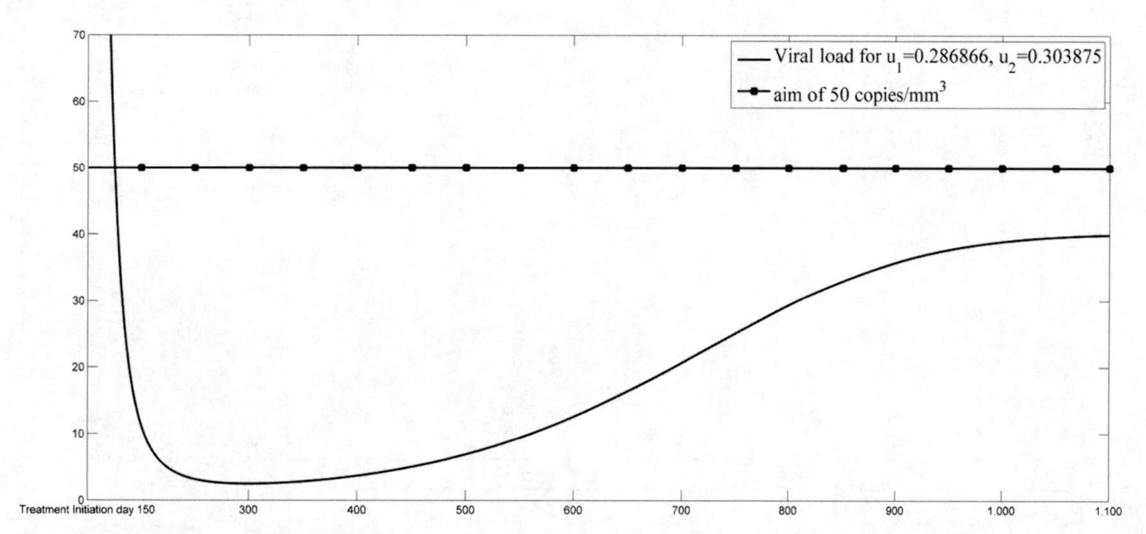

$$\dot{T}(t) = s - dT(t) - \beta T(t)v(t) \tag{9a}$$

$$\dot{T}^*(t) = \beta T(t)v(t) - m_2 T^*(t) \tag{9b}$$

$$\dot{v}(t) = \left(1 - u(t)\right) kT^*(t) - m_1 v(t) \tag{9c}$$

where the parameter *u(t)* denotes the effectiveness of the combined treatment. For this system the equilibrium is given by (assuming *u(t)* is constant)

$$\left(T_{eq_2} \quad T^*_{eq_2} \quad v_{eq_2}\right) = \left(\frac{m_1 m_2}{k\beta(1-u)} \quad \frac{s}{m_2} - \frac{dm_1}{k\beta(1-u)} \quad \frac{ks(1-u)}{m_1 m_2} - \frac{d}{\beta}\right) \tag{10}$$

From the above equation, solving for $v_{eq_2} < 50$ we find that the value of the input should be greater than 0.4912, in order for the equilibrium value of the viral load to be less than 50 copies/mm^3.

The system response for a single input model is shown in Figures 10 and 11. A notable difference that we observe though in contrast to the two input model (6) is that after treatment is interrupted, the viral load rises back up much faster than in the two input case, for medium drug effectiveness. By using a higher dosage, for example of 0.6, the viral load stays lower for more days, until day 500 approximately.

As with the two input system, initiating the system at a really early stage manages to suppress the high overshoot in the acute infection stage. In Figure 12, the treatment is initiated at day 10 and is kept for about a year. Of course, in both models presented here, using higher drug dosages (except of course

Figure 10. Viral load for the single input system

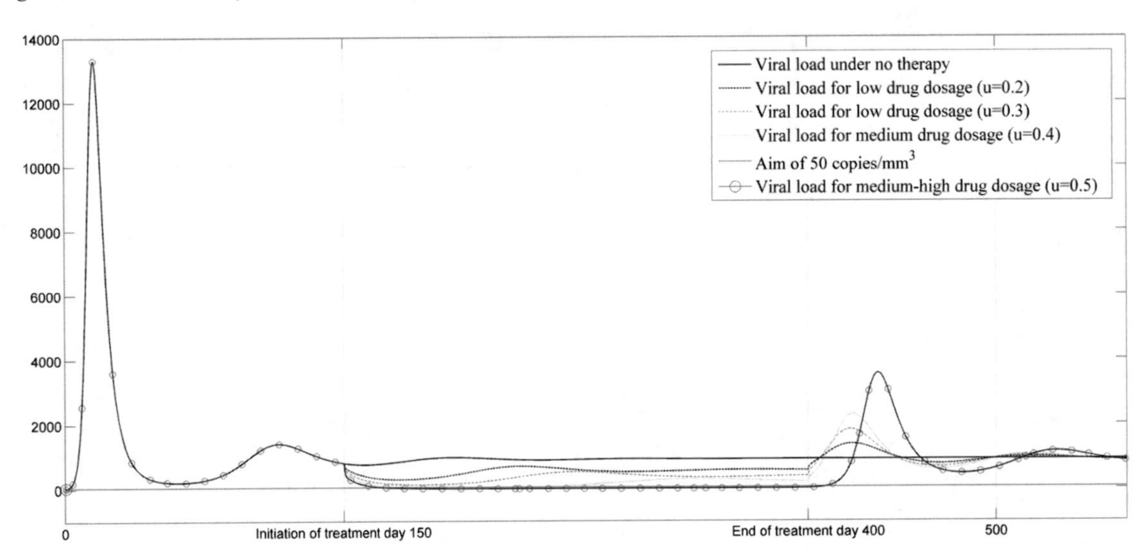

Figure 11. Viral load for the single input system (zoomed in)

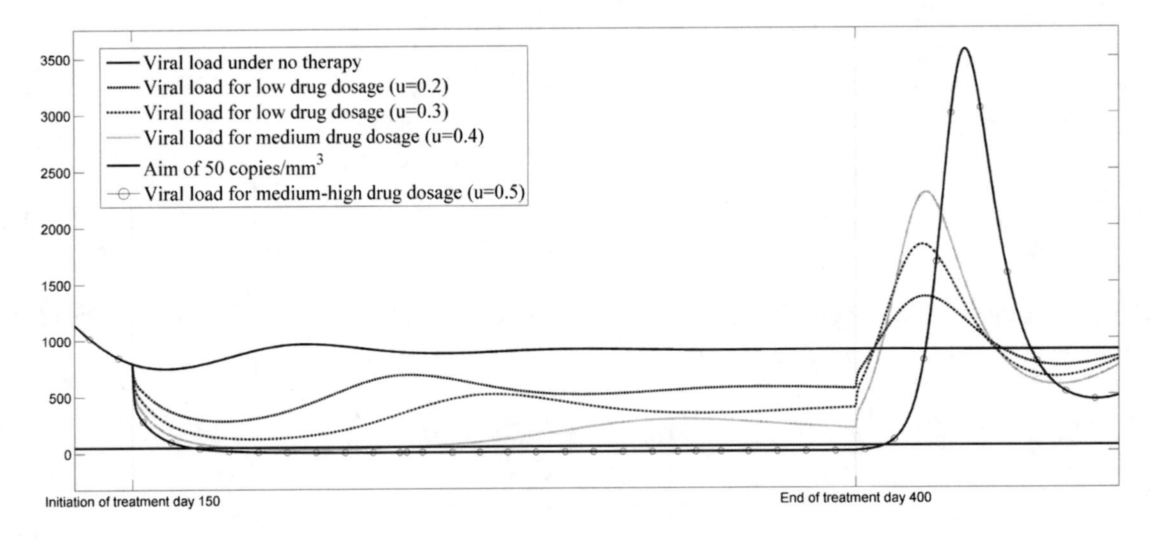

from the case where $u(t)=1$), cannot in any case result in the complete elimination of the infection. In all cases the virus will regress back up after the termination of the treatment. This simulation result mirrors the current available drug capabilities, since no cure exists for the virus.

3.3. Feedback Control

As seen in the previous two models the drugs are administered at a steady pace throughout the treatment. This is a good method of approach when the patient responds well to the treatment provided. Another effective approach would be to administer the drugs depending on the measurements of the Infected

Figure 12. Initiation of treatment at day 10 (single input system)

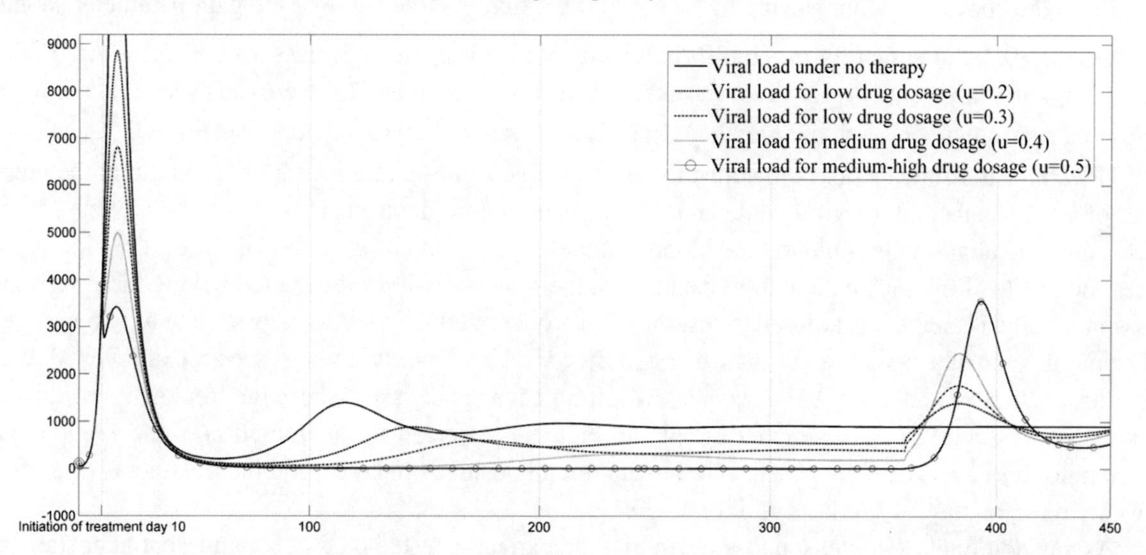

CD4+ cells and the viral load. This can be done through the technique of feedback linearization. The theory behind this method is to use a state feedback as an input in order to cancel out the nonlinearities of the system. This was showcased in (Barão & Lemos, 2007; Karagiannis et al. 2016; Mhawej et al. 2009; Mhawej et al. 2010; Moog et al. 2007; Radisavljevic-Gajic, 2009). It is easy to see that if we consider the system (6) with just the RTI drugs, a feedback of the form

$$u_1(t) = 1 - \frac{g}{\beta T(t)v(t)} \tag{11}$$

where g is a gain parameter, will linearize the system. The resulting system will be

$$\dot{T}(t) = s - dT(t) - g \tag{12a}$$

$$\dot{T}^*(t) = g - m_2 T^*(t) \tag{12b}$$

$$\dot{v}(t) = kT^*(t) - m_1 v(t) \tag{12c}$$

with equilibrium

$$\begin{pmatrix} T_{eq_2} & T^*_{eq_2} & v_{eq_2} \end{pmatrix} = \begin{pmatrix} \frac{s-g}{d} & \frac{w}{m_2} & \frac{kg}{m_1 m_2} \end{pmatrix} \tag{13}$$

From the above equation, solving for $v_{eq_2} < 50$, we find that the value of the gain parameter should be less than 0.288, in order for the equilibrium value of the viral load to be less than 50 copies/mm^3. For g=0.2304, the input and viral load for the system are shown in Figure 13. Here, it is seen that the input $u_1(t)$ starts from a very high dosage, then drops low after about 20 days and stabilizes at 0.5.

Now, in using state feedback to adjust the drug dosages, one should take into account that the number of CD4+ cells and the viral load cannot be measured continuously. This should be obvious, since it is unpractical and unfeasible to take blood samples from a patient each day. Besides, the aim of the treatment is to allow each patient to move on with their everyday lives, instead of having them visit the hospital daily. Usually, it is advised to test the CD4+ count and the viral load every one to two months. The monitoring of a patient can be done using just the viral load measurements, see for example (Alavez-Ramírez, 2015). In addition, the frequency of testing changes in cases where the treatment is adjusted or a new drug is taken. As a simple example, in Figure 14, we can see a simulation of the single input system for the case where the patient is tested and found positive on day 30 and the treatment starts after twenty days, on day 50 and lasts until day 300.

As an additional example, suppose again that the patient is tested on day 30, and treatment starts at day 50. But assume that at day 250, the effectiveness of the drugs starts to lower, from 0.5 to 0.2. This cannot be seen clearly on the tests taken at day 270 and 300 but only on day 330 the rise of the viral load can be seen from the blood tests and the treatment can be adjusted again to counteract this. This simulation is seen in Figure 15. Had the blood test been taken more sporadically, say for example every 60 days, then the viral load at day 360 would have been even higher than the one measured in Figure 15.

Thus, the issue of having constant measurements of the values of CD4+ cells and the viral load arises when considering the feedback control (11). Since having continuous measurements of these quantities may not be possible, a possible solution would be to use an observer to obtain estimations of these values. The parameters used for this observer could be computed using identification methods and be adjusted to a specific patient using age, gender, and other clinical data that can be available (Guedj et al. 2007; Xia & Moog, 2003; Xia, 2003).

Figure 13. Viral load and input for feedback linearization

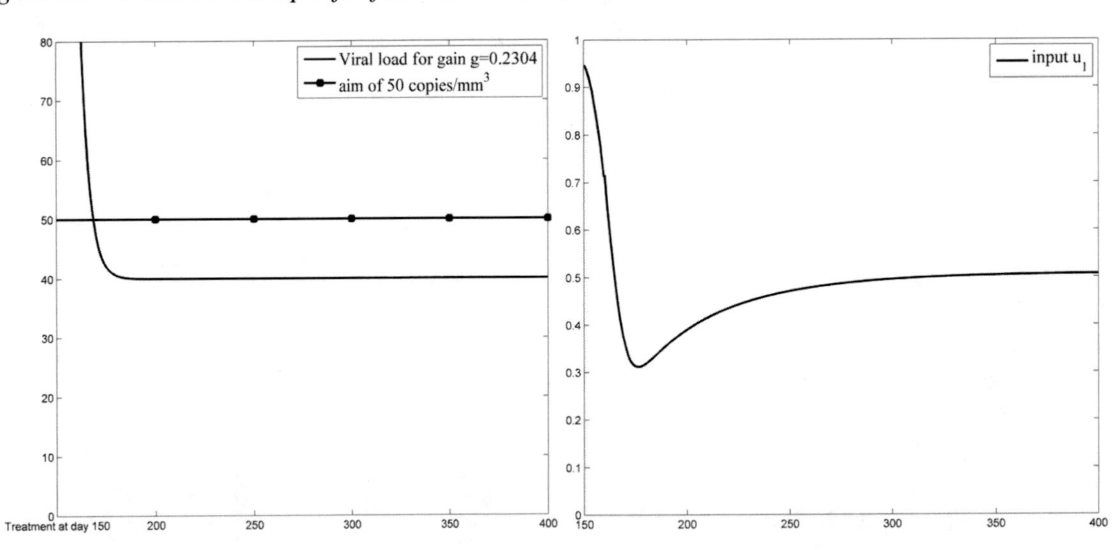

Figure 14. Test information taken each month

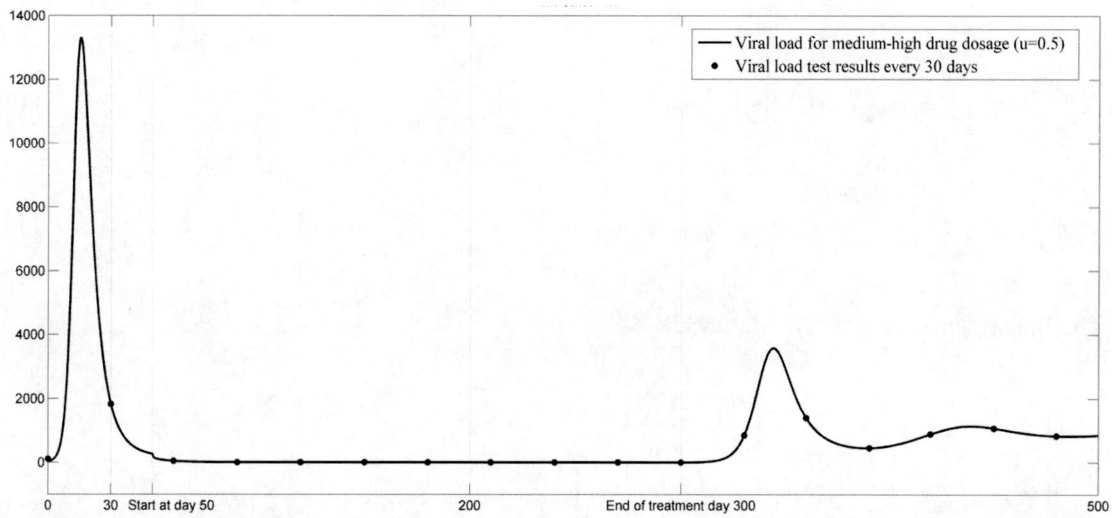

Figure 15. Test results are used to adjust the drug therapy

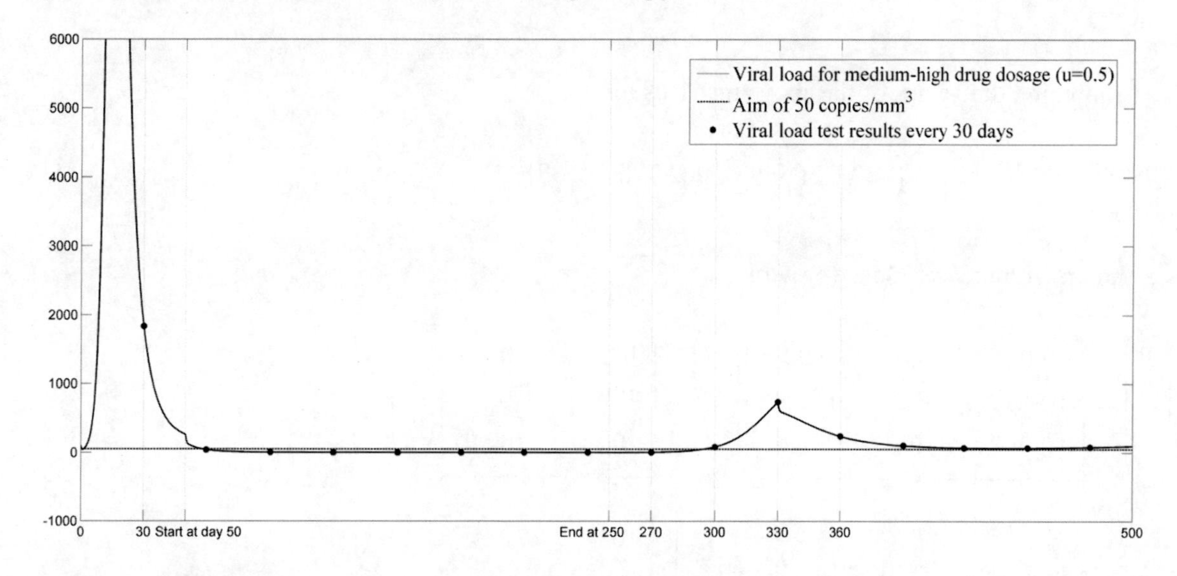

4. LINEARIZATION AROUND THE EQUILIBRIUM

The analysis of the nonlinear systems (1), (6) is a very complex and challenging task. For this reason, our aim is to determine the dynamical behavior of the system around its *equilibrium points*. As was seen in Section 2, the equilibrium point corresponding to an infected individual was stable. This, in combination with the *Hartman-Grobman theorem* (Sastry, 2013) guarantees that the linearization is possible and that the linearized system preserves the qualitative properties of the nonlinear system around the equilibrium. With the addition of inputs, we define

$$\tilde{f}_1(T,T^*,v,u_1,u_2) = s - dT(t) - (1-u_1)\beta T(t)v(t) \tag{14a}$$

$$\tilde{f}_2(T,T^*,v,u_1,u_2) = (1-u_1)\beta T(t)v(t) - m_2 T^*(t) \tag{14b}$$

$$\tilde{f}_3(T,T^*,v,u_1,u_2) = (1-u_2)kT^*(t) - m_1 v(t) \tag{14c}$$

The linearized system is (Khalil, 2002):

$$\begin{pmatrix} \dot{T} \\ \dot{T}^* \\ \dot{v} \end{pmatrix} = \begin{pmatrix} \frac{\partial \tilde{f}_1}{\partial T} & \frac{\partial \tilde{f}_1}{\partial T^*} & \frac{\partial \tilde{f}_1}{\partial v} \\ \frac{\partial \tilde{f}_2}{\partial T} & \frac{\partial \tilde{f}_2}{\partial T^*} & \frac{\partial \tilde{f}_2}{\partial v} \\ \frac{\partial \tilde{f}_3}{\partial T} & \frac{\partial \tilde{f}_3}{\partial T^*} & \frac{\partial \tilde{f}_3}{\partial v} \end{pmatrix} \begin{pmatrix} T \\ T^* \\ v \end{pmatrix} + \begin{pmatrix} \frac{\partial \tilde{f}_1}{\partial u_1} & \frac{\partial \tilde{f}_1}{\partial u_2} \\ \frac{\partial \tilde{f}_2}{\partial u_1} & \frac{\partial \tilde{f}_2}{\partial u_2} \\ \frac{\partial \tilde{f}_3}{\partial u_1} & \frac{\partial \tilde{f}_3}{\partial u_2} \end{pmatrix} \begin{pmatrix} u_1 \\ u_2 \end{pmatrix} \tag{15}$$

Computing the values of the above matrices for

$$\begin{pmatrix} T & T^* & v & u_1 & u_2 \end{pmatrix} = \begin{pmatrix} 240 & 21.6667 & 902.778 & 0 & 0 \end{pmatrix} \tag{16}$$

we end up with the state space system

$$\begin{gathered} \begin{pmatrix} \dot{T} \\ \dot{T}^* \\ \dot{v} \end{pmatrix} = \underbrace{\begin{pmatrix} -0.0417 & 0 & -0.0058 \\ 0.0217 & -0.24 & 0.0058 \\ 0 & 100 & -2.4 \end{pmatrix}}_{A} \begin{pmatrix} T \\ T^* \\ v \end{pmatrix} + \underbrace{\begin{pmatrix} 5.2 & 0 \\ -5.2 & 0 \\ 0 & -2166.67 \end{pmatrix}}_{B} \begin{pmatrix} u_1 \\ u_2 \end{pmatrix} \\ y = \underbrace{\begin{pmatrix} 0 & 0 & 1 \end{pmatrix}}_{C} \begin{pmatrix} T \\ T^* \\ v \end{pmatrix} \end{gathered} \tag{17}$$

where we chose the viral load as the measured output, although the number of infected CD4+ can also be chosen. The next step in the analysis of the state space system (17) is to compute its transfer function that gives the connection between the output and each input (Nise, 2015). It is computed as

$$G(s) = C\left(sI_3 - A\right)^{-1} B = \begin{pmatrix} \frac{\text{-520s-10.4}}{s^3 + 2.682s^2 + 0.1061s + 0.01242} & \frac{-2167s^2 - 610.4s - 21.68}{s^3 + 2.682s^2 + 0.1061s + 0.01242} \end{pmatrix} \tag{18}$$

The controllability matrix is given by

$$\mathcal{L} = \begin{pmatrix} B & AB & A^2B \end{pmatrix} = \begin{pmatrix} 5.2 & 0 & -0.216667 & 12.48 & 3.00423 & -30.472 \\ -5.2 & 0 & 1.36067 & -12.48 & -3.32645 & 33.2176 \\ 0 & -2166.67 & -520. & 5200. & 1384.07 & -13728. \end{pmatrix} \quad (19)$$

and has full rank, thus the system is controllable. Thus, the system can be compensated through the use of open or closed loop controllers.

If we consider the single input nonlinear system (9), as presented in the previous section, then following the same procedure we end up in the state space system (17), where the new matrix *B* consists of just the second column of the previous *B*. In that case the controllability matrix will be

$$\mathcal{L} = \begin{pmatrix} B & AB & A^2B \end{pmatrix} = \begin{pmatrix} 0 & 12.48 & -30.472 \\ 0 & -12.48 & 33.2176 \\ -2166.67 & 5200. & -13728. \end{pmatrix} \quad (20)$$

Although the linear model (17) is a simplification of (6) and only captures its dynamical qualities around the equilibrium, can be used as a basis for the demonstration of a plethora of problems of control systems engineering. Such topics include the state feedback of the system (17) and the computation of its gain margin, the design of PID controllers (Mousa et al. 2015; Nise, 2015) for the reduction of the viral load, the evaluation of the sampling time through Bode diagrams to decide the frequency in which the patient should be tested and many more.

5. DISCUSSION

Simulation Results

Overall, the most important result that should be derived from the simulations run on the model is that in all cases, the use of antiretroviral therapy cannot completely eliminate the virus. Thus, it is essential that drug administration should be planned for a long time horizon, since the aim is to suppress the viral load for as many years as possible. An early initiation of treatment can also suppress the viral overshoot and in addition give more options for scheduling the treatment plan for the patient. Moreover, it is seen that frequent and scheduled blood tests should be taken, in order to constantly observe the progression of the infection.

Termination of the treatment is not encouraged in any case, as the virus will be given the chance to become resistant to drugs. In cases where side effects from the drugs arise and the patient has to change the prescription, the effect of the new drugs should be monitored within a month after the change of treatment (Panel on Antiretroviral Guidelines for Adults and Adolescents, 2016).

Use of the Model in Higher Education

As mentioned in the introduction, the authors strongly believe that the subject of a dynamical model for the HIV infection can be used extensively in higher education. Each separate part of the above analysis can cleverly be integrated into courses evolving around the subjects of linear and nonlinear systems, dynamic systems in general and control systems engineering. Such courses can be found in any curriculum of Engineering, Mathematics and Biology departments of most universities. Our suggested points where this model can be integrated in such courses are the following:

1. Nonlinear models found in nature.
2. The dynamics of a nonlinear model:
   a. The role of initial conditions.
   b. Equilibrium points.
3. The design of nonlinear models in *Matlab*® and *Simulink*®.
4. Compensation and feedback control of nonlinear systems.
5. Linearization around the equilibrium.
6. Feedback control of linear systems.
7. Discretization of continuous time systems.
8. Continuous time systems with discrete time controls.

In each of these submodules, the proposed models can be used to illustrate the corresponding theory. In addition, if there is the possibility for cooperation among the different exact sciences departments and the Medical department and Health Care facilities of a university, these courses can be further enhanced by the simultaneous briefing of the students about the HIV prevention methods, thus raising awareness about the virus while simultaneously making the theory behind these courses much more intriguing.

6. CONCLUSION AND FUTURE WORK

We presented a fundamental nonlinear model that describes the HIV infection. The effect of antiretroviral treatment was studied under variable drug effectiveness. By choosing the desired values of the system's equilibrium, the appropriate input values can be computed. A simple feedback technique was also given which linearizes the system and the issues regarding its implementation were discussed. Then a linear state space model was developed to further simplify the dynamic behavior of the system and various control engineering problems where proposed like the design of controllers for its compensation. Every part of this work can be potentially integrated into the syllabus of linear and nonlinear dynamical systems courses and can be combined with the use of computer software like Matlab® (Moysis et al. 2017, 2015; Nise, 2015) to simulate the above models. One of the intentions of the first two authors is to organize open discussions and seminars to present this model to undergraduates at their department.

Further work on the field of HIV/AIDS infection constitutes the study of more complex nonlinear models (Alvarez-Ramirezet al. 2000; Callaway & Perelson, 2002; Ho & Ling 2010; Kramer, 1999; Perelson & Nelson, 1999; Shehata et al. 2017; Xia, 2007) that describe more accurately the complicated nature of the virus (by taking into account for example the antibody immune cells) and the effects of the treatment on other parts of the body like the liver. Fractional order models have also been described (Ding

& Ye, 2009) or models that describe HIV when other infections are also present in the body like malaria (Carvalho & Pinto, 2016), hepatitis (Moualeu et al. 2011) or tuberculosis (Gakkhar & Chavda, 2012). The problem of feedback linearization of the nonlinear system (Barão & Lemos, 2007; Karagiannis et al. 2016; Mhawej et al. 2009; Mhawej et al. 2010; Moog et al. 2007; Radisavljevic-Garij, 2009) and the use of time variant or even impulsive inputs for its control (Barão & Lemos, 2007; Mhawej et al. 2009; Mhawej et al. 2010; Rivadeneira & Moog, 2012) is also a subject for further study. A system dynamics approach can also be applied in further understanding the behavior of the HIV model (Azar, 2012) or other intelligent control approaches (Azar & Vaidyanathan, 2015a,b; Zhu & Azar, 2015)

ACKNOWLEDGMENT

The authors would like to acknowledge the editor in chief for his insightful comments that greatly improved the present work. They are also thankful to the anonymous reviewers for their comments.

REFERENCES

Alavez-Ramírez, J., Fuentes-Allen, J. L., López-Estrada, J., & Mata-Marín, J. A. (2015). Monitoring CD4+ cells using only viral load measurements. *Sky Journal of Medicine and Medical Sciences, 3*(7), 81-89.

Azar, A. T. (2012). System dynamics as a useful technique for complex systems. *International Journal of Industrial and Systems Engineering, 10*(4), 377–410. doi:10.1504/IJISE.2012.046298

Azar, A. T., & Vaidyanathan, S. (2015a). Handbook of Research on Advanced Intelligent Control Engineering and Automation. IGI Global. doi:10.4018/978-1-4666-7248-2

Azar, A. T., & Vaidyanathan, S. (2015b). *Computational Intelligence applications in Modeling and Control. Studies in Computational Intelligence* (Vol. 575). Springer-Verlag.

Barão, M., & Lemos, J. M. (2007). Nonlinear control of HIV-1 infection with a singular perturbation model. *Biomedical Signal Processing and Control, 2*(3), 248–257. doi:10.1016/j.bspc.2007.07.011

Barman, B., & Mukhopadhyay, A. (2015). Extracting Biological Significant Subnetworks from Protein-Protein Interactions Induced by Differentially Expressed Genes of HIV-1 Vpr Variants. [IJSDA]. *International Journal of System Dynamics Applications, 4*(4), 35–51. doi:10.4018/IJSDA.2015100103

Callaway, D. S., & Perelson, A. S. (2002). HIV-1 infection and low steady state viral loads. *Bulletin of Mathematical Biology, 64*(1), 29–64. doi:10.1006/bulm.2001.0266 PMID:11868336

Carvalho, A., & Pinto, C. M. (2016). A delay fractional order model for the co-infection of malaria and HIV/AIDS. *International Journal of Dynamics and Control*, 1-19.

Craig, I., & Xia, X. (2005). Can HIV/AIDS be controlled? Applying control engineering concepts outside traditional fields. *Control Systems, IEEE, 25*(1), 80–83. doi:10.1109/MCS.2005.1388805

Craig, I. K., Xia, X., & Venter, J. W. (2004). Introducing HIV/AIDS education into the electrical engineering curriculum at the University of Pretoria. *Education. IEEE Transactions on, 47*(1), 65–73.

Department of Internal Medicine, School of Medicine, Aristotle University of Thessaloniki. (2012). *Internal Medicine* (4th ed.). Thessaloniki, Greece: University Studio Press.

Ding, Y., & Ye, H. (2009). A fractional-order differential equation model of HIV infection of CD4+ T-cells. *Mathematical and Computer Modelling*, *50*(3), 386–392. doi:10.1016/j.mcm.2009.04.019

El-Sadr, W.M., Lundgren, J.D., & Neaton, J.D. (2006). CD4+ count-guided interruption of antiretroviral treatment. *New England Journal of Medicine, 355*(22), 2283-96.

Gakkhar, S., & Chavda, N. (2012). A dynamical model for HIV–TB co-infection. *Applied Mathematics and Computation*, *218*(18), 9261–9270. doi:10.1016/j.amc.2012.03.004

Gonçalves, P., & Kamdem, S. T. (2016). Reaching an AIDS-Free Generation in Côte d'Ivoire, Data Driven Policy Design for HIV/AIDS Response Programs: Evidence-Based Policy Design for HIV/AIDS Response Programs in Côte d'Ivoire. *International Journal of System Dynamics Applications*, *5*(1), 43–62. doi:10.4018/IJSDA.2016010104

Guedj, J., Thiébaut, R., & Commenges, D. (2007). Practical identifiability of HIV dynamics models. *Bulletin of Mathematical Biology*, *69*(8), 2493–2513. doi:10.100711538-007-9228-7 PMID:17557186

Hatzakis, A., Sypsa, V., Paraskevis, D., Nikolopoulos, G., Tsiara, C., Micha, K., ... Wiessing, L. (2015). Design and baseline findings of a large-scale rapid response to an HIV outbreak in people who inject drugs in Athens, Greece: The ARISTOTLE programme. *Addiction (Abingdon, England)*, *110*(9), 1453–1467. doi:10.1111/add.12999 PMID:26032121

Hellenic Center for Disease Control and Prevention. (2014, December). *HIV/AIDS Surveillance Report in Greece (Issue 29), Athens.* Retrieved from www.keelpno.gr

Hellenic Center for Disease Control and Prevention. (2015, October). *HIV infection: newest epidemiological data, Athens*. Retrieved from www.keelpno.gr.

Ho, C. Y. F., & Ling, B. W. K. (2010). Initiation of HIV therapy. *International Journal of Bifurcation and Chaos in Applied Sciences and Engineering*, *20*(04), 1279–1292. doi:10.1142/S0218127410026484 PMID:20543654

Jeffrey, A. M., Xia, X., & Craig, I. K. (2002). Controllability Analysis of the Chemotherapy of HIV/AIDS. *IFAC Proceedings Volumes, 35*(1), 127-132.

Jeffrey, A. M., Xia, X., & Craig, I. K. (2003). When to initiate HIV therapy: A control theoretic approach. *Biomedical Engineering. IEEE Transactions on*, *50*(11), 1213–1220. PMID:14619991

Joint United Nations Programme on HIV/AIDS (UNAIDS). (2014). *The gap report*. Geneva: UNAIDS.

Karagiannis, D., Radisavljevic-Gajic, V., & Ashrafiuon, H. (2016, October). Control of Human Immunodeficiency Virus (HIV) Dynamics With Parameter Uncertainties. In *ASME 2016 Dynamic Systems and Control Conference* (pp. V001T09A003-V001T09A003). American Society of Mechanical Engineers.

Khalil, H. K. (2002). *Nonlinear systems* (3rd ed.). Prentice Hall.

Kramer, I. (1999). Modeling the dynamical impact of HIV on the immune system: Viral clearance, infection, and AIDS. *Mathematical and Computer Modelling*, *29*(6), 95–112. doi:10.1016/S0895-7177(99)00057-6

Lodi, S., Phillips, A., Touloumi, G., Geskus, R., Meyer, L., Thiébaut, R., ... Porter, K. (2011). Time from human immunodeficiency virus seroconversion to reaching CD4+ cell count thresholds< 200,< 350, and< 500 cells/mm3: Assessment of need following changes in treatment guidelines. *Clinical Infectious Diseases*, *53*(8), 817–825. doi:10.1093/cid/cir494 PMID:21921225

Mayo Clinic. (2010). *Mayo Clinic Internal Medicine Review* (Greek edition). Thessaloniki, Greece: Rotonda Press.

Mhawej, M. J., Moog, C. H., & Biafore, F. (2009). The HIV dynamics is a single input system. In *13th International Conference on Biomedical Engineering* (pp. 1263-1266). Springer Berlin Heidelberg. 10.1007/978-3-540-92841-6_310

Mhawej, M. J., Moog, C. H., Biafore, F., & Brunet-Franois, C. (2010). Control of the HIV infection and drug dosage. *Biomedical Signal Processing and Control*, *5*(1), 45–52. doi:10.1016/j.bspc.2009.05.001

Moog, C. H., Ouattara, D. A., & Mhawej, M. J. (2007). Analysis of the HIV dynamics. *IFAC Proceedings Volumes, 40*(12), 379-386.

Moualeu, D. P., Mbang, J., Ndoundam, R., & Bowong, S. (2011). Modeling and analysis of HIV and hepatitis C co-infections. *Journal of Biological System*, *19*(04), 683–723. doi:10.1142/S0218339011004159

Mousa, M. E., Ebrahim, M. A., & Hassan, M. M. (2015). Stabilizing and swinging-up the inverted pendulum using PI and PID controllers based on reduced linear quadratic regulator tuned by PSO. *International Journal of System Dynamics Applications*, *4*(4), 52–69. doi:10.4018/IJSDA.2015100104

Moysis, L., Azar, A. T., Kafetzis, I., Tsiaousis, M., & Charalampidis, N. (2017). Introduction to Control Systems Design Using Matlab. *International Journal of System Dynamics Applications*, *6*(3), 130–170. doi:10.4018/IJSDA.2017070107

Moysis, L., Kafetzis, I., & Politis, M. (2016). Analysis of a Dynamical Model for HIV Infection with One or Two Inputs. *International Journal of System Dynamics Applications*, *5*(4), 83–100. doi:10.4018/IJSDA.2016100105

Moysis, L., Tsiaousis, M., Charalampidis, N., Eliadou, M., & Kafetzis, I. (2015). *An Introduction to Control Theory Applications with Matlab*. Retrieved from http://users.auth.gr/lazarosm/

Nikolopoulos, G. K., & Fotiou, A. (2015). "Integrated interventions are dead. Long live sustainable integrated interventions!"—Austerity Challenges the Continuation of Effective Interventions in the Field of Drug Use-Related Harm Reduction. *Substance Use & Misuse*, *50*(8-9), 1220–1222. doi:10.3109/10826084.2015.1042326 PMID:26361930

Nikolopoulos, G. K., Pavlitina, E., Muth, S. Q., Schneider, J., Psichogiou, M., Williams, L. D., ... Korobchuk, A. (2016). A network intervention that locates and intervenes with recently HIV-infected persons: The Transmission Reduction Intervention Project (TRIP). *Scientific Reports*, 6. PMID:27917890

Nikolopoulos, G. K., Sypsa, V., Bonovas, S., Paraskevis, D., Malliori-Minerva, M., Hatzakis, A., & Friedman, S. R. (2015). Big Events in Greece and HIV infection among people who inject drugs. *Substance Use & Misuse*, *50*(7), 825–838. doi:10.3109/10826084.2015.978659 PMID:25723309

Nise, N. S. (2015). *Control Systems Engineering* (7th ed.). John Wiley and Sons.

Nowak, M., & May, R. M. (2000). *Virus dynamics: Mathematical principles of immunology and virology: mathematical principles of immunology and virology*. Oxford University Press.

Panel on Antiretroviral Guidelines for Adults and Adolescents. (2016). *Guidelines for the use of antiretroviral agents in HIV-1-infected adults and adolescents.* Department of Health and Human Services. Retrieved from http://www.aidsinfo.nih.gov/ContentFiles/AdultandAdolescentGL.pdf

Perelson, A. S., & Nelson, P. W. (1999). Mathematical analysis of HIV-1 dynamics in vivo. *SIAM Review, 41*(1), 3–44. doi:10.1137/S0036144598335107

Perelson, A. S., & Ribeiro, R. M. (2013). Modeling the within-host dynamics of HIV infection. *BMC Biology, 11*(1), 96. doi:10.1186/1741-7007-11-96 PMID:24020860

Puhan, M. A., Van Natta, M. L., Palella, F. J., Addessi, A., & Meinert, C.. (2010). Excess mortality in patients with AIDS in the era of highly active antiretroviral therapy: Temporal changes and risk factors. *Clinical Infectious Diseases, 51*(8), 947–956. doi:10.1086/656415 PMID:20825306

Radisavljevic-Gajic, V. (2009). Optimal control of HIV-virus dynamics. *Annals of Biomedical Engineering, 37*(6), 1251–1261. doi:10.100710439-009-9672-7 PMID:19294513

Rivadeneira, P. S., & Moog, C. H. (2012). Impulsive control of single-input nonlinear systems with application to HIV dynamics. *Applied Mathematics and Computation, 218*(17), 8462–8474. doi:10.1016/j.amc.2012.01.071

Rivadeneira, P. S., Moog, C. H., Stan, G. B., Brunet, C., Raffi, F., Ferr, V., ... Ernst, D. (2014). Mathematical Modeling of HIV Dynamics After Antiretroviral Therapy Initiation: A Review. *BioResearch Open Access, 3*(5), 233–241. doi:10.1089/biores.2014.0024 PMID:25371860

Sastry, S. (2013). *Nonlinear systems: analysis, stability, and control* (Vol. 10). Springer Science Business Media.

Shehata, A. M., Elaiw, A. M., & Elnahary, E. K. (2017). Effect of antibodies and latently infected cells on HIV dynamics with differential drug efficacy in cocirculating target cells. *Journal of Computational Analysis and Applications, 22*(1).

Stephens, R. (2008). *The struggle for access to treatment for HIV/AIDS in India.* Socio Legal Information Cent.

Sypsa, V., Psichogiou, M., Paraskevis, D., Nikolopoulos, G., Tsiara, C., Paraskeva, D., ... Donoghoe, M. (2017). Rapid decline in HIV incidence among persons who inject drugs during a fast-track combination prevention program after an HIV outbreak in Athens. *The Journal of Infectious Diseases, 215*(10), 1496–1505. PMID:28407106

Tsang, M. A., Schneider, J. A., Sypsa, V., Schumm, P., Nikolopoulos, G. K., Paraskevis, D., ... Hatzakis, A. (2015). Network Characteristics of People Who Inject Drugs Within a New HIV Epidemic Following Austerity in Athens, Greece. *JAIDS Journal of Acquired Immune Deficiency Syndromes, 69*(4), 499–508. doi:10.1097/QAI.0000000000000665 PMID:26115439

World Health Organization. (2007). *WHO case definitions of HIV for surveillance and revised clinical staging and immunological classification of HIV-related disease in adults and children.* WHO.

Xia, X. (2003). Estimation of HIV/AIDS parameters. *Automatica, 39*(11), 1983–1988. doi:10.1016/S0005-1098(03)00220-6

Xia, X. (2007). Modelling of HIV infection: Vaccine readiness, drug effectiveness and therapeutical failures. *Journal of Process Control, 17*(3), 253–260. doi:10.1016/j.jprocont.2006.10.007

Xia, X., & Moog, C. H. (2003). Identifiability of nonlinear systems with application to HIV/AIDS models. *IEEE Transactions on Automatic Control, 48*(2), 330–336. doi:10.1109/TAC.2002.808494

Zhu, Q., & Azar, A. T. (2015). *Complex system modelling and control through intelligent soft computations. Studies in Fuzziness and Soft Computing* (Vol. 319). Springer-Verlag.

Chapter 13
A Novel Hyperchaotic System With Adaptive Control, Synchronization, and Circuit Simulation

Sundarapandian Vaidyanathan
Vel Tech University, India

Ahmad Taher Azar
Benha University, Egypt & Nile University, Egypt

Aceng Sambas
Universitas Muhammadiyah Tasikmalaya, Indonesia

Shikha Singh
Jamia Millia Islamia, India

Kammogne Soup Tewa Alain
Dschang University, Cameroon

Fernando E. Serrano
Central American Technical University (UNITEC), Honduras

ABSTRACT

This chapter announces a new four-dimensional hyperchaotic system having two positive Lyapunov exponents, a zero Lyapunov exponent, and a negative Lyapunov exponent. Since the sum of the Lyapunov exponents of the new hyperchaotic system is shown to be negative, it is a dissipative system. The phase portraits of the new hyperchaotic system are displayed with both two-dimensional and three-dimensional phase portraits. Next, the qualitative properties of the new hyperchaotic system are dealt with in detail. It is shown that the new hyperchaotic system has three unstable equilibrium points. Explicitly, it is shown that the equilibrium at the origin is a saddle-point, while the other two equilibrium points are saddle-focus equilibrium points. Thus, it is shown that all three equilibrium points of the new hyperchaotic system are unstable. Numerical simulations with MATLAB have been shown to validate and demonstrate all the new results derived in this chapter. Finally, a circuit design of the new hyperchaotic system is implemented in MultiSim to validate the theoretical model.

DOI: 10.4018/978-1-5225-4077-9.ch013

1. INTRODUCTION

The first experimental chaotic system was discovered by the American meteorologist E.N. Lorenz when he was studying weather patterns with a 3-D model (Lorenz, 1963). Characteristics of a chaotic system are: (1) dynamical instability, (2) topological mixing, and (3) dense periodic orbits (Hasselblatt & Katok, 2003). Dynamical instability is also known as the "butterfly effect", which means that a small change in initial conditions of system can create significant differences. This characteristic makes the chaotic system highly sensitive to initial conditions (Strogatz, 1994). Topologically mixing for a chaotic system refers to stretching and folding of the phase space, which means that the chaotic trajectory at the phase space will evolve in time so that each given area of this trajectory will eventually cover part of any particular region. Having dense periodic orbits means that the trajectory of a chaotic system can come arbitrarily close every possible asymptotic state. Hence, the future behavior of a chaotic system is quite complex and also unpredictable.

Chaos theory has several applications in science and engineering (Strogatz, 1994; Azar & Vaidyanathan, 2015a,b,c, 2016; Vaidyanathan & Volos, 2016; Azar et al., 2017a,b,c; Boulkroune et al, 2016a,b; Vaidyanathan et al, 2015a,b,c; Wang et al., 2017; Soliman et al., 2017; Tolba et al., 2017; Grassi et al., 2017; Ouannas et al., 2016a,b, 2017a,b,c,d,e,f,g,h,I,j; Singh et al., 2017; Vaidyanathan & Azar, 2015a,b,c,d, 2016a,b,c,d,e,f,g, 2017a,b,c). Some important applications of chaotic systems can be described as lasers (Donati & Hwang, 2012; Yuan, Zhang & Wang, 2013; Fen, 2017), neural networks (Potapov & Ali, 2000; Yang & Yuan, 2005; Kaslik & Sivasundaram, 2012; Akhmet & Fen, 2014; Przystalka & Moczulski, 2015; Vaidyanathan, 2015r; Fen & Fen, 2017; Bouallegue, 2017), memristors (Raj & Vaidyanathan, 2017; Pham et al., 2017; Vaidyanathan & Volos, 2017; Vaidyanathan, 2017b), chemical reactors (Vaidyanathan, 2015a,b,d,f,l), dynamo systems (Vaidyanathan, 2015c,e,p), fuzzy logic models (Yau & Shieh, 2008; Pai, Yau & Kuo, 2010; Li, 2011), biological systems (Vaidyanathan 2015g,j,k,n, 2017j), convection systems (Vaidyanathan, 2015i,o), DC motors (Rajagopal et al., 2017), mechanical systems (Vaidyanathan, 2017a,c,d,e,i), Tokamak systems (Vaidyanathan, 2015q), cardiology (Witte & Witte, 1991; Bozoki, 1997), oscillators (Vaidyanathan, 2015m, 2016a, 2016b, 2016c, 2016d, 2016e, 2016f, 2016g, 2017f, 2017g, 2017h; Vaidyanathan & Volos, 2015; Vaidyanathan & Boulkroune, 2016; Vaidyanathan & Pakiriswamy, 2016; Vaidyanathan & Rajagopal, 2016, 2017), voice encryption (Vaidyanathan et al., 2017), etc.

Hyperchaotic systems are chaotic systems equipped with two or more positive Lyapunov exponents. They have important applications in control and communication engineering (Vaidyanathan & Volos, 2016; Azar & Vaidyanathan, 2015a,b,c; Azar & Zhu, 2015; Zhu & Azar, 2015). Hyperchaotic system was first reported by Rössler in 1979. In the chaos literature, many hyperchaotic systems with interesting properties have been found (Rössler, 1979; Chen et al., 2007; Jia, 2007; Bao & Liu, 2008; Ghosh & Bhattacharya, 2010; Yu, Cai & Li, 2012). Hyperchaotic systems have applications in many areas such as cryptosystems (Wu, Bai & Kan, 2014; Hammami, 2015), secure communications (Hassan, 2014; He, Cai & Lin, 2016), encryption (Tong et al., 2015), etc.

In the control literature, many methods have been devised to regulate the state trajectories of a chaotic or hyperchaotic system with the help of feedback control laws. Some popular methods for chaos control can be listed as active control (Vaidyanathan, 2011a, 2011b, 2011c, 2012c), adaptive control (Vaidyanathan & Azar, 2016c,d,e,g, 2017b,c), backstepping control (Vaidyanathan, 2017c; Vaidyanathan & Idowu,

2016), sliding mode control (Vaidyanathan, 2012a, 2012b), etc. Many control methods have been also devised to synchronize the state trajectories of a pair of chaotic systems called master and slave systems asymptotically. Some popular methods for chaos synchronization can be listed as active control (Sarasu & Sundarapandian, 2011; Vaidyanathan & Pakiriswamy, 2011; Vaidyanathan & Rajagopal, 2011), adaptive control (Sarasu & Sundarapandian, 2012; Vaidyanathan & Rajagopal, 2012; Vaidyanathan & Pakiriswamy, 2013), backstepping control (Rasappan & Vaidyanathan, 2012; Shukla & Sharma, 2017), fuzzy logic control (Wang & Fan, 2015), sliding mode control (Sundarapandian & Sivaperumal, 2011; Vaidyanathan & Sampath, 2012), etc.

In this chapter, we derive a novel hyperchaotic system with a cubic nonlinearity and two quadratic nonlinearities. The phase portraits of the novel hyperchaotic system are depicted and the dynamical properties of the novel hyperchaotic system are discussed in detail. Explicitly, we show that the novel hyperchaotic system has three unstable equilibrium points. Thus, we exhibit that the novel hyperchaotic system has a self-excited attractor.

The rest of the chapter is organized as follows. A mathematical model of the new hyperchaotic system is proposed in Section 2. Dynamical properties of the new hyperchaotic system are detailed in Section 3. Adaptive control of the new hyperchaotic system is described in Section 4, while adaptive synchronization of a pair of identical new hyperchaotic systems is detailed in Section 5. Also, the circuit implementation of the new hyperchaotic system is presented in Section 6, which validates the theoretical hyperchaotic model. Finally, Section 7 contains the conclusions of this chapter.

2. A NEW HYPERCHAOTIC SYSTEM

In this section, we propose a novel 4-D hyperchaotic system, which is modelled by the following system of differential equations:

$$\begin{aligned} \dot{x}_1 &= a(x_2 - x_1) + bx_2x_3 + x_4 \\ \dot{x}_2 &= cx_2 - x_1x_3^2 \\ \dot{x}_3 &= -4x_3 + x_1x_2 \\ \dot{x}_4 &= 2x_1 + dx_4 \end{aligned} \tag{1}$$

In the system (1), x_1, x_2, x_3, x_4 are the state variables and a, b, c, d are positive constants, which are the parameters of the system. The system (1) has a cubic nonlinearity and two quadratic nonlinearities.

In this chapter, we show that the 4-D system (1) exhibits a strange hyperchaotic attractor for the parameter values

$$a = 32, \quad b = 17, \quad c = 15, \quad d = 0.3 \tag{2}$$

For numerical simulations, we take the initial value of the system (1) as

$$x_1(0) = 0.3, \quad x_2(0) = 0.3, \quad x_3(0) = 0.3, \quad x_4(0) = 0.3 \tag{3}$$

For the parameter values (2) and the initial conditions (3), the Lyapunov chaos exponents of the system (1) are numerically evaluated using Wolf's algorithm (Wolf et al., 1985) as

$$L_1 = 2.6494,\ L_2 = 0.3984,\ L_3 = 0,\ L_4 = -23.7478 \tag{4}$$

Since there are two positive Lyapunov exponents in the spectrum (4), we deduce that our new system (1) is hyperchaotic.

Figures 1-4 show 3-D views of the new hyperchaotic system (1) in (x_1, x_2, x_3), (x_1, x_2, x_4), (x_1, x_3, x_4) and (x_2, x_3, x_4) spaces, respectively.

Figures 5-8 show 2-D views of the new hyperchaotic system (1) in (x_1, x_2), (x_2, x_3), (x_3, x_4) and (x_1, x_4) planes, respectively.

From these figures, we deduce that the system (1) exhibits a *two-scroll* hyperchaotic attractor in R^4.

Figure 1. 3-D view of the new hyperchaotic system in (x_1, x_2, x_3) space

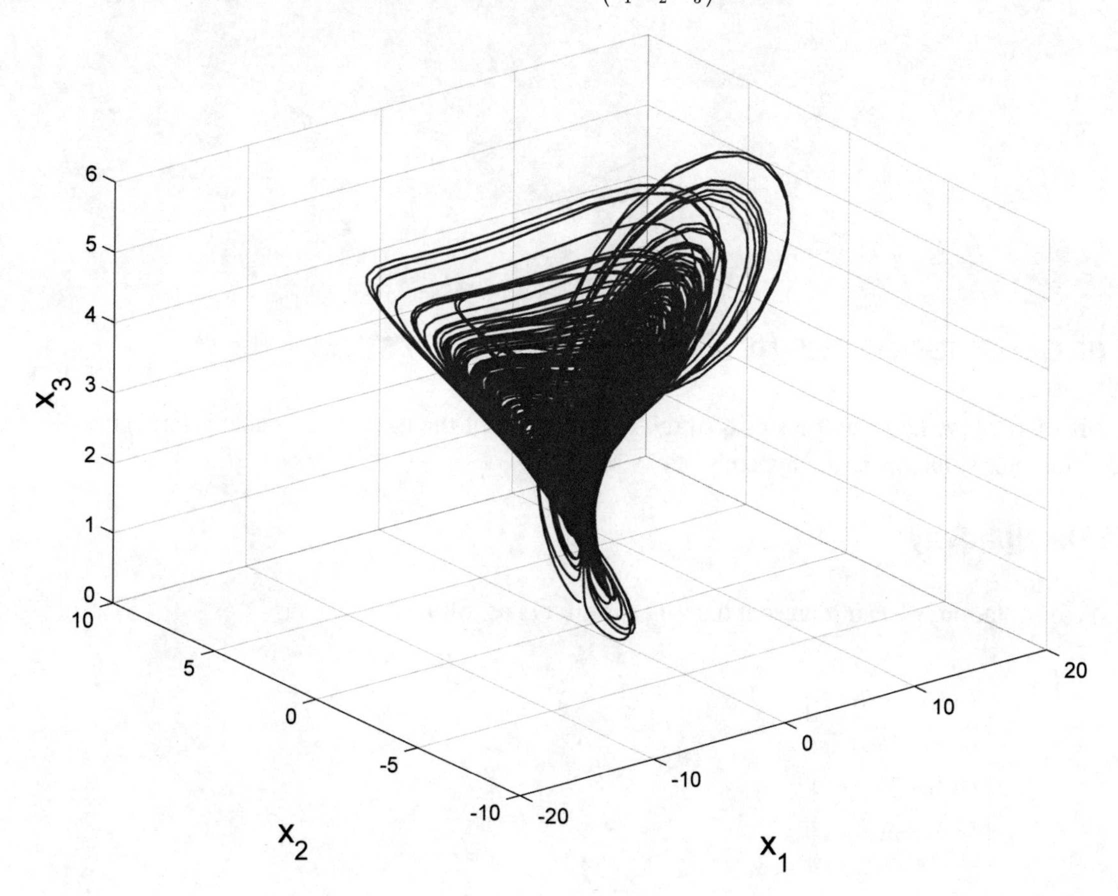

Figure 2. 3-D view of the new hyperchaotic system in (x_1, x_2, x_4) space

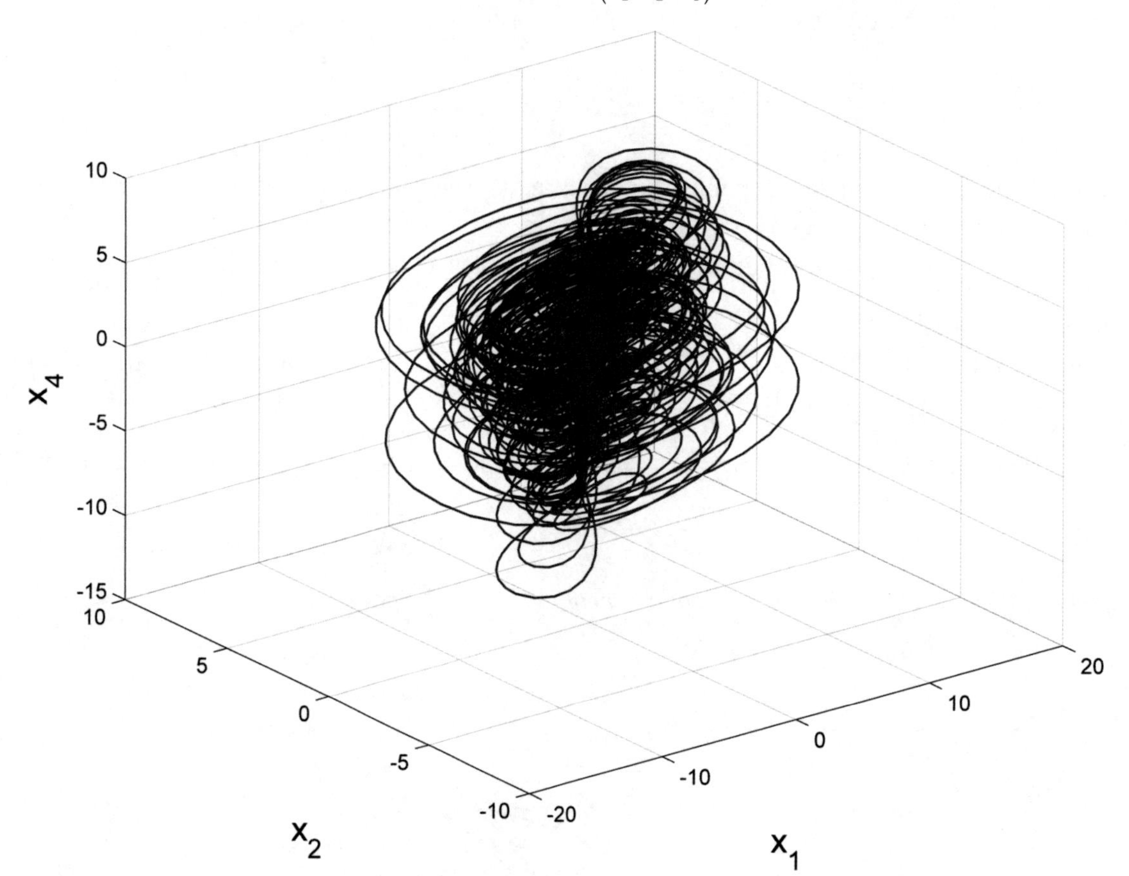

3. PROPERTIES OF THE NEW HYPERCHAOTIC SYSTEM

In this section, we describe various qualitative properties of the new hyperchaotic system (1). We take the parameter values as in the hyperchaotic case (2).

3.1 Dissipativity

In vector notation, we can represent the 4-D system (1) as follows:

$$\dot{x} = F(x) = \begin{bmatrix} f_1(x_1, x_2, x_3, x_4) \\ f_2(x_1, x_2, x_3, x_4) \\ f_3(x_1, x_2, x_3, x_4) \\ f_4(x_1, x_2, x_3, x_4) \end{bmatrix} \tag{5}$$

where

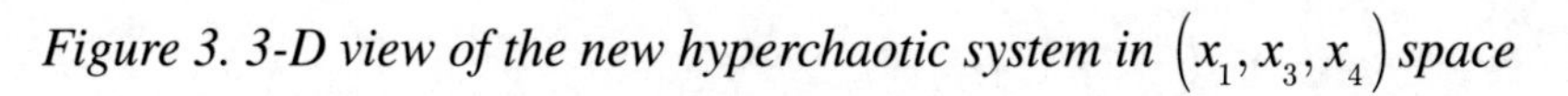

Figure 3. 3-D view of the new hyperchaotic system in (x_1, x_3, x_4) *space*

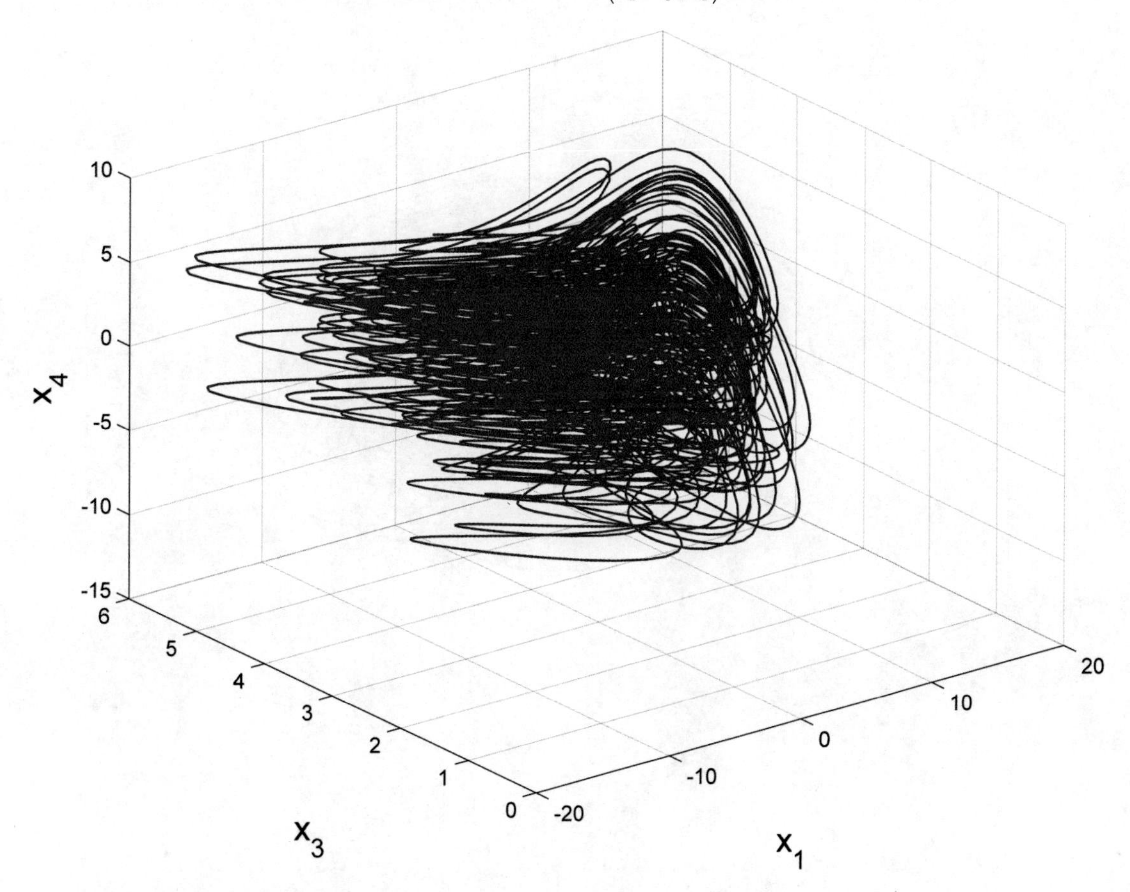

$$\begin{aligned} f_1(x_1, x_2, x_3, x_4) &= a(x_2 - x_1) + bx_2x_3 + x_4 \\ f_2(x_1, x_2, x_3, x_4) &= cx_2 - x_1x_3^2 \\ f_3(x_1, x_2, x_3, x_4) &= -4x_3 + x_1x_2 \\ f_4(x_1, x_2, x_3, x_4) &= 2x_1 + dx_4 \end{aligned} \tag{6}$$

In this section, the parameter values are taken as in the hyperchaotic case (2), i.e.

$$a = 32, \;\; b = 17, \;\; c = 15, \;\; d = 0.5 \tag{7}$$

The divergence of the vector field F is determined as follows:

$$\operatorname{div} F = \nabla \cdot F = \frac{\partial f_1}{\partial x_1} + \frac{\partial f_2}{\partial x_2} + \frac{\partial f_3}{\partial x_3} + \frac{\partial f_4}{\partial x_4} = -\zeta, \tag{8}$$

Figure 4. 3-D view of the new hyperchaotic system in (x_2, x_3, x_4) space

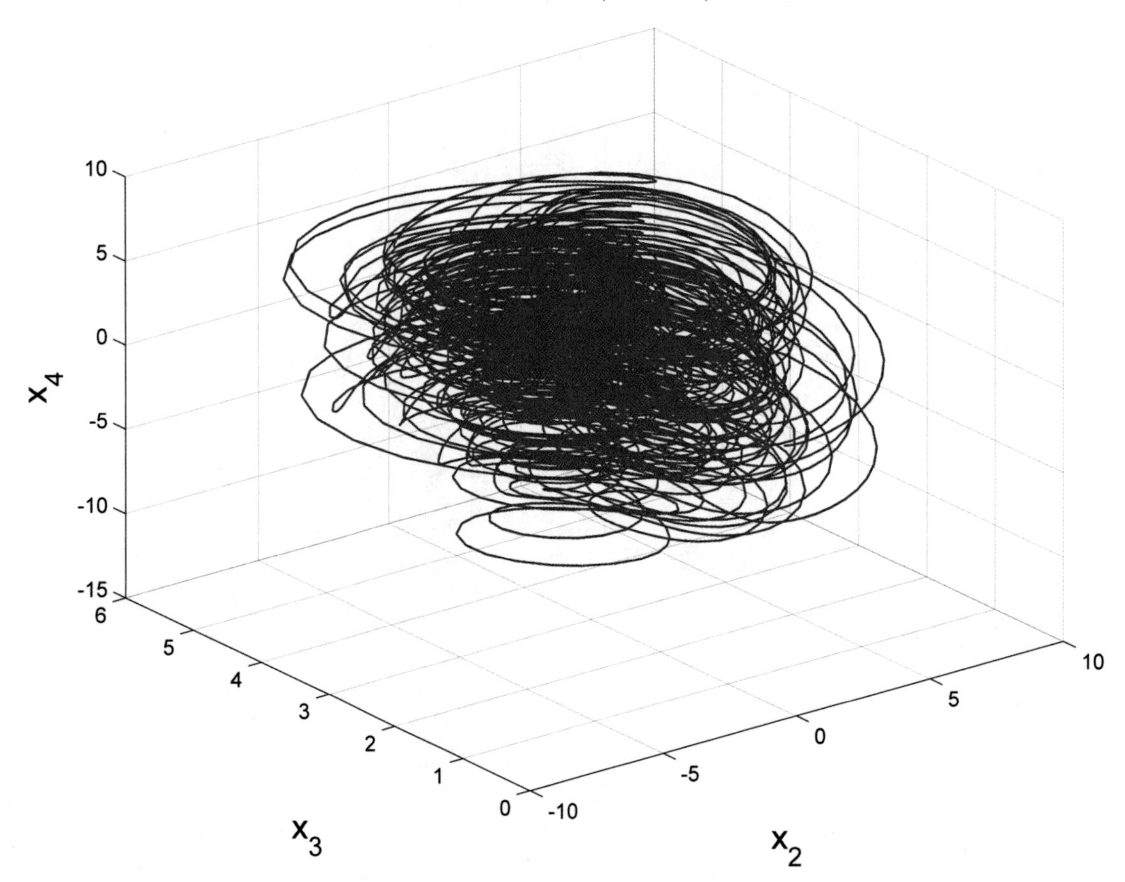

where

$$\zeta = a - c + 4 - d = 20.7 > 0. \tag{9}$$

We consider any region Ω in R^4 with a smooth boundary.

We define $\Omega(t) = \Phi_t(\Omega)$, where Φ_t is the flow of the vector field F. We represent the hypervolume of $\Omega(t)$ as $V(t)$.

By Liouville's theorem, we find that

$$\frac{dV}{dt} = \int_{\Omega(t)} (\text{div}\, F)\, dx_1 dx_2 dx_3 dx_4 = \int_{\Omega(t)} (-\zeta)\, dx_1 dx_2 dx_3 dx_4 = -\zeta V \tag{10}$$

Integrating the first order differential equation (10), we obtain the solution

Figure 5. 2-D view of the new hyperchaotic system in (x_1, x_2) plane

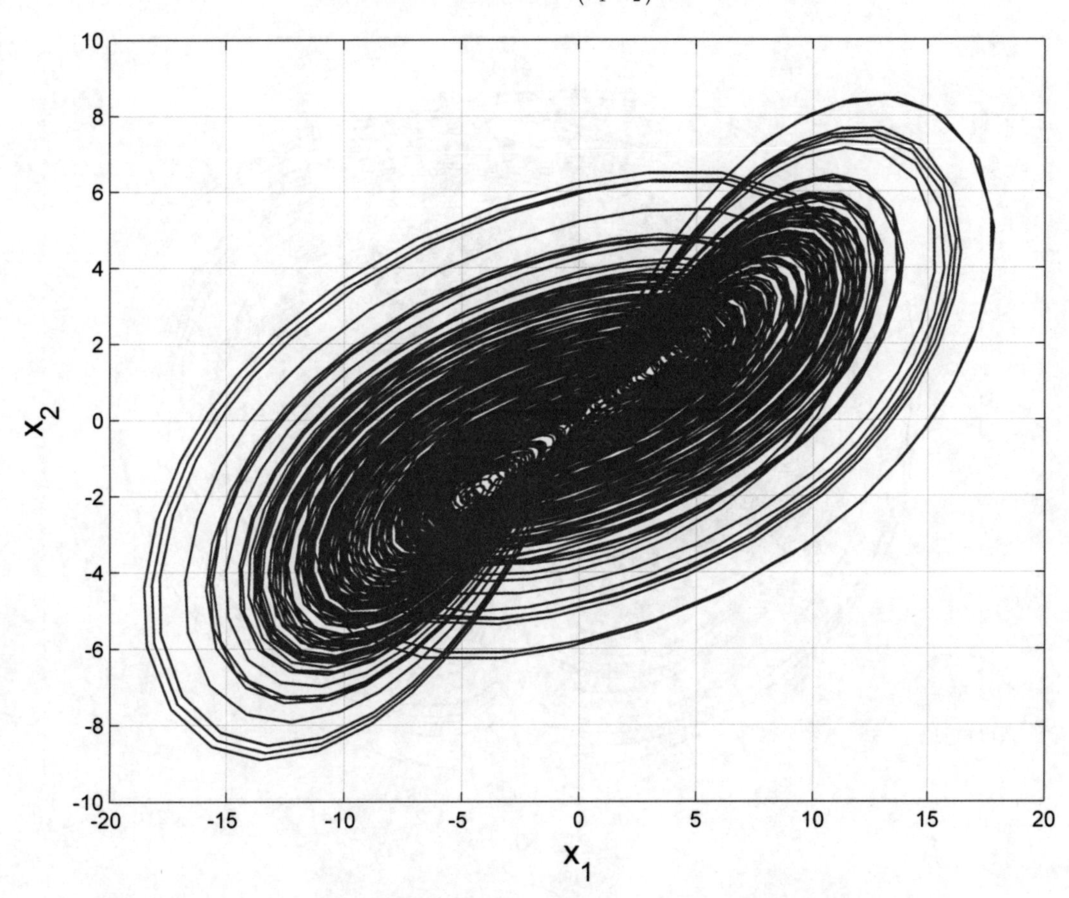

$$V(t) = V(0)\exp(-\zeta t) \tag{11}$$

Since $\zeta > 0$, it is immediate that the volume $V(t)$ shrinks to zero exponentially as $t \to \infty$.

Thus, the new 4-D hyperchaotic system (1) is dissipative.

Hence, the asymptotic motion of the novel 4-D hyperchaotic system (1) settles exponentially onto a set of measure zero, namely, a strange hyperchaotic attractor.

3.2 Symmetry

We consider a change of coordinates defined by

$$\begin{aligned} \xi_1 &= -x_1 \\ \xi_2 &= -x_2 \\ \xi_3 &= x_3 \\ \xi_4 &= -x_4 \end{aligned} \tag{12}$$

Figure 6. 2-D view of the new hyperchaotic system in (x_2, x_3) plane

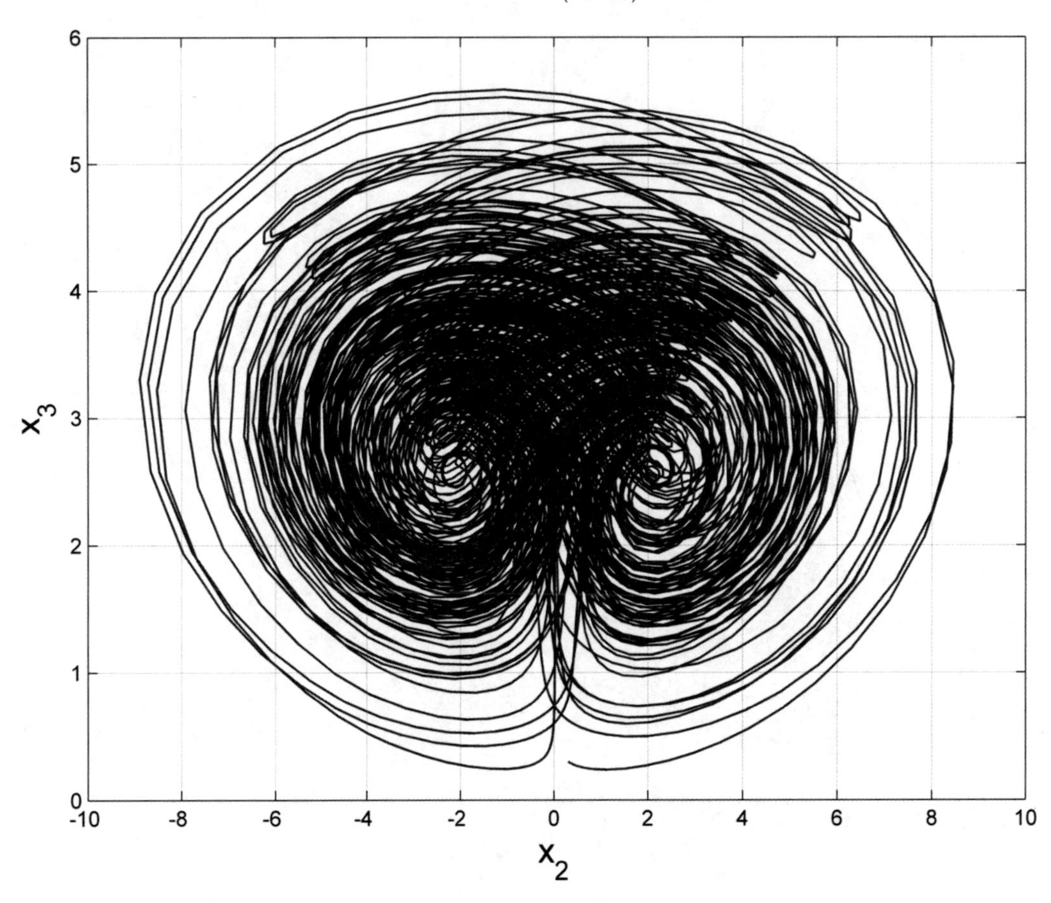

Under the change of coordinates (12), the new hyperchaotic system (1) becomes

$$\begin{aligned}
\dot{\xi}_1 &= a(\xi_2 - \xi_1) + b\xi_2\xi_3 + \xi_4 \\
\dot{\xi}_2 &= c\xi_2 - \xi_1\xi_3^2 \\
\dot{\xi}_3 &= -4\xi_3 + \xi_1\xi_2 \\
\dot{\xi}_4 &= 2\xi_1 + d\xi_4
\end{aligned} \tag{13}$$

Since the system (13) is the same as the system (1), we conclude that the system (1) is invariant under the change of coordinates (12). Hence, it follows that the new 4-D hyperchaotic system has rotation symmetry about the x_3 – axis. As a consequence, any non-trivial trajectory of the system (1) must have a twin-trajectory.

Figure 7. 2-D view of the new hyperchaotic system in (x_3, x_4) plane

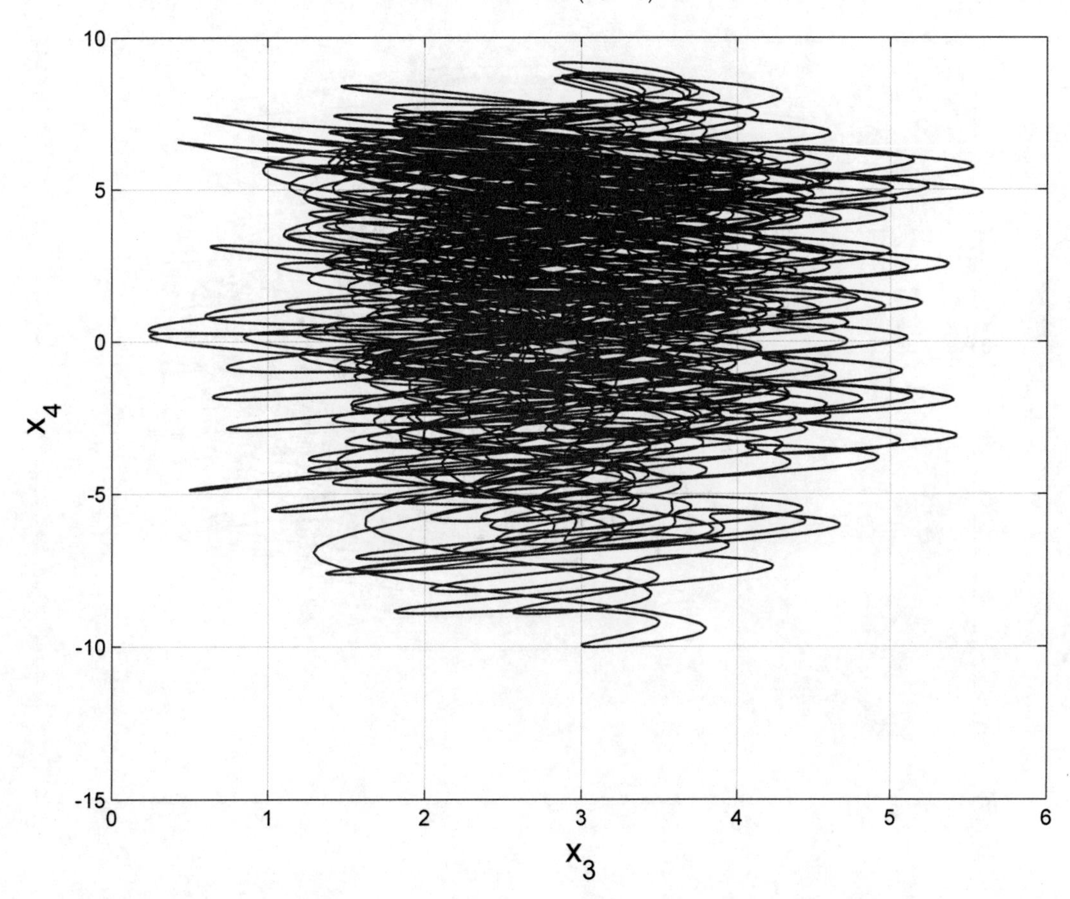

3.3 Invariance

It is easy to verify that the x_3 – axis is invariant under the flow of the hyperchaotic system (1). Hence, all orbits of the hyperchaotic system (1) starting on the x_3 – axis stay in the x_3 – axis for all values of time. Also, the invariant motion on the x_3 – axis is characterized by the 1-D dynamics

$$\dot{x}_3 = -4x_3 \tag{14}$$

which is globally exponentially stable.

3.4 Equilibrium Points

The equilibrium points of the new hyperchaotic system (1) are obtained by solving the following system of equations:

Figure 8. 2-D view of the new hyperchaotic system in (x_1, x_4) plane

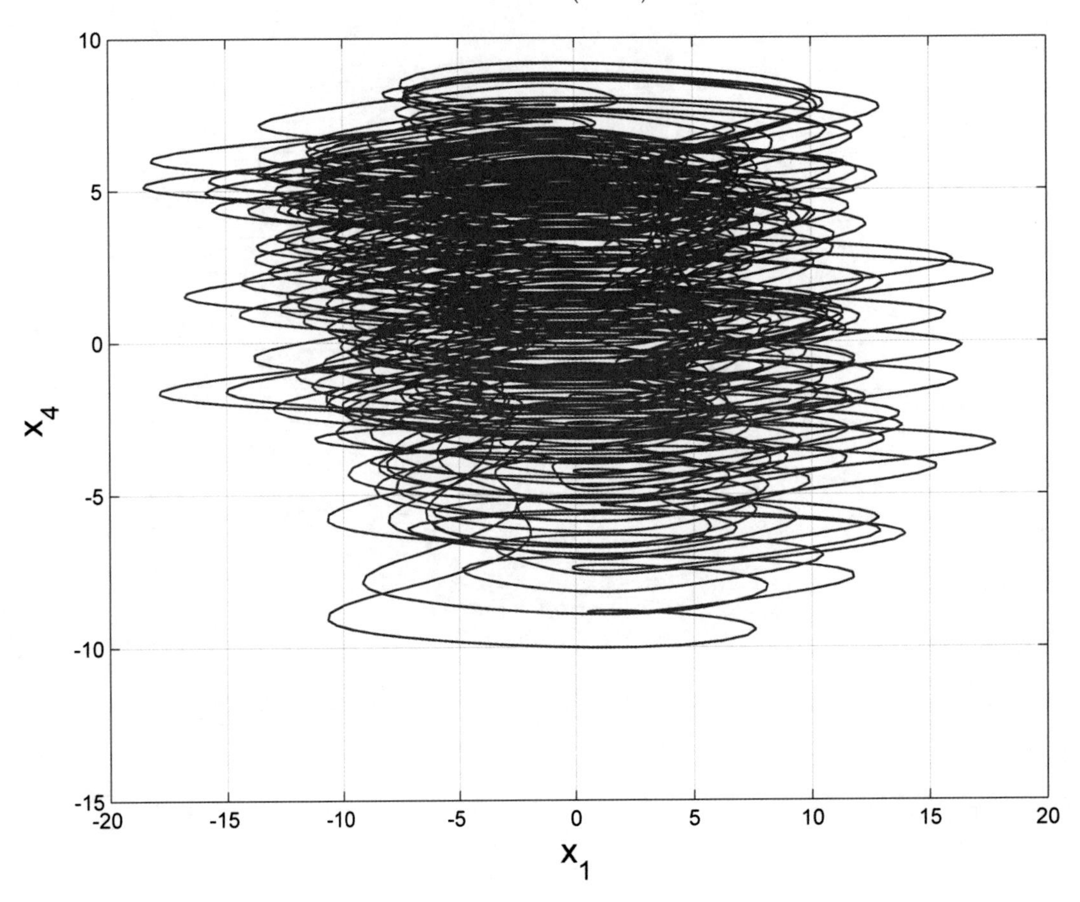

$$
\begin{aligned}
f_1(x_1, x_2, x_3, x_4) &= a(x_2 - x_1) + bx_2x_3 + x_4 = 0 \\
f_2(x_1, x_2, x_3, x_4) &= cx_2 - x_1x_3^2 = 0 \\
f_3(x_1, x_2, x_3, x_4) &= -4x_3 + x_1x_2 = 0 \\
f_4(x_1, x_2, x_3, x_4) &= 2x_1 + dx_4 = 0
\end{aligned}
\tag{15}
$$

We take the parameter values as in the hyperchaotic case (2).

Solving the system (15) with the parameter values in (2), we obtain three equilibrium points:

$$
E_0 = \begin{bmatrix} 0 \\ 0 \\ 0 \\ 0 \end{bmatrix}, \quad E_1 = \begin{bmatrix} -5.8800 \\ -2.4432 \\ 3.5916 \\ 39.2001 \end{bmatrix}, \quad E_2 = \begin{bmatrix} 5.8800 \\ 2.4432 \\ 3.5916 \\ -39.2001 \end{bmatrix} \tag{16}
$$

The Jacobian matrix of the new hyperchaotic system (1) at any point $x \in R^4$ is obtained as

$$J(x) = \begin{bmatrix} -32 & 32+17x_3 & 17x_2 & 1 \\ -x_3^2 & 15 & -2x_1x_3 & -1 \\ x_2 & x_1 & -4 & 0 \\ 2 & 0 & 0 & 0.3 \end{bmatrix} \quad (17)$$

We find that

$$J_0 = J(E_0) = \begin{bmatrix} -32 & 32 & 0 & 1 \\ 0 & 15 & 0 & -1 \\ 0 & 0 & -4 & 0 \\ 2 & 0 & 0 & 0.3 \end{bmatrix} \quad (18)$$

The eigenvalues of the matrix $J_0 = J(E_0)$ are numerically derived as

$$\lambda_1 = -4, \ \lambda_2 = -32.1037, \ \lambda_3 = 0.4973, \ \lambda_4 = 14.9063 \quad (19)$$

This shows that E_0 is a saddle-point. Hence, E_0 is unstable.
We also find that

$$J_1 = J(E_1) = \begin{bmatrix} -32 & 93.0572 & -41.5344 & 1 \\ -12.8996 & 15 & 42.2372 & -1 \\ -2.4432 & -5.8800 & -4 & 0 \\ 2 & 0 & 0 & 0.3 \end{bmatrix} \quad (20)$$

The eigenvalues of the matrix $J_1 = J(E_1)$ are numerically derived as

$$\lambda_1 = -24.6802, \ \lambda_2 = 0.2641, \ \lambda_{3,4} = 1.8581 \pm 31.9496\, i \quad (21)$$

This shows that E_1 is a saddle-focus point. Hence, E_1 is unstable.
Next, we find that

$$J_2 = J(E_2) = \begin{bmatrix} -32 & 93.0572 & 41.5344 & 1 \\ -12.8996 & 15 & -42.2372 & -1 \\ 2.4432 & 5.8800 & -4 & 0 \\ 2 & 0 & 0 & 0.3 \end{bmatrix} \quad (22)$$

The eigenvalues of the matrix $J_2 = J(E_2)$ are numerically derived as

$$\lambda_1 = -24.6802,\ \lambda_2 = 0.2641,\ \lambda_{3,4} = 1.8581 \pm 31.9496\, i \tag{21}$$

This shows that E_2 is a saddle-focus point. Hence, E_2 is unstable.

Since all the equilibrium points of the new hyperchaotic system (1) are unstable, it follows that it exhibits a self-excited hyperchaotic attractor.

3.5 Lyapunov Exponents and Kaplan-Yorke Dimension

We take the parameter values of the new hyperchaotic system (1) as in the hyperchaotic case (2) and the parameter values are taken as in (3). Then the Lyapunov exponents of the new hyperchaotic system (1) are numerically obtained for the parameter values (22) and the initial values (23) as

$$L_1 = 2.6494,\ L_2 = 0.3984,\ L_3 = 0,\ L_4 = -23.7478 \tag{22}$$

Thus, the system (1) is hyperchaotic since it has two positive Lyapunov exponents. Also, the system (1) is dissipative, since the sum of all Lyapunov exponents of the system (1) is negative. Figure 9 shows the Lyapunov exponents of the new hyperchaotic system (1).

Figure 9. Lyapunov exponents of the new hyperchaotic system (1)

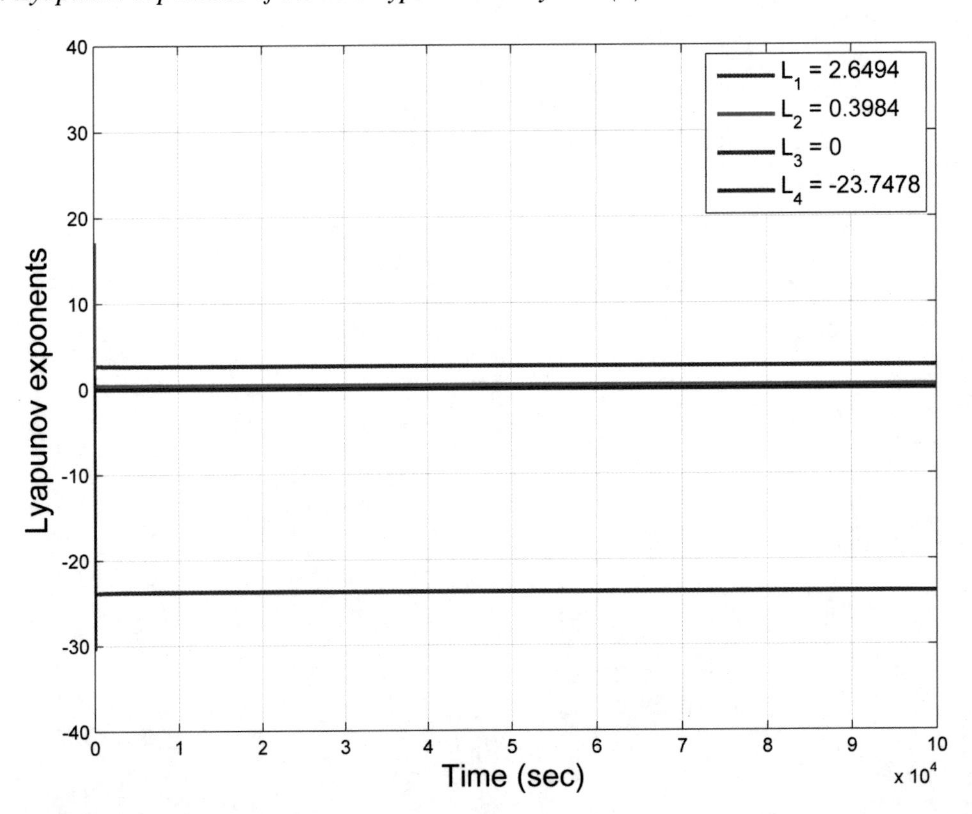

Also, the Kaplan-Yorke dimension of the new hyperchaotic system (1) is determined as

$$D_{KY} = 3 + \frac{L_1 + L_2 + L_3}{|L_4|} = 3.1283 \tag{23}$$

4. ADAPTIVE CONTROL OF THE NEW HYPERCHAOTIC SYSTEM

In this section, we derive a new adaptive control scheme for global stabilization of all the trajectories of the new hyperchaotic system with the help of Lyapunov stability theory. The importance of adaptive control scheme is that it helps practical implementation of state feedback law by using estimates of the unknown system parameters.

We consider the new hyperchaotic system with controls given by

$$\begin{aligned} \dot{x}_1 &= a(x_2 - x_1) + bx_2x_3 + x_4 + u_1 \\ \dot{x}_2 &= cx_2 - x_1x_3^2 - x_4 + u_2 \\ \dot{x}_3 &= -4x_3 + x_1x_2 + u_3 \\ \dot{x}_4 &= 2x_1 + dx_4 + u_4 \end{aligned} \tag{24}$$

In the system (24), x_1, x_2, x_3, x_4 are state variables, a, b, c, d are constant, unknown, parameters of the system and u_1, u_2, u_3, u_4 are adaptive controls to be designed using estimates of the unknown parameters.

We aim to solve the adaptive control problem by considering the adaptive feedback control law

$$\begin{aligned} u_1 &= -\hat{a}(t)(x_2 - x_1) - \hat{b}(t)x_2x_3 - x_4 - k_1x_1 \\ u_2 &= -\hat{c}(t)x_2 + x_1x_3^2 + x_4 - k_2x_2 \\ u_3 &= 4x_3 - x_1x_2 - k_3x_3 \\ u_4 &= -2x_1 - \hat{d}(t)x_4 - k_4x_4 \end{aligned} \tag{25}$$

In (25), k_1, k_2, k_3, k_4 are positive gain constants.

The closed-loop system is obtained by substituting (25) into (24) as

$$\begin{aligned} \dot{x}_1 &= [a - \hat{a}(t)](x_2 - x_1) + [b - \hat{b}(t)]x_2x_3 - k_1x_1 \\ \dot{x}_2 &= [c - \hat{c}(t)]x_2 - k_2x_2 \\ \dot{x}_3 &= -k_3x_3 \\ \dot{x}_4 &= [d - \hat{d}(t)]x_4 - k_4x_4 \end{aligned} \tag{26}$$

To simplify the closed loop system (26), we define the parameter estimation error as

$$\begin{aligned} e_a(t) &= a - \hat{a}(t) \\ e_b(t) &= b - \hat{b}(t) \\ e_c(t) &= c - \hat{c}(t) \\ e_d(t) &= d - \hat{d}(t) \end{aligned} \tag{27}$$

Substituting (27) into (26), the closed-loop gets simplified as

$$\begin{aligned} \dot{x}_1 &= e_a(x_2 - x_1) + e_b x_2 x_3 - k_1 x_1 \\ \dot{x}_2 &= e_c x_2 - k_2 x_2 \\ \dot{x}_3 &= -k_3 x_3 \\ \dot{x}_4 &= e_d x_4 - k_4 x_4 \end{aligned} \tag{28}$$

Differentiating the parameter estimation error (27) with respect to t, we get

$$\begin{aligned} \dot{e}_a(t) &= -\dot{\hat{a}}(t) \\ \dot{e}_b(t) &= -\dot{\hat{b}}(t) \\ \dot{e}_c(t) &= -\dot{\hat{c}}(t) \\ \dot{e}_d(t) &= -\dot{\hat{d}}(t) \end{aligned} \tag{29}$$

Next, we find an update law for parameter estimates using Lyapunov stability theory. Consider the quadratic Lyapunov function defined by

$$V(x_1, x_2, x_3, x_4, e_a, e_b, e_c, e_d) = \frac{1}{2}\left(x_1^2 + x_2^2 + x_3^2 + x_4^2 + e_a^2 + e_b^2 + e_c^2 + e_d^2\right) \tag{30}$$

It is clear that V is quadratic and positive definite on R^8.
Differentiating V along the trajectories of the systems (28) and (29), we get the following:

$$\dot{V} = -\sum_{i=1}^{4} k_i x_i^2 + e_a\left[x_1(x_2 - x_1) - \dot{\hat{a}}\right] + e_b\left[x_1 x_2 x_3 - \dot{\hat{b}}\right] + e_c\left[x_2^2 - \dot{\hat{c}}\right] + e_d\left[x_4^2 - \dot{\hat{d}}\right] \tag{31}$$

Next, we define an update law for the parameter estimates as follows:

$$\begin{aligned} \dot{\hat{a}} &= x_1(x_2 - x_1) \\ \dot{\hat{b}} &= x_1 x_2 x_3 \\ \dot{\hat{c}} &= x_2^2 \\ \dot{\hat{d}} &= x_4^2 \end{aligned} \tag{32}$$

Next, we state and prove the main result of this section.

Theorem 1. The new hyperchaotic system (24) with unknown system parameters is globally and exponentially stabilized for all initial conditions $x(0) \in R^4$ by the adaptive control law (25) and the parameter update law (32), where k_1, k_2, k_3, k_4 are positive constants.

Proof. The result is proved using Lyapunov stability theory (Khalil, 2002).

We consider the candidate Lyapunov function V defined by (28), which is a quadratic and positive definite function on R^8.

Next, we substitute the parameter update law (32) into (31).

Then the derivative of the Lyapunov function simplifies as follows:

$$\dot{V} = -k_1x_1^2 - k_2x_2^2 - k_3x_3^2 - k_4x_4^2 \tag{33}$$

which is a negative semi-definite function on R^8.

From Lyapunov stability theory (Khalil, 2002), it is clear that the state vector $x(t)$ and the parameter estimation error are both globally bounded.

Next, we define $k = \min\left\{k_1, k_2, k_3, k_4\right\}$.

From (33), it follows that

$$\dot{V} \leq -k\left\|x\right\|^2 \tag{34}$$

We can rewrite the inequality (34) as follows:

$$k\left\|x\right\|^2 \leq -\dot{V} \tag{35}$$

We integrate the inequality (35) from 0 to t. Then we obtain

$$k\int_o^t \left\|x(\tau)\right\|^2 d\tau \;\leq\; -\int_0^t \dot{V}(\tau)d\tau = V(0) - V(t) \tag{36}$$

From (36), it follows that $x(t) \in L_2$.

Using the closed-loop system (28), we can conclude that $\dot{x}(t) \in L_\infty$.

Applying Barbalat's lemma (Khalil, 2002), we can conclude that $x(t) \to 0$ exponentially as $t \to \infty$ for all initial conditions $x(0) \in R^4$.

This completes the proof. ■

Next, we apply classical fourth-order Runge-Kutta method to numerically solve systems of differential equations described in Theorem 1.

For the new hyperchaotic system (24), the parameter values are taken as in the hyperchaotic case (2), i.e.

$$a = 32, \;\; b = 17, \;\; c = 15, \;\; d = 0.3 \tag{37}$$

We take the feedback gains as

$$k_1 = 5, \;\; k_2 = 5, \;\; k_3 = 5, \;\; k_4 = 5 \tag{38}$$

The initial values of the hyperchaotic system (22) are taken as

$$x_1(0) = 4.6, \; x_2(0) = -5.2, \; x_3(0) = 3.7, \;\; x_4(0) = -8.1 \tag{39}$$

The initial values of the parameter estimates are taken as

$$\hat{a}(0) = 5.1, \; \hat{b}(0) = 3.8, \;\; \hat{c}(0) = 4.7, \; \hat{d}(0) = 2.2 \tag{40}$$

Figure 10 depicts the time-history of the controlled novel hyperchaotic system (24) when the adaptive control law (25) is applied.

Figure 10. Lyapunov exponents of the new hyperchaotic system (1)

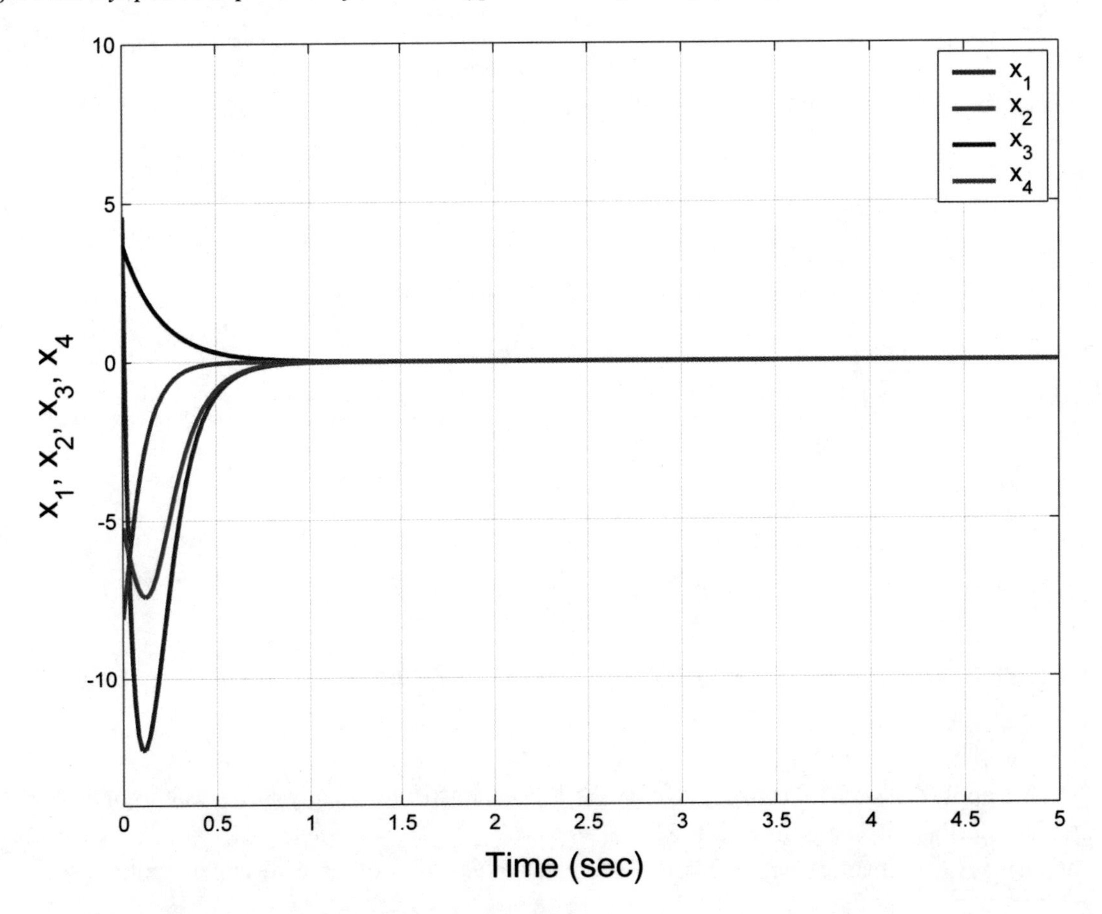

5. ADAPTIVE SYNCHRONIZATION OF THE NEW HYPERCHAOTIC SYSTEMS

In this section, we derive a new adaptive control scheme for the global synchronization of identical trajectories of a pair of new hyperchaotic systems (master and slave systems) with the help of Lyapunov stability theory. The importance of adaptive control scheme is that it helps practical implementation of state feedback law by using estimates of the unknown system parameters.

As the master system, we consider the new hyperchaotic system given by

$$\begin{aligned} \dot{x}_1 &= a(x_2 - x_1) + bx_2x_3 + x_4 \\ \dot{x}_2 &= cx_2 - x_1x_3^2 - x_4 \\ \dot{x}_3 &= -4x_3 + x_1x_2 \\ \dot{x}_4 &= 2x_1 + dx_4 \end{aligned} \tag{41}$$

In the system (41), x_1, x_2, x_3, x_4 are state variables, and a, b, c, d are constant, unknown, parameters of the system.

As the slave system, we consider the new hyperchaotic system with controls given by

$$\begin{aligned} \dot{y}_1 &= a(y_2 - y_1) + by_2y_3 + y_4 + u_1 \\ \dot{y}_2 &= cy_2 - y_1y_3^2 - y_4 + u_2 \\ \dot{y}_3 &= -4y_3 + y_1y_2 + u_3 \\ \dot{y}_4 &= 2y_1 + dy_4 + u_4 \end{aligned} \tag{42}$$

In the system (42), y_1, y_2, y_3, y_4 are state variables and u_1, u_2, u_3, u_4 are adaptive controls to be determined using estimates of the unknown parameters of the systems.

The synchronization error between the systems (41) and (42) is defined as follows:

$$\begin{aligned} e_1 &= y_1 - x_1 \\ e_2 &= y_2 - x_2 \\ e_3 &= y_3 - x_3 \\ e_4 &= y_4 - x_4 \end{aligned} \tag{43}$$

The error dynamics is obtained as follows:

$$\begin{aligned} \dot{e}_1 &= a(e_2 - e_1) + e_4 + b(y_2y_3 - x_2x_3) + u_1 \\ \dot{e}_2 &= ce_2 - e_4 - y_1y_3^2 + x_1x_3^2 + u_2 \\ \dot{e}_3 &= -4e_3 + y_1y_2 - x_1x_2 + u_3 \\ \dot{e}_4 &= 2e_1 + de_4 + u_4 \end{aligned} \tag{44}$$

Our goal in this section is to drive the synchronization errors to zero asymptotically as $t \to \infty$ for all values of $e(0) \in R^4$ with the help of adaptive controls based on the trajectories $x(t)$, $y(t)$ and estimates of the unknown system parameters.

We aim to solve the adaptive control problem by considering the adaptive feedback control law

$$\begin{aligned} u_1 &= -\hat{a}(t)(e_2 - e_1) - e_4 - \hat{b}(t)(y_2 y_3 - x_2 x_3) - k_1 e_1 \\ u_2 &= -\hat{c}(t) e_2 + e_4 + y_1 y_3^2 - x_1 x_3^2 - k_2 e_2 \\ u_3 &= 4e_3 - y_1 y_2 + x_1 x_2 - k_3 e_3 \\ u_4 &= -2e_1 - \hat{d}(t) e_4 - k_4 e_4 \end{aligned} \tag{45}$$

In (45), k_1, k_2, k_3, k_4 are positive gain constants.

The closed-loop system is obtained by substituting (45) into (44) as

$$\begin{aligned} \dot{e}_1 &= [a - \hat{a}(t)](e_2 - e_1) + [b - \hat{b}(t)](y_2 y_3 - x_2 x_3) - k_1 e_1 \\ \dot{e}_2 &= [c - \hat{c}(t)] e_2 - k_2 e_2 \\ \dot{e}_3 &= -k_3 e_3 \\ \dot{e}_4 &= [d - \hat{d}(t)] e_4 - k_4 e_4 \end{aligned} \tag{46}$$

To simplify the closed loop system (46), we define the parameter estimation error as

$$\begin{aligned} e_a(t) &= a - \hat{a}(t) \\ e_b(t) &= b - \hat{b}(t) \\ e_c(t) &= c - \hat{c}(t) \\ e_d(t) &= d - \hat{d}(t) \end{aligned} \tag{47}$$

Substituting (47) into (46), the closed-loop gets simplified as

$$\begin{aligned} \dot{e}_1 &= e_a(e_2 - e_1) + e_b(y_2 y_3 - x_2 x_3) - k_1 e_1 \\ \dot{e}_2 &= e_c e_2 - k_2 e_2 \\ \dot{e}_3 &= -k_3 e_3 \\ \dot{e}_4 &= e_d e_4 - k_4 e_4 \end{aligned} \tag{48}$$

Differentiating the parameter estimation error (47) with respect to t, we get

$$\begin{aligned} \dot{e}_a(t) &= -\dot{\hat{a}}(t) \\ \dot{e}_b(t) &= -\dot{\hat{b}}(t) \\ \dot{e}_c(t) &= -\dot{\hat{c}}(t) \\ \dot{e}_d(t) &= -\dot{\hat{d}}(t) \end{aligned} \tag{49}$$

Next, we find an update law for parameter estimates using Lyapunov stability theory.

Consider the quadratic Lyapunov function defined by

$$V(e_1,e_2,e_3,e_4,e_a,e_b,e_c,e_d)=\frac{1}{2}\left(e_1^2+e_2^2+e_3^2+e_4^2+e_a^2+e_b^2+e_c^2+e_d^2\right) \tag{50}$$

It is clear that V is quadratic and positive definite on R^8.

Differentiating V along the trajectories of the systems (48) and (49), we get the following:

$$\dot{V}=-\sum_{i=1}^{4}k_ie_i^2+e_a\left[e_1(e_2-e_1)-\dot{\hat{a}}\right]+e_b\left[e_1(y_2y_3-x_2x_3)-\dot{\hat{b}}\right]+e_c\left[e_2^2-\dot{\hat{c}}\right]+e_d\left[e_4^2-\dot{\hat{d}}\right] \tag{51}$$

Next, we define an update law for the parameter estimates as follows:

$$\begin{aligned}\dot{\hat{a}}&=e_1(e_2-e_1)\\ \dot{\hat{b}}&=e_1(y_2y_3-x_2x_3)\\ \dot{\hat{c}}&=e_2^2\\ \dot{\hat{d}}&=e_4^2\end{aligned} \tag{52}$$

Next, we state and prove the main result of this section.

Theorem 2. The new hyperchaotic systems (41) and (42) with unknown system parameters are globally and exponentially synchronized for all initial conditions $x(0), y(0)\in R^4$ by the adaptive control law (45) and the parameter update law (52), where k_1,k_2,k_3,k_4 are positive constants.

Proof. The result is proved using Lyapunov stability theory (Khalil, 2002).

We consider the candidate Lyapunov function V defined by (50), which is a quadratic and positive definite function on R^8.

Next, we substitute the parameter update law (52) into (51).

Then the derivative of the Lyapunov function simplifies as follows:

$$\dot{V}=-k_1e_1^2-k_2e_2^2-k_3e_3^2-k_4e_4^2 \tag{53}$$

which is a negative semi-definite function on R^8.

From Lyapunov stability theory (Khalil, 2002), it is clear that the error vector $e(t)$ and the parameter estimation error are both globally bounded.

Next, we define $k=\min\left\{k_1,k_2,k_3,k_4\right\}$.

From (53), it follows that

$$\dot{V}\le -k\left\|e\right\|^2 \tag{54}$$

We can rewrite the inequality (54) as follows:

$$k\|e\|^2 \leq -\dot{V} \tag{55}$$

We integrate the inequality (55) from 0 to t. Then we obtain

$$k\int_0^t \|e(\tau)\|^2 \, d\tau \ \leq \ -\int_0^t \dot{V}(\tau)d\tau = V(0) - V(t) \tag{56}$$

From (56), it follows that $e(t) \in L_2$.

Using the closed-loop error system (48), we can conclude that $\dot{e}(t) \in L_\infty$.

Applying Barbalat's lemma (Khalil, 2002), we can conclude that $e(t) \to 0$ exponentially as $t \to \infty$ for all initial conditions $e(0) \in R^4$.

This completes the proof. ■

Next, we apply classical fourth-order Runge-Kutta method to numerically solve systems of differential equations described in Theorem 2.

For the new hyperchaotic systems (41) and (42), the parameter values are taken as in the hyperchaotic case (2), i.e.

$$a = 32, \ \ b = 17, \ \ c = 15, \ \ d = 0.3 \tag{57}$$

We take the feedback gains as

$$k_1 = 5, \ \ k_2 = 5, \ \ k_3 = 5, \ \ k_4 = 5 \tag{58}$$

The initial values of the master system (41) are taken as

$$x_1(0) = 1.6, \ x_2(0) = 2.5, \ x_3(0) = 1.7, \ \ x_4(0) = 3.4 \tag{59}$$

The initial values of the slave system (42) are taken as

$$y_1(0) = 2.8, \ y_2(0) = 0.5, \ y_3(0) = 6.1, \ \ y_4(0) = 2.7 \tag{60}$$

The initial values of the parameter estimates are taken as

$$\hat{a}(0) = 1.4, \ \hat{b}(0) = 2.2, \ \ \hat{c}(0) = 3.8, \ \hat{d}(0) = 1.9 \tag{61}$$

Figures 11-14 show the complete synchronization of the new hyperchaotic systems (41) and (42).

Figure 15 shows the time-history of the synchronization errors e_1, e_2, e_3, e_4.

Figure 11. Synchronization of the states x_1 and y_1 of the new hyperchaotic systems

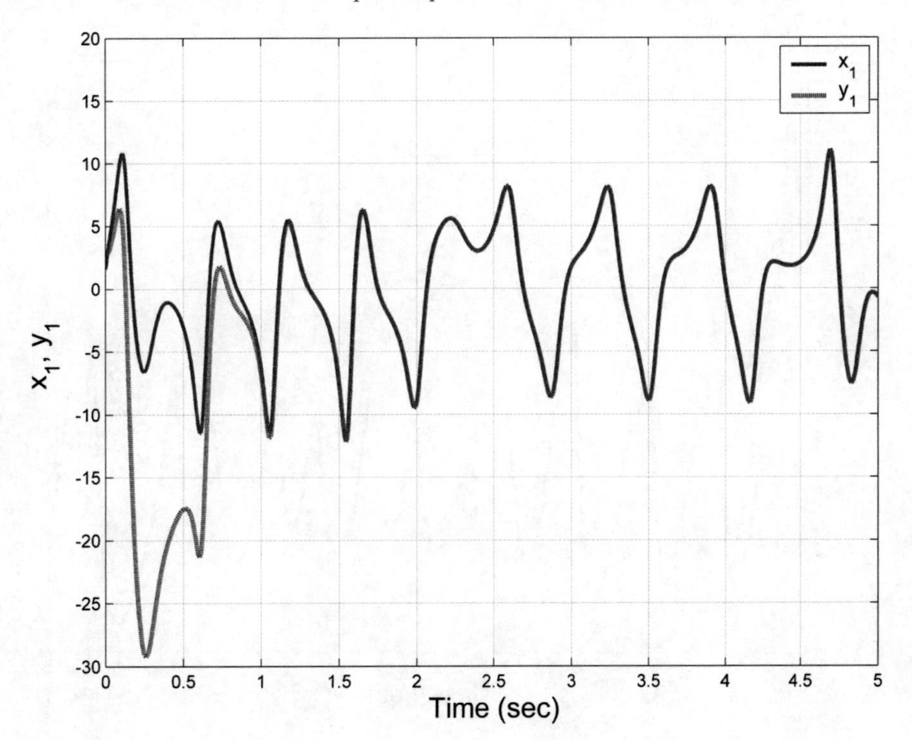

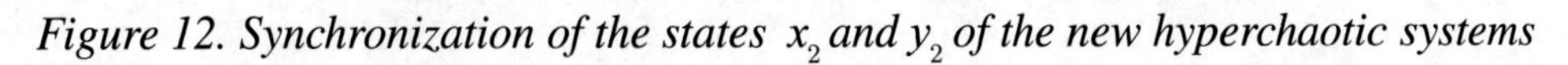

Figure 12. Synchronization of the states x_2 and y_2 of the new hyperchaotic systems

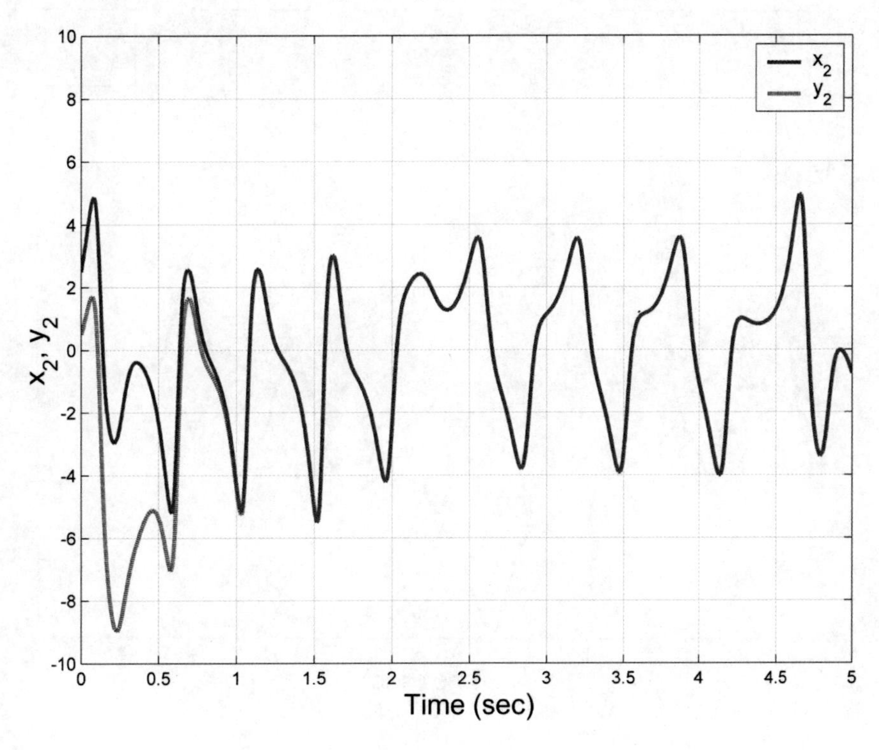

Figure 13. Synchronization of the states x_3 and y_3 of the new hyperchaotic systems

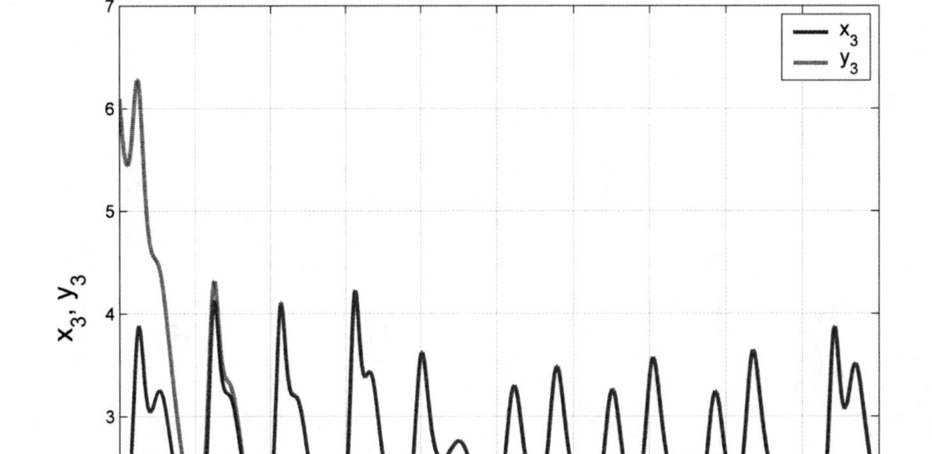

Figure 14. Synchronization of the states x_4 and y_4 of the new hyperchaotic systems

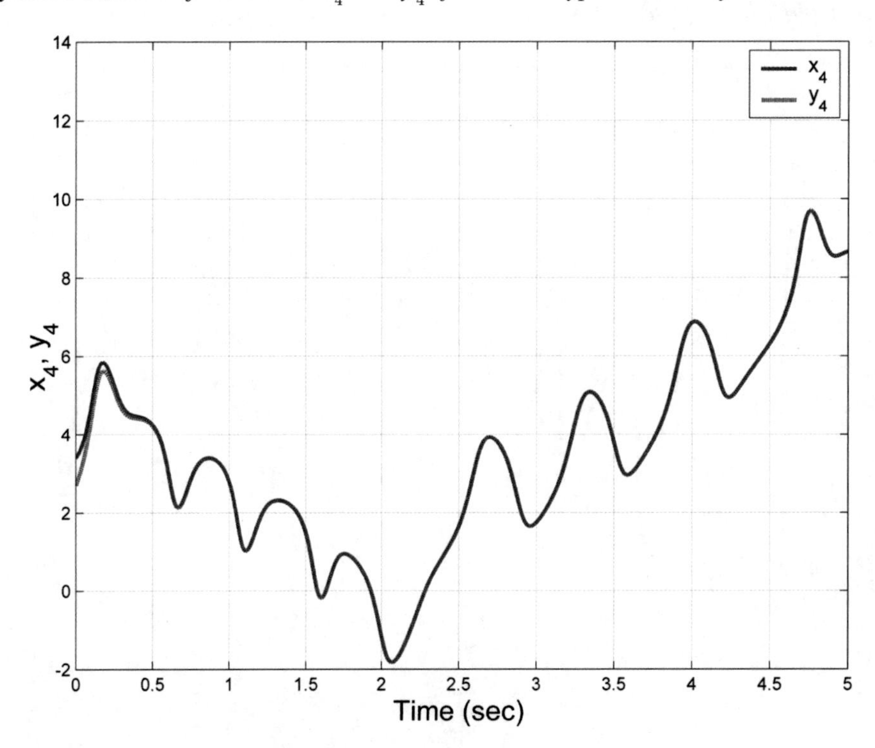

Figure 15. Time-history of the synchronization errors for the new hyperchaotic systems

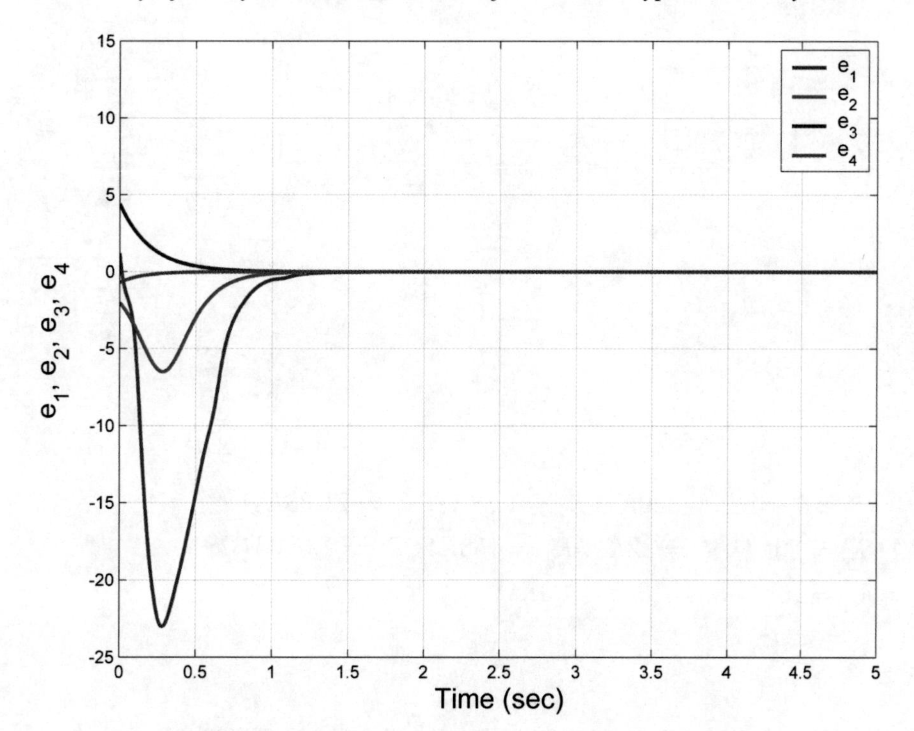

6. CIRCUIT IMPLEMENTATION OF THE NEW HYPERCHAOTIC SYSTEM

In this section, we describe the circuit implementation of the new hyperchaotic system (1) introduced in Section 2. Here, the electronic circuit design of the novel hyperchaotic system (1) is reported. The circuit designed shown in Figure 16, in which there are four integrators (U1A-U4A) with corresponding output voltages (VC1–VC4), three inverters (U5A-U7A) and four multipliers (AD633JN). The circuit equations, which are derived from Figure 16, have the following form:

$$\begin{cases} \dot{x}_1 = \dfrac{1}{C_1R_1}x_2 - \dfrac{1}{C_1R_2}x_1 + \dfrac{1}{10C_1R_3}x_2x_3 + \dfrac{1}{C_1R_4}x_4 \\ \dot{x}_2 = \dfrac{1}{C_2R_5}x_2 - \dfrac{1}{100C_2R_6}x_1x_3^{\,2} - \dfrac{1}{C_2R_7}x_4 \\ \dot{x}_3 = -\dfrac{1}{C_3R_8}x_3 + \dfrac{1}{10C_3R_9}x_1x_2 \\ \dot{x}_4 = \dfrac{1}{C_4R_{10}}x_1 + \dfrac{1}{C_4R_{11}}x_4 \end{cases} \tag{62}$$

We choose the values of the circuital elements as

Figure 16. Circuit design of the new hyperchaotic system (1)

$$\begin{cases} R_1 = R_2 = 10K\Omega, R_4 = R_7 = 320K\Omega, R_3 = 1.88K\Omega, R_5 = 21.33K\Omega, \\ R_6 = 3.2K\Omega, R_8 = 80K\Omega, R_9 = 32K\Omega, R_{10} = 160K\Omega, R_{11} = 1.066M\Omega \\ R_{12} = R_{13} = R_{14} = R_{15} = R_{16} = R_{17} = 100K\Omega \\ C_1 = C_2 = C_3 = 3.2nF \end{cases} \tag{63}$$

In Eq. (62), x_1, x_2, x_3, x_4 are corresponding the voltages at the capacitors (V_{C1}, V_{C2}, $V_{C3,}$ V_{C4}). The power supplies of all active devices are $\pm 15V_{DC}$. The MultiSIM projections of the novel hyperchaotic system (1) are presented in Figures 17-20. The MultiSIM results also show that the circuit model (62) can emulate the theoretical model (1).

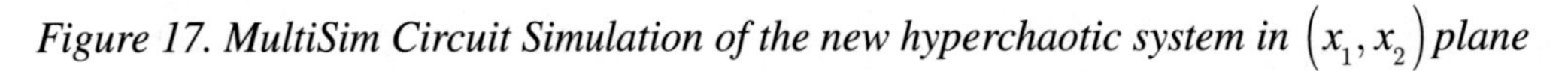

Figure 17. MultiSim Circuit Simulation of the new hyperchaotic system in (x_1, x_2) plane

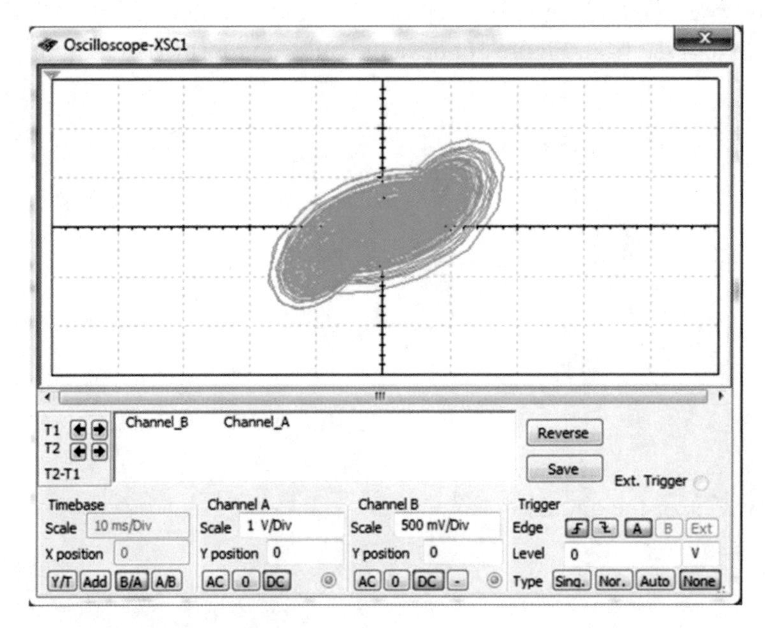

Figure 18. MultiSim Circuit Simulation of the new hyperchaotic system in (x_2, x_3) *plane*

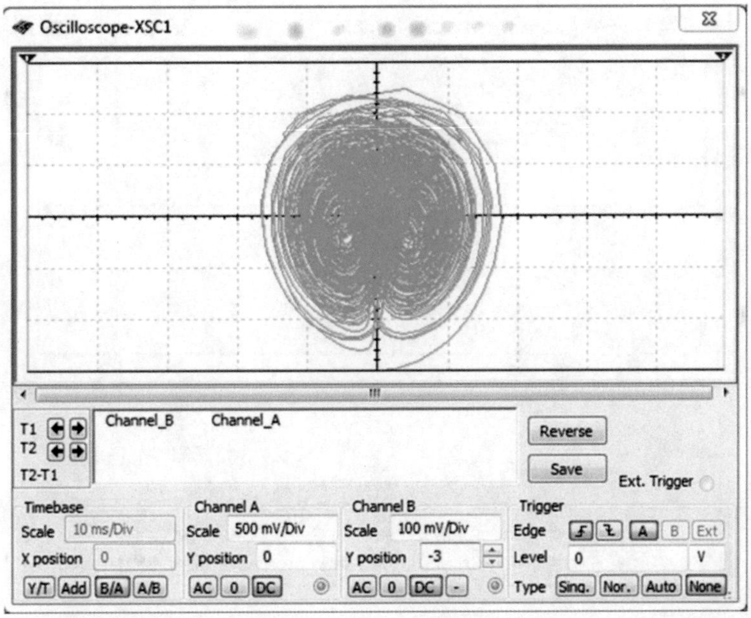

Figure 19. MultiSim Circuit Simulation of the new hyperchaotic system in (x_3, x_4) *plane*

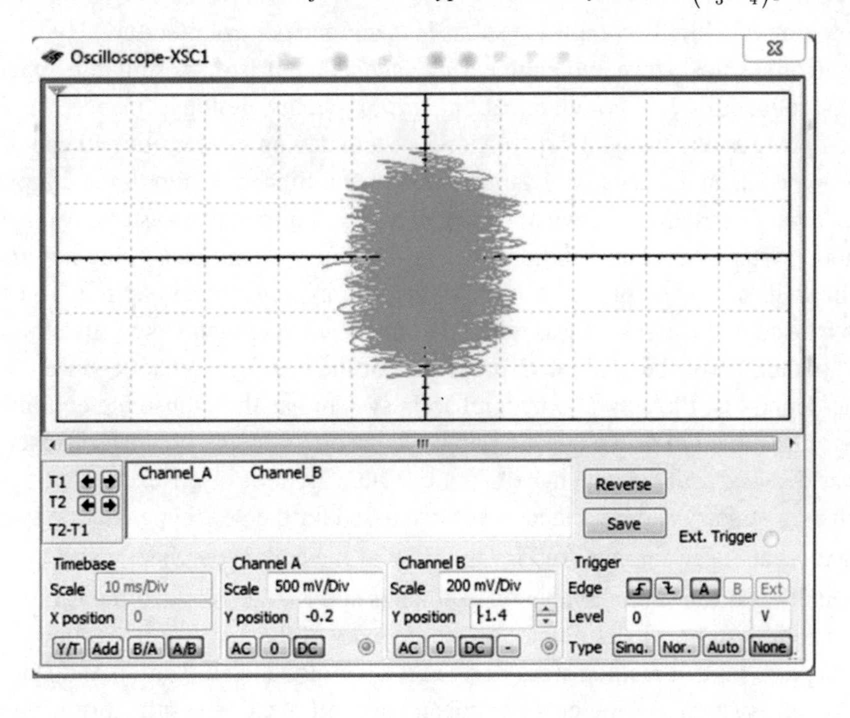

Figure 20. MultiSim Circuit Simulation of the new hyperchaotic system in (x_1, x_4) *plane*

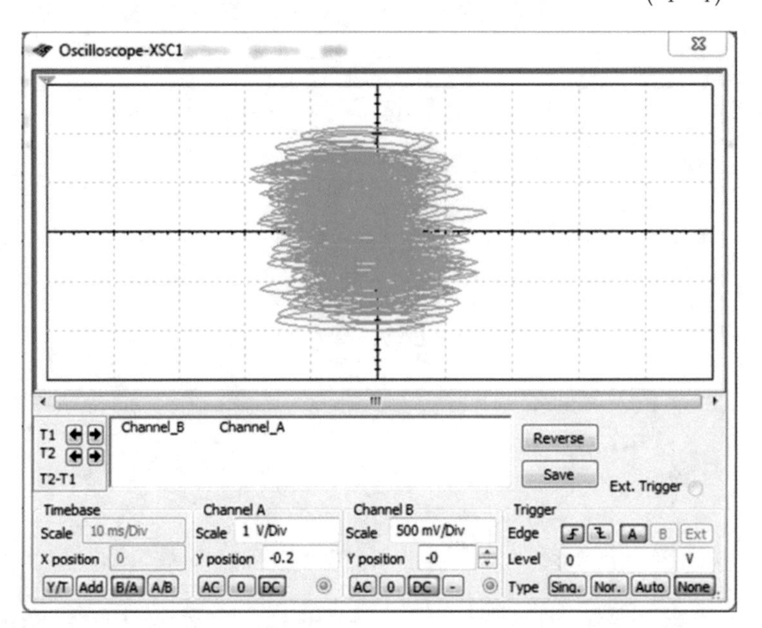

7. CONCLUSION

Hyperchaotic systems are highly complex systems in chaos and control literature. Hyperchaotic systems have many applications in science and engineering such as memristors, oscillators, chemical reactors, neural networks, robotics, secure communication, cryptosystems, biology, finance, etc. In this chapter, we described a new four-dimensional hyperchaotic system having two positive Lyapunov exponents, a zero Lyapunov exponent and a negative Lyapunov exponent. Since the sum of the Lyapunov exponents of the new hyperchaotic system is shown to be negative, it is a dissipative system. A novel feature of the new hyperchaotic system introduced in this work is that our system has a cubic nonlinearity and two quadratic nonlinearities. Several phase portraits of the new hyperchaotic system in 3-D spaces and 2-D planes were displayed in this work. It was noted that the new hyperchaotic system exhibits a two-scroll hyperchaotic attractor. Next, the qualitative properties of the new hyperchaotic system were dealt with in detail. It was found that the new 4-D hyperchaotic system has three unstable equilibrium points. In view of the new classification of the chaotic and hyperchaotic systems such as self-excited and hidden attractors, it was deduced that the new hyperchaotic system exhibits a self-excited attractor. Dynamical properties such as symmetry and invariance were discussed for the new hyperchaotic system. We found that the x_3 – axis is an invariant manifold for the flow of the new hyperchaotic system and the 1-D invariant flow is stable. Furthermore, Lyapunov exponents and Kaplan-Yorke dimension were derived for the new hyperchaotic system, which indicate the complexity of the new hyperchaotic system. Next, new results using adaptive control method were derived for the global stabilization and synchronization of the new hyperchaotic system. All the new control and synchronization results for the new hyperchaotic system were established using Barbalat's Lemma and Lyapunov stability theory. Numerical simulations with MATLAB were shown in detail to validate and demonstrate all the new results derived in this chapter. Finally, a circuit design of the new hyperchaotic system was implemented in MultiSim to validate the theoretical model.

REFERENCES

Akhmet, M., & Fen, M. O. (2014). Generation of cyclic/toroidal chaos by Hopfield neural networks. *Neurocomputing*, *145*, 230–239. doi:10.1016/j.neucom.2014.05.038

Azar, A. T., Ouannas, A., & Singh, S. (2017c). Control of New Type of Fractional Chaos Synchronization. *Proceedings of the International Conference on Advanced Intelligent Systems and Informatics 2017, 639*, 47-56.

Azar, A. T., & Vaidyanathan, S. (2015a). Handbook of Research on Advanced Intelligent Control Engineering and Automation. IGI Global. doi:10.4018/978-1-4666-7248-2

Azar, A. T., & Vaidyanathan, S. (2015b). *Computational Intelligence applications in Modeling and Control. Studies in Computational Intelligence* (Vol. 575). Springer-Verlag.

Azar, A. T., & Vaidyanathan, S. (2015c). *Chaos Modeling and Control Systems Design, Studies in Computational Intelligence* (Vol. 581). Springer-Verlag.

Azar, A. T., & Vaidyanathan, S. (2016). *Advances in Chaos Theory and Intelligent Control. Studies in Fuzziness and Soft Computing* (Vol. 337). Springer-Verlag. doi:10.1007/978-3-319-30340-6

Azar, A. T., Vaidyanathan, S., & Ouannas, A. (2017a). *Fractional Order Control and Synchronization of Chaotic Systems. Studies in Computational Intelligence* (Vol. 688). Springer-Verlag. doi:10.1007/978-3-319-50249-6

Azar, A.T., Volos, C., Gerodimos, N.A., Tombras, G.S., Pham, V.T., Radwan, A.G., ... Munoz-Pacheco, J.M. (2017b). A novel chaotic system without equilibrium: Dynamics, synchronization and circuit realization. *Complexity*. doi:10.1155/2017/7871467

Azar, A. T., & Zhu, Q. (2015). *Advances and Applications in Sliding Mode Control systems. Studies in Computational Intelligence* (Vol. 576). Springer-Verlag.

Bao, B. C., & Liu, Z. (2008). A hyperchaotic attractor coined from chaotic Lü system. *Chinese Physics Letters*, *25*(7), 2396–2399. doi:10.1088/0256-307X/25/7/018

Bouallegue, K. (2017). A new class of neural networks and its applications. *Neurocomputing*, *249*, 28–47. doi:10.1016/j.neucom.2017.03.006

Boulkroune, A., Bouzeriba, A., Bouden, T., & Azar, A. T. (2016a). Fuzzy Adaptive Synchronization of Uncertain Fractional-order Chaotic Systems. In A. T. Azar & S. Vaidyanathan (Eds.), *Advances in Chaos Theory and Intelligent Control. Studies in Fuzziness and Soft Computing* (Vol. 337). Springer-Verlag. doi:10.1007/978-3-319-30340-6_28

Boulkroune, A., Hamel, S., & Azar, A. T. (2016b). *Fuzzy control-based function synchronization of unknown chaotic systems with dead-zone input. Advances in Chaos Theory and Intelligent Control. Studies in Fuzziness and Soft Computing* (Vol. 337). Springer-Verlag.

Bozoki, Z. (1997). Chaos theory and power spectrum analysis in computerized cardiotocography. *European Journal of Obstetrics, Gynecology, and Reproductive Biology*, *71*(2), 163–168. doi:10.1016/S0301-2115(96)02628-0 PMID:9138960

Chen, Z., Yang, Y., Qi, G., & Yuan, Z. (2007). A novel hyperchaos system only with one equilibrium. *Physics Letters. [Part A]*, *360*(6), 696–701. doi:10.1016/j.physleta.2006.08.085

Donati, S., & Hwang, S. K. (2012). Chaos and high-level dynamics in coupled lasers and their applications. *Progress in Quantum Electronics*, *36*(2-3), 293–341. doi:10.1016/j.pquantelec.2012.06.001

Fen, M. O. (2017). Persistence of chaos in coupled Lorenz systems. *Chaos, Solitons, and Fractals*, *95*, 200–205. doi:10.1016/j.chaos.2016.12.017

Fen, M. O., & Fen, F. T. (2017). SICNNs with Li-Yorke chaotic outputs on a time scale. *Neurocomputing*, *237*, 158–165. doi:10.1016/j.neucom.2016.09.073

Ghosh, D., & Bhattacharya, S. (2010). Projective synchronization of new hyperchaotic system with fully unknown parameters. *Nonlinear Dynamics*, *61*(1-2), 11–21. doi:10.100711071-009-9627-4

Grassi, G., Ouannas, A., Azar, A. T., Radwan, A. G., Volos, C., Pham, V. T., . . . Stouboulos, I. N. (2017). *Chaos Synchronisation Of Continuous Systems Via Scalar Signal*. The 6th International Conference on Modern Circuits and Systems Technologies (MOCAST), Thessaloniki, Greece. 10.1109/MOCAST.2017.7937629

Hammami, S. (2015). State feedback-based secure image cryptosystem using hyperchaotic synchronization. *ISA Transactions*, *54*, 52–59. doi:10.1016/j.isatra.2014.05.027 PMID:25085481

Hassan, M. F. (2014). A new approach for secure communication using constrained hyperchaotic systems. *Applied Mathematics and Computation*, *246*, 711–730. doi:10.1016/j.amc.2014.08.029

Hasselblatt, B., & Katok, A. (2003). *A First Course in Dynamics: With a Panorama of Recent Developments*. Cambridge, UK: Cambridge University Press. doi:10.1017/CBO9780511998188

He, J., Cai, J., & Lin, J. (2016). Synchronization of hyperchaotic systems with multiple unknown parameters and its application in secure communication. *Optik (Stuttgart)*, *127*(5), 2502–2508. doi:10.1016/j.ijleo.2015.11.055

Jia, Q. (2007). Hyperchaos generated from the Lorenz chaotic system and its control. *Physics Letters. [Part A]*, *366*(3), 217–222. doi:10.1016/j.physleta.2007.02.024

Kaslik, E., & Sivasundaram, S. (2012). Nonlinear dynamics and chaos in fractional-order neural networks. *Neural Networks*, *32*, 245–256. doi:10.1016/j.neunet.2012.02.030 PMID:22386788

Khalil, H. K. (2002). *Nonlinear Systems*. Prentice Hall.

Li, S. Y. (2011). Chaos control of new Mathieu–van der Pol systems by fuzzy logic constant controllers. *Applied Soft Computing*, *11*(8), 4474–4487. doi:10.1016/j.asoc.2011.08.024

Lorenz, E. N. (1963). Deterministic nonperiodic flow. *Journal of the Atmospheric Sciences*, *29*(2), 130–141. doi:

Ouannas, A., Azar, A. T., & Abu-Saris, R. (2016a). A new type of hybrid synchronization between arbitrary hyperchaotic maps. *International Journal of Machine Learning and Cybernetics*. doi:10.100713042-016-0566-3

Ouannas, A., Azar, A. T., & Radwan, A. G. (2016b). *On Inverse Problem of Generalized Synchronization Between Different Dimensional Integer-Order and Fractional-Order Chaotic Systems*. The 28th International Conference on Microelectronics, Cairo, Egypt. 10.1109/ICM.2016.7847942

Ouannas, A., Azar, A. T., & Vaidyanathan, S. (2017f). On A Simple Approach for Q-S Synchronization of Chaotic Dynamical Systems in Continuous-Time. *Int. J. Computing Science and Mathematics*, *8*(1), 20–27.

Ouannas, A., Azar, A. T., & Vaidyanathan, S. (2017g). New Hybrid Synchronization Schemes Based on Coexistence of Various Types of Synchronization Between Master-Slave Hyperchaotic Systems. *International Journal of Computer Applications in Technology*, *55*(2), 112–120. doi:10.1504/IJCAT.2017.082868

Ouannas, A., Azar, A. T., & Vaidyanathan, S. (2017i). A Robust Method for New Fractional Hybrid Chaos Synchronization. *Mathematical Methods in the Applied Sciences*, *40*(5), 1804–1812. doi:10.1002/mma.4099

Ouannas, A., Azar, A. T., & Ziar, T. (2017h). *On Inverse Full State Hybrid Function Projective Synchronization for Continuous-time Chaotic Dynamical Systems with Arbitrary Dimensions*. Differential Equations and Dynamical Systems. doi:10.100712591-017-0362-x

Ouannas, A., Azar, A. T., Ziar, T., & Radwan, A. G. (2017d). *Study On Coexistence of Different Types of Synchronization Between Different dimensional Fractional Chaotic Systems. Studies in Computational Intelligence* (Vol. 688). Springer-Verlag.

Ouannas, A., Azar, A. T., Ziar, T., & Radwan, A. G. (2017e). *Generalized Synchronization of Different Dimensional Integer-order and Fractional Order Chaotic Systems. Studies in Computational Intelligence* (Vol. 688). Springer-Verlag.

Ouannas, A., Azar, A. T., Ziar, T., & Vaidyanathan, S. (2017a). *On New Fractional Inverse Matrix Projective Synchronization Schemes. Studies in Computational Intelligence* (Vol. 688). Springer-Verlag.

Ouannas, A., Azar, A. T., Ziar, T., & Vaidyanathan, S. (2017b). *Fractional Inverse Generalized Chaos Synchronization Between Different Dimensional Systems. Studies in Computational Intelligence* (Vol. 688). Springer-Verlag.

Ouannas, A., Azar, A. T., Ziar, T., & Vaidyanathan, S. (2017c). *A New Method To Synchronize Fractional Chaotic Systems With Different Dimensions. Studies in Computational Intelligence* (Vol. 688). Springer-Verlag.

Ouannas, A., Grassi, G., Azar, A. T., Radwan, A. G., Volos, C., Pham, V. T., . . . Stouboulos, I. N. (2017j). *Dead-Beat Synchronization Control in Discrete-Time Chaotic Systems*. The 6th International Conference on Modern Circuits and Systems Technologies (MOCAST), Thessaloniki, Greece. 10.1109/MOCAST.2017.7937628

Pai, N. S., Yau, H. T., & Kuo, C. L. (2010). Fuzzy logic combining controller design for chaos control of a rod-type plasma torch system. *Expert Systems with Applications*, *37*(12), 8278–8283. doi:10.1016/j.eswa.2010.05.057

Pham, V. T., Vaidyanathan, S., Volos, C., Wang, X., & Hoang, D. V. (2017). A hyperjerk memristive system with hidden attractors. *Studies in Computational Intelligence*, *701*, 59–80.

Pham, V. T., Vaidyanathan, S., Volos, C. K., Azar, A. T., Hoang, T. M., & Yem, V. V. (2017a). A Three-Dimensional No-Equilibrium Chaotic System: Analysis, Synchronization and Its Fractional Order Form. Studies in Computational Intelligence, 688, 449-470.

Potapov, A., & Ali, M. K. (2000). Robust chaos in neural networks. *Physics Letters. [Part A]*, *277*(6), 310–322. doi:10.1016/S0375-9601(00)00726-X

Przystalka, P., & Moczulski, W. (2015). Methodology of neural modelling in fault detection with the use of chaos engineering. *Engineering Applications of Artificial Intelligence*, *41*, 25–40. doi:10.1016/j.engappai.2015.01.016

Raj, B., & Vaidyanathan, S. (2017). Analysis of dynamic linear memristor device models. *Studies in Computational Intelligence*, *701*, 449–476.

Rajagopal, K., Vaidyanathan, S., Karthikeyan, A., & Duraisamy, P. (2017). Dynamic analysis and chaos suppression in a fractional order brushless DC motor. *Electrical Engineering*, *99*(2), 721–733. doi:10.100700202-016-0444-8

Rasappan, S., & Vaidyanathan, S. (2012). Hybrid synchronization of n-scroll Chua and Lur'e chaotic systems via backstepping control with novel feedback. *Archives of Control Sciences*, *22*(3), 343–365.

Rössler, O. (1979). An equation for hyperchaos. *Physics Letters. [Part A]*, *71*(2-3), 155–157. doi:10.1016/0375-9601(79)90150-6

Sarasu, P., & Sundarapandian, V. (2011). The generalized projective synchronization of hyperchaotic Lorenz and hyperchaotic Qi systems via active control. *International Journal of Soft Computing*, *6*(5), 216–223. doi:10.3923/ijscomp.2011.216.223

Sarasu, P., & Sundarapandian, V. (2012). Generalized projective synchronization of two-scroll systems via adaptive control. *International Journal of Soft Computing*, *7*(4), 146–156. doi:10.3923/ijscomp.2012.146.156

Shukla, M. K., & Sharma, B. B. (2017). Backstepping based stabilization and synchronization of a class of fractional order chaotic systems. *Chaos, Solitons, and Fractals*, *102*, 274–284. doi:10.1016/j.chaos.2017.05.015

Singh, S., Azar, A. T., Ouannas, A., Zhu, Q., Zhang, W., & Na, J. (2017). *Sliding Mode Control Technique for Multi-switching Synchronization of Chaotic Systems. 9th International Conference on Modelling, Identification and Control (ICMIC 2017)*, Kunming, China.

Soliman, N. S., Said, L. A., Azar, A. T., Madian, A. H., Radwan, A. G., & Ouannas, A. (2017). *Fractional Controllable Multi-Scroll V-Shape Attractor with Parameters Effect*. The 6th International Conference on Modern Circuits and Systems Technologies (MOCAST), Thessaloniki, Greece.

Strogatz, S. H. (1994). *Nonlinear Dynamics and Chaos: with Applications to Physics, Biology, Chemistry, and Engineering*. Perseus Books.

Sundarapandian, V., & Sivaperumal, S. (2011). Sliding controller design of hybrid synchronization of four-wing chaotic systems. *International Journal of Soft Computing*, *6*(5), 224–231. doi:10.3923/ijscomp.2011.224.231

Tolba, M. F., AbdelAty, A. M., Soliman, N. S., Said, L. A., Madian, A. H., Azar, A. T., & Radwan, A. G. (2017). FPGA implementation of two fractional order chaotic systems. *International Journal of Electronics and Communications*, *28*, 162–172. doi:10.1016/j.aeue.2017.04.028

Tong, X. J., Zhang, M., Wang, Z., Liu, Y., & Ma, J. (2015). An image encryption scheme based on a new hyperchaotic finance system. *Optik (Stuttgart)*, *126*(20), 2445–2452. doi:10.1016/j.ijleo.2015.06.018

Vaidyanathan, S. (2011a). Hybrid chaos synchronization of Liu and Lü systems by active nonlinear control. *Communications in Computer and Information Science*, *204*, 1–10. doi:10.1007/978-3-642-24043-0_1

Vaidyanathan, S. (2011b). Output regulation of Arneodo-Coullet chaotic system. *Communications in Computer and Information Science*, *133*, 98–107. doi:10.1007/978-3-642-17881-8_10

Vaidyanathan, S. (2011c). Output regulation of the unified chaotic system. *Communications in Computer and Information Science*, *198*, 1–9. doi:10.1007/978-3-642-22555-0_1

Vaidyanathan, S. (2012a). Global chaos control of hyperchaotic Liu system via sliding control method. *International Journal of Control Theory and Applications*, *5*(2), 117–123.

Vaidyanathan, S. (2012b). Sliding mode control based global chaos control of Liu-Liu-Liu-Su chaotic system. *International Journal of Control Theory and Applications*, *5*(1), 15–20.

Vaidyanathan, S. (2012c). Output regulation of the Liu chaotic system. *Applied Mechanics and Materials*, *110*, 3982–3989.

Vaidyanathan, S. (2015a). A novel chemical chaotic reactor system and its adaptive control. *International Journal of Chemtech Research*, *8*(7), 146–158.

Vaidyanathan, S. (2015b). Adaptive control design for the anti-synchronization of novel 3-D chemical chaotic reactor systems. *International Journal of Chemtech Research*, *8*(11), 654–668.

Vaidyanathan, S. (2015c). Adaptive control of Rikitake two-disk dynamo system. *International Journal of Chemtech Research*, *8*(8), 121–133.

Vaidyanathan, S. (2015d). Adaptive synchronization of novel 3-D chemical chaotic reactor systems. *International Journal of Chemtech Research*, *8*(7), 159–171.

Vaidyanathan, S. (2015e). Adaptive synchronization of Rikitake two-disk dynamo chaotic systems. *International Journal of Chemtech Research*, *8*(8), 100–111.

Vaidyanathan, S. (2015f). Anti-synchronization of chemical chaotic reactors via adaptive control method. *International Journal of Chemtech Research*, *8*(8), 73–85.

Vaidyanathan, S. (2015g). Anti-synchronization of the FitzHugh-Nagumo chaotic neuron models via adaptive control method. *International Journal of Pharm Tech Research*, *8*(7), 71–83.

Vaidyanathan, S. (2015h). Chaos in neurons and adaptive control of Birkhoff-Shaw strange chaotic attractor. *International Journal of Pharm Tech Research*, *8*(5), 959–963.

Vaidyanathan, S. (2015i). Global chaos synchronization of Rucklidge chaotic systems for double convection via sliding mode control. *International Journal of Chemtech Research*, *8*(8), 61–72.

Vaidyanathan, S. (2015j). Global chaos synchronization of the Lotka-Volterra biological systems with four competitive species via active control. *International Journal of Pharm Tech Research*, *8*(6), 206–217.

Vaidyanathan, S. (2015k). Hybrid chaos synchronization of the FitzHugh-Nagumo chaotic neuron models via adaptive control method. *International Journal of Pharm Tech Research*, *8*(8), 48–60.

Vaidyanathan, S. (2015l). Integral sliding mode control design for the global chaos synchronization of identical novel chemical chaotic reactor systems. *International Journal of Chemtech Research*, *8*(11), 684–699.

Vaidyanathan, S. (2015m). Output regulation of the forced Van der Pol chaotic oscillator via adaptive control method. *International Journal of Pharm Tech Research*, *8*(6), 106–116.

Vaidyanathan, S. (2015n). Sliding controller design for the global chaos synchronization of enzymes-substrates systems. *International Journal of Chemtech Research*, *8*(7), 89–99.

Vaidyanathan, S. (2015o). Sliding mode control of Rucklidge chaotic system for nonlinear double convection. *International Journal of Chemtech Research*, *8*(8), 25–35.

Vaidyanathan, S. (2015p). State regulation of Rikitake two-disk dynamo chaotic system via adaptive control method. *International Journal of Chemtech Research*, *8*(9), 374–386.

Vaidyanathan, S. (2015q). Synchronization of Tokamak systems with symmetric and magnetically confined plasma via adaptive control. *International Journal of Chemtech Research*, *8*(6), 818–827.

Vaidyanathan, S. (2015r). Synchronization of 3-cells cellular neural network (CNN) attractors via adaptive control method. *International Journal of Pharm Tech Research*, *8*(5), 946–955.

Vaidyanathan, S. (2016a). A highly chaotic system with four quadratic nonlinearities, its analysis, control and synchronization via integral sliding mode control. *International Journal of Control Theory and Applications*, *9*(1), 279–297.

Vaidyanathan, S. (2016b). A novel 3-D conservative chaotic system with a sinusoidal nonlinearity and its adaptive control. *International Journal of Control Theory and Applications*, *9*(1), 115–132.

Vaidyanathan, S. (2016c). A novel 3-D jerk chaotic system with three quadratic nonlinearities and its adaptive control. *Archives of Control Sciences*, *26*(1), 19–47. doi:10.1515/acsc-2016-0002

Vaidyanathan, S. (2016d). A novel hyperchaotic hyperjerk system with two nonlinearities, its analysis, adaptive control and synchronization via backstepping control method. *International Journal of Control Theory and Applications*, *9*(1), 257–278.

Vaidyanathan, S. (2016e). Analysis, adaptive control and synchronization of a novel 4-D hyperchaotic hyperjerk system via backstepping control method. *Archives of Control Sciences*, *26*(3), 311–338. doi:10.1515/acsc-2016-0018

Vaidyanathan, S. (2016f). Hyperchaos, adaptive control and synchronization of a novel 4-D hyperchaotic system with two quadratic nonlinearities. *Archives of Control Sciences*, *26*(4), 471–495. doi:10.1515/acsc-2016-0026

Vaidyanathan, S. (2016g). Mathematical analysis, adaptive control and synchronization of a ten-term novel three-scroll chaotic system with four quadratic nonlinearities. *International Journal of Control Theory and Applications*, *9*(1), 1–20.

Vaidyanathan, S. (2017a). A conservative hyperchaotic hyperjerk system based on memristive device. *Studies in Computational Intelligence*, *701*, 393–423.

Vaidyanathan, S. (2017b). A memristor-based hyperchaotic system with hidden attractor and its sliding mode control. *Studies in Computational Intelligence*, *709*, 343–369.

Vaidyanathan, S. (2017c). A new 3-D jerk chaotic system with two cubic nonlinearities and its adaptive backstepping control. *Archives of Control Sciences*, *27*(3), 365–395. doi:10.1515/acsc-2017-0026

Vaidyanathan, S. (2017d). Adaptive integral sliding mode controller design for the control and synchronization of a novel jerk chaotic system. *Studies in Computational Intelligence*, *709*, 393–417.

Vaidyanathan, S. (2017e). Adaptive integral sliding mode controller design for the control and synchronization of a rod-type plasma torch chaotic system. *Studies in Computational Intelligence*, *709*, 263–287.

Vaidyanathan, S. (2017f). Complete synchronization of chaotic systems via novel second order sliding mode control with an application to a novel three-scroll chaotic system. *Studies in Computational Intelligence*, *709*, 193–212.

Vaidyanathan, S. (2017g). Global stabilization of nonlinear systems via novel second order sliding mode control with an application to a novel highly chaotic system. *Studies in Computational Intelligence*, *709*, 171–191.

Vaidyanathan, S. (2017h). Novel second order sliding mode control design for the anti-synchronization of chaotic systems with an application to a novel four-wing chaotic system. *Studies in Computational Intelligence*, *709*, 213–234.

Vaidyanathan, S. (2017i). Super-twisting sliding mode control and synchronization of Moore-Spiegel thermo-mechanical chaotic system. *Studies in Computational Intelligence*, *709*, 451–470.

Vaidyanathan, S. (2017j). Super-twisting sliding mode control of the enzymes-substrates biological chaotic system. *Studies in Computational Intelligence*, *709*, 435–450.

Vaidyanathan, S., & Azar, A. T. (2015a). Anti-Synchronization of Identical Chaotic Systems using Sliding Mode Control and an Application to Vaidyanathan-Madhavan Chaotic Systems. In Advances and Applications in Sliding Mode Control systems. Springer-Verlag GmbH Berlin/Heidelberg. doi:10.1007/978-3-319-11173-5_19

Vaidyanathan, S., & Azar, A. T. (2015b). Hybrid Synchronization of Identical Chaotic Systems using Sliding Mode Control and an Application to Vaidyanathan Chaotic Systems. In Advances and Applications in Sliding Mode Control systems. Springer-Verlag GmbH Berlin/Heidelberg. doi:10.1007/978-3-319-11173-5_20

Vaidyanathan, S., & Azar, A. T. (2015c). Analysis, Control and Synchronization of a Nine-Term 3-D Novel Chaotic System. In Chaos Modeling and Control Systems Design. Springer-Verlag GmbH Berlin/Heidelberg. DOI doi:10.1007/978-3-319-13132-0_1

Vaidyanathan, S., & Azar, A. T. (2015d). Analysis and Control of a 4-D Novel Hyperchaotic System. In Chaos Modeling and Control Systems Design. Springer-Verlag GmbH Berlin/Heidelberg. DOI doi:10.1007/978-3-319-13132-0_2

Vaidyanathan, S., & Azar, A. T. (2016a). Takagi-Sugeno Fuzzy Logic Controller for Liu-Chen Four-Scroll Chaotic System. *International Journal of Intelligent Engineering Informatics*, *4*(2), 135–150. doi:10.1504/IJIEI.2016.076699

Vaidyanathan, S., & Azar, A. T. (2016b). *Dynamic Analysis, Adaptive Feedback Control and Synchronization of an Eight-Term 3-D Novel Chaotic System with Three Quadratic Nonlinearities. Studies in Fuzziness and Soft Computing* (Vol. 337). Springer-Verlag.

Vaidyanathan, S., & Azar, A. T. (2016c). *Qualitative Study and Adaptive Control of a Novel 4-D Hyperchaotic System with Three Quadratic Nonlinearities. Studies in Fuzziness and Soft Computing* (Vol. 337). Springer-Verlag.

Vaidyanathan, S., & Azar, A. T. (2016d). *A Novel 4-D Four-Wing Chaotic System with Four Quadratic Nonlinearities and its Synchronization via Adaptive Control Method. Advances in Chaos Theory and Intelligent Control. Studies in Fuzziness and Soft Computing* (Vol. 337). Springer-Verlag.

Vaidyanathan, S., & Azar, A. T. (2016e). *Adaptive Control and Synchronization of Halvorsen Circulant Chaotic Systems. Advances in Chaos Theory and Intelligent Control. Studies in Fuzziness and Soft Computing* (Vol. 337). Springer-Verlag.

Vaidyanathan, S., & Azar, A. T. (2016f). *Adaptive Backstepping Control and Synchronization of a Novel 3-D Jerk System with an Exponential Nonlinearity. Advances in Chaos Theory and Intelligent Control. Studies in Fuzziness and Soft Computing* (Vol. 337). Springer-Verlag.

Vaidyanathan, S., & Azar, A. T. (2016g). *Generalized Projective Synchronization of a Novel Hyperchaotic Four-Wing System via Adaptive Control Method. Advances in Chaos Theory and Intelligent Control. Studies in Fuzziness and Soft Computing* (Vol. 337). Springer-Verlag.

Vaidyanathan, S., Azar, A. T., & Ouannas, A. (2017a). *An Eight-Term 3-D Novel Chaotic System with Three Quadratic Nonlinearities, its Adaptive Feedback Control and Synchronization. Studies in Computational Intelligence* (Vol. 688). Springer-Verlag.

Vaidyanathan, S., Azar, A. T., & Ouannas, A. (2017c). *Hyperchaos and Adaptive Control of a Novel Hyperchaotic System with Two Quadratic Nonlinearities. Studies in Computational Intelligence* (Vol. 688). Springer-Verlag.

Vaidyanathan, S., Azar, A. T., Rajagopal, K., & Alexander, P. (2015b). Design and SPICE implementation of a 12-term novel hyperchaotic system and its synchronization via active control (2015). International Journal of Modelling *Identification and Control, 23*(3), 267–277. doi:10.1504/IJMIC.2015.069936

Vaidyanathan, S., & Boulkroune, A. (2016). A novel hyperchaotic system with two quadratic nonlinearities, its analysis and synchronization via integral sliding mode control. *International Journal of Control Theory and Applications*, *9*(1), 321–337.

Vaidyanathan, S., & Idowu, B. A. (2016). Adaptive control and synchronization of Chlouverakis-Sprott hyperjerk system via backstepping control. *Studies in Computational Intelligence*, *635*, 117–141.

Vaidyanathan, S., Idowu, B. A., & Azar, A. T. (2015c). Backstepping Controller Design for the Global Chaos Synchronization of Sprott's Jerk Systems. In Chaos Modeling and Control Systems Design. Springer-Verlag GmbH Berlin/Heidelberg. doi:10.1007/978-3-319-13132-0_3

Vaidyanathan, S., & Pakiriswamy, S. (2011). The design of active feedback controllers for the generalized projective synchronization of hyperchaotic Qi and hyperchaotic Lorenz systems. *Communications in Computer and Information Science*, *245*, 231–238. doi:10.1007/978-3-642-27245-5_28

Vaidyanathan, S., & Pakiriswamy, S. (2013). Generalized projective synchronization of six-term Sundarapandian chaotic systems by adaptive control. *International Journal of Control Theory and Applications*, *6*(2), 153–163.

Vaidyanathan, S., & Pakiriswamy, S. (2016). A five-term 3-D novel conservative chaotic system and its generalized projective synchronization via adaptive control method. *International Journal of Control Theory and Applications*, *9*(1), 61–78.

Vaidyanathan, S., & Rajagopal, K. (2011). Hybrid synchronization of hyperchaotic Wang-Chen and hyperchaotic Lorenz systems by active non-linear control. *International Journal of Systems Signal Control and Engineering Application*, *4*(3), 55–61.

Vaidyanathan, S., & Rajagopal, K. (2012). Global chaos synchronization of hyperchaotic Pang and hyperchaotic Wang systems via adaptive control. *International Journal of Soft Computing*, *7*(1), 28–37. doi:10.3923/ijscomp.2012.28.37

Vaidyanathan, S., & Rajagopal, K. (2016a). Adaptive control, synchronization and LabVIEW implementation of Rucklidge chaotic system for nonlinear double convection. *International Journal of Control Theory and Applications*, *9*(1), 175–197.

Vaidyanathan, S., & Rajagopal, K. (2016b). Analysis, control, synchronization and LabVIEW implementation of a seven-term novel chaotic system. *International Journal of Control Theory and Applications*, *9*(1), 151–174.

Vaidyanathan, S., & Rajagopal, K. (2017). LabVIEW implementation of chaotic masking with adaptively synchronised forced Van der Pol oscillators and its application in real-time image encryption. *International Journal of Simulation and Process Modelling*, *12*(2), 165–178. doi:10.1504/IJSPM.2017.083534

Vaidyanathan, S., Sambas, A., Mamat, M., & Sanjaya, W. S. M. (2017). Analysis, synchronisation and circuit implementation of a novel jerk chaotic system and its application for voice encryption. *International Journal of Modelling. Identification and Control*, *28*(2), 153–166. doi:10.1504/IJMIC.2017.085934

Vaidyanathan, S., & Sampath, S. (2012). Anti-synchronization of four-wing chaotic systems via sliding mode control. *International Journal of Automation and Computing*, *9*(3), 274–279. doi:10.100711633-012-0644-2

Vaidyanathan, S., Sampath, S., & Azar, A. T. (2015a). Global chaos synchronisation of identical chaotic systems via novel sliding mode control method and its application to Zhu system. International Journal of Modelling *Identification and Control*, *23*(1), 92–100. doi:10.1504/IJMIC.2015.067495

Vaidyanathan, S., & Volos, C. (2015). Analysis and adaptive control of a novel 3-D conservative no-equilibrium chaotic system. *Archives of Control Sciences*, *25*(3), 333–353. doi:10.1515/acsc-2015-0022

Vaidyanathan, S., & Volos, C. (2016). *Advances and Applications in Nonlinear Control Systems*. Berlin, Germany: Springer. doi:10.1007/978-3-319-30169-3

Vaidyanathan, S., & Volos, C. (2017). *Advances in Memristors, Memristive Devices and Systems*. Berlin, Germany: Springer. doi:10.1007/978-3-319-51724-7

Vaidyanathan, S., Zhu, Q., & Azar, A. T. (2017b). *Adaptive Control of a Novel Nonlinear Double Convection Chaotic System. Studies in Computational Intelligence* (Vol. 688). Springer-Verlag.

Wang, W., & Fan, Y. (2015). Synchronization of Arneodo chaotic system via backstepping fuzzy adaptive control. *Optik (Stuttgart)*, *126*(20), 2679–2683. doi:10.1016/j.ijleo.2015.06.071

Wang, Z., Volos, C., Kingni, S.T., Azar, A.T., & Pham, V.T. (2017). Four-wing attractors in a novel chaotic system with hyperbolic sine nonlinearity. *Optik - International Journal for Light and Electron Optics, 131*(2017), 1071-1078.

Witte, C. L., & Witte, M. H. (1991). Chaos and predicting varix hemorrhage. *Medical Hypotheses*, *36*(4), 312–317. doi:10.1016/0306-9877(91)90002-G PMID:1809849

Wolf, A., Swift, J. B., Swinney, H. L., & Vastano, J. A. (1985). Determining Lyapunov exponents from a time series. *Physica D. Nonlinear Phenomena*, *16*(3), 285–317. doi:10.1016/0167-2789(85)90011-9

Wu, X., Bai, C., & Kan, H. (2014). A new color image cryptosystem via hyperchaos synchronization. *Communications in Nonlinear Science and Numerical Simulation*, *19*(6), 1884–1897. doi:10.1016/j.cnsns.2013.10.025

Yang, X. S., & Yuan, Q. (2005). Chaos and transient chaos in simple Hopfield neural networks. *Neurocomputing*, *69*(1-3), 232–241. doi:10.1016/j.neucom.2005.06.005

Yau, H. T., & Shieh, C. S. (2008). Chaos synchronization using fuzzy logic controller. *Nonlinear Analysis Real World Applications*, *9*(4), 1800–1810. doi:10.1016/j.nonrwa.2007.05.009

Yu, H., Cai, G., & Li, Y. (2012). Dynamic analysis and control of a new hyperchaotic finance system. *Nonlinear Dynamics*, *67*(3), 2171–2182. doi:10.100711071-011-0137-9

Yuan, G., Zhang, X., & Wang, Z. (2013). Chaos generation in a semiconductor ring laser with an optical injection. *Optik (Stuttgart)*, *124*(22), 5715–5718. doi:10.1016/j.ijleo.2013.04.029

Section 2
Applications of Dynamical Systems

Chapter 14
Numerical Analysis for Vehicle Collision Mitigation and Safety Using Dynamics Control Systems

Mustafa Elkady
Lebanese International University, Lebanon & Ain Shams University, Lebanon

Muhammad Sheikh
University of Sunderland, UK

Kevin Burn
University of Sunderland, UK

ABSTRACT

The aim of this chapter is to investigate the effect of vehicle dynamics control systems (VDCS) on both the collision of the vehicle body and the kinematic behaviour of the vehicle's occupant in case of offset frontal vehicle-to-vehicle collision. The study also investigates the full-frontal vehicle-to-barrier crash scenario. A unique 6-degree-of-freedom (6-DOF) vehicle dynamics/crash mathematical model and a simplified lumped mass occupant model are developed. The first model is used to define the vehicle body crash parameters and it integrates a vehicle dynamics model with a vehicle front-end structure model. The second model aims to predict the effect of VDCS on the kinematics of the occupant. It is shown from the numerical simulations that the vehicle dynamics/crash response and occupant behaviour can be captured and analysed quickly and accurately. Furthermore, it is shown that the VDCS can affect the crash characteristics positively and the occupant behaviour is improved in the full and offset crash scenarios.

1. INTRODUCTION

Complex issues and problems can be easily discussed using the powerful methodology and computer simulation modelling which is the system dynamics. It is widely used to analyse a range of systems in, e.g. business, ecology, medical and social systems as well as engineering (Azar 2012). System dynamics research has been also used for several applications on mechanical engineering field. For example, a dy-

DOI: 10.4018/978-1-5225-4077-9.ch014

namic system as adaptive and self-controlling was made to solve the problem of the Active thruster control in AUV (Joshi and Talange, 2016). Another example, to solve the backlash problem, a frequency domain approach is implemented for the control of nonlinear system of any kind such as robotics, mechatronics, other kind of mechanisms, electrical motors etc (Azar and Serrano, 2016). To avoid derailment and hunting, and to improve ride comfort at high speed, forced/active steering bogie design was studied; the actively steered bogie was able to negotiate cant excess and deficiency (Samantaray and Pradhan, 2016).

Vehicle dynamics control systems (VDCS) exist on the most modern vehicles and play important roles in vehicle ride, stability, and safety (Khosravi, 2015). For example, Anti-lock brake system (ABS) is used to allow the vehicle to follow the desired steering angle while intense braking is applied (Yu et al., 2002; Morteza, et al, 2015; Siramdasu and Taheri, 2016). In addition, the ABS helps reducing the stopping distance of a vehicle compared to the conventional braking system. The Active suspension control system (ASC) is used to improve the quality of the vehicle ride and reduce the vertical acceleration (Yue et al., 1988; Alleyne and Hedrick, 1995; Jongsang, et al., 2015; Mirko, et al., 2016; Khan and Qamar, 2015). From the view of vehicle transportation safety, nowadays, occupant safety becomes one of the most important research areas and the automotive industry increased their efforts to enhance the safety of vehicles. Seat belts, airbags, and advanced driver assistant systems (ADAS) are used to prevent a vehicle crash or mitigate vehicle collision when a crash occurs.

To evaluate the crashworthiness, real crash tests or vehicle modelling are carried out. Due to the complexity and the high cost of crash tests, vehicle modelling is commonly used in the first stage of development. Vehicle modelling can be mainly classified as finite element and mathematical modelling. Finite element models of vehicles are increasingly used in preliminary design analysis, component design, and roadside hardware design (Belytschko, 1992). However, finite element modelling is also costly and slow in its simulation analysis. Mathematical modelling produces very quick results and it can be accurately used for unlimited numbers of different types of vehicles in case of vehicle-to-barrier crash tests (Kamal, 1970).

Using mathematical models in crash simulation is useful at the first design concept because rapid analysis is required at this stage. In addition, the well-known advantage of mathematical modelling provides a quick simulation analysis compared with FE models. Vehicle crash structures are designed to be able to absorb the crash energy and control vehicle deformations, therefore simple mathematical models are used to represent the vehicle front structure (Emori, 1968). In this model, the vehicle mass is represented as a lumped mass and the vehicle structure is represented as a spring in a simple model to simulate a frontal and rear-end vehicle collision processes. Also, other analyses and simulations of vehicle-to-barrier impact using a simple mass spring model were established by Kamal (1970) and widely extended by Elmarakbi & Zu (2005, 2007) to include smart-front structures. To achieve enhanced occupant safety, the crash energy management system was explored by Khattab (2010). This study, using a simple lumped-parameter model, discussed the applicability of providing variable energy-absorbing properties as a function of the impact speed.

In terms of the enhancing crash energy absorption and minimizing deformation of the vehicle's structure, a frontal structure consisting of two special longitudinal members was designed (Witteman & Kriens, 1998; Witteman, 1999). This longitudinal member system was divided to two separate systems: the first, called the crushing part, guarantees the desired stable and efficient energy absorption; the other, called the supporting part, guarantees the desired stiffness in the transverse direction. For high crash energy absorption and weight efficiency, new multi-cell profiles were developed (Kim, 2002). Various design aspects of the new multi-cell members were investigated and the optimization was carried out as an exemplary design guide. To absorb the kinetic energy in a low-speed collision an aluminium-carbon fibre-reinforced polymer hybrid crash management system is developed (Matheis and Eckstein, 2016). This system incorporates a braided tube in a metallic crash box and is designed as a suitable substitute for the crash management system.

The vehicle body pitch and drop at fontal impact is the main reason for the unbelted driver neck and head injury (Chang et al., 2006). Vehicle pitch and drop are normally experienced at frontal crash tests. They used a finite element (FE) method to investigate the frame deformation at full frontal impact and discussed the cause and countermeasures design for the issue of vehicle body pitch and drop. It found that the bending down of frame rails caused by the geometry offsets of the frame rails in vertical direction during a crash is the key feature of the pitching of the vehicle body.

1.1. Related Work

The most well-known pre-collision method is the advance driver assistant systems (ADAS). The aim of ADAS is to mitigate and avoid vehicle frontal collisions. The main idea of ADAS is to collect data from the road (i.e. traffic lights, other cars distances and velocities, obstacles, etc.) and transfer this information to the driver, warn the driver in danger situations (Jansson, et al., 2002; Fanxing, et al., 2015) and aide the driver actively in imminent collision. There are different actions may be taken when these systems detect that the collision is unavoidable. For example, the brake assistant system (BAS) (Tamura et al., 2001), the collision mitigation brake system (CMBS) (Sugimoto & Sauer, 2005) and electric steering activation system (Shah et al., 2015) were used to activate the braking instantly based on the behaviour characteristics of the driver, and relative position from the most dangerous other object for the moment.

The effect of vehicle braking on the crash and the possibility of using vehicle dynamics control systems to reduce the risk of incompatibility and improve the crash performance in frontal vehicle-to-barrier collision were investigated (Hogan & Manning, 2007). They proved that there is a slight improvement of the vehicle deformation once the brakes are applied during the crash. A multi-body vehicle dynamic model using ADAMS software, alongside with a simple crash model was generated in order to study the effects of the implemented control strategy.

Their study showed that the control systems were not able to significantly affect the vehicle dynamics in the offset barrier impact. In addition, it was found that in offset vehicle-to-vehicle rear-end collision, the ABS or direct yaw control (DYC) systems can stabilise the vehicle; however, these control systems affected each other and cannot work together at the same time.

The effect of vehicle dynamics control systems (VDCS) on both the collision of the vehicle body and the kinematic behaviour of the vehicle's occupant has been studied and the results showed that the VDCS can affect the crash characteristics positively and the occupant behaviour is improved (Elkady et al., 2016).

The main aim of this research is to investigate the effect of the VDCS on vehicle collision mitigation, enhance vehicle crash characteristics, and improve occupant biodynamics responses in case of 50% vehicle-to-vehicle offset and full frontal crash scenarios. To accomplish this study, a unique 6-Degree-of-Freedom (6-DOF) vehicle dynamics/crash mathematical model and a simplified lumped mass occupant model are developed.

This chapter is divided to six sections including this introduction. The second part of this chapter is the methodology which describes the vehicle dynamics/crash and the occupant models in details with their associated equations of motions. The third part presents the validations of the two modes while the forth section shows the numerical results of the simulation analysis. In the fifth part of this chapter, the modified control system using an integrated active and semi-active suspension control system is applied and its effect on the vehicle crash is discussed. Finally, the conclusion is presented in section six.

2. METHODOLOGY

A vehicle frontal collision can be divided into two main stages, the first one is a primary impact, and the second one is a secondary impact. The primary impact indicates the collision between the front-end structure of the vehicle and an obstacle (another vehicle or barrier). The secondary impact is the interaction between the occupant and the restraint system and/or the vehicle interior due to vehicle collisions.

2.1. Vehicle Dynamics/Crash Model

In this paper, a (6-DOF) vehicle dynamics/crash mathematical model, shown in Figure 1, has been developed to optimise the VDCS in impending impact at offset vehicle-to-vehicle crash scenarios for vehicle collision mitigation. The ABS and the ASC systems are co-simulated with a full car vehicle dynamic model and integrated with a front-end structure. It is worthwhile mentioning that vehicle components, which significantly affect the dynamics of a frontal impact, are modelled by lumped masses and nonlinear springs.

In this full-car model, the vehicle body is represented by lumped mass m and it has a translational motion in longitudinal direction (x axis), translational motion on vertical direction (z axis), pitching motion (around y axis), rolling motion (around x axis), and yawing motion in case of offset collision (around

Figure 1.

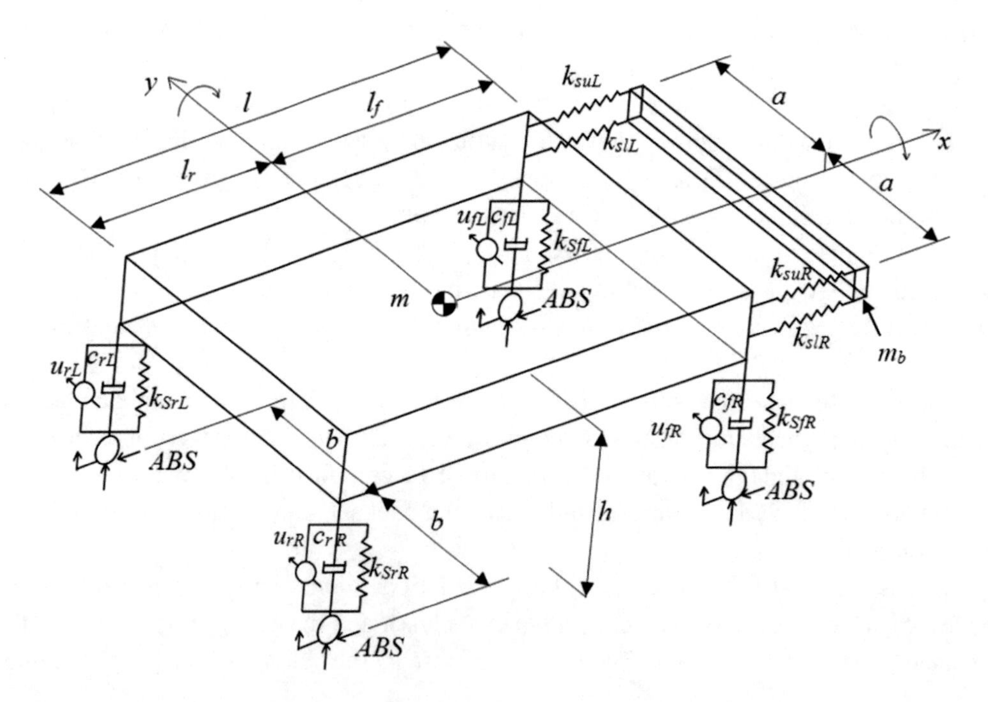

z axis at the point of impact). Four spring/damper units are used to represent the conventional vehicle suspension systems. Each unit has a spring stiffness k_S and a damping coefficient c. The subscripts f, r, R and L denote the front, rear, right and left wheels, respectively. The ASC system is co-simulated with the conventional suspension system to add or subtract an active force element u. The ABS is co-simulated with the mathematical model using a simple wheel model. The unsprung masses are not considered in this model and it is assumed that the vehicle moves in a flat-asphalted road, which means that the vertical movement of the tyres and road vertical forces can be neglected.

To represent the front-end structure of the vehicle, four non-linear springs with stiffness k_s are proposed: two springs represent the upper members (rails) and two springs represent lower members of the vehicle frontal structure. The subscript u denotes the upper rails while the subscript l denotes the lower rails. The bumper of the vehicle is represented by a lumped mass m_b and it has a longitudinal motion in the x direction and rotational motion for the non-impacted side of each bumper.

The general dimensions of the model are shown in Figure 1, where l_f, l_r, l and h represent the longitudinal distance between the vehicle's CG and front wheels, the longitudinal distance between the CG and rear wheels, the wheel base and the high of the CG from the ground, respectively. a is the distance between the centre of the bumper and the right/left frontal springs; b is the distance between the CG and right/left wheels.

The free body diagram of the mathematical model is shown in Figure 2, which represents the different internal and external forces applied on the vehicle body. F_s, F_S, F_b, F_z and F_f are front-end non-linear spring forces, vehicle suspension forces, braking forces, normal forces and friction forces between the tyres and the road due to vehicle yawing, respectively.

Figure 2.

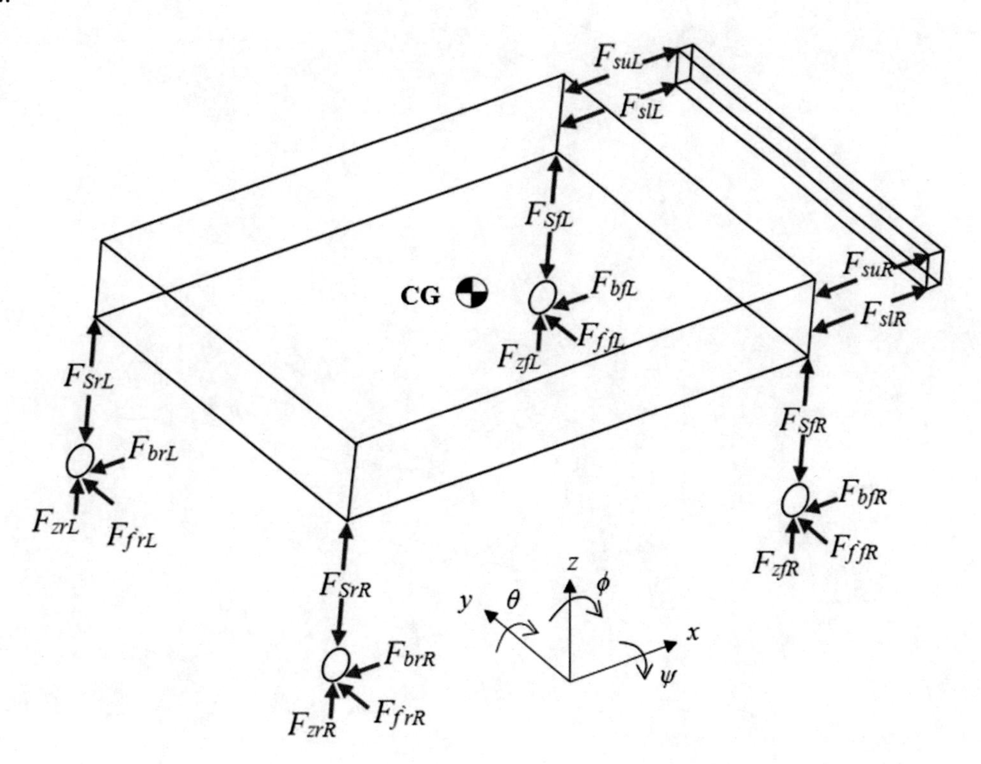

2.1.1. Equations of Motion of Vehicle-to-Vehicle Crash Scenario

The model in the case of offset frontal vehicle-to-barrier is thirteen DOF namely longitudinal and vertical movements, pitching, rolling and yawing motions for each vehicle body, the longitudinal movement of the two bumpers as one part, and the rotational motion for the non-impacted side of each bumper. The two bumpers of each vehicle are considered as lumped masses, and dealt as one mass to transfer the load from one vehicle to another. Figures 3 (a) and 3 (b) show the vehicle model before and after collision in case of offset frontal vehicle-to-vehicle crash scenario. The equations of motion of the mathematical model shown in Figure 3 are developed to study and predict the dynamic response of the primary impact of offset vehicle-to-vehicle crash scenario.

Figure 3.

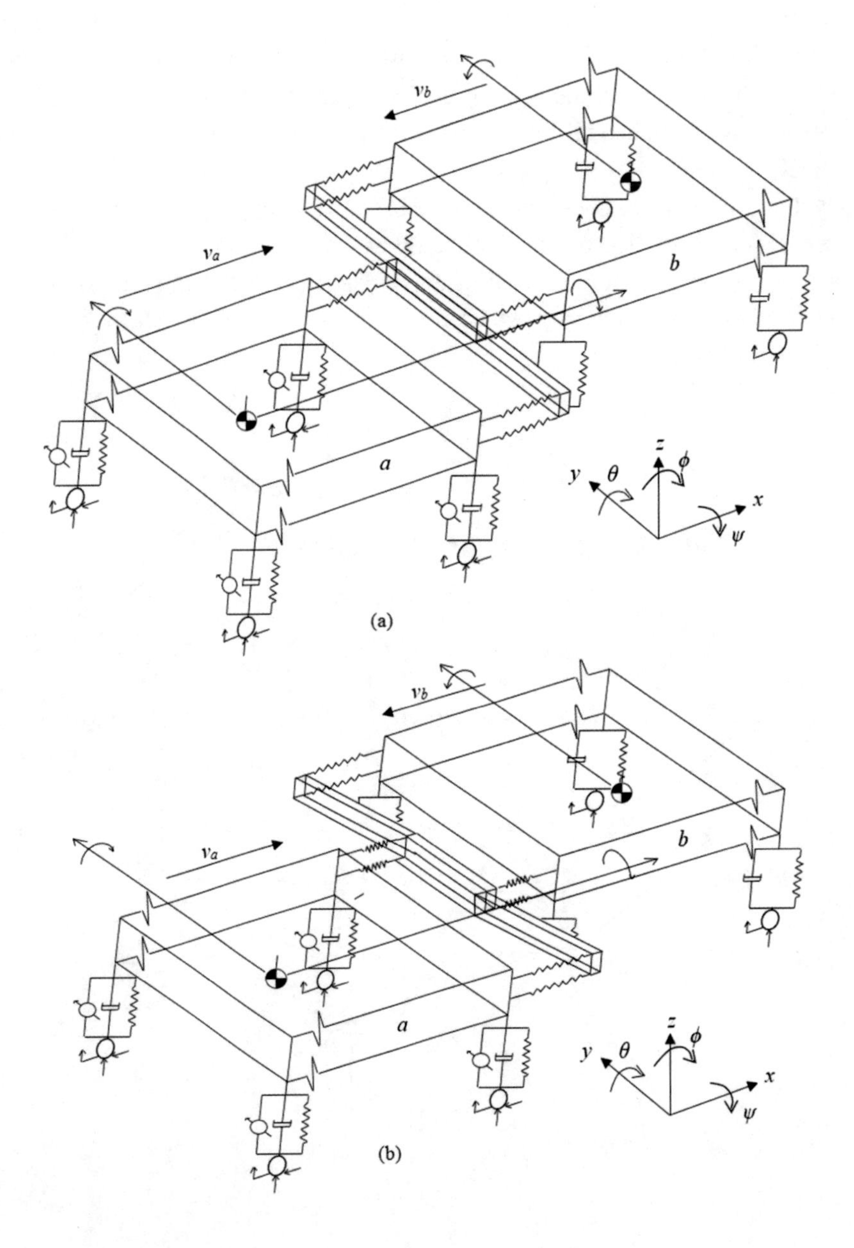

Figures 4 and 5 are used to describe the deformation of the front springs due to vehicle pitching around its CG and vehicle yawing around the point of impact for the two vehicles, respectively.

Figures 1 and 2 are also used to derive the equations of motion of the two vehicle models. The detailed equations of motion are presented as follows:

Figure 4.

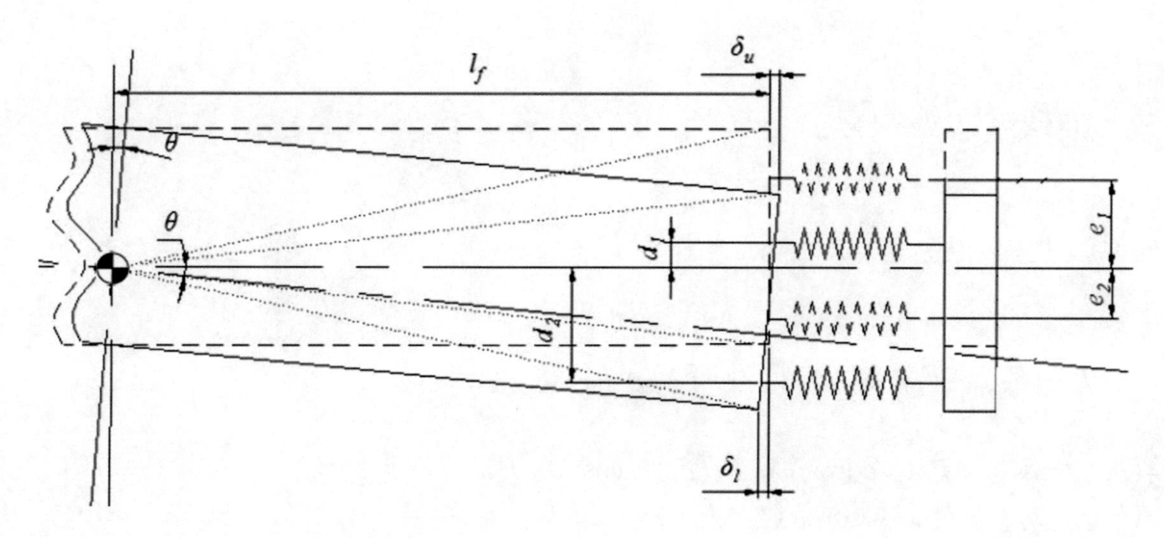

Figure 5.

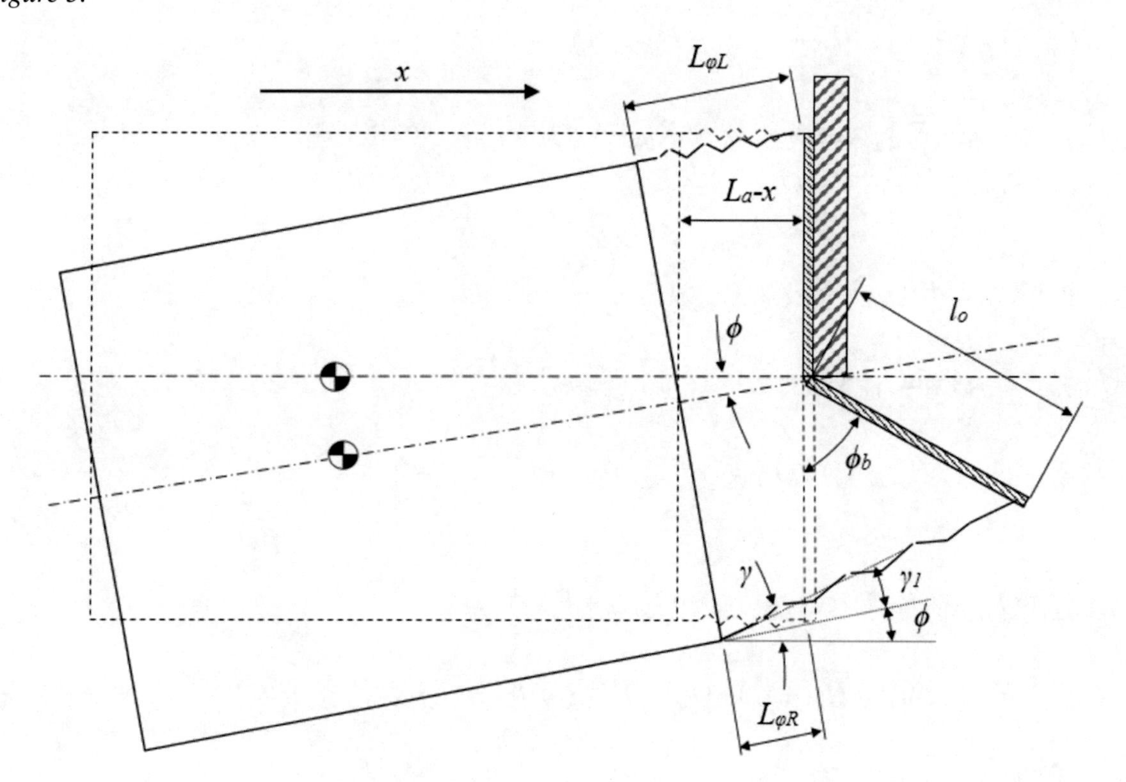

$$m_a \cdot \ddot{x}_a + (F_{suRa} + F_{slRa}) \cdot \cos\gamma_a + (F_{suLa} + F_{slLa}) \cdot \cos\varphi_a$$

$$+F_{bfRa} + F_{bfLa} + F_{brRa} + F_{brLa} = 0 \quad (1)$$

$$m_b \cdot \ddot{x}_b + (F_{suRb} + F_{slRb}) \cdot \cos\gamma_b + (F_{suLb} + F_{slLb}) \cdot \cos\varphi_b + F_{bfRb} + F_{bfLb} + F_{brRb} + F_{brLb} = 0 \quad (2)$$

$$m_a \cdot \ddot{z}_a + F_{SfRa} + F_{SfLa} + F_{SrRa} + F_{SrLa} = 0 \quad (3)$$

$$m_b \cdot \ddot{z}_b + F_{SfRb} + F_{SfLb} + F_{SrRb} + F_{SrLb} = 0 \quad (4)$$

$$I_{yya} \cdot \ddot{\theta}_a - (F_{SfRa} + F_{SfLa}) \cdot l_{fa} + (F_{SrRa} + F_{SrLa}) \cdot l_{ra}$$

$$+(F_{suRa} \cdot \cos\gamma_a + F_{suLa} \cdot \cos\varphi_a) \cdot d_{1a} - (F_{slRa} \cdot \cos\gamma_a + F_{slLa} \cdot \cos\varphi_a) \cdot d_{2a}$$
$$-(F_{bfRa} + F_{bfLa} + F_{brRa} + F_{brLa}) \cdot (z_a + h_a) = 0 \quad (5)$$

$$I_{yyb} \cdot \ddot{\theta}_b - (F_{SfRb} + F_{SfLb}) \cdot l_{fb} + (F_{SrRb} + F_{SrLb}) \cdot l_{rb}$$

$$+(F_{suRb} \cdot \cos\gamma_b + F_{suLb} \cdot \cos\varphi_b) \cdot d_{1b} - (F_{slRb} \cdot \cos\gamma_b + F_{slLb} \cdot \cos\varphi_b) \cdot d_{2b}$$
$$-(F_{bfRb} + F_{bfLb} + F_{brRb} + F_{brLb}) \cdot (z_b + h_b) = 0 \quad (6)$$

$$I_{zza} \cdot \ddot{\varphi}_a + (F_{suRa} + F_{slRa}) \cdot \cos\gamma_{1a} \cdot a_{oa} - (F_{suLa} + F_{slLa}) \cdot a_{ia}$$

$$-(F_{suRa} + F_{slRa}) \cdot \sin\gamma_{1a} \cdot (l_{aa} - x_a) + (F_{bfRa} + F_{brRa}) \cdot b_{oa} - (F_{bfLa} + F_{brLa}) \cdot b_{ia}$$

$$+(F_{ffRa} + F_{ffLa}) \cdot (l_{ba} - x_a) + (F_{frRa} + F_{frLa}) \cdot (l_a + l_{ba} - x_a) = 0 \quad (7)$$

$$I_{zzb} \cdot \ddot{\varphi}_b + (F_{suRb} + F_{slRb}) \cdot \cos\gamma_{1b} \cdot a_{ob} - (F_{suLb} + F_{slLb}) \cdot a_{ib}$$

$$-(F_{suRb} + F_{slRb}) \cdot \sin\gamma_{1b} \cdot (l_{ab} - x_b) + (F_{bfRb} + F_{brRb}) \cdot b_{ob} - (F_{bfLb} + F_{brLb}) \cdot b_{ib}$$

$$+(F_{ffRb}+F_{ffLb})\cdot(l_{bb}-x_b)+(F_{frRb}+F_{frLb})\cdot(l_b+l_{bb}-x_b)=0 \tag{8}$$

$$I_{xxa}\cdot\ddot{\psi}_a+(F_{SfLa}+F_{SrLa})\cdot b_{ia}-(F_{SfRa}+F_{SrRa})\cdot b_{oa}$$

$$-(F_{ffRa}+F_{ffLa}+F_{frRa}+F_{frLa})\cdot(z_a+h_a)-F_{suRa}\sin\gamma_{1a}\cdot e_{1a}+F_{slRa}\sin\gamma_{1a}\cdot e_{2a}=0 \tag{9}$$

$$I_{xxb}\cdot\ddot{\psi}_b+(F_{SfLb}+F_{SrLb})\cdot b_{ib}-(F_{SfRb}+F_{SrRb})\cdot b_{ob}$$

$$-(F_{ffRb}+F_{ffLb}+F_{frRb}+F_{frLb})\cdot(z_b+h_b)-F_{suRb}\sin\gamma_{1b}\cdot e_{1b}+F_{slRb}\sin\gamma_{1b}\cdot e_{2b}=0 \tag{10}$$

$$I_{zzba}\cdot\ddot{\varphi}_{ba}-(F_{suRa}+F_{slRa})\cos\gamma_a\cdot l_{oa}\cos\varphi_{ba}-(F_{suRa}+F_{slRa})\sin\gamma_a\cdot l_{oa}\sin\varphi_{ba}=0 \tag{11}$$

$$I_{zzbb}\cdot\ddot{\varphi}_{bb}-(F_{suRb}+F_{slRb})\cos\gamma_b\cdot l_{ob}\cos\varphi_{bb}-(F_{suRb}+F_{slRb})\sin\gamma_b\cdot l_{ob}\sin\varphi_{bb}=0 \tag{12}$$

$$m_c\cdot\ddot{x}_c+(F_{suRb}+F_{slRb})\cdot\cos\gamma_b+(F_{suLb}+F_{slLb})\cdot\cos\varphi_b$$
$$-(F_{suRa}+F_{slRa})\cdot\cos\gamma_a-(F_{suLa}+F_{slLa})\cdot\cos\varphi_a=0 \tag{13}$$

where subscript a denotes vehicle (a) which is equipped with the VDCS and a subscript b denotes vehicle (b) which is used in a free rolling case for all crash scenarios. It is assumed that the two vehicle bumpers are moved in the longitudinal direction of the x axis as one part and subscript c denotes the equivalent of the two bumpers. d_1 and d_2 represent the distance between the CG and the upper springs force and the lower springs force for each vehicle, respectively and can be calculated using Figure 4 as

$$d_{1a}=\sqrt{l_{fa}^2+e_{1a}^2}\cdot\sin(\tan^{-1}(\frac{e_{1a}}{l_{fa}})-\theta_a) \tag{14}$$

$$d_{1b}=\sqrt{l_{fb}^2+e_{1b}^2}\cdot\sin(\tan^{-1}(\frac{e_{1b}}{l_{fb}})-\theta_b) \tag{15}$$

$$d_{2a}=\sqrt{l_{fa}^2+e_{2a}^2}\cdot\sin(\tan^{-1}(\frac{e_{2a}}{l_{fa}})+\theta_a) \tag{16}$$

$$d_{2b} = \sqrt{l_{fb}^2 + e_{2b}^2} \cdot \sin(\tan^{-1}(\frac{e_{2b}}{l_{fb}}) + \theta_b) \tag{17}$$

where angles γ and γ_1 for each vehicle can also be calculated using Figure 5 as

$$\gamma_a = \tan^{-1}(\frac{l_{oa} - l_{oa}\cos\varphi_{ba}}{l_{oa} \cdot \sin\varphi_{ba} + l_{\varphi Ra} \cdot \cos\varphi_a}) \tag{18}$$

$$\gamma_b = \tan^{-1}(\frac{l_{ob} - l_{ob}\cos\varphi_{bb}}{l_{ob} \cdot \sin\varphi_{bb} + l_{\varphi Rb} \cdot \cos\varphi_b}) \tag{19}$$

$$l_{\varphi Ra} = \frac{(l_{aa} - x_a) - a_{oa}\sin\varphi_a}{\cos\varphi_a} \tag{20}$$

$$l_{\varphi Rb} = \frac{(l_{ab} - x_b) - a_{ob}\sin\varphi_b}{\cos\varphi_b} \tag{21}$$

$$\gamma_{1a} = \gamma_a - \varphi_a \tag{22}$$

$$\gamma_{1b} = \gamma_b - \varphi_b \tag{23}$$

The forces of the front-end springs are calculated using the general relationship between the force and deflection of a non-linear spring depicted in Figure 7 as follows:

$$F_{si} = k_{sij}\delta_i + F_{ij} \tag{24}$$

where k_s and δ represent the stiffness and the deflection of the front-end spring, respectively. The subscript i indicates the spring location (u_R: upper right spring, u_L: upper left spring, l_R: lower right spring and l_L: lower left spring) and the subscript j indicates different stages of the force-deformation characteristics as shown in Figure 7. The stiffness of the spring k_s and the force elements F_{ij} vary according to the different stages of the deflection δ and can be defined as follows:

$$k_{sij} = k_{si1}, \qquad F_{ij} = 0 \; 0 \le \delta < \delta_{i1} \tag{25}$$

$$k_{sij} = k_{si2}, \qquad F_{ij} = (k_{si1} - k_{si2})\delta_{i1}\ \delta_{i1} \le \delta < \delta_{i2} \tag{26}$$

$$k_{sij} = k_{si3}, \qquad F_{ij} = (k_{si1} - k_{si2})\delta_{i1} + (k_{si2} - k_{si3})\delta_{i2}\ \delta_{i2} \le \delta < \delta_{i3} \tag{27}$$

$$k_{sij} = k_{\sin},\ F_{ij} = (k_{si1} - k_{si2})\delta_{i1} + (k_{si2} - k_{si3})\delta_{i2} + \ldots$$

$$+(k_{si(n-1)} - k_{\sin})\delta_{i(n-1)}\ \delta \ge \delta_{(n-1)} \tag{28}$$

where the deformation of the front-end springs δ_i can be calculated using Figures 4 and 5 as follows:

$$\delta_{uR} = x + \delta_{\theta uR} + \delta_{\varphi uR} - \delta_b \tag{29}$$

$$\delta_{uL} = x + \delta_{\theta uL} - \delta_{\varphi uL} \tag{30}$$

$$\delta_{lR} = x - \delta_{\theta lR} + \delta_{\varphi lR} - \delta_b \tag{31}$$

$$\delta_{lL} = x - \delta_{\theta lL} - \delta_{\varphi lL} \tag{32}$$

where δ_θ, δ_φ and δ_b represent the deflection of the front end due to pitching, yawing and the bumper's rotation, respectively and can be calculated as

$$\delta_{\theta uR} = \delta_{\theta uL} = \sqrt{l_f^2 + e_1^2} \cdot \cos(\tan^{-1}(\frac{e_1}{l_f}) - \theta) - l_f \tag{33}$$

$$\delta_{\theta lR} = \delta_{\theta lL} = l_f - [\sqrt{l_f^2 + e_2^2} \cdot \cos(\tan^{-1}(\frac{e_2}{l_f}) + \theta)] \tag{34}$$

$$\delta_{\varphi uR} = \delta_{\varphi lR} = (l_a - x) - l_{\varphi R} \tag{35}$$

$$\delta_{\varphi uL} = \delta_{\varphi lL} = l_{\varphi L} - (l_a - x) \tag{36}$$

$$l_{\varphi L} = \frac{(l_a - x) + a_i \sin\varphi}{\cos\varphi} \tag{37}$$

$$\delta_b = \sqrt{(l_o - l_o \cos\phi_1)^2 + (l_o \cdot \sin\phi_1 + l_{\phi R} \cdot \cos\phi)^2} - l_{\phi R} \tag{38}$$

The suspension forces of the vehicle body can be written as follows:

$$F_{SfR} = k_{SfR}(z - l_f \cdot \sin\theta - b_o \cdot \psi) + c_{fR}(\dot{z} - l_f \cdot \dot{\theta} \cdot \cos\theta - b_o \cdot \dot{\psi}) - u_{fR} \tag{39}$$

$$F_{SfL} = k_{SfL}(z - l_f \cdot \sin\theta + b_i \cdot \psi) + c_{fL}(\dot{z} - l_f \cdot \dot{\theta} \cdot \cos\theta + b_i \cdot \dot{\psi}) - u_{fL} \tag{40}$$

$$F_{SrR} = k_{SrR}(z + l_r \cdot \sin\theta - b_o \cdot \psi) + c_{rR}(\dot{z} + l_r \cdot \dot{\theta} \cdot \cos\theta - b_o \cdot \dot{\psi}) - u_{rR} \tag{41}$$

$$F_{SrL} = k_{SrL}(z - l_r \cdot \sin\theta + b_i \cdot \psi) + c_{rL}(\dot{z} - l_r \cdot \dot{\theta} \cdot \cos\theta + b_i \cdot \dot{\psi}) - u_{rL} \tag{42}$$

where θ and ψ are the vehicle body pitching and rolling angles, respectively, and $\dot{z}$, $\dot{\theta}$ and $\dot{\psi}$ are the vehicle body vertical, pitching and rolling velocities, respectively. The ASC force elements (u) are applied in the vertical direction parallel to the existing conventional suspension system.

2.1.2. Forces Applied to the Vehicle

There are different types of forces which are applied on the vehicle body. These forces are generated by crushing the front-end structure, conventional suspension system due to the movement of the vehicle body and the active control systems such as the ABS and ASC. The free body diagram shown in Figure 2 illustrates these different forces and their directions.

To simulate the upper and lower members of the vehicle front-end structure, multi-stage piecewise linear force-deformation spring characteristics are considered. The non-linear springs used in the multi-body model (ADAMS) (Hogan & Manning, 2007) are taken to generate the n stage piecewise spring's characteristics as shown in Figure 6, while the general relationship between the force and the deflection, Figure 7, is used to calculate the force of the vehicle's front-end. The suspension forces of the vehicle body are also calculated and the detailed equations of these forces are mentioned in section 2.1.1.

Figure 6.

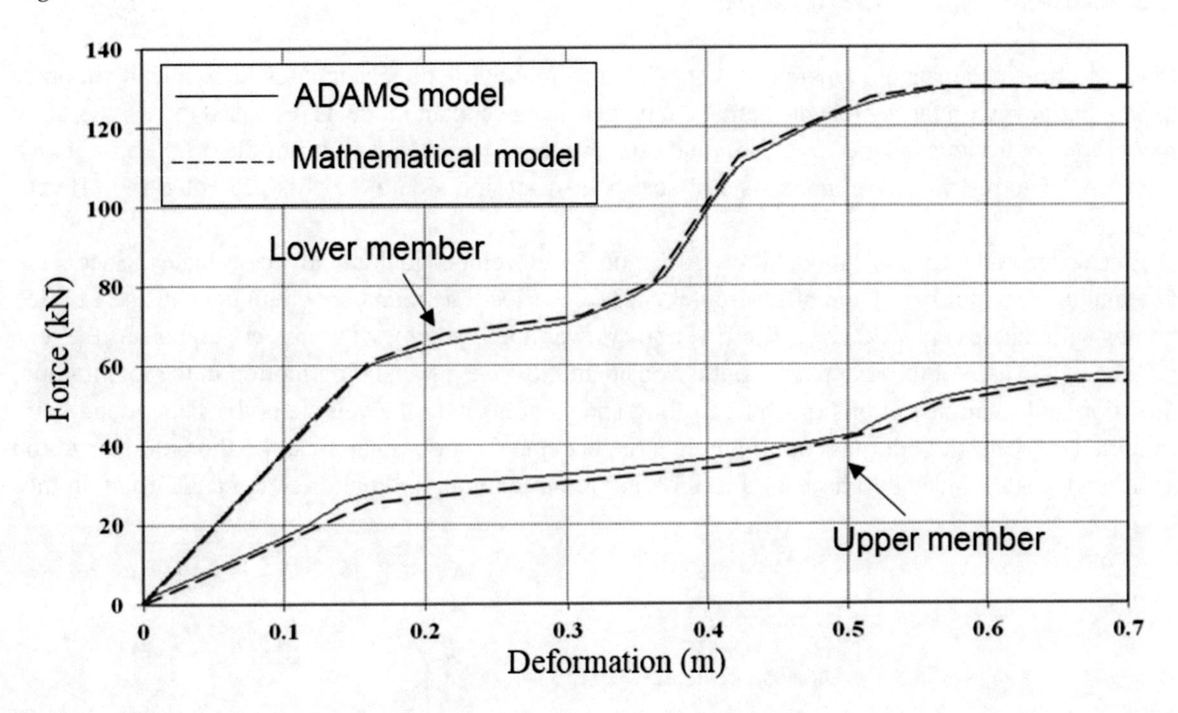

Figure 7.

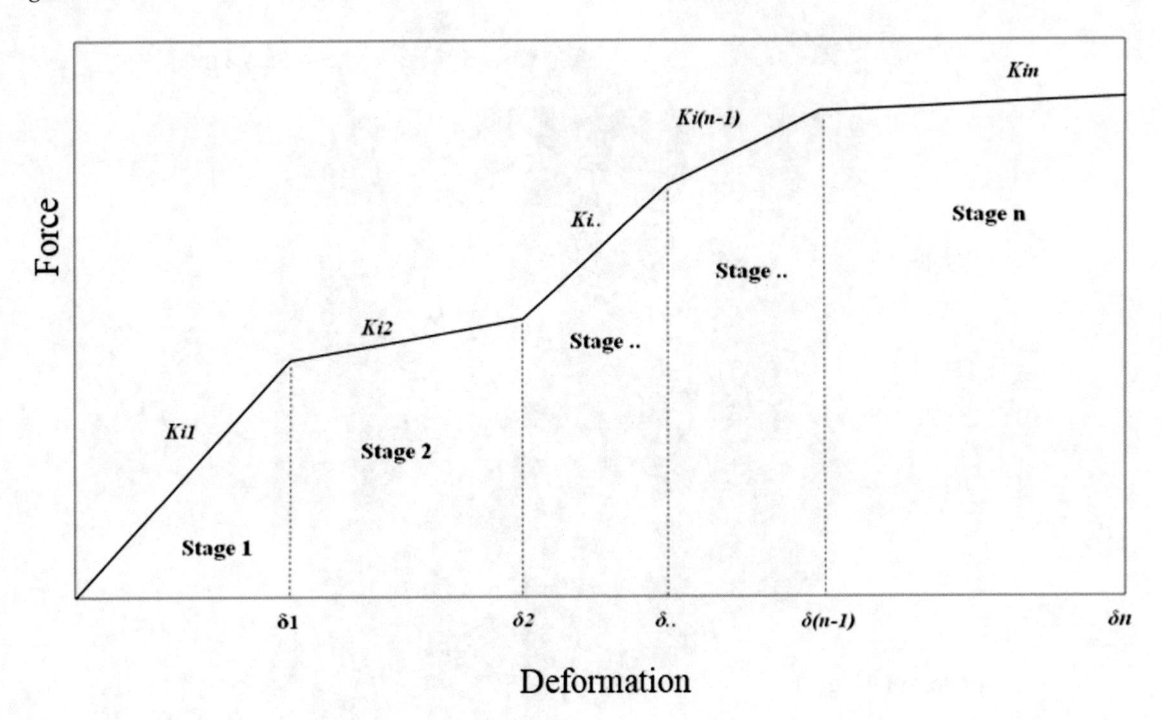

2.2. Multi-Body Occupant Model

In this section, occupant biodynamics is considered by modelling the occupant mathematically in order to be integrated with the vehicle mathematical model. The occupant model is proposed to be three-body model to capture its dynamic response, rotational events of the chest and head, due to different crash scenarios. The restraint system consists of seat belt, front and side airbags is presented by different spring-damper systems.

The occupant biodynamic model shown in Figure 8 is developed in this study to evaluate the occupant kinematic behaviour in full and offset frontal crash scenarios. The human body model consists of three bodies with masses m_1, m_2 and m_3. The first body (lower body/pelvis) with mass m_1, represents the legs and the pelvic area of the occupant and it is considered to have a translation motion in the longitudinal direction and rotation motions (pitching, rolling and yawing) with the vehicle body. The second body (middle body/chest), with mass m_2, represents the occupant's abdominal area, the thorax area and the arms, and it is considered to have a translation motion in the longitudinal direction and a rotation mo-

Figure 8.

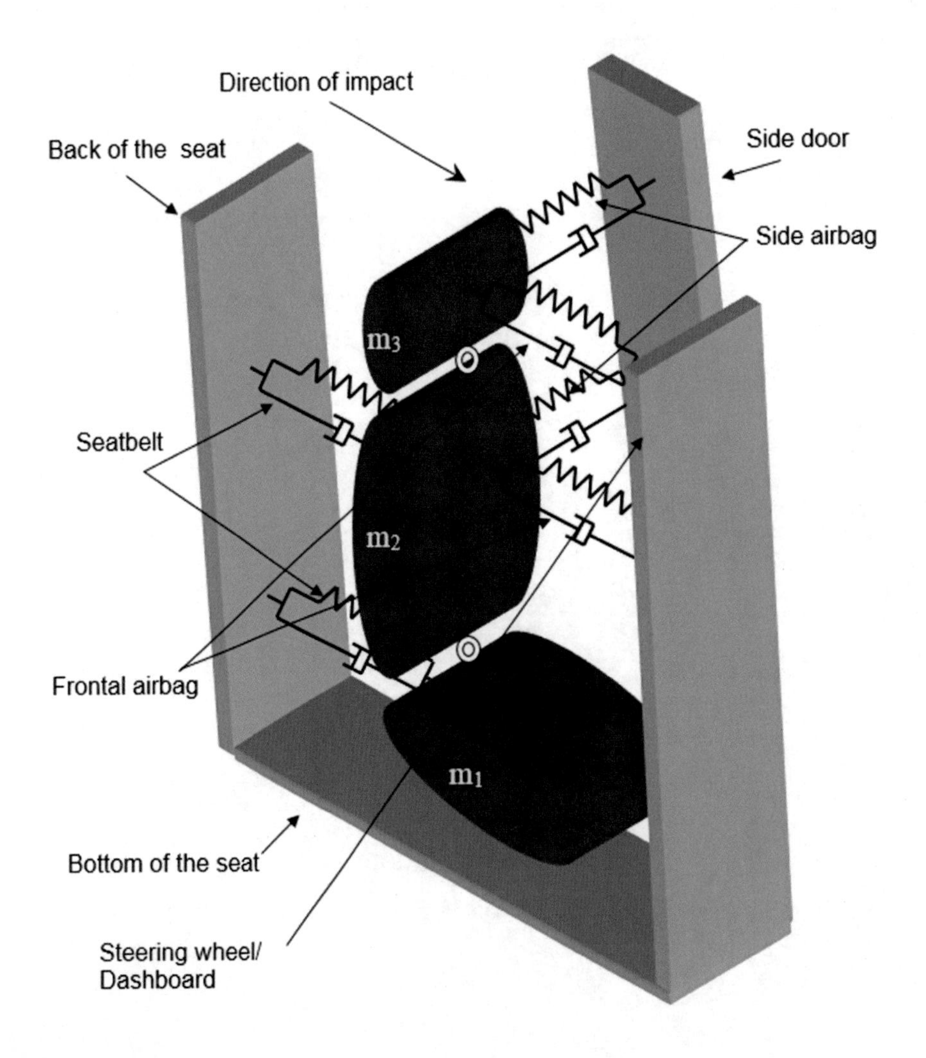

tion around the pivot between the lower and middle bodies (pivot 1). The third body (upper body/head), with mass m_3, represents the head and neck of the occupant and it is considered to have a translation motion in the longitudinal direction and a rotational motion around the pivot between the middle and upper bodies (pivot 2).

A rotational coil spring is proposed at each pivot to represent the joint stiffness between the pelvic area and the abdominal area and between the thorax area and the neck/head area. The seatbelt is represented by two linear spring-damper units between the compartment and the occupant. The frontal and side airbags are each represented by two linear spring-damper units.

2.2.1. Equation of Motion (EOM) of the Human Body Model

Figures 9 (a), (b), and (c) show the side, top and front views of the occupant model, respectively. For each figure, the positions of the occupant's three bodies are illustrated before and after the crash. Lagrange's equations are used to describe the general motions of the multi-body human model.

The general motions of the multi-body human model are described using Lagrange's equations as follows:

$$\frac{d}{dt}\left(\frac{\partial E}{\partial \dot{x}_1}\right)-\frac{\partial E}{\partial x_1}+\frac{\partial V}{\partial x_1}+\frac{\partial D}{\partial \dot{x}_1}=0 \tag{43}$$

$$\frac{d}{dt}\left(\frac{\partial E}{\partial \dot{\theta}_2}\right)-\frac{\partial E}{\partial \theta_2}+\frac{\partial V}{\partial \theta_2}+\frac{\partial D}{\partial \dot{\theta}_2}=0 \tag{44}$$

$$\frac{d}{dt}\left(\frac{\partial E}{\partial \dot{\theta}_3}\right)-\frac{\partial E}{\partial \theta_3}+\frac{\partial V}{\partial \theta_3}+\frac{\partial D}{\partial \dot{\theta}_3}=0 \tag{45}$$

$$\frac{d}{dt}\left(\frac{\partial E}{\partial \dot{\psi}_2}\right)-\frac{\partial E}{\partial \psi_2}+\frac{\partial V}{\partial \psi_2}+\frac{\partial D}{\partial \dot{\psi}_2}=0 \tag{46}$$

$$\frac{d}{dt}\left(\frac{\partial E}{\partial \dot{\psi}_3}\right)-\frac{\partial E}{\partial \psi_3}+\frac{\partial V}{\partial \psi_3}+\frac{\partial D}{\partial \dot{\psi}_3}=0 \tag{47}$$

where E, V and D are the kinetic energy, potential energy and the Rayleigh dissipation function of the system, respectively. x_1, θ_2, θ_3, ψ_2 and ψ_3 are the longitudinal movement of the occupant's lower body, the rotational angle of the occupant's middle body about y axis, the rotational angle of the occupant's

Figure 9.

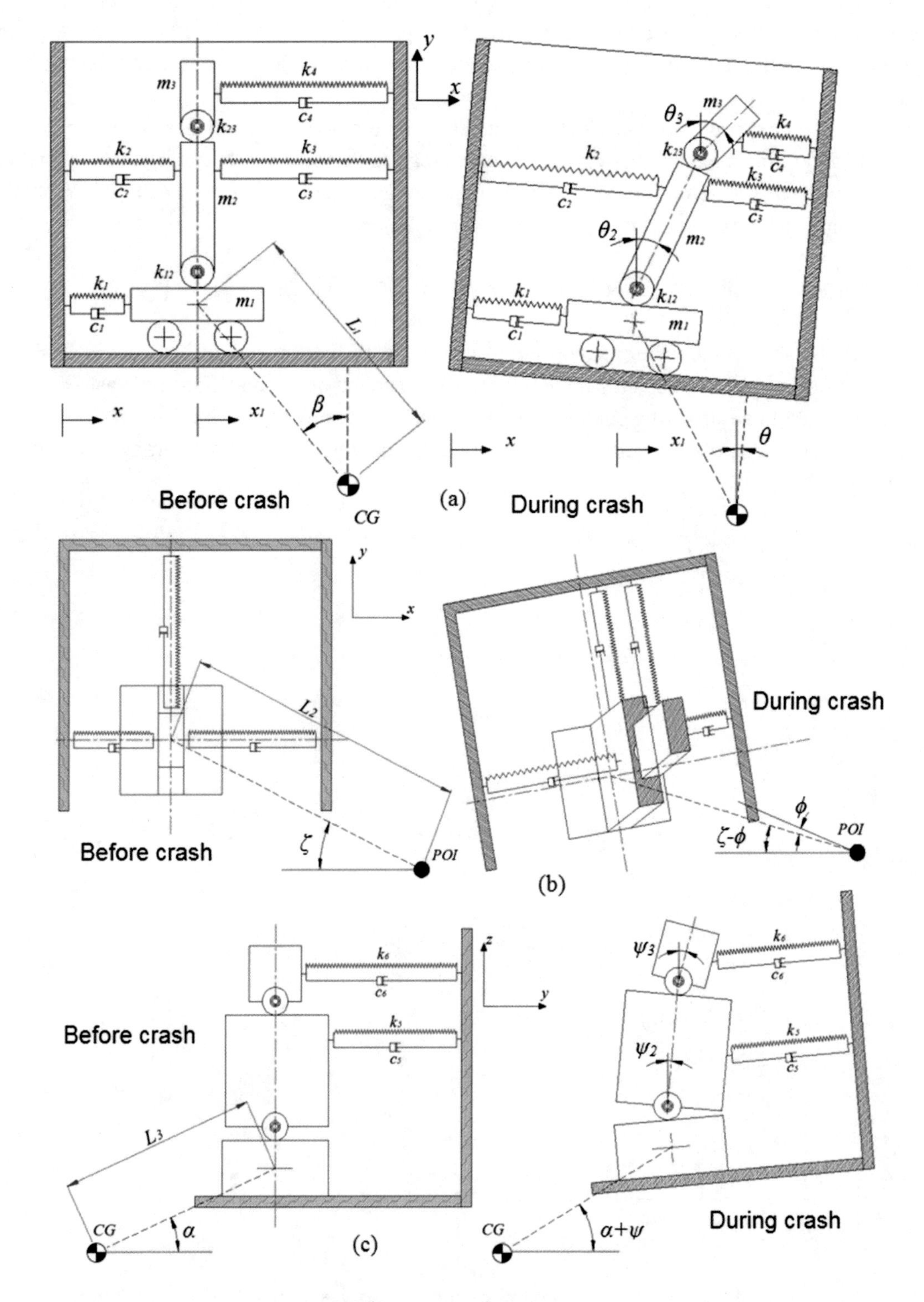
Before crash
During crash
(a)
CG
Before crash
During crash
(b)
POI
Before crash
During crash
(c)
CG

upper body about y axis, the rotational angle of the occupant's middle body about x axis and the rotational angle of the occupant's upper body about x axis, respectively. Hence, $\dot{x}_1$, $\dot{\theta}_2$, $\dot{\theta}_3$, $\dot{\psi}_2$ and $\dot{\psi}_3$ are their associated velocities, respectively.

The kinetic energy of the system can be written as:

$$E = \frac{m_1 \cdot v_1^2}{2} + \frac{m_2 \cdot v_2^2}{2} + \frac{m_3 \cdot v_3^2}{2} + \frac{I_1}{2} \cdot (\dot{\theta}^2 + \dot{\phi}^2 + \dot{\psi}^2)$$

$$+ \frac{I_2}{2} \cdot (\dot{\theta}_2^2 + \dot{\psi}_2^2) + \frac{I_3}{2} \cdot (\dot{\theta}_2^2 + \dot{\psi}_3^2) \quad (48)$$

where v_1, v_2 and v_3 are the equivalent velocities of the lower, middle and upper bodies of the occupant, respectively. I_1, I_2 and I_3 are the rotational moment of inertia of the lower, middle and upper bodies about the CG of each body, respectively. It is assumed that the rotational moment of inertia of each body around x, y and z axes are the same. $\dot{\theta}$, $\dot{\varphi}$ and $\dot{\psi}$ represent the vehicle body pitching, yawing and rolling velocities, respectively. The equivalent velocities of the three bodies of the occupant can be calculated as follows:

$$v_1^2 = \dot{X}_{m1}^2 + \dot{Y}_{m1}^2 + \dot{Z}_{m1}^2 \quad (49)$$

where the displacement of the lower body in x direction can be calculated using Figure 10 as

$$I_{zz} \cdot \ddot{\varphi} + (F_{suR} + F_{slR}) \cdot \cos\gamma_1 \cdot a_o - (F_{suL} + F_{slL}) \cdot a_i \quad (50)$$

The velocity of the lower body in x direction can be written as

$$\dot{X}_{m1} = \dot{x}_1 + L_1 \cdot \dot{\theta} \cdot \cos(\beta - \theta) - L_2 \cdot \dot{\phi} \cdot \sin(\zeta - \phi) \quad (51)$$

The displacement and velocity of the lower body in y direction can be calculated as

$$Y_{m1} = L_2 \cdot (\sin\zeta - \sin(\zeta - \phi)) + L_3 \cdot (\cos\alpha - co\,s(\alpha - \psi)) \quad (52)$$

$$\dot{Y}_{m1} = L_2 \cdot \dot{\phi} \cdot \cos(\zeta - \phi) + L_3 \cdot \dot{\psi} \cdot \sin(\alpha - \psi) \quad (53)$$

the displacement and velocity of the lower body in y direction can be calculated as

$$Z_{m1} = z + L_1 \cdot (\cos(\beta - \theta) - \cos\beta) + L_3 \cdot (\sin(\alpha + \psi) - \sin\alpha) \quad (54)$$

Figure 10.

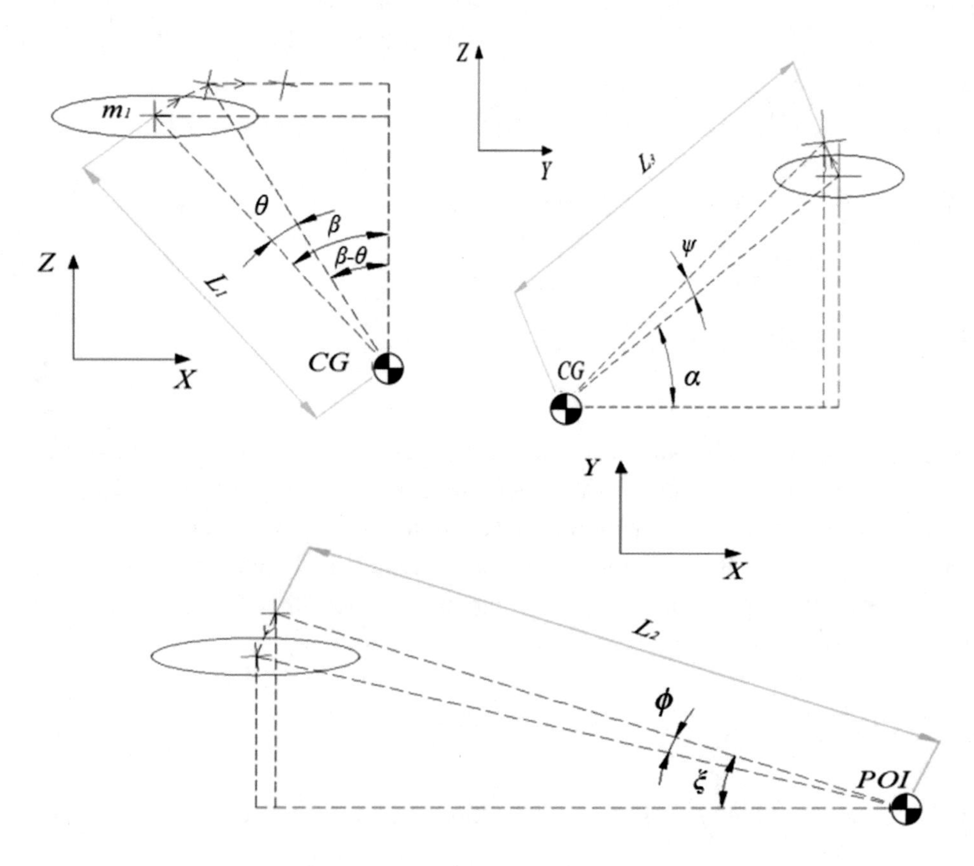

$$\dot{Z}_{m1} = L_1 \cdot \dot{\theta} \cdot \sin(\beta - \theta) + L_3 \cdot \dot{\psi} \cdot \cos(\alpha + \psi) \tag{55}$$

substituting equations 32, 34 and 36 in equation 30, the equivalent velocity of the lower body can be determined. By repeating the previous steps of these equations (from equation 30 to equation 36), the equivalent velocities of the middle and upper bodies can be calculated.

Where X_m is the resultant longitudinal displacement in *x* direction, Y_m is the resultant vertical displacement in *y* direction and Z_m is the resultant vertical displacement. (*1*: lower body, *2*: middle body and *3*: upper body). L_1 is the distance from the vehicle's *y* axis to the lower body's CG, L_2 is the distance between the point of impact and the CG of the lower body and L_3 is the distance from the vehicle's *x* axis to the lower body's CG. It is assumed that L_1, L_2 and L_3 are constant due to the insignificant change of their lengths during the crash. β, ξ, and α are the angles between the vertical centreline of the vehicle *z* axis and the line between the vehicle's *y* axis and the CG of the lower body (L_1); the angle between the longitudinal centreline of the vehicle *x* axis and the line between the point of impact and the CG of the lower body (L_2); and the angle between the vertical centreline of the vehicle *z* axis and the line between the vehicle's *x* axis and the CG of the lower body (L_3), respectively.

By substituting the equivalent velocities of the three bodies in equation 4.6, the kinetic energy can be written as follows:

$$E=\frac{1}{2}\cdot(m_1+m_2+m_3)\cdot\dot{x}_1^2+\frac{1}{2}\cdot(m_1+m_2+m_3)\cdot\dot{z}_1^2+\frac{1}{2}\cdot(m_1+m_2+m_3)\cdot L_1^2\dot{\theta}^2$$

$$+\frac{1}{2}\cdot(m_1+m_2+m_3)\cdot L_2^2\dot{\phi}^2+\frac{1}{2}\cdot(m_1+m_2+m_3)\cdot L_3^2\dot{\psi}^2+\left(\frac{m_2}{6}+\frac{m_3}{2}\right)\cdot l_2^2\cdot\theta_2^2$$

$$+\left(\frac{m_2}{6}+\frac{m_3}{2}\right)\cdot l_2^2\cdot\psi_2^2+\frac{m_3}{6}\cdot l_3^2\cdot\dot{\theta}_3^2+\frac{m_3}{6}\cdot l_3^2\cdot\dot{\psi}_3^2\frac{1}{2}+(m_1+m_2+m_3)\cdot L_1\cdot\dot{x}_1\cdot\dot{\theta}\cdot\cos(\beta-\theta)$$

$$-(m_1+m_2+m_3)\cdot L_2\cdot\dot{x}_1\cdot\dot{\phi}\cdot\sin(\zeta-\phi)$$

$$-(m_1+m_2+m_3)\cdot L_1\cdot L_2\cdot\dot{\theta}\cdot\dot{\phi}\cdot\cos(\beta-\theta)\cdot\sin(\zeta-\phi)$$

$$+(m_1+m_2+m_3)\cdot L_2\cdot L_3\cdot\dot{\phi}\cdot\dot{\psi}\cdot\cos(\zeta-\phi)\cdot\sin(\alpha+\psi)$$

$$+(m_1+m_2+m_3)\cdot L_1\cdot\dot{z}\cdot\dot{\theta}\cdot\sin(\beta-\theta)+(m_1+m_2+m_3)\cdot L_3\cdot\dot{z}\cdot\dot{\psi}\cdot\cos(\alpha+\psi)$$

$$-(m_1+m_2+m_3)\cdot L_1\cdot L_3\cdot\dot{\theta}\cdot\dot{\psi}\cdot\sin(\beta-\theta)\cdot\cos(\alpha+\psi)+\left(\frac{m_2}{2}+m_3\right)\cdot l_2\cdot\dot{x}_1\cdot\dot{\theta}_2\cdot\cos\theta_2$$

$$-\left(\frac{m_2}{2}+m_3\right)\cdot L_2\cdot l_2\cdot\dot{\phi}\cdot\dot{\psi}_2\cdot\cos(\zeta-\phi)\cdot\cos\psi_2$$

$$-\left(\frac{m_2}{2}+m_3\right)\cdot L_3\cdot l_2\cdot\dot{\psi}\cdot\dot{\psi}_2\cdot\sin(\alpha+\psi)\cdot\cos\psi_2-\left(\frac{m_2}{2}+m_3\right)\cdot l_2\cdot\dot{z}\cdot\dot{\theta}_2\cdot\sin\theta_2$$

$$-\left(\frac{m_2}{2}+m_3\right)\cdot l_2\cdot\dot{z}\cdot\dot{\psi}_2\cdot\sin\psi_2-\left(\frac{m_2}{2}+m_3\right)\cdot L_1\cdot l_2\cdot\dot{\theta}\cdot\dot{\theta}_2\cdot\sin(\beta-\theta)\cdot\sin\theta_2$$

$$-\left(\frac{m_2}{2}+m_3\right)\cdot L_1\cdot l_2\cdot\dot{\theta}\cdot\dot{\psi}_2\cdot\sin(\beta-\theta)\cdot\sin\psi_2$$

$$-\left(\frac{m_2}{2}+m_3\right)\cdot L_3\cdot l_2\cdot\dot{\psi}\cdot\dot{\theta}_2\cdot\cos(\alpha+\psi)\cdot\sin\theta_2$$

$$-\left(\frac{m_2}{2}+m_3\right)\cdot L_3\cdot l_2\cdot\dot{\psi}\cdot\dot{\psi}_2\cdot\cos(\alpha+\psi)\cdot\sin\psi_2+\left(\frac{m_2}{4}+m_3\right)\cdot l_2^2\cdot\dot{\theta}_2\cdot\dot{\psi}_2\cdot\sin\theta_2\cdot\sin\psi_2$$

$$+\frac{m_3}{2}\cdot l_3\cdot\dot{x}_1\cdot\dot{\theta}_3\cdot\cos\theta_3+\frac{m_3}{2}\cdot L_1\cdot l_3\cdot\dot{\theta}\cdot\dot{\theta}_3\cdot\cos(\beta-\theta)\cdot\cos\theta_3$$

$$-\frac{m_3}{2}\cdot L_2\cdot l_3\cdot\dot{\phi}\cdot\dot{\theta}_3\cdot\sin(\zeta-\phi)\cdot\cos\theta_3+\frac{m_3}{2}\cdot l_2\cdot l_3\cdot\dot{\theta}_2\cdot\dot{\theta}_3\cdot\cos\theta_2\cdot\cos\theta_3$$

$$-\frac{m_3}{2}\cdot L_2\cdot l_3\cdot\dot{\phi}\cdot\dot{\psi}_3\cdot\cos(\zeta-\phi)\cdot\cos\psi_3-\frac{m_3}{2}\cdot L_3\cdot l_3\cdot\dot{\psi}\cdot\dot{\psi}_3\cdot\sin(\alpha+\psi)\cdot\cos\psi_3$$

$$+\frac{m_3}{2}\cdot l_2\cdot l_3\cdot\dot{\psi}_2\cdot\dot{\psi}_3\cdot\cos\psi_2\cdot\cos\psi_3-\frac{m_3}{2}\cdot l_3\cdot\dot{z}\cdot\dot{\theta}_3\cdot\sin\theta_3-\frac{m_3}{2}\cdot l_3\cdot\dot{z}\cdot\dot{\psi}_3\cdot\sin\psi_3$$

$$-\frac{m_3}{2}\cdot L_1\cdot l_3\cdot\dot{\theta}_2\cdot\dot{\theta}_3\cdot\sin(\beta-\theta)\cdot\sin\theta_3-\frac{m_3}{2}\cdot L_1\cdot l_3\cdot\dot{\theta}\cdot\dot{\psi}_3\cdot\sin(\beta-\theta)\sin\psi_3$$

$$-\frac{m_3}{2}\cdot L_3\cdot l_3\cdot\dot{\psi}\cdot\dot{\theta}_3\cdot\cos(\alpha+\psi)\cdot\sin\theta_3-\frac{m_3}{2}\cdot L_3\cdot l_3\cdot\dot{\psi}\cdot\dot{\psi}_3\cdot\cos(\alpha+\psi)\cdot\sin\psi_3$$

$$+\frac{m_3}{2}\cdot l_2\cdot l_3\cdot\dot{\theta}_2\cdot\dot{\theta}_3\cdot\sin\theta_2\cdot\sin\theta_3+\frac{m_3}{2}\cdot l_2\cdot l_3\cdot\dot{\theta}_2\cdot\dot{\psi}_3\cdot\sin\theta_2\cdot\sin\psi_3$$

$$+\frac{m_3}{2}\cdot l_2\cdot l_3\cdot\dot{\psi}_2\cdot\dot{\theta}_3\cdot\sin\psi_2\cdot\sin\theta_3+\frac{m_3}{2}\cdot l_2\cdot l_3\cdot\dot{\psi}_2\cdot\dot{\psi}_3\cdot\sin\psi_2\cdot\sin\psi_3$$

$$+m_3\cdot l_3^2\cdot\dot{\theta}_3\cdot\dot{\psi}_3\cdot\sin\theta_3\cdot\sin\psi_3 \quad (56)$$

where l_2 and l_3 are the middle body and upper body lengths, respectively. Using Figure 9 the potential energy of the system can be written as

$$V=m_1\cdot g\cdot\left[h+z+L_1\cdot(\cos(\beta-\theta)-\cos\beta)\right]+m_2\cdot g\cdot[h+z+L_1\cdot(\cos(\beta-\theta)-\cos\beta)$$

$$+\frac{l_2}{2}\cdot\cos\theta_2-\frac{l_2}{2}\cdot(1-\cos\psi_2)]+m_3\cdot g\cdot[h+z+L_1\cdot(\cos(\beta-\theta)-\cos\beta)+l_2\cdot\cos\theta_2$$

$$-l_2 \cdot (1-\cos\psi_2) + \frac{l_3}{2} \cdot \cos\theta_3 - \frac{l_3}{2} \cdot (1-\cos\psi_3)] + \frac{1}{2} \cdot [F_{k1} \cdot \delta_1 + F_{k2} \cdot \delta_2 + F_{k3} \cdot \delta_3 + F_{k4} \cdot \delta_4$$

$$+F_{k5} \cdot \delta_5 + F_{k6} \cdot \delta_6 + F_{k12\theta} \cdot \delta_{12\theta} + F_{k12\psi} \cdot \delta_{12\psi} + F_{k23\theta} \cdot \delta_{23\theta} + F_{k23\psi} \cdot \delta_{23\psi}] \quad (57)$$

where h is the vehicle's CG height and z is the vertical displacement of the vehicle body. F_{k1}, F_{k2}, F_{k3}, F_{k4}, F_{k5} and F_{k6} are the forces generated from the lower seatbelt spring, the upper seatbelt spring, the lower frontal airbag spring, the upper frontal airbag spring, the lower side airbag spring, the upper side airbag spring, respectively. $F_{k12\theta}$ and $F_{k12\psi}$ are the forces generated from the rotational spring between the middle and lower body around y and x axes, respectively; $F_{k23\theta}$ and $F_{k23\psi}$ are the forces generated from the rotational spring between the upper and middle body around y and x axes, respectively. δ_1, δ_2, δ_3, δ_4, δ_5 and δ_6 represent the total deflection of the lower seatbelt spring, of the upper seatbelt spring, of the lower frontal airbag spring, of the upper frontal airbag spring, of the lower side airbag spring, of the upper side airbag spring, respectively. $\delta_{12\theta}$ and $\delta_{12\psi}$, $\delta_{23\theta}$ and $\delta_{23\psi}$ are the deflection of the rotational spring between the lower and middle body around y and x axes and deflection of the rotational spring between the middle and upper body around y and x axes, respectively.

The Rayleigh dissipation function can be written as follows:

$$\gamma_b = \tan^{-1}\left(\frac{l_{ob} - l_{ob}\cos\varphi_{bb}}{l_{ob} \cdot \sin\varphi_{bb} + l_{\varphi Rb} \cdot \cos\varphi_b}\right) \quad (58)$$

where F_{c1}, F_{c2}, F_{c3}, F_{c4}, F_{c5} and F_{c6} are the forces generated from the lower seatbelt, the upper seatbelt, the lower frontal airbag, the upper frontal airbag, the lower side airbag, and the upper side airbag dampers, respectively. $\dot{\delta}_1, \dot{\delta}_2, \dot{\delta}_3, \dot{\delta}_4, \dot{\delta}_5$ and $\dot{\delta}_6$ are the associated velocities of the δ_1, δ_2, δ_3, δ_4, δ_5 and δ_6, respectively.

The forces F_{ki} and F_{ci} (where i= 1, 2, ...) are calculated as

$$F_{ki} = k_i \cdot \delta_i \quad (59)$$

$$F_{ci} = c_i \cdot \dot{\delta}_i \quad (60)$$

In order to get the components of the equations 1, 2, 3, 4 and 5, the differentiations of the kinetic energy, potential energy and Rayleigh dissipation function are determined. To solve these equations, they need to be re-arranged in an integratable form and then rewritten in a matrix form as follows:

$$[A] \cdot [\ddot{B}] = [C] \quad (61)$$

where the $[\ddot{B}] = [\ddot{x}_1 \quad \ddot{\theta}_2 \quad \ddot{\theta}_3 \quad \ddot{\psi}_2 \quad \ddot{\psi}_3]^T$.

The final form then can be written as:

$$\left[\ddot{B}\right] = \left[A\right]^{-1} \cdot \left[C\right] \tag{62}$$

Different occupant bodies' responses (x_1, θ_2, θ_3, ψ_2 and ψ_3) can be determined by solving equation 62 numerically.

3. VALIDATION ANALYSIS

To ensure that the models are valid, provide accurate results and the dynamic responses of the vehicle body and the occupant are reliable, comparisons between the mathematical models, real test data and former finite element and multi-body models are carried out.

3.1. Validation of the Vehicle Dynamics/Crash Mathematical Model

The values of different parameters used in numerical simulations are given in Table 1 (Alleyne, 1997). The case of full frontal vehicle-to-barrier is used in this section to be compared with real test data and former multi-body model used ADAMS software. The numerical results (the velocity and, deceleration of the vehicle body and deformation of the front-end structure) of the two models (mathematical and ADAMS models) and the real results (TRL data, 1995) are depicted in Figures 11 to 13.

The lower initial speed of 15.1 m/s at the moment of impact of the ADAMS model as shown in Figure 11 is due to the effect of rolling resistance prior to impact (Hogan, 2008), while the initial speed of the mathematical model is adapted to be the same as the actual test impact speed. However, the post-impact velocity curve of the mathematical model is in a good correlation with both real test and ADAMS model results.

Figure 11.

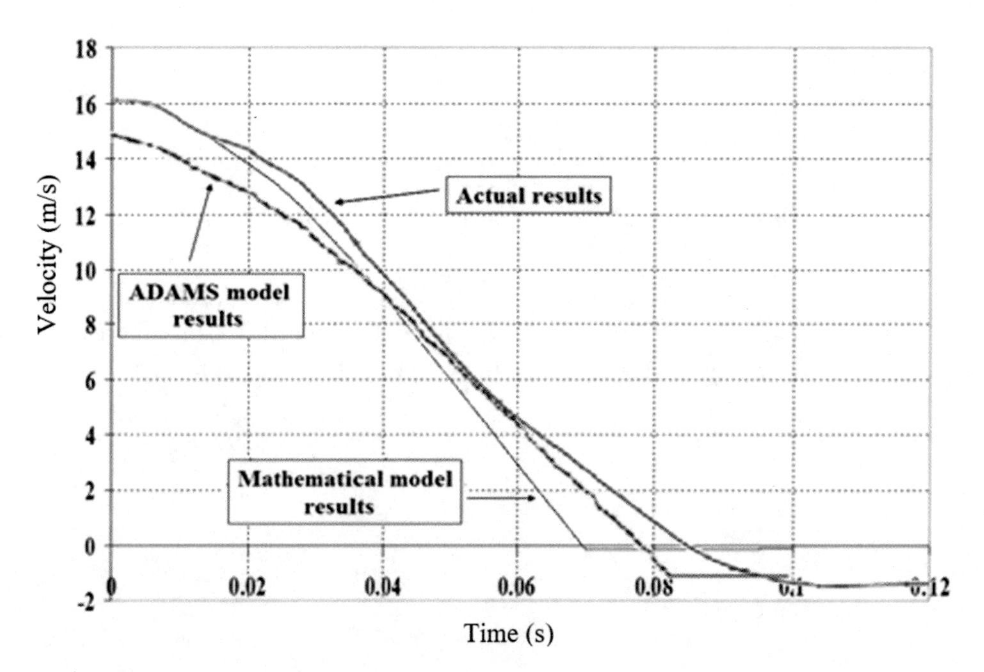

Figure 12.

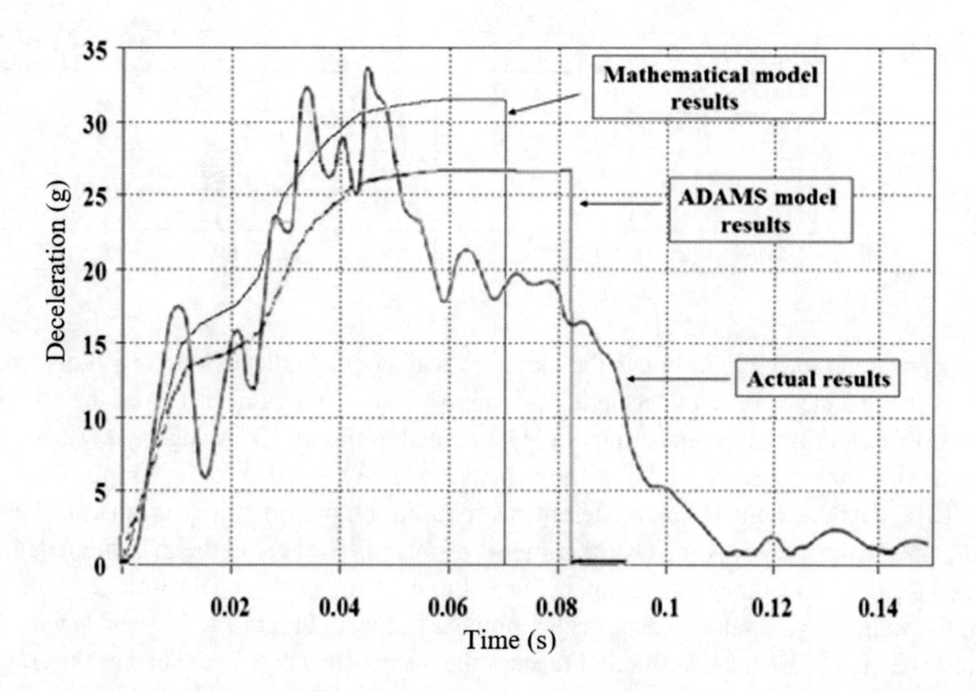

Figure 13.

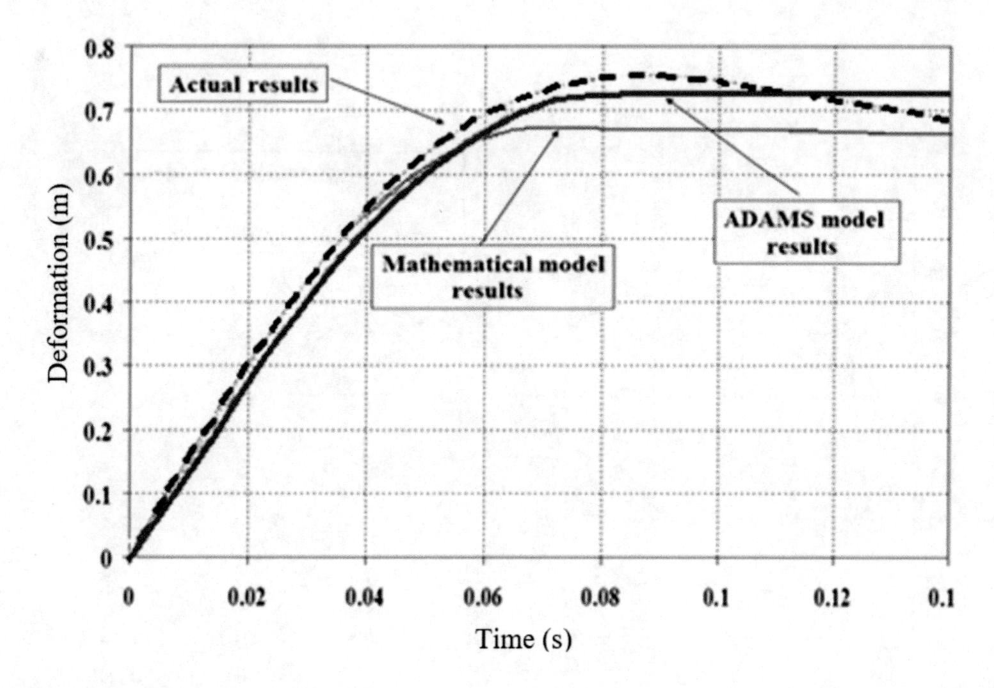

The decelerations of the vehicle body are shown in Figure 12. It is noticed that there is a high correlation between the mathematical model and the ADAMS model and mean results of the real test is observed. The sudden reduction of the vehicle deceleration at the end of the collision in both mathematical model and ADAMS results is due to the deactivation of the spring forces at this point (there is no

Table 1. The values of the different parameters, which are used in the simulations

Parameter	m	I_{yy}	I_{xx}	I_{zz}	I_{bzz}
Value	1200 kg	1490 kg.m^2	350 kg.m^2	1750 kg.m^2	40 kg.m^2
Parameter	$k_{SfR} = k_{SfL}$	$k_{SrR} = k_{SrL}$	$c_{fR} = c_{fL}$	$c_{rR} = c_{rL}$	l_f
Value	18.25 kN/m	13.75 kN/m	1100 N.s/m	900 N.s/m	1.185 m
Parameter	l_r	h	l_a	l_b	$b_i = b_o$
Value	1.58 m	0.452 m	1.2 m	0.85 m	0.8 m

recoil of the front-end springs). Although the mathematical model predicted a slightly higher value than ADAMS results, the mean value of deceleration is approximately the same as that of the actual results.

The deformation of the front-end structure is illustrated in Figure 13. A slightly lower value of the maximum deformation appeared in the mathematical model. This is due to the simplification of both mathematical and ADAMS models and different masses used compare to the real crash test. However, the trend in the three cases is approximately the same with small differences in the maximum deformation.

Figures 14 and 15 show the comparison between the mathematical model results and the ADAMS results for the vehicle's yaw velocity and acceleration. As shown in Figure 14, the vehicle yawing velocity is almost the same in both models until it reaches the maximum value (at the end of the crash). After the crash ended, the vehicle yaw becomes dependent on the maximum vehicle's pitch angle and the period during the rear wheels leave the ground. This describes the difference between the yaw velocity

Figure 14.

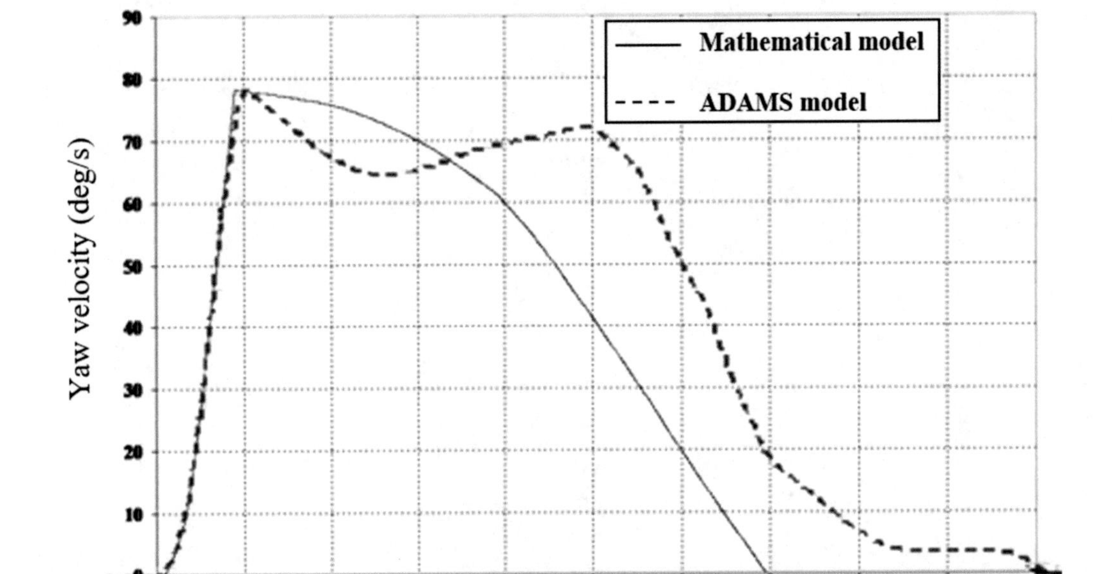

Figure 15.

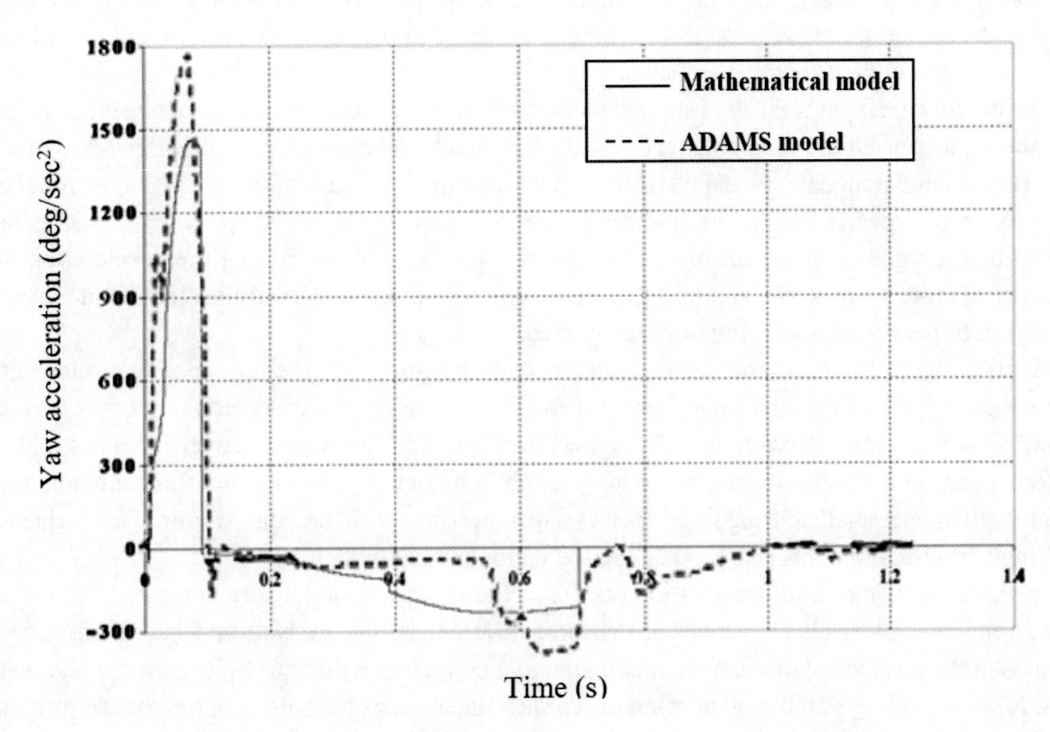

results of each model at the post-crash. While the maximum vehicle's yaw acceleration is slightly higher in ADAMS model than the mathematical model, a good correlation between both results is noted as shown in Figure 15.

3.2. Validation of the Occupant Kinematics Mathematical Model

The values of different parameters used in numerical simulations are given in Table 2. The values m_1, m_2, m_3, l_2, l_3, k_{12} and k_{23} have been taken from (Ilie & Tabacu, 2010). The robustness of the occupant model is confirmed by comparing its results with the former finite element human model (Marzougui

Table 2. The values of the different parameters, which are used in the simulations

Parameter	m_1	m_2	m_3	l_2	l_3	L_1	L_2	L_3	L_4
Value	26.68 kg	46.06 kg	5.52 kg	0.427 m	0.24 m	0.3 m	2.3 m	0.65 m	0.3 m
Parameter	L_5	L_6	L_7	L_8	L_9	β	ζ	α	γ
Value	0.35 m	0.45 m	0.55 m	0.97 m	1.1 m	30 deg	15 deg	23 deg	30 deg
Parameter	ε_1	ε_2	ρ_1	ρ_2	k_{12}	k_{23}	k_1	k_2	k_3
Value	15 deg	15 deg	35 deg	43 deg	380 Nm/rad	200 Nm/ rad	58860 N/m	39240 N/m	2500 N/m
Parameter	k_4	k_5	k_6	c_1, c_2, c_3, c_4, c_5, c_6		d_{s1}, d_{s2}	d_{s3}, d_{s4}	d_{s5}	d_{s6}
Value	2500 N/m	2500 N/m	2500 N/m	20% of the critical damping		0 m	0.05 m	0 m	0.05 m

et al., 1996) and crash test (Markusic, 1992). The same test conditions of the car and the occupant in the real test with an initial velocity of 48.3 km/hr was used in the finite element model and proposed mathematical model described in this paper.

To ensure that the input crash data applied to the dummy and the occupant in the finite element model match the input data in the mathematical model, the vehicle decelerations in all cases (mathematical model, finite element model and real test) are compared as depicted in Figure 16. The same initial crash conditions (initial speed of 48 km/hr, and free rolling crash scenario) are adapted in the mathematical model to be the same as in the FE model and the real test. It is observed that the deceleration of the mathematical model shows outstanding agreement with the real test and the finite element model results with respect to peak values and timing of the curves.

Similarly, Figure 17 shows the chest deceleration-time histories of the real test, finite element and mathematical models. The values and trends of the three different chest deceleration curves are well-matched. The maximum deceleration of the occupant chest in the mathematical model is a slightly lower compared to the real test data, while it is a slightly higher compared to the finite element model. In addition there is a small shifting in this peak value compared with the other results. This is due to the modelling simplification of the airbag used in the mathematical models.

In the same way, the head deceleration results of the occupant models are presented in Figure 18. Although the general trends and slopes of the three different results are well matched, there is a small difference in the peak value of the mathematical model compared with both finite element and real test results. A small shifting of the head deceleration peak value is also observed here for both finite element and mathematical models by different values compared with the real test data.

Figure 16.

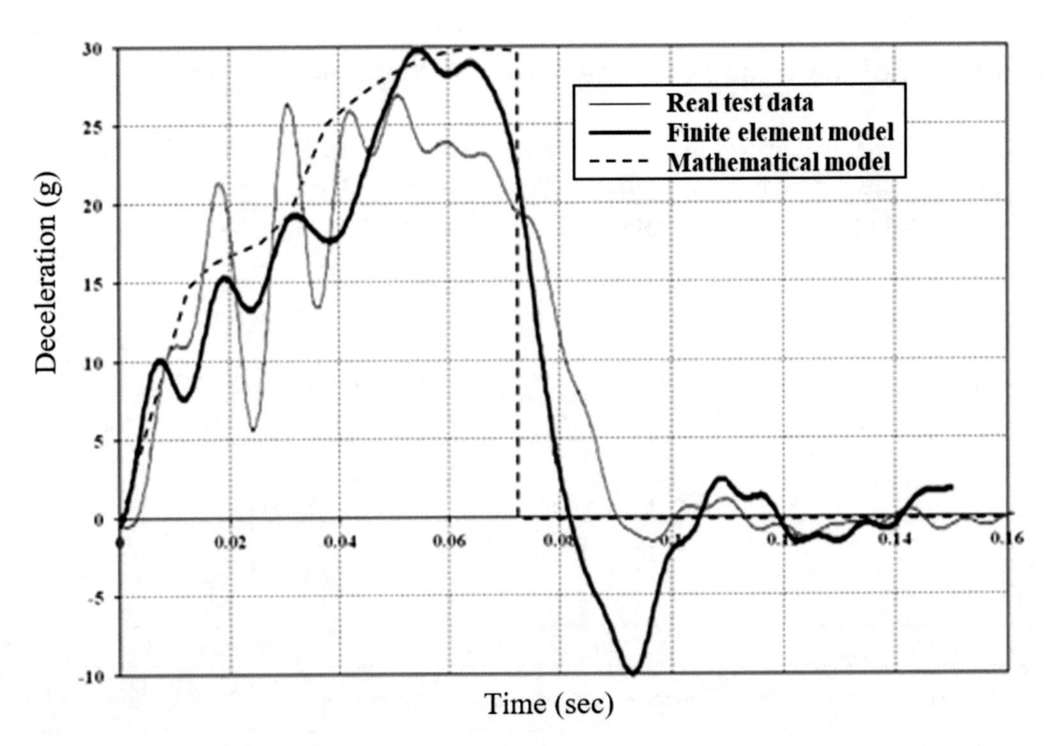

Figure 17.

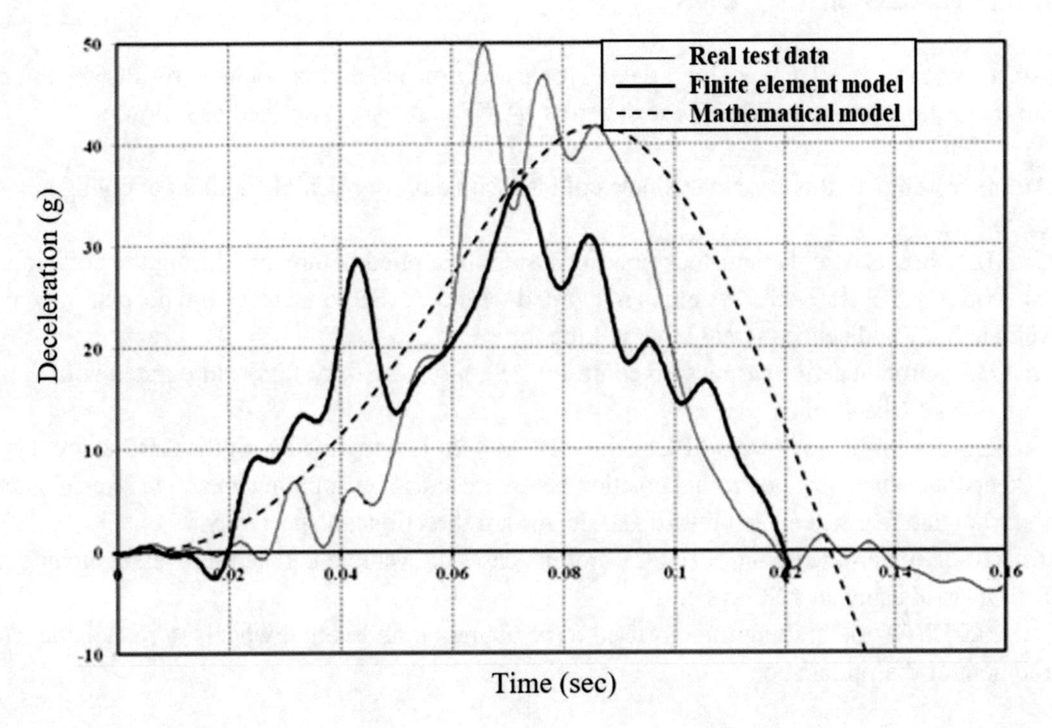

Figure 18.

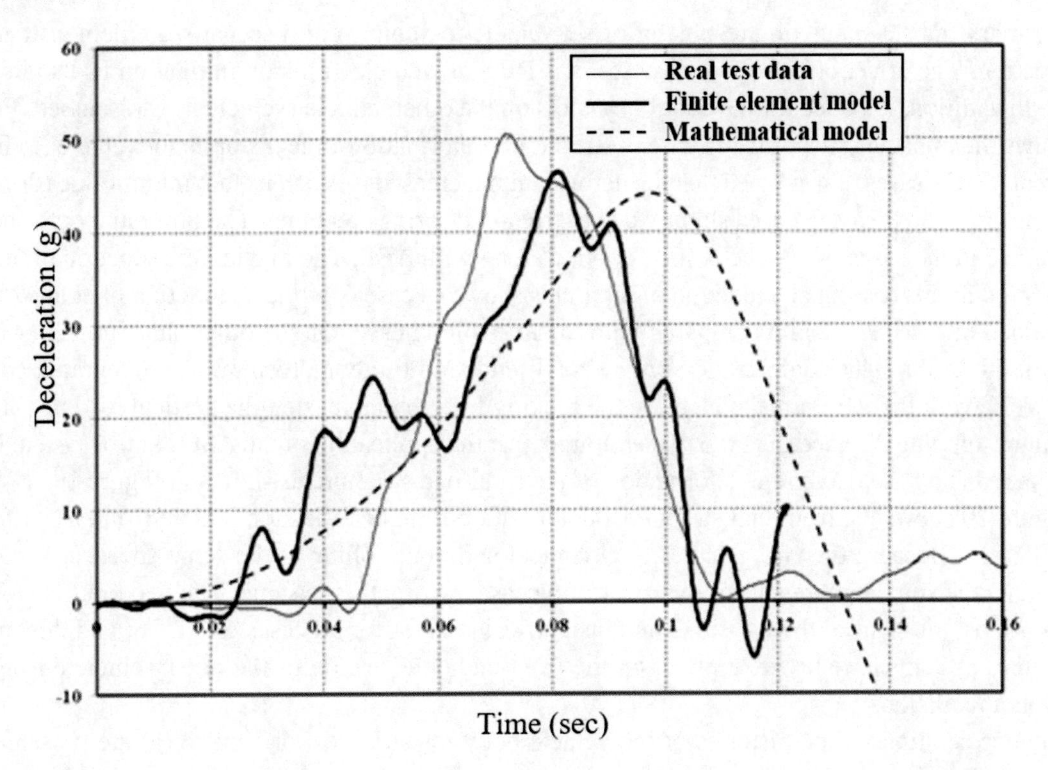

4. NUMERICAL SIMULATIONS

Seven different cases of VDCS are investigated in this section and their associated results are compared with the free rolling case scenario. These different VDCS cases are described as follows:

Case 1: Free rolling - in this case the vehicle collides with a barrier/vehicle without applying any types of control.
Case 2: ABS - in this case the anti-lock braking system is applied before and during the collision.
Case 3: ABS + ASC - the ASC system is integrated with the ABS to increase the normal force on the vehicle body and hence increase the braking force.
Case 4: ABS + frontal active suspension control (FASC) - the ASC system is integrated with the ABS on the front wheels only.
Case 5: ABS + anti-pitch control (APC) - the APC system is integrated with the ABS using the ACS to keep the vehicle in a horizontal position before the crash by applying an active force element on the front and rear wheels in upward and downward directions, respectively.
Case 6: ABS + under-pitch control (UPC) - in this case, the vehicle is taken a reverse pitching angle before crash using an ASC system.
Case 7: ABS DYC - the braking force is used to be applied to individual wheels to reduce the yawing moment of the vehicle body.

4.1. Primary Impact Results

The primary impact simulation results for offset vehicle-to-vehicle crash scenario are demonstrated in this section. The effect of the different cases of VDCS on vehicle collision mitigation is also investigated. In addition, the effect of the control systems on the other vehicle (vehicle b) is discussed. Figure 19 shows the impacted side of the front-end structure's deformation-time histories for vehicle (a) for all different VDCS cases. It is noticed that the deformation increased to reach its maximum value (different for each case) and then decreased slightly due to front-end springs rebound. The minimum deformation is obtained in the case 3 when the ASC is applied along with ABS. The maximum reduction of 50 mm is observed in this case and a reduction of 30 mm is shown in case 6, while a reduction of about 25 mm is obtained in cases 2, 4 and 5 compared with the free rolling case. On the other hand, case 7 (ABS + DYC) produced a higher deformation with a total reduction of about 15 mm. The integrated control of the ASC with the ABS aims to increase the braking force by increasing the vertical load to obtain a minimum stopping distance. It is worth mentioning that the application of the ASC control system (case 3) helps reducing the maximum deformation of the front-end structure as shown in Figure 19.

Figure 20 shows the front-end structure's deformation-time histories for vehicle (b) in all different VDCS cases. Because the two vehicles are identical and both collide at the same speed, it is clearly shown that the simulation results of the free rolling case are exactly the same. The maximum deformation is almost the same with very small and insignificant values for all cases of VDCS, and this means the control systems have no great effect on the front-end deformation of the other vehicle during the full-frontal collision.

The deceleration – time histories of the vehicle body for all cases for vehicle (a) are presented in Figure 21. The deceleration-time history can be divided to three stages. The first stage represents the increase of the vehicle's deceleration before the front left wheel reach the barrier. In this stage the highest

Figure 19.

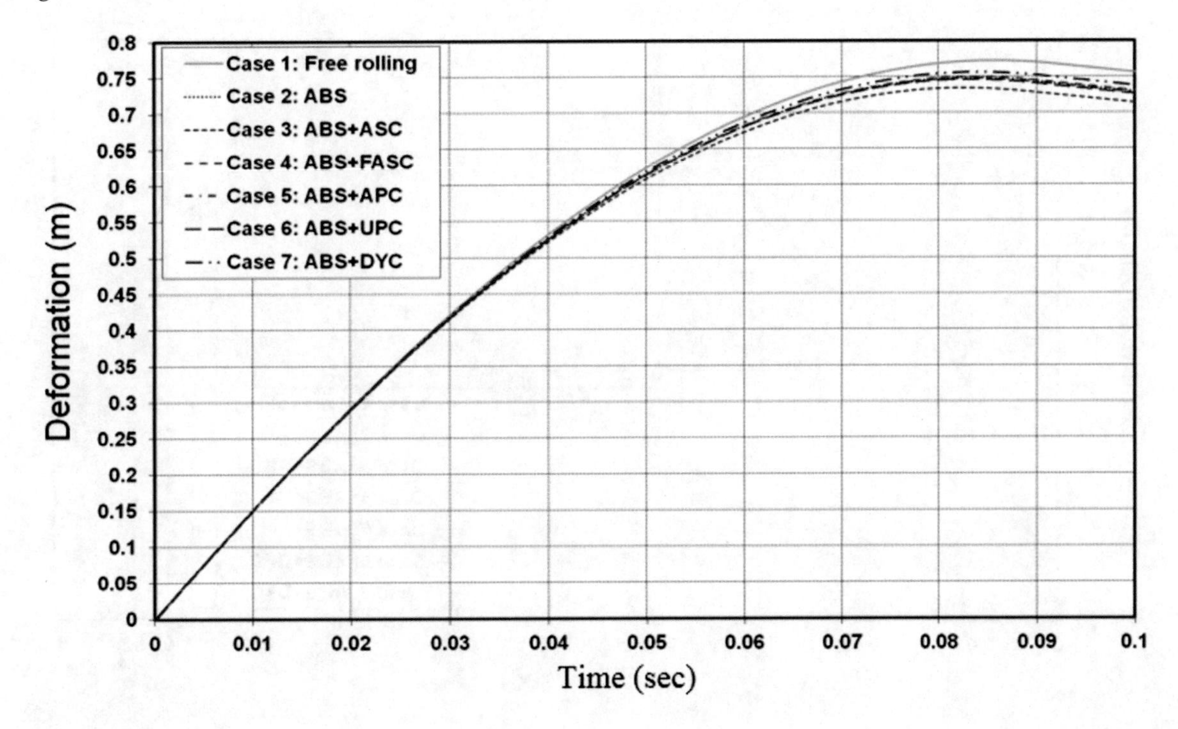

Figure 20.

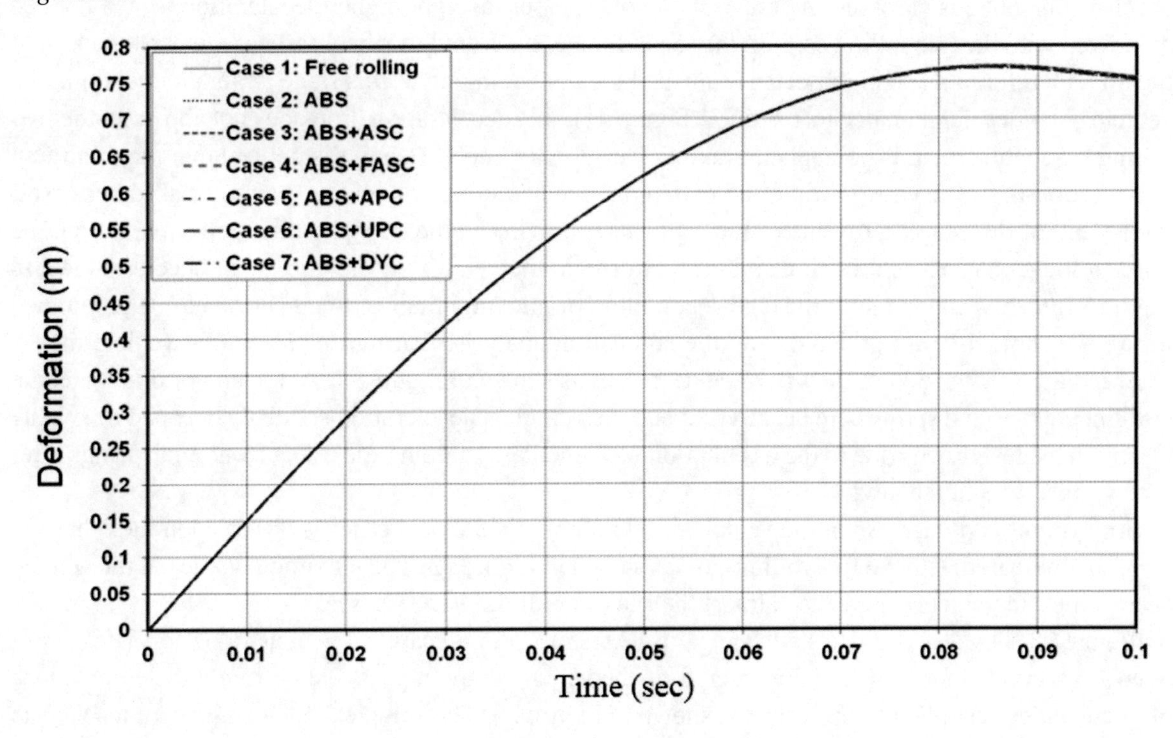

Figure 21.

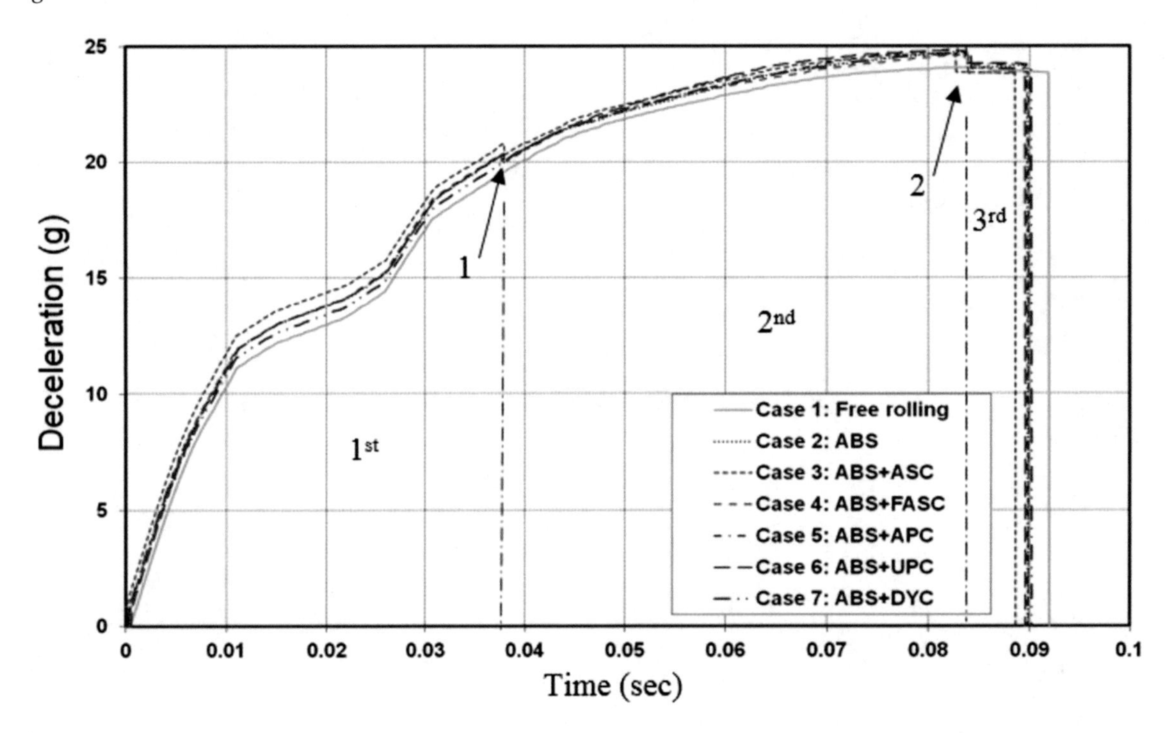

deceleration value is observed in case 3. In the other cases, a slight higher deceleration is also noticed compared with the free rolling case. In the second stage, the front left wheel reaches the barrier and stop moving, therefore its braking effects is vanished. At the beginning of this stage a rapid reduction in the vehicle body deceleration occurs (arrow 1, Figure 21); this deceleration drop does not appear in the free rolling case while there is no applied braking. During the second stage, it is noticed that the minimum deceleration is still in case 1, while the maximum deceleration is almost the same for all other cases. At the end of this stage, the vehicle stops and starts moving in the opposite direction. In addition, the braking force changes its direction and another drop in the vehicle deceleration is noticed as shown in Figure 21, (arrow 2). At the third stage, a condition of allowing the front-end springs to be rebounded for a very short time is applied during the simulation analysis. During this stage, the vehicle moves back and the deformation of the front-end decreases as shown in Figure 21. At the end of this stage, the non-linear front-end springs are deactivated and the vehicle's deceleration suddenly dropped to a value of zero. This fast drop is due to the assumption of immediate stopping the effect front-end springs after a very short time of rebound.

An insignificant increase of the vehicle deceleration in all VDCS cases is observed in the other vehicle (b) compared with the free rolling case as shown in Figure 22. The maximum values of the vehicle deceleration in vehicle (b) are also almost the same for all the VDCS cases.

Figure 23 shows the vehicle's pitch angle-time histories for all cases of vehicle (a). The VDCS is applied 1.5 second before the collision, therefore, the vehicle body impacts the barrier at different values of pitch angles according to each case as shown in Figure 23. The vehicle's pitch angle then reaches its maximum values (normally after the end of the crash) according to each case. Following this, the pitch angle reduced to reach negative values and then bounces to reach its steady-state condition. In the offset

Figure 22.

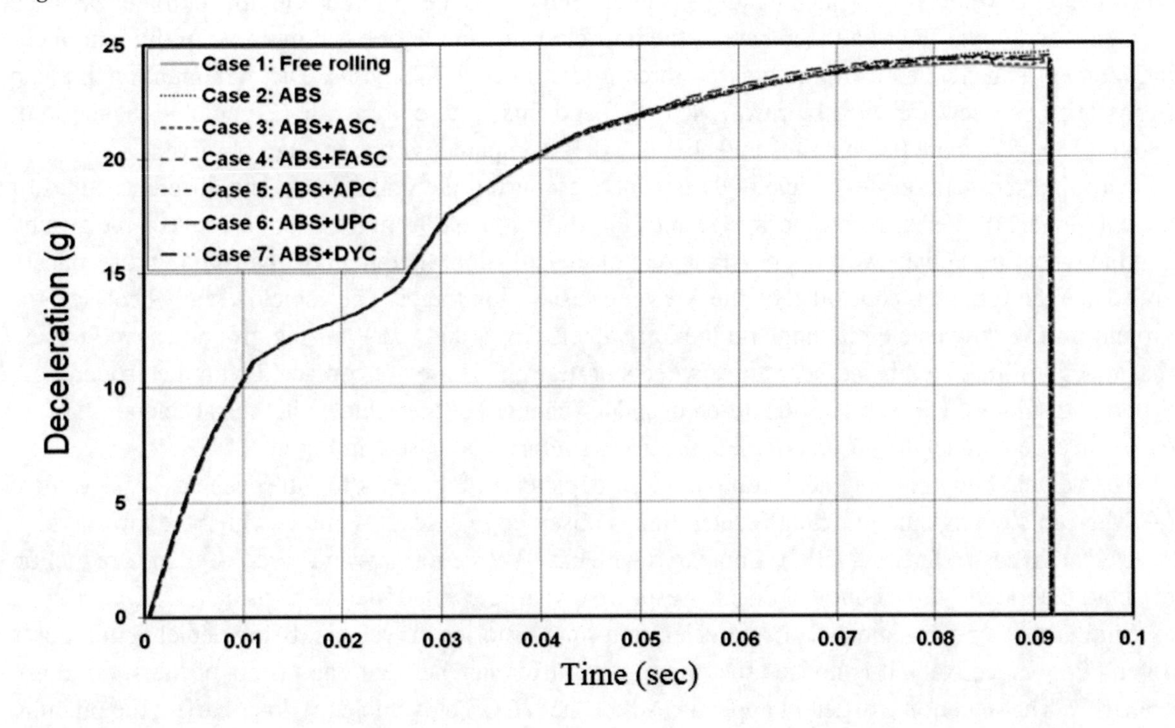

Figure 23.

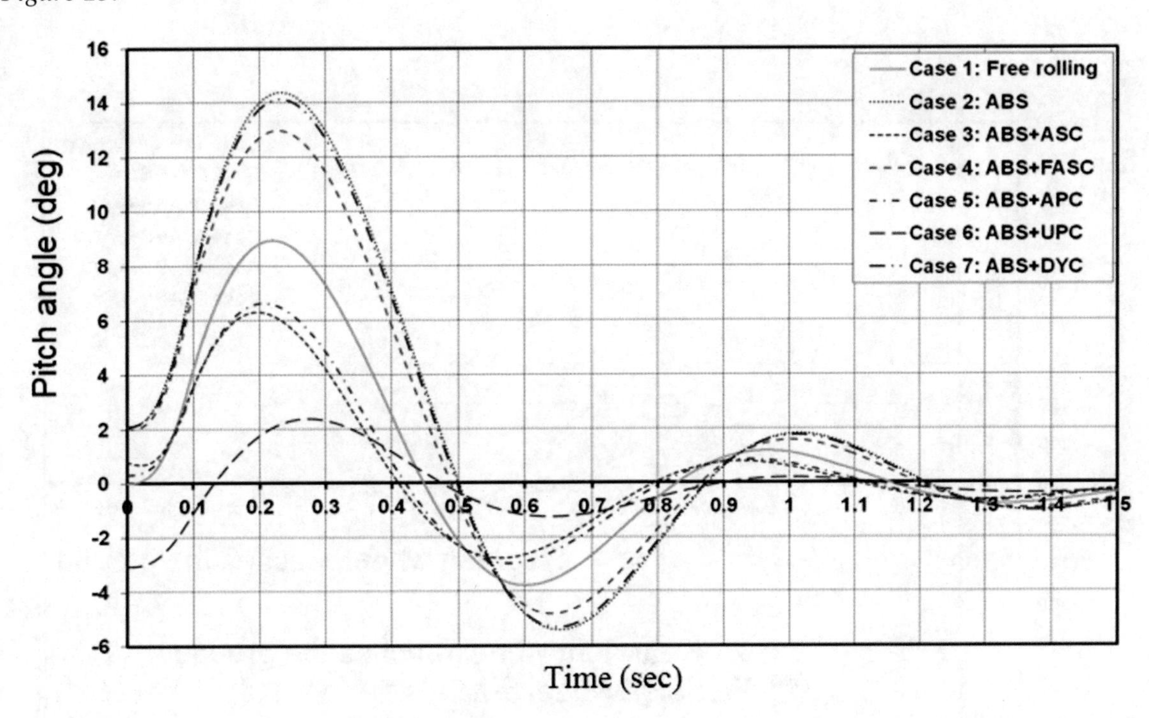

crash scenario, vehicle body pitching angle is generated due to the difference in impact forces between the upper and lower front-end members of the impacted side in the free rolling case. Additional pitching moment is generated from the braking force in the other VDCS cases. The maximum pitch angle is observed in case 2 followed by case 7, 4, 1, 5, 3 and finally case 6. In case 6, a notable reduction of about 6.5 deg compared with case 1 and about 12 deg, compared with case 2 are observed.

A rolling moment of the vehicle body is generated during the crash due to the different values of the component of the left frontal springs' forces in *y* direction and from the friction between the ground and the tyres due to the yaw motion. At the end of the collision, the pitching and rolling moments are ended and the vehicle is controlled by the tyres and suspension forces. The vehicle's rear wheels left the ground during the vehicle pitching and the left wheels (front and rear) left the ground as well during the vehicle rolling. At this moment, three wheels of the vehicle are not contacted with the ground with different distances. This explains the different sudden changes of the vehicle pitching acceleration when each wheel re-contact the ground (look at the arrows referred to case 1 in Figure 24).

The vehicle body pitching acceleration is also depicted in Figure 24 for all seven cases for vehicle (a). The vehicle maximum pitching acceleration is observed in cases 2, 4 and 7, whilst the lowest value is detected in case 6 (ABS + UPC). Compared with case 1 (free rolling) and case 2 (ABS), a reduction of about 670 deg/s2 and about 950 deg/s2, respectively, are obtained in case 6 (ABS + UPC).

Similarly, the pitch angle and pitch acceleration-time histories for vehicle (b) are depicted in Figures 25 and 26, respectively. It is noticed that there is no difference between the results of the seven crash scenarios. That means the different applied cases of the VDCS on vehicle (a) do not affect the pitching event of vehicle (b) in case of offset collision.

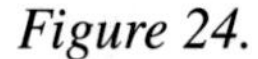
Figure 24.

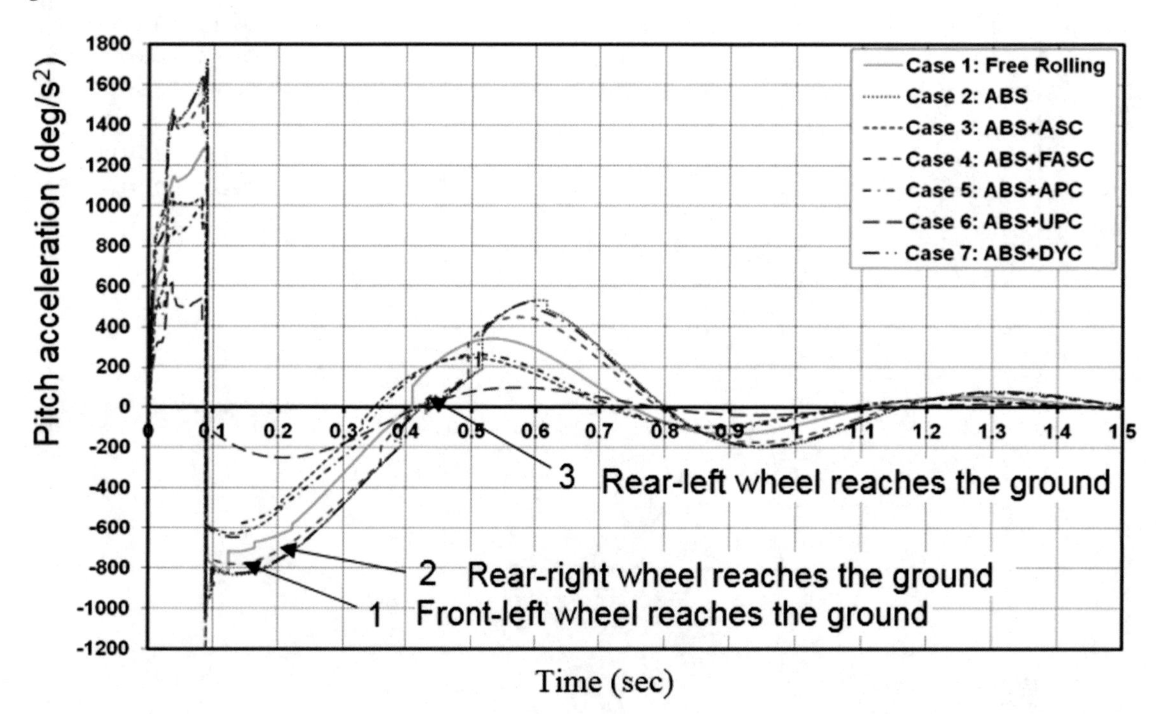

Figure 25.

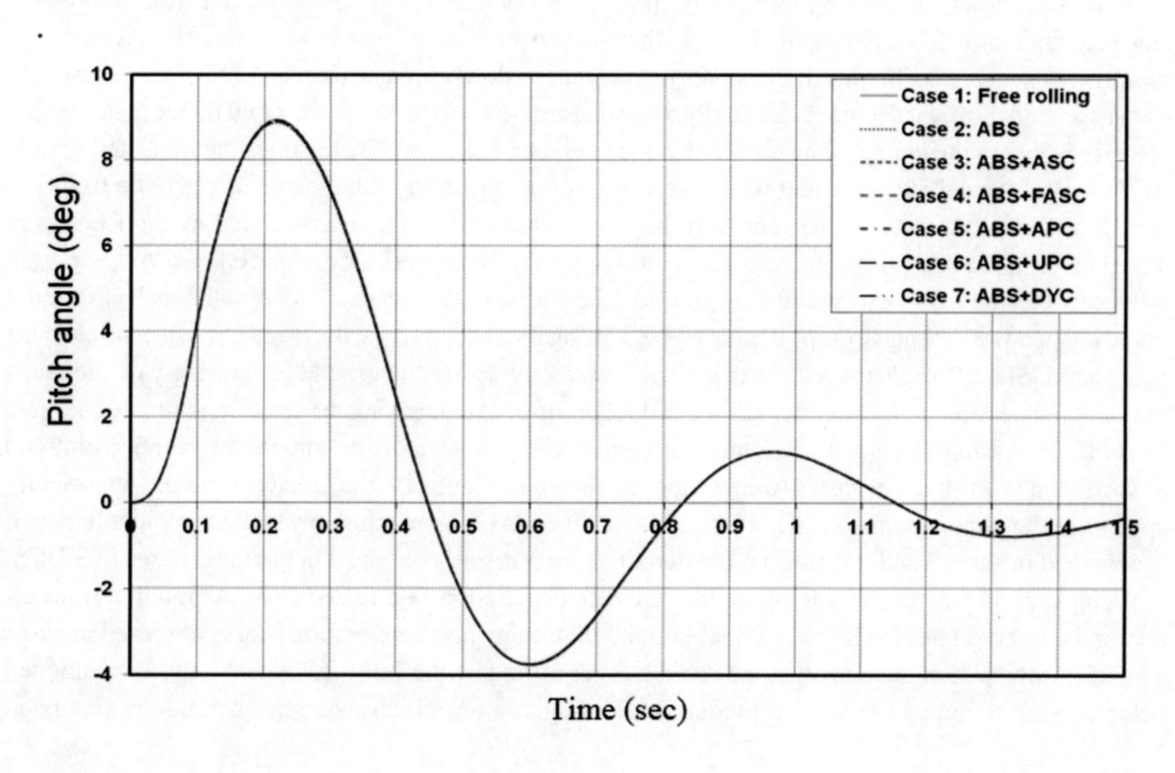

Figure 26.

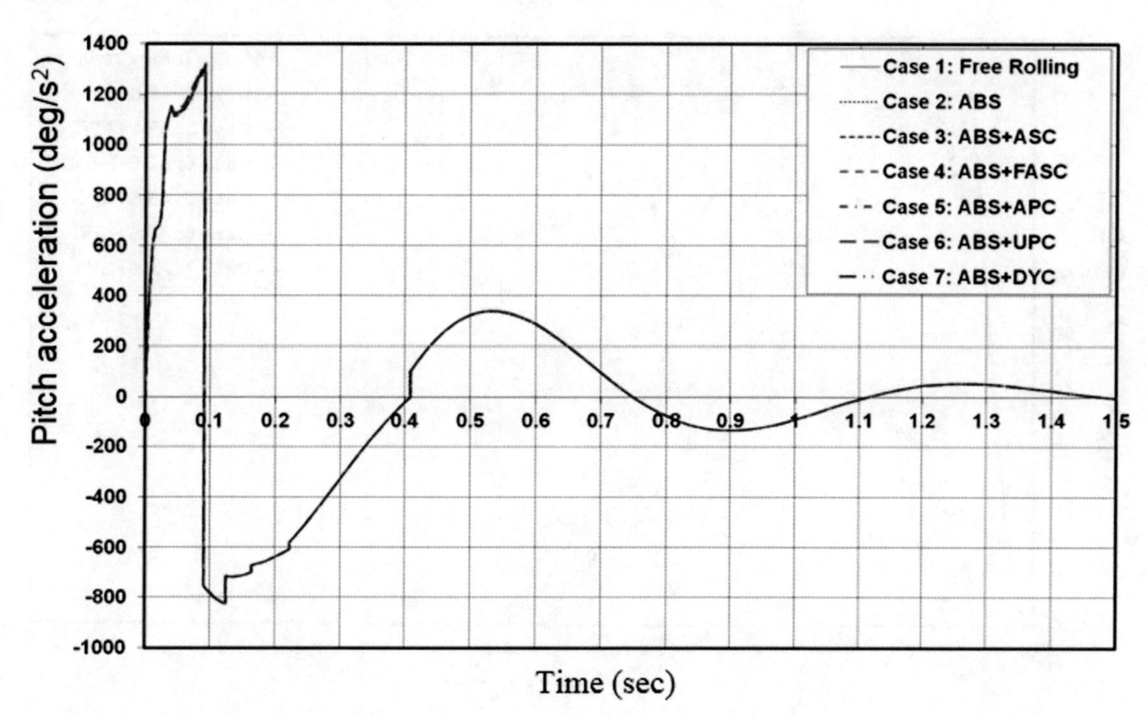

Figure 27 shows the vehicle yaw velocity-time histories for all seven cases of vehicle (a). The vehicle yaw velocity is equal to zero before the crash, then it changes in three different stages: firstly, it increases rapidly to reach its maximum value; secondly, it decreases slowly for a different period of time related to each case; and thirdly it decreases gradually to reach zero. In the first stage, the rapid increase in the yaw velocity is due to the high yawing acceleration (see Figure 28) caused by the one side impacted spring. At the end of the collision, the rear wheels left the ground due to the vehicle pitching and the front-left wheel left the ground due to the vehicle rolling and hence the vehicle is controlled by the front-right wheel only. In the second stage, the decrease in the vehicle's yaw velocity occurred due to the friction force between the front-rear tyre and the ground. The period of this stage is different for each case and it mainly depends on the maximum pitching angle. During the second stage, the front-left wheel re-contacts the ground. Stage 3 begins when the rear wheels start contacting the ground generating yaw moments in the opposite direction. This is causing a reduction of the vehicle yawing velocity with a higher rate than the decreasing of velocity rate in the second stage. Because of the maximum vehicle front-end deformation is observed in case 1 (free rolling) as shown in Figure 19, the greatest peak of yaw velocity appears in the same case as shown in Figure 27. A reduction of the maximum yawing velocity (10 deg/s) is observed in cases 3 and 6, while a reduction of about 5 deg/s is obtained in the other cases of VDCS.

Vehicle body yaw acceleration-time histories are depicted in Figure 28. The maximum yaw acceleration is observed in case 1 (free rolling) and the minimum yaw acceleration is also observed in cases 3 and 6. At the end of the collision, the vehicle is controlled by the front-left wheel only, as mentioned before, trying to hinder the yawing motion. Accordingly, a negative yawing acceleration is generated

Figure 27.

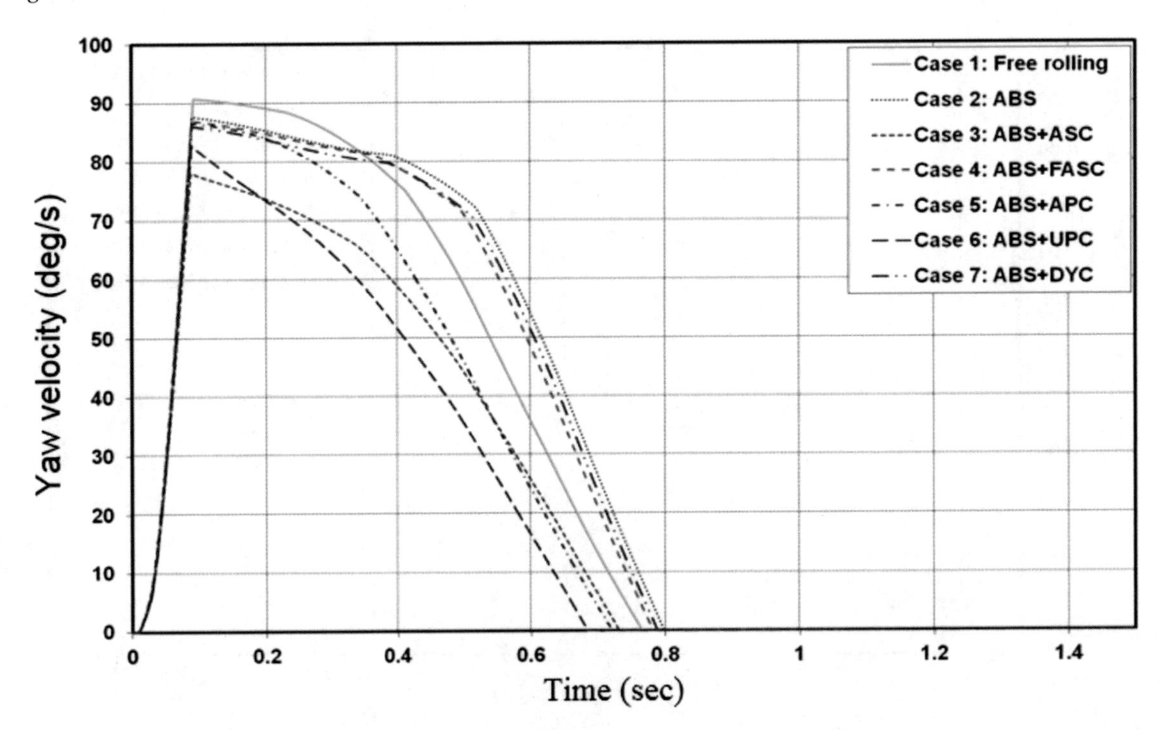

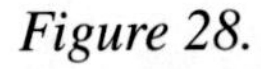

Figure 28.

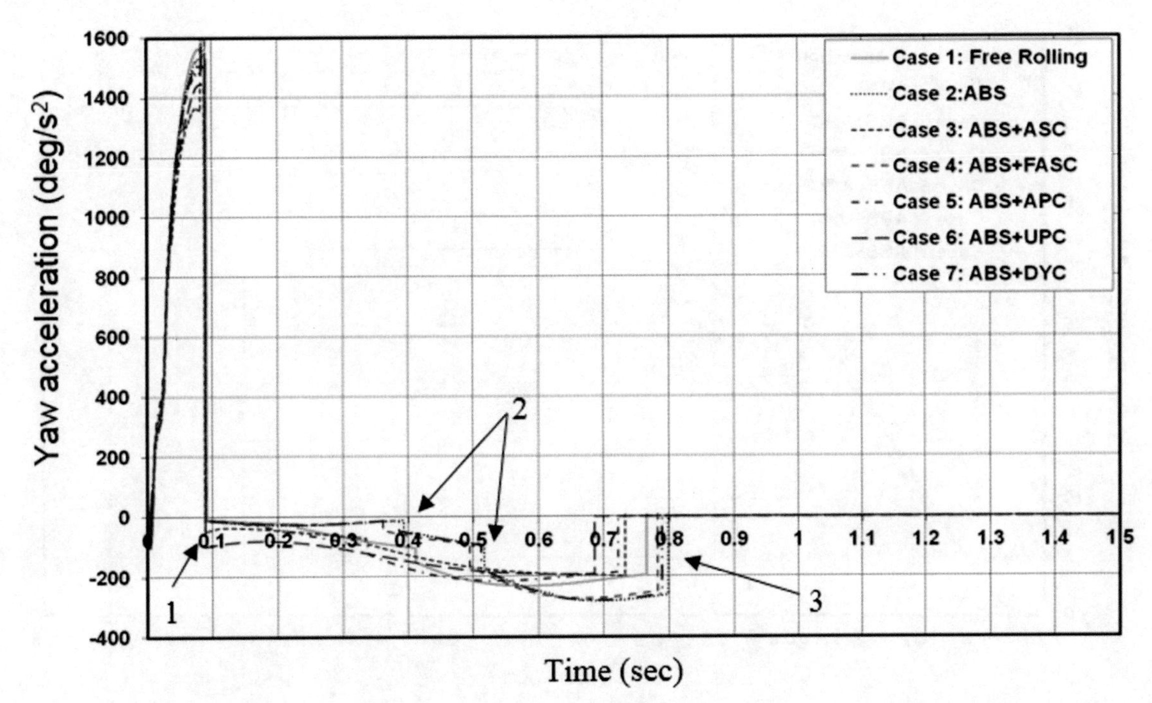

with different small values related to each case as shown in Figure 28 (arrow 1). These negative values of the vehicle yaw acceleration increase slowly with time producing two sudden drops of acceleration (arrow 2) once the right-rear wheel and the left-rear wheel re-contact the ground, respectively. These drops are not shown in case 6 because the rear wheels do not leave the ground in this case. When the vehicle yawing ends and the yaw speed reaches zero, the yaw acceleration returns to zero as well as shown in Figure 28 (arrow 3).

Figure 29 shows the vehicle body yaw angle – time histories for all cases of vehicle (a). It is found that the maximum yaw angle of 49.3 deg is noticed in case 2 (ABS) while the minimum yaw angle of 36.8 deg is noticed in case 6 (ABS + UP). The maximum value of the vehicle yaw angle depends on the maximum yaw acceleration and the vehicle pitch angle for each case. It is worth mentioning that reducing the maximum vehicle body yaw angle reduces the risk of the car side-impact by any obstacles on the road. Following the yawing analysis, it can be said that the best set of the vehicle dynamic control is to apply case 6 (ABS + UPC) since the minimum yaw angle and acceleration are obtained in this case.

The yawing event of the vehicle (b), which is not equipped by the VDCS, is affected by vehicle (a) once different control systems are applied. The maximum yaw velocity of the vehicle (b) is increased in all cases compared with the free rolling case, except in case 6, as shown in Figure 30. Figure 31 shows the yaw acceleration of the vehicle (b). It is observed that the maximum yaw acceleration is also increased in all cases compared with the free rolling case by different values related to each case. In the same manner, the maximum yaw angle of the vehicle (b) is increased in all cases by different values (from 1.5 to 2 deg) related to each case, except in case 6 as shown in Figure 32.

Figure 29.

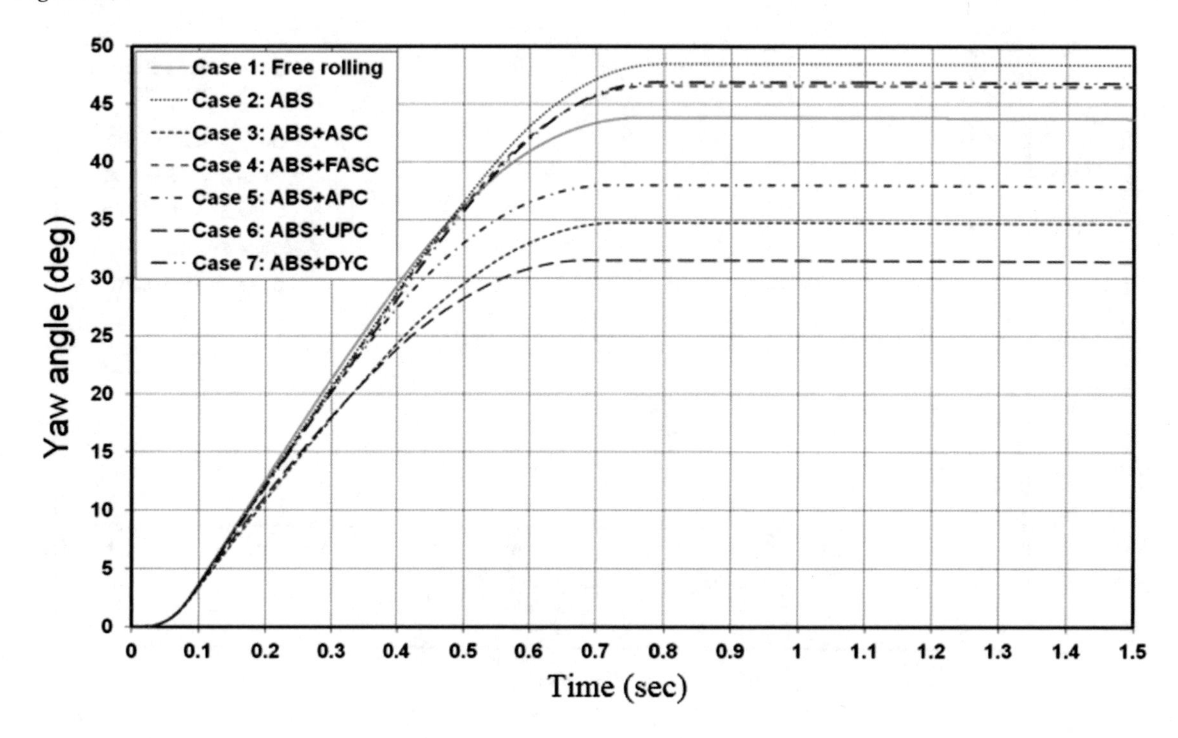

Figure 30.

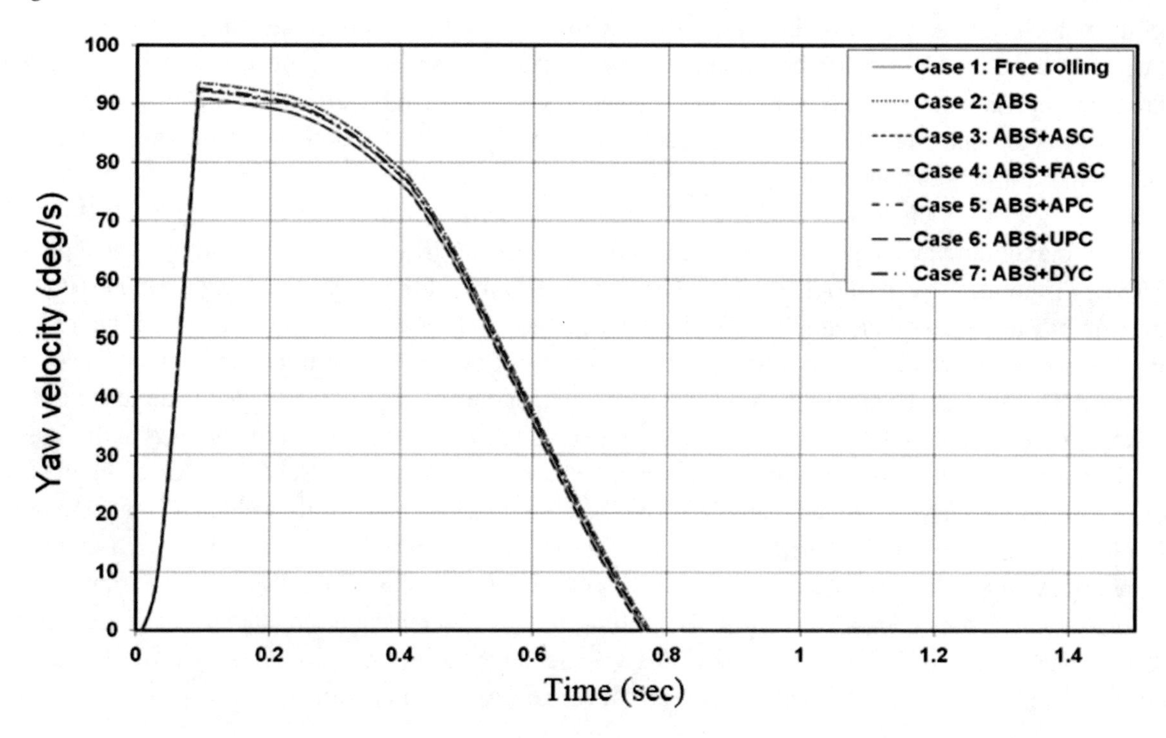

Figure 31.

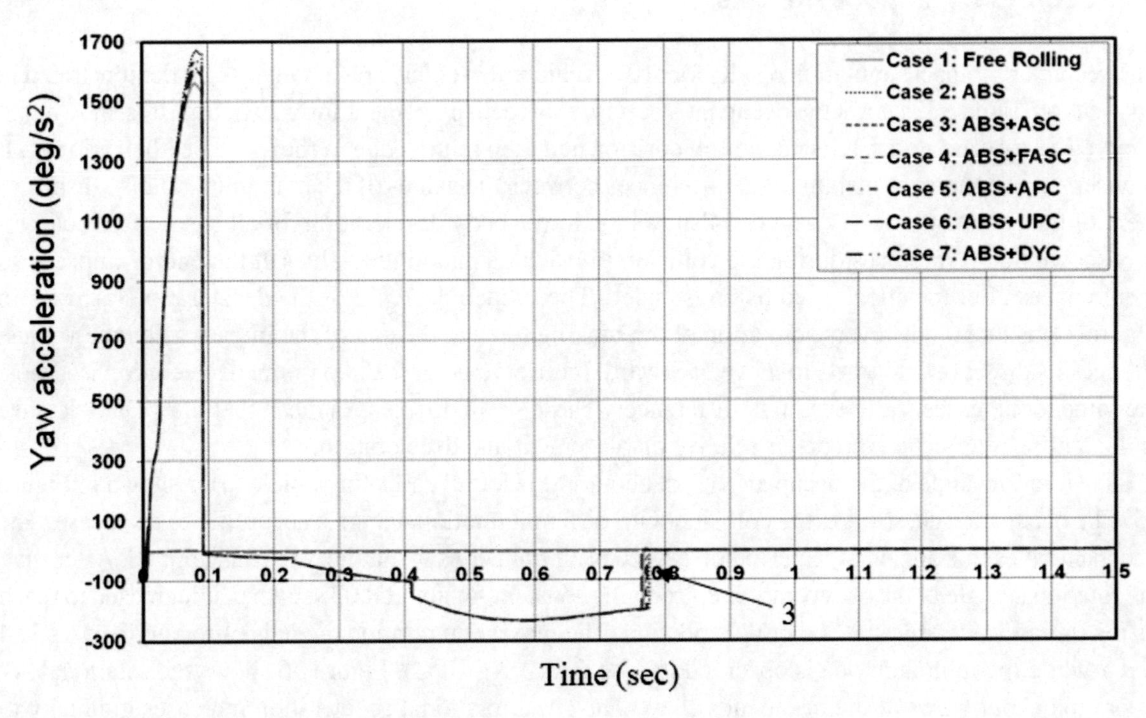

Figure 32.

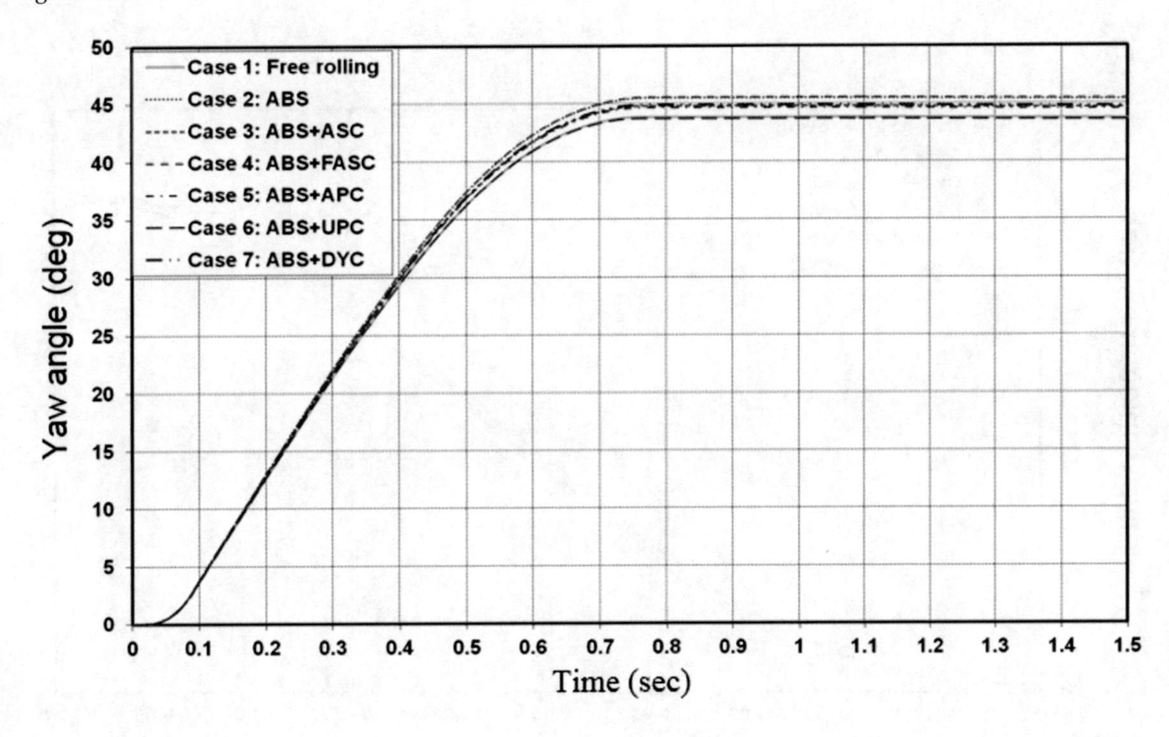

4.2. Secondary Impact Results

The secondary impact simulation results for offset vehicle-to-vehicle crash scenario are demonstrated in this section. Figure 33 shows the occupant's pelvis relative displacement for vehicle (a). It is shown that it increases forward to reach its maximum position and then returns due to the lower seatbelt springs. It is observed that there are insignificant differences between the values of the maximum relative displacement of the occupant's pelvis. Figure 34 shows the lower-body deceleration for all cases of vehicle (a). It is shown that it increases during the collision to reach its maximum values at the end of impact and then reduces after the effect of collision is ended. The sudden decrease of the deceleration (arrow 1 in Figure 34) is due to the reverse direction of the braking force at the end of the impact when the vehicle changes its direction and starts to move backward. It observed that the maximum deceleration is almost the same for all cases with very small differences. These small differences mean that the VDCS do have an insignificant effect on the pelvis relative displacement and deceleration.

The rotation angle of the occupant's chest about *y* axis for all cases for vehicle (a) is shown in Figure 35. The occupant's chest starts the collision with different rotational angles according to each case. The occupant takes this angle in the period of 1.5 sec prior collisions when the VDCS is applied. After that, the rotational angle of the occupant's chest remains constant for about 0.03 sec, then it increased to reach its maximum value after the end of the collision. The maximum rotation angle is observed in cases 2, 4 and 7 while the minimum one is observed in case 6 (ABS + UPC). Figure 36 shows the rotational acceleration about *y* axis of the occupant's chest. The chest rotational acceleration increases gradually to reach its maximum positive value and then reduces to reach its maximum negative value. The maximum

Figure 33.

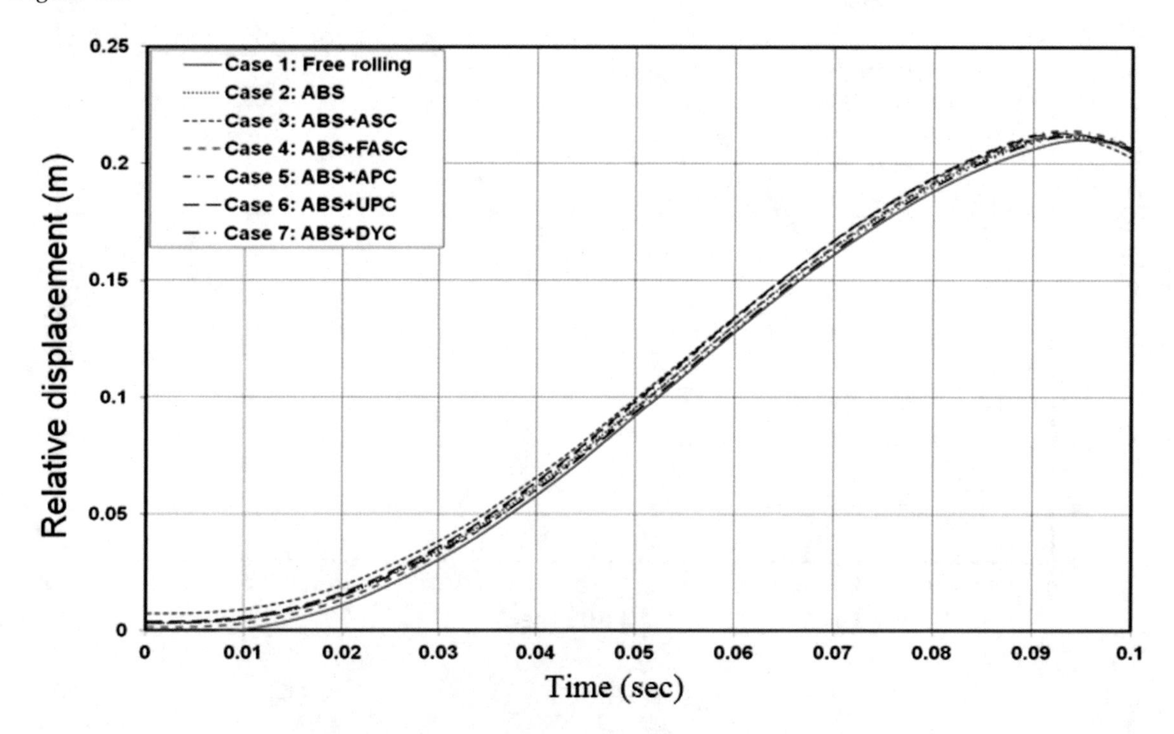

Figure 34.

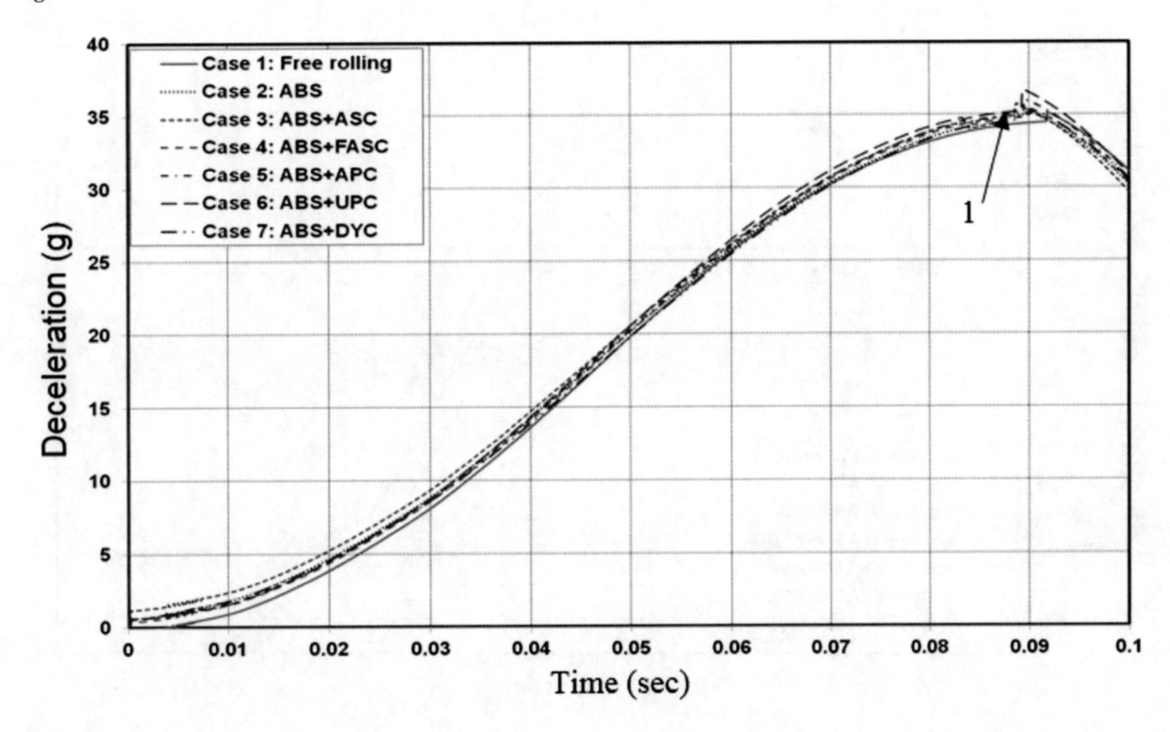

Figure 35.

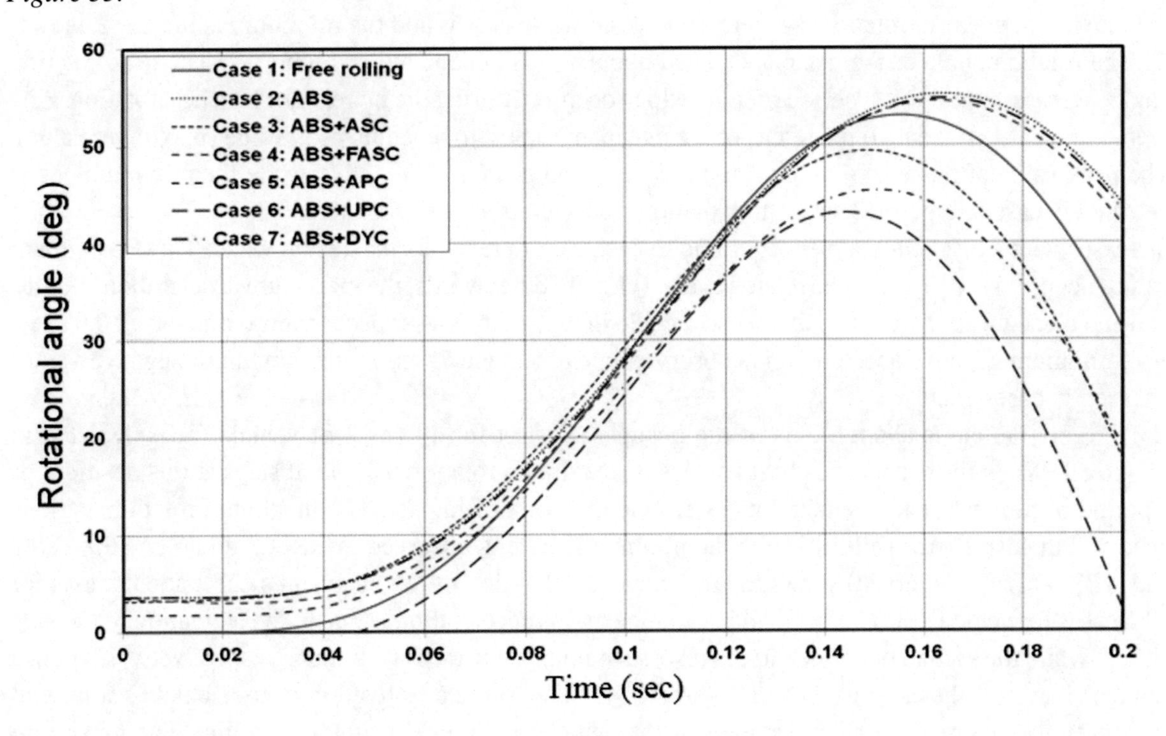

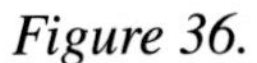

Figure 36.

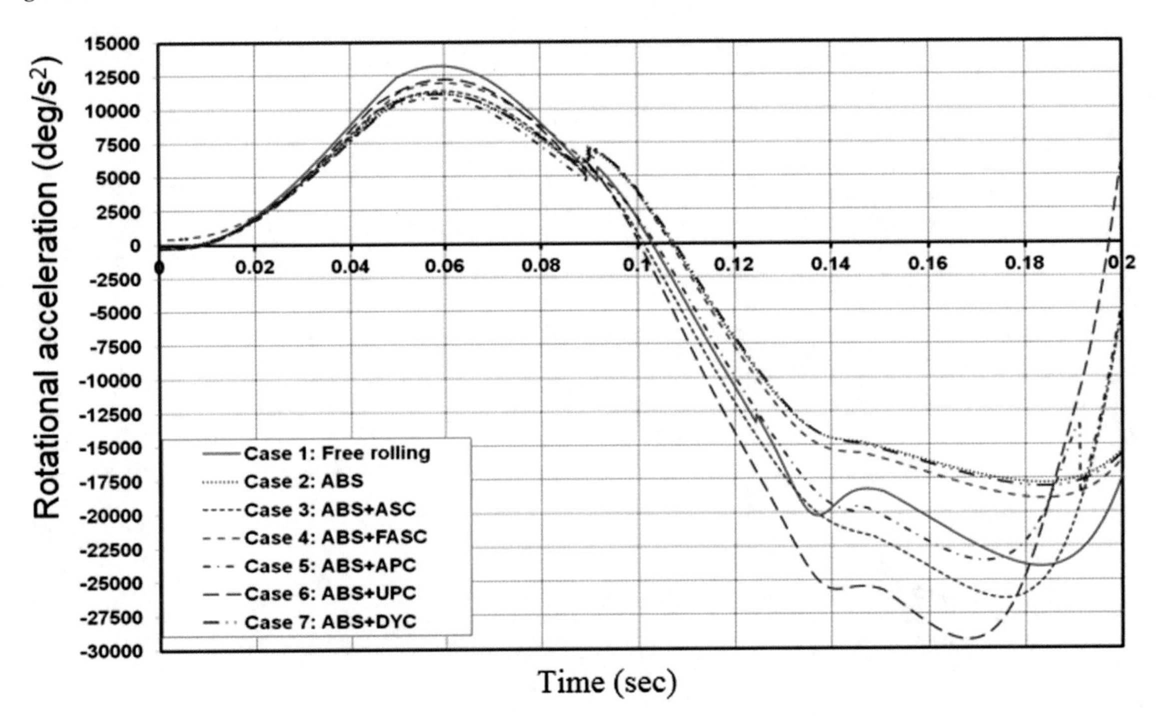

positive rotational acceleration is monitored in case 1 and the minimum one occurred in case 5, while the maximum negative rotational acceleration is shown in case 6 and the minimum is in case 2 and 7.

The rotation angle of the occupant's head about y axis is depicted in Figure 37. The head rotation angle increases rapidly for a period of time, which occurred during the increase of the chest rotation. And then, it increases fast due to the return of the occupant's chest to reach its peak value (maximum value). The peak value of the head rotational angle is observed in cases 2, 4 and 7, while the minimum one is detected in case 6. Figure 38 shows the rotational acceleration of the occupant's head. The acceleration increases with a different manner according to each case to reach its maximum value. These maximum values occurred in different time related to each case. In other words, the maximum acceleration in cases 1, 3 and 6 occurs approximately at 0.07 sec, while in the other cases it occurs approximately at 0.08 sec. The minimum negative acceleration is observed in cases 2 and 7, while the maximum negative values are seen in cases 1 and 6.

The rotation angle about x axis of the occupant's chest for all cases of vehicle (a) is depicted in Figure 39. When the occupant's chest reaches its maximum rotational angle, it stays at this position for a period of time while the vehicle rotates around the point of impact. The maximum rotation angle is observed in case 1 (free rolling) while the minimum angle is observed in cases 3 and 6 (ABS + ASC and ABS + UPC). Figure 40 shows the rotational acceleration of the occupant's chest about x axis for all 6 cases for vehicle (a). The first sudden change in this acceleration is due to the activation of the side airbag, while the second one is due to the reverse braking force (arrows 1 and 2, respectively). The third sudden change of the chest acceleration (arrow 3) is due to the deactivation of the vehicle's front-end springs, which causes a sudden decrease of the vehicle pitching, yawing and rolling. The maximum positive rotational acceleration of the occupant's chest about x axis is observed in cases 1 and 7, while

Figure 37.

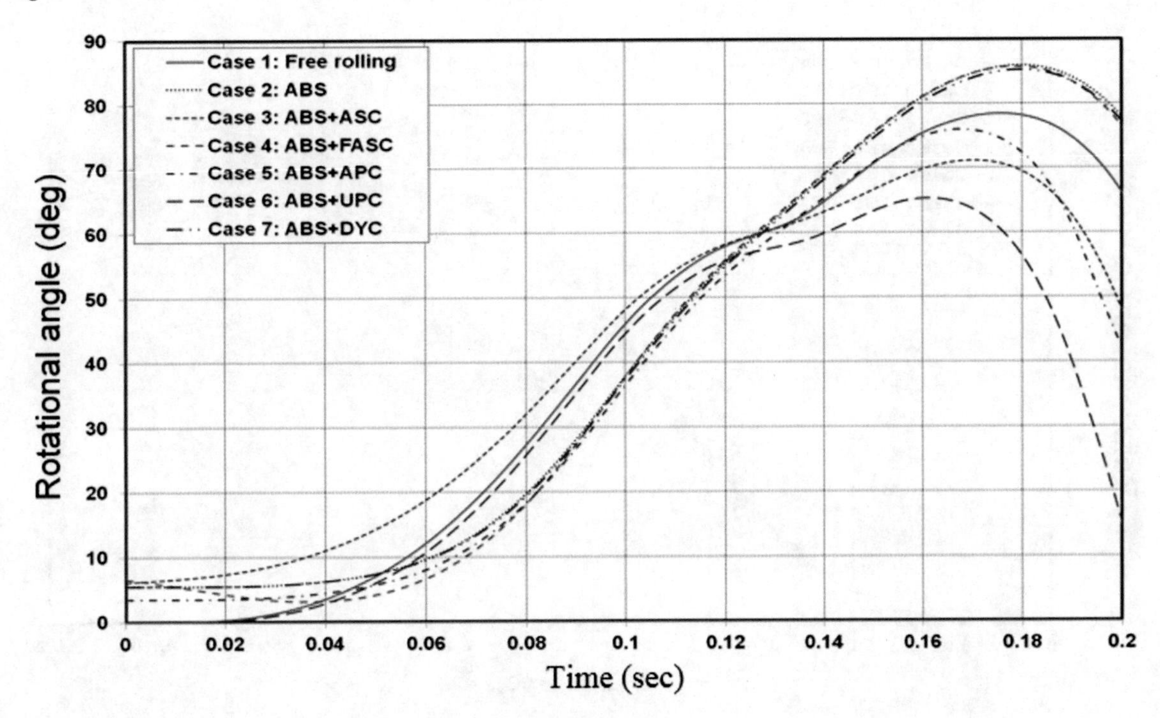

Figure 38.

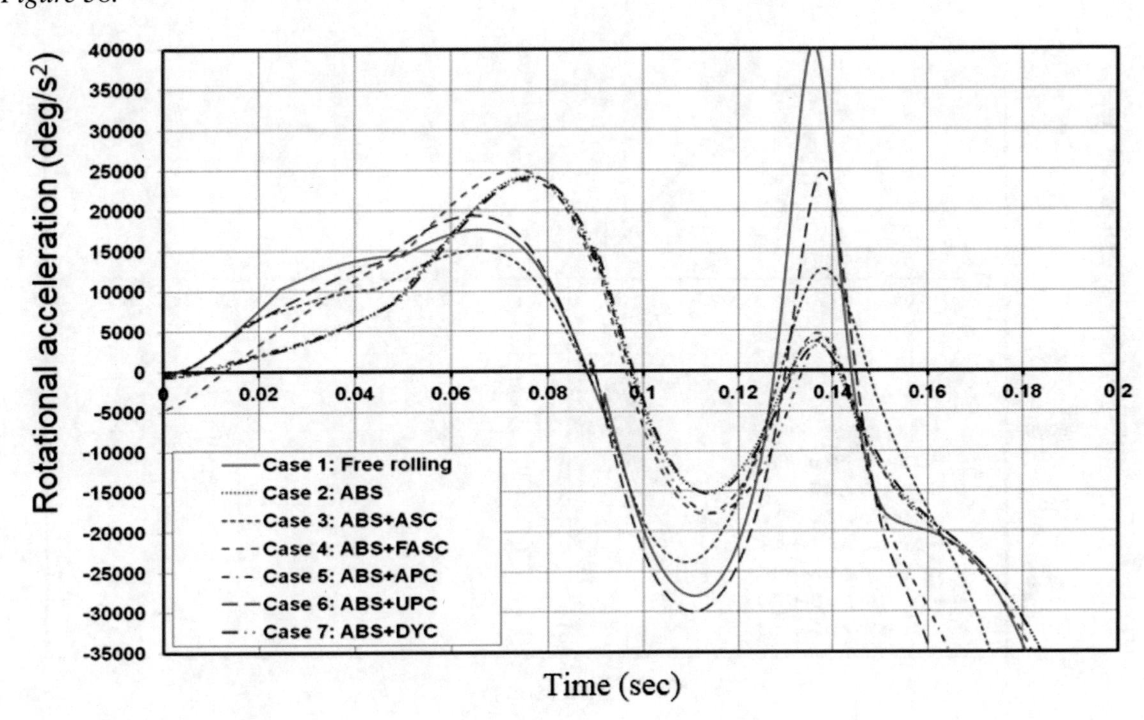

Figure 39.

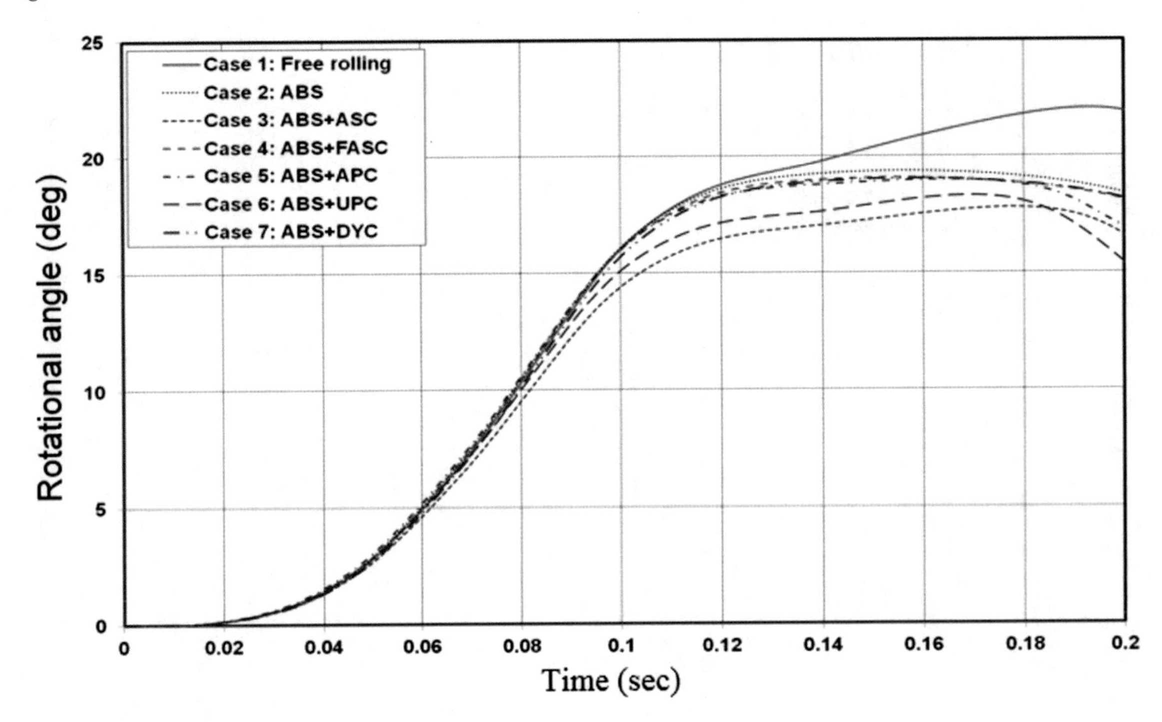

Figure 40.

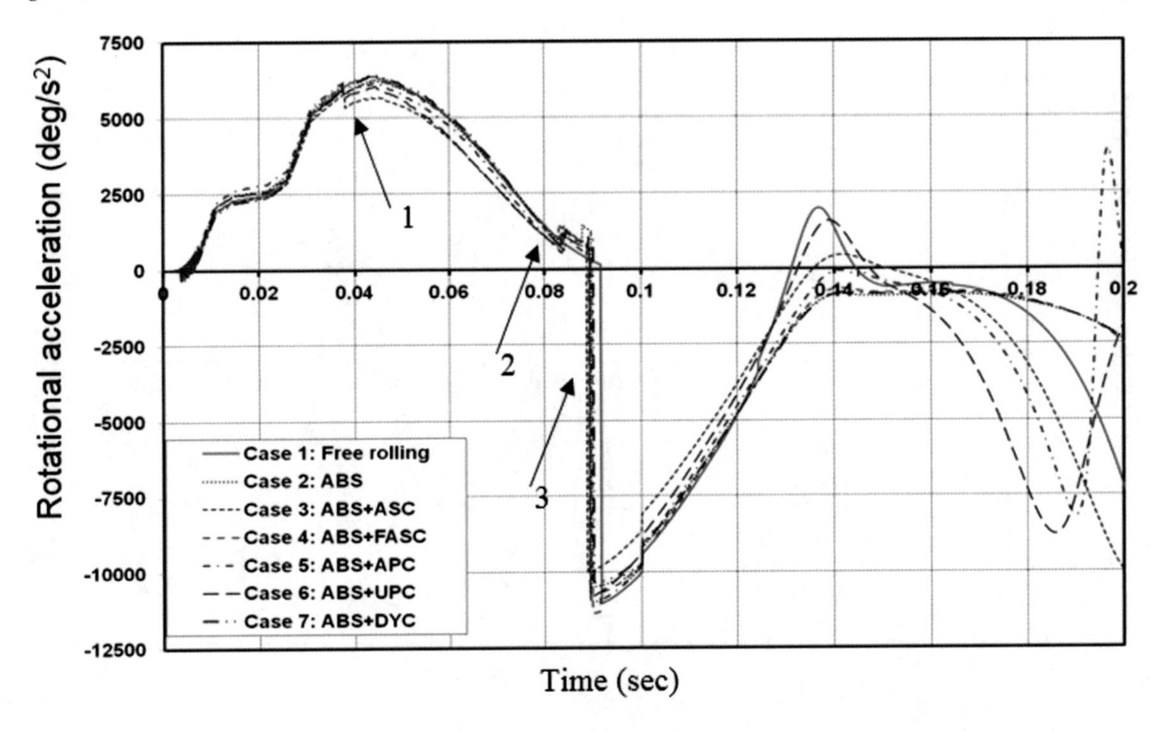

the minimum value occurs in cases 3. The maximum negative rotational acceleration happens in cases 1 and 4 and the minimum is observed in case 3. These negative acceleration values occur due to the force generated by the lower spring-damper system of the side airbag.

The rotation angle about x axis of the occupant's head for vehicle (a) is shown in Figure 41. At the beginning of the collision, while the chest takes a positive acceleration and starts rotating towards the vehicle's side door, the head takes a different negative small rotation value related to each case, all these values are close to 5 deg. The positive maximum value of the head rotational angle is observed in case 6, while the minimum peak angle is seen in cases 2, 3, 4 and 7. Figure 42 shows the rotational acceleration about x axis of the occupant's head for all cases. The effect of the reverse braking force is observed at the end of the collision (arrow 1 in Figure 42). The maximum positive acceleration (in the period from 0.06 to 0.1 sec) is almost the same for all cases, while the maximum negative acceleration (in the period from 0.1 to 0.16 sec), caused by the side airbag force, is observed in cases 1 with relatively a higher value. The minimum negative acceleration is detected in cases 2, 4, 5 and 7.

Figures 43 and 44 show the occupant's pelvis relative displacement and deceleration, respectively for vehicle (b). It is shown that the occupant's pelvis relative displacement and deceleration are insignificantly affected by the application of VDCS on the other vehicle (vehicle (a)). There are very small and insignificant increases, especially on the peak values, for all cases compared with the free rolling case.

Figures 45 and 46 show the occupant's chest rotational angle for vehicle (b) and its acceleration about y axis, respectively. It observed that there are no changes in the rotational angle; however, there are small variations among the different cases on the occupant's chest acceleration from 0.13 to 0.15 sec. These variations are also very small and insignificant.

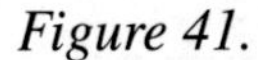
Figure 41.

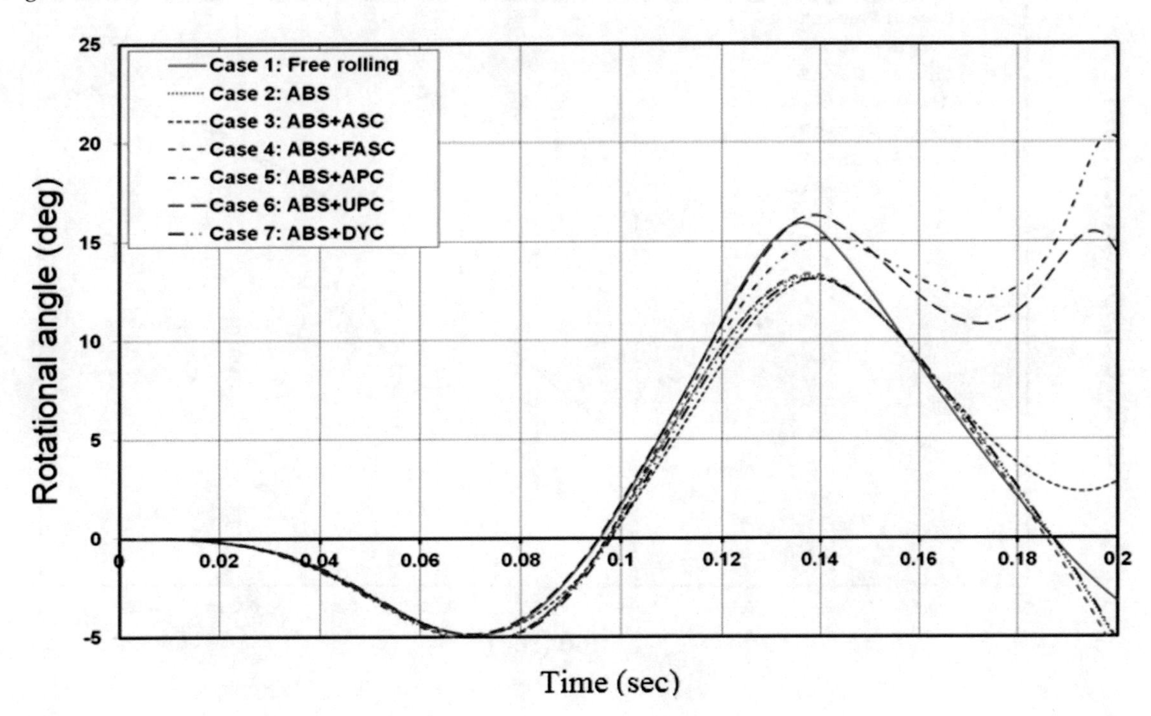

Figure 42.

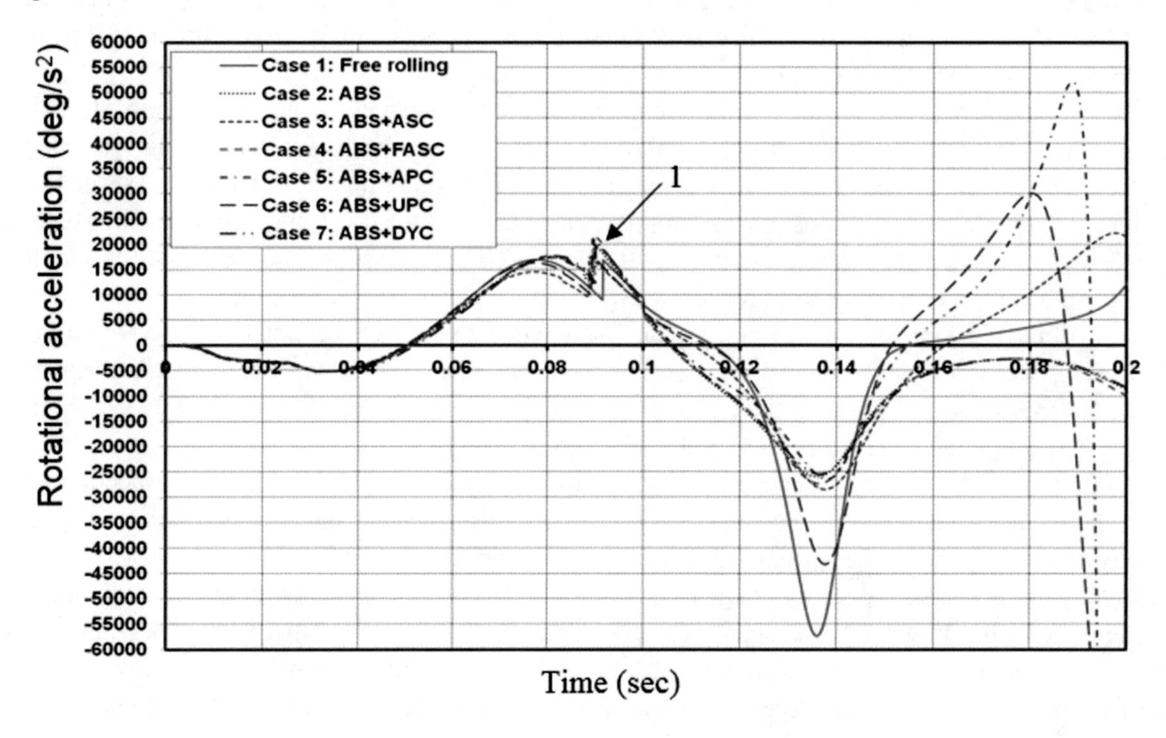

Figure 43.

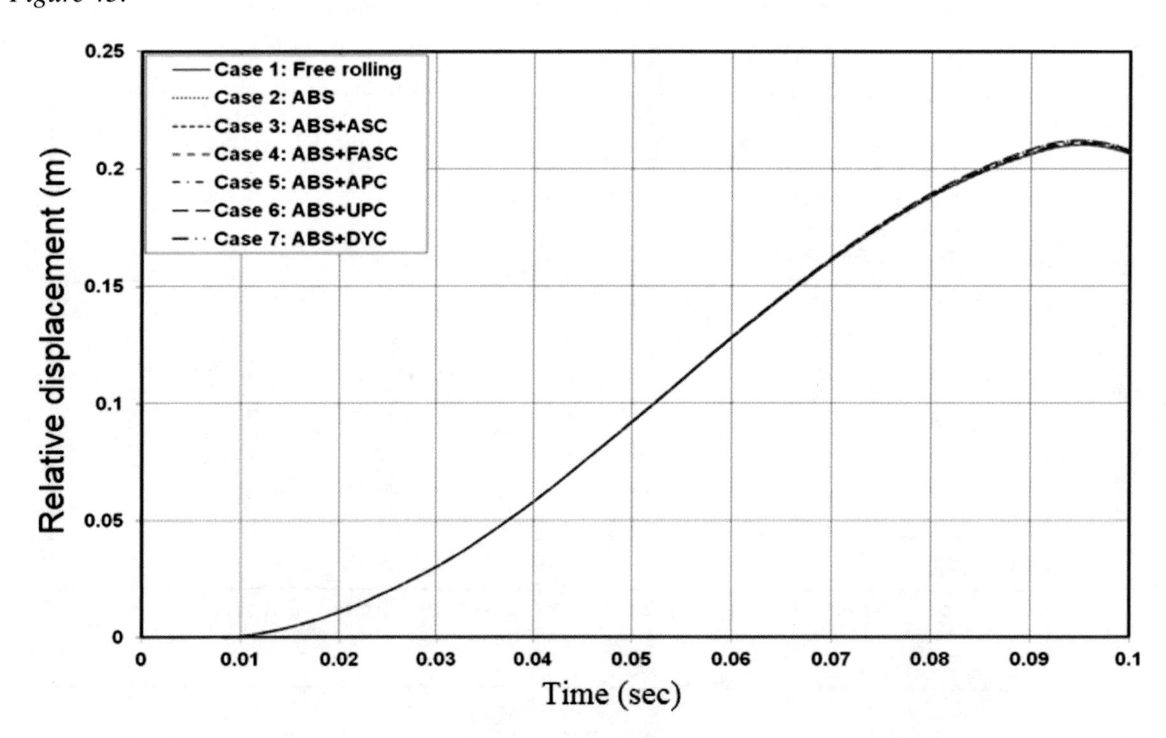

Figure 44.

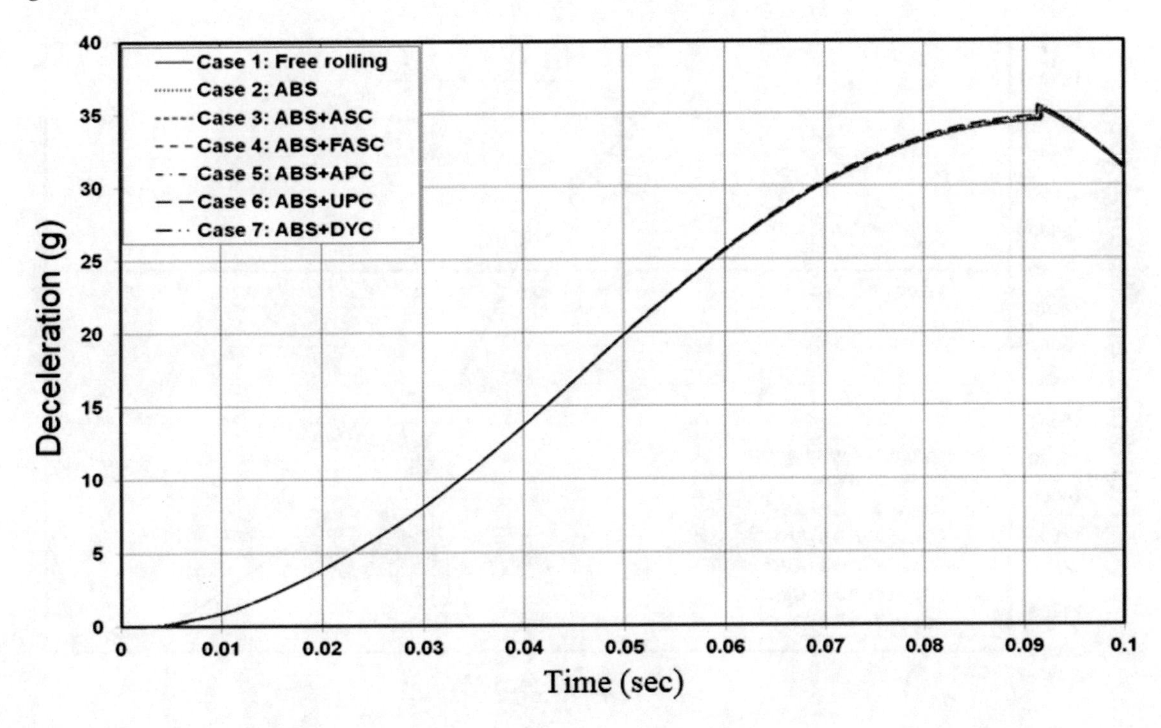

Figure 45.

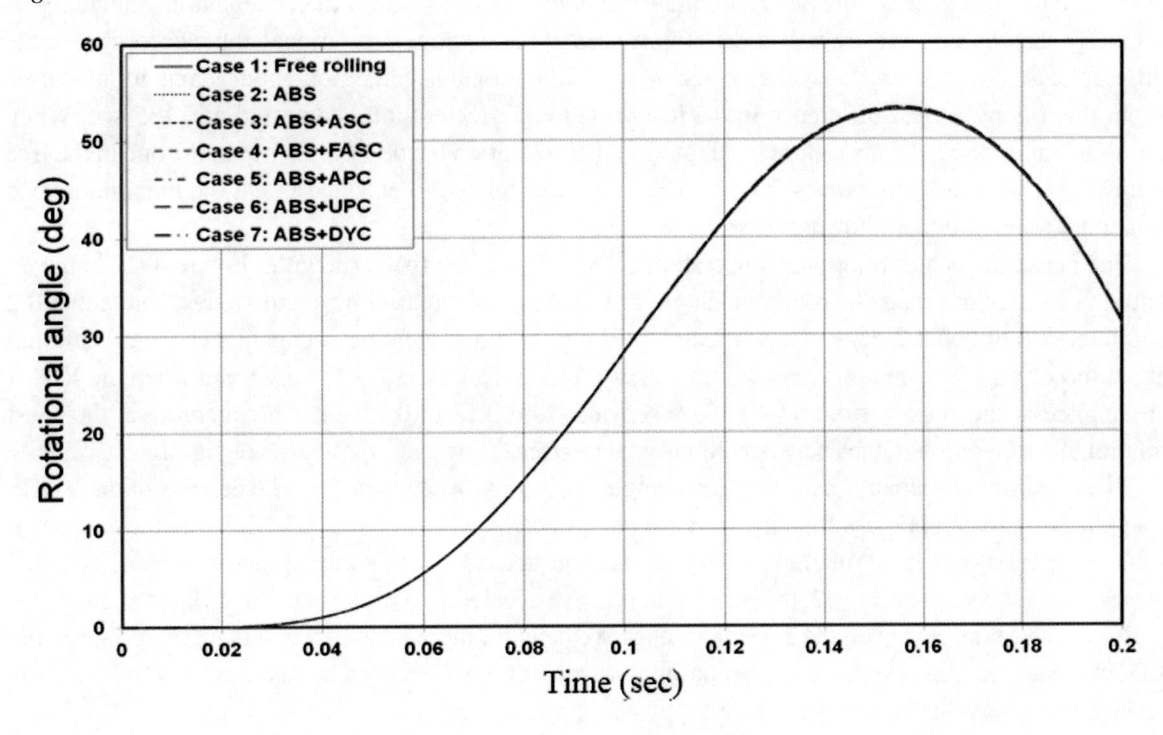

Figure 46.

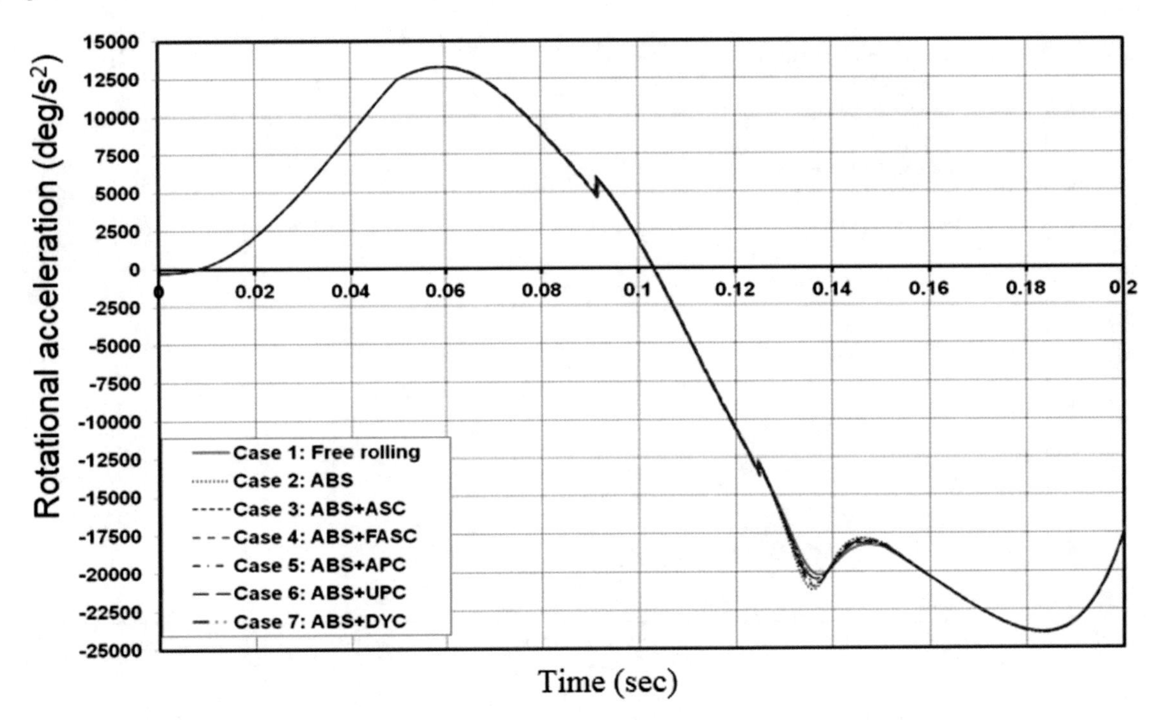

Figure 47 shows the occupant's head rotational angle about y axis for the occupant in vehicle (b). It is clearly shown that there are very small differences of the maximum rotational angle according to the different cases. Figure 48 shows the occupant's head rotational acceleration about y axis for all cases. From this figure, a clear difference in the head rotational acceleration is detected at 0.135 sec. When the VDCS is applied, the maximum head rotational acceleration becomes higher than the one in the free rolling case with different values from 5 to 15 kdeg/sec^2 related to each case; and the maximum head rotational acceleration is shown in case 2.

The occupant's chest rotational angle about x axis for vehicle (b) is shown in Figure 49. Compared with the free rolling case, the rotational angle of the chest is increased by small values from about 0.2 deg in case 6 to about 2 degs in cases 2 and 4. Figure 50 illustrates the occupant's chest acceleration about the x axis. Very small increases of the chest rotational acceleration are observed when the VDCS are applied at the periods from 0.04 to 0.09 sec and from 0.13 to 0.15 sec. This increase in the chest rotational acceleration ranges between 300 to 800 deg/sec2, however, these are not significant values.

The maximum occupant's head rotational angle about x axis is also increased when any of the VDCS is applied as shown in Figure 51. This increase ranges between 0.2 to 1 deg, and this is not a significant value. The maximum head rotational angle is observed in case 2, while the minimum value is detected in case 1. As shown in Figure 52, the maximum positive acceleration of the occupant's head about x axis is almost the same. However, the maximum negative head rotational acceleration is increased when the VDCS are applied. In case 6 the head rotational acceleration is increased by about 5 kdeg/s^2, while the highest increase value is observed in case 2 by about 15 kdeg/s^2.

Figure 47.

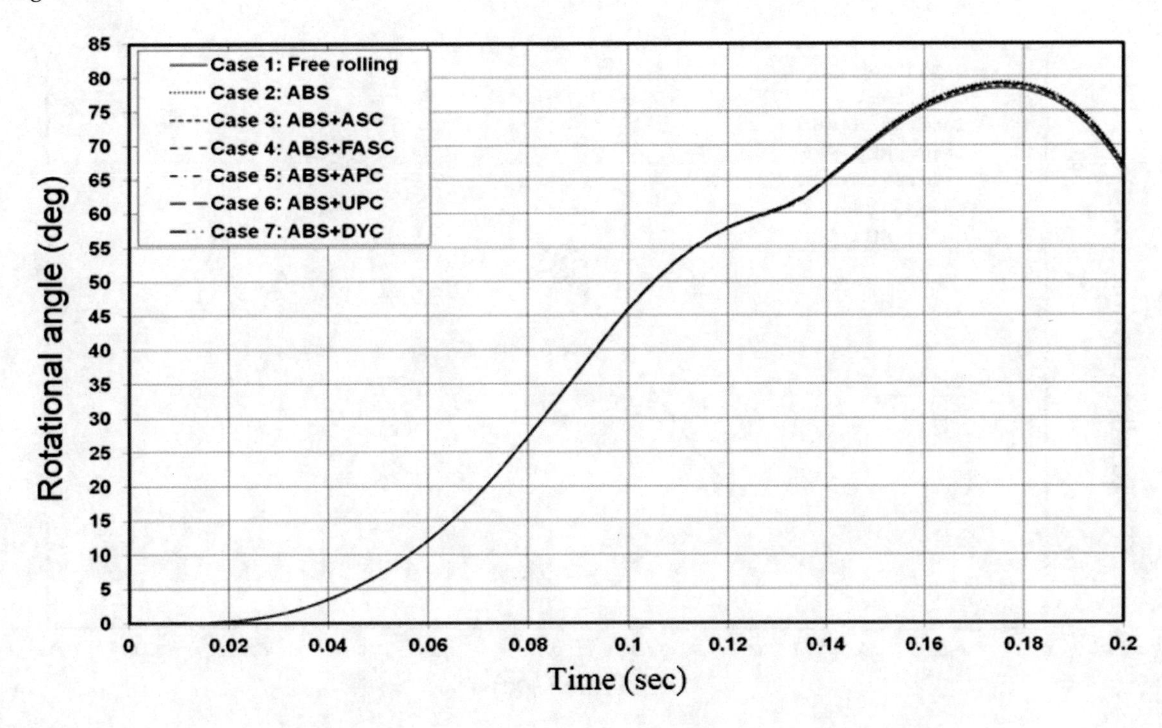

Figure 48.

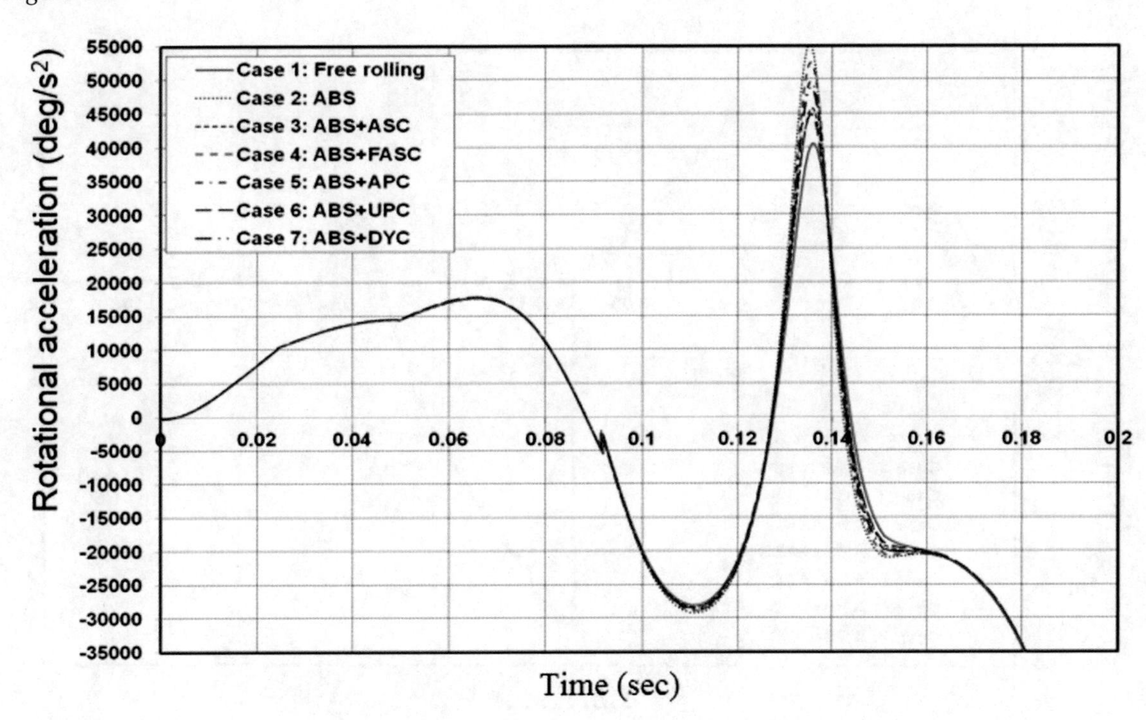

Figure 49.

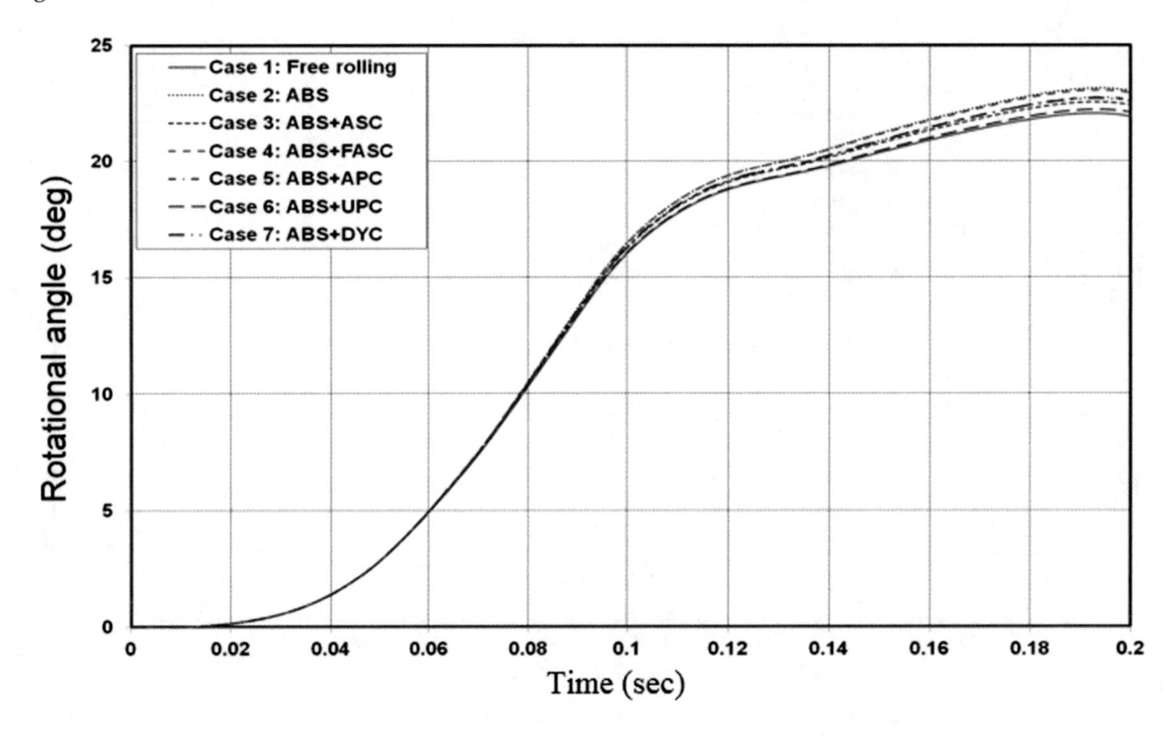

Figure 50.

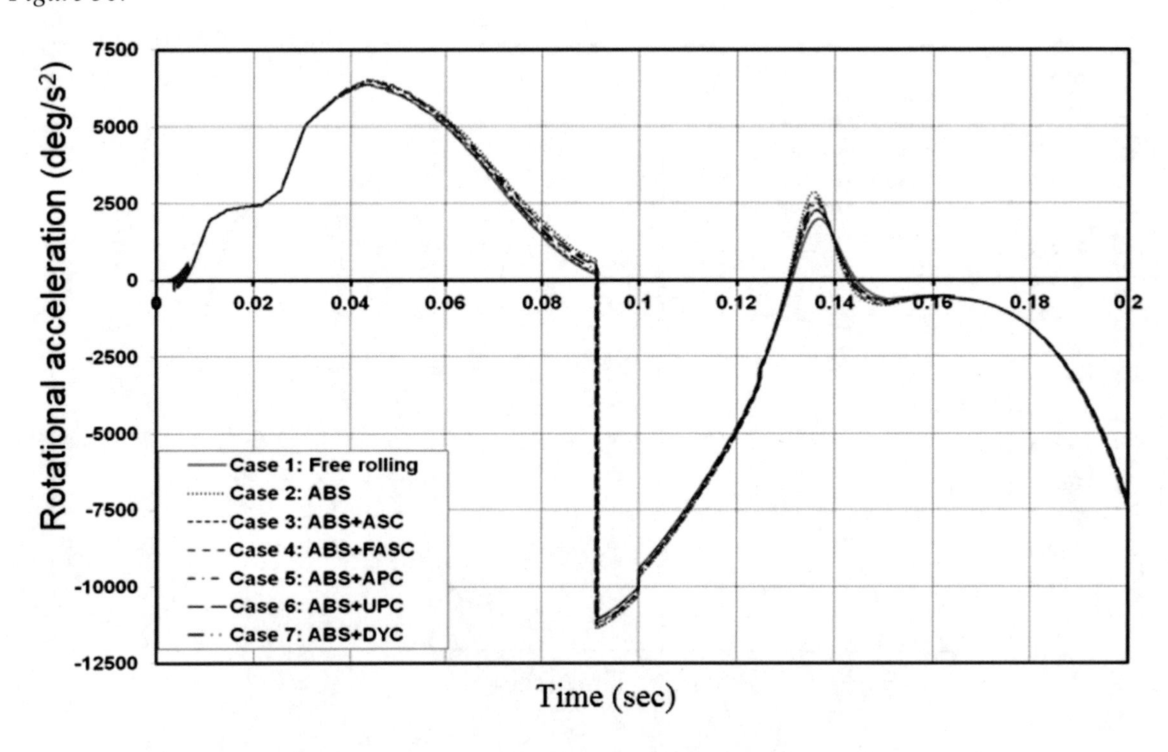

Figure 51.

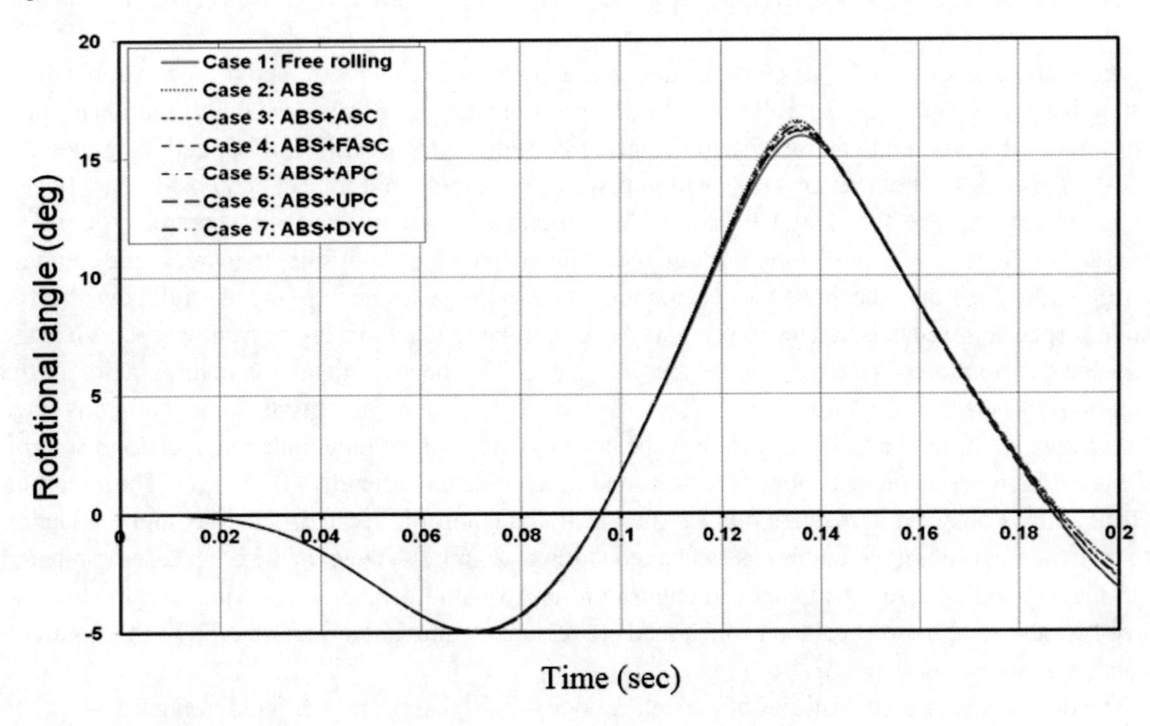

Figure 52.

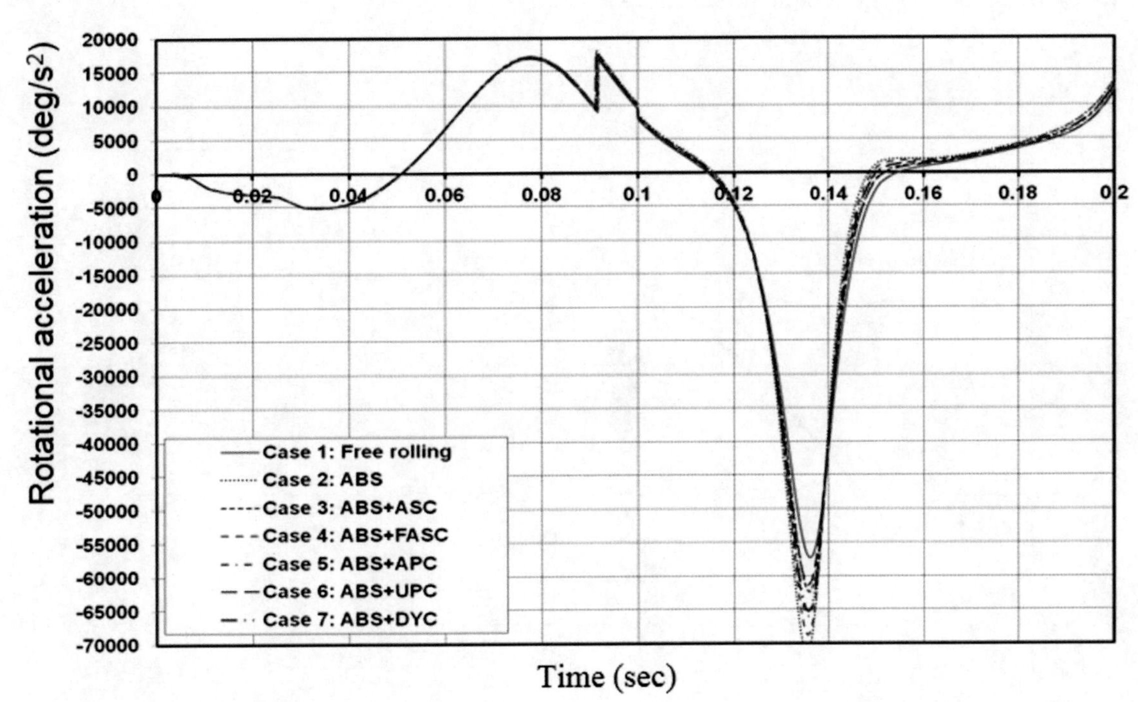

5. INTEGRATED ACTIVE AND SEMI-ACTIVE SUSPENSION CONTROL SYSTEM

Based on the previous results, a new technique of integrated active and semi-active suspension control system is proposed in the case of full frontal collision. Four cases have been used in this section to show the effect of the proposed control system namely: free rolling, ABS, ABS + UPC, and integrated AS + SAS. This new control system works within two stages; namely: pre-impact and post-impact stages. In the pre-impact stage, the fuzzy UPC controller is used for the active suspension control system. The semi-active suspension control system is utilized using an open loop controller to increase the damping coefficient of the front wheel to achieve a higher value. In the post-impact stage, the full power of the active suspension system is utilized to generate a maximum possible force on the front wheels, while the active suspension force on the rear wheel are deactivated. On the other hand, the main function of the semi-active suspension controller is to obtain the maximum damping ratio for the damper. In this stage of post impact, the active and semi-active suspension systems are working under an open loop control.

Figure 53 shows the deformation of the front-end structure for all different VDCS cases. The minimum deformation is obtained in the case 4 when the integrated control is applied. The maximum reduction of about 50 mm is observed in this case and a reduction of 20 mm is shown in the other cases compared with the free rolling case. The integrated control of the AS with the SAS helps to increase the braking force by increasing the vertical load which leads to reduce the maximum deformation of the front-end structure as shown in Figure 53.

The deceleration – time histories of the vehicle body for all cases are presented in Figure 54. In the first stage the highest deceleration value is observed in case 4. In the other cases, a slight higher deceleration is also noticed compared with the free rolling case. During the second stage, it is noticed that the deceleration is almost the same for all cases.

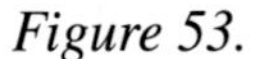

Figure 53.

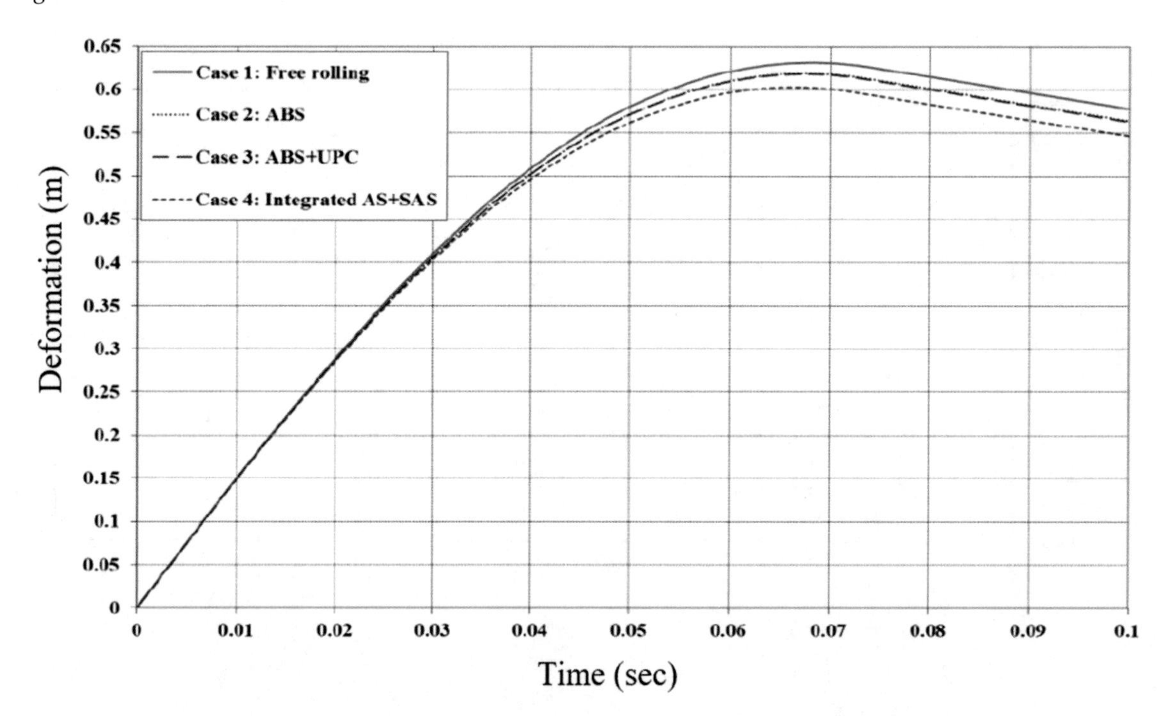

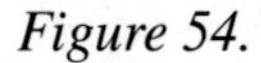

Figure 54.

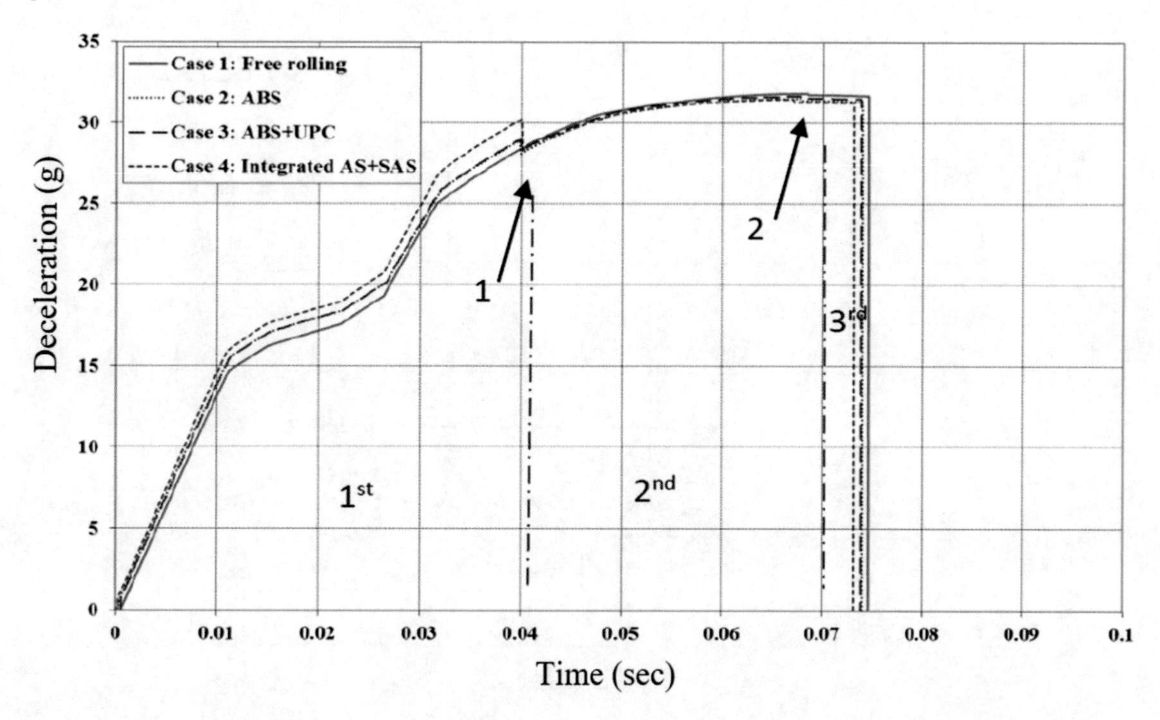

Figure 55 shows the vehicle's pitch angle-time histories for all cases. The maximum pitch angle is observed in case 2 followed by case 1, 3 and finally case 4. In case 3, a notable reduction of about 6.5 deg compared with case 1 and about 12 deg, compared with case 2 are observed. For case 4 (integrated control), there is an extra reduction in the vehicle's pitch angle with total reduction of about 8.5 deg compared with case 1 and about 14 deg, compared with case 2.

The vehicle body pitching acceleration is also depicted in Figure 56 for all cases. As shown in the Figure, the vehicle's maximum pitching acceleration occurs at the end of the collision and the greatest value of the maximum pitching acceleration is observed in cases 2 (ABS). In this case, the pitching acceleration is still higher than the value obtained in the free rolling case. The lowest value is detected in case 4 (Integrated control system). The reduction of the vehicle pitch acceleration in this case is also notable, it decreases from about 1900 deg/s2 in case of free rolling to about 950 deg/s2 in case 3and to about 600 deg/s2 in case 4. Because of the vehicle's rear wheels left the ground during the vehicle pitching, a sudden increase of the vehicle pitching acceleration is observed when the rear wheels re-contacted the ground (look at arrows 1 in Figure 56). This sudden increase in pitching acceleration is not existing in cases 3 and 4 because the rear wheels do not leave the ground in this cases.

6. CONCLUSION

Development of a new 6-DOF vehicle dynamics/crash mathematical model and three dimensional-three-mass occupant mathematical model have been represented to study the effect of vehicle dynamic control systems (VDCS) on vehicle crash at offset frontal vehicle-to-vehicle and full frontal vehicle-to-barrier

Figure 55.

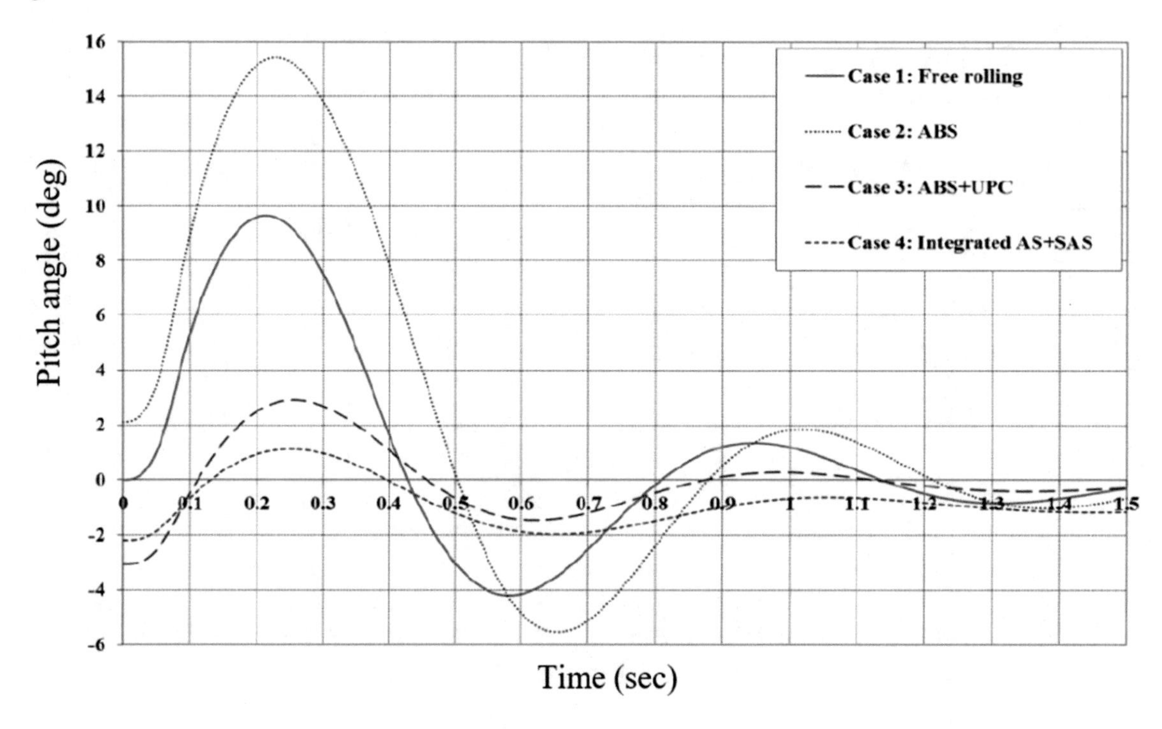

Figure 56.

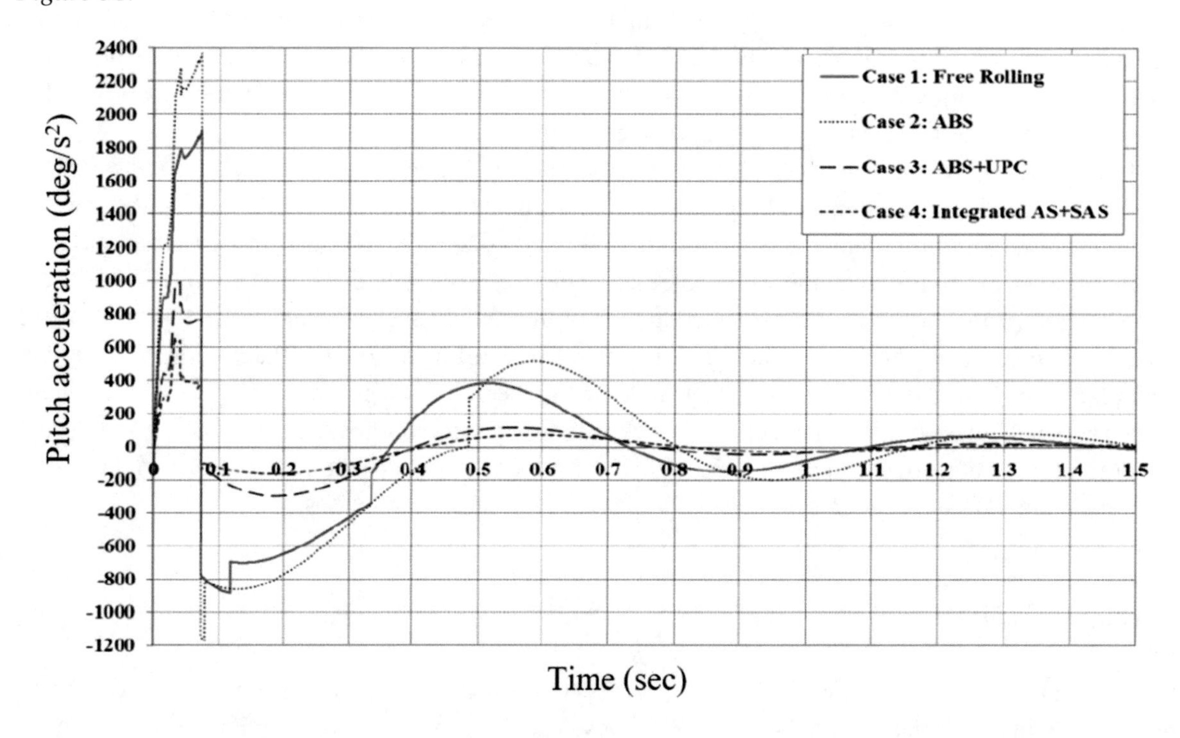

collisions. The models presented here would be very useful in the early design stages for assessing the crash worthiness performance of the vehicle and for selecting appropriate vehicle parameters. From the numerical simulations, it can be said that the VDCS can improve the vehicle crash situation and the occupant behaviour. The different cases applied in this paper have a different effect on the vehicle and its occupant. It is shown that the crash event gets worse related to the vehicle (b), based on higher values of vehicle deceleration, pitching angle and acceleration, etc. However, these higher values are very small and insignificant. In the case of frontal collision, the vehicle pitch angle and its acceleration are dramatically reduced when the UPC system is applied and more reductions obtained when the (AS and SAS) control system is used.

ACKNOWLEDGMENT

The authors would like to thank the Egyptian Government and the Faculty of Engineering, Ain Shams University for supporting this research.

We also acknowledge with sadness, the contribution of Prof. Dave Crolla who has passed away during the period of this research.

REFERENCES

Alleyne, A. (1997). Improved Vehicle Performance Using Combined Suspension and Braking Forces. *Vehicle System Dynamics*, *27*(4), 235–265. doi:10.1080/00423119708969330

Azar, A. T. (2012). System dynamics as a useful technique for complex systems. *International Journal of Industrial and Systems Engineering*, *10*(4), 377–410. doi:10.1504/IJISE.2012.046298

Azar, A. T., & Serrano, F. E. (2016). Stabilization of Mechanical Systems with Backlash by PI Loop Shaping. *International Journal of System Dynamics Applications*, *5*(3), 21–46. doi:10.4018/IJSDA.2016070102

Belytschko, T. (1992). On Computational Methods for Crashworthiness. *Computers & Structures*, *42*(2), 271–279. doi:10.1016/0045-7949(92)90211-H

Chang, J. M., Ali, M., Craig, R., Tyan, T., El-bkaily, M., & Cheng, J. (2006). *Important Modeling Practices in CAE Simulation for Vehicle Pitch and Drop.* SAE International, Warrendale, PA, SAE Technical Paper No. 2006-01-0124.

Elkady, M., Elmarakbi, A., MacIntyre, J., & Alhariri, M. (2016). Multi-Body Integrated Vehicle-Occupant Models for Collision Mitigation and Vehicle Safety using Dynamics Control Systems. *International Journal of System Dynamics Applications*, *5*(2), 80–122. doi:10.4018/IJSDA.2016040105

Elmarakbi, A., & Zu, J. (2005). Crashworthiness Improvement of Vehicle-to-Rigid Fixed Barrier in Full Frontal Impact using Novel Vehicle's Front-End Structures. *International Journal of Automotive Technology*, *6*(5), 491–499.

Elmarakbi, A., & Zu, J. (2007). Incremental Harmonic Balance Method for Analysis of Standard/Smart Vehicles-to-Rigid Barrier Frontal Collision. *International Journal of Vehicle Safety*, *2*(3), 288–315. doi:10.1504/IJVS.2007.015545

Emori, R. I. (1968). *Analytical Approach to Autombile Collisions*. SAE International, Warrendale, PA, SAE Technical Paper No. 680016.

Fanxing, M., Rob, G., Cristy, H., Mujthaba, A., & Charles, S. (2015). Dynamic Vibrotactile Signals for Forward Collision Avoidance Warning Systems. *Human Factors*, *57*(2), 329–346. doi:10.1177/0018720814542651 PMID:25850161

Hogan, I. (2008a). *The development of a vehicle collision mitigation control system through multibody modelling. FISITA World Automotive Congress*, Munich, Germany.

Hogan, I., & Manning, W. (2007). The Use of Vehicle Dynamic Control Systems for Automotive Collision Mitigation. *3rd Institution of Engineering and Technology Conference on Automotive Electronics,* 1-10.

Ilie, S., & Tabacu, Ş. (2010). Study of the Occupant's Kinematics during the Frontal Impact. Ann Oradea Univ. *Fascicle Managmt Technol Engng*, *6*(16), 542–551.

Jansson, J., Gustafsson, F., & Ekmark, J. (2002). *Decision Making For Collision Avoidance Systems*. SAE International, Warrendale, PA, SAE Technical Paper No. 2002-01-0403.

Jongsang, S., Donghoon, S., Kyongsu, Y., Seongjin, Y., Kihan, N., & Hyungjeen, C. (2015). Control of the motorized active suspension damper for good ride quality. Proc IMechE Part D. *Journal of Automobile Engineering*, *228*(11), 1344–1358.

Joshi, S., & Talange, D. B. (2016). Fault Tolerant Control of an AUV using Periodic Output Feedback with Multi Model Approach. *International Journal of System Dynamics Applications*, *5*(2), 41–62. doi:10.4018/IJSDA.2016040103

Kamal, M. M. (1970). *Analysis and Simulation of Vehicle to Barrier Impact*. SAE International, Warrendale, PA, SAE Technical Paper No. 700414.

Khan, L., & Qamar, S. (2015). *Online Adaptive Neuro-Fuzzy Based Full Car Suspension Control Strategy. Research Methods: Concepts*. Methodologies, Tools, and Applications.

Khattab, A. (2010). *Steering system and method for independent steering of wheels* (Ph.D. Thesis). The Department of Mechanical and Industrial Engineering, Concordia University, Montreal, Quebec, Canada.

Khosravi, A., Lachini, Z., & Sarhadi, P. (2015). Predictor-based model reference adaptive control for a vehicle lateral dynamics considering uncertainties. Proc IMechE Part I. *Journal of Systems and Control Engineering*, *229*(9), 797–807.

Kim, H.-S. (2002). New Extruded Multi-Cell Aluminum Profile For Maximum Crash Energy Absorption And Weight Efficiency. *Thin-walled Structures*, *40*(4), 311–327. doi:10.1016/S0263-8231(01)00069-6

Markusic, C. A. (1992). *Vehicle Safety Compliance Testing for Occupant Crash Protection, Windshield Mounting, Windshield Zone Intrusion, and Fuel System Integrity, Final Report of FMVSS NOS. 208, 212, 219, and 301 Compliance Testing*. Washington, DC: Department of Transportation.

Marzougui, D., Kan, C. D., & Bedewi, N. E. (1996). Development and Validation of an NCAP Simulation using LS-DYNA3D. FHWA/NHTSA National Crash Analysis Center, The George Washington University, Virginia Campus.

Matheis, R. & Eckstein, L. (2016). Aluminium-carbon fibre-reinforced polymer hybrid crash management system incorporating braided tubes. *International Journal of Automotive Composites, 2*(3-4), 330–355.

Mirko, Č., Joško, D., Li, X., Eric, T., & Davor, H. (2016). Optimisation of active suspension control inputs for improved vehicle ride performance. *Vehicle System Dynamics, 54*(7), 1004–1030. doi:10.1080/00423114.2016.1177655

Morteza, D., Caglar, S., Teoman, E., & Selim, S. (2015). Design of a multiple-model switching controller for ABS braking dynamics. *Transactions of the Institute of Measurement and Control, 37*(5), 582–595. doi:10.1177/0142331214546522

Samantaray, A. K., & Pradhan, S. (2016). Dynamic Analysis of Steering Bogies. Handbook of Research on Emerging Innovations in Rail Transportation Engineering, 524 – 579. doi:10.4018/978-1-5225-0084-1.ch021

Shah, J., Best, M., Benmimoun, A., & Ayat, M. (2015). Autonomous Rear-end Collision Avoidance Using an Electric Power Steering System. Proc IMechE Part D. *Journal of Automobile Engineering, 229*(12), 1638–1655. doi:10.1177/0954407014567517

Siramdasu, Y., & Taheri, S. (2016). Discrete tyre model application for evaluation of vehicle limit handling performance. *Vehicle System Dynamics, 54*(11), 1554–1573. doi:10.1080/00423114.2016.1220594

Sugimoto, Y., & Sauer, C. (2005). Effectiveness Estimation Method for Advanced Driver Assistance System and Its Application to Collision Mitigation Brake System. *Proceeding 19th International Technology Conference, Enhanced Safety Vehicles*, 1-8.

Tamura, M., Inoue, H., Watanabe, T., & Maruko, N. (2001). *Research on a Brake Assist System with a Preview Function*. SAE International, Warrendale, PA, SAE Technical Paper No. 2001-01-0357.

TRL. (1995). *Real Crash Test Data*. Retrieved from http://www.trl.co.uk

Witteman, W. J. (1999). *Improved Vehicle Crashworthiness Design by Control of the Energy Absorption for Different Collision Situations* (Ph.D. Thesis). Technische University.

Witteman, W. J., & Kriens, R. F. C. (1998). Modeling of an Innovative Frontal Car Structure: Similar Deceleration Curves at Full Overlap, 40 Percent Offset and 30 Degrees Collisions. *Proceedings of 16th International Technical Conference on the Enhanced Safety of Vehicles*, 194-212.

Yu, F., Feng, J. Z., & Li, J. (2002). A Fuzzy Logic Controller Design for Vehicle Abs with an On-Line Optimized Target Wheel Slip Ratio. *International Journal of Automotive Technology, 3*(4), 165–170.

Yue, C., Butsuen, T., & Hedrick, J. K. (1988). Alternative Control Laws for Automotive Active Suspensions. *American Control Conference*, 2373-2378.

Chapter 15
A Study on the Transportation Mode Choice Behaviour of Individuals With Different Socio-Economic Status

Arun Bajracharya
Heriot-Watt University Malaysia, Malaysia

ABSTRACT

This chapter presents a study on the transportation mode choice behaviour of individuals with different socio-economic status. A previously developed system dynamics model has been adopted by differentiating the population mass into upper, middle, and lower classes. The simulation experiments with the model revealed that generally the upper class individuals would be more inclined to use a private car (PC) instead of public transportation (PT) when their tendency is compared to middle and lower class individuals. It was also observed that lower class individuals would be more willing to use PT instead of PC when their tendency is compared to middle and upper class individuals. As such, it would be difficult to encourage the upper class individuals to use PT instead of PC, and it would be successively easier to do so in the case of middle and lower class individuals. However, the results also indicated that under certain different circumstances, the upper class individuals would also prefer to go for PT, and the lower class ones could prefer to own and use PC instead of PT.

INTRODUCTION

The increasing use of private cars for transportation is a persisting matter of concern in growing cities. In order to develop and maintain a functional and sustainable transportation system, it is better that excessive use of private cars be kept under control but it seems that there is little or no success in doing so in the cities around the world especially those which are growing rapidly. A large number of research works have been done to understand the tendency of choosing private car as a mode of transportation. In this research, a particular line of inquiry has been taken to understand how the socio-economic status of

DOI: 10.4018/978-1-5225-4077-9.ch015

individuals residing in and around city area affect their mode choice behaviour. It was found that personal or household income is a closest key construct that represents the socio-economic status of individuals. Generally, it has been reported that usage of personal cars in comparison to public transportation would rise with increasing income levels (Alqhatani et al., 2013; Luo et al., 2007; Paulley et al., 2006). However, there are numerous observations that clearly indicate that the relationship between socio-economic status and mode choice decision is still not very clear. For example, in AASHTO (2013) it is reported that increasing income level would not necessarily increase the use of private car in comparison to public transportation. Giuliano (2005) found that even low-income households used public transit for only small portion of their travel. Combs (2017) reported that public transit ridership by even lower wealth households did not increase even though public transit accessibility has been improved much for them.

A previously developed system dynamics model by the author has been used for this research (see Bajracharya, 2016 for the model, and Sterman (2000), Morecroft (2007) or Azar (2012) for details on the systems thinking and system dynamics approach). The model was used to study individual mode choice behaviour in the context of homogeneous population mass by taking Dubai as a case city. The model is not an agent based detail model, but it attempts to portray the micro behaviour that has potential to demonstrate the macro behaviour of population mass. The model takes the advantage of system dynamics that can demonstrate aggregate behaviour without the need to collect and use big data for simulation purpose (Pruyt, 2016). In this research, a change has been made in using the model by categorising population mass in terms of socio-economic status of individuals residing in a typical growing city. The core structure of the generic model has been retained as it is, and only the relevant parameter values have been altered to create the situations of heterogeneous socio-economic status of individuals.

In this chapter, first the description of the generic feedback loop and simulation model have been presented as it was done in Bajracharya (2016). Then the concept of heterogeneous socio-economic status of individuals has been explained and operationalised in terms of the values of relevant parameters in the model. The model was then used to do series of simulation experiments based on which some pertinent findings have been extracted and reported.

CONCEPTUAL FEEDBACK LOOP MODEL

Private Car Ownership and Usage

Private car (PC) in general would be a preferred choice for transportation in modern urban life if one can afford to own and use it. This proposition is largely supported by most of the literature in car psychology and behavioural mode choice. Private car is taken as a sovereign mode of transportation that can provide protection, convenience, flexibility and reliability to make private trips (Hiscock et al., 2002). There are other numerous literature (such as Innocenti et al., 2013; Gatersleben and Uzzell, 2007; Mann and Abraham, 2006; Steg et al., 2001) that describe why the concept of private car is intrinsically related to the attachment to consume its possession and use. In addition to that, there is a distinct set of theoretical arguments on why people own and use car. Steg (2005) and Steg et al. (2001) stated that private car ownership and use is strongly influenced by the whole set of instrumental, symbolic and affective motives. The instrumental argument suggests that private car is basically a means of transportation. People prefer to use it because it is taken as a safe, comfortable and superior means of transportation. The symbolic argument explains that the possession and use of private car exhibit one's social identity and status, and people generally desire to project one's status image in the society they live. The affective argument on the other hand highlights the fact that possession and use of private car would be closely related to one's emotional attachment and the attachment with pleasant feelings reinforce the desire to possess and use private car.

In Figure 1, the key motivational connotation to own and use private car has been represented by the construct "Desire to Own and Use PC". The link between the "Need to Own Private Car" and the "Desire to Own and Use PC" represents the instrumental motive of owning and using private car – the desire would increase if there is a real need to own car for personal and family use. Another link between the "Social Need" and the "Desire to Own and Use PC" depicts the "symbolic" motive of owning and using private car – the social need or the need to maintain one's identity and status in society would also influence the desire.

With a certain high level of desire, once one starts owning and using private car, an interesting perpetual phenomenon would take place. Driving one's own car provides a level of "Satisfaction with Driving" (Lupton, 2002) and such satisfaction increases the desire to keep owning and using private car. This will further increase the "Use of Private Car", enhance the "Satisfaction with Driving" experience and it in turn further escalates the desire itself. A positive attitude motivates car use and is further

Figure 1. The feedback loop model

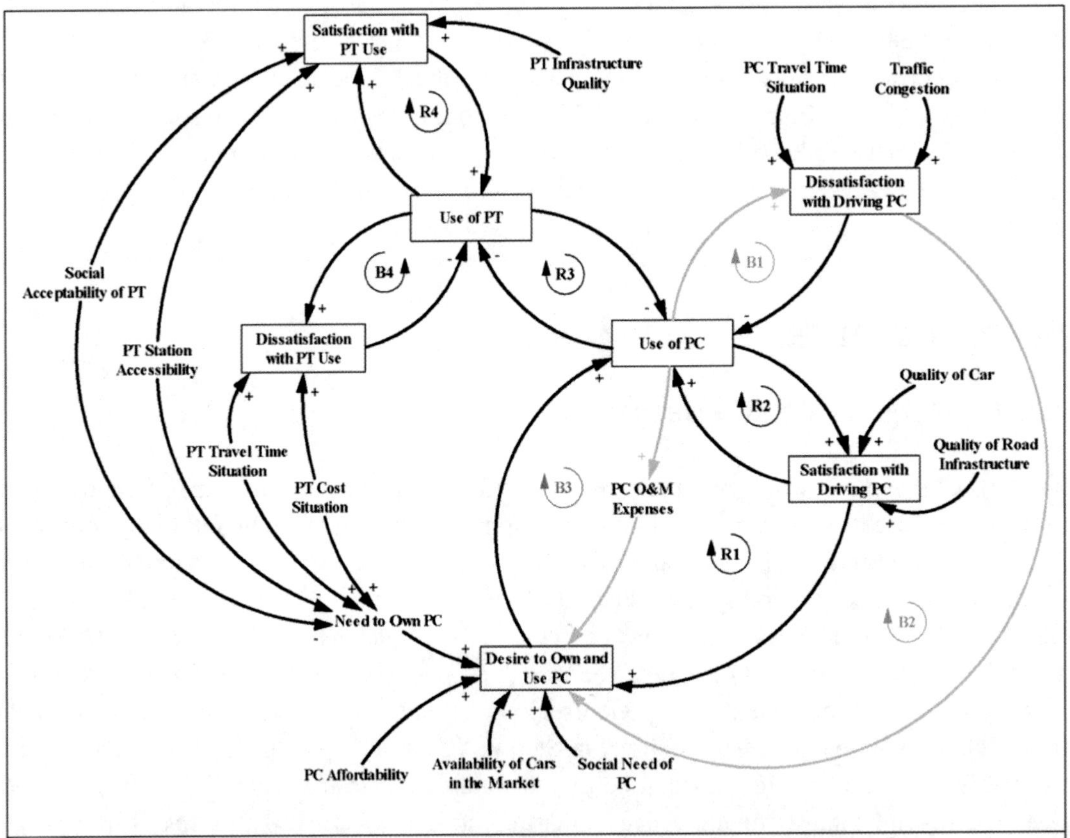

Note: PT → Public Transportation; PC → Private Car; O&M Expenses → Operations and Maintenance Expenses

strengthened by a positive outcome of the choice to use the car (Gärling et al., 2002). This particular perpetual dynamics has been presented in reinforcing loop R1 (Figure 1). The satisfaction with driving would not only escalate the desire to own and use private car, it would also urge the user to simply use the car more (Steg et al., 2001). This straight amplifier effect (Stardling et al., 2000) has been presented in reinforcing loop R2 (Figure 1). The perpetual effect (reinforcing loop R1) and the amplifier effect (reinforcing loop R2) in combination actually depict the "affective" motive that explains one of the reasons behind persistent car use.

While the three separate and distinct motives have been identified to explain the dependency on private car, it has also been observed that the three motives are interrelated (Steg, 2005; Steg et al., 2001). Studies indicate only limited insight into the extent to which affective and symbolic appraisals of the car help to predict car use and mode choice, and it has been reported that the relationship between instrumental, affective and symbolic aspects is often unclear (Gatersleben, 2007). Probably car use is influenced by other factors such as, for instance, situational constraints and intentions. Steg (2005) mentioned that future research should reveal whether and how situational characteristics and motives influence each other. In this research, an attempt has been made to explore other contextual factors and phenomenon that are interrelated to the three basic motives of car use.

Firstly, it has been reported that the "Private Car Affordability" would affect the "Desire to Own and Use Private Car" (Figure 1). Income and affordability is the primary impetus to automobile ownership, and it is used as the only explanatory variable in many car ownership forecast models (Dargay 2001; Dargay and Gately 1999). Another obvious factor is that if many car ownership options are there in the market and cars are easily available in various makes and models, such situation might also generate the desire to own and use car. Besides that, DeCorla-Souza (2000) observed that increase in demand for car use may result if there are improvements in road network. This implies another aspect that affect the private car use: if the "Quality of Road Infrastructure" and "Quality of Car" are better, the driving satisfaction would be high and it would enhance the affective desire to own and use car.

While comfortable car and good road infrastructure could provide satisfaction in driving, car driving would not necessarily be always pleasant. A level of dissatisfaction is also associated with car driving which could be worsened by the distance-wise travel time and traffic congestion (Gatersleben and Uzzell, 2007; Mann and Abraham, 2006; Anable, 2005). If one has to drive a long distance on daily routine basis, then it would definitely not be pleasant. Likewise, the routine of getting trapped into long grinding traffic jam would be one of the very unpleasant experiences. All these discomfort and dissatisfaction in car driving would directly discourage the car use as shown in balancing feedback loop B1 (Figure 1), and continuous experience of such discomfort and dissatisfaction would even decrease one's desire to own and use car as shown in balancing feedback loop B2 (Figure 1).

Another factor that would discourage one to own and use car is the operations and maintenance (O&M) expenses of car. Steg et al. (2001) found that O&M expenses of car is one of the most unattractive aspects of car use. Balancing feedback loop B3 (Figure 1) presents this issue, and the balancing feedback loop effect would be more pronounced when there are substantial car ownership hurdles in terms of car registration and renewal processes, car and road use taxes, parking charges and difficulties, fuel price/ surcharge, traffic fines, insurance charges, and other repair and maintenance expenses.

The two sets of reinforcing feedback loops (R1 and R2) would explain the phenomenon of perpetual increase in the use of private car whereas the three sets of balancing feedback loops (B1, B2 and B3) would indicate the possible situations that limit the car ownership and usage. In the situation, when an individual gets discouraged to own and use private car, the alternative mode for transportation would be public transportation (PT) provided that it is available. The understanding here is that the use of PT and private car are mutually exclusive at individual trip level. The number of trips made in PT excludes a person to use potentially available private car for the same trips or vice versa. This understanding is presented in the reinforcing feedback loop R3 (Figure 1). The loop is interestingly a reinforcing loop in the sense that the continuous preference in one mode reinforces the use of the same mode excluding the other mode. This loop would also help to explain the habitual behaviour with preferred, available and routinely used mode of transportation.

Public Transportation Choice and Usage

Similarly, as the private car, the use of public transportation (PT) would provide different experiences of riding satisfaction and dissatisfaction. It is natural that more riding satisfaction would encourage the use of PT and it is possible that it further provides instances of satisfactory rides. This reinforcing loop R4 (Figure 1) would thus explain the probable persistent use of PT ridership. On the other hand, instances of dissatisfactory ride would limit the use of PT as depicted by the balancing loop B4 (Figure 1).

The literature in the area of public transportation choice and usage mainly focus into different aspects of the quality of public transportation infrastructure and services. Lai and Chen (2011) stated that the perception of good service quality of public transit services enhances the higher value perception and satisfaction, and this would encourage travellers to continue to use the service. Hensher et al. (2003) and Konig (2002) asserted that the reliability (being on time) is a decisive factor in the choice and usage of public transportation. Outwater et al. (2011) listed reliability, real-time information, and modern transit and on-board amenities as significant attributes that distinguish premium transit services. Eboli and Mazzulla (2012) found that the quality determinants in public transportation could be summarised and listed as service availability, service reliability, comfort, cleanliness, safety, security, fare, information, customer care, and environmental impacts. They concluded that both subjective and objective measures on the determinants are necessary for evaluating the performance of transit service. Beirao and Cabral (2007) found that instead of the fare of public transportation, the reliability, travel time and comfort have a great impact on customer satisfaction. Wardman (2004) stated that in order to tempt car users it is essential to provide faster, more frequent and accessible services in PT. Spichkova and Hamilton (2016) concluded that additional and innovative features in PT system could be instrumental in stimulating the potential passengers to become actual ones.

In this research, different attributes of service quality have been summarised, and it is considered that they would be instrumental in affecting the satisfaction or dissatisfaction of PT use. The satisfaction of PT use would be enhanced if the PT stations are accessible, the PT infrastructure quality is good, and importantly if PT is socially acceptable. The dissatisfaction with PT on the other hand would be exacerbated if it takes longer trip time, for instance it takes long time to reach the PT station (access time), to wait at the station (wait time), to make the real travel (in vehicle travel time), to change carriers if needed (transit time), and to reach the final destination from the last station (egress time). The dissatisfaction would also be increased if the cost (say the fare) of using PT is significantly high.

The feedback loop model (Figure 1) also shows that if the PT travel time is longer, PT station accessibility is difficult, PT is perceptively costly, and if the PT use does not indicate the social "class" then there will be a real need to own private car and it would consequently develop a need based desire of car.

THE SIMULATION MODEL

The structure, constructs and parameters presented in the feedback loop model have been used to develop a simulation model. For the simulation purpose the constructs have been translated into respective stock, flow and auxiliary variables and they have been supplemented with other relevant variables for structural detailing. Besides that all the parameters in the feedback loop model have also been properly incorporated. Importantly the whole causal loop structure has been precisely retained for simulation.

In order to operationalise the simulation model, certain protocols have been adopted with some assumptions. First of all it is assumed that an individual would make certain average number of trips per day either using the PT or PC, or both, but the choice of mode would be mutually exclusive for the same trip. The average number of trips per day in the case of PC also includes the trips generated by the straight amplifier effect (indicated by the reinforcing loop R2 in Figure 1). All the other soft variables and parameters are quantified using the protocol of index measures that are good enough to provide ordinal comparisons (Saeed, 1994, 2004). An illustration on the variables and parameters has been presented in Table 1.

Table 1. Quantification of the Variables and Parameters

Variables/Parameters	Numerical Range	Meaning of the Range
Satisfaction with PT use Dissatisfaction with PT use Satisfaction with driving PC Dissatisfaction with driving PC	0 to any positive numerical value	0 means no satisfaction or no dissatisfaction at all, and higher positive values mean higher levels of the respective variables.
Quality of PT infrastructure Quality of road infrastructure Quality of car Social acceptability of PT PT station accessibility Need to own PC PC affordability Availability of cars in the market Social need of PC	0 to 1	0 means the total absence of the respective features and 1 means their maximum possible values. For e.g., 0 accessibility means not accessible at all and 1 means immediately accessible.
PT travel time situation	0.5 to 3	Perceptive comparison of the actual to expected time taken by PT for a trip. 0.5 means PT takes half the expected time and 3 means three times more than the expected time.
PT cost situation	0.5 to 2	Perceptive comparison of the actual to expected costs of making a trip on PT. 0.5 means PT costs half the expected amount and 2 means double the expected amount.
PC travel time situation	0.5 to 3	Perceptive comparison of the actual to expected time taken by PC for a trip. 0.5 means PC takes half the expected time and 3 means three times more than the expected time.
Traffic congestion	0 to 5	Perceptive comparison of the actual to expected traffic congestion experience in a trip. 0 means no congestion experience at all and 5 means five times more than the expected experience.
Actual O&M expenses for PC	1 to 5	Perceptive comparison of the actual to expected expenses for making daily trips on PC. 1 means exactly the expected amount and 5 means five times the expected amount.
Proportion of PT Ridership	0 to 1	Proportion of daily trips made in PT in comparison to the total daily trips. 0 means no trips were made in PT or all the trips were made in PC. 1 means all the trips were made in PT or no the trips were made in PC. It is assumed that the total number of (average) daily trips made in PT and PC are mutually exclusive and collectively exhaustive.

SIMULATION OF THE MODEL

Variation in socioeconomic status of population mass is almost a norm in any natural human settlements including modern cities. The existence of different categories of socioeconomic status of population mass have been observed and recognised since a long time. For example, Weber (1947) categorised it as working class, lower-middle class, intelligentsia, and upper class. Warner (1949) developed a class model in which population mass was divided into upper, middle and lower class with further sub-division of upper and lower sub classes under each of the three classes. Thompson and Hickey (2005) and Gilbert (2002) came up with new variations of Warner's class model, but there is not much change in the three main classes and their sub-divisions. In terms of distribution of the three main classes in different regions in the world, ADB (2010) reported that majority of population fall in middle and lower classes in developing world, and the observed pattern is such that the proportion of middle class and to some extent that of upper class have been steadily increasing across the globe (Rose, 2016).

Generally, the income, occupation, economic capacity, and social values differentiate the socioeconomic status of the population mass. Because of the difference in status, their tastes, preferences and perception would also be different, and it would get reflected in their consumption behaviour including the mode choice behaviour in transportation. In this research, mainly the three classes of population mass – upper, middle and lower class – have been considered and they have been represented in terms of their respective perception on the basic representative parameters (BRPs) used in the simulation model. The relative differences in the perception of the three classes on BRPs are shown in Table 2, and description on the quantified BRPs are given afterwards.

In the cities where mix of different classes of population reside, the quality and standard of public infrastructure and facilities would tend to reflect the standard of middle and lower class. As such the upper class individuals would perceive the "Quality of PT Infrastructure" and "Quality of Road Infrastructure" inferior than that is perceived by the middle and lower class individuals, and further it would also be true that in general, middle class individuals would perceive the qualities inferior in comparison to lower class individuals.

For the upper class individuals, the "PT Cost Situation" would not be worse than that they could afford, meaning that it would not be more than what they expect it to be. For the middle class individuals the perception about the "PT Cost Situation" would be slightly more expensive that they expect, and for the

Table 2. The quantified BRPs to differentiate the three classes

BRPs	Upper Class	Middle Class	Lower Class
Quality of PT Infrastructure	0.60	0.70	0.80
Quality of Road Infrastructure	0.70	0.80	0.90
PT Cost Situation	1.00	1.20	1.50
PC Affordability	1.00	0.80	0.40
Actual O&M Expenses for PC	1.00	1.20	2.00
Availability of Cars in the Market	0.80	0.80	0.80
Quality of Car	0.80	0.80	0.80
Social Need of PC	1.00	0.80	0.20

lower class ones it would be further more expensive than their expectation. Likewise regarding the "PC Affordability", the upper class individuals can readily afford the PC of their choice whereas the middle class ones would have little bit difficulty and the lower ones would think really seriously when they are taking a PC. Similar pattern of perception would also be true for the "Actual O&M Expenses for PC" – the upper class individuals could afford it, and it would be as per their expectation whereas the middle class ones would feel slightly more expensive and for the lower ones it would be far more expensive.

The "Availability of Cars in the Market" would be relatively sufficient for all the three classes. In the context of growing cities, car companies and dealers would have their good presence to serve the population, and different individuals in the three classes would have ample choice according to their tastes and preferences on the makes and models. Regarding the "Quality of Car", it is assumed that individuals in different classes would make optimal choice of their cars to their satisfaction, and yet they would always be looking for slightly better ones.

Regarding the "Social Need of PC", for the upper class individuals PC is almost like a must, whereas for the middle class ones the need would be quite high but not as much as that for the upper ones. The lower class ones on the other hand could live in their society even without a PC, but in the modern city life they would slightly feel the need of PC if affordable options are available for them.

Considering the above values of BRPs, numbers of simulation experiments were carried out with the purpose of validating the model with different combinations of parameter values including the extreme ones. After gaining confidence with the model, some selected combinations of the values of relevant parameters were considered to reflect different possible policy combinations that could be used in a typical context of growing city with different classes of residing population. In order to present some important outcomes, mainly the results of three sets of simulation runs with corresponding values of relevant parameters have been shown in Figures 2, 3 and 4. "Proportion of PT Ridership" has been chosen as the key representative variable to reflect the summative results of the simulation experiments. In each set, three simulation runs on the "Proportion of PT Ridership" are presented with different combinations of low, moderate or high values of the listed parameters to demonstrate the PT ridership patterns of upper, middle and lower class individuals.

The Effect of Social Acceptability of PT, PT Station Accessibility and PT Travel Time Situation on PT Ridership

The first set of simulation runs (SRs) as presented in Figure 2 show the effects of "Social Acceptability of PT", "PT Station Accessibility" and "PT Travel Time Situation" on PT ridership while fixing the "PC Travel Time Situation" and "Traffic Congestion" at a very comfortable level.

In Figure 2, on the part of upper class individuals, SR 1 shows that they would not prefer to use PT when social acceptability of PT is very low, PT station accessibility is very difficult, and PT travel time is very long. SR2 shows that this class of individuals would not prefer to use PT even though their social acceptability of PT is moderate, PT station is reasonably accessible, and PT travel time is relatively shorter than that in SR1. Further, SR3 shows that the upper class individuals would prefer to use PT for some time but they would not continue to use it even though their social acceptability is very high, PT station is quite nearby, and PT travel time is just 50% more than they expect.

On the part of middle class individuals, SR1 in Figure 2 shows that they would not prefer to use PT when social acceptability of PT is very low, PT station accessibility is very difficult, and PT travel time is very long. SR2 shows that they would use PT for some time but would not continue to use when their

Figure 2. The effect of social acceptability of PT, PT station accessibility and PT travel time situation of PT ridership

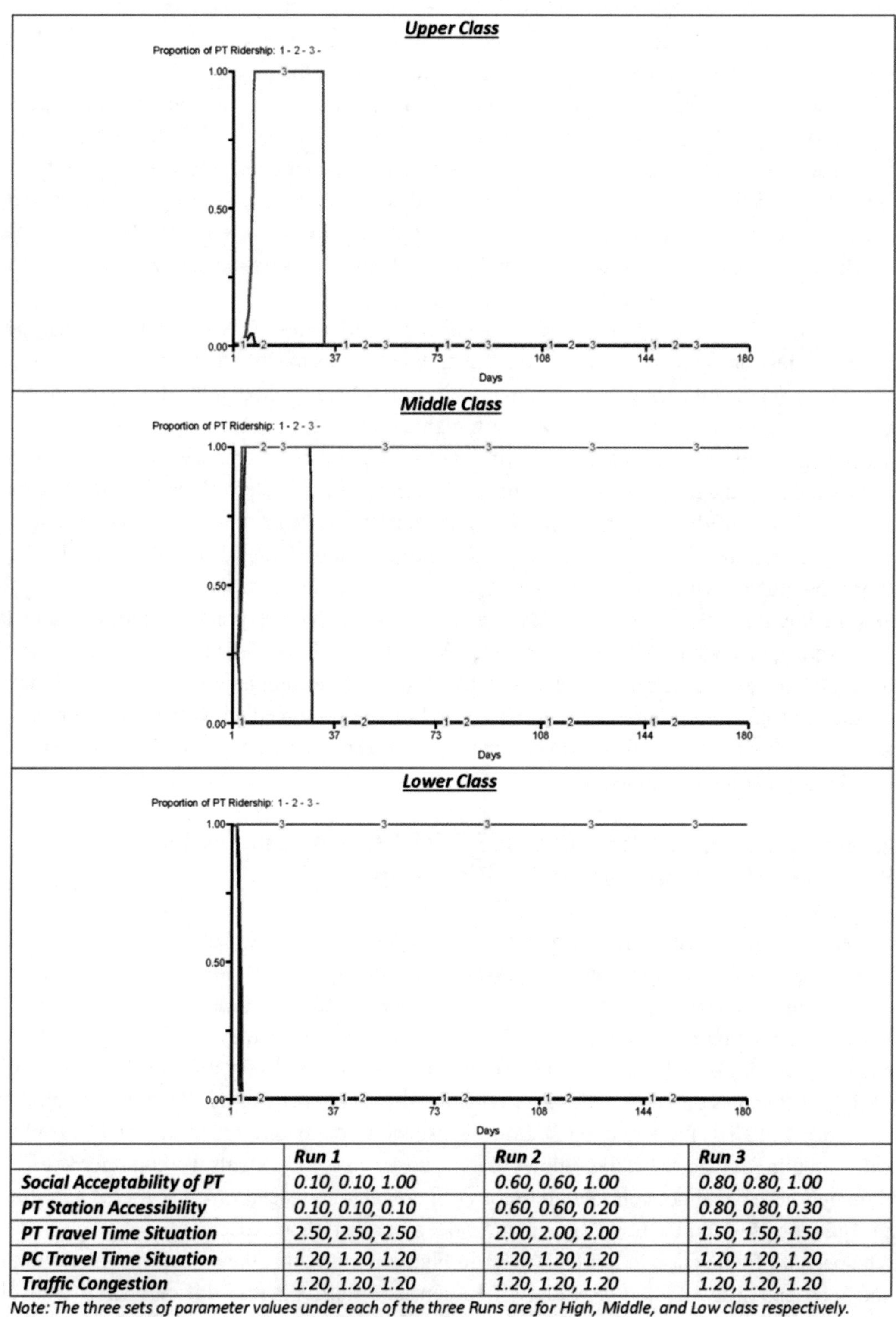

	Run 1	Run 2	Run 3
Social Acceptability of PT	0.10, 0.10, 1.00	0.60, 0.60, 1.00	0.80, 0.80, 1.00
PT Station Accessibility	0.10, 0.10, 0.10	0.60, 0.60, 0.20	0.80, 0.80, 0.30
PT Travel Time Situation	2.50, 2.50, 2.50	2.00, 2.00, 2.00	1.50, 1.50, 1.50
PC Travel Time Situation	1.20, 1.20, 1.20	1.20, 1.20, 1.20	1.20, 1.20, 1.20
Traffic Congestion	1.20, 1.20, 1.20	1.20, 1.20, 1.20	1.20, 1.20, 1.20

Note: The three sets of parameter values under each of the three Runs are for High, Middle, and Low class respectively.

social acceptability of PT is moderate, PT station is reasonably accessible, and PT travel time is relatively shorter than that in SR1. Further SR3 shows that this class of individuals would prefer and continue to use PT only when their social acceptability of PT is high, PT station is quite accessible, and PT travel time situation is reasonably acceptable.

The context for the lower class individuals is little bit different in that unlike the upper and middle class, their social acceptability of PT would be always very high. As such in Figure 2, SRs 1, 2, and 3 show the effects of only two parameters of PT station accessibility and PT travel time situations by considering very high social acceptability of PT for all the three runs. Another observation was that even low to moderate accessibility of PT station would be sufficient enough for the lower class individuals to prefer the PT use, but if it is very difficult to get access to PT station (that means if PT accessibility is very low) they would rather opt for PC instead of using PT. It was also observed that the change in PT travel time situation also affects the use of PT – it was found that longer travel time would discourage them to use PT for the long run.

The Effect of Traffic Congestion on PT Ridership

The second set of SRs as presented in Figure 3 shows mainly the effect of traffic congestion on PT ridership. For the upper class individuals, keeping the “Social Acceptability of PT”, “PT Station Accessibility”, “PT Travel Time Situation”, and “PC Travel Time Situation” at their very high levels, three SRs have been presented with successively good, worse and worst traffic congestion situations. At the good and even at the worse traffic congestion situations, PT ridership is dominated by PC ridership as shown in SRs 1 and 2. Because of the three relatively better PT related parameters, an individual would get attracted to PT for a while – for a longer duration with worse traffic congestion situations. However, the desire to own and use PC would still be more attractive with the “bearable” traffic congestion. But further, when the traffic congestion situation was turned to its worst level, the dissatisfaction with driving increases significantly and consequently even the high class individuals would find PT more attractive than to bear the daily grinding traffic woes.

For the middle class individuals, when the parameters “Social Acceptability of PT”, “PT Station Accessibility”, “PT Travel Time Situation”, and “PC Travel Time Situation” were kept at highly comfortable levels, it was found that they would prefer to use PT even though the level of traffic congestion is very low. Therefore, an experiment was done to know what if the “Social Acceptability of PT” and “PT Station Accessibility” were only moderate and the “PT Travel Time Situation”, and “PC Travel Time Situation” were at highly comfortable levels. The experiment results as presented in the three SRs for middle class individuals in Figure 3 show that they would use PT for a while – for a longer duration with worse traffic congestion situations, but eventually they would opt for their PC. Only when the traffic congestion becomes worse to bear with, they would use PT even though the PT station is only moderately accessible and their society have moderate acceptability of PT.

On the part of lower class individuals, it was found that even at moderate to fairly low accessibility of PT station and comfortable traffic congestion and travel time situation for PCs, they would prefer to use PT instead of PC. Therefore, a different experiment was carried out to learn about the behaviour of lower class individuals when the PT travel time situation was changed whereby PT station accessibility is fairly low, and the traffic congestion and PC travel time situation are comfortable. It was found that

Figure 3. The effect of traffic congestion on PT ridership

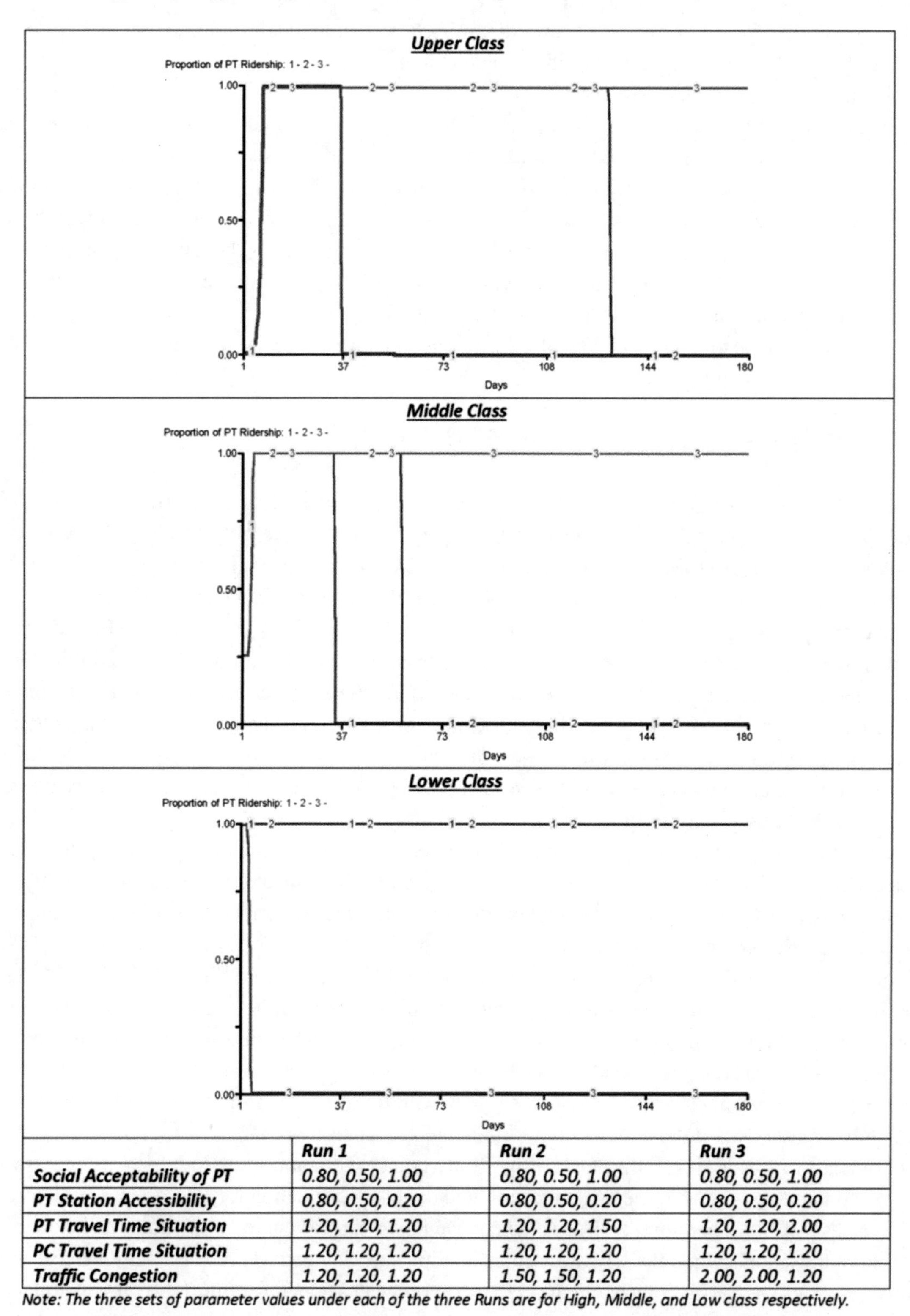

	Run 1	Run 2	Run 3
Social Acceptability of PT	0.80, 0.50, 1.00	0.80, 0.50, 1.00	0.80, 0.50, 1.00
PT Station Accessibility	0.80, 0.50, 0.20	0.80, 0.50, 0.20	0.80, 0.50, 0.20
PT Travel Time Situation	1.20, 1.20, 1.20	1.20, 1.20, 1.50	1.20, 1.20, 2.00
PC Travel Time Situation	1.20, 1.20, 1.20	1.20, 1.20, 1.20	1.20, 1.20, 1.20
Traffic Congestion	1.20, 1.20, 1.20	1.50, 1.50, 1.20	2.00, 2.00, 1.20

Note: The three sets of parameter values under each of the three Runs are for High, Middle, and Low class respectively.

in the situation of comfortable and even moderately longer PT travel time situation, they would prefer to use PT. Only when the PT travel time situation gets very long, they would opt for their PC instead of using PT.

The Effect of PC Affordability and Actual O&M Expenses for PC on PT Ridership

The third set of SRs as presented in Figure 4 shows mainly the effect of "PC Affordability" and "Actual O&M expenses for PC" on PT ridership. For the upper class individuals, keeping the "Social Acceptability of PT", "PT Station Accessibility", "PT Travel Time Situation", "PC Travel Time Situation", and "Traffic Congestion" at relatively better levels, three SRs have been presented with successively low, high and higher levels of "Actual O&M Expenses for PC". At the same time, it is assumed that the upper class individuals would be fully capable in affording PC. At low and even at high levels of O&M expenses it is observed that the PT ridership could not get sustained. An interesting observation is however there when O&M expenses are very high – the corresponding SR shows that although the PT ridership goes down for a certain time period, it again increases up, gets sustained for some time and then decreases, and the pattern repeats. A pattern of mixed mode choice has been observed in the situation of very high "Actual O&M Expenses for PC", that means even the upper class people would go for mixed mode if they feel that the O&M expenses are too high for them to bear with while other PT and PC related parameters are highly favourable.

For the middle class individuals, when the "Social Acceptability of PT" and "PT Station Accessibility" were kept at very high level, it was found that they would stick with PT ridership irrespective of high or low values of "PC Affordability" and "Actual O&M Expenses for PC". Therefore, another experiment was done by keeping the "Social Acceptability of PT" and "PT Station Accessibility" at moderate levels and the "PT Travel Time Situation", "PC Travel Time Situation", and "Traffic Congestion" at relatively better levels. With these, the three SRs have been presented with successively high, low and lower levels of PC affordability with respectively low, high and higher levels of O&M expenses. At low and even at high levels of O&M expenses it is observed that the PT ridership would not get sustained. When the O&M expenses increased to very high level, then it was found that the middle class individuals would go for mixed mode choice as it was observed with the high class individuals.

On the part of the lower class individuals, as they would have full "Social Acceptability of PT", even moderate level of "PT Station Acceptability" would attract them to stick with PT ridership irrespective of high or low values of "PC Affordability" and "Actual O&M Expenses for PC". That is why another experiment was carried out to test how this class of individuals would behave when the "PT Station Accessibility" is difficult and "PT Travel Time Situation" is moderate. Keeping "PC Travel Time Situation" and "Traffic Congestion" at very comfortable levels, it was found that at moderate levels of "PC Affordability" and "Actual O&M Expenses for PC", PT ridership would not get sustained. At lower level of "PC Affordability" and higher level of "Actual O&M Expenses for PC", the lower class individuals would go for mixed mode choice as it was observed with the high and middle class individuals. Further, when the "PC Affordability" is very low and the "Actual O&M Expenses for PC" is very high, the lower class individuals would prefer PT and continue to use it.

Figure 4. The effect of PC affordability and actual O&M expenses for PC on PT ridership

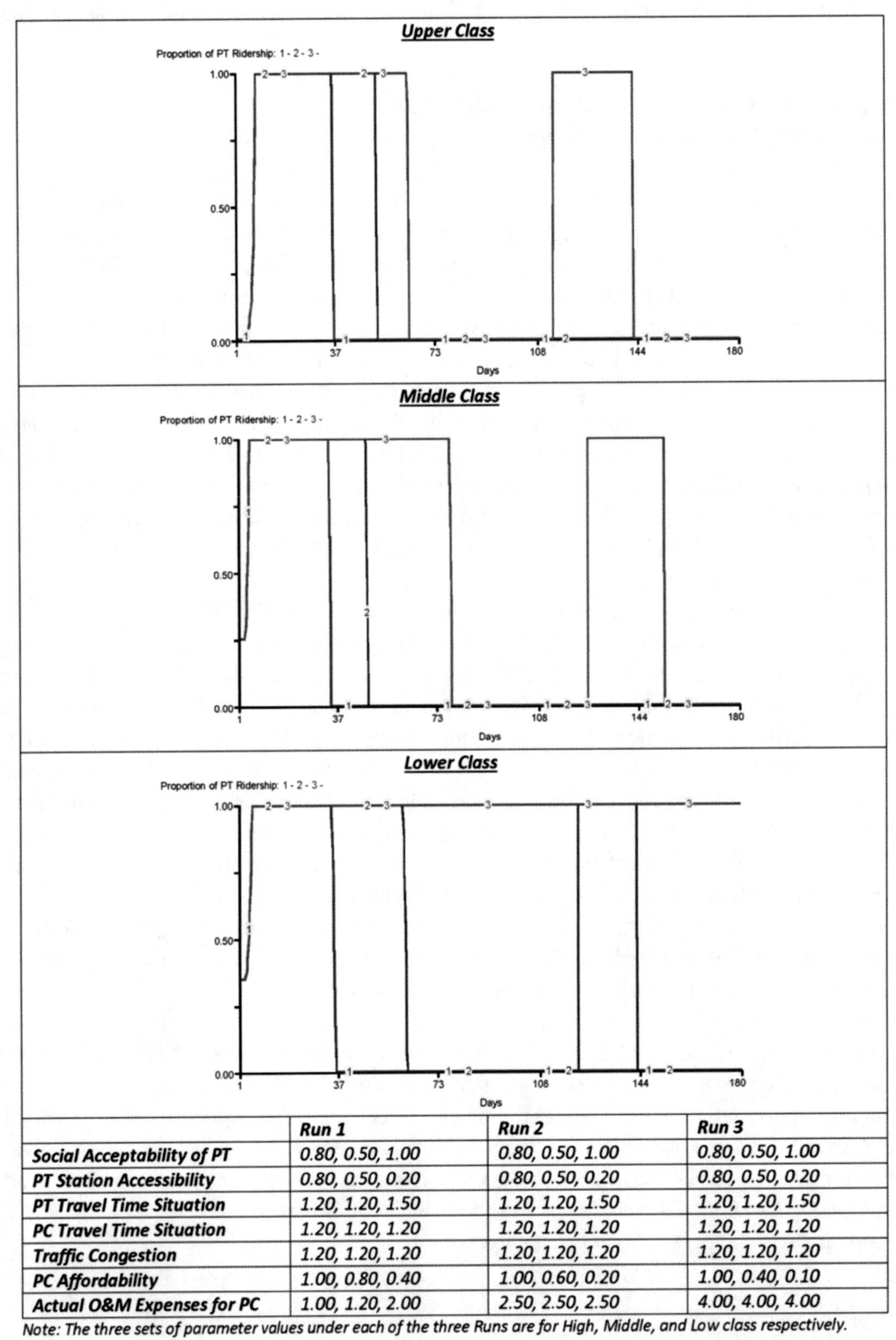

	Run 1	Run 2	Run 3
Social Acceptability of PT	0.80, 0.50, 1.00	0.80, 0.50, 1.00	0.80, 0.50, 1.00
PT Station Accessibility	0.80, 0.50, 0.20	0.80, 0.50, 0.20	0.80, 0.50, 0.20
PT Travel Time Situation	1.20, 1.20, 1.50	1.20, 1.20, 1.50	1.20, 1.20, 1.50
PC Travel Time Situation	1.20, 1.20, 1.20	1.20, 1.20, 1.20	1.20, 1.20, 1.20
Traffic Congestion	1.20, 1.20, 1.20	1.20, 1.20, 1.20	1.20, 1.20, 1.20
PC Affordability	1.00, 0.80, 0.40	1.00, 0.60, 0.20	1.00, 0.40, 0.10
Actual O&M Expenses for PC	1.00, 1.20, 2.00	2.50, 2.50, 2.50	4.00, 4.00, 4.00

Note: The three sets of parameter values under each of the three Runs are for High, Middle, and Low class respectively.

CONCLUSION

In this research, a set of previously developed causal feedback loop and simulation model have been used to understand how individuals with different socio-economic status would make mode choice decision in the context of growing cities. Generally it was found that the upper class individuals would be more inclined in using PC instead of PT when their tendency is compared to middle and lower class individuals. In the other way round, again generally it was also found that lower class individuals would be more willing to use PT instead of PC when their tendency is compared to middle and upper class individuals. These findings generally go along with the output and arguments given in general mode choice literature (for example, de Vasconcellos, 2005). However, the simulation experiments done in this research revealed a little bit more detail about the behavioural tendencies of individuals with different socio-economic status. The findings of the experiments are summarised under the two broader policy options that could be used to address the issue of excessive use of PCs.

Improving the PT Related Parameters

One set of broader policy measures is to attract individuals to use PT by improving the PT related parameters such as social acceptability of PT, accessibility to PT, and PT travel time situation. Social acceptability of PT could be improved by offering high class PT infrastructure, conducting media campaigns, and providing several incentives to use PT. Likewise, PT could be made more accessible by extending PT networks and serving catchment areas more closely. PT travel time situation could be improved by laying down and maintaining efficient and reliable PT system.

The findings revealed that this set of policy measures would not be effective for upper class individuals unless and until their PC travel time and traffic congestion are too difficult to bear with. The middle class individuals on the other hand would need very attractive PT related parameters for them to opt for the use of PT – just moderately attractive PT related parameters would not be sufficient for them to stick with using PT when PC related parameters are attractive. However, if they have attractive PT related parameters, they would go for PT even in the situation of very comfortable PC travel time and traffic situations. On the part of lower class individuals, it was observed that low and moderately attractive PT related parameters would be sufficient for them to go with PT even though PC related parameters are attractive. However, if the PT related parameters are too much less attractive for them, they would stick for PC provided that they could afford to purchase and maintain their class of PC.

Discouraging to own and use PC

Another set of broader policy measures is to discourage to own and use PC by making it less affordable to purchase and more expensive to own and maintain. This particular option has been adopted to curb the excessive usage of PCs. For example, in Singapore, the attractiveness of purchasing PC has been controlled by increasing the up-front costs of PC. At the same time, discriminant electronic road pricing and other ownership hurdles have also been created to discourage the ownership and usage of PC (Li et al. 2011 and Santos et al. 2004).

The findings of the simulation experiments showed that this set of policy measures also would not be effective for the upper class individuals. As they are affluent individuals, it is not likely that they won't be able to afford to purchase and maintain PC of their choice. O&M hurdles could be created but it would be less practical. In case, if O&M hurdles are created to the extent that even the upper class individuals feel the real heat, it was found that they would go for mixed mode provided that other PT and PC related parameters are highly favourable.

On the part of middle class individuals, it was found that with a moderate capacity to afford PC and high level of O&M expenses, they would not go for PT in the situation whereby their social acceptability of PT and PT station accessibility are at moderate levels, and PT and PC travel time situations and traffic congestion are relatively comfortable for them. However, in such situation they would go for mixed mode when O&M expenses are very high for them.

In the case of lower class individuals, it was found that if they have moderate level of PC affordability and O&M expenses to bear with, they would rather choose to use PC in the situation whereby PT station accessibility is difficult, PT travel time situation is moderate, and PC travel time situation and traffic congestion are at comfortable levels. In the similar situation when their PC affordability is low and O&M expenses are high they would go for mixed mode. However, if their PC affordability is very low and O&M expenses are very high, then they would prefer PT and continue to use it.

LIMITATIONS AND FURTHER RESEARCH

The strength of this research is the model that could demonstrate a different range of mode choice behaviour of the population mass divided into upper, middle and lower classes. The simulation results on the model showed that it is difficult to encourage the upper class individuals to use PT instead of PC, and it is successively easier in the case of middle and lower class individuals. The results also indicated that under certain circumstances the upper class individuals would also prefer to go for PT and the lower class ones could also stick with PC instead of using PT. However, the model was developed at individual level, and it is more conceptual, semi-empirical and highly parameter driven. If the behaviour of population clusters in different socio-economic classes are considered, then the study on interaction between the state of the city, consequent policy parameters, and the collective behaviour of the whole population classes would be much more insightful.

REFERENCES

AASHTO (2013). *Commuting in America 2013: The National Report on Commuting Patterns and Trends*. The American Association of State Highway and Transportation Officials. Publication Code: CA10-4.

ADB. (2010). *The Rise of Asia's Middle Class*. Retrieved from www.adb.org/sites/defailt/files/publication/27726/special-chapter-02.pdf

Alqhatani, M., Bajwa, S., & Setunge, S. (2013). Modelling the Influence of Socioeconomic and Land-Use Factors on Mode Choice: A Comparison of Riyadh, Saudi Arabia, and Melbourne, Australia. *International Journal of Environmental, Chemical, Ecological. Geological and Geophysical Engineering*, *7*(2), 91–103.

Anable, J. (2005). 'Complacent Car Addicts' or 'Aspiring Environmentalists'? Identifying Travel Behaviour Segments Using Attitude Theory. *Transport Policy*, *12*(1), 65–78. doi:10.1016/j.tranpol.2004.11.004

Azar, A. T. (2012). System Dynamics as a Useful Technique for Complex Systems. *International Journal of Industrial and Systems Engineering*, *10*(4), 377–410. doi:10.1504/IJISE.2012.046298

Bajracharya, A. (2016). Public Transportation and Private Car: A System Dynamics Approach in Understanding the Mode Choice. *International Journal of System Dynamics Applications*, *5*(2), 1–18. doi:10.4018/IJSDA.2016040101

Beirao, G., & Cabral, J. A. S. (2007). Understanding Attitudes Towards Public Transport and Private Car: A Qualitative Study. *Transport Policy*, *14*(6), 478–489. doi:10.1016/j.tranpol.2007.04.009

Combs, T. S. (2017). Examining Changes in Travel Patterns among Lower Wealth Households after BRT Investment in Bogota, Columbia. *Journal of Transport Geography*, *60*, 11–20. doi:10.1016/j.jtrangeo.2017.02.004

Dargey, J. M. (2001). The Effect of Income on Car Ownership: Evidence of Asymmetry. *Transportation Research Part A, Policy and Practice*, *35*(9), 807–821. doi:10.1016/S0965-8564(00)00018-5

Dargey, J. M., & Gately, D. (1999). Income's Effect on Car and Vehicle Ownership, Worldwide: 1960-2015. *Transportation Research Part A, Policy and Practice*, *33*(2), 101–138. doi:10.1016/S0965-8564(98)00026-3

de Vasconcellos, E. A. (2005). Transport Metabolism, Social Diversity and Equity: The Case of Sao Paulo, Brazil. *Journal of Transport Geology*, *13*(4), 329–339. doi:10.1016/j.jtrangeo.2004.10.007

DeCorla-Souza, P. (2000). Induced Highway Travel: Transportation Policy Implications for Congested Metropolitan Areas. *Transportation Quarterly*, *54*(2), 13–30.

Eboli, L., & Mazzulla, G. (2012). Performance Indicators for an Objective Measure of Public Transport Service Quality. *European Transport*, *51*(3), 1825–3997.

Gärling, T., Biel, A., & Gustafsson, M. (2002). The Human Interdependence Paradigm and its Application in Environmental Psychology. In R. Bechtel & A. Churchman (Eds.), *Handbook of Environmental Psychology* (pp. 85–94). New York: Wiley.

Gatersleben, B. (2007). Affective and Symbolic Aspects of Car Use. In T. Gärling & L. Steg (Eds.), *Threats from Car Traffic to the Quality of Urban Life* (pp. 219–233). Elsevier. doi:10.1108/9780080481449-012

Gatersleben, B., & Uzzell, D. (2007). Affective Appraisals of the Daily Commute: Comparing Perceptions of Drivers, Cyclists, Walkers and Users of Public Transport. *Environment and Behavior*, *39*(3), 416–431. doi:10.1177/0013916506294032

Gilbert, D. (2002). *The American Class Structure: In an Age of Growing Inequality*. Belmont, CA: Wadsworth.

Giuliano, G. (2005). Low Income, Public Transit and Mobility. *Transportation Research Record: Journal of the Transportation Research Board*, (1927): 55–62.

Hensher, D. A. (1998). The Imbalance between Car and Public Transport Use in Urban Australia: Why Does it Exist? *Transport Policy*, *5*(4), 193–204. doi:10.1016/S0967-070X(98)00022-5

Hiscock, R., Macintyre, S., Kearns, A., & Ellaway, A. (2002). Means of Transport and Ontological Security: Do Cars Provide Psycho-social Benefits to their Users? *Transportation Research Part D, Transport and Environment*, *7*(2), 119–135. doi:10.1016/S1361-9209(01)00015-3

Innocenti, A., Lattarulo, P., & Pazienza, M. G. (2013). Car Stickiness: Heuristics and Biases in Travel Choice. *Transport Policy*, *25*, 158–168. doi:10.1016/j.tranpol.2012.11.004

Konig, A. (2002). The Reliability of the Transportation System and its Influence on the Choice Behaviour. *Proceedings of the 2nd Swiss Transport Research Conference*.

Lai, W. T., & Chen, C. F. (2011). Behavioural Intentions of Public Transit Passengers – The Roles of Service Quality, Perceived Value, Satisfaction and Involvement. *Transport Policy*, *18*(2), 318–325. doi:10.1016/j.tranpol.2010.09.003

Li, M. Z. F., Lau, D. C. B., & Seah, D. W. M. (2011). Car ownership and Urban Transport Demand in Singapore. *Rivista Internazionale di Economia dei Trasporti*, *38*(1), 47–70.

Luo, X., Morimoto, A., Daimon, H., & Koike, H. (2007). A Study on Traffic Behaviour of High Income People in Asian Developing Countries. *Journal of the Eastern Asia Society for Transportation Studies*, *7*, 1222–1235.

Lupton, D. (2002). Road Rage: Drivers' Understandings and Experiences. *Journal of Sociology (Melbourne, Vic.)*, *38*(3), 275–290. doi:10.1177/144078302128756660

Mann, E., & Abraham, C. (2006). The Role of Affect in UK Commuters' Travel Mode Choices: An Interpretative Phenomenological Analysis. *British Journal of Psychology*, *97*(2), 155–176. doi:10.1348/000712605X61723 PMID:16613647

Morecroft, J. (2007). *Strategic Modelling and Business Dynamics. A Feedback Systems Approach*. Chichester, UK: John Wiley & Sons.

Outwater, M. L., Spitz, G., Lobb, J., Campbell, M., Sana, B., Pendyala, R., & Woodford, W. (2011). Characteristics of Premium Transit Services that Affect Mode Choice. *Transportation*, *38*(4), 605–623. doi:10.100711116-011-9334-0

Paulley, N., Balcombe, R., Mackett, R., Titheridge, H., Preston, J. M., Wardman, M. R., ... White, P. (2006). The demand for public transport: The effects of fares, quality of service, income and car ownership. *Transport Policy*, *13*(4), 295–306. doi:10.1016/j.tranpol.2005.12.004

Pruyt, E. (2016). Integrating Systems Modelling and Data Science: The Joint Future of Simulation and 'Big Data' Science. *International Journal of System Dynamics Applications*, *5*(1), 1–16. doi:10.4018/IJSDA.2016010101

Rose, S. J. (2016). *The Growing Size and Incomes of the Upper Middle Class*. Washington, DC: Urban Institute.

Saeed, K. (1994). *Development Planning and Policy Design*. Avebury.

Saeed, K. (2004). Designing an Environmental Mitigation Banking Institution for Linking the Size of Economic Activity to Environmental Capacity. *Journal of Economic Issues*, *38*(4), 909–937. doi:10.1080/00213624.2004.11506749

Santos, G., Li, W. W., & Koh, W. T. (2004). Transport Policies in Singapore. *Research in Transportation Economics*, *9*(1), 209–235. doi:10.1016/S0739-8859(04)09009-2

Spichkova, M., & Hamilton, M. (2016). Dynamic Decision Making System for Public Transport Routes. *International Journal of System Dynamics Applications*, *5*(3), 47–70. doi:10.4018/IJSDA.2016070103

Stardling, S. G., Meadows, M. L., & Beatty, S. (2000). Helping Drivers Out of Their Cars: Integrating Transport Policy and Social Psychology for Sustainable Change. *Transport Policy*, *7*(3), 207–215. doi:10.1016/S0967-070X(00)00026-3

Steg, L. (2005). Car Use: Lust and Must. Instrumental, Symbolic and Affective Motives for Car Use. *Transportation Research*, *39*(2), 147–162.

Steg, L., Vlek, C., & Slotegraaf, G. (2001). Instrumental-Reasoned and Symbolic-Affective Motives for using a Motor Car. *Transportation Research Part F: Traffic Psychology and Behaviour*, *4*(3), 151–169. doi:10.1016/S1369-8478(01)00020-1

Sterman, J. D. (2000). *Business Dynamics: Systems Thinking and Modelling for a Complex World*. New York: Irwin McGraw-Hill.

Thompson, W., & Hicky, J. (2005). *Society in Focus*. Boston: Pearson, Allyn & Bacon.

Wardman, M. (2004). Public Transport Values of Time. *Transport Policy*, *11*(4), 363–377. doi:10.1016/j.tranpol.2004.05.001

Warner, W. L., Meeker, M., & Eells, K. (1949). *Social Class in America: A Manual of Procedure for the Measurement of Social Status*. Chicago: Science Research Associates, Inc.

Weber, M. (1947). *The Theory of Social and Economic Organization*. New York: Oxford University Press.

Chapter 16
Enhancing Humanitarian Logistics and the Transportation of Relief Supplies:
Integrating System Dynamics and Vehicle Routing

Yesenia Cruz-Cantillo
University of Puerto Rico – Mayagüez, Puerto Rico

Carlos González-Oquendo
University of Puerto Rico – Mayagüez, Puerto Rico

ABSTRACT

This chapter describes a system dynamics model developed for forecasting, prioritization, and distribution of critical supplies during relief operations in case of a hurricane event, while integrating GIS information. Development of alternates' routes selection through vehicle routing procedures and the results incorporation into this system dynamics model allows decisions about the operation in case of a major catastrophe and any preparation for future events. The model developed is also able to (1) establish people's decision and transportation characteristics that determine evacuation time; (2) simulate the behavior of key variables due to the relation between hazard level and people's decision to evacuate; (3) estimate for each natural hazard level the time frequency to order and the order size of each relief supply to be needed in shelters and points of distribution; and (4) reveal which routes cause more delays during relief supplies distribution.

DOI: 10.4018/978-1-5225-4077-9.ch016

INTRODUCTION

Due to a wide variety of factors that influence emergency logistics, it becomes a challenge to optimize critical resource logistics and distribution during a hurricane event. Therefore, identifying, inventorying, dispatching, mobilizing, and transporting critical supplies throughout emergency relief operations are necessary to preserve life affected by these events.

System dynamics can account for the interrelations and dynamics of evacuated people, traffic flow, response time, inventory level, reorder points, transportation and supplies demand, among other elements. In addition, the creation of an information technology framework helping to collect data in real time about conditions of roads and supply levels in shelters and points of distribution during the event could effectively help improve the operations of the agencies in charge of emergency relief. This methodology allowed the integration of GIS information resulting from vehicle routing procedures run in TransCAD® that attempted to simulate the performance of relief supplies distribution.

The dynamic relief demands in affected areas and the immediate outcomes of humanitarian logistics aid intervention could in turn be used to decide how to adequately distribute necessary resources at their disposal. Which in turn will help to correct any mistakes in the dispatching to distribution centers and in turn to shelters and points of distribution. Development in hazardous areas and increase in a hurricane event are gradually more along with corresponding rises in traffic volumes. Therefore, traffic disruptions during critical commodities distribution in emergency relief, is an increasing problem, becoming costlier and more important to mitigate. The Dynamic Transportation and Humanitarian Logistics' Model (DTHL) considers the disaster implication in transportation for hurricanes (Cruz, 2013,2014). In addition, sensitivity analyses are illustrated to show how this integration took place and what were immediate results that contribute to the assessment of emergency relief operation in real time.

BACKGROUND

System Dynamics

The basis of system dynamics is to consider all "things" as a whole and comprehend how all the objects in the system interact with one another. The interactions between objects and people occurs through feedback loops, therefore, a change in one variable, influences other variables over time, and in turn impacts the original variable and so on (Forrester, 1961). System dynamics is interdisciplinary, and it is discussed in the theory of nonlinear dynamics and feedback control systems built on mathematics, physics, and engineering (Sterman, 2001). The understanding of the basic structure of a system, and the understanding of this behavior that it can generate is what system dynamics attempts to do (Azar, 2012).

System dynamics has been also employed in modelling distribution complex systems. Such is the case of modelling a newer healthcare supply network causal loop diagram where authors analyzed and predicted the growth pattern of a healthcare logistic network (Battini et al., 2013). The use of system dynamics can also be extended to mobile broadband market where authors modeled the dynamic behavior of wireless ecosystem (Thakker et al., 2013). And the dynamics of social care workforce could be comprehended through system dynamics through the identification of the key feedback loops and their use to analyze the adult social care system (Onggo, 2012). Other applications of system dynamics include: monitoring phases of new product development process (González et al., 2014), sustainable food security based on initiatives exclusive to the farmers (Oyo et al., 2016), and analyze daily calorie intake of the population in Ethiopia (Ayenew, 2015) among others.

System Dynamics and Humanitarian Logistics

Altay and Green (2006) observed that system dynamics, constraint programming, and soft operations research (OR) techniques were the practices less frequently used in the disaster operations management arena.

Gonçalves (2008), using system dynamics, provided an illustration of how managers in humanitarian relief organizations can model the behavior of complex systems.

Besiou et al. (2011) demonstrated the appropriateness of system dynamics to model the complexity of humanitarian logistics operations, including uncertainty, resource constraints, and interrelations of multiple factors, feedback loops, and time pressures.

System Dynamics and Resource Distribution

Ho et al. (2006) proposed seven (7) subsystems for urban disaster prevention. Transportation was identified as one of the most important subsystems because, during a disaster, the roads and railways are critical for delivery of emergency relief and supplies.

Ramezankhani and Najafiyazdi (2008) proposed a dynamic system aiming to simulate the activities in the zone after an earthquake that hit Southeastern Iran in 2003. Key parameters were selected with the purpose of setting up some post-disaster policies, which were then applied to the model and their effects were studied.

Cruz (2008) and Cruz et al. (2009) built a computer simulation model using system dynamics assisting in the decision-making process of the American Red Cross in resource allocation and measuring of client's satisfaction when a hurricane hits.

Logistics Modeling in Disaster Relief Operation

Balcik and Beamon (2008) developed a model that determines in the relief network locations and amount of the distribution centers and at each distribution center the number of relief commodities to be supplied.

A mixed integer dynamic programming model was developed by Wang, et al. (2008), for the single-commodity multi-mode transportation of emergency relief commodities.

Campbell et al. (2008) proved the potential impact of using new objective functions to reflect the relevant priorities in disaster relief using two alternative objective functions for traveling salesman problems and vehicle routing problems.

Zhu and Ji analyzed (2009) the subsystems that sustain emergency logistics which included provision for infrastructure, emergency transportation canal, network coordination, among others.

Afshar and Haghani (2009) developed a model that described the joined logistics operations in response to natural disasters. This is also the first model that described the special structure of FEMA's supply chain system.

Wohlgemuth et al. (2012) employed multi-stage mixed integer problem to evaluate the benefits of dynamic optimization anticipating varying travel and unknown orders in the emergency environment.

Bozorgi-Amiri et al. (2013) considered uncertainty to analyze disaster relief logistics and help in de decision making on resource allocation and facility location using multi-objective robust stochastic programming.

Voyer et al. (2015) aimed to understand systemic processes dynamics applied to humanitarian supply chain logistics and offered an operational approach to a short time horizon.

Victoria et al. (2015) found that a two-phase heuristic method based on multi-start iterated local search solved the cumulative capacitated vehicle routing problem with time-dependent demand in humanitarian logistics on small instances.

Camacho et al. (2015) optimized decisions associated with international aid distribution after a catastrophic disaster, employing a bi-level mathematical programming model for humanitarian logistics.

Duhamel et al. (2016) solved a multi-period location-allocation problem in post-disaster operations considering the impact of distribution in the population through a mathematical model and heuristics.

Puerto Rico Humanitarian Logistics During Emergencies

Puerto Rico Emergency Management Agency (PREMA) has commodities in its distribution centers to be spread to shelters and points of distribution (PODs) for the first 24 or 48 hours; with the scope of meeting needs those affected people in case of a national emergency. One of the organizational units of the Puerto Rico Department of Education (PRDOE) is the School Food Authority. Once the governor signs for an emergency declaration, the school authority has a responsibility to offer food service to refuges in shelters. Therefore, since the second day through last day the state of emergency remains, the school food authority oversees the feeding of affected people in shelters. Puerto Rico Department of Housing (PRDOH) oversees mass care, that is, in charge of managing five (5) shelters and two (2) PODs. PRDOE oversees feeding people in shelters (Ayala, 2006). DTHL model depicts the dynamics of humanitarian logistics operations for major emergency management agency PREMA, PRDOE and PRDOH in response to immediate aftermath of a hurricane event.

Emergency Management Operations Using TransCAD

TransCAD is a Geographic Information System (GIS) designed to store, display, manage, and analyze transportation data. It joins GIS and transportation modeling capabilities in a single integrated platform. It can be employed for all modes of transportation, at any scale or level of detail (Caliper Corporation, 2010).

Modali (2005) employed a gravity model for hurricane evacuation trip distribution using a look-up table of discrete friction factors calibrated using TransCAD.

TransCAD has been used to compare link flows of evacuation traffic using static traffic assignment with those acquired from dynamic traffic assignment and detected traffic counts (Andem, 2006).

A study using TransCAD revealed how the adapted inputs and existed portions of the four-step transportation planning model can be employed in place of the usual data demands of the software (Andrews, 2009).

TransCAD has been also used to improve the sequential logistics hurricane evacuation trip generation model (Cheng, 2010).

DTHL MODEL DEVELOPMENT

The DTHL Model incorporates different elements of the humanitarian supply chain system that interact with other factors to impact transportation and logistics decisions during extreme and/or unanticipated natural events. This section describes the chronological steps followed to develop the model.

Problem Articulation (Boundary Selection)

The model concentrates on a problem: Successful distribution of critical resources in emergency relief. Therefore, it is not attempting to model the whole complexity of the emergency-management system. The scope of this model is enclosed in the disaster relief operation system, specifically, in the transportation and the humanitarian logistics subsystems. The model will consider hurricane disaster events only and is specific for PREMA, PRDOE and PRDOH.

Conceptual Model

The conceptual model captures the essential concepts of the humanitarian logistics, transportation functions and requirements, and emergency relief operations in the figure of an information model. It is expressed as a composite structure diagram embracing the interactions point of the elements of each part of the system (Figure 1).

Formulation of Dynamic Hypotheses

Dynamic hypotheses were formulated to explain the reference mode behavior and should be consistent with the model's purpose. The three dynamic hypotheses for this research are:

Figure 1. The conceptual model: Dynamic Transportation and Humanitarian Logistics' (DTHL) model

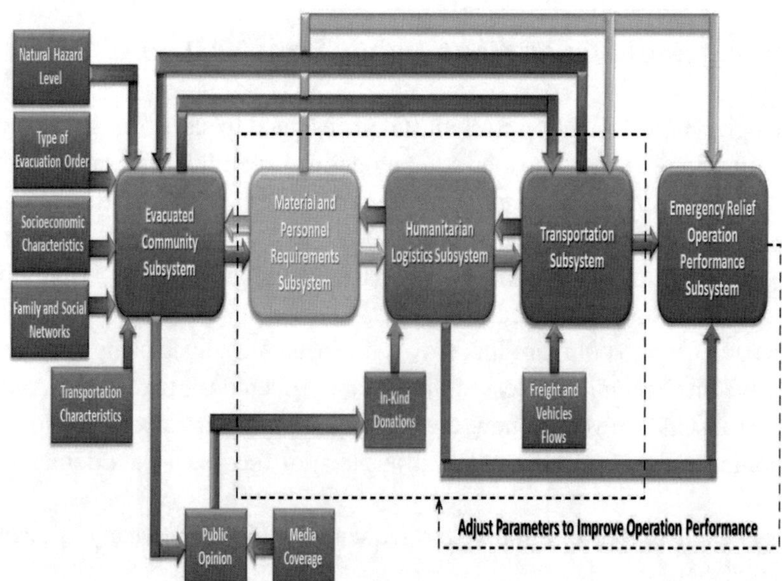

- **Hypothesis One:** The disposition for evacuation for affected communities in case of a hurricane event depends on natural hazard level, type of evacuation order, socioeconomic characteristics, family and social networks and travel characteristics. A sudden increment in the number of people that evacuate will produce larger numbers of vehicles in the road network and in turn get a poorer Level of Service. However, although traffic congestion affects driver satisfaction and influences his or her concern about road conditions, there will not be a significant reduction in people deciding to evacuate. That is, because people -in case of emergencies- usually try to reach a safe place.
- **Hypothesis Two:** The number of in-kind donations made by non-affected communities interferes with the efficient and reliable serving of critical supplies flow in the disaster site. An increasing in the in-kind donations flows will cause the number of volunteers of PRDOH allocated to deliver and serve critical supplies during first 24 hours (distributed by PREMA) to evacuees to be insufficient. That is, the greater the number of in-kind donations the greater the number of volunteers needed to deliver these donations, which in turn, will produce a delay in the 24 hours' critical commodities served at the shelters and points of distribution.
- **Hypothesis Three:** The use of alternate routes for the transport of critical commodities in case of an emergency, provide additional capacity to service primary route traffic for non-recurring congestion, specifically, the impact of a hurricane. The choosing of an alternate route and the incorporation in a vehicle routing procedure will affect the response time of the vehicles transporting critical supplies to shelters and point of distributions, minimizing or incrementing delays in the distribution of these commodities.

Therefore, model scenarios were created to illustrate the above hypotheses. Scenarios analysis would allow the analysis for accurate, efficient and reliable resource allocation and distribution, while considering the driver satisfaction, congestion roads, alternate routes, vehicle routing for optimal delivery and delivery priorities of the commodities during a hurricane disaster.

Mapping System Structure

Figures 2 through 4 exhibit a causal loop diagram of the system showing all possible set of causal relationships within this model. This diagram is fragmented in 4 parts with 22 nodes representing the joints between each one of them. *Positive Loops are self-reinforcing: they tend to reinforce or amplify whatever is happening in the system* (Sterman, 2000). As an example, the reinforcing loop R21 is a representation of how performance measures are useful to determine the need for alternate routes to minimize delays in delivery of critical supplies over time. The greater the number of critical supplies inventory in the shelter the greater the critical supplies served inside it. Therefore, the percentage of meals delivered in the shelter increases showing upright performance for delivery from both PREMA and PRDOE. This lead to a decrease in the need for the establishment of alternate routes to obtain optimal delivery of the critical supplies to shelters and PODs, and is an indicator that delivery delays are minimum.

The shorter the delays for delivery the greater the number of critical commodities arriving at the shelters and PODs. The greater the amount of arriving of supplies the greater the inventory in the shelters. Loop R22, is a representation of how the concern about the road conditions influence people that leave the disaster site. The greater the number of people leaving the disaster site the more the flow rate of vehicles on roads. Therefore, vehicles on the road in affected area increase, and in turn, the flow of

Figure 2. Causal-loop diagram: DTHL model-part 1

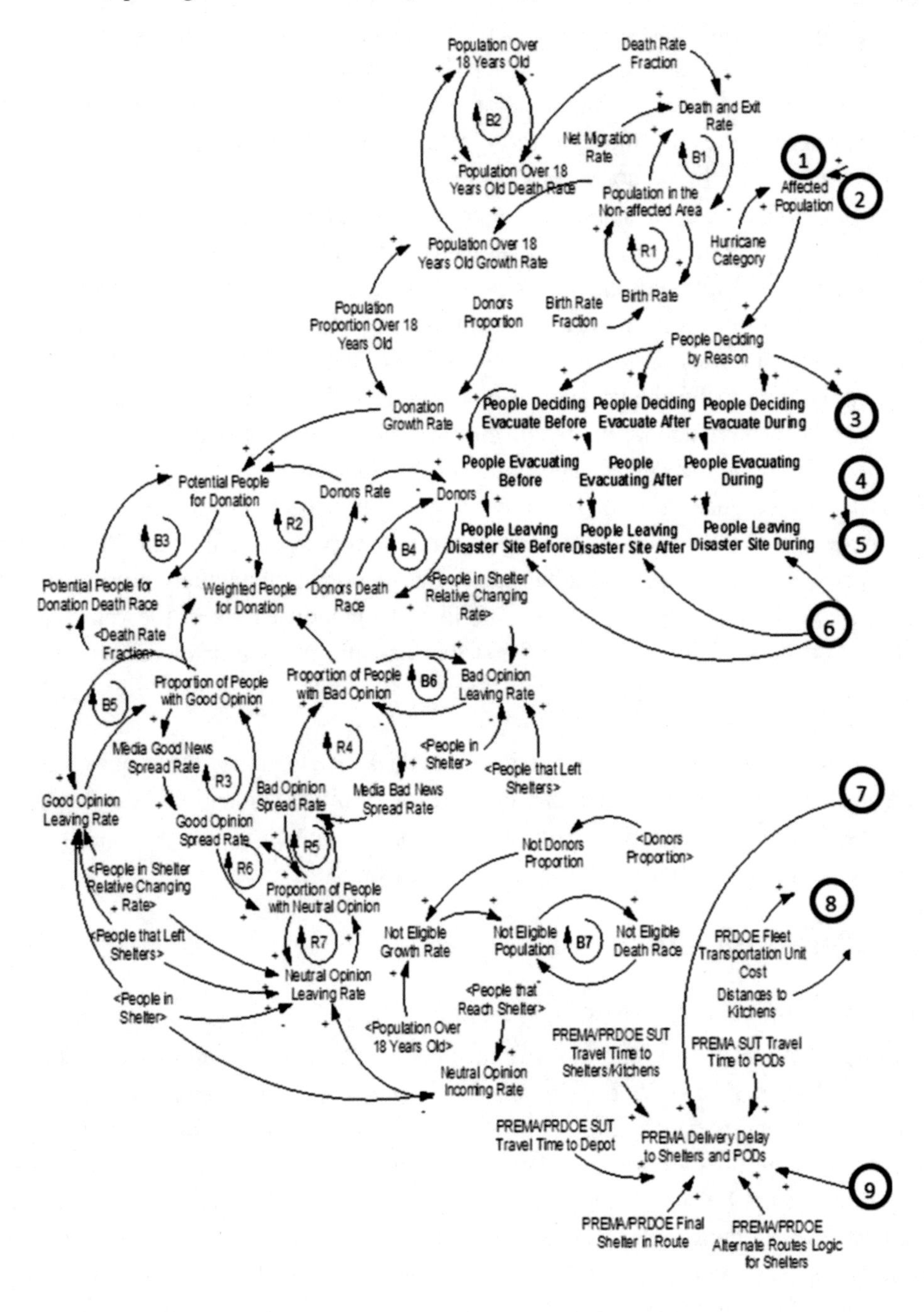

vehicles in the process of evacuation also increases. The higher flow of vehicles used in evacuation implies that the road capacity decreases and in turn, the level of service (LOS) gets worse. Traffic congestion increases because of lowering LOS and increasing volume to capacity ratio. Then, the greater the congestion perceived the greater the input rate of change in driver satisfaction. In turn, the driver satisfaction decreases. The above leads to more people with concern about road conditions and in turn, more people leave the disaster site.

Figure 3. Causal-loop diagram: DTHL model-part 2

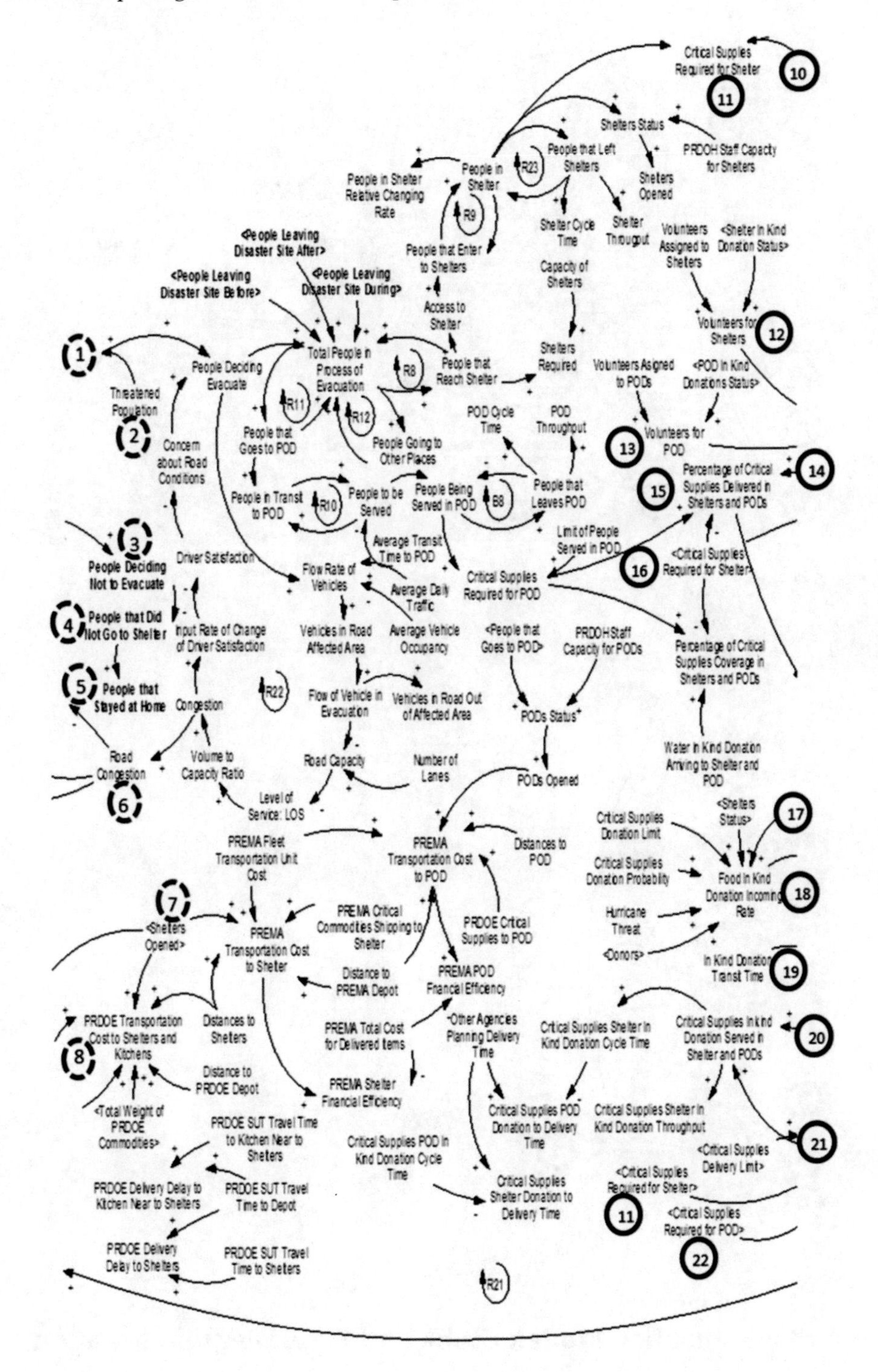

Figure 4. Causal-loop diagram: DTHL model-part 3

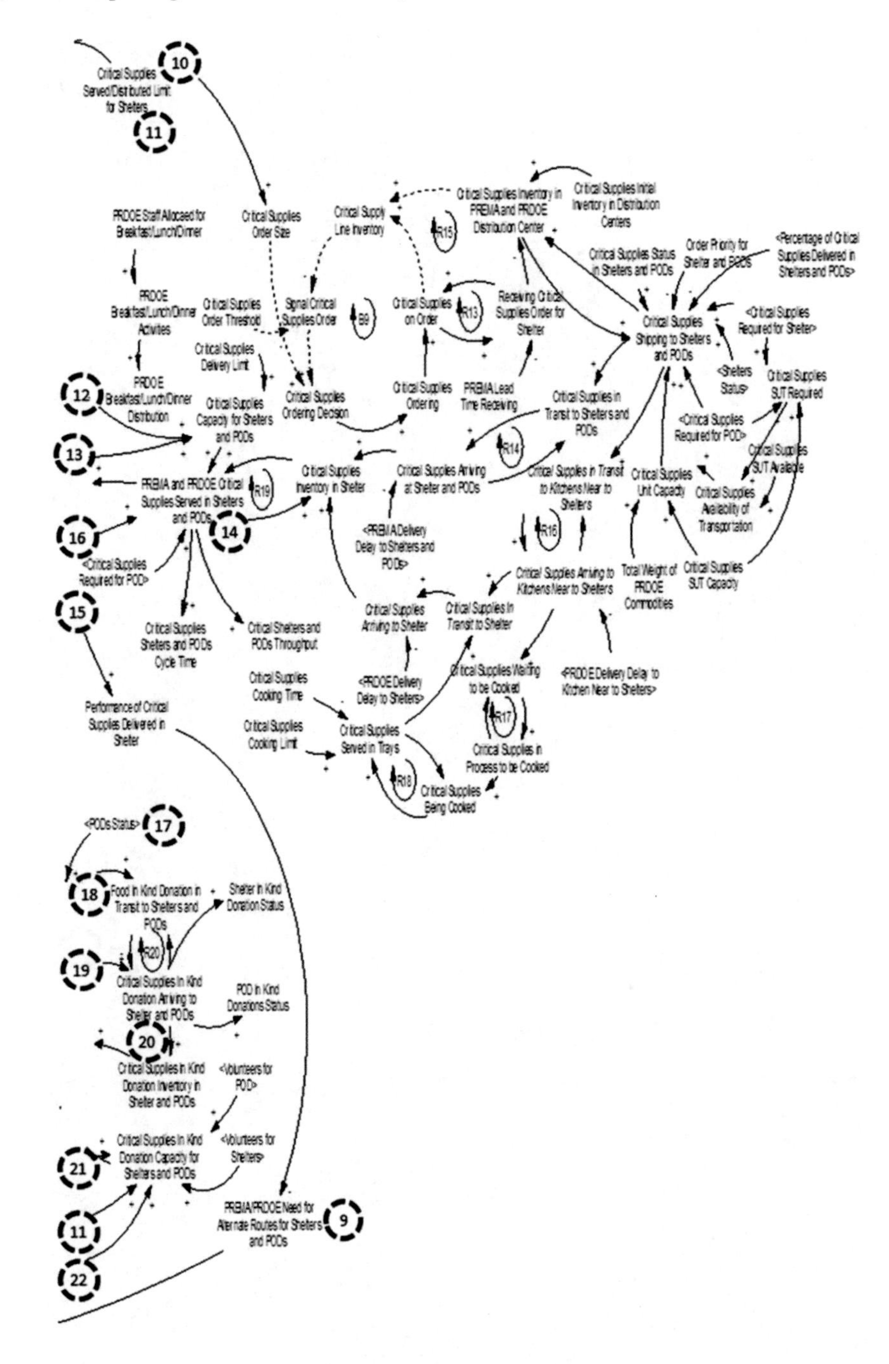

Formulation of a Simulation Model: Stock and Flow Diagram Notation

Causal loop diagram was converted into a simulation model with equations, parameters and initial conditions that were represented as a stock and flow structure. Formulation and modeling were made using Stella®. In appendix is detailed the most important equations of each subsystem of the model.

Evacuated Community Subsystem

When people go to a POD, the number of people attended, that is the number of people that picked up critical commodities depends on the number of volunteers in the facility, and the number of people each volunteer can serve in a period. This process reflects the proper characteristics of emergency procedures for the PREMA logistics (Figure 5).

Material and Personnel Requirements for Relief Subsystem

This sector frame has stocks, flows and converters that specify the opening, capacity and status of shelters and points of distribution, staff and volunteers that PREMA, PRDOH and PRDOE should deploy to the disaster site to meet the people's needs over time (Figure 6).

Transportation Subsystem

This sector frame shows the stocks, flows and converters displaying how level of service of the road influences driver satisfaction and in turn the people decisions will take concerning evacuation. This sector embraces distance and travel time variables imported from outputs of TransCAD. Therefore, it is possible to calculate transportation costs and delivery delays for PREMA and PRDOE over time (Figure 7).

Figure 5. Evacuated community subsystem

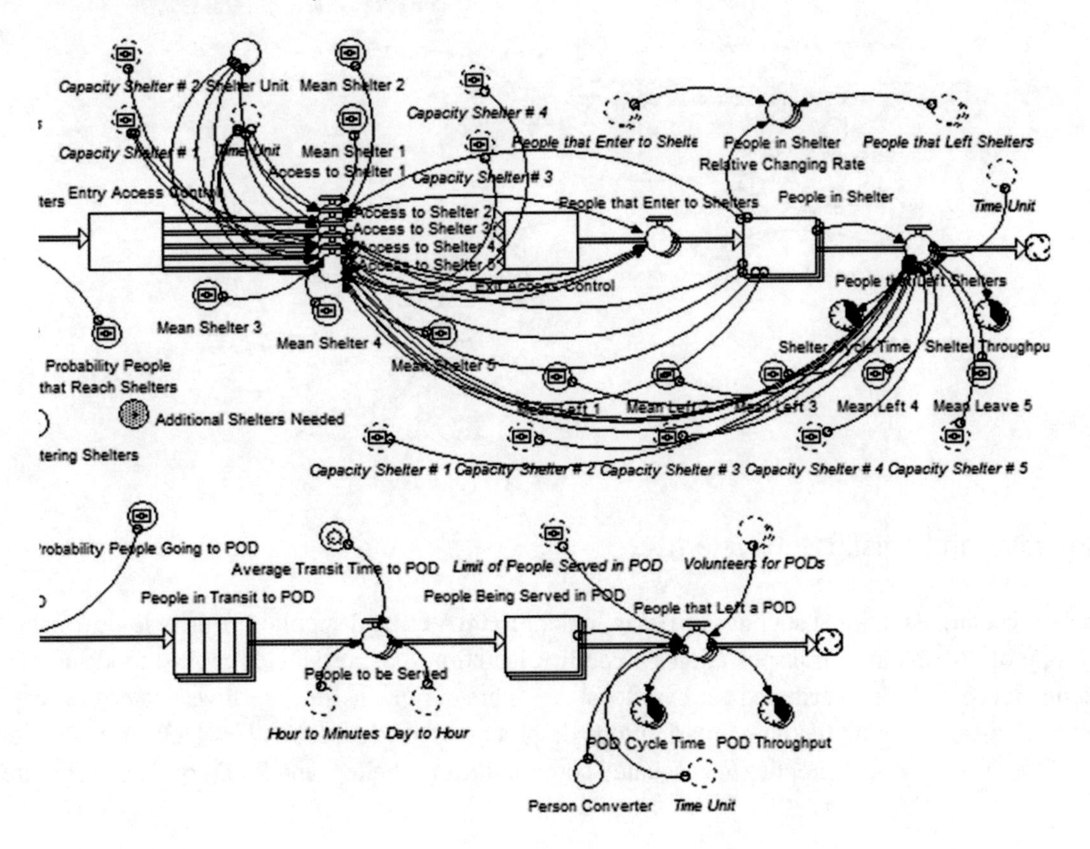

Figure 6. Material and personnel requirements for relief subsystem

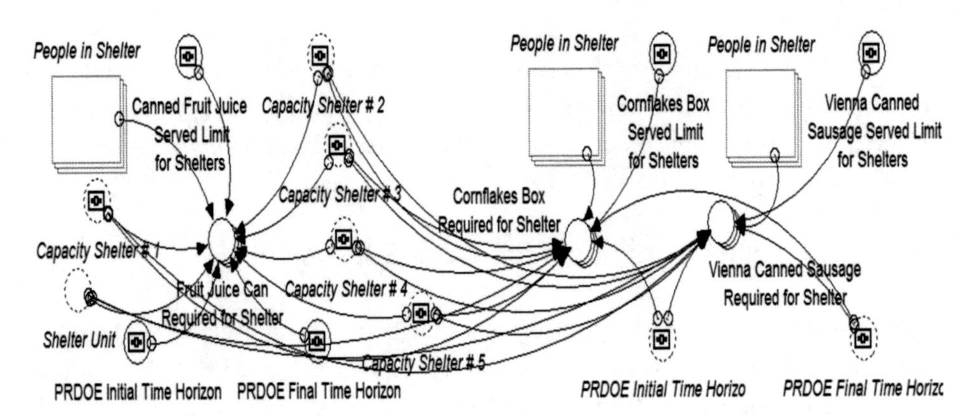

Figure 7. Transportation subsystem

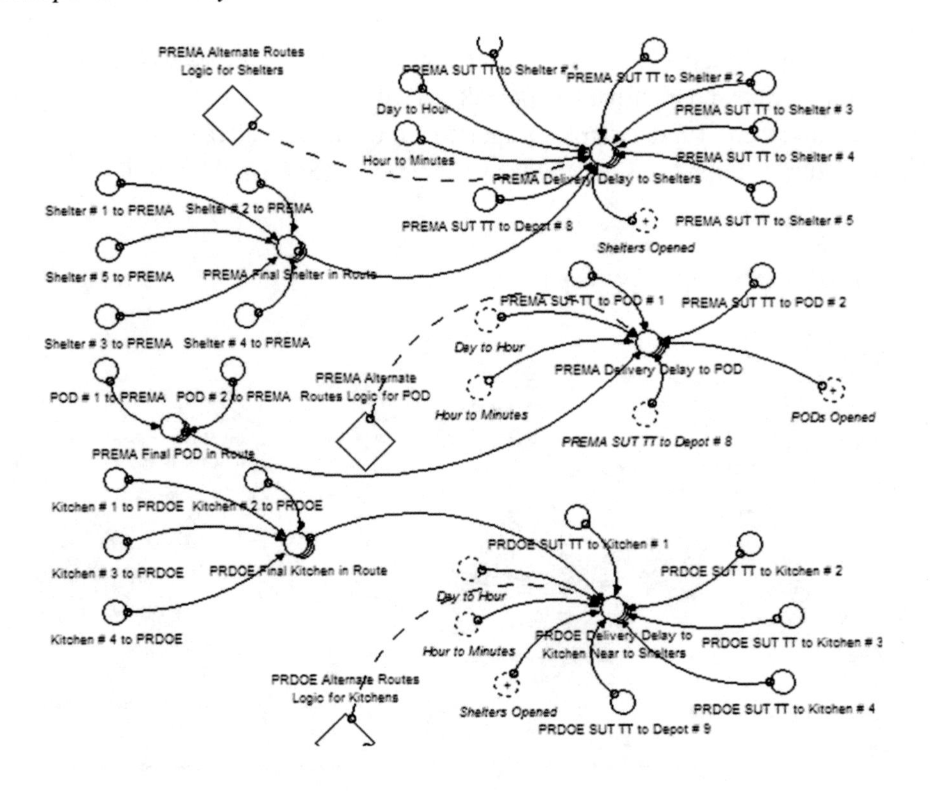

Humanitarian Logistic Subsystem

Level of inventories, critical supplies ordering logic, PREMA critical supplies priority logic for shelters and point of distributions, transportation availability, lead times, processing of cooked food and in kind donations received and distributed per evacuees' needs are defined as stocks, flows and converters. All these variables constitute the humanitarian logistic process that PREMA and PRDOE needs to define optimal deliver of critical supplies to evacuated communities in shelters and PODs over time (Figure 8).

Figure 8. Humanitarian logistics subsystem

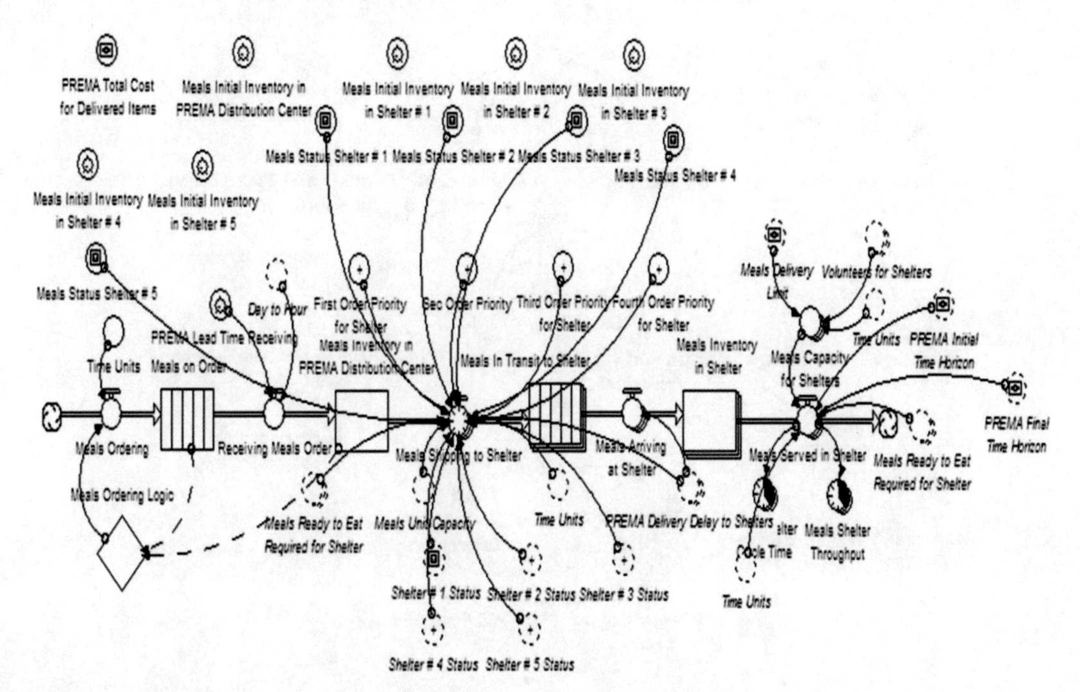

Emergency Relief Operation Performance Subsystem

This sector frame of the model is representing index calculation in form of converters. This performance measure will help PREMA and PRDOE get a sense of how well they are achieving their goals for the emergency relief operations and in turn, made the necessary corrections to improve it (Figure 9).

External Factors Stock and Flow Structure

Converters that describe socioeconomic characteristics, travel characteristics, level of natural hazard and family and social networks of the evacuated people are detailed in this sector frame. The variables that compose the socio-economics and demographics used as key variables to determine the disposition of people to evacuate or not were taken from a previous study (Cruz, 2008) (Cruz et al., 2009) (Figure 10).

System Dynamics and GIS Integration

DTHL model was built, incorporating the operational reports of Hurricane George, census data, FEMA and public databases, media and newspapers to parameterize the model. The model was built around five subsystems and could forecast critical commodities for allocation purposes, as well as to prioritize delivery of critical supplies during emergency relief operations. Levels of inventories, the time frequency for ordering and critical supplies order sizes can also be determined. Considering all the above restrictions of staff; the model was developed to solve a dynamic large scale multi-commodity and dynamic delivery vehicle routing problem with time windows contained in a time-space network of PREMA and PRDOE.

Figure 9. Emergency relief operation performance subsystem

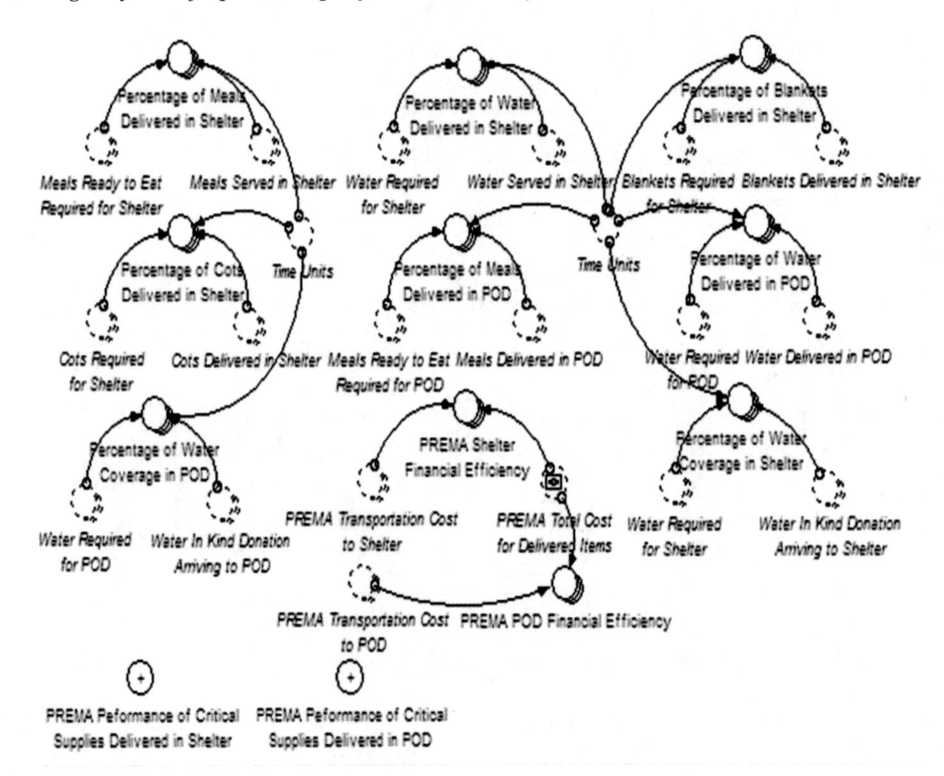

Figure 10. External factors stock and flow structure

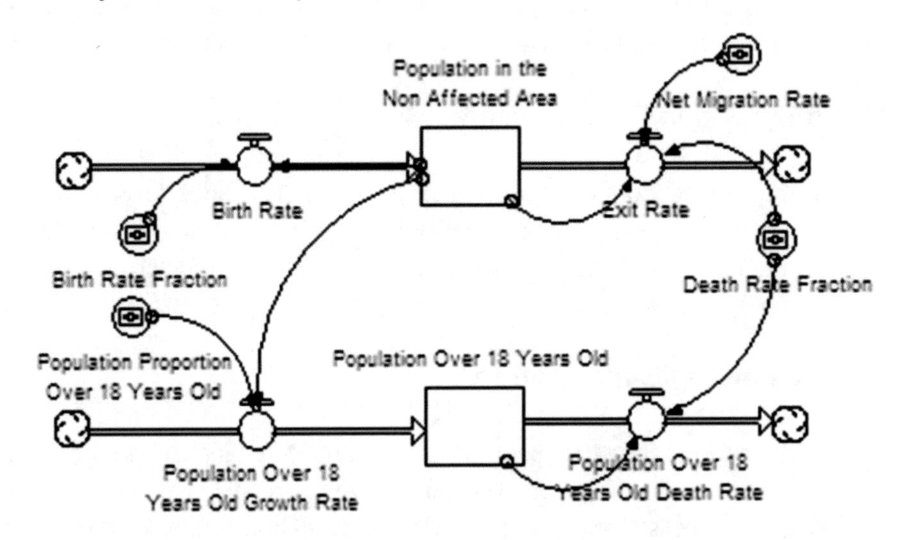

Once the Stella model was developed it was linked dynamically to Microsoft Excel® through variables related with distance and travel time.

Information about flood areas in western Puerto Rico was obtained from FEMA flood maps. In addition, Google Earth® was used to obtained information about location of PREMA and PRDOE distribution centers; facilities used as preventive shelters, kitchens and PODs. Distribution centers and facilities locations were marked in Google Earth. Afterward, using Imagery Toolbox from TransCAD, Google locations and images were added to TransCAD maps. Then the above information was utilized to create scenarios of flooded road networks and to delineate preliminary alternate routes, using TransCAD.

Field visual inspection was made with the aim to corroborate information obtained from TransCAD about paths between a set of origins and destinations. Distribution centers and facilities location, were also visited to verify the initial location obtained in Google Earth maps. As result of these inspections and verifications of distribution centers and facilities location, network adjustments were made during the field inspection. New routes were delineated and final alternate routes were defined.

TransCAD maps were created using several locations and networks as layers. Then vehicle routing process were run and vehicle routing matrices of distances and travel times were obtained, as well as optimal routes systems and vehicle routing itineraries to deliver critical supplies distribution during emergency relief operations. Those results and the vehicle routing itinerary were exported to Microsoft Excel.

Stella variables linked in Excel were combined to TransCAD results. Hence, simulation was run and results from outputs of simulation were used to feed TransCAD vehicle routing process (Figure 11).

Methodological Framework for Real Time Data Collection

The methodological framework adopts three modules: real time data collection, system structural diagram of information feeding and system dynamics, and GIS. The interactions of these modules will help to gather relevant real-time information for the emergency relief operation during the hurricane event, distribute this information and use it to forecast and prioritize the delivery of critical supplies from distribution centers to facilities used as shelters, kitchens and PODs (Figure 12).

Figure 11. Flowchart of interactions between System Dynamics and GIS

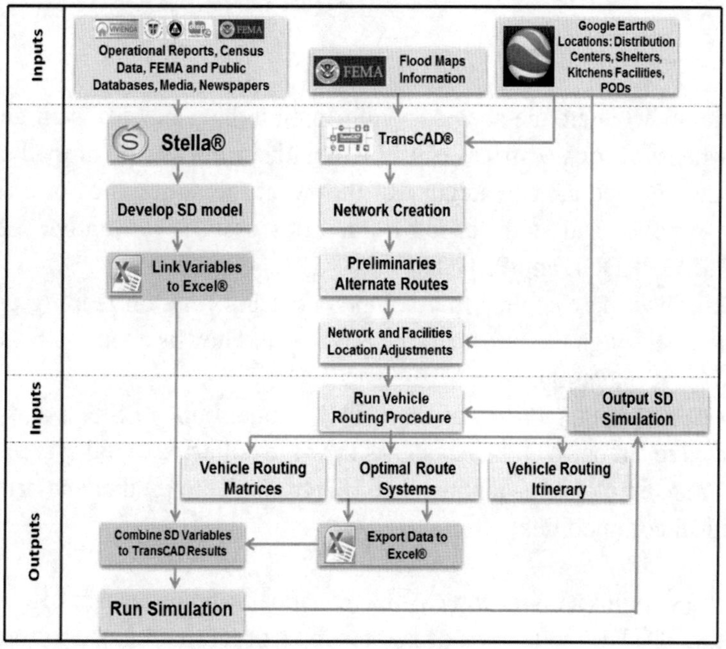

Figure 12. Information technology methodological framework flowchart

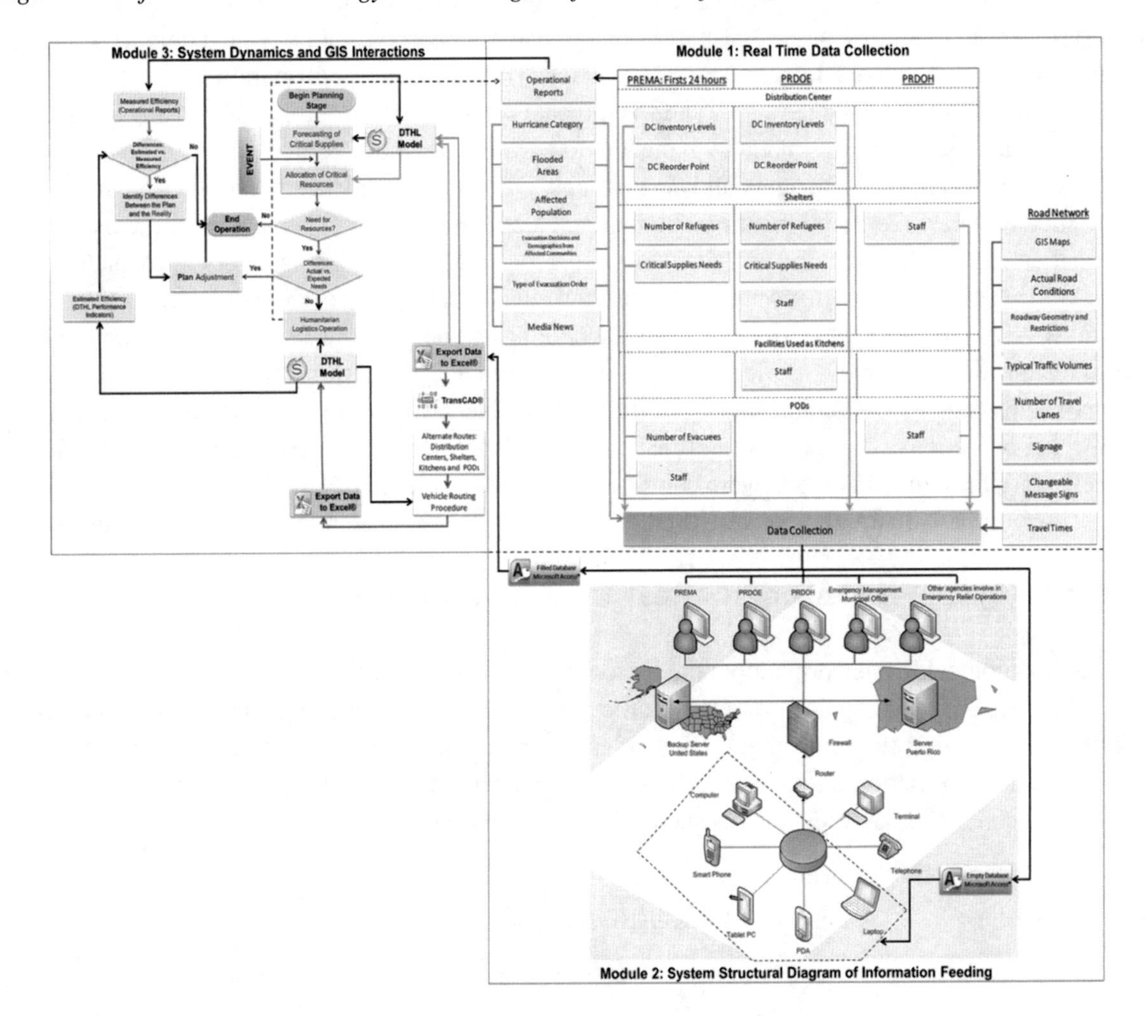

- **Module 1:** Exhibits what are the necessary information that agencies' staff need to collect in real time. That is, when a hurricane strikes is useful to gather information of road network; geographic conditions of the affected areas; category of the event; demographics of affected communities, media; critical supplies and staff needed in facilities used as preventive shelters, kitchens and PODs for PREMA, PRDOE and PRDOH.
- **Module 2:** Describes the elements that compose the information feeding process, that is, how information travels through the information network, and how is acquired by agencies involved in the emergency relief operation.
- **Module 3:** Depicts the interactions of the DTHL model built in Stella and the vehicle routing process generated in TransCAD; it also shows how the collected and disseminated information in modules 1 and 2 are employed as inputs to the DTHL model to predict and prioritize over time the delivery of critical commodities.

The planning process begins with the forecasting of critical supplies in case of a hurricane event. This planning made with the DTHL model, is a decision support tool that helped to forecast the amount of resources needed prior the events occurs (Module 3). This prediction can be made gathering information about hurricane category, flooded areas, affected population, demographic characteristics of affected communities, type of evacuation order and media news (Module 1). Knowing this information in advance, will help PREMA, PRDOE and PRDOH to know the amount of material and personnel resources needed to be prepositioned before the emergency relief process begins. In addition, initial inventories and order sizes from PREMA and PRDOE distribution centers can be also established, needed to have in stock in case a hurricane strike and the western area were affected.

Once the emergency is declared, allocation of critical resources (personnel and supplies) are made (Module 3).

Critical resources needed for the affected communities are established with the continuous monitoring of the number of refugees, critical supplies needs, number of evacuees and staff for PREMA; number of refugees, critical supplies need and staff for PRDOE; and staff for PRDOH. This information is usually collected as part of the agencies' operational reports (Module 1).

If there are no needs in the shelters and PODs to be met, then the humanitarian logistics operation is cancel. If needs for supplies are identified in shelters and PODs, then they proceed to detect whether there are or not differences between actual and expected needs. Expected needs are obtained with the planning tool: DTHL Model (Module 3).

If there are differences between actual and expected needs, then it is required to make adjustment to the original planning process. Therefore, it is necessary to change input parameters for Stella® Model, and run a simulation with new inputs. If no differences are identified then continue with the humanitarian logistic operation and deliver supplies and personnel, allocated previously, to shelters, facilities identified as kitchens and PODs. For each delivery, it becomes a priority, to find optimal alternate routes to minimize travel time (Module 3).

To respond dynamically to the delivery of critical supplies it is necessary to determinate alternate routes in case that the Puerto Rico Highway # 2 (known as PR-2) - which is the main route to communicate the western area of the island -, presents flooding in some segments. Having this purpose in mind, with this framework it will be possible to gather information related with actual road conditions, roadway geometry and restrictions, typical traffic volumes, number of travel lanes, signage, availability of changeable message signs, and travel time among others. This information, will depict a real-time panorama of the road network, which is going to be used to deliver the critical supplies (Module 1).

The above information is translated into a GIS Map using TransCAD, to create the new network with the real conditions at that precise moment. Using the network created, the locations of the facilities using as preventive shelters, kitchens and PODs, then the vehicle routing process is run. The vehicle routing process will provide an estimate of the vehicles' schedule for deliver, optimal routes, service times, travel times, distance, load, among other key information that will help to minimize deliver of commodities during relief operations (Module 3).

Data generated from the vehicle routing process can be exported to an Excel file and imported to the DTHL model. Variables related with travel time and distances are used as inputs for the system dynamics model. DTHL model helped to understand how the dynamic relationships between external factors, evacuation decisions and demographics from affected communities, resources requested, transportation measures and humanitarian logistics process interact with the variables of the vehicle routing process output. This affect the delivery of supplies to needed people over time and the dispatch priority in case of mixing products; and in turn, how this delay influences the efficiency of the total performance operation (Module 3).

Agencies involve in emergency relief, produce operational reports from the operation in course. These operational reports serve as new inputs collected in real time data collection framework, which will be used again to feed dynamically the DTHL model (Module 1). Operational reports can also be used as a source to measures the efficiency of the current operation.

The performance execution of the agencies involved in the humanitarian logistic process can be measures through three indicators: appeal coverage (percent of appeal coverage and percent of items delivered), donation-to-delivery time and financial efficiency.

DTHL model provides humanitarian logistical performance indicators that can also be used as estimated measures of the planned operation performance (Module 3). Using information for the real-time data collection framework allow us to determine these humanitarian logistics indicators for the real operation (Module 1). Both the estimated and the measured indicators can be compared and emergency managers to improve the knowledge of the entire emergency relief operation. When there are differences between the estimated and the measured indicators, managers must identify what are the differences between the plan and reality, which in turn, lead to the plan adjustment of the relief operation. If there are no differences between the two-humanitarian logistics efficiency performance measures, then the process ends (Module 3).

Vehicle routing process will be also enriched its results from run simulation of DTHL model and are used to predict new loads of critical commodities to be delivered to satisfy evacuees immediate needs. For that, results from Stella software, related to the predicted number of critical supplies needed in shelters, can be used as inputs in TransCAD software of loads of commodities to be delivered from distribution centers to shelters or kitchens or PODs. That can be achieved introducing Stella results in stop dataview of TransCAD, and with this information, run the vehicle routing process again (Module 3).

To make this process possible, all the information could be collected in real time using smart phones, tablets PC, personnel digital assistant (PDA) and laptops. IQ Mobile Tablet™ Mobile Software from RF Industries Inc., is an example of the newest option in the market, which provides a mobile software interface to public safety and private Computer Aided Dispatch (CAD) systems via RadioMobile's IQ Mobile Server. It also interfaces with applications such as CAD, mapping, among others via a tablet application. Those applications can be configured to operational needs (RF Industries, Inc., 2013).

The information is entered at Microsoft Access® database file, created previously. In case any none of these devices were available, agency staff can collect the information in paper forms, and then back in the agencies' offices, use computer and/or terminals to input the data into the Access database (Module 2).

All the gathered information is transmitted through the internet. If the internet services are down due to an electrical failure, damages caused by the event strike or any kind of problems with the electrical system; a telephone line for transmitting information promptly and for communication between agencies must be available (Module 2).

A router is used to connect to the internet and make the transmission possible. The firewall acts as a protection to the information network, preventing the attack of intruders. Then, the information is transmitted through internet mainly to a central server. Central served can be in Puerto Rico with one or several support servers in any location in the United States and its territories (Module 2).

Information transmitted is downloaded, processed and analyzed by managers of the agencies involve in the emergency relief operation. As servers are supported by each other, agencies can download the information directly from the servers where they are connected (Module 2). The information in Access database is exported to an Excel file, which will have several purposes through the modeling process of the operation (Module 3).

Policy Design and Results

To improve the dynamics of the model, testing alternatives and new decision policies were designed to help to generate the observable patterns of behavior for the system. DTHL model interface allowed the creation of several "what if" scenarios, which were significant to policy making.

Scenario 1: What If the Probability of People Evacuating Increased to 10%, 27.5%, 45%, 62.5% or 80%?

The simulation delivers what the Hypothesis 1 states, that is, the number of people evacuating increases even though people were concerned about the road conditions. Figures 13, 14 and 15 display the outputs of the simulation run for scenario 1. Line 1, represents the behavior of the variable with parameters established for initial conditions. Line 2, represents the behavior of the variable increased 10%; Line 3, shows the increased variable 32.5%; Line 4, displays the variable raised 55%; Line 5, presents the variable increased 77.5%; and Line 6, exhibits the variable raised 100%.

- **Probability increased to 10%:** in this case LOS is C and D (Figure 14) the first day and D and F during the second day, driver satisfaction is less than 38.36% (Figure 15), which implies that more people are concerned with the conditions of the roads. From Figure 13, it is easily perceived that the more the concern for the conditions of the roads the more people leaving the threatened area, and in turn the greater the increase in the flow of vehicles during evacuation. This proves the hypothesis that, although road conditions could be congested or damaged, people try to move to a safe place in case of a hurricane event.

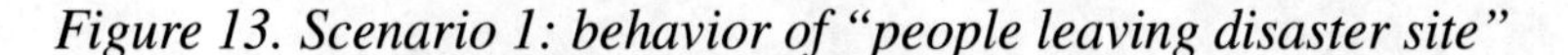

Figure 13. Scenario 1: behavior of "people leaving disaster site"

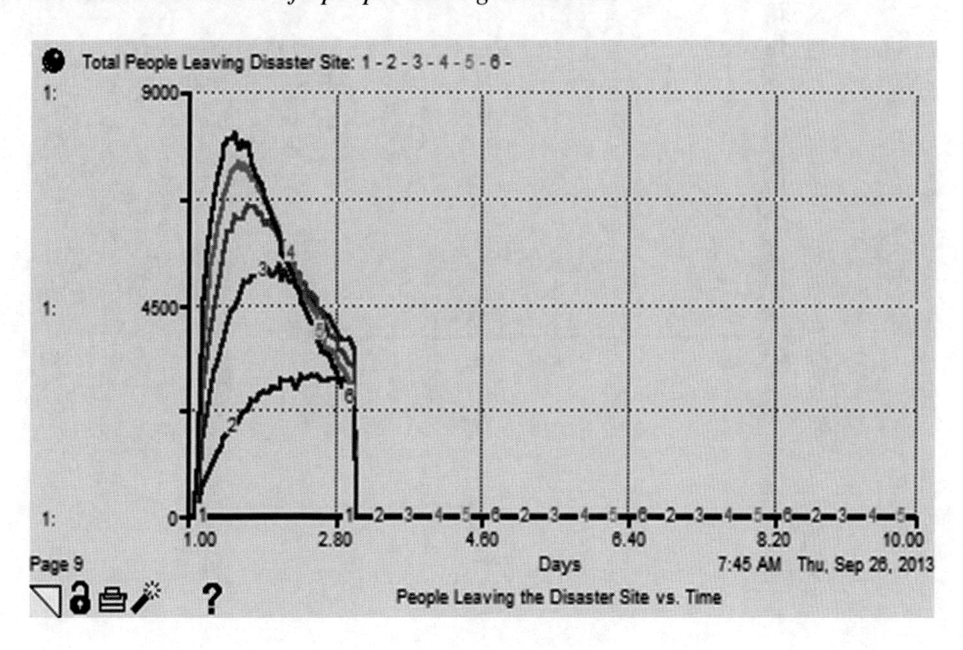

Figure 14. Scenario 1: behavior of "level of service"
Y-axis is representing level of service, being 1=A, 2=B, 3=C, 4=D and 5 or more=F.

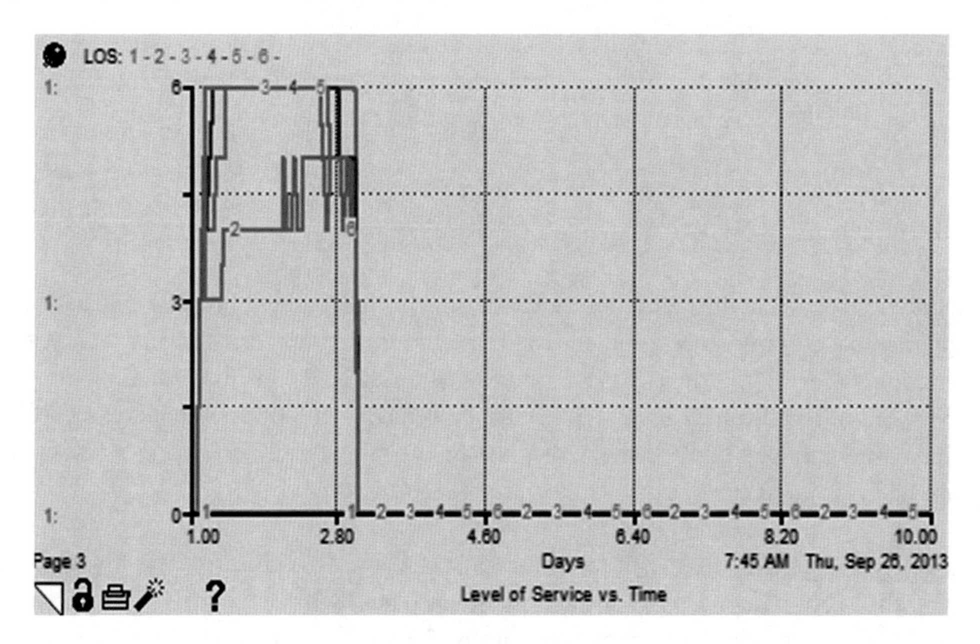

Figure 15. Scenario 1: behavior of "driver satisfaction"

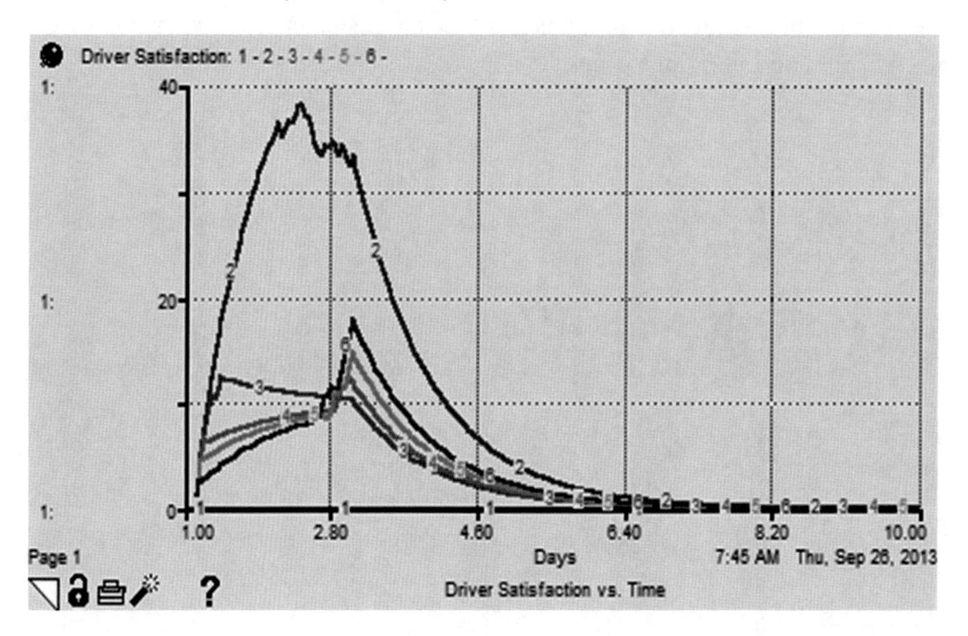

- **Probability increased to 80%:** in this case LOS is F was estimated for the first two days (Figure 12), driver satisfaction is less than 18.09% (Figure 15).

Scenario 2: What If the In-Kind Donations Rate Increase to 10%, 32.5%, 55%, 77.5% or 100%?

The simulation produces what the Hypothesis 2 states, that is, the number of critical commodities served to people in shelter decreases when the in-kind donation increase and more volunteers are needed to unload and distribute them.

Figures 16 and 17, displays the example of outputs of the simulation run for scenario 2. Line 1, represents the behavior of the variable with the parameters established in the initial conditions. Line 2, represents the behavior of the variable increased by 10%; Line 3, shows the increased variable to 32.5%; Line 4, displays the variable raised to a 55%; Line 5, presents the variable increased to 77.5%; and Line 6, exhibits the variable raised to 100%.

- **In-kind donations rate increased to 10%:** in this case, the greater the donations of bottles of water, the greater the number of volunteers needed to unload trucks and deliver donations to needed people in the shelters and PODs (Figure 16). Then, it can be appreciated that the number of bottles of water served in Recreation and Sports Palace decrease when in-kind donations increase (Figures 17). This proves the hypothesis that arrivals of in-kind donations reduce the number of critical commodities delivered to shelters and PODs. In this scenario, in-kind donations arrive to shelter in the afternoon of first day.

Figure 16. Scenario 2: behavior of "water in-kind donation arriving to recreation and sports palace"

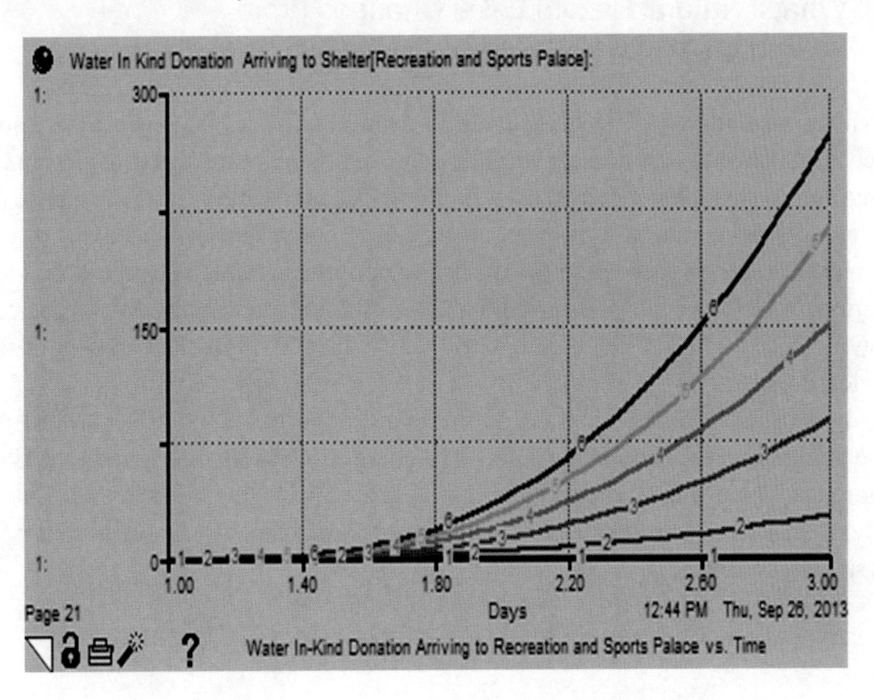

Figure 17. Scenario 2: Behavior of "Water Served in Recreation and Sports Palace"

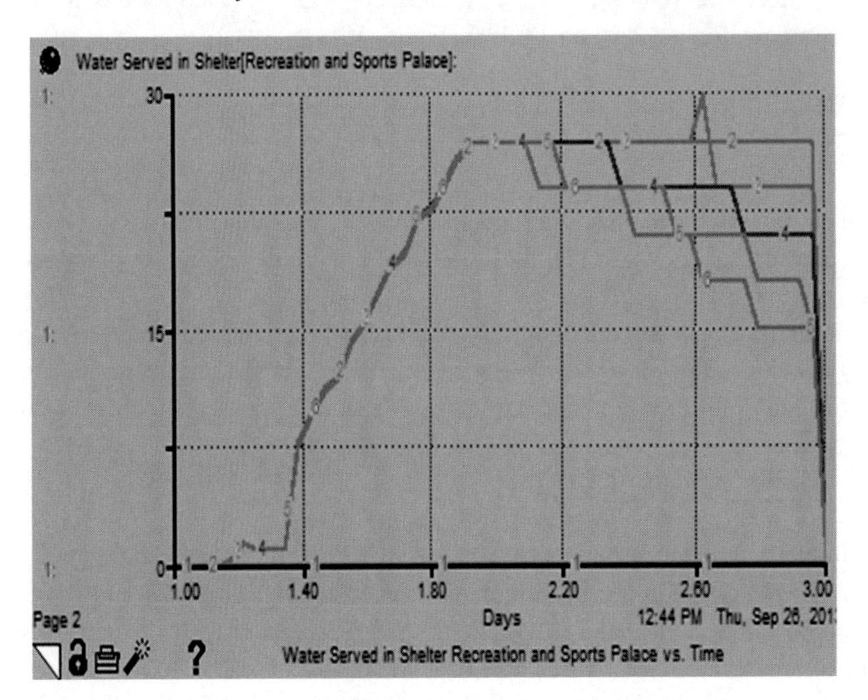

- **In-kind donations rate increased to 100%:** In this scenario, in-kind donations arrived at the shelter at the beginning of day one. The number of bottles of water served went from a range of 15 to 21 bottles per hour to a range of 15 to 18 bottles per hour.

Scenario 3: What If Natural Hazard Level Changes From Tropical Storm to Hurricane Category 1, 2, 3, 4 and 5?

In case the whole population of Mayaguez (92,996 people) will be threatened by a tropical storm or different levels of hurricanes, the number of people leaving the disaster site considering their economics and demographics characteristics is shown in Figure 18 and Tables 1 and 2. Line 1, represents the behavior of the variable in case of a tropical storm. Line 2, represents the behavior of the variable in case of a hurricane category 1. Line 3, shows the behavior of the variable in case of a hurricane category 2. Line 4, displays the behavior of the variable in case of a hurricane category 3. Line 5, presents the variable behavior in case of a hurricane category 4, and Line 6 exhibits the behavior of the variable in case of a hurricane category 5.

Analyzing by level of hazard, it is worth noting that Category 3 could affect 40,081 people, which 12,997 people could leave the disaster site and 4,419 could reach shelters. Therefore, a Category 3 hurricane will produce higher numbers of people that decide to leave the disaster site. That is consistent with the study of Land sea which states that a category 3 hurricane possesses a higher percentage of damage in case of occurrence.

Figure 18. Scenario 3: behavior of "people leaving the disaster site"

Total People Leaving Disaster Site: 1 - 2 - 3 - 4 - 5 - 6 -

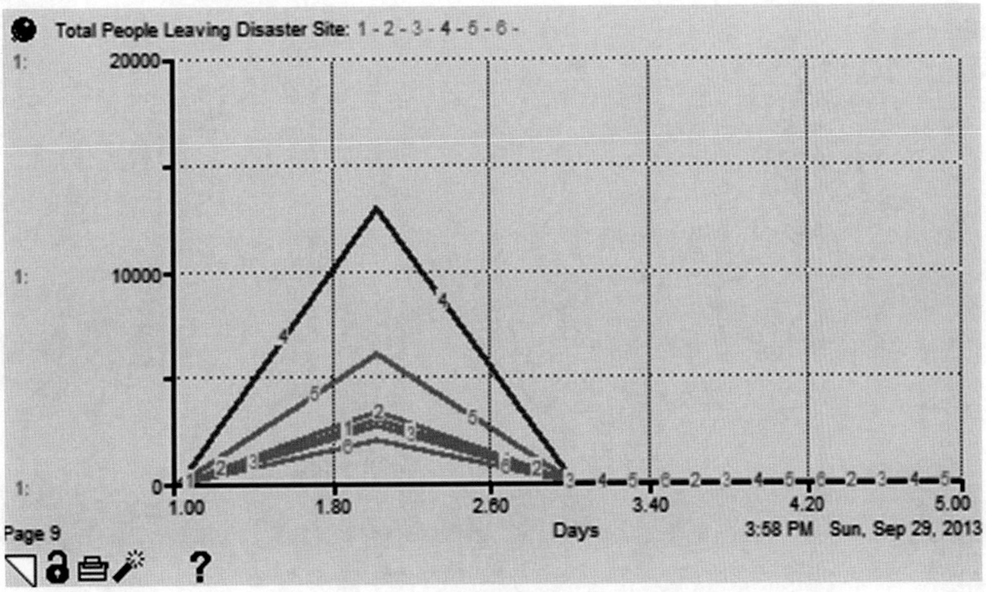

Table 1. Scenario 5: behavior of "people leaving the disaster site"

Days	Tropical Storm	Category 1	Category 2	Category 3	Category 4	Category 5
1	0	0	0	0	0	0
2	2955	3377	2684	12997	6091	2020

Table 2. Scenario 5: behavior of "people that reach shelter"

Days	Tropical Storm	Category 1	Category 2	Category 3	Category 4	Category 5
1	0	0	0	0	0	0
2	0	0	0	0	0	0
3	1005	1148	912	4419	2071	687

Figure 19 and Table 3, depict the number of shelters required for each level of the natural hazard. If a hurricane category 3 strikes the five (5) shelters in Mayagüez, there will not be enough to serve all the potential evacuated population. That means, to refugee the potential evacuated people will be necessary until 11 shelters in this scenario.

Table 3. Scenario 5: behavior of "shelters required"

Days	Tropical Storm	Category 1	Category 2	Category 3	Category 4	Category 5
1	0	0	0	0	0	0
2	0	0	0	0	0	0
3	2	3	2	11	5	2

Figure 19. Scenario 5: behavior of "shelters required"

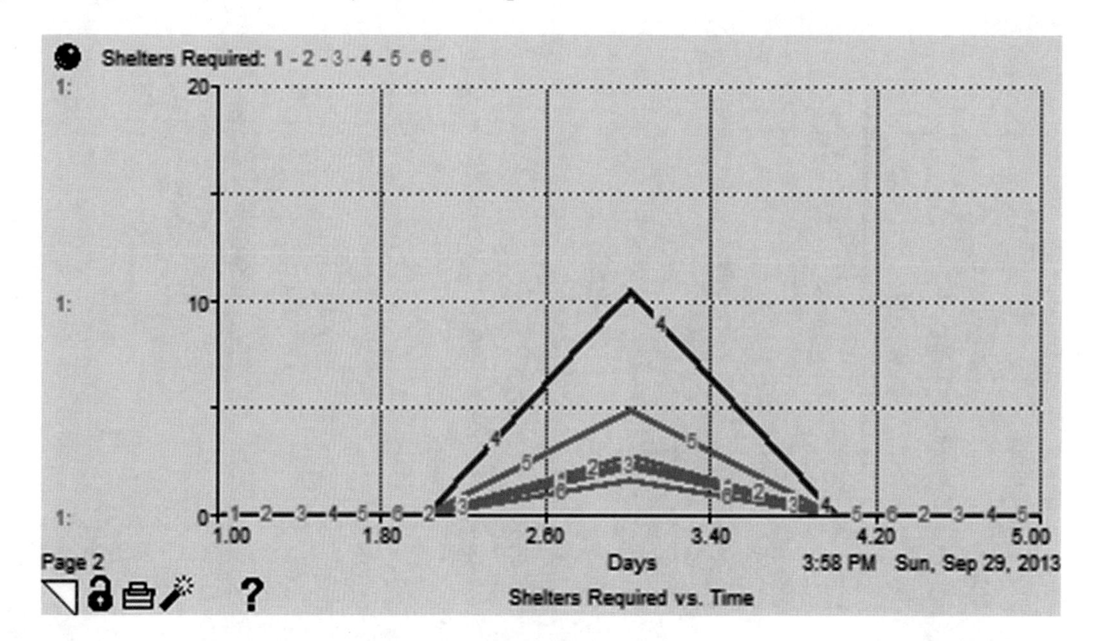

ISSUES, CONTROVERSIES, PROBLEMS

Boundaries

DTHL model can be particularized to some boundary, that is, because trying to model the complexity of the whole problem could lead to losing focus of the central situation, and weakening the attempt of reaching a solution for the complete problem.

GIS and System Dynamics Integration

A relevant limitation presented during this research, is related to the integration between GIS and System dynamics, that is, the consideration of what happened whether a route change was due to a flooding scenario and how the variables are influenced immediately by this change. DTHL model import variables related with vehicle routing procedure automatically and does not consider manual adjustments that reflect these changes.

Vehicle Routing and Schedules

DTHL contemplates PREMA vehicle routing and schedules for the delivery of critical commodities to Mayagüez shelters.

Methodology

DTHL model is specific for PREMA, PRDOE and PRDOH.

Truck Capacities

DTHL calculated truck capacities for PRDOE based on weight. Due to modeling restrictions, capacity based on volume was not considered. However, truck utilization was decreased to 62.81%, to compensate for this problem. That is, the truck gross weight was decreased from 15,920 pounds to 10,000 pounds in the input parameters.

SOLUTIONS AND RECOMMENDATIONS

Boundaries

Several research opportunities could be delineated to attempt for including more factors, relationships and variables that refine transportation and humanitarian logistics problem in Puerto Rico. Probabilities such as reasons to evacuate or not, people that going to other places, people that going to PODs, and people that reach shelters could be estimated in a future work.

GIS and System Dynamics Integration

If flooding conditions change in such a way, during the period shelters are opened, it is possible to change shortest routes for trucks and in turn consider shortest travel times. Integration between Stella and TransCAD could be made manually; that is, converting import variables to variables with sliders. Sliders, can be adjusted during the simulation.

Vehicle Routing and Schedules

PREMA vehicle routing and schedules for the delivery of critical commodities could include the analysis to all the municipalities of the western area that could be served by its distribution center. New interactions and relations built will enrich the evaluation of agencies involve in relief operations.

Methodology

This methodology could be spread over other agencies involved in relief operations and distributions of humanitarian aid. Knowledge, procedures and activities may differ between agencies and organizations; however, they share the same goal to provide relief to affected communities in case of emergency. With appropriate information, knowledge and data, the DTHL simulation model could be rearranged to cover more relief agencies and/or organizations and the analysis could also cover the entire island.

Truck Capacities

Further research could lead to incorporate loadability analysis in terms of volume to the system dynamic model.

FUTURE RESEARCH DIRECTIONS

The DTHL model welcomes improvements, in terms of the considerations of new variables and relationships that lead to the scope increase.

Probabilities for variables such as: reasons to evacuate or not, people going to other places, people that going to PODs, and people that reach shelters could be estimated in a future work. This will allow refining the model and in turn, resemble characteristics of the island population. Minor adjustments will allow that PREMA can forecast commodities ordering decision for future events per the evacuees needs over a period. This will allow PREMA the assessments of its inventory prepositioned in each distribution center.

Hazus methodology embraces models that estimate potential losses from earthquakes, floods, and hurricanes. It uses GIS technology to estimate physical, economic, and social impacts of disasters (FEMA, 2013). DTHL model could be modified, to attempt to consider Hazus Methodology to estimate probabilities of damage and in turn determines number of people affected by the disaster.

CONCLUSION

The DTHL model is a 451th order model constituted of 451 stocks, 266 flows, 702 converters and 19 decision diamonds. All above for a total of 1438 variables. The model is comprehensive enough for the understanding of the humanitarian logistic process, conceptualizing the system involved in humanitarian logistics and capturing variables related to transportation, performance measurements, materials and personnel requirements and evacuated community. It also contemplates some external factors that influence the dynamics of the system. In addition, the model establishes feedback structures, representing how several variable relationships are interrelated between each other affecting the dynamics and the performance of the whole operation. Then, DTHL Model is a decision tool that is capable to forecast and prioritize critical supplies distribution during emergency relief operations.

The development of an alternate route selection and the results incorporation into the system dynamics model could become a key component of the traffic incident and emergency management program for agencies such as The Puerto Rico Department of Transportation and Public Works (PRDOTPW), PREMA and PRDOE. Because it is important for these agencies to operate in case of a major catastrophe that closed a roadway section and to be prepared for any future event. Therefore, the alternate route criterion is setting the extent to which response time of the supplies emergency fleet may be affected by the alternate route. Since emergencies for a hurricane event, may cause road closures and an increase in traffic demand for the evacuation routes. This creates bottlenecks at capacity restrained locations that affect the distribution of critical supplies to communities affected by a disaster. Then, the alternate route becomes indispensable when a hurricane event makes a transportation facility unusable for an extended period. These new response times will be added to the DTHL model to appreciate the impact in the dynamics of the whole relief operation of the alternate routes addition.

Related to people concerns about road conditions over time were proven that although roads are congested showing a level of service from C and F in the scenario results, people leaves the disaster site. Driver satisfaction ranged from 12.46% to 38.36%. Associated with the behavior of in-kind donations over time it was demonstrated that the arrival of in-kind donations reduces the number of critical commodities delivered in shelters and PODs.

For a Category 3 hurricane, the number of actual shelters is not enough to attend to evacuees over time. If this level of hazard occurs, 40,081 people could be affected, in which 12,997 could leave the disaster site and 4,419 could reach shelters. Therefore, eleven shelters are needed to receive them. The amount of inventory in stock in PREMA and PRDOE are well calculated by agencies to attend Mayagüez evacuees' needs. The model provides the frequency to order and the order size over time for agency and for the type of commodities to replace distribution center inventories.

DTHL model can simulate the behavior of key variables making a relation between level of hazard and people decision to evacuate. From the analysis of the number of people that decides to evacuate regarding changes in hurricane level was inferred that Category 3 of a hurricane will produce the higher number of people that leave the disaster site. In addition, for each level of natural hazard, the time frequency to order and the order size of each relief supply to be needed in shelters and PODs could be estimated. The advance recognition in advance of people's decision to evacuate the disaster area could lead to a better PREMA and PRDOE planning to deliver the right number of critical commodities to meet needs of this population with the least delay as possible.

Humanitarian logistics activities of PREMA and PRDOE involves the management of transportation, single unit truck (SUT) schedules and distribution center inventories, as well as demand and supply planning, warehousing, materials handling, among others activities. The analysis of vehicle routing for the agencies involve in relief operations is crucial due to the establishment of the amount of transportation resources needed to distribute critical commodities to the right place with the least delay possible. Though, road conditions, access to the affected zone, road capacity, alternates routes, and travel times must be contemplated in the analysis of vehicle routing procedure, to plan transportation resources and schedules needed for the delivery of aid.

Sample menu given by School Food Authority is a clear example of one cultural aspect of the population in the area. Menus are prepared based on specific dietary needs common to islanders. DTHL simulation model shows the inventory of these products as well as commodities from PREMA and how variations in lead times affects inventory control in those distribution centers. In the analysis of the research problem, DTHL is proposed as a simulation model that established the relationships between transportation costs, delivery delays, SUT travel times, distance between origins (distribution centers) and destinations (shelters, kitchens and PODs), AADT, flow of vehicles, geometric characteristics of the road, road capacity, level of service, congestion, road conditions, driver satisfaction and (transportation factors); dietary needs, inventory levels, reorder points, order sizes, ordering decision, vehicles available and agencies transportation capacity (humanitarian aid factors); hazard level, donation probabilities, population threatened, non-affected population, reasons given for people for making the decision to evacuate or not, potential people for donation, and opinion made by people in shelters about the performance of the operation (environmental factors).

With the construction of the DTHL model it was also established how does the transportation demand and dynamic demand of critical resources during a natural disaster, paired with the humanitarian logistics characteristics, affecting the distribution of resources needed by the involved organizations. Some of the barriers facing by PREMA and PRDOE are the unpredictable and dynamic demand for critical commodities. In this research the most vital demand considered was MRE, water, blankets, cots and products to be cooked or served followed a sample menu from the School Food Authority. The uncertainty relies on the intrinsic characteristics of the Puerto Rico humanitarian logistics process such as, supply problems, vulnerability of road infrastructure and shelters and PODs demands fluctuations among others. Although lead times is low because agencies have inventory of commodities prepositioned on distribution centers, these inventories have high variations in demand, especially resources from PRDOE that must be shared with daily activities of schools.

DTHL model can be used to forecast supply and demand to reduce uncertainty and its negative effect on the system. By the estimation through sensitivity analysis of suitable number of volunteers and staff needed in activities of delivery, unload of trucks, cooking; the approximation of optimal cooking times, and in-kind donations handling, non-value-adding activities and waiting times can be reduced. The system dynamic model also provides output performance measures, which make radiography of how the agencies respond to a disaster or the ability they must meet the evacuated needs. Finally, methodological framework for real time data collection will also help to deal with lack of information during the disaster; and to reduce uncertainty, through gathering relevant real time information to the emergency relief operation during hurricane event, the distribution of this information and its use to forecast and prioritize delivery of critical supplies from distribution centers to shelters, kitchens and PODs.

TransCAD analysis through the logistic module, allowed the analysis of vehicle routing process for PREMA and PRDOE. The incorporation of GIS information in terms of routes, travel times and distances to the system dynamics model permit the analysis of the effect that a selection of one route over others had on the performance of delivered/served commodities in shelters, kitchens and PODs.

One of the practical contributions of this research is the analysis of the people's decision and travel characteristics that determine the timing of evacuation. This was demonstrated in the testing of hypothesis 1 that the number of people leaving the disaster site increases despite people concerns about the road conditions.

This research work shows to be worth to humanitarian logistics, transportation and system dynamics field illustrating contributions in a theoretical and practice framework. The system dynamic model developed that integrates GIS information resulting from a vehicle routing procedure run in TransCAD, attempt to simulate the performance of the relief operation of three agencies: PREMA, PRDOE and PRDOH, in relation with the distribution of relief supplies. A wide research review was conducted through humanitarian logistics' field, GIS, vehicle routing procedure, system dynamics among others, trying to model the complexity of the research problem. The developed system dynamic model proved to be a valuable planning tool that could help to decision makers and logisticians to anticipate, estimate, forecast, and prioritize the distribution of emergency supplies during a relief operation.

Finally, this research work contributes with a description of a methodological framework for real-time data collection during an emergency. This framework adopts three modules which join the information that agency's staff need to collect in real time; the elements that compose the information feeding process; and the interactions of the above modules with the system dynamics model (Stella®) and the vehicle routing procedure (TransCAD®).

REFERENCES

Afshar, A., & Haghani, A. (2009). Logistics Modeling in Large-Scale Disaster Relief Operations. *Transportation Research Board. Proceedings of the 89th Annual Meeting.*

Altay, N., & Green, W. G. III. (2006). OR/MS Research in Disaster Operations Management. *European Journal of Operational Research*, *175*(1), 475–493. doi:10.1016/j.ejor.2005.05.016

Andem, S. (2006). *A comparative Analysis of Hurricane Evacuation Traffic Conditions Using Static and Dynamic Traffic Assignments* (Published Ph.D. Dissertation). Louisiana State University.

Andrews, S. P. (2009). *Computer-Assisted Emergency Evacuation Planning Using TransCAD: Case Studies in Western Massachusetts* (Published Master Thesis). University of Massachusetts Amherst.

Ayala, W. (2006). *Puerto Rico Emergency Management Agency – Emergency Operational Plans*. Retrieved August 21, 2013 from http://www.uprm.edu/cde/public_main/slider/files_slider/presentaciones_foro/manejo_emergencias.pdf

Ayenew, M. M. (2015). The Dynamics of Food Insecurity in Ethiopia. *International Journal of System Dynamics Applications*, *4*(4), 17–34. doi:10.4018/IJSDA.2015100102

Azar, A. (2012). System Dynamics as a Useful Technique for Complex Systems. *International Journal of Industrial and Systems Engineering*, *10*(4), 377–410. doi:10.1504/IJISE.2012.046298

Balcik, B., & Beamon, B. (2008). Facility Location in Humanitarian Relief. *International Journal of Logistics. Research and Applications*, *11*(2), 101–121.

Battini, D., Faccio, M., Persona, A., & Sgarbossa, F. (2013). Modelling the Growing Process of Integrated Healthcare Supply Networks. *International Journal of System Dynamics Applications*, *2*(1), 1–13. doi:10.4018/ijsda.2013010101

Besiou, M., Stapleton, O., & Wassenhove, L. (2011). System Dynamics for Humanitarian Operations. *Journal of Humanitarian Logistics and Supply Chain Management*, *1*(1), 78–103. doi:10.1108/20426741111122420

Bozorgi-Amiri, A., Jabalameli, M. S., & Mirzapour Al-e-Hashem, S. M. (2013). A multi-objective robust stochastic programming model for disaster relief logistics under uncertainty. *OR-Spektrum*, *35*(4), 905–933. doi:10.100700291-011-0268-x

Caliper Corporation. (2010). *TransCAD Overview*. Retrieved June 10, 2010 from http://www.caliper.com/tcovu.htm

Camacho-Vallejo, J. F., González-Rodríguez, E., Almaguer, F. J., & González-Ramírez, R. G. (2015). A bi-level optimization model for aid distribution after the occurrence of a disaster. *Journal of Cleaner Production*, *105*, 134–145. doi:10.1016/j.jclepro.2014.09.069

Campbell, A. M., Vandenbussche, D., & Hermann, W. (2008). Routing for relief efforts. *Transportation Science*, *42*(2), 127–145. doi:10.1287/trsc.1070.0209

Cheng, G. (2010). *Dynamic Trip Distribution Models for Hurricane Evacuation* (Published Ph.D. Dissertation). Louisiana State University.

Cruz, Y. (2008). *Integrating Complex Evacuation Dynamics in Resources Allocation for Relief Operations* (Published Master thesis). University of Puerto Rico, Mayagüez.

Cruz, Y. (2013). *Dynamic Transportation and Humanitarian Logistics Model: A Decision Support Tool to Forecast and Prioritize Critical Supplies Distribution During Emergency Relief Operations* (Published Doctoral Dissertation). University of Puerto Rico, Mayagüez.

Cruz, Y. (2014). A System Dynamics Approach to Humanitarian Logistics and the Transportation of Relief Supplies. *International Journal of System Dynamics Applications*, *3*(3), 96–128. doi:10.4018/ijsda.2014070105

Cruz, Y., Medina, A., & Medin, J. (2009). Understanding the Role of Victims' Non-Discretionary Factors in Hurricane Evacuation Dynamics: a planning tool for disaster relief. *Proceedings of the 27th International Conference of the System Dynamics Society.*

Duhamel, C., Santos A., & Birregah B. (2016). Connecting a population dynamic model with a multi-period location-allocation problem for post-disaster relief operations. *Annals of Operations Research OR Confronting Crises*, 1-21. DOI: 10.1007/s10479-015-2104-1

Federal Emergency Management Agency. (2013). *The Federal Emergency Management Agency's (FEMA's) Methodology for Estimating Potential Losses from Disasters*. Retrieved October 2, 2013 from http://www.fema.gov/hazus

Forrester, J. (1961). *Industrial Dynamics*. Cambridge, MA: MIT Press.

Forrester, J. (1961). *What is System Dynamics?* Retrieved May 24, 2016 from http://systemdynamics.org.uk/about/

Gonçalves, P. (2008). *System Dynamics Modeling of Humanitarian Relief Operations* (MIT Sloan Working Paper No. 4704-08). Retrieved from Social Science Research Network Electronic Paper Collection: http://papers.ssrn.com/sol3/papers.cfm?abstract_id=1139817

González, D. B., & Salvador, M. R. (2014). Dynamic Modeling in New Product Development: The Case of Knowledge Management Enablers in a Food Product. *International Journal of System Dynamics Applications*, *3*(1), 111–134. doi:10.4018/ijsda.2014010106

Ho, Y., Lu, C., & Wang, H. (2006). Dynamic Model for Earthquake Disaster Prevention System: A Case Study of Taichung City, Taiwan. *Proceedings of the 24th International Conference of the System Dynamics Society.*

Landsea, C. (1992). *A climatology of Intense (or Major) Atlantic Hurricanes.* Fort Collins, CO: American Meteorological Society.

Modali, N. (2005). *Modeling Destination Choice and Measuring the Transferability of Hurricane Evacuation Patterns* (Published Master Thesis). Department of Civil and Environmental Engineering, Louisiana State University.

Onggo, S. (2012). Adult Social Care Workforce Analysis in England: A System Dynamics Approach. *International Journal of System Dynamics Applications*, *1*(4), 1–20. doi:10.4018/ijsda.2012100101

Oyo, B., & Kalema, B. M. (2016). A System Dynamics Model for Subsistence Farmers' Food Security Resilience in Sub-Saharan Africa. *International Journal of System Dynamics Applications*, *5*(1), 17–30. doi:10.4018/IJSDA.2016010102

Ramezankhani, A., & Najafiyazdi, M. (2008). A System Dynamics Approach on Post-Disaster Management: A Case Study of Bam Earthquake, December 2003. *Proceedings of the 26th International Conference of the System Dynamics Society.*

RF Industries Inc. (2013). *Software Provides Mobility for Emergency Workers. Product Announcements.* Retrieved December 5, 2013 from http://www.radiomobile.com/product-IQMobileTablet.html

Sterman, J. (2000). *Business Dynamics System Thinking and Modeling for a Complex World.* Boston, MA: Irwing McGraw-Hill.

Sterman, J. (2001). System Dynamics Modeling: Tools for Learning in a Complex World. *California Management Review Reprint Series*, *43*(4), 8–25. doi:10.2307/41166098

Thakker, R., Eveleigh, T., Holzer, T., & Sarkani, S. (2013). A System Dynamics Approach to Quantitatively Analyze the Effects of Mobile Broadband Ecosystem's Variables on Demands and Allocation of Wireless Spectrum for the Cellular Industry. *International Journal of System Dynamics Applications*, *2*(3), 73–93. doi:10.4018/ijsda.2013070105

Victoria, J. F., Afsar, H. M., & Prins, C. (2015). Vehicle Routing Problem with Time-Dependent Demand in humanitarian logistics. *International Conference on Industrial Engineering and Systems Management (IESM)*, 686-694.10.1109/IESM.2015.7380233

Voyer, J., Dean, M., & Pickles, C. (2015). Understanding Humanitarian Supply Chain Logistics with System Dynamics Modeling. System Dynamics Society. *Proceedings of the 33rd International Conference of the System Dynamics Society.*

Wang, S., Ma, Z., & Li, Z. (2008). A Dynamic Programming Model for Optimal Transportation of Emergency Relief Commodities in Natural Disasters. *American Society of Civil Engineers (ASCE)*, *211*(330), 1452-1457. DOI: 10.1061/40996(330)211

Wohlgemuth, S., Oloruntoba, R., & Clausen, U. (2012). Dynamic vehicle routing with anticipation in disaster relief. *Socio-Economic Planning Sciences*, *46*(4), 261–271. doi:10.1016/j.seps.2012.06.001

Zhu, C., & Ji, G. (2009). Emergency Logistics and the Distribution Model for Quick Response to Urgent Relief Demand. *Proceedings of the 6th International Conference on Service Systems and Service Management*. DOI: 10.1109/ICSSSM.2009.5174910

KEY TERMS AND DEFINITIONS

Alternate Routes: Routes used as other alternatives in case the main one is not available.

Humanitarian Logistics: Coordination of delivery efforts and critical commodities to affected communities in case of complex emergencies.

In-Kind Donations: Donations given as goods to people in affected areas.

Level of Service: Is a measure of the quality of traffic service.

Relief Supplies: Critical commodities delivered to people during emergency relief operations.

System Dynamics: Is a methodology that study the world as a unit in terms of causal relationships and interactions.

Vehicle Routing Procedure: A process employed to find the optimal group of routes for the delivery of relief supplies.

APPENDIX

Evacuated Community Subsystem

Inflows

$$\begin{aligned} Access\ to\ Shelter_1 = {} & IF\ People\ in\ Shelter_1 \geq Capacity_1 \\ & THEN\ 0 \\ & ELSE\ POISSON\left(\lambda_1\right) \end{aligned}$$

$$\begin{aligned} Access\ to\ Shelter_2 = {} & IF\ People\ in\ Shelter_1 \leq Capacity_1 \\ & THEN\ 0 \\ & ELSE\left(POISSON\left(\lambda_2\right) + People\ that\ Leave\ Shelter_1\right) \end{aligned}$$

$$\begin{aligned} Access\ to\ Shelter_3 = {} & IF\ People\ in\ Shelter_2 \leq Capacity_2 \\ & THEN\ 0 \\ & ELSE\left(POISSON\left(\lambda_3\right) + People\ that\ Leave\ Shelter_2\right) \end{aligned}$$

$$\begin{aligned} Access\ to\ Shelter_4 = {} & IF\ People\ in\ Shelter_3 \leq Capacity_3 \\ & THEN\ 0 \\ & ELSE\left(POISSON\left(\lambda_4\right) + People\ that\ Leave\ Shelter_3\right) \end{aligned}$$

$$\begin{aligned} Access\ to\ Shelter_5 = {} & IF\ People\ in\ Shelter_4 \leq Capacity_4 \\ & THEN\ 0 \\ & ELSE\left(POISSON\left(\lambda_5\right) + People\ that\ Leave\ Shelter_4\right) \end{aligned}$$

Stock

$Exit\ Access\ Control(t) = Exit\ Access\ Control\ (t - dt) + (Access\ to\ Shelter_1 + Access\ to\ Shelter_2 + Access\ to\ Shelter_3 + Access\ to\ Shelter_4 + Access\ to\ Shelter_5 - People\ that\ Enter\ to\ Shelter_1 - People\ that\ Enter\ to\ Shelter_2 - People\ that\ Enter\ to\ Shelter_3 - People\ that\ Enter\ to\ Shelter_4 - People\ that\ Enter\ to\ Shelter_5)*dt$

Outflows

$$People\ that\ Enter\ to\ Shelter_i = Access\ to\ Shelter_i$$

Material and Personnel Requirements for Relief Subsystem

$$Volunteers\ for\ Shelter_i \left[Delivery\ of\ Food\right] = IF\ Total\ in\_kind\ Donations\ Units_i = 0$$
$$THEN\ 0$$
$$ELSE$$

$$IF\ Total\ in\_kind\ Donations\ Units_i > 0.5$$
$$AND\ Total\ in\_kind\ Donations\ Units_i \leq 50$$
$$THEN \left(Volunteers\ Assigned\ Shelter_i * 0.9\right) / Shelters\ Opened$$
$$ELSE$$

$$IF\ Total\ in\_kind\ Donations\ Units_i > 51$$
$$AND\ Total\ in\_kind\ Donations\ Units_i \leq 100$$
$$THEN \left(Volunteers\ Assigned\ Shelter_i * 0.8\right) / Shelters\ Opened$$
$$ELSE$$

$$IF\ Total\ in\_kind\ Donations\ Units_i > 101$$
$$AND\ Total\ in\_kind\ Donations\ Units_i \leq 150$$
$$THEN \left(Volunteers\ Assigned\ Shelter_i * 0.7\right) / Shelters\ Opened$$
$$ELSE$$

$$IF\ Total\ in\_kind\ Donations\ Units_i > 151$$
$$AND\ Total\ in\_kind\ Donations\ Units_i \leq 200$$
$$THEN \left(Volunteers\ Assigned\ Shelter_i * 0.6\right) / Shelters\ Opened$$
$$ELSE$$

$$IF\ Total\ in_{kind}\ Donations\ Units_i > 201$$
$$AND\ Total\ in\_kind\ Donations\ Units_i \leq 300$$
$$THEN \left(Volunteers\ Assigned\ Shelter_i * 0.5\right) / Shelters\ Opened$$
$$ELSE$$

$$\left(Volunteers\ Assigned\ Shelter_i\right) / Shelters\ Opened$$

Transportation Subsystem

$$PREMA \mid PRDOE\ Performance\ of\ Critical\ Supplies\ Delivered\ in\ Shelter =$$
$$IF\ ARRAYMEAN\left(Percentage\ of\ Commodities\ Delivered\ in\ Shelter\right) \leq 70$$
$$THEN\ 1$$
$$ELSE\ 0$$

$$PREMA \mid PRDOE\ Need\ for\ Alternate\ Routes\ for\ Shelter =$$

$$IF\ PREMA \mid PRDOE\ Performace\ of\ Critical\ Supplies\ Delivered\ in\ Shelter = 1$$
$$THEN\ 1$$
$$ELSE\ 0$$

Humanitarian Logistic Subsystem

First Order Priority = IF Commodities Delivered to Shelter$_i$ *= 0 THEN 5 ELSE IF (MRE Del Sh =Water Del Sh AND MRE Del Sh=Blankets Del Sh AND MRE Del Sh =Cots Del Sh) AND (MRE R Sh=Water R Sh AND MRE R Sh=Blanket R Sh AND MRE R Sh =Cot R Sh) THEN 6 ELSE IF MIN(MRE Del Sh,WaterDel Sh,Blankets Del Sh,Cots Del Sh) =0 AND MAX(MRE R Sh,Water R Sh,Blanket R Sh,Cot R Sh) =MRE R Sh THEN 1 ELSE IF MIN(MRE Del Sh,WaterDel Sh,Blankets Del Sh,Cots Del Sh) =0 AND MAX(MRE R Sh,Water R Sh, Blanket R Sh, Cot R Sh) =Water R Sh THEN 2 ELSE IF MIN(MRE Del Sh,WaterDel Sh,Blankets Del Sh,Cots Del Sh) =0 AND MAX(MRE R Sh,Water R Sh,Blanket R Sh,Cot R Sh) =Blanket R Sh THEN 3 ELSE IF IN(MRE Del Sh,WaterDel Sh,Blankets Del Sh,Cots Del Sh) =0 AND MAX(MRE R Sh,Water R Sh,Blanket R Sh,Cot R Sh) =Cot R Sh THEN 4 ELSE IF MIN(MRE Del Sh,WaterDel Sh,Blankets Del Sh,Cots Del Sh) =MRE Del Sh AND MAX(MRE R Sh,Water R Sh,Blanket R Sh,Cot R Sh) =MRE R Sh THEN 1 ELSE IF MIN(MRE Del Sh,WaterDel Sh,Blankets Del Sh,Cots Del Sh) = WaterDel Sh AND MAX(MRE R Sh,Water R Sh,Blanket R Sh,Cot R Sh) =Water R Sh THEN 2 ELSE IF MIN(MRE Del Sh,WaterDel Sh,Blankets Del Sh,Cots Del Sh) =Blankets Del Sh AND MAX(MRE R Sh,Water R Sh,Blanket R Sh,Cot R Sh) =Blanket R Sh THEN 3 ELSE IF IN(MRE Del Sh,WaterDel Sh,Blankets Del Sh,Cots Del Sh) =Cots Del Sh AND MAX(MRE R Sh,Water R Sh,Blanket R Sh,Cot R Sh) =Cot R Sh THEN 4 ELSE 0*

$$Commodities\ Shipping\ to\ Shelter = IF\ PREMA\ Delivery\ Delay\ to\ Shelters = 0$$
$$THEN\ 0$$
$$ELSE$$

$$\begin{aligned}
&IF\ Commodities\ Status\ in\ Shelter_i = 1\\
&THEN\ IF\ Status\ in\ Shelter_i = 0\\
&THEN\ 0\\
&ELSE\\
&IF\ First\ |Second|\ Third\ |\ Fourth\ Order\ priority\ for\ Shelter_i = 1\\
&THEN\ \ (IF\ Commodities\ Required\ for\ Shelter_i > Commodities\ Unit\ Capacity\\
&THEN\ Commodities\ Unit\ Capacity\\
&ELSE\\
&Commodities\ Required\ for\ Shelter_i\ ELSE\ 0)\ ELSE\ 0
\end{aligned}$$

$$Where\ 1 = MRE, 2 = Water, 3 = Blankets, 4 = Cots, 5 = None, 6 = All$$

Emergency Relief Operation Performance Subsystem

$$\begin{aligned}
Percentage\ of\ Commodities\ Delivered\ in\ Shelter_i = &\ IF\ Commodities\ Required\ for\ Shelter < 1\\
&THEN\ 0\\
&ELSE
\end{aligned}$$

$$(Commodities\ Delivered\ in\ Shelter_i\ /\ Commodities\ Required\ in\ Shelter_i) * 100$$

Chapter 17
Logistics Improvement by Investment in Information Technology Using System Dynamics

Amrita Jhawar
Delhi Technological University, India

S. K. Garg
Delhi Technological University, India

ABSTRACT

In this era of globalization, adoption of information technology (IT) is one of the critical contributing factors of logistics companies' competitiveness and growth. This chapter investigates the investment in IT by an Indian-based logistics company on the logistics performance. Technologies like RFID, EDI, GPS/GIS, and ERP are chosen for improving processes like tracking and tracing, planning and forecasting, transportation automation, coordination with suppliers and customers, and decision optimization. Simulations are carried out using system dynamics modelling. The model is validated and sensitivity analysis is performed. Scenarios are generated under optimistic and pessimistic conditions.

INTRODUCTION

Information is a valuable logistics resource and IT plays a very important role to enhance logistics competitiveness. Many studies since the 1990s suggest the important role information technology plays in enhancing the effectiveness and efficiency of logistics management (Introna (1991); Schary (1991); Hammant (1995); Closs (1997); Loebbeck (1998)). Timely, accurate and well-managed information improves decision making and enhances effectiveness, efficiency and flexibility. Functional role of IT is transaction execution, collaboration and coordination and decision support (Nair et al., 2009). Bowersox et al. (2002) separated the functionality of ICT systems for logistics into four categories: strategic planning, decision analysis, management control and transaction systems. The various activities performed under the above functions and the benefits obtained through them are shown in Table 1.

DOI: 10.4018/978-1-5225-4077-9.ch017

Table 1. Role of IT in logistics management

Author	Benefits
Closs et al. (1997)	Accuracy, information sharing, timeliness, availability, internal connectivity, operating timeliness, usage driven formatting and flexibility
Lai et al. (2006)	Improving delivery speed and reliability, customer relations and order accuracy, higher cost advantage
Pokharel (2005)	Higher efficiency, cost savings, reduced data entry error and increased customer service level
Auramo et al. (2005)	Customer service, efficiency, information quality, planning collaboration for improving agility
Tseng et al. (2011)	Robust, seamless and resilient supply chain, enormous economic benefits, reduction in cost and time wastage, enhancing competitive advantage
Savitskie (2007)	logistic costs, inventory turnover, order fill capacity, product and order flexibility, delivery time, flexibility, customer satisfaction

Logistics is the work needed to move and position inventory within a company's supply chain management and is the process that creates value by timing and positioning inventory (Cruz-Cantillo, 2014). For a consistent and superior logistics performance, organizations should invest heavily in information technology and make it an integral part of the logistics process. The Indian logistics industry spends hardly 0.3% of its revenues on ICT as compared to 2-3% in developed countries and the need of the hour is 4-5% of revenues need to be ploughed back in ICT to advance quickly and generate competitive advantage (Srivastava and Chandra, 2013). Figure 1 shows the overall trend of investment in information technology by the Indian logistics players in the year 2010. As shown in figure 1, almost 50% of the players are investing less than ten lakh rupees and only 2.58% are investing more than 1 crore rupees. Hammant (1995) suggests that the pressure to invest in information technology is high and will increase with an increase in profits and the penalties of under investment or of poorly-thought-through investment is also very high.

The main objectives of the chapter are as follows:

1. To identify the technologies, which will maximize logistics performance?
2. To develop a dynamic model using system dynamics modelling for the investments in IT

Figure 1. Investments in IT by Indian logistics players in 2009 Source: Softlink, 2009

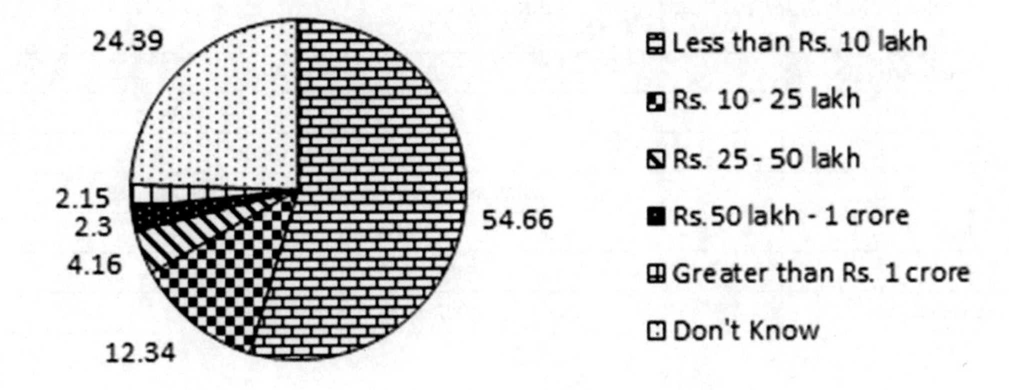

3. To evaluate the various investment plans and scenarios for the decision maker to formulate the investment strategy which best meets the requirements of the business.
4. To quantify the relationship between performances measures like logistics cost, delivery time, reliability, flexibility and safety and logistics performance.
5. To study the effect of improvement in logistics performance, if any, on the profit of the firm.

IDENTIFICATION OF TECHNOLOGIES FOR INVESTMENT

One of the utmost critical factors of effective logistics service is adequate information technology systems support, which changes the nature of operations performed by logistics organizations. Table 2 identified various technologies being used by logistics professionals.

EDI and RFID emerged as the two technologies that were addressed most often in SCM literature accounting 32% of all the articles in which IT is the primary focus (Hazen and Byrd, 2012). Also, logistics require a high level of organizational and inter-organizational communication systems such as RFID, EDI and ERP at various levels of the logistics chain for better coordination, planning and decision optimization. Coordination is the management of dependencies between activities and use of IT enhances it by reducing uncertainty in the supply chain, enhancing decision making and communication (Lewis and Talalayevsky, 2004). For automatic tracking of vehicles, freight, containers, etc., including location, speed and time can be measured with the help of GPS. Tracking and tracing concerns a process of determining the current and past locations (and other information) of a unique item or property. This information can be appropriately used by GIS for corrective actions. Although, there are innumerable technologies being used, the authors have considered the above mentioned five technologies to be studied further in this study. Table 3 explains the concept, purpose, benefits and application/empirical evidence of the five technologies identified in this chapter.

The five technologies shortlisted for the study will impact logistics processes like tracking and tracing, planning and forecasting, transportation and automation, coordination with suppliers and customers and decision optimization. These processes in turn will help to reduce the cost, reduce the delivery time, improve the reliability of logistics services, and improve the flexibility of logistics services and safety which will affect the logistics performance index.

Table 2. Various technologies used in logistics management

Author	Technologies Identified
Closs (2007)	ERP; WMS; TMS; SCEM; RFID; CPFR; CRM
LQ (2007)	RFID; EDI; GPS;ERP;CPFR
Nair et al. (2009)	EDI; Material Resource Planning; ERP; WMS; TMS; IMS; RFID
Vashisht (2013)	EDI;ERP;GPS; GIS
PwC (2013)	ERP; WMS;RFID; FMS;SS
Bhandari (2014)	RFID; EDI; GPS; GIS; ERP

Table 3. Technologies identified

1. RFID
Concept: 1. It is a term used for technologies utilizing radio waves for identifying individual items automatically and is designed to track items in the supply chain without requiring a line of sight (Mehrjerdi, 2010). 2. It is a technology that enables radio frequencies to send and receive data and from one or many RFID tags and an enabler system including antennas (Stefansson and Lumsden, 2009).
Purpose: 1. It is an automatic identification method to keep track and trace of moving objects within the logistics network (Lee et al., 2011) 2. It is used in the logistical planning and operation of supply chain processes in the manufacturing, distribution and retail industries, and has helped move its adoption into services such as security and access control, tracking, monitoring, and management (Cheung et al., 2008). 3. RFID has the potential to increase the level of visibility and communication, which can be used in decision making to eliminate non-value-adding activities, strengthening the competitiveness of the supply chain (Kumar et al., 2015). 4. It helps in transport network design by helping in making decisions on transportation modes, location, routes for shipping, type of mode to be used etc. (Jones and Chung, 2007).
Benefits: 1. Walmart believes RFID system can help in reducing labour costs, reduce inventory costs, reduce human errors, increasing revenues by limiting shortages, increasing overall efficiency and productivity of the supply chain (Mehrjerdi, 2013). 2. It is a data acquisition and storage method, which promises numerous supply chain benefits such as improved speed, accuracy, efficiency and security of information sharing (Kumar et al., 2015).
Application/Empirical Evidence: 1. P&G Company expects to cut its costs by $400 million a year by using RFID (Bhandari, 2014).
2. EDI
Concept: 1. EDI is defined as computer to computer exchange of structured data for automatic processing (Nair et. al., 2009). 2. It is the electronic transfer of structured data by agreed message standards from one computer application, with a minimum of human intervention, connecting all parties in a supply chain (Adebambo and Toyin, 2011).
Purpose: 1. It enhances efficient coordination of logistics systems and facilitates logistical integration (Larson and Kulchitsky, 1998).
Benefits: The main advantages of using EDI are to enter only informative needs on the computer system once, and then it is able to speed of transaction and to reduce cost and error rates, better customer service, reduced paper work, increased productivity, improved tracing and expediting, cost efficiency and improved billing (Nair et. al., 2009).
Application/Empirical Evidence: 1. Singapore has been noted as a leader in Paperless Trading, with its Trade Net System, a nationwide EDI System focused on the submission of regulatory documents (Toh et al., 2009).
3. & 4. GPS/GIS
Concept: 1. GIS is the software tool for visualization of spatial location of any entity on earth, in terms of physical maps of the surface of the earth, layout of the inner surface of the earth or a layout of streets or roads, which is stored in databases (Bhandari, 2014). 2. GPS provides the service of vehicles positioning. It could help the control centres to monitor and dispatch trucks. GIS provides the basic geographic database for the deliverers to enable to organise their routes easier and faster (Tseng et al., 2011).
Purpose: 1. GIS in integration with GPS is used in logistical operation for tracking and tracing of the consignment location to the extent of road or street in a particular city (Bhandari, 2014). 2. GPS technology has provided major breakthroughs in transportation management by vehicle tracking, determination of speed and waiting time (Prasanna and Hemalatha, 2012).
Benefits: 1. It increases service quality, relevance of information, traceability of products and also improves productivity (Saidi and Hammami, 2011). 2. The benefits of integrating GPS and GIS with advanced information systems are better service quality, reduced unnecessary trips, and increased loading rate (Tseng et al., 2011).

continued on following page

Table 3. Continued

Application/Empirical Evidence: 1. A decision support system using GPS and GIS reduced the ELR, which measures the efficiency and wastage of a route, by 20% in China (Hu and Sheng, 2014). 2. Use of IT in vehicles leads to fuel savings of 5%, reduction in accident damage by 50%, security, better maintenance and utilization of vehicle (Hammant, 1995).
5. ERP
Concept: 1. ERP systems have been touted to streamline organizational functions and processes by integrating enterprise-wide data and business processes (Katerattanakul et al., 2014). 2. ERP systems are software packages that integrate a number of business processes, such as manufacturing, supply chain, sales, finance, human resources, budgeting and customer service activities (Schniederjans and Yadav, 2013).
Purpose: 1. ERP is generally referred to as a cutting-edge information technology that helps the firm coordinate and integrate company-wide business processes, including sales, marketing, manufacturing, logistics, purchasing, accounting, and human resources management using a common database and shared management reporting tools (Hwang and Min, 2013). 2. If successfully implemented, ERP can create value in a number of different ways of integrating the firm's multifarious business activities into a single system, facilitating organizational standardization, increasing access to online and real time information, improving intra- and inter-organizational communication and collaboration, and enhancing decision-making capabilities (Hwang and Min, 2013).
Benefits: 1. The most significant benefits are cycle time reduction, faster information transactions, better financial management, laying the groundwork for electronic commerce, making tacit process knowledge explicit (transferring knowledge from an aging workforce into the enterprise system) (Adebambo and Toyin, 2011). 2. ERP systems are transaction based enterprise-wide information systems used for automating and integrating all activities and functions of a business (Hwang and Min, 2013).
Application/Empirical Evidence: 1. Companies such as Honeywell, Caterpillar, Procter and Gamble, GlaxoSmithKline, and others have made decisions to implement ERP systems across their end-to-end supply chains, from customer order management to supplier collaboration (Hwang and Min, 2013). 2. Hunton et al., (2003) conducted a longitudinal study of ERP system deployment effects on financial performance based on a sample of 63 companies. Results suggest that return on assets, ROI, and asset turnover of ERP adopters were significantly better than non-adopters. 3. The companies like Hindustan Lever, Colgate and Nestle have implemented ERP in their supply chain system, resulting in minimum inventory of raw material and finished goods and benefit in terms of cost reduction (Bhandari, 2014).

RESEARCH METHODOLOGY

The research methodology adopted in this chapter is as follows:

Model Assumptions

The following assumptions are made for carrying out the simulations

a. The activities are not interrelated to each other i.e. improvement in RFID does not affect EDI etc.
b. The effect of improvement in logistics processes is instantaneous and there is no time lag between investment and improvement.
c. After 12 quarters, if the profit increases by 3%, then the company will invest 1% of the investment amount every quarter.The existing profit percentage of the company is 10%. With every percentage improvement in LPI, profit will improve by 0.005.

Investment Plans

The investment plans need to be developed with respect to two aspects:

1. Proportion of investment in different technologies (Table 4).
2. Time phasing of the investment (Table 5).

More than fifteen combinations of different investment plans and quarter wise allocation of funds were proposed and simulated. The plans with maximum improvement were considered for further simulation.

In the equal focus plan (PA1), as shown in Table 4, 25% of total budgets are earmarked for RFID, 25% of EDI, 25% for GPS and 25% for ERP. Technologies like RFID and GPS directly impacts the automation of the transportation network like vehicle routing, fleet management, location of the product identification, etc. On the other hand, ERP and EDI will help more in improving in planning and forecasting, coordination and decision optimization. PA2 and PA3 are customized plans where investment combinations are done to test the effect of improvement in different technologies.

In the external focus plan (PA4), 50% investment is done EDI and ERP each to focus on better coordination between suppliers and customers which will lead to better planning and decision making. For better tracking and tracing, 25% investment in RFID, 25% investment in GPS and 50% investment in ERP is done in TT focus plan (PA5).

To achieve the maximum benefits, the investment in an area is further broken quarter wise. Since the present plan is for 3 years, the investment is divided into 12 quarterly periods.

Based on it, five plans are prepared and analysed as given in Table 5. In QAP1, 10% of the investment is done in first eight quarters and it was reduced to half in the last four quarters. Exactly opposite

Table 4. Investment Plans for Different Activities

Investment Plans		Investment in Activity (%)			
Code	**Description**	**RFID**	**EDI**	**GPS**	**ERP**
PA1	**Equal Focus Plan**	25	25	25	25
PA2	**Customized Plan I**	30	15	15	40
PA3	**Customized Plan II**	15	30	15	40
PA4	**External Focus Plan**	0	50	0	50
PA5	**TT Focus Plan**	25	0	25	50

Table 5. QAP as Percentage of Activity

QAP	Quarter wise Allocation of Funds (%)												
	1	**2**	**3**	**4**	**5**	**6**	**7**	**8**	**9**	**10**	**11**	**12**	**Total**
QAP1	10	10	10	10	10	10	10	10	5	5	5	5	100
QAP2	5	5	5	5	5	5	5	5	10	10	20	20	100
QAP3	25	0	0	25	0	0	25	0	0	25	0	0	100
QAP4	15	15	15	10	10	5	5	5	5	5	5	5	100

to this, in QAP2, 5% investment was done in first eight quarters and it was doubled in the last four quarters. In QAP3, 25% of the investment amount was invested every third quarter. More than 50% of the investment was done in QAP4, in the initial five quarters and 5% of the investment was made in every quarter afterwards.

Research Framework

As shown in Figure 2, investment in the five technologies will lead to improvement in logistics processes like tracking and tracing, planning and forecasting, transportation automation, coordination with suppliers and customers and decision optimization. This will lead to improvement in the performance measures like reduction in cost, reduction in delivery time, improvement in reliability, improvement in flexibility and improvement in safety. This will improve the logistics performance leading to improvement in profit. Improved profit will lead to more investment.

CAUSAL LOOP DIAGRAM

A model of a system is a tool used to study the behaviour of a system without having to experiment on the real system (Oyo and Kalema, 2016). System dynamics (SD) is a powerful methodology and computer simulation modelling technique for framing, understanding and discussing complex issues and problems (Azar, 2012). It has its origins in control engineering and management; the approach uses a perspective based on information feedback and delays to understand the dynamic behaviour of complex physical,

Figure 2. Research Framework

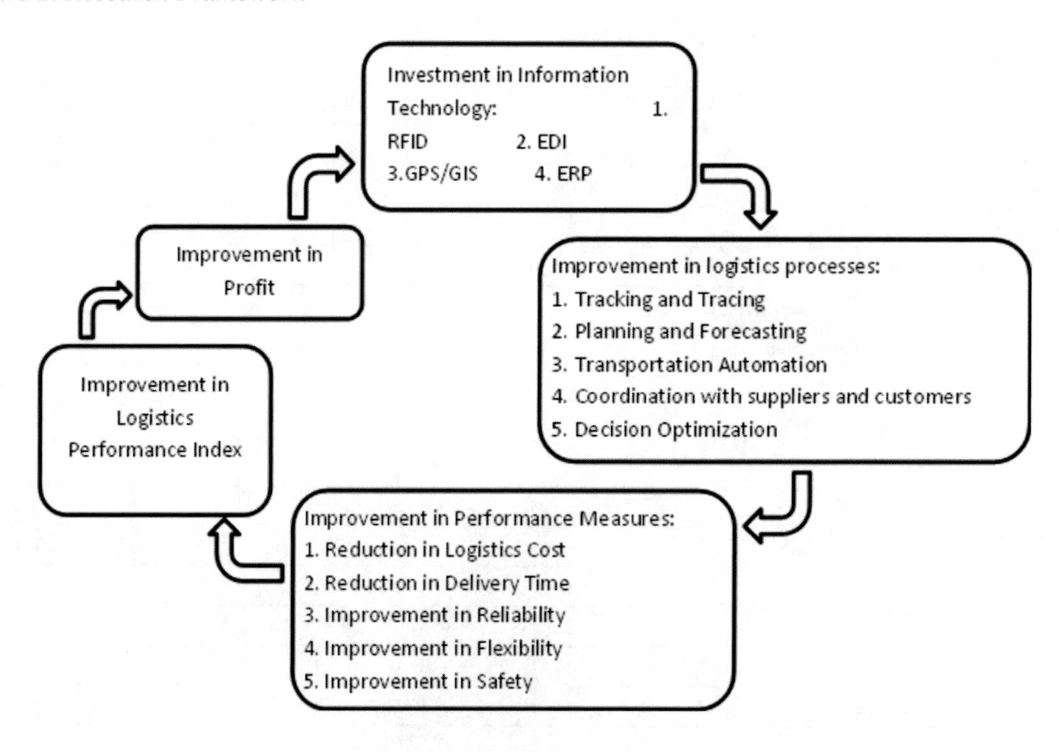

biological and social systems (Angerhofer, 2000). It is a computer-aided approach for analyzing and solving complex problems with a focus on policy analysis and design (Angerhofer, 2000).

The SD tools i.e. the Causal Loop Diagrams (CLD) and the stock and flow diagrams are powerful communication tools between the modeller and the policy makers and they offer means of experimenting with different scenarios (Mindila et al., 2016). The causal loop diagram in system dynamics focuses on the structure and behaviour of the systems composed of interacting feedback loops (Kiani et al., 2009). The causal loop diagram is an important tool which helps the modeller to conceptualize the real-world system in terms of feedback loops (Sachan et al., 2005). In a causal loop diagram, the arrows indicate the direction of influence, and the plus or minus sign the type of influence. All other things being equal, if a change in one variable generates a change in the same direction in the second variable, relative to its prior value, the relationship between the two variables is referred to as positive and the loop is known as reinforcing loop. If the change in the second variable takes place in the opposite direction, the relationship is negative (Forrester, 1985) and the loop is known as balancing loop. Logistics service providers will invest in IT (Reddy, 2012; Sahay and Mohan, 2003) to adopt technologies for improving logistics.

RFID

RFID was classified as one of the ten major innovation technologies in 2004 by CNN and one of the ten major IT technologies in 2005 by ZDNet (Lin, 2009). It possesses multiple advantages such as high storage capacity, remote and repeated reading, writing better data security and ability to read numerous tags simultaneously (Lin, 2009). It will help in tracking and tracing of pallets and shipments (Cheung et al., 2008); reduce amount of potential error and diminishes losses (Ginters and Martin- Gutierrez, 2013); enhances speed and accuracy (Bhandari, 2014); improvement in responsiveness, lean and agile logistics workflow (Lee et al., 2011); helps in order fulfilment and efficient WMS (Garcia et al., 2006) leading to reduction in cost, reduction in time and improvement in safety (Mehrjerdi, 2010). Error in warehouse can create several million in damages, even if component costs a few euros (Ginters and Martin-Gutierrez 2013). Although RFID implementations incur additional costs, it can make the supply chain continuously visible, thus reducing the production lead times to zero or almost negligible (Bhadrachalam et al, 2011). Therefore in Figure 3, the loop between investment in IT by LSP, RFID, tracking and tracing, logistics cost/logistics time, LPI and profit are balancing loops and the loop between investment in IT by LSP, RFID, tracking and tracing, safety/reliability/flexibility, LPI and profit are reinforcing loop.

By integrating RFID with ERP, efficient fleet management system can be created (PwC, 2013) leading to transportation automation. It is a key factor in good customer service affecting delivery, punctuality, timeliness accuracy and tracking (Ngai et al., 2008b). As synonyms to the word “reliability” is dependability, accuracy, constancy, fidelity and security, transportation automation improves reliability of the system. Thus, the loop between investment in IT by LSP, RFID and ERP, transportation automation, logistics time, LPI and profit is a balancing loop and the loop between investment in IT by LSP, RFID and ERP, transportation automation, reliability, LPI and profit is a reinforcing loop.

EDI

EDI can be defined as the computer to computer exchange of business information electronically in a structured format between business trading partners (Murphy and Daley, 1998). It helps companies to

Figure 3. Causal Loop Diagram for Investment in IT and its Effect on LPI

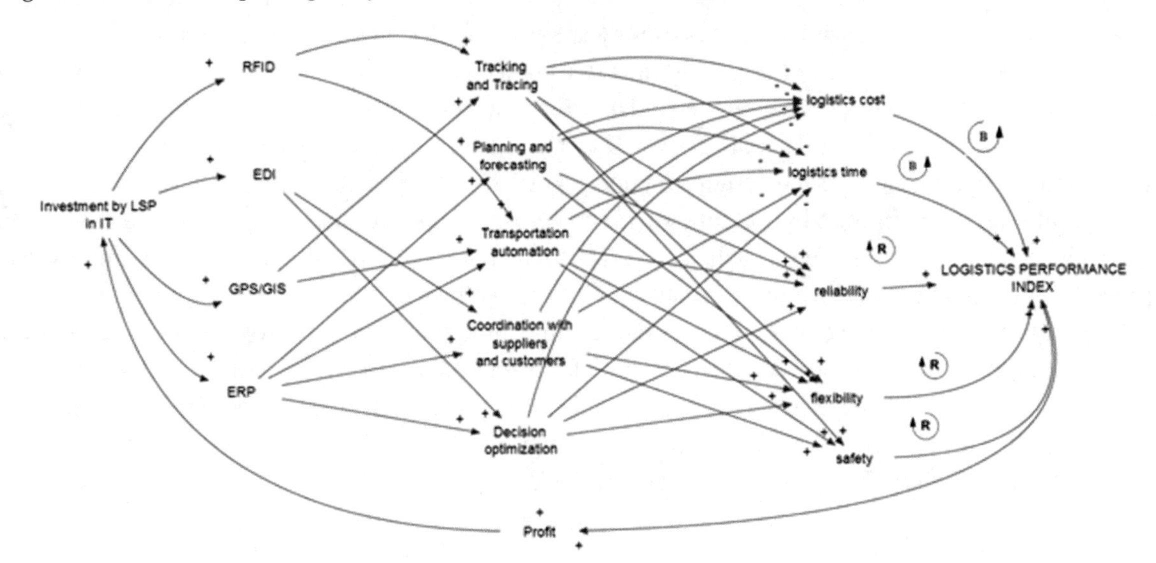

exchange commercial documents without human intervention (Ngai et al., 2008a). It enhances efficient coordination (Larson and Kulchitsky, 1998), which enhances decision making and communication facilitating better planning and forecasting leading to reduction in cost (Lewis and Talalayevsky, 2004), reduction in error, improvement in transaction, speed, better customer service and achieving cost efficiency (Nair et al., 2009); improvement in accuracy (Mulligan, 1996) and flexibility (Hazen and Byrd, 2012). Therefore in Figure 3, the loop between investments in IT, EDI, coordination with suppliers and customers/decision optimization, logistics cost/logistics time, LPI and profit are balancing loops. Also, the loop between investment in IT, EDI, coordination with suppliers and customers/decision optimization, reliability/flexibility/safety, LPI and profit is reinforcing loop.

GPS/GIS

The next important technology to be adopted by organization is GPS and GIS. It helps in supporting route scheduling and visualization (Hu and Sheng, 2014) leading to transportation automation and tracking and tracing. GPS tracking and IT enabling of vehicles no doubt will help in tracking, but tracking the welfare of human being who do this arduous work is undoubted more critical (Sethi, 2013). GPS and GIS combined with RFID will provide safety and better utilization of fleet. Also, it will reduce the ELR, which measures efficiency and wastage of a route. Use of IT in vehicles leads to fuel savings of 5%, reduction in accident damage by 50%, security, better maintenance and utilization of vehicle (Hammant, 1995). Therefore, huge cost and time savings, reduction in uncertainty and improvement in reliability, safety and flexibility cab be achieved through GPS and GIS.

Therefore, in Figure 3, the loop between investment in IT, GPS/GIS, tracking and tracing/ transportation automation, logistics cost/logistics time, LPI and profit are balancing loops. Also, the loop between investment in IT, GPS/GIS, tracking and tracing/transportation automation, reliability/flexibility/safety, LPI and profit are reinforcing loops.

ERP

ERP is business management software which integrates core business processes of an organization and facilitates information flow between all business functions and manages connections to outside stakeholders. It collects, store, manage and interpret data from many business activities like product planning, cost and development, manufacturing or service delivery, marketing and sales, inventory management and shipping and payment. ERP integrates all the business processes in order to improve efficiency of the organisation and enhanced supply chain performance (Koh et al, 2014).It improves operational decision making (Reddy, 2012), coordination, better planning and forecasting (Razi and Tarn, 2003) leading to reduction in cost (Burca et al., 2005), reduction in cycle time (Yang and Su, 2009), reduction in uncertainty (Lewis and Talalayevsky, 2004) leading to improvement in reliability and improvement in responsiveness (Closs and Savitskie, 2003) leading to improvement in flexibility (Daughtery and Pittman, 1995). Also, other systems like WMS, TMS, IMS, FMS and SS can be combined together with ERP to get a customized solution leading to accuracy, consistency, economies of scale and efficiency (LQ, 2007). Therefore, in Figure 3, the loop between investment in IT, ERP, planning and forecasting/ coordination with suppliers and customers/decision optimization, logistics cost/logistics time, LPI and profit are balancing loops. Also, the loop between investment in IT, ERP, planning and forecasting/ coordination with suppliers and customers/decision optimization, reliability/ flexibility, LPI and profit are reinforcing loops.

As shown in Figure 3, investment in RFID, GPS/GIS, EDI and ERP will lead to reduction in cost and time and improvement in reliability, flexibility and safety leading to improvement in LPI. LPI will improve the profit, as high logistics performance is associated with reliable operation, high asset productivity (Essays, 2013) and high profitability (Coyle et al., 2008) leading to more investments in IT.

STOCK AND FLOW DIAGRAM

The causal loop diagrams help to create the flow diagram, which is the ultimate diagramming aid that represents the feedback structure in terms of physical and information flows and stocks and is also known as stock and flow diagram. The important components used to develop the stock and flow diagram are shown in Table 6.

The stock and flow diagram shown in Figure 4, has been developed using STELLA 9.1.3 software. After developing the stock and flow diagram, the model has been simulated for 12 quarters, taking the value of DT (Delta Time) as 1. DT controls how frequently calculations are applied each unit of time and as they process will not change every unit of time, it is taken as 1 in this case.

CASE DESCRIPTION

The company is an Indian based medium sized logistics service provider having a turnover of Rs. 1200 crores with a profit of Rs. 150 crores in 2012-13. The manpower base of the company is fifteen thousand,

Table 6. Description of important system dynamics components

S.No.	Variable Name	Symbol	Description
1.	Level		It accumulates changes and is influenced by flow
2.	Auxiliary		A variable type, which contains calculations based on other variables
3.	Flow with rate		It influences levels. The flow is controlled by the connected rate variable, normally an auxiliary variable

Source: Jhawar et al., 2014

the majority of which is fleet staff. For improving the logistics performance, the company decided to invest Rs. 50 crores in the next three years.

Once the amount is earmarked and technologies and performance measures are identified, the company needs to have an implementation plan which will provide the quarter wise investment in each of the improvement area for the next 3 years. The following set of information was required for simulating the system:

a. The present level and the target level of the logistics processes in the case organization.
b. The present level and the target level of the performance measures in the case organization.
c. The improvement in the logistics processes with every one lakh investment.
d. The improvement in the performance measures with percent improvement in the logistics processes.
e. The improvement in LPI with one percent improvement in the performance measure.
f. The weightage of each performance measure on the LPI

To collect the above information, discussion was held with the executives of the company and the following information was collected for use in the study.

Existing and Target Values of Logistics Processes

The existing level of the logistics processes in given in Table 7. The target is taken as cent percent. Although, at present, IT is not used in the company at a very large extent, the above logistics processes are carried out with the help of mobile phones, internet etc. as most of the Indian organizations from the unorganized sector works in this manner.

Table 7. Existing and target levels of processes achieved from IT adoption

Processes	Existing (%)	Target (%)
Tracking and tracing	30	100
Planning and forecasting	60	100
Transportation automation	25	100
Coordination with suppliers and customers	55	100
Decision optimization	55	100

Existing and Target Values of Performance Measures

As discussed earlier, five performance measures considered for developing the LPI. 100% is considered as the target value for each of the performance measure as shown in Table 8. For cost, it is informed by the executives the logistics cost in their company is 63% more than the rest of the industry. Thus, logistics cost is taken as 163%. Similarly, the delivery time is 40% more than the industry and it is taken as 140%. 60% of the deliveries are consistent; therefore reliability of logistics services is 60%. Last minute changes cannot be incorporated in most of the deliveries and hence the flexibility of the system as measured by the executives is 55%. With the increase in accidents and damage to freight, safety is merely 52% in the case organization.

Improvement in Processes

The improvement in processes is measured through per lakh investment in the technology. For example, as shown in Table 9, per lakh investment in RFID and GPS/GIS will improve tracking and tracing by

Table 8. Values of Performance Measures

Performance Measures	Existing (%)	Best in Industry (%)
Logistics Cost	163	100
Delivery Time	140	100
Reliability of logistics services	60	100
Flexibility of logistics services	55	100
Safety	52	100

Table 9. Percentage improvement in processes by investing (Rs in Lakh) in technologies

Technology	Percentage change in benefits by per lakh investment in technology				
	TT	PF	TA	CO	DO
RFID	.006	-	.004	-	-
EDI	-	.007	-	.009	.008
GPS/GIS	.006	-	.007	-	-
ERP	-	.009	.005	.007	.006

(.006+.006) = 0.012. Therefore, tracking and tracing will become 30.012 with every one lakh investment. Similarly planning and forecasting will become 60.016, transportation automation will become 25.016, coordination with suppliers and customers will become 55.016 and decision optimization will become 55.014 with everyone lakh investment respectively.

Improvement in Performance Measures

With every one percent improvement in logistics processes, the percentage improvement in performance measures, is given in Table 10. For example, with percent improvement in processes, the logistics cost will be reduced by (.005+.009+.007+.006+.0065) =0.0335. Therefore, the logistics cost will be 162.9665 with every percent improvement in logistics processes. Similarly, delivery time will be 139.962, improvement in reliability will be 60.038, improvement in flexibility will be 55.0375 and improvement in safety will be 52.035.

The total improvement in performance measures is calculated using Table 10. The value obtained is used in equation 1 as percentage improvement in performance measure (k).

The rate of improvement in performance measures is given by equation 1.

$$\text{Rate of improvement in PM (t)} = \text{PM (t-dt)} + \left(\frac{PV - TV}{TV}\right) * k \ldots \quad (1)$$

where PM (t) is the value of performance measure in the next interval

PM (t-dt) is the value of performance measure at the last interval
PV = Present Value
TV = Target Value
k = percentage improvement in performance measure

Improvement in LPI

LPI is the weighted score of the five performance measures considered in this study. The weight of the each of the five inputs is arrived by using pair wise comparison technique (PCT). Inputs of PCT are

Table 10. Percentage change in performance measure by percentage improvement in processes

Processes	Improvement in Performance measure (in %) by improvement (in %) in Processes				
	Reduction in Cost	Reduction in Time	Improvement in Reliability	Improvement in Flexibility	Improvement in Safety
TT	.005	.007	.009	.0095	.008
PF	.009	.0095	.009	.008	.006
TA	.007	.008	.008	.007	.009
CO	.006	.0075	.007	.006	.007
DO	.0065	.006	.005	.007	.005

taken in discussion with the executives of the company. Initially, when no investment is done, the LPI for the company is calculated using equation 2.

$$LPI = [(\frac{PV - TV}{TV})*w_1+(\frac{PV - TV}{TV})*w_2+(\frac{TV - PV}{TV})*w_3+(\frac{TV - PV}{TV})*w_4+(\frac{TV - PV}{TV})*w_5]*100 \quad (2)$$

Where PV = Present value

TV = Target Value
$W_{1\text{-}5}$ = weight of each performance measure

Using equation 2, the LPI for the case organization is calculated as follows:

$$LPI=[(\frac{163-100}{100})*.35+(\frac{140-100}{100})*.25+(\frac{100-60}{100})*.15+(\frac{100-55}{100})*.15+(\frac{100-52}{100})*.1]*100$$

LPI = 0.22 + 0.1 + 0.06+ 0.07 + 0.05

LPI = 0.50 *100

LPI = 50

The present value and target value are used from Table 8 and the weight of each performance measure is taken from Table 11. Therefore, the existing value of LPI for the case organization is 50 and the target value is 100, that is the best in industry.

With every percent improvement in the performance measure after investment, percentage improvement in LPI is given in Table11. For example, if cost improves by 1%, then percentage improvement in LPI will be 0.0007. Therefore, the total improvement in LPI will be the product of percentage improvement in LPI through improvement in logistics cost and weight in LPI for logistics cost i.e. total improvement will be 0.000245 for every percentage improvement in logistics cost. Similarly, improvement in LPI for every percentage improvement in delivery time will be 0.000125; improvement in LPI for every per-

Table 11. Improvement and contribution in LPI by each performance measure

Performance Measures	Improvement in LPI (%)	Weight in LPI (%)
Logistics Cost	.0007	.35
Delivery Time	.0005	.25
Reliability of logistics services	.00035	.15
Flexibility of logistics services	.00035	.15
Safety	.00035	.1

Figure 4. Stock and flow diagram for investment in information technology

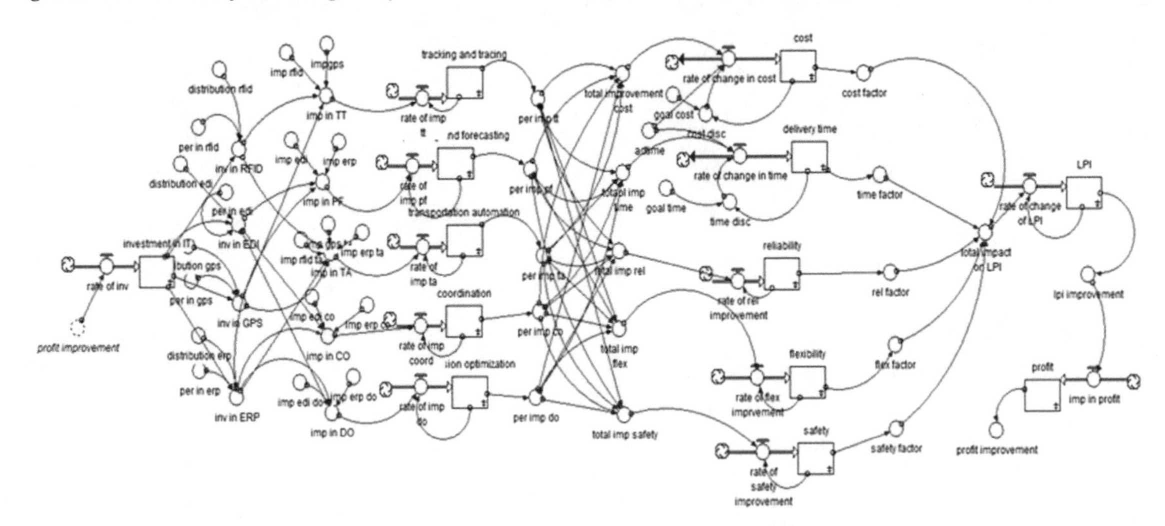

centage improvement in reliability and flexibility will be 0.0000525 and for safety it will be 0.000025. Therefore, the total improvement in LPI, for percent improvement in performance measures is 0.0004475.

Improvement in Profit

The existing profit percentage of the company is 10%. With every percentage improvement in LPI, profit will improve by 0.005.

MODEL VALIDATION

The validation results are shown in Table 12. The ultimate aim of a system dynamics models is to test different management policies, it is necessary to generate confidence in the model so that it can be used for policy recommendations. Khanna et al. (2008) accepted the model at a percent deviation of 10%. Since maximum variation has been observed to be around 6 percent, the SD model fairly replicates the dynamic behaviour and thus validates the interrelationships.

Table 12. Validation Results

Performance Measures	Percentage Change based on calculations	Results based on SD model	Percent deviation from system dynamics prediction
Logistics Cost	162.9	162.42	-0.29
Delivery Time	138.9	139.59	-0.49
Reliability of Services	61.3	64.64	5.16
Flexibility of Services	56.7	60.09	5.64
Safety	53.5	57.16	6.4

RESULTS AND DISCUSSION

The LPI results are shown in Figure 5. LPI reached the highest value in the external focus plan (PA4), with a value of 50.95. The second highest value of 50.8 was for customized plan II (PA3), followed by PA2, PA5 and PA1. Further simulations will be carried out with base as PA3 and PA4. In phase 2, the quarter-wise allocation of funds as a percentage of total investment in the activity is shown in Table 13.

Quarter Wise Allocation With Base as Semi Focus Plan (PA3)

Simulations runs were carried out by taking base PA3 as selected above and quarter wise investment as the percentage of total investment from Table 13.

The results for quarter wise investment for PA3 is shown in Figure 6. LPI reached highest with a value of 51.58 in QAP4, where 10 to 15% investment is done more in initial quarters and 5% investment is done 6th quarter onwards. The second highest value of LPI is 50.96 through QAP1, in which 10% investment is done in initial quarters and 5% investment is done in last four quarters.

Figure 5. Results for LPI for Alternative Investment Plans in Activities

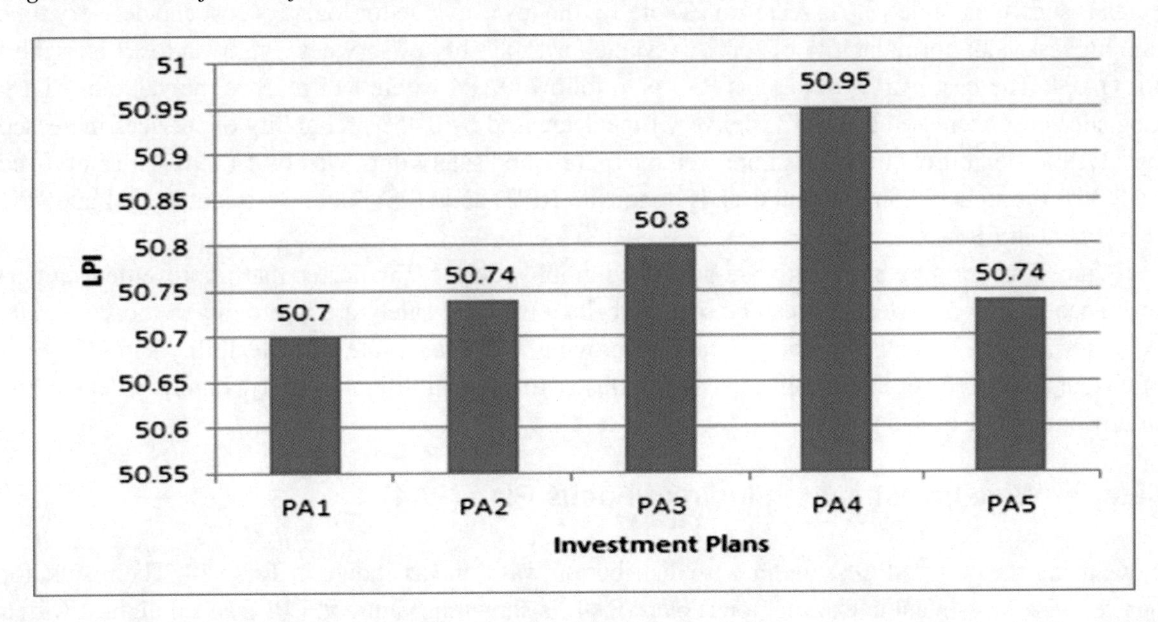

Table 13. Results for performance measures with quarter wise investment in PA3

QAP	Logistics Cost	Delivery Time	Reliability of services	Flexibility of services	Safety	LPI
QAP1	162.19	139.43	66.05	61.63	58.60	50.96
QAP2	162.54	139.67	63.59	58.93	55.91	50.49
QAP3	162.30	139.51	65.30	60.80	57.58	50.80
QAP4	162.10	139.37	66.71	62.36	59.33	51.18

Figure 6. Results for LPI for quarter wise investment in PA3

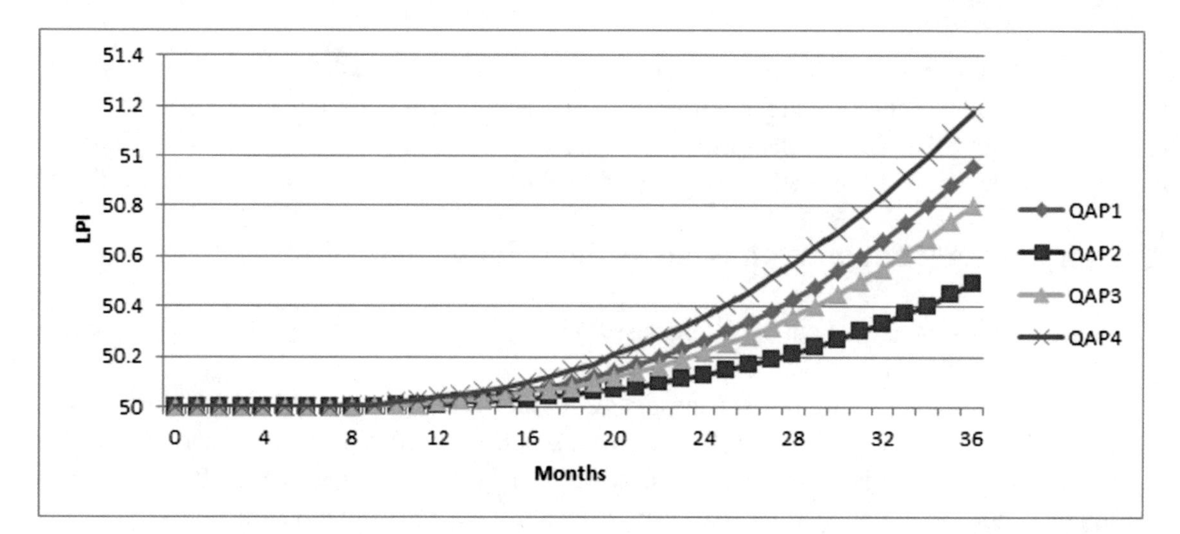

After evaluating, the results for QAP1 to QAP4 with base as PA3, the result of performance measures is shown in Table 13. As seen from Table 13, the lowest value for logistics cost and delivery time and highest value for reliability of services, value for flexibility of services, safety and LPI is highest for QAP4. The best plan with base as PA3 is to follow QAP4 where LPI reaches the value of 51.18. Logistics cost decreased by 0.55%, delivery time decreased by 0.45%, reliability of services increased by 11.18%, flexibility of services improved by 13.38% and safety improved by 14.09%. LPI improved by 2.36% through 15% investment each is done with RFID and GPS, 30% investment in EDI and 40% investment in ERP.

Figure 7 and Figure 8 are software generated graphs. Figure 7 indicates that improvement in performance measures is steady. It can be seen that flexibility and safety are improving at the same rate. Also, for initial 12 months reliability is also improving at the same rate with flexibility and safety but after that improvement in reliability is slightly faster than flexibility and safety. Figure 8 depicts the improvement in LPI and profit.

Quarter Wise Investment in Indirect Focus Plan (PA4)

Now, using the base as PA4, quarter wise distribution was done as shown in Table 14. The results for quarter wise investment in external focus plan (PA4) is shown in Figure 9. LPI reached highest with a value of 51.40 in QAP4. The second highest value of LPI is 51.13 through QAP1.

After evaluating, the results for QAP1 to QAP5 with base as PA4, the result of performance measures is shown in Table 14. As seen from Table 14, the lowest value for logistics cost and delivery time and highest value for reliability of services, value for flexibility of services, safety and LPI is highest for QAP4. The best plan with base as PA4 is to follow QAP4 where LPI reaches the value of 51.40. Logistics cost decreased by 0.7%, delivery time decreased by 0.56%, reliability of services increased by 13.21%, flexibility of services improved by 15.85% and safety improved by 16.28%. LPI improved by 2.8% through 50% investment in EDI and 50% investment in ERP respectively.

Figure 7. Results for performance measure for quarter wise investment in PA3-QAP4

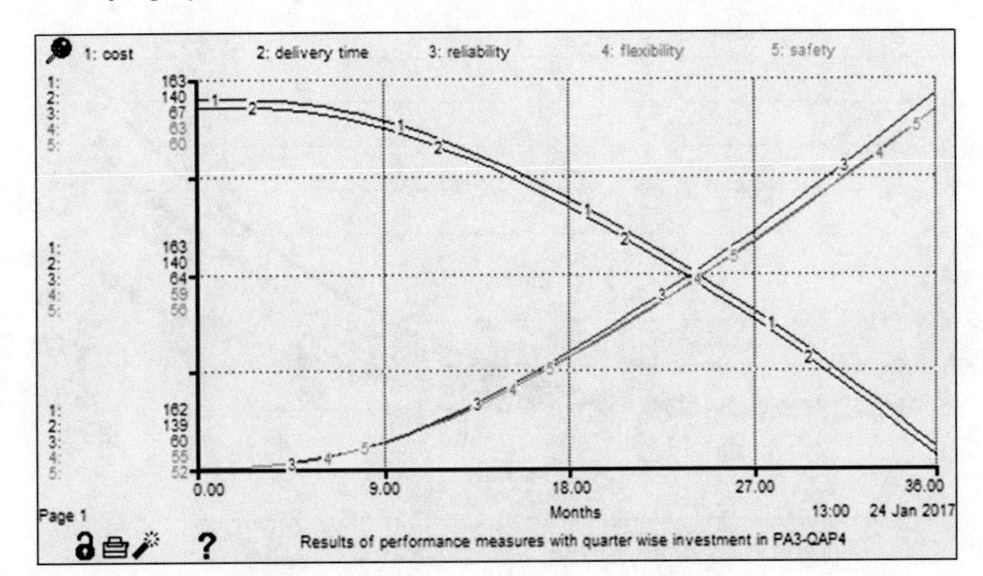

Figure 8. Results for LPI and profit improvement for quarter wise investment in PA3-QAP4

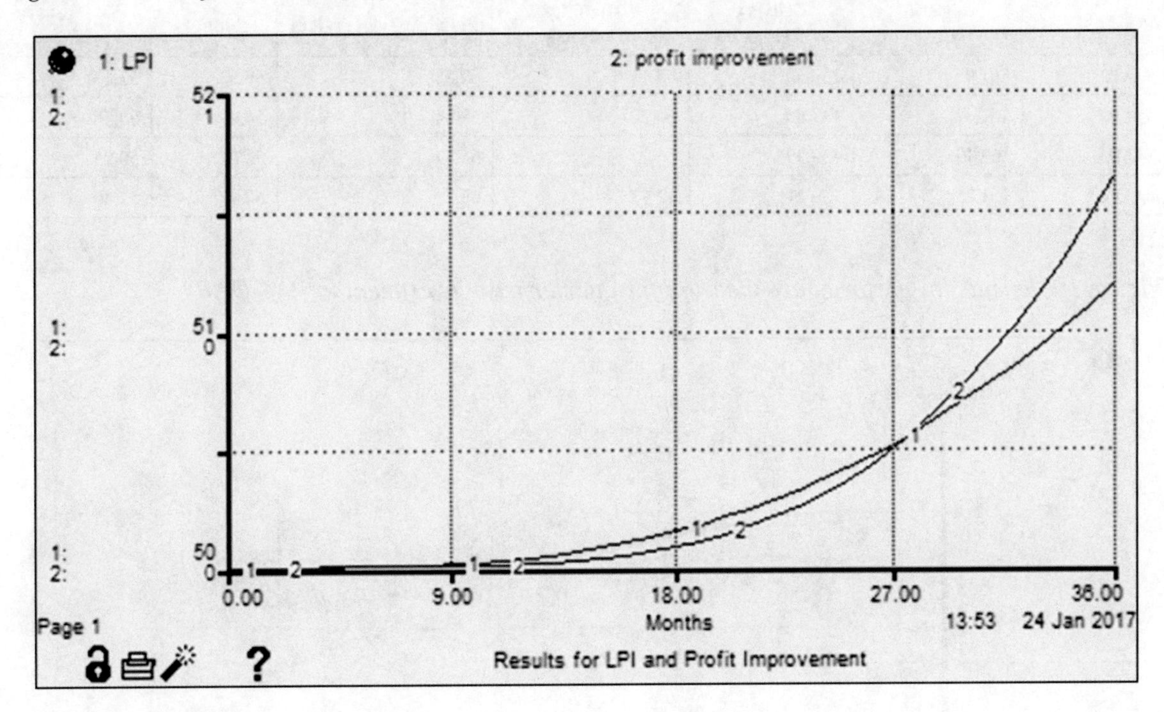

Figure 10 and Figure 11 are software generated graphs. Figure 10 indicates that improvement in performance measures is steady. Also, for initial 12 months reliability is improving at the same rate with flexibility and safety but after that improvement in reliability is slightly faster than flexibility and safety. Unlike Figure 7, flexibility is improving at a faster rate than safety. Also, improvement in LPI and profit is better than Figure 8, indicating that PA4 is a better plan than PA3.

Figure 9. Results for LPI for quarter wise investment in PA4

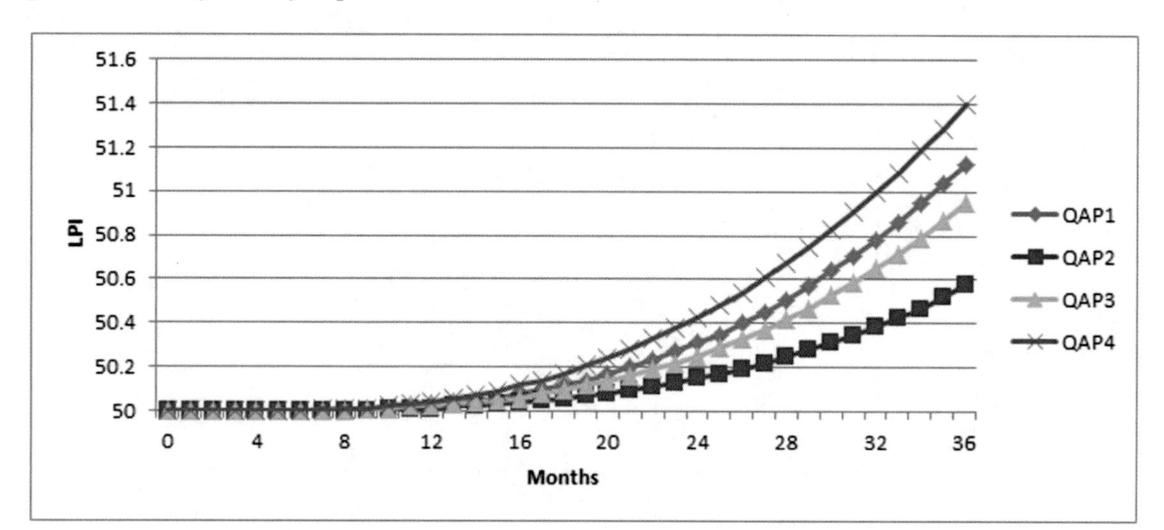

Table 14. Results for performance measures with quarter wise investment in PA4

QAP	Logistics Cost	Delivery Time	Reliability of services	Flexibility of services	Safety	LPI
QAP1	161.98	139.30	67.15	62.86	59.63	51.13
QAP2	162.42	139.60	64.22	59.64	56.49	50.58
QAP3	162.12	139.39	66.25	61.87	58.67	50.95
QAP4	161.85	139.21	67.93	63.72	60.47	51.40

Figure 10. Results for performance measure for quarter wise investment in PA4-QAP4

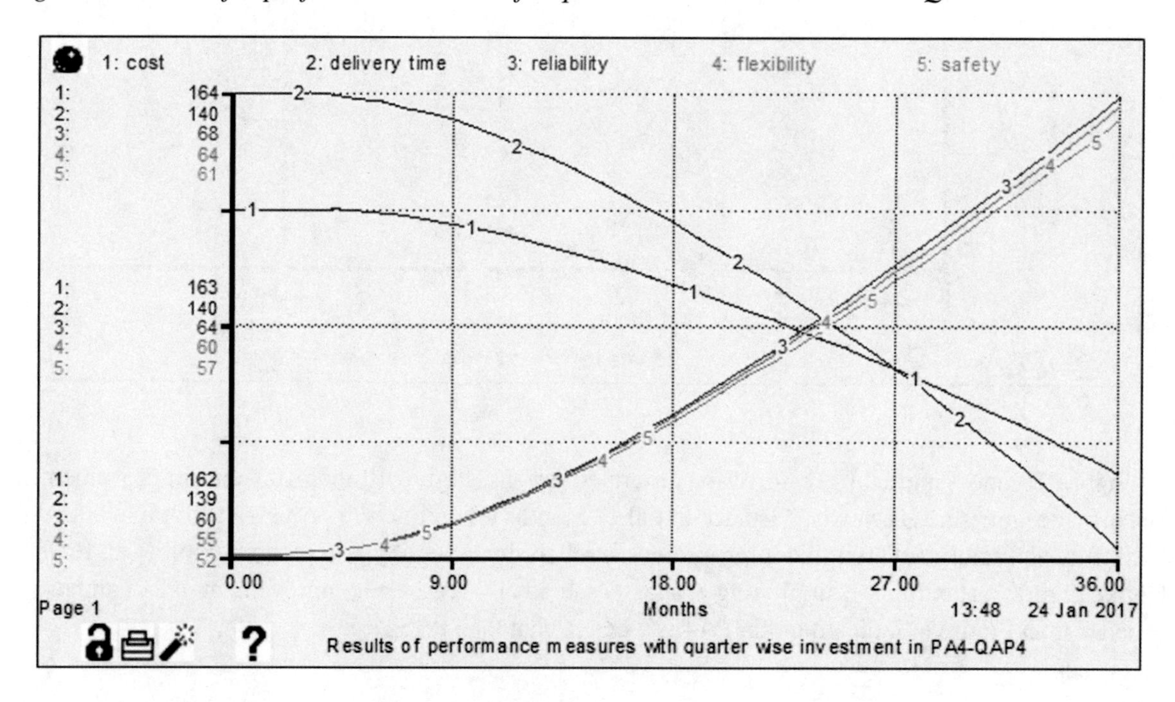

Figure 11. Results of LPI and profit improvement with quarter wise investment in PA4-QAP4

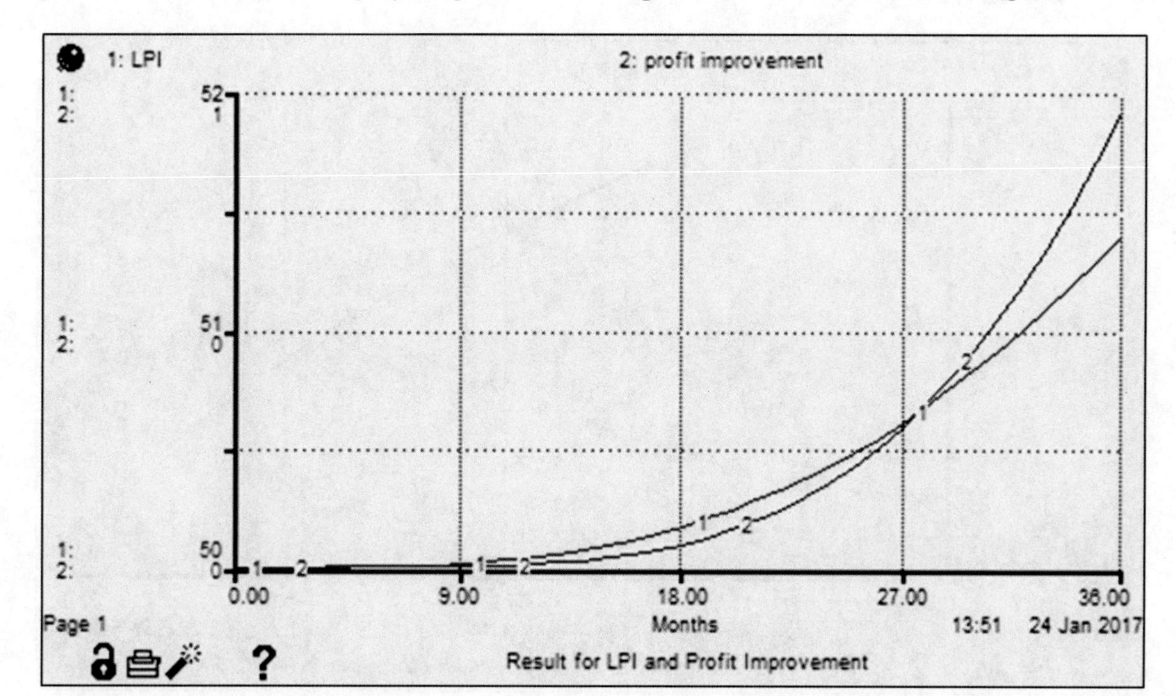

Year Wise Improvement in Performance Measures in PA4-QAP4

To understand the exact amount of investment and time required by the company to achieve significant results, PA4-QAP4 was further simulated by increasing the investment amount by 10%, when profit improvement will be more that 3% as it was decided by the company initially. The results are shown in Table 15.

From Figure 12, it can be observed that improvement in reliability is the slowest but after 25 months, its starts improving and exceeds improvement in flexibility and safety. Improvement in flexibility and safety is steady, but improvement in flexibility is more than improvement in safety. Reduction is cost and reduction in time is almost simultaneous. From Figure 13, profit improvement reaches 3% between 58 months to 60 months, indicating that 10% of the initial amount invested must have started getting added to the investment amount.

Table 15. Year Wise Improvement in Performance Measures

Months	Logistics Cost	Delivery Time	Reliability of services	Flexibility of services	Safety	LPI	PI
36	161.85	139.21	67.93	63.72	60.47	51.40	0.48
48	161.12	138.71	72.24	68.48	65.17	53.10	1.49
60	160.22	138 .10	76.77	73.50	70.21	55.69	3.51

Figure 12. Results for Performance Measures for Year Wise Investment in PA4-QAP4

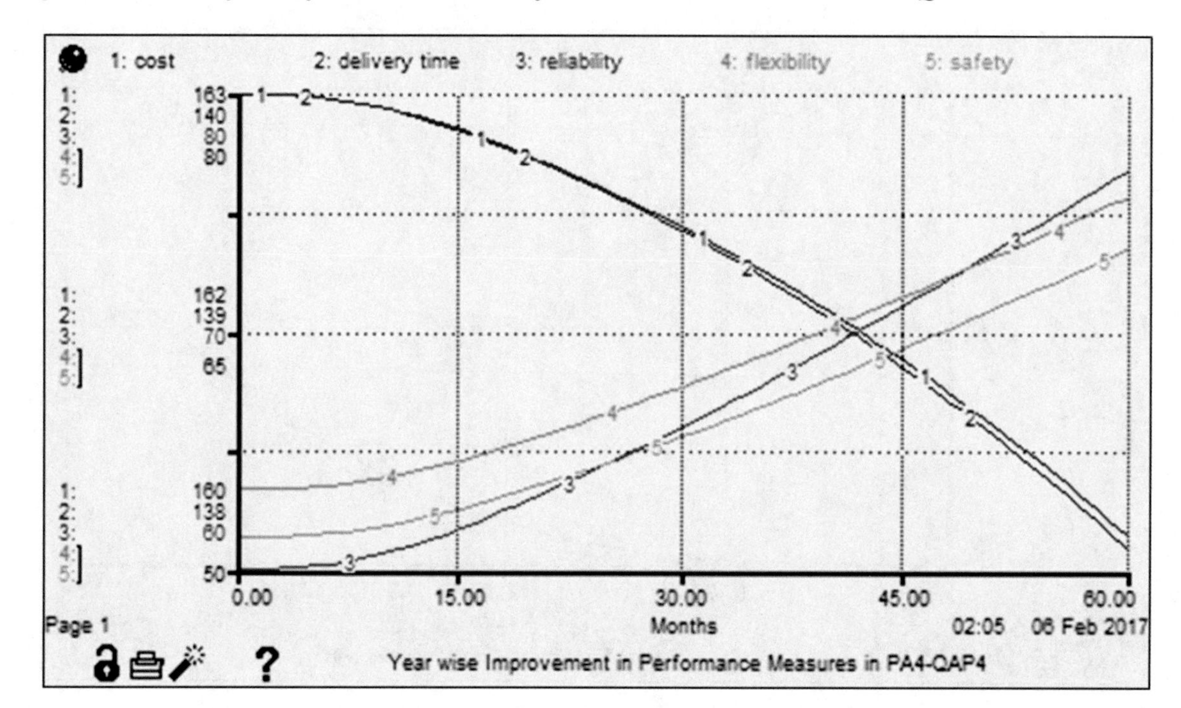

Figure 13. Results for LPI and Profit Improvement for Year Wise Investment in PA4-QAP4

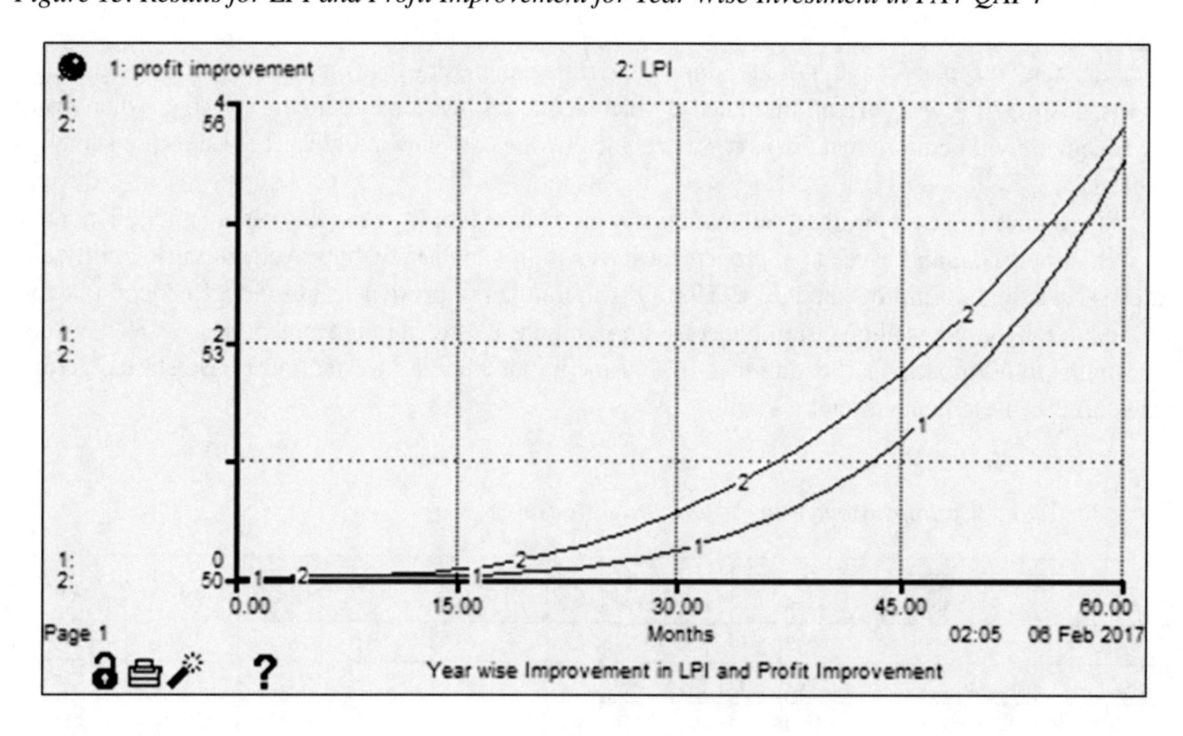

Sensitivity Analysis

Sensitivity analysis is carried out for developing faith in the model and to check the sturdiness of the model. If the model appears to be too sensitive to reasonable changes in the model, the model based conclusions are difficult to be relied on because sensitive models are not much help as a policy tool (Sushil, 1993). Sensitivity analysis was performed by taking investment as decision variable from Rs. 50 crores to Rs. 5000 crores.

Figure 14 displays the input with for sensitivity analysis in the Stella software. The decision variable is the input to the selected (value) window. In the start and end tab, the initial and final value for the decision variable is entered. The user can select the number of runs for the simulation. After selecting and inputting all required data, the set button chooses different values for the decision variables according to the number of runs selected.

Figure 14. Input window for sensitivity analysis in Stella software

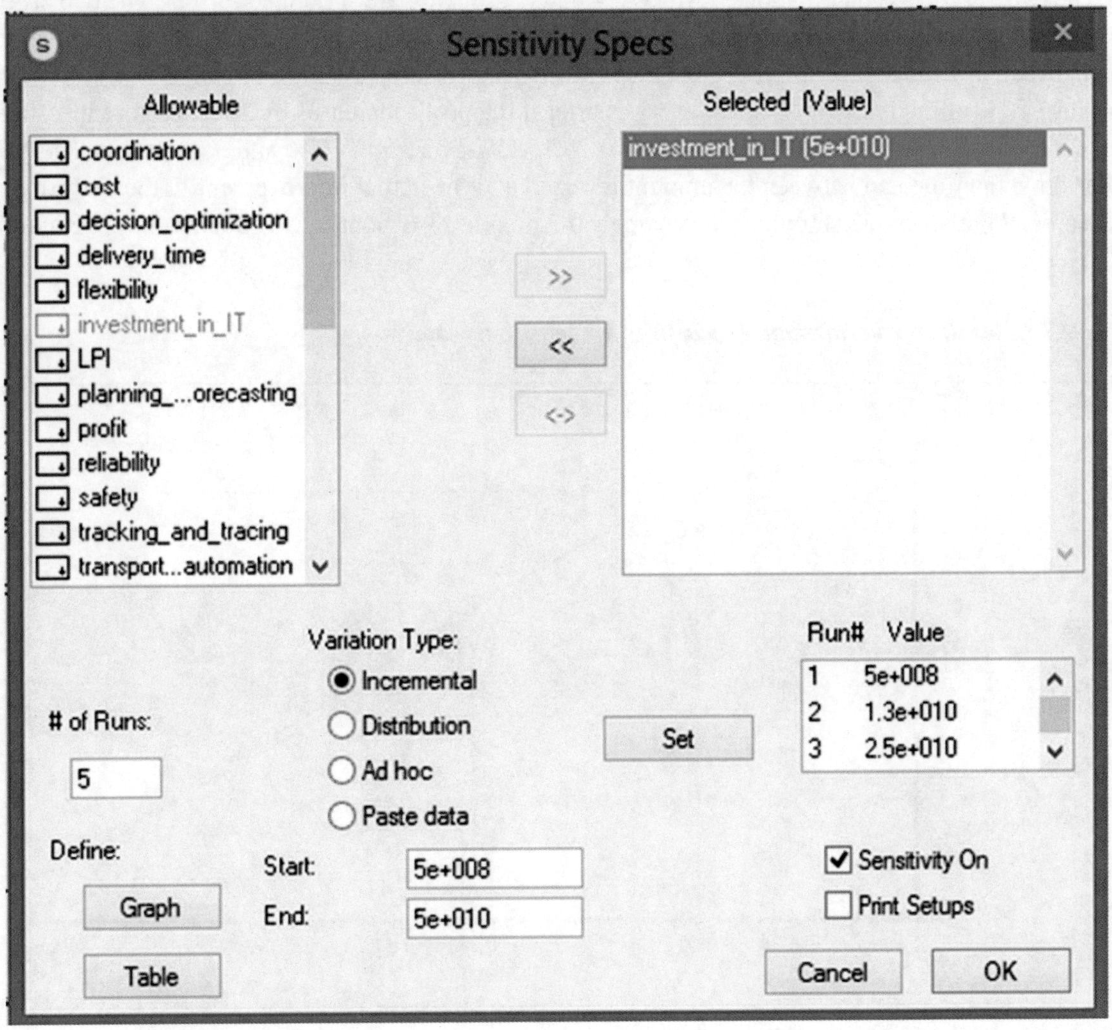

Figure 15 and Figure 16 depict the result of sensitivity analysis. As the maximum value for the decision variable is too large the performance measures have reached the target values in a short period of time. From Figure 15, it can be seen that reliability reaches 100 in around 15 months, flexibility and safety reaches its target values in around 18 months. Reduction in cost and time reached a minimum value of 115 and 105 respectively. From Figure 16, it can be seen that LPI reaches its target value in 15 months and profit is about 50% in 36 months. From the results, it can be seen that the model does not display any abnormal behaviour and it is found suitable for scenario generation or policy formulation.

Scenario Generation

Once a valid model with improved policy structure is obtained after sensitivity analysis, it can be used to create generate different types of scenario for future. Various managerial options regarding different policy and system parameters can be considered and their impact on the dynamic response of the model can be taken as a future scenario (Sushil, 1993). The four scenarios considered for further evaluation are shown in Table 16.

The two best plans combinations, PA3-QAP4 and PA4-QAP4 are simulated further. The two criteria considered for scenario generation are percentage investment after improvement in profit and the time gap between investment and improvement in performance measures. As the company has decided that it will invest 1% of the initial investment every quarter if the profit increases by 3%, therefore investment percentage is divided into four slots namely 0-25%, 25%-50%, 50%-75% and 75%-100%. The other criterion is the time gap between the amount invested and the actual improvement in the performance measures. It is also divided into four slots namely 0-3 months, 3-6 months, 6-9 months and 9-12 months.

Figure 15. Results for performance measures for sensitivity analysis

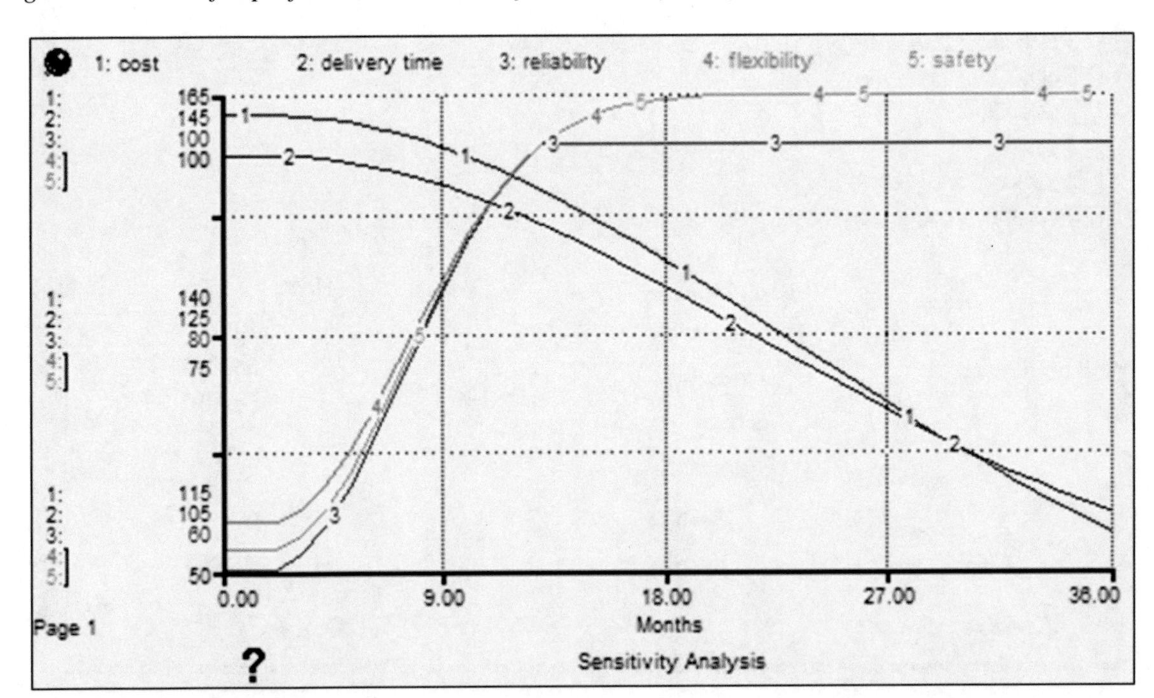

Figure 16. Results for LPI and profit improvement for sensitivity analysis

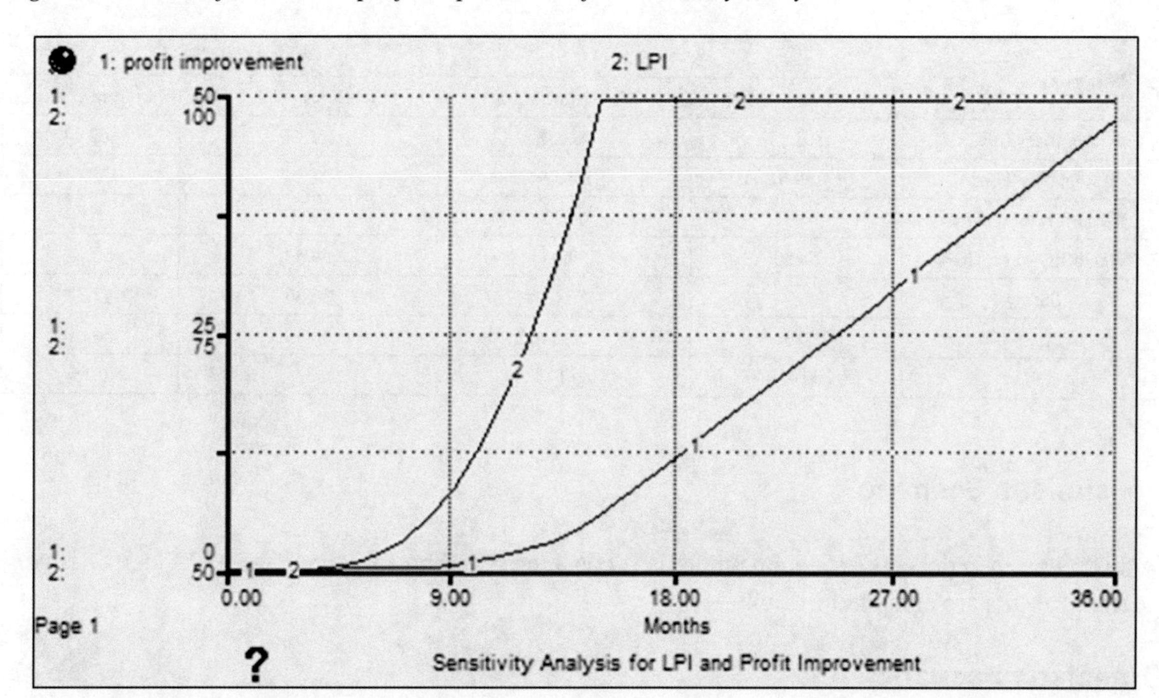

Table 16. Scenario Generation

Scenario	Percentage investment after improvement in profit	Time gap between investment and improvement in performance measures (months)
Highly Pessimistic	0-25	9-12
Pessimistic	25-50	6-9
Optimistic	50-75	3-6
Highly Optimistic	75-100	0-3

Highly Pessimistic Scenario

In this scenario, the maximum time delay and minimum profit percentage are considered. In the base model, no time delay is taken into consideration. But in real environment, delays are natural and a lot many factors influence them. Delays may be caused due to human errors, people reluctant to change or taking the initiative of the company in a negative manner, improper installation, improper use of technology etc. Therefore, a maximum delay of 12 months and minimum delay of 9 months is considered in this case. Delay duration will be generated randomly for every run between the maximum and minimum duration. Also, what if the company does not invest the decided amount back even if the profit is achieved. Therefore, a minimum of zero percentage and a maximum of 25% are considered of the invested amount. The percentage investment will be generated randomly for every run. Results are compiled in Table 17.

Table 17. Highly Pessimistic Scenario Result

Performance Measure	PA3-QAP4		PA4-QAP4	
	Minimum Value	Maximum Value	Minimum Value	Maximum Value
Logistics Cost	162.45	162.55	162.30	162.44
Logistics Time	139.61	139.69	139.52	139.61
Reliability of services	63.47	64.23	64.10	65
Flexibility of services	58.50	59.64	59.50	60.49
Safety	55.78	56.61	56.36	57.32
LPI	50.36	50.52	50.43	50.61
PI	0.08	0.12	0.09	0.15

Pessimistic Scenario

In this scenario, a delay of six to nine months is considered and profit percentage of 25 to 50% is considered. Results are compiled in Table 18.

Optimistic Scenario

Assuming that the investments in the areas chosen are yielding the desired results, in this scenario, a delay of three to six months is considered and profit percentage of 50 to 75% is considered. Results are compiled in Table 19.

Highly Optimistic Scenario

In this scenario, a delay of zero to three months is considered and profit percentage of 75% to 100% is considered. Results are compiled in Table 20.

Table 18. Pessimistic Scenario Result

Performance Measure	PA3-QAP4		PA4-QAP4	
	Minimum Value	Maximum Value	Minimum Value	Maximum Value
Logistics Cost	162.34	162.45	162.16	162.30
Logistics Time	139.54	139.61	139.43	139.52
Reliability of services	64.23	65.03	65	65.94
Flexibility of services	59.64	60.51	60.83	61.53
Safety	56.61	57.48	57.32	59.33
LPI	50.52	50.70	50.61	50.83
PI	0.12	0.19	0.15	0.23

Table 19. Optimistic Scenario Result

Performance Measure	PA3-QAP4		PA4-QAP4	
	Minimum Value	Maximum Value	Minimum Value	Maximum Value
Logistics Cost	162.22	162.34	162.01	162.16
Logistics Time	139.48	139.54	139.32	139.43
Reliability of services	65.03	65.86	65.94	66.92
Flexibility of services	60.51	61.42	61.53	62.60
Safety	57.48	58.39	58.33	59.38
LPI	50.70	50.92	50.83	51.09
PI	0.19	0.29	0.23	0.34

Table 20. Highly Optimistic Scenario Result

Performance Measure	PA3-QAP4		PA4-QAP4	
	Minimum Value	Maximum Value	Minimum Value	Maximum Value
Logistics Cost	162.10	162.22	161.85	162.01
Logistics Time	139.37	139.45	139.21	139.32
Reliability of services	65.86	66.71	66.92	67.93
Flexibility of services	61.42	62.36	62.60	63.72
Safety	58.39	59.33	59.38	60.47
LPI	50.92	51.18	51.09	51.40
PI	0.29	0.41	0.34	0.48

Figure 17 depicts the improvement in profit in PA3-QAP4 under all the four scenarios. Profit improvement is slowest in highly pessimistic scenario, which will start around 71 months. It is the fastest in the highly optimistic scenario, which will start around 59 months.

Similarly, profit improvement in PA4-QAP4 is slowest in highly pessimistic scenario (Figure 18), which will start around 67 months. It is the fastest in the highly optimistic scenario, which will start around 58 months. Circumstances differ from time to time and businesses get affected by many exogenous factors which are beyond the control of the company. So, managers need to implement the investment strategies keeping in mind the repercussions of any delay.

CONCLUSION

In this chapter, the improvement in logistics performance is studied by making investments in information technology, which has become a necessity in today's business arena. System dynamics are used as a tool to demonstrate the impact of investment in information technology on the logistics performance index. The developed model will allow companies to simulate the investment environment and to understand the impact of investment on performance measures like cost, time, reliability, flexibility and safety and also the time frame and the technology in which the investment will reap maximum benefits.

Figure 17. Improvement in Profit in PA3-QAP4

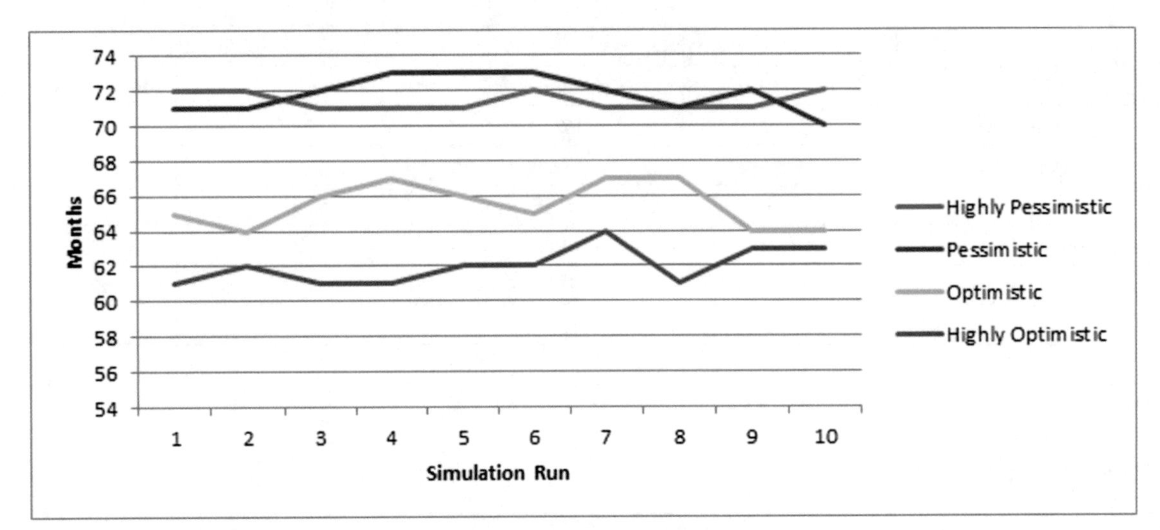

Figure 18. Improvement in Profit in PA4-QAP4

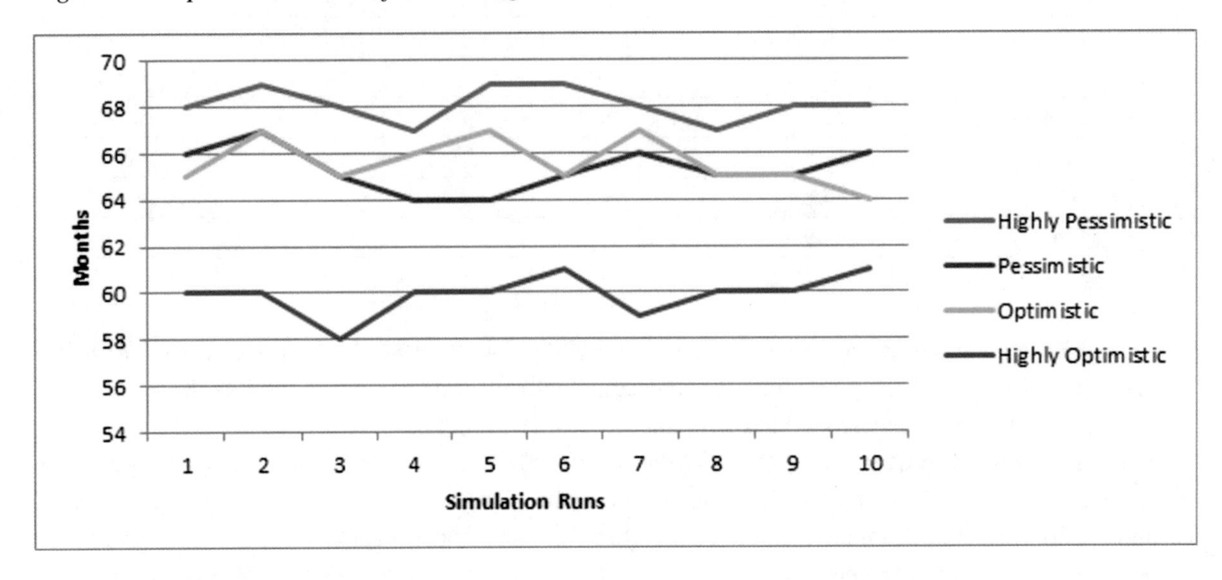

Out of the five plans proposed, two plans which reaped maximum benefits were external focus plan (PA4) and customized plan II (PA3). The plans were further simulated by doing investment quarter wise. The best quarter wise investment plan is QAP4, where 65% investment is one in initial 5 quarters and rest in remaining 7 quarters.

In the external focus plan, 50% investment in done in EDI and 50% investment in ERP. After following QAP4, cost reduced by 0.70%, time reduced by 0.56%, reliability improved by 13.21%, flexibility improved by 15.85% and safety by 16.28%. LPI improved by 2.8%.

In the customized plan II, 15% investment was done in RFID, 30% investment was done in EDI, 15% investment in GPS and 40% investment in ERP. After following QAP4, cost reduced by 0.55%, time reduced by 0.45%, reliability improved by 11.18%, flexibility improved by 13.38% and safety by 14.09%. LPI improved by 2.36%.

Profit improvement will start after approximately after 5 years under highly optimistic scenario where time gap between investment and improvement in performance measures is only up to 3 months and percentage investment after improvement in profit is 75 to 100%.

By comparing both the plans, it can be observed that highest investment is done in ERP. Therefore, companies should focus on maximizing investment in ERP. Also, Indian companies need to invest heavily in IT to achieve competitive advantage and to face the fierce competition posed by foreign competitors. Also, the maximum improvement is observed in flexibility and safety. It can be observed that the value of LPI and other performance measures have not increased considerably by investment in IT. LPI is governed by various several other factors like infrastructure, government regulations and skilled work force. Improvement in these factors also is a must to study the impact of LPI improvement at the organization and country level.

MANAGERIAL IMPLICATIONS

The biggest role of the manager is to identify the right technology for the organization. As implementation of the technology requires huge investment, adopting the right technology will be the key to ease logistics processes. Also, the company will have to bear huge losses if a wrong technology is chosen or the implementation is faulty.

Any technology chosen comes with many features and upgradations. It becomes the duty of manager to ensure that completely utilization of technology is happening. Return on investment on IT is a slow process and before implementation all the steps of business process reengineering should be carried out.

After the successful implementation of the technology identified, the employees should be trained for the same. Proper training program may assist acceptance of the technology by the users. It will also build employee's confidence to use particular technology and lead to employee satisfaction. Employees should be informed and explained why a particular technology is being implemented and how it will affect their work and the company goals. Without such knowledge, unfamiliarity and uncertainty will lead to opposition, lack of involvement and eventual disassociation by the employee. Therefore, training programs should not only provide exposure to technical aspect of the system, but also resolve whatever concerns and question users might have about proposed implementation

A technology offers hundreds of services, so there are innumerable ways to misuse it. Managers have to keep constant attention to avoid misuse of the technology. Vast information is available with employee and can be used against company's interests. Many times fear of being replaced or removed due to automation affects the work of employee. To keep the employee motivated after implementation of the technology and to clear doubts regarding the same becomes the role of the manager. If necessary, retraining can be arranged for employees who are either reluctant or not able to properly use the technology. So the role of manager is very important to successfully choose, implement, train/retrain and upgrade the technology.

REFERENCES

Adebambo, S., & Toyin, A. (2011). Analysis of Information and Communication Technologies (ICT) Usage on Logistics Activities of Manufacturing Companies in Southwestern Nigeria. *Journal of Emerging Trends in Economics and Management Science*, *2*(1), 68–74.

Angerhofer, B. J., & Angelides, M. C. (2000). System dynamics modelling in supply chain management: research review. *Simulation Conference, 2000. Proceedings. Winter*, 1, 342-351. 10.1109/WSC.2000.899737

Auramo, J., Kauremaa, J., & Tanskanen, K. (2005). Benefits of IT in supply chain management: An explorative study of progressive companies. *International Journal of Physical Distribution & Logistics Management*, *35*(2), 82–100. doi:10.1108/09600030510590282

Azar, A. T. (2012). System dynamics as a useful technique for complex systems. *International Journal of Industrial and Systems Engineering*, *10*(4), 377–410. doi:10.1504/IJISE.2012.046298

Bhadrachalam, L., Chalasani, S., & Boppana, R. V. (2011). Impact of RFID technology on economic order quantity models. *International Journal of Productivity and Quality Management*, *7*(3), 325–357. doi:10.1504/IJPQM.2011.039351

Bhandari, R. (2014). Impact of Technology on Logistics and Supply Chain Management. *IOSR Journal of Business and Management.*

Bowersox, D. J., Closs, D. J., & Cooper, M. B. (2002). *Supply chain logistics management* (Vol. 2). New York: McGraw-Hill.

Burca, S., Fynes, B., & Marshall, D. (2005). Strategic technology adoption: Extending ERP across the supply chain. *Journal of Enterprise Information Management*, *18*(4), 427–440. doi:10.1108/17410390510609581

Calza, F., & Passaro, R. (1997). EDI network and logistics management at Unilever-Sagit. *Supply Chain Management*, *2*(4), 158–170. doi:10.1108/13598549710191322

Carrasco, N. (2011). Quantifying public transport reliability in Zurich. *Swiss Transport Research Conference (SRTC).*

Cheung, Y., Choy, K., & Lau, W. (2008). The Impact of RFID Technology on the Formulation of Logistics Strategy. *PICMET Proceedings*, 1673-1680.

Closs, D. J., Goldsby, T. J., & Clinton, S. R. (1997). Information technology influences on world class logistics capability. *International Journal of Physical Distribution & Logistics Management*, *27*(1), 4–17. doi:10.1108/09600039710162259

Closs, D. J., & Savitskie, K. (2003). Internal and External Logistics Information Technology Integration. *International Journal of Logistics Management*, *14*(1), 63–76. doi:10.1108/09574090310806549

Coyle, J., Langley, C., Gibson, B., Novack, R., & Bardi, E. (2008). *Supply chain management: A logistics perspective*. Cengage Learning.

Cruz-Cantillo, Y. (2014). A System Dynamics Approach to Humanitarian Logistics and the Transportation of Relief Supplies. *International Journal of System Dynamics Applications*, *3*(3), 96–126. doi:10.4018/ijsda.2014070105

Daughtery, P. J., & Pittman, P. H. (1995). Utilization of time-based strategies creaoyleting distribution flexibility/responsiveness. *International Journal of Operations & Production Management*, *15*(2), 54–60. doi:10.1108/01443579510080418

Deloitte. (2012). *Logistics sector present situation and way forward.* Retrieved June 25, 2014, from http://www.lopdf.net/get/1leUkOr0QJWTW9JztLEH9qyrxz-d5wvIqXI8xGDCcw0,/Logistics-Sector-Present-situation-and-way-forward.pdf

Essays, U. K. (2013). *Relationship between Financial Performance and Logistics Performance Business Essay.* Retrieved July 11, 2014, from http://www.ukessays.com/essays/business/relationship-between-financial-performance-and-logistics-performance-business-essay.php

Folinas, D. K., & Daniel, E. H. (2012). Estimating the impact of ERP Systems on Logistics System. *International Journal of Enterprise Information Systems*, *8*(3), 1–14. doi:10.4018/jeis.2012070101

Forrester, J. W. (1961). *Industrial Dynamics*. Cambridge, MA: MIT Press.

Forrester, J. W. (1985). *Industrial Dynamics*. Cambridge, MA: MIT Press.

Garcia, A., Chang, Y. S., & Valverde, R. (2006). Impact of new identification and tracking technologies on a distribution centre. *Computers & Industrial Engineering*, *51*(3), 542–552. doi:10.1016/j.cie.2006.08.013

Ginters, E., & Martin-Gutierrez, J. (2013). Low cost augmented reality and RFID application for logistics items visualization. *Procedia Computer Science*, *26*, 3–13. doi:10.1016/j.procs.2013.12.002

Hammant, J. (1995). Information technology trends in logistics. *Logistics Information Management*, *8*(6), 32–37. doi:10.1108/09576059510102235

Hazen, B., & Byrd, T. (2012). Toward creating competitive advantage with logistics information technology. *International Journal of Physical Distribution & Logistics Management*, *42*(1), 8–35. doi:10.1108/09600031211202454

Hu, Z. H., & Sheng, Z. H. (2014). A decision support system for public logistics information service management and optimization. *Decision Support Systems*, *59*, 219–229. doi:10.1016/j.dss.2013.12.001

Hunton, J. E., Lippincott, B., & Reck, J. L. (2003). Enterprise resource planning systems: Comparing firm performance of adopters and nonadopters. *International Journal of Accounting Information Systems*, *4*(3), 165–184. doi:10.1016/S1467-0895(03)00008-3

Hwang, W., & Min, H. (2013). Assessing the impact of ERP on supplier performance. *Industrial Management & Data Systems*, *113*(7), 1025–1047. doi:10.1108/IMDS-01-2013-0035

Introna, L. (1991). The Impact of Information Technology on Logistics. *International Journal of Physical Distribution & Logistics Management*, *21*(5), 32–37. doi:10.1108/EUM0000000000387

Jhawar, A., Garg, S., & Khera, S. (2014). Analysis of the Skilled Work Force Effect on the Logistics Performance Index- Case study from India. *Logistics Research*, *7*(1). Retrieved on July 20, 2014 from, http://www.springer.com/alert/urltracking.do?id=L4b9b5f4Mf81ec8Sb106a2e

Jones, E. C., & Chung, C. A. (2007). *RFID in logistics: a practical introduction*. CRC Press. doi:10.1201/9781420009361

Katerattanakul, P., Lee, J. J., & Hong, S. (2014). Effect of business characteristics and ERP implementation on business outcomes. *Management Research Review*, *37*(2), 186–206. doi:10.1108/MRR-10-2012-0218

Khanna, V. K., Vrat, P., Sahay, B., & Shankar, R. (2008). *TQM Planning, Design and Implementation*. New Delhi: New Age International Publishers.

Kiani, B., Shirouyehzad, H., Khoshsaligheh Bafti, F., & Fouladgar, H. (2009). System dynamics approach to analysing the cost factors effects on cost of quality. *International Journal of Quality & Reliability Management*, *26*(7), 685–698. doi:10.1108/02656710910975750

Koh, S., Ganesh, K., Pratik, V., & Anbuudayasankar, S. (2014). Impact of ERP implementation on supply chain performance. *International Journal of Productivity and Quality Management*, *14*(2), 196–227. doi:10.1504/IJPQM.2014.064476

Kumar, S., Heustis, D., & Graham, J. M. (2015). The future of traceability within the U.S. food industry supply chain – a business case. *International Journal of Productivity and Performance Management*, *64*(1), 129–146. doi:10.1108/IJPPM-03-2014-0046

Lai, F., Zhao, X., & Wang, Q. (2006). The impact of information technology on the competitive advantage of logistics firms in China. *Industrial Management & Data Systems*, *106*(9), 1249–1271. doi:10.1108/02635570610712564

Larson, P. D., & Kulchitsky, J. D. (1999). Logistics improvement programs the dynamics between people and performance. *International Journal of Physical Distribution & Logistics Management*, *29*(2), 88–102. doi:10.1108/09600039910264687

Lee, C., Ho, W., Ho, G., & Lau, H. (2011). Design and development of logistics workflow systems for management with RFID. *Expert Systems with Applications*, *38*(5), 5428–5437. doi:10.1016/j.eswa.2010.10.012

Leon, A. (2008). *Enterprise resource planning*. New Delhi: Tata McGraw-Hill Education.

Lewis, I., & Talalayevsky, A. (2004). Improving the interorganizational supply chain through optimization of information flows. *Journal of Enterprise Information Management*, *17*(3), 229–237. doi:10.1108/17410390410531470

Lin, L. (2009). An integrated framework for the development of radio frequency identification technology in the logistics and supply chain management. *Computers & Industrial Engineering*, *57*(3), 832–842. doi:10.1016/j.cie.2009.02.010

Loebbecke, P., & Powell, P. (1998). Competitive Advantage from IT in Logistics: The Integrated Transport Tracking System. *International Journal of Information Management*, *18*(1), 17–27. doi:10.1016/S0268-4012(97)00037-6

LQ. (2007). An Interview with John Motley. *Logistics Quarterly*, *13*(4), 12-14. Retrieved on May 22, 2015 from, http://www.logisticsquarterly.com/issues/13-4/LQ_13-4.pdf

Mehrjerdi, Z. (2010). Coupling RFID with supply chain to enhance productivity. *Business Strategy Series*, *11*(2), 107–123. doi:10.1108/17515631011026434

Mehrjerdi, Z. (2013). A framework for Six-Sigma driven RFID-enabled supply chain systems. *International Journal of Quality & Reliability Management*, *30*(2), 142–160. doi:10.1108/02656711311293562

Mindila, A., Rodrigues, A., McCormick, D., & Mwangi, R. (2016). ICT Powered Strategic Flexibility System Dynamic Model: A Pillar for Economic Development in Micro and Small Enterprises. *International Journal of System Dynamics Applications*, *3*(1), 90–110. doi:10.4018/ijsda.2014010105

Mulligan, R. (1998). EDI in foreign trade Case studies in utilisation. *International Journal of Physical Distribution & Logistics Management*, *28*(9/10), 794–804. doi:10.1108/09600039810248172

Murphy, P. R., & Daley, J. M. (1999). EDI benefits and barriers comparing international freight forwarders and their customers. *International Journal of Physical Distribution & Logistics Management*, *29*(3), 207–216. doi:10.1108/09600039910268700

Nair, P., Venkitaswamy, R., & Anbudayashankar, S. (2009). Overview of Information Technology Tools for Supply Chain Management. *CSI Communications*, *33*(9), 20–27.

Ngai, E. W. T., Lai, K. H., & Cheng, T. C. (2008a). Logistics information systems: The Hong Kong experience. *International Journal of Production Economics*, *113*(1), 223–234. doi:10.1016/j.ijpe.2007.05.018

Ngai, E. W. T., Moon, K. L. K., Riggins, F. J., & Yi, C. Y. (2008b). RFID research: An academic literature review (1995 -2005) and future research directions. *International Journal of Production Economics*, *112*(2), 510–520. doi:10.1016/j.ijpe.2007.05.004

Oyo, B., & Kalema, B. M. (2016). A System Dynamics Model for Subsistence Farmers' Food Security Resilience in Sub-Saharan Africa. *International Journal of System Dynamics Applications*, *5*(1), 17–30. doi:10.4018/IJSDA.2016010102

Pokharel, S. (2005). Perception on information and communication technology perspectives in logistics. *Journal of Enterprise Information Management*, *18*(2), 136–149. doi:10.1108/17410390510579882

Prasanna, K. R., & Hemalatha, M. (2012). RFID GPS and GSM based logistics vehicle load balancing and tracking mechanism. *Procedia Engineering*, *30*, 726–729. doi:10.1016/j.proeng.2012.01.920

PwC. (2013). *Leveraging IT Transforming the T&L sector*. Retrieved on May 1, 2015 from, http://www.pwc.in/en_IN/in/assets/pdfs/publications/2013/it-print.pdf

Razi, M. A., & Tarn, M. F. (2003). An applied model for improving inventory management in ERP systems. *Logistics Information Management*, *16*(2), 114–124. doi:10.1108/09576050310467250

Reddy, M. (2012). Status of supply chain management in India. *International Journal of Emerging Technology and Advanced Engineering*, *2*(7), 429–432.

Ringsberg, H. A., & Mirzabeiki, V. (2013). Effects on logistic operations from RFID-and EPCIS-enabled traceability. *British Food Journal*, *116*(1), 104–124. doi:10.1108/BFJ-03-2012-0055

Sachan, A., Sahay, B., & Sharma, D. (2005). Developing Indian grain supply chain cost model: A system dynamics approach. *International Journal of Productivity and Performance Management*, *54*(3), 187–205. doi:10.1108/17410400510584901

Sahay, B. S., Vrat, P., & Jain, P. K. (1996). Long term fertilizer demand, production and imports in India-A system dynamics approach. *System Dynamics: An International Journal of Policy Modelling*, *8*(1&2), 19–45.

Sahay, S., & Mohan, R. (2003). Supply chain management practices in Indian industry. *International Journal of Physical Distribution and Management*, *36*(9), 666–689. doi:10.1108/09600030610710845

Saidi, S., & Hammami, S. (2011). The role of transport and logistics to attract foreign direct investment in the developing countries. *Logistics (LOGISTIQUA) 4th International Conference on IEEE*, 484-489.

Savitskie, K. (2007). Internal and external logistics information technologies: The performance impact in an international setting. *International Journal of Physical Distribution & Logistics Management*, *37*(6), 454–468. doi:10.1108/09600030710763378

Schary, P., & Coakley, J. (1991). Logistics Organization and the Information System. *International Journal of Logistics Management*, *2*(2), 22–29. doi:10.1108/09574099110804715

Schniederjans, D., & Yadav, S. (2013). Successful ERP implementation: An integrative model. *Business Process Management Journal*, *19*(2), 364–398. doi:10.1108/14637151311308358

Sethi, J. (2013). *Supply Chain 2020*. Retrieved on June 1, 2015 from, https://www.mycii.in/KmResource-Application/40789.FinalFlashDriveEdition12013.pdf

Softlink. (2009). *Adoption of IT in Indian Logistic Sector – 2009*. Retrieved on June 15, 2015 from http://www.softlinkglobal.com/resources/Expert%20Opinion/Adoption_of_IT_In_Logistics.aspx?Type=resources

Srivastav, S. K., & Chandra, S. (2013). *A road map for internal reforms and other actions required to enhance exports in logistic services from India*. Retrieved on June 10, 2015 from http://www.iimidr.ac.in/iimi/images/faculty/omqt/LogisticsServicesExportsIndia_ConceptPaper.pdf

Stefansson, G., & Lumsden, K. (2009). Performance issues of Smart Transportation Management systems. *International Journal of Productivity and Performance Management*, *58*(1), 54–70.

Sushil. (1993). *System Dynamics A practical approach for managerial problems.* Wiley Easter Limited.

Toh, K., Nagel, P., & Oakden, R. (2009). A business and ICT architecture for a logistics city. *International Journal of Production Economics*, *122*(1), 216–228. doi:10.1016/j.ijpe.2009.05.021

Tseng, M., Wu, K., & Nguyen, T. (2011). Information technology in supply chain management: A case study. *Procedia: Social and Behavioral Sciences*, *25*, 257–272. doi:10.1016/j.sbspro.2011.10.546

Vashisht, A., & Uppal, A. (2013). Case of Logistics and Information System (LIS) Vis a Vis Mc Donald's. *Scholars World-International Refereed Multidisciplinary Journal of Contemporary Research*, *1*(2), 127–132.

Xiangqiang, K. (2006). The Application of GIS/GPS in Logistics Distribution. *Value Engineering*, *11*, 31.

Yang, C., & Su, Y. (2009). The relationship between benefits of ERP systems implementation and its impacts on firm performance of SCM. *Journal of Enterprise Information Management*, *22*(6), 722–752. doi:10.1108/17410390910999602

APPENDIX

Equations for Base Run Model for Investment in Information Technology

coordination(t) = coordination(t - dt) + (rate_of_imp_coord) * dt

INIT coordination = 55

INFLOWS:

rate_of_imp_coord =

((100-coordination)/100)*(imp_in_CO)

cost(t) = cost(t - dt) + (rate_of_change_in_cost) * dt

INIT cost = 163

INFLOWS:

rate_of_change_in_cost = (cost_disc/adtime)*total_improvement_cost

decision_optimization(t) = decision_optimization(t - dt) + (rate_of_imp_do) * dt

INIT decision_optimization = 55

INFLOWS:

rate_of_imp_do =

((100-decision_optimization)/100)*(imp_in_DO)

delivery_time(t) = delivery_time(t - dt) + (rate_of_change_in_time) * dt

INIT delivery_time = 140

INFLOWS:

rate_of_change_in_time = (time_disc/adtime)*totaol_imp_time

flexibility(t) = flexibility(t - dt) + (rate_of_flex_imprvement) * dt

INIT flexibility = 55

INFLOWS:

rate_of_flex_imprvement = if(flexibility>=100) then 0 else (((100-flexibility)/100)*total_imp_flex)

investment_in_IT(t) = investment_in_IT(t - dt) + (rate_of_inv) * dt

INIT investment_in_IT = 2000000000

INFLOWS:

rate_of_inv = pulse(if (profit_improvement>=3) then (.01*500000000) else 0,36,1)

LPI(t) = LPI(t - dt) + (rate_of_change__of_LPI) * dt

INIT LPI = 50

INFLOWS:

rate_of_change__of_LPI = if (LPI<=95) then (total_impact__on_LPI*LPI) else 0

planning_and_forecasting(t) = planning_and_forecasting(t - dt) + (rate_of__imp_pf) * dt

INIT planning_and_forecasting = 60

INFLOWS:

rate_of__imp_pf =

((100-planning_and_forecasting)/100)*(imp_in_PF)

profit(t) = profit(t - dt) + (imp_in_profit) * dt

INIT profit = 10

INFLOWS:

imp_in_profit = lpi_improvement*.002

reliability(t) = reliability(t - dt) + (rate_of_rel__improvement) * dt

INIT reliability = 60

INFLOWS:

rate_of_rel__improvement = if(reliability>=95) then 0 else (((100-reliability)/100)*(total_imp_rel))

safety(t) = safety(t - dt) + (rate_of_safety_improvement) * dt

INIT safety = 52

INFLOWS:

rate_of_safety_improvement = if(safety>=100) then 0 else (((100-safety)/100)*total_imp_safety)

tracking_and_tracing(t) = tracking_and_tracing(t - dt) + (rate_of_imp_tt) * dt

INIT tracking_and_tracing = 30

INFLOWS:

rate_of_imp_tt =

((100-tracking_and_tracing)/100)*(imp_in_TT)

transportation_automation(t) = transportation_automation(t - dt) + (rate_of__imp_ta) * dt

INIT transportation_automation = 25

INFLOWS:

rate_of__imp_ta =

((100-transportation_automation)/100)*(imp_in_TA)

adtime = 12

cost_disc = (goal_cost-cost)/goal_cost

cost_factor = (((init(cost)-cost)/init(cost))*100)*.0007

distribution_edi = pulse(.0833,1,1)/3

distribution_erp = pulse(.0833,1,1)/3

distribution_gps = pulse(.0833,1,1)/3

distribution_rfid = pulse(.0833,1,1)/3

flex_factor = (((flexibility-init(flexibility))/init(flexibility))*100)*.00035

goal_cost = 100

goal_time = 100

impgps = .006

imp_edi = .007

imp_edi_co = .009

imp_edi_do = .008

imp_erp = .009

imp_erp_co = .007

imp_erp_do = .006

imp_erp_ta = .005

imp_gps_ta = .007

imp_in_CO = (((inv_in_EDI/100000)*imp_edi_co)+(inv_in_erp/100000)*imp_erp_co)/100

imp_in_DO = (((inv_in_edi/100000)*imp_edi_do)+(inv_in_ERP/100000)*imp_erp_do)/100

imp_in_PF = (((inv_in_edi/100000)*imp_edi)+(inv_in_erp/100000)*imp_erp)/100

imp_in_TA = ((((inv_in_RFID/100000)*imp_rfid_ta)+(inv_in_GPS/100000)*imp_gps_ta)+((inv_in_ERP/100000)*imp_erp_ta))/100

imp_in_TT = ((((inv_in_RFID/100000)*imp_rfid)+(inv_in_GPS/100000)*impgps))/100

imp_rfid = .006

imp_rfid_ta = .004

inv_in_EDI = pulse((distribution_edi*investment_in_IT*per_in_edi),1,1)

inv_in_ERP = pulse((distribution_erp*investment_in_IT*per_in_erp),1,1) inv_in_GPS = pulse((distribution_gps*investment_in_IT*per_in_gps),1,1)

inv_in_RFID = pulse((distribution_rfid*investment_in_IT*per_in_rfid),1,1)

lpi_improvement = ((LPI-init(LPI))/init(LPI))*100

per_imp_co = ((coordination-init(coordination))/init(coordination))*100

per_imp_do = ((decision_optimization-init(decision_optimization))/init(decision_optimization))*100

per_imp_pf = ((planning_and_forecasting-init(planning_and_forecasting))/init(planning_and_forecasting))*100

per_imp_ta = ((transportation_automation-init(transportation_automation))/init(transportation_automation))*100

per_imp_tt = ((tracking_and_tracing-init(tracking_and_tracing))/init(tracking_and_tracing))*100

per_in_edi = .25

per_in_erp = .25

per_in_gps = .25

per_in_rfid = .25

profit_improvement = ((profit-init(profit))/init(profit))*100

rel_factor = (((reliability-init(reliability))/init(reliability))*100)*.00035

safety_factor = (((safety-init(safety))/init(safety))*100)*.00025

time_disc = (goal_time-delivery_time)/goal_time

time_factor = (((init(delivery_time)-delivery_time)/init(delivery_time))*100)*.0005

total_impact__on_LPI = (cost_factor*.35+flex_factor*.15+rel_factor*.15+safety_factor*.1+time_factor*.25)

total_improvement_cost = per_imp_co*.006+per_imp_do*.0065+per_imp_pf*.009+per_imp_ta*.007+per_imp_tt*.005

total_imp_flex = per_imp_co*.006+per_imp_do*.007+per_imp_pf*.008+per_imp_ta*.007+per_imp_tt*.0095 total_imp_rel = per_imp_co*.007+per_imp_do*.005+per_imp_pf*.009+per_imp_ta*.008+per_imp_tt*.009

total_imp_safety = per_imp_co*.007+per_imp_do*.005+per_imp_pf*.006+per_imp_ta*.009+per_imp_tt*.008

totaol_imp_time = per_imp_co*.0075+per_imp_do*.006+per_imp_pf*.0095+per_imp_ta*.008

+per_imp_tt*.007

Chapter 18
Re-Conceptualizing Smallholders' Food Security Resilience in Sub-Saharan Africa:
A System Dynamics Perspective

Benedict Oyo
Gulu University, Uganda

Billy Mathias Kalema
Tshwane University of Technology, South Africa

Isdore Paterson Guma
Gulu University, Uganda

ABSTRACT

Smallholder African systems operate in harsh environments of climate changes, resource scarcity, environmental degradation, market failures, and weak public and/or donor support. The smallholders must therefore be prepared to survive by self-provisioning. This chapter examines the nature of vulnerability of smallholders' food security caused by above conditions in the context of system dynamics modelling. The results show that smallholders co-exist whereby the non-resilient households offer labor to the resilient households for survival during turbulent seasons irrespective of the magnitude of external shocks and stressors. In addition, non-resilient households cannot be liberated by external handouts but rather through building their capacity for self-reliance. Using simulation evidence, this chapter supports the claim that in the next decade only resilient households will endure the extreme situations highlighted above. Future research that employs similar systems-based methods are encouraged to explore how long-term food security among smallholders can be sustained.

DOI: 10.4018/978-1-5225-4077-9.ch018

INTRODUCTION

Food security systems undergo rapid changes in response to high food demands from the rising population. The world population is estimated to rise by 70% by 2050 (Tsolakis & Srai, 2017) and this creates pressure on the agricultural systems to match future food production needs. This corresponding increase in food production however, is required in an environment of food security stressors such as: food price volatility due to competition of food for feeding and biofuels (Hubbard and Hubbard, 2013; Pruyt & De Sitter, 2008); climate change and extreme weather conditions (Tadesse et al., 2014); and dietary norms characterized by consumption of food beyond physical need (Sage, 2013). In the context of Africa, other challenges to food security systems include; resource scarcity (e.g. land and inputs), environmental degradation (e.g. declining soil fertility, deforestation, and surface water eutrophication), market failures and weak public/donor support and policy initiatives.

In light of the aforementioned food security stressors, poor nations such as those in sub Saharan Africa are likely to be most affected. For instance, the number of people suffering from hunger in sub Saharan Africa only reduced by a small margin from an estimated 239 million in 2010 (Sasson, 2012) to 226 million in 2016 (FAO, 2017). With this decrease of about 13%, there is no doubt that the millennium development goal number one "*to half extreme poverty and hunger by 2015*" could not be achieved. The current emphasis on sustainable development goals (SDGs) with SDG2 focusing on "*ending hunger, achieving food security and improved nutrition and promoting sustainable agriculture by 2030*", provides renewed opportunity for more effective food security interventions to be undertaken. In addition, agricultural led development is fundamental to cutting hunger, reducing poverty (by 70% in rural areas), generating economic growth, reducing the burden of food imports and opening the way to an expansion of export markets (NEPAD, 2002).

The latest commitment to ending hunger and achieving food security in Africa is pronounced in the 2014 Malabo Declaration on "*Accelerated Agricultural Growth and Transformation for Shared Prosperity and Improved Livelihoods*". Accordingly, African Heads of State and Government pledged, among other goals, to end hunger by 2025, focusing on the triple targets of increased production, reduced losses and waste and improved nutrition (FAO, 2017).

In essence, food security issues in sub Saharan Africa have equal measures of fears and hopes. The fears are backed by undesired realities such as: un-met commitments, e.g., the 10% national budgets expenditure on agriculture as was agreed under Maputo Declaration of 2003 but has not been realized by majority of the signatory countries (Harvey et al. 2014); an estimated 218 million people are undernourished and about 153 million people aged 15 and above suffer severe food insecurity (FAO, 2016); only about 1.6% farmland is irrigated compared to 40% of farmland irrigated in Asia (Sasson, 2012); 80% of people surviving below the poverty threshold living in rural areas and have increasing difficulties in feeding themselves (Tyler and Grahame, 2013); and so on. On the other hand, the hopes are underscored by cross-sectorial policies and programmes for elimination of food insecurity and hunger such as: African Development Bank's (AfDB) 'Feed Africa' strategy to enhance a competitive and inclusive agribusiness sector that creates wealth, improves lives and protects the environment (AfDB, 2016); having at least 25 million farm households in Africa practicing Climate Smart Agriculture (CSA) as one of the targets set in the Malobo Declaration for 2025; and of course the overarching sustainable development agenda for 2030.

As the magnitude and impact of crises and disasters increase aggravated by the overexploitation of natural resources and climate change, more and more households, communities and governments in Africa are less able to absorb, recover and adapt, making them increasingly vulnerable to future shocks (FAO, 2017). In addition, past research has studied the sub-domains of food production, food security and livelihood separately, and yet these sub-domains are interlinked and need to be studied as a whole. At the core, the interactional effects of smallholders' food production affects their food security and as a result their livelihoods. Viewed differently or rather as a feedback, smallholders with better livelihoods, i.e., resilient households produce adequate food and store their surplus for future needs. In an ideal farming cycle, seeds preserved from previous harvest are used for new season planting and previous stored food is consumed until a subsequent harvest is got. However, in case of a shock, such as an extended dry season, non-resilient households run-out of previous food stocks and even consume seeds meant for future planting, leaving them food insecure and at the mercy of external handouts. This depicts the food security system as a complex system which is characterized by interconnected and interdependent elements (Oyo & Kalema, 2016; Tittonell, 2014; Walters et al., 2016) and dynamic feedback processes (Ayenew, 2015; Oyo & Kalema, 2016). Hence this study sought to examine food security and resilience at smallholder housholds from the perspective of systems science and in particular system dynamics. System dynamics is adopted due to its ability to describe and simulate dynamically complex issues through the structural identification of feedback, and in many cases, delay processes that drive system behavior (Sterman, 2000; Zhu and Azar, 2015). A detailed precept on the importance of system dynamics to this study is given in a later section of this chapter.

The rest of this chapter presents the problem and objective of this study, this is followed by the case household resilience. Subsequently, system dynamics modeling is discussed by several sub-topics including: related system dynamics models, reference modes, the extended resilience model, model simulations and analysis. The chapter ends with a concluding section and directions for future work. Since this chapter extends previous work of Oyo and Kalema (2016), definition of key terms such as food security, system dynamics modeling, and resilience, are not explicitly repeated here but are appropriately handled in their respective sections.

Problem

Smallholder African systems always operate under non-conducive circumstances (Tittonell, 2014). In such extreme situations: changing climate, resource scarcity (e.g. land and inputs), environmental degradation (e.g. declining soil fertility, deforestation, and surface water eutrophication), market failures and weak public or donor support and policy initiatives, farmers or households must be prepared to survive by self-provisioning. As such, smallholder livelihood strategies are determined by their resilience to stressors and shocks and even recurrent shocks in their food systems. This implies various levels of food security that should be investigated, documented and pursued in future livelihood initiatives.

Objective

The interactional effects for food production, food preservation and livelihood in non-conducive smallholders' environments need to be studied in order to generate better understanding of the desired support initiatives for the specific households. To help generate this understanding, techniques from systems science, such as system dynamics are necessary to provide richer representation of the complex, dynamic, and adaptive processes involved in achieving food security at smallholders level. This study therefore investigates the various levels of smallholders' food security and provides simulation evidence for more effective support initiatives.

THE CASE FOR HOUSEHOLD RESILIENCE

Resilience is the capacity over time of a person, household or other aggregate unit to avoid failures (e.g. poverty, hunger) in the face of various stressors and in the wake of myriad shocks. If and only if that capacity is and remains high, then the unit is resilient (Walker et al., 2006). The concept of resilient households has become important in exploring sustainable agriculture and food security amidst a number of threats arising from: climate change, soil exhaustion, market failures, resource scarcity (e.g land and inputs), and so on. As these threats persist, the resulting recurrent shocks can be mitigated if the household is resilient.

A household may be considered a complex adaptive system when the survival of a household as a system depends less on the stability of its individual components than on its ability to maintain self-organization in the face of stress and shock, in other words on its resilience (Alinovi, Mane & Romano, 2010). In a resilient household, change can create opportunity for innovation and development (Gonzalez & Salvado, 2014). For instance, rice failures due to declining annual rainfall in a rice growing community should cause resilient households to diversify into more drought resistant varieties such as upland rice, thereby maintain or increasing productivity. On the other hand, the non-resilient households will resort to unsustainable appeals for food aid while persisting on the previous failing variety. At the same time, studies have shown that smallholder farmers living below the poverty line are difficult to liberate externally as the acute need for money leaves them with no option but to sell their harvest as soon as it leaves the field without realistic consideration of future food/seeds need (Lukyamuzi, Ngubiri & Okori, 2015; Mindila et al., 2014; Oyo, 2013).

In effect, resilient households are conscious about the future and will ensure that sufficient land and inputs (seeds, labour, fertilizers, etc) for the next planting season are reserved. The non-resilient households, however, trade future planting prospects less on their provisions but more on external input handouts. As such food production by non-resilient households may decline not because of soil exhaustion or inadequate access to land or climate change but because these farmers are planting less as seeds for planting are either scarcely available or unaffordable or because of delays in external seeds handouts.

Application of the concept of resilience to household food security therefore seems promising as it emphasizes households' capability to absorb the negative effects of unpredictable shocks, thereby enabling smallholders to be food secure irrespective of food productivity fluctuations. In addition, subsistence farming has always been a vulnerable enterprise due to a number of known factors that will not be reiterated here. As these factors escalate, farmers tend to endure because of their resilience through a variety of risk-coping strategies. Most importantly, successful subsistence farming occurs when external support from government, donors and NGOs complement household's self-provisioning initiatives. As such, the kind of external support should vary from one household to another.

Following from the above analysis on the effect of stressors and shocks on household farming systems, it emerges that resilient households are less vulnerable and can maintain food production compared to non-resilient households irrespective of the magnitude or frequency of stressors and shocks. This can be graphically represented as in Figure 1.

Figure 1 depicts that households generally can be food secure when there are low/no turbulences (stressors and shocks) in their farming systems. However, when the turbulences exceed a certain minimum threshold, resilient households endure and eventually attain long-term food security while the non-resilient households collapse into chronic food insecurity (Oyo & Kalema, 2016). In real-life, the resilient and non-resilient households are common. Tittonell (2014) presents an interesting case in Kenya whereby wealthier households (in this case resilient households) are always self-sufficient and able to store maize surpluses, and sell them at peak prices before the next harvest, or use them to pay for hired labor. On the other hand, poorer households (in this case non-resilient households) according to Tittonell (2014) fail to achieve self-sufficiency as they often sell their maize immediately after harvest, when prices are the lowest, and buy food the rest of the year. These feedbacks keep poorest households trapped in chronic food insecurity as demonstrated in Figure 1. Similar cases have been reported in Uganda (cf. Guma et al., 2016; Oyo, Kaye & Nkalubo, 2014).

Chronic Food Insecurity

Chronic food insecurity in the context of Figure 1 occurs in non-resilient households that fail to meet their minimum food production due to increases in stressors and shocks in their farming systems. As such, these households resort to survival strategies that further escalate their vulnerability such as: eating less food, reducing the number of meals per day, purchasing food, changing diet, selling assets to buy food,

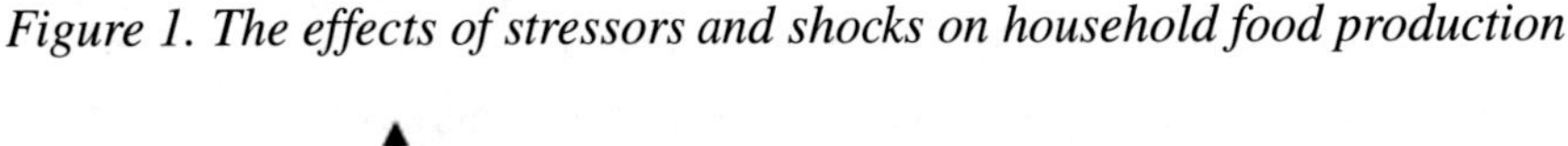

Figure 1. The effects of stressors and shocks on household food production

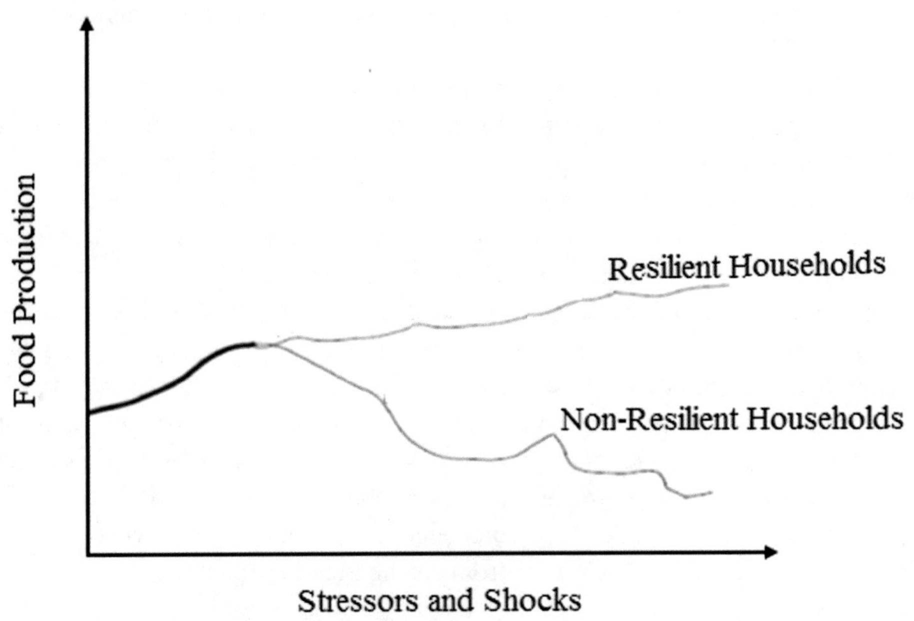

borrowing money for food, receiving food from relatives or the community, increasing consumption of wild plants and animals, leasing land to other farmers, taking children out of school, and receiving food aid from government/charity organizations. Ultimately, such households become chronically food insecure and cannot cope with recovery measures that may require diversifying to high yielding varieties and associated input requirements such as: fertilizers, pesticides and irrigation. They resort to providing cheap labor for credit from the resilient/wealthier households (cf. Tittonell, 2014).

Long-Term Food Security

Resilient households achieve long-term food security despite turbulences because the stressors and shocks create opportunities for innovation and development rather than chronic failures. Most importantly resilient households prepare for future shocks. For instance, resilient household enjoy the ideal farming cycle, whereby seeds preserved from previous harvest are used for new season planting and previous stored food is consumed until a subsequent harvest is got. They also endure a turbulent cycle where shocks in the farming system, such as an extended dry season or a plague, would cause non-resilient households to exhaust their previous food stocks and even consume seeds meant for future planting, leaving them food insecure and at the mercy of external handouts. The resilient households take necessary risks, make necessary sacrifices and investments to mitigate stressors and shocks and as such are able to:

- Preserve seeds for future planting seasons only use them for the intended purpose;
- Store food for future household needs in case of turbulences in projected production;
- Using soil conservation methods like mulching, contour farming to maintain optimal yields;
- Apply small-scale irrigation initiatives especially for vegetables and fruit farming;
- Invest in agriculture through improved seeds, fertilizers, pesticides, ox plough, and extension services to improve yields;
- Sell processed produce that yield higher returns;
- Diversify farming practices by integrating livestock with crop production;
- Have access to adequate land for producing food that matches the needs of the household.

Judging from the above characteristics, resilient households engage in farming for their livelihood and therefore are able to thrive in all circumstances.

The Effect of Climate

Climate variability has both direct and indirect impacts on food security and human health. The overall availability of food shows some correlation with climate variability (Thornton et al., 2014). The study by Lloyd et al. (2011) builds upon previous work of Nelson (2009) to show clearly that climate change and increased climate variability has a direct impact on food production (Lloyd et al., 2011; Nelson, 2009). Ahmed et al. (2011) also used a modeling approach to estimate how changes in climate variability affects crop yields and hence poverty rates in Tanzania. These effects as projected to the early 2030s show that future climate scenarios with the largest increases in climate volatility rendered Tanzanians increasingly vulnerable to poverty through its impact on the production of staple grains.

The impacts of changes in climate variability and extremes will affect food security in the future because of the socio-economic and political context in which humans live. Thus, vulnerability to climate change is highly differentiated across geography, income levels, type of livelihood, and governance arrangements, among other things (Thornton et al., 2014). The vulnerability can be evaluated with a range of different outcomes such as food security or household income. Vulnerability can be viewed in terms of multiple and dynamic factors and hence, need to take a synthetic approach to translate the sectoral impacts of changes in climate and climate variability into consequences for people. Food security is a particularly important developmental outcome that is highly vulnerable to climate change. This vulnerability is a product of climate change impacts on food systems, affecting food availability, as well as economic and social impacts that affect food utilization, access to food and the stability of food security (Nelson, 2009).

We now extend this discussion (climate change effect and food security typology) in the context of system dynamics modeling in the next section.

THE SYSTEM DYNAMICS PERSPECTIVE

System dynamics (SD) is a powerful methodology and computer simulation modeling technique for structuring, understanding and discussing complex issues and problems (Azar, 2012). It is extensively used to analyse a range of systems in business, ecology, medical and social systems as well as engineering. System dynamics is a collection of elements that continually interact over time to form a unified whole (Azar & Vaidyanathan, 2015; Luna-Reyes & Andersen, 2003). Dynamics refers to change over time. System dynamics is, therefore, a methodology used to understand how systems change over time. It presents a means to describe and simulate dynamically complex issues through the structural identification of feedback, and in many cases, delay processes that drive system behavior (Sterman, 2000; Zhu & Azar, 2015). In the context of modelling, system dynamics modelling generally takes on two complimentary forms: qualitative and quantitative modelling. Qualitative modeling takes the form of causal loop diagrams (CLD) that represent dynamic interaction of the system modeled (Luna-Reyes & Andersen, 2003; Oyo, Williams & Barendsen, 2009). Quantitative modelling builds on the CLD by representing the factors studied as stocks, flows and converters, from which model simulation runs are made. The stocks, flows and causal links consist of interconnecting set of differential and algebraic equations developed from a broad range of relevant empirical data (Homer & Hirsch, 2006). Stocks are fundamental to a system and represent the basic quantities that change in a system. For example, a stock may show household income levels. Flows designate rates and determine what goes in or comes out of a stock. They symbolize physical or information flows. Relating to the household income stock, the corresponding flow (out-flow) is the expenditure that drains the income. Converters hold information which is either fixed (constants) or variable quantities because they depend directly or indirectly on stocks (Azar, 2012; Sterman, 2000). The combination of these building blocks is a dynamic system because the stocks, flows and converters may change over time. In this study both qualitative and quantitative models for food security issues at smallholder levels are built and discussed.

Since smallholder systems are turbulent, have multiple levels and forms of interaction between actors, operate in inefficient financial markets, and have deviations from rational expectations, they are better studied using systems approaches like system dynamics. Indeed in system dynamics terms, the practices leading to the smallholders' food security resilience is characterized in terms of identifiable stocks and flows. As pointed out by Stave and Kopainsky (2014), any given stock might be sustainable if the flows in and out of the stock are the same. In the same manner, the agricultural production cycle from planting, harvesting, post harvesting, consumption and sale of surplus food, consists of several stocks that can be maintained by managing the inflows and outflows. Resilience in this cycle is achievable by considering adaptation strategies that would minimize any disturbances arising from sudden large changes to the outflows (cf. Azar, 2012; Hammond & Dubé, 2012; Hassanien et al., 2015). For example, extended rains beyond the harvesting period would limit sunshine that is needed for drying the harvested crops and the farmers' response would be to process the raw food itself.

Furthermore, the dynamics of food production and hence food security and livelihoods are interlinked, and need to be studied as a whole. The interactional effect of food production for smallholders need to be studied in order to investigate appropriate strategies that could improve their production/livelihoods. As such, food security and livelihood issues are complex and a thorough understanding of the underlying relationships is necessary. To help generate this understanding, conceptual and simulation models are necessary. To this end, this study extends the preliminary system dynamics smallholders' resilience model (see Oyo & Kalema, 2016) by improving the stocks and flows and discussing model behaviors.

Related System Dynamics Models

Oyo (2013) analyses system dynamics models for food security over the period 2001-2011 and finds that these models are more qualitative than quantitative based. Interestingly, none of the models reviewed focused on Africa's situations. Between 2011 and 2016, however, system dynamics models for agricultural development and food security in sub-Saharan Africa have been studied at an impressive rate. The reminder of this section focuses on these recent studies. Oyo and Kalema (2016) present a preliminary system dynamics model for exploring the effect of subsistence farmers' resilience on their food security; Kopainsky et al. (2012) examine sustainable food security policies in sub-Saharan African countries from social dynamics perspective, maintaining that social dynamics override adoption of effective food security policies. In the same study area scope, Saldarriaga et al. (2013) explore stakeholders' views on dynamic complexity of climate change, agriculture and food security.

Other studies have focused on individual sub-Saharan African countries such as: Oyo (2013) on system dynamics model for food security and livelihood at subsistence farmer level in the Uganda with emphasis on seed banking; Guma, Rwashana and Oyo's (2016) model that extend Oyo's (2013) seed banking model by providing generic analysis of household food security circumstances; Ayenew and Kopainsky (2014) on food insecurity issues using system dynamics simulation model for the effects of population, food production and markets in Ethiopia; and Ayenew's (2015) model that extends the latter model by examining the influence of natural endowment on food security in different regions in Ethiopia.

Farmers Resilience Model

The resilience model is premised on the understanding that empowerment initiatives of the smallholders are effective when led by the smallholders themselves. The argument here is that smallholders' level of self-provisioning or rather resilience is more important than their dependence on the volatile external support from government and other development partners. In real-life, however, there are variations on the extent to which smallholders can take charge of their affairs, leading to four different manifestations of food security, including; chronic food insecurity, long-term food insecurity, long-term food security and stable food security (Oyo & Kalema, 2016). Accordingly, chronic food insecurity occurs when smallholders have low resilience and external support is negligible. In this case, the farmers are unable to meet their minimum food production requirements over a sustained period of time. As such, the farmers resort to copying strategies that further escalate their vulnerability such as: eating less food, reducing the number of meals per day, purchasing food, changing diet, selling assets to buy food, borrowing money for food, receiving food from relatives or the community, increasing consumption of wild plants and animals, leasing land to other farmers, taking children out of school, and receiving food aid from government/charity organizations (Oyo & Kalema, 2016). In this case, increasing external support may alleviate the problem only for a short period of time, but in the farmers remain food insecure in their life-time. Again, over dependence on external intervention without self-provisioning initiatives leads to short lived food security but long term food insecurity. In this scenario, farmers rely on constant flow of seeds for planting and other basic inputs without which their production capacity falls below minimum levels required for provision of household food needs. This results into food insecurity in the long-term or rather a better-before-worse behavior.

Details of long-term food security and stable food security can be found in Oyo and Kalema (2016) and most importantly the system dynamics smallholders' resilience model makes the following policy suggestions:

- Separation of production of food for cash and production of food for consumption as these are different goals and in some cases having unique requirements. For cash crops, production and processing need to be addressed concurrently, while for food crops, focus should be placed on production, postharvest handling and storage;
- Building capacity for crop production at both family level and community level, whereby the basic production requirements such as: access to land, preservation of seeds for future seasons and provision of human labor, are handled at family level. Other expensive production inputs such as acquiring high-yielding seed varieties, ensuring integrated pest management, and supporting small-scale irrigation, are addressed at community level;
- Reducing waste and losses right from crop planting to food consumption. For instance, knowledge of seeds spacing is critical in avoiding planting excess seeds per unit land area.
- Ensuring functional markets for processed food and not raw food.

Seed Banking Model

Seed banking is a holistic approach for empowerment of smallholder farmers through preserving seeds for future planting, diversifying into higher value crops and saving money from sale of surplus crops concurrently (Oyo, 2013). This ensures that smallholders do not lack the quantity and quality of seeds they need during planting seasons as well as access their savings to invest in necessary farm inputs for higher productivity. In effect, seed banking services are provided by a seed bank which is a community based organization that also offers agro-processing, agricultural produce marketing and extension services (Oyo, 2013). The seed banking model therefore studied production and earnings from smallholders in eastern Uganda and revealed the following:

1. That the relationship between production and profitability is not linear when dealing with unprocessed crops at the grassroots whose prices cannot be determined by market forces.
2. That smallholders living below the poverty line are difficult to liberate as the acute need for money leaves them with no option but to sell their harvest as soon as it leaves the field without realistic

consideration of future food/seeds need. Smallholders are most likely to continue selling their yields at a loss unless new structures for fair food prices are provided.

3. That crop production by smallholders may decline not because of soil fertility or climatic change issues but because farmers are planting less as seeds for planting are either scarcely available or unaffordable.
4. That the poverty levels among the smallholders will continue to increase as they resort to selling their livestock and charcoal to buy food when their food reserves are empty. At the same time, the smallholders have no capacity to replace livestock sold or trees lost from subsequent crop harvests due to the challenge highlighted in c) above.

The above revelations point to the need to support smallholders through seed banking whereby the seed bank buys harvested crops from farmers at competitive prices, processes them and sells the processed crops for profit, while maintaining a threshold amount of money that is converted into improved seeds and other farm inputs accessible by the farmers during the planting season.

Household Food Security Model

Guma et al. (2016) investigate food security challenges and examine policies for improving livelihood at household levels. This model extends Oyo's (2013) seed banking model by exploring the general household food security circumstances, i.e, explaining how a balance between food stock, seeds preserved, crop sales and consumption can be attained. The model is conceptualized in four sectors. The first sector (land and inputs) examines the effect of population change cropland and capacity of land to sustain farming need. The second sector (crop production) tracks the dynamics of yields under varying farming situations. Thirdly, the sales and income sector that investigates real-life circumstances of sales because of need for cash or sales from the surplus harvested crops. The fourth and last sector (food consumption) examines food consumption in the context of family size and nutritional values. Overall, the insights from the model include the following:

- That increase in population decreases land per person for cultivation, which limits the capacity for food production. As a result, farmers resort to more drastic measures such as deforestation and wetlands encroachment which in the long-term cause adverse climate changes that affect food production.
- That climate change has a more profound effect than other factors such as soil exhaustion, volatile markets and pests and diseases. This is because changes in climate (reduction in rainfall periods) has reduced crop planting frequency from three seasons to two seasons and in some cases to one season per year. As a result farmers are neither able to produce for their basic household food needs nor produce for their livelihoods.

Arising from their study, Guma et al. (2016) make an interesting conclusion that wealthier households are always food secure. They store food surpluses at the end of the farming season and sell them at peak prices before the next season or use their food in exchange for labor from the poorer households that are in need of food. In contrast, the poorer households often sell their crops immediately after harvest, when prices are the lowest, and buy food the rest of the year.

Socio-Ecological Model

Saldarriaga et al. (2013) explore stakeholders' views on dynamic complexity of climate change, agriculture and food security. They explain that climate change will lead to significant yield reductions in maize in sub Saharan Africa. Achieving food security and adaptation to climate change is a serious challenge to food systems as there is growing demand from population. Saldarriaga et al. (2013) argue that food systems are social-ecological systems that consist of bio-physical and social factors which are linked through feedback mechanisms. These mechanisms determine the development of food system outcomes such as food security, environmental welfare and social welfare over time. The focus of their analysis is on three components of food security. 1) Food availability as the amount, type and quality of food a unit has at its disposal to consume, either through local production, distribution, or exchange for money, labor or other items of value. 2) Access to food in terms of the affordability of food that is available (how well allocation mechanisms such as markets and government policies work) and whether consumers can meet their food preferences. 3) Utilization of food as the ability to consume and benefit from food. Saldarriaga et al. (2013) further test these propositions on small scale farmers' circumstances and found little evidence to suggest benefits by such farmers.

The Ethiopian Food Insecurity Model

Ayenew and Kopainsky (2014) contend that Ethiopia is the largest recipient of food aid in Sub-Saharan Africa arising. Their food security model therefore sought to examine the underlying problems causing food insecurity in Ethiopia and test policy options that could alleviate food insecurity. Their model was structured in three sectors, namely; population, food production and market dynamics. The model shows that in the past, both availability of food and access to food constrained the actual food consumption of the population. In addition, there were gaps in food production and food purchasing power of the population. Ayenew and Kopainsky (2014) further argued that degraded land contributed considerably to the poor average productivity of the land and recommended policies tied to land rehabilitation and capacity building for skilled use of agricultural inputs such as improved seeds, fertilizers and pesticides.

Ayenew (2015) extended their previous model (Ayenew & Kopainsky, 2014) by adding rainfall dynamics. This was driven by the fact that agriculture being the main economic activity of Ethiopia relies heavily on rainfall. Ethiopians is and the key characteristic of Ethiopian agriculture is its dependence on rainfall. Due to limited rainfall which in some cases is erratic, Ayenew (2015) recommends integration of irrigation practices in the entire Ethiopian farming system.

Judging from the literature discussed here, it is clear that research on food security issues in sub-Saharan Africa using system dynamics modeling is slowly gaining prominence with the first published work dating 2012. This study therefore adds to this growing body of knowledge by providing a deeper analysis of the effect of resilience on the different categories of smallholders using simulations.

Dynamic Patterns of Food Security Issues

In order to appreciate the importance of system dynamics in examining food security problems, reference real-life behavior is important. In the context of this research, yields for major foods (cereals, roots and tubers) in selected countries in sub-Saharan Africa over the last five decades provide a relevant reference behavior. This is shown in Figure 2. Aware that the population in sub-Saharan Africa has been steadily

Figure 2. Trends in yields of cereals, roots and tubers for selected countries in sub-Saharan Africa

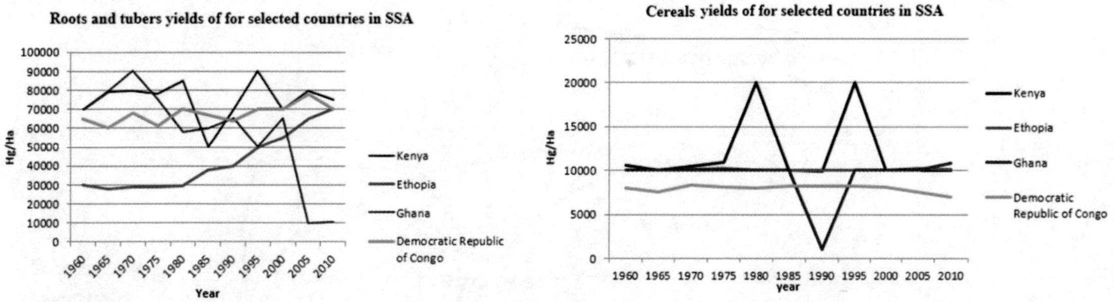

increasing over the last several decades, the demand for food and hence food yields should have equally had risen steadily. The mismatch however, points to the need to investigate and experiment systemic solutions that strengthen self-reliance of the farmers.

Trends in Figure 2 have in some cases been associated with climate change effect (Morton, 2007; Thornton et al., 2007; Walker et al., 2010). This is supported by the growing consensus that changes in climate variability and extremes will affect food security in the future because of the socio-economic and political context in which humans live (Ahmed et al., 2011; Llyod et al., 2011). At the same time, vulnerability to climate change is highly differentiated across geography, income levels, type of livelihood, and governance arrangements, among other things (Thornton et al., 2014).

Model Scope

The focus of the model is to experiment the two unique food security scenarios, i.e., long-term food security and chronic food insecurity arising from the nature of household resilience as already discussed. Since the model is meant for sub-Saharan Africa's subsistence farmers' situations, the paper presents underlying feedback for food security and food insecurity scenarios with emphasis on resilience susceptibility at household level as shown in Figure 3.

Figure 3 is the basic feedback loops depicting food security scenarios (R loops) and food insecurity scenarios (B loops). In the context of this research, chronic food insecurity arises when elements comprised in the B loops and those interfacing with B loops are ignored by the respective households. This occurs under the following household circumstances:

- Selling raw food more than processed food;
- Failing to preserve seeds for future seasons;
- Experiencing food shortages because of low food productivity as well as food losses in the garden, at harvest, and during post-harvest handling and storage;
- Planting less crops due to lack of capacity to invest in basic inputs (seeds, pesticides, land, irrigation);
- Failing to investment in extension services.

Figure 3. Basic feedbacks for food security

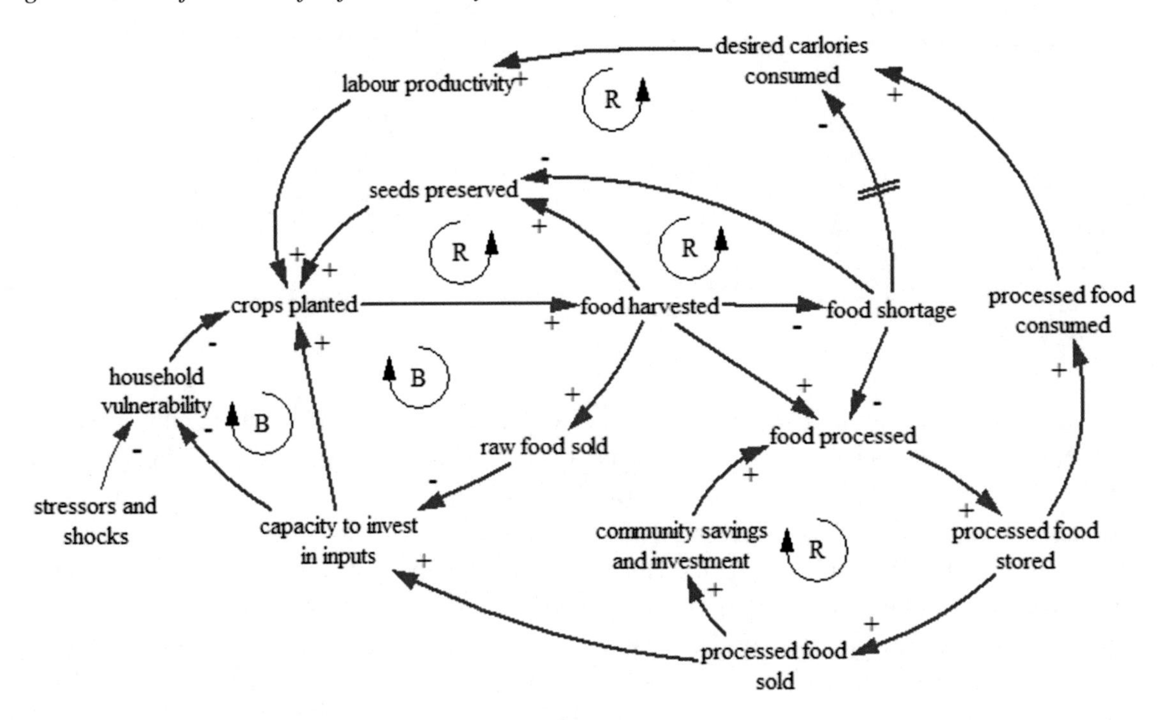

Model Stocks and Flows

The corresponding stocks and flows for the basic feedbacks in Figure 3 is given in Figure 4. The stocks and flows focus on the effect of resilience on household food security. Essentially, the resilience is measured from the capacity of households to invest in inputs. In terms of modelling, this capacity arises from the nature in which households manage the contention of selling raw food versus processed food as well as food storage to minimize food shortages.

Vulnerability Analysis of Households

In the context of this paper, two simulation runs contrasting resilient and non-resilient households are given in Figure 5 and Figure 6 respectively. The basic feedbacks in Figure 3 depict stressors and shocks as an exogenous variable and as such, it only deepens the vulnerability of non-resilient households. In other words, the absence of stressors and shocks does not imply that smallholders can be food secure. For instance, selling unprocessed or raw food than the higher value processed foods limits the capacity of households to provide inputs they need to be food secure. This is depicted in Figure 5 for resilient households where increase in capacity to provide inputs decreases vulnerability of the households thereby enabling such households to achieve long-term food security even in cases of stressors and recurrent stressors.

The resilient households as depicted in Figure 5 have the following characteristics:

Figure 4. Stocks and flows for household vulnerability analysis

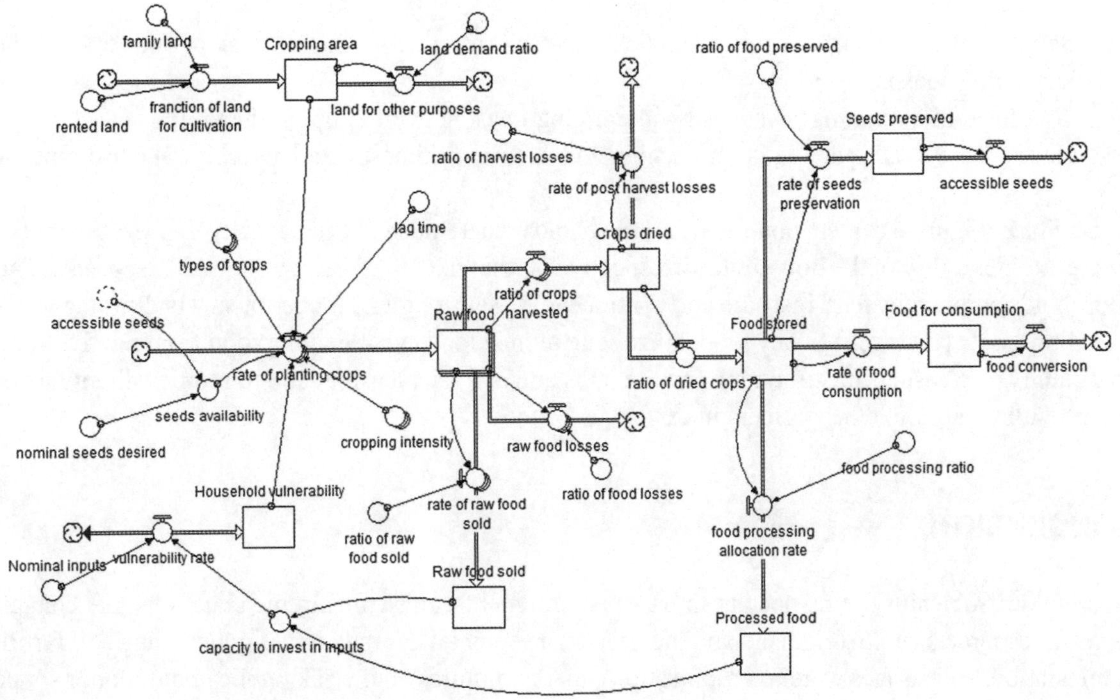

Figure 5. Analysis of vulnerability for resilient household

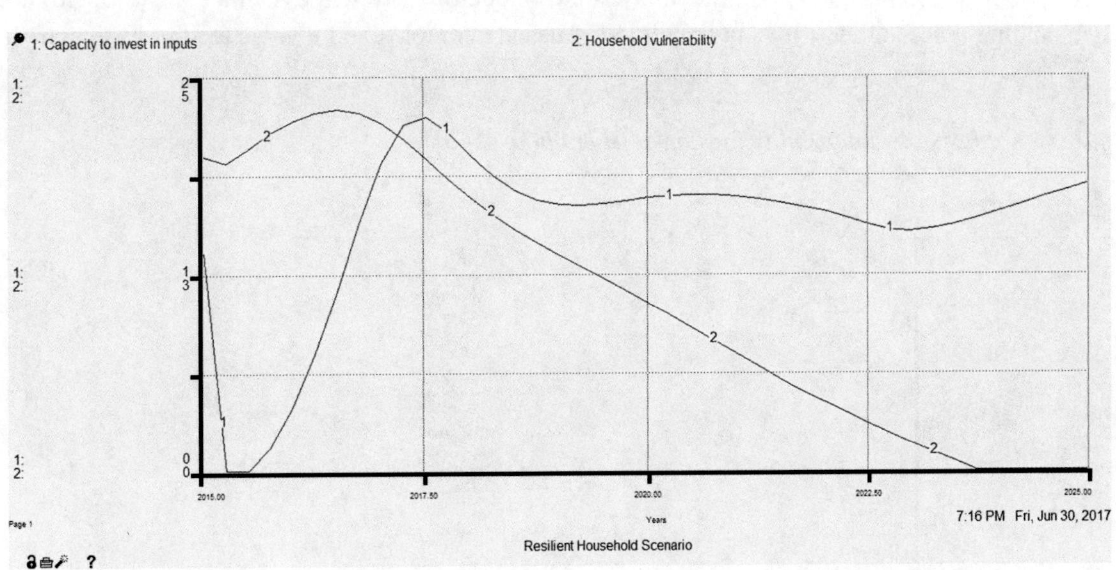

- Preserve seeds for future planting seasons;
- Store food for future household needs in case of turbulences in projected production;
- Use effective farming practices like mulching, contour farming;
- Apply small-scale irrigation initiatives;

- Invest in agriculture through improved seeds, fertilizers, pesticides, ox ploughs, and extension services;
- Sell processed produce whenever applicable or sell stored crops during peak periods towards next harvesting season;
- Use diversified farming practices by integrating livestock with crop production;
- Have access to adequate land for farming and water for domestic and agricultural consumption.

Similarly Figure 6 depicts non-resilient households where decrease in capacity to provide inputs increases vulnerability of the households irrespective of whether stressors and shocks exist or not. These households chronically food insecure and continue to exist through a number of survival strategies such as selling assets (livestock) to buy food, borrowing money for food, receiving food from relatives or the community, increasing consumption of wild plants and animals, leasing land to more resilient farmers, and providing labor to other farmers in exchange for food.

CONCLUSION

Smallholder African systems operate in harsh environments. In such extreme situations like changing climate, resource scarcity (e.g. land and inputs), environmental degradation (e.g. declining soil fertility, deforestation, and surface water eutrophication), market failures, and weak public and/or donor support initiatives, farmers or households must be prepared to survive by self-provisioning. This study examined the nature of vulnerability of smallholders' food security caused by extreme conditions in their farming environments, in the context of system dynamics modelling. System dynamics was adopted on the understanding that food security and livelihood issues are complex and involve feedbacks that are best

Figure 6. Analysis of vulnerability for non-resilient household

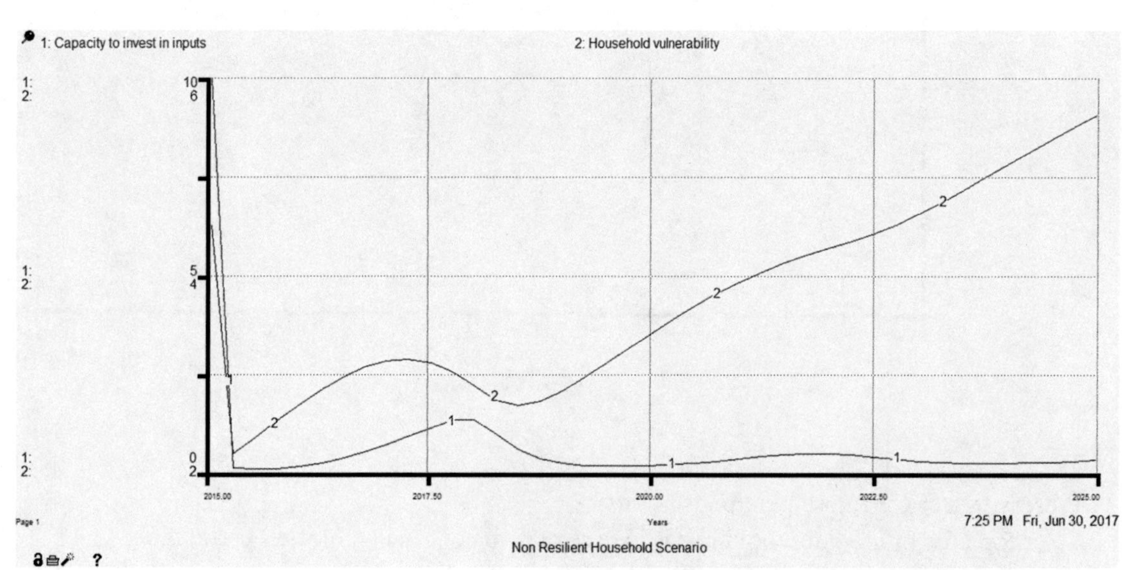

studied using such a systems science method. As such, a system dynamics simulation model was developed and used to explore the effects of shocks and stressors on resilient and non-resilient households. These effects were further linked to chronic food insecurity and long-term food security manifestations in non-resilient households and resilient households respectively.

This study further made and supported the claim that long-term food security of smallholder farmers stems from building resilience, short of which renders the farmers susceptible to chronic food insecurity. The study also maintained that the effect of stressors and shocks on household farming systems is less severe for resilient households than non-resilient households. A conceptual representation based on this insight was provided in Figure 1 and confirmed by simulation results in Figure 5 and Figure 6. In essence the study has demonstrated that smallholders generally can be food secure when there are low or no turbulences (stressors and shocks) in their farming systems. However, when the turbulences exceed a certain minimum threshold, resilient households endure and eventually attain long-term food security while the non-resilient households collapse into chronic food insecurity. In addition, the diversity of households in the continuum of resilient to non-resilient households requires that smallholder households are not treated as equal but rather be support according to their specific levels of vulnerability. At the same time, the possible manifestations of food security or insecurity among households, i.e, chronic food insecurity, long-term food insecurity, long-term food security and stable food security provide clear categorization of households' vulnerability for effective external intervention.

Due to weak external support to households in most African countries, the smallholder households have continued to co-exist amongst themselves whereby the non-resilient households offer cheap labor to the resilient households for income and livelihood. This dependence is responsible for chronic food insecurity among non-resilient households. Several examples that support this claim have been made in the text and will not be reiterated here. However, it is plausible to note that non-resilient households require support programs that enable them become self-reliant rather than handouts when shocks and stressors escalate their prevailing bottom line livelihood. On the other hand, despite multiple shocks and stressors, whether endogenous or exogenous, rural households seem to have regulatory feedbacks and self-organized adaptability that prevent a large majority of smallholders from collapsing. Several buffering mechanisms exit at community level such as local rules or traditions that preserve households irrespective of the magnitude of shocks in their environment.

FUTURE RESEARCH

The literature presents two types of food insecurity and two types of food security at smallholders' levels including; chronic food insecurity, and long-term food insecurity as well as long-term food security and stable food security. This research identified chronic food insecurity and long-term food security as the most prominent manifestations among smallholders and holistically studied them, including developing a corresponding simulation model. Further research should therefore explore the occurrence of long-term food insecurity and stable food security by building on the insights of chronic food insecurity, and long-term food insecurity as presented in this chapter.

REFERENCES

AfDB (2016). *Strategy for Agricultural Transformation in Africa 2016-2025*. Author.

Ahmed, S. A., Diffenbaugh, N. S., Hertel, T. W., Lobell, D. B., Ramankutty, N., Rios, A. R., & Rowhani, P. (2011). Climate volatility and poverty vulnerability in Tanzania. *Global Environmental Change*, *21*(1), 46–55. doi:10.1016/j.gloenvcha.2010.10.003

Alinovi, L., Mane, E., & Romano, D. (2010). Measuring Household Resilience to Food Insecurity: Application to Palestinian Households. In R. Benedetti, M. Bee, G. Espa, & F. Piersimoni (Eds.), *Agricultural Survey Methods*. Chichester, UK: John Wiley & Sons, Ltd. doi:10.1002/9780470665480.ch21

Ayenew, M. M. (2015). The Dynamics of Food Insecurity in Ethiopia. *International Journal of System Dynamics Applications*, *4*(4), 17–34. doi:10.4018/IJSDA.2015100102

Ayenew, M. M., & Kopainsky, B. (2014, July). *Food Insecurity in Ethiopia: Population, Food Production and Market*. Paper presented at the 32nd International Conference of the System Dynamics Society, Delft, The Netherlands.

Azar, A. T. (2012). System Dynamics as a useful Technique for Complex Systems. *International Journal of Industrial and Systems Engineering*, *10*(4), 377–410. doi:10.1504/IJISE.2012.046298

Azar, A. T., & Vaidyanathan, S. (2015). *Computational Intelligence applications in Modeling and Control. Studies in Computational Intelligence* (Vol. 575). Springer-Verlag.

Baiphethi, M. N., & Jacobs, P. T. (2009). The contribution of subsistence farming to food security in South Africa. *Agrekon*, *48*(4), 459–482. doi:10.1080/03031853.2009.9523836

Codjoe, S., & Owusu, G. (2011). Climate change/variability and food systems: Evidence from the Afram Plains, Ghana. *Regional Environmental Change*, *11*(4), 753–765. doi:10.100710113-011-0211-3

Fan, S., Brzeska, J., Keyzer, M., & Halsema, A. (2013). *From Subsistence to Profit: Transforming Smallholder Farms*. IFPRI Food Policy Report. Doi:.10.2499/9780896295582

FAO. (2016). *Regional overview of food insecurity in Africa*. Accessed May 2017 from www.fao.org/3/a-i4635e.pdf

FAO. (2017). Regional overview of food security and nutrition in Africa 2016. The challenges of building resilience to shocks and stressors. Accra, Ghana: FAO.

Gonzalez, D. B. Q., & Salvado, M. R. (2014). Dynamic Modeling in New Product Development: The Case of Knowledge Management Enablers in a Food Product. *International Journal of System Dynamics Applications*, *3*(1), 111–134. doi:10.4018/ijsda.2014010106

Haggblade, S., & Hazell, P. B. R. (2010). *Successes in African Agriculture: Lessons for the future*. IFPRI Issue Brief 63. Retrieved from http://www.ifpri.org/sites/default/files/publications/ib63.pdf

Hammond, R. A., & Dubé, L. (2012). A systems science perspective and transdisciplinary models for food and nutrition security. *Proceedings of the National Academy of Sciences of the United States of America*, *109*(31), 1235–12363. doi:10.1073/pnas.0913003109 PMID:22826247

Harvey, C. A., Rakotobe, Z. L., Rao, N. S., Dave, R., Razafimahatratra, H., Rabarijohn, R. H., ... MacKinnon, J. L. (2014). Extreme vulnerability of smallholder farmers to agricultural risks and climate change in Madagascar. *Philosophical Transactions of the Royal Society of London. Series B, Biological Sciences*, *369*(1639), 20130089. doi:10.1098/rstb.2013.0089 PMID:24535397

Hassanien, A. E., Azar, A. T., Snasel, V., Kacprzyk, J., & Abawajy, J. H. (2015). *Big Data in Complex Systems: Challenges and Opportunities*. Springer-Verlag. doi:10.1007/978-3-319-11056-1

Kopainsky, B., Tröger, K., Derwisch, S., & Ulli-Beer, S. (2012). Designing Sustainable Food Security Policies in Sub-Saharan African Countries: How Social Dynamics Over-Ride Utility Evaluations for Good and Bad. *Systems Research and Behavioral Science*, *29*(6), 575–589. doi:10.1002res.2140

Lloyd, S. J., Kovats, R. S., & Chalabi, Z. (2011). Climate change, crop yields and under-nutrition: Development of a model to quantify the impacts of climate scenarios on child under-nutrition. *Environmental Health Perspectives*, *119*(12), 1817–1823. doi:10.1289/ehp.1003311 PMID:21844000

Lukyamuzi, A., Ngubiri, J., & Okori, W. (2015). Towards harnessing phone messages and telephone conversations for prediction of food crisis. *International Journal of System Dynamics Applications*, *4*(4), 1–16. doi:10.4018/IJSDA.2015100101

Luna-Reyes, L. F., & Andersen, D. L. (2003). Collecting and analyzing qualitative data for system dynamics: Methods and models. *System Dynamics Review*, *19*(4), 271–296. doi:10.1002dr.280

Mindila, A., Rodrigues, A., McCormick, D., & Mwangi, R. (2014). ICT powered strategic flexibility system dynamics model: A pillar for economic development in micro and small enterprises. *International Journal of System Dynamics Applications*, *3*(1), 90–110. doi:10.4018/ijsda.2014010105

Morton, J. F. (2007). The impact of climate change on smallholder and subsistence agriculture. *Proceedings of the National Academy of Sciences of the United States of America*, *104*(50), 19680–19685. doi:10.1073/pnas.0701855104 PMID:18077400

Nelson, G. C. (2009). *Climate Change: Impact on Agriculture and Costs of Adaptation*. Washington, DC: International Food Policy Research Institute.

Oyo, B. (2013, May). *A System Dynamics analysis of seed banking effectiveness for Empowerment of Small Holder Farmers*. Paper presented at the IST-Africa Conference, Nairobi, Kenya.

Oyo, B., & Kalema, B. M. (2016). A System Dynamics model for subsistence farmers' food security resilience in Sub-Saharan Africa. *International Journal of System Dynamics Applications*, *5*(1), 17–30. doi:10.4018/IJSDA.2016010102

Oyo, B., Kaye, M., & Nkalubo, N. (2014). Re-Conceptualisation of Agriculture Information System for Uganda. *Transaction on Electrical and Electronic Circuits and Systems*, *4*(2), 39–44.

Oyo, B., Williams, D., & Barendsen, E. (2009). *Integrating Action Research and System Dynamics: Towards a Generic Process Design for Participative Modeling*. Paper presented at the 2009 Hawaii International Conference on System Sciences.

Saldarriaga, M., Kopainsky, B., & Alessi, S. M. (2013, July). *Knowledge analysis in coupled social-ecological systems. What do stakeholders in sub Saharan Africa know about the dynamic complexity of climate change, agriculture and food security?* Paper presented at the 31st International Conference of the System Dynamics Society, Cambridge, MA.

Stave, K. A., & Kopainsky, B. (2014, July). *Dynamic thinking about food system vulnerabilities in highly developed countries: Issues and initial analytic structure for building resilience.* Paper presented at the 32nd International Conference of the System Dynamics Society, Delft, The Netherlands.

Thornton, P. K., Ericksen, P. J., Herrero, M., & Challinor, A. J. (2014). Climate variability and vulnerability to climate change: A review. *Global Change Biology*, *20*(11), 3313–3328. doi:10.1111/gcb.12581 PMID:24668802

Thornton, P.K., Jones, P.G., Ericksen, P.J., & Challinor, A.J. (2011). Agriculture and food systems in sub-Saharan Africa in a 40C+ world. *Phil. Trans. R. Soc. A, 369*(1934), 117–136. doi:10.1098/rsta.2010.0246

Tittonell, P. (2014). Livelihood strategies, resilience and transformability in African agroecosystems. *Agricultural Systems*, *126*, 3–14. doi:10.1016/j.agsy.2013.10.010

Tsolakis, N., & Srai, J. S. (2017). *A System Dynamics Approach to Food Security through Smallholder Farming in the UK.* Academic Press.

Walker, B. H., Anderies, J. M., Kinzig, A. P., & Ryan, P. (2006). Exploring resilience in social-ecological systems through comparative studies and theory development: Introduction to the special issue. *Ecology and Society*, *11*(1), 12. doi:10.5751/ES-01573-110112

Walker, B. H., Sayer, J., Andrew, N. L., & Campbell, B. (2010). Should enhanced resilience be an objective of natural resource management research for developing countries? *Crop Science*, *50*(Supplement_1), 10–19. doi:10.2135/cropsci2009.10.0565

Walters, J. P., Archer, D. W., Sassenrath, G. F., Hendrickson, J. R., Hanson, J. D., Halloran, J. M., ... Alarcon, V. J. (2016). Exploring agricultural production systems and their fundamental components with system dynamics modelling. *Ecological Modelling*, *333*, 51–65. doi:10.1016/j.ecolmodel.2016.04.015

Zhu, Q., & Azar, A. T. (2015). *Complex system modelling and control through intelligent soft computations. Studies in Fuzziness and Soft Computing* (Vol. 319). Springer-Verlag.

Chapter 19
Computational Model for the Study of Fontan Circulation

Alejandro Talaminos-Barroso
University of Seville, Spain

Laura María Roa-Romero
University of Seville, Spain

Javier Reina-Tosina
University of Seville, Spain

ABSTRACT

In this chapter, the design and development of a computational model of the cardiovascular system is presented for patients who have undergone the Fontan operation. The model has been built from a physiological basis, considering some of the mechanisms associated to the cardiovascular system of patients with univentricular heart disease. Thus, the model allows the prediction of some hemodynamic variables considering different physiopathological conditions. The original conditions of the model are changed in the Fontan procedure and these new dynamics force the hemodynamic behaviours of the different considered variables. The model has been proved considering the classic Fontan procedure and the techniques from the lateral tunnel and the extracardiac conduit. The results compiled knowledge of several cardiovascular surgeons with many years of experience in such interventions, and have been validated by using other authors' data. In this sense, the participation of a multidisciplinary team has been considered as a key factor for the development of this work.

INTRODUCTION

The incidence of Congenital Heart Diseases (CHD) is approximately 1% of total births (Masoller et al., 2016), assuming that the main cause of death in children is due to congenital defects (Parnell et al., 2017) and resulting in a high cost in hospitalization due to the necessary surgical interventions. The significant progress in the diagnosis, prevention and treatment of CHD has made possible that the vast majority of patients who suffer this type of disease reach the adult stage (Biglino et al., 2017). However, in most cases, CHD cannot be cured and treatments are more palliative than corrective (Ferguson et al., 2016).

DOI: 10.4018/978-1-5225-4077-9.ch019

Within the wide variety of CHD illnesses, tricuspid atresia is considered one of the most complex and critical types. It is estimated that the emergence of this malformation of the heart occurs on approximately 1 out of every 10000 births (Bangash et al., 2016), although the true prevalence is not known (Rao et al., 2012). Tricuspid atresia is determined by the absence of the tricuspid valve and the small size of the right ventricle. This physical defect does not allow blood to be pushed to the lungs in a normal way, thus leading to a poorly oxygenated blood and the apparition of cyanosis.

In 1971, Francis M. Fontan presented a surgical correction for the tricuspid atresia (Fontan et al., 1971). This intervention became the most common treatment over time used for congenital malformations that are characterized for the presence of a single ventricle. It is usually based on the realization of three interventions during the first years of the patient, with the objective of providing an appropriate delivery of oxygen to the peripheral system without overloading the ventricle (Corsini et al., 2014). The classic Fontan procedure or atriopulmonary anastomosis (APC) is currently obsolete (Hazinski, 2013). The most current techniques are based on intracardiac total cavopulmonary connection or lateral tunnel (ELT), or the extracardiac conduit (ECC) (Bartelse et al., 2016). Health institutions carrying out this kind of interventions are usually specialized on these last two techniques. As a consequence, several works have been proposed (Clifford et al., 2015; Ravishankar et al., 2016; Trusty et al., 2016) with the objective of comparing both techniques from a postoperative hemodynamics perspective, and to assess the prevalence of arrhythmias and functional status for patients.

Despite the improvements accomplished in the last decades with the Fontan procedure, the postoperative consequences remain a long-term concern (Sakamoto et al., 2016). First, a progressive circulatory failure is caused in some patients, resulting in a pathophysiological status that is not currently sufficiently understood (Cheng et al., 2016). Furthermore, other problems can arise, such as the cognitive impairment (Tyagi et al., 2016), the chronic venous congestion (Opotowsky et al., 2017) or the appearance of kidney diseases such as cirrhosis or hepatic dysfunction (Opotowsky et al., 2016).

Therefore, it is necessary to invest efforts to search for new treatments, prevention techniques and surgical improvements to help to achieve a better diagnosis and the most suitable treatment for congenital heart diseases so as to increase the patient's life and improve the quality of life at large. New research lines emerging from technological advances in the last years, such as the use of 3D electrocardiograms (Agarwal et al., 2016), magnetic resonance imaging (Marvao et al., 2016), anatomical and geometric characterizations (Quarteroni et al., 2016), medical image analysis (Ahmed et al., 2015; Wong et al., 2017), speedometers for microparticles, computational techniques based on big data (Pruyt et al., 2016) for the analysis of large amount of clinical data or computational models (Hose et al., 2017; Moysis et al., 2016).

Computational modeling has been proved to be a useful resource for the analysis and comprehension of the complex biological mechanisms within the cardiovascular system. It also helps to supplement other experimental studies to understand the cardiovascular physiopathology and to generate biomedical and knowledge (Mindila et al., 2014). In this sense, computational modeling is an alternative to methods such as experimentation with animals, a technique that is not always possible to execute due to ethical considerations (Biglino et al., 2017), costs, and regulations (Mukherjee et al., 2016). Furthermore, the results obtained are not always satisfactory because each animal possesses different reactions and physiology. Others advantages of computational modeling are associated to their allowing the simulation in different pathophysiological conditions with a simple variation in the parameters described by the model (Sack et al., 2016). In order to assess the causes for the failure of the Fontan procedure it is necessary to have a deep knowledge about the different mechanisms underlying cardiac physiology, such as anatomy of the heart, details of the surgical intervention, cardiac images, hemodynamic status in patients, functional status of other organs and metabolic functions (Carvalho et al., 2017). The aim of this work is a model-based study of the dynamic behaviour associated with some hemodynamic variables in the practice of different techniques and alternatives to the Fontan procedure. The proposed model allows the prediction, heartbeat by heartbeat or on average term, of some hemodynamic variables from the cardiovascular system. The integration of this model with other clinical tools can help to provide a better understanding of the pathophysiological behaviour associated with the failure of the Fontan procedure.

The remainder of this paper is organized as follows. Related work is discussed briefly in Section II; in Section III, the structural model and the steps followed for the model construction are described; Section IV contains a description of the experiments conducted by computer simulation; a discussion of the results is contained in Section V; finally, some concluding remarks are drawn in Section VI.

RELATED WORK

The physiological complexity of cardiovascular dynamics has been approached historically from different perspectives of mathematical modeling, considering different temporal and spatial scales (Alfio et al., 2017) to limit the problem to a specific context. A traditional way to face the study of the cardiovascular system is from an hemodynamic point of view (Chen et al., 2015), being based primarily on pressure-volume relationships of each of the vascular chambers that constitute the cardiovascular system. This type of models allows the obtaining of the dynamic behaviors of some hemodynamic variables, which are difficult to measure in clinical practice. They can serve as an aid to the diagnosis and prevention of heart disease. In addition, its low computational cost allows the hemodynamic models to have a great flexibility to simulate different experiences in a wide range of diseases and therapies. The results can be displayed in real time from virtually any computing-capable device, including a smartphone (Doshi et al., 2016). Finally, model customization is also an important factor that can be considered, since hemodynamic models usually require a minimum set of initial parameters that can be estimated from a specific patient. (Garcia-Canadilla et al., 2015).

Focusing on computer models that address congenital heart pathologies, recent studies (Biglino et al., 2017; Pennati et al., 2013; Petukhov et al., 2016) have tried to simulate the hemodynamic behaviors of different congenital disorders considering the complete cardiovascular system as an electrical circuit composed mainly of the heart, the systemic circulation and the pulmonary circulation. Due to the great variability of CHD types, these models are very useful because of their great flexibility to easily establish different routes of connection between compartments, adapting their physiological structure to a particular pathological state.

Regarding Fontan's circulation, other studies (Liang et al., 2014; Molfetta et al., 2016) try to model this particular configuration of connections through a lumped-parameter circuit of the cardiovascular system. Validation is performed afterwards by comparing pulmonary artery and vena cava flows with experimental data collected from the literature (Corsini et al., 2014), or by a hemodynamic analysis of some variables in the Fontan circulation and others in the normal biventricular circulation. Once the model is sufficiently validated and tested, some studies (Shimizu et al., 2016) attempt to theoretically demonstrate different technical improvements to existing surgical interventions, in order to evaluate possible improvements in post-operative hemodynamic evolution and to avoid the failure of Fontan.

On the other hand, alternative models focus on more specific aspects of the hemodynamic evolution associated with Fontan's circulation, for example on the Glenn's procedure (Kung et al., 2013), on the post-operative evolution of the fenestration procedure (Sughimoto et al., 2017), or on the regurgitation of the tricuspid valve (Pant et al., 2016). Even some models have also focused on the simulation of physical activity in adult patients who have this type of pathologies (Van De Bruaene et al., 2015; Watrous et al., 2017). Finally, there are other more general tools (Delorme et al., 2017; Luffel et al., 2016) based on computer models developed specifically for the clinician, which aid in the planning and optimization of heart surgery interventions in children.

Other computer models provide a broader view, allowing to simulate the hemodynamic effects derived from the impact of heart diseases or clinical interventions through their personalization to the patient, including the Fontan circulation. An example of such initiatives is the BioGears project, which is a source-free computer tool that includes mathematical models of a wide variety of physiological systems, including the cardiovascular system among them. Numerous research works have emerged from this software, including virtual surgical intervention schedules (Potter et al., 2017) or the analysis of the dynamic behavior of different types of physiological variables based on the simulation of some specific medications (Clipp et al., 2016). Finally, one of the most important initiatives in computational modeling is the Physiome Project. It offers a simulation environment called JSim with different types of models in physiology and biomedicine. Regarding cardiac physiology, the model presented for PhysioNet (Clifford et al., 2015) includes three mayor components: a lumped-parameter model of the pulsatile heart and circulation, a short-term regulatory system and a model of resting physiologic perturbation (respiration, autoregulation of local vascular beds and higher brain center activity).

However, the building of models still needs to allow more customization from factors associated to the patient physiology and also to provide a comprehensive view about cardiovascular system from a hemodynamic perspective, assuming effects of different drugs, pathophysiological conditions and surgical operations.

In the next section, the structure of the proposed model and the methodology followed, are presented. The relationships and functions constitutions between the different parameters, variables and state variables are expressed, as well as the new compartments included in the model with respect to previous work. Finally, the modular design is drawn as a fundamental requirement from the early phases of model development.

METHODS AND MATERIALS

The methodology used for the construction of the proposed structural model has been the following: development of the structure of the model, quantification of the relations established, codification in a high-level language, validation of the model considering the data provided by other authors, and predictions conducted by computer simulation.

The volumes of the different compartments have been considered as the state variables of the model, regarding resistance and capacitance as the constitutive relations. Mitral, tricuspid, aortic and pulmonary valves have been modeled as valves that open or close depending on the blood pressure variations at both sides of the valve. This way, state variables are expressed through ordinary differential equations. The relationships between the different flows, functions constitutions, blood pressures and state variables have been established by resistance functions of capacitance.

The proposed computational model for the cardiovascular system has been designed as a lumped-parameter fluid circuit that is divided into four compartments: left heart, right heart, pulmonary circulation and systemic circulation. Furthermore, these four compartments are composed of different cavities accounting for the heart ventricles and the atrium and arteries, veins and blood capillaries. The blood flowing along the circulatory system is modeled by fluid flows that determine the measured blood flowing between the different cavities.

A more comprehensive overview of the internal structure of the model is detailed in a previous work (Talaminos et al., 2014), although new modifications were introduced in this paper to give the model a wider vision about the different pathophysiological conditions that can be simulated before and after the Fontan procedure.

Thus, the pulmonary artery was developed with three new capacitors by adding the truncus pulmonalis (C_{ap}), the right branch of the pulmonary artery (C_{apr}) and the left one (C_{apl}). The truncus pulmonalis pressure (P_{ap}), the right pulmonary artery pressure (P_{apr}), the left pulmonary artery pressure (P_{apl}) and the branch pulmonary blood flows ($\dot{Q}_{ap1}$, $\dot{Q}_{ap2}$, $\dot{Q}_{apr}$, $\dot{Q}_{apl}$) were added to the same extent. All these variables are illustrated in Figure 1, which shows P_{cp} y C_{cp} as the pulmonary capillary pressure and the pulmonary capillary capacitance, respectively.

Flows and pressures in the right and left pulmonary arteries were considered as equal since the pulmonary resistance on the left side (R_{ap1}) and on the right side (R_{ap2}) were assumed to take the same value. In this way, two resistances have been defined for the left lung (R_{apl}) and the right lung (R_{apr}).

The venous system has been modeled through the superior vena cava (SVC) and the inferior vena cava (IVC). In the model, these two new compartments have been included by the insertion of the superior venous capacitance (C_{vss}), the inferior venous capacitance (C_{vsi}), as well as their respective pressures (P_{vss} and P_{vsi}), as shown in Figure 2. Moreover, both veins include their respective resistance as well, such as the superior venous resistance (R_{vss}) and the inferior venous resistance (R_{vsi}). As shown in

Figure 1. Structure of the model for the truncus pulmonalis and the right and left pulmonary arteries

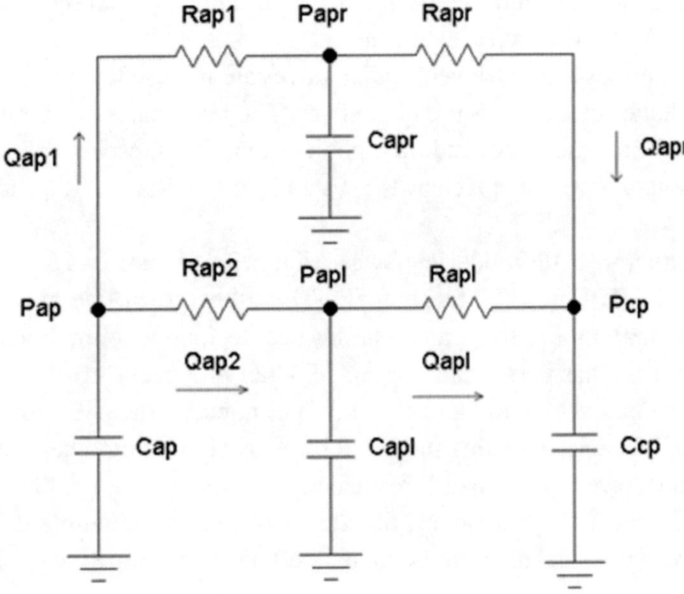

Figure 2. Structure of the model for the superior and inferior cava veins

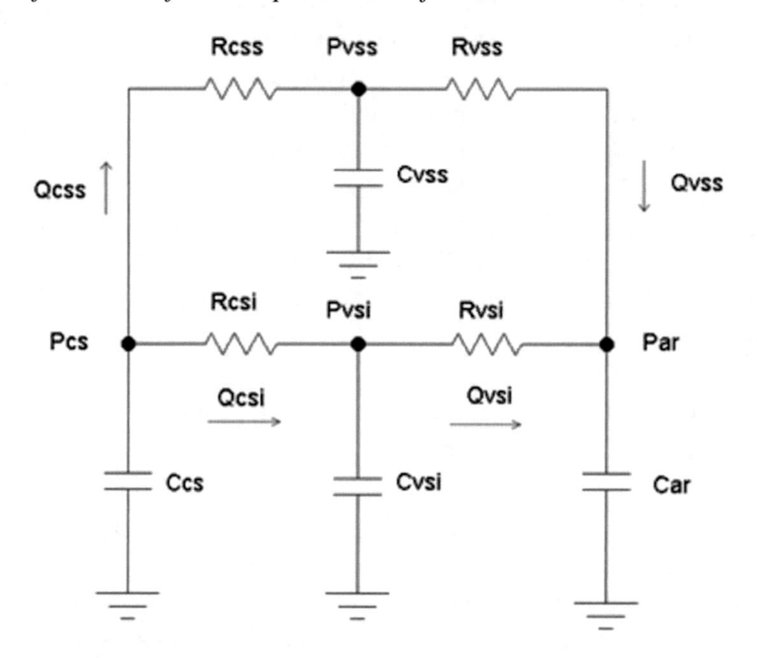

Figure 2 the model also accounts for the systemic capillary pressure (P_{cs}), the systemic capillary volume (C_{cs}), the superior systemic capillary resistance (R_{css}), which are related to the neck and the head, and the inferior systemic capillary resistance (R_{csi}), which is related to the trunk and limbs. Finally, different flows associated with these connections have been added, including the superior systemic capillary flow ($\dot{Q}_{css}$), the inferior systemic capillary flow ($\dot{Q}_{csi}$), the superior systemic venous flow ($\dot{Q}_{vss}$) and the inferior systemic venous flow ($\dot{Q}_{vsi}$).

Furthermore, new flow connections among atrial and ventricles were added in to the model, such as the foramen ovale and the interventricular septum. To this aim, an atrial septal defect resistance (R_{ia}) and a ventricular septal defect (R_{iv}) have been considered.

On the other hand, the four heart atrioventricular valves are represented within the model as a valve and a resistor that facilitates or obstructs the blood flow. The resistances of mitral and tricuspid valves are considered as the left resistance (R_l) and the right resistance (R_r) respectively, while the resistances of the aortic and pulmonary valves are given by the systemic left resistance (R_{ls}) and the right pulmonary resistance (R_{rp}).

The physiological structure of the model is shown in Figure 3, considering a pre-operative status before the Fontan procedure for ELT and ECC techniques. The dashed green line indicates the bidirectional Glenn shunt or hemi-Fontan procedure, a previous surgical technique to the Fontan procedure used to temporarily improve ventricular performance. Hemi-Fontan procedure involves rerouting circulation such that the superior vena cava drains into the right pulmonary artery. Besides, different functions implemented in the model can change this structural basis by simulating other initial pathophysiological conditions, surgical interventions and different changes to the existing Fontan procedure techniques.

Concerning the ELT and ECC techniques, the model is configured with a cavopulmonary bypass between the superior vena cava and the right pulmonary artery, resembling the bidirectional Glenn shut.

Figure 3. Components of the initial physiological structural basis of the cardiovascular system model for the univentricular heart in pre-operative status for ELT and ECC techniques

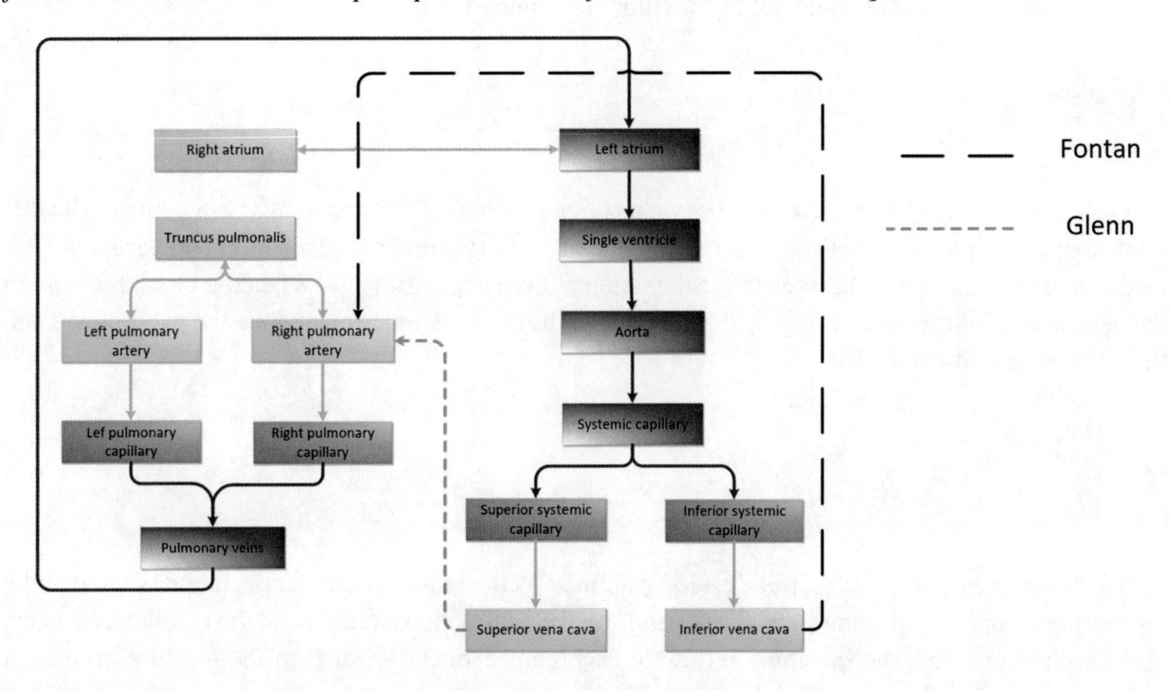

On the other hand, for the APC technique, superior and inferior cava veins are joined directly to the right atrium. Furthermore, the aperture in the interatrial septum was considered for the three techniques.

As aforementioned, the blood volumes in each compartment are considered as state variables of the model (Table 1) and are normally expressed by ordinary differential equations.

Table 1. State variables considered in the model

State variable	Acronym
Left atrial volume	Val
Left ventricle volume	Vvl
Systemic arterial volume	Vas
Systemic capillary volume	Vcs
Superior systemic venous volume	Vvss
Inferior systemic venous volume	Vvsi
Right atrial volume	Var
Right ventricle volume	Vvr
Truncus pulmonalis volume	Vap
Left pulmonary arterial volume	Vapl
Right pulmonary arterial volume Pulmonary capillary volume Pulmonary venous volume	Vapr Vcp Vvp

This way, the blood volumes of a given compartment are defined as the difference between the magnitude of blood flow in ($\dot{Q}_e$) and out ($\dot{Q}_s$) within the compartment:

$$\frac{dV}{dt} = \dot{Q}_e - \dot{Q}_s$$

Generally, the flow ($\dot{Q}$) circulating between compartments is determined by the quantity of the difference of blood pressures between the origin compartment (P_1) and the destination compartment (P_2), mediated by a resistance (R) associated to the union of both compartments. When the blood pressure in the destination compartment is higher than the one in the origin compartment, then the valve closes and the flow through it is zero:

$$\dot{Q} = \begin{cases} \left(P_1 - P_2\right)/R, & P_1 > P_2 \\ 0, & P_1 \leq P_2 \end{cases}$$

The blood pressure in each cardiac cavity is defined by the relation between the blood volume in the compartment and its capacitance, which depends on the contraction strength and the cardiac frequency.

In each interaction, the incoming inflow to each compartment is equal to the outflow from each compartment. Thus, the model is based on the mass conservation law, which considers the blood as a Newtonian fluid and circulates in the different compartments of the cardiovascular system. The blood flowing along the circulatory system is modeled by fluid flows which determine the measured blood flow between the different cavities.

From an implementation point of view, the model has been developed using the Matlab® computing environment for system simulation, employing the modified Euler method with an integration period of one millisecond. Simulations have been performed heartbeat by heartbeat, which presents a distinguishing aspect with respect to other works (Yang & Saucerman, 2011).

The model is based on the aforementioned physiological structural basis. However, different functions can be established to change this structure depending on some pathophysiological change or new anatomical condition after surgery. In particular, two types of functions have been defined: on the one hand, those affecting the model structure at the beginning of the simulation, and on the other hand, those concerning the pathophysiological change or surgical condition.

Table 2 shows a list of the functions implemented in the model, which can be referred to the beginning of the situation (B), during the pathophysiological change or surgical condition (C) or at both specific conditions (B and C). Furthermore, one or more parameters are passed to each function, thus allowing a more personalized operation.

A brief summary of each function and the corresponding parameters is described next:

- **Initial_Condition:** This function should be invoked at the beginning of the simulation. The parameters are the patient's age (*age*), gender (*gender*), height (*height*) and weight (*weight*). With these values, the model will calculate the total blood volume of from the Body Mass Index (BMI), which can be obtained by Haycock's formula.

Table 2. Functions implemented in the model to simulate different pathophysiological conditions before the intervention (P) and during the operation (F).

Function	P	F
Initial_Condition (age, height, weight)	X	
Previous_interventions (interventions [] {Glenn, arteriovenous_fistula})	X	
Pulmonary_valve (valve_obstruction)	X	X
Aortic_valve (valve_obstruction)	X	X
Mitral_valve (valve_obstruction)	X	X
Tricuspid_valve (valve_obstruction)	X	X
Foramen_ovale (size)	X	X
Right_ventricle_size (size)	X	X
Fontan_procedure (procedure {APC,ELT,ECC}, conduit_resistance)		X
Fenestrated_Fontan (size)		X

- **Previous_Interventions:** This function will receive an enumerated array (*interventions*) with the interventions the patient has undergone before the simulation. If this function is not called at the beginning, no intervention is considered.
- **X_Valve:** Where X can refer to the pulmonary, aortic, mitral and tricuspid valves. This function allows to define the degree of obstruction of each of these valves, where the variable *valve_obstruction* can take the following values depending on the status of the valve:
    - 0: Totally closed valve (atresia). There is no blood flow in any direction between the compartments that separate the valve.
    - (0,1): Valve stenosis. The valve has a small orifice area. The obstruction will be more severe and the regurgitation will be higher with values close to zero. However, the obstruction will be milder and the blood regurgitation will be lower with values close to one.
    - 1: Normal valve.
    - (1, 2): Valve insufficiency. The valve has a normal orifice area but there is possibility of regurgitation. With values close to one the blood regurgitation will be lower, while with values close to two, the blood regurgitation will be higher.
    - 2: Severe valve insufficiency. The valve has a normal orifice area but remains open during all the cardiac cycle, thus the backflow of blood towards the previous compartment is very high.
- **Foramen_ovale:** This function states whether the foramen ovale should be opened or closed before and after the intervention. The size parameter will define the degree of openness of the orifice, values ranging from 0 (totally closed) to 1 (totally opened).
- **Right_ventricle_size (size):** This function allows defining the size of the right ventricle within the model. The size is customized using the variable size, with values ranging from 0 (congenital heart disease univentricular heart type) to 1 (right ventricle of normal size).
- **Fontan_procedure:** This function allows specifying the Fontan procedure to be simulated. This is a mandatory function to invoke. As parameters, it receives an enumeration type whose values can be APC, ELT or ECC, defining the technique that has to be simulated afterwards. Also, the parameter conduit_resistance will define the resistance associated with the conduit used during the intervention.

- **Fenestrated_Fontan:** This function allows indicating the degree of fenestration carried out in the Fontan procedure. The parameter size takes values from 0 (there is no fenestration) to 1 (there is fenestration and the blood flows free from the conduit to the right atrium).

The model has been built in a functional modular way (see Figure 4) in order to include new knowledge that could force the model's hemodynamic behaviors and simulate other pathophysiological conditions.

The results obtained from the model are presented in the following section. First, a validation has been made by using other authors' data and the provided knowledge of several cardiovascular surgeons. Once the dynamics are verified that are realistic and that the structure of the model is robust and stable, some experiments by simulation with different Fontan techniques are conducted.

RESULTS

The model has been validated with data collected from the literature of patients with tricuspid atresia (Klimes et al., 2007), aged from 19.0±7.9. Therefore, the validation has been made considering the flows in the SVC, IVC, left pulmonary artery (LPA) and right pulmonary artery (RPA) for post-operative status in the APC technique. Table 3 shows the values for these flows measured in L/min•m2.

Experiments lasted 100 seconds. The first 50 seconds belong to the Fontan pre-operative status, while the other 50 seconds belong to the post-operative status. The times specified are considered sufficient to reach the stabilization in the pre- and post-operative status of the hemodynamic variables calculated in the model.

Figure 4.

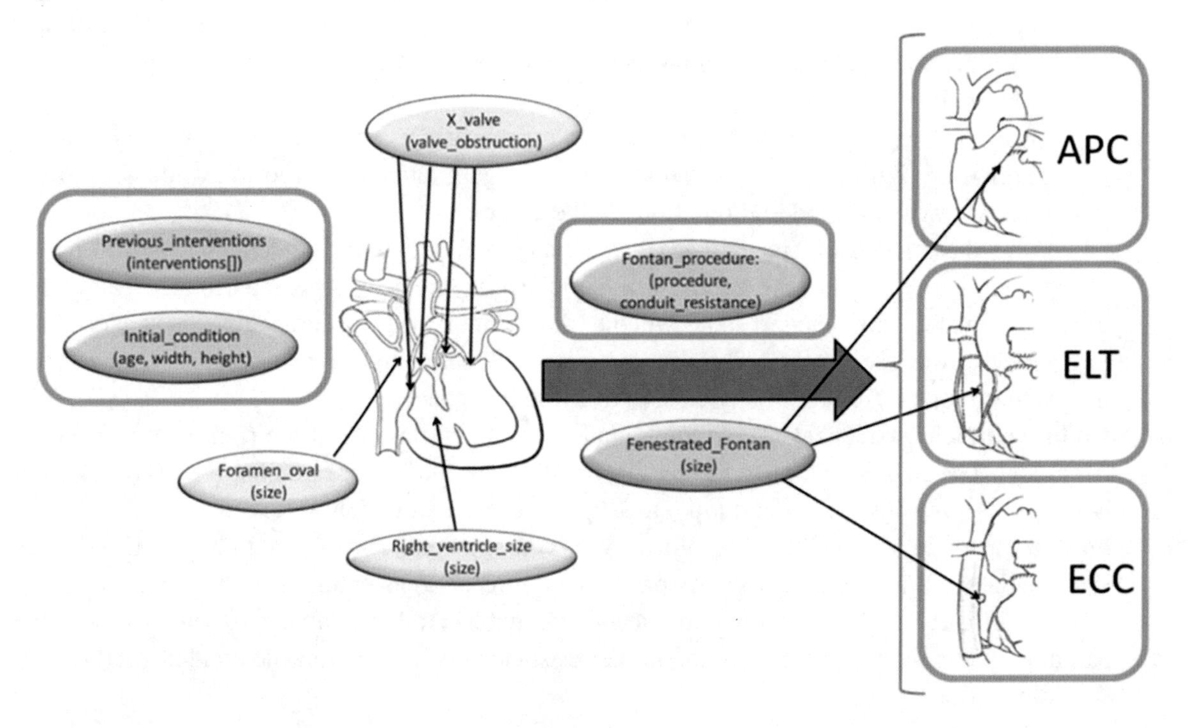

Figure 5 shows the results of the simulations of the different flows for the SVC, IVC, LPA, RPA using the APC technique of the Fontan procedure, where the horizontal axis represents the number of heartbeats.

Alternatively, Figure 6 shows the results of the simulations of the different flows for SVC, IVC, LPA, RPA using the ELT technique of the Fontan procedure. From the hemodynamic point of view, there are few differences between the flows for the ELT and ECC techniques.

On the other hand, the pressures of the left and right atrium are shown in Figure 7 and 8, considering APC and ECC techniques, respectively.

Finally, Figure 9 shows a simulation that includes three clearly differentiated phases: pre-operative status, post-operative status without fenestration and post-operative with fenestration. This figure shows the atrial pressures in these three phases. As it can be seen, after the fenestration there is an increase of the pressure in both atria caused by the incoming flow from the extra cardiac conduit.

The following section discusses the results obtained based on the hemodynamics of the simulated surgical intervention techniques, including advantages and differences between them. Finally, a brief discussion about fenestration and its importance is also presented.

DISCUSSION

For the validation of patients with APC, the flows in the LPA and the RPA have been considered identical and therefore, the same amount of blood is conducted to each lung. However, (Klimes et al., 2007) shows that the flow in the LPA is lower than in the RPA, possibly due to occurrence of stenosis in any of the pulmonary branches for the patients studied.

Figure 5. Simulation of the SVC, IVC, LPA, RPA flows (L/min·m2) in the Fontan procedure using the APC technique

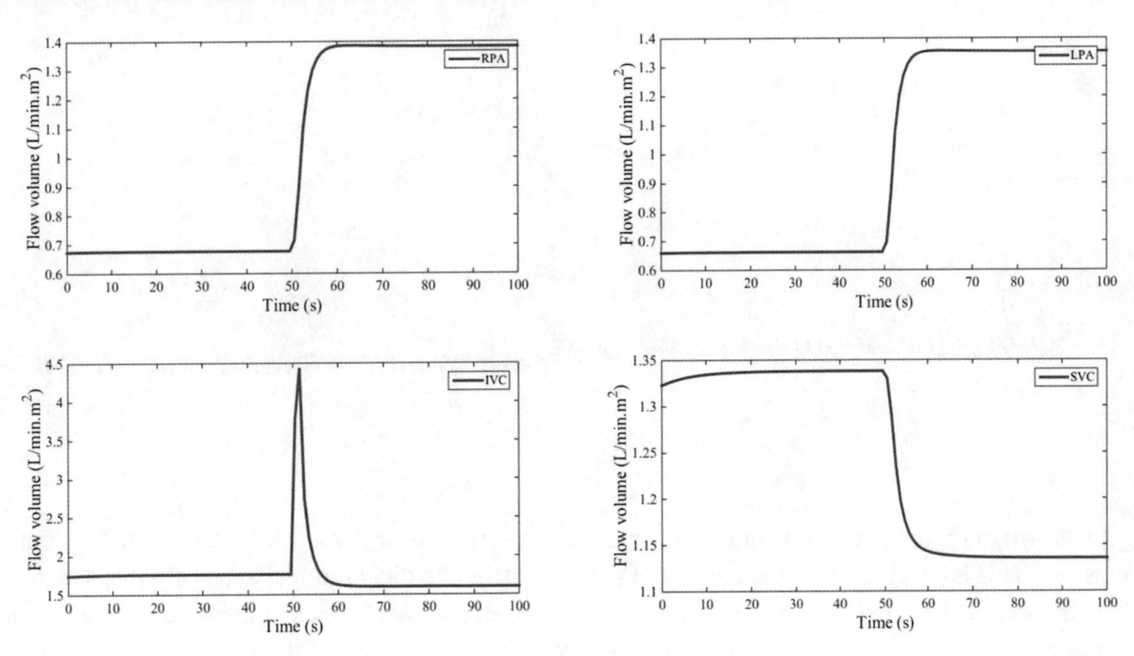

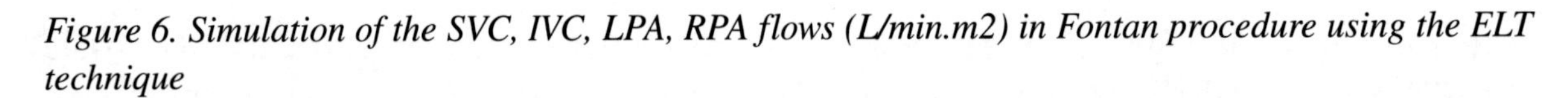

Figure 6. Simulation of the SVC, IVC, LPA, RPA flows (L/min.m2) in Fontan procedure using the ELT technique

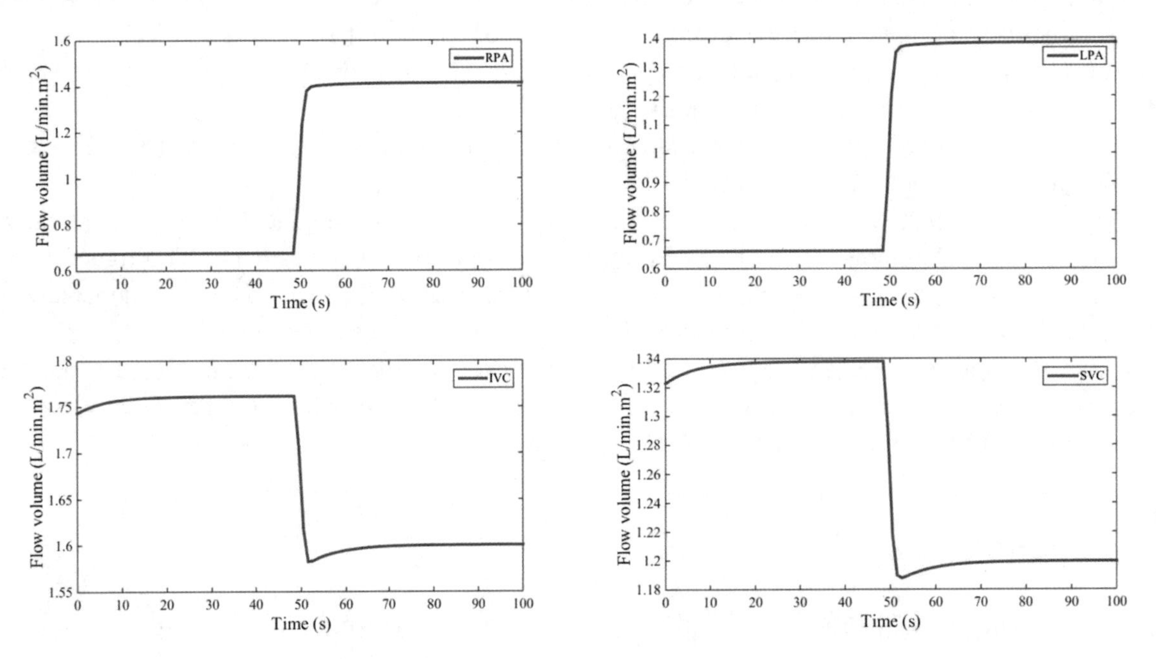

Figure 7. Right atrial pressure (Par) and left atrial pressure (Pal) in a Fontan procedure using the APC technique

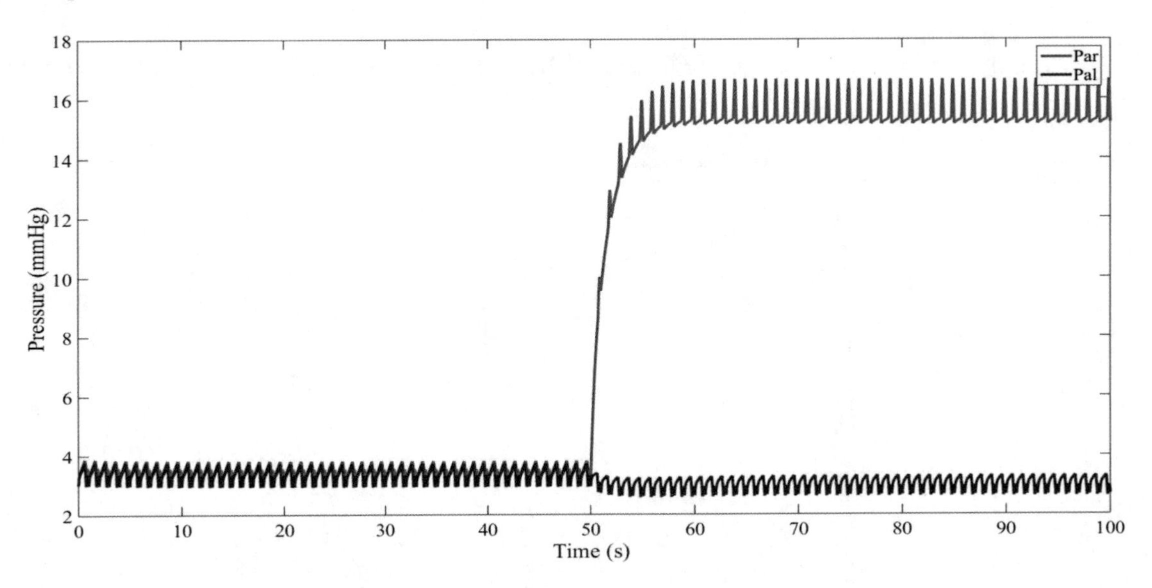

As shown in Figure 5, the flow in both the right and left pulmonary artery increases after the Fontan procedure. This is because of the connection of the right atrium to the pulmonary artery, which channels all the blood from the inferior vena cava to the pulmonary artery. After the closing of the foramen ovale, the pulmonary circulation remains totally isolated from the systemic circulation.

Figure 8. Right atrial pressure (Par) and left atrial pressure (Pal) in a Fontan procedure using the ECC technique

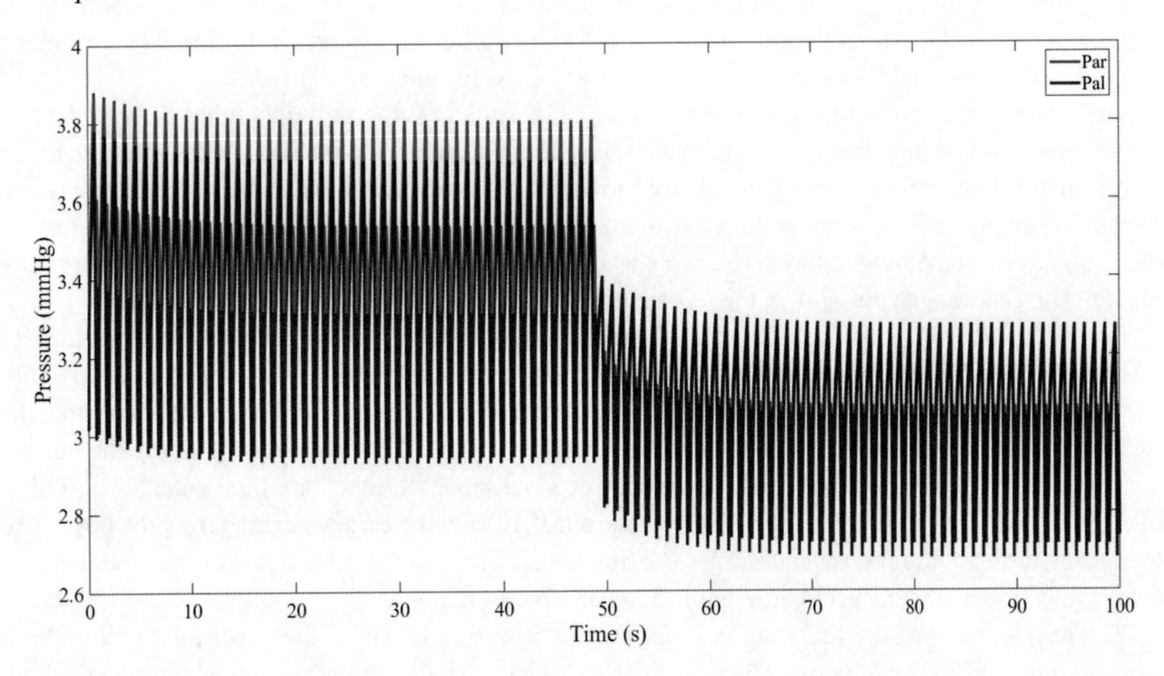

Figure 9. Right atrial pressure (Par) and left atrial pressure (Pal) in a Fontan procedure using the ECC technique with fenestration

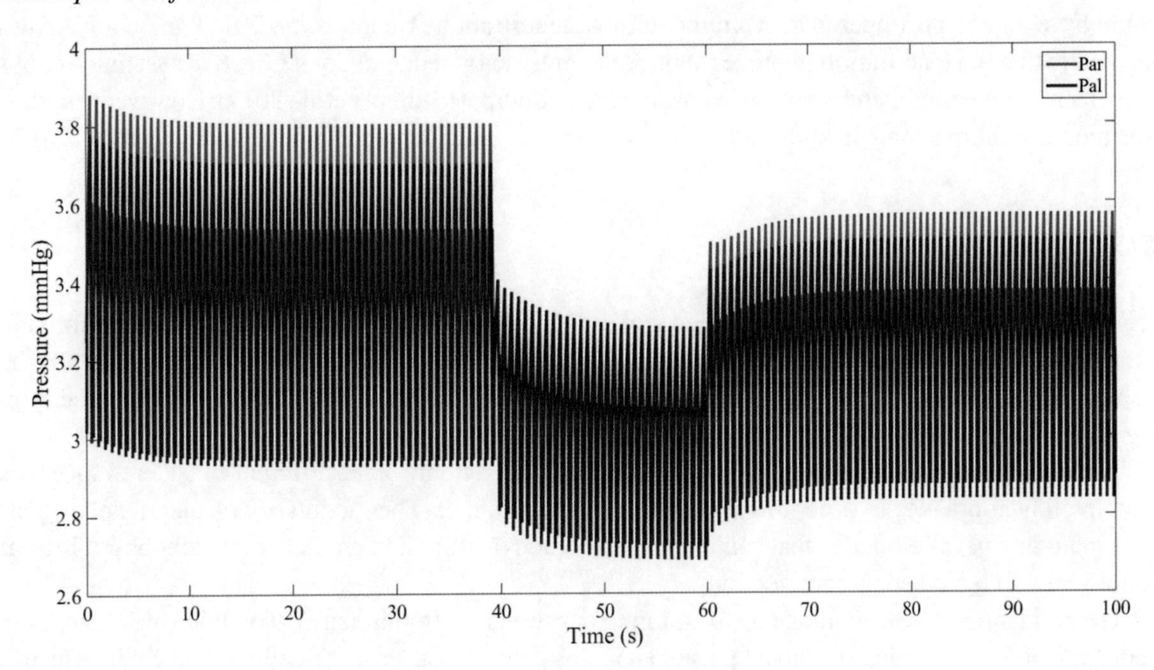

Also, an increase of the pressure in the right atrium takes place due to the influence of the pressure of the pulmonary artery, causing a slight decrease in the cava vein flow. This increase in the right atrial pressure (Figure 7) is one of the reasons that leads to the failure of the Fontan for the APC technique and this is what led to the introduction of the ELT and ECC techniques.

After the Fontan procedure for the ELT and ECC techniques, the only incoming flow in the left atrium is the one coming from the pulmonary veins. This contributes to the drop of the pressure in the left atrial as it is shown in Figure 8 and also to the drop of the pressure in the single ventricle. However, the saturation increases given that there is no mixture of poorly oxygenated blood. On the other hand, the right atrium remains as a blood reservoir whose single entry is the foramen ovale, so its pressure remains the same as the pressure in the left atrium.

The advantages of using the ELT or ECC techniques have been widely studied in the literature. In this regard, the ELT technique has shown short and long-term excellent results (Islam et al., 2016), with a reduced risk of developing thromboembolic complications (Hirsch et al., 2008). On the other hand, the ECC technique presents significant advantages compared to the ELT technique, including the normal preservation of the ventricle pressure, the absence of atrial septal defect suture lines and the possibility of avoiding the cardiopulmonary bypass (Brown et al., 2010) and the cardiac arrest during the operation. Regarding the arrhythmias, several studies (Carins et al., 2016; Li et al., 2017) have compared their appearance in both techniques and different results have been obtained.

The development of the fenestration during the intervention is one of the experiments carried out from the simulations that took place in the validation. The fenestration is carried out when there is a high pressure in the pulmonary artery and a low cardiac output or elective. Currently, the development or not of the fenestration still remains controversial (Zou et al., 2016) and the clinical consequences are not completely understood (Fan et al., 2017). Although there are improvements in the early post-operative results, complications arose later, especially due to the drop of the oxygen saturation. Although a patient could have a good post-operative evolution without fenestration (Huang et al., 2017), there are studies that claim that the fenestration improves ventricular preload by reducing total effective systemic venous vascular resistance and thereby improving overall cardiac output (Stumper et al., 2017). However, fenestration requires a stronger medication and higher costs in the staged procedures period (Huang et al., 2017).

CONCLUSION

A useful, easy to use and low-cost simulation tool has been developed. The model allows to obtain through simulation several hemodynamic phenomena that take place in the pre and post-operative stages of the Fontan Procedure. The participation of a multidisciplinary team has been considered as a key factor in the development of this work.

The simulations allowed to explain the hemodynamic behaviours of the different considered variables seen in clinical practice in order to validate the results obtained. The modularity of the model also allows including new knowledge that could force the hemodynamics and predict other pathophysiological conditions and hypothetical interventions.

The results obtained encourage us to continue our research. In this sense, new lines of research are being pursued, considering the model presented in this paper. First, a user-friendly graphical interface is being developed with the aim of providing a tool to surgeons to assist for the planning of cardiovascular procedures, to researchers as a complement to animal experimentation, as well as to students for a better understanding of cardiovascular dynamics. On the other hand, a cellular automaton of the electrical conduction system of the heart is being designed, contributing to improve the results of the hemodynamic model through a computer coupling. Other line of future work includes the exploitation of the model and the experimentation of new modifications in the already existing Fontan techniques for the treatment of the hypoplastic right ventricle syndrome. The predictions of some hemodynamic variables in these simulations could help to avoid the failure of the current Fontan procedure.

ACKNOWLEDGMENT

This work was supported in part by the Fundación Progreso y Salud (Junta de Andalucía), under Grants PI-0010-2013 y PI-0041-2014, in part by the Fondo de Investigaciones Sanitarias, Instituto de Salud Carlos III, under Grants PI15/00306 and DTS15/00195, and in part by the CIBER de Bioingeniería, Biomateriales y Nanomedicina (CIBER-BBN), under Grants INT-2-CARE, NeuroIBC, y ALBUMARK.

REFERENCES

Agarwal, S., Krishnamoorthy, V., & Pratiher, S. (2016). ECG signal analysis using wavelet coherence and s-transform for classification of cardiovascular diseases. *2016 International Conference on Advances in Computing, Communications and Informatics (ICACCI)*, 2765-2770. 10.1109/ICACCI.2016.7732481

Ahmed, T., Pathan, A.-S. K., & Ahmed, S. S. (2015). Learning Algorithms for Anomaly Detection from Images. *International Journal of System Dynamics Applications*, *4*(3), 43–69. doi:10.4018/IJSDA.2015070103

Bangash, S. K., Pathan, I. H., & Zaki, S. B. (2016). Total Cavopulmonary Connection for Functionally Single Ventricle without Cardiopulmonary Bypass Support. *Journal of the College of Physicians and Surgeons--Pakistan*, *26*(10), 855–857. PMID:27806817

Bartelse, S., Roche, S. L., Williams, W. G., Silversides, C., Wald, R., Oechslin, E., ... Hickey, E. J. (2016). Abstract 20112: Lateral Tunnel and Extra-Cardiac Fontan Operations Have Equivalent Early and Late Outcomes in the Modern Era. *Circulation*, *134*(Suppl 1), A20112–A20112.

Biglino, G., Capelli, C., Bruse, J., Bosi, G. M., Taylor, A. M., & Schievano, S. (2017). Computational modelling for congenital heart disease: How far are we from clinical translation? *Heart (British Cardiac Society)*, *103*(2), 98–103. doi:10.1136/heartjnl-2016-310423 PMID:27798056

Brown, J. W., Ruzmetov, M., Deschner, B. W., Rodefeld, M. D., & Turrentine, M. W. (2010). Lateral tunnel Fontan in the current era: Is it still a good option? *The Annals of Thoracic Surgery*, *89*(2), 556–562, discussion 562–563. doi:10.1016/j.athoracsur.2009.10.050 PMID:20103341

Carins, T. A., Shi, W. Y., Iyengar, A. J., Nisbet, A., Forsdick, V., Zannino, D., ... d'Udekem, Y. (2016). Long-term outcomes after first-onset arrhythmia in Fontan physiology. *The Journal of Thoracic and Cardiovascular Surgery*, *152*(5), 1355–1363.e1. doi:10.1016/j.jtcvs.2016.07.073 PMID:27751239

Carvalho, J. S., & Api, O. (2017). Fetal Heart Disease. In J. W. Roos-Hesselink & M. R. Johnson (Eds.), *Pregnancy and Congenital Heart Disease* (pp. 3–21). Springer International Publishing. doi:10.1007/978-3-319-38913-4_1

Chen, W. W., Gao, H., Luo, X. Y., & Hill, N. A. (2016). Study of cardiovascular function using a coupled left ventricle and systemic circulation model. *Journal of Biomechanics*, *49*(12), 2445–2454. doi:10.1016/j.jbiomech.2016.03.009 PMID:27040388

Cheng, A. L., Takao, C. M., Wenby, R. B., Meiselman, H. J., Wood, J. C., & Detterich, J. A. (2016). Elevated Low-Shear Blood Viscosity is Associated with Decreased Pulmonary Blood Flow in Children with Univentricular Heart Defects. *Pediatric Cardiology*, *37*(4), 789–801. doi:10.100700246-016-1352-4 PMID:26888364

Clifford, G. D., Silva, I., Moody, B., Li, Q., Kella, D., Shahin, A., … Mark, R. G. (2015). The PhysioNet/Computing in Cardiology Challenge 2015: Reducing false arrhythmia alarms in the ICU. 2015 Computing in Cardiology Conference (CinC), 273-276. doi:10.1109/CIC.2015.7408639

Clipp, R. B., Bray, A., Metoyer, R., Thames, M. C., & Webb, J. B. (2016). Pharmacokinetic and pharmacodynamic modeling in BioGears. *2016 38th Annual International Conference of the IEEE Engineering in Medicine and Biology Society (EMBC)*, 1467-1470. 10.1109/EMBC.2016.7590986

Corsini, C., Baker, C., Kung, E., Schievano, S., Arbia, G., Baretta, A., ... Dorfman, A. (2014). An integrated approach to patient-specific predictive modeling for single ventricle heart palliation. *Computer Methods in Biomechanics and Biomedical Engineering*, *17*(14), 1572–1589. doi:10.1080/10255842.2012.758254 PMID:23343002

Delorme, Y. T., Rodefeld, M. D., & Frankel, S. H. (2017). Multiblock high order Large Eddy Simulation of powered Fontan hemodynamics: Towards computational surgery. *Computers & Fluids*, *143*, 16–31. doi:10.1016/j.compfluid.2016.10.032 PMID:28649147

Doshi, D., & Burkhoff, D. (2016). Cardiovascular Simulation of Heart Failure Pathophysiology and Therapeutics. *Journal of Cardiac Failure*, *22*(4), 303–311. doi:10.1016/j.cardfail.2015.12.012 PMID:26703246

Fan, F., Liu, Z., Li, S., Yi, T., Yan, J., Yan, F., ... Wang, Q. (2017). Effect of Fenestration on Early Postoperative Outcome in Extracardiac Fontan Patients with Different Risk Levels. *Pediatric Cardiology*, *38*(4), 643–649. doi:10.100700246-016-1561-x PMID:28116475

Ferguson, M., & Kovacs, A. H. (2016). An Integrated Adult Congenital Heart Disease Psychology Service. *Congenital Heart Disease*, *11*(5), 444–451. doi:10.1111/chd.12331 PMID:26918262

Fontan, F., & Baudet, E. (1971). Surgical repair of tricuspid atresia. *Thorax*, *26*(3), 240–248. doi:10.1136/thx.26.3.240 PMID:5089489

Garcia-Canadilla, P., Crispi, F., Cruz-Lemini, M., Triunfo, S., Nadal, A., Valenzuela-Alcaraz, B., ... Bijnens, B. H. (2015). Patient-specific estimates of vascular and placental properties in growth-restricted fetuses based on a model of the fetal circulation. *Placenta*, *36*(9), 981–989. doi:10.1016/j.placenta.2015.07.130 PMID:26242709

Hazinski, M. F. (2013). *Nursing Care of the Critically Ill Child*. Elsevier Health Sciences.

Hirsch, J. C., Goldberg, C., Bove, E. L., Salehian, S., Lee, T., Ohye, R. G., & Devaney, E. J. (2008). Fontan operation in the current era: A 15-year single institution experience. *Annals of Surgery*, *248*(3), 402–410. doi:10.1097/SLA.0b013e3181858286 PMID:18791360

Hose, D. R., & Doyle, B. J. (2017). Modelling of the Cardiovascular System. In P. R. Hoskins, P. V. Lawford, & B. J. Doyle (Eds.), *Cardiovascular Biomechanics* (pp. 193–205). Springer International Publishing; doi:10.1007/978-3-319-46407-7_10

Huang, L., Schilling, C., Dalziel, K. M., Xie, S., Celermajer, D. S., McNeil, J. J., ... d'Udekem, Y. (2017). Hospital Inpatient Costs for Single Ventricle Patients Surviving the Fontan Procedure. *The American Journal of Cardiology*, *120*(3), 467–472. doi:10.1016/j.amjcard.2017.04.049 PMID:28583678

Islam, M. Z., Rahim, A. A., Hasan, K. A., & Ahsan, S. I. (2016). Intracardiac Lateral Tunnel Fontan by using Right Atrial Wall. *Cardiovascular Journal*, *9*(1), 68–72. doi:10.3329/cardio.v9i1.29547

Klimes, K., Abdul-Khaliq, H., Ovroutski, S., Hui, W., Alexi-Meskishvili, V., Spors, B., ... Gutberlet, M. (2007). Pulmonary and caval blood flow patterns in patients with intracardiac and extracardiac Fontan: A magnetic resonance study. *Clinical Research in Cardiology; Official Journal of the German Cardiac Society*, *96*(3), 160–167. doi:10.100700392-007-0470-z PMID:17180575

Kung, E., Baretta, A., Baker, C., Arbia, G., Biglino, G., Corsini, C., ... Migliavacca, F. (2013). Predictive modeling of the virtual Hemi-Fontan operation for second stage single ventricle palliation: Two patient-specific cases. *Journal of Biomechanics*, *46*(2), 423–429. doi:10.1016/j.jbiomech.2012.10.023 PMID:23174419

Li, D., Fan, Q., Hirata, Y., Ono, M., & An, Q. (2017). Arrhythmias After Fontan Operation with Intra-atrial Lateral Tunnel Versus Extra-cardiac Conduit: A Systematic Review and Meta-analysis. *Pediatric Cardiology*, *38*(4), 873–880. doi:10.100700246-017-1595-8 PMID:28271152

Liang, F., Senzaki, H., Kurishima, C., Sughimoto, K., Inuzuka, R., & Liu, H. (2014). Hemodynamic performance of the Fontan circulation compared with a normal biventricular circulation: A computational model study. *American Journal of Physiology. Heart and Circulatory Physiology*, *307*(7), H1056–H1072. doi:10.1152/ajpheart.00245.2014 PMID:25063796

Luffel, M., Sati, M., Rossignac, J., Yoganathan, A. P., Haggerty, C. M., Restrepo, M., ... Fogel, M. A. (2016). SURGEM: A solid modeling tool for planning and optimizing pediatric heart surgeries. *Computer Aided Design*, *70*, 3–12. doi:10.1016/j.cad.2015.06.018

Marvao, A., de, Meyer, H., Dawes, T., Francis, C., Shi, W., & Bai, W. (2016). Development of integrated high-resolution three-dimensional MRI and computational modelling techniques to identify novel genetic and anthropometric determinants of cardiac form and function. *Lancet*, *387*, S36. doi:10.1016/S0140-6736(16)00423-2

Masoller, N., Sanz-Cortés, M., Crispi, F., Gómez, O., Bennasar, M., Egaña-Ugrinovic, G., ... Gratacós, E. (2016). Mid-gestation brain Doppler and head biometry in fetuses with congenital heart disease predict abnormal brain development at birth. *Ultrasound in Obstetrics & Gynecology: The Official Journal of the International Society of Ultrasound in Obstetrics and Gynecology*, *47*(1), 65–73. doi:10.1002/uog.14919 PMID:26053596

Mindila, A., Rodrigues, A., McCormick, D., & Mwangi, R. (2014). An Adaptive ICT-Enabled Model for Knowledge Identification and Management for Enterprise Development. *International Journal of System Dynamics Applications*, *3*(1), 71–89. doi:10.4018/ijsda.2014010104

Molfetta, A. D., Amodeo, A., Fresiello, L., Filippelli, S., Pilati, M., Iacobelli, R., ... Ferrari, G. (2016). The use of a numerical model to simulate the cavo-pulmonary assistance in Fontan circulation: A preliminary verification. *Journal of Artificial Organs*, *19*(2), 105–113. doi:10.100710047-015-0874-5 PMID:26545595

Moysis, L., Kafetzis, I., & Politis, M. (2016). Analysis of a Dynamical Model for HIV Infection with One or Two Inputs. *International Journal of System Dynamics Applications*, *5*(4), 83–100. doi:10.4018/IJSDA.2016100105

Mukherjee, S., Mukhopadhyay, D., & Das, P. (2016). Usefulness of Animal Simulator Software in teaching Amphibian Physiology Practical for 1st Prof MBBS Students. *Journal of Contemporary Medical Education*, *4*(1), 21–25. doi:10.5455/jcme.20160107115900

Opotowsky, A. R., Baraona, F., Landzberg, M., Wu, F., McCausland, F., Owumi, J., ... Waikar, S. (2016). Kidney Dysfunction in Patients with a Single Ventricle Fontan Circulation. *Journal of the American College of Cardiology, 67*(13), 898.

Opotowsky, A. R., Baraona, F. R., Causland, F. R. M., Loukas, B., Landzberg, E., Landzberg, M. J., ... Waikar, S. S. (2017). Estimated glomerular filtration rate and urine biomarkers in patients with single-ventricle Fontan circulation. *Heart (British Cardiac Society)*, *103*(6), 434–442. doi:10.1136/heartjnl-2016-309729 PMID:27670967

Pant, S., Corsini, C., Baker, C., Hsia, T.-Y., Pennati, G., & Vignon-Clementel, I. E. (2016). Data assimilation and modelling of patient-specific single-ventricle physiology with and without valve regurgitation. *Journal of Biomechanics*, *49*(11), 2162–2173. doi:10.1016/j.jbiomech.2015.11.030 PMID:26708918

Parnell, A. S., & Correa, A. (2017). Analyses of trends in prevalence of congenital heart defects and folic acid supplementation. *Journal of Thoracic Disease*, *9*(3), 495–500. doi:10.21037/jtd.2017.03.16 PMID:28449454

Pennati, G., Corsini, C., Hsia, T.-Y., & Migliavacca, F. (2013). Computational fluid dynamics models and congenital heart diseases. *Frontiers in Pediatrics*, *1*. doi:10.3389/fped.2013.00004 PMID:24432298

Petukhov, D. S., & Telyshev, D. V. (2016). A Mathematical Model of the Cardiovascular System of Pediatric Patients with Congenital Heart Defect. *Biomedical Engineering*, *50*(4), 229–232. doi:10.100710527-016-9626-y

Pironet, A., Dauby, P. C., Chase, J. G., Docherty, P. D., Revie, J. A., & Desaive, T. (2016). Structural identifiability analysis of a cardiovascular system model. *Medical Engineering & Physics*, *38*(5), 433–441. doi:10.1016/j.medengphy.2016.02.005 PMID:26970891

Potter, L., Arikatla, S., Bray, A., Webb, J., & Enquobahrie, A. (2017). *Physiology informed virtual surgical planning: A case study with a virtual airway surgical planner and BioGears* (Vol. 10135, p. 101351T-101351T-10). 10.1117/12.2252510

Pruyt, E. (2016). Integrating Systems Modelling and Data Science: The Joint Future of Simulation and 'Big Data' Science. *International Journal of System Dynamics Applications*, *5*(1), 1–16. doi:10.4018/IJSDA.2016010101

Quarteroni, A., Lassila, T., Rossi, S., & Ruiz-Baier, R. (2017). Integrated Heart—Coupling multiscale and multiphysics models for the simulation of the cardiac function. *Computer Methods in Applied Mechanics and Engineering*, *314*, 345–407. doi:10.1016/j.cma.2016.05.031

Quarteroni, A., Veneziani, A., & Vergara, C. (2016). Geometric multiscale modeling of the cardiovascular system, between theory and practice. *Computer Methods in Applied Mechanics and Engineering*, *302*, 193–252. doi:10.1016/j.cma.2016.01.007

Rao & Alapati. (2012). Tricuspid Atresia in the Neonate. *Neonatology Today*, *7*(5), 1–12.

Ravishankar, C., Gerstenberger, E., Sleeper, L. A., Atz, A. M., Affolter, J. T., Bradley, T. J., ... Newburger, J. W. (2016). Factors affecting Fontan length of stay: Results from the Single Ventricle Reconstruction trial. *The Journal of Thoracic and Cardiovascular Surgery*, *151*(3), 669–675.e1. doi:10.1016/j.jtcvs.2015.09.061 PMID:26519244

Sack, K. L., Davies, N. H., Guccione, J. M., & Franz, T. (2016). Personalised computational cardiology: Patient-specific modelling in cardiac mechanics and biomaterial injection therapies for myocardial infarction. *Heart Failure Reviews*, *21*(6), 815–826. doi:10.100710741-016-9528-9 PMID:26833320

Sakamoto, T., Nagashima, M., Hiramatsu, T., Matsumura, G., Park, I.-S., & Yamazaki, K. (2016). Fontan circulation over 30 years. What should we learn from those patients? *Asian Cardiovascular & Thoracic Annals*, *24*(8), 765–771. doi:10.1177/0218492316667771 PMID:27563102

Schiavazzi, D. E., Kung, E. O., Marsden, A. L., Baker, C., Pennati, G., Hsia, T.-Y., ... Dorfman, A. L. (2015). Hemodynamic effects of left pulmonary artery stenosis after superior cavopulmonary connection: A patient-specific multiscale modeling study. *The Journal of Thoracic and Cardiovascular Surgery*, *149*(3), 689–696.e3. doi:10.1016/j.jtcvs.2014.12.040 PMID:25659189

Shimizu, S., Kawada, T., Une, D., Fukumitsu, M., Turner, M. J., Kamiya, A., ... Sugimachi, M. (2016). Partial cavopulmonary assist from the inferior vena cava to the pulmonary artery improves hemodynamics in failing Fontan circulation: A theoretical analysis. *The Journal of Physiological Sciences; JPS*, *66*(3), 249–255. doi:10.100712576-015-0422-3 PMID:26546008

Stumper, O., & Penford, G. (2017). Catheter hemodynamic assessment of the univentricular circulation. *Annals of Pediatric Cardiology*, *10*(2), 167–174. doi:10.4103/apc.APC_160_16 PMID:28566825

Sughimoto, K., Asakura, Y., Brizard, C. P., Liang, F., Fujiwara, T., Miyaji, K., & Liu, H. (2017). Impact of the location of the fenestration on Fontan circulation haemodynamics: A three-dimensional, computational model study. *Cardiology in the Young*, 1–6. doi:10.1017/S1047951117000099 PMID:28376950

Talaminos, A., Roa, L. M., Álvarez, A., & Reina, J. (2014). Computational Hemodynamic Modeling of the Cardiovascular System. *International Journal of System Dynamics Applications*, *3*(2), 81–98. doi:10.4018/ijsda.2014040106

Trusty, P. M., Restrepo, M., Kanter, K. R., Yoganathan, A. P., Fogel, M. A., & Slesnick, T. C. (2016). A pulsatile hemodynamic evaluation of the commercially available bifurcated Y-graft Fontan modification and comparison with the lateral tunnel and extracardiac conduits. *The Journal of Thoracic and Cardiovascular Surgery*, *151*(6), 1529–1536. doi:10.1016/j.jtcvs.2016.03.019 PMID:27056758

Tyagi, M., Fteropoulli, T., Hurt, C. S., Hirani, S. P., Rixon, L., Davies, A., ... Newman, S. P. (2016). Cognitive dysfunction in adult CHD with different structural complexity. *Cardiology in the Young*, 1–9. doi:10.1017/S1047951116001396 PMID:27751192

Van De Bruaene, A., Claessen, G., La Gerche, A., Kung, E., Marsden, A., De Meester, P., ... Gewillig, M. (2015). Effect of respiration on cardiac filling at rest and during exercise in Fontan patients: A clinical and computational modeling study. *IJC Heart & Vasculature*, *9*, 100–108. doi:10.1016/j.ijcha.2015.08.002 PMID:28785717

Watrous, R. L., & Chin, A. J. (2017). Model-Based Comparison of the Normal and Fontan Circulatory Systems—Part III: Major Differences in Performance With Respiration and Exercise. *World Journal for Pediatric & Congenital Heart Surgery*, *8*(2), 148–160. doi:10.1177/2150135116679831 PMID:28329460

Wong, K. K. L., Wang, D., Ko, J. K. L., Mazumdar, J., Le, T.-T., & Ghista, D. (2017). Computational medical imaging and hemodynamics framework for functional analysis and assessment of cardiovascular structures. *Biomedical Engineering Online*, *16*(1), 35. doi:10.118612938-017-0326-y PMID:28327144

Yang, J. H., & Saucerman, J. J. (2011). Computational Models Reduce Complexity and Accelerate Insight Into Cardiac Signaling Networks. *Circulation Research*, *108*(1), 85–97. doi:10.1161/CIRCRESAHA.110.223602 PMID:21212391

Zou, M., Wang, Y., Cui, H., Ma, L., Yang, S., Xia, Y., ... Chen, X. (2016). Outcomes of total cavopulmonary connection for single ventricle palliation. *Journal of Thoracic Disease*, *8*(1), 43–51. doi:10.3978/j.issn.2072-1439.2016.01.41 PMID:26904211

Compilation of References

AASHTO (2013). *Commuting in America 2013: The National Report on Commuting Patterns and Trends*. The American Association of State Highway and Transportation Officials. Publication Code: CA10-4.

Ababei, C., & Marculescu, R. (2000). Low-power realizations of secure chaotic communication Schemes. In: *Proceedings of the IEEE Asia-Pacific Conference on Circuits and Systems*, 30–33. 10.1109/APCCAS.2000.913397

Abbou, A., Nasser, T., Mahmoudi, H., Akherraz, M., & Essadki, A. (2012). dSPACE IFOC Fuzzy Logic Controller Implementation for Induction Motor Drive. *Journal of Electrical Systems*, *8*(3), 317–327.

Abdel Aziz, M. S., El Samahy, M., Hassan, M. A., & El Bendary, F. (2016). Applications of ANFIS in Loss of Excitation Faults Detection in Hydro-Generators. *International Journal of System Dynamics Applications*, *5*(2), 63–79. doi:10.4018/IJSDA.2016040104

Abdel Aziz, M. S., Elsamahy, M., Hassan, M. A., & Bendary, F. M. (2017). Enhancement of Turbo-Generators Phase Backup Protection Using Adaptive Neuro Fuzzy Inference System. *International Journal of System Dynamics Applications*, *6*(1), 58–76. doi:10.4018/IJSDA.2017010104

Abdel Aziz, M. S., Elsamahy, M., Moustafa Hassan, M. A., & Bendary, F. M. A. (2017). A novel study for hydro-generators loss of excitation faults detection using ANFIS. *International Journal of Modelling and Simulation*, *37*(1), 36–45.

Abu-Seada, H. F., Mansor, W. M., Bendary, F. M., Emery, A. A., & Moustafa Hassan, M. A. (2013). Application of Particle Swarm Optimization in Design of PID Controller for AVR System. *International Journal of System Dynamics Applications*, *2*(3), 1–17. doi:10.4018/ijsda.2013070101

Adam, A. A., Gulez, K., & Erdogan, N. (2007, August). Minimum torque ripple algorithm with fuzzy logic controller for DTC of PMSM. In *International Conference on Intelligent Computing* (pp. 511-521). Springer. 10.1007/978-3-540-74171-8_51

Adams, R. J., & Baron, J. R. (1998). Loop Shaping to Improve the Multi-variable Phase Margin. *Proceedings of the 37th IEEE Conference on Decision & Control.* DOI: 10.1109/CDC.1998.757872

ADB. (2010). *The Rise of Asia's Middle Class*. Retrieved from www.adb.org/sites/defailt/files/publication/27726/special-chapter-02.pdf

Adebambo, S., & Toyin, A. (2011). Analysis of Information and Communication Technologies (ICT) Usage on Logistics Activities of Manufacturing Companies in Southwestern Nigeria. *Journal of Emerging Trends in Economics and Management Science*, *2*(1), 68–74.

AfDB (2016). *Strategy for Agricultural Transformation in Africa 2016-2025*. Author.

Afshar, A., & Haghani, A. (2009). Logistics Modeling in Large-Scale Disaster Relief Operations. *Transportation Research Board. Proceedings of the 89th Annual Meeting.*

Agarwal, S., Krishnamoorthy, V., & Pratiher, S. (2016). ECG signal analysis using wavelet coherence and s-transform for classification of cardiovascular diseases. *2016 International Conference on Advances in Computing, Communications and Informatics (ICACCI)*, 2765-2770. 10.1109/ICACCI.2016.7732481

Agbossou, K., Chahine, R., Hamelin, J., Laurencelle, F., Anouar, A., St-Arnaud, J. M., & Bose, T. K. (2001). Renewable energy systems based on hydrogen for remote applications. *Journal of Power Sources*, *96*(1), 168–172. doi:10.1016/S0378-7753(01)00495-5

Agbossou, K., Kolhe, M., Hamelin, J., & Bose, T. K. (2004). Performance of a stand-alone renewable energy system based on energy storage as hydrogen. *IEEE Transactions on Energy Conversion*, *19*(3), 633–640. doi:10.1109/TEC.2004.827719

Aghababa, M. P. (2012). Finite-time chaos control and synchronization of fractional-order nonautonomous chaotic (hyperchaotic) systems using fractional nonsingular terminal sliding mode technique. *Nonlinear Dynamics*, *69*(1-2), 247–267. doi:10.100711071-011-0261-6

Ahammad, T., Beig, A. R., & Al-Hosani, K. (2013, May). An improved direct torque control of induction motor with modified sliding mode control approach. In Electric Machines & Drives Conference (IEMDC), 2013 IEEE International (pp. 166-171). IEEE. doi:10.1109/IEMDC.2013.6556249

Ahmad, I., Saaban, A. B., Ibrahim, A. B., Shahzad, M., & Al-Sawalha, M. M. (2016a). Reduced-order synchronization of time-delay chaotic systems with known and unknown parameters. *Optik-International Journal for Light and Electron Optics*, *127*(13), 5506–5514. doi:10.1016/j.ijleo.2016.02.078

Ahmad, I., Shafiq, M., Saaban, A. B., Ibrahim, A. B., & Shahzad, M. (2016b). Robust finite-time global synchronization of chaotic systems with different orders. *Optik-International Journal for Light and Electron Optics*, *127*(19), 8172–8185. doi:10.1016/j.ijleo.2016.05.065

Ahmed, S., Tarek, B., & Djemai, N. (2013). Economic Dispatch Resolution using Adaptive Accelerated Coefficients based PSO considering Generator Constraints. *International Conference on Control, Decision and Information Technologies (CoDIT'13).*

Ahmed, S. A., Diffenbaugh, N. S., Hertel, T. W., Lobell, D. B., Ramankutty, N., Rios, A. R., & Rowhani, P. (2011). Climate volatility and poverty vulnerability in Tanzania. *Global Environmental Change*, *21*(1), 46–55. doi:10.1016/j.gloenvcha.2010.10.003

Ahmed, T., Pathan, A.-S. K., & Ahmed, S. S. (2015). Learning Algorithms for Anomaly Detection from Images. *International Journal of System Dynamics Applications*, *4*(3), 43–69. doi:10.4018/IJSDA.2015070103

Ai, Y., Wang, Y., & Marrten, K. (2010). Modelling and control of six-phase induction machine under special current waveform. *International Journal of Modelling, Identification and Control*, *10*(1), 4–11. doi:10.1504/IJMIC.2010.033838

Akhmet, M., & Fen, M. O. (2014). Generation of cyclic/toroidal chaos by Hopfield neural networks. *Neurocomputing*, *145*, 230–239. doi:10.1016/j.neucom.2014.05.038

Alavez-Ramírez, J., Fuentes-Allen, J. L., López-Estrada, J., & Mata-Marín, J. A. (2015). Monitoring CD4+ cells using only viral load measurements. *Sky Journal of Medicine and Medical Sciences, 3*(7), 81-89.

Aleksandr, L., & Pogromsky, A. Y. (1998). *Introduction to control of oscillations and chaos* (Vol. 35). World Scientific.

Ali, A., Ebrahim, M.A., & Hassan, M.M. (2015). Control of Single Area Power System Based on Evolutionary Computation Techniques. *MEPCON*, *16*, 19.

Ali, A. B. H., Khalgui, M., & Ahmed, S. B. (2012). UML-based design and validation of intelligent agents-based reconfigurable embedded control systems. *International Journal of System Dynamics Applications, 1*(1), 17–38. doi:10.4018/ijsda.2012010102

Ali, A. M., Ebrahim, M. A., & Hassan, M. M. (2016). Automatic Voltage Generation Control for Two Area Power System Based on Particle Swarm Optimization. *Indonesian Journal of Electrical Engineering and Computer Science*, *2*(1), 132–144. doi:10.11591/ijeecs.v2.i1.pp132-144

Ali, M. M., & Hassan, M. A. (2012). Parameter Identification Using ANFIS for Magnetically Saturated Induction Motor. *International Journal of System Dynamics Applications, 1*(2), 28–43. doi:10.4018/ijsda.2012040103

Alinovi, L., Mane, E., & Romano, D. (2010). Measuring Household Resilience to Food Insecurity: Application to Palestinian Households. In R. Benedetti, M. Bee, G. Espa, & F. Piersimoni (Eds.), *Agricultural Survey Methods*. Chichester, UK: John Wiley & Sons, Ltd. doi:10.1002/9780470665480.ch21

Allaoua, B., Abdessalam, A., Brahim, G., & Abdelfatah, N. (2008). The efficiency of Particle Swarm Optimization applied on Fuzzy Logic DC motor speed control. *Serbian Journal of Electrical Engineering*, *5*(2), 247–262. doi:10.2298/SJEE0802247A

Alleyne, A. (1997). Improved Vehicle Performance Using Combined Suspension and Braking Forces. *Vehicle System Dynamics*, *27*(4), 235–265. doi:10.1080/00423119708969330

Alqhatani, M., Bajwa, S., & Setunge, S. (2013). Modelling the Influence of Socioeconomic and Land-Use Factors on Mode Choice: A Comparison of Riyadh, Saudi Arabia, and Melbourne, Australia. *International Journal of Environmental, Chemical, Ecological. Geological and Geophysical Engineering*, *7*(2), 91–103.

Altay, N., & Green, W. G. III. (2006). OR/MS Research in Disaster Operations Management. *European Journal of Operational Research*, *175*(1), 475–493. doi:10.1016/j.ejor.2005.05.016

Amini, M., Davarpanah, M., & Sanaye-Pasand, M. (2015). A novel approach to detect the synchronous generator loss of excitation. *IEEE Transactions on Power Delivery*, *30*(3), 1429–1438. doi:10.1109/TPWRD.2014.2370763

Amjady, N., & Nasiri-Rad, H. (2009). Nonconvex economic dispatch with AC constraints by a new real coded genetic algorithm. *Power Systems' IEEE Transactions on*, *24*(3), 1489–1502.

Anable, J. (2005). 'Complacent Car Addicts' or 'Aspiring Environmentalists'? Identifying Travel Behaviour Segments Using Attitude Theory. *Transport Policy*, *12*(1), 65–78. doi:10.1016/j.tranpol.2004.11.004

Andem, S. (2006). *A comparative Analysis of Hurricane Evacuation Traffic Conditions Using Static and Dynamic Traffic Assignments* (Published Ph.D. Dissertation). Louisiana State University.

Andrews, S. P. (2009). *Computer-Assisted Emergency Evacuation Planning Using TransCAD: Case Studies in Western Massachusetts* (Published Master Thesis). University of Massachusetts Amherst.

Andronov, A., Vitt, A.A., & Khaikin, S.E. (2011). *Theory of Oscillators.* Dover Publications.

Angerhofer, B. J., & Angelides, M. C. (2000). System dynamics modelling in supply chain management: research review. *Simulation Conference, 2000. Proceedings. Winter*, 1, 342-351. 10.1109/WSC.2000.899737

Ang, K. H., Chong, G. C. Y., & Li, Y. P. I. D. (2005). Control system analysis, design, and technology. *IEEE Transactions on Control Systems Technology*, *13*(4), 559–576. doi:10.1109/TCST.2005.847331

Antoniewicz, P., & Kazmierkowski, P. (2008). Virtual-flux-based predictive direct power control of AC/DC converters with online inductance estimation. *IEEE Transactions on Industrial Electronics*, *55*(12), 4381–4390. doi:10.1109/TIE.2008.2007519

Auramo, J., Kauremaa, J., & Tanskanen, K. (2005). Benefits of IT in supply chain management: An explorative study of progressive companies. *International Journal of Physical Distribution & Logistics Management*, *35*(2), 82–100. doi:10.1108/09600030510590282

Ayala, W. (2006). *Puerto Rico Emergency Management Agency – Emergency Operational Plans*. Retrieved August 21, 2013 from http://www.uprm.edu/cde/public_main/slider/files_slider/presentaciones_foro/manejo_emergencias.pdf

Ayenew, M. M., & Kopainsky, B. (2014, July). *Food Insecurity in Ethiopia: Population, Food Production and Market*. Paper presented at the 32nd International Conference of the System Dynamics Society, Delft, The Netherlands.

Ayenew, M. M. (2015). The Dynamics of Food Insecurity in Ethiopia. *International Journal of System Dynamics Applications*, *4*(4), 17–34. doi:10.4018/IJSDA.2015100102

Azar, A. T., & Serrano, F. E. (2014). Robust IMC-PID tuning for cascade control systems with gain and phase margin specifications. *Neural Computing and Applications, 25*(5), 983-995. DOI: 10.1007/s00521-014-1560-x

Azar, A. T., & Serrano, F. E. (2015a). Stabilization and Control of Mechanical Systems with Backlash. IGI Global. doi:10.4018/978-1-4666-7248-2.ch001

Azar, A. T., & Serrano, F. E. (2015b). Design and Modeling of Anti Wind Up PID Controllers. In Complex system modelling and control through intelligent soft computations (vol. 319, pp. 1-44). Springer-Verlag. doi:10.1007/978-3-319-12883-2_1

Azar, A. T., & Serrano, F. E. (2015c). Adaptive Sliding mode control of the Furuta pendulum. In Studies in Computational Intelligence (vol. 576, pp. 1-42). Springer-Verlag GmbH Berlin/Heidelberg. doi:10.1007/978-3-319-11173-5_1

Azar, A. T., & Serrano, F. E. (2015d). Deadbeat Control for Multivariable Systems with Time Varying Delays. In Chaos Modeling and Control Systems Design (vol. 581, pp. 97-132). Springer-Verlag GmbH Berlin/Heidelberg. DOI doi:10.1007/978-3-319-13132-0_6

Azar, A. T., & Vaidyanathan, S. (2015a). Handbook of Research on Advanced Intelligent Control Engineering and Automation. Hershey, PA: IGI Global. doi:10.4018/978-1-4666-7248-2

Azar, A. T., Kumar, J., Kumar, V., & Rana, K. P. S. (2017d) Control of a Two Link Planar Electrically-Driven Rigid Robotic Manipulator Using Fractional Order SOFC. *Proceedings of the International Conference on Advanced Intelligent Systems and Informatics 2017, 639*, 47-56.

Azar, A. T., Kumar, J., Kumar, V., & Rana, K. P. S. (2017d) Control of a Two Link Planar Electrically-Driven Rigid Robotic Manipulator Using Fractional Order SOFC. Proceedings of the International Conference on Advanced Intelligent Systems and Informatics 2017, Advances in Intelligent Systems and Computing series, Vol. 639, pp 47-56. Springer-Verlag, Germany.

Azar, A. T., Kumar, J., Kumar, V., & Rana, K. P. S. (2017d). Control of a Two Link Planar Electrically-Driven Rigid Robotic Manipulator Using Fractional Order SOFC. *Proceedings of the International Conference on Advanced Intelligent Systems and Informatics 2017, 639*, 47-56.

Azar, A. T., Ouannas, A., & Singh, S. (2017c) Control of New Type of Fractional Chaos Synchronization. Proceedings of the International Conference on Advanced Intelligent Systems and Informatics 2017, Advances in Intelligent Systems and Computing series, Vol. 639, pp 47-56. Springer-Verlag, Germany.

Azar, A. T., Ouannas, A., & Singh, S. (2017c). Control of New Type of Fractional Chaos Synchronization. *Proceedings of the International Conference on Advanced Intelligent Systems and Informatics 2017, 639*, 47-56.

Azar, A. T., Volos, C., Gerodimos, N. A., Tombras, G. S., Pham, V. T., Radwan, A. G., ... Munoz-Pacheco, J. M. (2017b). A novel chaotic system without equilibrium: Dynamics, synchronization and circuit realization. *Complexity*. doi:10.1155/2017/7871467

Azar, A.T. (2013). Fast neural network learning algorithms for medical applications. *Neural Computing and Applications, 23*(3-4), 1019-1034. DOI: 10.1007/s00521-012-1026-y

Azar, A.T., & El-Said, S.A. (2013). Probabilistic neural network for breast cancer classification. *Neural Computing and Applications, 23*(6), 1737-1751. DOI: 10.1007/s00521-012-1134-8

Azar, A.T., & El-Said, S.A. (2013). Superior Neuro-Fuzzy Classification Systems. *Neural Computing and Applications, 23*(1), 55-72. DOI: 10.1007/s00521-012-1231-8

Azar, A. T. (2010a). *Fuzzy Systems*. Vienna, Austria: IN-TECH.

Azar, A. T. (2010b). Adaptive Neuro-Fuzzy Systems. In A. T. Azar (Ed.), *Fuzzy Systems*. Vienna, Austria: IN-TECH. doi:10.5772/7220

Azar, A. T. (2012). Overview of Type-2 Fuzzy logic systems. *International Journal of Fuzzy System Applications*, *2*(4), 1–28. doi:10.4018/ijfsa.2012100101

Azar, A. T. (2012a). System Dynamics as a Useful Technique for Complex Systems. *International Journal of Industrial and Systems Engineering*, *10*(4), 377–410. doi:10.1504/IJISE.2012.046298

Azar, A. T., & El-Said, S. A. (2013). Superior neuro-fuzzy classification systems. *Neural Computing & Applications*, 1–18.

Azar, A. T., & Serrano, F. E. (2016a) Robust control for asynchronous switched nonlinear systems with time varying delays. *Proceedings of the International Conference on Advanced Intelligent Systems and Informatics 2016*, 533, 891-899. 10.1007/978-3-319-48308-5_85

Azar, A. T., & Serrano, F. E. (2016b). Stabilization of Mechanical Systems with Backlash by PI Loop Shaping. *International Journal of System Dynamics Applications*, *5*(3), 20–47. doi:10.4018/IJSDA.2016070102

Azar, A. T., & Vaidyanathan, S. (2015a). *Chaos Modeling and Control Systems Design, Studies in Computational Intelligence* (Vol. 581). Springer-Verlag.

Azar, A. T., & Vaidyanathan, S. (2015a). *Chaos Modeling and Control Systems Design.* Springer-Verlag.

Azar, A. T., & Vaidyanathan, S. (2015b). *Computational Intelligence applications in Modeling and Control. In Studies in Computational Intelligence* (Vol. 575). Springer-Verlag.

Azar, A. T., & Vaidyanathan, S. (2015b). *Computational Intelligence Applications in Modeling and Control. In Studies in Computational Intelligence* (Vol. 575). Springer-Verlag.

Azar, A. T., & Vaidyanathan, S. (2015b). *Computational Intelligence applications in Modeling and Control. Studies in Computational Intelligence* (Vol. 575). Springer-Verlag.

Azar, A. T., & Vaidyanathan, S. (2015c). *Chaos Modeling and Control Systems Design. In Studies in Computational Intelligence* (Vol. 581). Springer-Verlag.

Azar, A. T., & Vaidyanathan, S. (2016). *Advances in Chaos Theory and Intelligent Control. In Studies in Fuzziness and Soft Computing* (Vol. 337). Springer-Verlag. doi:10.1007/978-3-319-30340-6

Azar, A. T., Vaidyanathan, S., & Ouannas, A. (2017a). *Fractional Order Control and Synchronization of Chaotic Systems. In Studies in Computational Intelligence* (Vol. 688). Springer-Verlag. doi:10.1007/978-3-319-50249-6

Azar, A. T., & Zhu, Q. (2015). *Advances and Applications in Sliding Mode Control systems. In Studies in Computational Intelligence* (Vol. 576). Germany: Springer-Verlag.

Azar, A. T., & Zhu, Q. (2015). *Advances and Applications in Sliding Mode Control systems. Studies in Computational Intelligence* (Vol. 576). Springer-Verlag.

Aziz, M. A., Hassan, M. M., & Zahab, E. A. (2011, September). Applications of ANFIS in high impedance faults detection and classification in distribution networks. In *Diagnostics for Electric Machines, Power Electronics & Drives (SDEMPED), 2011 IEEE International Symposium*, (pp. 612-619). IEEE.

Aziz, M. A., Hassan, M. A., & Zahab, E. A. (2011, October). *An Artificial Intelligence Based Approach for High Impedance Faults Analysis in Distribution Networks under Different Loading Conditions*. In *The 21st International conference on Computer Theory and Applications*, Alexandria, Egypt.

Aziz, M. A., Hassan, M. M., & El-Zahab, E. A. (2012). An artificial intelligence based approach for high impedance faults analysis in distribution networks. *International Journal of System Dynamics Applications*, *1*(2), 44–59. doi:10.4018/ijsda.2012040104

Aziz, M. A., Hassan, M. M., & Zahab, E. A. (2012). High-impedance faults analysis in distribution networks using an adaptive neuro fuzzy inference system. *Electric Power Components and Systems*, *40*(11), 1300–1318. doi:10.1080/15325008.2012.689418

Aziz, M. S. E. D. A., Elsamahy, M., Moustafa, M., & Bendary, F. (2016). Detecting the Loss of Excitation in Hydro Generators Using a Neuro-Fuzzy Technique. The Annals of "Dunarea De Jos". *University of Galati*, *39*(1), 34–43.

Aziz, M. S. E. D. A., Elsamahy, M., Moustafa, M., & Bendary, F. (2016). Loss of Excitation Detection in Hydro-Generators Based on ANFIS Approach Using Positive Sequence Components. *The XIX IEEE International Conference on Soft Computing and Measurements SCM'2016*, 309-312. 10.1109/SCM.2016.7519765

Aziz, M. S. E. D. A., Elsamahy, M., Moustafa, M., & Bendary, F. (2016). Loss of Excitation Faults Detection in Hydro-Generators Using an Adaptive Neuro Fuzzy Inference System. *Indonesian Journal of Electrical Engineering and Computer Science*, *1*(2), 300–309. doi:10.11591/ijeecs.v1.i2.pp300-309

Baader, M., Depenbrock, U., & Gierse, G. (1992). Direct self-control (DSC) of inverter-fed induction machine: A basis for speed control without speed measurement. *IEEE Transactions on Industry Applications*, *28*(3), 581–588. doi:10.1109/28.137442

Babu, T. S., Rajasekar, N., & Sangeetha, K. (2015). Modified particle swarm optimization technique based maximum power point tracking for uniform and under partial shading condition. *Applied Soft Computing*, *34*, 613–624. doi:10.1016/j.asoc.2015.05.029

Baghli, L. (1999). *Contribution à la Commande de la Machine Asynchrone, Utilisation de la Logique Floue, des Réseaux de Neurones et des Algorithmes Génétiques* (Thèse de Doctorat). Département de Génie Electrique Université Henri Poincaré, Nancy-I.

Bagley, R. L., & Calico, R. A. (1991). Fractional order state equations for the control of viscoelastically damped structures. *Journal of Guidance, Control, and Dynamics*, *14*(2), 304–311. doi:10.2514/3.20641

Bahgaat, N. K. (2013). *Artificial intelligent based controller for frequency control in power systems* (Ph.D. thesis). Faculty of Engineering at Al- Azhar University, Cairo, Egypt.

Bahgaat, N. K., El-Sayed, M. I., Moustafa Hassan, M. A., & Bendary, F. A. (2014). Load Frequency Control in Power System via Improving PID Controller Based on Particle Swarm Optimization and ANFIS Techniques. International Journal of System Dynamics Applications, 3(3), 1-24.

Bahgaat, N. K., El-Sayed, M. I., Moustafa Hassan, M. A., & Bendary, F. A. (2015). *'Application of Some Modern Techniques in Load Frequency Control in Power Systems', Chaos Modeling and Control Systems Design* (Vol. 581). Springer-Verlag.

Baiphethi, M. N., & Jacobs, P. T. (2009). The contribution of subsistence farming to food security in South Africa. *Agrekon*, *48*(4), 459–482. doi:10.1080/03031853.2009.9523836

Bajracharya, A. (2016). Public Transportation and Private Car: A System Dynamics Approach in Understanding the Mode Choice. *International Journal of System Dynamics Applications*, *5*(2), 1–18. doi:10.4018/IJSDA.2016040101

Balcik, B., & Beamon, B. (2008). Facility Location in Humanitarian Relief. *International Journal of Logistics. Research and Applications*, *11*(2), 101–121.

Bangash, S. K., Pathan, I. H., & Zaki, S. B. (2016). Total Cavopulmonary Connection for Functionally Single Ventricle without Cardiopulmonary Bypass Support. *Journal of the College of Physicians and Surgeons--Pakistan*, *26*(10), 855–857. PMID:27806817

Bao, B. C., & Liu, Z. (2008). A hyperchaotic attractor coined from chaotic Lü system. *Chinese Physics Letters*, *25*(7), 2396–2399. doi:10.1088/0256-307X/25/7/018

Bao, H., & Cao, J. (2015). Projective synchronization of fractional-order memristor-based neural networks. *Neural Networks*, *63*, 1–9. doi:10.1016/j.neunet.2014.10.007 PMID:25463390

Barão, M., & Lemos, J. M. (2007). Nonlinear control of HIV-1 infection with a singular perturbation model. *Biomedical Signal Processing and Control*, *2*(3), 248–257. doi:10.1016/j.bspc.2007.07.011

Barman, B., & Mukhopadhyay, A. (2015). Extracting Biological Significant Subnetworks from Protein-Protein Interactions Induced by Differentially Expressed Genes of HIV-1 Vpr Variants. [IJSDA]. *International Journal of System Dynamics Applications*, *4*(4), 35–51. doi:10.4018/IJSDA.2015100103

Barreiro, A., & Baños, A. (2006). Input output stability of systems with backlash. *Automatica*, *42*(6), 1017–1024. doi:10.1016/j.automatica.2006.02.017

Bartelse, S., Roche, S. L., Williams, W. G., Silversides, C., Wald, R., Oechslin, E., ... Hickey, E. J. (2016). Abstract 20112: Lateral Tunnel and Extra-Cardiac Fontan Operations Have Equivalent Early and Late Outcomes in the Modern Era. *Circulation*, *134*(Suppl 1), A20112–A20112.

Battini, D., Faccio, M., Persona, A., & Sgarbossa, F. (2013). Modelling the Growing Process of Integrated Healthcare Supply Networks. *International Journal of System Dynamics Applications*, *2*(1), 1–13. doi:10.4018/ijsda.2013010101

Becker, G., & Packard, A. (1994). Robust performance of linear parametrically varying systems using parametrically-dependent linear feedback. *Systems & Control Letters*, *23*(3), 205–215. doi:10.1016/0167-6911(94)90006-X

Behagi. (1992). Piece-wise Linear Modeling of Solid-state Varactor-tuned Microwave Oscillators. *Proceedings of the IEEE Frequency Control Symposium*, 415–519.

Beirao, G., & Cabral, J. A. S. (2007). Understanding Attitudes Towards Public Transport and Private Car: A Qualitative Study. *Transport Policy*, *14*(6), 478–489. doi:10.1016/j.tranpol.2007.04.009

Belytschko, T. (1992). On Computational Methods for Crashworthiness. *Computers & Structures*, *42*(2), 271–279. doi:10.1016/0045-7949(92)90211-H

Ben Hariz, M., Bouani, F., & Ksouri, M. (2012). Robust controller for uncertain parameters systems. *ISA Transactions*, *51*(5), 632–640. doi:10.1016/j.isatra.2012.04.007 PMID:22749294

Ben Hariz, M., Bouani, F., & Ksouri, M. (2014). Implementation of a fixed low order controller on STM32 microcontroller. *International Conference on Control, Engineering and Information Technologies (CEIT)*, 244-252.

Ben Hariz, M., Chagra, W., & Bouani, F. (2013). Controllers design for MIMO systems with time response specifications. *International Conference on Control, Decision and Information Technologies (CoDIT)*, 573-578. 10.1109/CoDIT.2013.6689607

Ben Hariz, M., Chagra, W., & Bouani, F. (2014). Synthesis of Controllers for MIMO Systems with Time Response Specifications. *International Journal of System Dynamics Applications*, *3*(3), 25–52. doi:10.4018/ijsda.2014070102

Ben Smida, M., & Sakly, A. (2016). A Comparative Study of Different MPPT Methods for Grid-Connected Partially Shaded Photovoltaic Systems. *International Journal of Renewable Energy Research*, *6*(3).

Bendjedia, M., Ait-Amirat, Y., Walther, B., & Berthon, A. (2007, September). Sensorless control of hybrid stepper motor. In *Power Electronics and Applications, 2007 European Conference on* (pp. 1-10). IEEE.

Benmouyal, G. (2007). *The impact of synchronous generators excitation supply on protection and relays*. Schweitzer Engineering Laboratories, Inc., Tech. Rep. TP6281-01, 20070912.

Bentsman, J., Orlov, Y., & Aguilar, L. T. (2013). *Nonsmooth H-infinity Output Regulation with Application to a Coal-Fired Boiler/Turbine Unit with Actuator Deadzone. 2013 American Control Conference (ACC)*, Washington, DC. DOI: 10.1109/ACC.2013.6580434

Besiou, M., Stapleton, O., & Wassenhove, L. (2011). System Dynamics for Humanitarian Operations. *Journal of Humanitarian Logistics and Supply Chain Management*, *1*(1), 78–103. doi:10.1108/20426741111122420

Bevrani, H. (2009). *Robust power system frequency control*. Brisbane, Australia: Springer Science and Business Media, LLC. doi:10.1007/978-0-387-84878-5

Bhadrachalam, L., Chalasani, S., & Boppana, R. V. (2011). Impact of RFID technology on economic order quantity models. *International Journal of Productivity and Quality Management*, *7*(3), 325–357. doi:10.1504/IJPQM.2011.039351

Bhandari, R. (2014). Impact of Technology on Logistics and Supply Chain Management. *IOSR Journal of Business and Management*.

Bharatirajal, C., Raghu, S., Jeevananthan, S., & Latha, R. (2011). *Implementation of variable structure DTC-SVM based VWF for an induction motor drive using FPGA-SPARTEN III*. Academic Press.

Bhati, S., & Nitnawwre, D. (2012). Genetic Optimization Tuning of an Automatic Voltage Regulator System. *International Journal of Scientific Engineering and Technology*, *1*, 120–124.

Bhatt, V. K., & Bhongade, S. (2013). Design Of PID Controller In Automatic Voltage Regulator (AVR) System Using PSO Technique. *International Journal of Engineering Research and Applications*, *3*(4), 1480–1485.

Bhim, S., Pradeep, J., Mittal, A. P., & Gupta, J. R. P. (2008). Torque Ripples Minimization of DTC IPMSM Drive for the EV Propulsion System using a Neural Network. *Journal of Power Electronics*, *8*(1), 23–34.

Biglino, G., Capelli, C., Bruse, J., Bosi, G. M., Taylor, A. M., & Schievano, S. (2017). Computational modelling for congenital heart disease: How far are we from clinical translation? *Heart (British Cardiac Society)*, *103*(2), 98–103. doi:10.1136/heartjnl-2016-310423 PMID:27798056

Bimal, & Bos, K. (1994). Expert system, fuzzy logic, and neural network applications in power electronics and motion control. *Proceedings of the IEEE, 82*(8), 1303 – 1323.

Bjork, K., Lindberg, P., & Westerlund, T. (2003). Some convexifications in global optimization of problems containing signomial terms. *Computers & Chemical Engineering, 27*(5), 669–679. doi:10.1016/S0098-1354(02)00254-5

Blackburn, J. L., & Domin, T. J. (2015). *Protective relaying: principles and applications*. CRC press.

Bose, B. (2001). *Artificial neural network applications in power electronics*. The 27th Annual Conférence of the IEEE Industrial Electronics Society, Denver, CO. 10.1109/IECON.2001.975533

Bose. (2002). Modern power electronics and AC drives. Academic Press.

Bossoufi, B., Karim, M., Silviu, I., & Lagrioui, A. (2011, June). FPGA-based implementation by direct torque control of a PMSM machine. In Compatibility and Power Electronics (CPE), 2011 7th International Conference-Workshop (pp. 464-469). IEEE.

Bossoufi, B., Karim, M., Lagrioui, A., Taoussi, M., & Derouich, A. (2015). Observer backstepping control of DFIG-Generators for wind turbines variable-speed: FPGA-based implementation. *Renewable Energy, 81*, 903–917. doi:10.1016/j.renene.2015.04.013

Bouafia, A., & Krim, F. (2008). A fuzzy-Logic-Based Controller for Three-Phase PWM Rectifier with Unity Power Factor Operation. J. *Electrical Systems, 4*(1), 36–50.

Bouafia, A., Krim, F., & Gaubert, J. P. (2009). Fuzzy-Logic-Based Switching State Selection for Direct Power Control of Three-Phase PWM Rectifier. *IEEE Transactions on Industrial Electronics, 56*(6), 1984–1992. doi:10.1109/TIE.2009.2014746

Bouallegue, K. (2017). A new class of neural networks and its applications. *Neurocomputing, 249*, 28–47. doi:10.1016/j.neucom.2017.03.006

Bouchakour, S. (2005). *Commande Directe de Puissance d'un Convertisseur AC/DC Triphasé Sans Capteurs de Tension*. Memory of Magister Ecole Militaire Polytechnique Algeria.

Boukhnifer, M., & Ferreira, A. (2005). H Infinity Loop Shaping for Stabilization and Robustness of a Tele-Micromanipulation System. *IEEE/RSJ International Conference on Intelligent Robots and Systems. Intelligent Robots and Systems*, 778-783.

Boulkroune, A., Bouzeriba, A., Bouden, T., & Azar, A. T. (2016a). Fuzzy Adaptive Synchronization of Uncertain Fractional-order Chaotic Systems. In A. T. Azar & S. Vaidyanathan (Eds.), *Advances in Chaos Theory and Intelligent Control. Studies in Fuzziness and Soft Computing* (Vol. 337). Springer-Verlag. doi:10.1007/978-3-319-30340-6_28

Boulkroune, A., Bouzeriba, A., Bouden, T., & Azar, A. T. (2016a). *Fuzzy Adaptive Synchronization of Uncertain Fractional-order Chaotic Systems. In Studies in Fuzziness and Soft Computing* (Vol. 337, pp. 681–697). Springer-Verlag.

Boulkroune, A., Hamel, S., & Azar, A. T. (2016b). *Fuzzy control-based function synchronization of unknown chaotic systems with dead-zone input. Advances in Chaos Theory and Intelligent Control. Studies in Fuzziness and Soft Computing* (Vol. 337). Springer-Verlag.

Boulkroune, A., Hamel, S., & Azar, A. T. (2016b). *Fuzzy control-based function synchronization of unknown chaotic systems with dead-zone input. In Advances in Chaos Theory and Intelligent Control* (Vol. 337). Springer-Verlag.

Boulkroune, A., Hamel, S., & Azar, A. T. (2016b). *Fuzzy control-based function synchronization of unknown chaotic systems with dead-zone input. In Advances in Chaos Theory and Intelligent Control. Studies in Fuzziness and Soft Computing* (Vol. 337). Springer-Verlag.

Boulkroune, A., Hamel, S., & Azar, A. T. (2016b). *Fuzzy control-based function synchronization of unknown chaotic systems with dead-zone input. In Studies in Fuzziness and Soft Computing* (Vol. 337, pp. 699–718). Springer-Verlag.

Boussak, M., & Jarray, K. (2006). A high-performance sensorless indirect stator flux orientation control of induction motor drive. *IEEE Transactions on Industrial Electronics*, *53*(1), 41–49. doi:10.1109/TIE.2005.862319

Bowersox, D. J., Closs, D. J., & Cooper, M. B. (2002). *Supply chain logistics management* (Vol. 2). New York: McGraw-Hill.

Bozoki, Z. (1997). Chaos theory and power spectrum analysis in computerized cardiotocography. *European Journal of Obstetrics, Gynecology, and Reproductive Biology*, *71*(2), 163–168. doi:10.1016/S0301-2115(96)02628-0 PMID:9138960

Bozorgi-Amiri, A., Jabalameli, M. S., & Mirzapour Al-e-Hashem, S. M. (2013). A multi-objective robust stochastic programming model for disaster relief logistics under uncertainty. *OR-Spektrum*, *35*(4), 905–933. doi:10.100700291-011-0268-x

Brandstetter, P., Kuchar, M., & Vinklarek, D. (2006, July). Estimation techniques for sensorless speed control of induction motor drive. In *Industrial Electronics, 2006 IEEE International Symposium on* (Vol. 1, pp. 154-159). IEEE.

Brisolara, L. C. B., Kreutz, M. E., & Carro, L. (2009). UML as front-end language for embedded systems design. In Behavioral Modeling for Embedded Systems and Technologies: Application for Design and Implementation (pp. 1–23). Hershey, PA: IGI Global.

Brogan, W. L. (2005). *Modern Control Theory*. Prentice Hall.

Brown, J. W., Ruzmetov, M., Deschner, B. W., Rodefeld, M. D., & Turrentine, M. W. (2010). Lateral tunnel Fontan in the current era: Is it still a good option? *The Annals of Thoracic Surgery*, *89*(2), 556–562, discussion 562–563. doi:10.1016/j.athoracsur.2009.10.050 PMID:20103341

Buja, G., Casadei, D., & Serra, G. (1997, July). Direct torque control of induction motor drives. In *Industrial Electronics, 1997. ISIE'97., Proceedings of the IEEE International Symposium on* (*Vol. 1*, pp. TU2-TU8). IEEE. 10.1109/ISIE.1997.651717

Burca, S., Fynes, B., & Marshall, D. (2005). Strategic technology adoption: Extending ERP across the supply chain. *Journal of Enterprise Information Management*, *18*(4), 427–440. doi:10.1108/17410390510609581

Caliper Corporation. (2010). *TransCAD Overview*. Retrieved June 10, 2010 from http://www.caliper.com/tcovu.htm

Callaway, D. S., & Perelson, A. S. (2002). HIV-1 infection and low steady state viral loads. *Bulletin of Mathematical Biology*, *64*(1), 29–64. doi:10.1006/bulm.2001.0266 PMID:11868336

Calza, F., & Passaro, R. (1997). EDI network and logistics management at Unilever-Sagit. *Supply Chain Management*, *2*(4), 158–170. doi:10.1108/13598549710191322

Camacho-Vallejo, J. F., González-Rodríguez, E., Almaguer, F. J., & González-Ramírez, R. G. (2015). A bi-level optimization model for aid distribution after the occurrence of a disaster. *Journal of Cleaner Production*, *105*, 134–145. doi:10.1016/j.jclepro.2014.09.069

Campbell, A. M., Vandenbussche, D., & Hermann, W. (2008). Routing for relief efforts. *Transportation Science*, *42*(2), 127–145. doi:10.1287/trsc.1070.0209

Carins, T. A., Shi, W. Y., Iyengar, A. J., Nisbet, A., Forsdick, V., Zannino, D., ... d'Udekem, Y. (2016). Long-term outcomes after first-onset arrhythmia in Fontan physiology. *The Journal of Thoracic and Cardiovascular Surgery*, *152*(5), 1355–1363.e1. doi:10.1016/j.jtcvs.2016.07.073 PMID:27751239

Carrasco, N. (2011). Quantifying public transport reliability in Zurich. *Swiss Transport Research Conference (SRTC).*

Carvalho, A., & Pinto, C. M. (2016). A delay fractional order model for the co-infection of malaria and HIV/AIDS. *International Journal of Dynamics and Control*, 1-19.

Carvalho, J. S., & Api, O. (2017). Fetal Heart Disease. In J. W. Roos-Hesselink & M. R. Johnson (Eds.), *Pregnancy and Congenital Heart Disease* (pp. 3–21). Springer International Publishing. doi:10.1007/978-3-319-38913-4_1

Casadei, D., Profum, F., Serra, G., & Tani, A. (2002). FOC and DTC: Two viable schemes for induction motors torque control. *IEEE Transactions on Power Electronics*, *17*(5), 779–787. doi:10.1109/TPEL.2002.802183

Casadei, D., Serra, G., & Tani, K. (2000). Implementation of a direct control algorithm for induction motors based on discrete space vector modulation. *IEEE Transactions on Power Electronics*, *15*(4), 769–777. doi:10.1109/63.849048

Celik, A. N. (2002). Optimization and techno-economic analysis of autonomous photovoltaic–wind hybrid energy systems in comparison to single photovoltaic and wind systems. *Energy Conversion and Management*, *43*(18), 2453–2468. doi:10.1016/S0196-8904(01)00198-4

Cha, H. J., & Enjeti, P. N. (2003, June). A three-phase AC/AC high-frequency link matrix converter for VSCF applications. In *Power Electronics Specialist Conference, 2003. PESC'03. 2003 IEEE 34th Annual* (Vol. 4, pp. 1971-1976). IEEE.

Chandrasekaran, V., Dalley, B., Ned Mohan, S. K., & Posbergh, T. (2013). Low Cost FPGA Based Replacement for dSPACE Units in the Electric Drives Laboratory. Laboratory to accompany 4701. *Simulink-based simulations of electric machines/drives in applications such as energy conservation and motion control in robotics*. Retrieved from http://cusp.umn.edu/Napa_2013/Friday/Tom_P_Napa.pdf

Chang, J. M., Ali, M., Craig, R., Tyan, T., El-bkaily, M., & Cheng, J. (2006). *Important Modeling Practices in CAE Simulation for Vehicle Pitch and Drop*. SAE International, Warrendale, PA, SAE Technical Paper No. 2006-01-0124.

Chapuis, Y. A. (1996). *Contrôle directe du couple d'une machine asynchrone par l'orientation de son flux statorique* (Doctoral thesis). INP-Grenoble, France.

Chen, L., Fang, K. L., & Hu, Z. F. (2005, August). A scheme of fuzzy direct torque control for induction machine. In *Machine Learning and Cybernetics, 2005. Proceedings of 2005 International Conference on* (*Vol. 2*, pp. 803-807). IEEE.

Chen, B., & Joos, G. (2008). Direct power control of active filters with averaged switching frequency regulation. *IEEE Transactions on Power Electronics*, *23*(6), 2729–2737. doi:10.1109/TPEL.2008.2004958

Chen, C. H., Hong, C. M., & Ou, T. C. (2012). Hybrid fuzzy control of wind turbine generator by pitch control using RNN. *International Journal of Ambient Energy*, *33*(2), 56–64. doi:10.1080/01430750.2011.630754

Cheng, G. (2010). *Dynamic Trip Distribution Models for Hurricane Evacuation* (Published Ph.D. Dissertation). Louisiana State University.

Cheng, A. L., Takao, C. M., Wenby, R. B., Meiselman, H. J., Wood, J. C., & Detterich, J. A. (2016). Elevated Low-Shear Blood Viscosity is Associated with Decreased Pulmonary Blood Flow in Children with Univentricular Heart Defects. *Pediatric Cardiology*, *37*(4), 789–801. doi:10.100700246-016-1352-4 PMID:26888364

Cheng, G. (1997). *Genetic Algorithms and Engineering Design*. New York: Wiley.

Chen, S., & Joos, G. (2001) Direct Power Control of Three Active filer with Minimum Energy Storage Components. *APEC 2001. Sixteenth Annual IEEE Applied Power Electronics Conference and Exposition*. DOI: 10.1109/APEC.2001.911703

Chen, W. W., Gao, H., Luo, X. Y., & Hill, N. A. (2016). Study of cardiovascular function using a coupled left ventricle and systemic circulation model. *Journal of Biomechanics*, *49*(12), 2445–2454. doi:10.1016/j.jbiomech.2016.03.009 PMID:27040388

Chen, Z., Yang, Y., Qi, G., & Yuan, Z. (2007). A novel hyperchaos system only with one equilibrium. *Physics Letters. [Part A]*, *360*(6), 696–701. doi:10.1016/j.physleta.2006.08.085

Cheung, Y., Choy, K., & Lau, W. (2008). The Impact of RFID Technology on the Formulation of Logistics Strategy. *PICMET Proceedings*, 1673-1680.

Chowdhury, M. A., Hosseinzadeh, N., & Shen, W. X. (2012). Smoothing wind power fluctuations by fuzzy logic pitch angle controller. *Renewable Energy*, *38*(1), 224–233. doi:10.1016/j.renene.2011.07.034

Chul, C., & Dennis, L. (1996). Effectiveness of a geometric programming algorithm for optimization of machining economics models. *Computers & Operations Research*, *23*(10), 957–961. doi:10.1016/0305-0548(96)00008-1

Chyung, D. H. (1992). Output Feedback Controller for Systems Containing a Backlash. *Proceedings of the 31st Conference on Decision and Control*. 10.1109/CDC.1992.371218

Cichowlas, M., Malinowski, M., Kazmierkowski, P., Sobczuk, D., & Pou, J. (2005). Active filtering function of three-phase PWM boost rectifier under different line voltage conditions. *IEEE Transactions on Industrial Electronics*, *52*(2), 410–419. doi:10.1109/TIE.2005.843915

Clerc, M., & Kennedy, J. (2002). The particle swarm-explosion, stability, and convergence in a multidimensional complex space. *IEEE Transactions on Evolutionary Computation*, *6*(1), 58–73. doi:10.1109/4235.985692

Clifford, G. D., Silva, I., Moody, B., Li, Q., Kella, D., Shahin, A., … Mark, R. G. (2015). The PhysioNet/Computing in Cardiology Challenge 2015: Reducing false arrhythmia alarms in the ICU. 2015 Computing in Cardiology Conference (CinC), 273-276. doi:10.1109/CIC.2015.7408639

Clipp, R. B., Bray, A., Metoyer, R., Thames, M. C., & Webb, J. B. (2016). Pharmacokinetic and pharmacodynamic modeling in BioGears. *2016 38th Annual International Conference of the IEEE Engineering in Medicine and Biology Society (EMBC)*, 1467-1470. 10.1109/EMBC.2016.7590986

Closs, D. J., Goldsby, T. J., & Clinton, S. R. (1997). Information technology influences on world class logistics capability. *International Journal of Physical Distribution & Logistics Management*, *27*(1), 4–17. doi:10.1108/09600039710162259

Closs, D. J., & Savitskie, K. (2003). Internal and External Logistics Information Technology Integration. *International Journal of Logistics Management*, *14*(1), 63–76. doi:10.1108/09574090310806549

Codjoe, S., & Owusu, G. (2011). Climate change/variability and food systems: Evidence from the Afram Plains, Ghana. *Regional Environmental Change*, *11*(4), 753–765. doi:10.100710113-011-0211-3

Coello, C. A. C., Pulido, G. T., & Lechuga, M. S. (2004). Handling multiple objectives with particle swarm optimization. *IEEE Transactions on Evolutionary Computation*, *8*(3), 256–279. doi:10.1109/TEVC.2004.826067

Combs, T. S. (2017). Examining Changes in Travel Patterns among Lower Wealth Households after BRT Investment in Bogota, Columbia. *Journal of Transport Geography*, *60*, 11–20. doi:10.1016/j.jtrangeo.2017.02.004

Constant, L. (2000). *Modélisation de Dispositifs Electriques par Réseaux de Neurones en Vue de L'émulation Temps Réel* (Thesis Doctorate). Toulouse, France.

Corsini, C., Baker, C., Kung, E., Schievano, S., Arbia, G., Baretta, A., ... Dorfman, A. (2014). An integrated approach to patient-specific predictive modeling for single ventricle heart palliation. *Computer Methods in Biomechanics and Biomedical Engineering*, *17*(14), 1572–1589. doi:10.1080/10255842.2012.758254 PMID:23343002

Costa, A., Barbosa, P., Gomez, L., Ramalho, F., Figueiredo, J., & Junior, A. (2010). Properties preservation in distributed execution of Petri nets models. Emerging Trends in Technological Innovation, 314, 241-250. doi:10.1007/978-3-642-11628-5_26

Costa, A., & Gomes, L. (2009). Petri net partitioning using net splitting operation. In *Proceedings of the 7th IEEE International Conference on Industrial Informatics*, (pp. 204-209). 10.1109/INDIN.2009.5195804

Coyle, J., Langley, C., Gibson, B., Novack, R., & Bardi, E. (2008). *Supply chain management: A logistics perspective.* Cengage Learning.

Craig, I. K., Xia, X., & Venter, J. W. (2004). Introducing HIV/AIDS education into the electrical engineering curriculum at the University of Pretoria. *Education. IEEE Transactions on*, *47*(1), 65–73.

Craig, I., & Xia, X. (2005). Can HIV/AIDS be controlled? Applying control engineering concepts outside traditional fields. *Control Systems, IEEE*, *25*(1), 80–83. doi:10.1109/MCS.2005.1388805

Cruz, Y. (2008). *Integrating Complex Evacuation Dynamics in Resources Allocation for Relief Operations* (Published Master thesis). University of Puerto Rico, Mayagüez.

Cruz, Y. (2013). *Dynamic Transportation and Humanitarian Logistics Model: A Decision Support Tool to Forecast and Prioritize Critical Supplies Distribution During Emergency Relief Operations* (Published Doctoral Dissertation). University of Puerto Rico, Mayagüez.

Cruz, Y. (2014). A System Dynamics Approach to Humanitarian Logistics and the Transportation of Relief Supplies. *International Journal of System Dynamics Applications*, *3*(3), 96–128. doi:10.4018/ijsda.2014070105

Cruz, Y., Medina, A., & Medin, J. (2009). Understanding the Role of Victims' Non-Discretionary Factors in Hurricane Evacuation Dynamics: a planning tool for disaster relief. *Proceedings of the 27th International Conference of the System Dynamics Society*.

Dargey, J. M. (2001). The Effect of Income on Car Ownership: Evidence of Asymmetry. *Transportation Research Part A, Policy and Practice*, *35*(9), 807–821. doi:10.1016/S0965-8564(00)00018-5

Dargey, J. M., & Gately, D. (1999). Income's Effect on Car and Vehicle Ownership, Worldwide: 1960-2015. *Transportation Research Part A, Policy and Practice*, *33*(2), 101–138. doi:10.1016/S0965-8564(98)00026-3

Darrell, W. (2005). *A Genetic Algorithm Tutorial* [Report]. Computer Science Department, Colorado State University.

Daughtery, P. J., & Pittman, P. H. (1995). Utilization of time-based strategies creaoyleting distribution flexibility/responsiveness. *International Journal of Operations & Production Management*, *15*(2), 54–60. doi:10.1108/01443579510080418

De Morais, A. P., Cardoso, G., & Mariotto, L. (2010). An innovative loss-of-excitation protection based on the fuzzy inference mechanism. *IEEE Transactions on Power Delivery*, *25*(4), 2197–2204. doi:10.1109/TPWRD.2010.2051462

de Vasconcellos, E. A. (2005). Transport Metabolism, Social Diversity and Equity: The Case of Sao Paulo, Brazil. *Journal of Transport Geology*, *13*(4), 329–339. doi:10.1016/j.jtrangeo.2004.10.007

DeCorla-Souza, P. (2000). Induced Highway Travel: Transportation Policy Implications for Congested Metropolitan Areas. *Transportation Quarterly*, *54*(2), 13–30.

Deloitte. (2012). *Logistics sector present situation and way forward.* Retrieved June 25, 2014, from http://www.lopdf.net/get/1leUkOr0QJWTW9JztLEH9qyrxz-d5wvIqXI8xGDCcw0,/Logistics-Sector-Present-situation-and-way-forward.pdf

Delorme, Y. T., Rodefeld, M. D., & Frankel, S. H. (2017). Multiblock high order Large Eddy Simulation of powered Fontan hemodynamics: Towards computational surgery. *Computers & Fluids*, *143*, 16–31. doi:10.1016/j.compfluid.2016.10.032 PMID:28649147

Deng, W. H., & Li, C. P. (2005). Synchronization of chaotic fractional Chen system. *Journal of the Physical Society of Japan*, *74*(6), 1645–1648. doi:10.1143/JPSJ.74.1645

Department of Internal Medicine, School of Medicine, Aristotle University of Thessaloniki. (2012). *Internal Medicine* (4th ed.). Thessaloniki, Greece: University Studio Press.

Ding, Y., & Ye, H. (2009). A fractional-order differential equation model of HIV infection of CD4+ T-cells. *Mathematical and Computer Modelling*, *50*(3), 386–392. doi:10.1016/j.mcm.2009.04.019

Donati, S., & Hwang, S. K. (2012). Chaos and high-level dynamics in coupled lasers and their applications. *Progress in Quantum Electronics*, *36*(2-3), 293–341. doi:10.1016/j.pquantelec.2012.06.001

Doshi, D., & Burkhoff, D. (2016). Cardiovascular Simulation of Heart Failure Pathophysiology and Therapeutics. *Journal of Cardiac Failure*, *22*(4), 303–311. doi:10.1016/j.cardfail.2015.12.012 PMID:26703246

Du, H., Zeng, Q., & Wang, C. (2008). Function projective synchronization of different chaotic systems with uncertain parameters. *Physics Letters. [Part A]*, *372*(33), 5402–5410. doi:10.1016/j.physleta.2008.06.036

Du, H., Zeng, Q., & Wang, C. (2009). Modified function projective synchronization of chaotic system. *Chaos, Solitons, and Fractals*, *42*(4), 2399–2404. doi:10.1016/j.chaos.2009.03.120

Duhamel, C., Santos A., & Birregah B. (2016). Connecting a population dynamic model with a multi-period location-allocation problem for post-disaster relief operations. *Annals of Operations Research OR Confronting Crises*, 1-21. DOI: 10.1007/s10479-015-2104-1

Eberhart, R. C., & Shi, Y. (1998). Comparison between genetic algorithms and particle swarm optimization. *Proc. IEEE Int. Conf. Evol. Comput.*, 611–616.

Eboli, L., & Mazzulla, G. (2012). Performance Indicators for an Objective Measure of Public Transport Service Quality. *European Transport*, *51*(3), 1825–3997.

Ebrahimi, S. Y., & Ghorbani, A. (2016). Performance comparison of LOE protection of synchronous generator in the presence of UPFC. *Engineering Science and Technology, an International Journal, 19*(1), 71-78.

El-Ghazaly, G. (2012). Adaptive Synchronization of Unknown Chaotic Systems Using Mamdani Fuzzy Approach. *International Journal of System Dynamics Applications*, *1*(3), 122–138. doi:10.4018/ijsda.2012070104

Elizondo, D., Hoogenboom, G., & McClendon, R. W. (1994). Development of a neural network model to predict daily solar radiation. *Agricultural and Forest Meteorology*, *71*(1-2), 115–132. doi:10.1016/0168-1923(94)90103-1

Elkady, M., Elmarakbi, A., MacIntyre, J., & Alhariri, M. (2016). Multi-Body Integrated Vehicle-Occupant Models for Collision Mitigation and Vehicle Safety using Dynamics Control Systems. *International Journal of System Dynamics Applications*, *5*(2), 80–122. doi:10.4018/IJSDA.2016040105

Elmarakbi, A., & Zu, J. (2005). Crashworthiness Improvement of Vehicle-to-Rigid Fixed Barrier in Full Frontal Impact using Novel Vehicle's Front-End Structures. *International Journal of Automotive Technology*, *6*(5), 491–499.

Elmarakbi, A., & Zu, J. (2007). Incremental Harmonic Balance Method for Analysis of Standard/Smart Vehicles-to-Rigid Barrier Frontal Collision. *International Journal of Vehicle Safety*, *2*(3), 288–315. doi:10.1504/IJVS.2007.015545

Elmore, W. A. (2003). *Protective relaying: theory and applications* (Vol. 1). CRC Press. doi:10.1201/9780203912850

El-Sadr, W.M., Lundgren, J.D., & Neaton, J.D. (2006). CD4+ count-guided interruption of antiretroviral treatment. *New England Journal of Medicine, 355*(22), 2283-96.

Elsamahy, M., Faried, S. O., & Ramakrishna, G. (2010, July). Impact of midpoint STATCOM on the coordination between generator distance phase backup protection and generator capability curves. *Power and Energy Society General Meeting*, 1-7. 10.1109/PES.2010.5590134

Emori, R. I. (1968). *Analytical Approach to Autombile Collisions*. SAE International, Warrendale, PA, SAE Technical Paper No. 680016.

Enany, T. A., Wahba, W. I., & Hassan, M. A. (2014). A Remote and Sensorless Stator Winding Temperature Estimation Method for Thermal Protection for Induction Motor. *International Journal of System Dynamics Applications*, *3*(3), 53–72. doi:10.4018/ijsda.2014070103

Escalante, M. F., Vannier, J. C., & Arzandé, A. (2002). Flying capacitor multilevel inverters and DTC motor drive applications. *IEEE Transactions on Industrial Electronics*, *49*(4), 809–815. doi:10.1109/TIE.2002.801231

Escobar, G., Stankovic, A., Carrasco, M., Galvan, E., & Ortega, R. (2003). Analysis and design of direct power control (DPC) for a three phase synchronous rectifier via output regulation subspaces. *IEEE Transactions on Power Electronics*, *18*(3), 823–830. doi:10.1109/TPEL.2003.810862

Essays, U. K. (2013). *Relationship between Financial Performance and Logistics Performance Business Essay*. Retrieved July 11, 2014, from http://www.ukessays.com/essays/business/relationship-between-financial-performance-and-logistics-performance-business-essay.php

Ezzat, M. A., & El-Karamany, A. S. (2012). Fractional thermoelectric viscoelastic materials. *Journal of Applied Polymer Science*, *124*(3), 2187–2199. doi:10.1002/app.35243

Fakhry, A. M., Ammar, M. E., & Hassan, M. M. (2016). Two Area Load Frequency Control Based On Evolutionary. *Computing Techniques*.

Fan, S., Brzeska, J., Keyzer, M., & Halsema, A. (2013). *From Subsistence to Profit: Transforming Smallholder Farms*. IFPRI Food Policy Report. Doi:.10.2499/9780896295582

Fan, F., Liu, Z., Li, S., Yi, T., Yan, J., Yan, F., ... Wang, Q. (2017). Effect of Fenestration on Early Postoperative Outcome in Extracardiac Fontan Patients with Different Risk Levels. *Pediatric Cardiology*, *38*(4), 643–649. doi:10.100700246-016-1561-x PMID:28116475

Fanxing, M., Rob, G., Cristy, H., Mujthaba, A., & Charles, S. (2015). Dynamic Vibrotactile Signals for Forward Collision Avoidance Warning Systems. *Human Factors*, *57*(2), 329–346. doi:10.1177/0018720814542651 PMID:25850161

FAO. (2016). *Regional overview of food insecurity in Africa*. Accessed May 2017 from www.fao.org/3/a-i4635e.pdf

FAO. (2017). Regional overview of food security and nutrition in Africa 2016. The challenges of building resilience to shocks and stressors. Accra, Ghana: FAO.

Farret, F. A., & Simoes, M. G. (2006). *Integration of alternative sources of energy*. John Wiley & Sons.

Fay, G., Schwoerer, T., & Keith, K. (2010). *Alaska isolated wind-diesel systems: performance and economic analysis*. Prepared for Alaska Energy Authority and Denali Commission, Institute of Social and Economic Research, University of Alaska, Anchorage.

Federal Emergency Management Agency. (2013). *The Federal Emergency Management Agency's (FEMA's) Methodology for Estimating Potential Losses from Disasters*. Retrieved October 2, 2013 from http://www.fema.gov/hazus

Fekik, A., Denoun, H., Benamrouche, N., Benyahia, N., Zaouia, M., & Haddad, S. (2015a) Comparative study of PI and FUZZY DC- voltage control for Voltage Oriented Control-PWM rectifier. *The 14th International Conference on Circuits, Systems, Electronics, Control & Signal Processing 2015.*

Fekik, A., Denoun, H., Benamrouche, N., Benyahia, N., Badji, A., & Zaouia, M. (2016*)* Comparative Analysis of Direct Power Control and Direct power control with space vector modulation of PWM rectifier. 4th IEEE *International Conference on Control Engineering & Information Technology (CEIT-2016).* 10.1109/CEIT.2016.7929058

Fekik, A., Denoun, H., Benamrouche, N., Benyahia, N., & Zaouia, M. (2015b). A Fuzzy Logic Based Controller For Three Phase PWM Rectifier With Voltage Oriented Control Strategy. *International Journal of Circuits, Systems and Signal Processing*, *9*, 412–419.

Fekik, A., Denoun, H., Benamrouche, N., Benyahia, N., Zaouia, M., Badji, A., & Vaidyanathan, S. (2017). Improvement of the Performances of the Direct Power Control Using Space Vector Modulation of Three Phases PWM-Rectifier. *International Journal of Control Theory and Applications*, *10*, 125–137.

Fen, M. O. (2017). Persistence of chaos in coupled Lorenz systems. *Chaos, Solitons, and Fractals*, *95*, 200–205. doi:10.1016/j.chaos.2016.12.017

Fen, M. O., & Fen, F. T. (2017). SICNNs with Li-Yorke chaotic outputs on a time scale. *Neurocomputing*, *237*, 158–165. doi:10.1016/j.neucom.2016.09.073

Ferguson, M., & Kovacs, A. H. (2016). An Integrated Adult Congenital Heart Disease Psychology Service. *Congenital Heart Disease*, *11*(5), 444–451. doi:10.1111/chd.12331 PMID:26918262

Ferreira, S., Haffner, F., Pereira, L. F., & Moraes, F. (2003, September). Design and prototyping of direct torque control of induction motors in FPGAs. In Integrated Circuits and Systems Design, 2003. SBCCI 2003. Proceedings. doi:10.1109/SBCCI.2003.1232814

Feudel, U. (2008). Complex dynamics in multistable systems. *International Journal of Bifurcation and Chaos in Applied Sciences and Engineering*, *18*(06), 1607–1626. doi:10.1142/S0218127408021233

Field, R. J., & Györgyi, L. (1993). *Chaos in chemistry and biochemistry.* World Scientific. doi:10.1142/1706

Fischer, J. R., González, S. A., Carugat, I., Herrán, M. A., Judewicz, M. G., & Carrica, D. O. (2014). Robust predictive control of grid-tied converters based on direct power control. *IEEE Transactions on Power Electronics*, *29*(10), 5634–5643. doi:10.1109/TPEL.2013.2294919

Fitch, J. W., Zachariah, K. J., & Farsi, M. (1999). Turbo generator Self-Tuning Automatic Voltage Regulator. *IEEE Transactions on Energy Conversion*, *14*(3), 843–848. doi:10.1109/60.790963

Folinas, D. K., & Daniel, E. H. (2012). Estimating the impact of ERP Systems on Logistics System. *International Journal of Enterprise Information Systems*, *8*(3), 1–14. doi:10.4018/jeis.2012070101

Fontan, F., & Baudet, E. (1971). Surgical repair of tricuspid atresia. *Thorax*, *26*(3), 240–248. doi:10.1136/thx.26.3.240 PMID:5089489

Forrester, J. (1961). *What is System Dynamics?* Retrieved May 24, 2016 from http://systemdynamics.org.uk/about/

Forrester, J. (1961). *Industrial Dynamics.* Cambridge, MA: MIT Press.

Gabor, D. (1947). Theory of Communication. *Journal of the Institution of Electrical Engineers*, *94*(73), 429–441.

Gagnon, E., Pomerleau, A., & Desbiens, A. (1998). Simplified, ideal or inverted decoupling? *ISA Transactions*, *37*(4), 265–276. doi:10.1016/S0019-0578(98)00023-8

Gaing, Z. L. (2004). 'A Particle Swarm Optimization approach for optimum design of PID controller in AVR system. *Energy Conversion. IEEE Transactions on*, *19*(2), 384–391.

Gaing, Z. L. (2004). A Particle Swarm Optimization approach for optimum design of PID controller in AVR system. *Energy Conversion. IEEE Transactions on*, *19*(2), 384–391.

Gakkhar, S., & Chavda, N. (2012). A dynamical model for HIV–TB co-infection. *Applied Mathematics and Computation*, *218*(18), 9261–9270. doi:10.1016/j.amc.2012.03.004

Gao, Z. W., & So, A. T. (2003). A general doubly coprime factorization for descriptor systems. *Systems & Control Letters*, *49*(3), 213–224. doi:10.1016/S0167-6911(02)00325-0

Garcia, A., Chang, Y. S., & Valverde, R. (2006). Impact of new identification and tracking technologies on a distribution centre. *Computers & Industrial Engineering*, *51*(3), 542–552. doi:10.1016/j.cie.2006.08.013

Garcia-Canadilla, P., Crispi, F., Cruz-Lemini, M., Triunfo, S., Nadal, A., Valenzuela-Alcaraz, B., ... Bijnens, B. H. (2015). Patient-specific estimates of vascular and placental properties in growth-restricted fetuses based on a model of the fetal circulation. *Placenta*, *36*(9), 981–989. doi:10.1016/j.placenta.2015.07.130 PMID:26242709

Gargantini, A., Riccobene, E., & Scandurra, P. (2009). Model-driven design and ASM validation of embedded systems. In Behavioral Modeling for Embedded Systems and Technologies: Application for Design and Implementation (pp. 24–54). Hershey, PA: IGI Global.

Gärling, T., Biel, A., & Gustafsson, M. (2002). The Human Interdependence Paradigm and its Application in Environmental Psychology. In R. Bechtel & A. Churchman (Eds.), *Handbook of Environmental Psychology* (pp. 85–94). New York: Wiley.

Garrido, J., Vazquez, F., & Morilla, F. (2012). Centralized multivariable control by simplified decoupling. *Journal of Process Control*, *22*(6), 1044–1062. doi:10.1016/j.jprocont.2012.04.008

Gatersleben, B. (2007). Affective and Symbolic Aspects of Car Use. In T. Gärling & L. Steg (Eds.), *Threats from Car Traffic to the Quality of Urban Life* (pp. 219–233). Elsevier. doi:10.1108/9780080481449-012

Gatersleben, B., & Uzzell, D. (2007). Affective Appraisals of the Daily Commute: Comparing Perceptions of Drivers, Cyclists, Walkers and Users of Public Transport. *Environment and Behavior*, *39*(3), 416–431. doi:10.1177/0013916506294032

Geyer, T., & Quevedo, E. (2015). Performance of multistep finite control set model predictive control for power electronics. *IEEE Transactions on Power Electronics*, *30*(3), 1633–1644. doi:10.1109/TPEL.2014.2316173

Ge, Z. M., & Li, S. Y. (2011). Chaos generalized synchronization of new Mathieu-VAN der POL systems with new Dufng-VAN der POL systems as functional system by GYC partial region stability theory. *Applied Mathematical Modelling*, *35*(11), 5245–5264. doi:10.1016/j.apm.2011.03.022

Ge, Z. M., & Ou, C. Y. (2007). Chaos in a fractional order modified Duffing system. *Chaos, Solitons, and Fractals*, *34*(2), 262–291. doi:10.1016/j.chaos.2005.11.059

Ghandhari, M. (2008). *Dynamic Analysis of Power Systems. PART II*. Royal Institute of Technology.

Gharsellaoui, H., Khalgui, M., & Ahmed, S. B. (2013). Reconfiguration of synchronous real-time operating system. *International Journal of System Dynamics Applications*, *2*(1), 114–132. doi:10.4018/ijsda.2013010106

Gholinezhad, J., & Noroozian, R. (2012, February). Application of cascaded H-bridge multilevel inverter in DTC-SVM based induction motor drive. In Power Electronics and Drive Systems Technology (PEDSTC), (pp. 127-132). IEEE.

Gholinezhad, J., & Noroozian, R. (2013). Analysis of cascaded H-bridge multilevel inverter in DTC-SVM induction motor drive for FCEV. *Journal of Electrical Engineering & Technology*, *8*(2), 304–315. doi:10.5370/JEET.2013.8.2.304

Ghosh, D., & Bhattacharya, S. (2010). Projective synchronization of new hyperchaotic system with fully unknown parameters. *Nonlinear Dynamics*, *61*(1-2), 11–21. doi:10.100711071-009-9627-4

Ghoudelbourk, S., Dib, D., Omeiri, A., & Azar, A. T. (2016). MPPT Control in wind energy conversion systems and the application of fractional control (PIα) in pitch wind turbine. International Journal of Modelling. *Identification and Control*, *26*(2), 140–151. doi:10.1504/IJMIC.2016.078329

Gilbert, D. (2002). *The American Class Structure: In an Age of Growing Inequality*. Belmont, CA: Wadsworth.

Ginters, E., & Martin-Gutierrez, J. (2013). Low cost augmented reality and RFID application for logistics items visualization. *Procedia Computer Science*, *26*, 3–13. doi:10.1016/j.procs.2013.12.002

Giuliano, G. (2005). Low Income, Public Transit and Mobility. *Transportation Research Record: Journal of the Transportation Research Board*, (1927): 55–62.

Glück, T., Eder, A., & Kugi, A. (2013). Swing-up control of a triple pendulum on a cart with experimental validation. *Automatica*, *49*(3), 801–808. doi:10.1016/j.automatica.2012.12.006

Gonçalves, P. (2008). *System Dynamics Modeling of Humanitarian Relief Operations* (MIT Sloan Working Paper No. 4704-08). Retrieved from Social Science Research Network Electronic Paper Collection: http://papers.ssrn.com/sol3/papers.cfm?abstract_id=1139817

Gonçalves, P., & Kamdem, S. T. (2016). Reaching an AIDS-Free Generation in Côte d'Ivoire, Data Driven Policy Design for HIV/AIDS Response Programs: Evidence-Based Policy Design for HIV/AIDS Response Programs in Côte d'Ivoire. *International Journal of System Dynamics Applications*, *5*(1), 43–62. doi:10.4018/IJSDA.2016010104

González, D. B., & Salvador, M. R. (2014). Dynamic Modeling in New Product Development: The Case of Knowledge Management Enablers in a Food Product. *International Journal of System Dynamics Applications*, *3*(1), 111–134. doi:10.4018/ijsda.2014010106

Gorenflo, R., & Mainardi, F. (1997). Fractional calculus: Integral and differential equations of fractional order. In A. Carpinteri & F. Mainardi (Eds.), *Fractals and fractional calculus in continuum mechanics*. Springer. doi:10.1007/978-3-7091-2664-6_6

Grabowski, P. Z., Kazmierkowski, M. P., Bose, B. K., & Blaabjerg, F. (2000). A simple direct-torque neuro-fuzzy control of PWM-inverter-fed induction motor drive. *IEEE Transactions on Industrial Electronics*, *47*(4), 863–870. doi:10.1109/41.857966

Grassi, G., Ouannas, A., Azar, A. T., Radwan, A. G., Volos, C., Pham, V. T., . . . Stouboulos, I. N. (2017). *Chaos Synchronisation Of Continuous Systems Via Scalar Signal*. The 6th International Conference on Modern Circuits and Systems Technologies (MOCAST), Thessaloniki Greece. 10.1109/MOCAST.2017.7937629

Grigorenko, I., & Grigorenko, E. (2003). Chaotic dynamics of the fractional Lorenz system. *Physical Review Letters*, *91*(3), 034101. doi:10.1103/PhysRevLett.91.034101 PMID:12906418

Grobelna, L., Grobelny, M., & Adamski, M. (2014). Model checking of UML activity diagrams in logic controllers design. *Proceedings of the 9th International Conference on Dependability and Complex System*, 233-242. 10.1007/978-3-319-07013-1_22

Guedj, J., Thiébaut, R., & Commenges, D. (2007). Practical identifiability of HIV dynamics models. *Bulletin of Mathematical Biology*, *69*(8), 2493–2513. doi:10.100711538-007-9228-7 PMID:17557186

Guo, J., Yao, B., Chen, Q., & Wu, X. (2009). High Performance Adaptive Robust Control for Nonlinear System with Unknown Input Backlash. *Proceedings of the 48th IEEE Conference on Decision and Control, 2009 held jointly with the 2009 28th Chinese Control Conference*. 10.1109/CDC.2009.5399543

Haddad, W. M., & Chellaboina, V. (2008). *Nonlinear Dynamical Systems and Control - a Lyapunov Based Approach*. Princeton University Press.

Hadji, S., Gaubert, J. P., & Krim, F. (2014, October). Experimental analysis of genetic algorithms based MPPT for PV systems. *In Renewable and Sustainable Energy Conference (IRSEC), 2014 International* (pp. 7-12). IEEE. 10.1109/IRSEC.2014.7059887

Haggblade, S., & Hazell, P. B. R. (2010). *Successes in African Agriculture: Lessons for the future*. IFPRI Issue Brief 63. Retrieved from http://www.ifpri.org/sites/default/files/publications/ib63.pdf

Hamid, A., & Abdul-Rahman, T. K. (2010). Short Term Load Forecasting Using an Artificial Neural Network Trained by Artificial Immune System Learning Algorithm in Computer Modeling and Simulation (UKSim). *IEEE, 12th International Conference on*, 408-413.

Hammami, S. (2015). State feedback-based secure image cryptosystem using hyperchaotic synchronization. *ISA Transactions*, *54*, 52–59. doi:10.1016/j.isatra.2014.05.027 PMID:25085481

Hammant, J. (1995). Information technology trends in logistics. *Logistics Information Management*, *8*(6), 32–37. doi:10.1108/09576059510102235

Hammond, R. A., & Dubé, L. (2012). A systems science perspective and transdisciplinary models for food and nutrition security. *Proceedings of the National Academy of Sciences of the United States of America*, *109*(31), 1235–12363. doi:10.1073/pnas.0913003109 PMID:22826247

Hariz, M. B., & Bouani, F. (2016). Synthesis and Implementation of a Fix Low Order Controller on an Electronic System. *International Journal of System Dynamics Applications*, *5*(4), 42–63. doi:10.4018/IJSDA.2016100103

Hartley, T. T., Lorenzo, C. F., & Killory, Q. H. (1995). Chaos in a fractional order Chua's system. *IEEE Trans. CAS-I*, *42*(8), 485–490. doi:10.1109/81.404062

Harvey, C. A., Rakotobe, Z. L., Rao, N. S., Dave, R., Razafimahatratra, H., Rabarijohn, R. H., ... MacKinnon, J. L. (2014). Extreme vulnerability of smallholder farmers to agricultural risks and climate change in Madagascar. *Philosophical Transactions of the Royal Society of London. Series B, Biological Sciences*, *369*(1639), 20130089. doi:10.1098/rstb.2013.0089 PMID:24535397

Hassan, F. R. (2013). Modified Direct Torque Control using Algorithm Control of Stator Flux Estimation and Space Vector Modulation Based on Fuzzy Logic Control for Achieving High Performance from Induction Motors. *Journal of Power Electronics*, *13*(3), 369–380. doi:10.6113/JPE.2013.13.3.369

Hassanien, A. E., Azar, A. T., Snasel, V., Kacprzyk, J., & Abawajy, J. H. (2015). *Big Data in Complex Systems: Challenges and Opportunities*. Springer-Verlag. doi:10.1007/978-3-319-11056-1

Hassanien, A. E., Tolba, M., & Azar, A. T. (2014). *Advanced Machine Learning Technologies and Applications: Second International Conference, AMLTA 2014*. Springer-Verlag GmbH Berlin/Heidelberg. 10.1007/978-3-319-13461-1

Hassanien, A.E., Moftah, H.M., Azar, A.T., & Shoman, M. (2014). MRI Breast cancer diagnosis hybrid approach using adaptive Ant-based segmentation and Multilayer Perceptron neural networks classifier. *Applied Soft computing, 14*(Part A), 62-71.

Hassan, M. F. (2014). A new approach for secure communication using constrained hyperchaotic systems. *Applied Mathematics and Computation*, *246*, 711–730. doi:10.1016/j.amc.2014.08.029

Hasselblatt, B., & Katok, A. (2003). *A First Course in Dynamics: With a Panorama of Recent Developments*. Cambridge, UK: Cambridge University Press. doi:10.1017/CBO9780511998188

Hatzakis, A., Sypsa, V., Paraskevis, D., Nikolopoulos, G., Tsiara, C., Micha, K., ... Wiessing, L. (2015). Design and baseline findings of a large-scale rapid response to an HIV outbreak in people who inject drugs in Athens, Greece: The ARISTOTLE programme. *Addiction (Abingdon, England)*, *110*(9), 1453–1467. doi:10.1111/add.12999 PMID:26032121

Hazen, B., & Byrd, T. (2012). Toward creating competitive advantage with logistics information technology. *International Journal of Physical Distribution & Logistics Management*, *42*(1), 8–35. doi:10.1108/09600031211202454

Hazinski, M. F. (2013). *Nursing Care of the Critically Ill Child*. Elsevier Health Sciences.

He, J., Cai, J., & Lin, J. (2016). Synchronization of hyperchaotic systems with multiple unknown parameters and its application in secure communication. *Optik (Stuttgart)*, *127*(5), 2502–2508. doi:10.1016/j.ijleo.2015.11.055

Hellenic Center for Disease Control and Prevention. (2014, December). *HIV/AIDS Surveillance Report in Greece (Issue 29), Athens.* Retrieved from www.keelpno.gr

Hellenic Center for Disease Control and Prevention. (2015, October). *HIV infection: newest epidemiological data, Athens*. Retrieved from www.keelpno.gr.

Hensher, D. A. (1998). The Imbalance between Car and Public Transport Use in Urban Australia: Why Does it Exist? *Transport Policy*, *5*(4), 193–204. doi:10.1016/S0967-070X(98)00022-5

Herrmann, R. (2011). *Fractional calculus* (1st ed.). World Scientific publishing Co. doi:10.1142/8072

Hippe, P. (1994). Strictly Doubly Coprime Factorizations and all Stabilizing Compensators Related to Reduced-order Observer. *Automatica*, *30*(12), 1955–1959. doi:10.1016/0005-1098(94)90056-6

Hirsch, J. C., Goldberg, C., Bove, E. L., Salehian, S., Lee, T., Ohye, R. G., & Devaney, E. J. (2008). Fontan operation in the current era: A 15-year single institution experience. *Annals of Surgery*, *248*(3), 402–410. doi:10.1097/SLA.0b013e3181858286 PMID:18791360

Hiscock, R., Macintyre, S., Kearns, A., & Ellaway, A. (2002). Means of Transport and Ontological Security: Do Cars Provide Psycho-social Benefits to their Users? *Transportation Research Part D, Transport and Environment*, *7*(2), 119–135. doi:10.1016/S1361-9209(01)00015-3

Hmidet, A., Dhifaoui, R., & Hasnaoui, O. (2010). Development, implementation and experimentation on a dSPACE DS1104 of a direct voltage control scheme. *Journal of Power Electronics*, *10*(5), 468–476. doi:10.6113/JPE.2010.10.5.468

Ho, C. Y. F., & Ling, B. W. K. (2010). Initiation of HIV therapy. *International Journal of Bifurcation and Chaos in Applied Sciences and Engineering*, *20*(04), 1279–1292. doi:10.1142/S0218127410026484 PMID:20543654

Hogan, I., & Manning, W. (2007). The Use of Vehicle Dynamic Control Systems for Automotive Collision Mitigation. *3rd Institution of Engineering and Technology Conference on Automotive Electronics,* 1-10.

Hogan, I. (2008a). *The development of a vehicle collision mitigation control system through multibody modelling*. *FISITA World Automotive Congress*, Munich, Germany.

Holtz, J. (1994). Pulsewidth modulation for electronic power conversion. *Proceedings of the IEEE*, *82*(8), 1194–1214. doi:10.1109/5.301684

Hose, D. R., & Doyle, B. J. (2017). Modelling of the Cardiovascular System. In P. R. Hoskins, P. V. Lawford, & B. J. Doyle (Eds.), *Cardiovascular Biomechanics* (pp. 193–205). Springer International Publishing; doi:10.1007/978-3-319-46407-7_10

Ho, Y., Lu, C., & Wang, H. (2006). Dynamic Model for Earthquake Disaster Prevention System: A Case Study of Taichung City, Taiwan. *Proceedings of the 24th International Conference of the System Dynamics Society*.

Huang, L., Schilling, C., Dalziel, K. M., Xie, S., Celermajer, D. S., McNeil, J. J., ... d'Udekem, Y. (2017). Hospital Inpatient Costs for Single Ventricle Patients Surviving the Fontan Procedure. *The American Journal of Cardiology*, *120*(3), 467–472. doi:10.1016/j.amjcard.2017.04.049 PMID:28583678

Hu, J., Zhu, J., Zhang, Y., Platt, G., Ma, Q., & Dorrell, D. G. (2013). Predictive direct virtual torque and power control of doubly fed induction generators for fast and smooth grid synchronization and flexible power regulation. *IEEE Transactions on Power Electronics*, *28*(7), 3182–3194. doi:10.1109/TPEL.2012.2219321

Hung, J. C. (2013). Modified particle swarm optimization structure approach to direction of arrival estimation. *Applied Soft Computing*, *13*(1), 315–320. doi:10.1016/j.asoc.2012.08.006

Hunton, J. E., Lippincott, B., & Reck, J. L. (2003). Enterprise resource planning systems: Comparing firm performance of adopters and nonadopters. *International Journal of Accounting Information Systems*, *4*(3), 165–184. doi:10.1016/S1467-0895(03)00008-3

Hussein, H. T., Ammar, M. E., & Hassan, M. M. (2017). Three Phase Induction Motor's Stator Turns Fault Analysis Based on Artificial Intelligence. *International Journal of System Dynamics Applications*, *6*(3), 1–19. doi:10.4018/IJSDA.2017070101

Hu, Z. H., & Sheng, Z. H. (2014). A decision support system for public logistics information service management and optimization. *Decision Support Systems*, *59*, 219–229. doi:10.1016/j.dss.2013.12.001

Hwang, W., & Min, H. (2013). Assessing the impact of ERP on supplier performance. *Industrial Management & Data Systems*, *113*(7), 1025–1047. doi:10.1108/IMDS-01-2013-0035

Ichise, M., Nagayanagi, Y., & Kojima, T. (1971). An analog simulation of non-integer order transfer functions for analysis of electrode process. *Journal of Electroanalytical Chemistry and Interfacial Electrochemistry*, *33*(2), 253–265. doi:10.1016/S0022-0728(71)80115-8

Idkhajine, L., Monmasson, E., & Maalouf, A. (2010, July). Extended Kalman filter for AC drive sensorless speed controller-FPGA-based solution or DSP-based solution. In *Industrial Electronics (ISIE), IEEE International Symposium on* (pp. 2759-2764). IEEE.

Idris, N. R. N., & Yatim, A. H. M. (2004). Direct torque control of induction machines with constant switching frequency and reduced torque ripple. *IEEE Transactions on Industrial Electronics*, *51*(4), 758–767. doi:10.1109/TIE.2004.831718

Ilie, S., & Tabacu, Ş. (2010). Study of the Occupant's Kinematics during the Frontal Impact. Ann Oradea Univ. *Fascicle Managmt Technol Engng*, *6*(16), 542–551.

Ingemar, E. O. (1983). *Electric Energy Systems Theory*. London: McGraw Hill Book Company.

Innocenti, A., Lattarulo, P., & Pazienza, M. G. (2013). Car Stickiness: Heuristics and Biases in Travel Choice. *Transport Policy*, *25*, 158–168. doi:10.1016/j.tranpol.2012.11.004

Introna, L. (1991). The Impact of Information Technology on Logistics. *International Journal of Physical Distribution & Logistics Management*, *21*(5), 32–37. doi:10.1108/EUM0000000000387

Iqbal, S., Bhatti, A. I., Akhtar, M., & Ullah, S. (2007). Design and Robustness Evaluation of an H Infinity Loop Shaping Controller for a 2DOF Stabilized Platform. *Proceedings of the European Control Conference. Proceedings of the European Control Conference 2007*, 2098-2104.

Ishaque, K., Salam, Z., Shamsudin, A., & Amjad, M. (2012). A direct control based maximum power point tracking method for photovoltaic system under partial shading conditions using particle swarm optimization algorithm. *Applied Energy*, *99*, 414–422. doi:10.1016/j.apenergy.2012.05.026

Islam, M. Z., Rahim, A. A., Hasan, K. A., & Ahsan, S. I. (2016). Intracardiac Lateral Tunnel Fontan by using Right Atrial Wall. *Cardiovascular Journal*, *9*(1), 68–72. doi:10.3329/cardio.v9i1.29547

Ismail, A. (2006). Improving UAE power systems control performance by using combined LFC and AVR. *7th UAE University Research Conference*, 50-60.

Ismail, M. M. (2012). Applications of ANFIS and Fuzzy Algorithms for Improvement of the DTC Performance for the Three Phase Saturated Model of Induction Motor. *International Journal of System Dynamics Applications*, *1*(3), 54–83. doi:10.4018/ijsda.2012070102

Ismail, M. M., Abdel Fattah, H. A., & Bhagat, A. (2012). Adaptive Output Feedback Voltage-Based Control of Magnetically-Saturated Induction Motors. *International Journal of System Dynamics Applications*, *1*(3), 1–53. doi:10.4018/ijsda.2012070101

Ismail, M. M., & Hassan, M. M. (2012). Using positive and negative sequence components of currents and voltages for high impedance fault analysis via ANFIS. *International Journal of System Dynamics Applications*, *1*(4), 132–157. doi:10.4018/ijsda.2012100106

Ismail, M. M., & Moustafa Hassan, M. A. (2012). Load Frequency Control Adaptation Using Artificial Intelligent Techniques for One and Two Different Areas Power System. *International Journal of Control, Automation, and Systems*, *1*(1), 12–23.

Jakubowska, A., & Szymczak, M. (2016). Electronic realizations of fractional-order elements: II. Simulation studies. Poznan University of Technology Academic Journals. *Electrical Engineering*, (85): 149–159.

Jang, J. O., Lee, P. G., Chung, H. T., & Jeon, G. J. (2003). Output Backlash Compensation of Systems Using Fuzzy Logic. *Proceedings of the 2003 American Control Conference*. 10.1109/ACC.2003.1243449

Jansson, J., Gustafsson, F., & Ekmark, J. (2002). *Decision Making For Collision Avoidance Systems*. SAE International, Warrendale, PA, SAE Technical Paper No. 2002-01-0403.

Jeffrey, A. M., Xia, X., & Craig, I. K. (2002). Controllability Analysis of the Chemotherapy of HIV/AIDS. *IFAC Proceedings Volumes, 35*(1), 127-132.

Jeffrey, A. M., Xia, X., & Craig, I. K. (2003). When to initiate HIV therapy: A control theoretic approach. *Biomedical Engineering. IEEE Transactions on, 50*(11), 1213–1220. PMID:14619991

Jevtovic, B. T., & Matauvsek, M. R. (2010). PID controller design of TITO system based on ideal decoupler. *Journal of Process Control*, *20*(7), 869–876. doi:10.1016/j.jprocont.2010.05.006

Jhawar, A., Garg, S., & Khera, S. (2014). Analysis of the Skilled Work Force Effect on the Logistics Performance Index- Case study from India. *Logistics Research*, *7*(1). Retrieved on July 20, 2014 from, http://www.springer.com/alert/urltracking.do?id=L4b9b5f4Mf81ec8Sb106a2e

Jiang, S., Ji, Z., & Shen, Y. (2014). A novel hybrid particle swarm optimization and gravitational search algorithm for solving economic emission load dispatch problems with various practical constraints. *Electrical Power and Energy Systems*, *55*(1), 628–644. doi:10.1016/j.ijepes.2013.10.006

Jiang, W. (2010) Sliding-mode Control of Single-phase PWM Rectifier for DC Microgrid Applications. *International Conference on Computer and Electrical Engineering*, 53, 82-90. DOI: 10.7763/IPCSIT.2012.V53.No.1.82

Jia, Q. (2007). Hyperchaos generated from the Lorenz chaotic system and its control. *Physics Letters. [Part A]*, *366*(3), 217–222. doi:10.1016/j.physleta.2007.02.024

Jidin, A. B., Idris, N. R. B. N., Yatim, A. H. B. M., Elbuluk, M. E., & Sutikno, T. (2012). A wide-speed high torque capability utilizing overmodulation strategy in DTC of induction machines with constant switching frequency controller. *IEEE Transactions on Power Electronics*, *27*(5), 2566–2575. doi:10.1109/TPEL.2011.2168240

Jing, Z., & Wen, C. (2007). Adaptive Inverse Control of a Magnetic Suspension System with Input Backlash. *16th IEEE International Conference on Control Applications*. DOI: 10.1109/CCA.2007.4389423

Jin, L., & Kim, Y. C. (2008). Fixed, low-order controller design with time response specifications using non-convex optimization. *ISA Transactions*, *47*(4), 429–438. doi:10.1016/j.isatra.2008.05.001 PMID:18606409

Joint United Nations Programme on HIV/AIDS (UNAIDS). (2014). *The gap report*. Geneva: UNAIDS.

Jones, E. C., & Chung, C. A. (2007). *RFID in logistics: a practical introduction*. CRC Press. doi:10.1201/9781420009361

Jongsang, S., Donghoon, S., Kyongsu, Y., Seongjin, Y., Kihan, N., & Hyungjeen, C. (2015). Control of the motorized active suspension damper for good ride quality. Proc IMechE Part D. *Journal of Automobile Engineering*, *228*(11), 1344–1358.

Jordehi, A. R. (2016). Maximum power point tracking in photovoltaic (PV) systems: A review of different approaches. *Renewable & Sustainable Energy Reviews*, *65*, 1127–1138. doi:10.1016/j.rser.2016.07.053

Joshi, P., & Arora, S. (2017). Maximum power point tracking methodologies for solar PV systems – A review. *Renewable & Sustainable Energy Reviews*, *70*, 1154–1177. doi:10.1016/j.rser.2016.12.019

Joshi, S., & Talange, D. B. (2016). Fault Tolerant Control of an UAV Using Periodic Output Feedback with Multi Model Approach. *International Journal of System Dynamics Applications*, *5*(2), 41–62. doi:10.4018/IJSDA.2016040103

Kaboli, S., Zolgbadri, M. R., & Emadi, A. (2003). Hysteresis Band Determination of Direct Torque Controlled Induction Motor Drives with Torque Ripple and Motor-Inverter Loss Considerations. *IEEE 34th annual, power electronics specialist conference*, (Vol. 3, pp. 1107-1111). IEEE.

Kamal, M. M. (1970). *Analysis and Simulation of Vehicle to Barrier Impact*. SAE International, Warrendale, PA, SAE Technical Paper No. 700414.

Kamel, T. S., El-Morshedy, A. K., & Moustafa, M. A. (2009). *A novel approach to distance protection of transmission lines using adaptive neuro fuzzy inference system* (Doctoral dissertation). Cairo University.

Kamel, T. S., Hassan, M. M. A., & El-Morshedy, A. (2011). An ANFIS based distance relay protection for transmission lines in EPS. *International Journal of Innovations in Electrical Power Systems*.

Kamel, T. S., Moustafa, M. A. & El-Morshedy, A. K. (2009). Application of Artificial Intelligent Approach in Distance Relay for Transmission line Protection. *The International Scientific & Technical Conference' Actual Trends in Development of Power System Protection and Automation*, 28-36.

Kamel, T. S., Moustafa Hassan, M. A., & El-Morshedy, A. (2012). Advanced distance protection technique based on multiple classified ANFIS considering different loading conditions for long transmission lines in EPS. International Journal of Modelling. *Identification and Control*, *16*(2), 108–121. doi:10.1504/IJMIC.2012.047119

Kammogne, S. T., & Fotsin, H. B. (2011). Synchronization of modified Colpitts oscillators with structural perturbations. *Physica Scripta*, *83*(6), 065011. doi:10.1088/0031-8949/83/06/065011

Kammogne, S. T., Fotsin, H. B., Kontchou, M., & Louodop, P. (2013). A robust observer design for passivity-based synchronization of uncertain modifed Colpitts oscillators and circuit simulation. *Asian Journal of Science and Technology*, *5*(1), 29–41.

Kang, J. W., & Sul, S. K. (2001). Analysis and prediction of inverter switching frequency in direct torque control of induction machine based on hysteresis bands and machine parameters. *IEEE Transactions on Industrial Electronics*, *48*(3), 545–553. doi:10.1109/41.925581

Kantaros, Y., & Zavlanos, M. M. (2016). Distributed communication-aware coverage control by mobile sensor networks. *Automatica*, *63*, 209–220. doi:10.1016/j.automatica.2015.10.035

Kanungo, B. M. (2009). A Direct Torque Controlled Induction Motor with Variable Hysteresis Band. *11th International Conference on Computer Modelling and Simulation*, 405-410.

Karagiannis, D., Radisavljevic-Gajic, V., & Ashrafiuon, H. (2016, October). Control of Human Immunodeficiency Virus (HIV) Dynamics With Parameter Uncertainties. In *ASME 2016 Dynamic Systems and Control Conference* (pp. V001T09A003-V001T09A003). American Society of Mechanical Engineers.

Karamanakos, P., Geyer, T., Oikonomou, N., Kieferndorf, F., & Manias, S. (2014). Direct model predictive control: A review of strategies that achieve long prediction intervals for power electronics. *IEEE Industrial Electronics Magazine*, *8*(1), 32–43. doi:10.1109/MIE.2013.2290474

Kaslik, E., & Sivasundaram, S. (2012). Nonlinear dynamics and chaos in fractional-order neural networks. *Neural Networks*, *32*, 245–256. doi:10.1016/j.neunet.2012.02.030 PMID:22386788

Katerattanakul, P., Lee, J. J., & Hong, S. (2014). Effect of business characteristics and ERP implementation on business outcomes. *Management Research Review*, *37*(2), 186–206. doi:10.1108/MRR-10-2012-0218

Kengne, J., Negou, A. N., & Tchiotsop, D. (2017). Antimonotonicity, chaos and multiple attractors in a novel autonomous memristor-based jerk circuit. *Nonlinear Dynamics*, *88*(4), 2589–2608. doi:10.100711071-017-3397-1

Kengne, J., Njitacke, T., & Fotsin, H. B. (2016b). Coexistence of multiple attractors and crisis route to chaos in autonomous third order Duffing-Holmes type chaotic oscillators. *Communications in Nonlinear Science and Numerical Simulation*, *36*, 29–44. doi:10.1016/j.cnsns.2015.11.009

Kengne, J., Njitacke, Z. T., & Fotsin, H. B. (2016a). Dynamical analysis of a simple autonomous jerk system with multiple attractors. *Nonlinear Dynamics*, *83*(1-2), 751–765. doi:10.100711071-015-2364-y

Kennedy, J., & Eberhart, R. C. (1995). A new optimizer using particle swarm theory. *Proc. of 6th International symposium Micro machine Human Sci.*, 39-43.

Kennedy, M. P. (1994). Chaos in the Colpitts Oscillator. *Fundamental Theory and Applications*, *41*(11), 771–778.

Khalifa, F., Moustafa Hassan, M. A., Abul-Haggag, O., & Mahmoud, H. (2015). The Application of Evolutionary Computational Techniques in Medium Term Forecasting. In *MEPCON'2015*. Mansoura, Egypt: Mansoura University.

Khalil, H. K. (2002). *Nonlinear systems* (3rd ed.). Prentice Hall.

Khalil, H. K. (2002). *Nonlinear Systems*. Prentice Hall.

Khan, A., & Bhat, M. A. (2016). Hyper-chaotic analysis and adaptive multi-switching synchronization of a novel asymmetric non-linear dynamical system. *International Journal of Dynamics and Control*, 1–11.

Khan, A., & Shikha, S. (2017a) Combination synchronization of genesio time delay chaotic system via robust adaptive sliding mode control. *International Journal of Dynamics and Control*, 1–10. DOI: 10.1007/s40435-017-0339-1

Khan, A., & Shikha. (2016) Hybrid function projective synchronization of chaotic systems via adaptive control. *International Journal of Dynamics and Control*, 1–8. DOI: 10.1007/s40435-016-0258-6

Khan, A., & Tyagi, A. (2016). Analysis and hyper-chaos control of a new 4-d hyper-chaotic system by using optimal and adaptive control design. *International Journal of Dynamics and Control*. doi:10.1007/s40435-016-0265-7

Khan, A., & Bhat, M. A. (2017). Multi-switching combination–combination synchronization of non-identical fractional-order chaotic systems. *Mathematical Methods in the Applied Sciences*, *40*(15), 5654–5667. doi:10.1002/mma.4416

Khan, A., Khattar, D., & Prajapati, N. (2017a). Adaptive multi switching combination synchronization of chaotic systems with unknown parameters. *International Journal of Dynamics and Control*. doi:10.100740435-017-0320-z

Khan, A., Khattar, D., & Prajapati, N. (2017b). Reduced order multi switching hybrid synchronization of chaotic systems. *Journal of Mathematical and Computational Science*, *7*(2), 414.

Khan, A., & Pal, R. (2013). Complete synchronization, anti-synchronization and hybrid synchronization of two identical parabolic restricted three body problem. *Asian Journal of Current Engineering and Maths*, *2*(2), 118–126.

Khan, A., & Shahzad, M. (2013). Synchronization of circular restricted three body problem with lorenz hyper chaotic system using a robust adaptive sliding mode controller. *Complexity*, *18*(6), 58–64. doi:10.1002/cplx.21459

Khan, A., & Shikha. (2017b). Combination synchronization of time-delay chaotic system via robust adaptive sliding mode control. *Pramana*, *88*(6), 91. doi:10.100712043-017-1385-0

Khan, A., & Shikha. (2017c). Increased and reduced order synchronisations between 5d and 6d hyperchaotic systems. *Indian Journal of Industrial and Applied Mathematics*, *8*(1), 118–131. doi:10.5958/1945-919X.2017.00010.X

Khan, L., & Qamar, S. (2015). *Online Adaptive Neuro-Fuzzy Based Full Car Suspension Control Strategy. Research Methods: Concepts*. Methodologies, Tools, and Applications.

Khanna, V. K., Vrat, P., Sahay, B., & Shankar, R. (2008). *TQM Planning, Design and Implementation*. New Delhi: New Age International Publishers.

Khare, A., & Rangnekar, S. (2013). A review of particle swarm optimization and its applications in solar photovoltaic system. *Applied Soft Computing*, *13*(5), 2997–3006. doi:10.1016/j.asoc.2012.11.033

Khattab, A. (2010). *Steering system and method for independent steering of wheels* (Ph.D. Thesis). The Department of Mechanical and Industrial Engineering, Concordia University, Montreal, Quebec, Canada.

Kheriji, A., Bouani, F., & Ksouri, M. (2011). A GGP approach to solve non convex min-max predictive controller for a class of constrained MIMO systems described by state-space models. *International Journal of Control, Automation, and Systems*, *9*(3), 452–460. doi:10.100712555-011-0304-2

Khosravi, A., Lachini, Z., & Sarhadi, P. (2015). Predictor-based model reference adaptive control for a vehicle lateral dynamics considering uncertainties. Proc IMechE Part I. *Journal of Systems and Control Engineering*, *229*(9), 797–807.

Kiani, B., Shirouyehzad, H., Khoshsaligheh Bafti, F., & Fouladgar, H. (2009). System dynamics approach to analysing the cost factors effects on cost of quality. *International Journal of Quality & Reliability Management*, *26*(7), 685–698. doi:10.1108/02656710910975750

Kiani-B, A., Fallahi, K., Pariz, N., & Leung, H. (2009). A chaotic secure communication scheme using fractional chaotic systems based on an extended fractional Kalman filter. *Commun. Nonlinear Sci.*, *14*(3), 863–879. doi:10.1016/j.cnsns.2007.11.011

Kilbas, A. A., Srivastava, H. M., & Trujillo, J. J. (2006). Theory and applications of fractional differential equations, vol. 204. North-Holland mathematics studies. Elsevier.

Kim, D. H., & Cho, J. H. (2006). A Biologically Inspired Intelligent PID Controller Tuning for AVR Systems. *International Journal of Control, Automation, and Systems*, *4*, 624–636.

Kim, H.-S. (2002). New Extruded Multi-Cell Aluminum Profile For Maximum Crash Energy Absorption And Weight Efficiency. *Thin-walled Structures*, *40*(4), 311–327. doi:10.1016/S0263-8231(01)00069-6

Kim, S.-M., Pereira, J. A., Lopes, V. Jr, Turra, A. E., & Brennan, M. J. (2017). Practical active control of cavity noise using loop shaping: Two case studies. *Applied Acoustics*, *121*, 65–73. doi:10.1016/j.apacoust.2016.12.004

Kim, Y. C., Keel, L. H., & Bhattacharyya, S. P. (2003). Transient response control via characteristic ratio assignment. *IEEE Transactions on Automatic Control*, *48*(12), 2238–2244. doi:10.1109/TAC.2003.820153

Kim, Y., Kim, K., & Manabe, S. (2004). Sensitivity of time response to characteristic ratios. *Proceeding of the 2004 American Control Conference Boston*, 2723-2728.

Kızılkaya, M. Ö., & Gülez, K. (2016). Feed-Forward Approach in Stator-Flux-Oriented Direct Torque Control of Induction Motor with Space Vector Pulse-Width Modulation. *Journal of Power Electronics*, *16*(3), 994–1003. doi:10.6113/JPE.2016.16.3.994

Klimes, K., Abdul-Khaliq, H., Ovroutski, S., Hui, W., Alexi-Meskishvili, V., Spors, B., ... Gutberlet, M. (2007). Pulmonary and caval blood flow patterns in patients with intracardiac and extracardiac Fontan: A magnetic resonance study. *Clinical Research in Cardiology; Official Journal of the German Cardiac Society*, *96*(3), 160–167. doi:10.100700392-007-0470-z PMID:17180575

Koh, S., Ganesh, K., Pratik, V., & Anbuudayasankar, S. (2014). Impact of ERP implementation on supply chain performance. *International Journal of Productivity and Quality Management*, *14*(2), 196–227. doi:10.1504/IJPQM.2014.064476

Kongnam, C., & Nuchprayoon, S. (2010). A particle swarm optimization for wind energy control problem. *Renewable Energy*, *35*(11), 2431–2438. doi:10.1016/j.renene.2010.02.020

Konig, A. (2002). The Reliability of the Transportation System and its Influence on the Choice Behaviour. *Proceedings of the 2nd Swiss Transport Research Conference.*

Kopainsky, B., Tröger, K., Derwisch, S., & Ulli-Beer, S. (2012). Designing Sustainable Food Security Policies in Sub-Saharan African Countries: How Social Dynamics Over-Ride Utility Evaluations for Good and Bad. *Systems Research and Behavioral Science*, *29*(6), 575–589. doi:10.1002res.2140

Koronovskii, A. A., Moskalenko, O. I., Shurygina, S. A., & Hramov, A. E. (2013). Generalized synchronization in discrete maps. new point of view on weak and strong synchronization. *Chaos, Solitons, and Fractals*, *46*, 12–18. doi:10.1016/j.chaos.2012.10.004

Ko, S. H., Lee, S. R., Dehbonei, H., & Nayar, C. V. (2006). Application of voltage-and current-controlled voltage source inverters for distributed generation systems. *IEEE Transactions on Energy Conversion*, *21*(3), 782–792. doi:10.1109/TEC.2006.877371

Kouro, S., Bernal, R., Miranda, H., Silva, C. A., & Rodríguez, J. (2007). High-performance torque and flux control for multilevel inverter fed induction motors. *IEEE Transactions on Power Electronics*, *22*(6), 2116–2123. doi:10.1109/TPEL.2007.909189

Kramer, I. (1999). Modeling the dynamical impact of HIV on the immune system: Viral clearance, infection, and AIDS. *Mathematical and Computer Modelling*, *29*(6), 95–112. doi:10.1016/S0895-7177(99)00057-6

Krim, S., Gdaim, S., Mtibaa, A., & Mimouni, M. F. (2016). FPGA Contribution in Photovoltaic Pumping Systems: Models of MPPT and DTC-SVM Algorithms. *International Journal of Renewable Energy Research*, *6*(3), 866–879.

Kumar, A., & Gupta, R. (2013). Compare the results of Tuning of PID controller by using PSO and GA Technique for AVR system. *International Journal of Advanced Research in Computer Engineering & Technology*, *2*(6).

Kumar, D. V. (1998). Intelligent controllers for automatic generation control. *TENCON' 98. IEEE Region, 10 International Conference on Global Connectivity in Energy, Computer, Communication and Control*, *2*, 557-574.

Kumar, S., Heustis, D., & Graham, J. M. (2015). The future of traceability within the U.S. food industry supply chain – a business case. *International Journal of Productivity and Performance Management*, *64*(1), 129–146. doi:10.1108/IJPPM-03-2014-0046

Kung, E., Baretta, A., Baker, C., Arbia, G., Biglino, G., Corsini, C., ... Migliavacca, F. (2013). Predictive modeling of the virtual Hemi-Fontan operation for second stage single ventricle palliation: Two patient-specific cases. *Journal of Biomechanics*, *46*(2), 423–429. doi:10.1016/j.jbiomech.2012.10.023 PMID:23174419

Lai, F., Zhao, X., & Wang, Q. (2006). The impact of information technology on the competitive advantage of logistics firms in China. *Industrial Management & Data Systems*, *106*(9), 1249–1271. doi:10.1108/02635570610712564

Lai, W. T., & Chen, C. F. (2011). Behavioural Intentions of Public Transit Passengers – The Roles of Service Quality, Perceived Value, Satisfaction and Involvement. *Transport Policy*, *18*(2), 318–325. doi:10.1016/j.tranpol.2010.09.003

Lai, Y. S., & Chen, J. H. (2001). A new approach to direct torque control of induction motor drives for constant inverter switching frequency and torque ripple reduction. *IEEE Transactions on Energy Conversion*, *16*(3), 220–227. doi:10.1109/60.937200

Lalouni, S., Rekioua, D., Rekioua, T., & Matagne, E. (2009). Fuzzy logic control of stand-alone photovoltaic system with battery storage. *Journal of Power Sources*, *193*(2), 899–907. doi:10.1016/j.jpowsour.2009.04.016

Lamamra, K., Azar, A. T., & Ben Salah, C. (2017). *Chaotic system modelling using a neural network with optimized structure. Studies in Computational Intelligence* (Vol. 688). Springer-Verlag.

Lamterkati, J., Khafallah, M., & Ouboubker, L. (2014a). A New DPC for Three-phase PWM rectifier with unity power factor operation. *International Journal of Advanced Research in Electrical Electronics and Instrumentation Engineering*, *3*(4), 8273–8285.

Lamterkati, J., Khafallah, M., & Ouboubker, L. (2014b). Comparison of PI and Fuzzy logic DC-Link Voltage Controller for DPC PWM-Rectifier. *International Journal of Enhanced Research in Science Technology & Engineering*, *3*(4), 321–332.

Landsea, C. (1992). *A climatology of Intense (or Major) Atlantic Hurricanes*. Fort Collins, CO: American Meteorological Society.

Larrinaga, S. A., Vidal, M. A. R., Oyarbide, E., & Apraiz, J. R. T. (2007). Predictive control strategy for DC/AC converters based on direct power control. *IEEE Transactions on Industrial Electronics*, *54*(3), 1261–1271. doi:10.1109/TIE.2007.893162

Larson, P. D., & Kulchitsky, J. D. (1999). Logistics improvement programs the dynamics between people and performance. *International Journal of Physical Distribution & Logistics Management*, *29*(2), 88–102. doi:10.1108/09600039910264687

Laskin, N. (2000). Fractional market dynamics. *Physica A*, *2875*(3), 482–492. doi:10.1016/S0378-4371(00)00387-3

Lee, C., Ho, W., Ho, G., & Lau, H. (2011). Design and development of logistics workflow systems for management with RFID. *Expert Systems with Applications*, *38*(5), 5428–5437. doi:10.1016/j.eswa.2010.10.012

Lekhchine, S., Bahi, T., & Soufi, Y. (2013). Direct Torque Control of Dual Star Induction Motor. *International Journal of Renewable Energy Research*, *3*(1), 121–125.

Leon, A. (2008). *Enterprise resource planning*. New Delhi: Tata McGraw-Hill Education.

Lepuschitz, W., Zoitl, A., Vallee, M., & Merdan, M. (2011). Toward self-reconfiguration of manufacturing systems using automation agents. *IEEE Transactions on Systems, Man, and Cybernetics. Part C*, *41*(1), 52–69.

Lequesne, D. (2006). Régulation PID Analogique-numérique-floue. Paris: Hermès, Lavoisier.

Lewis, I., & Talalayevsky, A. (2004). Improving the interorganizational supply chain through optimization of information flows. *Journal of Enterprise Information Management*, *17*(3), 229–237. doi:10.1108/17410390410531470

Li, C., Chen, A & Ye, J. (2011). Numerical approaches to fractional calculus and fractional ordinary differential equation. *J. Comput. Phys.*, *230*(9), 3352–3368. doi:.2011.01.03010.1016/j.jcp

Liang, F., Senzaki, H., Kurishima, C., Sughimoto, K., Inuzuka, R., & Liu, H. (2014). Hemodynamic performance of the Fontan circulation compared with a normal biventricular circulation: A computational model study. *American Journal of Physiology. Heart and Circulatory Physiology*, *307*(7), H1056–H1072. doi:10.1152/ajpheart.00245.2014 PMID:25063796

Liberti, L., & Maculan, N. (2006). *Global Optimization From Theory to Implementation*. Springer.

Li, C. P., & Peng, G. J. (2004). Chaos in Chen's system with a fractional order. *Chaos Solit. Frac.*, *22*(2), 443–450.

Li, C., Gong, Z., Qian, D., & Chen, Y. (2010). On the bound of the Lyapunov exponents for the fractional differential systems. *Chaos (Woodbury, N.Y.)*, *20*(1), 013127. doi:10.1063/1.3314277 PMID:20370282

Li, D., Fan, Q., Hirata, Y., Ono, M., & An, Q. (2017). Arrhythmias After Fontan Operation with Intra-atrial Lateral Tunnel Versus Extra-cardiac Conduit: A Systematic Review and Meta-analysis. *Pediatric Cardiology*, *38*(4), 873–880. doi:10.100700246-017-1595-8 PMID:28271152

Li, F., & Yao, C. (2016). The infinite-scroll attractor and energy transition in chaotic circuit. *Nonlinear Dynamics*, *84*(4), 2305–2315. doi:10.100711071-016-2646-z

Li, G.-H. (2007). Modified projective synchronization of chaotic system. *Chaos, Solitons, and Fractals*, *32*(5), 1786–1790. doi:10.1016/j.chaos.2005.12.009

Li, H., Liao, X., & Luo, M. (2012). A novel non-equilibrium fractional-order chaotic system and its complete synchronization by circuit implementation. *Nonlinear Dynamics*, *68*(1-2), 137–149. doi:10.100711071-011-0210-4

Li, M. Z. F., Lau, D. C. B., & Seah, D. W. M. (2011). Car ownership and Urban Transport Demand in Singapore. *Rivista Internazionale di Economia dei Trasporti*, *38*(1), 47–70.

Lindberg, E. (2004). Is the Quadrature Oscillator a Multivibrator? *IEEE Circuits & Devices Magazine*, *20*(6), 23–28. doi:10.1109/MCD.2004.1364772

Lin, L. (2009). An integrated framework for the development of radio frequency identification technology in the logistics and supply chain management. *Computers & Industrial Engineering*, *57*(3), 832–842. doi:10.1016/j.cie.2009.02.010

Li, S. Y. (2011). Chaos control of new Mathieu–van der Pol systems by fuzzy logic constant controllers. *Applied Soft Computing*, *11*(8), 4474–4487. doi:10.1016/j.asoc.2011.08.024

Liu, J., Wu, P., Bai, H., & Huang, X. (2004, June). Application of fuzzy control in direct torque control of permanent magnet synchronous motor. In *Intelligent Control and Automation, 2004. WCICA 2004. Fifth World Congress on* (Vol. 5, pp. 4573-4576). IEEE.

Liu, Y. D., Wang, Z. P., Zheng, T., Tu, L. M., Su, Y., & Wu, Z. Q. (2013, December). A novel adaptive loss of excitation protection criterion based on steady-state stability limit. *Power and Energy Engineering Conference (APPEEC), IEEE PES Asia-Pacific*, 1-5. 10.1109/APPEEC.2013.6837140

Liu, L., Meng, X., & Liu, C. (2016). A review of maximum power point tracking methods of PV power system at uniform and partial shading. *Renewable & Sustainable Energy Reviews*, *53*, 1500–1507. doi:10.1016/j.rser.2015.09.065

Liu, S., Ai, H., Lin, Z., & Meng, Z. (2017). Analysis of vibration characteristics and adaptive continuous perturbation control of some torsional vibration system with backlash. *Chaos, Solitons, and Fractals*, *103*, 151–158. doi:10.1016/j.chaos.2017.06.001

Liu, Y. H., Chen, J. H., & Huang, J. W. (2015). A review of maximum power point tracking techniques for use in partially shaded conditions. *Renewable & Sustainable Energy Reviews*, *41*, 436–453. doi:10.1016/j.rser.2014.08.038

Li, Y., Chen, Y. Q., Podlubny, I., & Cao, Y. (2008). Mittag-Leffler stability of fractional order nonlinear dynamic system. *Automatica*, *45*(8), 1965–1969. doi:10.1016/j.automatica.2009.04.003

Li, Z. W., Wu, N. O., & Zhou, M. C. (2012). Deadlock control of automated manufacturing systems based on Petri nets – a literature review. *IEEE Transactions on Systems, Man, and Cybernetics. Part C*, *42*(4), 437–462.

Llor, A., Allard, B., Lin-Shi, X., & Retif, J. M. (2004, June). Comparison of DTC implementations for synchronous machines. In *Power Electronics Specialists Conference, 2004. PESC 04. 2004 IEEE 35th Annual* (Vol. 5, pp. 3581-3587). IEEE. 10.1109/PESC.2004.1355109

Lloyd, S. J., Kovats, R. S., & Chalabi, Z. (2011). Climate change, crop yields and under-nutrition: Development of a model to quantify the impacts of climate scenarios on child under-nutrition. *Environmental Health Perspectives*, *119*(12), 1817–1823. doi:10.1289/ehp.1003311 PMID:21844000

Lodi, S., Phillips, A., Touloumi, G., Geskus, R., Meyer, L., Thiébaut, R., ... Porter, K. (2011). Time from human immunodeficiency virus seroconversion to reaching CD4+ cell count thresholds< 200,< 350, and< 500 cells/mm3: Assessment of need following changes in treatment guidelines. *Clinical Infectious Diseases*, *53*(8), 817–825. doi:10.1093/cid/cir494 PMID:21921225

Loebbecke, P., & Powell, P. (1998). Competitive Advantage from IT in Logistics: The Integrated Transport Tracking System. *International Journal of Information Management*, *18*(1), 17–27. doi:10.1016/S0268-4012(97)00037-6

Lokriti, A., Salhi, I., Doubabi, S., & Zidani, Y. (2013). Induction motor speed drive improvement using fuzzy IP-self-tuning controller. A real time implementation. *ISA Transactions*, *52*(3), 406–417. doi:10.1016/j.isatra.2012.11.002 PMID:23317661

Lorenz, E. N. (1963). Deterministic nonperiodic flow. *Journal of the Atmospheric Sciences*, *29*(2), 130–141. doi:

LQ. (2007). An Interview with John Motley. *Logistics Quarterly*, *13*(4), 12-14. Retrieved on May 22, 2015 from, http://www.logisticsquarterly.com/issues/13-4/LQ_13-4.pdf

Luffel, M., Sati, M., Rossignac, J., Yoganathan, A. P., Haggerty, C. M., Restrepo, M., ... Fogel, M. A. (2016). SURGEM: A solid modeling tool for planning and optimizing pediatric heart surgeries. *Computer Aided Design*, *70*, 3–12. doi:10.1016/j.cad.2015.06.018

Lukyamuzi, A., Ngubiri, J., & Okori, W. (2015). Towards harnessing phone messages and telephone conversations for prediction of food crisis. *International Journal of System Dynamics Applications*, *4*(4), 1–16. doi:10.4018/IJSDA.2015100101

Luna-Reyes, L. F., & Andersen, D. L. (2003). Collecting and analyzing qualitative data for system dynamics: Methods and models. *System Dynamics Review*, *19*(4), 271–296. doi:10.1002dr.280

Luo, X., Morimoto, A., Daimon, H., & Koike, H. (2007). A Study on Traffic Behaviour of High Income People in Asian Developing Countries. *Journal of the Eastern Asia Society for Transportation Studies*, *7*, 1222–1235.

Lupton, D. (2002). Road Rage: Drivers' Understandings and Experiences. *Journal of Sociology (Melbourne, Vic.)*, *38*(3), 275–290. doi:10.1177/144078302128756660

Luyben, W. L. (1970). Distillation decoupling. *AIChE Journal. American Institute of Chemical Engineers*, *16*(2), 198–203. doi:10.1002/aic.690160209

Lyden, S., & Haque, M. E. (2015). Maximum Power Point Tracking techniques for photovoltaic systems: A comprehensive review and comparative analysis. *Renewable & Sustainable Energy Reviews*, *52*, 1504–1518. doi:10.1016/j.rser.2015.07.172

Machado, J. T., Kiryakova, V., & Mainardi, F. (2011). Recent history of fractional calculus. *Communications in Nonlinear Science and Numerical Simulation*, *16*(3), 1140–1153. doi:10.1016/j.cnsns.2010.05.027

Maharjan, L., Inoue, S., & Akagi, H. (2008). A transformerless energy storage system based on a cascade multilevel PWM converter with star configuration. *IEEE Transactions on Industry Applications*, *44*(5), 1621–1630. doi:10.1109/TIA.2008.2002180

Mahmoud, G. M., & Mahmoud, E. E. (2010). Complete synchronization of chaotic complex nonlinear systems with uncertain parameters. *Nonlinear Dynamics*, *62*(4), 875–882. doi:10.100711071-010-9770-y

Mainieri, R., & Rehacek, J. (1999). Projective synchronization in three-dimensional chaotic systems. *Physical Review Letters*, *82*(15), 3042–3045. doi:10.1103/PhysRevLett.82.3042

Malinowski, M., & Kazmierkowski, M.P. (2000). *Simulation Study of Virtual Flux Based Direct Power Control for Three-Phase PWM Rectifiers*. 26th Annual Confjerence of the IEEE Industrial Electronics Society, Nagoya, Japan. DOI: 10.1109/IECON.2000.972411

Malinowski, M., Jasinski, M., & Kazmierkowski, P. (2004). Simple Direct power control of three phase PWM rectifier using space vector modulation (DPC-SVM). *IEEE Transactions on Industrial Electronics*, *51*(2), 447–454. doi:10.1109/TIE.2004.825278

Malinowski, M., Kaz'mierkowski, M. P., Hansen, S., Blaabjerg, F., & Marques, G. D. (2001). Virtual flux based direct power control of three-phase PWM rectifiers. *IEEE Transactions on Industry Applications*, *37*(4), 1019–1027. doi:10.1109/28.936392

Malinowski, M., Kazmierkowski, M. P., & Trzynadlowski, A. M. (2003). A Comparative Study of Control Techniques for PWM Rectifiers in AC Adjustable Speed Drives. *IEEE Transactions on Power Electronics*, *18*(6), 1390–1396. doi:10.1109/TPEL.2003.818871

Mamdoohi, G., Abas, A. F., & Samsudin, K. (2012). Implementation of genetic algorithm in an embedded microcontroller based polarization control system. *Engineering Applications of Artificial Intelligence*, *25*(4), 869–873. doi:10.1016/j.engappai.2012.01.018

Mann, E., & Abraham, C. (2006). The Role of Affect in UK Commuters' Travel Mode Choices: An Interpretative Phenomenological Analysis. *British Journal of Psychology*, *97*(2), 155–176. doi:10.1348/000712605X61723 PMID:16613647

Mansour. (2012). *Development of advanced controllers using adaptive weighted PSO algorithm with applications* (M.Sc Thesis). Faculty of Engineering, Cairo University, Cairo, Egypt.

Mansour. (2012). *Development of advanced controllers using adaptive weighted PSO algorithm with applications* (M.Sc. Thesis). Faculty of Engineering, Cairo University, Cairo, Egypt.

Maranas, C., & Floudas, C. (1997). Global optimization in generalized geometric programming. *Computers & Chemical Engineering*, *21*(4), 351–369. doi:10.1016/S0098-1354(96)00282-7

Markusic, C. A. (1992). *Vehicle Safety Compliance Testing for Occupant Crash Protection, Windshield Mounting, Windshield Zone Intrusion, and Fuel System Integrity, Final Report of FMVSS NOS. 208, 212, 219, and 301 Compliance Testing*. Washington, DC: Department of Transportation.

Marvao, A., de, Meyer, H., Dawes, T., Francis, C., Shi, W., & Bai, W. (2016). Development of integrated high-resolution three-dimensional MRI and computational modelling techniques to identify novel genetic and anthropometric determinants of cardiac form and function. *Lancet*, *387*, S36. doi:10.1016/S0140-6736(16)00423-2

Marzougui, D., Kan, C. D., & Bedewi, N. E. (1996). Development and Validation of an NCAP Simulation using LS-DYNA3D. FHWA/NHTSA National Crash Analysis Center, The George Washington University, Virginia Campus.

Masoller, N., Sanz-Cortés, M., Crispi, F., Gómez, O., Bennasar, M., Egaña-Ugrinovic, G., ... Gratacós, E. (2016). Mid-gestation brain Doppler and head biometry in fetuses with congenital heart disease predict abnormal brain development at birth. *Ultrasound in Obstetrics & Gynecology: The Official Journal of the International Society of Ultrasound in Obstetrics and Gynecology*, *47*(1), 65–73. doi:10.1002/uog.14919 PMID:26053596

Masoum, M. A. S., Seyed, M., Badejani, M., & Kalantar, M. (2010). *Optimal placement of hybrid PV-wind systems using genetic algorithm*. IEEE 2010 Innovative Smart Grid Technologies (ISGT), Gaithersburg, MD. DOI: 10.1109/ISGT.2010.5434746

Matheis, R. & Eckstein, L. (2016). Aluminium-carbon fibre-reinforced polymer hybrid crash management system incorporating braided tubes. *International Journal of Automotive Composites, 2*(3-4), 330–355.

Matignon, D. (1998). Stability properties for generalized fractional differential systems. Proc. of Fractional Differential Systems, 5, 145-158. doi:10.1051/proc:1998004

Matignon, D. (1996). Stability results of fractional differential equations with applications to control processing. In *IMACS* (pp. 963–968). Lille, France: IEEE–SMC.

Mayo Clinic. (2010). *Mayo Clinic Internal Medicine Review* (Greek edition). Thessaloniki, Greece: Rotonda Press.

McFarlane, D., & Glover, K. (1992). A Loop Shaping Design Procedure Using H Infinity Synthesis. *IEEE Transactions on Automatic Control*, *37*(6), 759–769. doi:10.1109/9.256330

Meghni, B., Dib, D., & Azar, A. T. (2017b). A Second-order sliding mode and fuzzy logic control to Optimal Energy Management in PMSG Wind Turbine with Battery Storage. *Neural Computing & Applications*, *28*(6), 1417–1434. doi:10.100700521-015-2161-z

Meghni, B., Dib, D., Azar, A. T., Ghoudelbourk, S., & Saadoun, A. (2017a). *Robust Adaptive Supervisory Fractional order Controller For optimal Energy Management in Wind Turbine with Battery Storage. In Studies in Computational Intelligence* (Vol. 688, pp. 165–202). Springer-Verlag.

Meghni, B., Dib, D., Azar, A. T., Ghoudelbourk, S., & Saadoun, A. (2017a). *Robust Adaptive Supervisory Fractional order Controller For optimal Energy Management in Wind Turbine with Battery Storage. Studies in Computational Intelligence* (Vol. 688). Springer-Verlag.

Meghni, B., Dib, D., Azar, A. T., & Saadoun, A. (2017c). *Effective Supervisory Controller to Extend Optimal Energy Management in Hybrid Wind Turbine under Energy and Reliability Constraints. International Journal of Dynamics and Control*. doi:10.100740435-016-0296-0

Mehrjerdi, Z. (2010). Coupling RFID with supply chain to enhance productivity. *Business Strategy Series*, *11*(2), 107–123. doi:10.1108/17515631011026434

Mehrjerdi, Z. (2013). A framework for Six-Sigma driven RFID-enabled supply chain systems. *International Journal of Quality & Reliability Management*, *30*(2), 142–160. doi:10.1108/02656711311293562

Mekki, H., Boukhetala, D., & Azar, A. T. (2015). Sliding Modes for Fault Tolerant Control. In Advances and Applications in Sliding Mode Control systems (vol. 576, pp. 407-433). Springer-Verlag GmbH Berlin/Heidelberg. doi:10.1007/978-3-319-11173-5_15

Melkou, L., & Hamerlain, M. (2014). Classical sliding and generalized variable structure controls for a manipulator robot arm with pneumatic artificial muscles. *International Journal of System Dynamics Applications*, *3*(1), 47–70. doi:10.4018/ijsda.2014010103

Messaif, I., Berkouk, E. M., & Saadia, N. (2007, December). Ripple reduction in DTC drives by using a three-level NPC VSI. In *Electronics, Circuits and Systems, 2007. ICECS 2007. 14th IEEE International Conference on* (pp. 1179-1182). IEEE. 10.1109/ICECS.2007.4511206

Mezache, A., & Betto, K. (1997). *Estimation et Commande d'un Réacteur de Fabrication de Pâte a Papier par les Réseaux de Neurones Flous. Memory of Engineer*. University of Constantine.

Mhawej, M. J., Moog, C. H., & Biafore, F. (2009). The HIV dynamics is a single input system. In *13th International Conference on Biomedical Engineering* (pp. 1263-1266). Springer Berlin Heidelberg. 10.1007/978-3-540-92841-6_310

Mhawej, M. J., Moog, C. H., Biafore, F., & Brunet-Franois, C. (2010). Control of the HIV infection and drug dosage. *Biomedical Signal Processing and Control*, *5*(1), 45–52. doi:10.1016/j.bspc.2009.05.001

Miller, K. S., & Ross, B. (1993). *Introduction to the Fractional Calculus and Fractional Differential Equations*. New York: John Wiley.

Mindila, A., Rodrigues, A., McCormick, D., & Mwangi, R. (2014). An Adaptive ICT-Enabled Model for Knowledge Identification and Management for Enterprise Development. *International Journal of System Dynamics Applications*, *3*(1), 71–89. doi:10.4018/ijsda.2014010104

Mindila, A., Rodrigues, A., McCormick, D., & Mwangi, R. (2016). ICT Powered Strategic Flexibility System Dynamic Model: A Pillar for Economic Development in Micro and Small Enterprises. *International Journal of System Dynamics Applications*, *3*(1), 90–110. doi:10.4018/ijsda.2014010105

Mirko, Č., Joško, D., Li, X., Eric, T., & Davor, H. (2016). Optimisation of active suspension control inputs for improved vehicle ride performance. *Vehicle System Dynamics*, *54*(7), 1004–1030. doi:10.1080/00423114.2016.1177655

Mnasser, A., Bouani, F., & Ksouri, M. (2014). Neural networks predictive controller using an adaptive control rate. *International Journal of System Dynamics Applications*, *3*(3), 127–147. doi:10.4018/ijsda.2014070106

Modali, N. (2005). *Modeling Destination Choice and Measuring the Transferability of Hurricane Evacuation Patterns* (Published Master Thesis). Department of Civil and Environmental Engineering, Louisiana State University.

Mohandes, M. K. S. R. M., Balghonaim, A., Kassas, M., Rehman, S., & Halawani, T. O. (2000). Use of radial basis functions for estimating monthly mean daily solar radiation. *Solar Energy*, *68*(2), 161–168. doi:10.1016/S0038-092X(99)00071-7

Molfetta, A. D., Amodeo, A., Fresiello, L., Filippelli, S., Pilati, M., Iacobelli, R., ... Ferrari, G. (2016). The use of a numerical model to simulate the cavo-pulmonary assistance in Fontan circulation: A preliminary verification. *Journal of Artificial Organs*, *19*(2), 105–113. doi:10.100710047-015-0874-5 PMID:26545595

Mondal, S. K., Pinto, J. O. P., & Bose, B. K. (2002). A Neural-Network-Based Space-Vector PWM Controller for a three-Level Voltage-Fed Inverter Induction Motor Drive. *Industry Applications. IEEE Transactions on.*, *38*(3), 660–669.

Monmasson, E., & Cirstea, M. N. (2007). FPGA design methodology for industrial control systems—A review. *IEEE Transactions on Industrial Electronics*, *54*(4), 1824–1842. doi:10.1109/TIE.2007.898281

Monmasson, E., Idkhajine, L., Cirstea, M. N., Bahri, I., Tisan, A., & Naouar, M. W. (2011). FPGAs in industrial control applications. *IEEE Transactions on Industrial Informatics*, *7*(2), 224–243. doi:10.1109/TII.2011.2123908

Moog, C. H., Ouattara, D. A., & Mhawej, M. J. (2007). Analysis of the HIV dynamics. *IFAC Proceedings Volumes, 40*(12), 379-386.

Morecroft, J. (2007). *Strategic Modelling and Business Dynamics. A Feedback Systems Approach*. Chichester, UK: John Wiley & Sons.

Mori, M. (1975). *The Three-eyed Beatles*. Presented at the International Ocean Exposition, Okinawa, Japan.

Morteza, D., Caglar, S., Teoman, E., & Selim, S. (2015). Design of a multiple-model switching controller for ABS braking dynamics. *Transactions of the Institute of Measurement and Control*, *37*(5), 582–595. doi:10.1177/0142331214546522

Morton, J. F. (2007). The impact of climate change on smallholder and subsistence agriculture. *Proceedings of the National Academy of Sciences of the United States of America*, *104*(50), 19680–19685. doi:10.1073/pnas.0701855104 PMID:18077400

Moualeu, D. P., Mbang, J., Ndoundam, R., & Bowong, S. (2011). Modeling and analysis of HIV and hepatitis C co-infections. *Journal of Biological System*, *19*(04), 683–723. doi:10.1142/S0218339011004159

Mousa, M. E., Ebrahim, M. A., & Hassan, M. A. M. (2015). Stabilizing and swinging-up the inverted pendulum using PI and PID controllers based on reduced linear quadratic regulator tuned by PSO. *International Journal of System Dynamics Applications*, *4*(4), 52–69. doi:10.4018/IJSDA.2015100104

Moysis, L., Tsiaousis, M., Charalampidis, N., Eliadou, M., & Kafetzis, I. (2015). *An Introduction to Control Theory Applications with Matlab*. Retrieved from http://users.auth.gr/lazarosm/

Moysis, L., Azar, A. T., Kafetzis, I., Tsiaousis, M., & Charalampidis, N. (2017). Introduction to Control Systems Design Using Matlab. *International Journal of System Dynamics Applications*, *6*(3), 130–170. doi:10.4018/IJSDA.2017070107

Moysis, L., Kafetzis, I., & Politis, M. (2016). Analysis of a Dynamical Model for HIV Infection with One or Two Inputs. *International Journal of System Dynamics Applications*, *5*(4), 83–100. doi:10.4018/IJSDA.2016100105

Mozina, C. J. (2010, March). Coordinating generator protection with transmission protection and generator control—NERC standards and pending requirements. *Protective Relay Engineers, 2010 63rd Annual Conference for IEEE*, 1-12.

Mozina, C. J., Reichard, M., Bukhala, Z., Conrad, S., Crawley, T., Gardell, J., . . . Johnson, G. (2008, June). Coordination of generator protection with generator excitation control and generator capability. *Pulp and Paper Industry Technical Conference, 2008. PPIC 2008. Conference Record of 2008 54th Annual IEEE*, 62-76.

Mukherjee, S., Mukhopadhyay, D., & Das, P. (2016). Usefulness of Animal Simulator Software in teaching Amphibian Physiology Practical for 1st Prof MBBS Students. *Journal of Contemporary Medical Education*, *4*(1), 21–25. doi:10.5455/jcme.20160107115900

Mulligan, R. (1998). EDI in foreign trade Case studies in utilisation. *International Journal of Physical Distribution & Logistics Management*, *28*(9/10), 794–804. doi:10.1108/09600039810248172

Murphy, P. R., & Daley, J. M. (1999). EDI benefits and barriers comparing international freight forwarders and their customers. *International Journal of Physical Distribution & Logistics Management*, *29*(3), 207–216. doi:10.1108/09600039910268700

Musa, B. U., Kalli, B. M., & Kalli, S. (2013). Modeling and Simulation of LFC and AVR with PID Controller. *International Journal of Engineering Science Invention*, *2*, 54–57.

Myaing, A., & Dinavahi, V. (2011, July). FPGA-based real-time emulation of power electronic systems with detailed representation of device characteristics. In *Power and Energy Society General Meeting, 2011 IEEE* (pp. 1-11). IEEE.

Naglaa & Hassan. (2016). Swarm Intelligence PID Controller Tuning for AVR System. Springer-Verlag.

Naglaa, K., Bahgaat, El-Sayed, M.I., Moustafa Hassan, M.A., & Bendary, F.A. (2013). Artificial Intelligence Based Controller for Load Frequency Control in Power System. *Al-Azhar University Engineering sector, 8*(28), 1215-1226.

Naglaa, K., Bahgaat, El-Sayed, M.I., Moustafa Hassan, M.A., & Bendary, F.A. (2014). Load Frequency Control in Power System via Improving PID Controller Based on Particle Swarm Optimization and ANFIS Techniques. *International Journal of System Dynamics Applications, 3*(3), 1-24.

Naglaa, K., Bahgaat, El-Sayed, M.I., Moustafa Hassan, M.A., & Bendary, F.A. (2014a). Load Frequency Control in Power System via Improving PID Controller Based on Particle Swarm Optimization and ANFIS Techniques. *International Journal of System Dynamics Applications.*

Naglaa, K., Bahgaat, El-Sayed, M.I., Moustafa Hassan, M.A., & Bendary, F.A. (2014b). Control of Load Frequency on Power System Based on Particle Swarm Optimization Techniques and ANFIS. *Al-Azhar University Engineering sector, 9*(30), 287-294.

Naglaa, K., Bahgaat, El-Sayed, M.I., Moustafa Hassan, M.A., & Bendary, F.A. (2015). Application of Some Modern Techniques in Load Frequency Control in Power Systems. Chaos Modeling and Control Systems Design, 581, 163-211.

Naglaa, K., Bahgaat, El-Sayed, M.I., Moustafa Hassan, M.A., & Bendary, F.A. (2015). Application of Some Modern Techniques in Load Frequency Control in Power Systems. In Computational Intelligence applications in Modeling and Control. Springer-Verlag.

Naglaa, K., Bahgaat, El-Sayed, M.I., Moustafa Hassan, M.A., & Bendary, F.A. (2016). Load Frequency Control Based on Evolutionary Techniques in Electrical Power Systems. Springer-Verlag.

Nahid-Mobarakeh, B., Meibody-Tabar, F., & Sargos, F. M. (2004). Mechanical sensorless control of PMSM with online estimation of stator resistance. *IEEE Transactions on Industry Applications*, *40*(2), 457–471. doi:10.1109/TIA.2004.824490

Naik, R.S., ChandraSekhar, K., & Vaisakh, K. (2005). Adaptive PSO based optimal fuzzy controller design for AGC equipped with SMES and SPSS. *Journal of Theoretical and Applied Information Technology, 7*(1), 8-17.

Nair, P., Venkitaswamy, R., & Anbudayashankar, S. (2009). Overview of Information Technology Tools for Supply Chain Management. *CSI Communications*, *33*(9), 20–27.

Nand, K. (1995). Geometric programming based robot control design. *Computers & Industrial Engineering*, *29*(1), 631–635.

Naouar, M. W., Monmasson, E., Naassani, A. A., & Slama-Belkhodja, I. (2013). FPGA-based dynamic reconfiguration of sliding mode current controllers for synchronous machines. *IEEE Transactions on Industrial Informatics*, *9*(3), 1262–1271. doi:10.1109/TII.2012.2220974

Naouar, M. W., Monmasson, E., Naassani, A. A., Slama-Belkhodja, I., & Patin, N. (2007). FPGA-based current controllers for AC machine drives—A review. *IEEE Transactions on Industrial Electronics*, *54*(4), 1907–1925. doi:10.1109/TIE.2007.898302

Nehrir, M. H., LaMeres, B. J., Venkataramanan, G., Gerez, V., & Alvarado, L. A. (2000). An approach to evaluate the general performance of stand-alone wind/photovoltaic generating systems. *IEEE Transactions on Energy Conversion*, *15*(4), 433–439. doi:10.1109/60.900505

Nehrir, M. H., & Wang, C. (2009). *Modeling and control of fuel cells: Distributed generation applications* (Vol. 41). John Wiley & Sons. doi:10.1109/9780470443569

Nelson, G. C. (2009). *Climate Change: Impact on Agriculture and Costs of Adaptation*. Washington, DC: International Food Policy Research Institute.

Nema, P., Nema, R. K., & Rangnekar, S. (2009). A current and future state of art development of hybrid energy system using wind and PV-solar: A review. *Renewable & Sustainable Energy Reviews*, *13*(8), 2096–2103. doi:10.1016/j.rser.2008.10.006

Ngai, E. W. T., Lai, K. H., & Cheng, T. C. (2008a). Logistics information systems: The Hong Kong experience. *International Journal of Production Economics*, *113*(1), 223–234. doi:10.1016/j.ijpe.2007.05.018

Ngai, E. W. T., Moon, K. L. K., Riggins, F. J., & Yi, C. Y. (2008b). RFID research: An academic literature review (1995 -2005) and future research directions. *International Journal of Production Economics*, *112*(2), 510–520. doi:10.1016/j.ijpe.2007.05.004

Nikolopoulos, G. K., & Fotiou, A. (2015). "Integrated interventions are dead. Long live sustainable integrated interventions!"—Austerity Challenges the Continuation of Effective Interventions in the Field of Drug Use-Related Harm Reduction. *Substance Use & Misuse*, *50*(8-9), 1220–1222. doi:10.3109/10826084.2015.1042326 PMID:26361930

Nikolopoulos, G. K., Pavlitina, E., Muth, S. Q., Schneider, J., Psichogiou, M., Williams, L. D., ... Korobchuk, A. (2016). A network intervention that locates and intervenes with recently HIV-infected persons: The Transmission Reduction Intervention Project (TRIP). *Scientific Reports*, 6. PMID:27917890

Nikolopoulos, G. K., Sypsa, V., Bonovas, S., Paraskevis, D., Malliori-Minerva, M., Hatzakis, A., & Friedman, S. R. (2015). Big Events in Greece and HIV infection among people who inject drugs. *Substance Use & Misuse*, *50*(7), 825–838. doi:10.3109/10826084.2015.978659 PMID:25723309

Nise, N. S. (2015). *Control Systems Engineering* (7th ed.). John Wiley and Sons.

Noguchi, T., Tomiki, H., Kondo, S., & Takahashi, I. (1998). Direct power control of PWM converter without power-source voltage sensors. *IEEE Transactions on Industry Applications*, *34*(3), 473–479. doi:10.1109/28.673716

Nordin, M., & Gutman, P.-O. (2002). Controlling mechanical systems with backlash—a survey. *Automatica*, *38*(10), 1633–1649. doi:10.1016/S0005-1098(02)00047-X

Nowak, M., & May, R. M. (2000). *Virus dynamics: Mathematical principles of immunology and virology: mathematical principles of immunology and virology*. Oxford University Press.

Ogunnaike, B., & Harmor, W. (1994). *Process Dynamics, Modelling and Control*. New York: Oxford University Press.

Onggo, S. (2012). Adult Social Care Workforce Analysis in England: A System Dynamics Approach. *International Journal of System Dynamics Applications*, *1*(4), 1–20. doi:10.4018/ijsda.2012100101

Opotowsky, A. R., Baraona, F., Landzberg, M., Wu, F., McCausland, F., Owumi, J., … Waikar, S. (2016). Kidney Dysfunction in Patients with a Single Ventricle Fontan Circulation. *Journal of the American College of Cardiology*, *67*(13), 898.

Opotowsky, A. R., Baraona, F. R., Causland, F. R. M., Loukas, B., Landzberg, E., Landzberg, M. J., ... Waikar, S. S. (2017). Estimated glomerular filtration rate and urine biomarkers in patients with single-ventricle Fontan circulation. *Heart (British Cardiac Society)*, *103*(6), 434–442. doi:10.1136/heartjnl-2016-309729 PMID:27670967

Ortega, M., Restrepo, J., Viola, J., Gimenez, M. I., & Guzman, V. (2005, November). Direct torque control of induction motors using fuzzy logic with current limitation. In *Industrial Electronics Society, 2005. IECON 2005. 31st Annual Conference of IEEE* (pp. 6-pp). IEEE. 10.1109/IECON.2005.1569107

Ott, E., Grebogi, C., and Yorke, J. A. (1990). Controlling chaos. *Physical Review Letters*, *64*(11), 1196-1199.

Ouannas, A., Azar, A. T., & Radwan, A. G. (2016b) On Inverse Problem of Generalized Synchronization Between Different Dimensional Integer-Order and Fractional-Order Chaotic Systems. *The 28th International Conference on Microelectronics*. 10.1109/ICM.2016.7847942

Ouannas, A., Grassi, G., Azar, A. T., Radwan, A. G., Volos, C., Pham, V. T., . . . Stouboulos, I. N. (2017j). *Dead-Beat Synchronization Control in Discrete-Time Chaotic Systems*. The 6th International Conference on Modern Circuits and Systems Technologies (MOCAST), Thessaloniki, Greece. 10.1109/MOCAST.2017.7937628

Ouannas, A., Azar, A. T., & Abu-Saris, R. (2016a). A new type of hybrid synchronization between arbitrary hyperchaotic maps. *International Journal of Machine Learning and Cybernetics*. doi:10.100713042-016-0566-3

Ouannas, A., Azar, A. T., & Vaidyanathan, S. (2017f). On A Simple Approach for Q-S Synchronization of Chaotic Dynamical Systems in Continuous-Time. *Int. J. Computing Science and Mathematics*, *8*(1), 20–27.

Ouannas, A., Azar, A. T., & Vaidyanathan, S. (2017g). New Hybrid Synchronization Schemes Based on Coexistence of Various Types of Synchronization Between Master-Slave Hyperchaotic Systems. *International Journal of Computer Applications in Technology*, *55*(2), 112–120. doi:10.1504/IJCAT.2017.082868

Ouannas, A., Azar, A. T., & Vaidyanathan, S. (2017i). A Robust Method for New Fractional Hybrid Chaos Synchronization. *Mathematical Methods in the Applied Sciences*, *40*(5), 1804–1812. doi:10.1002/mma.4099

Ouannas, A., Azar, A. T., & Ziar, T. (2017h). *On Inverse Full State Hybrid Function Projective Synchronization for Continuous-time Chaotic Dynamical Systems with Arbitrary Dimensions*. Differential Equations and Dynamical Systems. doi:10.100712591-017-0362-x

Ouannas, A., Azar, A. T., Ziar, T., & Radwan, A. G. (2017d). *Study On Coexistence of Different Types of Synchronization Between Different dimensional Fractional Chaotic Systems. In Studies in Computational Intelligence* (Vol. 688, pp. 637–669). Springer-Verlag.

Ouannas, A., Azar, A. T., Ziar, T., & Radwan, A. G. (2017d). *Study On Coexistence of Different Types of Synchronization Between Different dimensional Fractional Chaotic Systems. Studies in Computational Intelligence* (Vol. 688). Springer-Verlag.

Ouannas, A., Azar, A. T., Ziar, T., & Radwan, A. G. (2017e). *Generalized Synchronization of Different Dimensional Integer-order and Fractional Order Chaotic Systems. In Studies in Computational Intelligence* (Vol. 688, pp. 671–697). Springer-Verlag.

Ouannas, A., Azar, A. T., Ziar, T., & Radwan, A. G. (2017e). *Generalized Synchronization of Different Dimensional Integer-order and Fractional Order Chaotic Systems. Studies in Computational Intelligence* (Vol. 688). Springer-Verlag.

Ouannas, A., Azar, A. T., Ziar, T., & Vaidyanathan, S. (2017a). *On New Fractional Inverse Matrix Projective Synchronization Schemes. In Studies in Computational Intelligence* (Vol. 688, pp. 497–524). Springer-Verlag.

Ouannas, A., Azar, A. T., Ziar, T., & Vaidyanathan, S. (2017a). *On New Fractional Inverse Matrix Projective Synchronization Schemes. Studies in Computational Intelligence* (Vol. 688). Springer-Verlag.

Ouannas, A., Azar, A. T., Ziar, T., & Vaidyanathan, S. (2017b). *Fractional Inverse Generalized Chaos Synchronization Between Different Dimensional Systems. In Studies in Computational Intelligence* (Vol. 688, pp. 525–551). Springer-Verlag.

Ouannas, A., Azar, A. T., Ziar, T., & Vaidyanathan, S. (2017b). *Fractional Inverse Generalized Chaos Synchronization Between Different Dimensional Systems. Studies in Computational Intelligence* (Vol. 688). Springer-Verlag.

Ouannas, A., Azar, A. T., Ziar, T., & Vaidyanathan, S. (2017c). *A New Method To Synchronize Fractional Chaotic Systems With Different Dimensions. In Studies in Computational Intelligence* (Vol. 688, pp. 581–611). Springer-Verlag.

Ouannas, A., Azar, A. T., Ziar, T., & Vaidyanathan, S. (2017c). *A New Method To Synchronize Fractional Chaotic Systems With Different Dimensions. Studies in Computational Intelligence* (Vol. 688). Springer-Verlag.

Oustaloup, A., Sabatier, J., Lanusse, P., Malti, R., Melchior, P., Moreau, X., & Moze, M. (2008). An overview of the CRONE approach in system analysis, modeling and identification, observation and control. *Proc. of the 17th World Congress IFAC*, 14254–14265. 10.3182/20080706-5-KR-1001.02416

Outwater, M. L., Spitz, G., Lobb, J., Campbell, M., Sana, B., Pendyala, R., & Woodford, W. (2011). Characteristics of Premium Transit Services that Affect Mode Choice. *Transportation*, *38*(4), 605–623. doi:10.100711116-011-9334-0

Oyo, B. (2013, May). *A System Dynamics analysis of seed banking effectiveness for Empowerment of Small Holder Farmers.* Paper presented at the IST-Africa Conference, Nairobi, Kenya.

Oyo, B., Williams, D., & Barendsen, E. (2009). *Integrating Action Research and System Dynamics: Towards a Generic Process Design for Participative Modeling*. Paper presented at the 2009 Hawaii International Conference on System Sciences.

Oyo, B., & Kalema, B. M. (2016). A System Dynamics Model for Subsistence Farmers' Food Security Resilience in Sub-Saharan Africa. *International Journal of System Dynamics Applications*, *5*(1), 17–30. doi:10.4018/IJSDA.2016010102

Oyo, B., Kaye, M., & Nkalubo, N. (2014). Re-Conceptualisation of Agriculture Information System for Uganda. *Transaction on Electrical and Electronic Circuits and Systems*, *4*(2), 39–44.

Pai, N. S., Yau, H. T., & Kuo, C. L. (2010). Fuzzy logic combining controller design for chaos control of a rod-type plasma torch system. *Expert Systems with Applications*, *37*(12), 8278–8283. doi:10.1016/j.eswa.2010.05.057

Paithankar. T. G., & Bhide S. R. (2003). *Fundamentals of Power System Protection*. Prentice-Hall of India Private Limited.

Panel on Antiretroviral Guidelines for Adults and Adolescents. (2016). *Guidelines for the use of antiretroviral agents in HIV-1-infected adults and adolescents.* Department of Health and Human Services. Retrieved from http://www.aidsinfo.nih.gov/ContentFiles/AdultandAdolescentGL.pdf

Panigrahi, B. K., Ravikumar Pandi, V., & Das, S. (2008). Adaptive particle swarm optimization approach for static and dynamic economic load dispatch. *Energy Conversion and Management*, *49*(6), 1407–1415. doi:10.1016/j.enconman.2007.12.023

Pant, S., Corsini, C., Baker, C., Hsia, T.-Y., Pennati, G., & Vignon-Clementel, I. E. (2016). Data assimilation and modelling of patient-specific single-ventricle physiology with and without valve regurgitation. *Journal of Biomechanics*, *49*(11), 2162–2173. doi:10.1016/j.jbiomech.2015.11.030 PMID:26708918

Parnell, A. S., & Correa, A. (2017). Analyses of trends in prevalence of congenital heart defects and folic acid supplementation. *Journal of Thoracic Disease*, *9*(3), 495–500. doi:10.21037/jtd.2017.03.16 PMID:28449454

Patel, S., Stephan, K., Bajpai, M., Das, R., Domin, T. J., Fennell, E., ... King, H. J. (2004). Performance of generator protection during major system disturbances. *IEEE Transactions on Power Delivery*, *19*(4), 1650–1662. doi:10.1109/TPWRD.2003.820613

Paulley, N., Balcombe, R., Mackett, R., Titheridge, H., Preston, J. M., Wardman, M. R., ... White, P. (2006). The demand for public transport: The effects of fares, quality of service, income and car ownership. *Transport Policy*, *13*(4), 295–306. doi:10.1016/j.tranpol.2005.12.004

Pecora, L. M., & Carroll, T. L. (1990). Synchronization in chaotic systems. *Physical Review Letters*, *64*(8), 821–825. doi:10.1103/PhysRevLett.64.821 PMID:10042089

Pennati, G., Corsini, C., Hsia, T.-Y., & Migliavacca, F. (2013). Computational fluid dynamics models and congenital heart diseases. *Frontiers in Pediatrics*, *1*. doi:10.3389/fped.2013.00004 PMID:24432298

Perelson, A. S., & Nelson, P. W. (1999). Mathematical analysis of HIV-1 dynamics in vivo. *SIAM Review*, *41*(1), 3–44. doi:10.1137/S0036144598335107

Perelson, A. S., & Ribeiro, R. M. (2013). Modeling the within-host dynamics of HIV infection. *BMC Biology*, *11*(1), 96. doi:10.1186/1741-7007-11-96 PMID:24020860

Petukhov, D. S., & Telyshev, D. V. (2016). A Mathematical Model of the Cardiovascular System of Pediatric Patients with Congenital Heart Defect. *Biomedical Engineering*, *50*(4), 229–232. doi:10.100710527-016-9626-y

Pham, V. T., Vaidyanathan, S., Volos, C. K., Azar, A. T., Hoang, T. M., & Yem, V. V. (2017a). A Three-Dimensional No-equilibrium chaotic system: Analysis, synchronization and its fractional order form. Studies in Computational Intelligence, 688, 449-470.

Pham, V. T., Vaidyanathan, S., Volos, C. K., Azar, A. T., Hoang, T. M., & Yem, V. V. (2017a). A Three-Dimensional No-Equilibrium Chaotic System: Analysis, Synchronization and Its Fractional Order Form. Studies in Computational Intelligence, 688, 449-470.

Pham, V. T., Vaidyanathan, S., Volos, C., Wang, X., & Hoang, D. V. (2017). A hyperjerk memristive system with hidden attractors. *Studies in Computational Intelligence*, *701*, 59–80.

Pham, V.-T., Vaidyanathan, S., Volos, C. K., Azar, A. T., Hoang, T. M., & Van Yem, V. (2017). *A Three-Dimensional No-equilibrium chaotic system: Analysis, synchronization and its fractional order form. In Studies in Computational Intelligence* (Vol. 688, pp. 449–470). Springer-Verlag.

Pham, V., Trillion, Q., Zheng, Z. Y., Fei, L., & Viet-dung, D. (2016). A DTC Stator Flux Algorithm for the Performance Improvement of Induction Traction Motors. *Journal of Power Electronics*, *16*(2), 572–583. doi:10.6113/JPE.2016.16.2.572

Pironet, A., Dauby, P. C., Chase, J. G., Docherty, P. D., Revie, J. A., & Desaive, T. (2016). Structural identifiability analysis of a cardiovascular system model. *Medical Engineering & Physics*, *38*(5), 433–441. doi:10.1016/j.medengphy.2016.02.005 PMID:26970891

Pokharel, S. (2005). Perception on information and communication technology perspectives in logistics. *Journal of Enterprise Information Management*, *18*(2), 136–149. doi:10.1108/17410390510579882

Porn, R., Bjork, K., & Westerlund, T. (2008). Global solution of optimization problems with signomial parts. *Discrete Optimization*, *5*(1), 108–120. doi:10.1016/j.disopt.2007.11.005

Potapov, A., & Ali, M. K. (2000). Robust chaos in neural networks. *Physics Letters. [Part A]*, *277*(6), 310–322. doi:10.1016/S0375-9601(00)00726-X

Potter, L., Arikatla, S., Bray, A., Webb, J., & Enquobahrie, A. (2017). *Physiology informed virtual surgical planning: A case study with a virtual airway surgical planner and BioGears* (Vol. 10135, p. 101351T-101351T-10). 10.1117/12.2252510

Poultangari, I., Shahnazi, R., & Sheikhan, M. (2012). RBF neural network based PI pitch controller for a class of 5-MW wind turbines using particle swarm optimization algorithm. *ISA Transactions*, *51*(5), 641–648. doi:10.1016/j.isatra.2012.06.001 PMID:22738782

Prasanna, K. R., & Hemalatha, M. (2012). RFID GPS and GSM based logistics vehicle load balancing and tracking mechanism. *Procedia Engineering*, *30*, 726–729. doi:10.1016/j.proeng.2012.01.920

Pruyt, E. (2016). Integrating Systems Modelling and Data Science: The Joint Future of Simulation and 'Big Data' Science. *International Journal of System Dynamics Applications*, *5*(1), 1–16. doi:10.4018/IJSDA.2016010101

Przystalka, P., & Moczulski, W. (2015). Methodology of neural modelling in fault detection with the use of chaos engineering. *Engineering Applications of Artificial Intelligence*, *41*, 25–40. doi:10.1016/j.engappai.2015.01.016

PSCAD/EMTDC User's Manual. (2003). Manitoba HVDC Research Centre.

Puhan, M. A., Van Natta, M. L., Palella, F. J., Addessi, A., & Meinert, C.. (2010). Excess mortality in patients with AIDS in the era of highly active antiretroviral therapy: Temporal changes and risk factors. *Clinical Infectious Diseases*, *51*(8), 947–956. doi:10.1086/656415 PMID:20825306

PwC. (2013). *Leveraging IT Transforming the T&L sector*. Retrieved on May 1, 2015 from, http://www.pwc.in/en_IN/in/assets/pdfs/publications/2013/it-print.pdf

Pyragas, K. (1996). Weak and strong synchronization of chaos. *Physical Review E: Statistical Physics, Plasmas, Fluids, and Related Interdisciplinary Topics*, *54*(5), R4508–R4511. doi:10.1103/PhysRevE.54.R4508 PMID:9965792

Quarteroni, A., Lassila, T., Rossi, S., & Ruiz-Baier, R. (2017). Integrated Heart—Coupling multiscale and multiphysics models for the simulation of the cardiac function. *Computer Methods in Applied Mechanics and Engineering*, *314*, 345–407. doi:10.1016/j.cma.2016.05.031

Quarteroni, A., Veneziani, A., & Vergara, C. (2016). Geometric multiscale modeling of the cardiovascular system, between theory and practice. *Computer Methods in Applied Mechanics and Engineering*, *302*, 193–252. doi:10.1016/j.cma.2016.01.007

Radisavljevic-Gajic, V. (2009). Optimal control of HIV-virus dynamics. *Annals of Biomedical Engineering*, *37*(6), 1251–1261. doi:10.100710439-009-9672-7 PMID:19294513

Rahmati, A., Arasteh, M., Farhangi, S., & Abrishamifar, A. (2011). Flying Capacitor DTC Drive with Reductions in Common Mode Voltage and Stator Overvoltage. *Journal of Power Electronics*, *11*(4), 512–519. doi:10.6113/JPE.2011.11.4.512

Rajagopal, K., Vaidyanathan, S., Karthikeyan, A., & Duraisamy, P. (2017). Dynamic analysis and chaos suppression in a fractional order brushless DC motor. *Electrical Engineering*, *99*(2), 721–733. doi:10.100700202-016-0444-8

Rajasekaran, V., Aranda, J., & Casals, A. (2014). Recovering planned trajectories in robotic rehabilitation therapies under the effect of disturbances. *International Journal of System Dynamics Applications*, *3*(2), 34–49. doi:10.4018/ijsda.2014040103

Raj, B., & Vaidyanathan, S. (2017). Analysis of dynamic linear memristor device models. *Studies in Computational Intelligence*, *701*, 449–476.

Rajkumar, R. K., Ramachandaramurthy, V. K., Yong, B. L., & Chia, D. B. (2011). Techno-economical optimization of hybrid pv/wind/battery system using Neuro-Fuzzy. *Energy*, *8*(36), 5148–5153. doi:10.1016/j.energy.2011.06.017

Rakesh, P. (2003). *AC Induction Motor Fundamentals*. Microchip Technology Inc, AN887, DS00887A, 1-24.

RamaSudha, K., Vakula, V.S., & Shanthi, R.V. (2010). PSO Based Design of Robust Controller for Two Area Load Frequency Control with Nonlinearities. *International Journal of Engineering Science*, *2*(5), 1311–1324.

Ramesh, T., Panda, A. K., & Kumar, S. S. (2015). MRAS speed estimator based on type-1 and type-2 fuzzy logic controller for the speed sensorless DTFC-SVPWM of an induction motor drive. *Journal of Power Electronics*, *15*(3), 730–740. doi:10.6113/JPE.2015.15.3.730

Ramezankhani, A., & Najafiyazdi, M. (2008). A System Dynamics Approach on Post-Disaster Management: A Case Study of Bam Earthquake, December 2003. *Proceedings of the 26th International Conference of the System Dynamics Society*.

Ramli, M. A. M., Twaha, S., Ishaque, K., & Al-Turki, Y. A. (2017). A review on maximum power point tracking for photovoltaic systems with and without shading conditions. *Renewable & Sustainable Energy Reviews*, *67*, 144–159. doi:10.1016/j.rser.2016.09.013

Rao & Alapati. (2012). Tricuspid Atresia in the Neonate. *Neonatology Today*, *7*(5), 1–12.

Rao, K., Vaghela, D. J., & Gojiya, M. V. (2016, July). Implementation of SPWM technique for 3-Φ VSI using STM32F4 discovery board interfaced with MATLAB. In *Power Electronics, Intelligent Control and Energy Systems (ICPEICES), IEEE International Conference on* (pp. 1-5). IEEE.

Rasappan, S., & Vaidyanathan, S. (2012a). Global chaos synchronization of WINDMI and Coullet chaotic systems by backstepping control. *Far East Journal of Mathematical Sciences*, *67*(2), 265–287.

Rasappan, S., & Vaidyanathan, S. (2012b). Synchronization of hyperchaotic Liu system via backstepping control with recursive feedback. *Communications in Computer and Information Science*, *305*, 212–221. doi:10.1007/978-3-642-32112-2_26

Rasappan, S., & Vaidyanathan, S. (2012c). Hybrid synchronization of n-scroll Chua and Lur'e chaotic systems via backstepping control with novel feedback. *Archives of Control Sciences*, *22*(3), 343–365.

Rasappan, S., & Vaidyanathan, S. (2013). Hybrid synchronization of n-scroll Chua circuits using adaptive backstepping control design with recursive feedback. *Malaysian Journal of Mathematical Sciences*, *7*(2), 219–246.

Rasappan, S., & Vaidyanathan, S. (2014). Global chaos synchronization of WINDMI and Coullet chaotic systems using adaptive backstepping control design. *Kyungpook Mathematical Journal*, *54*(1), 293–320. doi:10.5666/KMJ.2014.54.2.293

Ravishankar, C., Gerstenberger, E., Sleeper, L. A., Atz, A. M., Affolter, J. T., Bradley, T. J., ... Newburger, J. W. (2016). Factors affecting Fontan length of stay: Results from the Single Ventricle Reconstruction trial. *The Journal of Thoracic and Cardiovascular Surgery*, *151*(3), 669–675.e1. doi:10.1016/j.jtcvs.2015.09.061 PMID:26519244

Razi, M. A., & Tarn, M. F. (2003). An applied model for improving inventory management in ERP systems. *Logistics Information Management*, *16*(2), 114–124. doi:10.1108/09576050310467250

Razminia, A., Majd, V. J., & Baleanu, D. (2011). Chaotic incommensurate fractional order Rössler system: Active control and synchronization. *Advances in Difference Equations*, *15*. doi:10.1186/1687-1847-2011-15

Reddy, M. (2012). Status of supply chain management in India. *International Journal of Emerging Technology and Advanced Engineering*, *2*(7), 429–432.

Reddy, T. B., Reddy, B. K., Amarnath, J., Rayudu, D. S., & Khan, M. H. (2006, April). Sensorless direct torque control of induction motor based on hybrid space vector pulsewidth modulation to reduce ripples and switching losses-A variable structure controller approach. In *Power India Conference*. IEEE.

Reeves, C. R., & Rowe, J. E. (2002). *Genetic algorithm Principles and perspective, A Guide to GA theory*. Kluwer Academic Publishers.

Reisi, A. R., Moradi, M. H., & Jamasb, S. (2013). Classification and comparison of maximum power point tracking techniques for photovoltaic system: A review. *Renewable & Sustainable Energy Reviews*, *19*, 433–443. doi:10.1016/j.rser.2012.11.052

RF Industries Inc. (2013). *Software Provides Mobility for Emergency Workers. Product Announcements*. Retrieved December 5, 2013 from http://www.radiomobile.com/product-IQMobileTablet.html

Rhea, R. (2004). A new class of oscillators. *IEEE Microwave Magazine*, *5*(2), 72–83. doi:10.1109/MMW.2004.1306839

Ringsberg, H. A., & Mirzabeiki, V. (2013). Effects on logistic operations from RFID-and EPCIS-enabled traceability. *British Food Journal*, *116*(1), 104–124. doi:10.1108/BFJ-03-2012-0055

Rivadeneira, P. S., & Moog, C. H. (2012). Impulsive control of single-input nonlinear systems with application to HIV dynamics. *Applied Mathematics and Computation*, *218*(17), 8462–8474. doi:10.1016/j.amc.2012.01.071

Rivadeneira, P. S., Moog, C. H., Stan, G. B., Brunet, C., Raffi, F., Ferr, V., ... Ernst, D. (2014). Mathematical Modeling of HIV Dynamics After Antiretroviral Therapy Initiation: A Review. *BioResearch Open Access*, *3*(5), 233–241. doi:10.1089/biores.2014.0024 PMID:25371860

Rodriguez, J., Pontt, J., Kouro, S., & Correa, P. (2003, June). Direct torque control with imposed switching frequency and torque ripple minimization in an 11-level cascaded inverter. In *Power Electronics Specialist Conference, 2003. PESC'03. 2003 IEEE 34th Annual* (Vol. 2, pp. 501-506). IEEE. 10.1109/PESC.2003.1218106

Rodriguez-Linan, M. C., & Heath, W. P. (2017). Backlash compensation for plants with saturating actuators. *Proceedings of the Institution of Mechanical Engineers. Part I, Journal of Systems and Control Engineering*, *231*(6), 471–480. doi:10.1177/0959651817692471

Romeral, L., Arias, A., Aldabas, E., & Jayne, M. G. (2003). Novel direct torque control (DTC) scheme with fuzzy adaptive torque-ripple reduction. *IEEE Transactions on Industrial Electronics*, *50*(3), 487–492. doi:10.1109/TIE.2003.812352

Rosenblum, M. G., Pikovsky, A. S., & Kurths, J. (1996). Phase synchronization of chaotic oscillators. *Physical Review Letters*, *76*(11), 1804–1807. doi:10.1103/PhysRevLett.76.1804 PMID:10060525

Rosenblum, M. G., Pikovsky, A. S., & Kurths, J. (1997). Phase synchronization in driven and coupled chaotic oscillators. *IEEE Transactions on circuits and Systems I. Fundamental Theory and Applications*, *44*(10), 874–881.

Rose, S. J. (2016). *The Growing Size and Incomes of the Upper Middle Class*. Washington, DC: Urban Institute.

Rössler, O. (1979). An equation for hyperchaos. *Physics Letters. [Part A], 71*(2-3), 155–157. doi:10.1016/0375-9601(79)90150-6

Runzi, L., Yinglan, W., & Shucheng, D. (2011). Combination synchronization of three classic chaotic systems using active backstepping design. *Chaos (Woodbury, N.Y.), 21*(4), 043114. doi:10.1063/1.3655366 PMID:22225351

Sachan, A., Sahay, B., & Sharma, D. (2005). Developing Indian grain supply chain cost model: A system dynamics approach. *International Journal of Productivity and Performance Management, 54*(3), 187–205. doi:10.1108/17410400510584901

Sack, K. L., Davies, N. H., Guccione, J. M., & Franz, T. (2016). Personalised computational cardiology: Patient-specific modelling in cardiac mechanics and biomaterial injection therapies for myocardial infarction. *Heart Failure Reviews, 21*(6), 815–826. doi:10.100710741-016-9528-9 PMID:26833320

Saeed, K. (1994). *Development Planning and Policy Design*. Avebury.

Saeed, K. (2004). Designing an Environmental Mitigation Banking Institution for Linking the Size of Economic Activity to Environmental Capacity. *Journal of Economic Issues, 38*(4), 909–937. doi:10.1080/00213624.2004.11506749

Sahay, B. S., Vrat, P., & Jain, P. K. (1996). Long term fertilizer demand, production and imports in India-A system dynamics approach. *System Dynamics: An International Journal of Policy Modelling, 8*(1&2), 19–45.

Sahay, S., & Mohan, R. (2003). Supply chain management practices in Indian industry. *International Journal of Physical Distribution and Management, 36*(9), 666–689. doi:10.1108/09600030610710845

Saidi, S., & Hammami, S. (2011). The role of transport and logistics to attract foreign direct investment in the developing countries. *Logistics (LOGISTIQUA) 4th International Conference on IEEE*, 484-489.

Sakamoto, T., Nagashima, M., Hiramatsu, T., Matsumura, G., Park, I.-S., & Yamazaki, K. (2016). Fontan circulation over 30 years. What should we learn from those patients? *Asian Cardiovascular & Thoracic Annals, 24*(8), 765–771. doi:10.1177/0218492316667771 PMID:27563102

Salami, A., Jadid, S., & Ramezani, N. (2006). The Effect of load frequency controller on load pickup during restoration. *Power and Energy Conference, PECon'06, IEEE International*, 225-228. 10.1109/PECON.2006.346651

Saldarriaga, M., Kopainsky, B., & Alessi, S. M. (2013, July). *Knowledge analysis in coupled social-ecological systems. What do stakeholders in sub Saharan Africa know about the dynamic complexity of climate change, agriculture and food security?* Paper presented at the 31st International Conference of the System Dynamics Society, Cambridge, MA.

Salem, A., Hassan, M. M., & Ammar, M. E. (2014). Tuning PID Controllers Using Artificial Intelligence Techniques Applied To DC-Motor and AVR System. *Asian Journal of Engineering and Technology, 2*(2).

Samantaray, A. K., & Pradhan, S. (2016). Dynamic Analysis of Steering Bogies. Handbook of Research on Emerging Innovations in Rail Transportation Engineering, 524 – 579. doi:10.4018/978-1-5225-0084-1.ch021

Samko, S. G., Klibas, A. A., & Marichev, O. I. (1993). *Fractional integrals and derivatives: theory and applications*. Gordan and Breach.

Sampath, S., & Vaidyanathan, S. (2016). Hybrid synchronization of identical chaotic systems via novel sliding control method with application to Sampath four-scroll chaotic system. *International Journal of Control Theory and Applications, 9*(1), 221–235.

Sandoval, R., Guzman, A., & Altuve, H. J. (2007, March). Dynamic simulations help improve generator protection. *Power Systems Conference: Advanced Metering, Protection, Control, Communication, and Distributed Resources, 2007. PSC 2007*, 16-38. 10.1109/PSAMP.2007.4740896

Sanila, C. M. (2012). Direct Torque Control of Induction Motor With Constant Switching Frequency. In *IEEE International Conference on Power Electronics, Drives and Energy Systems* (pp. 1-6). Bengaluru, India: IEEE. 10.1109/PEDES.2012.6484352

Sanjuan, S. (2010). Voltage Oriented Control of Three-Phase Boost PWM Converters Design, simulation and implementation of a 3-phase boost battery Charger. Chalmers University of Technologie.

Santos, G., Li, W. W., & Koh, W. T. (2004). Transport Policies in Singapore. *Research in Transportation Economics*, *9*(1), 209–235. doi:10.1016/S0739-8859(04)09009-2

Sarafian, G., & Kaplan, B.-Z. (1993). A New approach to the modeling of the dynamics of RF VCOs and Some of Its Practical Implications. *IEEE Transactions on Circuits and Systems–Fundamental Theory and Applications*, *40*(12), 895–901. doi:10.1109/81.269030

Sarasu, P., & Sundarapandian, V. (2011a). Active controller design for generalized projective synchronization of four-scroll chaotic systems. *International Journal of Systems Signal Control and Engineering Application*, *4*(2), 26–33.

Sarasu, P., & Sundarapandian, V. (2011b). The generalized projective synchronization of hyperchaotic Lorenz and hyperchaotic Qi systems. *International Journal of Soft Computing*, *6*(5), 216–223. doi:10.3923/ijscomp.2011.216.223

Sarasu, P., & Sundarapandian, V. (2012a). Adaptive controller design for the generalized projective synchronization of 4-scroll systems. *International Journal of Systems Signal Control and Engineering Application*, *5*(2), 21–30.

Sarasu, P., & Sundarapandian, V. (2012b). Generalized projective synchronization of two-scroll systems via adaptive control. *International Journal of Soft Computing*, *7*(4), 146–156. doi:10.3923/ijscomp.2012.146.156

Sarasu, P., & Sundarapandian, V. (2012c). Generalized projective synchronization of three-scroll chaotic systems via adaptive control. *European Journal of Scientific Research*, *72*(4), 504–522.

Saravanan, S., & Babu, R. (2016). Maximum power point tracking algorithms for photovoltaic system – A review. *Renewable & Sustainable Energy Reviews*, *57*, 192–204. doi:10.1016/j.rser.2015.12.105

Sastry, S. (2013). *Nonlinear systems: analysis, stability, and control* (Vol. 10). Springer Science Business Media.

Savitskie, K. (2007). Internal and external logistics information technologies: The performance impact in an international setting. *International Journal of Physical Distribution & Logistics Management*, *37*(6), 454–468. doi:10.1108/09600030710763378

Schary, P., & Coakley, J. (1991). Logistics Organization and the Information System. *International Journal of Logistics Management*, *2*(2), 22–29. doi:10.1108/09574099110804715

Schiavazzi, D. E., Kung, E. O., Marsden, A. L., Baker, C., Pennati, G., Hsia, T.-Y., ... Dorfman, A. L. (2015). Hemodynamic effects of left pulmonary artery stenosis after superior cavopulmonary connection: A patient-specific multiscale modeling study. *The Journal of Thoracic and Cardiovascular Surgery*, *149*(3), 689–696.e3. doi:10.1016/j.jtcvs.2014.12.040 PMID:25659189

Schniederjans, D., & Yadav, S. (2013). Successful ERP implementation: An integrative model. *Business Process Management Journal*, *19*(2), 364–398. doi:10.1108/14637151311308358

Schöbel, A., & Scholz, D. (2014). A solution algorithm for non-convex mixed integer optimization problems with only few continuous variables. *European Journal of Operational Research*, *232*(1), 266–275. doi:10.1016/j.ejor.2013.07.003

Seborg, D. E., Edgar, T. F., & Mellichamp, D. A. (1989). *Process Dynamics & Control*. New York: John Wiley and Sons.

Seo, J. H., Im, C. H., Heo, C. G., Kim, J. K., Jung, H. K., & Lee, C. G. (2006). Multimodal function optimization based on particle swarm optimization. *IEEE Transactions on Magnetics*, *42*(4), 1095–1098. doi:10.1109/TMAG.2006.871568

Serrano, F. E., & Flores, M. A. (2015). C++ Library for Fuzzy Type-2 Controller Design With Particle Swarm Optimization Tuning. IEEE CONCAPAN 2015, Tegucigalpa, Honduras.

Servet Kiran, M., Gunduz, M., & Kaan Baykan, O. (2012). A novel hybrid algorithm based on particle swarm and ant colony optimization for finding the global minimum. *Applied Mathematics and Computation*, *219*(1), 1515–1521. doi:10.1016/j.amc.2012.06.078

Sethi, J. (2013). *Supply Chain 2020*. Retrieved on June 1, 2015 from, https://www.mycii.in/KmResourceApplication/40789.FinalFlashDriveEdition12013.pdf

Seyedmahmoudian, M., Mekhilef, S., Rahmani, R., Yusof, R., & Asghar Shojaei, A. (2014). Maximum power point tracking of partial shaded photovoltaic array using an evolutionary algorithm: A particle swarm optimization technique. *Journal of Renewable and Sustainable Energy, 6*(2), 1-13.

Shabib, G., Abdel Gayed, M., & Rashwan, A. M. (2010). Optimal Tuning of PID Controller for AVR System using Modified Particle Swarm Optimization. *Proceedings of the 14th International Middle East Power Systems Conference (MEPCON'10).*

Shahin, M., Saied, E., Moustafa Hassan, M. A., Liang, A., & Bendary, F. (2014). Voltage Swell Mitigation Using Flexible AC Transmission Systems Based on Evolutionary Computing Methods. *International Journal of System Dynamics Applications*, *3*(3), 73–95. doi:10.4018/ijsda.2014070104

Shah, J., Best, M., Benmimoun, A., & Ayat, M. (2015). Autonomous Rear-end Collision Avoidance Using an Electric Power Steering System. Proc IMechE Part D. *Journal of Automobile Engineering*, *229*(12), 1638–1655. doi:10.1177/0954407014567517

Shahverdiev, E., Sivaprakasam, S., & Shore, K. (2002). Lag synchronization in time-delayed systems. *Physics Letters. [Part A]*, *292*(6), 320–324. doi:10.1016/S0375-9601(01)00824-6

Shaiek, Y. B., Smida, M., Sakly, A., & Mimouni, M. F. (2013). Comparison between conventional methods and GA approach for maximum power point tracking of shaded solar PV generators. *Solar Energy*, *90*, 107–122. doi:10.1016/j.solener.2013.01.005

Sharaf, A. M., & Lie, T. T. (1994). ANN based pattern classification of synchronous generator stability and loss of excitation. *IEEE Transactions on Energy Conversion*, *9*(4), 753–759. doi:10.1109/60.368331

Sharma, A., Shrimali, M., Prasad, A., Ramaswamy, R., & Feudel, U. (2011). Phase-flip transition in relay-coupled nonlinear oscillators. *Physical Review. E*, *84*(016226), 1–5. PMID:21867292

Shehata, A. M., Elaiw, A. M., & Elnahary, E. K. (2017). Effect of antibodies and latently infected cells on HIV dynamics with differential drug efficacy in cocirculating target cells. *Journal of Computational Analysis and Applications*, *22*(1).

Shereen, A. (2016). Classification of EEG Signals for Motor Imagery based on Mutual Information and Adaptive Neuro Fuzzy Inference System. *International Journal of System Dynamics Applications*, *5*(4), 64–82. doi:10.4018/IJSDA.2016100104

Shi, Z. (2010). *Investigation on generator loss of excitation protection in generator protection coordination*. Academic Press.

Shi, Z. P., Wang, J. P., Gajic, Z., Sao, C., & Ghandhari, M. (2012). The comparison and analysis for loss of excitation protection schemes in generator protection. *Developments in Power Systems Protection, 11th International Conference on IET*, 1-6. 10.1049/cp.2012.0071

Shimizu, S., Kawada, T., Une, D., Fukumitsu, M., Turner, M. J., Kamiya, A., ... Sugimachi, M. (2016). Partial cavopulmonary assist from the inferior vena cava to the pulmonary artery improves hemodynamics in failing Fontan circulation: A theoretical analysis. *The Journal of Physiological Sciences; JPS*, *66*(3), 249–255. doi:10.100712576-015-0422-3 PMID:26546008

Shin, S., Choi, C., Youm, J., Lee, T., & Won, C. (2012). Position Control of PMSM using Jerk-Limited Trajectory for Torque Ripple Reduction in Robot Applications. *IECON - 38th Annual Conference on IEEE Industrial Electronics Society*, 2400 – 2405. DOI: 10.1109/IECON.2012.6388868

Shinskey, F. G. (1988). *Process Control Systems: Application, Design and Adjustment*. New York: McGraw- Hill.

Shukla, M. K., & Sharma, B. B. (2017). Backstepping based stabilization and synchronization of a class of fractional order chaotic systems. *Chaos, Solitons, and Fractals*, *102*, 274–284. doi:10.1016/j.chaos.2017.05.015

Silva, E. I., & Erraz, D. A. (2006). An LQR Based MIMO PID Controller Synthesis Method for Unconstrained Lagrangian Mechanical Systems. *Proceedings of the 45th IEEE Conference on Decision & Control. Decision and Control*. 10.1109/CDC.2006.377348

Silva, E., Campos-Rebelo, R., Hirashima, T., Moutinbo, F., Malo, P., Costa, A., & Gomes, L. (2014). Communication support for Petri nets based distributed controllers. *Proceedings of the 2014 IEEE International Symposium on Industrial Electronics*, 1111-1116. 10.1109/ISIE.2014.6864769

Singh, S., Azar, A. T., Ouannas, A., Zhu, Q., Zhang, W., & Na, J. (2017). Sliding Mode Control Technique for Multi-switching Synchronization of Chaotic Systems. *9th International Conference on Modelling, Identification and Control (ICMIC 2017)*, Kunming, China.

Siramdasu, Y., & Taheri, S. (2016). Discrete tyre model application for evaluation of vehicle limit handling performance. *Vehicle System Dynamics*, *54*(11), 1554–1573. doi:10.1080/00423114.2016.1220594

Sivaprakasam, A., & Manigandan, T. (2013). Novel Switching Table for Direct Torque Controlled Permanent Magnet Synchronous Motors to Reduce Torque Ripple. *Journal of Power Electronics*, *13*(6), 939–954. doi:10.6113/JPE.2013.13.6.939

Si, W., Dong, X., & Yang, F. (2017). Adaptive neural prescribed performance control for a class of strict-feedback stochastic nonlinear systems with hysteresis input. *Neurocomputing*, *251*, 35–44. doi:10.1016/j.neucom.2017.04.017

Skogestad, S. (2003). Simple analytic rules for model reduction and PID controller tuning. *Journal of Process Control*, *13*(4), 291–309. doi:10.1016/S0959-1524(02)00062-8

Skogestad, S., & Postlethwaite, I. (2006). *Multivariable Feedback Control: Analysis and Design*. New York: John Wiley and Sons.

Softlink. (2009). *Adoption of IT in Indian Logistic Sector – 2009*. Retrieved on June 15, 2015 from http://www.softlink-global.com/resources/Expert%20Opinion/Adoption_of_IT_In_Logistics.aspx?Type=resources

Soliman, N. S., Said, L. A., Azar, A. T., Madian, A. H., Radwan, A. G., & Ouannas, A. (2017). *Fractional Controllable Multi-Scroll V-Shape Attractor with Parameters Effect*. The 6th International Conference on Modern Circuits and Systems Technologies (MOCAST), Thessaloniki, Greece.

Song, Z., Tian, Y., Chen, W., Zou, Z., & Chen, Z. (2016). Predictive duty cycle control of three-phase active-front-end rectifier. *IEEE Transactions on Power Electronics*, *31*(1), 698–710. doi:10.1109/TPEL.2015.2398872

Sood, P., Lipo, T., & Hansen, I. (1987, March). A versatile power converter for high frequency link systems. In Applied Power Electronics Conference and Exposition, 1987 IEEE (pp. 249-256). IEEE. doi:10.1109/APEC.1987.7067159

Soufyane Benyoucef, A., Chouder, A., Kara, K., & Silvestre, S. (2015). Artificial bee colony based algorithm for maximum power point tracking (MPPT) for PV systems operating under partial shaded conditions. *Applied Soft Computing*, *32*, 38–48.

Soundarrajan, A., & Sumathi, S. (2010). *Particle Swarm Optimization Based LFC and AVR of Autonomous Power Generating System*. IAENG International Journal of Computer Science.

Spichkova, M., & Hamilton, M. (2016). Dynamic Decision Making System for Public Transport Routes. *International Journal of System Dynamics Applications*, *5*(3), 47–70. doi:10.4018/IJSDA.2016070103

Srirattanawichaikul, W., Kumsuwan, Y., & Premrudeepreechacharn, S. (2010). Reduction of torque ripples in direct torque control for induction motor drives using decoupled amplitude and angle of stator flux control. *ECTI Trans. on Electrical Engineering, Electronics, and Communications*, *8*(2), 187–196.

Srivastav, S. K., & Chandra, S. (2013). *A road map for internal reforms and other actions required to enhance exports in logistic services from India*. Retrieved on June 10, 2015 from http://www.iimidr.ac.in/iimi/images/faculty/omqt/LogisticsServicesExportsIndia_ConceptPaper.pdf

Stardling, S. G., Meadows, M. L., & Beatty, S. (2000). Helping Drivers Out of Their Cars: Integrating Transport Policy and Social Psychology for Sustainable Change. *Transport Policy*, *7*(3), 207–215. doi:10.1016/S0967-070X(00)00026-3

Stave, K. A., & Kopainsky, B. (2014, July). *Dynamic thinking about food system vulnerabilities in highly developed countries: Issues and initial analytic structure for building resilience*. Paper presented at the 32nd International Conference of the System Dynamics Society, Delft, The Netherlands.

Stefansson, G., & Lumsden, K. (2009). Performance issues of Smart Transportation Management systems. *International Journal of Productivity and Performance Management*, *58*(1), 54–70.

Steg, L. (2005). Car Use: Lust and Must. Instrumental, Symbolic and Affective Motives for Car Use. *Transportation Research*, *39*(2), 147–162.

Steg, L., Vlek, C., & Slotegraaf, G. (2001). Instrumental-Reasoned and Symbolic-Affective Motives for using a Motor Car. *Transportation Research Part F: Traffic Psychology and Behaviour*, *4*(3), 151–169. doi:10.1016/S1369-8478(01)00020-1

Stephens, R. (2008). *The struggle for access to treatment for HIV/AIDS in India*. Socio Legal Information Cent.

Sterman, J. (2000). *Business Dynamics System Thinking and Modeling for a Complex World*. Boston, MA: Irwing McGraw-Hill.

Sterman, J. (2001). System Dynamics Modeling: Tools for Learning in a Complex World. *California Management Review Reprint Series*, *43*(4), 8–25. doi:10.2307/41166098

Sterman, J. D. (2000). *Business Dynamics: Systems Thinking and Modelling for a Complex World*. New York: Irwin McGraw-Hill.

Stoyanov, L. (2011). *Etude de différentes structures de systèmes hybrides à sources d'énergie renouvelables* (Doctoral dissertation). Université Pascal Paoli.

Strogatz, S. H. (1994). *Nonlinear Dynamics and Chaos: with Applications to Physics, Biology, Chemistry, and Engineering*. Perseus Books.

Stumper, O., & Penford, G. (2017). Catheter hemodynamic assessment of the univentricular circulation. *Annals of Pediatric Cardiology, 10*(2), 167–174. doi:10.4103/apc.APC_160_16 PMID:28566825

Sughimoto, K., Asakura, Y., Brizard, C. P., Liang, F., Fujiwara, T., Miyaji, K., & Liu, H. (2017). Impact of the location of the fenestration on Fontan circulation haemodynamics: A three-dimensional, computational model study. *Cardiology in the Young*, 1–6. doi:10.1017/S1047951117000099 PMID:28376950

Sugimoto, Y., & Sauer, C. (2005). Effectiveness Estimation Method for Advanced Driver Assistance System and Its Application to Collision Mitigation Brake System. *Proceeding 19th International Technology Conference, Enhanced Safety Vehicles*, 1-8.

Sundarapandian, V., & Sivaperumal, S. (2011). Sliding controller design of hybrid synchronization of four-wing chaotic systems. *International Journal of Soft Computing, 6*(5), 224–231. doi:10.3923/ijscomp.2011.224.231

Sun, H., Abdelwahab, A., & Onaral, B. (1984). Linear approximation of transfer function with a pole of fractional power. *IEEE Transactions on Automatic Control, 29*(5), 441–444. doi:10.1109/TAC.1984.1103551

Sun, J., Cui, G., Wang, Y., & Shen, Y. (2015). Combination complex synchronization of three chaotic complex systems. *Nonlinear Dynamics, 2*(79), 953–965. doi:10.100711071-014-1714-5

Suresh, R., & Sundarapandian, V. (2013). Global chaos synchronization of a family of n-scroll hyperchaotic Chua circuits using backstepping control with recursive feedback. *Far East Journal of Mathematical Sciences, 73*(1), 73–95.

Sushil. (1993). *System Dynamics A practical approach for managerial problems.* Wiley Easter Limited.

Suvire, G. O., & Mercado, P. E. (2012). Active power control of a flywheel energy storage system for wind energy applications. *IET Renewable Power Generation, 6*(1), 9–16. doi:10.1049/iet-rpg.2010.0155

Swidenbank, E., Brown, M. D., & Flynn, D. (1999). Self-Tuning Turbine Generator Control for Power Plant. *Mechatronics, 9*(5), 513–537. doi:10.1016/S0957-4158(99)00009-4

Sypsa, V., Psichogiou, M., Paraskevis, D., Nikolopoulos, G., Tsiara, C., Paraskeva, D., ... Donoghoe, M. (2017). Rapid decline in HIV incidence among persons who inject drugs during a fast-track combination prevention program after an HIV outbreak in Athens. *The Journal of Infectious Diseases, 215*(10), 1496–1505. PMID:28407106

Tabakhi, S., Moradi, P., & Akhlaghian, F. (2014). An unsupervised feature selection algorithm based on ant colony optimization. *Engineering Applications of Artificial Intelligence, 32*(1), 112–123. doi:10.1016/j.engappai.2014.03.007

Taher, M., & Abdeljawad, M. (2013). A new modular strategy for action sequence automation using neural networks and hidden Markov models. *International Journal of System Dynamics Applications, 2*(3), 18–35. doi:10.4018/ijsda.2013070102

Taib, N., Rekioua, T., & François, B. (2010). *An improved fixed switching frequency direct torque control of induction motor drives fed by direct matrix converter.* arXiv preprint arXiv:1004.1745.

Takahashi, I., & Noguchi, T. (1986). A new quick-response and high-efficiency control strategy of an induction motor. *IEEE Transactions on Industry Applications, 22*(5), 820–827. doi:10.1109/TIA.1986.4504799

Talaminos, A., Roa, L. M., Álvarez, A., & Reina, J. (2014). Computational Hemodynamic Modeling of the Cardiovascular System. *International Journal of System Dynamics Applications, 3*(2), 81–98. doi:10.4018/ijsda.2014040106

Tamás, T. (2015). The joy of transient chaos. *Chaos, 25*(2015). doi: 1728710.1063/1.49

Tambay, S. R., & Paithankar, Y. G. (2005, June). A new adaptive loss of excitation relay augmented by rate of change of reactance. *Power Engineering Society General Meeting*, 1831-1835. 10.1109/PES.2005.1489421

Tammam, M. A. (2011). *Multi objective genetic algorithm controllers Tuning for load frequency control in Electric power systems* (M. Sc. Thesis). Faculty of Engineering at Cairo University, Cairo, Egypt.

Tamura, M., Inoue, H., Watanabe, T., & Maruko, N. (2001). *Research on a Brake Assist System with a Preview Function*. SAE International, Warrendale, PA, SAE Technical Paper No. 2001-01-0357.

Tang, Y., & Fang, J.-A. (2010). Synchronization of n-coupled fractional order chaotic systems with ring connection. *Commun. Nonlinear Sci.*, *15*(2), 401–412. doi:10.1016/j.cnsns.2009.03.024

Tao, G., & Kokotovic, P. V. (1993a). Adaptive Control of Systems with Backlash. *Automatic*, *29*(2), 323–335. doi:10.1016/0005-1098(93)90126-E

Tao, G., & Kokotovic, P. V. (1993b). Continuous-time Adaptive Control of Systems with Unknown Backlash. In *Proceedings of the American Control Conference*. IEEE.

Tao, G., & Kokotovik, P. (1995). Adaptive Control of Systems with Unknown Output Backlash. *IEEE Transactions on Automatic Control*, *40*(2), 326–330. doi:10.1109/9.341803

Tavazoei, M. S., & Haeri, M. (2007). Unreliability of frequency-domain approximation in recognizing chaos in fractional-order systems. *IET Signal Processing*, *1*(4), 171–181. doi:10.1049/iet-spr:20070053

Tavazoei, M. S., & Haeri, M. (2008). Limitations of frequency domain approximation for detecting chaos in fractional order systems. *Nonlinear Analysis*, *69*(4), 1299–1320. doi:10.1016/j.na.2007.06.030

Texas Instruments Europe. (1997). *Sensorless Control with Kalman Filter on TMS320 Fixed-Point DSP.* TI. Literature no. BPRA057.

Thakker, R., Eveleigh, T., Holzer, T., & Sarkani, S. (2013). A System Dynamics Approach to Quantitatively Analyze the Effects of Mobile Broadband Ecosystem's Variables on Demands and Allocation of Wireless Spectrum for the Cellular Industry. *International Journal of System Dynamics Applications*, *2*(3), 73–93. doi:10.4018/ijsda.2013070105

Thompson, W., & Hicky, J. (2005). *Society in Focus*. Boston: Pearson, Allyn & Bacon.

Thornton, P.K., Jones, P.G., Ericksen, P.J., & Challinor, A.J. (2011). Agriculture and food systems in sub-Saharan Africa in a 40C+ world. *Phil. Trans. R. Soc. A*, *369*(1934), 117–136. doi:10.1098/rsta.2010.0246

Thornton, P. K., Ericksen, P. J., Herrero, M., & Challinor, A. J. (2014). Climate variability and vulnerability to climate change: A review. *Global Change Biology*, *20*(11), 3313–3328. doi:10.1111/gcb.12581 PMID:24668802

Tierno, J. E., Kim, K. Y., Lacy, S. L., & Bernstein, D. S. (2000). Describing Function Analysis of an Anti-Backlash Controller. *Proceedings of the American Control Conference*. 10.1109/ACC.2000.877005

Tittonell, P. (2014). Livelihood strategies, resilience and transformability in African agroecosystems. *Agricultural Systems*, *126*, 3–14. doi:10.1016/j.agsy.2013.10.010

Toh, K., Nagel, P., & Oakden, R. (2009). A business and ICT architecture for a logistics city. *International Journal of Production Economics*, *122*(1), 216–228. doi:10.1016/j.ijpe.2009.05.021

Tolba, M. F., AbdelAty, A. M., Soliman, N. S., Said, L. A., Madian, A. H., Azar, A. T., & Radwan, A. G. (2017). FPGA implementation of two fractional order chaotic systems. *International Journal of Electronics and Communications*, *28*, 162–172. doi:10.1016/j.aeue.2017.04.028

Toledo, C. F. M., Oliveira, L., & França, P. M. (2014). Global optimization using a genetic algorithm with hierarchically structured population. *Journal of Computational and Applied Mathematics*, *261*, 341–351. doi:10.1016/j.cam.2013.11.008

Tomohiro, N., Shinji, D., & Masami, F. (2014). Position Sensorless control of PMSM with a low-frequency signal injection. *International Power Electronics Conference (IPEC-Hiroshima - ECCE ASIA)*, 3079 – 3084. DOI: 10.1109/IPEC.2014.6870124

Tong, X. J., Zhang, M., Wang, Z., Liu, Y., & Ma, J. (2015). An image encryption scheme based on a new hyperchaotic finance system. *Optik (Stuttgart)*, *126*(20), 2445–2452. doi:10.1016/j.ijleo.2015.06.018

TRL. (1995). *Real Crash Test Data*. Retrieved from http://www.trl.co.uk

Trusty, P. M., Restrepo, M., Kanter, K. R., Yoganathan, A. P., Fogel, M. A., & Slesnick, T. C. (2016). A pulsatile hemodynamic evaluation of the commercially available bifurcated Y-graft Fontan modification and comparison with the lateral tunnel and extracardiac conduits. *The Journal of Thoracic and Cardiovascular Surgery*, *151*(6), 1529–1536. doi:10.1016/j.jtcvs.2016.03.019 PMID:27056758

Tsai, J. (2009). Treating free variables in generalized geometric programming problems. *Computers & Chemical Engineering*, *33*(1), 239–243. doi:10.1016/j.compchemeng.2008.08.011

Tsai, J., Lin, M., & Hu, Y. (2007). On generalized geometric programming problems with non positive variables. *European Journal of Operational Research*, *178*(1), 10–19. doi:10.1016/j.ejor.2005.11.037

Tsang, M. A., Schneider, J. A., Sypsa, V., Schumm, P., Nikolopoulos, G. K., Paraskevis, D., ... Hatzakis, A. (2015). Network Characteristics of People Who Inject Drugs Within a New HIV Epidemic Following Austerity in Athens, Greece. *JAIDS Journal of Acquired Immune Deficiency Syndromes*, *69*(4), 499–508. doi:10.1097/QAI.0000000000000665 PMID:26115439

Tseng, M., Wu, K., & Nguyen, T. (2011). Information technology in supply chain management: A case study. *Procedia: Social and Behavioral Sciences*, *25*, 257–272. doi:10.1016/j.sbspro.2011.10.546

Tsolakis, N., & Srai, J. S. (2017). *A System Dynamics Approach to Food Security through Smallholder Farming in the UK*. Academic Press.

Tyagi, M., Fteropoulli, T., Hurt, C. S., Hirani, S. P., Rixon, L., Davies, A., ... Newman, S. P. (2016). Cognitive dysfunction in adult CHD with different structural complexity. *Cardiology in the Young*, 1–9. doi:10.1017/S1047951116001396 PMID:27751192

Ucar, A., Lonngren, K. E., & Bai, E.-W. (2008). Multi-switching synchronization of chaotic systems with active controllers. *Chaos, Solitons, and Fractals*, *38*(1), 254–262. doi:10.1016/j.chaos.2006.11.041

Uddin, M., Mekhilef, S., Mubin, M., Rivera, M., & Rodriguez, J. (2014). Model predictive torque ripple reduction with weighting factor optimization fed by an indirect matrix converter. *Electric Power Components and Systems*, *42*(10), 1059–1069. doi:10.1080/15325008.2014.913739

Uddin, M., Mekhilef, S., Rivera, M., & Rodriguez, J. (2015). Imposed weighting factor optimization method for torque ripple reduction of IM fed by indirect matrix converter with predictive control algorithm. *Journal of Electrical Engineering & Technology*, *10*(1), 227–242. doi:10.5370/JEET.2015.10.1.227

Usta, Ö., Musa, M. H., Bayrak, M., & Redfern, M. A. (2007). A new relaying algorithm to detect loss of excitation of synchronous generators. *Turkish Journal of Electrical Engineering and Computer Sciences*, *15*(3), 339–349.

Utsumi, Y., Hoshi, N., & Oguchi, K. (2006). Comparison of FPGA-based Direct Torque Controllers for Permanent Magnet Synchronous Motors. *Journal of Power Electronics*, *6*(2), 114–120.

Vaidyanathan, S., & Azar, A. T. (2015a) Anti-Synchronization of Identical Chaotic Systems using Sliding Mode Control and an Application to Vaidyanathan-Madhavan Chaotic Systems. In Advances and Applications in Sliding Mode Control systems (vol. 576, pp. 527-547). Springer-Verlag GmbH Berlin/Heidelberg. doi:10.1007/978-3-319-11173-5_19

Vaidyanathan, S., & Azar, A. T. (2015b). Hybrid Synchronization of Identical Chaotic Systems using Sliding Mode Control and an Application to Vaidyanathan Chaotic Systems. In Advances and Applications in Sliding Mode Control systems (vol. 576, pp. 549-569). Springer-Verlag GmbH Berlin/Heidelberg. doi:10.1007/978-3-319-11173-5_20

Vaidyanathan, S., & Azar, A. T. (2015c). Analysis, Control and Synchronization of a Nine-Term 3-D Novel Chaotic System. In Chaos Modeling and Control Systems Design (vol. 581, pp. 3-17). Springer-Verlag GmbH Berlin/Heidelberg. DOI doi:10.1007/978-3-319-13132-0_1

Vaidyanathan, S., & Azar, A. T. (2015d). Analysis and Control of a 4-D Novel Hyperchaotic System. In Chaos Modeling and Control Systems Design (vol. 581, pp. 19-38). Springer-Verlag GmbH Berlin/Heidelberg. DOI doi:10.1007/978-3-319-13132-0_2

Vaidyanathan, S., Idowu, B. A., & Azar, A. T. (2015c). Backstepping Controller Design for the Global Chaos Synchronization of Sprott's Jerk Systems. In Chaos Modeling and Control Systems Design (vol. 581, pp. 39-58). Springer-Verlag GmbH Berlin/Heidelberg. doi:10.1007/978-3-319-13132-0_3

Vaidyanathan, S. (2011). Hybrid chaos synchronization of Liu and Lü systems by active nonlinear control. *Communications in Computer and Information Science*, *204*, 1–10. doi:10.1007/978-3-642-24043-0_1

Vaidyanathan, S. (2011b). Output regulation of Arneodo-Coullet chaotic system. *Communications in Computer and Information Science*, *133*, 98–107. doi:10.1007/978-3-642-17881-8_10

Vaidyanathan, S. (2011c). Output regulation of the unified chaotic system. *Communications in Computer and Information Science*, *198*, 1–9. doi:10.1007/978-3-642-22555-0_1

Vaidyanathan, S. (2012). Adaptive controller and synchronizer design for the Qi-Chen chaotic system. *Lecture Notes of the Institute for Computer Sciences. Social-Informatics and Telecommunications Engineering*, *85*, 124–133.

Vaidyanathan, S. (2012a). Global chaos control of hyperchaotic Liu system via sliding control method. *International Journal of Control Theory and Applications*, *5*(2), 117–123.

Vaidyanathan, S. (2012b). Sliding mode control based global chaos control of Liu-Liu-Liu-Su chaotic system. *International Journal of Control Theory and Applications*, *5*(1), 15–20.

Vaidyanathan, S. (2012c). Output regulation of the Liu chaotic system. *Applied Mechanics and Materials*, *110*, 3982–3989.

Vaidyanathan, S. (2015a). A novel chemical chaotic reactor system and its adaptive control. *International Journal of Chemtech Research*, *8*(7), 146–158.

Vaidyanathan, S. (2015a). Adaptive synchronization of novel 3-D chemical chaotic reactor systems. *International Journal of Chemtech Research*, *8*(7), 159–171.

Vaidyanathan, S. (2015b). Adaptive control design for the anti-synchronization of novel 3-D chemical chaotic reactor systems. *International Journal of Chemtech Research*, *8*(11), 654–668.

Vaidyanathan, S. (2015b). Synchronization of 3-cells cellular neural network (CNN) attractors via adaptive control method. *International Journal of Pharm Tech Research*, *8*(5), 946–955.

Vaidyanathan, S. (2015c). Adaptive control of Rikitake two-disk dynamo system. *International Journal of Chemtech Research*, *8*(8), 121–133.

Vaidyanathan, S. (2015c). Chaos in neurons and synchronization of Birkhoff-Shaw strange chaotic attractors via adaptive control. *International Journal of Pharm Tech Research, 8*(6), 1–11.

Vaidyanathan, S. (2015d). Output regulation of the forced Van der Pol chaotic oscillator via adaptive control method. *International Journal of Pharm Tech Research, 8*(6), 106–116.

Vaidyanathan, S. (2015e). Adaptive control of the FitzHugh-Nagumo chaotic neuron model. *International Journal of Pharm Tech Research, 8*(6), 117–127.

Vaidyanathan, S. (2015e). Adaptive synchronization of Rikitake two-disk dynamo chaotic systems. *International Journal of Chemtech Research, 8*(8), 100–111.

Vaidyanathan, S. (2015f). Anti-synchronization of chemical chaotic reactors via adaptive control method. *International Journal of Chemtech Research, 8*(8), 73–85.

Vaidyanathan, S. (2015f). Global chaos synchronization of the forced Van der Pol chaotic oscillators via adaptive control method. *International Journal of Pharm Tech Research, 8*(6), 156–166.

Vaidyanathan, S. (2015g). Anti-synchronization of the FitzHugh-Nagumo chaotic neuron models via adaptive control method. *International Journal of Pharm Tech Research, 8*(7), 71–83.

Vaidyanathan, S. (2015h). Chaos in neurons and adaptive control of Birkhoff-Shaw strange chaotic attractor. *International Journal of Pharm Tech Research, 8*(5), 959–963.

Vaidyanathan, S. (2015i). Global chaos synchronization of Rucklidge chaotic systems for double convection via sliding mode control. *International Journal of Chemtech Research, 8*(8), 61–72.

Vaidyanathan, S. (2015j). Global chaos synchronization of the Lotka-Volterra biological systems with four competitive species via active control. *International Journal of Pharm Tech Research, 8*(6), 206–217.

Vaidyanathan, S. (2015k). Hybrid chaos synchronization of the FitzHugh-Nagumo chaotic neuron models via adaptive control method. *International Journal of Pharm Tech Research, 8*(8), 48–60.

Vaidyanathan, S. (2015l). Integral sliding mode control design for the global chaos synchronization of identical novel chemical chaotic reactor systems. *International Journal of Chemtech Research, 8*(11), 684–699.

Vaidyanathan, S. (2015n). Sliding controller design for the global chaos synchronization of enzymes-substrates systems. *International Journal of Chemtech Research, 8*(7), 89–99.

Vaidyanathan, S. (2015o). Sliding mode control of Rucklidge chaotic system for nonlinear double convection. *International Journal of Chemtech Research, 8*(8), 25–35.

Vaidyanathan, S. (2015p). State regulation of Rikitake two-disk dynamo chaotic system via adaptive control method. *International Journal of Chemtech Research, 8*(9), 374–386.

Vaidyanathan, S. (2015q). Synchronization of Tokamak systems with symmetric and magnetically confined plasma via adaptive control. *International Journal of Chemtech Research, 8*(6), 818–827.

Vaidyanathan, S. (2016a). A highly chaotic system with four quadratic nonlinearities, its analysis, control and synchronization via integral sliding mode control. *International Journal of Control Theory and Applications, 9*(1), 279–297.

Vaidyanathan, S. (2016a). Mathematical analysis, adaptive control and synchronization of a ten-term novel three-scroll chaotic system with four quadratic nonlinearities. *International Journal of Control Theory and Applications, 9*(1), 1–20.

Vaidyanathan, S. (2016b). A novel 3-D conservative chaotic system with a sinusoidal nonlinearity and its adaptive control. *International Journal of Control Theory and Applications*, *9*(1), 115–132.

Vaidyanathan, S. (2016b). An eleven-term novel 4-D hyperchaotic system with three quadratic nonlinearities, analysis, control and synchronization via adaptive control method. *International Journal of Control Theory and Applications*, *9*(1), 21–43.

Vaidyanathan, S. (2016c). A novel 3-D conservative chaotic system with a sinusoidal nonlinearity and its adaptive control. *International Journal of Control Theory and Applications*, *9*(1), 115–132.

Vaidyanathan, S. (2016c). A novel 3-D jerk chaotic system with three quadratic nonlinearities and its adaptive control. *Archives of Control Sciences*, *26*(1), 19–47. doi:10.1515/acsc-2016-0002

Vaidyanathan, S. (2016d). A novel 3-D jerk chaotic system with two quadratic nonlinearities and its adaptive backstepping control. *International Journal of Control Theory and Applications*, *9*(1), 199–216.

Vaidyanathan, S. (2016e). A novel hyperchaotic hyperjerk system with two nonlinearities, its analysis, adaptive control and synchronization via backstepping control method. *International Journal of Control Theory and Applications*, *9*(1), 257–278.

Vaidyanathan, S. (2016e). Analysis, adaptive control and synchronization of a novel 4-D hyperchaotic hyperjerk system via backstepping control method. *Archives of Control Sciences*, *26*(3), 311–338. doi:10.1515/acsc-2016-0018

Vaidyanathan, S. (2016f). A highly chaotic system with four quadratic nonlinearities and its adaptive backstepping control. *International Journal of Control Theory and Applications*, *9*(1), 279–297.

Vaidyanathan, S. (2016f). Hyperchaos, adaptive control and synchronization of a novel 4-D hyperchaotic system with two quadratic nonlinearities. *Archives of Control Sciences*, *26*(4), 471–495. doi:10.1515/acsc-2016-0026

Vaidyanathan, S. (2016g). Hybrid synchronization of the generalized Lotka-Volterra three-species biological systems via adaptive control. *International Journal of Pharm Tech Research*, *9*(1), 179–192.

Vaidyanathan, S. (2016h). Anti-synchronization of novel coupled Van der Pol conservative chaotic Systems via adaptive control method. *International Journal of Pharm Tech Research*, *9*(2), 106–123.

Vaidyanathan, S. (2016i). Anti-synchronization of enzymes-substrates biological systems via adaptive backstepping control. *International Journal of Pharm Tech Research*, *9*(2), 193–205.

Vaidyanathan, S. (2016j). Anti-synchronization of Duffing double-well chaotic oscillators via integral sliding mode control. *International Journal of Chemtech Research*, *9*(2), 297–304.

Vaidyanathan, S. (2016k). Global chaos regulation of a symmetric nonlinear gyro system via integral sliding mode control. *International Journal of Chemtech Research*, *9*(2), 462–469.

Vaidyanathan, S. (2016l). Anti-synchronization of 3-cells cellular neural network attractors via integral sliding mode control. *International Journal of Pharm Tech Research*, *9*(1), 193–205.

Vaidyanathan, S. (2016n). Global chaos control of the generalized Lotka-Volterra three-species system via integral sliding mode control. *International Journal of Pharm Tech Research*, *9*(4), 399–412.

Vaidyanathan, S. (2016o). Analysis, control and synchronization of a novel highly chaotic system with three quadratic nonlinearities. In *Advances and Applications in Nonlinear Control Systems* (pp. 211–234). Springer. doi:10.1007/978-3-319-30169-3_11

Vaidyanathan, S. (2017a). A conservative hyperchaotic hyperjerk system based on memristive device. *Studies in Computational Intelligence*, *701*, 393–423.

Vaidyanathan, S. (2017b). A memristor-based hyperchaotic system with hidden attractor and its sliding mode control. *Studies in Computational Intelligence*, *709*, 343–369.

Vaidyanathan, S. (2017c). A new 3-D jerk chaotic system with two cubic nonlinearities and its adaptive backstepping control. *Archives of Control Sciences*, *27*(3), 365–395. doi:10.1515/acsc-2017-0026

Vaidyanathan, S. (2017d). Adaptive integral sliding mode controller design for the control and synchronization of a novel jerk chaotic system. *Studies in Computational Intelligence*, *709*, 393–417.

Vaidyanathan, S. (2017e). Adaptive integral sliding mode controller design for the control and synchronization of a rod-type plasma torch chaotic system. *Studies in Computational Intelligence*, *709*, 263–287.

Vaidyanathan, S. (2017f). Complete synchronization of chaotic systems via novel second order sliding mode control with an application to a novel three-scroll chaotic system. *Studies in Computational Intelligence*, *709*, 193–212.

Vaidyanathan, S. (2017g). Global stabilization of nonlinear systems via novel second order sliding mode control with an application to a novel highly chaotic system. *Studies in Computational Intelligence*, *709*, 171–191.

Vaidyanathan, S. (2017h). Novel second order sliding mode control design for the anti-synchronization of chaotic systems with an application to a novel four-wing chaotic system. *Studies in Computational Intelligence*, *709*, 213–234.

Vaidyanathan, S. (2017i). Super-twisting sliding mode control and synchronization of Moore-Spiegel thermo-mechanical chaotic system. *Studies in Computational Intelligence*, *709*, 451–470.

Vaidyanathan, S. (2017j). Super-twisting sliding mode control of the enzymes-substrates biological chaotic system. *Studies in Computational Intelligence*, *709*, 435–450.

Vaidyanathan, S., & Azar, A. T. (2016). Takagi-Sugeno Fuzzy Logic Controller for Liu-Chen Four-Scroll Chaotic System. *International Journal of Intelligent Engineering Informatics*, *4*(2), 135–150. doi:10.1504/IJIEI.2016.076699

Vaidyanathan, S., & Azar, A. T. (2016a). *Adaptive Control and Synchronization of Halvorsen Circulant Chaotic Systems. In Advances in Chaos Theory and Intelligent Control. Studies in Fuzziness and Soft Computing* (Vol. 337, pp. 225–247). Springer-Verlag.

Vaidyanathan, S., & Azar, A. T. (2016b). *Dynamic Analysis, Adaptive Feedback Control and Synchronization of an Eight-Term 3-D Novel Chaotic System with Three Quadratic Nonlinearities. In Studies in Fuzziness and Soft Computing* (Vol. 337, pp. 155–178). Springer-Verlag.

Vaidyanathan, S., & Azar, A. T. (2016b). *Dynamic Analysis, Adaptive Feedback Control and Synchronization of an Eight-Term 3-D Novel Chaotic System with Three Quadratic Nonlinearities. Studies in Fuzziness and Soft Computing* (Vol. 337). Springer-Verlag.

Vaidyanathan, S., & Azar, A. T. (2016c). *Generalized Projective Synchronization of a Novel Hyperchaotic Four-Wing System via Adaptive Control Method. Advances in Chaos Theory and Intelligent Control. In Studies in Fuzziness and Soft Computing* (Vol. 337, pp. 275–296). Springer-Verlag.

Vaidyanathan, S., & Azar, A. T. (2016c). *Qualitative Study and Adaptive Control of a Novel 4-D Hyperchaotic System with Three Quadratic Nonlinearities. In Studies in Fuzziness and Soft Computing* (Vol. 337, pp. 179–202). Springer-Verlag.

Vaidyanathan, S., & Azar, A. T. (2016c). *Qualitative Study and Adaptive Control of a Novel 4-D Hyperchaotic System with Three Quadratic Nonlinearities. Studies in Fuzziness and Soft Computing* (Vol. 337). Springer-Verlag.

Vaidyanathan, S., & Azar, A. T. (2016d). *A Novel 4-D Four-Wing Chaotic System with Four Quadratic Nonlinearities and its Synchronization via Adaptive Control Method. Advances in Chaos Theory and Intelligent Control. In Studies in Fuzziness and Soft Computing* (Vol. 337, pp. 203–224). Springer-Verlag.

Vaidyanathan, S., & Azar, A. T. (2016d). *A Novel 4-D Four-Wing Chaotic System with Four Quadratic Nonlinearities and its Synchronization via Adaptive Control Method. Advances in Chaos Theory and Intelligent Control. Studies in Fuzziness and Soft Computing* (Vol. 337). Springer-Verlag.

Vaidyanathan, S., & Azar, A. T. (2016d). A novel 4-d four-wing chaotic system with four quadratic nonlinearities and its synchronization via adaptive control method. In *Advances in Chaos Theory and Intelligent Control* (pp. 203–224). Springer. doi:10.1007/978-3-319-30340-6_9

Vaidyanathan, S., & Azar, A. T. (2016d). *A Novel 4-D Four-Wing Chaotic System with Four Quadratic Nonlinearities and its Synchronization via Adaptive Control Method. In Advances in Chaos Theory and Intelligent Control* (Vol. 337). Springer-Verlag.

Vaidyanathan, S., & Azar, A. T. (2016e). *Adaptive Control and Synchronization of Halvorsen Circulant Chaotic Systems. Advances in Chaos Theory and Intelligent Control. In Studies in Fuzziness and Soft Computing* (Vol. 337, pp. 225–247). Springer-Verlag.

Vaidyanathan, S., & Azar, A. T. (2016e). *Adaptive Control and Synchronization of Halvorsen Circulant Chaotic Systems. Advances in Chaos Theory and Intelligent Control. Studies in Fuzziness and Soft Computing* (Vol. 337). Springer-Verlag.

Vaidyanathan, S., & Azar, A. T. (2016e). *Adaptive Control and Synchronization of Halvorsen Circulant Chaotic Systems. In Advances in Chaos Theory and Intelligent Control* (Vol. 337). Springer-Verlag.

Vaidyanathan, S., & Azar, A. T. (2016f). *Adaptive Backstepping Control and Synchronization of a Novel 3-D Jerk System with an Exponential Nonlinearity. Advances in Chaos Theory and Intelligent Control. Studies in Fuzziness and Soft Computing* (Vol. 337). Springer-Verlag.

Vaidyanathan, S., & Azar, A. T. (2016f). *Adaptive Backstepping Control and Synchronization of a Novel 3-D Jerk System with an Exponential Nonlinearity. In Advances in Chaos Theory and Intelligent Control* (Vol. 337, pp. 249–274). Springer-Verlag.

Vaidyanathan, S., & Azar, A. T. (2016g). *Generalized Projective Synchronization of a Novel Hyperchaotic Four-Wing System via Adaptive Control Method. Advances in Chaos Theory and Intelligent Control. Studies in Fuzziness and Soft Computing* (Vol. 337). Springer-Verlag.

Vaidyanathan, S., & Azar, A. T. (2016g). *Generalized Projective Synchronization of a Novel Hyperchaotic Four-Wing System via Adaptive Control Method. In Advances in Chaos Theory and Intelligent Control* (Vol. 337, pp. 275–296). Springer-Verlag.

Vaidyanathan, S., Azar, A. T., & Ouannas, A. (2017a). *An Eight-Term 3-D Novel Chaotic System with Three Quadratic Nonlinearities, its Adaptive Feedback Control and Synchronization. In Studies in Computational Intelligence* (Vol. 688, pp. 719–746). Springer-Verlag.

Vaidyanathan, S., Azar, A. T., & Ouannas, A. (2017a). *An Eight-Term 3-D Novel Chaotic System with Three Quadratic Nonlinearities, its Adaptive Feedback Control and Synchronization. Studies in Computational Intelligence* (Vol. 688). Springer-Verlag.

Vaidyanathan, S., Azar, A. T., & Ouannas, A. (2017c). *Hyperchaos and Adaptive Control of a Novel Hyperchaotic System with Two Quadratic Nonlinearities. In Studies in Computational Intelligence* (Vol. 688, pp. 773–803). Springer-Verlag.

Vaidyanathan, S., Azar, A. T., & Ouannas, A. (2017c). *Hyperchaos and Adaptive Control of a Novel Hyperchaotic System with Two Quadratic Nonlinearities. Studies in Computational Intelligence* (Vol. 688). Springer-Verlag.

Vaidyanathan, S., Azar, A. T., Rajagopal, K., & Alexander, P. (2015b). Design and SPICE implementation of a 12-term novel hyperchaotic system and its synchronization via active control (2015). International *Journal of Modelling, Identification and Control, 23*(3), 267–277. doi:10.1504/IJMIC.2015.069936

Vaidyanathan, S., & Boulkroune, A. (2016). A novel hyperchaotic system with two quadratic nonlinearities, its analysis and synchronization via integral sliding mode control. *International Journal of Control Theory and Applications, 9*(1), 321–337.

Vaidyanathan, S., & Idowu, B. A. (2016). Adaptive control and synchronization of Chlouverakis-Sprott hyperjerk system via backstepping control. *Studies in Computational Intelligence, 635*, 117–141.

Vaidyanathan, S., & Pakiriswamy, S. (2011). The design of active feedback controllers for the generalized projective synchronization of hyperchaotic Qi and hyperchaotic Lorenz systems. *Communications in Computer and Information Science, 245*, 231–238. doi:10.1007/978-3-642-27245-5_28

Vaidyanathan, S., & Pakiriswamy, S. (2013). Generalized projective synchronization of six-term Sundarapandian chaotic systems by adaptive control. *International Journal of Control Theory and Applications, 6*(2), 153–163.

Vaidyanathan, S., & Pakiriswamy, S. (2016). A five-term 3-D novel conservative chaotic system and its generalized projective synchronization via adaptive control method. *International Journal of Control Theory and Applications, 9*(1), 61–78.

Vaidyanathan, S., & Rajagopal, K. (2011). Hybrid synchronization of hyperchaotic Wang-Chen and hyperchaotic Lorenz systems by active non-linear control. *International Journal of Systems Signal Control and Engineering Application, 4*(3), 55–61.

Vaidyanathan, S., & Rajagopal, K. (2012). Global chaos synchronization of hyperchaotic Pang and hyperchaotic Wang systems via adaptive control. *International Journal of Soft Computing, 7*(1), 28–37. doi:10.3923/ijscomp.2012.28.37

Vaidyanathan, S., & Rajagopal, K. (2016a). Adaptive control, synchronization and LabVIEW implementation of Rucklidge chaotic system for nonlinear double convection. *International Journal of Control Theory and Applications, 9*(1), 175–197.

Vaidyanathan, S., & Rajagopal, K. (2016b). Analysis, control, synchronization and LabVIEW implementation of a seven-term novel chaotic system. *International Journal of Control Theory and Applications, 9*(1), 151–174.

Vaidyanathan, S., & Rajagopal, K. (2017). LabVIEW implementation of chaotic masking with adaptively synchronised forced Van der Pol oscillators and its application in real-time image encryption. *International Journal of Simulation and Process Modelling, 12*(2), 165–178. doi:10.1504/IJSPM.2017.083534

Vaidyanathan, S., Sambas, A., Mamat, M., & Sanjaya, W. S. M. (2017). Analysis, synchronisation and circuit implementation of a novel jerk chaotic system and its application for voice encryption. *International Journal of Modelling. Identification and Control, 28*(2), 153–166. doi:10.1504/IJMIC.2017.085934

Vaidyanathan, S., & Sampath, S. (2012). Anti-synchronization of four-wing chaotic systems via sliding mode control. *International Journal of Automation and Computing, 9*(3), 274–279. doi:10.100711633-012-0644-2

Vaidyanathan, S., Sampath, S., & Azar, A. T. (2015a). Global chaos synchronisation of identical chaotic systems via novel sliding mode control method and its application to Zhu system. International Journal of Modelling. *Identification and Control, 23*(1), 92–100. doi:10.1504/IJMIC.2015.067495

Vaidyanathan, S., & Volos, C. (2015). Analysis and adaptive control of a novel 3-D conservative no-equilibrium chaotic system. *Archives of Control Sciences, 25*(3), 333–353. doi:10.1515/acsc-2015-0022

Vaidyanathan, S., & Volos, C. (2016). *Advances and Applications in Nonlinear Control Systems*. Berlin, Germany: Springer. doi:10.1007/978-3-319-30169-3

Vaidyanathan, S., & Volos, C. (2017). *Advances in Memristors, Memristive Devices and Systems*. Berlin, Germany: Springer. doi:10.1007/978-3-319-51724-7

Vaidyanathan, S., Zhu, Q., & Azar, A. T. (2017b). *Adaptive Control of a Novel Nonlinear Double Convection Chaotic System. In Studies in Computational Intelligence* (Vol. 688, pp. 357–385). Springer-Verlag.

Vaidyanathan, S., Zhu, Q., & Azar, A. T. (2017b). *Adaptive Control of a Novel Nonlinear Double Convection Chaotic System. Studies in Computational Intelligence* (Vol. 688). Springer-Verlag.

Valdez, F., Melin, P., & Castillo, O. (2014). Modular Neural Networks architecture optimization with a new nature inspired method using a fuzzy combination of Particle Swarm Optimization and Genetic Algorithms. *Information Sciences*, *270*(20), 143–153. doi:10.1016/j.ins.2014.02.091

Van De Bruaene, A., Claessen, G., La Gerche, A., Kung, E., Marsden, A., De Meester, P., ... Gewillig, M. (2015). Effect of respiration on cardiac filling at rest and during exercise in Fontan patients: A clinical and computational modeling study. *IJC Heart & Vasculature*, *9*, 100–108. doi:10.1016/j.ijcha.2015.08.002 PMID:28785717

Vashisht, A., & Uppal, A. (2013). Case of Logistics and Information System (LIS) Vis a Vis Mc Donald's. *Scholars World-International Refereed Multidisciplinary Journal of Contemporary Research*, *1*(2), 127–132.

Vazquez, J., & Salmeron, P. (2003). Active power filter control using neural network technologies. *IEE Proceedings. Electric Power Applications*, *150*(2), 139–145. doi:10.1049/ip-epa:20030009

Vazquez, S., Leon, J. I., Franquelo, L. G., Rodriguez, J., Young, H., Marquez, A., & Zanchetta, P. (2014). Model predictive control: A review of its applications in power electronics. *IEEE Industrial Electronics Magazine*, *8*(1), 16–31. doi:10.1109/MIE.2013.2290138

Vazquez, S., Sanchez, J., Carrasco, J., Leon, J., & Galvan, E. (2008). A model-based direct power control for three-phase power converters. *IEEE Transactions on Industrial Electronics*, *55*(4), 1647–11657. doi:10.1109/TIE.2008.917113

Vechiu, I. (2005). *Modélisation et analyse de l'intégration des énergies renouvelables dans un réseau autonome* (Doctoral dissertation). Université du Havre.

Victoria, J. F., Afsar, H. M., & Prins, C. (2015). Vehicle Routing Problem with Time-Dependent Demand in humanitarian logistics. *International Conference on Industrial Engineering and Systems Management (IESM)*, 686-694.10.1109/IESM.2015.7380233

Vijay Kumar, V., Rao, V. S. R., & Chidambaram, M. (2012). Centralized PI controllers for interacting multivariable processes by synthesis method. *ISA Transactions*, *51*(3), 400–409. doi:10.1016/j.isatra.2012.02.001 PMID:22405751

Vittek, J., Bris, P., Štulrajter, M., Makyš, P., Comnac, V., & Cernat, M. (2008). Chattering free sliding mode control law for the drive employing PMSM position control. *International Conference on Optimization of Electrical and Electronic Equipment*, 115-120. 10.1109/OPTIM.2008.4602466

Vittek, J., Stulrajter, M., Makys, P., Vavrus, V., Dodds, J. S., & Perryman, R. (2005). Near-time-optimal position control of an actuator with PMSM. *European Conference on Power Electronics and Applications*, *21*(2), 1-10. DOI: 10.1109/EPE.2005.219516

Vlachogiannis, J. G., & Lee, K. Y. (2009). Economic load dispatch - A comparative study on heuristic optimization techniques with an improved coordinated aggregation based PSO. *Power Systems. IEEE Transactions on*, *24*(2), 991–1001.

Voyer, J., Dean, M., & Pickles, C. (2015). Understanding Humanitarian Supply Chain Logistics with System Dynamics Modeling. System Dynamics Society. *Proceedings of the 33rd International Conference of the System Dynamics Society*.

Walker, B. H., Anderies, J. M., Kinzig, A. P., & Ryan, P. (2006). Exploring resilience in social-ecological systems through comparative studies and theory development: Introduction to the special issue. *Ecology and Society*, *11*(1), 12. doi:10.5751/ES-01573-110112

Walker, B. H., Sayer, J., Andrew, N. L., & Campbell, B. (2010). Should enhanced resilience be an objective of natural resource management research for developing countries? *Crop Science*, *50*(Supplement_1), 10–19. doi:10.2135/cropsci2009.10.0565

Walters, J. P., Archer, D. W., Sassenrath, G. F., Hendrickson, J. R., Hanson, J. D., Halloran, J. M., ... Alarcon, V. J. (2016). Exploring agricultural production systems and their fundamental components with system dynamics modelling. *Ecological Modelling*, *333*, 51–65. doi:10.1016/j.ecolmodel.2016.04.015

Wang, S., Ma, Z., & Li, Z. (2008). A Dynamic Programming Model for Optimal Transportation of Emergency Relief Commodities in Natural Disasters. *American Society of Civil Engineers (ASCE)*, *211*(330), 1452-1457. DOI: 10.1061/40996(330)211

Wang, Y., Li, H., & Shi, X. (2006, November). Direct torque control with space vector modulation for induction motors fed by cascaded multilevel inverters. In *IEEE Industrial Electronics, IECON 2006-32nd Annual Conference on* (pp. 1575-1579). IEEE. 10.1109/IECON.2006.347240

Wang, Z., Volos, C., Kingni, S. T., Azar, A. T., & Pham, V. T. (2017). Four-wing attractors in a novel chaotic system with hyperbolic sine nonlinearity. *Optik - International Journal for Light and Electron Optics, 131*(2017), 1071-1078.

Wang, Z., Volos, C., Kingni, S. T., Azar, A. T., & Pham, V. T. (2017). Four-wing attractors in a novel chaotic system with hyperbolic sine nonlinearity. Optik - International Journal for Light and Electron Optics, 131(2017): 1071-1078.

Wang, Z., Volos, C., Kingni, S.T., Azar, A.T., & Pham, V.T. (2017). Four-wing attractors in a novel chaotic system with hyperbolic sine nonlinearity. *Optik - International Journal for Light and Electron Optics, 131*(2017), 1071-1078.

Wang, C., & Su, J. P. (2004). A new adaptive variable structure control for chaotic synchronization and secure communication. *Chaos, Solitons, and Fractals*, *20*(5), 967–977. doi:10.1016/j.chaos.2003.10.026

Wang, F., & Liu, C. (2007). Synchronization of unified chaotic system based on passive control. *Physica D. Nonlinear Phenomena*, *225*(1), 55–60. doi:10.1016/j.physd.2006.09.038

Wang, L., & Singh, C. (2009). Multicriteria design of hybrid power generation systems based on a modified particle swarm optimization algorithm. *IEEE Transactions on Energy Conversion*, *24*(1), 163–172. doi:10.1109/TEC.2008.2005280

Wang, Q. W. (2003). *Decoupling Control.* New York: Springer-Verlag.

Wang, W. (2002). *Principle and Application of Electric Power Equipment Protection. China Electric*. Power Press.

Wang, W., & Fan, Y. (2015). Synchronization of Arneodo chaotic system via backstepping fuzzy adaptive control. *Optik (Stuttgart)*, *126*(20), 2679–2683. doi:10.1016/j.ijleo.2015.06.071

Wang, Z., Volos, C., Kingni, S. T., Azar, A. T., & Pham, V.-T. (2017). Four-wing attractors in a novel chaotic system with hyperbolic sine nonlinearity. *Optik-International Journal for Light and Electron Optics*, *131*, 1071–1078. doi:10.1016/j.ijleo.2016.12.016

Wardman, M. (2004). Public Transport Values of Time. *Transport Policy*, *11*(4), 363–377. doi:10.1016/j.tranpol.2004.05.001

Warner, W. L., Meeker, M., & Eells, K. (1949). *Social Class in America: A Manual of Procedure for the Measurement of Social Status*. Chicago: Science Research Associates, Inc.

Watrous, R. L., & Chin, A. J. (2017). Model-Based Comparison of the Normal and Fontan Circulatory Systems—Part III: Major Differences in Performance With Respiration and Exercise. *World Journal for Pediatric & Congenital Heart Surgery*, *8*(2), 148–160. doi:10.1177/2150135116679831 PMID:28329460

Weber, M. (1947). *The Theory of Social and Economic Organization*. New York: Oxford University Press.

Weischedel, K., & McAvoy, T. J. (1980). Feasibility of decoupling in conventionally controlled distillation columns. *Industrial & Engineering Chemistry Fundamentals*, *19*(4), 379–384. doi:10.1021/i160076a010

Wigren, T. (2017). Loop-Shaping Feedback and Feedforward Control for Networked Systems With Saturation and Delay. *Asian Journal of Control*, *19*(4), 1329–1349. doi:10.1002/asjc.1442

Witte, C. L., & Witte, M. H. (1991). Chaos and predicting varix hemorrhage. *Medical Hypotheses*, *36*(4), 312–317. doi:10.1016/0306-9877(91)90002-G PMID:1809849

Witteman, W. J. (1999). *Improved Vehicle Crashworthiness Design by Control of the Energy Absorption for Different Collision Situations* (Ph.D. Thesis). Technische University.

Witteman, W. J., & Kriens, R. F. C. (1998). Modeling of an Innovative Frontal Car Structure: Similar Deceleration Curves at Full Overlap, 40 Percent Offset and 30 Degrees Collisions. *Proceedings of 16th International Technical Conference on the Enhanced Safety of Vehicles*, 194-212.

Wohlgemuth, S., Oloruntoba, R., & Clausen, U. (2012). Dynamic vehicle routing with anticipation in disaster relief. *Socio-Economic Planning Sciences*, *46*(4), 261–271. doi:10.1016/j.seps.2012.06.001

Wolf, A., Swift, J. B., Swinney, H. L., & Vastano, J. A. (1985). Determining Lyapunov exponents from a time series. *Physica D. Nonlinear Phenomena*, *16*(3), 285–317. doi:10.1016/0167-2789(85)90011-9

Wong, C. C., An Li, S., & Wang, H. (2009). Optimal PID Controller Design for AVR System. *Tamkang Journal of Science and Engineering*, *12*(3), 259–270.

Wong, K. K. L., Wang, D., Ko, J. K. L., Mazumdar, J., Le, T.-T., & Ghista, D. (2017). Computational medical imaging and hemodynamics framework for functional analysis and assessment of cardiovascular structures. *Biomedical Engineering Online*, *16*(1), 35. doi:10.118612938-017-0326-y PMID:28327144

World Health Organization. (2007). *WHO case definitions of HIV for surveillance and revised clinical staging and immunological classification of HIV-related disease in adults and children*. WHO.

Wu, H., Wang, L., Wang, Y., Niu, P., & Fang, B. (2016). Global Mittag-Leffler projective synchronization for fractional-order neural networks: An LMI-based approach. *Advances in Difference Equations*, *2016*(1), 132. doi:10.118613662-016-0857-8

Wu, N. Q., & Zhou, M. C. (2009). *System Modeling and Control with Resource-oriented Petri Nets*. New York: CRC Press.

Wu, X., Bai, C., & Kan, H. (2014). A new color image cryptosystem via hyperchaos synchronization. *Communications in Nonlinear Science and Numerical Simulation*, *19*(6), 1884–1897. doi:10.1016/j.cnsns.2013.10.025

Wu, Z., & Fu, X. (2013). Combination synchronization of three different order nonlinear systems using active backstepping design. *Nonlinear Dynamics*, *3*(73), 1863–1872. doi:10.100711071-013-0909-5

Xiangqiang, K. (2006). The Application of GIS/GPS in Logistics Distribution. *Value Engineering*, *11*, 31.

Xia, X. (2003). Estimation of HIV/AIDS parameters. *Automatica*, *39*(11), 1983–1988. doi:10.1016/S0005-1098(03)00220-6

Xia, X. (2007). Modelling of HIV infection: Vaccine readiness, drug effectiveness and therapeutical failures. *Journal of Process Control*, *17*(3), 253–260. doi:10.1016/j.jprocont.2006.10.007

Xia, X., & Moog, C. H. (2003). Identifiability of nonlinear systems with application to HIV/AIDS models. *IEEE Transactions on Automatic Control*, *48*(2), 330–336. doi:10.1109/TAC.2002.808494

Xu, R. (2009). *Loss of field protection and its impact on power system stability* (Doctoral dissertation). Washington State University.

Yang, C., & Su, Y. (2009). The relationship between benefits of ERP systems implementation and its impacts on firm performance of SCM. *Journal of Enterprise Information Management*, *22*(6), 722–752. doi:10.1108/17410390910999602

Yang, H., Zhou, W., Lu, L., & Fang, Z. (2008). Optimal sizing method for stand-alone hybrid solar–wind system with LPSP technology by using a genetic algorithm. *Solar Energy*, *82*(4), 354–367. doi:10.1016/j.solener.2007.08.005

Yang, J. H., & Saucerman, J. J. (2011). Computational Models Reduce Complexity and Accelerate Insight Into Cardiac Signaling Networks. *Circulation Research*, *108*(1), 85–97. doi:10.1161/CIRCRESAHA.110.223602 PMID:21212391

Yang, T., & Chua, L. O. (1997). Impulsive stabilization for control and synchronization of chaotic systems: Theory and application to secure communication. *IEEE Transactions on Circuits and Systems. I, Fundamental Theory and Applications*, *44*(10), 976–988. doi:10.1109/81.633887

Yang, T., Jian-an, F., & Qingying, M. (2009). On the exponential synchronization of stochastic jumping chaotic neural networks with mixed delays and sector-bounded non-linearities. *Neurocomputing*, *72*(7–9), 1694–1701.

Yang, X. S., & Yuan, Q. (2005). Chaos and transient chaos in simple Hopfield neural networks. *Neurocomputing*, *69*(1-3), 232–241. doi:10.1016/j.neucom.2005.06.005

Yasuda, G. (1971). *A Fundamental Study on Reproduction - Application of Graph Theory to Self-Reproducing Processes* (Master thesis). The University of Tokyo, Tokyo, Japan.

Yasuda, G. (2015). Distributed coordination architecture for cooperative task planning and execution of intelligent multi-Robot systems. In Handbook of Research on Advanced Intelligent Control Engineering and Automation (pp. 407-426). Hershey PA: IGI Global. doi:10.4018/978-1-4666-7248-2.ch015

Yasuda, G. (2016). Design and implementation of distributed autonomous coordinators for cooperative multi-robot systems. *International Journal of System Dynamics Applications*, *5*(4), 1–15. doi:10.4018/IJSDA.2016100101

Yau, H. T., & Shieh, C. S. (2008). Chaos synchronization using fuzzy logic controller. *Nonlinear Analysis Real World Applications*, *9*(4), 1800–1810. doi:10.1016/j.nonrwa.2007.05.009

Yoshida, H., Kawata, K., Fukuyama, Y., Takayama, S., & Nakanishi, Y. (2000). A particle swarm optimization for reactive power and voltage control considering voltage security assessment. *IEEE Transactions on Power Systems*, *15*(4), 1232–1239. doi:10.1109/59.898095

Youb, L., & Craciunescu, A. (2009). Direct torque control of induction motors with fuzzy minimization torque ripple. In *Proceedings of the world congress on engineering and computer science* (*Vol. 2*, pp. 713-717). Academic Press.

Yousry, A. (2009). Torque Ripple Minimization for Induction Motor Driven by a Photovoltaic Inverter. *Journal of Power Electronics*, *9*(5), 679–690.

Yuan, G., Zhang, X., & Wang, Z. (2013). Chaos generation in a semiconductor ring laser with an optical injection. *Optik (Stuttgart)*, *124*(22), 5715–5718. doi:10.1016/j.ijleo.2013.04.029

Yue, C., Butsuen, T., & Hedrick, J. K. (1988). Alternative Control Laws for Automotive Active Suspensions. *American Control Conference*, 2373-2378.

Yu, F., Feng, J. Z., & Li, J. (2002). A Fuzzy Logic Controller Design for Vehicle Abs with an On-Line Optimized Target Wheel Slip Ratio. *International Journal of Automotive Technology*, *3*(4), 165–170.

Yu, H., Cai, G., & Li, Y. (2012). Dynamic analysis and control of a new hyperchaotic finance system. *Nonlinear Dynamics*, *67*(3), 2171–2182. doi:10.100711071-011-0137-9

Yu, J., Hu, C., Jiang, H., & Fan, X. (2014). Projective synchronization for fractional neural networks. *Neural Networks*, *49*, 87–95. doi:10.1016/j.neunet.2013.10.002 PMID:24184824

Zaimeddine, R., & Undeland, T. (2010, June). DTC control schemes for induction motor fed by three-level NPC-VSI using space vector modulation. In *Power Electronics Electrical Drives Automation and Motion (SPEEDAM), 2010 International Symposium on* (pp. 966-971). IEEE. 10.1109/SPEEDAM.2010.5545036

Zegaoui, A., Aillerie, M., Petit, P., Sawicki, J. P., Charles, J. P., & Belarbi, A. W. (2011). Dynamic behaviour of PV generator trackers under irradiation and temperature changes. *Solar Energy*, *85*(11), 2953–2964. doi:10.1016/j.solener.2011.08.038

Zhang, Y., Yang, H., & Li, Z. (2013, October). A simple SVM-based deadbeat direct torque control of induction motor drives. In *Electrical Machines and Systems (ICEMS), 2013 International Conference on* (pp. 2201-2206). Academic Press.

Zhang, H., Lewis, F. L., & Das, A. (2011). Optimal design for synchronization of cooperative systems: State feedback, observer and output feedback. *IEEE Transactions on Automatic Control*, *56*(8), 1948–1952. doi:10.1109/TAC.2011.2139510

Zhang, H., Ma, X.-K., & Liu, W.-Z. (2004). Synchronization of chaotic systems with parametric uncertainty using active sliding mode control. *Chaos, Solitons, and Fractals*, *21*(5), 1249–1257. doi:10.1016/j.chaos.2003.12.073

Zhang, Y., Xie, W., Li, Z., & Zhang, Y. (2013). Model predictive direct power control of a PWM rectifier with duty cycle optimization. *IEEE Transactions on Power Electronics*, *28*(11), 5343–5351. doi:10.1109/TPEL.2013.2243846

Zhang, Y., Zhu, J., Guo, Y., Xu, W., Wang, Y., & Zhao, Z. (2009, September). A sensorless DTC strategy of induction motor fed by three-level inverter based on discrete space vector modulation. *In Power Engineering Conference, 2009. AUPEC 2009. Australasian Universities* (pp. 1-6). IEEE.

Zhan, Z. H., Zhang, J., Li, Y., & Chung, H. S. H. (2009). Adaptive particle swarm optimization. *IEEE Transactions on Systems, Man, and Cybernetics. Part B, Cybernetics*, *39*(6), 1362–1381. doi:10.1109/TSMCB.2009.2015956 PMID:19362911

Zhou, J., Er, M. J., & Wen, C. (2005). Adaptive Control of Nonlinear Systems with Uncertain Dead-zone Nonlinearity. *Proceedings of the 44th IEEE Conference on Decision and Control, and the European Control Conference*. DOI: 10.1109/CDC.2005.1582254

Zhou, S.-L., Han, P., Wang, D.-F., & Liu, Y.-Y. (2004). A Kind of Multivariable PID Design Method for Chaos System using H infinity loop shaping design procedure. *Proceedings of the Third International Conference on Machine Learning and Cybernetics. Machine Learning and Cybernetics*. DOI: 10.1109/ICMLC.2004.1382294

Zhou, Y., Xiao, K., Wang, Y., Liang, A., & Hassanien, A. E. (2013). A PSO-inspired multi-robot map exploration algorithm using frontier-based strategy. *International Journal of System Dynamics Applications*, *2*(2), 1–13. doi:10.4018/ijsda.2013040101

Zhu, C., & Ji, G. (2009). Emergency Logistics and the Distribution Model for Quick Response to Urgent Relief Demand. *Proceedings of the 6th International Conference on Service Systems and Service Management*. DOI: 10.1109/ICSSSM.2009.5174910

Zhu, Q., & Azar, A. T. (2015). *Complex system modelling and control through intelligent soft computations. In Studies in Fuzziness and Soft Computing* (Vol. 319). Springer-Verlag.

Zhu, Q., & Azar, A. T. (2015). *Complex System Modelling and Control through Intelligent Soft Computations. In Studies in Fuzziness and Soft Computing* (Vol. 319). Springer-Verlag.

Zhu, Q., & Azar, A. T. (2015). *Complex system modelling and control through intelligent soft computations. Studies in Fuzziness and Soft Computing* (Vol. 319). Springer-Verlag.

Zhuxiang, D., Tao, L., & Yu, W. (2016). *Adaptive synchronization of the fractional order chaotic system based on passive control. 2016 Chinese Control and Decision Conference (CCDC)*, Yinchuan, China. 10.1109/CCDC.2016.7531689

Zidani, F., & Said, R. N. (2005). Direct torque control of induction motor with fuzzy minimization torque ripple. *Journal of Electrical Engineering-Bratislava*, *56*(7/8), 183.

Zou, M., Wang, Y., Cui, H., Ma, L., Yang, S., Xia, Y., ... Chen, X. (2016). Outcomes of total cavopulmonary connection for single ventricle palliation. *Journal of Thoracic Disease*, *8*(1), 43–51. doi:10.3978/j.issn.2072-1439.2016.01.41 PMID:26904211

About the Contributors

Ahmad Taher Azar has received the M.Sc. degree (2006) in System Dynamics and Ph.D degree (2009) in Adaptive Neuro-Fuzzy Systems from Faculty of Engineering, Cairo University (Egypt). He is currently assistant professor, Faculty of computers and information, Benha University, Egypt. Dr. Azar is the Editor in Chief of International Journal of System Dynamics Applications (IJSDA) published by IGI Global, USA. Also, he is the Editor in Chief of International Journal of Intelligent Engineering Informatics (IJIEI), Inderscience Publishers, Olney, UK. Dr. Ahmad Azar has worked in the areas of Control Theory & Applications, Process Control, Chaos Control and Synchronization, Nonlinear control, Computational Intelligence and has authored/coauthored over 190 research publications in peer-reviewed reputed journals, book chapters and conference proceedings. He is an editor of many Books in the field of Fuzzy logic systems, modeling techniques, control systems, computational intelligence, Chaos modeling and Machine learning. Dr. Ahmad Azar is closely associated with several international journals as a reviewer. He serves as international programme committee member in many international and peer-reviewed conferences. Dr Ahmad Azar is currently Senior member in IEEE, Chair of IEEE Computational Intelligence Society (CIS) Egypt Chapter and Vice chair of IEEE Computational Intelligence Society Interdisciplinary Emergent Technologies Task Force. Also, he is the Vice-president (North) of System dynamics Africa Regional Chapter and an Academic Member of IEEE Systems, Man, and Cybernetics Society Technical Committee on Computational Collective Intelligence.

Sundarapandian Vaidyanathan has received the Doctor of Science (D.Sc.) degree (1996) in the Department of Electrical and Systems Engineering from Washington University, St. Louis, Missouri, U.S.A. He is currently the Professor and Dean, Research and Development Centre at Vel Tech University, Avadi, Chennai, India. Dr. Sundarapandian is the Associate Editor of two journals published by IGI Global, USA entitled International Journal of System Dynamics Applications (IJSDA) and International Journal of Rough Sets and Data Analysis (IJRSDA). He has published over 130 Scopus-indexed research publications and five books. He is an active researcher in the areas of Chaos and Control and constructed many novel chaotic and hyperchaotic systems in the chaos literature. He has given many plenary lectures in International Conferences on Control Engineering, Computer Science and information Technology. Dr. Sundarapandian's research interests include: Control Systems, Dynamical Systems, Stability Theory, Chaos Theory, Computational Science, Mathematical Modelling, Optimal Control, Robotics, Operations Research and Intelligent Control.

* * *

Ngo Mouelas Adèle Mohammed Ahmed is a member of the Egyptian electric code committee, an expert at the General Authority of the Urban Planning in Cairo, also an associate professor at the Electrical Engineering Dept., Faculty of Engineering, Al Azhar University). He received my B.Sc. in Electrical Powers and Machines field in 1997. In 2000, he was assigned as a Demonstrator then received my M.Sc. in the Electrical Power and Machines from Al Azhar University in 2003 and was appointed within the same Dept. as an assistant lecturer. In 2006, he have awarded my PhD degree and appointed as assistant professor at the same year. Finally in 2012, He was ranked to an associate professor. he supervised 2 PhD and 15 Master theses; he has 8 publications in local and international journals. Now he has interest in studying controlling and stability of electrical power systems, power generating and economics, and the use of intelligent systems in controlling.

Mohammad Al-Hariri is Research Assistant in the Department of Computing, Engineering and Technology and a PhD student in Automotive Engineering in the University of Sunderland. His research interests lie in the area of safety in passenger-vehicle. His current work focuses on developing a novel controller for vehicles dynamic systems aiming for better energy absorption resulting from vehicle frontal crashes.

Kammogne Soup Tewa Alain received the BSc degree in Physics from the University of Dschang, Cameroon in 2005, the MSc in electronics from the same university in 2008 and the PhD degree in electronic and control theory in 2012. He was awarded the DIPES II from the High Teacher College of Bambili, Cameroon. He is currently an Assistant Lecturer at the University of Dschang and National Polytechnic of Bamenda. His research interests are in the areas of nonlinear systems, focusing on chaos control, robust control, noises analysis and their potential applications to secure communication, biological systems and power electronics.

Mohamed Salah El-Din Ahmed Abdel Aziz received the BSc and MSc degrees in electrical engineering from Cairo University, Cairo, Egypt, in 2008 and 2011, respectively. Furthermore, he obtained recently his PhD degree in electrical engineering from faculty of engineering (Shoubra branch), Benha University, Egypt, in 2017. He works at Dar Al-Handasah (shair and Partners), Cairo office, as an electrical engineer. He published more than ten articles in international journals and conferences in addition to authoring a book in the field of power system protection. His research interests focus on High Impedance faults analysis, generators loss of excitation protection, and generator phase backup protection. He is also a reviewer in some International Scientific Journals.

Antonio Álvarez, M.D., graduated from the Faculty of Medicine of the University of Seville in 1976. He specialised in cardiovascular surgery at Virgen del Rocío University Hospital (Seville), having also the chance to complete his medical training in congenital heart surgery at La Paz University Hospital (Madrid). He has developed his entire professional career at Virgen del Rocío University Hospital where he mainly focused on paediatric heart surgery. To a lesser extent he has also cultivated adult heart surgery. In this last field, he had the opportunity to participate in the start-up and development of the heart transplantation programme. His main centres of interest cover early correction of congenital heart defects, anatomic correction of transposition of the great arteries (TGA) and surgical repair of univentricular heart.

Throughout his medical praxis he has taken part in the surgical treatment of more than five thousands children with congenital heart defects. He has been invited as a speaker to many panel discussions and participated in numerous conferences. He is author to relevant academic publications within his field, having been awarded several prizes in recognition for his scientific production.

Naglaa K. Bahgaat received the B.Sc., M.Sc. and PhD in 1999 and 2009 and 2014 respectively, in Electrical Engineering and Machine Dept. from Ain Shams University, Egypt. She is Registered Ph.D. in electrical engineering at Al-Azhar University since 2009; She is working at Modern Academy for Engineering and technology as Assistant Lecturer at Computer Dept. and from 2014 till now she working at Faculty of Engineering, Canadian International College (CIC), 6 October City. Her research interested includes Control Systems, Fuzzy Logic, and Artificial intelligence techniques in protection, control, and safety of power systems. She published 4 scientific papers international journal. And 3 chapters in Springer Books.

Arun Bajracharya is a Senior Assistant Professor in Construction Project Management at Heriot-Watt University in Malaysia. He has a Master's Degree in Infrastructure Planning and Management (1998) from the Asian Institute of Technology, Thailand and he holds a PhD in Construction and Project Management (2009) from the National University of Singapore. Dr Arun has research interests in system dynamics modelling, innovation management, transport policies, project finance and project dynamics. He has more than 16 years of experience with the tool of system dynamics, and he is interested in teaching application of the tool in the areas of construction, infrastructure and project management.

Maher Ben Hariz has received his B.Sc. degree (2008) in Electronic and computer science, his M.Sc. (2010) and Ph.D degree (2015) in Electronic from Faculty of Sciences of Tunis, Tunis El Manar University (Tunisia). He is a member of the Analysis, Conception and Control Systems laboratory at the National Engineering School of Tunis. His research interests include robust control of linear and nonlinear systems, and implementation of control algorithms.

Mouna Ben Smida was born in 1985. She received the B.S., M.S., and Dr.Eng. degrees in electrical engineering from National engineering school of Monastir, Tunisia, in 2008, 2010, and 2016,respectively. Her current research interests include renewable energy integration, electric power and energy systems, power system reliability, and computational intelligence.

Nacereddine Benamrouche received his BSc degree in Electrical Engineering in 1985 from the University of Tizi Ouzou, Algeria. He then received his PhD in Electrical Engineering from The University of Sheffield, U.K in 1990. He worked as a teaching assistant at the University of Leeds in 1990/1991, and as a Head of Department in Najran Technical College of Technology, Saudi Arabia, from 2000-2004. He is currently a professor at the Electrical Engineering Department, University of Tizi-Ouzou, Algeria, where he is director of a research laboratory (Laboratoire des Technologies avancées du Génie Electrique LATAGE). He did occupy the chair of Vice Chancellor to postgraduate studies and research at the same University from 2007 to 2010. He also chaired the scientific board for the electrical engineering department for many years. His research interests include electrical machines and drives, power electronics, control systems and renewable energy particularly photovoltaic.

Fahmy Bendary obtained B. Sc electrical power and machines engineering from Ain Shams university at 1966. He has got M.Sc. in electrical engineering from Cairo University at 1979. He has been granted his PhD. in automatic control and its applications to electrical power systems from Paris XL University, France at 1984. He worked as Lecturer at Military Technical College, Cairo from 1984 till 1990. He was Associate Professor in Zagazig University from 1991 till 2003. He worked as full professor of automatic control since 1995 till now. He has joind Faculty of engineering (Shoubra), Banha university from 2003 till now. His main interest is power systems analysis, optimization and control. He has also supervised about 10 PhD and 25 M.Sc Theses, and published 60 scientific papers in journals and international conferences. He is currently a member of CIRED and CIGRE Councils.

Nabil Benyahia received the BSC degree in electrical engineering from the University of Bejaia, Algeria, in 2002, and the Magister and PhD. degrees in electrical engineering from the same university, in 2005 and 2014, respectively. In 2009, he joined the Department of Electrical Engineering, University of Tizi-Ouzou, as an Assistant-Professor, and in 2014. His current research interests include power electronics, electrical machines and drives, fuel cell modeling, hybrid system based renewable energy, and storage system.

Muzaffar Ahmad Bhat is currently working as a research scholar in the department of Mathematics at the Jamia Millia Islamia in India. He has participated in several international conferences and has published several papers in various international journals. His research interest fields are: chaos control, chaos synchronization, nonlinear dynamical systems.

Faouzi Bouani received the M.S. degree in electrical engineering from the University of Tunis, High Normal School of Technical Education (ex. ENSET) in 1992, the Ph.D. degree and the "Habilitation universitaire" in electrical engineering both from Tunis El Manar University, National Engineering School of Tunis, Tunisia, in 1997 and 2007, respectively. He was an Associate Professor in three academic institutions at Tunisia (from 1993 to 2007). He joined the National Engineering School of Tunis, from 2008, where he is currently a professor of automatic control. He has authored or co-authored several journal and conference papers in the area of linear, nonlinear and robust model predictive control. He is the author of a book about predictive control based on artificial neural networks, with CPU editor, in 2015. His current research interests include robust and nonlinear predictive control, intelligent control systems and neural networks control.

Kevin Burn was born in Alnwick, UK, in 1962. His qualifications include degrees from Newcastle University (BSc Mechanical Engineering, 1984, PhD in Teleoperation and Control, 1994), and Durham University (MEng, 1986). He is currently a Senior Lecturer at the University of Sunderland, where his main areas of research interest are in system identification and automatic control of industrial processes, robotic control, intelligent systems design and fuzzy control, mathematical modelling of engineering systems, and vehicle dynamic control systems design. Dr Burn is a Chartered Engineer and a Member of the Institution of Mechanical Engineers.

Wassila Chagra is an associate professor at El Manar Preparatory Institute for Engineering Studies (IPEIT). She received her M.Sc. degree from the "Ecole Supérieure des Sciences et Techniques de Tunis" in 1995. She received her Ph.D. thesis degree in 2001 from the National Engineering School of

Tunis (ENIT). She is a member of the Analysis, Conception and Control Systems laboratory at ENIT. Her research interests include communication channel equalization and the computational intelligence techniques in the field of automatic control.

Yesenia Cruz is an Industrial Engineering (2000) from the Faculty of Engineering at Universidad del Atlántico, Colombia. She has received a M.S. degree in Quality Systems (2009), a M.E. in Transportation Engineering (2013) and Ph.D. degree in Transportation Engineering (2014), from the Faculty of Engineering at the University of Puerto Rico at Mayagüez Campus. She has six years of experience in the development, evaluation and implementation of quality management systems using ISO 9000 standards; and the statistical analysis applied to various production processes and services. She has worked in several manufacturing and service companies and has 12 years of experience in research and teaching. She is currently a Transport Consultant with almost 3 years of experience. She has made research in the fields of system dynamics, humanitarian logistics, education in the engineering field, vehicle routing, data mining, transition zones, infrastructure evaluation and highways operation.

Hakim Denoun received his BSc degree in Electrical Engineering in 1997 from the University of Tizi Ouzou, Algeria, and the D.E.A (Academic year) degree from Paris 6, France and the Magister degree from Polytechnic School, Algiers, Algeria in 1998 and 2001 respectively. He received his PhD degree in Electrical Engineering from The University of Mouloud Mammeri, Tizi-Ouzou .He is a researcher in laboratory (Laboratoire des Technologies avancées du Génie Electrique LATAGE) and a senior lecturer at the same university. He has published articles, and participates in many international scientific conferences. His research interests include electrical machines and drives, power electronics and control systems.

Mustafa Elkady is an assistant professor of Mechanical Engineering at Lebanese International University (LIU). He received a competition grant from the Egyptian Government (~ £100,000 -3 years) for his PhD. He obtained his PhD in mechanical engineering at the Department of Computing, Engineering and Technology, university of Sunderland, UK (2012). Prior to this he was a teaching assistant in Mechanical Engineering at the Automotive Department, Ain Shams University, Egypt. He obtained his Master degree in Automotive Engineering at Ain Shams University, Egypt (2004). Prior to this he was a Demonstrator in Mechanical Engineering at the Automotive Department, Ain Shams University. His research interests include mathematical modeling analysis, advanced dynamics, vehicle dynamics, crashworthiness, vehicle safety and impact biomechanics, vehicle engine controls and energy-efficient using light weight materials. His research outcomes are realized as evident from his over 20 publications, he has published the book (Enhancement of Vehicle Crash/Occupant Safety:Mathematical Modelling), Lambert.

Ahmed Mohamed Elmarakbi obtained his PhD in Mechanical Engineering from the University of Toronto, Canada (2004). After successful postdoctoral fellowships in Canada and Japan, he moved to the University of Sunderland, UK in 2007, where he is, currently, Professor of Automotive Composites. His research interests lie in the area of energy-efficient and safe vehicles (EESVs) including advanced composite materials, including Graphene, for automotive applications and low carbon vehicles. His work outcomes are recognised both nationally and internationally as evident from his 70+ Plenary Lectures, invited talks and presentations; 130+ peer-reviewed research papers. Most recently (2013), he has published the book: "Advanced Composite Materials for Automotive Applications: Structural Integrity and Crashworthiness", Wiley, UK. He has 15 years of experience managing national and international projects, including multi-disciplinary collaborative projects with Europe, USA, Canada, China, Japan, and Brazil. He has received many prestigious awards and grants world-wide, including EU Graphene Flagship, Horizon2020, EPSRC, NSERC, JSPS, OGS, FP7, and several fellowships. He is expert reviewer for FP7 and EPSRC; member of several professional bodies; editorial-board member of high-impact international journals; organiser of international conferences and reviewer for conferences and many high-impact journals. He is also founder Editor-in-Chief of 'International Journal of Automotive Composites'. He has an extensive track record of collaboration with the automotive industry and world-class academic institutions over the last 15 years and he is currently a member of the EU Graphene Flagship.

Arezki Fekik was born in Tizi-Ouzou,Algeria, on May 20, 1990. He received the B.Sc. M.Sc. degrees in electrical engineering from Mouloud Mammeri University, Tizi-Ouzou, Algeria, in 2011 and 2013, respectively. He is currently pursuing the Ph.D. degree at the LATAGE laboratory, Mouloud Mammeri University, Tizi-Ouzou. His research interests include the application of modern control methods (Fuzzy Petri nets…) to AC/DC converters and Multicellular chopper. His research interests include power converters, power electronics and control systems

Suresh Garg is currently working as Pro Vice chancellor at Delhi Technological University. He obtained his M. Tech and PhD degree in Industrial Engineering from Indian Institute of Technology, Delhi. He has published more than 90 papers in international/national journals and proceedings of international and national conferences. He visited USA and Chile to present papers and interact with faculty. His research area includes SCM, TQM, Knowledge management, Innovation and creativity, Productivity, JIT, quantitative techniques and FMS.

Soufien Gdiam received the degree in Electrical Engineering from National School of Engineering of Sfax, Tunisia in 1998. In 2007 he received his M.S degree in electronic and real-time informatic from Sousse University and received his PhD degree in Electrical Engineering in 2013 from ENIM, Tunisia. His current research interests include rapid prototyping and reconfigurable architecture for real-time control applications of electrical system.

Carlos J. González-Oquendo received his Master's Degree in Electrical Engineering specialized in Telecommunications and Electronics with a major in Applied Math from the University of Puerto Rico at Mayaguez Campus in 2009. Since 2000, he has been working as an Instructor and Professor, offering a variety of courses in different disciplines such as engineering, applied math, programming, electronics and avionics. He was hired as an Assistant Professor at The Eastern University at Carolina Campus, Puerto Rico. He is currently the Engineering Coordinator at the Department of Engineering Technology and Aerospace Sciences. He has written several lab manuals for different courses of electronics. His interest and project are related to: Probability and Statistics, Stochastic and Random Processes, Math and Physical Modelling, Signal and Image Processing, Control Systems, and Embedded Systems. He is formally the author of a technical paper (https://www.ll.mit.edu/HPEC/agendas/proc09/Day1/PA05_Goenaga-Rodriguez_abstract.pdf) for the MIT HPEC (High Performance Embedded Computing) 2009 conference (https://www.ll.mit.edu/HPEC/agendas/proc09/agenda.html).

Isdore Guma is a Lecturer at the Department of Computer Science, Gulu University. He holds Diploma in Science Technology Physics-Kyambogo University and Bachelors of Science (Computer Science)-Gulu University. Attained Master of Science in Information Systems at Makerere University with special interest in System Dynamics.

Mohamed Lamine Hamida was born in Ain El Hammam, Algeria. He received his diploma in electrical engineering from the Mouloud Mammeri University, Tizi-Ouzou, Algeria, in June 2013. He also received his master thesis degree in electrical engineering on September 2015. He is currently doing his PhD thesis researches in the theme of control of multicell converter. His research interests include power converters, power electronics and control systems.

Mohamed A. Moustafa Hassan (S. Member IEEE): received the B.Sc., M.Sc. and Ph.D. in 1977, 1982, and 1988 respectively, in Electrical Engineering, from Cairo University, Egypt. Since 1977, He joined the faculty of Electrical Engineering at Cairo University, Egypt as a Teaching staff. During his PhD research program, He visited Department of Electrical Engineering, BUGH - Wuppertal funded by DAAD, Germany for the academic years of 1984 to 1987. During the academic years of 1989 to 1992, he was a Visiting Scholar in the Department of Electrical Engineering, at The University of Calgary, CANADA, funded partially by CIDA. He is currently a Professor of control of Power Systems at Cairo University. He was working as Vice Dean for ITEC Alamieria (Funded via EDF, Egyptian Ministry Cabinet) Cairo Egypt (from Sept 2012 till Fe 2014), and Vice Dean for graduate Studies at FISCS October 6 University, Giza Egypt (for the Academic Year 2014/2015). His research activities include Control Systems, Fuzzy Logic, and ANN, Artificial intelligence techniques in protection, control, and safety of power systems. He published c.a. 115 scientific papers in International Journals and International Conferences. He is also a reviewer in some International Scientific Journals (IJSDA, IJMIC, EPSC).

Fotsin Hilaire Bertrand Amrita Jhawar received her B.E (Industrial Engineering) in 2005 and M. Tech (Industrial Engineering) in 2008 from Shri Ramdeobaba Kamla Nehru Engineering College, Nagpur. She has submitted her PhD to Delhi School of Management, Delhi Technological University and awaiting result. Her areas of expertise include Industrial Engineering, Supply Chain Management and Operations Research. She has to her credit 2 national publications, 5 international publications, 3 papers in an international conference and 2 papers in national conference.

Ioannis Kafetzis is a Masters student at Aristotle University of Thessaloniki and currently in pursuit of a PhD. He finished his bachelors in Aristotle University of Thessaloniki and got accepted in the Masters program the same year. His interests include System and Control Theory and Matrix Theory.

Billy Mathias Kalema holds a Doctor of Technology specializing in Information Systems. He is the Head of department Informatics at Tshwane University of Technology South Africa. He has supervised and examined several postgraduate studies at both masters and doctoral level and has spoken in various international conferences, PhD symposiums, seminars and workshops. He is a member of the Association of Information Systems (AIS), Institute of Electrical and Electronics Engineers (IEEE); Information Society for Africa (IST-Africa) and the International Association of Computer Science and Information Technology (IACSIT). He serves on several technical committees as an Editorial board member and peer reviewer for both journals and conferences and has published widely on ERPs, E-learning,

ICT4Education and MOOCs. His current and future research plans revolve around the practical application of research in daily life by putting IT to use especially for the economically and technologically disadvantaged developing countries.

Saber Krim received the degree in Electrical Engineering from National School of Engineering of Monastir (ENIM), Tunisia in 2011. In 2013 he received his M.S degree in electrical Engineering from Monastir University, Tunisia and received his PhD degree in Electrical Engineering in 2016 from ENIM, Tunisia. His current research interests include rapid prototyping and reconfigurable architecture for real-time control applications of electrical system.

John MacIntyre is the Dean of the Faculty of Applied Sciences, and Pro Vice Chancellor at the University of Sunderland. He has worked at the University of Sunderland since 1992, having graduated from the University with a First Class Honours Degree in Combined Science (Computer Science and Physiology). He then went on to complete a PhD in applied artificial intelligence, focussing on the use of neural networks in predictive maintenance, which was awarded in 1996. During the 1990s John established a research centre – the Centre for Adaptive Systems – at the University, which became recognised by the UK government as a Centre of Excellence for applied research in adaptive computing and artificial intelligence. The Centre undertook many projects working with and for external organisations in industry, science and academia, and for three years ran the Smart Software for Decision Makers programme on behalf of the Department of Trade and Industry. He has successfully supervised PhDs in fields ranging from neural networks, hybrid systems, and bioinformatics through to lean manufacturing, predictive maintenance, and business and maintenance strategies. He went on to become Associate Dean, and then Dean, of the School of Computing, Engineering and Technology, covering Computer Science and Engineering; in 2008 he became the Dean of the Faculty of Applied Science, and in 2010 Pro Vice Chancellor of the University.

Mohamed Faouzi Mimouni received his Mastery of Science and DEA from ENSET, Tunisia in 1984 and 1986, respectively. In 1997, he obtained his Doctorate Degree in Electrical Engineering from ENSET, Tunisia. He is currently Full Professor of Electrical Engineering with Electrical Department at the National School of Engineering of Monastir. His specific research interests are in the area Power Electronics, Motor Drives, Solar and Wind Power generation. Dr. Med Faouzi MIMOUNI has authored/coauthored over 100 papers in international journals and conferences. He served on the technical program committees for several international conferences.

Lazaros Moysis is a PhD Student at the Department of Mathematics, Aristotle University of Thessaloniki, Greece. He received his Bachelor degree in 2011 and his Master degree in 2013. His research interests include the theory of control systems, linear systems, descriptor and higher order systems of differential or difference equations and matrix theory. He has published works in international journals and conferences, as well as some free tutorials on Matlab and Latex. He is an IEEE member. His personal ResearchGate profile is https://www.researchgate.net/profile/Lazaros Moysis.

Abdellatif Mtibaa is currently Professor in Micro-Electronics and Hardware Design with Electrical Department at the National School of Engineering of Monastir and Head of Circuits Systems Reconfigurable ENIM-Group at Electronic and microelectronic Laboratory. He holds a Diploma in Electrical

Engineering in 1985 and received his PhD degree in Electrical Engineering in 2000. His current research interests include System on Programmable Chip, high level synthesis, rapid prototyping and reconfigurable architecture for real-time multimedia applications. Dr. Abdellatif Mtibaa has authored/coauthored over 150 papers in international journals and conferences. He served on the technical program committees for several international conferences. He also served as a co-organizer of several international conferences.

Benedict Oyo obtained his PhD in Information Systems in 2012. His areas of interest are System Dynamics, Speech Recognition, Open Educational Resources (OERs), Massive Open Online Courses (MOOCs) and Technology Usage. He manages an integrated OER and MOOCs platform at www.mwalimu.ug.

Marios Politis received a Medical Doctor (MD), from Medical School of Aristotle University of Thessaloniki. Current position: Resident of Family Medicine, General Hospital of Thessaloniki ''G. Papanikolaou''.

Javier Reina-Tosina was born in Seville, Spain. He received the Telecomm. Eng. and Doctor degrees from the University of Seville, Seville, Spain, in 1996 and 2003, respectively. Since 1997, he has been with the Department of Signal Theory and Communications, University of Seville, where he is currently Associate Professor. His research interests include the integration of information technologies in biomedicine, intelligent devices for homecare, and bioelectromagnetics.

Laura M. Roa received the Ph.D. degree (cum laude) from the University of Seville, Spain. She is a Full Professor at the University of Seville. Her research interests include multiscale computational modeling for multimodal diagnosis, arquitectures for the integration of social/health services, intelligent devices for ehealth, and bioelectromagnetics. Prof. Roa is a Fellow of the Institute of Electrical and Electronics Engineers, Fellow of the American Institute for Medical and Biological Engineering, the International Academy for Medical and Biological Engineering Sciences, Fellow of the European Alliance for Medical and Biological Engineering & Science, and a member of the Royal Medical Academy of Seville, Spain.

Aceng Sambas is currently a Lecturer at the Muhammadiyah University of Tasikmalaya, Indonesia since 2015. He received his MSc in Mathematics from the Universiti Sultan Zainal Abidin (UniSZA), Malaysia in 2015. His current research focuses on dynamical systems, chaotic signals, electrical engineering, computational science, signal processing, robotics, embedded systems and artificial intelligence.

Muhammad Sheikh completed his B.S Electronics engineering in 2008 and MSc Electrical engineering from Staffordshire University, UK in 2011 and now working towards his PhD from University of Sunderland UK. Muhammad's primary research area is Energy storage systems and he published paper title "Voltage balancing of supercapacitor string using rectifier diode" in an international journal in 2014. New emerging battery technologies and need to make them efficient and safe drag him to do further research on energy storage systems and he chose to investigate unseen conditions of batteries after crash/collision so in his PhD Muhammad is working on project, "State of Charge dependent Thermal Runaway Detection of Lithium-Ion Battery". Muhammad is developing his teaching profile and actively participated in "Preparing to teach" course held in university of Sunderland. Muhammad is currently working as research associate in university of Sunderland.

Shikha Singh is currently working as a assistant professor in the department of Mathematics at Delhi University in India. She participated in several international conferences and has published several papers in various international journals. Her research interest fields are: chaos control, chaos synchronization, nonlinear dynamical systems.

Alejandro Talaminos was born in Zafra (Badajoz), Spain. He received the Telecomm. Eng. degree in 2009 from the University of Extremadura, Spain, and he is currently working in Seville, Spain, toward the Ph.D. degree at the Biomedical Engineering Group. His current research interests include Multiscale computational modeling for multimodal diagnosis and distributed computing.

Gen'ichi Yasuda joined Information Science and Control Engineering Course in Department of Mechanical Engineering, Faculty of Engineering, at Nagasaki Institute of Applied Science, Japan as a Research Assistant, in 1983. He was a Professor in Department of Mechanical Engineering during 1996-2005, a Professor in Department of Human and Computer Intelligence, Faculty of Informatics during 2005-2010, and also a Professor in Division of Instrument and Control, Department of Electronics and Information Technology, Graduate School of Engineering during 1996-2010. He is now a Guest Professor at Nagasaki Institute of Applied Science. He is a recipient of CACS International Automatic Control Conference Best Paper Award in 2009. He also served as session chairman in many international conferences. He originated the frontier researches on non-centralized systems and grouping robots as a doctoral dissertation at Tokyo Institute of Technology since 1971.

Mustapha Zaouia was born in Tizi-Ouzou, Algeria. He received Magister degree from Polytechnic School, Algiers, Algeria in 2001and the PhD degree in the Mouloud Mammeri University of Tizi-Ouzou, Algeria. He is Assistant Professor. His research interest include electrical machines and drives, the electromagnetic-mechanical modelling, numerical simulation of electromagnetic machines particularly the linear machines and permanent-magnet machines applied to the electrical and hybrid vehicles.

Index

T

V

W

X

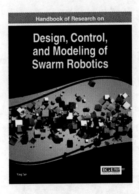

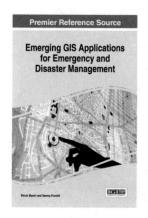

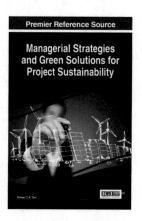

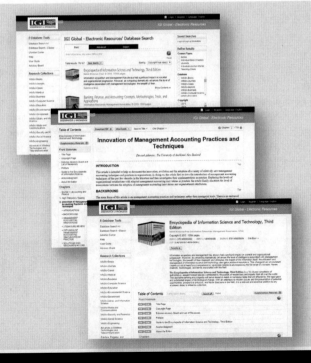

Printed in the United States
By Bookmasters